INTERNATIONAL HANDBOOK ON THE ECONOMICS OF ENERGY

T0305575

International Handbook on the Economics of Energy

Edited by

Joanne Evans

Lecturer in Economics, Surrey Energy Economics Centre (SEEC), Department of Economics, University of Surrey, UK

and

Lester C. Hunt

Professor of Energy Economics, Surrey Energy Economics Centre (SEEC), Department of Economics, University of Surrey, UK

Edward Elgar
Cheltenham, UK • Northampton, MA, USA

Published by
Edward Elgar Publishing Limited
The Lypiatts
15 Lansdown Road
Cheltenham
Glos GL50 2JA
UK

Edward Elgar Publishing, Inc.
William Pratt House
9 Dewey Court
Northampton
Massachusetts 01060
USA

Paperback edition 2011

A catalogue record for this book
is available from the British Library

Library of Congress Control Number: 2009930863

ISBN 978 1 84270 352 6 (cased)
      978 0 85793 825 1 (paperback)

Typeset by Servis Filmsetting Ltd, Stockport, Cheshire
Printed and bound in Great Britain by T. J. International Ltd, Padstow

Contents

v

List of contributors

Grant Allan is Research Fellow, funded through the EPSRC SuperGen Marine Energy Research Consortium, Fraser of Allander Institute and Department of Economics, University of Strathclyde, Glasgow, Scotland.

Chris Bataille is Adjunct Professor, School of Resource and Environmental Management, Simon Fraser University and Director, MKJA Inc., Vancouver, Canada.

Seth Blumsack is Assistant Professor of Energy Policy and Economics, Department of Energy and Mineral Engineering, Pennsylvania State University, University Park, PA, USA.

Getúlio Borges da Silveira is Associate Professor, Instituto de Economia – Universidade Federal do Rio de Janeiro, Brazil.

Adilson de Oliveira is Professor, Instituto de Economia – Universidade Federal do Rio de Janeiro and Director of the High Studies Brazilian College, Universidade Federal do Rio de Janeiro, Brazil.

Paul Ekins is Professor of Energy and Environment Policy, UCL Energy Institute, University College London, UK.

Joanne Evans is Lecturer in Economics, Surrey Energy Economics Centre (SEEC), Department of Economics, University of Surrey, Guildford, UK.

Mehdi Farsi is Senior Scientist and Lecturer, Centre for Energy Policy and Economics (CEPE), Department of Management, Technology and Economics, ETH Zurich, Switzerland and Lecturer at the Department of Economics, University of Lugano, Switzerland.

Massimo Filippini is Professor of Economics/Energy Economics, Department of Management, Technology and Economics, ETH Zurich and Department of Economics, University of Lugano, Switzerland. He is also the Co-Director of the Centre for Energy Policy and Economics (CEPE), ETH Zurich, Switzerland.

Roger Fouquet is Ikerbasque Research Professor, Basque Centre for Climate Change (BC3), Bilbao, Spain.

Christoph W. Frei is Secretary General at the World Energy Council and Titulary Professor and Advisor to the President of the Swiss Federal Institute of Technology, Lausanne, Switzerland.

Dalton Garis is Associate Professor of Economics and Petroleum Market Behaviour, The Petroleum Institute, Abu Dhabi, United Arab Emirates.

Lullit Getachew is a Senior Economist, Pacific Economics Group, Madison, WI, USA.

Michelle Gilmartin is a PhD student, funded through the EPSRC SuperGen Marine

Energy Research Consortium, Fraser of Allander Institute and Department of Economics, University of Strathclyde, Glasgow, Scotland.

Richard L. Gordon is Professor Emeritus of Mineral Economics, Pennsylvania State University, University Park, PA, USA.

Paul W. Graham is Theme Leader, Energy Futures, Commonwealth Scientific and Industrial Research Organisation (CSIRO) Energy Technology, Newcastle, Australia.

Lorna A. Greening is an Energy and Environmental Economics Consultant, Los Alamos, NM, USA.

Lester C. Hunt is Professor of Energy Economics, Surrey Energy Economics Centre (SEEC), Department of Economics, University of Surrey, Guildford, UK.

Hillard G. Huntington is Executive Director of the Energy Modeling Forum, Stanford University, Stanford, CA, USA.

Mark Jaccard is Professor, School of Resource and Environmental Management, Simon Fraser University, Vancouver, Canada.

Ramachandran Kannan is a Research Scientist, Paul Scherrer Institute, Switzerland.

Claudia Kemfert is Professor and Head of the Department of Energy Transportation and Environment, Deutsches Institut für Wirtschaftsforschung (DIW), Berlin and Humboldt University, Berlin, Germany.

Luciano Losekann is Associate Professor, Faculdade de Economia – Universidade Federal Fluminense, Rio de Janeiro, Brazil.

Mark N. Lowry is a Partner, Pacific Economics Group, Madison, WI, USA.

Reinhard Madlener is Full Professor of Energy Economics and Management and Director of the Institute for Future Energy Consumer Needs and Behavior (FCN), E.ON Energy Research Center, RWTH Aachen University, Aachen, Germany.

Peter McGregor is Professor of Economics and Director of the Fraser of Allander Institute and a member of the Department of Economics, University of Strathclyde, Glasgow.

Kenneth B. Medlock III is Fellow in Energy Studies, James A. Baker III Institute for Public Policy and Adjunct Professor, Department of Economics, Rice University, Houston, TX, USA.

Carole Nakhle is Associate Lecturer, Surrey Energy Economics Centre (SEEC), Department of Economics, University of Surrey, Guildford, UK.

Dmitri Perekhodtsev is Managing Consultant, LECG Consulting SAS, Paris, France.

André Plourde is Professor of Economics, Department of Economics, University of Alberta, Edmonton, Canada.

Luke J. Reedman is a Research Scientist, Energy Futures, Commonwealth Scientific and Industrial Research Organisation (CSIRO) Energy Technology, Newcastle, Australia.

Ronald D. Ripple is Professor of Energy Economics, Curtin Business School, Curtin University of Technology, Perth, Australia.

Juan Rosellón is Professor, Centro de Investigación y Docencia Económicas (CIDE), División de Economia, Mexico and Research Associate, Dresden University of Technology (TU Dresden), Department of Business Management and Economics, Chair of Energy Economics and Public Sector Management, Germany.

David L. Ryan is Professor of Economics, Director of the Canadian Building Energy End-Use Data and Analysis Centre (CBEEDAC) and Fellow of the Institute for Public Economics, Department of Economics, University of Alberta, Edmonton, Canada.

Harry Saunders is Managing Director, Decision Processes Incorporated, Danville, CA, USA.

Steve Sorrell is Senior Fellow in the Sussex Energy Group, SPRU (Science and Technology Policy Research), University of Sussex, Brighton, UK.

Neil Strachan is Reader in Energy Economics and Modelling at the UCL Energy Institute, University College London, UK.

Ian Sue Wing is Associate Professor, Department of Geography and Environment, Boston University, Boston, MA, USA.

J. Kim Swales is Professor of Economics and Head of the Department of Economics, University of Strathclyde, Glasgow, Scotland.

Truong Truong is Research Professor, Deutsches Institut für Wirtschaftsforschung (DIW), Berlin, Germany and Honorary Professor in Sustainable Transport Systems, Institute of Transport and Logistics Studies (ITLS), Faculty of Economics and Business, The University of Sydney, NSW, Australia.

Karen Turner is Senior Lecturer, Fraser of Allander Institute and Department of Economics, University of Strathclyde, Glasgow, Scotland.

W.D. Walls is Professor of Economics, Department of Economics, University of Calgary, Alberta, Canada.

Thomas Weyman-Jones is Professor of Industrial Economics, Department of Economics, Loughborough University, UK.

Denise Young is Associate Professor, Department of Economics and Associate Director of the Canadian Building Energy End-Use Data and Analysis Centre (CBEEDAC), University of Alberta, Edmonton, Canada.

Introduction
Joanne Evans and Lester C. Hunt

Energy security, the impact of energy use on the environment, fuel prices and fuel poverty are all issues at the forefront of public attention. The economics of energy is a vital element which contributes to our understanding of these complex issues and influences policy makers' thinking as energy policy is determined.

This handbook reviews the key aspects and research issues in the economics of energy. It brings together a collection of contributions from international experts (both practitioners and academics) in the economics of energy, which synthesise the current literature and provide an analysis of the key issues. The handbook covers historical aspects of the economics of energy and the important topical research and policy issues of the day with the focus very much on the 'economics of energy' and subsequent policy. Aiming to be accessible to final-year undergraduates and postgraduate students studying the economics of energy, as well as practitioners in industry and government, the handbook summarises the current state of knowledge and provides an insightful commentary. The handbook starts with a historical prospective of energy and associated public policy issues, followed by an overview of the economics of energy supply and demand. The economics of energy efficiency including the 'rebound effect' are discussed, and then various energy economics modelling techniques are presented. Key issues associated with the various energy markets are addressed in turn: oil, coal, natural gas and electricity. The book concludes with a focus on contemporary energy policy issues.

In Chapter 1, Fouquet considers the history of energy use and the global economy in starting from the evolution of agrarian economies and discussing the attempts in Europe to overcome the limits in organic energy systems and the first successful transition to a fossil-fuel economy in Britain. Fouquet also considers the long-term trends in the global energy system and different energy policies through time. In Chapter 2, Weyman-Jones provides an overview of the theory of 'energy economics', arguing that this is really just a phrase used for convenience given that there is no such commodity as 'energy'; it is really the 'economics of fuel markets'. Weyman-Jones analyses resource allocation in capital-intensive fuel industries covering the nature of short- and long-run marginal cost of energy supply, the process of investment decision making, the design of efficient price mechanisms, and the market conditions that are frequently found in the fuel industries.

In Chapter 3, Medlock reviews the economics of energy supply considering the way in which energy sources are allocated through space and time. He outlines and develops the economists' model of optimal extraction of depletable resources that is used to examine a range of energy economics issues; and assesses the worth of such models by analysing 'firm behaviour' and 'peak oil'. In Chapter 4, Gordon examines the theory and practice of energy policy, considering examples of energy programmes that he argues were ill advised, reviewing the errors in policies in search of energy security. For the US, Gordon considers policies that have attempted to alter energy choices and those with an environmental focus, whereas for Western Europe and Japan he considers the reluctance of governments to accept the uneconomic position of coal.

In Chapter 5, Medlock turns his attention to the theory of energy demand, highlighting that energy is a *derived* demand, required in order to obtain energy services such as heating, lighting, automotive power and so on. He discusses energy accounting, the relationship between energy use and economic development and the issues of structural and technological change, before going on to consider the micro foundations of energy demand and the elasticity of energy demand. In Chapter 6, Ryan and Plourde focus on the empirical modelling of energy demand. They consider the historical development of empirical models of energy demand from single-equation models to systems approaches, the implications of non-stationarity of appropriate data series on empirical models of energy demand, and the issues associated with allowing for asymmetric price responses in empirical models of energy demand.

The next few chapters focus on energy efficiency and the 'rebound effect' (where an increase in energy efficiency reduces the price of the energy service, resulting in an increase in demand for energy that moderates any energy saving). In Chapter 7, Allan et al. analyse the economics of energy efficiency, given the arguments that improvements in energy efficiency are important for meeting sustainability and security of supply goals. Allan et al. adopt an analytical approach to investigate the impact of an improvement in energy efficiency in a stylised open economy, aiming to identify and clarify the nature of the various system-wide factors that can affect the change in energy use that accompanies improvements in energy efficiency. In Chapter 8, Saunders presents the theoretical foundations of the rebound effect in order to explore the 'subtle' relationship between energy efficiency and energy consumption. He develops a simplified, but rigorous, theoretical framework for understanding the relationship, highlighting that the potential rebound impact is unknown but could be significant and have important policy impacts. In Chapter 9, Sorrell further examines the definitions and estimation of the rebound effect, highlighting that there are a range of mechanisms that may induce the rebound effect or even 'backfire' (where the introduction of certain types of energy efficiency results in an overall increase in energy demand). He clarifies the definition of direct, indirect and economy-wide rebound effects, highlights the methodological challenges associated with quantifying such effects, and summarises the estimates of rebound that are currently available. Sorrell concludes that rebound effects are significant, but they need not make energy efficiency policies ineffective in reducing energy demand.

In Chapter 10, Ryan and Young present an application of modelling the energy savings and environmental benefits from energy policies and new technologies. Drawing primarily on examples from the residential sector, they develop empirical microeconomic modelling approaches to evaluate the outcomes of policies that focus on the adoption of new technologies as a means of reducing energy demand and/or improving environmental quality, assessing the strengths and weaknesses of the various approaches.

The following few chapters consider a range of energy economy models used by energy analysts and energy policy makers. In Chapter 11, Greening and Bataille provide an overview of technology-orientated 'bottom-up' models of energy, focusing on the efforts to embed economic dynamics in bottom-up models by increasing their behavioural realism and macroeconomic completeness, as well as the possibility of including sufficiently large amounts of technological detail in existing macroeconometric or computable general equilibrium (CGE) frameworks. Greening and Bataille therefore discuss simulation models and hybridisation. They demonstrate that bottom-up models have become increasingly more detailed and sophisticated in the way they handle technology choice and represent the dynamics of the energy system, in addition to increasing their capabilities for simulating the relationship between the physical stock and the wider economy. One particular type of model reviewed by Greening and Bataille is the MARKAL model (MARKet ALlocation model), which is a bottom-up dynamic, linear programming optimisation model. MARKAL is a commonly used model for energy policy analysis and in Chapter 12, Kannan et al. consider MARKAL further by detailing the development of a UK MARKAL model. Kannan et al. present indicative results to demonstrate MARKAL's strengths, range of outputs, and how MARKAL deals with uncertainties between alternative energy pathways.

In Chapter 13, Jaccard investigates the combining of 'top-down' and 'bottom-up' energy economy models, exploring public policy efforts to influence the direction of technological evolution, known as 'induced technological change' (ITC). He explores the ideal attributes of ITC policy models, noting the deficiencies and strengths of conventional approaches before explaining some recent modelling innovations that attempt to combine the best qualities of competing conventional models and parameter estimation. Jaccard then considers a specific ITC as an example of the challenge to provide a real-world empirical basis for estimating the response to ITC policies, and concludes that there remains considerable uncertainty concerning future responses of consumers and businesses to ITC policies. In Chapter 14, Sue Wing provides an exposition of CGE modelling for analysing energy and climate policies in order to 'de-mystify' the CGE approach. By developing the general algebraic framework of a CGE model from microeconomic principles, Sue Wing demonstrates how such a model might be calibrated using actual data, solved for the equilibrium values of economic variables, and the equilibrium perturbed by introducing price and quantity distortions; hence demonstrating how the economy-wide impact of energy and climate policies might be analysed. In Chapter 15, Kemfert and Truong survey energy–economy–environment modelling. Recent modelling has attempted to integrate climate, ecosystem and economic impacts into a single framework of so-called integrated assessment modelling (IAM), and Kemfert and Truong provide an overview of such models covering the theoretical backgrounds, the methodologies and model designs.

The following chapters focus on different fuels. In Chapter 16, Huntington evaluates the contributions of several strands in the energy security literature that emphasise the US oil security problem; however, the methodologies and basic principles also apply to many European and Asian countries. Huntington reviews and discusses three key economic issues central to the discussion of oil security: the oil import premium, the risk of oil supply interruptions, and the vulnerability of the economy to an oil disruption. In Chapter 17, Nakhle discusses the challenges inherent in designing and implementing an appropriate petroleum tax system aimed at achieving an appropriate balance between both government and industry interests. She recognises that there are no uniform solutions to these challenges; nevertheless, she argues that variety, flexibility and a readiness to adapt and evolve are the key requirements. In Chapter 18, Garis investigates the behaviour of petroleum markets beyond supply–demand fundamentals, arguing that there are circumstances where traders reject these in petroleum markets in favour of psychological characteristics and trader expectations. Garis conducts a behaviour analysis to show how petroleum market prices behave under various scenarios in order to try to understand why, at various times, the supply–demand fundamentals are ignored. In Chapter 19, Gordon plots the history of the coal industry and the world coal market, highlighting that in the twentieth century coal moved from being a general-use fuel to primarily being used for electricity generation – with all the associated environmental implications. Following the historical review, Gordon examines coal trade patterns and US policy before concluding with a brief discussion of the uncertain future of coal.

The opening up to markets, competition, alternate market structures, and incentives in electricity and gas industries is the focus of a number of following chapters. In Chapter 20, Walls provides an overview of the issues around the opening up of gas and electricity markets, as the industries are increasingly being regulated by 'market forces'. Walls argues that the transition for natural gas to markets was easier in the US than it might have been; however, due to the complexity of balancing supply and demand, the introduction of market-based allocation mechanisms has proved to be far more difficult for electricity. In Chapter 21, Weyman-Jones presents a summary of the key theoretical ideas underpinning the incentive regulation of energy networks. He outlines the main regulatory principles and tools employed and the different regulatory models and mechanisms that are applied in the real world: price-cap, revenue-cap, sliding scale, and yardstick competition.

In Chapter 22, Getachew and Lowry also explore the regulation of transmission and distribution in the developed world. Using the US as a case study, they demonstrate the importance of scale economies to illustrate the factors that affect the electricity industry in the developed world, going on to discuss the use of incentive-based regulation in the US, Canada, Europe, and the Pacific Region. In Chapter 23, Getachew explores the market structure of electricity networks in the developed world, presenting the various ways in which power industry restructuring by separating the natural monopoly activities of distribution and transmission from the competitive sectors has been instituted in the US, Canada, Western European countries, Japan, Australia and New Zealand. Getachew highlights the various transmission service arrangements that have been put in place across the developed world, concluding that the restructuring of the power industry is far from finished. In Chapter 24, Rosellón reviews incentive mechanisms for electricity transmission expansion, arguing that the economic analysis of electricity markets has typically concentrated on short-term issues whereas investment in transmission capacity is long term in nature, as well as stochastic. He discusses the two main disparate analytical approaches to transmission investment (the incentive regulation hypothesis and the merchant approach) before offering insights into how to build a more comprehensive approach that combines both mechanisms.

In Chapter 25, Farsi and Filippini review and discuss the empirical measurement of the productive efficiency of electricity and gas distribution. Following a review of production theory and the concepts of economies of scale and scope, they illustrate the different statistical approaches used to measure efficiency in the distribution sectors of electricity and gas (benchmarking), providing a selection of previous empirical studies. This is followed by a short discussion of actual benchmarking practice undertaken and a short case study of Switzerland. Farsi and Filippini conclude that the measurement of efficiency is a contentious issue, so it is important to try to measure the efficiency from several angles, applying a number of models with different assumptions.

Perekhodtsev and Blumsack review wholesale electricity markets and generators' incentives in Chapter 26, outlining the critical properties of the markets applied in different wholesale electricity markets around the world. Highlighting the three design characteristics of 'market design rules', 'market power' and 'resource adequacy and capacity mechanisms', Perekhodtsev and Blumsack conclude that the poor design of electricity markets may increase significantly the cost of electricity to customers and that no market has managed to overcome all the identified problems. In Chapter 27, Losekann et al. discuss security of supply in large hydropower systems. They use a simulation model to apply the 'missing money problem' to Brazil and conclude that if the issue of energy storage incentive is not adequately addressed the system is likely to run into security of supply problems – despite capacity payments to ensure an abundant supply of generation capacity.

In Chapter 28, Blumsack and Perekhodtsev turn their attention to electricity retail competition, discussing the transition from regulated monopoly pricing to competition. By reviewing the various retail electricity market models across the world, they highlight that there is no widely accepted way to design such markets, and conclude by offering a set of policy prescriptions for successful retail electricity markets. In Chapter 29, Reedman and Graham consider emissions trading and the convergence of electricity and transport markets in Australia. Following an examination of the relative cost of greenhouse gas (GHG) abatement in the Australian electricity and transport sectors, they employ a partial equilibrium model to formulate three emission reduction scenarios. Some of their key findings include the need for emission permit prices to be significantly higher in order to achieve rapid and deep GHG emission abatement targets and that without further measures, the combined electricity and transport sectors will be unable to meet aggressive cuts in GHG emissions in the short term.

The fundamental purpose for derivatives is to facilitate risk mitigation and to aid in price discovery of the underlying asset, and in Chapter 30 Ripple provides historical background on the introduction of derivatives, futures, forwards, options and other financial instruments into the energy markets, which assist market participants with their risk mitigation needs. Ripple outlines the underlying economics of these instruments and their markets with some examples of how such instruments might be employed, providing an analysis of the evolution of both price volatility and the relative roles of hedgers and investors/speculators in these markets.

Some of the major themes and strands of research on the economics of energy supply and use in developing countries are presented by Madlener in Chapter 31, highlighting the literature on: the relationship between energy consumption and economic growth; the relationship between rapid fossil-fuel price rises on development; and interfuel substitution. Madlener concludes by predicting an increase in research activity on the impact of energy price rises on the sustainable development of developing countries, while indicating that the issues of equity and energy poverty should also be addressed.

The final two chapters examine energy policy from very different perspectives. In Chapter 32, Frei presents an example of the use of 'energy visions' analysis to consider alternative routes that energy policy might take in the future to address the twin problems of energy security and climate change. Using a combination of economics, and Weber's classifications of social behaviour, Frei builds 'energy visions' that investigate different possible futures to aid the thinking of policy makers. In Chapter 33, Weyman-Jones takes a different perspective considering the current key issues in the design of energy policy.[1] Recognising that energy policy is the attempt to correct the three market failures of asymmetric information, market power and externality, Weyman-Jones focuses on the positive economics of market power and externality (the normative economic policy towards asymmetric information being covered in Chapter 21). He therefore critically analyses a number of key contemporary energy policy issues including the social cost of carbon, carbon permits versus taxes, integrated assessment models, and the UK Stern Review of the economics of climate change.

We hope that the wide spectrum of issues and techniques in this Handbook, as well as the depth of analysis, makes the economics of energy accessible to all those who are interested in understanding the current issues in energy economics. We would like thank all who contributed a chapter (or in some cases two or even three chapters) to this volume – even the late ones that we had to chase – the Handbook is the richer for each contribution. Finally, our thanks also to Matthew Pitman of Edward Elgar, who originally persuaded us to undertake this project, and also to the publishing team.

Note

1. In Chapter 4, Gordon considers the energy policy as previously designed, whereas in Chapter 33 Weyman-Jones considers the key energy policy issues currently faced by energy economists.

1 A brief history of energy
Roger Fouquet[1]

1 The Importance of History

Energy has been fundamental to human survival and growth. At a basic level, the concentration of energy is the basis of life itself. For millions of years, animals have dedicated much of their lives to collecting sufficient energy in the form of food to survive. Success in this endeavour has enabled the human population to grow spectacularly over the last ten thousand years.

The concentration of other (non-agricultural) forms of energy has allowed humankind to create increasingly elaborate surroundings and complex societies. More energy, more efficiently consumed provided greater amounts of heat, power, transport and light (Fouquet 2008). Most would agree that, overall, this has improved the population's quality of life.

Human economies – the production, exchange and consumption of goods and services – are driven by refinements in ways of capturing and harnessing energetic resources. The growth of economies has been closely linked with the availability, extraction, distribution and use of energy. Indeed, there is a close relationship between energy consumption and economic development (see, for instance, Judson et al. 1999). Thus, to study this relationship is to partially investigate the processes of economic growth and development, to identify the likely changes in energy requirements and to consider the possible environmental implications of energy usage.

Due to a lack of statistical information, many economists trying to study this relationship have focused at a point-in-time picture of energy and GDP, using cross-sectional data. However, there have been many attempts to identify the crucial steps in the history of energy (see, for instance, Cottrell 1955; Cipolla 1962; Wrigley 1988; Smil 1994 and Fouquet 2008). This is another briefer effort, benefiting from some of the latest research on the topic.

First, this chapter looks at the evolution of agrarian economies, tied to the fruits of direct solar energy supplies. Then, there is a discussion of the limits that were faced in organic energy systems, with an emphasis on attempts to overcome them in Europe. The following section reviews the first successful transition to a fossil-fuel economy, in Britain. This then leads to an analysis of past and current trends in the global modern energy system. There is a brief discussion of the different energy policies through time, and a section on issues raised by environmental pollution related to energy. The final section tries to draw conclusions about the past ten thousand years of energy use in the global economy.

2 Energy in an Agricultural World

Life on Earth ultimately depends on solar energy. The sun provides on average 1366 watts (W) per square metre per second, which is roughly 170 000 terawatts (TW) on Earth, equivalent to 128000000 million tonnes of oil equivalent (mtoe) per year (Ruddiman 2001). Plants capture and convert some of this energy through photosynthesis, providing the base for animal food chains.

Early humans tended to live nomadic existences following the rhythm of seasonal plant growth. As gatherers of food, humans needed a large area of land within which to find sufficient food to meet their roughly 2000 kilocalories (kcal) daily requirement. The introduction of agriculture, as a way of directing the growth of plants, generally increased the amount of food yielded on a plot of land, allowing for an increase in population density. While there is great uncertainty and debate about the drivers for its permanent adoption, considerable evidence shows that agriculture in various forms co-existed with hunter–gatherer lifestyles for extended periods of time (Boserup 1965; Cowan and Watson 1992; Smil 1994, p. 23).

Twelve thousand years ago, the human population on Earth numbered about four million. Most cultivations at the time were 'slash and burn'. Burning the vegetation created a temporarily fertile soil, which could be cultivated for a few years. As the nutrients in the soil became depleted, the community moved on to the next settlement.

By about 7000 years ago, the population had increased to five million. It is unclear which was cause and which was effect, yet, with the rise in population came a decline in 'slash and burn' and an intensification of more permanent agricultural activities (Boserup 1965). In the next two thousand years, major innovations radically improved agricultural yields: irrigation, animals, the plough, the wheel and metals were introduced. These are likely to have helped support the 15 million inhabitants living 5000 years ago. Over the next three thousand years, the population rose between 170 and 250 million (Malanima 2003, p. 80).

In many of the main centres of population, winters were mild, as humans lived sufficiently close to the equator. This reduced the need to protect from the cold and to create a warmer inner climate to survive. Thus, for many early communities fire, which was discovered more than 500000 years ago, was used mainly for cooking – heat provided the vital role of improving food's calorific and nutritional value (ibid., p. 80).

Yet, the ability to use fire for warmth enabled settlements to gradually spread to more temperate climates. In pre-industrial Europe, where populations faced harsh winters, large quantities of crop residue, dung and especially wood were needed for domestic heating. This could reach 10 kg of wood or 30000 kcal per day in the colder regions, which was at least three-quarters of a household's energy requirements – the majority of the rest was for animal fodder and food (ibid., p. 75).

As well as cooking food and keeping humans warm, fire created light, which improved protection and safety. Heat enabled materials to be transformed, too, which was essential for many industrial activities. In other words, the gradual improvements in the taming and directing of fire enabled humans to generate more useful heat and light, increasing human populations and pushing the boundaries of human inhabitation away from the equator – with better tools and greater protection.

The expanding population had lived and their communities been bound by the flow of energy generated directly and indirectly from solar radiation. By the sixteenth century, about one-eighth of the world's surface area was under continuous cultivation (ibid., p. 63). By that time, the population density was above 5–10 people per square kilometre. The main centres of continuous agriculture and, therefore, population were in Asia

(South, South-East and Far East), in the Middle East, Egypt and North Africa, in Europe and in Central America (ibid., p. 65).

But the density of populations varied considerably according to the types of agriculture. For instance, in Japan, more than 850 inhabitants could live in 1 sq km; in China, nearly 500; in India, 270; and in Europe, only 60 people (ibid., p. 72). In Asia, more people cultivated the land, allowing for more-intensive farming and higher yields. Dense populations implied that labour was in large supply and wages low, encouraging intensification. In such concentrated activities, animals and machines could be harmful, and little incentive would have existed to develop animal- or machine-based innovations. Thus, the more-intensive farming led to little incentive for technical innovation and, therefore, the lowest standards of living (ibid., p. 74).

In Europe, more land providing lower yields (and implying fewer people could survive) were more suited for animals. Although animals required considerable fodder, they were able to perform certain menial and hard tasks with more power. Oxen and later horses ploughed the earth for humanity – also freeing up human effort for other activities and increasing crop yields by providing manure as a fertiliser. Their power was also being increasingly harnessed in commercial and industrial activities, and for transportation (Langdon 2003).

3 The Limits of the Organic Energy Economy

Evidence in England at the end of the eleventh century indicates that there was one animal (probably an ox) for every two people. In many locations across Europe, the horse replaced the ox as the source of power. A series of technological improvements in horse management during the Middle Ages led to a spectacular increase in draught horses (Langdon 1986, p. 19). The nailed horseshoe protected hooves, reducing splinters, and became common around the ninth century. The harness increased the animal's productivity – until its introduction, a metal bar was placed across the horse's chest and windpipe, strangulating it, and reducing its efficiency by about 80 per cent (Mokyr 1990, p. 36).

Another way in which humans helped generate more food was through the harnessing of other sources of energy. Water and wind power were directed towards the crushing of grains, in particular. The waterwheel was invented about 2500 years ago and, by the end of the Roman Empire, had made its way across Europe to become an established source of power for crushing grain, fulling cloth, tanning leather, smelting and shaping iron and sawing wood where sufficient demand existed for these goods (Reynolds 1983). The expansion of watermills and then windmills, which diffused through Europe in the twelfth century, drove down the cost of producing flour and bread (Langdon 2005). Yet, claims of an industrial power revolution in the medieval era (Carus-Wilson 1941) may have been exaggerated given that, certainly in Britain, work from animals provided considerably more power than water- or windmills (Fouquet 2008).

Despite improvements in the ability to generate more power, the rapid growth in human population in Europe about one thousand years ago led to dramatic pressures on the land. Yields were dropping as less-fertile lands were being exploited. Forests were being encroached upon to provide more agricultural output. This tension between uses of land tended to favour agriculture, which could often generate faster returns, especially when food prices were rising. The late medieval period in Europe saw the first examples of 'energy policy' to address the problem of woodfuel supply (Hatcher 1993; Warde 2003, p. 585).

While the pressures were relieved by the collapse of European populations in the middle of the fourteenth century as a result of the Black Death, they returned by the sixteenth century. Agricultural yields increased considerably in Western Europe from the fifteenth century (Smil 1994, p. 75). Wind power also provided a partial solution by reducing the costs of shipping crops from sources of supply to those of demand (Maddison 2003, p. 47).

More food also led to a rise in the population, which put growing pressure on land both for agricultural and forestry products. Europe was caught in a tension between increasing supply of energy sources and growing demand.

Holland provided a first (partial) success at extricating the economy from the limits of land and creating a modern and industrial economy. By the beginning of the sixteenth century, only one-quarter of the workforce was involved in agriculture, with another 12 per cent in fisheries and 3 per cent in peat digging; 38 per cent were in industrial activities, especially textiles, metalwork and brewing; the rest provided mostly trade and transport services (van Zanden 2003, p. 1016).

A series of agricultural crises in the fourteenth and fifteenth centuries drove the populations towards the urban centres. This generated a large labour force able to work in fisheries and the brewing and textile industries, and to generate economies of scale (and possible learning effects) in production, making its products cheap. The Dutch maritime tradition and its improving ability to harness winds on its sailing ships meant that these products were competitive across much of Europe (ibid., p. 1019). A large trade developed with cities in the Baltic which could supply agricultural products in return, reducing land pressures in Holland (van Zanden 2003, p. 1022).

Holland had managed to remove the land problem through importing grain and exporting high-value goods. The economy flourished in the sixteenth and seventeenth centuries. To manage this transition to an industrial economy it depended on a reliable fuel for heating. The damp countryside of parts of the Low Countries (that is, present Netherlands and Belgium) created large quantities of peat. The Flemish cities, such as Antwerp and Bruges, had already been exploiting these sources of energy in the thirteenth century. Given the slow rate of growth of peat in the soil, it was a non-renewable source of energy. The Flemish cities used up their local sources of peat and had to start importing from nearby areas, such as Brabant and even Holland. Similarly, during the sixteenth century, supplies of peat near Amsterdam were being heavily exploited (either for local uses or export) and started to dwindle. Especially after the crisis of the 1620s, large quantities of peat were available in other parts of the Netherlands that could be imported to Holland and the more urban areas along the wide network of canals of the Low Countries (ibid., p. 1025).

An organic economy can only use energy at the rate at which direct and indirect solar energy can be converted into valuable services. The example of the Dutch Golden Age reflects that solutions could be found to the problem of organic energy supply, but that they were only temporary. The Dutch Golden Age was driven by wind (for transport) and peat (for heat). Peat's supply was dependent on the availability of land, but was a reserve of more concentrated fuel than traditional biomass fuels. In other words, it

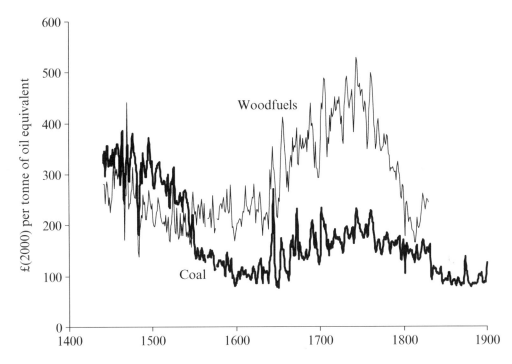

Source: Fouquet (2008).

Figure 1.1   *The price of coal and woodfuels in the United Kingdom (£(2000) per toe), 1440–1900*

was an intermediary between an organic and a mineral fuel. However, had the Dutch economy continued to grow so rapidly with such a large dependence on peat, it would have eventually faced land limits as the reserves were used up, and then its solution would have been to import a more concentrated form of energy with deeper reserves from abroad, which it eventually did by importing coal from Britain in the eighteenth century (van den Wouden 2003, p. 463).

4   The Transition to Fossil Fuels

In Britain, the solution to the tension was found through the use of mineral fuels (Cipolla 1962; Wrigley 1988; Warde 2007; Fouquet 2008). It has been argued that a woodfuel crisis imposed a heavy burden on the British economy in the sixteenth century, forcing an energy transition (Nef 1926). While there may have been localised shortages, the evidence available (Hatcher 2003 and Figure 1.1) puts in question a nationwide crisis at that time. It appears that the substitution towards coal was due to favourable prices of coal for heating, especially in urban centres (Fouquet 2008).

    While there may not have been a woodfuel crisis in the sixteenth century, the introduction of coal did reduce the burden imposed by a constrained land on a growing population. Later, between the 1650s and the 1740s, real woodfuel prices did rise substantially, encouraging certain users and industries to make the transition to coal. It enabled the economy and especially industrial activity to expand to an extent impossible if limited to biomass. For instance, one estimate suggests that by 1800, had the British economy been dependent on woodfuel, a surface area of land equivalent to Britain would have had to be coppiced every year to meet the energy requirements (Wrigley 1988).

Yet, in the same way that the production of biomass energy provided a flow of resources, the extraction of mineral resources created a flow. The stock of reserves was converted into a flow, through the carriage of coal vans and later trains full of coal. In other words, extraction rates and supply infrastructure determined the flow of energy.

In medieval times, many of the British coal seams lay under Church land. Henry VIII's (1509–47) Reformation meant that land owned by the Catholic Church was up for sale. An impetus for the expansion of the coal industry was the transfer of land ownership from the Bishop of Durham to the merchants of Newcastle in the sixteenth century. While the Church had mined coal, the land and what lay beneath it was exploited more vigorously in commercial hands (Hatcher 1993).

The coal industry began to open many more mines and expand to meet the growing demands for heating. From the fifteenth to the end of the seventeenth century, the coal-mining industry grew from a niche business to one of the major generators of wealth in the North-East of England. Around 1500, production was 27000 toe (tonnes of oil equivalent), and increased to about 1.5 million toe in 1700 (ibid.).

As demand grew in the seventeenth century, however, coal supplies were initially inadequate and fuel prices started to rise (see Figure 1.1). A series of transformations helped the coal industry adapt and become one of the pillars of the British economy. First, the development of pumps to remove water from mines enabled much greater depths to be achieved. In the eighteenth century, this was achieved most successfully by using the recently developed steam engines. At the time, steam engines were highly inefficient, burning large quantities of coal. Since coal was very cheap at the pit mouth, inefficiency was of little concern. Their great use for pumping water in coal mines enabled steam engine manufacturers to improve their efficiency and reduce both their operating and capital costs (Kanefsky 1979).

Second, Britain discovered that its vast energy reserves were not limited to the North-East. A number of regions started to compete with the Newcastle trade. The coal industry transformed itself from a localised business to one of the leading sectors of the economy. Third, transport routes were dramatically improved. The improvements to rivers and building of canals enabled industrial regions to reduce the cost of heating services. Also, along the coast, economies of scale were achieved by increasing the size of ships carrying the goods (Hatcher 1993).

However, the switch to coal was not a simple case of reacting to a lack of land and its products. The substitution towards coal had begun in the sixteenth century for certain industries and households. Instead of fossil fuels spectacularly resolving an energy crisis and driving an Industrial Revolution in Britain, the energy transition was a gradual process, lasting more than two hundred years. It depended on industries finding a solution and it being commercially viable. For instance, in the iron industry, the technological solution introduced by Abraham Darby in 1709 that enabled coal, in the form of coke, to be used was not adopted for over fifty years. It required substantial improvements in the efficiency of coke-smelting before it became cheaper than traditional charcoal-based iron (Hyde 1973; King 2005).

By the eighteenth century, many industries had found ways of using coal rather than woodfuels and had adopted them for heating purposes. The improvements in agricultural productivity in the eighteenth century had pushed much of the labour force to the urban centres, which expanded greatly (Campbell 2003). This population needed to keep warm and also use coal, as few had access to wood. In 1500, the British economy used roughly the same amount of energy for heating and power. By 1800, three-quarters of its energy requirements were for heating services – in households, buildings and industry (Fouquet 2008).

Heating services had made the transition from organic to fossil fuels by the beginning of the nineteenth century. Wind and water for power services, although significant, only provided one-tenth of the total power in 1800. Power and transport services (apart from at sea) depended mostly on food and fodder and were still stuck in the organic energy system at the beginning of the nineteenth century (Fouquet 2008).

The means of making the transition to fossil fuels for both power and transport already existed and were used in niche markets. The steam engine and coal had been used to pump water out of mines since the early eighteenth century. During the nineteenth century, its adoption in the cotton industry began the transition for power services (von Tunzelmann 1978), and railways and steam ships enabled the switch for transport services (Harley 1988). By 1900, steam engines provided two-thirds of all power services. By then, railways carried more than 90 per cent of goods and steam ships provided about 80 per cent of all freight services at sea (Fouquet 2008).

The growing demand for coal in the nineteenth century created new concerns about the scarcity of coal (see, for example, Jevons 1865) and the threat of higher prices (Church 1987). However, with only small technical improvements in production methods, coal supply in Britain again managed to expand to meet the growing demand, keeping prices stable throughout much of the nineteenth century (Figure 1.2). This was due to large and accessible reserves, a diversity of types and qualities of coal, a big labour force to draw from and improving means of transportation. For example, in 1830, there were around 100 000 miners, by 1870, nearly 400 000 and by 1913, over one million (Church 1989, p. 12).

Taking a longer-run perspective, it is interesting to see the periods of abundance and scarcity. In the sixteenth and early seventeenth centuries, supply expanded and demand found new uses for coal. For the next hundred years, demand outstripped supply, which had to catch up. It did, ensuring resource abundance, driving down the price, and encouraging the creation of new demands for coal. Demand expanded to meet the large supply (Fouquet 2008).

One of the problems associated with the production and supply of energy resources is that they often require long-term investments. For the British coal industry, there was, at times, a delay between the signal of scarcity and the change in flow of resources resulting from higher investment in extraction, hiring more miners and finding new seams. This created price volatility but no upward trend in the long run.

As few economies had sufficient land and woodfuel resources to meet the large heating demands necessary to industrialise, in the nineteenth century, many countries discovered large coal reserves and followed Britain's lead. Thus, coal provided the source of

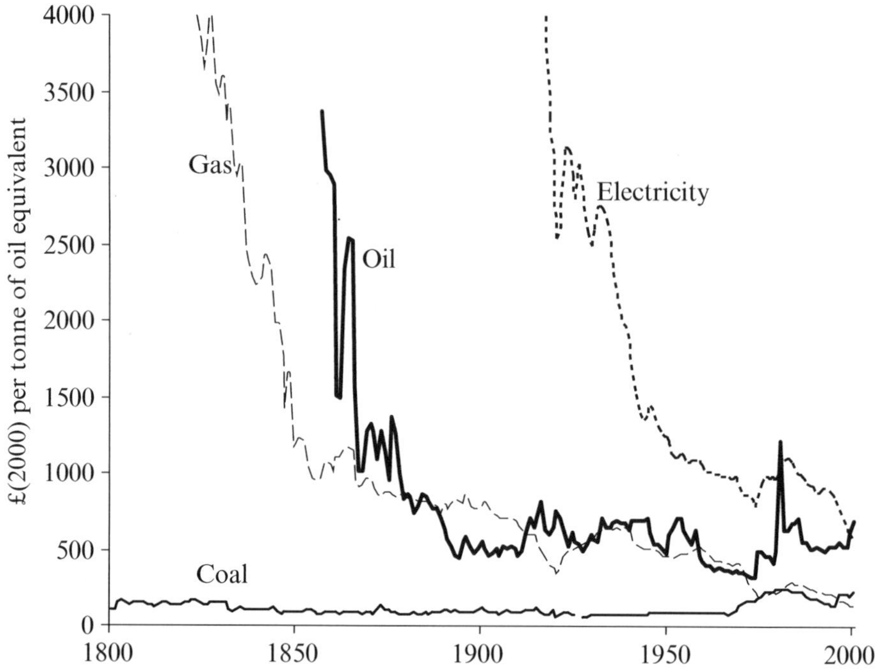

Source: Fouquet (2008).

*Figure 1.2   The price of energy sources in the United Kingdom (£(2000) per toe),
1800–2000*

transition from organic to fossil fuels for industrialising economies, especially in the USA, Germany and other European countries (Schurr and Netschert 1960; Sieferle 2001; Gales et al. 2007).

For instance, in 1850, less than 10 per cent of the USA's energy requirements were met by coal. In 1910, fossil fuels provided 90 per cent of energy needs (Schurr and Netschert 1960, p. 145). The energy transition in the USA took about 60 years, whereas in Britain the same transition took two hundred years, between 1600 and 1800 (Fouquet and Pearson 2003, p. 103). This indicates that, as more of the 'new' energy-using technology is available, the speed of the transition increases. Nevertheless, energy transitions will always be limited by the process of the scrapping of old technologies and the setting up of infrastructure associated with the new energy system.

5   Modern Energy Systems

Coal met energy requirements in many economies into the second half of the twentieth century (Schurr and Netschert 1960; Gales et al. 2007; Fouquet 2008). But, while coal production globally continued to grow into the twentieth century, the fragmentation of supply also reflected its jeopardy as the dominant energy source (Etemad et al. 1991).

The introduction of new energy sources in the nineteenth century provided the next phase in the history of energy. 'Town' gas (derived from coal), petroleum and electricity all started as sources of energy in the emerging market of lighting (Fouquet and Pearson 2003). Their success in the lighting market and the dramatic decline in their prices (see Figure 1.2) encouraged use in other energy service markets where they increasingly ousted coal.

The first oilfields to be exploited on a large scale were in Pennsylvania, in the North-East of the United States, in the 1860s. By the 1880s, one company, Standard Oil, emerged as the main refiner and supplier of petroleum products. It managed to control product quality and prices, providing stability to the oil lighting customer in a volatile market (Yergin 1991).

The introduction and adoption of the internal combustion engine at the beginning of the twentieth century meant that petroleum products were to be used in the much larger market for transport services. The decline in the price of cars between the two world wars led to a huge growth in the demand for gasoline. As Standard Oil was broken up as a result of North American anti-trust laws and more suppliers entered the market, the price of petroleum products gradually fell between the 1930s and early 1970s (see Figure 1.2).

Especially after the Second World War, global production and consumption of oil grew rapidly as the demand for private transport soared and oil began to be used for other services, such as heating and even electricity generation (Figure 1.3). By the early 1970s, despite being the largest oil producer in the world, the USA's consumption exceeded its supply for the first time. This implied that its companies no longer had the ability to increase output to control and stabilise oil prices.

Instead, the Saudi Arabian oil industry had this privilege. As part of OPEC (the Organization of Petroleum Exporting Countries), and in response to North American and European policies in the Middle East, it began to limit supply and raise prices, which led to the oil shock of 1973. This was followed by other fears about supply from the Middle East in 1979 and 1980, triggered by the Revolution in Iran and its war with Iraq, driving the prices up further (Yergin 1991).

The mid-1980s and 1990s saw a glut of oil as many countries drove up or began oil production (see Figure 1.3). With low prices and rapidly expanding developing economies, especially in Asia, consumption increased substantially. The beginning of the twenty-first century saw a return to higher oil prices, due to the growing world demand and the political instability in the Middle East, still the main oil exporting region. But, by the end of the first decade of the twenty-first century, as the global economy has entered a recession, oil prices have fallen again, allowing energy companies to expand their reserves and infrastructure.

Concerns about security of energy supply in the 1960s and 1970s had generated a series of different reactions among importing governments. Some tried to forge strong political ties with countries that had reserves. Others searched and found oil. Many also focused on developing other energy sources.

Gas had initially been produced from coal and used for lighting. It lit up the streets of industrialising nations in the middle of the nineteenth century. In the late nineteenth century, competition from electricity had forced lamp manufacturers to improve the efficiency of their products and gas suppliers to find alternative uses for theirs. The efficiency improvements delayed the uptake of electricity in many countries. The search for new uses also led to the adoption of gas as a smoke-free heating fuel (Thorsheim 2002).

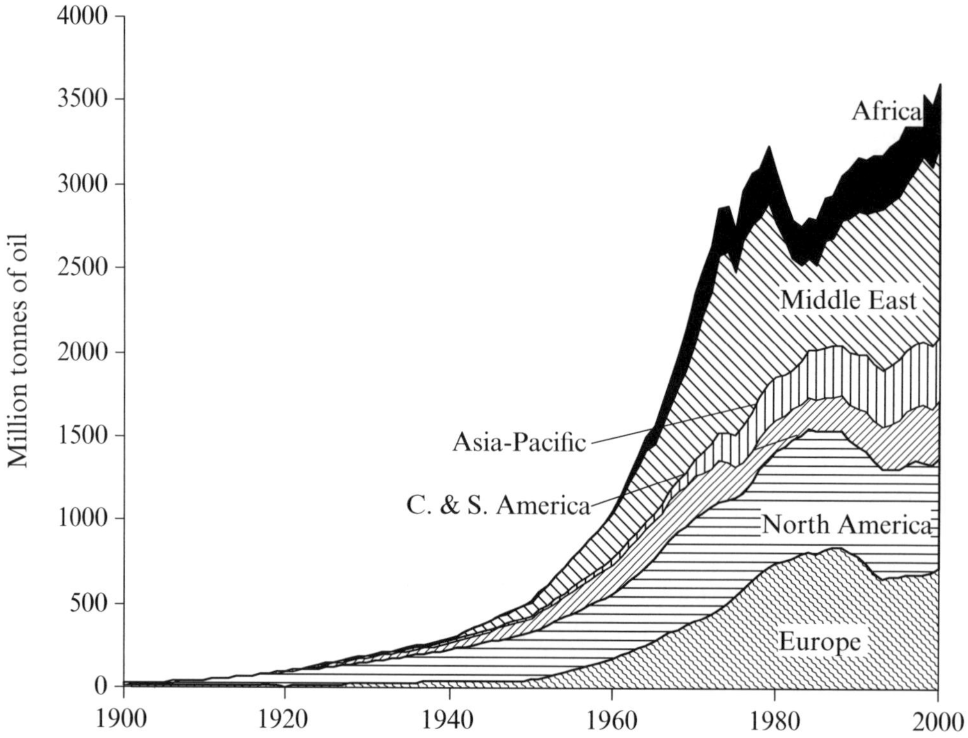

Sources: Mitchell (2003) and BP (2007).

Figure 1.3   World petroleum production by region (mtoe), 1850–2000

'Natural' gas (that is, not converted from coal) tended to be found during the extraction of oil. Often, the gas had been simply burnt at source as it had little market value. Threats relating to oil security of supply had encouraged consumers to start using gas for heating purposes and producers to pipe it to the growing sources of demand. After the oil shocks of the 1970s, the gas market increased rapidly, representing 21 per cent of the global energy market in 2000 (Figure 1.4).

Electricity had been used predominantly for lighting at the end of the nineteenth century. Its use in urban transport services and for industrial power needs had enabled the price of electricity to fall. After all, a power station generating electricity for times of darkness had excess capacity during the day time. Thus, finding uses for electricity throughout the day spread the capital costs.

The electrification of the global economy has radically altered many aspects of productive activities. While electricity could extend and replace human effort like steam engines did, it could provide the services in an easier, more flexible and safer environment. Machines had been driven by a single central steam engine, through a series of shafts and belts. The engine could stop, halting all work; a worker could stop working, implying wasted power; or a taught belt could snap, risking life and limb. An electrical machine allowed each worker to be in control of his or her equipment (Nye 1999). The

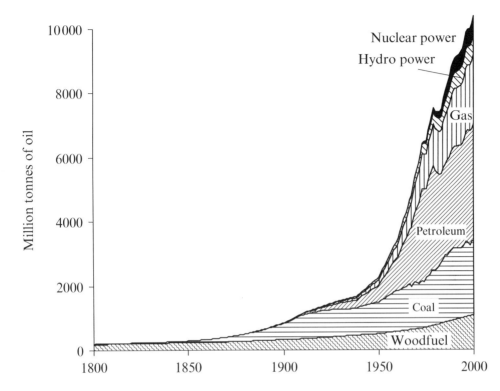

Sources: Etemad et al. (1991), Maddison (1995, 2003) and BP (2007).

Figure 1.4   World primary energy consumption by type (mtoe), 1800–2000

ease and flexibility of electricity in the provision of power and lighting encouraged the electrification of much of the world's economies (Rosenberg 1998).

Before the 1960s, much of the electricity was generated from coal. Oil increased its share of power generation, until the oil shocks of the 1970s. Where possible, many economies had sought to harness hydropower. After the Second World War, a desire for cheap electricity had led many governments along the path of supporting a civil nuclear power programme. While in a few countries, it has provided an important share of their electricity, higher expected costs and safety concerns have stunted nuclear power's growth. In 2000, hydro and nuclear power each provided nearly 6 per cent of global primary energy consumption (see Figure 1.4).

6   The Global Need for Energy

In the twenty-first century, changes in energy supply or demand in one region will have repercussions across the whole planet. Increasingly, the global economy consumes energy in a single and integrated market. Thus, it is worth considering global trends in energy consumption.

From a global perspective, the slow energy transition from woodfuel to coal began in

Table 1.1   Total primary energy consumption (in mtoe) and annual growth rate (from year in previous column)

	1820	1870	1913	1939	1973	2000	2006
Consumption	225	397	1214	1713	6417	10392	12029
Growth rate (%)		1.1	2.6	1.17	4.0	1.8	2.5

Source: See Figure 1.4.

the second half of the nineteenth century. In 1900, woodfuel was estimated to have still provided nearly 40 per cent of the global energy needs. By 1950, fossil fuels met 75 per cent of the total, and in 2000, they provided an estimated 78 per cent. Perhaps the most surprising information is the resilience of biomass fuels, still meeting an estimated 10 per cent of energy requirements around the world (see Figure 1.4).

In 1870, the global economy consumed less than 400 mtoe. It had reached more than 1200 mtoe by 1913, reflecting the industrialisation of numerous Western economies and the growth in coal use. The annual rate of growth was 2.6 per cent (Table 1.1). In 1939, consumption had risen modestly to just over 1700 million. Then, the global economy expanded dramatically up to 1973, reaching nearly 6500 mtoe, rising at a spectacular 4.0 per cent per year. The oil crises slowed the global economy's expansion, yet it is about 13000 mtoe level at the end of the first decade of the twenty-first century.

While a global picture hides much of the detail between countries and regions, to understand the dramatic growth in world energy consumption, it is worth observing per capita use and energy intensity. Per capita energy consumption has increased in two distinct phases: first, it rose from about 1850 up to 1913 and, then, between 1939 and 1979. Current global energy consumption per person has hardly changed since then (Figure 1.5).

Energy intensity, however, shows a more complex path. It fell in the first half of the nineteenth century. This may have reflected the high value placed on manufactured products in the early phases of industrialisation – so, early industrialisation, although using large quantities of energy, generated important increases in GDP. Then, between 1850 and 1913, the heat-intensive activities for heavy industries drove up energy intensity. It has been falling since then, especially after 1979.

7   The Evolution of Energy Policies

The role of government in influencing energy markets has changed dramatically over the last two hundred years. Historically, governments of agrarian and rural economies focused only marginally on 'modern' forms of energy. Governments have had other priorities. Their principal objectives have been the maintenance of power and peace. Peace often was tied in with ensuring that the population had sufficient food to eat, so, attempts were made to stabilise agricultural markets. Ultimately, however, the state was a relatively small body with limited economic influence (Jupp 2006).

In many cases, governments have introduced economic policies, such as new institutions or taxation schemes, with major implications for energy markets. These decisions were rarely concerned with the impact on the energy market, and were often modified

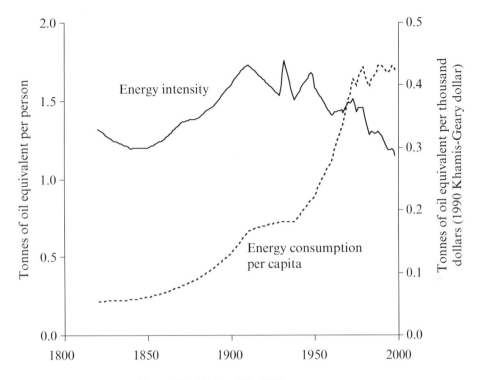

Sources: Etemad (1991), Maddison (1995, 2003) and BP (2007).

Figure 1.5 *World primary fossil fuel and biomass energy consumption per capita and energy intensity, 1820–2000*

or revoked with abrupt changes in incentives for the markets. Apart from a few bans on using particular forests in times of concern about the availability of wood, energy markets tended to follow their own course, disturbed but not disrupted by government (Fouquet 2008).

The transition away from biomass fuels, dependent on land for production, towards fossil fuels, gradually led to an increased involvement of the state in energy markets. The nineteenth and twentieth centuries saw the formation of a number of large energy supply companies, first, of coal and then, oil. During the nineteenth century, coal companies focused on the extraction and distribution process in the industrialising countries, and were subject to only minimal government influence. For instance, the main intervention of government upon the coal industry in the nineteenth century was to improve safety conditions and minimise the death toll relating to mining accidents (ibid.).

In the first half of the twentieth century, cases of supply shortages and of poorly integrated systems (especially among electricity companies) highlighted some potential drawbacks of unregulated competition. Following the Second World War, and the experience of extreme dependence on energy in fuelling and powering the war effort, many countries chose to nationalise their oil and electricity companies. Much of the energy was supplied, therefore, through public monopolies (Chick 2007).

The 1980s saw the rebirth of energy market liberalisation, starting in the United Kingdom (Newbery 1996). This saw the dismantling of the monopolistic structure of energy production and supply. At the beginning of the twenty-first century economies are still involved in this process, such as efforts to promote competition in the Single European Market.

Energy markets traditionally worked with little governance. Nation-states began to appreciate the importance of managing markets to avoid abuses and to promote specific objectives. Certain markets, such as the oil markets, are already fully integrated international markets. For natural gas and electricity, pipelines and interconnections have enabled much of the globe to be linked. Most main energy sources can be moved around to meet the short-term changes in supply and demand. Given the global reach of the energy markets, no organisation is in a position to oversee and potentially regulate them. Thus, they experienced a brief period of being managed, but have slipped the grasp of the policy maker and have become stronger than any individual country's government. The question is whether there will be sufficient belief that the global energy market needs to be managed, and whether an international energy regulator, beyond the European Union, develops.

8   Energy and Its Environmental Effects

One example, which may be the precursor to other supra-national bodies dealing with energy issues, is the United Nations Framework Convention on Climate Change (UNFCCC). It has attempted to coordinate efforts to minimise the impact of greenhouse gas emissions on the climate. The Kyoto Protocol, the agreement on target emissions and mechanisms for potentially meeting them, acts as a modest step towards international cooperation and regulation of environment-related energy behaviour.

The environmental problems of energy production and combustion have existed for hundreds of years. Local and national legislation on air pollution banning the burning of coal in certain areas was introduced as early as the thirteenth century (Brimblecombe 1987). Individual countries have suffered the burden of local energy-inflicted air pollution. For instance, one estimate of the health damage related to smoke placed it at one-quarter of Britain's GDP at the end of the nineteenth century (Fouquet 2008).

There have been international organisations addressing transboundary effects of acid rain. Yet, the efforts of the Kyoto Protocol appear to be on a larger scale, because the perceived implications of inaction are greater and more irreversible.

The Agricultural Revolution probably led to considerable deforestation, which meant that less carbon was absorbed by nature. While this effect on the global climate may have been relatively minor, as far more carbon is trapped in the oceans than in plant life, it was the beginning of an anthropogenic influence on climate (Ruddiman 2005). Since fossil fuels have been burnt and since the Industrial Revolution, the global economy has also been generating and adding to naturally occurring carbon dioxide emissions. The relatively rapid increase in the consumption of fossil fuels and, at the beginning of the twenty-first century, its addition of more than 7 billion tonnes of carbon dioxide each year is having an effect on greenhouse gas concentrations and, therefore, on the Earth's climate (IPCC 2007).

Having industrialised first, heavily dependent on coal, Europe has been the largest polluter in history (Figure 1.6). Given that greenhouse gases act as stocks of pollutants, it is worth identifying the burden imposed by different regions. By 2000, Europe was responsible for about 115 000 billion tonnes of carbon accumulated. North America added 87 000 billion tonnes. It also surpassed Europe in annual contributions in 1999 – and stood at more than 1.8 billion tonnes per year in 2004. Yet, the largest emitter (since 1994) is the Asia-Pacific region, responsible for 2.7 billion tonnes in 2004 (Marland et al. 2007). Since 1990, its annual growth rate has been 4.2 per cent. The Asia-Pacific region's historical addition of carbon to the atmosphere is just under 50 000 billion tonnes – 42 per cent of it, after 1990.

At the beginning of the nineteenth century, renewable energy sources met an estimated 95 per cent of all energy needs around the globe. At the beginning of the twentieth century, it fell to about 38 per cent and down to 16 per cent at the dawn of the twenty-first century.

While the amount of annual solar radiation on Earth is 12 800 times greater than world energy consumption in 2000, without an abrupt transformation of the global energy system, this trend is likely to continue. Investments in renewable energy sources are growing rapidly. However, the incentives do not favour a reduction in the use of fossil fuels. There still exist large reserves of easily extracted fossil fuels. However, without a significant increase in renewable energy sources and a major decline in the use of fossil fuels, global emissions will continue to rise, perhaps faster than they have since 1950.

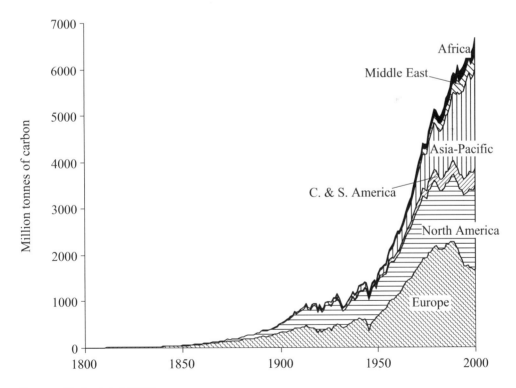

Source: Marland et al. (2007).

Figure 1.6   World carbon dioxide emissions by region, 1800–2000

9 Concluding Remarks

This chapter has tried to provide a very broad perspective on the history of energy use. It focused on the economic forces at work driving trends in energy use, and some of the key technologies that altered these trends. It inevitably ignored many important developments in the history of energy (see Smil 1994 for more detail), yet, it tries to tie the past with the present condition and possible future paths.

Humankind started its story as just another animal consuming the fruits of solar energy. Over the last ten thousand years, the human population has managed to achieve radical changes in its ability to harness energy sources, through a series of technological, managerial and institutional transformations. The Agricultural Revolution enabled humans to intensify agricultural productivity and, therefore, the quantity of energy in the form of food. Over thousands of years, a series of major refinements radically increased agricultural productivity and output, which coincided with step-jumps in the population level.

The Industrial Revolution allowed humankind to remove the land constraints for non-agricultural energy sources. As a result of numerous technological innovations, the shift from an organic- to a fossil-fuel-based economy first led to a huge growth in the consumption of energy for heating purposes, such as iron and other metals, and then, in the generation of power, transport and light (Nordhaus 1997; Fouquet and Pearson 2006; Fouquet 2008).

Central to these developments was the major transformations of the energy system and, in particular, the diversification of energy sources. The large-scale exploitation of coal, petroleum, natural gas, hydroelectricity and uranium and the vast networks of distribution, which began in the nineteenth century and extended to much of the human world in the twentieth century, has led to another leap in energy use. From the beginning of the nineteenth century to the end of the twentieth century, the global economy has managed to harness fifty times more (non-agricultural) primary energy. Given the rise in population, this implies that each person on earth is able to consume eight times more energy (see Figure 1.5).

Naturally, there are large differences in per capita consumption, today. For instance, in 2006, the average person in North America consumed about 7 toe of primary energy; a person in India used around half of one tonne. And, despite substantial increases within developing economies lately – in China, per capita consumption increased from 0.2 tonnes in 1965 to 1.5 in 2006 – a large gap between countries and between regions remains (BP 2007).

Yet, at the beginning of the twenty-first century, energy markets need to be considered not only at a local, national or even regional level, but also as a single global entity. As the overall world economy becomes more integrated, so do energy markets. Coal, petroleum and increasingly natural gas and even electricity markets are dependent on the dynamics of demand and supply around the world. It is probable that phases of abundance and scarcity of energy resources that have implied periods of wealth and of strife in individual cities, countries or continents of the past will now affect the whole world. To minimise these periods of strife – as well as to address other issues, such as to contain abuses of market power as fewer, larger companies seek to control the global market – a single world energy market regulator might be sought.

The focus on the world economy is even more pertinent in relation to environmental problems. Waste assimilation of atmospheric pollution acts at a global level. The global rate of pollution is beyond the planet's assimilation capacity. This global scarcity is starting to signal the need for unified action. The Kyoto Protocol has begun a process of trading the rights to emit carbon dioxide, closely linking the world energy markets to international tradable permit schemes (Fischer 2005). Perhaps, in a not too distant future, the supply of permits will be dictated by the chairman of a global carbon reserve, whose role it is to manage naturally released and anthropogenic greenhouse gas emissions to stabilise the Earth's climate.

Since the Agricultural Revolution, the story of humankind has been transformed by its ability to harness energy. Economies and societies have faced a perpetual cycle of abundance and scarcity along a series of stages of rising consumption of energy and its services. Each new phase of scarcity leads to new pressures and outcomes. Today, scarcity in relation to energy acts on two fronts – on resources and on pollution assimilation. The pressure (whether market prices or articles from climatologists appearing in newspapers) on the economy or politicians will lead to new outcomes and probably some solutions. These may well be the stepping-stones for the next 'stage' in humankind's ability to harness energy.

Note

1. I would like to thank John Langdon for drawing my attention to the many papers on the history of energy in Cavaciocchi (2003).

References

Boserup, E. (1965), *The Conditions of Agricultural Growth: The Economics of Agrarian Change Under Population Pressure*, Allen and Unwin, London.

Brimblecombe, P. (1987), *The Big Smoke: A History of Air Pollution in London Since Medieval Times*, Methuen, London.

British Petroleum (BP) (2007), 'BP Statistical Review of World Energy', available at: http://www.bp.com/productlanding.do?categoryId=6848&contentId=7033471 (accessed 12 July 2008).

Campbell, B.M.S. (2003), 'The uses and exploitation of human power from the thirteenth to the eighteenth century', in Cavaciocchi (ed.), pp. 183–212.

Carus-Wilson, E.M. (1941), 'An industrial revolution of the thirteenth century', *Economic History Review*, **11**, 1–18.

Cavaciocchi, S. (ed.) (2003), *Economia e Energia*, Le Monnier, Florence.

Chick, M. (2007), *Electricity and Energy Policy in Britain, France and the United States since 1951*, Edward Elgar, Cheltenham, UK and Northampton, MA, USA.

Church, R. (1987), *The History of the British Coal Industry, Vol. 3: 1830–1913*, Clarendon Press, Oxford.

Church, R. (1989), 'Production, employment and labour productivity in the British coalfields, 1830–1913: some reinterpretations', *Business History*, **31**, 7–27.

Cipolla, C.M (1962), *The Economic History of World Population*, Pelican Books, London.

Cottrell, W.F. (1955), *Energy and Society: The Relation Between Energy, Social Change, and Economic Development*, McGraw-Hill, London.

Cowan, C.W. and P.J. Watson (1992), *The Origins of Agriculture*, Smithsonian Institute Press, Washington, DC.

Etemad, B., J. Luciani, P. Bairoch and J.-C. Toutain (1991), *World Energy Production 1800–1985*, Librairie Droz, Geneva.

Fischer, C. (2005), 'Project-based mechanisms for emissions reductions: balancing trade-offs with baselines', *Energy Policy*, **33**(14), 1807–23.

Fouquet, R. (2008), *Heat, Power and Light: Revolutions in Energy Services*, Edward Elgar, Cheltenham, UK and Northampton, MA, USA.

Fouquet, R. and P.J.G. Pearson (2003), 'Five centuries of energy prices', *World Economics*, **4**(3), 93–119.
Fouquet, R. and P.J.G. Pearson (2006), 'Seven centuries of energy services: the price and use of lighting in the United Kingdom (1300–2000)', *The Energy Journal*, **27**(1), 139–77.
Gales, B., A. Kander, P. Malanima and M. Rubio (2007), 'North versus South: energy transition and energy intensity in Europe over 200 years', *European Review of Economic History*, **11**(2), 219–53.
Harley, C.K. (1988), 'Ocean freight rates and productivity, 1740–1913: the primacy of mechanical invention reaffirmed', *Journal of Economic History*, **48**(4), 851–76.
Hatcher, J. (1993), *The History of the British Coal Industry*, Vol. I, Clarendon Press, Oxford.
Hatcher, J. (2003), 'The emergence of a mineral-based energy economy in England, c.1550–c.1850', in Cavaciocchi (ed.), pp. 483–504.
Hyde, C.K. (1973), 'The adoption of coke-smelting by the British iron industry, 1709–1790', *Explorations in Economic History*, **10**, 400–407.
IPCC (2007), 'Climate Change 2007: The Physical Science Basis', Contribution of Working Group I to the Fourth Assessment Report of the Intergovernmental Panel on Climate Change, edited by S. Solomon, D. Qin, M. Manning, Z. Chen, M. Marquis, K.B. Averyt, M. Tignor and H.L. Miller (eds), Cambridge University Press, Cambridge, and New York.
Jevons, W.S. (1865), *The Coal Question*, Macmillan, London.
Jones, C.L. (1989), 'Coal, gas and electricity', in R. Pope (ed.), *Atlas of British Economic and Social History since 1700*, Routledge, London, pp. 68–95.
Judson, R., R. Schmalensee and T. Stoker (1999) 'Economic development and the structure of the demand for commercial energy', *The Energy Journal*, **20**(2), 29–58.
Jupp, P. (2006), *The Governing of Britain, 1688–1848*, Routledge, London.
Kanefsky, J.W. (1979), 'The diffusion of power technology in British industry, 1760–1870', PhD thesis, University of Exeter.
King, P. (2005), 'The production and consumption of bar iron in early modern England and Wales', *Economic History Review*, **58**(1), 1–33.
Langdon, J. (1986), *Horses, Oxen and Technological Innovation: The Use of Draught Animals in English Farming from 1066 to 1500*, Cambridge University Press, Cambridge.
Langdon, J. (2003), 'The use of animal power from 1200 to 1800', in Cavaciocchi (ed.), pp. 213–22.
Langdon, J. (2005), *Mills in the Medieval Economy: England 1300–1540*, Oxford University Press, Oxford.
Maddison, A. (1995), *Monitoring the World Economy*, OECD Publications, Paris.
Maddison, A. (2003), 'Growth accounts, technological change, and the role of energy in western growth', in Cavaciocchi (ed.), pp. 43–60.
Malanima, P. (2003), 'Energy system in agrarian societies: the European deviation', in Cavaciocchi (ed.), pp. 61–100.
Marland, G., T.A. Boden and R.J. Andres (2007), 'Global, regional, and national CO_2 emissions', in *Trends: A Compendium of Data on Global Change*, Carbon Dioxide Information Analysis Center, Oak Ridge National Laboratory, US Department of Energy, Oak Ridge, TN.
Mitchell, B.R (2003), *International Historical Statistics (Volumes 1–3), 1750–1988*, Macmillan, Basingstoke.
Mokyr, J. (1990), *Levers of Riches: Technological Creativity and Economic Progress*, Oxford University Press, Oxford.
Nef, J.U. (1926), *The Rise of the British Coal Industry*, Vols I–II, Routledge, London.
Newbery, D. (1996), 'The restructuring of UK energy industries: what have we learned?', in G. MacKerron and P.J.G. Pearson (eds), *The UK Energy Experience: A Model or a Warning?*, Imperial College Press, London, pp. 1–30.
Nordhaus, W.D. (1997), 'Do real output and real wage measures capture reality? The history of lighting suggests not', in T.F. Bresnahan and R. Gordon (eds), *The Economics of New Goods*, Chicago University Press, Chicago, IL.
Nye, D.E. (1999), *Consuming Power: A Social History of American Energies*, MIT Press, Cambridge, MA and London.
Reynolds, T.S. (1983), *Stronger than A Hundred Men: A History of the Vertical Water Wheel*, Johns Hopkins University Press, Baltimore, MD.
Rosenberg, N. (1998), 'The role of electricity in industrial development', *The Energy Journal*, **19**(2), 7–24.
Ruddiman, W.F. (2001), *Earth's Climate: Past and Future*, W.H. Freeman, London.
Ruddiman, W.F. (2005), *Plows, Plagues and Petroleum: How Humans Took Control of Climate*, Princeton University Press, Princeton, NJ and Oxford.
Schurr, S. and B. Netschert (1960), *Energy in the American Economy, 1850–1975*, Johns Hopkins University Press, Baltimore, MD.
Sieferle, R.P. (2001), *The Subterranean Forest: Energy Systems and the Industrial Revolution*, White Horse Press, Cambridge.
Smil, V. (1994), *Energy in World History*, Westview Press, Boulder, CO.

Thorsheim, P. (2002), 'The paradox of smokeless fuels: gas, coke and the environment in Britain, 1813–1949', *Environment and History*, **8**, 381–401.

Unger, R. (1984), 'Energy sources for the Dutch Golden Age', *Research in Economic History*, **9**, 221–52.

van den Wouden, A. (2003), 'Sources of energy in the Dutch Golden Age', in Cavaciocchi (ed.), pp. 445–68.

van Zanden, J.L. (2003), 'The ecological constraints of an early modern energy economy: the case of Holland 1350–1800', in Cavaciocchi (ed.), pp. 1011–30.

von Tunzelmann, G.N. (1978), *Steam Power and British Industrialisation until 1860*, Clarendon Press, Oxford.

Warde, P. (2003), 'Forests, energy and politics in the early-modern German states', in Cavaciocchi (ed.), pp. 585–98.

Warde, P. (2007), *Energy Consumption in England and Wales (1560–2000)*, Consiglio Nazionele delle Ricerche, Istituto di studi sulle Società del Mediterraneo, Napoli.

Wrigley, E.A. (1988), *Continuity, Chance and Change: The Character of the Industrial Revolution in England*, Cambridge University Press, Cambridge.

Yergin, D.H (1991), *The Prize: The Epic Quest for Oil, Money and Power*, Simon & Schuster, London.

2 The theory of energy economics: an overview
Thomas Weyman-Jones

1 Introduction

In reality there is no such subject as energy economics, because energy, although a meaningful concept in the physics or engineering sense, is not a commodity that can be bought and sold in the marketplace. However, individual fuels (primary and secondary electricity, natural gas, oil, coal) can be bought and sold; in this context, primary electricity includes renewable sources and nuclear power. Therefore 'energy economics' is really the economics of fuel markets, and the phrase: energy economics is used for convenience to represent all the useful economic concepts which arise in studying different fuels. The energy industries are organised in different ways in different countries; many are investor owned, especially in the USA and the UK, but state ownership is also common. Many are characterised by economies of scale and hence have considerable market power, which usually leads to them being regulated. Fuels are widely traded in solid, liquid and gaseous form, and are transported all over the world in tankers, pipes and wires.

In some of these fuel markets we can see that it is cheaper to have one company do all the business rather than many. Examples are the national power and gas grid companies engaged in the activity of bulk transmission of electric power and natural gas. Such companies are traditionally referred to as public utilities (although there is no presumption that they are or should be owned by the state). Because these companies are believed to operate most cheaply or efficiently when there is only one of them in each market we call them 'natural monopolies' (that is, the traditional public utilities: water, gas, electricity, telecommunications, have the characteristics known as natural monopoly even when they are not statutory monopolies). Consequently there is a wide public interest in the possibility of regulating their behaviour, and the economics of regulation becomes an intrinsic part of energy economics.[1]

The format of this chapter follows from these fundamental ideas. It begins by looking at the basic economic ideas of resource allocation in capital-intensive fuel industries with emphasis on the nature of cost–benefit analysis of fuel investment decisions, and the consequent implications for efficient market pricing. The topics covered here include the nature of short- and long-run marginal cost of energy supply, the process of investment decision making, and the design of efficient price mechanisms in industries where storage of the product is very costly, and in industries where delivery of the product through a grid differs from the economic activity of creating the product. Both of these features are critical characteristics of the energy industries. When such characteristics stem from the fact that the industry delivers its output through a network of wires or pipes, analysts often use the alternative description: network industries. This is followed by a discussion of the market conditions that are frequently found in the fuel industries.

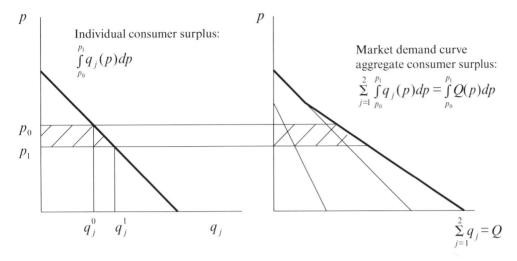

Figure 2.1   Individual and aggregate consumer surplus

2   Cost–Benefit Analysis and Market Structure

A considerable part of energy economics and policy is concerned with optimal resource allocation which is normative rather than positive economics. However, a normative economics approach can be useful to understand market outcomes. This is because a competitive market will mimic the allocation of resources that is achieved in a welfare-maximising model. For that reason, a useful way to simulate the behaviour of a competitive market equilibrium is to characterise the equilibrium through welfare analysis[2] (Mas-Colell et al. 1995, pp. 630–31). Therefore, cost–benefit analysis is a useful building block because it conveniently describes a route to an optimal allocation of resources. In fact cost–benefit analysis has a stronger property as well: the conventional economics approach to efficient resource allocation, the Pareto criterion,[3] is unable to offer policy recommendations when there are losers as well as winners from a policy change. A fundamental tool of cost–benefit analysis is the individual consumer's demand curve which expresses the quantity demanded of any commodity (good or service) as a negative function of its price:

$$q = q(p); \quad q'(p) < 0.$$

This is illustrated in the left-hand panel of Figure 2.1, for one consumer labelled: j. In the figure, the price has fallen from p_0 to p_1 and quantity demanded has risen as a result from q_j^0 to q_j^1. The demand curve expresses the consumer's willingness to pay for different units of a commodity, with the marginal willingness to pay for additional units falling as more units are consumed. The area left of the demand curve but above the price actually being charged at present is called the 'consumer surplus', and it is the willingness to pay for so many units of a commodity minus the amount actually paid for those units, using the traditional Marshallian definition.

When the price of a commodity falls, the consumer obtains additional consumer surplus. In Figure 2.1 (left-hand panel):

$$CS_j = \int_{p''}^{p'} q_j(p)\,dp.$$

Note that this is measurable as an amount of money, and can be measured from an empirically estimated demand function. If the compensated demand function has been measured, that is, the demand function based only on the substitution effect of a price change after compensating for the income effect, an alternative definition is: consumer surplus is the amount of real income a consumer would pay to be as well off after a fall in price as he/she would be if the price had not fallen; this is Hicks's compensating variation definition of consumer surplus.

To arrive at the market demand curve for a commodity, horizontal summation of the individual demand curves of different persons or households, (j) is used:

$$Q(p) = \sum_{1}^{J} q_j(p).$$

Horizontal summation is illustrated in the right-hand panel of Figure 2.1, and is required when the consumption of the good in question by person 1 reduces the amount available for person 2. Such goods (the majority) are called 'private goods'.

The area left of the market demand curve and above the price charged is then the aggregate consumer surplus from consumption of the commodity at the prevailing market price, p^*:

$$CS = \int_{p^*}^{\infty} Q(p)\,dp.$$

This is interpreted as one part of the gross benefit from supply of the commodity at the price p^* and is the economist's universal measure of aggregate consumer welfare. It represents the sum of all persons' compensating variation measures of consumer surplus.

The supplier's revenue is: pQ, and the cost of supplying a commodity is given by the *cost function*:

$$C = C(Q); \quad C'(Q) \equiv \text{Marginal Cost } (MC) > 0.$$

Marginal cost is a forward-looking measure, and represents the change in total cost that would be observed if the level of output were to change by one unit. Aggregate producer surplus is the other part of the gross benefit from supply of the commodity, and this is the area left of the supply curve and below the price charged for the product. The supply curve of a product to a market is the horizontal summation of the marginal cost curves of the individual firms so that producer surplus,[4] written π is:

$$\pi = pQ(p) - C[Q(p)].$$

Then the net economic welfare, $W(p^*)$ from supplying the commodity at a price of p^* is the taken to be the unweighted sum of aggregate consumer surplus (CS) plus aggregate producer surplus π, that is, total revenue minus the cost of supply, $C(Q)$:

$$W(p) = CS + \pi = \left[\int_{p^*}^{\infty} Q(p)\,dp\right] + \{p^*Q(p) - C[Q(p)]\}.$$

The cost–benefit analysis of microeconomic economic policy therefore requires the choice of p^* to maximise this objective with first-order condition depending on the slope[5] of the aggregate market demand curve, $dQ/dp = Q'(p)$:

$$\frac{dW}{dp} = \left(\frac{dCS}{dp}\right) + \left(\frac{d\pi}{dp}\right) = [-Q(p^*)] + \{Q(p^*) + [p^* - C'(Q)]Q'(p^*)\} = 0,$$

and simplifying:

$$\frac{dW}{dp} = \left(p - \frac{dC}{dQ}\right)\frac{dQ}{dp} = (p - MC)\frac{dQ}{dp} = 0,$$

which requires that price should equal marginal cost: $p^* = C'(Q)$. This coincides with the condition for a Pareto optimum, but it is derived by allowing for winners and losers, with the winners gaining enough to sufficiently compensate the losers,[6] and hence is consistent only with the potential Pareto criterion; this is the basis of cost–benefit analysis. In turn, this leads to the prediction that a sufficiently competitive market will choose the socially optimal behaviour of marginal cost pricing. The problem of economic regulation is whether a given market can be expected to be sufficiently competitive. As shown above, the standard social welfare function adopted for policy choices in energy economics is based on unweighted consumer and producer surplus. For energy policy that leads to discrete changes a useful approximation to the consequent welfare change is:

$$\Delta W = \tfrac{1}{2}(p - MC)\Delta Q.$$

It is immediately clear that a necessary condition for the policy to be desirable according to the potential Pareto criterion is that after the policy change there are no further welfare gains, $\Delta W = 0$, in other words, price equals marginal cost. But who gets what when there is a policy change? Conventional cost–benefit does not weight these gains differently, but different weights to reflect social preferences for one group in society *vis-à-vis* another is always a possibility.

What happens when there are large fixed costs to setting up an energy company, for example, the installation of a distribution network: total cost is $C = F + cQ$? This is illustrated in Figure 2.2, where average cost lies above marginal cost because the role of fixed costs is never entirely absent irrespective of the volume of output. Marginal cost pricing at the optimal output Q^* leads to losses, and consequently no firm will enter the industry to supply the commodity, despite the fact that at every output below Q^*, willingness to pay for the product exceeds the total cost, including fixed cost, of supplying it.

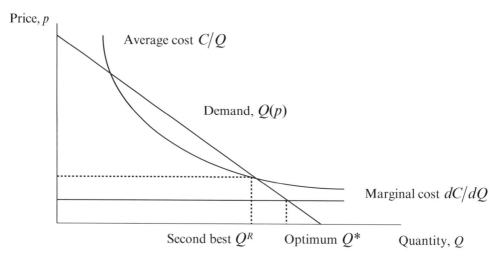

Figure 2.2   First- and second-best allocations for natural monopoly

Try average cost pricing, in this case a specific example of the more general idea of Ramsey pricing. The second-best outcome is at $Q^R(p^R)$ which is the solution to the problem:

$$\max W(p) = CS + \pi = \left[\int_{p*}^{\infty} Q(p)\,dp \right] + \{p^*Q(p) - C[Q(p)]\},$$

such that:

$$p * Q(p) - C[Q(p)] \geq 0.$$

Since there are equal weights on consumer and producer surplus, social welfare improves for every fall in price that gives a monetary transfer from producer to consumer until the constraint is just satisfied. Therefore lower price with an implied welfare gain of $\{p - C'[Q(p)]\} Q'(p)$ until $p^R = C[Q(p^R)]/Q(p^R)$.

3   The Social Discount Rate in Cost–Benefit Analysis

The passage of time is regarded as one of the most important issues in an economic decision since it affects the delay with which benefits arrive and costs can be postponed. The discount rate, i, measures the loss of interest on cash flows that arrive one year from now and so cannot be invested until then. The procedure of discounted cash flow analysis states that the standard formula for net present value (NPV) (including both negative and positive cash flows, where each cash flow is assumed to occur at the *beginning* of the year) is:

$$NPV = x_0 + \frac{x_1}{1 + i} + \frac{x_2}{(1 + i)^2} + \ldots + \frac{x_t}{(1 + i)^t} + \ldots + \frac{x_T}{(1 + i)^T} = \sum_{t=0}^{t=T} \frac{x_t}{(1 + i)^t}.$$

Projects with a positive net present value are worth doing. A useful version of the present value formula occurs when the cash flow is expected to be the same in every year: $(x/i)[1 - (1 + i)^{-T}]$. This is the net present value of an annuity.

What is the appropriate choice for the discount rate i in cost–benefit analysis? There are two suggested solutions for the choice of social discount rate (SDR): the social time preference rate (STP), and the social opportunity cost of capital (SOC).

Begin with a social welfare function that depends on the level of consumption in different periods: $W = \phi(C_0, C_1, \ldots)$. This weights the levels of total consumption for society in each period (t) (including the distribution among individuals, j). One example of this social welfare function is:

$$W = \sum_t \sum_j \delta(t) U_j(C_{jt}),$$

where:

$$U_j(C_{jt}) = \frac{1}{1 - \eta} C_{jt}^{1 - \eta}.$$

If society consisted of a single individual, $j = 1$, who is assumed to have diminishing marginal utility, then a specific example of the social welfare function could be:

$$W = 2\sqrt{C_0} + 2\sqrt{C_1}.$$

This example is a special case corresponding to $\delta(t) = 1$ and $\eta = \frac{1}{2}$. More generally, this is an example where the present and future generations are weighted exactly equally:

$$\delta(0) = \delta(1) = \cdots = \delta(t) = \cdots = 1.$$

Note that this example has the property that when present and future consumption is the same, the marginal social welfare of consumption is the same, so that the marginal rate of substitution between present and future consumption is unity. Consequently in this case the generational weights will not affect the fundamental choice of the social discount rate. Figure 2.3 illustrates this example by using the property of 45° lines, and it can be seen that society's preference for present over future consumption is represented by the slope of the welfare contour:

$$dC_1/dC_0 = -[(\partial W/\partial C_0)/(\partial W/\partial C_1)] = -1 = -C_1/C_0 \Leftrightarrow C_1 = C_0.$$

Another special example of the social welfare function corresponds to $\eta = 1$. It plays a major role in the UK government report on the economics of climate change (Stern 2006).

$$W = \sum_t \sum_j \delta(t) \ln C_{jt}.$$

In Figure 2.4, the consumption possibility frontier represents the rate at which present consumption can be turned into future consumption in the economy's

Consumption next period, C_1

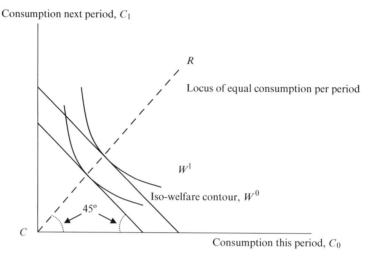

Figure 2.3   Equal welfare weights for current and future consumption

Consumption next period, C_1

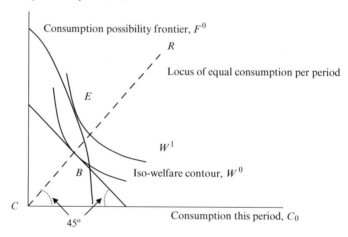

Figure 2.4   Positive marginal social return to capital requires lower consumption in the current period even when there are equal welfare weights for current and future consumption

production of real national income, that is, the rate of return to saving and investment. Consider a simple derivation of this frontier for two periods: this period is $t = 0$ and next period is $t = 1$. Suppose the economy starts with a capital stock of K_0 and that the maximum output available for consumption is $f(K)$. The fundamental constraint limits the sum of total consumption over the two periods to the total output available from the capital stock. Period 1's capital, K_1, is equal to the initial stock plus any saving (that is, output – consumption) done in period 0. Assume for the present that capital does not wear out.

The constrained optimisation model for choosing the social discount rate is shown below:

$$\max W = \phi(C_0, C_1)$$

$$\text{s.t. } C_0 + C_1 = f(K_0) + f[K_0 + f(K_0) - C_0].$$

The Lagrangean function is:

$$L = \phi(C_0, C_1) + \lambda(C_0 + C_1 - \{f(K_0) + f[K_0 + f(K_0) - C_0]\}),$$

with first-order conditions:

$$\partial L / \partial C_0 = \partial \phi / \partial C_0 + \lambda[1 + f'(K_1)] = 0,$$

$$\partial L / \partial C_1 = \partial \phi / \partial C_1 + \lambda = 0,$$

$$\partial L / \partial \lambda = (C_0 + C_1 - \{f(K_0) + f[K_0 + f(K_0) - C_0]\}) = 0.$$

Eliminating λ yields the tangency condition:

$$\frac{\partial \phi / \partial C_0}{\partial \phi / \partial C_1} = [1 + f'(K_1)].$$

This is shown at point E in Figure 2.4, where:

$$dC_1 / dC_0 = -[(\partial W / \partial C_0)/(\partial W / \partial C_1)] = -[1 + f'(K)] \Leftrightarrow C_1 > C_0.$$

In general, therefore, the social discount rate should be different from zero, because otherwise the marginal product of capital is treated as zero. The implication of discounting the future to reflect that positive return to capital is that society should refrain from consumption today to build up capital for the future.

The equilibrium condition can be rearranged to give:

$$\frac{\partial \phi / \partial C_0}{\partial \phi / \partial C_1} = 1 + \left(\frac{\partial \phi / \partial C_0 - \partial \phi / \partial C_1}{\partial \phi / \partial C_1} \right) = [1 + f'(K_1)].$$

The left-hand side can be expanded further:

$$1 + \left(\frac{\partial \phi / \partial C_0 - \partial \phi / \partial C_1}{\partial \phi / \partial C_1} \right) = 1 + \left(\frac{\partial \phi / \partial C_0 - \partial \phi / \partial C_1}{dC} \frac{C}{\partial \phi / \partial C_1} \frac{dC}{C} \right).$$

If it is assumed that the weights on intergenerational consumption are constant at $\delta(t) = 1$, then this expression representing the left-hand side of the equilibrium condition can be interpreted as:

$$1 + \left(\frac{dMU}{dC} \frac{C}{MU} \frac{dC}{C} \right) = 1 + (\eta \Delta \log C),$$

where η is the elasticity of the marginal utility of consumption:

$$\eta = (dMU/dC)(C/MU),$$

and $\Delta \log C$ is the growth rate of consumption.

However, for reasons to be explored later in the context of Stern (2006), economists sometimes do assume that generations are weighted differently, that is, that there is a positive rate of pure time preference resulting in the discounting of the welfare of a future population, that is,

$$\delta(t) = 1/(1 + \delta)^t.$$

In this case the social welfare function would be written in the form:

$$W = U(C_0) + [U(C_1)/(1 + \delta)].$$

The slope of the welfare contour must take account of this intergenerational rate of pure time preference, so that the social time preference rate becomes:

$$-\frac{dC_1}{dC_0} = (1 + \eta \Delta \log C)(1 + \delta) \approx (1 + \delta + \eta \Delta \log C).$$

The right-hand side of the equilibrium condition can also be expanded:

$$1 + f'(K)$$

$$= 1 + \{f'(K)[f(K)/K]K/f(K)\} = 1 + (\Delta \log Y/\Delta \log K)(Y/K) = 1 + (\alpha Y/K).$$

In this expression, $f(K) \equiv Y$ is the real income producible by the capital stock, and α is the elasticity of real national income with respect to capital. The common tangent slope at E in Figure 2.4 is the discount factor to be applied to socially desirable investments:

$$1 + SDR = 1 + [\delta + \eta(\Delta \log C)] = 1 + (\alpha Y/K),$$

that is,

$$SDR = STP = SOC.$$

The left-hand side of the basic equilibrium condition is the rate of social time preference, *STP*, while the right-hand side is the rate of social opportunity cost of capital, *SOC*. Note that neither side allows for risk, because each individual social investment project is assumed to have returns per head of the population that are small relative to and uncorrelated with national income.

Estimating this discount factor is problematic. Suppose, which can usually be expected to be the case, that the economy is not at an efficient equilibrium, but is at a point such as B in Figure 2.4, where the economy is underinvesting (that is, overconsuming) for next year compared with point E. Here the *STP* rate, the left-hand side of the equilibrium condition, is given by the flatter slope of the welfare contour compared with the *SOC* rate, the right-hand side of the equilibrium condition, which is given by the steeper slope of the production possibility frontier. Using either of these two rates to compute the social discount rate will result in an error: when there is underinvestment: $STP < SDR < SOC$.

Now that the essential building blocks of cost–benefit analysis have been established, the optimal allocation of resources in energy economics can be investigated.

4 Marginal Cost and Investment Decisions in Energy Supply

The application of cost–benefit analysis in energy economics was pioneered at Électricité de France in the 1950s (see Boiteux 1960). It came into English economics through the work of Turvey (1967, 1971) at the UK Electricity Council and subsequently spread worldwide through the work of Turvey and Anderson (1977), and Rees (1984). Other important theoretical contributions have been made by Crew and Kleindorfer (1979) (uncertainty and pricing), Littlechild (1970) (non-linear programming models), Wenders (1976) (tariff schedule implications) and Bohn et al. (1983) (spot and real-time pricing), among others. The textbook model needs to be amended to take account of capital-intensive energy production, transmission and distribution (Berrie, 1983; Stoft 2002). A principal distinction is between output and capacity to produce output. Both are measured in the same units: electricity = kilowatt-hours per hour (= kilowatts); gas: therms per day; oil: barrels per day or tonnes per year; coal: tonnes per year; renewables: tonnes of oil equivalent per year (that is, the amount of heat generated that is the same as the amount generated by burning 1 tonne of oil).

Assume that one unit of plant and equipment is used to produce one unit of output, and that it costs £c per period to hire this plant. Alternatively it costs £c per period to repay with interest the loan used to buy the plant. Once installed, it costs £r per period to operate 1 unit of plant to produce 1 unit of output. Note that r is the running or operating cost of 1 unit of power production; c is capacity cost of 1 unit of power production. Operating cost is constant up to the level of capacity installed, then it is infinite because no more capacity is available. Figure 2.5 illustrates this.

In this model:

$$SRMC = \begin{cases} r \text{: demand} \ \leq \ \text{capacity} \\ \infty \text{: demand} \ > \ \text{capacity} \end{cases}$$

$$LRMC = r + c.$$

The *SRMC* (short-run marginal cost) curve shifts to the right whenever more capacity is installed, and it always intersects *LRMC* (long-run marginal cost) from below, as shown in Figure 2.5.

Optimal resource allocation using cost–benefit analysis therefore requires:

1. Set price, $p = SRMC$ to ration demand to capacity, or to make maximum use of spare capacity: $p = m$, where m is whatever level of *SRMC* intersects the demand curve.

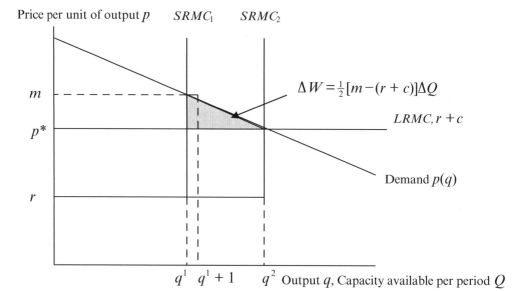

Figure 2.5   Single-period marginal net benefit of increasing capacity by 1 unit and by
ΔQ = q² − q¹ units

2.   Compute the net benefit of changing capacity, and invest in or scrap capacity until
the net benefit has been used up:

$$\Delta W = \tfrac{1}{2}(p - LRMC)\Delta q = \tfrac{1}{2}[m - (r + c)]\Delta q = 0.$$

This net benefit for a discrete change in capacity is shown as the shaded triangle of consumer and producer surplus[7] in Figure 2.5. At this point:

$$p^* = SRMC = LRMC.$$

It is often convenient to work in terms of a single unit change in capacity: $\Delta q = 1$ and
in this case the net benefit is illustrated in Figure 2.5 by the rectangular sliver with base
equal to $q^1 + 1 - q^1$. The marginal net benefit of 1 unit of capacity is:

$$dW/dp = (p - LRMC)(dq/dp) = [m - (r + c)](dq/dp).$$

Now think of a single unit of capacity and suppose it lasts for T years. The net present
value of installing that unit over its life is:

$$NPV = \sum_{t=0}^{t=T} \frac{[m - (r + c)]}{(1 + i)^t},$$

and the optimal decision is to invest if $NPV > 0$. An alternative expression uses the total
cost of installing 1 unit of capacity instead of the periodic repayment:

$$NPV = -C + \sum_{t=0}^{t=T} \frac{(m-r)}{(1+i)^t}.$$

In the energy industry it is customary to write this in the reverse as net effective cost of capacity (*NEC*):

$$NEC = C - \sum_{t=0}^{t=T} \frac{(m-r)}{(1+i)^t},$$

and invest if $NEC < 0$.

The *NEC* is the cost of installing 1 unit of capacity less the lifetime opportunity cost savings of having that unit and therefore not having to ration demand. Note the ingredients required in this recipe: (i) forecast of the market-clearing price of energy up to T years ahead (m), (ii) choice of discount rate, (i), and (iii) forecast of the technically efficient operating cost of capacity up to T years ahead.

This has led to a well-known controversy. If demand fluctuates or is uncertain, then *SRMC* pricing may become very volatile and scrapping and investment policy may show many changes of direction. Some economists have suggested setting price = *LRMC* all the time, and using non-price rationing, or maintaining surplus capacity to match demand with supply. This was the UK Treasury view in the 1970s–1980s for the electricity supply industry. The two opposing viewpoints are represented by Munasinghe and Warford (1982) and Newbery (1985). The analysis just completed sets out the essence of the merchant investment model of electricity and gas production. It proceeds as if each capacity investment decision is taken separately by a different competitive firm or merchant. This is the model that lies at the core of many major studies of power plant investment such as MIT (2004).

Much policy analysis of individual power plant and renewable technology decisions takes the merchant investor approach but it is not clear how to compare different technology choices in this model. The net present value criterion applies to a single plant type but different plant types may have different lifetime durations. One solution for comparing different plant types uses a system-based approach discussed later in this chapter. Another solution to this comparison problem which can be applied to the merchant investor problem is to use the annuitised *NEC*s for different technologies (Rees 1973).[8] Imagine $s = 1 \ldots S$ different technologies, with different lives: $T(s)$. Compute the annuity factor for each, that is, the annual constant sum for which the present value is equal to the *NEC* (or *NPV*) of the corresponding technology:

$$A \left\{ C^s - \sum_{t=0}^{t=T(s)} [(m_t^s - r_t^s)/(1+i)^t] \right\} = (i \times NEC^s)/[1 - (1+i)^{-T(s)}].$$

Note the appropriate value for m_t^s varies with the type of capacity being evaluated. Choose the technology with the lowest annuitised *NEC* or highest annuitised *NPV*.

Another approximation used in many studies of energy investments, is based on levelised discounted cost. The purpose is to obtain an equivalent energy price (expressed in terms of gas or electricity or oil and so on) for each technology. This ignores system implications, and in effect treats each separate capacity investment as a mini-supply industry of its own. It asks what constant price through time, $\bar{p}$, would allow a plant operating independently to break even?

$$\sum_{t=1}^{t=T(s)} [\overline{p}^s q_t^s/(1 + i)^t] = C^s + \sum_{t=1}^{t=T(s)} [r_t^s q_t^s/(1 + i)^t],$$

so that the levelised discounted cost, *LDC* is:

$$\overline{p}^s = \frac{C^s + \sum_{t=1}^{t=T(s)} [r_t^s q_t^s/(1 + i)^t]}{\sum_{t=1}^{t=T(s)} [q_t^s/(1 + i)^t]},$$

that is, the present value of lifetime costs relative to the present value of lifetime energy delivered.

Figure 2.5 has become the most widely used investment tool by energy regulators, and governments, although not necessarily by energy utilities. Many widely publicised studies of electricity generation costs, for example, calculate *LDC* for different plant types and then recommended on the basis of lowest *LDC*.

There are several objections to this method of cost evaluation, although its ease of use and apparent financial soundness makes it very popular:

1. The forecast of energy refers to that generated by the plant, not the demand on the system so it assumes that the plant will largely maintain its position in the merit order of relative operating costs.
2. The calculation takes no account of the mix of other plant types on the system, and does not calculate running cost savings relative to these other plant types.
3. The calculation directly compares plants with different lives.

All of these factors mean that *LDC* expresses what the average discounted price of electricity would be in a hypothetical situation in which all of a utility's generating system was converted to the plant in question. *LDC* is logically coherent as an accounting calculation, but whether it is economically relevant to cost-minimising plant choice is another question.

5   Peak-load Pricing

The analysis can be extended to cover several periods of demand when energy cannot be stored from one period to the next. The critical idea is that a period – day, week, month, year – is composed of a cycle of subperiods each with its own demand schedule. For example, in electricity supply a 24-hour day consists of two demand subperiods: daytime peak demand and night-time off-peak demand. In telecoms we might distinguish weekday from weekend calls in a 7-day cycle of subperiods. Gas demand fluctuates between summer and winter. Figure 2.6 assumes two subperiods of equal length in each cycle for convenience, labelled with superscript 1 for off-peak demand and superscript 2 for peak demand. The lower demand curve ($p^1(q)$ corresponding to the prices labelled p_0^1 and p_1^1) represents off-peak demand, and it lies entirely below the upper demand curve ($p^2(q)$ corresponding to the prices labelled p_0^2 and p_1^2) which represents peak demand).

The cost assumptions are a development of those used earlier. The critical aspect of

Price per unit of output *p*

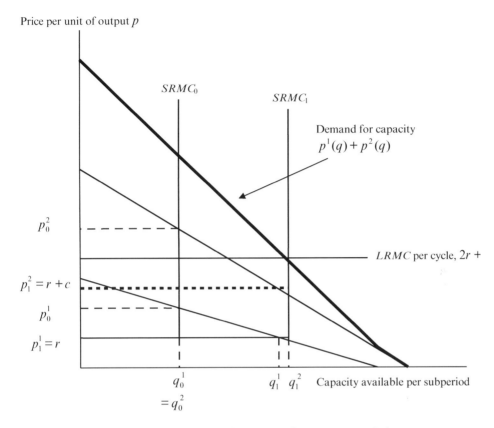

Figure 2.6 Two-period peak and off-peak pricing when capacity is below optimum:
$p_0^1 + p_0^2 > 2r + c$, and at the optimum: $p_1^1 + p_1^2 = 2r + c$

capacity is that it is available for both peak and off-peak demand. These demands are not rivals for the same capacity. This is called the 'public good nature of peak demand' and allows us to sum the demand curves for each subperiod vertically to obtain a demand for capacity curve for the cycle of subperiods.

Once installed, it costs £r per subperiod to operate 1 unit of plant for 1 subperiod to produce 1 unit of output per subperiod. Capacity that produces 1 unit of output for the whole cycle incurs £$2r$ operating cost. The investment rule requires that price $= LRMC = 2r + c$, but price for the cycle is a hypothetical concept constructed by summing the peak and off-peak demand curves vertically to represent the demand for capacity curve: $p^1(q) + p^2(q)$. Now the pricing rule requires that demand is rationed to capacity in each subperiod, by charging a price equal to or greater than operating cost, r:

$$p^1 = r + k_1,$$

$$p^2 = r + k_2.$$

The investment rule requires that the vertical summation of the peak and off-peak prices should cover $LRMC = 2r + c$ for the cycle of subperiods:

$$p^1 + p^2 = (r + k_1) + (r + k_2) = 2r + c \Rightarrow k_1 + k_2 = c.$$

The general properties of the solution are clear from Figure 2.6. Two different positions are illustrated. With the upper limit to capacity given by the $SRMC_0$ curve, the prices which ration demand to capacity are p_0^1 in the off-peak period, and p_0^2 in the peak period. At this point both prices exceed operating cost, and each subperiod's demand makes a contribution to capacity cost, the capacity payment (k_1 or k_2, with $k_2 > k_1$). The distances $p_0^1 - r$ and $p_0^2 - r$ represent these capacity payments in Figure 2.6 when capacity is limited along $SRMC_0$. However, $SRMC_0$ is not an equilibrium outcome; there is a positive net benefit to increasing capacity, represented in Figure 2.6 by the fact that the vertically summed demand for capacity curve $p^1(q) + p^2(q)$ intersects $LRMC$ further to the right at a capacity level represented by $SRMC_1$. The willingness to pay for an extra unit of capacity at the margin exceeds the marginal cost of another unit of capacity. This net benefit is captured by expanding capacity until $p^1(q) + p^2(q) = 2r + c$, and at this level the prices which ration demand to capacity are p_1^1 in the off-peak period, and p_1^2 in the peak period. Figure 2.6 illustrates two different possible shapes for the demand profile and the distribution of capacity payments across periods. At the initial capacity level represented by $SRMC_0$, both off-peak and peak prices exceed the operating cost in order to ration demand to capacity. This has the effect of removing the actual peak in demand and the resulting load profile is flat with the same power consumption in both subperiods: $q_0^1 = q_0^2$. However, in this example, it is the strength of peak demand that generates most of the positive net benefit of expanding capacity. When this has occurred, the optimal prices are such that all of the capacity cost is recovered from the peak period: $p_1^2 = r + c$ while the off-peak demand covers operating cost only: $p_1^1 = r$. A consequence of this is that the load profile is no longer flat and an actual peak in consumption has occurred: $q_1^1 < q_1^2$.

Another useful way of thinking of the issue is this. If the only way of meeting peak demand is to build more capacity, the difference between the peak and off-peak prices must equal the willingness to pay for more capacity at the peak less the willingness to pay for more capacity in the off-peak period: $k_2 - k_1 \leq c$.

6   A Simplified Spot Pricing Model with and without Random Demand

An important model of energy markets such as gas and electricity is the competitive spot pricing equilibrium where the corresponding welfare-maximising equilibrium is analysed using Kuhn–Tucker nonlinear programming analysis (similar to classical Lagrangean optimisation) to construct a simple model. A much more detailed review of this topic is contained in the masterly survey paper by Crew et al. (1995), who, in particular, discuss the issue of modelling actual rather than planned consumer surplus.

$B(y_t)$ is the aggregate benefit function, associated with demand of y in period t.

Assume that the marginal benefit of electricity at a given level of consumption is its market price, $B'(y_t^*) = p_t$. The aggregate benefit could be the consumer surplus plus the revenue component of producer surplus:

$$B(y_t) = \int_0^{y_t^*} p_t(y_t)\,dy_t,$$

that is, the area under the inverse demand function $p_t(y_t)$. Net welfare benefit is then $B(y_t) - Cost$. Assume that there is a finite value for the aggregate benefit of the first unit of consumption: $B(0) = V^*$. This is taken as the willingness to pay to avoid loss of consumption, and in energy market terms is the *value of lost load*.

x_t is the load produced in period t which may differ from the demand y_t,
q is the capacity installed for all periods $t = 1 \ldots T$,
e_t is the excess of demand over output load available in period t, so that
$e_t \equiv y_t - x_t$; therefore e_t is the random variable in the model when uncertainty of demand is permitted,
r_t is the operating cost of output per unit in period t, and
β is the unit cost of new capacity installed; installed capacity is $q^* = q/a$ where a is availability of capacity.

When there is no uncertainty, the standard model for one plant and many equal length subperiods is:

$$\max W = \sum_{t=1}^{t=T} B(y_t) - \sum_{t=1}^{t=T} r_t x_t - \beta q,$$

subject to the demand constraints: $x_t \geq y_t$, $t = 1 \ldots T$ with dual variables: m_t and the capacity constraints: $x_t \leq q$, $t = 1 \ldots T$ with dual variables: k_t. The Lagrangean is:

$$L = \sum_{t=1}^{t=T} B(y_t) - \sum_{t=1}^{t=T} r_t x_t - \beta q + \sum_{t=1}^{t=T} m_t(x_t - y_t) + \sum_{t=1}^{t=T} k_t(q - x_t)$$

The firm chooses to maximise net economic benefit with respect to y_t, x_t, q, because it chooses capacity, price and output simultaneously, but not independently. The necessary conditions are:

$$\partial L/\partial y_t = p(y_t) - m_t \leq 0, \quad y_t(\partial L/\partial y_t) = 0, \quad t = 1 \ldots T,$$

$$\partial L/\partial x_t = -r_t + m_t - k_t \leq 0, \quad x_t(\partial L/\partial x_t) = 0, \quad t = 1 \ldots T,$$

$$\partial L/\partial q = \beta - \sum_t k_t \leq 0, \quad q(\partial L/\partial q) = 0,$$

$$\partial L/\partial m_t = x_t - y_t \geq 0, \quad m_t(\partial L/\partial m_t) = 0, \quad t = 1 \ldots T,$$

$$\partial L/\partial k_t = q - x_t \geq 0, \quad k_t(\partial L/\partial k_t) = 0, \quad t = 1 \ldots T.$$

Assume an interior optimum: $y_t, x_t, q > 0$, then these conditions are written:

$p_t = m_t$: price equals marginal cost on the system,
$m_t = r_t + k_t$: system marginal cost equals operating cost plus capacity payment, and
$\sum_t k_t = \beta$: sum of periodic capacity payments equals the cost of capacity.

These conditions apply to a span of time periods that could cover one day or a cycle of subperiods, but they generalise to optimisation over many years with the addition of a discount factor; for example, to make an investment decision compare the present value of lifetime capacity payments to the lifetime capacity cost:

$$\sum_t [k_t/(1 + i)^t] = \beta.$$

The conditions also generalise to many different types of capacity: $s = 1 \ldots S$ with the addition of an appropriate subscript, and an aggregated form of the demand constraint:

$$\sum_{s+1}^{s=S} x_{st} - y_t \geq 0.$$

Then, for example, the marginal cost calculation is:

$$m_{1t} = r_{1t} + k_{1t} = \ldots = m_{st} = r_{st} + k_{st} = m_{St} = r_{St} + k_{St}.$$

This last result is illustrated in Figure 2.7, which is based on Turvey (1971).

In the figure, five different types (or vintages) of capacity are shown with installed values of $Q_1 \ldots Q_5$. They are arrayed in ascending order of operating cost to represent the idea of the merit order of plant dispatch. Critically the long-run marginal cost is no longer immediately obvious. Since the optimisation solves the pricing and investment model simultaneously, the system marginal cost is a measure of both short- and long-run marginal cost.

With uncertainty, model specification is particularly important. The basic idea in this model is to penalise the proximity of load to available capacity, and this can be demonstrated in a very simple setting. Load shedding or the use of unsatisfied demand is now included in the model. In particular, it is necessary to distinguish between potential demand associated with the current price and the actual load which can be delivered. This simple model is based on Stoft (2002, p.136).[9] It uses the concept of lost load, served load and states that the sum of the two is defined as load: $y_t \equiv x_t + e_t$. The difference between potential demand and actual load can now be positive: $e_t \equiv y_t - x_t$, and this random variable has a known probability density function, $f(e_t)$. The cumulative distribution function defines the probability of any given size of outage:

$$F(e_t^*) = \int_{-\infty}^{e_t^*} f(e_t) de_t = \text{prob}(e_t \leq e_t^*),$$

and two values are of interest: the probability of non-positive outage (no load shedding), $F(0)$, and the probability of positive outage: $1 - F(0)$.

The cost of load which is shed is: V^* per unit of $y_t - x_t = e_t$, that is, the value of lost

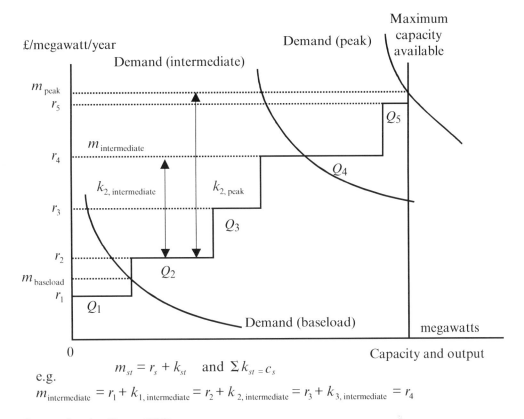

$$m_{st} = r_s + k_{st} \quad \text{and} \quad \Sigma k_{st = c_s}$$

e.g.

$$m_{\text{intermediate}} = r_1 + k_{1,\text{intermediate}} = r_2 + k_{2,\text{intermediate}} = r_3 + k_{3,\text{intermediate}} = r_4$$

Source: Based on Turvey (1971).

Figure 2.7 Multiplant and multiperiod marginal cost of energy generation

load. The demand constraints of the certainty model remain: $x_t - y_t \geq 0$; however, they will have shadow prices that include the probability that the constraint is binding. The constraint may be violated if load shedding is allowed, and then this is penalised by an additional term in costs that again reflects the probability of this occurring, that is, the probability of lost load: $1 - F(0)$. The problem has the Lagrangean function:

$$L = \sum_{t=1}^{t=T} B(y_t) - \sum_{t=1}^{t=T} r_t x_t - \beta q - \sum_{t=1}^{t=T} [1 - F(0)] V^*(y_t - x_t)$$

$$+ \sum_{t=1}^{t=T} [m_t F(0)](x_t - y_t) + \sum_{t=1}^{t=T} k_t(q - x_t).$$

Note how the demand constraints have been replaced by an expression composed of two terms: the first records positive outages: $y_t - x_t \equiv e_t > 0$ which are associated with an expected monetary cost, $[1 - F(0)]V^*$, and the second records non-positive outages with an expected shadow cost: $F(0)m_t$. The necessary conditions for this simplified statement of the problem read:

$$\partial L/\partial y_t = p(y_t) - [1 - F(0)]V^* - F(0)m_t \le 0, \quad y_t(\partial L/\partial y_t) = 0, \quad t = 1 \ldots T,$$

$$\partial L/\partial x_t = -r_t + [1 - F(0)]V^* + F(0)m_t - k_t \le 0, \quad x_t(\partial L/\partial x_t) = 0, \quad t = 1 \ldots T,$$

$$\partial L/\partial q = \beta - \sum_t k_t \le 0, \quad q(\partial L/\partial q) = 0,$$

$$\partial L/\partial[F(0)m_t] = x_t - y_t \ge 0, \quad F(0)m_t\{\partial L/\partial[F(0)m_t]\} = 0, \quad t = 1 \ldots T,$$

$$\partial L/\partial k_t = q - x_t \ge 0, \quad k_t(\partial L/\partial k_t) = 0, \quad t = 1 \ldots T.$$

Assume an interior optimum: $y_t, x_t, q > 0$, then these conditions can now be interpreted in a simple way. Refer to the probability of positive outage as loss of load probability, *LOLP*:

$$LOLP \equiv 1 - F(0),$$

and refer to short-run marginal cost as system marginal price, *SMP*:

$$SMP \equiv m_t.$$

Then:

$$p_t = [1 - F(0)](V^* - m_t) + m_t = LOLP(V^* - SMP) + SMP$$

$$= LOLP \times V^* + (1 - LOLP) \times SMP.$$

That is, the spot price equals the loss of load probability times the value of lost load plus the probability of maintaining load times the system marginal price. System marginal price is the cost of the marginal production unit and equals operating cost plus capacity payment. The capacity payments sum to the cost of capacity:

$$\sum_t k_t = \beta: \text{sum of periodic capacity payments equals the cost of capacity,}$$

but each now has two components which depend on the loss of load probability:

$$k_t = [1 - F(0)](V^* - r)_t + F(0)(m_t - r_t).$$

These are the standard results in the spot pricing literature: in each half hour the efficient spot price equals:

marginal generation cost + marginal capital cost . . . no uncertainty case,
weighted average of marginal generation and outage costs . . . uncertainty case.

Outages are modelled as output from non-existent capacity which has zero capacity cost but a very high operating (outage) cost. An important qualification remains, however. The model with certainty has a set of *ex ante* price relationships that will automatically be realised in practice because uncertainty is absent. This is not the case in the model with uncertainty; the *ex ante* relationships are based on the maximisation of expected net welfare benefit, but the actual *ex post* realisation will be different. To handle the divergences between expected values of the variables and their realisations there should also exist an *ex post* balancing market. Thus the uncertainty model outlines the equilibrium before trading, but the real-time spot market must allow instantaneous adjustment of *ex ante* values to realised outcomes.

7   Energy Market Architecture

The analysis to this point gives an insight into the price relationships at the efficient allocation of resources. However, the welfare maximisation model has been used only as a means of simulating the competitive outcome. The mechanism for achieving this outcome still relies on competitive markets rather than centralised regulation, as the issue of capacity payments highlights. In the uncertainty model the capacity payment which covers the cost of building new capacity depends on the strength of demand at the peak relative to the system marginal price. In early applications of spot pricing with investor-owned producing firms, many market designs arranged for separate capacity payments with regulator-determined value of lost load in addition to system marginal price recovery.[10] However, such a regulated market architecture is open to abuse of market power if a producer with sufficient capacity can increase loss of load probability by withdrawing nominated capacity availability at the last moment. Consequently, during the years after 2000, many spot markets such as that of the UK moved away from a pool with separate capacity payments. The efficient spot market outcome was left to competitive entrants to make offers and bids to supply through individual negotiated contracts with a balancing market to adjust realised values to *ex ante* planned supply and demand. The mechanism for spreading the risk of faulty contracting is an active market in financial options related to spot and forward electricity and gas contracts (Stoft 2002; Wolak 2006). In the UK case, it is arguable that the stimulus to a more efficient wholesale market after the disappearance of the capacity payments system owes as much if not more to competitive entry by new generators as it did to the evolution of new trading and contracting arrangements (Evans and Green 2005). Consequently, it is important to keep in mind that the structure of the welfare maximisation model is not a guide to market architecture; it simulates the competitive outcome, but it is still the mechanism of free entry and exit in response to profit incentives that implements the spot pricing equilibrium.

Joskow (2006) has suggested some practical critical ingredients for liberalised electricity markets on the basis of several years of international experience. In Table 2.1, Joskow's architecture for energy market reform to replace public or state-owned utilities (POUs) with investor-owned utilities (IOUs) is summarised. Several of the ideas raised in Joskow's table are considered below, including the rate of entry into energy markets, and access to networks. Wholesale market spot prices can even be signalled to retail consumers with the option of a fixed price tariff instead.

8   Competition in Wholesale Energy Markets

In UK energy markets a classic case study of the competition in wholesale power markets concerns the trading arrangements for electricity in England and Wales. The analysis of

Table 2.1   Architecture for energy market reform

Component	Policy	Objectives
a. IOUs	Privatise state-owned utilities	High-powered incentives, non-political objectives, hard budget constraints
b. Separation	Vertical separation of generation, transmission, distribution and supply	Barriers to cross-subsidisation, and discrimination against access
c. Demerger	Horizontal demerger of generation	Wholesale market competition
d. Integration	Horizontal integration of transmission	Single *independent* system operator for system reliability and economic standards
e. Wholesale market	Voluntary public wholesale spot energy and operating reserve markets	Support for real-time supply–demand balancing, economic trading, quick response to outages
f. Demand-side response	Develop active demand-side institutions	Consumer demand-side response to wholesale prices
g. Access	Promote efficient access to transmission network	Efficient competitive production and exchange, and allocates scarce transmission capacity among competing users
h. Unbundling	Unbundle retail tariffs into retail power supply and delivery charges	Competition in supply separate from regulated (natural monopoly) distribution and transmission
i. Economic procurement	Benchmark supply costs for small consumers	Yardstick for supply by distribution company where small consumers not open to competition
j. Independent regulation	Independent regulatory authority with expert staff	Performance-based regulation using good information to regulate for distribution and transmission, e.g., yardstick competition
k. Transition	Transition from POUs to IOUs	Mechanisms compatible with competitive markets

Source: Joskow (2006).

Green and Newbery (1992) suggested that the small number and concentrated size of the original market participants led to a Nash equilibrium in supply schedules (offer curves) that produced large efficiency losses. They suggested that firms used market power to manipulate the availability of capacity in order to push up capacity payments, and increase the marginal price of electricity. This produces the *policy implication* that divestment of plant and enhanced competitive entry is required to improve competition in electricity generation, but a difficulty with the analysis of markets with a finite number of firms is to determine the optimal number in the market. Many oligopoly models use the Nash equilibrium for a Cournot game in which firms choose output quantities to maximise profit, taking the quantity of output from rivals as given. Powell (1993) used such a model to show that forward contract commitments would reduce the ability of firms to exercise spot market power. In power markets, however, it is often more interesting to focus on price-setting behaviour. In a two-player Bertrand game each duopolist chooses his/her price, taking the other's price as given: for example, for duopolist 1, where π, p, c, q are respectively profit, price, marginal cost and output, the model states:

$$\max_{\{P_1: \text{ given } p_2\}} \pi_1 = (p_1 - c)q_1.$$

Here, a pure strategy Nash equilibrium has five properties (Rasmusen 1994), where market demand is written $p = a - bQ$, and c is marginal cost (the same for each firm):

if $p_1 < p_2$, then $q_1 = Q = (a - p_1)/b$ and $q_2 = 0$;
if $p_2 < p_1$, then $q_2 = Q = (a - p_2)/b$ and $q_1 = 0$;
if $p_1 = p_2 = p$, then $q_1 + q_2 = Q = (a - p)/b$;
neither deviates and the unique equilibrium is where $p_1 = p_2 = c$.

The essence is that the lower-price duopolist captures the whole market. Prices cannot differ because the higher-price duopolist can respond by shaving price sufficiently to capture the other's market share. This stops when each has shaved price to marginal cost. Any division of the market is then a Nash equilibrium because each just breaks even while any deviation of price from marginal cost will mean zero or negative profits.

In a classic paper, Klemperer and Meyer (1989) described a way of extending the Cournot and Bertrand models. Instead of saying that players must choose either quantity or price as the strategic variable, they argued that each firm would look for its profit-maximising supply *curve* relating quantity to price. Hence this is called a 'supply function' model. Here the Nash equilibrium strategies consist not of a set of outputs or a set of prices but a set of supply functions stating how much each firm will supply for any given market price: $q_i = q_i(p)$. There have been several applications of this model, particularly to markets where a small number of firms participate in auctions to supply a product and each firm's bid consists of both a nominated supply quantity and a price that is required for that supply to be available. This is very relevant to the nature of spot energy markets where energy producers bid in supplies and prices to a daily market organised by an independent system operator, as envisaged in the Joskow architecture. Note that there is an additional problem with auctions because the difficulty of monitoring the firms' signals to each other and the transparency of any firm cheating tend to encourage cartel bidding. The version of the Klemperer–Meyer model used here is that of Green (1996) and Green and Newbery (1992). Green's (1996) model is restricted to linear supply functions.

Market demand is $D = q_1 + q_2$ and market demand is a function of market price: $D = D(P)$. Each firm thinks of the market price as its strategic variable and recognises that its share of market demand is the difference between total demand and the other firm's share: $q_1 \equiv D - q_2$ and $q_2 \equiv D - q_1$. It takes as given the other firm's supply function: $q(P)$. In the derivation, note that this identity holds:

$$\frac{dq_1}{dP} \equiv \frac{dD(P)}{dP} - \frac{dq_2}{dP}.$$

Firm 1:

$$\max_{P,\,q_2(P)\,given} \pi_1 = Pq_1 - TC(q_1) = P(D - q_2) - TC(q_1)$$

so $\dfrac{d\pi_1}{dP} = (D - q_2) + (P - MC_1)\left(\dfrac{dD}{dP} - \dfrac{dq_2}{dP}\right) = 0$

solve: $q_1 = (P - MC_1)\left(-\dfrac{dD}{dP} + \dfrac{dq_2}{dP}\right),$

and Firm 2:

$$\max_{P,\,q_1(P)\,given} \pi_2 = Pq_2 - TC(q_2) = P(D - q_1) - TC(q_2)$$

so $\dfrac{d\pi_2}{dP} = (D - q_1) + (P - MC_2)\left(\dfrac{dD}{dP} - \dfrac{dq_1}{dP}\right) = 0$

solve: $q_2 = (P - MC_2)\left(-\dfrac{dD}{dP} + \dfrac{dq_1}{dP}\right).$

These are a pair of simultaneous differential equations, so the solutions take the form of equations: $q = q(P)$ rather than numbers. Now we restrict our search for the solutions to linear supply curves of the form: $q = \beta P$. We assume linear marginal cost curves: $MC_i = c_i q_i$ and a linear market demand curve:

$$D = a - bP \Rightarrow \frac{dD(P)}{dP} = -b.$$

Our differential equation response functions are:

$$\beta_1 P = (P - c_1\beta_1 P)(b + \beta_2)$$

$$\beta_2 P = (P - c_2\beta_2 P)(b + \beta_1),$$

but P can be cancelled:

$$\beta_1 = (1 - c_1\beta_1)(b + \beta_2)$$

$$\beta_2 = (1 - c_2\beta_2)(b + \beta_1).$$

The problem now is to solve for β_1 and β_2, the slope of each firm's best response supply function with respect to the P axis. Market supply is then the horizontal summation of the individual supply curves: $\beta_1 P + \beta_2 P = (\beta_1 + \beta_2)P$. The critical question asked by Green and Newbery is this: will the market supply curve approximate the competitive industry marginal cost curve (what they call the 'Bertrand curve') or will it approximate the cartel monopoly bidding curve? Even more interesting is this question: how many

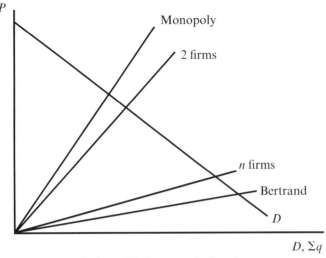

Nash equilibrium supply functions

Source: Green and Newbery (1992).

Figure 2.8 Green and Newbery power spot market model

new entrants are needed to ensure that the market supply curve is close to the Bertrand curve? The effect of adding more firms is to make the market supply curve steeper with respect to the price axis, that is, flatter with respect to the quantity axis:

$$\beta_1 P + \cdots + \beta_n P = \left(\sum_{i=1}^{i=n} \beta_i \right) P,$$

but it also increases the number of equations to be solved simultaneously:

$$\beta_i = (1 - c_i \beta_i)\left(b + \sum_{j \neq i}^{n} \beta_j \right), \ i = 1 \ldots n.$$

The effect is shown in Figure 2.8. The steepest supply function is the bidding curve for a monopoly firm, and the least steep supply schedule is that corresponding to a number of firms which behave as if they comprise a Bertrand–Nash equilibrium in supply schedules. As the number of firms entering the market increases, each maximising profit while taking the bidding supply schedule of the others as given, the aggregate of the supply schedules moves closer to the efficient Bertrand equilibrium schedule.

How many firms are needed for efficient resource allocation? Green and Newbery (1992) simulated the UK spot electricity market shortly after privatisation in 1990, and argued that with five or more players of equal scale, the aggregate Nash equilibrium supply schedule hardly differed from the Bertrand equilibrium supply schedule in terms of the estimated deadweight welfare loss. Consequently, although efficiency of outcome required more than simply splitting the incumbent monopolist into two separate players,

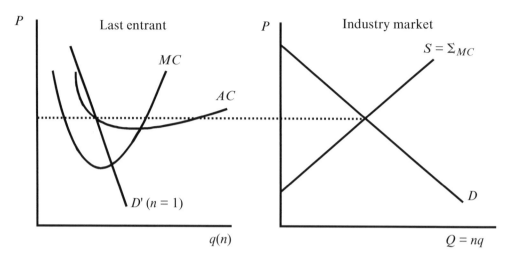

Figure 2.9   Incentive to new entry

nevertheless a feasible and finite number of entrants would deliver an outcome relatively close to a competitive equilibrium.

9   What Determines the Optimal Degree of Entry to Market?

A simple model of the optimal number of firms in an industry is given by Armstrong et al. (1994, p. 107). This is explained below.

The aggregate output of an industry is $Q = nq$ where n is the number of firms and q is the average output per firm. Generally we expect the average output per firm to fall as the number of firms rises. Trading off producer surplus against consumer surplus suggests that the net economic benefit of an extra entrant to an industry is:

Profit of last entrant + effect of last entrant in lowering price towards marginal cost.

The first term accrues to the producer while the second accrues to the consumers
    The net benefit can be zero for two reasons. First, if both terms are zero and n is very large, that is, if there are constant or decreasing returns to scale then the gain from more entry is zero when both the last entrant's profit is zero, and price equals marginal cost. Second, if the two terms are non-zero but cancel out when n is small. If there are increasing returns to scale (or fixed costs are important), then when entry has pushed profit down to zero, this implies $P = AC > MC$. The second term is negative and entry is excessive. The more important the fixed costs, or increasing returns to scale, the lower should be n. Figure 2.9 illustrates. First assume that demand is large relative to the output of a single firm. This means start with the diagram on the right and ignore the demand curve labelled D' in the left diagram. If demand is large enough (D) then free entry leads to $P = MC > AC$ and further entry incentives exist until $P = AC = MC$. Now instead assume that the output of one firm is large relative to the market demand. Ignore the diagram on the right and assume that market demand is: D'. If minimum

efficient scale is high relative to market demand (D') then entry should stop when $P = AC > MC$.

The formal analysis of the effect on a firm's output as the number of firms rises is given by:

$$\frac{dq(n)}{dn} = q'(n) < 0,$$

$$\frac{dW}{dn} = \pi_n + (P - MC)nq'(n) \; (>0) \; + \; [(>0) \times (<0)].$$

Here π_n is the profit of the last entrant, and the second term is the effect of an extra firm in reducing the $P - MC$ gap. The optimal number of firms is:

$$n = -\frac{q(P_n - AC_n)}{q'(n)(P_n - MC_n)}.$$

10   The Access Pricing Problem

The Joskow (2006) architecture argues for vertical de-integration of different aspects of power supply, but there is a link between vertical integration and the important topic of access pricing. In vertical integration the key question is the determination of the price of input charged to a downstream firm by the upstream firm. In access pricing, one firm owns the network for distributing the commodity to the final consumers. It could but need not be vertically integrated. However, there is now another firm, the third party, which wishes to supply the commodity to some of these final customers. It can obtain the commodity as input (the third party might be an upstream firm) but must use the available network owned by the downstream firm. The downstream firm can charge for access to this network. The access charge must cover the network costs associated with the customers which the third-party firm detaches from the network owner. These costs may be very difficult to measure separately. What is the marginal opportunity cost of access that will form the basis of an efficient access price? Baumol and Sidak's (1994) efficient component pricing rule argues that the marginal opportunity cost of access is the profit forgone by the network owner in permitting the third party to detach some customers that the downstream firm would otherwise supply. In principle, profit per customer is calculable, but it will be difficult to distinguish the fraction which covers network costs from the fraction which reflects the downstream firm's market power. The access pricing problem is discussed in detail by Armstrong et al. (1994).

Facilitating competition in the electricity and gas industries requires non-discriminatory open access to the transmission and distribution network, for all producers and suppliers. Identify an incumbent network owner (firm 1) and a competitive supplier (firm 2). Given that mce_1 describes the incumbent's marginal cost of energy, then its price for final downstream supply is:

$$P_1 = mce_1 + ica + \pi,$$

where ica is the incremental cost of access provision, and π shows the profit mark-up to ensure financial viability Therefore the price of access is:

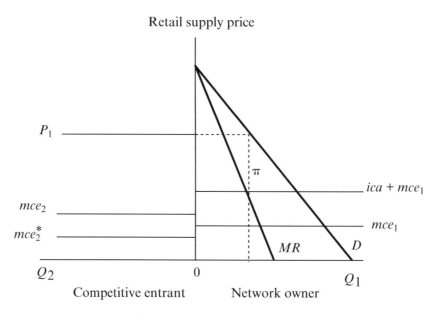

Figure 2.10   Unbundling products for access pricing

$$P_a = ica + \pi = ica + [P_1 - (mce_1 + ica)],$$

and this describes a version of the efficient component pricing rule (ECPR) (Vickers 1997). The competitive supplier will only enter the market if it has a lower marginal cost of energy, mce_2^* than the incumbent (Figure 2.10), but entry is inefficient at an entrant's energy source cost of mce_2. ECPR therefore discourages inefficient entry because the new supplier not only has to pay an access charge, it also has to pay the opportunity cost of access which includes the incumbent's lost profit. The model allows us to unbundle services, in this case distribution and supply. The ECPR model identifies efficient entry conditions, but assumes that regulatory issues are resolved elsewhere. Figure 2.10 shows efficient entry where the network owner is an unregulated monopolist.

Product differentiation can exist in the supply market, as in any other competitive market. Vickers extends the model to write:

$$P_a = ica + \sigma[P_1 - (mce_1 + ica)],$$

where σ is the displacement ratio, defined as the ratio of (a change in output sales for the incumbent with respect to the access price) to (a change in supply of access to new entrants with respect to the access price).

Three assumptions are made about the displacement ratio to ensure unity: homogeneous products; fixed coefficients technology (one unit of output requires one unit of access); and no bypass (the incumbent supplies all access via its distribution network). The first of these assumptions may be relaxed. Consequently when the demand for access by a new entrant increases by 1 unit, the incumbent will not see a 1 unit reduction in

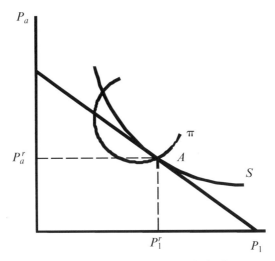

Efficiency gain from global price cap

Source: Derived from Vickers (1997).

Figure 2.11   Global price cap

demand for its product, because of customer inertia, brand loyalty, and the like, inducing $\sigma < 1$. Product differentiation will lower the access price relative to homogeneous products.

The regulatory issue of the network owner's profitability remains. Laffont and Tirole (1996) have suggested a global price cap in which the intermediate good (access) is treated as a final good and included in the computation of the price cap. This treats access and supply symmetrically in a Ramsey pricing framework. Laffont and Tirole contrast this with 'the general view that intermediate and final goods are to be treated asymmetrically' (pp. 244–5).

The efficiency gain of using the global price cap suggested by Laffont and Tirole can be neatly illustrated in Figure 2.11, which is derived from Vickers (1997). The final price and the access price are displayed on the horizontal and vertical axes. Separately regulated price caps are shown at point A as P_a^r and P_1^r. This pair of prices will generally lie on an iso-profit contour labelled π, and an indifference curve of consumer surplus labelled S. Consumer surplus improvements are represented by S contours closer to the origin, while profit gains to the firm are represented by π contours further from the origin. All of the area above the profit contour and below the consumer surplus contour represents price pairs which are more efficient than the pair at A. We can construct a global price cap: $wP_a + (1 - w)P_1 = \overline{P}$ through point A such that points between the locus and the π contour are more efficient than A without the consumer paying more in aggregate than at A. If the weights are proportional to the actual quantities consumed at A, the locus will be tangential to the S contour at A. Any chosen combination in the area between the locus and the profit contour will approximate to a more efficient entry-access allocation than the one implied by the separate price caps, and will yield a Ramsey pricing outcome. The incumbent will concentrate where it has a comparative advantage, reflecting Bertrand entry in ECPR.

A regulator may opt for maximum price limits to protect customers who will initially not benefit from competition. For access pricing this has the following effect, reflecting what Laffont and Tirole describe as the general asymmetric approach:

$$P_1 \leq \overline{P_1} \text{ and } P_a \leq \overline{P_a},$$

where the access price cap is determined by the distribution and transmission price controls. Firms would be expected to publish indicative charges well in advance of implementation, and efficiency requires that these are the same for each entrant to a particular supply market.

Access pricing may need floors and ceilings to prevent inefficient suppliers entering the market or to prohibit barriers to entry. Without use of a global price cap, Vickers worries about the distortion arising from partial regulation, a special case of this. If the access price is regulated, $P_1 - P_a$ will widen, increasing productive inefficiency, as less efficient rivals enter the market. To prevent predatory pricing, on the other hand, as a result of some competitive energy costs being allocated to the regulated business, suggests a constraint such as:

$$P - a \geq MC_1.$$

However, if a firm's distribution and supply business were separated into two companies, each with its own terms of license the possibility of cross-subsidy would no longer arise.

11   Conclusions

This chapter has attempted to make a broad survey of the theoretical core ideas in energy economics. The initial discussion used the idea of Pareto-efficient outcomes and social cost–benefit analysis to establish the benchmark competitive and efficient allocations of energy resources. An important ingredient is the choice of social discount rate which was first explained in terms of an optimal saving and growth model. The core ideas of efficient resource allocation were then applied to investments in new energy supply and capacity, and this was shown to be intimately related to the idea of marginal cost pricing. The measurement of marginal cost in multiple plants and multiple time period investment planning models of energy supply followed and was demonstrated in a spot pricing model with uncertainty. Having described the ideas of efficient resource allocation in an energy context, attention turned to the practical implementation in real-world energy markets. An architecture for efficient energy markets was suggested by Joskow (2006), and this was used as a context to investigate the role of entry by investor-owned firms into energy markets. Feasible competition was demonstrated with a finite number of entrants, but care is necessary in determining the optimal market design. One important aspect of this is the access pricing problem since much of energy supply is delivered through pipes and wires.

Notes

1. Incentive regulation of energy industries is treated in Chapter 21.
2. The fundamental theorems of welfare economics state that (i) every competitive equilibrium is a Pareto optimum, and (ii) for every Pareto optimum there is a competitive equilibrium.
3. The Pareto criterion states that an allocation of resources is optimal if no person can be made better off without making another worse off.
4. Since producer surplus is the difference between revenue and the area under the curve representing the horizontal summation of the marginal cost curves, it strictly excludes fixed cost and therefore is less than economic profit.
5. Strictly this should be the slope of the aggregate of the compensated demand curves.
6. There is no assumption that compensation is actually paid, otherwise the Pareto criterion itself would be satisfied.
7. In Figure 2.5, additional producer surplus from this capacity to change is zero, since the long-run marginal cost is constant.
8. Rees demonstrates that this is equivalent to comparing the NEC of consecutive programmes of identical investments in the different technologies where the investment programmes have a common lifetime factor.
9. Stoft (2002, pp. 48 and 136) discusses economic demand as the amount of power that would be consumed if the system were operating normally for all consumers. Shed load is included as part of demand.
10. The UK Pool market after privatisation, 1990–2000 is an example of this. Many US power markets remained in this situation subsequently (Joskow 2006; Wolak 2006).

References

Armstrong, M., S. Cowan and J. Vickers (1994), *Regulatory Reform: Economic Analysis and British Experience*, Cambridge, MA: MIT Press.

Baumol, W.J. and G. Sidak (1994), *Toward Competition in Local Telephony*, Cambridge, MA: MIT Press.

Berrie, T. (1983), *Power System Economics*, London: Peregrinus on behalf of Institution of Electrical Engineers.

Bohn, R., F. Schweppe and M. Caramanis (1983), 'Using spot pricing to co-ordinate deregulated utilities, customers and generators', in J. Plummer (ed.), *Electric Power Strategic Issues*, Arlington, VA: Public Utility Reports Inc., 265–82.

Boiteux, M. (1960), 'Peak load pricing', *Journal of Business*, **33**, 157–79.

Crew, M., C. Fernando and P. Kleindorfer (1995), 'The theory of peak load pricing: a survey', *Journal of Regulatory Economics*, **8**, 215–48.

Crew, M. and P. Kleindorfer (1979), *Public Utility Economics*, New York: St. Martin's Press.

Evans, J.E. and R. Green (2005), 'Why did British electricity prices fall after 1998?', Department of Economics Discussion Paper 05-13, University of Birmingham.

Green, R. (1996), 'Increasing competition in the British electricity spot market', *Journal of Industrial Economics*, **44**(2), 205–16.

Green, R. and D. Newbery (1992), 'Competition in the British electricity spot market', *Journal of Political Economy*, **100**(5), 929–53.

Joskow, Paul L. (2006), 'Introduction to electricity sector liberalization: lessons learned from cross-country studies', in F. Sioshansi and W. Pfaffenberger (eds), *Electricity Market Reform: An International Perspective*, Amsterdam: Elsevier, 1–32.

Klemperer, P. and M. Meyer (1986), 'Supply function equilibria in oligopoly under uncertainty', *Econometrica*, **57**(6), November, 1243–77.

Laffont, J.-J. and J. Tirole (1996), 'Creating competition through interconnection: theory and practice', *Journal of Regulatory Economics*, **10**(3), 227–56.

Littlechild, S.C. (1970), 'Marginal cost pricing with joint costs', *Economic Journal*, **80**(318), June, 323–35.

Mas-Colell, A., M.D. Whinston and J.R. Green (1995), *Microeconomic Theory*, Oxford: Oxford University Press.

MIT (2004), 'MIT report on Nuclear Power', Massachusetts Institute of Technology, Cambridge, MA.

Munasinghe, M. and J. Warford (1982), *Electricity Pricing*, Washington, DC: World Bank.

Newbery, D. (1985), 'Pricing policy', in R. Belgrave and M. Cornell (eds), *Energy Self Sufficiency for the UK?*, Aldershot: Gower, 77–113.

Powell, A. (1993), 'Trading forward in an imperfect market: the case of electricity in Britain', *Economic Journal*, **103**(417), 444–53.

Rasmusen, E. (1994), *Games and Information: An Introduction to Game Theory*, 2nd edn, Oxford: Blackwell.
Rees, R. (1973), *The Economics of Investment Analysis*, Civil Service College Occasional Papers, London: Her Majesty's Stationery Office.
Rees, R. (1984), *Public Enterprise Economics*, 2nd edn, London: Weidenfeld & Nicholson.
Stern, N. (2006), *Stern Review on the Economics of Climate Change*, London: H.M. Treasury.
Stoft, S. (2002), *Power System Economics: Designing Markets for Electricity*, New York: IEEE Press Wiley-Interscience.
Turvey, R. (1967), *Optimal Pricing and Investment in Electricity Supply*, London: Allen & Unwin.
Turvey, R. (1971), *Economic Analysis and Public Enterprises*, London: Allen & Unwin.
Turvey, R. and D. Anderson (1977), *Electricity Economics*, Washington, DC: World Bank.
Vickers, J. (1997), 'Regulation, competition and the structure of prices', *Oxford Review of Economic Policy*, **1**, 15–26.
Wenders, J.T. (1976), 'Peak load pricing in the electric utility industry', *Bell Journal of Economics*, **7**(1), Spring, 232–41.
Wolak, F.A. (2006), 'Why the United States has yet to benefit from electricity industry re-structuring (and what can be done to change this)', Western Power Trading Forum, New York Meeting, July 11, available at: http://www.stanford.edu/~wolak/ (accessed August 21 2008).

3 The economics of energy supply
Kenneth B. Medlock III

1 Introduction

The economics of energy supply are concerned with the manner in which energy resources are allocated through space and time. Generally, energy resources can be classified as either depletable or non-depletable.[1] A resource is considered depletable when the sum over time of all possible production is finite, or the stock of the resources is not replaceable in a reasonable timeframe. Crude oil, natural gas, and coal – fossil fuels – are examples of depletable resources. A resource is considered non-depletable if its stock can be replenished within a reasonable timeframe. Non-depletable energy resources include geothermal, wind, and solar.

Heretofore, energy economists have been concerned with the allocation of *depletable* resources, primarily because fossil fuels have been the principal source of energy. Hotelling (1931) was the first of many theoretical studies of optimal depletion rates and associated pricing rules, as well as empirical studies aimed at testing the validity of theory.[2] Application of Hotelling's well-known '*r*-percent' rule in the late 1970s and early 1980s contributed to many analysts incorrectly predicting that oil prices would rise to ever higher levels over the next couple of decades. However, the fault for the inaccuracy of such a prediction lies not in the basic theoretical framework. Rather, an apparent underappreciation of many factors that influence energy markets – such as technological change in the extractive industries, the development of lower-cost alternatives, expansion of the resource base through exploration activities, uncertainty in reserve assessments, and various demand-side responses to higher prices – are largely responsible.

The value of the theory of the extraction of depletable resources lies not in its capability to predict market *outcomes*. In fact, it is well known that the Hotelling rule is insufficient in that regard. Rather, the value lies in the framework itself. Specifically, the framework presented by Hotelling established the importance of intertemporal arbitrage and set a useful starting point for analysis of the extraction of depletable resources. However, the basic framework must be expanded upon to include the many facets and uncertainties that characterize the resource extraction industry in order to be useful in a predictive sense. In particular, temporal trade-offs are crucial to maximizing the value of assets in industries characterized by large capital investments, such as the energy industry, but geologic, economic and technological uncertainties expose such decisions to varying degrees of risk. This, in turn, perturbs outcomes from a deterministic path, and can therefore result in highly variable outcomes.

This chapter proceeds by presenting the basic framework used by economists to examine the optimal extraction of depletable resources in Section 2. A conceptual framework for analyzing issues such as 'peak oil', resource nationalization, resource taxation, monopoly control and cartel behavior, the transition to alternative energy sources, and the future of long-term energy prices, lies in the theory of depletable resources. Some extensions to this model are presented in Section 3. In assessing the practical worth of theoretical models, Sections 4 and 5 consider firm behavior. Section 6 concludes.

2   A Simple Model of Extraction of a Depletable Resource

Economic models of the extraction of a depletable resource involve maximizing the present value of a resource. There are various assumptions that can be made regarding things such as cost of development, the size of the resource, and whether or not the market is a monopoly or is perfectly competitive. Uncertainty about costs, market prices, and resource quantity can also be varied. Each of these potential adjustments to the basic model lends important insights, but they all ultimately begin with the conceptual framework considered by Hotelling.

The basic model
The type of problem considered by Hotelling is one in which a firm seeks to maximize the present value of profits from extraction of a depletable resource. More formally, we begin with a known finite stock of resource, Q, from which production, q_t, can commence at cost, $c(q_t)$, for all time periods, t. The resource remaining at the beginning of each period is given as R_t. Output can be sold into a perfectly competitive market at price, p_t. We then have,

$$\max_q \sum_{t=0}^{T} \beta^t [p_t q_t - c(q_t)],$$

subject to the constraints:

$$R_{t+1} - R_t = -q_t, c, q, R \geq 0, \forall t,$$

where β is the rate at which future profits are discounted. β is equal to $1/(1 + r)$ with r being a risk-adjusted rate of interest. The first constraint describes the evolution of the remaining resource. Assuming that there is no value to the resource in any period beyond T, then exhaustion of the resource is optimal so that $R_{T+1} = 0$ (leaving the resource in the ground would in effect be like leaving money uncollected). This allows us to write our problem to be solved as:

$$\max_{q, \lambda} V = \sum_{t=0}^{T} \beta^t [p_t q_t - c(q_t)] + \lambda \left(\overline{Q} - \sum_{t=0}^{T} q_t \right),$$

where the constraint $R_{t+1} - R_t = -q_t$ has been replaced with $\overline{Q} - \sum_{t=0}^{T} q_t$ because the resource is completely exhausted at time T.[3] The first-order condition for a maximum is then given as:

$$\frac{\partial V}{\partial q} = \beta^t (p_t - c_{q,t}) - \lambda = 0,$$

where c_q denotes the derivative of cost with respect to quantity extracted. The first-order condition must be true for all time periods. The term λ is the shadow price of the resource, or the incremental value to the resource owner of adding an additional unit of resource. It is also the scarcity rent associated with depleting the resource. Note also that if T is unknown and must be determined optimally, λ will be indexed by t. Such a case arises when, for example, the cost of extraction is made a function of the remaining resource – we shall consider this case below.

It follows from the above first-order condition that:

$$\beta^0(p_0 - c_{q,0}) = \ldots = \beta^t(p_t - c_{q,t}) = \beta^{t+1}(p_{t+1} - c_{q,t+1}) = \ldots, \tag{3.1}$$

so that the rents associated with extraction must rise at the rate of interest:

$$(p_{t+1} - c_{q,t+1}) = (1 + r)(p_t - c_{q,t}). \tag{3.2}$$

In other words, extraction will occur so that the present value of the activity is the same in all periods. If costs are assumed to be zero, then we have the famous 'r-percent' rule,

$$p_{t+1} = (1 + r)p_t. \tag{3.3}$$

The intuition behind the result is rather elegant. If condition (3.2) were to be violated, then the resource owner could move production either forward or backward in time and do better. For example, assume that $(p_{t+1} - c_{q,t+1}) > (1 + r)(p_t - c_{q,t})$. The producer would opt to shift production into the future in order to increase overall profit. But, the dynamics of many sellers dictates that if all producers behaved similarly, the price in period $t + 1$ would be driven down, and the price in period t would be driven up. This would occur until condition (3.2) was satisfied. By similar logic, if the inequality is reversed, producers will shift production to the current period until the equality is restored. Therefore, optimizing the value of the resource requires that the present value of the marginal profit in each period be the same.

From the first-order condition, we can show that price is a simple mark-up over the marginal cost of extraction. For example, solving for p_t, we have:

$$p_t = (1 + r)^t \lambda + c_{q,t}. \tag{3.4}$$

The first term on the right-hand side of equation (3.4) is the mark-up over marginal extraction cost and is referred to as the 'marginal user cost' (MUC), and the second term is the 'marginal extraction cost' (MEC). Thus, equation (3.4) stipulates that the price at any given point in time must equal *total* marginal cost of extraction, or the opportunity cost plus the cost of incremental production. This follows because $MUC_t = (1 + r)^t \lambda$, meaning that the marginal user cost is directly related to the shadow value of the resource, λ, and reflects the opportunity cost of extraction. In other words, once the resource has been extracted it cannot be used for profit at a later date. Thus, the resource owner must be fairly compensated for the decision to extract today and forgo the marginal value of extracting tomorrow.

Equation (3.4) is depicted graphically in Figure 3.1 for the special case of constant marginal extraction cost, that is, $- c_{q,t} = \bar{c}$ for all t. The vertical sum of MUC and MEC is simply the price of the resource. As illustrated, we see that the price of the resource

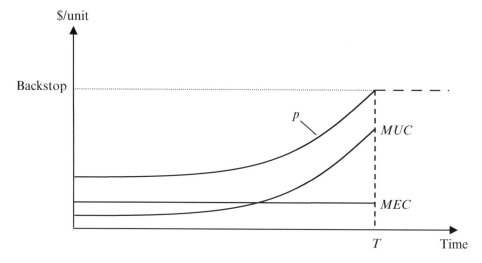

Note: The marginal user cost of the resource is related to its shadow value. It rises at the rate of interest, reflecting an economically efficient level of compensation for its use. The price is the vertical sum of marginal user cost and marginal extraction cost, the latter of which is held constant in this illustration. The resource is no longer used when its price reaches the price of some alternative, or backstop.

Figure 3.1   The 'optimal' price path of a depletable resource (with constant extraction costs)

will rise until it reaches some alternative, or 'backstop', price. This can be a new energy resource that is non-depletable, or it could even be another higher-cost depletable resource. Thus, depletion eventually leads to a transition, which is why depletable resources are often called 'transition fuels'.[4]

The nature of marginal extraction cost is very important in characterizing resource depletion. Not pictured is the case where extraction costs are rising through time. If this is the case, the opportunity cost of extracting a unit of resource diminishes so that MUC falls (see Heal 1976 and Oren and Powell 1985). Moreover, the transition to a new source of energy arises due to prohibitive costs rather than physically running out.

The backstop has an important role in these types of models. It establishes the terminal value, or the long-run price at which demand for the depletable resource goes to zero. If the backstop price is lowered, then the user cost of the resource also falls. This follows because solution of λ reveals that it is a function of the resource price in the final time period, which should equal the backstop price. In particular, recursive substitution in equation (3.4) indicates that $\lambda = \beta^T (p_T - c_{q,T})$. If p_T is known, as would be the case if the backstop price is just the full marginal cost of, say, solar energy, then λ is also known. Note that if p_T falls, so does λ. It then follows from equation (3.3) that the price in all periods is lower. Note also that a lower backstop price exerts a similar influence on λ as a lower discount factor (higher interest rate).

An Example with Linear Demand
If we have an expression for demand, we can eliminate λ from equation (3.4) and solve expressly for the optimal price path and extraction path. For example, given a linear

inverse demand function of the form $p_t = a - bq_t$, because the resource is depletable there is some period T such that $p_T = a$ where demand falls to zero. Furthermore, if the firm is a price-taker[5] in this market, we can simply substitute this into equation (3.1), expand the term β and rearrange terms to show that:

$$p_t = (1 + r)^{t-T}(a - c_{q,T}) + c_{q,t}. \tag{3.5}$$

Thus, we have as above that price is a mark-up over marginal extraction cost. Note that $MUC_t = (1 + r)^{t-T}(a - c_{q,T})$ in this formulation. The parameter a is referred to as the 'choke' price, or maximum willingness to pay. It establishes a value for the last unit of resource extracted. If there are multiple fuels, the choke establishes the price at which the market transitions to either an alternative fuel or some backstop technology.

To solve for q_t, we simply need to substitute equation (3.5) into the linear inverse demand equation to find $a - bq_t = (1 + r)^{t-T}(a - c_{q,T}) + c_{q,t}$, which can be solved for q_t to yield:

$$q_t = \frac{a}{b} - \frac{(1 + r)^{t-T}(a - c_{q,T}) + c_{q,t}}{b}.$$

Note that as $t \to T$ it must also be true that $q_t \to 0$. This follows because at time T, $c_{q,T} = a$ so that $q_t = 0$.

Because costs are constant through time, as in the depiction in Figure 3.1, then we have *physical* resource exhaustion. But, if costs are increasing through time, perhaps due to resource depletion, we will have *economic* exhaustion.[6] Economic exhaustion results when costs rise to the point that the resource is no longer profitable to extract. Thus, there is still resource physically remaining at the point of exhaustion. In either case, at time T we will transition to an alternative, or backstop, resource, whose price in this example is just equal to a.

Comparative statics on the optimal solutions for p and q reveal some important variable relationships. For example,

- increasing the interest rate lowers price and raises extraction in the current period; and
- lowering the price of the backstop, a, tends to lower price and increase extraction in all periods.

These are important considerations because, for instance, they have implications for conservation and technological innovation in alternative energy resources. In particular, if innovation reduces the cost of a backstop, the result herein suggests that the depletable resource will be consumed more rapidly. Intuitively, this follows because any resource left in the ground will be worthless after the transition to the backstop and the firm is seeking to maximize the rents from the resource. Thus, profit-maximizing behavior here actually results in more rapid depletion of the resource.

However, if the cost of the backstop is tied to the cost of capital, then the result can actually be quite different. In particular, a higher interest rate could lower extraction and decelerate depletion if an increase in the interest rate raises the cost of the backstop and hence the choke price of the depletable resource (see Farzin 1984). This is counter to the result obtained when the backstop price is exogenous.

Monopoly production in the simple model

We can extend the basic model to consider the case of a monopolist resource owner rather than a firm acting in a perfectly competitive market. In fact, this has been of special interest given the nature of world crude oil markets, and has been considered by many authors within the context of the models they develop (see, for example, Stiglitz 1976). In a market characterized by imperfect competition, the resource owner's extraction decisions influence price, much as the production decisions of the Organization of Petroleum Exporting Countries (OPEC) influence the global crude oil price. In the case of the monopolist operating in the simplest of worlds, it can be shown that the production will be scheduled so that discounted marginal revenue, MR, is equal in every period, or $MR_{t+1} = (1 + r)MR_t$. Interestingly, if demand is constant elasticity, such that $p_t = aq_t^{-b}$, then marginal revenue is $-abq_t^{-b}$, yielding $aq_{t+1}^{-b} = (1 + r)aq_t^{-b}$, or $p_{t+1} = (1 + r)p_t$, which is the solution in the perfectly competitive case. This follows from the fact that revenues are the same for any point along a constant elasticity demand curve, so the monopolist cannot do any better by restricting production. Thus, the resulting optimal price and extraction paths are unchanged from the competitive case.

If, however, elasticity is not constant, as is the case in the example above with linear demand, then the resource owner will raise price in the current period by constraining the level of production. This results in the resource lasting longer, leading to the rather famous conclusion that 'the monopolist is the conservationist's friend'. However, the monopoly producer is not acting out of conservation ethic. Rather, the goal is to maximize monopoly profit.

Empirical evidence and the simple model

Reality is the benchmark by which theory is tested, and aggregate data do not typically support the predictions of the simple model presented above. Equations (3.2) and (3.4) indicate that the resource rents should rise at the rate of interest and that the resource price should reflect scarcity rent and the marginal cost of extraction. The measure of interest to economists is generally that of resource scarcity, and there has been much discourse in the economic literature regarding the appropriate measure of resource scarcity (cost, price, and rent). For example, Brown and Field (1978) argue that considering only the resource price or the extraction costs is not sufficient. They argue instead that the resource rents are more appropriate, but given data difficulties suggest the marginal discovery cost as an adequate proxy. Halvorsen and Smith (1984) contend that vertical integration in firms in the extractive industries can render rents to be an inadequate measure of scarcity. More recently, Farzin (1995) considers the influence of innovation and contends that resource rents are the best measure of scarcity.

Although it has been argued that resource rents are the best indicator of scarcity, and hence should be considered rather than price in assessing the validity of the Hotelling framework, it is still useful to examine the history of depletable resource prices. Figure 3.2 plots the US domestic first purchase price of crude oil from 1950 to 2006. We see that the price of crude oil – a depletable resource – has fluctuated widely in the past 40 years, with periods of both rapid increase and decrease. This sort of price path is not consistent with the type of pattern depicted in Figure 3.1. Moreover, this is not unique to crude oil price, as prices of other commodities have also exhibited significant variation over time.

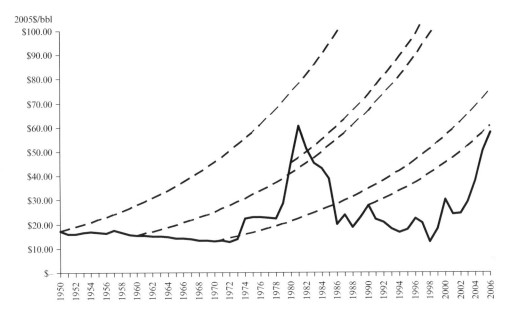

2005$/bbl

Note: The price of crude oil (in real 2005 dollars) does not conform to the path predicted by a simple *r*-percent rule. Depicted in the figure are the future price paths as predicted by the *r*-percent rule beginning at different points in time. The observation that actual oil prices deviate from the predicted paths has brought with it criticism of Hotelling's basic framework for analyzing the extraction of a depletable resource.

Source: Energy Information Administration.

Figure 3.2   US domestic first purchase crude oil price and the 'r-percent' rule

Also depicted in Figure 3.2 are several Hotelling-type 'predicted' price paths. Each path is constructed beginning in 10-year increments from 1950 through 1990 using an interest rate of 5 percent. The Hotelling-type paths so constructed are for illustrative purposes only, but it is obvious that the price of crude oil has not conformed to something such as the *r*-percent rule. This does not necessarily mean, however, that the basic model has no value. Rather, it simply needs to be generalized. We therefore need to understand why the basic framework fails to adequately explain reality.

3   Some Necessary Complications to the Simple Model

The pricing rule described by equation (3.3), and all of the subsequent analysis, is valid for very specific assumptions. In fact, these assumptions are somewhat limiting in terms of how they depict reality. Some of the more crucial assumptions are:

- extraction costs are a function only of current extraction;
- the total quantity of resource Q_0 is known;
- there is no uncertainty; and
- extraction, marketing, and, if allowed, exploration investment, all occur in an incremental manner.

While relaxing these assumptions can bring us closer to reality, anything we do from here is ultimately built upon a single premise – the resource owner will arbitrage production through time in order to maximize the net present value of the resource. This is the value of the Hotelling model. In effect, the finite resource is an asset. As with any asset, the owner wishes to maximize its value. If the resource is extracted too fast, it will drive down price and lower current revenue. If the resource is extracted too slowly, revenue will increase today but be sacrificed tomorrow. In either case, the sum of all revenues through time will not be maximized. Thus, production will be scheduled so that the asset (the resource in the ground) bears its highest return (see, for example, Pindyck 1980; Oren and Powell 1989; Krautkraemer 1998 and Krautkraemer and Toman 2004 for a short summary of the literature).[7]

Extraction costs

In the basic model, extraction costs are assumed to be affected only by current extraction. While such a formulation does allow for excluding short-run adjustment costs, other important factors such as reserve dependency and cost-reducing technological change are not included. Generalization to include these variable influences is possible through modification of the cost function, and the outcome of such modifications can be distinctly different from those given from the simple model above.

In the case where costs can increase as the resource is depleted, it can be shown that the resource is *economically* exhausted if a backstop is present. Specifically, if we specify cost to be a function of the level of reserves R_t in time period t so that $c_t = c(q_t, R_t)$ such that $c_R < 0$ and $c_{RR} > 0$, then when reserves are large, costs are lower. But as reserves fall, costs escalate at an increasing rate. Under such assumptions, exhaustion is a direct function of how difficult and costly it is to access the remaining resource. This is akin to a well operator capping a well when deliverability falls and it becomes too costly to continue production. Note, however, just as in reality, if there is a technological innovation that reduces the cost of extracting those marginal resources, then development will continue so long as it is profitable to do so. The technique of water-driven enhanced recovery is one such innovation that enables the extraction of marginal resources at an acceptable cost. Another is directional drilling, which also lowers costs by reducing the number of individual wells needed to extract a given amount of resource. Including such innovations is an additional complication to the model, but it can be done.

It is also possible to incorporate additional short-run costs through geologic operating constraints that govern production for a given level of reserves. For example, if reserves in any period are given as R_t, then production in that period might be given as $q_t = \delta(\,\cdot\,)R_t$, where $\delta(\,\cdot\,) \in [0, 1]$. Moreover, $\delta(\,\cdot\,)$, which can be thought of as the rate of well productivity, can be a function of variable inputs that allow the amount of production from a given level of reserves to change with things such as labor inputs or use of enhanced recovery techniques. Of course, these variable inputs come with a cost, so the resource owner must consider those costs when determining the optimal level of production. Moreover, if capacity constraints exist that drive up the short-run cost of employment of these variable factors, there will be some feasible maximum value of $\delta(\,\cdot\,)$ that the resource owner would be willing to accept.

Still further modifications of the cost function to allow the short-run cost escalation associated with exploration and development are possible. For example, if costs escalate at an increasing rate with greater production, such that $c_q > 0$ and $c_{qq} > 0$, it is possible to capture the notion that if operators 'rush to drill', perhaps to capture rents from near-term high prices, input costs will escalate reflecting shortages of rigs, equipment and personnel. If binding, this will serve to limit the maximum extraction that will feasibly occur in any one period. Note that this possibility is in the basic model where costs are a function of extraction, $c(q_t)$.

An Example with Reserve-dependent Costs
Pindyck (1978) examined a case in which extraction costs rise with resource depletion. This involves first generalizing the cost function so that cost is influenced by the remaining resource. Such a problem is posed as:

$$\max_q \sum_{t=0}^{T} \beta^t [p_t q_t - c(q_t, R_t)],$$

subject to the constraints:

$$R_{t+1} - R_t = -q_t, \quad c, q, R \geq 0, \forall\, t.$$

Note, as before the first constraint indicates that reserves decrease with extraction, but now the effect of depletion explicitly influences the cost function, $c(q_t, R_t)$. As before, future profits are discounted at the rate β, and T is the period in which production of the depletable resource ceases.

Our problem is written as:

$$\max_{q,R,\lambda} V = \sum_{t=0}^{T} \beta^t \{ [p_t q_t - c(q_t, R_t)] + \lambda_t(-R_{t+1} + R_t - q_t) \},$$

with first-order conditions given as:

$$\frac{\partial V}{\partial q} = p_t - c_{q,t} - \lambda_t = 0, \tag{3.6}$$

$$\frac{\partial V}{\partial R} = -\lambda_{t-1} + \beta(-c_{R,t} + \lambda_t) = 0 \tag{3.7}$$

and the constraint.

From equations (3.6) and (3.7) it can be shown that the price of the resource is a mark-up over marginal extraction cost:

$$p_t = c_{q,t} + \sum_{n=1}^{T-t} \beta^n(-c_{R,t+n}), \tag{3.8}$$

where $T - t$ is the remaining number of periods.[8] The term

$$\sum_{n=1}^{T-t} \beta^n(-c_{R,t+n})$$

is the marginal user cost of the resource, and is the sum of the remaining marginal contributions to cost (in present value terms) that arise from the resource being depleted. Because $c_{R,t} < 0$, reflecting the idea that a larger reserve base lowers cost, the price of the resource should begin well above marginal extraction cost and fall toward it as $t \rightarrow T$, holding all else constant. This follows because

$$\lambda_t = \sum_{n=1}^{T-t} \beta^n (-c_{R,t+n}),$$

from (3.6) and (3.7), and since the resource has no value when production ceases in period T, $\lambda_T = 0$. Therefore, it must be that $p_T = c_{q,T}$, so depletion implies that marginal extraction cost approaches price, or alternatively that rents diminish to zero.

Equations (3.6) and (3.7) together also give the condition that:

$$(p_t - c_{q,t}) = (1 + r)(p_{t-1} - c_{q,t-1}) + c_{R,t}, \tag{3.9}$$

which is similar to equation (3.2) from above but with the additional term $c_{R,t}$. Thus, for any $c_{R,t} < 0$, equation (3.9) implies that the rents from extraction rise at some rate less than the rate of interest. Moreover, as long as $|c_{R,t}|$ continues to increase, we will reach a point at which the resource is economically exhausted, so that:

$$(1 + r)(p_{T-1} - c_{q,T-1}) = c_{R,T-1} \Rightarrow p_T = c_{q,T},$$

which is simply a restatement of the result in the preceding paragraph.

A Comment on Resource Heterogeneity and Non-constant Costs

An important implication of both equations (3.2) and (3.9) is that when costs are non-constant, the highest rent resources will be extracted first. If costs are non-constant it is possible to think of the problem in terms of there being multiple constant cost heterogeneous depletable resource deposits, each with different costs from the other deposits. Because the entire stock of the resource is known and there is no uncertainty regarding cost of extraction, the resource owner will schedule production so that the first deposit produced will be the lowest-cost deposit, with subsequent production being ordered so that the next deposit produced has the lowest cost of the remaining deposits.

Illustration of this concept is done with an example in which there are two time periods and two resource deposits. For example, consider that there are two oil deposits – A and B – that can be extracted in either period 1 at price $p_1 = \$75$ or period 2 at price $p_2 = \$85$. Each deposit has a different but constant cost, with $c_A = \$15$ and $c_B = \$2$. In addition, assume that the prevailing interest rate on investments of similar risk is 15 percent, there are only two periods, and if a deposit is developed in one period it is used up so that it is not available in another period. The rent from producing deposit A in period 1 is $R_{1A} = p_1 - c_A = \$60$, and the rent from producing deposit B in period 1 is $R_{1B} = p_1 - c_A = \$73$. The rents in period 2 are $R_{2A} = \$70$ and $R_{2B} = \$83$. Therefore, we see that the return to waiting to develop deposit A in period 2 is $(R_{2A} - R_{1A})/R_{1A} = 16.7$ percent and the return to waiting to develop deposit B is 13.7 percent. Obviously, the resource owner will prefer to wait to develop deposit A because the return to doing so is better than could be done by developing today and investing the proceeds at 15 percent. However, deposit *B* will be developed today, so that the rent collected can be invested at 15 percent. Note that this intertemporal profit-maximizing behavior results in deposit *B* being developed in period 1 and deposit *A* being developed in period 2. Thus, the highest rent resource is developed first.

This example is, of course, only illustrative of the principle. In practice, a firm would use its own internal rate of return on invested capital, a number which can vary across firms. The internal rate of interest used on invested capital could also vary across deposits, reflecting different project risks, and across time, reflecting a firm's financial status. For example, on projects in regions of the world where government is not stable, the fully risked required rate of return could be quite high, a factor that could result in a low-cost deposit being produced later than some higher-cost projects in more stable regions. The interest rate may also vary temporally if a firm is, for example, at risk of defaulting on debt. In this case, the firm may accelerate production from known deposits in order to increase cash flows. Such behavior is consistent with a very high rate of discount on future production, which follows because, in the absence of cash flows, the firm might not be around to reap the benefit of future production.

Exploration

Incorporating the discovery of new resources through exploratory effort is another significant and necessary alteration of the basic model. If extraction costs are reserve dependent then producers will have an incentive to expand their reserve base through exploration effort as they deplete existing reserves. This, in turn, may allow the firm to expand production, especially if reserves expand enough so that extraction costs fall. Exploration, however, becomes increasingly costly as depletion occurs, so the firm must consider this in evaluating the optimal level of exploration effort. Pindyck (1978), Arrow and Chang (1982) and others have considered models with this characteristic, and a review of the literature can be found in Cairns (1990). It can be demonstrated that if the initial stock of reserves is small, price can follow a 'U-shaped' pattern, as producers initially expand their production through the discovery of relatively cheap and large deposits of the resource, then ultimately see declines as the total demonstrated resource (all past production plus current proved reserves) approaches its technical limit, $\overline{Q}$.

In order to allow the resource owner to expand reserves through exploration activities, we can modify the models presented above by incorporating an investment decision for the resource owner. For example, we can modify the producer's objective to include a function describing investment in exploration activity, such that investment cost is increasing in the 'level of effort' in exploration and the demonstrated resource to date. The problem so posed stipulates that ramping up exploration investment in the near term becomes increasingly costly, reflecting short-run scarcity of qualified geologists and other technical personnel as well as any short-run constraints on equipment. By allowing exploration investment to also be a function of demonstrated resource, depletion renders exploration investment increasingly costly in the longer term so that as the resource is depleted, greater effort is required to maintain a given reserve base.

When we incorporate exploration activity, the resource owner must weigh the decision to invest in exploration, which may or may not prove to be successful in expanding reserves if we also include some probability of success, against allocating funds to current production activities. Thus, the total marginal cost of investing in exploration must equal the net present value of the marginal benefits to the resource owner. In other words, the price of the resource must compensate the resource owner for the marginal cost of extraction, the marginal cost of expanding (or at least offsetting the decline of) the reserve base, and the opportunity cost arising from reduced *future* exploration success and subsequent extraction. Expected future prices will, therefore, be a crucial determinant of the level of exploration effort. The initial foray into exploration can lead to lower prices, particularly if discoveries outpace depletion. But, since the investment cost of exploration rises as the total stock of resource is depleted, we shall eventually have a cessation of production with some more expensive resource remaining in the ground, assuming of course that there is a backstop technology.

Uncertainty

A major criticism of most models of optimal extraction of a depletable resource is that they are 'perfect foresight' in nature. In particular, the dynamic optimization framework used in such models allows all future prices to influence the current outcome, meaning we typically solve for optimal *paths*. In addition, the basic models generally do not incorporate uncertainty. If, however, uncertainty is a fundamental feature of the underlying data-generating process, then an absence of stochastic features in any theoretical model could render it to be fatally flawed.

If uncertainty is included, the resource owner's decisions must be based on *expected* market conditions, and the problem becomes one of investment under uncertainty, where the investment is in optimization of the value of the asset through exploration and production. Therefore, the extraction and price paths can be affected in many ways. Uncertainty can be introduced through future price, demand, exploration success, the cost of exploration and production, and the cost of a backstop resource. In addition, technological innovations can provide a source of uncertainty acting through each of the aforementioned channels.

Uncertainty in demand can, in principle, lead to some periods in which demand growth is unexpectedly high or unexpectedly low, which can lead to varied outcomes, especially in the presence of short-run constraints on production, which can arise when there is geologic uncertainty. In general, uncertainty about future demand will cause resource owners to shift production into the current period. In effect, the risk associated with demand (or absence of it) in the future will cause the resource owner to discount future cash flows more heavily, meaning that current production looks more attractive. This will tend to lower price in the current period and facilitate more rapid exhaustion of the resource. Moreover, this effect can be exacerbated as we move to the extreme case in which demand is at risk of evaporating very rapidly, perhaps due to the development of a new low-cost backstop technology.

Another concern involves geologic uncertainty and the relative cost ordering of deposits. The model with exploration (described above) typically assumes that reserves are found in order of ascending cost. This leads us to the result that deposits will be found and extracted in order from least to greatest cost, or that the easiest prospects are mined first. However, this result is an oversimplification. There are many characteristics of a resource deposit – such as size, depth and rock porosity – that affect cost, and there is often uncertainty about the nature of the deposit until wells have been drilled.

In addition, because there is also uncertainty about the location of deposits, resources are not necessarily *discovered* in order of ascending cost (see, for example, Livernois and Uhler 1987 and Swierzbinski and Mendelsohn 1989). As a result, resources are not necessarily discovered and developed in order of ascending cost. If we allow for a stochastic discovery process, the resulting price path can be highly variable, with periods of rising prices possibly followed by prolonged periods of falling prices.

Uncertainty in technological innovation is yet another source of uncertainty. If cost-reducing technological changes occur in unexpected discrete increments, then the result-ing impact on price can be quite substantial. The adoption of 3-D seismic technology by the oil industry resulted in significant cost reductions by improving the accuracy of exploration activity and facilitating the discovery of resources that had yet to be identi-fied. Similarly, directional drilling techniques lowered per unit costs of development by allowing a greater amount of resource to be extracted with fewer wells. The effect of these types of innovations can vary. If they are expected, then price should rise continuously (see Swierzbinski and Mendelsohn 1989) as resource owners will adjust their behavior in accordance with the availability of the new technology. But, if the innovations are unex-pected, some *ex post* suboptimal investments may be made (particularly those immedi-ately preceding the innovation) and price may rise and fall through time.

Production constraints and 'lumpy' capital investment
The basic framework for examining the optimal extraction of depletable resources does not account for the high capital intensity of development. The exploration and produc-tion process is, in general, very capital intensive. Moreover, the capital investments generally occur in large discrete 'lumps'. As such, a firm's decision to devote very large sums of money to the development of a resource deposit will hinge on the perceived profitability of the venture. Thus, as in all the preceding cases, expected future prices is a crucial determinant of the flow of capital, but, unlike in the preceding cases, so is the size of the upfront fixed cost.

Capital investments in the extractive industries, once made, are typically not revers-ible. This is because the capital equipment employed in oil- and gasfield development, for instance, is not easily transferred to some alternative activity once in place. As a result, if there is any uncertainty regarding future prices, investments will be made at a slower pace than if they were reversible. This can result in a short-run supply curve that is rela-tively inelastic. Moreover, prices can be very volatile in the short run, especially if the market is operating near its productive capacity and demand surges unexpectedly. It may be optimal for resource owners to hold some spare capacity in this case in order to meet such unexpected demand surges, but doing so depends on the fixed cost of development, the frequency and severity of unexpected demand increases, and the expected volatility of near-term prices.

Figure 3.3 illustrates the effect of short-run constraints on deliverability. In principle, deliverability is a function of the quantity of proven reserves, geologic considerations that govern the rate at which proved reserves can be produced, such as natural decline, and possibly some other variable inputs such as labor and applied technology. The horizontal axis in the first graph in Figure 3.3 represents the demonstrated resource to date, $Q_t = \sum_{n=0}^{t-1} q_n + R_t$, which is the sum of all production through the current period plus the stock of proved reserves. The cost of developing reserves is along the vertical

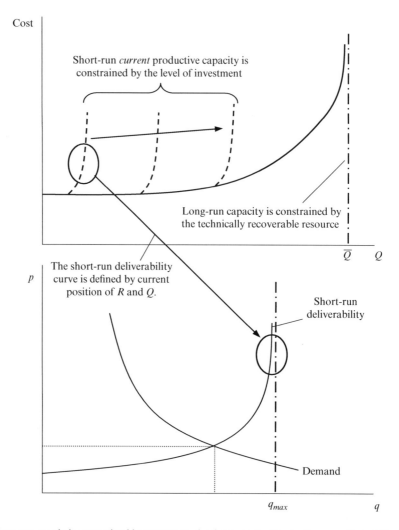

Note: Short-run supply is constrained by current productive capacity. Productive capacity is defined by the level of reserves at time *t*, so it is a reflection of past exploration success and cumulative production to date, and some combination of variable inputs such as labor. The long-run outcome is the eventual adoption of a backstop technology as the resource is depleted.

Figure 3.3   An illustration of short-run constraints on productive capacity

axis. So, the short-run cost curves indicate that there is limited ability to expand reserves within a period, but such is not the case in the long run until the technical resource limit is reached.

   As above, we can let $q_t = \delta(\cdot)R_t$ where $\delta(\cdot) \in [0, 1]$ and specify some functional relation governing exploration investment that results in expansion of R_t through new discoveries. Since deliverability in any period is a function of R and possibly some other variable inputs, the maximum feasible production would be some fraction of the stock of proved reserves. Thus, there is a short-run supply curve associated with every Q_t and it is constrained by the maximum production that can occur for a given R_t. The resource owner, in the long run, can invest in reserve additions, which results in a movement along the long-run cost curve. With every such investment there will be a new relevant short-run cost curve that extends upward from the long-run cost curve, and hence a new short-run deliverability curve.

If the investments that result in reserve additions occur in 'lumps', and those investments are irreversible, then unanticipated changes in market conditions can result in short-run constraints becoming binding, potentially resulting in dramatic swings in price. If, however, reserve additions and the necessary capital outlay can be incrementally small, then adjustment to unexpected changes in market conditions can be made incrementally. This will tend to limit the degree to which short-run constraints are binding. In either case, if we eliminate uncertainty from the mix so that no unanticipated changes can occur, then reserve additions are 'timed' so that deviations from the long-run path are minimized. In this case, the resource owner will invest in anticipation of the need for capacity because not doing so leaves some unrealized gain and is therefore suboptimal.

Implications for the resource price

Representations of the price paths that result from the optimal solution of models discussed indicated above are indicated in Figure 3.4. The price path in Panel 3, which follows from the most complicated of the models considered herein, suggests that these models may be capable of depicting the type of pricing behavior realized historically. In particular, if extraction costs depend on the size of reserve, firms engage in exploration to find new prospects, there is uncertainty, there is technological innovation, and capital investments are lumpy, then prices can move up and down without any clear trajectory, at least for a while.

The result in Figure 3.4 indicates that a properly posed theoretical model may be capable of explaining past observation. It should also be pointed out that even in Panel 3, prices will ultimately rise to the price of the backstop. Thus, only if there is innovation that reduces the cost of the backstop will the long-run price not rise substantially. Even then, if the technical resource limits are approached without firms being aware, prices could still rise dramatically especially if there are any constraints involved in transitioning to the alternative resource.

4   Firm Behavior

The preceding sections outline the basic framework, as well as some of the modifications to that framework, that economists use to analyze the optimal extraction and price of a depletable resource. It is important to understand that such frameworks, regardless of the level of complication, are an abstraction from reality. One of the benefits of developing such models is to understand how various things might influence the 'optimal' path. In assessing the value of these models, therefore, it is worthwhile considering how individual firms actually behave. More specifically, is there anything in the observed behavior of producers of depletable resources – such as oil and gas, for example – that suggests there is value in the theory of the optimal extraction of depletable resources?

To begin, we must consider what a firm actually does when determining whether or not to explore, develop and market a depletable resource deposit. Typically, the

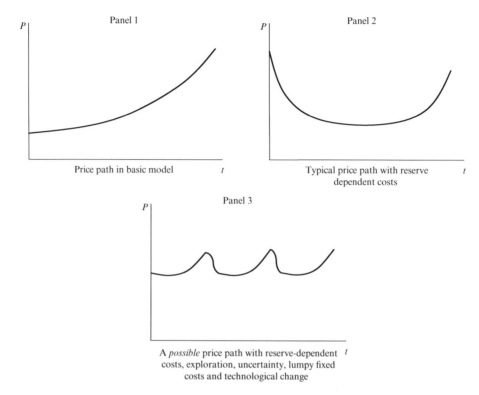

Note: The price paths indicated are for illustration only. Panel 1 depicts the optimal price path in the basic model. As we move from the upper-left quadrant to the lower-right quadrant, we increase the degree of modification to the basic model. Panel 3 indicates that price can rise and fall through time without any particular underlying trend. However, as we ultimately approach exhaustion, the price will rise toward the backstop price.

Figure 3.4   Optimal price paths under different model assumptions

exploration and development phase is the most capital-intensive phase of a project. A firm must spend large sums of money in the finding and development phase of a project, prior to ever realizing any cash inflow from production of the resource. Moreover, this upfront expenditure is an investment for which the firm hopes to earn a suitable rate of return. Therefore, the firm must expect future prices to be high enough so that the project indeed earns a suitable rate of return on the upfront initial investment. Indeed, Chermak and Patrick (2001) used panel data covering 29 natural gas wells to find evidence that producer behavior is consistent with the theory of depletable resources.

Typically, firms have multiple such investment opportunities at any given time. In fact, within a firm, there are usually a number of project teams that focus on various opportunities of differing scale. Sometimes these teams may be differentiated by the type of resource developments (oil versus gas, for example) they are seeking opportunities in, or they may be differentiated along regional lines. In any case, the firm as a whole must decide how to allocate a limited amount of capital to a suite of potential projects to which it has access.

To illustrate, consider the following. A firm must determine whether to develop an oilfield. Initial seismic testing indicates that there is oil in place, but there are additional fixed costs that must be incurred prior to any actual production. Namely, the expected ultimate recovery (EUR) of the prospective project and the maximum production rate is still unknown, so a 'wildcat' well must be drilled and additional seismic work done in order to determine the reservoir pressure and gauge potential productivity. Then, once the EUR and expected production rate are established, if the project is deemed profitable, production infrastructure must be put in place. All of these steps require significant capital expenditure, but no positive cash flow will be generated until after the final step.

In practice, the firm will typically construct a discounted cash flow model to determine the profitability of such a project. This amounts to determining if the sum of future cash flows over some predetermined time period, discounted at some discount rate reflecting the project risk and the firm's internal required rate of return, is sufficient to 'pay' for the upfront capital outlay plus a return.[9] If the sum of discounted cash flows is sufficient, then the firm will shortlist the project for development. It must then be compared to other projects that also satisfy the profitability criteria, and the most profitable projects are the ones that are chosen. Note that this process results in the highest rent investment opportunities available to the firm being taken first. Of course, if we aggregate across all firms, then it may be that some projects with very different costs are developed at the same time, particularly when capital is not perfectly mobile.

The firm's assessment of profitability is highly dependent on expected future prices. In fact, if a project is deemed not to earn a suitable rate of return, it may still be developed at some later date, especially if prices rise or costs fall, perhaps due to a technological breakthrough. But, note that this means that the firm is simply shifting production from a high-cost project into the future until either prices rise or costs fall so that its development will bear a suitable rate of return. This shift of production can also occur if the firm decides to sell the rights to the field to another firm. The firm selling the project is increasing its perceived value because, perhaps, it has expectations about future market conditions that differ from those of the firm that is willing to buy the mineral rights. Regardless, the firm is behaving much in the manner prescribed by the basic framework analyzed by Hotelling – by 'delaying' production in this manner, firms in the extractive industries engage in intertemporal arbitrage. This is an important point, in particular, because it suggests that we ought to look at the theoretical framework as being predictive of *behavior* rather than *outcomes*. There are simply too many unknowns and too much heterogeneity across resource deposits and the firms that mine them for theory as it currently stands to provide much in the way of predicting outcomes.

5   A Comment on Peak Oil

To begin, it is worth pointing out that, in general, rising prices do not necessarily mean we are running out of crude oil. (This, in fact, is what makes the issue of 'peak oil' so contentious and interesting.) Rising prices may simply mean that demand is currently accelerating faster than supply. This can happen due to a mismatch in producer and consumer incentives to invest in new capital, and may have nothing to do with resource availability. For example, a period of low prices will discourage expansion of productive capacity on the part of resource owners, especially if they expect prices to remain

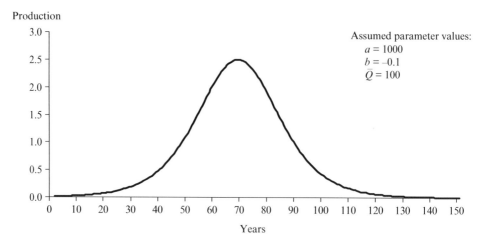

Production

Note: The Hubbert curve is constructed using a logistics curve, giving it a bell shape. The implication is that once half of the resource is consumed, a peak in production will occur and decline will commence.

Figure 3.5   The Hubbert curve and 'peak oil'

low for some time. Consumers, however, respond to low prices by increasing demand in the current period. Demand also grows in future periods if consumers expect low prices to persist because they may favor attributes of capital equipment other than efficiency. This can subsequently lead to a period of high prices as demand grows and supply is constrained in the short term.

Hubbert (1956) correctly predicted that US oil production would peak by 1970. The so-called 'Hubbert curve' is now widely used in the analysis of peaking production of conventional petroleum in other countries and on a global scale. According to the Hubbert curve, the production of a finite resource, when viewed over time, will resemble an inverted U, or a bell curve. This follows from the technical limits of exploitation. 'Peak oil' is the term used to describe the situation where the rate of oil production reaches its absolute maximum and begins to decline. A depiction of the Hubbert curve is given in Figure 3.5.

The Hubbert curve is not based in depletable resource theory as discussed above. Rather, it is a physical descriptive of the production life of a depletable resource. It is based on a logistics curve similar to:

$$Q_t = \frac{\overline{Q}}{1 + ae^{bt}},$$

(3.10)

where Q_t is cumulative production to date, $\overline{Q}$ is the recoverable resource, and the parameters a and b are fitted parameters. One obvious flaw in this simple formulation is that the parameters a and b are themselves functions of other variables that reflect structural elements of the market, such as price, development and extraction cost, and the cost of a backstop technology. Thus, if these effects are not taken into account, any estimation of equation (3.10), or its derivative, is biased.

Such criticism notwithstanding, an increasing number of analysts are increasingly concerned with the ability of current known *conventional* oil and gas resources to meet rapidly increasing global demand.[10] In fact, predictions in the Association for the Study of Peak Oil (ASPO) Newsletters have recently reported that global conventional crude oil production will peak in 2010.[11] There is concern on this issue because without a low-cost alternative, a peak in production will lead to rapidly rising prices and global economic malaise. The leading indicators for such a crisis include:

- diminishing production capacity and well productivity;
- constraints on equipment and personnel for exploration and development, which comes about from having to drill an increased number of wells to sustain a given level of production; and
- declining exploration success.

Each of these leading indicators is a facet of a depletable resource model that includes reserve-dependent costs and exploration.

Data reveal that well productivity is indeed in decline in many of the major producing regions around the world, and the early 2000s have been characterized by rapid increases in drilling costs due to scarcity of rigs and qualified personnel. In addition, although there is general agreement that new discoveries will occur, they will be increasingly costly – a notion that is consistent with the model of exploration discussed above. Thus, the leading indicators of peak oil, as of the early twenty-first century, appear to be upon us.

A major contention, however, with forecasts of an imminent peak can also be found in the theory above. Specifically, if there is uncertainty about the location and quality of new deposits and new technological breakthroughs that reduce the costs of developing resources in more difficult environments, then a peak may yet be some years away. In particular, if these sorts of factors come to bear, then production may yet be able to expand, albeit at potentially higher prices. In fact, the run-up in price in the early 2000s could be precisely the impetus needed to spur the exploration effort and technological innovation that would allow production to expand.

Of note is the fact that technological change, in particular, makes the problem of assessing peak oil problematic because it is difficult to capture in empirical analysis. Changes in technology are structural changes, and historical data do not bear witness to that which has yet to occur. So a prediction based on historical data can be upset if a technological innovation occurs, thereby changing the variable relationships in the underlying model.

So-called 'above ground' factors are also often mentioned by those who contend that a peak in oil production is not imminent. Geopolitical factors limit access by firms in the extraction industries to certain areas of the world, such as the Middle East and Russia, where there may be an abundance of yet to be discovered relatively low-cost crude oil. However, if we are to take those factors as given, then geopolitics effectively reduce $\bar{Q}$. Thus, geopolitics may in fact be the bearer of a production peak. If true, then only if those barriers are removed will the effective $\bar{Q}$ approach its technical maximum. In fact, economic incentive should result in those barriers being dropped because any resource that remains untapped is worthless. However, a more complicated model of resource extraction would have to incorporate political variables that carry their own costs. In such a case, it is possible to imagine a world in which the political costs of a country opening up its resources to the international community outweigh the economic benefits, so that the resource indeed remains untapped.

Even if peak oil is imminent, the predictions of ever higher prices may not be accurate. Theory tells us that if there is uncertainty in demand, then production should be accelerated, and it should be done as rapidly as possible if there is potential for demand to completely evaporate. This would tend to lower prices in the short term. Could this happen? To the extent that it can, yes. Higher prices encourage demand-side innovation. Increases in energy efficiency and the adoption of alternative technologies serve to reduce demand for crude oil. The importance of this cannot be underestimated given the trends seen following the oil crises of the late 1970s and early 1980s. If a demand-side innovation in the face of high prices were to encourage yet again improvements in energy efficiency and wider-scale adoption of alternative technologies, then long-term production could in fact decline, even if there is a low-cost major deposit of crude oil yet to be discovered. Timing is everything.

This brings up a final point. Crude oil is a finite resource. We shall eventually consume less of it. This is an inescapable truth. But, the reasons for production decline and movement to alternative (backstop) energy resources can be many. Moreover, the timing of the peak is a subject that is still debated. Unfortunately, the theory of depletable resources can be used to support either hypothesis if the 'right' assumptions are made. Thus, theory can suggest what to expect when a peak seems imminent, and what is needed (and at what cost) to prolong high rates of production and hence avoid a peak. But, it cannot tell us with certainty when the actual peak will occur.

6   Final Remarks

The finiteness of a depletable resource is the single most important feature in determining how it should be used and what its value should be. In fact, this assumption is the backbone of Hotelling's so-called '*r*-percent' rule. In examining the ability of the basic Hotelling model to explain observed prices, however, it is clear that other factors must play a role or the theory is simply inadequate.

Factors such as exploration, technology that reduces the cost or increases the success rate of exploration, technology that lowers the cost of extraction, technology that alters demand for the depletable resource (such as efficiency improvement or alternative energy), uncertainty in the rate at which these new technologies may be adopted, uncertainty in the size and location of resource deposits, and the lumpiness of capital investments in the extractive industries are all important for understanding how a firm may behave under different conditions. In fact, these other factors appear to have at least as much, if not more, bearing on the observed price paths of depletable commodities such as crude oil. This can be especially true when these factors are combined.

The modifications presented herein are not an exhaustive list of the types of alterations that can be made to the basic model. For example, we can use the basic framework to examine the effect of taxation on resource development (see, for example, Dasgupta and Heal 1979) to aid in determining, perhaps, an optimal tax strategy. We can also study the behavior of firms in the extractive industries that have multiple social welfare and other objectives to meet, such as might be the case with a national oil company, to determine what something like resource nationalization means for supply and price (see Hartley and Medlock 2008). We can also investigate the effects of resource scarcity on economic welfare and how welfare is influenced by perceived benefits to conservation (see, for example, Krautkraemer 1985). In principle, the theoretical framework lends itself to the study of many problems in which a depletable resource is present.

Depletable energy resources are by their very nature, transition fuels. Eventually, their cost will rise, reflecting various degrees of scarcity. This will promote a transition to a different energy source, perhaps one that is non-depletable. At that point, economic models of capital investment and provision of energy services that do not need to incorporate long-run depletability constraints will be adequate for explaining the behavior of energy producers, thus simplifying the microeconomic analysis of such firms. But, by most accounts economic activity will be dependent on depletable energy resources for the foreseeable future. So, understanding the behaviors that result in the provision of those supplies is crucial. Moreover, the transition to the next regime, one in which depletable energy resources are no longer consumed, will be of increasing interest, especially if a global peak in production is imminent.

Notes

1. 'Renewable' and 'non-renewable' are often used in place of 'non-depletable' and 'depletable', respectively.
2. It is more correct to note Gray (1914) as it pre-dates Hotelling's paper. Gray showed that the present value of marginal revenue must be equal in all periods when extraction is positive. Hotelling's paper is most often noted as it employed some more modern techniques (calculus of variations) to demonstrate the principle and considered several deviations from the continuous, competitive case.
3. The problem presented here is a variant of the 'cake-eating' model of resource extraction where firm profits have replaced the general notion of social utility in the objective function.
4. A concise discussion of 'depletion pressures' and what they mean for transitioning to different fuels is found in Hartwick (2004).
5. The case where the firm's production decision influences the market price will be considered below.
6. The case of rising extraction costs due to resource depletion is considered below.
7. Virtually all theoretical papers raise these issues. Frequently cited papers are listed at the end of the chapter.
8. Recursive substitution in (3.7) reveals

$$\lambda_t = \sum_{n=1}^{T-t} \beta^n (-c_{R,t+n})$$

   because $\beta^{T-t}\lambda_T = 0$ since the resource is valueless once production ceases.
9. Of course there are many other parameters that must be included in the project analysis, such as tax and royalty rates and operating costs.
10. *Conventional* oil production is usually distinguished from *unconventional* oil production because extraction techniques used in unconventional oil production are generally more costly and use technically different extraction methods. In addition, the stock of non-conventional crude oil is estimated to be much larger than the remaining conventional stock.
11. The production profile is published monthly in the ASPO newsletter. The peak here is determined by summing 'Regular Oil' and 'Deepwater' and 'Polar' oil from the 'Other' category.

References

Arrow, K.J. and S. Chang (1982), 'Optimal pricing, use, and exploration of uncertain natural resource stocks', *Journal of Environmental Economics and Management*, **9**: 1–10.

Association for the Study of Peak Oil (ASPO) Newsletter (October 2007), available at: http://www.aspo-ireland.org/index.cfm/page/newsletter (accessed November 2007).

Brown, Jr., G.M. and B.C. Field (1978), 'Implications of alternative measures of natural resource scarcity', *Journal of Political Economy*, **86**(2), Part 1: 229–43.

Cairns, R.D. (1990), 'The economics of exploration for nonrenewable resources', *Journal of Economic Surveys*, **4**: 361–95.
Chermak, J.M. and R.H. Patrick (2001), 'A microeconomic test of the theory of exhaustible resources', *Journal of Environmental Economics and Management*, **42**: 82–103.
Dasgupta, P.S. and G.M. Heal (1979), *Economic Theory and Exhaustible Resources*, Cambridge: Cambridge University Press.
Energy Information Administration, United States Department of Energy, Washington, DC, available at: www.eia.doe.gov (accessed November 2007).
Farzin, Y.H. (1984), 'The effect of the discount rate on depletion of exhaustible resources', *Journal of Political Economy*, **92**: 841–51.
Farzin, Y.H. (1995), 'Technological change and the dynamics of resource scarcity measures', *Journal of Environmental Economics and Management*, **29**: 105–20.
Gray, L.C. (1914), 'Rent under the assumption of exhaustibility', *Quarterly Journal of Economics*, **28**: 466–89.
Halvorsen, R. and T.R. Smith (1984), 'On measuring natural resource scarcity', *Journal of Political Economy*, **92**: 954–64.
Hartley, P. and K.B. Medlock III (2008), 'A model of the operation and development of a national oil company', *Energy Economics*, **30**(5), September: 2459–85.
Hartwick, J. (2004), 'Depletion and valuation of energy resources', in Cutler J. Cleveland (ed.), *The Encyclopedia of Energy*, London: Elsevier Academic Press, pp. 771–80.
Heal, G. (1976), 'The relationship between price and extraction cost for a resource with a backstop technology', *Bell Journal of Economics*, **7**(2): 371–8.
Hotelling, H. (1931), 'The economics of exhaustible resources', *Journal of Political Economy*, **39**: 137–75.
Hubbert, M.K. (1956), 'Nuclear energy and fossil fuels', paper presented to the Spring Meeting of the Southern District Division of Production, American Petroleum Institute, San Antonio, TX, March 8, Publication No. 95, Houston: Shell Development Company, Exploration and Production Research Division, available at: http://www.hubbertpeak.com/hubbert/ (accessed November 2007).
Krautkraemer, J.A. (1985), 'Optimal growth, resource amenities, and the preservation of natural environments', *Review of Economic Studies*, **52**: 153–70.
Krautkraemer, J.A. (1998), 'Nonrenewable resource scarcity', *Journal of Economic Literature*, **36**(4): 831–42.
Krautkraemer, J.A. and M.A. Toman (2004), 'Economics of energy supply', in Cutler J. Cleveland (ed.), *The Encyclopedia of Energy*, London: Elsevier Academic Press, pp. 91–102.
Livernois, J.R. and R.S. Uhler (1987), 'Extraction costs and the economics of nonrenewable resources', *Journal of Political Economy*, **95**(1): 195–203.
Oren, S.S. and S.G. Powell (1985), 'Optimal supply of a depletable resource with a backstop technology: Heal's theorem revisited', *Operations Research*, **33**(2): 277–92.
Oren, S.S. and S.G. Powell (1989), 'The transition to nondepletable energy: social planning and market models of capacity expansion', *Operations Research*, **37**(3): 373–83.
Pindyck, R.S. (1978), 'The optimal exploration and production of nonrenewable resources', *Journal of Political Economy*, **86**(5): 841–61.
Pindyck, R.S. (1980), 'Uncertainty and exhaustible resource markets', *Journal of Political Economy*, **88**(6): 1203–25.
Stiglitz, J.E. (1976), 'Monopoly and the rate of extraction of exhaustible resources', *American Economic Review*, **66**: 655–61.
Swierzbinski, J.E. and R. Mendelsohn (1989), 'Exploration and exhaustible resources: the microfoundations of aggregate models', *International Economic Review*, **30**(1): 175–86.

4 The theory and practice of energy policy
Richard L. Gordon

1 Introduction

At least since early in the twentieth century, many governments have intervened heavily and largely disastrously in the production, processing, and distribution of energy. A vast literature has arisen on these efforts. This chapter presents examples of such programs and states the conceptual reasons why the programs were ill advised. Discussion begins in Section 2 with a review of the errors committed in the name of seeking energy security. The analysis in Section 3 focuses on the United States because of its large size and long, well-documented history of wide-ranging interference. In Section 4, attention is given to policies directed solely at altering energy choice and to those that have a specific environmental focus. An analysis of the stress in current US energy policy of performance standards is presented in Section 5. Section 6 focuses on the way Western European and Japan resisted overwhelming evidence that their coal industries had become profoundly uneconomic. Section 7 concludes.

2 The Theory of Energy Intervention

It has become routine in the economics literature to distinguish between the public interest and public choice theories of intervention. The former presumes that policy is designed to correct the departures from the assumptions of pure competition that economists term 'market failures'. Public choice responds to the obvious lack of market-failure rationales for many or even most interventions by observing interest-group pressures for aid and the circumstances under which these efforts are rewarded. Others have suggested that politicians possess and employ slack that allows them to express their ideological preferences. A further influence is the unexpected-consequences effect; after a policy is legislated, administrative and judicial review can and has produced interpretations that probably were unexpected by the legislators.

The focus of this section is on the market-failure concept that perniciously dominated energy debates, the issue of security of supply.[1] This issue is often used by protectionists to pressure the politically influential. Protection based on nostalgia is particularly prevalent in Germany where coal protection was justified on the grounds that it was preserving a once great industry.

The political instability of oil suppliers produces much hysteria, but little useful policy advice. The 2008 posturing among US politicians (regardless of party affiliation) about ending the 'addiction to oil' led to assorted ideas of how to micromanage energy consumption and promote alternatives to imported oil. The available alternatives have problematic aspects including politicians' reluctance to reverse limitations on the development of the promising offshore oil and gas resources. Preference is given more to unconventional and thus more risky alternatives such as ethanol from agricultural sources. To date, the danger from a reliance on imports has been of temporary disruption of supplies due to local crisis. This is a manageable problem that free-market institutions could handle if not thwarted by intervention.

Eliminating or even sharply reducing oil imports is not a sensible response to such short-term disruptions. It is premature to postulate and respond to longer-term supply disruptions. Indeed, it is hard to conceive of plausible long-term threats. Oil is more easily extracted, transported, transformed, and utilized than any other fuel. These rival energy sources can overcome the drawbacks but only at a cost. It is the height of that cost that prevents the energy transitions.

Political visions of what drives oil markets are invalid, diplomacy will not provide solutions, and access to oil is neither a problem nor best treated by special arrangements. Appraisal depends radically upon which model of exporting-country behavior is adopted. Thus, debate over an economic versus a political model of exporter behavior is examined and updated. In particular, attention is given to whether the rise of Islamic fundamentalism changes anything of substance.

Broadly, a long-standing conflict prevails between those who believe that world oil supply is primarily driven by the conventional economic objective of wealth maximization and those who believe that political influences are dominant. Neither view should be pushed to its logical limits. Proponents of the economic view generally recognize that at least one important departure from wealth maximization has arisen. The rhetoric of the 1970s pushed most members of the Organization of Petroleum Exporting Countries (OPEC) to nationalize fully the oil industry. Given the prior efforts to ensure that its nationals secured training in petroleum-industry management and the ability to hire managers, the ability to operate was not undermined. However, investment decision making was harmfully altered. With foreign contractors, stress was on undertaking profitable investments in capacity maintenance and addition. With nationalization, the funds became part of a national pool, and oil investments had to compete with other national plans. The effects of this on the industry illustrate the fallacy of reliance on allegedly superior governmental investment skills.

One clear consequence of an economics-based view of oil is that if oil policy is governed by national self-interest, the engagement with producers so beloved among politicians is a waste of time. Exporting, if profitable, will be undertaken whatever foreign diplomats may suggest. More complex considerations relate to possible consequences of dealing with imported oil. Theories have proliferated on ways to counteract monopolistic behavior of oil exporters and on alleged macroeconomic effects of oil shocks.

Nixon's call for energy independence in the 1974 Project Independence initiative proved infeasible when analyzed by the old US Federal Energy Administration (1974). Its well-designed (but necessarily very oversimplified) 1974 model nicely quantified what experienced energy observers sensed. The nature of petroleum use with its heavy concentration in the transportation sector makes substitution extremely expensive.

Conversely, the so-called political theory is more like a managerial-slack model of firm behavior. The countries supposedly have sufficiently limited objectives that they sacrifice opportunities for wealth maximization. This view has the same inherent implausibility as the slack theories that it resembles.[2]

More critically, the key example cited of this sort of behavior, the purported Arab oil boycott of 1973, implied no such thing. Selective boycotts are infeasible as once oil hits the high sea its destination cannot be controlled, and in addition shifts of suppliers are possible. The Adelman (1972, 1993, and 1995) analysis of world oil argues that production reductions were motivated more by a desire to force oil prices up than by a desire to punish anyone for support of Israel.

The lineup at gas stations in the United States was due to the imposition of price controls on gasoline and their enforcement by rigid rules for distribution. This is classic. Price controls always affect their price-rise limitation role by thwarting the role of price fully to allocate supply. Messy rules must be imposed to deal with the excess of the quantity demanded over the amount available.

Further evidence is provided by the effects of the critical revolutions in Iraq, Libya, and Iran in which rulers 'friendly to the West' were replaced by hostile leaders. Aside from the later years of Saddam Hussein's rule in Iraq, these hostile rulers were at least as dedicated as their predecessors to maintenance of oil supplies. Even Saddam Hussein's attacks on Iran in 1979 and Kuwait in 1991 had wealth-maximizing aspects. To be sure, the moves were motivated by ancient grudges. However, the effort could also be construed as an oil grab based on ill-conceived beliefs that more oil wealth could be secured cheaply.

The infamous oil negotiations in 1971 first with Libya and then in Tehran with the Middle Eastern producers were the nadir of this process of political dealing and the great turning point for world oil.[3] Reporters from *Forbes* learned that the State Department, apparently under the leadership of James Akins, its long-time energy adviser and cooperation advocate, pushed through a deal allowing oil-price rises (*Forbes* 1976). Akins (1973) contended that the deal prevented even larger rises. Adelman (1973) argued that the timidity would unleash efforts more vigorously to raise oil prices closer to a monopoly profit-maximizing level. This fostered price-rigging policies that would have been avoided had the demands been resisted. He later noted that perhaps the outcome could have arisen in any case (Adelman, 1995). The 1973–74 oil-price rises were the realization of Adelman's warnings.[4] More broadly, Adelman (1995) argues that the special relation with Saudi Arabia is a sham; Saudi Arabia, as should be expected, does what is in its economic interest, which rarely means doing what the US wants. Calls for dialog and cooperation remain.

The oil dependence of these countries has been critical as most possess nothing else that can produce significant incomes. Others have become so dependent on oil that other industries lie fallow, as for example in Venezuela. The key is that maximizing wealth and spending the income is far more rewarding than capricious political manipulation of markets.

The rise of Islamic fundamentalism more extreme than in Iran supposedly profoundly alters the situation. At least two critical implicit assumptions are made. First, it is inferred from the willingness of such fundamentalists to harm fellow Muslims that they would take the ultimate step of dooming Islamic nations by ceasing oil production. Second, it is presumed that these fundamentalists have good prospects of assuming power in many oil-producing states. A possible third tacit assumption is that the suicide strategy could not be resisted as with the suicidal stinging scorpion in many jokes. While all this might occur, it appears far too wild a possibility to be the core of national energy policies. Moreover, it is unlikely that any good strategy exists to prepare for this situation. No vision of oil-exporter restraint from wealth maximization implies either that good relations are needed to ensure supply or that the exporters are susceptible to cajoling.

A key variant of the political-motivation viewpoint is the search for 'access' to oil. In markets governed by economic principles, access is secured by paying the prevailing market price. This is true whatever the state of competition in the market. With textbook pure competition, every one is a price taker, buying or selling goods and services at the prevailing market price. With imperfect competition, some sellers and buyers may affect the price, but sellers will still sell to all at whatever price results from the interaction.[5]

Political theories argue that these tendencies can be overridden, as the maneuvering to secure rights to develop oil in the Middle East illustrates. Other forms of deals have arisen. No evidence exists that these arrangements have ever affected allocations. Neither the economics nor the politics are favorable. The oil companies, the exporting country, and the country with 'access' all face enormous pressures not to indulge in favoritism. By definition, favoritism is bad for the producing companies and countries. Favoritism can only mean selling to less remunerative outlets. Even the consuming countries suffer the consequences of diversion from what may be actual or potential allies.

None of this has prevented pursuit of special relations. The first important case was the British government's purchase of the company (the predecessor of today's BP) developing Iranian oil resources.[6] The key symbolic start of the US's embrace of the political-relations approach to oil was President Roosevelt's 1945 detour to meet Saudi Arabian king Ibn Saud. France and Japan are other examples of futile efforts to establish special relations with oil producers. Chinese efforts simply repeat past errors.

In sum, the economic view of oil advocated here holds for the primacy of economic goals, recognizes that this generates vast revenues that may be and indeed often are misused, and that the feasible options open to the United States and other major oil consumers are limited to avoiding incentives to rig markets. It is fantasy to believe that other countries can redirect the policies of oil exporters. Price restraint is totally against exporter interests. Redirecting governance or use of the funds is beyond the power of other countries.

Adelman (1972) on one side and the US Cabinet Task Force on Oil Import Control (1970) on the other agreed that the main concern was ensuring vigorous competition in oil, which was not the case at that time. For decades, a conflict has prevailed between the protectionist forces in US policy and what promotes vigorous competition. As with all protectionism, policy makers pursue a balanced approach, seeking as much shelter as possible. The result is a messy, overly prolonged erosion of the amount of domestic activity protected. From the exporters' side, this is a discouraging situation. No matter how hard they try, they are limited in their ability to sell. Competing makes little sense, and attention turns to market rigging.

Neglect of the importance of competition made cartelization easier, and public policy should foster as much as possible a pro-competitive environment. Since 1971, the oil-exporting countries have secured sharply higher but widely fluctuating prices. This may be due to a simple tightening of demand–supply balances. However, many analysts see some form of cartel-like behavior; what Adelman (1980) identifies as a clumsy cartel. The crux of the clumsiness argument is that the states are far from united on strategy, and it is unclear which of the OPEC countries participate in output restriction. Also, whoever the participants, they face great uncertainty about how far they can go. Thus, prices have fluctuated widely and wildly. The clearest advice for consuming states is that they do nothing to obstruct the flow of the oil trade. The biggest danger of imports is the hysteria about them and the market-disrupting measures proposed as cures.[7]

3 The Phases of US Energy Policy

Until the oil turmoil of 1973, the United States slowly accumulated its energy programs. In the first phase from about 1920 to 1973, policies with the glaring exception of natural-gas price regulation aided at least parts of the oil and gas industry. From 1973 to 1980, emphasis shifted to limiting petroleum-company profits and micromanaging most aspects of energy. The profit controls were killed in the 1980s, but micromanagement has strengthened since 1991.

The first major US energy policy, special mineral tax provisions, arose during the implementation of federal income taxes (McDonald 1963; Brannon 1974 and 1975; and Bradley 1995). These provisions were initially enacted only for oil and gas, but later were extended to all minerals. These provisions governed allowable 'expense' deductions in determining taxable income. Two forms of cost recovery were allowed. The first was 'cost depletion'. This was conventional depreciation accounting under a different name. The firm charged off over time the actual expenses of acquiring and developing the mineral. The second approach set write-off allowances as a percentage of sales income. The starting point was specifying the allowance rate for a given mineral. From 1926 to 1969, the rate on oil and gas was 27.5 percent. This meant that every year an allowance of 27.5 percent of sales revenues from oil and gas production could be deducted from taxable income. However, a limit of 50 percent of the net income of each property was set. Moreover, the allowance was shared between the operator and the landowner. The operator secured the allowance on the value net of royalties, and the royalty recipient received an allowance on the royalty.

In 1932, the allowance was extended to all minerals and raised in 1954. Uranium got an allowance of 23 percent, lowered to 22 percent in 1969; coal, 10 percent. The oil and gas allowance was reduced to 22 percent in 1969. In 1975, the oil and gas allowance was removed from integrated firms, foreign production, and fields transferred. For other producers, the allowance was reduced in stages to 15 percent from 1975 to 1984 with a faster cut for primary production than for secondary and tertiary. The law limited the amount of oil that could receive the allowance.

The provisions were perpetually controversial. They seemed yet another arbitrary tax break for a politically important industry. Efforts to prove otherwise proved futile. The provisions, for example, were not a good way to deal with tax treatment of unusually risky investments in industries with high capital/output ratios. Thus, a drastic reduction was imposed during the 1970s turmoil.

A more intrusive intervention resulted from the combination of massive oil discoveries and the great depression. Oil-producing states in desperation adopted programs of production control (see Lovejoy and Homan 1967; McDonald 1971; and Bradley 1995). In many key states such as Texas, the specific approach was 'market-demand prorationing'. The process involved setting maximum allowable production rates for individual oil wells, often on the basis of rules with no economic or technological basis. Then using US Bureau of Mines and other estimates, the state regulatory agencies would estimate 'market demand' – tacitly at the then-prevailing price, although price was never mentioned and in the Texas case demand was treated as unrelated to price. An estimate of expected production from the small wells exempt from production control was made and the remainder was allocated ('prorated' in the terminology of the implementation) to the remainder of the wells. The effect was to create a class of many small producers producing little but politically potent. The program became a way to protect these small producers from the competition of larger ones. The existence of protection implies the economic inferiority of the small wells.

The policies were an inferior cure to a problem in US property law. Under that law, mineral rights initially belonged to the owner of the surface. That owner could sell the rights separately or retain them in a subsequent sale of surface rights. Oil- and gasfields, however, normally underlie multiple properties. Efficient utilization requires that the owners pool ('unitize' in industry jargon) these rights so that the inter-property effects were properly accounted for. To aggravate matters, US courts adopted the 'law of capture' doctrine previously employed regarding the rights to wandering wild animals. Landowners and their oil and gas rights leasers were free to extract all they could, and counteraction was the only recourse.

This raised formidable transaction costs to unitization. The standard view is that these barriers were insuperable, although some suggest that they could have been overcome (see Libecap and Wiggins 1984, 1985; Wiggins and Libecap 1985). All observers agree that unitization is superior to market-demand prorationing for the usual reasons for preferring a private solution to a state-imposed one. Thus, state stimulus to unitization was the preferred option. The only debate was about how much stimulus was needed. The states agreed, and by law or fiat instituted unitization. Prorationing survived because the rent seekers had such political clout.

The strong expansion after World War II of Middle-Eastern and Venezuelan production predictably put massive pressure on this system. Pressures arose to curtail imports of oil into the United States (see Bohi and Russell 1978; Bradley 1995). After various informal efforts, President Eisenhower then instituted a mandatory oil-import quota program. Eisenhower used a national defense justification reflecting prevailing law that made defense the only allowable basis. This program set the model for subsequent programs. For most of the country, imports were set at a specific percentage of expected consumption. Initially the quotas were allocated on the basis of historical levels of imports, but a transition was made to a sliding scale such that the smaller the refinery the larger the percentage of capacity was allocated as a quota. The West coast was treated differently; imports were set at the difference between expected consumption and expected domestic production in the region. Throughout its history, the program was characterized by battles both between consuming and producing states over the level of imports and among actual and potential importers over quota allocation. For example, quotas were given to refineries in Puerto Rico and the Virgin Islands to promote economic development. A program-ending threat emerged in the late 1960s when Armand Hammer of Occidental Petroleum proposed grants of import quotas for a refinery to be built in Michiasport, Maine. Then President Johnson was identified with Texas oil interests and (preoccupied with the war) deferred to Nixon, his successor.

Nixon commissioned a Cabinet Task Force (1970) to undertake a *serious* study which suggested that the program was best replaced by tariffs. Nixon was unwilling to accept the proposals; the massive rise in world-oil prices developed (due, Adelman has argued, to ineptitude in US policy); then the quotas were ended.

A third major US energy policy of the period arose from a series of political missteps in natural gas (see MacAvoy 1962, 2001, 2007; Breyer and MacAvoy 1974). The 1938 Natural Gas Act was designed primarily to regulate interstate pipelines. Production was exempt. However, aborted action led to placing the sale of natural gas under federal regulation. Congress grappled unsuccessfully in both the Truman and Eisenhower administrations with eliminating uncertainties about what the law meant. In the absence of that clarification, the US Supreme Court decided, in defiance of economic principles and common sense, that selling natural gas was marketing and distinct from production. Thus, regulation of field prices of natural gas was required.

This was a regulator's nightmare. The standard approach of securing production-cost data and calculating the break-even price was unworkable. The calculations would have been analytic nonsense since gas is often produced jointly with oil, and allocation of joint costs is economically invalid. Only the market determines what portion of total cost is recovered from jointly produced product. Regulators often ignore such realities. However, what could not be ignored was that the number of gas producers vastly exceeded the number of entities typically handled by a regulatory agency. Decades would have passed before the relevant agency, the Federal Power Commission (FPC), cleared its backlog.

The FPC hit on a two-tier price ceiling system for each gas-producing region. Gas produced in association with oil was given a ceiling lower than that produced separately. This too was a recipe for ruin. If the ceilings had been set at the average for viable wells, then the above-average cost portion was automatically made unprofitable. A trade-off between excess profits and production loss had to be made.

With the oil crisis came a frenzy of new regulatory efforts (Kalt 1981; Bradley 1995). Concern focused on preventing domestic energy producers from benefiting from the rise in world oil prices. Between 1973 and 1979, a succession of laws was enacted to limit energy price increases. With oil, the approach was price controls combined with entitlements to low-priced oil. Under the system, transfers among refiners smoothed out differences in supply sources. Refiners with above-average use of the lower-priced portion of price-controlled domestic crude oil made payments that were transferred to those with below-average access. Undiluted, the system would have made the weighted average of domestic and imported crude oil prices the marginal cost to refiners. This stimulus to imports was offset somewhat by the introduction of yet another smaller-producers' bias; smaller refineries received proportionally more compensation than larger ones. Another complication was that the rules allowed adding US$0.05 to the price of oil upon transfer to a reseller; Bradley (1995) argues that the whole benefit of entitlements was lost through undertaking a 'daisy-chain' of resales numerous enough to eliminate the difference between domestic and imported oil prices.

Carter's second round of energy laws in 1980 included passage of an oil excise tax misleadingly called an 'excess-profits' tax. Domestic crude-oil production was divided into four categories, and the tax applied to three of these. In each case of application, the tax applied to the difference between actual prices and a base set in the law. That base differed among tiers, and tier three had a greater escalation rate than the others. The tax rates differed between tiers one and two; for both, the rate on integrated oil companies was higher than on those that were independent. The tier three rate was 30 percent, the tier two rate for those who were independent.

This is the quintessence of simplicity compared to the price-ceiling rules of the 1978 Natural Gas Policy Act, which established eight categories of natural gas with differences in the base-year ceiling, its escalation, and when, if ever, the controls expired.

All these systems have been dismantled. President Reagan ended oil-price controls shortly after inauguration, and Congress repealed the windfall profits tax in 1987. Natural gas controls ended in 1989.

From the first post-turmoil energy act of 1974, The US Congress has imposed a mix of requirements, subsidies, loan programs, and research and development to alter energy choices on the basis of assorted theories about why market decisions about energy options might be inefficient. This is another example of how bad regulation begets more bad regulation. The best of several bad explanations for this heavy-handed and capricious intervention is that it was an exceedingly crude way to offset underpricing due to price controls. These efforts have persisted and indeed multiplied. The last three major US energy bills, in the presidencies of the first and second George Bush, contain virtually nothing else since price controls are now recognized as counterproductive by enough politicians to prevent their imposition. No realm of energy use including very indirect ones has escaped attention. Thus, motor vehicles are subject to the much-studied corporate automobile fleet efficiency (CAFE) standard. Similar efficiency standards are imposed on major household and commercial energy-using devices. Looser loophole-filled rules tried to encourage electric utilities and other large energy users to shift away from oil and natural gas to coal. Subsidies were given at various times to the use of solar and windpower.[8]

Research programs were devised for numerous energy options. The great fiasco in the realm was Carter's creation of the Synthetic Fuels Corporation, which was to effect development of the energy alternatives such as extracting oil from shale, long known as possessing the physical ability to provide a large amount of energy and converting coal to a liquid or a gas. The perennial drawback is that, even after massive rises in oil prices, these alternative technologies are prohibitively expensive. Rises in oil prices similar to those that prevailed were previously thought sufficient to recover synthetic fuel costs. Subsequent efforts better to characterize the prospects uncovered the optimism of prior estimates. The Synthetic Fuel Corporation's main accomplishment was a coal gasification plant in North Dakota that has passed into the hands of an electricity generation and transmission cooperative that kept it alive in part though infusion of new aid. The Corporation was shut down in 1985.

The efforts at controlling large-scale energy use are also of particular interest. The fuel-choice mandates proved either fruitless or redundant. The electric power industry was in the process of greatly increasing its oil use prior to the price spikes. Enough of the plans made then came to fruition that electric power oil use rose through 1978. Then a large-scale decline arose. All the industry's adaptation options came into use. New coal and nuclear plants came on line in heavily oil-dependent regions, particularly the Middle Atlantic states. Switches to gas were made, particularly in California and Florida. Coal-using utilities, particularly American Electric Power, in the Midwest transmitted a large amount of electricity to eastern utilities.

Carter's 1978 initiatives had buried in them an initiative that led to large increases in natural gas use by the electric-utility industry. A provision in the Public Utility Regulatory Policy Act encouraged state regulators to set rates at which electric utilities would purchase electricity from alternative energy sources produced by companies outside the industry. While most of the options were true alternatives such as solar and wind, the law included under its glorified new name of cogeneration the old practice of sale of surplus energy from large independent facilities. The creation of new cogeneration facilities was the principal effect of the law.

4   Environmental Policy

Energy is profoundly affected by the rise of extensive environmental policies. US air pollution laws created multi-tiered, complex, and periodically tightened regulations. By 1990, three different approaches were adopted: goals for overall air quality, restrictions on the emissions from new plants, as well as a program targeted at reducing emissions in the most heavily polluting existing electric power plants. The overall goals specify the allowable concentrations in the atmosphere of the pollutants with which the law is concerned. States must establish implementation plans (SIPs) to ensure meeting these goals. Failure to do so makes a region a nonattainment area subject to specific pollution-reduction requirements.

A federal court decided that the preamble to the law that called for maintaining air quality required 'prevention of significant deterioration' (PSD) in areas in compliance with the rules. Widespread failure to meet SIP goals and the vagueness of the PSD mandate were treated in the 1977 Clean Air Act Amendments. The country was separated into nonattainment areas in which actions must be taken to comply and PSD regions in which increases in pollution were to be limited to amounts specified in the law. Continued nonattainment inspired further remedial legislation in 1990. Three different PSD limits were set. The law required that numerous types of areas such as national parks and national forests be limited to the lowest or second-lowest pollution increase allowance. All other areas were to adopt at least the middle norm unless governors requested application of the least-stringent limits.

The new source rules originally imposed stricter emission controls on new facilities. The justification stressed that the cost of incorporating controls into a newly designed plant was less than that of adding controls to an old plant. The disincentives to adding and operating new plants were ignored. The initial rules clearly produced considerable fuel shifting. Western coal was heavily used in such producing states as Illinois and Indiana and in states such as Minnesota that previously relied on Illinois coal. Pressures arose to restrict shifting. Therefore, US law was changed in 1977 to favor using cleanup devices preferably with the coals previously burned over shifting to low sulfur coals. The 1977 Clean Air Act Amendments reflected this by requiring use of best available control technology (BACT) for preventing the discharge of pollution. Since some cleanup was necessary, the advantage of shifting to a cleaner fuel was at least diminished.

Shortly after the passage of the act, much publicity was given to the dangers of acid rain. The emphasis was on damage to lakes and forests in the Northeast United States and Canada. However, the available data indicate that the loss to damage of such lakes and forests was far smaller than the costs of reducing pollution, and some evidence suggested that cheaper solutions such as deacidifying lakes were available. Attention turned instead to effects on health and damage to other property. These, however, were the damages that supposedly had been properly controlled under the prior laws. Acid rain was a disguise for claims that the prior legislation was inadequately stringent.

The Reagan administration was sufficiently skeptical about the acid rain problem that it successfully opposed action throughout its eight years. The Bush administration decided just as the studies on impacts became available that the time for action had come and so proposed a new law, and agreed to accept the legislation enacted in 1990 requiring that by January 1, 2000, electric power plants reduce sulfur dioxide by ten million tons (from 1980 levels) and nitrogen oxide emissions be reduced by two million tons by assigning reduction targets to affected plants in two stages. This law is highly intrusive. The acid rain section contains over 50 pages of provisions for determining how the burden of reductions should be shared. The law lists and sets pollution-reduction allocations for specific units at 111 power plants. These plants were to undertake the reductions in the first phase of the program. They were the ones with the highest emission rates in 1985. The law encourages cheaper abatement by allowing the polluters opportunities to buy offsets to their activities.

Paradoxically Congress first extended the command and control approach by requiring emission reductions in plants named in the law. Then a concession to market forces was added by allowing trade of the pollution permits. A vigorous market in permits arose and greatly alleviated the problems of compliance.

Environmental economists frequently condemn the inefficiencies of enforcement policies selected. The adoption of BACT has been widely characterized as reflecting an unholy alliance of environmentalists and eastern high-sulfur coal producers. PSD is criticized as concentrating too much effort on the least critical problems and excessively discouraging relocation as an abatement measure. Taking advantage of unused ability to absorb pollution may at times be the least harmful response.

5   Consumption Control

The policies to reduce energy consumption, promote new technologies, and develop scientific and engineering capabilities were initially ill-advised ways to respond to the alleged underpricing of oil. Continuation of this sort of command and control intervention is now deprived of its 'offset-to-price-controls' excuse. New alibis were needed, and economic theory is quite up to the challenge. An old but tired rationale and a new but suspect one exist. The old idea is that capital markets hedge risks inadequately; the new is that imperfect information may cloud economic choices.

The key imperfect capital market argument is that a decline of oil production is impending but private investors are not correctly anticipating this development (which is unlikely). It employs a concept of market failure that the free market will not establish enough procedures to hedge risks and thus will produce inefficiently low levels of investment. The Coase (1960) warning that the costs of establishing activities be considered is the critical analytic response to the criticism. Every possible risk is not hedged simply because most of them are too small to justify establishing protective measures. Since World War II, there has been a steep rise in the array of new financial instruments. In the United States, mutual-fund companies have introduced a stunning variety of options that differ in extent of active management, whether stocks or bonds are involved, what countries are included, in what sectors of the economy investments are made, and where the shares are traded. Consequently there has been a rise of futures markets in energy.

To believe that governments are better anticipators of the future than private investors ignores the vast record demonstrating the contrary. Moreover, better anticipation is not identical to slowing the decline of oil. Economic analysis shows that oil production may be slowed because of increased incentives not to produce. However, this can be counteracted by the increased incentives to invest in and operate new producing capacity (Gordon 1965). More precisely, the economic interpretation of inadequate concern for the future is the use of too high a rate of interest to evaluate the worth of future incomes to current investors (net present value).

The assertion that consumers are inadequately informed about energy options is also dubious. This is an argument with weak theoretic support and unacceptable empirical analyses.

The relevant models are of questionable validity, and energy choice is not a good example of where the concepts are most likely to be applicable. The ideas are part of a new effort to discover ways in which market outcomes are unsatisfactory.[9] The proliferation has at least two bases. One is the pressure to develop new ideas. Another is a desire to counter the influential onslaught on older market-failure ideas. Discontent with these old ideas has become vigorous since at least the 1970s. Doubts have arisen about the ability to determine conclusively that a problem prevails. Questions also emerged about the ability to prevent mistaken accusations of a need. Further concerns relate to the ability to devise a satisfactory remedy.

The newer theories show that certain situations may or may not produce unsatisfactory performance due to various sources of market failure. Thus, the identification, possible misuse, and remedy-design problems are worse than with the older theories. The theories relevant to energy choice are clear examples of such unmanageably complex rationales for intervention.

Such unconventional economic theories treat intervention to regulate private decisions such as those about energy consumption. In the theoretic literature, most treatments appear as discussions of the implications of imperfect information. However, Spulber (1989) presented an analysis of what he called 'internalities' to relate these theories to the persistence of government regulation of purely private transactions. The cases he treats are more straightforward than the libertarian interventionist analyses that Whitman (2006) also terms 'internalities'. Whitman does not cite Spulber.

Spulber (1989) presents his analysis in two parts. The first begins by showing that no inefficiency arises if the standard assumption of pure competition with complete information prevails. The usual types of market imperfections need not cause inefficient harm to participants in a transaction. The second part deals with the inefficiencies that might arise with various types of knowledge gaps by the participants. Spulber is quite careful to recognize both that private alternatives to public intervention exist and that the prospects for public design of efficient interventions are dubious. Information provision is probably preferable to directly regulating transactions. Spulber does not go far enough. All too many of the analyses that he cites postulate problems that are unlikely to arise. To cite a particularly clear case, Spulber notes Akerlof's market for lemons article (1970). However, Bond (1982) examines the used-truck market suggesting that mechanisms existed to appraise used-truck quality.[10]

There are a massive number of allegations of neglected opportunities economically to reduce energy consumption. However, none of the proponents has experience in implementing energy choices. Moreover, the assertions are undermined by claims that even large-scale energy users are ill-informed despite ample evidence of energy concerns of such major consumers. Thus, the invalidity of these studies seems more plausible. Moreover, the theories apply to actions where the relevant knowledge is difficult for one party to the transaction to secure. This does not apply to energy choice. Consumers can readily determine the energy-use characteristics of all the energy-using equipment that they purchase. It is impossible to know what the private response to the pressure of higher energy prices would have been. However, once information problems had been solved, the second stage of performance mandates violates basic economic principles of the optimal way choices should be made. No one can be a better judge of what is best than a well-informed consumer; both government institutes with a mandate to reduce energy consumption and private groups advocating a reduction in energy use are suspect. In short, performance standards can be very bad economics.

A notable review of electric-utility energy-conservation programs by Joskow and Marron (1992) showed serious flaws in how the benefits of these programs were calculated. The central element of consumption control, CAFE, is widely but not universally criticized as an undesirable way to intervene. The main problems are effects of the standards on other aspects of automobile performance such as safety (Crandall and Graham 1989) and the incentives to increase automobile use from the higher mileage and thus lower per mile travel cost (Kleit 2004). A further drawback was establishing more-stringent rules for automobiles than for light trucks. As should have been expected, this spurred the substitution of light trucks for automobiles. In addition, new types of trucks with properties more like automobiles emerged. The literature on CAFE suggests that the case critically depends on massive consumer neglect of the value of fuel savings. For example, Fischer et al. (2007) show that with consumer awareness, CAFE is redundant and has negative effects if it diverts investment from improving other characteristics of motor vehicles. Nevertheless, they feel that a modest tightening of CAFE may be beneficial as there are other benefits that the analysis did not capture. These benefits, however, seem more speculative than the consumer ignorance arguments about which Fischer et al. were properly skeptical.

6   The Reluctant Retreat from Coal after 38 Years

World War I caused upheaval in both large and small world institutions. Among the lesser changes were those in the coal industry. From the end of the war, revival of the industry was hampered by the great depression of the 1920s and World War II.

After World War II, the three chief European coal-producing countries drastically reorganized their coal industries and embarked on ambitious programs for reviving the industries (see Gordon, 1963, 1965, 1970, 1987 and 1992a, and International Energy Agency annual). Britain and France nationalized. West German deNazification involved breaking up a heavily coal-owning steel firm into three separate companies. Each got some mines, and the rest were given a newly created independent coal company. Less ambitious plans arose elsewhere and in one case, Belgium, the need for contraction quickly became evident.

In 1950, French advocates of European unification decided that a small step involving a few critical sectors would be the best way to start. To implement this idea, then French foreign minister Robert Schuman proposed a European Coal and Steel Community to coordinate activities in these allegedly critical areas.

The Community began operating in 1952 and quickly encountered the problem that still plagues European unification, the resistance of individual countries to coordinated action. By the late 1950s, the uncompetitiveness of European coal was becoming evident. Extant and subsequently emerging rivals such as Middle East, North African, and later European North Sea oil, North Sea and Russian gas, coal from the United States, Australia, and South Africa, and nuclear power added up to an irresistible competitive threat. The oil-price rises of the 1970s did not help. Continued rises in European coalmining costs and the emergence of new rivals worsened the competitive position of European coal. Similar competitive problems and a reluctance to allow them to work arose in Japan.

For many reasons, European governments and Japan adopted programs of gradual adjustment. Part of the motivation was reluctance to face up to the refutation of at least four decades of advocacy of a strong coal industry. Another influence was the political commitments made to the mine workers. An obligation was felt, not merely to protect their income, but to do so by preserving their jobs in the coal industry.

The responses ranged from ending Dutch coal production in 1974 to particularly stubborn resistance by the Germans. Belgian production ceased in 1992; Italian in 1994; Japanese in 2002; and French in 2004. In 2007, German production was 24 million tonnes; British 17 million tonnes; Spanish, 11 million tonnes. All these countries took over the cost of worker pensions and various costs of mine closings. The prevalent practice was simply to subsidize losses not covered by these specific aids. The key exceptions were Germany and Britain where special arrangements were made with the steel and electric power industries.

The British arrangement was government ownership of the steel, electric power, and coal industries. Then in 1988, steel was privatized; electricity followed in 1989. Both newly freed customers sought and obtained freedom from British coal. The privatization of British Coal then left the industry to fend for itself, and it shrank greatly from 96 million tonnes in 1989 to 17 million tonnes in 2007.

The Germans relied on a complex set of programs. Two objectives were set. First, all domestic steel industry coal needs and some needs elsewhere in Western Europe were to be met by German coal. Second, a specific amount of German hard coal would be used to generate electricity. The first program was straightforward. A subsidy related to the difference between German costs and the world price was paid on all coal purchases of the German steel industry and a specified amount of export sales. European Community pressures led to the phaseout of the export subsidy. German industry objections led to elimination of a requirement that it pay 5 percent of the cost differential.

The electricity coal program was based on a contract with the coal industry by utility and industrial generators of electricity. This contract was signed in 1980 and called for a gradual increase in the amount of hard coal used through the duration to 1995. Part of the excess over world prices of what was paid to German suppliers was financed by a tax on electricity sales. The electricity generators had to absorb the difference. Other countries had exerted pressure on utilities to buy coal domestically, but at least some of the cost was covered from general tax revenues. With the end of the special arrangements and the electricity tax, direct subsidies became the policy.

The Germans followed the standard practice in coal protectionism of making pledges to maintain current levels of coal production. Regularly, the cost of complying with these programs proved prohibitive. New lower goals were set with claims that these could be sustained. Further adjustments became necessary, including a 1991 proposal calling for a gradual reduction in the output of German hard coal from about 70 million tonnes in 1990 to 50 million tonnes by 2005. (Actual 2005 production was 28 million tonnes according to the Statistik der Kohlenwirtschaft annual.) Preservation was rationalized by the same security of supply arguments that have prevailed since the start of the coal crisis.

7   Conclusions on Energy Policy

Whether protecting or persecuting domestic energy industries, governments in the United States, Western Europe, and Japan have adversely skewed the market outcomes. At least in the nonenvironmental realm, interference has arisen despite the existence of well-functioning markets. Environmental regulations largely have been badly designed, and critics come from every school of economic analysis. The progress made in dismantling the interference is threatened at least in the United States by a new focus on the addiction to oil. The tired arguments of the 1970s are reappearing. The present review thus seeks to recall the record as a reminder that the new hysteria simply duplicates the old. Rather than superior insight, politicians seem to have short memories.

Notes

1. See Gordon (1983 and 1992b) for earlier treatments of these issues.
2. Hicks's (1935) statement that a quiet life is the best monopoly profit is the classic statement of the view. Subsequently, many variant models of behavior were proposed. In contrast, Williamson (1967) developed an analysis of the behavior of managers able to divert profits from stockholders. He points out that the best strategy generally is to maximize profits and then divert the money to themselves in wages and fringes. Only when that fringe is hiring of employees who add to sales, but by less than their costs, are the firm's output decisions altered.
3. Adelman's works (1972, 1993 and 1995) are relevant. Sampson's (1975) is a useful supplement. *Forbes* (1976) did a remarkable reporting job that showed how the State Department blindly fostered acquiescence with oil-country demands. State seems to have felt that this was the least worst possible outcome, but *Forbes* feels that State overestimated the strength and resolve of the producing countries. State characteristically failed to comprehend the importance of preserving competition.
4. His later survey of world oil developments documents the movements of world oil prices. Akins (1973) is a rebuttal of Adelman without citing Adelman. Akins, in turn, is the key figure in the Adelman (1995) critique of the cooperation-based approach to world oil.
5. A further complication, once but now no longer potentially important in oil, is the ability to discriminate – that is, to charge different prices for the same product on different sales.
6. This story appears in every one of the many histories of world oil of which the most celebrated example is Yergin (1991).
7. Among the additional writings relevant to this topic are Bohi and Montgomery (1982), Bradley (1989), Bohi (1990), Bohi and Toman (1995), Taylor and Van Doren (2005, 2006, and 2007), and Gholz and Press (2007),
8. The 1992 law contained the quintessence of overregulation – the curious stretch to regulation of the water flows in showerheads and toilets. (The toilet standards, however, undermine themselves by necessitating more flushes.)
9. These efforts and their refutation have reached the point where an anthology (Cowan and Crampton, 2003) has appeared. This is a sequel to Cowan (1988), dealing with the older theories. Both start with examples of the assertions of failure and go on to present articles criticizing the claims.

10. Cowan and Crampton make Akerlof (1970) one of their four examples of new thinking; two others are from Stiglitz (1994, 1999), who has generated many models of peculiar markets that are inefficient; David (2001) generated the fourth. The Nobel prizes awarded to Akerlof and Stiglitz prove novelty, not validity. Bond was one of the refuting articles in the anthology.

References

Adelman, M.A. (1972), *The World Petroleum Market*, Baltimore: Johns Hopkins University Press for Resources for the Future.

Adelman, M.A. (1973), 'Is the oil shortage real? Oil companies as OPEC tax-collectors', *Foreign Policy*, **9**, 69–107. Reprinted in Adelman 1993, Reading 15, 329–57.

Adelman, M.A. (1980), 'The clumsy cartel', *The Energy Journal*, **1**(1) (January), 43–53. Reprinted in Adelman, 1993, Reading 19, 407–16.

Adelman, M.A. (1993), *The Economics of Petroleum Supply: Papers by M.A. Adelman 1962–1993*, Cambridge, MA: MIT Press.

Adelman, M.A. (1995), *The Genie out of the Bottle: World Oil since 1970*, Cambridge, MA: MIT Press.

Akerlof, George A. (1970), 'The market for "lemons": qualitative uncertainty and the market mechanism', *Quarterly Journal of Economics*, **84**, 488–500.

Akins, James E. (1973), 'The oil crisis: this time the wolf is here', *Foreign Affairs*, **51**(2) (April), 462–90.

Bohi, Douglas R. (1990), *Energy Price Shocks and Macroeconomic Performance*, Washington: Resources for the Future.

Bohi, Douglas R. and W. David Montgomery (1982), *Oil Prices, Energy Security, and Import Policy*, Washington: Resources for the Future.

Bohi, Douglas R. and Milton Russell (1978), *Limiting Oil Imports: An Economic History and Analysis*, Baltimore: Johns Hopkins University Press, for Resources for the Future.

Bohi, Douglas R. and Michael A. Toman (1995), *Energy Security as a Basis for Energy Policy*, Boston: Kluwer Academic (also available free from American Petroleum Institute).

Bond, Eric W. (1982), 'A direct test of the "lemons" model: the market for used pickup trucks', *American Economic Review*, **72**(4) (September), 836–40.

Bradley, Robert L., Jr (1989), *The Mirage of Oil Protection*, Lanham: University Press of America.

Bradley, Robert L., Jr (1995), *Oil, Gas and Government: The U.S. Experience*, Lanham: Rowman & Littlefield.

Brannon, Gerard M. (1974), *Energy Taxes and Subsidies*, Cambridge, MA: Ballinger.

Brannon, Gerard M. (ed.) (1975), *Studies in Energy Tax Policy*, Cambridge, MA: Ballinger.

Breyer, Stephen G. and Paul W. MacAvoy (1974), *Energy Regulation by the Federal Power Commission*, Washington: Brookings Institution.

Coase, Ronald H. (1960), 'The problem of social costs', *Journal of Law and Economics*, **3** (October), 1–44.

Cowan, Tyler (1988), *The Theory of Market Failure: A Critical Examination*, Fairfax: George Mason University Press.

Cowan, Tyler and Eric Crampton (eds) (2003), *Market Failure or Success: The New Debate*, Cheltenham, UK and Northampton, MA, USA: Edward Elgar for the Independent Institute.

Crandall, Robert W. and John G. Graham (1989), 'The effects of fuel economy standards on automobile safety', *Journal of Law and Economics*, **38**(1) (April), 97–118.

David, Paul A. (2001), 'Path dependence and its critics and the quest for historical economics', in P. Garrouste and S. Ioannides (eds), *Evolution and Path Dependence in Economic Ideas: Past and Present*, Cheltenham, UK and Northampton, MA, USA: Edward Elgar, pp. 15–40.

Fischer, Caroline, Winston Harrington and Ian W.H. Parry (2007), 'Should automobile fuel economy standards be tightened?', *The Energy Journal*, **28**(4), 1–29.

Forbes (1976), 'Don't blame the oil companies, blame the State Department', April 15, 69–74.

Gholz, Eugene and Daryl G. Press (2007), 'Energy alarmism: the myths that make America worry about oil', Cato Institute Policy Analysis 589, April 5.

Gordon, Richard L. (1963), 'Coal price regulation in the European Community', *Journal of Industrial Economics*, **10**(3) (July), 188–203.

Gordon, Richard L. (1965), 'Energy policy in the European Community', *Journal of Industrial Economics*, **13**(3) (June), 219–34.

Gordon, Richard L. (1970), *The Evolution of Energy Policy in Western Europe: The Reluctant Retreat from Coal*, New York: Praeger Special Studies in International Economics and Development.

Gordon, Richard L. (1983), 'The economics of optimal self-sufficiency and energy independence, mineral wars and soft energy paths', *Materials and Society*, **7**(2), 225–35.

Gordon, Richard L. (1987), *World Coal: Economics, Policies and Prospects*, Cambridge: Cambridge University Press.

Gordon, Richard L. (1992a), 'EEC hard coal in a restructured Europe', *Coping with the Energy Future: Markets and Regulations*, proceedings of the 15th Annual International Conference, International Association for Energy Economics, H-21–H-28.
Gordon, Richard L. (1992b), 'Energy intervention after Desert Storm', *The Energy Journal*, **13**(3), 1–15.
Hicks, J.R. (1935), 'Annual survey of economic theory: the theory of monopoly', *Econometrica*, **3**, 1–20. Reprinted in George J. Stigler and Kenneth E. Boulding (eds) (1952), *Readings in Price Theory*, Homewood, Il: Richard D. Irwin, 361–83.
International Energy Agency, annual, *Energy Policies and Programmes of IEA Countries*, Paris: Organisation for Economic Co-operation and Development.
Joskow, Paul L. and Donald B. Marron (1992), 'What does a negawatt really cost? Evidence from utility conservation programs', *The Energy Journal*, **13**(4), 41–74.
Kalt, Joseph (1981), *The Economics and Politics of Oil Price Regulation: Federal Policy in the Post-Embargo Era*, Cambridge, MA: MIT Press.
Kleit, Andrew N. (2004), 'Impacts of long-range increases in the corporate average fuel economy (CAFE) standard', *Economic Inquiry*, **42**, 279–94.
Libecap, Gary D. and Steven N. Wiggins (1984), 'Contractual responses to the common pool problem: prorationing of crude oil production', *American Economic Review*, **74**(1) (March), 87–98.
Libecap, Gary D. and Steven N. Wiggins (1985), 'The influence of private contractual failure on regulation: the case of oil field unitization', *Journal of Political Economy*, **93**(4) (August), 690–714.
Lovejoy, Wallace F. and Paul T. Homan (1967), *Economic Aspects of Oil Conservation Regulation*, Baltimore: Johns Hopkins Press for Resources for the Future.
MacAvoy, Paul W. (1962), *Price Formation in Natural Gas Fields*, New Haven: Yale University Press.
MacAvoy, Paul W. (2001), *The Natural Gas Market Sixty Years of Regulation and Deregulation*, New Haven: Yale University Press.
MacAvoy, Paul W. (2007), *The Unsustainable Costs of Partial Deregulation*, New Haven: Yale University Press.
McDonald, Stephen L. (1963), *Federal Tax Treatment of Income from Oil and Gas*, Washington: Brookings Institution.
McDonald, Stephen L. (1971), *Petroleum Conservation in the United States: An Economic Analysis*, Baltimore: Johns Hopkins Press for Resources for the Future.
Sampson, Anthony (1975), *The Seven Sisters: The Great Oil Companies and the World They Shaped*, New York: Viking Press.
Spulber, Daniel F. (1989), *Regulation and Markets*, Cambridge, MA: MIT Press.
Statistik der Kohlenwirtschaft e. V., annual, *Zahlen zur Kohlenwirtschaft*, Essen: Statistik der Kohlenwirtschaft.
Stiglitz, Joseph E. (1994), *Whither Socialism?*, Cambridge, MA: MIT Press.
Stiglitz, Joseph E. (1999), 'Toward a general theory of wage and price rigidities and economic fluctuations', *American Economic Review*, **89**(2), 75–80.
Taylor, Jerry and Peter Van Doren (2005), 'The case against the strategic petroleum reserve', Cato Institute Policy Analysis 555, November 21.
Taylor, Jerry and Peter Van Doren (2006), 'Economic amnesia: the case against oil price controls and windfall profit taxes', Cato Institute Policy Analysis 561, January 1.
Taylor, Jerry and Peter Van Doren (2007), 'Don't increase federal gasoline taxes – abolish them', Cato Institute Policy Analysis 598, August 7.
US Cabinet Task Force on Oil Import Control (1970), *The Oil Import Question: A Report on the Relationship of Oil Imports to the National Security*, Washington: US Government Printing Office.
US Federal Energy Administration (1974), *Project Independence Report*, Washington.
Whitman, Glen (2006), 'Against the new paternalism: internalities and the economics of self-control', Cato Institute Policy Analysis 563, February 22.
Wiggins, Steven N. and Gary D. Libecap (1985), 'Oil field unitization: contractual failure in the presence of imperfect information', *American Economic Review*, **75**(3) (June), 368–85.
Williamson, Oliver E. (1967), *The Economics of Discretionary Behavior: Managerial Objectives in the Theory of the Firm*, Chicago: Markham (earlier edn, Englewood Cliffs: Prentice-Hall, 1964).
Yergin, Daniel (1991), *The Prize: The Epic Quest for Oil, Money, and Power*, New York: Simon & Schuster.

5 Energy demand theory
Kenneth B. Medlock III

1 Introduction

Energy is crucial to the improvement of social and economic welfare. It is necessary to continued economic activity in modern industrialized nations, and its absence would result in cessation of economic growth and diminishing standards of living. In fact, in developing nations a lack of modern energy services is a principal cause of low levels of economic and social development. Access to electricity promotes social development and improved welfare by allowing greater access to information via computer, radio and television, cleaner means of storing and preparing food, and the attainment of heating and cooling services.

Over the last two centuries there has been unprecedented economic growth and radical improvements in standards of living. A major contributing factor has been the replacement of manpower with mechanical power through the development of new technologies. This has provided new opportunities and facilitated significant improvements in productivity. One example of this is the invention of the internal combustion engine and motor vehicle, which along with the consumption of crude oil products, has provided a more expedient means of transporting people and goods, thus creating growth opportunities by connecting markets and facilitating trade.

The demand for energy is a *derived* demand inasmuch as energy's value is determined by its ability to provide some set of desired services. In particular, when combined with energy-using capital, energy facilitates the provision of goods and services in industry and in the household. Therefore, energy consumption at the individual, household and/ or firm level is the result of a set of simultaneous decisions involving the quantity and type of capital equipment to purchase – where capital type is differentiated by technological characteristics such as efficiency and type of fuel input – and the rate of capital utilization.

Demand in the long and short runs is complicated by many factors. Economic development itself leads to changes in the structure of output that can alter the manner in which demand grows relative to income. Moreover, factors such as technological change and the effect of energy prices on the composition, efficiency and utilization of deployed capital must also be considered, not to mention the influence that policy can have on demand by altering costs. Understanding these influences is vital to developing informed, intelligent policies aimed at dealing with some of the world's most pressing problems, such as climate change and access to affordable energy services.

Today's modern economy thrives on the consumption of fossil fuels. According to the US Energy Information Administration, global primary energy demand increased at an average annual rate of 2.0 percent from 1980 to 2005, and this demand has been met primarily by fossil fuels. In 2005, petroleum comprised 36.6 percent of total energy use, followed by coal at 26.5 percent, and natural gas at 23.3 percent. It is likely that fossil fuels will continue to make up a dominant share of total primary energy use well into the future.

Despite this conjecture of fossil fuel's dominance, the composition of energy demand has not been constant over time, nor will it be as we move forward. Today's technologies and capital stocks are tuned to converting fossil fuels, rather than some other energy source, into some useful energy service, but yesterday's technology and very likely tomorrow's technologies will be different. In the United States, for example, wood was the primary source of energy consumption through the late-1800s. However, with industrialization coal emerged as the dominant source of primary energy due to its relative availability, the efficiency with which it could be used to achieve a given energy service, and the development of new technologies. Ever since, these factors and others, such as relative prices, technology, economic structure and environmental considerations, have shaped the composition of energy demand.

In order to convey a clear understanding of the energy data typically used in demand analysis, this chapter begins with a discussion of energy accounting in Section 2. The macroeconomic relationship between energy use and economic development is discussed in Sections 3 and 4, with specific attention to structural and technological change. This allows for a framework to think about, for example, the manner in which policies might best promote macro-level energy demand reductions through targeting efficiency improvements in particular industries or economic sectors. In Section 5 the microeconomic foundations of energy demand are presented, with a focus on the relationship between energy and capital. Elasticity of energy demand is discussed in Sections 6 and 7. Section 8 concludes.

2   Energy Accounting

Energy balance tables are useful data reporting tools. They allow the researcher to track the total energy required to facilitate final consumption by sector and fuel type. Raw energy commodities such as crude oil, coal and wet natural gas must typically be converted to some other form prior to being marketable to end-users. For example, raw crude oil is generally converted into products such as gasoline and heating oil, and wet natural gas is typically processed into natural gas liquids, other potentially useful products such as CO_2 for carbonation of beverages, and dry natural gas, the latter of which can be consumed directly or used to generate electricity.

The energy conversion industries, such as refining and electricity generation, convert primary energy inputs to products for final consumption. Energy balance tables are a means of accounting for the conversion of primary energy for final consumption. Figure 5.1 illustrates the general flow of energy balance tables. Total primary energy requirement (TPER) is the quantity of energy necessary to produce the energy for total final consumption (TFC). TPER is greater than TFC due to the energy expended in the conversion, transmission and distribution activities. Moreover, the difference between TPER and TFC, referred to as conversion and distribution losses, can vary across countries depending upon a number of factors, such as which fuels are used and how efficient the conversion processes are.

In less-developed countries, waste and other forms of biomass are often used to provide

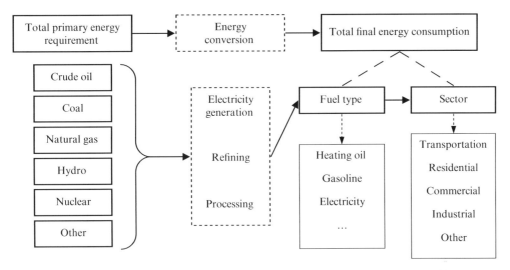

Note: Total primary energy requirement is the energy required to meet total final consumption. Some energy is expended in the energy conversion industries.

Figure 5.1   Typical structure of energy balance tables

heat for cooking and other purposes. However, there is often no record of a transaction of sale for these forms of *non-commercial* energy, because they are not traded in the same manner as *commercial* forms of energy such as crude oil, coal and natural gas. This can make it difficult to measure consumption accurately. As a result of this deficiency, it is common to consider only commercial energy use in empirical studies of energy demand, especially in studies that include developing and less-developed economies.

3   The Energy–Capital Relationship

The demand for energy is a derived demand. Energy is an input, along with capital, to provide a set of energy services, such as producing steam, driving certain industrial processes, and also to provide transportation services.

In general, because energy consumption depends on the energy efficiency and utilization rate of installed capital and the scale of the operation, we can write the following expression for energy use:

$$E = \frac{u}{\varepsilon}K, \tag{5.1}$$

where E denotes energy use, u denotes capacity utilization of capital, ε denotes the energy efficiency of capital, and K denotes the capital stock. Importantly, this relationship is equipment specific, and there is one such relationship for each type of capital equipment. It is a gross oversimplification to aggregate capital stocks and energy when considering the relationship between energy and capital.

Equation (5.1) is an identity because the units simplify to energy $\equiv$ energy. In principle, we can consider the energy service derived from a specific type of capital and energy source, but as an illustration, consider the case of motor fuel consumption. Efficiency is expressed as miles per gallon (or kilometers per liter), capital utilization is expressed as miles per vehicle (or kilometers per vehicle), and units of capital stock is expressed as the number of motor vehicles. This yields gallons $\equiv$ [(miles/vehicle)/(miles/gallon)] · vehicles, which simplifies to gallons $\equiv$ gallons.

Note that the service derived from vehicle ownership and the consumption of gallons of fuel is miles. Thus, it is possible to rearrange the above equation so that it is possible to see the amount of fuel consumption required to achieve a given level of transportation service. In particular,

$$\text{miles} \equiv \left(\frac{\text{miles}}{\text{gallon}}\right) \cdot \left(\frac{\text{gallons}}{\text{vehicle}}\right) \cdot \text{vehicles}.$$

Thus, we can increase the amount of transportation service per vehicle by increasing either fuel efficiency or fuel use per vehicle, *ceteris paribus*.

The capital utilization rate denotes the service rendered by capital equipment, such as miles driven per vehicle, thus energy use is positively related to capital utilization. However, we also see that as efficiency increases, the energy required per unit of service declines. According to the US Federal Highway and Traffic Safety Administration, the on-road fuel efficiency of a passenger vehicle, on average, increased from about 14.3 miles per gallon in 1978 to about 20.2 miles per gallon in 1990. During the same period, motor vehicle stocks increased from about 150 million to 194 million and motor vehicle utilization increased from about 9500 miles per vehicle to 11 100 miles per vehicle. Had efficiency remained constant *ceteris paribus*, the increase in capital and utilization would have resulted in a considerable increase in fuel use. However, the gains in efficiency more than offset the increases in other variable, resulting in a decrease in motor fuel use from 7412 thousand barrels per day to 7235 thousand barrels per day. Clearly, efficiency gains offset increased utilization and growing vehicle stocks thereby mitigating increased fuel consumption.

4   Energy Demand in the Long Run

Economic structure and technology are critical determinants of energy demand. At the macro level, each influences energy intensity, where energy intensity is defined as the quantity of energy consumed per unit of economic output. Regarding economic structure, as an economy develops it will generally become more service oriented. To the extent that a unit of service output requires less energy input than a unit of manufacturing output, energy intensity will decline. Regarding technology, as more energy-efficient capital is deployed, the energy requirements for a given level of output decline, thus allowing economic activity to expand without an increase in energy demand.

Empirical evidence supports the notion that energy intensity ultimately declines as economies develop. As an example, Figure 5.2 illustrates the energy intensity for the US from 1880 through 2005 plotted against per capita income in the top graph, and against time in the bottom one. Also indicated is the industrial share of GDP as an indicator of economic structure over time. Clearly, the trend in energy intensity is downward, indicating lower energy consumption per dollar of GDP.

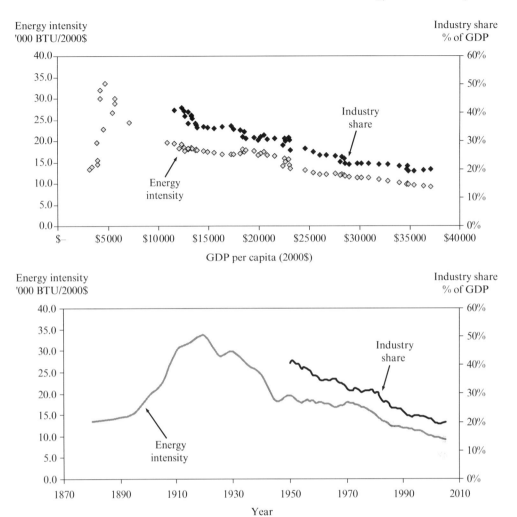

Note: Energy intensity rises then declines as per capita income rises. Changing economic structure and improvements in technology are the primary drivers of this phenomenon. Industry share is only graphed from 1950 through 2005 due to data limitations.

Sources: US Energy Information Administration, US Bureau of Economic Analysis.

Figure 5.2   Trends in energy intensity in the US (1880–2005)

Indeed, several authors have used econometric analysis to show that the energy intensity of an economy resembles an inverted U-shape across increasing levels of per capita income (see, for example, Medlock and Soligo 2001). This arises from structural and technological change.

During the course of economic development, changes in the structure of GDP will lead to rising then declining energy intensity. Specifically, industrialization results in large increases in commercial energy use. Then, as economies move into the post-industrial

Energy intensity

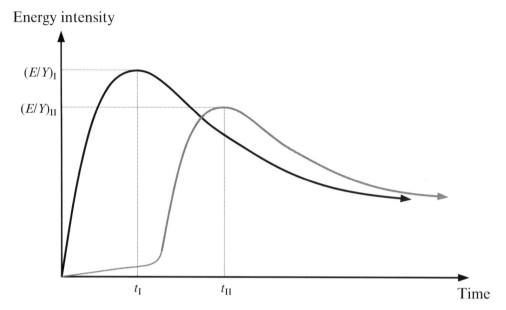

Note: Consider two countries, I and II. Assume Country I develops more rapidly than Country II. All else equal, the energy intensity of Country I reaches its peak (t_I, $(E/Y)_I$) before Country II reaches its peak (t_{II}, $(E/Y)_{II}$) because Country II benefits from the technologies developed as Country I progressed. Structural change yields the inverted U-shape of energy intensity we see in both countries.

Figure 5.3   *Dematerialization and energy intensity*

phase of economic development, the service sector grows faster than other sectors and energy demand grows at a slower rate for given increases in GDP. This pattern is consistent with the theory of *dematerialization*, which is 'the reduction of raw material (energy and material) intensity of economic activities, measured as the ratio of material (or energy) consumption in physical terms to gross domestic product in deflated constant terms' (Bernardini and Galli 1993, p. 432).

There are two basic premises of the theory of dematerialization as it pertains to energy (note that the theory was originally developed with regard to other raw material inputs). The first is that energy intensity initially increases then decreases with increasing GDP. The second is that the later in time economic growth occurs, the lower the maximum intensity of use of energy will be. These concepts are illustrated in Figure 5.3. It is important to note here that declining energy intensity does not imply that energy demand declines, only that energy demand grows more slowly than output.

Economic structure
Changing economic structure has a pronounced influence on energy use. In general, as economies develop they move from being more rural and agricultural based to urban and industrial then service based. At the same time, consumer wealth is also rising, thereby raising demand for things such as light manufactures and financial and leisure services. These structural changes in consumption and production result in changes in the structure of the deployed capital stock. This, in turn, will promote changes in energy

consumption and energy intensity. At higher levels of economic development, energy intensity declines as the service sector grows relative to other sectors.

To illustrate how structural change can lead to changes in energy intensity, consider a three-sector economy (denoted as sectors A, I and S). Total energy consumption is given as the sum of energy use across all sectors, $E = E_A + E_I + E_S$. The energy intensity in each sector i can be given as E_i/Y_i, where Y_i is the output of sector i. Total output is given as $Y = Y_A + Y_I + Y_S$. Total energy intensity can be written as:

$$\frac{E}{Y} = \frac{E_A + E_I + E_S}{Y}$$

$$= \frac{E_A}{Y_A} \cdot \frac{Y_A}{Y} + \frac{E_I}{Y_I} \cdot \frac{Y_I}{Y} + \frac{E_S}{Y_S} \cdot \frac{Y_S}{Y}$$

$$= \frac{E_A}{Y_A} \cdot \theta_A + \frac{E_I}{Y_I} \cdot \theta_I + \frac{E_S}{Y_S} \cdot \theta_S, \tag{5.2}$$

where θ_i is the sector i share of total output. Thus, total energy intensity is a share-weighted sum of energy intensity of each sector. Also, by definition $\theta_A + \theta_I + \theta_S = 1$.

Assume that the energy intensity of each sector can be ordered such that:

$$\frac{E_A}{Y_A} < \frac{E_S}{Y_S} < \frac{E_I}{Y_I}.$$

It follows that if sector I grows faster than sector A, holding the output share of sector S constant, energy intensity will increase. To see this, we can take the derivative of equation (5.2) with respect to the output share of industry:

$$\frac{d(E/Y)}{d\theta_I} = -\left(\frac{E_A}{Y_A} \cdot \frac{d\theta_A}{d\theta_I} + \frac{E_S}{Y_S} \cdot \frac{d\theta_S}{d\theta_I} \right) + \frac{E_I}{Y_I} > 0. \tag{5.3}$$

We know (5.3) is positive because:

$$\left| \frac{E_A}{Y_A} \cdot \frac{d\theta_A}{d\theta_I} + \frac{E_S}{Y_S} \cdot \frac{d\theta_S}{d\theta_I} \right| < \frac{E_I}{Y_I},$$

which follows from the fact that $E_A/Y_A < E_S/Y_S < E_I/Y_I$ and $\Delta\theta_A + \Delta\theta_S + \Delta\theta_I = 0$. Thus, the impact on energy intensity of the aggregate shift to industry is positive. We can also show, in a similar manner, that growth in the less energy-intensive sectors results in declining energy intensity.

Reality is not as simple as the above example. Specifically, technological progress also causes sector-specific energy intensity to change over time. However, as the example illustrates, technological change is not necessary for total energy intensity to change over time.

Technological change
The second of the ideas central to the theory of dematerialization is that technological progress effectively lowers the peak energy intensity of an economy. Thus, for a given economy, the later in time it develops the lower its energy requirements will be. This is

because the diffusion of newer technologies and the economic/environmental lessons learned in the industrialized world contribute to lowering the maximum energy intensity of developing nations.

Combining equations (5.1) and (5.2) yields an expression that can be useful in understanding the influence of technology:

$$\frac{E}{Y} = \frac{(u_A/\varepsilon_A) \cdot K_A}{Y_A} \cdot \theta_A + \frac{(u_I/\varepsilon_I) \cdot K_I}{Y_I} \cdot \theta_I + \frac{(u_S/\varepsilon_S) \cdot K_S}{Y_S} \cdot \theta_S. \tag{5.4}$$

From equation (5.4) we can see that an increase in energy efficiency in any sector i, for instance through the adoption of a new technology, will lead to a decline in the energy intensity of sector i, and hence overall energy intensity. This is apparent by simply differentiating equation (5.4) with respect to energy efficiency in sector i:

$$\frac{d(E/Y)}{d\varepsilon_I} = -\frac{(u_I/\varepsilon_I^2) K_I}{Y_I} \cdot \theta_I < 0.$$

Notably, the impact of the technological change will have the greatest impact if it occurs in the sector with the largest share of total output. This has implications for the design of any policy directed at lowering energy intensity through raising energy efficiency. In addition, since the second derivative of equation (5.4) is positive, the negative effect on energy intensity is increasing with the innovation. Thus, any innovation in the industrial sector that occurs in one country can have a substantial impact on energy intensity in countries that develop later in time, provided the technology is transferable.

In general, the time dependency of energy intensity suggests that developing countries may never realize the energy intensities seen in countries in Western Europe and the US during the earlier part of the twentieth century. Therefore, long-term forecasts, and hence policy, should be developed accordingly.

A comment on the energy–income relationship
Asymmetry in the relationship between energy and income has been discussed in the economic literature. It has been observed that an increase in GDP will lead to an increase in energy demand, but a decrease in GDP will not necessarily have an equal and opposite effect on energy demand (see, for example, Huntington 1998). Equations (5.1) and (5.2) are important to understanding why this asymmetry arises.

First, some periods of economic expansion (recession) may be characterized by growth (contraction) in certain sectors that do not grow (contract) in other periods of expansion (recession). If a particular period of economic expansion is characterized by growth in a sector of the economy that is very energy intensive, then that period of economic growth will be associated with high energy demand growth. But, if a period of economic contraction hits a sector of the economy that is less energy intensive, then energy demand will not fall by as much as it increased during the period of economic expansion. Therefore, the structure of the economy and the manner in which growth occurs can lead to asymmetry in the energy–income relationship.

Asymmetry can arise in another way as well. If a period of economic contraction and subsequent expansion occur in the same sector, the changes in energy demand may still not be symmetric. For example, if the energy efficiency of the capital stock increases between the periods of contraction and expansion, then the size of the increase in energy consumption during the period of expansion will not match the size of the decrease in energy consumption during the preceding period of economic contraction.

Energy intensity versus energy efficiency

Consider two countries with the same level of per capita income, country A and country B, and assume $(E/Y)_A > (E/Y)_B$. Since *energy intensity* is higher in country A, it is a common mistake to assume that *energy efficiency* is higher in country B. While this may indeed be true, it does not necessarily follow. In particular, the economic structure of countries A and B may be very different. For example, country A may specialize in the production of oil and gas resources or some industrial commodity such as steel. These activities are by nature very energy intensive. Country B, by contrast, may specialize in wine production or global financial services, neither of which is very energy intensive by comparison. If these two countries engage in trade with each other, it is possible that the law of comparative advantage has yielded the most efficient allocation of resources across both countries. Each nation, therefore, may be employing state-of-the-art technologies that maximize energy efficiency. But, energy intensity will not reveal this structural difference.

In fact, if country A began producing the goods and services currently produced in country B, and country B began producing the goods and services currently produced in country A, the end result would likely be lower economic efficiency, and perhaps lower energy efficiency. Thus, it is important to account for the structural differences across countries when comparing energy efficiency at the aggregate level.

5 Modeling Energy Demand

The decision to consume energy involves three simultaneous choices – the choice to invest in capital stocks, the choice of a particular type of capital stocks, and the choice of a rate of capital utilization. These choices all lead to a desired amount of energy service, which is what motivated the choices in the first place. Note that this means there is an investment decision involved in the attainment of energy services. Accordingly, models that incorporate dynamic investment behavior are suited to capture both the short- and long-run responses of energy demand to changes in economic variables. Static models that do not incorporate such behavior are nevertheless widely utilized, and they can be valuable in understanding full-adjustment variable response. In what follows, a static model of the firm and a dynamic model of the household are presented. In fact, the reader can verify that the cases not presented, that of the household in the static model and the firm in a dynamic model, are not too dissimilar from the problems that are presented herein, with the exception being that there is an obvious required change in terminology. We limit ourselves to the problems below in the interest of brevity.

A static model of the representative firm

The problem of the firm is generally taken to be one of profit maximization, or cost minimization for a given level of output. The firm must purchase energy and all other inputs to production of its output. Accordingly, the firm's demand for energy can be shown to be a function of its output and the price of all inputs, including of course energy.

To demonstrate, consider a representative firm that minimizes costs, C, for a given level of output, $\overline{Q}$. Output is a function of capital, K, labor, L, energy, E, and materials, M, so that $Q = f(K, L, E, M)$. Costs are the sum of payments to the factors of production, $C = rK + wL + p_E E + p_M M$, where r is rent payment to capital, w is the wage paid to labor, p_E is the price of energy, and p_M is the price of material inputs. The firm's problem is then given as:

$$\min_{K,L,E,M} C$$

subject to:

$$\overline{Q} = f(K, L, E, M);$$

$$C = rK + wL + p_E E + p_M M;$$

$$E \equiv \frac{u}{\varepsilon} K.$$

Equation (5.1) enters the set of constraints, and can be used to simplify the firm's problem by substitution where appropriate. This results in a restatement of the firm's problem:

$$\min_{K,L,M,u,\varepsilon} \left(r + p_E \frac{u}{\varepsilon} \right) K + wL + p_M M + \phi \varepsilon + \lambda \left[\overline{Q} - f\left(K, L, \frac{u}{\varepsilon} K, M \right) \right].$$

where ϕ is the cost of efficiency improvement. Solution of the first-order conditions for a maximum for this problem reveals that the firm will choose inputs of K, L, M and ε and a rate of utilization of capital, u, so that the marginal values in production are equal.

It can be shown that the general function for the firm's energy demand is given as:

$$E^* = E(\overline{Q}, r, w, p_E, p_M). \tag{5.5}*$$

Thus, the firm weighs the price of all possible factor inputs when choosing the amount of energy it consumes.[1]

Note that the full cost of capital incorporates the energy cost of utilization $p_E(u/\varepsilon)$. This is important when considering changes in variables such as energy price because it means that the firm can only adjust its utilization rate of installed capital in the short run, when capital and technology are fixed. Thus, the short-run expression describing the firm's energy demand simplifies to:

$$E^{*sr} = E(\overline{Q}, w, p_E, p_M, \overline{K}, \overline{\varepsilon}),$$

because the function is conditional on a given level of energy efficiency and stock of capital. In the long run, the firm can adjust both capital and technology, so that the demand function takes the more general form of equation (5.5). Therefore, the full response to a change in energy prices may take the form of reduced capacity utilization in the short run *transitioning* to the turnover of capital stocks in favor of higher levels of efficiency in the long run. Although this transition cannot be captured in the static framework, comparative statics in these problems can be a useful tool for understanding the short- and long-run impacts of a rise in energy prices, for example.

The above problem, because it is a static representation of energy demand, disregards the intertemporal aspects of the choices an energy consumer faces when choosing the type of capital, utilization of capital, and efficiency of capital. A more general approach would allow for a dynamic specification of demand and thus allow for an analysis of the *transition* from the short to the long run.

A dynamic model of the household

Dynamic models of energy demand incorporate the intertemporal choices that a consumer, or firm, must make when maximizing a particular objective function over some time horizon. Such models capture the idea that the decision to consume energy is made jointly with the decision to purchase and maintain energy-using capital equipment, the latter of which is an investment problem. Moreover, dynamic models allow analysis of the transition that occurs from one state to another in response to changes in particular variables. This latter point is important because understanding the potential adjustment costs associated with an energy tax, for example, is important to policy makers and consumers alike.

In this exposition, we shall focus on the individual, or household, problem. However, the results herein translate to the problem of the firm. First, consider the problem of a utility-maximizing representative consumer.[2] Energy is assumed to be proportional to the service it provides, and therefore, consumer utility is affected by energy demand. Denoting time with the subscript t, the consumer seeks to maximize the discounted present value of lifetime utility,

$$\sum_{t=0}^{T} \beta^t U(C_t, E_t),$$

subject to a constraint that purchases of energy, E_t, purchases of other consumption goods, C_t, purchases, I_t, of capital stocks, K_t, and savings, S_t, in each period cannot exceed this period's income, Y_t, plus the return on last period's savings, $(1 + r)S_{t-1}$. Capital stocks are assumed to depreciate at some rate δ, savings earn a rate of return r, the discount rate is such that $0 < \beta < 1$, and all initial conditions are given.

The consumer's problem is therefore formulated as:

$$\max_{C,E,S} \sum_{t=0}^{T} \beta^t U(C_t, E_t),$$

subject to:

$$p_{C,t}C_t + p_{E,t}E_t + p_{K,t}I_t + S_t \leq Y_t + (1 + r)S_{t-1};$$

$$E_t \equiv \frac{u_t}{\varepsilon_t}K_t;$$

$$I_t = K_t - (1 - \delta)K_{t-1};$$

$$C_t, u_t, K_t \geq 0 \quad t = 1, \ldots, T,$$

where $p_{i,t}$ is the price of good i at time t, and all initial values are given. Note that equation (5.1) from above is incorporated into the consumer's problem via the second constraint, which is how the relationship between energy and capital is accounted for. In fact, equation (5.1) can be substituted into the utility function and the budget constraint to simplify the consumer's problem.

The first-order conditions for a maximum for this consumer's problem yield:

$$U_K \frac{u_t^*}{\varepsilon_t} = U_Z \left[p_{E,t} \frac{u_t^*}{\varepsilon_t} + p_{K,t} - p_{K,t+1} \left(\frac{1 - \delta}{1 + r} \right) \right],$$

where the star denotes an optimal value. Thus, the consumer will allocate income among purchases of energy, capital, savings and all other goods such that the marginal value of the energy services attained from the capital stock is equal to the marginal value of consumption of all other goods. In addition, because the consumer is ultimately interested in energy services (including heating, cooking, transportation and manufacturing), the decision is conditional on, among other things, the energy cost of capital utilization.

In the above expression, the term in brackets on the right-hand side,

$$\mu_{K,t} = p_{E,t} \frac{u_t^*}{\varepsilon_t} + p_{K,t} - p_{K,t+1} \left(\frac{1 - \delta}{1 + r} \right), \tag{5.6}$$

is defined as the 'user cost', μ_K, of the capital stock. The first term in equation (5.6), $p_{E,t}(u_t^*/\varepsilon_t)$, indicates that the consumer chooses user cost to the extent that capital utilization is a choice variable. Note that if the optimal choice of utilization were such that $u_t^* = 0$, equation (5.6) becomes $p_{K,t} - p_{K,t+1}[(1 - \delta)/(1 + r)]$, which is the *rental price* $(p_{R,t})$ of owning capital equipment.[3] In addition, we can see from equation (5.6) that an increase in the price of energy need not lead to an increase in the cost of obtaining energy services. For example, if price doubles, but efficiency also doubles, the net effect on consumer behavior should be zero because $p_{E,t}(u_t^*/\varepsilon_t)$ will not change.

The full set of first-order conditions for this consumer's problem yield a system of simultaneous equations that can be solved for each of the choice variables. Once solutions are obtained for K_t^* and u_t^*, for a given ε_t, we can use equation (5.1) to solve for energy consumption. Thus, the optimal level of energy demand is *derived* from the optimal capital utilization rate, optimal size of the capital stock, and efficiency. Energy demand can therefore be expressed as a function of the user cost of capital, capital stocks and capacity utilization. In general, it can be shown that user cost is a function of energy price, energy efficiency, and the rental price of capital. Furthermore, capital stocks are a function of the rental price of capital and income, and capacity utilization is a function of energy price and income. This allows us to write a general function describing energy demand as:

$$E_t^* = E(Y_t, p_{Z,t}, p_{E,t}, p_{R,t}, \varepsilon_t). \tag{5.7}$$

To fully understand the value of the dynamic framework, consider the case of an increase in energy price, perhaps through the introduction of a tax. In the short run, the full response of increased efficiency may be exceedingly costly, resulting in a reduction in capital stock utilization. Generally, this is associated with a reduction in economic activity, so it is not a desirable effect. Thus, in the case of a tax on energy designed to reduce consumption, the short-run effects of lowered capacity utilization can be mitigated through promotion of more rapid adoption of more energy-efficient technologies, perhaps through subsidies. However, such an approach would only be recommended if the normal adjustment period for the consumer to adopt higher fuel efficiency were sufficiently long such that the subsidy actually promoted a more economically efficient outcome.

Given the influence of efficiency on the cost of achieving an energy service, the consumer would in principle like to have energy efficiency be as large as possible. If, in fact, we allow efficiency to be a choice variable, as in the static case, the preceding discussion would be altered, and equation (5.7) would be modified. Although not done here, the problem would require some distinction of types of capital stocks through the use of an additional set of constraints. In such a problem, since energy-efficient technology is typically embodied in the capital stock, increasing fuel efficiency occurs with capital stock purchases. If the cost of capital investment is increasing with efficiency, then the consumer will choose some level of energy efficiency that reflects his/her preferences and budget constraint. Tishler (1983) developed a model in which consumers could choose between different motor vehicle characteristics when making vehicle purchases, one of which was fuel efficiency. It was shown that choice across multiple fuel efficiencies allows the consumer to increase efficiency if energy prices rise in order to prevent the user cost of capital from rising.

In the above examples we made some simplifying assumptions deserving of comment. First, we denoted energy as a single commodity. Relaxation of this constraint would allow the consumer to choose between different energy commodities and different types of capital with the goal of satisfying multiple energy service demands. Second, it is possible to further complicate the consumer's problem by including multiple energy services, and hence multiple types of capital equipment and fuel sources. This simply expands the choices available for achieving a particular energy service, and would result in, for example, natural gas prices appearing in an electricity demand function as consumers choose between natural gas and electric appliances. To the extent that multiple fuels are available for other energy services, such as diesel or gasoline for transportation, this issue extends into many other choices as well.

Other variables not included in the above analyses, such as weather, can also influence energy demand by changing a desired amount of energy service in response to a change in weather. Weather-driven movements in energy demand that occur with shifting seasonal patterns are typically short run in nature, and consumer response will vary depending on the timeframe under consideration. One particularly short-run phenomenon of interest is *extreme* cold or hot weather, for example, which can lead to dramatic short-term increases in energy service demands. For example, an extremely cold winter usually brings with it a temporary increase in demand for natural gas and heating oil as the demand for heating service rises. If capital and technology are fixed in the short run, the consumer can respond by increasing the utilization rate of existing capital, to the extent possible, in order to increase the heating service attained from a given stock of capital. In the long run, however, if extreme cold becomes the norm, the consumer may opt to increase the size and efficiency of the pertinent stock of capital.

6   The Elasticity of Energy Demand

There are a large number of empirical studies that have estimated the income elasticity and price elasticity of energy demand. There is a great deal of interest in these elasticities because they are vital when forecasting energy demand.

The income elasticity of energy demand is defined as the percentage change in energy demand resulting from a 1 percent change in income, *holding all else constant*:

$$\varepsilon_Y = \frac{\%\Delta E}{\%\Delta Y} = \frac{\partial E}{\partial Y} \cdot \frac{Y}{E},$$

where E denotes energy demand and Y denotes income, often measured as GDP. A good portion of the empirical literature had long reported the income elasticity of energy demand to be close to one. However, several recent papers have indicated that this may be greatly overstated for industrialized countries, particularly in light of the evidence that energy intensity is inversely related to economic development (see, for example, Galli 1998; Judson et al. 1999; and Medlock and Soligo 2001). This is important because it is desirable to account for any nonlinearity in the income elasticity resulting from economic growth and structural change, especially when forecasting.

The own-price elasticity of energy demand is similarly defined, being the percentage change in energy demand given a 1 percent change in the price of energy *holding all else constant*:

$$\varepsilon_P = \frac{\%\Delta E}{\%\Delta P} = \frac{dE}{dP} \cdot \frac{P}{E},$$

where P denotes the price of energy. Note that 'own' price is used here to indicate that 'cross'-price elasticities are also often estimated. This practice is more prevalent in cases where the demand for a particular fuel source is being modeled, such as natural gas, when there is a competing fuel source alternative, such as residual fuel oil.

The own-price elasticity is often used as an indicator of the impact of various policies aimed at conservation, such as energy taxes or subsidies. For example, it is possible to approximate the reduction in carbon emissions if an accurate estimate of price elasticity is in hand – a given tax will influence some reduction in energy demand, which, in turn, will cause emissions to decline. Knowing the price elasticity, therefore, can allow for an educated, objective assessment of the size of the tax to be instituted for a desired reduction in emissions.

In general, income and price elasticities of energy demand are the rules of thumb that help direct energy policy. Unfortunately, as can be seen in a review of the economic literature on the matter, there is no consensus regarding the appropriate value of income and/or price elasticity. The disagreement ultimately centers on the model specification that is chosen by the researcher in his or her study. Moreover, some of the differences in specification come about simply because it can be very difficult to isolate the effects of changes in things such as in technology, capital stock composition and utilization, economic structure, and energy policy. Each of these variables can, in finite samples, have very different levels of relevance and importance in a given country or region in a given period.

An oft-used specification for energy demand used in empirical studies is the log-linear demand equation given as:

$$\ln E_t^* = \alpha_0 + \alpha_1 \ln Y_t + \alpha_2 \ln p_{E,t} + \alpha_3 \ln X_t, \tag{5.8}$$

where E^* is the 'optimal' long-run quantity of energy demanded, Y is income, p_E is energy price, X is a variable or set of variables that may influence demand, and α_i are coefficients to be estimated. The variable X can play a very important role in obtaining valid estimates of the α_i parameters (we shall return to this point below). Variables such as population and capital stocks may be included as independent variables, as well as other parameters such as weather and the price of alternative fuels. The last two are particularly important when modeling the demand for individual fuels for which consumption is seasonal.

A demand specification such as equation (5.8) implies a function of the form $E_t^* = \alpha_0 Y_t^{\alpha_1} p_t^{\alpha_2} X_t^{\alpha_3}$, and can be thought of as an approximation of the 'true' demand function whose general form is given by equations (5.5) or (5.7). While such approximations are often necessary, they can lead to substantial variation in published results since parameter estimates are sensitive to model specification.

Equation (5.8) can be estimated to directly yield an income elasticity, α_1, and a price elasticity, α_2. Usually, however, lagged endogenous variables, or lags in income and price, are included to capture the fact that capital stock turnover and/or habit persistence may create delays in demand adjustment to changes in the exogenous variables. One popular means of capturing this is to assume the existence of a partial adjustment mechanism of the form $(\ln E_t - \ln E_{t-1}) = \gamma(\ln E_t^* - \ln E_{t-1})$ where $\gamma \in [0, 1]$ is the speed of adjustment. By substitution of the left-hand-side variable in equation (5.8), we have the following equation to be estimated:

$$\ln E_t = \gamma\alpha_0 + \gamma\alpha_1 \ln Y_t + \gamma\alpha_2 \ln p_{E,t} + \gamma\alpha_3 \ln X_t + (1 - \gamma)\ln E_{t-1}, \tag{5.9}$$

where α_i is the long-run elasticity of variable i, and $\gamma\alpha_i$ are the short-run elasticities.

An econometric specification such as (5.9) is easily estimated using standard procedures, such as ordinary least squares (OLS), and yields elasticities directly. However, such models are *constant elasticity* formulations, and elasticity may not be constant. In fact, the notion of declining income elasticity with increasing income is at the heart of the dematerialization principle discussed above. It is possible, however, to specify an equation to be estimated that incorporates nonlinearity in all or some of the included variables. Spline-knot functions and functions with quadratic terms are two such methods that have been employed.

Equation (5.9) allows one to capture the influence of changes in the composition of capital stocks over time (through the variable X). This is an important aspect of energy demand models as it could alter energy required per unit output and result in asymmetric demand responses to changes in variables such as income and price. Recognizing this, it is possible to estimate the functions describing each of the variables in equation (5.1), then using the results to derive an estimate of energy demand. In fact, this has been done by Johansson and Schipper (1997) with regard to forecasting long-term motor fuel demand in several countries. While the systems approach to estimating energy elasticities can be more cumbersome than the single-equation approach, it has an advantage because it takes into consideration the simultaneous set of decisions that must be made when determining energy consumption. Such an approach borders on an alternative class of models in which the first-order conditions from a theoretical modeling framework are directly estimated. Thus, the 'true' demand function is derived by solving the consumer/producer maximization problem. Then the resulting simultaneous system of equations can be estimated. Of course, even these approaches are not immune from potential mis-specification. Specifically, one must specify utility functions or production functions to obtain an analytical solution.

There are numerous specifications/approaches that can be considered when estimating energy demand functions and some are more appropriate than others for answering particular questions. Nevertheless, regardless of the specification chosen, a strong understanding of the economic drivers is crucial to empirical analysis. Moreover, while the issues surrounding an appropriate specification can be difficult to resolve, there are some pitfalls that can and should be avoided. For example, when estimating an income elasticity of energy demand it is not correct to simply divide the percentage change in energy demand by the percentage change in income. Moreover, it is not correct to estimate a simple bivariate linear regression of demand on income. Both of these approaches are common mistakes often made by energy analysts since they ignore the affects of other variables on energy demand. This leads to statistically biased results.

To illustrate this point, we must recognize that the very definition of elasticity includes a *ceteris paribus* qualifier. For example, as stated above, the income elasticity of energy demand is the percentage change in energy demand given a 1 percent change in income, *holding all else constant*. Thus, if we seek an estimate of income elasticity, we must account for all other variables that influence demand as well. For example, US gasoline consumption increased at 1.33 percent per year from 1980 through 2005. During the same period, growth of US real income (measured in 2000US$) averaged 3.07 percent per year. A naive approximation of the income elasticity of demand for crude oil would be 0.43 (= 0.0133/0.0307). However, if we consider that other variables also changed during this time, for instance, real gasoline prices decreased at an average annual rate of 0.5 percent, then our naive estimate is likely incorrect.

A comparison of two simple linear regression models of gasoline consumption highlights the importance of including all relevant factors. For example, using annual data, covering the 1980–2005 period, on gasoline consumption from the US Energy Information Administration and data for real GDP obtained from the US Bureau of Economic Analysis, a simple model of gasoline demand regressed on income yields the following:

$$\ln G_t = \underset{(38.20)}{4.92} + \underset{(31.24)}{0.45}\ln Y_t, \tag{5.10}$$

where:

G_t = gasoline consumption,
Y_t = GDP (in real 2000US$),

with $R^2 = 0.976$ and t-values in parentheses. Since the variables are in natural logarithms, the coefficient on income, 0.45, is interpreted as the income elasticity of gasoline demand. This result holds because

$$\frac{\partial \ln G}{\partial \ln Y} = \frac{\partial G}{\partial Y} \cdot \frac{Y}{G}.$$

By contrast, given the relationship between energy and capital (see above), we may choose to include other variables in the regression analysis. Specifically, if we allow utilization of vehicles at the aggregate level to be a function of income, price, and population, then gasoline consumption can be estimated as a function of income, price, population, the vehicle stock, and fuel efficiency. Using annual data, covering the 1980–2005 period, on gasoline consumption and gasoline price from the US Energy Information Administration, data for real GDP obtained from the US Bureau of Economic Analysis, data on vehicle stocks and motor vehicle on-road fuel efficiency from the US Federal Highway and Traffic Safety Administration, we can estimate the following model:

$$\ln G_t = \underset{(-0.81)}{-1.71} + \underset{(1.46)}{0.16 \ln Y_t} - \underset{(-1.50)}{0.02 \ln P_t} + \underset{(1.24)}{0.25 \ln POP_t} + \underset{(3.66)}{0.61 \ln V_t} - \underset{(-7.64)}{0.45 \ln \varepsilon_t}, \tag{5.11}$$

where:

G_t = gasoline consumption,
Y_t = GDP (in real 2000US$),
V_t = no. of motor vehicles,
ε_t = fuel efficiency,
POP_t = population,
P_t = gasoline price (in real 2000US$),

with $R^2 = 0.996$ and t-values in parentheses. Again, since the variables are in natural logarithms, the estimated coefficients are interpreted as elasticities. The income elasticity in this case is now 0.16, or almost one-third of the value estimated in the simple bivariate model. Thus, both the naive approximation and the simple bivariate model yield an income elasticity that is overstated.

The preceding example pertains only to gasoline demand in the US, but similar examples using data for other countries or different end-uses can also be constructed. Moreover, to the extent that we can construct a reduced form of (5.11), we may indeed opt to estimate a model that is more parsimonious than (5.11). However, even (5.10) omits variables that would be included in a reduced form of (5.11) and leads to biased parameter estimates. It is important to note that the above example is meant to be illustrative. Using different datasets, different time periods or different model specifications can lead to different results. In fact, there are more complicated models of motor fuel demand estimated in the economic literature (see, for example, Small and Van Dender 2007) that utilize simultaneous equations specifications or panel datasets.

More generally, if we take energy demand to be a function of income, price, and another n variables, say X_n, then, the total derivative of energy demand is given as:

$$dE = \frac{\partial E}{\partial Y} dY + \frac{\partial E}{\partial P} dP + \frac{\partial E}{\partial X_1} dX_1 + \ldots.$$

If we hold all factors but income constant, the above equation reduces to $dE = (\partial E/\partial Y)\,dY$. Multiplying both sides by $(1/DY) \cdot (Y/E)$ yields:

$$\frac{dE}{dY} \cdot \frac{Y}{E} = \frac{\partial E}{\partial Y} \cdot \frac{Y}{E},$$

which is precisely the definition of income elasticity of energy demand. But, we only obtain this result when we hold all variables except income constant. If we relax the assumption of all other variables held constant and repeat the steps above, we end up with an additional term on the right-hand side of the above equation (indicated in square brackets below):

$$\frac{dE}{dY} \cdot \frac{Y}{E} = \frac{\partial E}{\partial Y} \cdot \frac{Y}{E} + \left[\left(\frac{\partial E}{\partial P} \cdot dP \cdot \frac{1}{dY} \frac{Y}{E} \right) + \left(\frac{\partial E}{\partial X_1} \cdot dX_1 \cdot \frac{1}{dY} \frac{Y}{E} \right) + \ldots \right].$$

The term in square brackets effectively contaminates the estimated coefficients. If, therefore, we seek an estimate of income elasticity, we cannot ignore the other relevant variables as it introduces a bias similar to the term in square brackets. Using a biased estimate of elasticity can lead to serious problems when forecasting future demand. Thus, it is important to recognize that many variables influence energy use, and those variables must be taken into consideration.

7 A Further Comment on the Effects of Price Changes

The long- and short-run effects of energy price changes on demand can be difficult to separate. This is largely because energy demand is predicated on ownership of energy-using capital, and the decision to purchase energy-using capital is made simultaneously with a choice of some level of energy efficiency and some planned rate of utilization of capital. Therefore, expectations about future prices are very important to the decision set. If prices are expected to be very high in the future, the cost-saving effect of higher energy efficiency may carry a greater weight. If, however, the expectation is for low prices, then the benefit of paying for increased efficiency is not as great, and the consumer may opt for other qualities in the capital stock.

One example of this pertains to a consumer's decision to purchase and operate a motor vehicle in the interest of obtaining transportation service. If fuel prices rise, the degree to which an individual reduces the distance he/she drives will alter his/her fuel consumption. This, for a given change in price, gives us some idea of the price elasticity of demand, once all other influences are taken into account. Because it is difficult to turn over vehicle stocks quickly in the interest of raising efficiency (there is usually a fixed cost to doing so), only the consumer's decision regarding utilization affects price responsiveness in the short run. In the long run, however, the consumer may buy a more fuel-efficient vehicle, which will tend to reduce fuel consumption regardless of price and the amount of driving. As a result of this behavior, the short-run price elasticity tends to be relatively small when compared to the long-run price elasticity which is enabled by the greater flexibility in capital and technology.

Not only is the short-run price elasticity smaller than the long-run price elasticity, but the demand response is asymmetric.[4] In other words, rising energy prices will tend to reduce growth in macroeconomic output and energy demand, but falling prices will not necessarily have an equal and opposite effect (see, for example, Gately and Huntington

2002). This asymmetry in price response, or so-called 'imperfect price-reversibility', comes about due to changes in the characteristics of the capital stock. In particular, rising energy prices give an incentive to increase energy efficiency, which can be done by either retrofitting or replacing installed capital. Once this is done, however, the investment will not be undone if energy prices fall.

Examination of equation (5.1) can provide basic insight into the nature of imperfect price reversibility. In the short run, an increase in energy price causes the user cost of capital to rise, which follows from equation (5.6). Since capital and technology are fixed, the consumer should respond by adjusting the utilization rate of capital. The resulting decline in capital utilization will reduce energy demand, and also influence a reduction in economic activity. In the long run, capital and technology can change. Accordingly, an increase in efficiency will still yield a decrease in energy demand, but the macroeconomic response to energy price increases in the long run becomes less clear. More specifically, improvements in energy efficiency can cause asymmetry in the responsiveness of demand to price by preventing energy use from rising by much when energy prices decline.

Investments that result in greater energy efficiency also lower the impact of future price increases because increasing efficiency lowers the user cost of energy-using capital. The US experience in the motor fuels market over the past 30+ years is evidence of the type of dynamic described above. Figure 5.4 reveals that average fuel efficiency of passenger vehicles in the US was basically constant from 1960 to 1978. Throughout this period, oil prices were relatively stable, and vehicle utilization (measured as miles per vehicle) grew steadily. Things were very different following the oil-price shocks of the 1970s and early 1980s, as there was an immediate decrease in vehicle utilization, reflecting the short-run response of consumers to higher prices. Through the 1980s and early 1990s, however, the average on-road efficiency of motor vehicles in the US increased substantially. In fact, from 1978 to 1992, the on-road efficiency of motor vehicle increased from about 13 to 20 miles per gallon – a greater than 50 percent improvement. These efficiency gains offset the effect of falling prices, which contributed to increased vehicle stocks and greater vehicle utilization. Thus, in the long run, the high prices in the 1970s and early 1980s prompted substantial change in the characteristics of the vehicle fleet.

In general, if technology changes in response to high prices, any particular subsequent price increase will not have the same effect as a previous increase in price of the same magnitude. This follows from the effects of higher efficiency on user cost. For example, assume that there is a price increase in time period 1. The effect on demand, given in equation (5.6), will be realized through the change in user cost, which is given as:

$$\frac{\partial \mu}{\partial p_E} = \frac{u}{\varepsilon} + \frac{1}{\varepsilon}\frac{\partial u}{\partial p_E},$$

recognizing utilization is a function of price. However, we shall have a smaller change in user cost if we allow technology to change, or:

$$\frac{u}{\varepsilon} + \frac{1}{\varepsilon}\frac{\partial u}{\partial p_E} > \frac{u}{\varepsilon} + \frac{1}{\varepsilon}\frac{\partial u}{\partial p_E} - \frac{u}{\varepsilon^2}\frac{\partial \varepsilon}{\partial p_E}.$$

Thus, a given change in price at some future date will affect user cost less than a current change in price of the same magnitude. As a result, future price changes will have to be ever larger to obtain the same reduction in demand realized from past price increases.

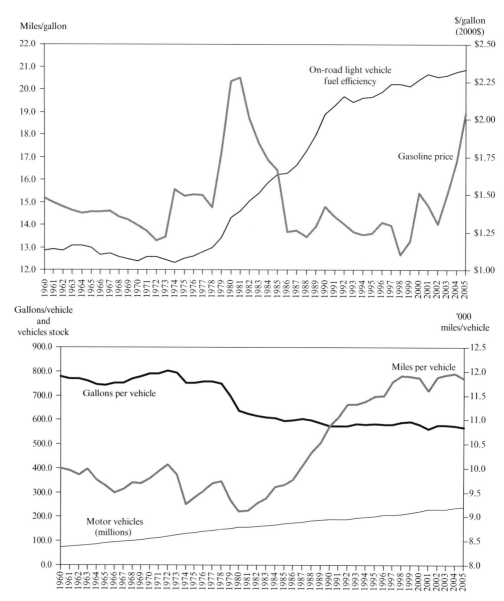

Note: Energy prices for transportation increased substantially from 1974 through 1982. Motor vehicle utilization declined initially, but a long-run increase in on-road motor vehicle fleet efficiency ultimately reduced user costs. As a result, there has been an increase in motor vehicle utilization but a decrease in fuel use per vehicle, and hence the cost of achieving a given transportation service.

Source: Energy Information Administration.

Figure 5.4   US fuel prices, vehicles, efficiency and use (1960–2005)

8   Final Remarks

The demand for energy is a *derived* demand. When combined with some stock of energy-consuming capital, energy use facilitates the provision of goods and services. Moreover, because an energy service is what is ultimately demanded, the final decision to use energy at the individual, household and/or firm level is the result of simultaneous actions regarding the quantity of capital equipment, the efficiency of capital equipment, the type of fuel input, and the rate of capital utilization.

These microeconomic considerations have a bearing on patterns of energy use at the aggregate level. In particular, as economic development progresses, production and consumption patterns change, partly due to changes in economic structure. This structural change results in changes in the type of capital employed and hence energy-use patterns. For example, growth in the financial service sector of an economy may result in more computer purchases, which will in turn result in an increase in the demand for electricity in the service sector as a whole. Such changes mean that rates of growth of energy demand for a given rate of economic growth will likely change through time, thereby having implications for energy security and environmental policy. In addition, factors such as technological change and the effect of energy prices on the composition, efficiency and utilization of deployed capital must also be considered in order to understand the manner in which demand may evolve. Such an understanding allows policy makers to consider the biggest 'bang-for-buck' when debating options for promoting energy security of environmental goals. If, for example, the transportation sector dominates crude oil use then policies aimed at promoting efficiency in that sector specifically will likely have the biggest impact on crude oil consumption, thus leading to a more cost-effective outcome than targeting sectors where oil is only a marginal fuel.

When modeling demand statistically, appropriate specification is important because it influences estimated demand elasticities. A misspecified model could render elasticity estimates that suggest a course of action that is inappropriate. For example, if policy targets a demand reduction through the implementation of a tax in a sector where price elasticity is very low, then the policy is unlikely to achieve its stated goal. This can, in turn, result in large costs being imposed on consumers without an offsetting benefit. As another example, suppose income elasticity is overestimated due to misspecification. Policy makers might adopt a very aggressive tax on energy use in the hope of reducing demand for a given projection of economic growth, even though the tax is not necessary. Again, the result will be large costs to consumers without an offsetting benefit. Such could be the case if the income elasticity of demand is assumed to be constant when it actually declines as income rises.

Energy is intimately intertwined with discussions of policy because of its importance to economic and social progress. At the national and local levels of government, forecasting is an essential part of developing a sound energy policy. In the private sector, corporate planners use forecasts of demand for the development of strategic outlooks and business plans. Public utilities use demand outlooks to develop and justify strategies to local public utility commissions and government regulators for the fulfillment of public service obligations. More generally, energy security concerns arise due to the energy–economy link that is supported by an abundance of empirical research demonstrating a strong negative correlation between energy prices and macroeconomic performance in energy-importing countries (see, for example, Hamilton 1983; Mork et al. 1994 and Ferderer 1996). Because of this, policy is often concerned with maintaining security of supply at a reasonable price.

In addition to energy security, the environment is at the forefront of energy policy debates. In both cases, trying to limit energy demand growth without detriment to economic welfare is a key goal. Regarding the environment in particular, fuel choice is very important. The relative prices of energy commodities impact on both long- and short-run energy consumption by influencing fuel switching and potentially investment behavior. Thus, environmental policy is often focused on making cleaner fuels more attractive to consumers. Unfortunately, environmental concerns can be at odds with resource cost and availability. For example, a large indigenous coal endowment will typically render coal relatively inexpensive so that it will be consumed in large quantities. But, coal is notoriously dirty, so unless its environmental costs are great enough, little will be done to abate its use. In fact, this helps to explain why coal dominates the energy composition in a country such as China, where the desire for continued rapid economic growth appears to outweigh environmental concerns, at least presently.

In general, theory is very important in forecasting and analyzing energy demand trends because it provides (or at least should) the underpinning of the development of suitable models that ultimately facilitate policy formulation. If policy is to promote cost-effective solutions to problems it addresses, then appropriate specification of energy demand models is vital. This point has at no time been more important than the present, when the formulation of strategies to combat climate change is at the forefront of policy discussions. This pressure comes in the face of high global energy prices and strong economic growth from developing countries, two factors which should promote swift decisive actions aimed at abating energy demand (or more precisely, fossil-fuel demand) growth while attempting to avoid harming macroeconomic health.

Notes

1. Note that the dual to the firm's problem is one of profit maximization, and the conclusions herein are not subject to the approach taken.
2. Medlock and Soligo (2002) formulated a similar problem to that presented herein with application to motor vehicle stocks and motor fuel consumption.
3. This follows from Diewert (1974).
4. For example, if a Δ_P increase in price results in a Δ_D decrease in demand, asymmetry exists when a Δ_P decrease in price does not result in a Δ_D decline in demand.

References

Bernardini, O. and R. Galli (1993), 'Dematerialization: long-term trends in the intensity of use of materials and energy', *Futures*, May: 431–48.
Bureau of Economic Analysis, United States Department of Commerce, available at: www.bea.gov (accessed October 2007).
Diewert, W.E. (1974), 'Intertemporal consumer theory and the demand for durables', *Econometrica*, **42**: 497–516.
Energy Information Administration, United States Department of Energy, available at: www.eia.doe.gov (accessed October 2007).
Federal Highway and Traffic Safety Administration, United States Department of Transportation, available at: www.fhtsa.gov (accessed October 2007).
Ferderer, J.P. (1996), 'Oil price volatility and the macroeconomy', *Journal of Macroeconomics*, Winter: 1–26.

Galli, R. (1998), 'The relationship between energy intensity and income levels: forecasting long term energy demand in Asian emerging countries', *The Energy Journal*, **19**(4): 85–105.

Gately, D. and H. Huntington (2002), 'The asymmetric effects of changes in price and income on energy and oil demand', *The Energy Journal*, **23**(1): 19–55.

Hamilton, J.D. (1983), 'Oil and the macroeconomy since World War II', *Journal of Political Economy*, **91**(2): 228–48.

Huntington, H. (1998), 'Crude oil prices and U.S. economic performance: where does the asymmetry reside?', *The Energy Journal*, **19**(4): 107–32.

Johansson, O. and L. Schipper (1997), 'Measuring the long-run fuel demand of cars: separate estimations of vehicle stock, mean fuel intensity, and mean annual driving distance', *Journal of Transport Economics and Policy*, **31**(3): 277–92.

Judson, R., R. Schmalensee and T. Stoker (1999), 'Economic development and the structure of the demand for commercial energy', *The Energy Journal*, **20**(2): 29–58.

Medlock III, K.B. and R. Soligo (2001), 'Economic development and end-use energy demand', *The Energy Journal*, **22**(2): 77–105.

Medlock III, K.B. and R. Soligo (2002), 'Car ownership and economic development with forecasts to 2015', *Journal of Transport Economics and Policy*, **36**(2): 163–88.

Mork, K., H.T. Mysen and O. Olsen (1994), 'Macroeconomic responses to oil price increases and decreases in seven OECD countries', *The Energy Journal*, **15**(4): 19–35.

Small, K.A. and K. Van Dender (2007), 'Fuel efficiency and motor vehicle travel: the declining rebound effect', *The Energy Journal*, **28**(1): 25–51.

Tishler, A. (1983), 'The demand for cars and gasoline: a simultaneous approach', *European Economic Review*, **10**: 271–87.

6 Empirical modelling of energy demand
*David L. Ryan and André Plourde**

1 Introduction

One of the consequences of the first world oil shock in the early 1970s was a marked increase in the empirical modelling of energy demand. There appear to be at least four primary motivations for this. First, there is the question of the magnitude of demand responses as a result of price changes and income changes that may occur. Clearly these responses can have important implications for policy analysis, since any type of tax would generally raise the price and hence affect demand, as would increases in income, perhaps as a country develops. Second, there is a general interest in forecasting or predicting future energy needs, and such forecasts are generally anchored in knowledge of what has happened in the past, how past demand behaviour depends on various factors and expectations about how those factors might change in the future. Third, while energy seldom plays the same role in economic analysis as labour and capital, there is a general understanding that without energy there would be no production, so that issues of the extent to which energy can be substituted in the production (or other) process have become an important consideration. Fourth, with increasing concern over greenhouse gas (GHG) emissions and climate change, which tend to be largely associated with energy production and consumption, questions of how demand for energy can be curtailed, or converted to forms associated with fewer emissions have received increased prominence.

Driven by such considerations as computing power, data availability, and even the background and training of the original analysts, early attempts at modelling energy demand were, at least in today's terms, relatively simplistic. However, all these factors have evolved over time, and as a result energy demand models and modelling have changed considerably over the past three to four decades, although perhaps somewhat surprisingly, versions of those simplistic early models are still found in many recent energy demand modelling exercises.

The purpose of this chapter is to review empirical models of energy demand, with a view to explaining the key features of the models and estimation methodology.[1] To do this, the models are considered in the context of the data that were available at particular times, and the extent to which previous models might have appeared to be no longer adequate as more data accumulated, technology improved, and the questions of interest evolved. Of course different data are available in different jurisdictions, and it is not possible to analyze all these datasets. Thus, in the empirical illustrations considered here we focus primarily on applications using data for Canada and the United States, and point out some important applications to data from other Organisation for Economic Co-operation and Development (OECD) countries.

A point to emphasize is that there is no single 'right' approach to modelling energy demand. Models differ according to various circumstances, and the model that might be applicable in one setting may be totally inappropriate in another. While it is not possible in a limited space to consider the many variations of model specifications that have been developed by different authors, our aim is to provide a feel for some of the major types of models that have been considered, and the reasons for their development.

The plan of the remainder of this chapter is as follows. In Section 2 we consider early approaches to model specification and estimation, particularly the focus on a single fuel and the functional specification in which all variables are in (natural) logarithms. Systems of equations approaches to modelling energy demand, both at the macroeconomic and microeconomic levels, are reviewed in Section 3. In Section 4 we address the issue of the implications for energy demand modelling and estimation of the potential non-stationarity of many of the relevant data series. The possibility of asymmetric demand responses to energy price changes, and issues associated with the specification and estimation of models that allow such behaviour are considered in Section 5. Section 6 summarizes and concludes.

2 Early Approaches to Modelling and Estimation

As illustrated in Chapter 5, an early and common specification of energy demand equations is:

$$\ln E = \beta_1 + \beta_2 \ln P + \beta_3 \ln Y + e, \tag{6.1}$$

where E represents energy (or an energy source such as oil or electricity) consumption, P represents its price, Y represents a measure of income or aggregate economic activity, e is a stochastic error term, and the β_js are unknown parameters – with β_2 and β_3 representing the constant (own-) price and income elasticities, respectively. Of course, convenience of interpretation is not a particularly good reason for specifying the model in logarithms, and ideally the functional form would be evaluated against other alternatives, as was considered later in several studies (for example, Chang and Hsing, 1991). However, in fairness, estimation of nonlinear functions that nest linear and log-linear specifications required increased computing power, and in these early approaches, little attention was paid to evaluating alternative functional specifications using model diagnostics, such as autocorrelation in the error term that might exist with one particular function but not with another. In addition, if all the variables in (6.1) were in linear form rather than natural logarithms, the price elasticity would be obtained as $\beta_2(P/E)$, and therefore would no longer be constant over the sample. Although the elasticity in this case could readily be evaluated using the sample means, or at some other point, or presented for a range of values of P and E, such an approach was not widely adopted. Also, while the estimated standard error, $s\hat{e}(\hat{\beta}_2)$, of the estimated parameter on $\ln P$ in the log-linear function, $\hat{\beta}_2$, yields an estimate of the standard error of the price elasticity, in a linear specification this would not be the case, so that unless both E and P are treated as non-random, in which case the standard error of the price elasticity would be given by $s\hat{e}(\hat{\beta}_2)(P/E)$, determination of an estimated standard error for the elasticity (using the estimated E in place of actual data) would require nonlinear methods (such as the delta method defined in Greene, 2008: 68) that were not as easily implemented in the 1970s and early 1980s.

Apart from these computational issues, there are other drawbacks of log-linear functional forms, including their generally not being consistent with optimizing behaviour, as outlined in more detail in Section 3. In some cases authors attempted to rectify the constancy of the elasticity by altering the model specification (Dias-Bandaranaike and Munasinghe, 1983) but generally such ad hoc approaches only serve to introduce additional problems (Plourde and Ryan, 1985). Perhaps the most problematical aspect of the specification in (6.1), however, was not the functional form, but the lack of any dynamic structure. Many authors, within an energy context and in other circumstances, have noted the need to allow for long-run responses to differ from short-run ones (for example, Berndt et al., 1981 – hereinafter, BMW, 1981). To the extent that the capital stock in place requires energy to operate, or requires a certain source of energy, the substitution that might be expected due to an energy price increase first requires a change in the capital stock, and such changes often cannot be enacted instantaneously. In such circumstances, the long-run response to a price increase would be expected to exceed the short-run response, since in the long run greater substitution possibilities will be available as the capital stock is changed. Again, empirical evidence of the need for such dynamics may have shown up in the model diagnostics – in terms of evidence that the errors were autocorrelated – had such diagnostics been obtained. The simplest dynamic specification, which BMW and others refer to as first-generation models, simply includes a lagged dependent variable as an explanatory variable. Thus, with time subscripts added, the model specification in (6.1) is replaced by:

$$\ln E_t = \gamma_1 + \gamma_2 \ln P_t + \gamma_3 \ln Y_t + \gamma_4 \ln E_{t-1} + e_t, \qquad (6.2)$$

where E_{t-1} is energy consumption in the previous period, and the unknown parameters are now represented by γ_js, for reasons that will become apparent below.

   With the specification in (6.2), the effect of a price (or income change) is now different in the short and long run. Specifically, in the short run, the price elasticity would be γ_2, the coefficient on $\ln P_t$ as before. Typically, the long run is defined as the period sufficiently long to have enabled all adjustments to have taken place, so that $E = E_t = E_{t-1} (= E_{t-2} = E_{t-3} = \cdots)$. Substituting this equality into (6.2), grouping terms, and then taking the derivative, the long-run price elasticity is given by $\partial \ln E / \partial \ln P = \gamma_2 / (1 - \gamma_4)$. In this case there is no avoiding the use of nonlinear methods to obtain an estimated standard error for estimated elasticity. Typically these standard errors were simply not calculated, and it was merely noted that the long- and short-run elasticities were different, with the magnitude of the (negative) long-run value typically exceeding (in absolute value terms) the magnitude of the (negative) short-run value, provided that $0 < \gamma_4 < 1$.

   One of the main criticisms levelled at the model specification in (6.2) was that it was purely ad hoc in nature. Indeed, the so-called second- and third-generation models that we consider in the next section were developed largely in response to this criticism. Despite this criticism, there are a number of possible justifications – or perhaps rationalizations – for the introduction of the lagged dependent variable in (6.2). These include a partial adjustment or stock adjustment model, whereby, perhaps due to the need to introduce different capital equipment, a desired change in energy consumption could not be satisfied in the current period. Thus, in (6.1), the dependent variable $\ln E_t$ would be replaced by the desired energy consumption, $\ln E_t^*$, so that this equation would now model how *desired* energy consumption responds to changes in price and income, and the coefficients in this model, the β_js, would be interpreted as indicating the long-run responses of energy demand to changes in the explanatory factors. However, due to technological constraints, actual consumption could only partially adapt to this desired level via the relationship:

$$\ln E_t - \ln E_{t-1} = \theta(\ln E_t^* - \ln E_{t-1}), 0 \le \theta \le 1, \tag{6.3}$$

where the parameter θ represents the speed of adjustment, with $\theta = 0$ indicating no adjustment in the current period, $\theta = 1$ indicating instantaneous adjustment, and values between these two extremes indicating partial adjustment. Substituting (6.1), which now represents $\ln E_t^*$, into (6.3) and rearranging yields the model in (6.2), where $\gamma_j = \theta\beta_j, j = 1, 2, 3$, and $\gamma_4 = (1 - \theta)$, and therefore $\gamma_j/(1 - \gamma_4) = \beta_j$, the long-run effects.

Of course, this is not the only possible way to rationalize the lagged dependent variable that appears in (6.2). For example, in (6.1), the terms $\beta_2 \ln P_t$ and $\beta_3 \ln Y_t$ could be replaced by geometric lags, that is, an infinite distributed lag where the coefficients decline geometrically. Thus, for example, in (6.1), $\beta_2 \ln P_t$ would be replaced by:

$$\beta_2(\ln P_t + \lambda \ln P_{t-1} + \lambda^2 \ln P_{t-2} + \lambda^3 \ln P_{t-3} + \cdots),$$

where $0 < \lambda < 1$, while $\beta_3 \ln Y_t$ would be replaced by:

$$\beta_3(\ln Y_t + \lambda \ln Y_{t-1} + \lambda^2 \ln Y_{t-2} + \lambda^3 \ln Y_{t-3} + \cdots),$$

so that β_2 and β_3 would represent short-run effects of changes in P and Y, respectively, while the corresponding long-run effects (when $P_t = P_{t-1} = P_{t-2} = \cdots$, and $Y_t = Y_{t-1} = Y_{t-2} = \cdots$) would be given by:

$$\beta_2(1 + \lambda + \lambda^2 + \cdots) = \beta_2/(1 - \lambda)$$

and

$$\beta_3(1 + \lambda + \lambda^2 + \cdots) = \beta_3/(1 - \lambda).$$

Hence the effect of a price or income change has an immediate effect as well as an effect in each subsequent period that is always smaller than the effect in all preceding periods. Making these substitutions yields an equation that includes infinite lags on the explanatory variables, although relatively few parameters. To obtain an estimating equation, a Koyck transformation is used. Specifically, we calculate $(\ln E_t - \lambda \ln E_{t-1})$, so that all the lag terms cancel, resulting in an estimating equation that has the same form as in (6.2) where $\gamma_1 = \beta_1(1 - \lambda)$, $\gamma_j = \beta_j, j = 2, 3$, and $\gamma_4 = \lambda$, and $\gamma_j/(1 - \gamma_4) = \beta_j/(1 - \lambda)$ would yield the long-run effects.

A different type of rationalization for the inclusion of lagged values of energy consumption, as well as possibly lagged values of the other explanatory variables, is outlined by Bentzen and Engsted (2001). Here the primary motivation concerns the properties of the estimators and their standard errors. As we discuss in more detail in Section 4, a problem with estimating models like (6.1) in a time-series context is that if the variables are non-stationary (trending), the regressions may be spurious. However, if appropriate lags of all the variables are included in (6.2), and there is a unique long-run (cointegrating) relationship among the variables being studied, then the model written in levels form as in (6.2) remains valid and asymptotically valid hypothesis testing can be conducted in the usual way.

Regardless of the rationalization that is used to justify the inclusion of the lagged dependent variable as an explanatory variable in (6.2), the modelling is ad hoc, with no justification for the lag structure based on any real consideration of economic behaviour. Additional criticisms of this approach were provided by BMW (1981). Generalizations of these dynamic structures to what BMW refer to as second- and third-generation models typically involve systems of equations rather than a single equation, so that the interrelationships between different inputs (such as labour, capital, energy and materials), or between different sources of energy, can be explicitly recognized. These types of models are considered in the next section.

While it may be attractive to think of the evolution of models as occurring due to theoretical developments, if there were not some perceived problem with the application of the simpler models it would certainly seem less likely that the more sophisticated models would be developed and receive relatively widespread acceptance. After all, arguably one of the most cherished aspects of modelling is parsimony, the ability to abstract from reality with models that are relatively simple and involve few parameters. Indeed, it could be argued that this criterion, parsimony, was one of the key factors resulting in widespread use of the log-linear specification, and one which maintains this simple specification as a workhorse of energy demand analysis even today. Therefore, it seems likely that there were some empirical problems that were perceived with the simpler specifications in (6.1) and (6.2) that resulted in the push to develop alternative specifications that were typically more complex. For example, BMW in an empirical comparison show that the single-equation partial-adjustment specification yields elasticity estimates that are unacceptably large in the long run.

3   Systems of Equations Approaches

Perhaps the most significant breakthrough in terms of econometric modelling in general, but particularly in modelling demand relationships, was the introduction of the transcendental logarithmic (translog) function by Christensen et al. (1973). Until this point, energy demand analysis predominantly involved a single-equation approach. The idea of a single aggregate function from which demand functions for individual goods or inputs could be derived and estimated was developed much earlier with the work of Stone (1954) and others. However, the aggregate function in these cases was usually a utility function, and the systems of demand equations referred predominantly to complete descriptions of consumer expenditures. On the production side, there was only a limited set of production functions from which a set of input demand equations could be derived, particularly the Cobb–Douglas and constant elasticity of substitution (CES) specifications. However, these were typically specified with two inputs – labour and capital – and were very restrictive. The main advantage of the translog form, like other flexible functional form specifications that followed, was that it could approximate an arbitrary function to the second order, that is, it had sufficient parameters to avoid imposing restrictions on the first and second derivatives of the function, the first derivatives being the demands, and the second derivatives being the price effects, which are the major component of the price elasticities. In addition, it could readily be used in applications with almost any number of inputs or commodities, thus allowing examination of the interrelationships between the demands for various energy sources.

BMW (1981) distinguish two types of multi-equation approaches, which they refer to as second- and third-generation models. Second-generation models are anchored in a framework in which interrelated demands for multiple energy sources are determined simultaneously using a static optimization approach. In much the same way as with the single-equation models reviewed in the previous section, dynamics are introduced in a relatively ad hoc manner, often through the subsequent addition of lagged terms to the demand equations derived from this static optimization process. In contrast, third-generation models are explicitly based on a dynamic optimization approach that incorporates adjustment costs. The dynamic adjustment processes are thus an integral part of the model specification. While the move from first- to second-generation models involved increased complexity in terms of both specification and estimation, the added complexity resulting from the further extension to third-generation models was far greater. This proved to be a significant drawback of third-generation models in empirical applications, as alluded to by BMW, who anticipated the continued use of first- and second-generation models in energy demand analysis.

Since different approaches have characterized the development of energy demand modelling of production and consumption, reflecting the different issues that have arisen in each context, we examine these two areas separately.

Production-side modelling
Formulations of energy demand have also been incorporated in models designed to provide representations of the interaction between energy and the economy and for policy analysis. Initially, two different approaches to dealing with energy demand within such models emerged. One of these, the 'bottom-up' approach, is discussed in later chapters. The second approach, which is the focus here draws more heavily on economics. A key characteristic of this approach is its treatment of energy as a factor of production within a representation of output production. The so-called 'top-down' approach implemented in production-side models shied away from including much technological detail and instead focused on using economics-inspired relationships that were typically estimated econometrically using data for the relevant variables. Energy demand was determined through the production relationship and the demands for individual energy sources, to the extent that these were even considered, were typically determined by splitting total energy demand through econometrically estimated relationships.

Key early contributors in this area, such as Hudson and Jorgenson (1974), took advantage of the development of flexible functional forms for production functions. In its most common form, this approach views energy (E) as an input that is combined with physical capital (K), labour (L), and materials (M) to yield the output of a sector of the economy (for example, manufacturing or subsectors of manufacturing) or of the economy as a whole. In some applications, materials are assumed to be part of what is modelled as being 'produced' and thus only three factors of production are explicitly taken into consideration (for example, Christodoulakis and Kalyvitis, 1997).

The standard approach begins with a representation of the production process:

$$y = g(K, L, E, M),\tag{6.4}$$

where y is a measure of real output and $g(\cdot)$ is a functional form for production. As noted earlier, conventional specifications for $g(\cdot)$, such as the Cobb–Douglas and CES forms, imposed strong restrictions – especially on the elasticities of substitution between inputs – which were relaxed with the introduction of flexible functional forms such as the generalized Leontief (Diewert, 1971) and translog (Christensen et al., 1973) production functions. Although some authors (for example, Chang, 1994) have proceeded to estimate the parameters of the production function directly, a far more common approach has been to start with a representation of production, invoke assumptions of cost-minimizing behaviour on the part of firms, and derive the dual cost function. Using this cost function, a system of consistent factor demand equations can be derived and their parameters subsequently estimated. By far the most commonly adopted specification using this approach is the (nonhomothetic) translog cost function:

$$\ln C = \alpha_0 + \sum_j \alpha_j \ln p_j + \tfrac{1}{2}\sum_j\sum_k \gamma_{jk}\ln p_j \ln p_k + \alpha_y \ln y + \tfrac{1}{2}\gamma_{yy}(\ln y)^2$$
$$+ \sum_j \gamma_{jy}\ln p_j \ln y,\tag{6.5}$$

where the subscripts j and k index the n inputs ($j, k = 1, \ldots, n$), p refers to the factor (input) prices, y is output, and C is cost. In some cases (for example, Binswanger, 1974), an allowance for technological progress is included in the specification by appending terms to (6.5) to yield:

$$\ln C^* = \ln C + \alpha_t \ln t + \tfrac{1}{2}\alpha_{tt}(\ln t)^2 + \sum_j \gamma_{jt}\ln p_j \ln t,\tag{6.6}$$

where t is a time trend. Applying the logarithmic form of Shephard's lemma (Diewert, 1974) to (6.5), the cost share equation for the ith input is obtained as the derivative of $\ln C$ with respect to the logarithm of the ith price, $\ln p_i$. This yields the following system of factor demand equations:

$$s_i = \alpha_i \ln p_i + \sum_j \gamma_{ij}\ln p_j + \gamma_{iy}\ln y, \quad i,j = 1,\ldots,n,\tag{6.7}$$

where s_i is the cost share of the ith input and $\gamma_{ij} = \gamma_{ji}$ ($i, j = 1, \ldots, n$). Adding-up of the share equations (that is, the requirement that the shares sum to unity), requires the following parameter restrictions:

$$\sum_i \alpha_i = 1,\tag{6.8}$$

$$\sum_i \gamma_{ij} = 0, j = 1, \ldots, n,\tag{6.9}$$

and

$$\sum_i \gamma_{iy} = 0.\tag{6.10}$$

Linear homogeneity in prices, which is required for the cost function to be well-behaved, requires the additional restriction that $\sum_j \gamma_{ij} = 0$, $i = 1, \ldots, n$, but since $\gamma_{ij} = \gamma_{ji}$, this additional restriction is automatically satisfied through (6.9).[2] Thus, the term $\sum_{j=1}^{n} \gamma_{ij} \ln p_j$ in (6.7) can be rewritten as $\sum_{j=1}^{n-1} \gamma_{ij} \ln(p_j/p_n)$. A necessary and sufficient condition for the cost function to be homothetic is that $\gamma_{iy} = 0$, $i = 1, \ldots, n$, in which case the terms involving output $(\ln y)$ would not appear in the share equations in (6.7). Returns to scale (RTS), which can be computed as $1/(\partial \ln C/\partial \ln y)$, are given by:

$$RTS = 1 \Big/ \Big(\alpha_y + \sum_j \gamma_{jy} \ln p_j + \gamma_{yy} \ln y \Big), \qquad (6.11)$$

so that output is homogeneous of a constant degree $(1/\alpha_y)$ if, in addition to the homotheticity conditions, $\gamma_{yy} = 0$, while constant returns to scale requires the additional restriction that $\alpha_y = 1$. Note that (6.11) involves some parameters that do not appear in the share equations, so that estimation of RTS would require estimation of the cost function (usually jointly with the system of share equations).

In general the estimated parameters are of little direct interest, the attention focused instead on price and substitution elasticities. For the translog model, the price elasticities can be calculated from the estimated parameters using the relationship:

$$\eta_{ij} = (\gamma_{ij} + s_i s_j - s_i \omega_{ij})/s_i, \qquad i, j = 1, \ldots, n, \qquad (6.12)$$

where $\omega_{ij} = 1$ if $i = j$, and $\omega_{ij} = 0$ otherwise. In terms of elasticities of substitution between the inputs, as outlined by Broadstock et al. (2007), there are several alternative definitions in common use, although the majority of existing empirical studies use the Allen–Uzawa elasticity of substitution (AES). For the translog cost function, the AESs are obtained as:

$$\sigma_{ij} = C(\partial^2 C/\partial p_i \partial p_j) / [(\partial C/\partial p_i)(\partial C/\partial p_j)]$$

$$= (\gamma_{ij} + s_i s_j - s_i \omega_{ij})/(s_i s_j), \qquad (6.13)$$

with positive signs for the AESs indicating substitutes and negative signs indicating complements. Of course, since these elasticities depend on the shares (and should be evaluated using estimated values of these shares), they differ for each observation.

The approach outlined above proved to be fertile ground for the development and empirical implementation of flexible functional forms in energy demand analysis. The early, influential work of Berndt and Wood (1975) is a clear example of a paper that both enhanced our appreciation of the usefulness of flexible functional forms in empirical applications and furthered our understanding of the role of energy in the production process. Within a short period after this paper had appeared, a number of other contributions pushed further explorations of factor substitution possibilities by, among others, using alternative functional forms (for example, Magnus, 1979) and pooled data from a number of different countries (for example, Griffin and Gregory, 1976). While not universally obtained in these kinds of empirical applications, estimation results often suggested that energy and capital were complements in production. However, Field and

Grebenstein (1980), for example, showed that the definition (and thus the measure) of 'capital' used could influence the conclusion as to whether a complementary or substitutability relationship existed between capital and energy. In their comprehensive review of empirical estimates of the elasticity of substitution between energy and capital, Broadstock et al. (2007) find that even the choice of the definition of the elasticity of substitution is open to question, and that the scope for substitution between these two factors might be expected to vary widely across sectors, levels of aggregation, and time periods, with estimates of this substitution elasticity often depending largely on the methodology and assumptions used. While commenting on the lack of consensus that has been obtained on this issue, their general conclusion is that energy and capital are typically found to be either complements or weak substitutes.

Fuss (1977) extended the work of Berndt and Wood (1975) by showing that if certain separability conditions are invoked, it is possible to apply a two-stage optimization approach and obtain, not only a representation of factor demands (including energy), but also consistent expressions of the demands for individual energy sources or fuels. However, this extension comes at a cost: the separability conditions needed to support the two-stage budgeting approach also imply that there can be no level effects in the consistent representations of the demands for energy sources, and thus real output cannot appear in the individual share equations. A survey of the relevant literature indicates that this lesson has not been heeded in a number of contributions. Further details on weak separability and its implications are provided below in a consumer demand context.[3]

Another direction explored in this literature has been to restrict the substitution possibilities across factors of production – and especially that between capital and energy – in the modelling efforts. This has typically involved the grouping of energy and capital as a 'bundle' within the overall production representation:

$$y = f[(K, E), L, M], \qquad (6.14)$$

where, by construction, capital and energy would be substitutes within the bundle, and then complements within the overall representation of the structure of production. Berndt and Wood (1979) and Helliwell et al. (1987) are examples of contributions that adopted this kind of approach.

The notion of treating energy as a factor of production has also been overwhelmingly adopted in efforts to model entire economies. Today, many – if not most – macroeconometric models the world over incorporate a KLEM-type of approach to modelling aggregate (or sectoral) production. Similarly, numerous computable general equilibrium (CGE) models also use a KLEM representation to incorporate energy as a distinct factor of production[4] (see Chapter 14, for example).

Consumer energy demand models and modelling[5]
In addition to flexible functional forms, probably the key development that enhanced modelling and estimation of systems of equations for different types of energy, or different energy sources, was the empirical implementation of the assumption of weak separability. This assumption is a necessary and sufficient condition for two-stage budgeting. Consider, for example, aggregate energy demand which comprises demand for oil products, natural gas, and electricity (and possibly other products such as wood,

propane, and so on, which can readily be included in particular applications where they are relevant). With two-stage budgeting, a consumer can be viewed as first determining the allocation of his/her budget to various aggregates – such as food, clothing, energy, and so on – and then for each of these aggregates, determining expenditures on the various items within that aggregate. At each stage, only certain variables are relevant to the decision making. Thus, at the first stage, the consumer would require information on the total budget and the prices of each aggregate – the price of 'food', the price of 'clothing', the price of 'energy', and so on. Focusing on the energy group, at the second stage all that would be required is total expenditure on energy and the prices of each of the different types of energy that comprise the group. Thus, in specifying demands for individual types of energy, food prices, whether for the group as a whole or for individual food items, are not relevant, and neither are prices of or expenditures on any other good, or group of goods, outside of those contained in the group of energy products. Further, while both stages of the budget allocation process can be considered, there is no need to do so, and attention can be limited just to one group at the second stage, that is, in the context that is relevant here, just to the determination of demands for different sources of energy. Of course one drawback with this approach is that the 'income' variable now becomes total expenditure on energy, so that rather than income elasticities, the corresponding measures that are obtained in this case are energy expenditure elasticities for the demands for the various energy sources.

Even with the development of the translog function and utilization of the weak separability assumption, there was one more key component in facilitating the specification and estimation of systems of energy demand equations. A difficulty with many utility function specifications, especially flexible specifications like the translog, is that the derived demand equations for any one good have the quantities of other goods as explanatory variables. Clearly, since utility is maximized by choosing the quantities subject to the budget constraint, these quantities are endogenous, resulting in difficulties in estimation of the resulting system of demand equations (McLaren, 1982). However, with the use of duality theory, it was realized that alternative representations of preferences that did not have this drawback could be utilized. Specifically, substituting the optimized demands into the utility function yields the indirect utility function which is a function of prices and income. Thus, analysts could start with a translog (or alternative flexible) specification of the indirect utility function and derive demand equations using Roy's identity (Diewert, 1974). Although demand equations derived from the translog indirect utility function were estimated in a number of papers, a serious drawback of this specification was that the resulting system of expenditure share equations was nonlinear, and this presented significant estimation difficulties in the 1970s and early 1980s.

Analogously with the translog cost function used on the production side, an 'ideal' specification for consumer demands, at least in terms of having linear expenditure equations that could be relatively easily estimated, would appear to have been a translog expenditure function. Demand equations could be obtained from an expenditure function, which depends only on prices and the level of utility, by differentiating with respect to each price, with the unobserved utility level subsequently substituted out using the relationship that the cost function must equal total expenditure.[6] The difficulty with adapting the translog cost function for use in a consumer rather than a production context is the appearance of the output level in the cost function, and, due to its interaction with prices, in the resulting share equations. However, if the cost function is homothetic these interaction terms do not appear, so that output would not be included as a determinant of the cost shares which would now depend (linearly) only on the logarithms of prices.[7] Since output, a variable that has no corresponding measure in the consumer context, does not appear here, these share equations could also be readily estimated in a consumer setting. Unfortunately, since the only explanatory variables in this specification are prices, it would mean that the expenditure shares would not depend on, and therefore would not change with changes in, total expenditure. This is a very strong assumption for which there appears to be little empirical support and which in any event would need to be tested. This drawback was not resolved until the expenditure or cost function corresponding to the almost ideal demand system (AIDS) was introduced by Deaton and Muellbauer (1980). Since that time, the AIDS model (and several variants of it) has become the most common way to specify systems of consumer demand equations, including those for energy sources.

The AIDS model is based on the expenditure function:

$$\ln E_t(u_t, p_t) = \alpha_0 + \sum_j \alpha_j \ln p_{jt} + \frac{1}{2} \sum_j \sum_k \gamma_{jk} \ln p_{jt} \ln p_{kt} + u_t \beta_0 \prod_j p_{jt}^{\beta_j}, \quad (6.15)$$

where u_t is household utility in period t, $p_t = (p_{1t}, \ldots, p_{nt})$ is the vector of prices prevailing in period t, and $\alpha_j, \beta_j, \gamma_{jk}$ are parameters, where $j, k = 1, \ldots, n$, with n in the current context being the number of energy sources. Based on the assumption of expenditure-minimizing behaviour on the part of households, a system of share equations describing residential demands for the various energy sources is derived from (6.15) using Shephard's lemma and equating $E_t(u_t, p_t)$ with observed per household energy expenditures.

Applying the logarithmic form of Shephard's lemma, the expenditure share equation for the ith good is obtained as the derivative of $\ln C$ with respect to the logarithm of the ith price, $\ln p_i$. Equating $E_t(u_t, p_t)$ with observed total expenditure on the group of goods in question, such as per household energy expenditures, the following system of expenditure share equations is obtained:

$$s_{it} = \alpha_i + \sum_k \gamma_{ik} \ln p_{kt} + \beta_i \ln (E_t / P_t), \quad (6.16)$$

where:

s_{it} is the expenditure share of the ith energy source in period t,
p_{kt} is the price of the kth energy source in period t,
E_t is the observed per household expenditure on residential energy in period t, and

$$\ln P_t = \alpha_0 + \sum_k \alpha_k \ln p_{kt} + \frac{1}{2} \sum_j \sum_k \gamma_{jk} \ln p_{jt} \ln p_{kt}. \quad (6.17)$$

In practice, the parameter α_0 can be difficult to estimate, and is sometimes set to zero, or to the minimum level of expenditure in the sample. An alternative formulation, which simplifies the empirical analysis by avoiding both the difficulty of empirically identifying α_0, and the estimation difficulties associated with the nonlinear specification that results when (6.17) is substituted into (6.16), involves replacing the nonlinear price index (6.17) with the Stone price index, $\ln P_t^* = \sum_k s_{kt} \ln p_{kt}$, where s_{kt} is the expenditure share for the kth energy source in period t. This yields the popular linear approximation to the almost ideal demand system (or LAIDS), which has been estimated frequently in empirical demand applications (Buse, 1994).

It is often the case in studies of residential energy demand that there is a need to include additional variables in the specification. Specifically, while the expenditure function from which the demand (share) equations are derived is a function only of the relevant prices and total expenditure, it may be conditioned on a number of other factors. For example, in a residential context, energy demands are known to be dependent on weather conditions, since these affect the need for space heating and cooling, which are typically the major end uses in the residential sector. The extent of weather-induced need for space heating and cooling (for example, Dunstan and Schmidt, 1988) can be incorporated in the model by including heating degree-days (*hdd*) and cooling degree-days (*cdd*) as additional explanatory variables. In the specification in (6.16), with $\ln P_t$ replaced by $\ln P_t^*$, this is equivalent to specifying the parameter α_i as a linear function of (the logarithms of) these variables:[8]

$$\alpha_i = \alpha_i^* + c_i \ln hdd_t + d_i \ln cdd_t, \tag{6.18}$$

where c_i and d_i ($i = 1, \ldots, n$) are additional parameters to be estimated. Other conditioning variables may also be included in the share equations by modifying (6.18). However, in some cases there are other alternatives. For example, in a residential context it might be expected that energy demand by a household would increase with household size. While household size could be included as an additional variable in (6.18), and hence in the share equations, the number of parameters to be estimated increases by n for every variable added. In the case of household size this is sometimes avoided by defining the quantity of energy and expenditure in per capita terms by dividing household values for these variables by household size.

With all these modifications incorporated, the LAIDS share equations have the following linear form:

$$s_{it} = \alpha_i + \sum_k \gamma_{ik} \ln p_{kt} + \beta_i \ln (E_t / P_t^*) + c_i \ln hdd_t + d_i \ln cdd_t, \tag{6.19}$$

where, in addition to the previous definitions:

P_t^* is the Stone price index, defined as: $\ln P_t^* = \sum_k s_{kt} \ln p_{kt}$,
hdd_t is heating degree-days in period t (for example, degree-days below 18° Celsius),
cdd_t is cooling degree-days in period t (for example, degree-days above 18° Celsius).

Another consideration with the specification of these expenditure share equations concerns dynamics. As noted in Section 2, energy demands do not always respond instantaneously to changes in prices for a variety of reasons, and this is typically captured by including lagged energy consumption terms in the single-equation specification. A similar approach can be used with a system of expenditure share equations, although it is more common in this case to include lagged expenditure shares. Specifically, expenditure shares in the current period are assumed to adjust only partially to their desired level from the previous (last period) level:[9]

$$s_t - s_{t-1} = \Lambda^* (s_t^* - s_{t-1}),$$
(6.20)

where $s_t = (s_{1t}, \ldots, s_{nt})'$ is a vector of the expenditure shares of the n different energy sources in period t, s_t^* is a vector of desired shares derived from expenditure-minimizing behaviour (for example, as specified in (6.19)), and Λ^* is an $(n \times n)$ matrix of adjustment coefficients with λ_{ij}^* being the (i, j) element. In the simplest form of this specification Λ^* is a constant, diagonal matrix, so that the adjustment for each energy source depends only on its own desired and previous levels:

$$s_{it} - s_{it-1} = \lambda_{ii}^* (s_{it}^* - s_{it-1}).$$
(6.21)

Rearranging (6.21) yields:

$$s_{it} = \lambda_{ii}^* s_{it}^* + (1 - \lambda_{ii}^*) s_{it-1},$$
(6.22)

where s_{it}^* is given by the right-hand side of (6.19). Since all the terms on the right-hand side of (6.19) involve parameters, $\lambda_{ii}^* s_{it}^*$ just means that all the parameters in (6.19) are multiplied by λ_{ii}^*. In practice, this need not be explicitly incorporated in the equation, as whether the parameters that are estimated are α_i, β_i, γ_{ik}, and so on, or $\alpha_i^* = \lambda_{ii}^* \alpha_i$, $\beta_i^* = \lambda_{ii}^* \beta_i$, $\gamma_{ik}^* = \lambda_{ii}^* \gamma_{ik}$, and so on, makes no difference to the estimation. Thus, defining $\lambda_i = (1 - \lambda_{ii}^*)$ for notational convenience, the expenditure share equations for the LAIDS model incorporating the dynamic specification in (6.22) have the form:

$$s_{it} = \alpha_i + \sum_k \gamma_{ik} \ln p_{kt} + \beta_i \ln (E_t / P_t^*) + c_i \ln hdd_t + d_i \ln cdd_t + \lambda_i s_{it-1},$$
(6.23)

whereas if the full specification in (6.20) is used rather than (6.22), then the last term in (6.23) would be replaced by $\sum_j \lambda_{ij} s_{jt-1}$, where $\lambda_{ij} = (1 - \lambda_{ii}^*)$ if $i = j$, and $\lambda_{ij} = -\lambda_{ij}^*$ otherwise. Note that in this latter case, since the lagged shares sum to unity, only $(n - 1)$ of the n lagged shares can be included in each equation.

When estimating the equation system in (6.23), adding-up of the share equations (that is, the requirement that the shares sum to unity) requires the following parameter restrictions:

$$\lambda_i = \lambda, i = 1, \ldots, n,$$
(6.24)

$$\sum_i \alpha_i + \lambda = 1,$$
(6.25)

$$\sum_i \beta_i = \sum_i c_i = \sum_i d_i = 0,$$
(6.26)

and

$$\sum_i \gamma_{ik} = 0, k = 1, \ldots, n.$$
(6.27)

The first of three parametric restrictions requires that in (6.23), the lagged own-share in each equation has the same coefficient. In other words, the speed of adjustment is restricted to be the same across all energy sources. This restriction arises because the sum of the lagged shares is unity, so that

$$\sum_{i=1}^{n} \lambda_i s_{it-1} = \sum_{i=1}^{n-1} (\lambda_i - \lambda_n) s_{it-1} + \lambda_n,$$

and for this to be constant in different time periods (observations), it must be independent of the shares, which can only occur if (6.24) holds. As a result of (6.24), $\sum_{i=1}^{n} \lambda_i s_{it-1} = \lambda$, so that the sum of the shares adding to 1 now results in the restriction in (6.25). The restriction that the lagged share in each equation must have the same coefficient can be avoided by using (6.20) and therefore including $(n-1)$ of the lagged shares in each equation by replacing $\lambda_i s_{it-1}$ in (6.23) by $\sum_{j=1}^{n-1} \lambda_{ij} s_{jt-1}$, in which case the parameter restrictions in (6.24) and (6.25) are replaced by:

$$\sum_{i} \lambda_{ij} = 0, j = 1, \ldots, (n-1), \tag{6.24a}$$

and

$$\sum_{i} \alpha_i = 1. \tag{6.25a}$$

Although the prices and expenditure in share equations such as (6.23) are typically expressed in nominal terms, if the demands satisfy the homogeneity condition (that is, they are homogeneous of degree zero in prices and total expenditure or total cost), so that a scaling of all prices and total expenditure does not affect the quantities that are demanded, then in (6.23):

$$\sum_{k=1}^{n} \gamma_{ik} = 0. \tag{6.28}$$

In this case the term $\sum_{k=1}^{n} \gamma_{ik} \ln p_{kt}$ in (6.23) can be rewritten as $\sum_{k=1}^{n-1} \gamma_{ik} \ln(p_{kt}/p_{nt})$. Consequently, any common price index that is used to convert nominal prices to real prices will cancel out when the price ratio terms (p_{kt}/p_{nt}) are calculated. Hence, with homogeneity imposed it does not matter whether real rather than nominal prices and expenditure are used. Since the homogeneity condition follows directly from the adding-up condition – that the sum of expenditures on (or costs of) each energy source equals total expenditure on (or cost of) energy – it is typically expected to hold in demand systems such as (6.23) and would often be imposed.

A second set of conditions that would be expected to hold in demand systems such as (6.23) are what we refer to as the 'standard symmetry conditions', namely:

$$\gamma_{ik} = \gamma_{ki} (i, k = 1, \ldots, n). \tag{6.29}$$

These conditions are required for identification purposes, and follow from the fact that the price term in (6.23), $\sum_{k=1}^{n} \gamma_{ik} \ln p_{kt}$, is obtained as the derivative with respect to the logarithm of the ith price of a cross-product term such as $\frac{1}{2}(\sum_{j=1}^{n} \sum_{k=1}^{n} \gamma_{jk}^* \ln p_j \ln p_k)$ that appears in the cost or expenditure function, such as (6.15). Technically this derivative equals $\sum_{k=1}^{n} \frac{1}{2}(\gamma_{ik}^* + \gamma_{ki}^*)\ln p_{kt}$, but since γ_{ik}^* and γ_{ki}^* always appear in the additive form $(\gamma_{ik}^* + \gamma_{ki}^*)/2$, neither is separately identified, so that this term is simply redefined as γ_{ik}, and by definition, $\gamma_{ik} = \gamma_{ki}$ $(i, k = 1, \ldots, n)$. In many circumstances (including here) these standard symmetry conditions are equivalent to the conditions required for Slutsky symmetry to hold, where the Slutsky symmetry conditions are the requirement that the derivative of the compensated demand for the ith good with respect to the jth price is equal to the derivative of the jth compensated demand with respect to the ith price, in other words that the second derivatives of the cost or expenditure function are the same regardless of the order in which the derivatives are taken. However, we emphasize here that (6.29) are just identification conditions so that they would generally be imposed on (6.23). It is also important to note that due to the adding-up condition (the sum of the shares summing to 1), as reflected in the parametric restrictions in (6.24) through (6.27), the imposition of the standard symmetry conditions in (6.29) means that the homogeneity condition (6.28) will automatically be satisfied.

Since the parameter estimates themselves have little direct interpretation, interest generally centres on the estimated price responses that are determined from the parameter estimates and data. For the LAIDS model, the price elasticities for the various energy sources (using either the real or relative price specifications) can be calculated from the estimated parameters using the relationship:[10]

$$\eta_{ik} = \gamma_{ik}/s_i - \beta_i s_k/s_i - \omega_{ik}, \tag{6.30}$$

where $\omega_{ik} = 1$ if $i = k$, and $\omega_{ik} = 0$ otherwise. Income (or total expenditure) elasticities can be calculated using:

$$\eta_{iE} = 1 + \beta_i/s_i. \tag{6.31}$$

Since these elasticities depend on the shares (and should be evaluated using estimated values of these shares), they differ for each observation. A common practice is to present estimated elasticities evaluated at the sample means for the explanatory variables, but this has a number of drawbacks. First, the point where each variable equals its sample mean is not necessarily even closely related to any of the sample observations. More importantly, one of the main advantages of using flexible functional forms as opposed to a single-equation linear in logarithms energy demand equation is that the elasticities are not assumed to be constant, and indeed will generally vary throughout the sample. Over time, price responsiveness may be changing quite extensively, but this information is lost if price elasticities are evaluated only at the sample mean. Thus, a recommended approach would be to calculate elasticities at each sample point, although they may be presented only for selected observations, such as every ten years or matching certain periods in energy demand evolution (pre-OPEC – Organization of Petroleum Exporting Countries – and so on). Of course, estimated elasticities for all observations in the sample could easily be presented using a graphical approach. Ideally, in order to evaluate the significance of the elasticities, estimated standard errors for the elasticities should be calculated using the delta method mentioned earlier, and in a graphical approach, confidence bounds for the elasticities could be included.

Finally, while we have focused here predominantly on model specification, in terms of estimation – both of consumer- and production-side relationships – it is worth noting the importance, particularly when using time-series data, of examining the model diagnostics and appropriately remedying any problems that are detected. Autocorrelation is a common problem with energy demand models but many authors do not test for its presence (or at least do not report the results of such tests) even though they often conduct and report on an extensive battery of tests on various other (structural) aspects of the model specification. At a minimum, the presence of auto-correlation will mean that the estimated standard errors used in these test procedures are incorrect, potentially leading to misleading results. Furthermore, autocorrelation of the errors is a particular problem when the model specification includes lagged values of the dependent variable as an explanatory variable. In this case, in a single-equation context, ordinary least squares (OLS) estimators are likely to be inconsistent. In a systems of equations context, the use of maximum likelihood estimation does not resolve this problem if the autocorrelation in the error structure is not explicitly incorporated in the likelihood function. Of course, autocorrelation may itself be a symptom of other problems with the specification, including the possibility that the model being estimated is spurious. Approaches to dealing with this issue are considered in the following section.

4   Non-stationarity and Implications for Energy Demand Modelling and Estimation

For some time, empirical modellers have worried about the fact that when using time-series data, the variables often exhibited strong trends. As a result, when one of these variables, such as energy demand, was regressed on others, such as price and income, a strong relationship might be found just because of the trends that were present in the variables. In the late 1970s and early 1980s this led to a series of papers questioning whether the results of empirical time-series estimations were actually useful, or should just be regarded as spurious (for example, Hendry, 1980). Typical evidence of such spurious regressions would be reflected in very good fit statistics, such as R^2 close to 1.0, and very low values of the Durbin–Watson statistic, indicating strong autocorrelation, with an autocorrelation coefficient often relatively close to 1.0. While the initial response to these concerns was to conduct extensive diagnostic testing, later a more common approach involved testing whether variables were indeed non-stationary, and to deal with identified non-stationarity through differencing of variables and estimation of short-run models or via estimation of cointegration relationships and/or error correction models (ECMs). Subsequently, various other approaches were also adopted. The remainder of this section focuses on the different methodologies that have been used in the context of energy demand models and modelling. A more detailed discussion of many of these issues is contained in Hendry and Juselius (2000, 2001).

If unit root tests reveal that certain variables are non-stationary but can be converted to stationarity by first- or higher-order differencing, that is they are integrated of order one (I(1)) or higher, while other variables may be stationary without the need for differencing (I(0)), then these stationary variables can be included in a model that can be estimated by standard means. For example, if energy consumption E, income Y, and energy price P, are all I(1), while a weather variable W is I(0), then a valid relationship that could be estimated is:

$$\Delta \ln E_t = \beta_1 + \beta_2 \Delta \ln P_t + \beta_3 \Delta \ln Y_t + \beta_4 W_t + \varepsilon_t, \quad (6.32)$$

where $\Delta \ln E_t = (E_t - E_{t-1})$, and $\Delta \ln P_t$ and $\Delta \ln Y_t$ are defined analogously. In this framework, the coefficients can only be interpreted as capturing short-run effects, since in the long run all the differenced variables would equal zero so that (6.32) would be vacuous. An approach that has been used to deal with this issue in a number of studies involves estimation of an ECM. Specifically, even though E, Y, and P may all be I(1), there may be one (or more) cointegrating relationship among these variables such that the error term in this relationship is itself stationary. This cointegrating relationship is viewed as representing the long-run or equilibrium relationship, so that the residuals from this relationship represent the deviations from equilibrium. Since – if a cointegrating relationship exists – these residuals are I(0), the lagged value of these residuals, interpreted as the deviation from equilibrium in the previous period, and denoted as EC_{t-1} to refer to the *E*rror that needs to be *C*orrected in subsequent periods, may be included in (6.32). In practice a two-step process (the Engle–Granger procedure) is frequently used, where (following unit root tests to verify the non-stationarity of the variables) OLS estimation of (6.1) yields estimated residuals, $\hat{e}_t$, which (after being confirmed as a stationary series) are then lagged and included as an additional regressor in (6.32), in which case $EC_{t-1} = \hat{e}_{t-1}$. This yields the ECM, so named because the change in energy consumption in any period is partly in response to the error (deviation from equilibrium) in the previous period:

$$\Delta \ln E_t = \beta_1 + \beta_2 \Delta \ln P_t + \beta_3 \Delta \ln Y_t + \beta_4 W_t + \beta_5 EC_{t-1} + \varepsilon_t. \quad (6.33)$$

In this case, the coefficients β_2, β_3, and β_4 would be interpreted as short-run effects, while β_5 would represent the speed of adjustment to equilibrium values. Of course, the possibility of non-instantaneous responses of the dependent variable to any of the explanatory variables may still arise, and this can be accommodated by including lagged values of these explanatory variables and/or of the dependent variable in the right-hand side of (6.33), such as, for example, in Silk and Joutz (1997), with the resulting model estimated using standard methods.

As noted by Bentzen and Engsted (1993), the first step of the Engle–Granger procedure described above has a number of drawbacks, including possibly severe bias on the parameter estimates of the long-run relationship (6.1) in small samples, the lack of invariance of the estimates in this long-run relationship to the variable that is (arbitrarily) chosen as the 'dependent' variable, and the fact that there may be up to $(p-1)$ stationary linear relationships among the p non-stationary variables, but of course only one is estimated. An alternative multivariate approach, developed by Johansen (1988, 1991), and applied by Johansen and Juselius (1990), that avoids these drawbacks is explained and applied in an energy context by Bentzen and Engsted (1993) and by Silk and Joutz (1997). Specifically, the p non-stationary I(1) variables are assembled into a vector x_t which is modelled as a vector autoregressive (VAR) system:

$$x_t = \Pi_0 + \Pi_1 x_{t-1} + \cdots + \Pi_k x_{t-k} + \varepsilon_t, \quad (6.34)$$

where Π_0 is a $(p \times 1)$ vector of constant terms while Π_i are $(p \times p)$ coefficient matrices at different lags. This system is reparameterized in error correction form as:

$$\Delta x_t = \Pi_0 + \Gamma_1 \Delta x_{t-1} + \cdots + \Gamma_{k-1} \Delta x_{t-k+1} + \Pi x_{t-k} + \varepsilon_t, \qquad (6.35)$$

where:

$$\Gamma_i = -I + \Pi_1 + \cdots + \Pi_i, \; i = 1, \ldots, (k-1), \qquad (6.36)$$

$$\Pi = -I + \Pi_1 + \cdots + \Pi_k. \qquad (6.37)$$

Cointegration among the variables in x_t means that the matrix Π should have reduced rank $r < p$, in which case it can be partitioned as $\Pi = -\alpha\beta'$, where α is a ($p \times r$) matrix of speed of adjustment coefficients (error correction parameters), while β is the ($p \times r$) matrix of cointegrating vectors (coefficients of the long-run relationships). Thus, the rank of Π can be used to determine the number of cointegrating relationships. Tests for cointegration and maximum likelihood estimation of β are based on a series of regressions and reduced-rank regressions, as explained in Bentzen and Engsted (1993), which can be accessed in various econometric software packages. Interestingly, both Bentzen and Engsted (1993) and Silk and Joutz (1997) find evidence of only one cointegrating relationship. Subsequently, they use the lagged residuals from the cointegrating relationship to form the error correction term and estimate (6.33), supplemented with additional lags of the first-differenced variables.

A possible problem with the above approaches arises if the sample size is small, since the unit root and cointegration tests are less reliable in these circumstances, and the resulting regression estimates are not robust (Mah, 2000). In interpreting whether a sample is small here, the relevant concern is the length of the period covered rather than just the number of observations (for example, Hakkio and Rush, 1991). An approach which avoids these problems and has better small-sample properties is based on the autoregressive distributed lag (ARDL) framework outlined in Pesaran and Shin (1999), and applied in an energy demand context by Narayan and Smyth (2005). With this approach, the first step is to specify the ECM in (6.33) as an ARDL model by including lags of the dependent variable and of the potentially non-stationary explanatory variables on the right-hand side. In addition, instead of estimating using a two-step process, the error correction term, EC_{t-1} in (6.33) is replaced by its components, where, from the long-run relationship in (6.1):

$$EC_{t-1} = e_{t-1} = (\ln E_{t-1} - \beta_1 - \beta_2 \ln P_{t-1} - \beta_3 \ln Y_{t-1}). \qquad (6.38)$$

This yields an ECM that has the form:

$$\Delta \ln E_t = \beta_1^* + \beta_{1A} t + \sum_{i=0}^{p} \beta_{2i} \Delta \ln P_{t-i} + \sum_{j=0}^{q} \beta_{3j} \Delta \ln Y_{t-j} + \sum_{k=1}^{r} \beta_{4k} \Delta \ln E_{t-k} + \beta_5^* W_t$$
$$+ \beta_6^* \ln E_{t-1} + \beta_7^* \ln P_{t-1} + \beta_8^* \ln Y_{t-1} + \varepsilon_t, \qquad (6.39)$$

where t is a time trend. Note that in this case, no pre-testing is done to determine whether any of the variables E, P, and Y are non-stationary, or whether there is a cointegrating relationship. Rather, (6.39) is simply estimated and the hypothesis that $\beta_6^* = \beta_7^* = \beta_8^* = 0$ is examined using a standard F-statistic, although this F-test has a non-standard distribution. Pesaran et al. (2001) provide critical values that enable a bounds test to be conducted. Regardless of the integration/cointegration status of the variables, if the calculated F is below the lower bound, then the null hypothesis of no cointegration cannot be rejected while if it is above the upper bound, this same hypothesis is rejected. However, if the test statistic falls between the bounds, the result is inconclusive and resolution of this uncertainty would require knowledge of the order of integration of the underlying variables.[11]

Narayan and Smyth (2005) estimate the ECM in (6.39) alternately using each of the potentially cointegrated variables as the 'dependent' variable. Based on a calculated F-test statistic that lies above the upper bound for one of their specifications, they conclude that there is a long-run cointegrating relationship among the variables in the original model. Although it would appear that all the relevant information is obtained once the parameter estimates are obtained for (6.39) and the existence of the long-run relationship is confirmed, Narayan and Smith proceed further. Specifically, they next estimate the long-run relationship as an ARDL model (the model in (6.2) with distributed lags on all the explanatory variables including the lagged dependent variable), and then obtain the short-run coefficients from the standard ECM in (6.33), using the lagged estimated errors from the estimated ARDL long-run relationship.

An alternative approach to the use of cointegration analysis, or the ECMs as specified above, is to use a structural time series model (STSM). This approach, argued by Harvey (1997) as being superior to a cointegration approach, has been applied in an energy demand context in a series of papers emanating from the Surrey Energy Economics Centre (SEEC) in the UK (Hunt et al., 2000, 2003a, 2003b; Hunt and Ninomiya, 2003, 2005; Dimitropoulos et al., 2005; Al-Rabbaie and Hunt, 2006). One of the main advantages of such models is that they allow for trends that are not necessarily linear and deterministic. As Harvey (1997) notes, to the extent that this is the case, analysis that begins by detrending the data by regressing variables on time will render all subsequent analysis invalid. The STSM model is also well suited to dealing with seasonality that is not deterministic and linear, that is, that is not well represented by the inclusion of seasonal dummy variables; such a model is considered by Hunt and Ninomiya (2003). A particular feature of the STSM is that a 'standard' model with a linear deterministic trend and seasonal dummy variables is a special case of the STSM. For illustrative purposes we consider an STSM version of the model in (6.1):

$$\ln E_t = \mu_t + \beta_2 \ln P_t + \beta_3 \ln Y_t + e_t, \tag{6.40}$$

where:

$$\mu_t = \mu_{t-1} + \gamma_{t-1} + \nu_t, \quad \text{where } \nu_t \sim N(0, \sigma_\nu^2), \tag{6.41}$$

$$\gamma_t = \gamma_{t-1} + \omega_t, \quad \text{where } \omega_t \sim N(0, \sigma_\omega^2). \tag{6.42}$$

Here (6.41) and (6.42) represent the level and slope of the trend, respectively. In the context of energy demand models, Hunt and Ninomiya (2005) refer to μ_t as the 'underlying energy demand trend' (UEDT). If the so-called 'hyperparameters', σ_ν^2 and σ_ω^2, are both zero, then the model in (6.40)–(6.42) reverts to a model with a deterministic linear trend:[12]

$$\ln E_t = \beta_1 + \gamma t + \beta_2 \ln P_t + \beta_3 \ln Y_t + e_t. \tag{6.43}$$

To conclude their specification, Hunt and Ninomiya allow for dynamic effects by including polynomial distributed lags on $\ln E, \ln P,$ and $\ln Y$. Estimation of the specification in (6.40)–(6.42), modified in this way, is accomplished using maximum likelihood estimation, with the Kalman filter used to obtain the optimal estimates of the last-period values of the level and slope of the trend, while a smoothing algorithm of the Kalman filter is used to obtain optimal estimates of the trend components. While this approach may seem particularly complex compared to, for example, a two-step ECM, as Harvey (1997) notes, it is not necessary to understand the Kalman filter in order to conduct this analysis as the entire procedure has been implemented in a 'user-friendly form' in the STAMP econometric software package.

To decide on the final specification for their STSM, Hunt and Ninomiya (2005) test down (consecutively omit lagged terms that are insignificant) from a general distributed lag formulation while ensuring that the residuals do not exhibit evidence of autocorrelation, heteroskedasticity, or non-normality. Applying their model to data for the UK and Japan, the authors found that the seasonal and trend components are indeed stochastic, that models that have a linear deterministic trend or no trend are rejected, and that the preferred model using the STSM framework was more parsimonious than using the cointegration approach, which tended to yield models that did not satisfy all the diagnostic tests in some cases.

5 Asymmetric Demand Responses to Price Changes[13]

Oil demand behaviour in the late 1980s provided a new set of puzzles for empirical energy researchers. During the 1970s, sharp and sustained increases in world oil prices resulted in significant reductions in the consumption of oil products in industrialized countries. For example, between 1973 and 1982, per capita use of oil products for non-transport use in the United States fell by 30.7 per cent. Based on this experience, it might have been expected that the sharp and sustained decreases in world oil prices that occurred in the second half of the 1980s would be accompanied by *increases* in oil consumption. However, the response in the demand for this energy source was, at best, sluggish, with per capita oil use for non-transport purposes in the US actually falling by 3.8 per cent in the decade that followed the sharp decreases of world oil prices in 1986.[14] These effects were generally pervasive across all sectors, and for many countries, as is demonstrated in Figure 6.1 which, based on the data used in Ryan and Plourde (2002), portrays the natural logarithm of real (1990) per gigajoule oil prices in local currency units for Canada, the United States, the UK, France, and Japan, and Figure 6.2, which shows the natural logarithm of per capita oil consumption (petajoules per thousand people) in these same countries using these same data. As these figures show, while increases in the real price of oil products were accompanied by reductions in consumption until the mid-1980s, the ensuing drop in real prices did not lead to a resurgence in oil consumption levels. Indeed, during the period from the mid-1980s to 1998, per capita oil consumption has generally continued to fall except in Japan where it has tended to remain static.

To explain this apparent asymmetric pattern of demand responses to oil price increases and decreases it is useful to recall that energy sources (or fuels) – such as electricity, natural gas, and oil products – are not of intrinsic value to consumers. Rather, they are

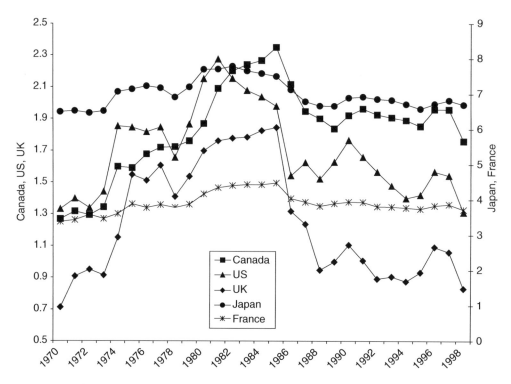

Source: Based on Ryan and Plourde (2002).

Figure 6.1   Natural logarithm of real oil price

used in conjunction with certain types of capital equipment (some of it energy using, such as furnaces, air conditioners, motors, and so on; and some of it in the nature of a substitute, such as insulation) to provide energy-related services (such as hot or cold air for space heating or cooling, hot water, and so on), and it is these services that are valued by consumers. Three characteristics of the energy-using equipment are of particular interest: much of it is long-lived, much of it is fuel specific, and its technical characteristics tend to be fixed. The fact that it is long-lived means that, once installed, energy-using equipment tends to have a useful life that spans many years, often decades. In addition, much of this equipment can only be used in conjunction with a single, specific energy source to produce energy-related services. Finally, each type of energy-using equipment tends to embody a technology that specifies a given level of energy use per unit of services produced. The key consequence of all these characteristics is that they limit the scope available to consumers to respond to energy price changes.

A sustained period of high energy prices will encourage consumers to change the stock of energy-using capital (for example, by purchasing more energy-efficient appliances) and to substitute capital for energy (for example, by installing insulation). It will also encourage manufacturers to improve the energy efficiency of capital equipment, thereby reducing the quantity of energy needed to produce a given level of energy-related services. At the same time, one might also expect governments to act and modify building codes and standards

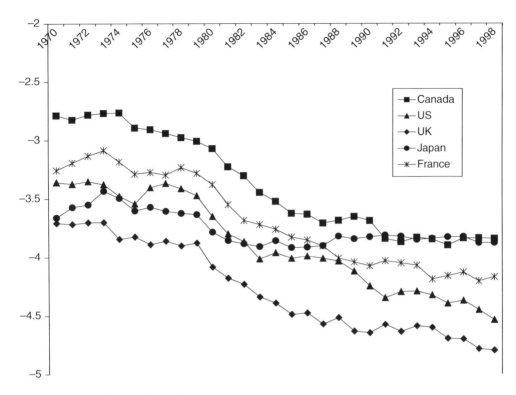

Source: Based on Ryan and Plourde (2002).

Figure 6.2 Natural logarithm of per capita oil consumption

applied to energy-using equipment in directions that encourage greater energy efficiency, for example. Indeed, both of these types of development were observed in most industrialized countries following the world oil price increases of the 1970s. As the time period during which high energy prices are experienced lengthens, one would expect these types of adjustment to become more and more pervasive, with a resulting sustained fall in energy consumption (or, at least, in the consumption of the energy source whose price had risen).

Now, if such a period were followed by a sharp (and sustained) decrease in energy prices, the same factors that shaped responses to higher energy prices would come into play, and initial adjustments would focus on changes – this time, increases – in the intensity of use of the existing energy-using equipment. But, the average remaining useful life of this equipment would likely be longer than that in use at the time when the preceding price increases occurred, since those price increases would have accelerated equipment replacement rates. While the lower energy prices would clearly dampen incentives for energy-saving technological progress, realized technological gains – especially in terms of energy efficiency – would not be reversed. In addition, it seems rather unlikely that government policy initiatives – such as changes in building codes and appliance standards – aimed at achieving greater energy efficiency introduced in response to the higher energy prices would now be reversed as energy prices fell. For example, building codes and equipment standards would generally not be modified to encourage greater energy consumption in response to lower energy prices.

On this basis, the responsiveness of energy demand to a (sustained) price decrease would be expected to be relatively weaker (in absolute value terms) than that of a (sustained) energy price increase that occurred earlier. Under some conditions, this could be observed for energy as a whole (if energy prices rose relative to those of other goods and services, for example), or for specific energy sources, or both. This is the starting point for a number of empirical assessments of the changing nature of the responsiveness of energy demand to energy price variations. Given the evolution of world oil prices since the early 1970s, much of this work has focused on the demand for oil.

Early attempts to explain the observed sluggish response of oil demand were predominantly based on the models that had been developed for agricultural applications (for example, Bye, 1986; Watkins and Waverman, 1987; Gately and Rappoport, 1988; Shealy, 1990; Brown and Phillips, 1991). The approach adopted by Dargay (1992) for the first time allowed for separate identification within a single-equation framework of different responses to price increases and price decreases as well as to the maximum price. This approach was further refined by Gately (1992), who demonstrated that these three effects could be captured through a respecification of the price variable. Specifically, current price was represented as the sum of the maximum price to date, cumulative price decreases, and cumulative price increases that do not establish a new maximum. Empirical implementation of this framework allows for straightforward testing of the existence of asymmetric responses to price changes, since evidence that the coefficients of the three price component series are not the same would indicate that there are different responses to variations in these three price components.

Beginning with the simple dynamic single-equation log-linear specification in (6.2), where energy, E, is usually defined as per capita oil consumption, the energy price, P, refers to the real price of oil and the income variable, Y, is typically expressed in real per capita terms, the approach popularized by Dargay (1992) and Gately (1992) allows for asymmetric responses by replacing the logarithm of the real price term by a number of 'components' that sum up to the original (logarithmic) price series. Three such component series are generated: the maximum historical values of the natural log of real prices (a non-decreasing series), *cumulative* sub-maximum recoveries in the natural log of real prices (a non-decreasing, non-negative series), and *cumulative* decreases (or cuts) in the natural log of real price (a non-increasing, non-positive series). This data transformation process yields the following breakdown into three component series for the natural logarithm of the *real* price of oil, $\ln(rpoil_t)$:

$$\ln(rpoil_t) = \max\,[\ln(rpoil_t)] + cut[\ln(rpoil_t)] + rec[\ln(rpoil_t)], \qquad (6.44)$$

where:

$$\max[\ln(rpoil_t)] = \max\,[\ln(rpoil_1), \ln(rpoil_2), \ldots, \ln(rpoil_t)\,];$$
$$cut[\ln(rpoil_t)] = \Sigma_{m=1}^{t} \min\,(0, \{\max[\ln(rpoil_{m-1})] - \ln(rpoil_{m-1})\}$$
$$- \{\max[\ln(rpoil_m)] - \ln(rpoil_m)\});$$
$$rec[\ln(rpoil_t)] = \Sigma_{m=1}^{t} \max\,(0, \{\max[\ln(rpoil_{m-1})] - \ln(rpoil_{m-1})\}$$
$$- \{\max[\ln(rpoil_m)] - \ln(rpoil_m)\}).$$

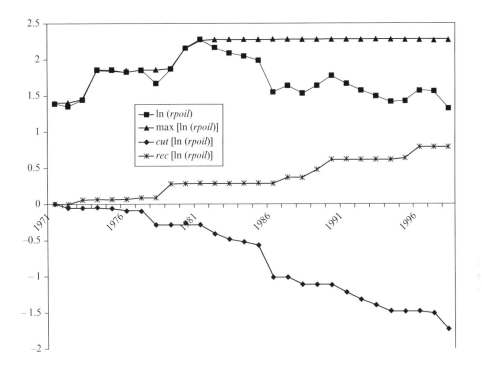

Source: Based on Ryan and Plourde (2002).

Figure 6.3 Decomposition of natural logarithm of US real oil price

Figure 6.3 shows the nature of this price decomposition for the natural logarithm of the US real price of oil based on the price series displayed in Figure 6.1.

Based on the decomposition in (6.44), $\ln(rpoil_t)$ would be replaced in the oil demand equation by the three components $\max[\ln(rpoil_t)]$, $cut[\ln(rpoil_t)]$, and $rec[\ln(rpoil_t)]$, and each of these terms would be permitted to have a different coefficient. Thus, the specification in (6.2) would be replaced by:

$$\ln(qoilpc_t) = \beta_1^* + \beta_2^* \ln(rgdppc_t) + \beta_{3A}^* \max[\ln(rpoil_t)] + \beta_{3B}^* cut[\ln(rpoil_t)]$$

$$+ \beta_{3C}^* rec[\ln(rpoil_t)] + \beta_4^* \ln(qoilpc_{t-1}) + e_t^*, \tag{6.45}$$

where $qoilpc$ represents the quantity of oil consumed per capita and $rgdppc$ is real GDP per capita, a measure of income. A test for symmetry of price responses then involves testing whether the coefficients on the three components of $\ln(rpoil_t)$ are the same, that is, whether:

$$\beta_{3A}^* = \beta_{3B}^* = \beta_{3C}^*. \tag{6.46}$$

This approach has been implemented in a series of papers (for example, Gately, 1993a, 1993b; Hogan, 1993; Dargay and Gately, 1994, 1995; Haas and Schipper, 1998; Gately and Huntington, 2002), which have provided quantitative measures of the extent of the asymmetry that is present in demand responses in a number of different settings, including for various sectors of the economy and across different countries. Interestingly, in a majority of studies where the possibility of non-stationarity of the time series variables has been implicitly or explicitly considered when examining asymmetry (Dargay, 1992; Gately, 1993b; Dargay and Gately, 1997), evidence of asymmetric demand responses to price changes remains, although Ryan and Plourde (2002) do not find this to be the case for all of the countries they examine.

Walker and Wirl (1993), and more recently, Griffin and Schulman (2005) consider an alternative explanation of the observed asymmetric responses to energy price changes, one that is explicitly based on the role of technological change.[15] In particular, Griffin and Schulman argue that the asymmetric price model is inappropriate as it produces intercept shifts in the demand function purely in response to price volatility so that what is in fact energy-saving technical change is attributed to price asymmetry. They also note that the parameter estimates in the asymmetric price response model are not robust across different sample periods as the components of the price decompositions are dependent on the starting point of the sample period. Griffin and Schulman estimate a fixed-effects single-equation energy demand model for a panel of OECD countries, and in that way can allow for technical change via a set of dummy variables for each year in their sample period rather than by simply including a time trend which, as noted earlier, may be inappropriate. They find that the price elasticities in the asymmetry model are affected by the inclusion of the time dummies, and conclude therefore that price volatility is serving as a surrogate for technical change. However, they do not formally test which model is preferred, an omission that is remedied by Huntington (2006) who shows that the model with the price decomposition and time dummies is statistically preferred to the model with time dummies but no price decomposition. In other words, even allowing for technological progress through the time dummies, there still appears to be evidence of asymmetric demand responses to price changes. Using a similar methodology, Adeyemi and Hunt (2007) obtain an analogous result for industrial energy demand, although when they use a non-nested testing approach they are unable to reject either the model without asymmetry or the model without time trends. An obvious extension here would be to incorporate the possibility of asymmetric price responses in a structural time-series model that allows for a stochastic trend, such as the model of Hunt and Ninomiya (2003) described in the previous section. Preliminary results using such an approach (Adeyemi et al., 2008) suggest that both the UEDT and asymmetric demand responses have a role to play in explaining energy demand.

In all the analyses described above, the focus is on oil as a single fuel (or on total energy use), so that the empirical framework always utilizes a single-equation specification. Proceeding in this manner gives rise to a number of unresolved issues. In particular, the omission of any explicit allowance for inter-fuel substitution means that the effects of changes in the prices of alternative energy forms are not taken into consideration. Consequently, it is not possible to determine whether inter-fuel substitution accounts for any of the asymmetric effects detected in studies of oil demand and thus whether any such effects can be found once these substitution possibilities have been taken into account. On a similar note, the issue of whether this type of asymmetry can be identified for other energy sources is not addressed. Finally, as noted in an earlier section of this chapter, the single-equation approach does not take into consideration the inter-related demands for various alternative energy sources when allowing for asymmetric responses to energy price changes.

To address these limitations, Ryan and Plourde (2007) adopt a systems approach to modelling the interrelated demands for multiple energy sources. Thus, as described in an earlier section, spending on any one energy source – including oil – is seen as part of the overall pattern of energy expenditures. Possible asymmetries are captured via a generalization, introduced in Ryan and Plourde (2002), of the price decomposition popularized by Dargay and Gately. Ryan and Plourde (2007) also analyze the consequences of these decompositions on some standard properties of demand systems (homogeneity and symmetry), and consider an alternative decomposition based on relative prices that largely avoids these consequences. They provide an empirical application using the LAIDS model involving three energy sources (electricity, natural gas, and oil products) with data from the residential sector for the province of Ontario (Canada) over the period from 1962 to 1994, which incorporates subperiods with sharp and sustained increases and decreases in world oil prices and in North American natural gas prices. Their results suggest that demands for these three energy sources were characterized by asymmetric responses to price changes, even after allowing for inter-fuel substitution.

6 Summary and Conclusion

In this chapter, we have reviewed empirical energy demand models in the context of the historical evolution of the approaches that have been used. The literature on this topic has blossomed and it is not possible to consider all of the many different models and modelling approaches that have been used.[16] Rather, we have attempted to explain some of the key features of the models and estimation methodology – which tend to be inexorably linked – as well as how these have evolved over time and, where possible, suggesting at least partial explanations for this evolution.

Many types of developments in energy demand models and modelling have been highlighted in the preceding sections. As Sections 2 and 3 make clear, a *first* set of contributions to the literature have sought to strengthen the theoretical underpinnings of energy demand analysis from an economics perspective. Early contributions focused on straightforward specifications of single-equation models of the demand for specific energy sources or energy as a whole. An extension of this approach consisted of adding some form of dynamic adjustment mechanism to the representation of demand patterns. In either case, the theoretical properties of the resulting contributions were not particularly satisfying, in the sense that it was difficult to link the approaches adopted to standard economic representations of producer and consumer behaviour.

The development of the translog and other types of flexible functional forms made it easier for researchers to strengthen the theoretical underpinnings of energy demand modelling. It was thus possible simultaneously to adopt a multi-fuel approach to the portrayal of energy demand and to embed this portrayal in an approach that found its roots in the standard optimization framework adopted in economics. The resulting systems models have been more complicated to specify and estimate than their single-equation predecessors, and the interpretation of the various coefficients is often less straightforward. As we have also argued, theoretical rigour has other costs as well. Notably, it imposes some restrictions on the choice of functional forms, relationships among coefficients, and even limits the choice of variables than can be included in the equations to be estimated.

It has proven difficult to extend the theoretically more rigorous approaches to include dynamic adjustment processes that are grounded in assumed optimization behaviour. For instance, research efforts involving third-generation models of the type noted by BMW (1981) have effectively ceased, and models involving more ad hoc specifications of the dynamic adjustment patterns have continued to characterize systems approaches to energy demand modelling.

A *second* set of contributions has sought to address an important shortcoming of the economics-inspired efforts, namely the role of technology in driving energy use. The demand for energy is a derived demand: energy sources are only useful to the extent that these are combined with energy-using capital equipment to produce services demanded by producers and consumers.

As far as what we have called 'production-side modelling' is concerned, bottom-up approaches typically include much in the way of technological detail, but much less in the way of economic structure. Top-down approaches, on the other hand, draw much from economic principles while offering weaker representations of technologies, their energy-using characteristics, and evolution over time. A number of researchers have recognized and acted on this obvious lacuna, and developed hybrid models that seek to embody the relative strengths of both bottom-up and top-down approaches into more complete and integrated representations of energy demand. It should be clear that in these cases, increases in computing power experienced over the last decades have made this advancement in modelling strategy much easier to achieve.

A key insight of the asymmetry work, reviewed in Section 5, is that the process of adjustment to energy price changes (especially, price reductions) is constrained by factors that are not explicitly included in the models that are specified and estimated to address the issue. However, the 'words' used to motivate the possible existence of such asymmetric effects almost invariably include descriptions of the role of energy-using equipment: improved energy efficiency characteristics embodied in such equipment during periods of high and rising energy prices will not be reversed as these prices subsequently fall, and thus proportionately smaller (in absolute value) changes in energy use are to be expected when prices do fall.

Instead of using information on factors believed to be at the root of the hypothesized asymmetric effects, contributors to this literature rely on re-specifications of the energy price variables in the context of models akin to those reviewed in Sections 2 and 4 to identify those types of effect. As with the models of Section 2, early contributions in this area focused on single-equation, double-logarithmic model specifications with ad hoc dynamic formulations. Some more recent contributions have adopted the systems approach characteristic of the models reviewed in Section 3 and thus generalized the analysis of asymmetric responses to price changes to the case of multiple energy sources within a framework of analysis consistent with assumed optimization behaviour on the part of end-users of energy. Here again, ad hoc specifications of the dynamic adjustment processes are used in empirical implementation. In general, asymmetric effects are detected in both single-equation and systems approaches.

A *third* set of contributions highlighted in this chapter can be described as applications of atheoretical approaches to energy demand analysis. Here, time-series methods are used to tease out relationships and response patterns in energy data. As the discussion in Section 4 indicates, increasingly sophisticated econometric tools have been brought to bear on these issues. Modelling of the dynamic adjustment processes, while not based in standard optimization approaches, has progressed noticeably since the 1990s. Through the application of these methods, rich dynamic response patterns of energy demand have been identified and provide a different perspective on the asymmetry issues discussed earlier. Most of the contributions, however, have remained within a single-equation, single-energy-source context. Application of the techniques used in these approaches to cases involving multiple energy sources will no doubt increase our understanding of the evolution of the demand for energy.

As we argued in the Introduction to this chapter, one of the conclusions to draw from this review is that there is no single 'right' way to model energy demand. The diversity of approaches adopted has acted not only to deepen our understanding of the key drivers of energy demand, but also to shed some light on specific issues, such as the possibly asymmetric nature of responses to energy price changes. As we move forward, it would be useful to keep in mind the fact that, in the overwhelming majority of situations, energy use requires a complementary piece of capital equipment to yield something of value to producers and consumers. Lags in adjustment are thus inevitable, thereby making energy demand an inherently dynamic process. As the discussion in this chapter has made clear, we still have much to learn about the nature of and the key factors driving the dynamic adjustment patterns observed in energy consumption data, and still much to do to enhance our modelling of these phenomena. Another area where additional research effort is needed relates to the interaction between technology and energy use, and especially in the evolution of this interaction over time. Much progress has been made in energy demand models and modelling, and much remains to be done.

Notes

* We are indebted to Matthew Hansen for excellent research assistance and to Natural Resources Canada for funding provided through the Canadian Building Energy End-Use Data and Analysis Centre (CBEEDAC).
1. This chapter is in the tradition of earlier contributions such as Hartman (1979) and Bohi and Zimmerman (1984).
2. These symmetry conditions are discussed in more detail in the next subsection.
3. In view of the usefulness and implications of the weak separability assumption, a number of authors have sought to test it. In the context of the translog, Berndt and Christensen (1973) devised a test based on the AES, but as shown by Blackorby et al. (1977) and Denny and Fuss (1977), such a test is more restrictive than intended, and this problem is not solved by choosing among alternative flexible functional forms. Woodland (1978) develops an alternative approach.
4. Later chapters discuss the use of CGE models as well as attempts to combine the 'bottom-up' and 'top-down' approaches.
5. Some material in this section is based on Ryan and Plourde (2007).
6. See, for example, Diewert (1974). Alternatively, the logarithmic form of Shephard's lemma can be used to derive the budget share equations as the derivative of the logarithm of expenditure with respect to the logarithm of price.
7. As noted earlier, as shown by Fuss (1977), homotheticity is an implication of the weak separability assumption in the production context.
8. There is no real need to take logarithms of *hdd* and *cdd*, even though other explanatory variables appear in logarithmic form. These variables can often take quite large values, and the use of logarithms reduces the scale.

9.　A number of criticisms have been levelled at the use of partial adjustment formulations in energy demand analysis. BMW (1981) indicate that partial adjustment mechanisms are not based on optimizing behaviour, and that the resulting estimated long-run elasticities do not necessarily exceed their corresponding short-run values. Instead, they propose a model with endogenous adjustment. Hogan (1989) also identifies a potential misspecification that results when the partial adjustment process is expressed in terms of expenditure shares rather than quantities. In the alternative specification that Hogan suggests, the coefficients of the lagged shares are themselves functions of prices.
10.　See Buse (1994) for an evaluation of the various possible elasticity expressions that can be used with the LAIDS model. The expression in (6.30) is the most widely used for the price elasticity and, according to Buse's results, is marginally the best. Buse finds the income elasticity as defined in (6.31) to be superior to other alternatives.
11.　Pesaran et al. (2001) note that this test is not appropriate if there may be more than one long-run relationship between the potentially non-stationary variables.
12.　There has been a long history of, and debate about, the merits of using a linear time trend to represent technical progress in energy demand models. For example, Beenstock and Willcocks (1981) argue that while not entirely satisfactory, it is better than ignoring technical progress, while Kouris (1983) argues that technical progress is mainly price induced and its dynamic impact cannot be adequately captured by a simple linear time trend. See Hunt et al. (2003b) for more on this issue.
13.　Some material in this section is based on Ryan and Plourde (2004, 2007).
14.　The data used in these calculations were taken from Tables 1.5 and 2.1 of US Department of Energy (1999).
15.　For an earlier discussion of the possible role of technology (and other factors) in giving rise to these asymmetries, see Sweeney with Fenechel (1986).
16.　Some particular omissions, due to space constraints, are: the 'joint modelling' of which energy-using equipment to use and how intensely to utilize it (some examples being Dubin and McFadden, 1984; Vaage, 2000 and Nesbakken, 2001); and 'conditional demand analysis' to determine energy end-use for particular activities when available data only indicate aggregate energy consumption (some examples being Parti and Parti, 1980; Bernard and Lacroix, 2005 and Ryan and Liu, 2006).

References

Adeyemi, O.I. and L.C. Hunt (2007), 'Modelling OECD industrial energy demand: asymmetric price responses and energy-saving technical change', *Energy Economics*, **29** (4), 693–709.
Adeyemi, O.I., D.C. Broadstock, M. Chitnis, L.C. Hunt and G. Judge (2008), 'Asymmetric price responses and the underlying energy demand trend: are they substitutes or complements? Evidence from modelling OECD aggregate energy demand', Surrey Energy Economics Discussion Paper 121, Surrey Energy Economics Centre (SEEC), Department of Economics, University of Surrey, Guildford.
Al-Rabbaie, A. and L.C. Hunt (2006), 'OECD energy demand: modelling underlying energy demand trends using the structural time series model', Surrey Energy Economics Discussion Paper 114, Surrey Energy Economics Centre (SEEC), Department of Economics, University of Surrey, Guildford.
Beenstock, M. and P. Willcocks (1981), 'Energy consumption and economic activity in industrialized countries', *Energy Economics*, **3** (4), 225–32.
Bentzen, J. and T. Engsted (1993), 'Short- and long-run elasticities in energy demand: a cointegration approach', *Energy Economics*, **15** (1), 9–16.
Bentzen, J. and T. Engsted (2001), 'A revival of the autoregressive distributed lag model in estimating energy demand relationships', *Energy*, **26** (1), 45–55.
Bernard, J.-T. and G. Lacroix (2005), 'Conditional demand analysis: tests for homoskedasticity and uniformity', mimeo, GREEN, Department of Economics, Laval University, June.
Berndt, E.R. and L.R. Christensen (1973), 'The translog function and the substitution of equipment, structures, and labor in U.S. manufacturing 1929–68', *Journal of Econometrics*, **1** (1), 81–113.
Berndt, E.R., C.J. Morrison and G.C. Watkins (BMW) (1981), 'Dynamic models of energy demand: an assessment and comparison', in E.R. Berndt and B.C. Field (eds), *Modelling and Measuring Natural Resource Substitution*, Cambridge, MA: MIT Press, pp. 259–89.
Berndt, E.R. and D.O. Wood (1975), 'Technology, prices, and the derived demand for energy', *Review of Economics and Statistics*, **57** (3), 259–68.
Berndt, E.R. and D.O. Wood (1979), 'Engineering and econometric interpretations of energy–capital complementarity', *American Economic Review*, **69** (3), 342–54.
Binswanger, H.P. (1974), 'The measurement of technical change biases with many factors of production', *American Economic Review*, **64** (5), 964–76.

Blackorby, C., D. Primont and R.R. Russell (1977), 'On testing separability restrictions with flexible functional forms', *Journal of Econometrics*, **5** (2), 195–209.

Bohi, D.R. and M.B. Zimmerman (1984), 'An update on econometric studies of energy demand behavior', *Annual Review of Energy*, **9**, 105–54.

Broadstock, D.C., L.C. Hunt and S. Sorrell (2007), 'UKERC review of evidence for the rebound effect – Technical Report 3: Elasticity of Substitution Studies', UK Energy Research Centre Working Paper UKERC/WP/TPA/2007/011, October, available at: http://www.ukerc.ac.uk/Downloads/PDF/07/0710Rebo undEffect/0710Techreport3.pdf (accessed 26 February 2009).

Brown, S.P.A. and K.R. Phillips (1991), 'U.S. oil demand and conservation', *Contemporary Policy Issues*, **9** (1), 67–72.

Buse, A. (1994), 'Evaluating the linearized almost ideal demand system', *American Journal of Agricultural Economics*, **76** (4), 781–93.

Bye, T. (1986), 'Non-symmetric responses in energy demand', in *Proceedings of the Eighth Annual International Conference of the International Association of Energy Economists*, Washington, DC: IAEE, pp. 354–8.

Chang, H.S. and Y. Hsing (1991), 'The demand for residential electricity: new evidence on time-varying elasticities', *Applied Economics*, **23** (7), 1251–6.

Chang, K.-P. (1994), 'Capital–energy substitution and the multi-level CES production function', *Energy Economics*, **16** (1), 22–6.

Christensen, L.R., D.W. Jorgenson and L.J. Lau (1973), 'Transcendental logarithmic production frontiers', *Review of Economics and Statistics*, **55** (1), 28–45.

Christodoulakis, N.M. and S.C. Kalyvitis (1997), 'The demand for energy in Greece: assessing the effects of the Community Support Framework 1994–1999', *Energy Economics*, **19** (4), 393–416.

Dargay, J.M. (1992), 'The irreversible effects of high oil prices: empirical evidence for the demand for motor fuels in France, Germany and the U.K.', in D. Hawdon (ed.), *Energy Demand: Evidence and Expectations*, London: Surrey University Press, pp. 165–82.

Dargay, J.M. and D. Gately (1994), 'Oil demand in the industrialized countries', *The Energy Journal*, **15** (Special Issue), 39–67.

Dargay, J.M. and D. Gately (1995), 'The imperfect price reversibility of non-transport oil demand in the OECD', *Energy Economics*, **17** (1), 59–71.

Dargay, J.M. and D. Gately (1997), 'The demand for transportation fuels: imperfect price reversibility?', *Transportation Research B*, **31** (1), 71–82.

Deaton, A. and J. Muellbauer (1980), 'An almost ideal demand system', *American Economic Review*, **70** (3), 312–26.

Denny, M. and M. Fuss (1977), 'The use of approximation analysis to test for separability and the existence of consistent aggregates', *American Economic Review*, **67** (3), 404–18.

Dias-Bandaranaike, R. and M. Munasinghe (1983), 'The demand for electricity services and the quality of supply', *The Energy Journal*, **4** (2), 49–71.

Diewert, W.E. (1971), 'An application of the Shephard duality theorem: a generalized Leontief production function', *Journal of Political Economy*, **79** (3), 481–507.

Diewert, W.E. (1974), 'Applications of duality theory', in M. Intriligator and D. Kendrick (eds), *Frontiers of Quantitative Economics*, Vol. 2, Amsterdam: North-Holland, pp. 106–71.

Dimitropoulos, J., L.C. Hunt and G. Judge (2005), 'Estimating underlying energy demand trends using UK annual data', *Applied Economics Letters*, **12**, 239–44.

Dubin, J.A. and D.L. McFadden (1984), 'An econometric analysis of residential electric appliance holdings and consumption', *Econometrica*, **52** (2), 345–62.

Dunstan, R.H. and R.H. Schmidt (1988), 'Structural changes in residential energy demand', *Energy Economics*, **10** (3), 206–12.

Field, B.C. and C. Grebenstein (1980), 'Substituting for energy in US manufacturing', *Review of Economics and Statistics*, **62** (2), 207–12.

Fuss, M.A. (1977), 'The demand for energy in Canadian manufacturing: an example of the estimation of production structures with many inputs', *Journal of Econometrics*, **5** (1), 89–116.

Gately, D. (1992), 'Imperfect price-reversibility of U.S. gasoline demand: asymmetric responses to price increases and declines', *The Energy Journal*, **13** (4), 179–207.

Gately, D. (1993a), 'The imperfect price-reversibility of world oil demand', *The Energy Journal*, **14** (4), 163–82.

Gately, D. (1993b), 'Oil demand in the US and Japan: why the demand reductions caused by the price increases of the 1970s won't be reversed by the price declines of the 1980s', *Japan and the World Economy*, **5** (4), 295–320.

Gately, D. and H. Huntington (2002), 'The asymmetric effects of changes in price and income on energy and oil demand', *The Energy Journal*, **23** (1), 19–55.

Gately, D. and P. Rappoport (1988), 'Adjustment of U.S. oil demand to the price increases of the 1970s', *The Energy Journal*, **9** (2), 93–107.

Greene, W.H. (2008), *Econometric Analysis*, 6th edn, Upper Saddle River, NJ: Pearson Prentice-Hall.

Griffin, J.M. and P.R. Gregory (1976), 'An intercountry translog model of energy substitution responses', *American Economic Review*, **66** (5), 845–57.

Griffin, J.M. and C.T. Schulman (2005), 'Price asymmetry in energy demand models: a proxy for energy-saving technical change', *The Energy Journal*, **26** (2), 1–21.

Haas, R. and L. Schipper (1998), 'Residential energy demand in OECD countries and the role of irreversible energy efficiency improvements', *Energy Economics*, **20** (4), 421–42.

Hakkio, C.S. and M. Rush (1991), 'Cointegration: how short is the long-run?', *Journal of International Money and Finance*, **10** (4), 571–81.

Hartman, R.S. (1979), 'Frontiers in energy demand modeling', *Annual Review of Energy*, **4**, 433–66.

Harvey, A.C. (1997), 'Trends, cycles, and autoregressions', *Economic Journal*, **107** (440), 192–201.

Helliwell, J.F., M.E. MacGregor, R.N. McRae, A. Plourde and A. Chung (1987), 'Supply oriented macroeconomics: the MACE model of Canada', *Economic Modelling*, **4** (3), 318–40.

Hendry, D.F. (1980), 'Econometrics: alchemy or science?', *Economica*, **47** (188), 387–406.

Hendry, D. and K. Juselius (2000), 'Explaining cointegration analysis: Part I', *The Energy Journal*, **21** (1), 1–42.

Hendry, D. and K. Juselius (2001), 'Explaining cointegration analysis: Part II', *The Energy Journal*, **22** (1), 75–120.

Hogan, W.W. (1989), 'A dynamic putty–semi-putty model of aggregate energy demand', *Energy Economics*, **11** (1), 53–69.

Hogan, W.W. (1993), 'OECD oil demand dynamics: trends and asymmetries', *The Energy Journal*, **14** (1), 125–57.

Hudson, E.A. and D.W. Jorgenson (1974), 'U.S. energy policy and economic growth, 1975–2000', *Bell Journal of Economics and Management Science*, **5** (2), 461–514.

Hunt, L.C., G. Judge and Y. Ninomiya (2000), 'Modelling technical progress: an application of the stochastic trend model to UK energy demand', Surrey Energy Economics Discussion Paper 99, Surrey Energy Economics Centre (SEEC), Department of Economics, University of Surrey, Guildford.

Hunt, L.C., G. Judge and Y. Ninomiya (2003a), 'Underlying trends and seasonality in UK energy demand: a sectoral analysis', *Energy Economics*, **25** (1), 93–118.

Hunt, L.C., G. Judge and Y. Ninomiya (2003b), 'Modelling underlying energy demand trends', in L.C. Hunt (ed.), *Energy in a Competitive Market: Essays in Honour of Colin Robinson*, Cheltenham, UK and Northampton, MA, USA: Edward Elgar, pp. 140–74.

Hunt, L.C. and Y. Ninomiya (2003), 'Unravelling trends and seasonality: a structural time series analysis of transport oil demand in the UK and Japan', *The Energy Journal*, **24** (3), 63–96.

Hunt, L.C. and Y. Ninomiya (2005), 'Primary energy demand in Japan: an empirical analysis of long-term Trends and future CO_2 emissions', *Energy Policy*, **33** (11), 1409–24.

Huntington, H.G. (2006), 'A note on price asymmetry as induced technical change', *The Energy Journal*, **27** (3), 1–7.

Johansen, S. (1988), 'Statistical analysis of cointegration vectors', *Journal of Economic Dynamics and Control*, **12** (2–3), 231–54.

Johansen, S. (1991), 'Estimation and hypothesis testing of cointegration vectors in Gaussian vector autoregressive models', *Econometrica*, **59** (6), 1551–80.

Johansen, S. and K. Juselius (1990), 'Maximum likelihood estimation and inference on cointegration – with applications to the demand for money', *Oxford Bulletin of Economics and Statistics*, **52** (2), 169–210.

Kouris, G. (1983), 'Energy consumption and economic activity in industrialized economics: a note', *Energy Economics*, **5** (3), 207–12.

Magnus, J.R. (1979), 'Substitution between energy and non-energy inputs in the Netherlands, 1950–1974', *International Economic Review*, **20** (2), 465–84.

Mah, J.S. (2000), 'An empirical examination of the disaggregated import demand of Korea – the case of information technology products', *Journal of Asian Economics*, **11** (2), 237–44.

McLaren, K.R. (1982), 'Estimation of translog demand systems', *Australian Economic Papers*, **21** (39), 392–406.

Narayan, P.K. and R. Smyth (2005), 'The residential demand for electricity in Australia: an application of the bounds testing approach to cointegration', *Energy Policy*, **33** (4), 467–74.

Nesbakken, R. (2001), 'Energy consumption for space heating: a discrete–continuous approach', *Scandinavian Journal of Economics*, **103** (1), 165–84.

Parti, M. and C. Parti (1980), 'The total and appliance-specific conditional demand for electricity in the household sector', *Bell Journal of Economics*, **11** (1), 309–21.

Pesaran, M.H. and Y. Shin (1999), 'An autoregressive distributed lag modelling approach to cointegration analysis', in S. Strom (ed.), *Econometrics and Economic Theory in the 20th Century: The Ragnar Frisch Centennial Symposium*, Cambridge: Cambridge University Press, pp. 371–413.

Pesaran, M.H., Y. Shin and R.J. Smith (2001), 'Bounds testing approaches to the analysis of level relationships', *Journal of Applied Econometrics*, **16** (3), 289–326.

Plourde, A. and D.L. Ryan (1985), 'On the use of double-log forms in energy demand analysis', *The Energy Journal*, **6** (4), 105–13.

Ryan, D.L. and R. Liu (2006), 'Conditional demand analysis revisited: evaluating residential end-use energy consumption in Canada', Canadian Building Energy End-Use Data and Analysis Centre Research Report, CBEEDAC 2007–RP-09.

Ryan, D.L. and A. Plourde (2002), 'Smaller and smaller? The price responsiveness of nontransport oil demand', *Quarterly Review of Economics and Finance*, **42** (2), 285–317.

Ryan, D.L. and A. Plourde (2004), 'Modelling sluggish price responses in energy demand models: a critical evaluation of alternative methodologies', in M. Filippini, E. Jochem and D. Spreng (eds), *Modelling in Energy Economics and Policy*, Proceedings of the 6th European Conference of the International Association for Energy Economics, Zurich: Swiss Association for Energy Economics.

Ryan, D.L. and A. Plourde (2007), 'A systems approach to modelling asymmetric demand responses to energy price changes', in W.A. Barnett and A. Serletis (eds), *Functional Structure Inference*, Amsterdam: Elsevier, pp. 183–224.

Shealy, M.T. (1990), 'Oil demand asymmetry in the OECD', in *Energy Supply/Demand Balances: Options and Costs*, Proceedings of the 12th Annual North American Conference of the International Association for Energy Economics, Washington, DC: IAEE, pp. 154–65.

Silk, J.I. and F.L. Joutz (1997), 'Short and long-run elasticities in US residential electricity demand: a cointegration approach', *Energy Economics*, **19** (4), 493–513.

Stone, J.R.N. (1954), 'Linear expenditure systems and demand analysis: an application to the pattern of British demand', *Economic Journal*, **64** (255), 511–27.

Sweeney, J.L. with D.A. Fenechel (1986), 'Price asymmetries in the demand for energy', in *Proceedings of the Eighth Annual International Conference of the International Association for Energy Economists*, Washington, DC: IAEE, pp. 218–22.

US Department of Energy (1999), *Annual Review of Energy 1998*, DOE/EIA-0384(98), Washington, DC: Energy Information Administration.

Vaage, K. (2000), 'Heating technology and energy use: a discrete/continuous choice approach to Norwegian household energy demand', *Energy Economics*, **22** (6), 649–66.

Walker, I.O. and F. Wirl (1993), 'Irreversible price-induced efficiency improvements: theory and empirical application to road transportation', *The Energy Journal*, **14** (4), 183–205.

Watkins, G.C. and L. Waverman (1987), 'Oil demand elasticities: the saviour as well as the scourge of OPEC?', in *The Changing World Energy Economy*, Papers and Proceedings of the Eighth Annual North American Conference of the International Association of Energy Economists, Cambridge, MA: IAEE, pp. 223–7.

Woodland, A.D. (1978), 'On testing weak separability', *Journal of Econometrics*, **8** (3), 383–98.

7 Economics of energy efficiency
Grant Allan, Michelle Gilmartin, Peter McGregor,
*J. Kim Swales and Karen Turner**

1 Overview

Improvements in energy efficiency are seen as a key mechanism for reducing energy dependence and meeting sustainability and security of supply goals (Sorrell, 2007; Stern, 2007). However, there is dispute about the way in which the economy responds to such efficiency improvements. An increase in energy efficiency reduces the price of energy, measured in efficiency units, and this has output, income and substitution effects that tend to mitigate, and possibly to offset totally, any energy saving. Mitigation is labelled as 'rebound' and an increase in energy use as 'backfire'.

Rebound and backfire involve system-wide effects that are difficult to quantify and track. In this chapter we adopt a purely analytical approach that investigates the impact of an improvement in energy efficiency in a stylised open economy. The aim is pedagogic: that is, to identify and clarify the nature of the various system-wide factors that can affect the change in energy use that accompanies improvements in energy efficiency.

Section 2 explains the small open economy model used and the resource, technology and sustainability problems that it faces. Section 3 introduces improvements in energy efficiency into the model and discusses measures of energy productivity. Section 4 analyses the way in which energy use will be affected by improvements in energy efficiency. Section 5 discusses how tax policy can adjust the profit-maximising energy use after improvements in energy efficiency. Section 6 extends the simple model in three ways so as to analyse variations in the price elasticity of demand for the product, the elasticity of substitution in the production function and the elasticity of supply of non-energy inputs. Section 7 discusses improved energy efficiency in consumption. Section 8 concludes.

2 A Small Stylised Open Economy: Resource, Technology and Sustainability Constraints

We illustrate the issues raised by concern over energy efficiency using a simple stylised model of a small open economy. This approach is adopted so as to illustrate the underlying issues that might be obscured in more practical and detailed studies.

In this model the economy produces an output Q of a single commodity by means of a fixed amount of local resources, N, and homogeneous energy used in production, E_P. This output is either consumed locally or exported and energy is wholly imported at a fixed international price. The price of output is taken as the numeraire, so the price of energy is given as p_E. The difference between the output of the economy and the energy imports is a surplus generated in production, S, available for consumption, C. Initially we focus only on production and assume that consumption consists of the local output or non-energy imports. This assumption is relaxed in Section 7.

The relationship between local resources, energy inputs and output is determined, initially at least, by a well-behaved production function. This implies the following. First, with no energy input, there is no output. Second, with fixed amounts of other inputs, an increase in energy use will generate additional output but at a diminishing rate. Third, there are constant returns to scale. The model can therefore be specified as:

$$S = C = Q - p_E E_P, \tag{7.1}$$

$$Q = Q(N, E_P), \tag{7.2}$$

where:

$$N = \overline{N},$$

and

$$Q(N, 0) = 0, \frac{\partial Q}{\partial E_P} > 0, \frac{\partial^2 Q}{\partial E_P^2} < 0.$$

This model is illustrated in Figure 7.1. The upper half, Figure 7.1a, represents total output and total energy cost as a function of the level of energy inputs. The production frontier $Q(E_P)$ shows the maximum output available for each energy input, on the assumption that there is a fixed input of local resources and a given well-behaved technology. Points on the production frontier are technically efficient: technical inefficiency is represented by points below and to the right of the production frontier. For any such points, there are possible movements to the frontier that will both generate higher output and use lower energy inputs.

The corresponding maximum consumption levels that are associated with given energy inputs (and resource and technology constraints) are presented in the lower half of the figure, Figure 1b. In such a simple model, the government's aim would normally be to maximise consumption.[1] This is achieved for an energy input where the marginal product of energy just equals the price, so that $(\partial Q/\partial E_P) = p_E$. This corresponds to point A in Figures 7.1a and b, with an output of Q^* and consumption C^*. This rule would apply in a centralised command economy whose aim is to maximise consumption, but would also be the outcome from a decentralised perfectly competitive economy with no market failures, since the equality of the marginal product of energy and the energy price would maximise profits.

However, sustainability issues typically drive current concerns over energy use. That is to say, the present level of energy consumption is thought to be unsustainable. The view that society might value an outcome that differs from the competitive one is represented by the notion of a social welfare function (*SWF*) (Bergson, 1938; Samuelson, 2004). In this case, the *SWF* would incorporate consumption as a positive component, but energy use as a negative component.[2]

Imagine that sustainability involves a minimum consumption level, $\underline{C}$, and a maximum

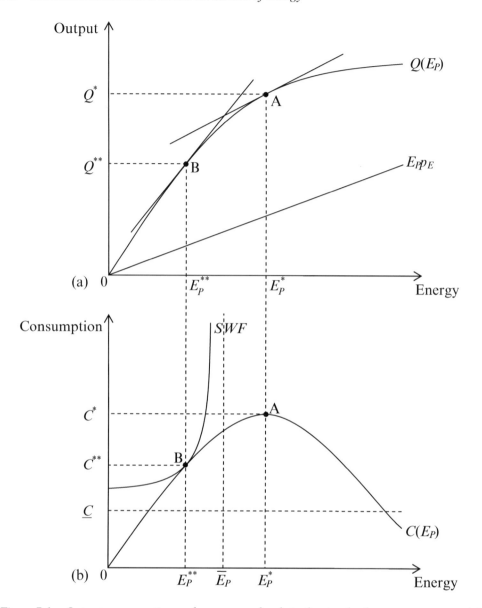

Figure 7.1   Output, consumption and energy-use levels in the standard open economy model

energy use in production $\bar{E}_P$. Within the energy input, commodity output space defined by:

$$C > \underline{C},\ 0 < E_P < \bar{E}_P,$$

there are a family of convex iso-*SWF* curves where each curve represents combinations of consumption and energy use that produce the same combined level of social welfare.

Social welfare will be maximised, here implicitly incorporating sustainability considerations, where the consumption curve in Figure 7.1b is just tangent to the highest iso-*SWF* curve. This is shown as point B in Figures 7.1a and b and implies an output and consumption of Q^{**} and C^{**}, where $Q^{**} < Q^*$ and $C^{**} < C^*$.

Figures 7.1a and b suggest that with fixed resources and technology, achieving technical and allocative efficiency implies sacrificing some consumption.[3] In a decentralised market system this can be achieved through setting a tax on energy use, so as to make the price of energy equal to the slope of the production frontier at B.[4] Of course, incorporating sustainability involves giving positive weight to the utility of future generations. The idea that this requires less consumption for present generations meets some political resistance. The question that is addressed in this chapter is whether changes in energy efficiency can aid the attainment of sustainable goals.

3 Energy Efficiency and Energy Productivity

The concept of energy efficiency used here is the notion of energy-augmenting technical change. In this framework, an improvement in energy efficiency means an increase in the effective productive services generated by a given amount of energy inputs. This can be conveniently thought of as inputs of energy measured in efficiency units, F, where:

$$F = nE. \tag{7.3}$$

An improvement in energy efficiency, or alternatively energy-augmenting technical change, is represented by an increase in n. The idea of measuring energy inputs in efficiency units is similar to the engineering notion of useful work, where an improvement in energy efficiency is measured as an increase in useful work performed by a given energy input (Patterson, 1996; Sorrell and Dimitropoulos, 2008). In this chapter, where we discuss changes in energy use, the implicit assumption is that this is measured in natural units. Where energy is measured in efficiency units, this will be referred to explicitly.

There is a convenient way of analysing the impact of energy-augmenting technical progress. In the conventional production function, the energy input measured in natural units, E_P, can be simply replaced with the same input measured in efficiency units. That is to say, equation (7.2) in the model presented in Section 2 can be replaced by equation (7.4):

$$Q = Q(N, F_P) = Q(N, nE_P). \tag{7.4}$$

Where energy inputs are still measured in natural units, this has the effect of moving the production frontier upwards and to the left, still anchored at the origin, as shown later in Figure 7.3a. A central characteristic of an improvement in energy efficiency is that a given output can now be produced with the same level of other inputs but less energy. Also, with a conventional well-behaved production function, a higher output can be generated with the same energy and non-energy inputs.

It is important to draw a distinction between this measure of energy efficiency and the more straightforward measure of energy productivity, Π. This is the average output per unit of energy input, so that:

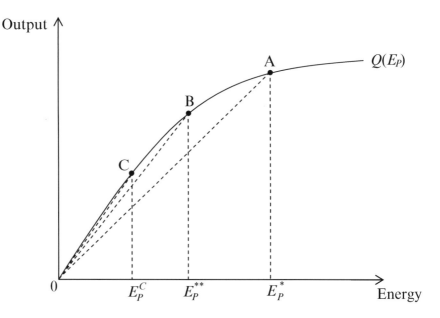

Figure 7.2   Energy productivity

$$\Pi = \frac{Q}{E_P}. \qquad (7.5)$$

The key point is that energy productivity is determined by a combination of energy efficiency and the ratio of energy to local resources used in production.

Figure 7.2 shows the production frontier from Figure 7.1a and identifies the
consumption-maximising point A, the welfare-maximising point B and a further point
C. At each point the slope of the line from the origin measures energy productivity: the
steeper that slope, the higher the energy productivity. Clearly, moving from A to B shows
a measured increase in the energy productivity, but this is unrelated to any change in
energy efficiency. The production frontier has not shifted. The increase in energy productivity comes about as a result of the change in the ratio of energy inputs in production.
Further, the fewer energy inputs are employed, with an unchanged technology, the higher
the energy productivity will be: point C has a higher measured energy productivity than
A or B. With a constant supply of local resources and no change in energy efficiency, an
increase in energy productivity necessarily implies a reduction in total output.

4   Increased Energy Efficiency and Energy Use

Figures 7.3a and b show the effect on production and consumption of an increase in
energy efficiency in the simple model outlined in Section 2. The proportionate increase in
energy efficiency is $\dot{n}$. The figures are constructed for a particular Cobb–Douglas form of
the production function.[5] This means that equation (7.4) can be written as:

$$Q = AN^{1-\alpha}F_P^{\alpha} = BF_P^{\alpha} = BE_{pn}^{\alpha}n^{\alpha}, \qquad (7.6)$$

where $A,B > 0$, $1 > \alpha > 0$.[6] A is a general productivity parameter, and α a distributional parameter. With marginal productivity factor pricing, α is the share of energy costs in total output. Many of the characteristics of the Cobb–Douglas production function are replicated for other well-behaved functions. However, other characteristics are specific and these will be clearly distinguished in the discussion.

Figure 7.3a shows how an increase in energy efficiency shifts the production frontier outwards, allowing the same output to be produced with less energy. The figure has been constructed so that the sustainable level of energy use can now be achieved with no change in output. The impact on the trade-off between consumption and energy use is even more favourable: if output remains constant with lower energy inputs and unchanged prices, consumption can rise. Sustainability can be achieved with a fall in energy use and a simultaneous increase in consumption.[7] However, a key issue in the literature is: will an increase in energy efficiency in itself lead to a reduction in energy use (Jevons, 1865; Brookes, 1978; Khazzoom, 1980; Saunders, 1992)?

As we observed in Section 2, in this simple model the output that would be derived from the free market mechanism will be the one that maximises consumption. The improvement in energy efficiency will allow an increase in consumption. However, with prices constant there is no guarantee that such an increase in consumption will be accompanied by a reduction in energy use. For a well-behaved production function, the increase in energy efficiency reduces the price of energy in efficiency units and increases the price of local resources. In general this increases the profit-maximising input of energy in efficiency units, so that there must be a degree of rebound. That is to say, in this basic variant of the model the use of energy, measured in natural units, cannot fall by the full amount of the increase in energy efficiency.

For backfire, in the present model the general issue is straightforward. If at the initial consumption-optimising energy use, $E^*_{P,1}$, the efficiency improvement increases the marginal productivity of energy, then the market equilibrium energy use (in natural units) will rise. With a well-behaved production function there seems no strong a priori reason for ruling this out. Moreover, in the Cobb–Douglas case, this condition will always hold.

Under the Cobb–Douglas production function, using the marginal productivity condition and equation (7.6), the profit-maximising energy use, E^*_P, is given as:

$$\left(\frac{\alpha B}{p_E}\right)^{\frac{1}{1-\alpha}} n^{\frac{\alpha}{1-\alpha}} = E^*_P, \tag{7.7}$$

so that the proportionate change in energy use, $\dot{E}_P$, is:

$$\dot{E}_P = \dot{n}\left(\frac{\alpha}{1-\alpha}\right) > 0. \tag{7.8}$$

Note that the growth in energy use is positively related to the growth in energy efficiency. More especially, from equations (7.6) and (7.8), the growth in output will be equal to the growth of energy inputs, so the energy productivity will remain unchanged, though energy efficiency has improved.

This result is illustrated in Figure 7.3a. The reaction to the increase in energy efficiency is an equal proportionate expansion in output and energy use, with the profit- (and

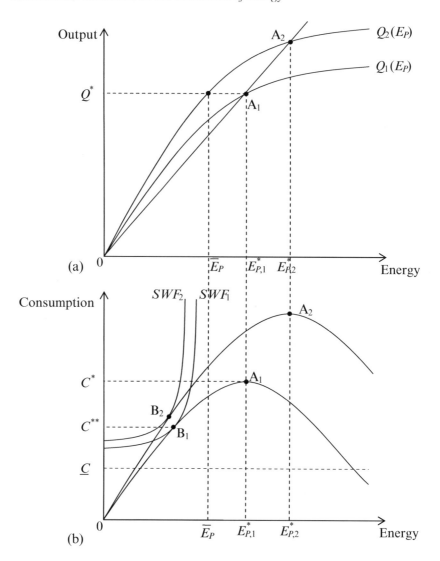

Figure 7.3   The impact of an increase in energy efficiency on output, consumption and energy use

consumption-)maximising energy use increasing from $E^*_{P,1}$ to $E^*_{P,2}$. The supply of local resources is fixed and fully employed.

5   Price Changes within the Model

As has been argued in Section 2, the limitations to using improved energy efficiency to achieve sustainability targets stem from the increased choice presented by such improvements. The increase in energy efficiency allows greater consumption and encourages greater energy use, measured in efficiency units. One response to this is that the

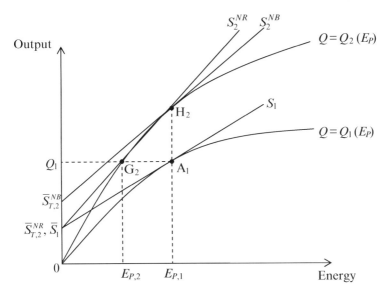

Figure 7.4   The effect of energy taxation on output and energy use

government could use tax or subsidy policy to change the prices faced by producers so as to bring about a more appropriate allocation of resources. That is to say, if energy use is too high after the introduction of improvements in energy efficiency, the government could place an appropriate tax on energy to improve the allocative efficiency of the market mechanism in the attainment of sustainability goals.[8]

At present the model has only one price, p_E, which is the price of energy relative to the domestically produced good. This price is fixed in international markets. However, it will be useful to introduce the post-tax price of energy, p_T, defined as:

$$p_T = tp_E, \tag{7.9}$$

where t is the ratio of the post- to pre-tax energy price. Where t is unity, there is no tax. Values of t less than 1 imply a subsidy, and greater than 1 imply a tax. In this model the tax is raised simply to adjust for externalities and not in order to finance public goods. The revenues would therefore be redistributed to the local population.

The use of tax policy combined with an improvement in energy efficiency is shown in Figure 7.4. It is perhaps appropriate here to discuss in a bit more detail the maximising procedure involved. With no taxes, the surplus (income) paid to local resources from production is given by equation (7.1). Rearranging equation (7.1) implies that the combinations of production and energy inputs that would generate any specific local resource income, $\overline{S}$, are given by the a positively sloped straight line:

$$Q = p_E E_P + \overline{S}. \tag{7.10}$$

These are iso-income curves. They have a slope equal to the energy price level and the constant term, which is the intercept on the Q axis, equals the value of the income. In

Figures 7.1a and 7.2a the consumption-maximising output, which is also the competitive equilibrium, is identified as the point on the relevant production frontier just tangent to the highest iso-income curve.

Where the government introduces a tax on energy this has two implications. First the iso-income curves that determine production choice in a market economy change to:

$$Q = p_T E_P + \overline{S}_T. \tag{7.11}$$

With the introduction of a tax, the slope is now steeper and equals the post-tax price, p_T. The income earned by local resources, $\overline{S}_T$, is net of tax. Second, some of the income generated in production now goes to the government in tax revenue for redistribution. This tax income equals $E_P p_E (t - 1)$.

The presence of rebound effects reduces the effectiveness of energy efficiency improvements in meeting energy-saving targets. In Figure 7.4, as in Figure 7.3a, energy efficiency improvements shift the production frontier outwards from $Q_1(E_P)$ to $Q_2(E_P)$. The energy use is initially at the consumption-maximising point $E_{P,1}$, producing output Q_1. With no tax, the figure is constructed such that energy use will rise in line with energy efficiency. To reduce rebound effects to zero, energy taxes should be introduced so that the income-maximising output remains constant. This implies that the input of energy in efficiency units remains constant, so that the reduction in energy use in natural units is the full extent of the improvement in energy efficiency.

The necessary tax adjustment can be derived using equation (7.7), but using the post-tax price of energy, as given in equation (7.9). The international price for energy, p_E, and the production function parameters α and B are taken to be fixed, so that:

$$\frac{\alpha}{1 - \alpha} \dot{n} - \frac{\dot{t}}{1 - \alpha} = \dot{E}_P, \tag{7.12}$$

where the dot notation again represents proportionate changes. For no rebound effects, the fall in the energy demand is to equal the improvement in energy efficiency, so that:

$$\dot{E}_P = -\dot{n}. \tag{7.13}$$

Substituting equation (7.13) into (7.12) gives the result that:

$$\dot{t} = \dot{n}. \tag{7.14}$$

This no-rebound result is illustrated in Figure 7.4 by pivoting the highest iso-income curve, S_2^{NR}, around the point on the Q axis, $\overline{S}_1$, until it is tangent to the new production frontier at G_2. The income-maximising output remains unchanged at Q_1, but energy use falls from $E_{P,1}$ to $E_{P,2}$.

Although equation (7.14) has been derived for the particular Cobb–Douglas production function, the result is general. To totally neutralise any rebound effects in production from increased energy efficiency, the proportionate increase in the post-tax price of energy must be the same as the proportionate increase in energy efficiency. There are two practical problems with this result. The first is that as energy efficiency increases, in order to remove all rebound effects, the tax on energy has to increase monotonically. To prevent any rebound effects, the absolute level of present consumption forgone will increase over time.

A second problem is that the post-tax income received by local productive resources remains unchanged after the efficiency improvement. The output is unaffected, as is the post-tax price of energy in efficiency units. There is an increase in consumption, but this is generated solely by the redistributed increase in tax revenue. However, improvements in energy efficiency will generally require the commitment of resources by the production sector, in the form of investment in research and development, for example. In order to motivate firms to introduce the required efficiency improvements in the face of positive costs of innovation, the government must be able to commit to continuously increasing energy taxation at the appropriate rate. There are clear credibility problems in implementing such a strategy (Leicester, 2005)

It is of interest also to consider, in the Cobb–Douglas case, what the tax policy should be if backfire is to be avoided. Again using equation (7.12) but in this case setting $\dot{E}$ equal to zero gives:

$$\dot{t} = \alpha \dot{n}. \tag{7.15}$$

This lower change in the tax rate means that the income-maximising position shifts from G_2 to H_2 along the production frontier $Q_2(E_P)$. The no-backfire highest iso-income curve is now S_2^{NB}, with a production income rising to $\bar{S}_{T,2}^{NB}$.

The result given in equation (7.15) is specific for the Cobb–Douglas production function. However, it shows that even where a competitive market outcome would otherwise generate backfire, an appropriate tax policy can engineer an outcome where consumption rises, income to local resources increases but energy use in production falls. Again, in the Cobb–Douglas case this requires tax changes in the range:

$$\dot{n} > \dot{t} > \alpha \dot{n}. \tag{7.16}$$

6   Modifications to the Model

The model at present imposes values for three key elasticities: the elasticity of demand for exports, η; the elasticity of substitution in the production of the domestic good, σ; and the elasticity of supply of the local resource, λ. In this section we investigate the effect of varying these parameters. In the case of an open economy, both the elasticity of export demand and the elasticity of substitution are shown to be key determinants of the size of rebound effects. These effects are also magnified where the supply of local resources is more elastic.

Elasticity of demand for exports
It is common to focus on the elasticity of substitution as being the key parameter in the analysis of the impact of changes in energy efficiency. However, we begin here by considering the elasticity of demand for the commodity. At present the small-country

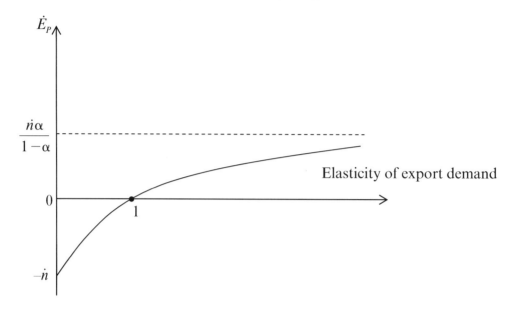

Figure 7.5   The relationship between profit-maximising energy use and the elasticity of export demand

assumption is made: that is, that the economy faces the law of one price in international markets. However, this is an extreme assumption, which effectively imposes a demand function that is infinitely elastic. But if the output price has to fall to sell higher levels of output, the price ratio between energy inputs and local output becomes endogenous. Specifically, the price of energy relative to the numeraire good, the locally produced output, will rise. This price change restricts the increase in energy demand.

The general relationship between proportionate changes in the product price and quantity demanded is given as:

$$\dot{Q} = \eta \dot{p}_E,$$ (7.17)

where η is the price elasticity of demand, given a positive sign here. Note that the product price is the numeraire. Using equation (7.17), together with equations (7.6) and (7.7), produces the result:

$$\dot{E}_P = \frac{\alpha(\eta - 1)\dot{n}}{(1 - \alpha)\eta + \alpha}.$$ (7.18)

The relationship between the proportionate change in energy use and the demand elasticity is given in Figure 7.5. Where demand is completely inelastic, so that $\eta = 0$, there is no rebound: energy demand in production falls the full amount of the efficiency change: $\dot{E}_P = -\dot{n}$. Where product demand is relatively inelastic, so that $1 > \eta > 0$, there is a reduction in energy demand, but by less than the increase in energy efficiency. Some rebound occurs. Finally, where demand for the product is elastic, with the price elasticity of demand taking a value greater than unity, energy use increases with an improvement in energy efficiency. Backfire occurs in this elasticity range, and as $\eta \to \infty$, $\dot{E}_P \to [\alpha/(1-\alpha)]\dot{n}$.

Clearly the value of the elasticity of export demand is important for determining the way that energy use in production responds to an increase in energy efficiency. The more elastic the demand, the greater is the output response to the efficiency improvement and the higher the probability of getting backfire.

Elasticity of substitution in production
There is a very large literature relating to the relationship between energy efficiency, energy use and the elasticity of substitution in production (Broadstock et al., 2007; Saunders, 2008). In a two-factor production function, the elasticity of substitution, σ, is the responsiveness of the ratio of the inputs to changes in the relative input prices. If the elasticity of substitution is high, it is relatively easy to substitute one input for the other, whereas if the elasticity of substitution is low, substitution is difficult.

The previous sections of this chapter have used the Cobb–Douglas production function, which has an elasticity of substitution equal to unity. Greater analytical scope is available with a constant elasticity of substitution (CES) production function, where the impact of varying the substitution elasticity in production can be investigated (Varian, 1992). Such a production function has a CES between inputs but this elasticity figure can take any non-negative value.

A side relationship of the CES function gives the cost-minimising input intensity as:

$$\left(\frac{p_N}{p_F} \frac{\phi}{1-\phi}\right)^{\sigma} = \frac{F_P}{N},$$ (7.19)

where p_N and p_F are the prices of local resources and energy, measured in efficiency units, ϕ is a distribution parameter and σ is the elasticity of substitution, where $0 < \sigma < \infty$.

The increase in the energy efficiency generates a reduction in the price of energy, measured in efficiency units, of $\dot{n}$. The price of output is constant so that, for small changes, an improvement in energy efficiency generates a proportionate increase in the price of the local resources that is given by:

$$\dot{p}_N = \frac{\alpha \dot{n}}{(1-\alpha)}.$$ (7.20)

In our standard model, local resources, N, are fixed and ϕ is a parameter, so that using equations (7.19) and (7.20) produces:

$$\dot{F}_P = \sigma(\dot{p}_N - \dot{p}_F) = \frac{\sigma \dot{n}}{(1-\alpha)}.$$ (7.21)

Equation (7.21) gives the demand for energy in efficiency units. In order to convert this to the change in energy demand in natural units, we subtract the percentage increase in energy efficiency, so that:

$$\dot{E}_P = \dot{F}_P - \dot{n} = \frac{(\sigma + \alpha - 1)\dot{n}}{(1-\alpha)}.$$ (7.22)

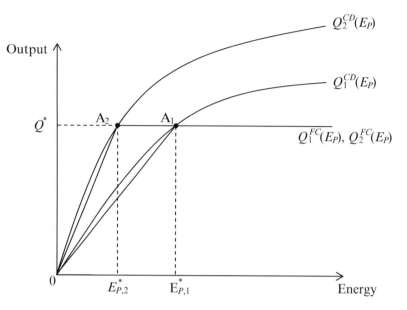

Figure 7.6   An increase in energy efficiency with the fixed coefficients production function

From equation (7.22) it is clear that the extent of the change in energy use will depend on the value of the elasticity of substitution, σ. If the value of the elasticity of substitution is zero, there is no rebound effect in production: the fall in energy use is equal to the increase in energy efficiency, $\dot{n}$. Where the elasticity of substitution lies within the range: $1 - \alpha > \sigma \geq 0$, then there is rebound but not backfire: energy use will fall but by less than the extent of the efficiency improvement. For values of $\sigma \geq 1 - \alpha$, energy use does not fall as energy efficiency increases. This is the parameter range over which backfire occurs. Note that the Cobb–Douglas function, with an elasticity equal to unity, always lies within this range.

In the literature there is often the implicit assumption that a lower elasticity of substitution in production is desirable, in that this reduces rebound effects. However, it does so only by offering policy makers more restricted options. Figure 7.6 presents the zero elasticity of substitution production frontier. This is derived from a fixed coefficients production function, where the inputs per unit of output for both the local resource and energy, measured in efficiency units, are fixed. There is no flexibility concerning the resource intensity of production. The input intensities are therefore invariant to changes in input prices. The line $Q_1^{FC}(E_P)$ represents the initial production frontier, where the superscript identifies the production function as having fixed coefficients.

This initial fixed coefficients (zero elasticity) production frontier comprises two linear segments: the straight line from the origin to the point A_1, which is associated with the maximum output, Q^*, and the horizontal line as subsequent increases in energy fail to increase output.[9] Compare the fixed coefficients $Q_1^{FC}(E_P)$ and Cobb–Douglas (unitary elasticity) production function $Q_1^{CD}(E_P)$ that goes through the same optimal point A_1. Also assume that A_1 is initially the profit-maximising point in the Cobb–Douglas case.

A key observation is that the Cobb–Douglas production function gives a greater range of production options. At no level of energy input does the output from the fixed coefficient, zero elasticity, production function generate a greater output than that from the Cobb–Douglas production function.

If there is an increase in energy efficiency, the fixed coefficients production function shifts to the left, with the maximum output still at Q^*, but with energy inputs reduced by $\dot{n}$. The profit-maximising point has moved to A_2. However, note that where the same efficiency improvement is imposed in the Cobb–Douglas production function the frontier also goes through point A_2. However, in the Cobb–Douglas case, this will not be the allocation chosen in a free market as it is not the new profit-maximising point. The point can be made more generally: a conventional well-behaved production function offers possibilities that are technically ruled out with the fixed coefficients production function. However, as we argued in Section 5, with a Cobb–Douglas (or any other well-behaved production function), the government can bring the economic system back to the zero rebound state at A_2 through the appropriate tax policy. Further, if the government wished to reduce energy use below $E_{P,2}^*$, it can do so with a smaller reduction in output and consumption, the higher the elasticity of substitution.

Supply of other factors

One comment concerning the standard economic approach is that the changes generated by improvements in energy efficiency are small. As noted in Section 2, in a competitive economy, the parameter α is the share of energy costs in total output. From equations (7.6) and (7.8), with our standard open economy model, the increase in energy use and output resulting from even a large increase in energy efficiency is modest. If energy costs are 5 per cent of total inputs, a 50 per cent increase in energy efficiency will generate a 2.6 per cent increase in output and energy use.

However, in the model at present, all non-energy inputs are provided locally with a supply elasticity of zero. But if non-energy inputs have a positive supply elasticity, the impact of increased energy efficiency can be much greater. For example, in analysing energy use, it is very common to use the KLEM production function, where inputs of capital, labour and materials are identified as K, L and M. For the constant returns to scale Cobb–Douglas case, equation (7.6) is amended to:

$$Q = AF_P^\alpha K^\beta M^\gamma L^{1-\alpha-\beta-\gamma}. \tag{7.23}$$

Imagine that in this case, the capital and materials inputs, such as energy, are supplied in international markets at fixed prices. Setting the marginal products of these inputs equal to their prices generates:

$$\frac{K}{Q} = \frac{\beta}{p_K}, \frac{M}{Q} = \frac{\gamma}{p_M}, \tag{7.24}$$

where p_K and p_M are the prices of capital and materials, respectively. Substituting these results into equation (7.23) and rearranging produces:

$$Q = DE_P^{\frac{\alpha}{1-\beta-\gamma}} n^{\frac{\alpha}{1-\beta-\gamma}}. \tag{7.25}$$

Equation (7.25) is in a form comparable to equation (7.6) except that the coefficients on the energy and energy efficiency terms E_P and n are increased.[10] This means that in the standard Cobb–Douglas case discussed in Section 4, an energy improvement of $\dot{n}$ now generates an increase in energy use given by:

$$\dot{E}_P = \frac{\alpha \dot{n}}{1 - \alpha - \beta - \gamma}. \tag{7.26}$$

Using the same numerical example of a 50 per cent improvement in efficiency, if the combined energy, capital and material costs made up 75 per cent of the total costs, the increase in output and energy use would now be 10 per cent.

A second consideration concerns the supply of the local input. If we again take the KLEM production function with labour as the only non-imported input, the proportionate increase in the price of labour as the price of energy, measured in efficiency units, falls is:

$$\dot{p}_L = \frac{\alpha \dot{n}}{1 - \alpha - \beta - \gamma}. \tag{7.27}$$

With an elasticity of labour supply equal to λ, the increase in employment is given as:

$$\dot{L} = \frac{\alpha \lambda \dot{n}}{1 - \alpha - \beta - \gamma}. \tag{7.28}$$

The change in the energy demand identified in equation (7.26) is driven by the increase in energy use per unit of the local resource (now labour). Incorporating the increase in labour supply implies summing the expressions in equations (7.26) and (7.28), producing:

$$\dot{E}_P = \frac{\alpha(1 + \lambda)\dot{n}}{1 - \alpha - \beta - \gamma}. \tag{7.29}$$

From equations (7.29) and (7.8), the effect of incorporating the elasticity of supply of non-energy inputs multiplies the proportionate increase in energy use by a factor of $[(1 + \lambda)(1 - \alpha)]/(1 - \alpha - \beta - \gamma) > 1$. The supply-augmented increase in output and energy use could therefore be substantially higher than the unadjusted calculation.

7   Consumption

Up to this point we have analysed only the effect of an improvement in energy efficiency in production on subsequent energy use in production. We now turn to the impact of changes in energy efficiency on the consumption demand for energy. We consider two cases. In the first, the improvement in energy efficiency occurs only in the production sector. In the second, the improvement in energy efficiency occurs only in the consumption sector.

The impact of improvements in energy efficiency in production on energy use in consumption

In those variants of the small open economy model where all commodity prices remain constant, it is straightforward to analyse the impact on consumption of an increase in energy efficiency in production.[11] Real local income increases as a result of the rise in the return to the local resource. The proportionate change in energy use in consumption, $\dot{E}_C$, is then given as the product of the proportionate change in real income and the income elasticity of demand for energy, ψ.

In the most basic model outlined in Section 4, with a Cobb–Douglas production function and no augmented supply effects, the proportionate increase in income is given by equation (7.20). The proportionate increase in consumption demand for energy, $\dot{E}_C$, is then:

$$\dot{E}_C = \dot{n}\left(\frac{\alpha}{1-\alpha}\right)\psi = \dot{E}_P\psi. \tag{7.30}$$

This increase in consumption demand does not come from higher energy expenditure in consumption partly or wholly replacing lower expenditure on energy in production. Rather it stems from the expansion in output, and the subsequent rise in the price for the services of the fixed local input, that the improvement in productive efficiency creates. This increases local income and energy use for local consumption.

The proportionate rise in total energy use, $\dot{E}_T$, is the weighted sum of the proportionate changes in consumption and production demand. The weights are the initial production and consumption energy use. For an initial output, Q, these initial absolute energy use levels are:

$$E_P = \frac{\alpha Q}{p_E}, \quad E_C = \frac{(1-\alpha)\mu Q}{p_E}, \tag{7.31}$$

where μ is the share of energy in total consumer expenditure. Using equations (7.8), (7.30) and (7.31):

$$\dot{E}_T = \dot{E}_P\left[\frac{\alpha + (1-\alpha)\mu\psi}{\alpha + (1-\alpha)\mu}\right] = \frac{\alpha[\alpha + (1-\alpha)\mu\psi]\dot{n}}{(1-\alpha)[\alpha + (1-\alpha)\mu]}. \tag{7.32}$$

In this case, equation (7.32) implies that whether the proportionate change in total energy use is greater or less than the proportionate change in energy use in production depends solely on the value of the income elasticity of demand for energy in consumption. Where the income elasticity of demand, ψ, is greater than unity, total energy use grows faster than energy use in production. Also if the absolute change in total energy use in the production sector, ΔE_P, is compared to the corresponding change in use in consumption, ΔE_C, the absolute increase in energy use in consumption is greater if:

$$(1-\alpha)\mu\psi > \alpha. \tag{7.33}$$

This inequality would hold with a relatively high share of energy in consumption ($\mu > \alpha$) and/or a relatively high income elasticity of demand for energy ($\psi > 1$). Essentially, in the basic open economy case with the Cobb–Douglas production function, changes in consumption demand for energy substantially reinforce the backfire effect identified in the production demand for energy.

It is also of interest to investigate the effect of incorporating the consumption demand for energy where the elasticity of substitution in production differs from unity, as in Section 6. Here equations (7.20), (7.22) (7.30) and (7.31) generate the following result:

$$\dot{E}_T = \frac{\alpha\dot{n}[(\sigma + \alpha - 1) + (1 - \alpha)\mu\psi]}{(1 - \alpha)[\alpha + (1 - \alpha)\mu]}. \tag{7.34}$$

First, even where the elasticity of substitution in production, σ, is zero, so that there is no rebound in production, with energy use falling in production by $\dot{n}$, there is some rebound as a result of increased consumption. This is represented by the second term in the brackets in equation (7.34).

Second, the range of values of σ over which the change in aggregate energy use is positive with an increase in energy efficiency in production is given by:

$$\sigma > (1 - \alpha)(1 - \mu\psi). \tag{7.35}$$

Therefore, using equations (7.22) and (7.35), there are a range of substitution elasticities:

$$1 - \alpha > \sigma > (1 - \alpha)(1 - \mu\psi), \tag{7.36}$$

where there is no backfire when the impact on energy use in production is considered on its own but where there is backfire once the impact on the demand for energy in consumption is incorporated.

Where the other adjustments to the standard model introduced in Section 6 are considered, these have implications for the extent of the increase in energy use in consumption. First, the more expansionary supply-side implications of relaxing the fixity of non-energy inputs will have a positive impact on consumption demand, as well as energy demand in production. Second, where the price of the commodity falls as output expands, there will be a more complex reaction, especially if the locally produced domestic product is a major part of the local consumption bundle. However, even here, there will be a rise in real income associated with introduction of the improvement in energy efficiency that should stimulate consumer energy demand.

The impact of energy efficiency improvements in consumption

In this subsection the assumption is made that the improvement in efficiency occurs solely in the use of energy for consumption purposes. In the standard version of the model, where local resources are fixed and fully employed, there is no feedback running from changes in consumption to changes in production: locally produced commodities that are not sold on the local market are exported at the same, internationally determined price.

In that case an improvement in energy efficiency in consumption generates a corresponding reduction in the price of energy measured in efficiency units. The consumption of energy, in efficiency units, is expected to rise as the price falls, so that rebound is expected:

$$\dot{F}_C = \tau\dot{n}, \tag{7.37}$$

where τ is the price elasticity of consumption demand, given a positive sign. To convert to the change in electricity use in natural units, subtract the efficiency gain, so that:

$$\dot{E}_C = \tau\dot{n} - \dot{n} = (\tau - 1)\dot{n}. \tag{7.38}$$

If the price elasticity of demand for energy is greater than unity, the proportionate increase in demand is greater than the proportionate reduction in price so that the total expenditure on energy will rise as the price, measured in efficiency units, falls. Where this occurs, backfire takes place for energy use in consumption.

Where the supply of non-energy inputs is not fixed, as discussed in Section 6, and labour is the only non-imported input, improvements in energy efficiency in consumption will increase the real wage. This leads to an expansion in the supply of labour and therefore affects energy use in both the production and consumption spheres. As argued above, a proportionate rise in energy efficiency in consumption of $\dot{n}$ generates a similar proportionate fall in the price of energy to consumers, measured in efficiency units. This produces an increase in the real wage equal to $\dot{n}\mu$, and the corresponding increase in labour supply equals $\dot{n}\mu\lambda$. The impact of the expansion in supply of the local resource is an equal proportionate increase in energy use in production.[12] The proportionate change in total energy use, incorporating supply-side impacts, from an increase in energy efficiency in consumption is therefore:

$$\dot{E}_{T,CS} = \dot{n}\mu\left[\frac{\lambda\alpha + (1 - \alpha - \beta - \gamma)(\tau - 1)}{\alpha + \mu(1 - \alpha - \beta - \gamma)}\right]. \tag{7.39}$$

The labour-supply effects always add to the demand for energy, even where the direct effect of the energy efficiency improvement in consumption identified in equation (7.38) is negative (that is, where consumer demand for electricity is inelastic). Also the value the labour supply elasticity can be large if migration effects are important.

8   Conclusion

In this chapter we identify the impact of changes in energy efficiency in a stylised small open economy model. The aim is pedagogic. We have four main themes. The first is that an improvement in energy efficiency will have system-wide effects. This means that in order to analyse the impact on energy use we need to model all the key interactions within the economy.

Second, a change in efficiency in the use of energy inputs increases the options open to the economy. The actual outcome will depend upon which of those options is chosen. Therefore in considering the effect of an improvement in energy efficiency, allocative efficiency, as well as technical efficiency, is under scrutiny.

Third, the existence of an important export sector in small open economies means that the conditions facing this sector are crucial in determining the subsequent energy use that follows from an improvement in energy efficiency. The impact of increased efficiency on competitiveness is an important stimulus to the aggregate economy and therefore to energy use. In particular, we show that the elasticity of demand for the export sector's output is as important as the elasticity of substitution in production in the analysis of the impact of improvements in energy efficiency on energy use.

Fourth, while analysing an economy in which energy inputs are assumed to be freely available at the existing international price, we identify the implication of varying the elasticities of supply of the other inputs. Any increase in the ease of supply of other inputs generally increases the impact of improved energy efficiency in production and also leads to an interaction between improved efficiency in energy use in consumption and the level of energy used in production.

Appendix 7A   The Production Frontier with Zero Elasticity of Substitution

The rationale for the linear, jointed production frontier where elasticity of substitution is zero is straightforward. If the required input of local resources per unit of output is θ_N then the maximum output, Q^*, is given by:

$$Q^* = \frac{\overline{N}}{\theta_N}. \tag{7A.1}$$

To attain the maximum output, the energy supply must lie in the range:

$$E_P \geq E_P^* = Q^*\theta_E = \frac{\overline{N}\theta_E}{\theta_N}, \tag{7A.2}$$

where θ_E is the required input of energy per unit of output. If total energy inputs are below E_P^*, production is constrained. Any increase in energy, ΔE_P, that relaxes that constraint generates additional output equal to $\Delta E_P/\theta_E$. The slope of the production frontier between the origin and A_1 is therefore $1/\theta_E$. However, once the total energy input reaches E_P^*, further increases in energy inputs have no impact on output as the level of local resources forms the binding constraint on production. Finally, with parametric prices if production is profitable at all, maximum profitability will be attained initially at A_1.

Notes

*   The research in this chapter is funded by the Engineering and Physical Science Research Council (EPSRC) through the SuperGen Marine Energy Research Consortium (grant reference: EP/E040136/1) and the Sustainable Hydrogen Energy Consortium (grant reference: EP/E040071/1). Karen Turner acknowledges support from the Economic and Social Research Council (ESRC) through the First Grants scheme (grant reference: RES_061_25_0010) on the research programme titled 'An empirical general equilibrium analysis of the factors that govern the extent of energy rebound effects in the UK economy'.
1.   Specifically, there are no issues concerning the distribution of income among individuals.
2.   Essentially lower present energy use represents increased welfare for future generations.
3.   Allocative efficiency involves making the best choice of inputs and scale of production among the technically efficient alternatives. To reach overall economic efficiency, the outcome must be both technically and allocatively efficient.
4.   In this case the tax is simply to change the prices facing producers and would be distributed back to consumers.
5.   The Cobb–Douglas production function has the characteristic that the elasticity of substitution between the inputs equals unity. This is discussed in greater detail in Section 6.
6. $B = AN^{1-\alpha}$, so that where the general productivity and the natural resource input is fixed, B is a constant.
7.   Although as drawn in Figure 7.3b social welfare would be maximised with a small drop in consumption.
8.   Similar goals could be played by physical restrictions, though in this simple model these would be expected to act very much in the same way as price signals.
9.   The form of the production frontier with zero elasticity of substitution is explained in greater detail in Appendix 7A.
10. $D = \{AL^{1-\alpha-\beta-\gamma}[(\beta/p_K)^\beta(\gamma/p_M)^\lambda]\}^{1/(1-\beta-\gamma)}$. Where the domestic labour supply and the prices of capital and materials are fixed in international markets, D is a constant.
11. These are the variants where the law of one price holds in the export sector.
12. In this case the consumption elasticity of demand is a general equilibrium measure which incorporates the

effects of the additional income generated by the expanded labour supply stimulated by the increase in the real wage.

References

Bergson, A. (1938), 'A reformulation of certain aspects of welfare economics', *Quarterly Journal of Economics*, **52** (2), 310–34.
Broadstock, D.C., L. Hunt and S. Sorrell (2007), 'Technical Report 2: Elasticity of Substitution studies', working paper for UKERC (Energy Research Centre) Review of Evidence for the Rebound Effect, ref: UKERC/WP/TPA/2007/011, October.
Brookes, L. (1978), 'Energy policy, the energy price fallacy and the role of nuclear energy in the UK', *Energy Policy*, **6** (2), 94–106.
Jevons, W.S. (1865), *The Coal Question, An Inquiry Concerning the Progress of the Nation, and the Probable Exhaustion of Our Coal Mines*, Reprinted 1906, London: Macmillan.
Khazzoom, D.J. (1980), 'Economic implications of mandated efficiency in standards for household appliances', *The Energy Journal*, **1** (4), 21–39.
Leicester, A. (2005), 'Fuel taxation', Institute for Fiscal Studies, Briefing Note No. 55, available at: http://www.ifs.org.uk/bns/bn55.pdf (accessed 26 February 2009).
Patterson, M.G. (1996), 'What is energy efficiency: concepts, indicators and methodological issues', *Energy Policy*, **24** (5), 377–90.
Samuelson, P. (2004), 'Abram Bergson: a biographical memoir by Paul Samuelson', *National Academy of Sciences, Biographical Memoirs*: Volume 84, Washington, DC.
Saunders, H.D. (1992), 'The Khazzoom–Brookes postulate and neoclassical growth', *The Energy Journal*, **13** (4), 131–48.
Saunders, H.D. (2008), 'Fuel conserving (and using) production functions', *Energy Economics*, **30** (5), 2184–235.
Sorrell, S. (2007), 'The rebound effect: an assessment of the evidence for economy-wide energy savings from improved energy efficiency', report published by the Sussex Energy Group for the Technology and Policy Assessment function of the UKERC (Energy Research Centre), October.
Sorrell, S. and J. Dimitropoulos (2008), 'The rebound effect: microeconomic definitions, limitations and extensions', *Ecological Economics*, **65** (3), 636–49.
Stern, N. (2007), *The Economics of Climate Change*, Cambridge: Cambridge University Press.
Varian, H. (1992), *Microeconomic Analysis*, 3rd edn, New York: W.W. Norton.

8 Theoretical foundations of the rebound effect
Harry Saunders

1 Introduction

The relationship between energy efficiency and energy consumption is a surprisingly subtle one. In this chapter, we present a highly simplified but nonetheless rigorous picture of a standard theoretical economic framework for understanding this relationship. The intent is to give the reader a solid foundation for informed analysis of policy issues related to energy efficiency. To keep things concrete, along the way we connect the discussion to the question of demand-side global warming remedies, which, as one might expect, depend heavily on the link between energy efficiency and energy consumption.

2 Energy–Economy Interactions – the Basics

We begin with the simplest possible way to look at energy efficiency in an economy. Suppose we have an economy that produces a certain amount of GDP with a certain amount of energy. We can characterize this economy by the following equation:

$$Y = f(R, E).$$

In this equation, Y represents 'real output', which you can think of as being GDP although strictly speaking there is a slight difference if you are an economist.[1] E represents the amount of energy used in producing this real output and R represents the quantity of other inputs used (capital, labor, materials and so on).

Were we looking only at an instant in time, we would not even need this equation to understand the relationship between energy and output – energy's efficiency in being able to produce output would be adequately characterized by the E/Y ratio. But in general we will want to know how and why this ratio might differ for different economies and how it might differ over time, for example, due to gains in energy efficiency technology. For this we need the mathematical depiction.

Hogan and Manne (1977) developed a beautifully simple way to look at this question, which is shown in Figure 8.1. The figure shows that reducing the energy input to an economy does not result in a one-for-one loss in output. Here we hold the quantity of other inputs, R, fixed. The exact shape of this curve will depend of course on how we characterize the function f, but it can be shown that all functions honoring the standard so-called 'regularity' conditions economists insist on will have this same basic shape. The good news from this is that if one wishes to reduce the energy used by an economy, one need not sacrifice a proportional amount of economic activity, or 'output' as we call it here.

The figure also says that the E/Y ratio can be reduced. If we begin with the point at

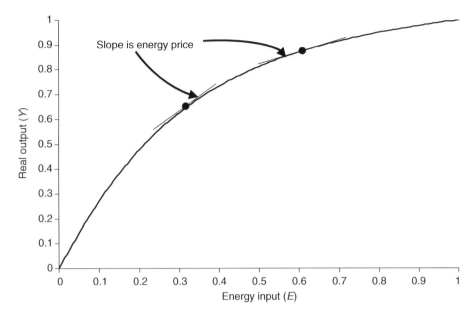

Figure 8.1 Economic output versus energy input

the upper right-hand extreme of this curve, which we can think of as the starting point of the E/Y ratio (E value on the x-axis; Y value on the y-axis), we see movement to the left causes this ratio to go down compared to the starting point. There is, in other words, an energy efficiency gain. The E/Y ratio is often called the 'energy intensity'.

Movement along this curve involves technology change. But it is a change arising from altering deployment of the array of technologies already existing. A simple example is substituting more building insulation for heating oil use in your home. Both technologies exist; you are just altering the proportions of their use. We later explain how this curve changes when new technologies are introduced.

The role of energy price in creating energy efficiency gains

An increase in energy price will cause movement along this curve. The way the economist will look at this is the following.

Pick a point along this curve. At this point, draw a tangent line. The slope of this line is a numerical quantification of how much additional output can be created if we increase energy input a little bit. Economists call this the 'marginal productivity of energy', and it can be shown that in a perfectly competitive economy where producers maximize profits, this marginal productivity must quantitatively equal the energy price.

We see that the slope of the curve increases as we move to the left. This reflects the commonsense notion that as energy price increases, the use of energy input will go down, as will the E/Y ratio. An increased energy price, in other words, increases energy efficiency.

However, it also reduces output. With fixed supply of other inputs, a reduction in energy input will reduce output, although not in a one-for-one fashion, as we have seen.

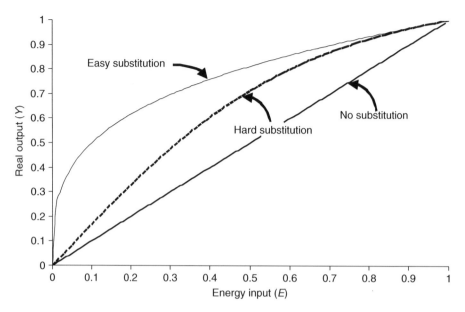

Figure 8.2   The importance of substitution potential

This has implications for global warming remedies. A favored remedy of economists is a global carbon tax. Such a tax, by increasing the energy price, would indeed reduce energy consumption and increase energy efficiency, but it would come at the cost of reduced economic welfare (that is, reduced economic activity). An argument commonly made is that this is economic welfare construed too narrowly. Global warming, the argument goes, carries with it present and future costs that are not reflected in economic mechanisms and these 'externalities' must be forced to become 'internal' if overall welfare-maximizing conditions are to be achieved. A carbon tax is seen as a way to do this without excessive distortion of economic signals. Even so, as we see from the Hogan–Manne curve, it comes at the cost of economic welfare in the narrower, near-term sense and the argument is easily made that the global warming debate must recognize this if it is to be an honest debate.

The role of substitution potential
Hogan and Manne had more to say about what drives the magnitudes of these effects. Figure 8.2 illustrates. We see three curves in this figure. The top curve depicts the output/energy input relationship if substitution is easy – that is, if producers can readily substitute other inputs for energy by choosing a different combination of existing technologies. Think of an old shack to which you are adding insulation where there was none: a big reduction in energy use is possible with a relatively small increase in insulation; if insulation is relatively inexpensive it will have a reasonably modest impact on your wealth. Likewise, this curve says that if such easy substitution is possible economy-wide, the reduction in output will be relatively small for a given decrease in energy use. Also, recalling the discussion above, we can see that this substitution will come with a relatively small increase in energy price. By way of further example, a petrochemical producer may

find it possible to readily reduce fuel consumption by investing in an inexpensive auto-mated control system – and economic to do so given a modest increase in energy price – but future economic plant expansions will be of marginally smaller scale because of the added expense. And so on.

If, on the other hand, substitution is more difficult, we have the situation depicted by the second curve from the top. We see that a given reduction in energy input has a larger negative effect on output than in the case of the top curve. Further, it requires a larger increase in energy price. Similarly, the bottom curve shows the extreme case where there is no substitution potential at all – a reduction in energy input causes a one-for-one reduc-tion in output. This corresponds to a highly simplistic depiction of the economy called by economists 'Leontief production', which we shall shortly have occasion to re-visit.

A subtlety arises here. While it is true that if substitution is easy a given reduction in energy input requires a smaller energy price increase and has a less negative effect on eco-nomic output, it is on the contrary true that a given increase in energy price will reduce economic output more if substitution is easy. Stated in concrete terms, a given carbon tax will have a larger negative economic impact if substitution is easier, but a smaller tax will be required to achieve a specific energy use target if substitution is easier (see Box 8.1).

So those are the basics: an energy input reduction reduces economic output, but not one for one; an energy price increase reduces energy input and increases its efficiency; the output cost to an economy of a reduction in energy input depends on how easy it is to substitute other inputs for energy.

We now turn to the question of what happens when new energy efficiency technologies appear on the scene.

Further reading on this section
The seminal idea underlying Figures 8.1 and 8.2 was developed by Hogan and Manne (1977). This reference gives further mathematical detail and discussion.

3   Energy–Economy Interactions with New Technology

The above analysis suggests how an economy might evolve given the existing array of technologies – the existing set of possibilities for combining economic inputs to produce economic output. But the core topic of this chapter – so-called energy consumption 'rebound' – has to do with what happens to energy consumption when *new* technology is developed aimed at reducing energy use.

For this, we need to extend the Hogan–Manne model. To keep things concrete, we could think of what happens when we introduce a new space heating technology that is very energy efficient. Let us say heat pump technology has only now been invented and it allows a building to be heated to the same comfort level but using only half the fuel of an older-style furnace. The simplest way to depict this is with a multiplier:

$$E_{Old} = \tau E_{New}.$$

Stated this way, τ is the engineering efficiency gain that will result in the provision of the same amount of energy services as previously, E_{Old}, with a reduced amount of physi-cal energy E_{New}. We can also think of E_{Old} as being 'effective' energy supply. We initialize

BOX 8.1   CARBON TAXES, EMISSIONS TRADING AND
SUBSTITUTION POTENTIAL

As described in the main text, if energy price rises (as through a carbon tax)
energy use will be reduced, and the easier it is for producers to substitute other
inputs for energy the smaller the tax that will be needed to achieve a given

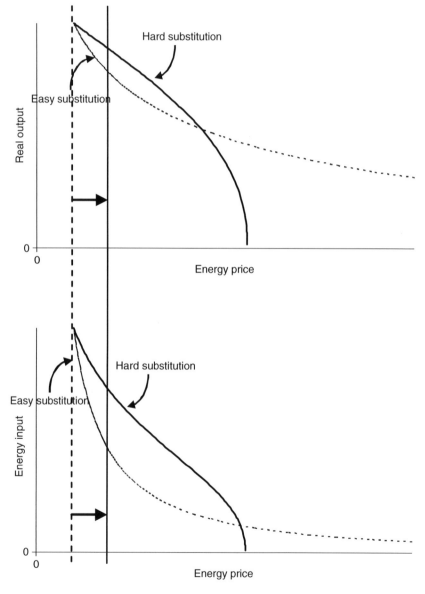

Carbon taxes, emissions trading and substitution potential

energy reduction. Thus, if one's goal is to reduce energy use via a carbon tax (or more precisely, to reduce carbon emissions from energy use via a carbon tax), one hopes that easy substitution is possible in the real-world economy. If this is the case, the economic cost of achieving any energy use target will be lower.

But it is also true that if substitution is easy, a given level of energy price increase (via a carbon tax) will likely cause a *greater* loss in economic activity than if substitution is hard. This may seem counterintuitive, but the figure illustrates. If the energy price starts out at a level corresponding to the dashed line running through both panels of the figure and is then increased to a level illustrated by the solid line, you can see that with easy substitution economic output is reduced more than it would be with hard substitution (top panel). Of course this energy price increase will also lead to a lower energy use (lower panel).

(You can also see that this conclusion can be reversed if the energy price rise is large enough (farther to the right in the upper panel), but at least for small enough energy price rises this will be the case. Very far to the right the hard substitution sector would suffer outright collapse, so we ignore this in the discussion following.)

The policy consequences are therefore this: if one thinks of the substitution potential of the *economy as a whole*, one hopes that substitution potential is easy if one wishes to reduce energy use to some specific target level – this will require a smaller carbon tax and will result in less loss of economic output. *But* if one imagines that substitution potential may be different for different sectors of the economy (likely the case in general), a uniform carbon tax applied to all sectors will hurt more those sectors that deliver the greatest reduction in energy use. This curious result would likely strike most as unfair. Fairness notions aside, it may run counter to welfare maximization, since in general one should be able to find for any target reduction in energy use a combination of differentially applied carbon taxes resulting in less loss of output than one would obtain with a uniformly applied tax, whichever sector may be thereby favored.

This suggests a possible policy solution that would apply different levels of carbon tax to different sectors. Whether this is a practical policy remedy is a political, not an economic question.

An alternative scheme for reducing carbon emissions is emissions trading or 'cap and trade'. In a 'cap-and-trade' scheme, governments set an overall limit on carbon emissions (in our simpler world here, on energy use) and firms are allowed to trade among themselves permits that in total represent this overall limit.

But in terms of their impact on output a carbon tax and emissions trading are identical. To see this, consider an economy composed of two sectors, one characterized by easy substitution (Sector A) and the other by hard substitution (Sector B). With emissions trading, the two sectors will trade permits until the marginal value of buying or selling the last permit is equal to zero for firms in both sectors. The marginal value to each is the added output that could be produced with an added increment of energy (its marginal productivity) less the 'effective' price of that energy (that is, including the permit cost). For a potential permit buyer, the effective energy price to produce another unit of output is the actual energy price plus the cost of the associated permit; for a potential permit seller it is the actual energy price plus the 'opportunity cost' or forgoing a sale of that permit. In equilibrium, then, this scheme acts exactly like a carbon tax – energy price plus an added cost.

The situation once again becomes that illustrated in the above figure: at a given effective energy price, which is equal for Sector A and Sector B, the total energy used economy-wide is the sum of the two energy inputs shown in the bottom panel where the vertical line intersects the energy input lines. As before, however, we see that the easy substitution Sector A suffers greater output loss than the hard substitution Sector B, in this case via total energy input being reduced by an emissions cap.

So as before this suggests a possible policy solution that discriminates between high and low substitution potential sectors, with different emissions caps on each. But again as before, whether this is a practical policy remedy is a political, not an economic question. (A final note: firms will generally prefer the cap-and-trade scheme since proceeds from sales of permits may stay in the private sector, unlike a carbon tax. However, if permits are initially auctioned off with proceeds to the government, this advantage will be reduced and may disappear altogether.)

the analysis at the point $\tau = 1$. So if $\tau = 1.25$, only $1/1.25 = 0.8$, or 80 percent of the physical energy needed previously will be needed to produce the same energy services. In the case of our heat pump we see that $\tau = 2$, indicating that it uses half the physical energy of the older furnace.

Now we modify the equation we used before as follows:

$$Y = f(R, \tau E).$$

What we want to ask is what happens to energy use and output as τ changes. Figure 8.3 illustrates. The figure shows two curves. The bottom curve is the same one we have seen before, although we have adjusted the scales to 'zoom in' on an initial starting point, indicated by the black dot at the base of the arrow. Since this is the same curve that we have seen before, it is the curve where we set $\tau = 1$. The top curve shows our equation when τ is greater than unity and so represents the energy/output combinations that are allowed with our more efficient energy technology. In economics terms, we see that the space of production possibilities has expanded – we can now produce more output with the same amount of energy and other inputs R, irrespective of the level of energy input.

The black arrow shows how the equilibrium energy/output combination changes given our new technology if energy price stays the same. The point on the upper curve indicated with a second black dot is the point where the slope of this curve equals the slope of the bottom curve at our starting point. Recalling that the slope equals the energy price, we see that the two points therefore represent points of equal energy price.

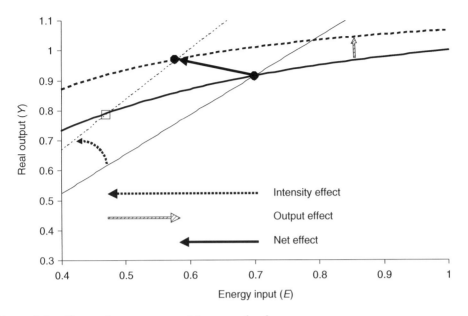

Figure 8.3   Change in energy use with new technology

We see that the net change in energy input is composed of two effects. The first effect is the change in energy 'intensity', which we have encountered before in the guise of the E/Y ratio. The two straight lines show how the equilibrium E/Y ratio changes from the first point to the second. These lines both go through the zero point, so their (inverse) slopes are the points' respective E/Y ratios. We see that the second line is the first line rotated leftward, indicating that the E/Y ratio, or intensity, has gone down as a result of the new technology.

But this intensity gain does not simply result in the new equilibrium being a point on the lower curve where the second straight line intersects it (indicated by the square). Instead, the expansion of output possibilities additionally shifts the lower curve upward, and the new equilibrium will be at the point where the second straight line intersects the upper curve. This is what we call the 'output' effect.

The net effect on energy will be a combination of the two effects. The dashed arrow near the bottom of the chart shows what would be the effect on energy if the intensity effect were the only result of the technology gain. The grey arrow shows the offsetting effect on energy due to the output effect. The resultant of these two effects is the 'net effect' indicated by the black arrow. We see, in other words, 'rebound'.

Energy consumption rebound
With all this in hand, we are finally in a position to address the rebound question. Focusing attention on the black arrow of Figure 8.3, we show in Figure 8.4 its range of possible configurations. The bold black arrow is a reference. It shows the change in the equilibrium point if there is a one-for-one reduction in energy input due to the technology; that is, if a certain percentage gain in energy efficiency translates into the same percentage reduction in energy use.

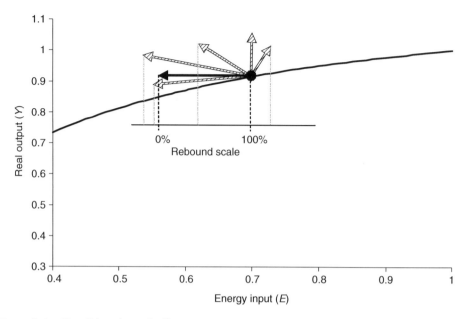

Figure 8.4   Possible rebound effects

More specifically, this is the equilibrium shift associated with so-called Leontief production, which we encountered above. For Leontief production, an *x* percent improvement in energy efficiency creates an *x* percent reduction in energy input and results in no change in output. This is the mental model that many policy makers have historically adopted when thinking about energy efficiency gains. But it is a far too simplistic model.

Nonetheless, it gives us a reference point for defining rebound quantitatively. If such a result were to occur, we would naturally be inclined to say that there has been no rebound in energy use arising from the technology gain. Therefore, we say there is 'zero' rebound, as indicated on Figure 8.4 (on the rebound scale). And if rebound were enough to completely recover energy use, so that energy use is unchanged, we would quite naturally think of that as 100 percent rebound. This is shown in the figure at the 100 percent rebound level on the rebound scale, and we can see that the starting and ending points are identical with respect to the quantity of energy used. This could occur even alongside an increase in output, as shown by the vertical arrow.

Similarly, if an arrow leads to a value on the rebound scale that is greater than 100 percent, we say that rebound is sufficient to cause 'backfire'. An arrow with a value on the rebound scale of 40 percent would indicate that 40 percent of the energy reduction you would have expected from the efficiency gain is lost, and so would be called '40 percent rebound'.

All the arrow types shown in the figure are legitimate arrows. The economist will want to see that they lie on points reflecting legitimate functional forms.

Indeed, choice of functional form (the *f* in our $Y = f(R, \tau E)$ equation) matters greatly to what arrow types will be legitimate, but well-known functions meeting the so-called 'regularity' requirements of economists can be shown to exhibit all the behaviors suggested in Figure 8.4. (Somewhat curiously, other well-known functions meeting these same requirements and otherwise considered suitable for economic analysis can exhibit only backfire, and so are said to be 'rebound inflexible'.)

Some functions allow for a legitimate arrow (like the one reaching farthest leftward in Figure 8.4) that exhibits an energy reduction so severe that it actually exceeds the energy efficiency gain; that is to say, energy use declines on a greater than one-for-one basis with efficiency, so a 1 percent gain in efficiency (that is, in τ) leads to, say, a 2 percent reduction in energy use. This is rebound of the 'super-conservation' type. At present, it is not known whether super-conservation, or backfire, are real-world phenomena. Or indeed, to what extent rebound actually occurs. Chapter 9 in this volume by Steve Sorrell addresses the question of what happens in reality. But standard economic theory cannot disallow either backfire or super-conservation and rebound seems to be a relatively straightforward consequence of the theory.

Given a functional form, the parameters of that form turn out to matter to how the arrow will behave. Overwhelmingly, it would appear, the parameters that matter are those that reflect the substitution potential among inputs, the same determining characteristic that we met before. In that case, substitution potential determined the relationship between reducing energy input and losing output, and easier substitution made this trade-off less onerous. But here we have a kind of opposite effect. That is, greater ease of substitution means greater rebound, and so the energy use one might wish to curb becomes more forceful. The distinction arises because of the difference between existing and new technology. If substitution is easy, existing technology provides a correspondingly less painful response to a carbon tax. Yet if it is indeed easy, new energy efficiency technology creates more energy use than if it is hard.

As before, this has implications for the global warming debate. If one's goal is to reduce energy use, this creates a dilemma regarding what to hope for by way of ease of substitution in real economies. If substitution is easy, a carbon tax would be less onerous than if it is difficult. As we have seen, with easy substitution, energy use can be reduced more easily and with less loss of output, and the carbon tax needed will be smaller. But if substitution is easy, rebound becomes more forceful in driving up energy use. On the other hand, if substitution is difficult, a carbon tax becomes more onerous, but rebound is quantitatively less.

There are further potential implications to the global warming debate at levels below the global economy and even individual economies. Substitution is likely to be more or less easy among different sectors of any economy. If one's goal is to reduce carbon emissions by reducing energy use, one would ideally like to see new energy efficiency technology advance in sectors where substitution is difficult and rebound is small, and a carbon tax applied to sectors where substitution is easy and the output loss is therefore small. Said in reverse, a carbon tax applied where substitution is difficult carries greater loss of economic activity, but new technologies applied where substitution is easy creates the greatest rebound. Whether it is practical for governments to regulate around these different effects is another question.

A final note on this section: we so far have been treating technology efficiency gains as specific to energy. In reality, efficiency gains can be expected for all inputs, not just energy. Even new efficient technologies targeted at reducing energy use often have effects on the other inputs. The news here from an energy conservation perspective is not especially good. In general, increases in the efficiency of other inputs increases rebound. The rebound effects we have been discussing, in other words, will be understated. This makes the rebound question all the more critical in crafting policy aimed at reducing energy use.

So, the conclusions: new energy efficiency technology has a twofold effect. First, it expands the space of production possibilities and 'drags up' energy use. Second, by making energy appear less expensive, it causes energy to be attractive to substitute in place of other inputs, thus tempering the reduction in the E/Y ratio that otherwise might be expected. Also, such technology can cause energy use to go up or down, across a range from super-conservation (greater than one-for-one reduction in energy use) to backfire (outright increase in energy use). And the ease with which inputs can be substituted for one another is a key determinant of rebound – the easier the substitution, the greater the rebound.

Further reading on this section
The first broad overview of rebound issues was the volume edited by Schipper (2000). A highly comprehensive and more recent overview is the report to policy makers by Sorrell (2007). A recent in-depth look at the role of substitution elasticity in the context of rebound appears in Broadstock et al. (2007). Another comprehensive source is Herring and Sorrell (2008). See Saunders (1992, 2005) for a discussion of the relationship between rebound and substitution elasticity and for a discussion of how increases in the efficiency of non-energy inputs increases rebound.

4 Energy–Economy Interactions – Time Dynamics

So far we have dealt with what economists call a 'comparative statics' picture of how energy efficiency affects energy use – looking at two static equilibrium points at different points in time and observing the differences. From it, we can gain intuition about how energy efficiency gains can affect energy use over time, but we have not been explicit about the time dynamics of getting from situation A to situation B. Here we correct that shortcoming.

Fortunately, neoclassical growth theory, created in its modern form by Robert Solow, provides an ideal tool for addressing this issue. Neoclassical growth theory is an elegant and powerful theory. First, it applies irrespective of the functional form chosen for f, provided only that this function honors the standard regularity conditions economists like to see.

Second, the theory is very commonsensical. But to see this, we first have to extend our model to be more explicit than we have so far been about the other inputs. In particular, we have to decompose what we have called R into capital and labor components (K and L). Our new equation (called a 'production function') becomes:

$$Y = f(K, L, E).$$

The neoclassical growth picture is this: labor supply L is assumed to grow over time due to natural population growth. Being an input to the production function, this labor growth increases output over time. Labor is, in fact, the primary engine of this growth.

But an equally necessary input to that growth is capital, both capital for growth and capital for replacement. As we shall see, energy, too, is a necessary input to that output growth. But let us begin with capital.

In the theory, new supply of capital (that is, 'investment') comes from setting aside some of the output created and putting it back into new production capacity, new physical capital assets, instead of just consuming it all. This is assumed to occur via consumers 'saving' some of their income and putting it into investment instead of consumption. In its simplest form, the amount of output consumers so save is depicted as follows:

$$I = sY,$$

where I is the amount set aside for investing in new (and replacement) capital, and s is consumers' 'savings rate'. The new amount of capital input to production of output Y is the old amount of capital plus this new investment:

$$K_{New} = K_{Old} + I,$$

where K_{Old} has had subtracted from it capital that needs replacing.

Solow showed that this simple set of assumptions leads to an interesting and remarkable dynamic. That is, for any suitably 'regular' functional form f, if labor grows at the rate r, output and capital will also grow at this rate (provided that producers maximize profits). Further, if the prices of other inputs such as energy are assumed fixed, they, too, will grow at this same rate. The rate r is independent of the savings rate s, although the level of output at any point depends on s. Two further consequences of the Solow growth model are that the rate of return to capital equals r in equilibrium and wages remain fixed. Additionally, consumption per worker (consumption being that portion of output that is not saved), which is neoclassical growth theory's natural measure of economic welfare, remains fixed, in alignment with wages remaining fixed.

So everything is aligned: output, all the inputs, and consumption grow together at the fixed rate r. Capital return is fixed at r and wages are fixed as well. From this, we can also see that the E/Y ratio remains fixed for all time, since all inputs, including energy, grow at the same rate as output.

But now we need to re-do our static analysis to see what happens if energy price changes, and if new energy efficiency technology is introduced.

Time dynamics with existing technology
We first focus on the first question. It is easiest to begin by assuming that there is a one-time increase in energy price (say, because of a universally adopted carbon tax) and ask what happens to the E/Y ratio when this occurs. The result is depicted in Figure 8.5. We see that the E/Y ratio declines to some fixed value. This will be the ratio corresponding to the values of E and Y from Figure 8.1, resulting from a leftward movement along that figure's curve due to an energy price rise, as discussed previously. However, we see that the decline to this equilibrium E/Y ratio does not occur all at once even though the price rise is instantaneous. The reason is rigidity of capital. Recall that movement along the Figure 8.1 curve is accompanied by substitution – points on this curve represent different 're-assemblies' of the inputs given existing technology, but it takes time for the inputs to

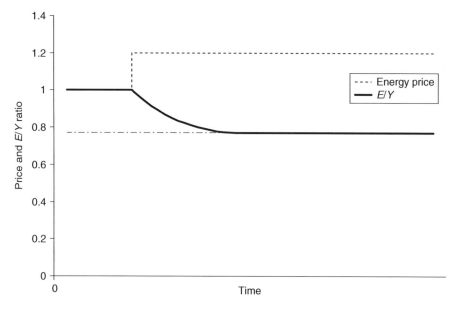

Figure 8.5   Time dynamic of the E/Y *ratio with an energy price increase*

be disassembled and reassembled according to the possibilities represented by the function f.

In particular, it takes time for the capital stock to turn over, for new capital to replace old capital in place as it deteriorates or 'depreciates' out of the economy. Until this happens, there will be capital in place that requires relatively fixed combinations of the inputs, so the efficiency gain will not be fully realized until this capital is displaced. Figure 8.1, recall, represents two 'snapshots' in time reflecting equilibrium combinations of the inputs. So even though the quantity of capital input may be the same in the two static equilibria, the capital in each case will be configured differently with respect to the quantity of energy each requires. The new equilibrium condition will reflect, in other words, a certain substitution of capital for energy, depending on both the ease of substitution and the size of the energy price increase.

To depict the resulting time dynamic for energy use, we need additionally to know how Y changes. This is shown in Figure 8.6. We can see that there is a reduction in real output Y, but its long-term growth rate does not change.

The resulting time dynamic of energy use is simply the multiplicative combination of E/Y with Y ($E \equiv (E/Y)\,Y$), and is shown in Figure 8.7. So, we see that a one-time increase in energy price does not alter the long-term energy demand growth rate. (The path of energy demand is not precisely parallel to the path that would occur in the absence of the energy price increase, but the growth rate is the same.)

One surprise arising from this result is that any fixed energy price over time is fundamentally problematic. The inability of a one-time energy price increase to alter at all the underlying long-term energy demand growth rate has a rather profound consequence. In a global economy reliant on an exhaustible energy supply, energy price must inevitably rise over time if demand is to match that supply – unless and

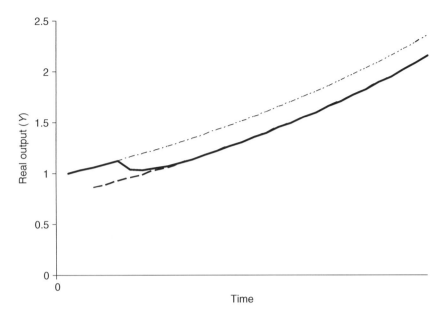

Figure 8.6   Time dynamic of real output Y *with an energy price increase*

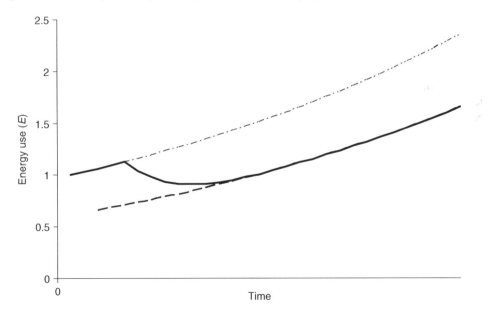

Figure 8.7   Time dynamic of energy use E *with an energy price increase*

until, of course, renewable resources are developed that economically fill the gap. Further, as we have seen, rising energy price reduces output, or economic activity. So the neoclassical growth model would say that failure to find such non-exhaustible supply has a direct and consequential economic disbenefit to the global economy.

The common presumption of economists is that when price rises enough, such supply will be economically forthcoming; but if that price is high, output will have suffered accordingly.

The conclusions: one-time energy price increases eventually lead to a reduced and stable E/Y ratio conforming to that of our previous 'comparative statics' description. They also lead to a reduction in real output Y and energy use E. However, the long-term growth *rate* of both Y and E is unaltered by a one-time energy price increase. The time dynamic of reaching this long-term equilibrium depends on the rate of turnover in capital stock.

Time dynamics with new technology

All this presumes existing technology, and specifically that no improvement in energy efficiency is forthcoming. So we have to ask how this picture changes given new energy efficiency technology. We can refer to Figures 8.3 and 8.4 to see the possible long-term equilibrium changes in E/Y and Y given a one-time improvement in energy efficiency. Figure 8.8 shows some of these possibilities. Unlike the case with an energy price increase, the evolution of the E/Y ratio in response to a one-time increase in energy efficiency is not an automatic decrease. For all the reasons discussed in connection with Figure 8.4, the long-term equilibrium E/Y ratio can be higher or lower than without the technology gain. Also, the change in the level of Y (although not its growth rate) can be larger or smaller.

The resulting time dynamic of energy use is shown in Figure 8.9. Here we see several possible time paths for energy use depending on the degree of rebound, which, as we have seen in the static cases, can range from super-conservation to backfire, and depends on the ease of substitution among inputs. As with an energy price increase, a one-time energy efficiency technology gain does not alter the long-term growth rate of energy demand.

If the energy efficiency gain increases real output Y, there will also be an increase in the wage rate and consumption per worker.

However, continuing technology improvements can change the story. If substitution is difficult and rebound is accordingly small, continuing improvements can result in a sustained reduction in energy use, depending on how the rate of technology improvement compares with the underlying growth of labor input. In contrast, if substitution is easy and rebound is large enough to cause backfire, continuing technology improvements will result in an increased growth rate of energy use.

This has obvious implications for global warming policy. If substitution is easy, a carbon tax or its equivalent will come at relatively small cost to economic output and will have a relatively larger effect on reducing energy use, as we have already seen. But, ironically, if substitution is easy, ongoing improvements in energy efficiency will cause relatively large rebound and could even increase the energy use growth rate.

The conclusions: a one-time improvement in energy efficiency technology can either reduce or increase energy use, but will not alter its underlying long-term growth rate. Such an improvement does increase economic welfare, ignoring 'external' costs of emissions. A continuing improvement in energy efficiency can either stabilize/reduce energy use or increase its growth rate. Once again, the time dynamic of reaching this long-term equilibrium depends on the rate of turnover in capital stock.

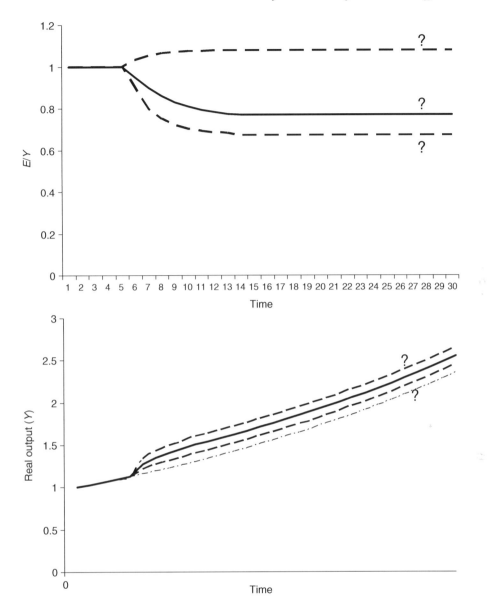

Figure 8.8 Time dynamic of the E/Y ratio and real output Y with an energy efficiency technology gain

Further reading on this section

The modern theory of neoclassical growth was developed by Solow (1956). This contribution earned him a Nobel Prize. A general mathematical development of rebound and neoclassical growth theory is Sorrell and Dimitropoulos (2007). For more detail on the economic effects of a one-time energy price increase, see Saunders (1984a).

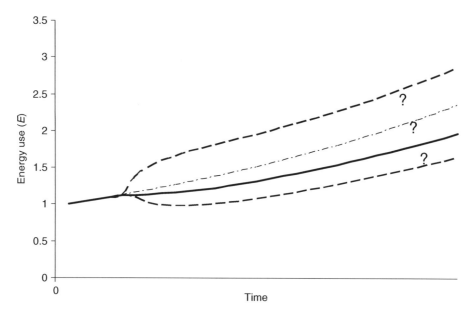

Figure 8.9   Time dynamic of energy use E *with an energy efficiency technology gain*

Demonstration that a one-time energy price increase does not alter energy demand growth rate can be found in Saunders (1984b). For a discussion of rebound effects within neoclassical growth theory, see Saunders (1992). This source also delineates the importance for rebound of the elasticity of substitution and the role of efficiency gains for non-energy inputs.

5   A Dual View

So far we have told the rebound story from the perspective of producers in the economy. Thus, we have seemed to ignore the role of consumers. For many, intuition is better served by considering the consumption side of the equation, which is, after all, what drives producers' actions. But to tell the story from the consumers' side, we first have to build a bridge. Since consumer choice is driven by the relative prices of the goods and services provided by producers, the bridge must allow us to speak in terms of the prices of various outputs from production processes. It is easiest to begin by retaining our assumption of a single output; later we relax this assumption.

In fact, economic theory provides two distinctly different but exactly equivalent ways of looking at the production process. That is, the description we have given so far can be replaced by an equivalent (or what is called a 'dual') description of everything we have discussed but cast in terms of costs, prices, and income.

The core of this 'dual' approach involves describing what has gone before using a 'cost function' instead of a production function. So in place of the production function we have been using, we introduce a function to characterize the price of economic output Y:

$$c = g(p_R, p_E).$$

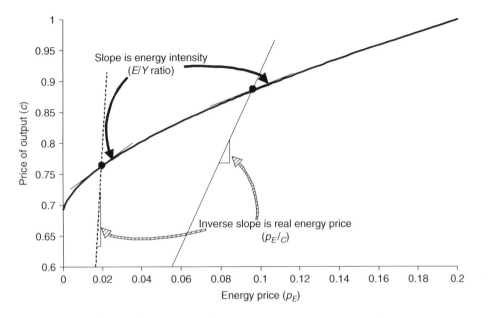

Figure 8.10   Dual view of Figure 8.1 (output price versus energy price)

For our single output economy, c is the cost to produce this output good, or GDP bundle, if you wish. More specifically, it is the unit cost of the last or 'marginal' unit of production and so is equal to the price paid for it by consumers in a competitive economy. The cost to produce this marginal unit depends, as indicated in the equation, on the prices of the inputs to production (here shown as p_E, the price of energy, and p_R, the price of the other inputs, which we have aggregated together as before to temporarily simplify things).

It can be shown that the function f from before is 'dual' to the function g. That is, if one chooses a functional form for f, there is then some function g that completely mimics the economic behavior of f. More specifically, if one somehow measures the parameters of f, the parameters of g are automatically determined (and vice versa); and any analysis one does using the functional form g will deliver the same results as if one had used f. To illustrate, let us recreate Figure 8.1 from this new, dual perspective.

Figure 8.10 contains all the same information as Figure 8.1, but is based on a plot of output price (cost of producing the marginal increment of Y) against energy price. The slope of this cost curve corresponds to the E/Y ratio, and the inverse slope of a line drawn from the origin to any point is the ratio of energy price to the price of output. This latter ratio is referred to as the 'real' price of energy (energy price relative to the total cost of a GDP 'bundle'). By comparison, in Figure 8.1 the slope of the curve was the real energy price and the slope of a line drawn from the origin to any point was the E/Y ratio. Here, if the cost function g is the 'dual' of the production function f used in Figure 8.1, the values of the E/Y ratio and real energy prices will all be numerically identical.

To illustrate, we see in Figure 8.10 that an increase in energy price rotates the straight line rightward and increases output price. We see that a consequence of this rotation is that the energy intensity, the E/Y ratio (the slope of the curve), will go down as expected.

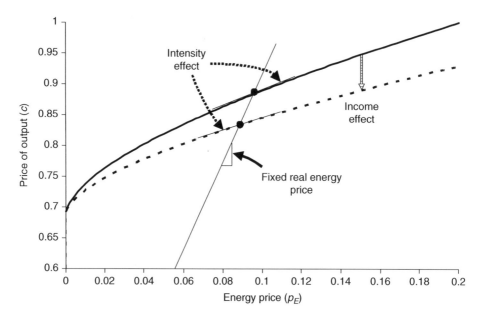

Figure 8.11   Dual view of Figure 8.3 (effect of a new energy efficiency technology)

The equivalent of Figure 8.2 can also be created and again, the results will match exactly: if E is reduced, greater ease of substitution will result in less loss of output; and a given real energy price increase will reduce the E/Y ratio more than if substitution is hard.

Similarly, Figure 8.3 has a counterpart, but in this case it is instructive to look at it explicitly. But for completeness in the comparison to what has gone before, we need to know that energy efficiency gains are equivalently introduced into the dual cost function as follows:

$$c = g\left(p_R, \frac{p_E}{\tau}\right).$$

Application of this approach gives us Figure 8.11, the counterpart to Figure 8.3. The top curve in Figure 8.11 is the same curve as that of Figure 8.10 where we have set $\tau = 1$. The bottom curve reflects the situation where energy efficiency is increased ($\tau > 1$). We see for this particular production/cost function that energy intensity is reduced (the slope of the curve goes down) when we increase energy efficiency τ if real energy price stays constant (that is, the equilibrium will lie on the straight line through the origin depicting fixed real energy price). But unlike in Figure 8.3, here we see that the energy efficiency gain reduces the overall cost of output for every energy price.

This builds our bridge to the consumption side: if the technology gain reduces the output price, common sense says that consumers' income will allow them to purchase more output (shown in the figure as the 'income effect'). Thus, this dual view tells us something new, or at least not obvious. What is now needed is a way to relate output and income more directly.

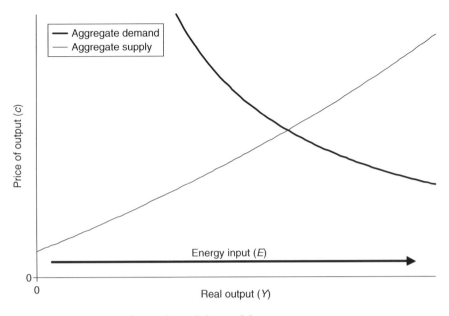

Figure 8.12   Economy-wide supply and demand for output

Further reading on this section
An excellent starting point for understanding the duality between production and cost functions is Diewert (1982). Proof that energy-augmenting technology gains can be introduced to the dual cost function as in the equation above (for constant returns to scale functions) can be found in Saunders (2005).

6   Output versus Income

Knowing now that the c of Figures 8.10 and 8.11 is the price consumers pay for the output Y created by producers shown in Figures 8.1–4, we can use this knowledge to relate output to income.

A standard way to look at the relationship between output and income at the economy-wide level is to revert to the depiction of supply/demand curves familiar to many from microeconomics. In the economy-wide world, these curves are called 'aggregate supply' and 'aggregate demand' curves. Figure 8.12 shows what this looks like. The aggregate supply curve depicts the set of possible combinations of Y and c for given levels of inputs. In fact, there will be a whole family of supply curves corresponding to different ratios of inputs (or, equivalently, different ratios of input prices). But for any input combination, there will be a unique combination of Y and c, as we have seen from the 'duality' of Figures 8.1 and 8.10. The particular aggregate supply curve shown is only an example, but it allows us to illustrate how output and income can be related. Usually this curve is shown as upwardly sloped, indicating that the production process is what is called 'diminishing returns to scale'. But whatever its exact shape, the effects we describe below will have the same character.

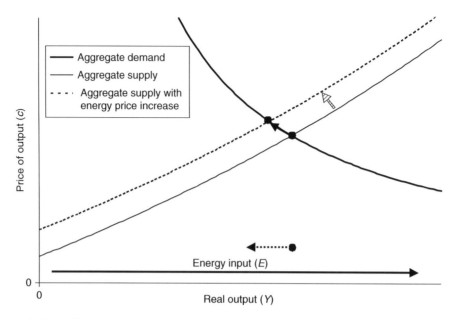

Figure 8.13   Effect of an energy price increase

The aggregate demand curve is a curve of constant income. Income is simply the product cY, since Y is the total product produced in the economy (and therefore the total product demanded in the economy) and c is the price paid for one unit of Y. Of course, the total product demanded is distributed between consumption and investment (we are ignoring government consumption). Naturally, if income increases (if the aggregate demand curve shifts rightward), more output can be profitably produced, although the price of that output will go up. A technical note that nonetheless has bearing on our discussion: when we speak of 'constant income' we are really speaking of what economists will call constant 'nominal' income; clearly for points farther right on the constant nominal income curve, consumers benefit from a higher level of real economic output, if it can be profitably supplied. The economic terminology would have it that points farther right on the curve, while always reflecting a constant nominal income, correspond to a higher 'real' income, which must, in fact always equal 'real' output in any equilibrium condition.

In this combined picture of income and output, we can see the results of an increase in energy price and an increase in energy efficiency, both of which we have examined before.

An increase in energy price shifts the aggregate supply curve upward and leftward, because it decreases profitable output possibilities (as we saw in Figure 8.1) and increases the associated output prices (as we saw in Figure 8.10.) This is shown in Figure 8.13. With fixed nominal income, we see that the energy price increase shifts the equilibrium: it reduces real output, reduces energy input, and increases the price of output – all effects we have seen before, but now visible on one figure.

With an improvement in energy efficiency, again the story is what we have seen. This is shown in Figure 8.14. An energy efficiency increase shifts the aggregate supply curve rightward and downward, because it increases output possibilities (Figure 8.3) and

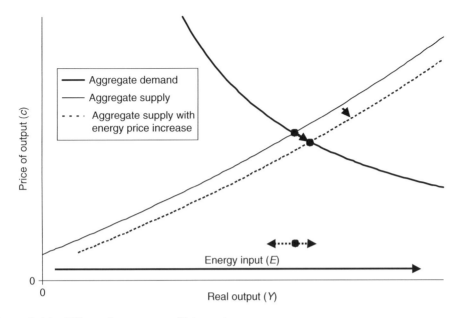

Figure 8.14   Effect of an energy efficiency increase

decreases the associated output price (Figure 8.11). We see that the result, given fixed nominal income, is an increase in real output (and real income) and also a reduction in the price of output. (A terminology note: for this economy-wide picture where we are thinking of the output as GDP 'bundles', economists sometimes refer to the price of output, c, as the 'GDP deflator'.) Finally, we see that this energy efficiency improvement has an uncertain effect on energy use, for all the reasons discussed previously.

So we can now draw some conclusions. We can combine the so-called 'primal' picture of energy and the economy, with its reliance on physical quantities of Y and E, with its equivalent dual picture that relies on costs and prices, to create an aggregate supply/aggregate demand picture for an economy considered to be producing a single output that we can think of as a GDP bundle of goods and services. In this world, an energy price increase reduces real output and real income, increases the price of output, and reduces energy use; in contrast, an energy efficiency improvement increases real output and real income, reduces the price of output, and can either increase or decrease energy use, depending largely on the ease with which other inputs to production can be substituted for energy.

7   Multiple Products and Consumer Preferences

To this point we have relied on one glaringly simplistic assumption: there is only one good/service produced in one giant, global economy and consumers treat this 'GDP bundle' as if it carried a single price. This assumption has been necessary to lay the economic foundation and get us to a point where we understand the fundamentals of energy–economy interactions. But clearly if we hope to make the theory remotely practical, we need to bring it at least one step closer to reality by considering more than one good/service.

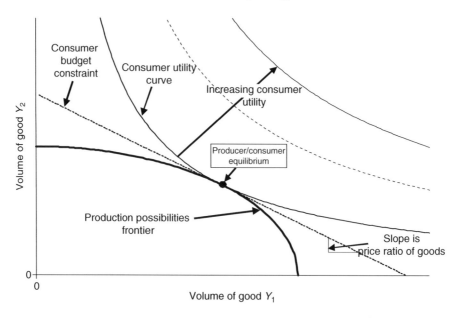

Figure 8.15   Producer/consumer equilibrium with two goods

Economic theory allows this, and the picture it paints is quite comprehensible. We begin by considering only two goods/services. (The extension to multiple goods/services is highly intuitive, once the principles are understood.)

We first look at the problem from the consumer side. The intuition is that a consumer faces a choice in selecting the amount of good/service 1 (call it good Y_1) he/she will buy relative to the amount of good/service 2 (call it good Y_2) he/she will buy. The total amount of both goods he/she will buy is constrained by his/her budget (his/her income). We can imagine that this choice will depend on the prices of the two goods. As we have seen, or at least can intuit, the prices of these goods will depend in part on the production possibilities represented in the function f, or as we now would depict it, the production possibilities represented in some new function f' that accommodates two outputs instead of one. But the prices will also depend on how much of each type of good consumers want – or more explicitly, on how consumers will trade off the benefits they see of one versus the other. Economists depict this trade-off according to what is called a 'utility curve'. Typically, the combination of production possibilities and consumer preferences is depicted in Figure 8.15. It is important to know that economic theory allows the aggregation of multiple producers and multiple consumers to generate a picture that looks in the aggregate like Figure 8.15. Another piece of information providing context is that often practitioners consider the goods Y_1 and Y_2 to be aggregated outputs from individual sectors of the economy, or simply, 'products'.

Figure 8.15 is noisy and contains a lot of information. But it is not as intimidating as it first appears. It shows, first, a production possibilities frontier – the result of our new function f' that now considers the trade-offs made by producers in the economy between production of product Y_1 and product Y_2 given a particular 'endowment' of the inputs E and R. In this particular depiction we see that if more inputs are allocated to product

Y_1 we will get more of it than if we allocate these same inputs to product Y_2. But what determines the actual realized quantities of the two products (the point indicated as the 'producer/consumer equilibrium') is consumer preferences.

Each consumer utility curve shows the combinations of the two products that would result in consumers realizing a fixed level of satisfaction, or 'utility'. The shaded utility curves to the upper right illustrate that consumers would prefer more of both to less of both. But their income – their budget – constrains how much of each they can afford. How much of each product they can afford depends on the prices of the products, of course. Consumers interact with producers to 'negotiate' these prices. But economic theory reveals that there will be an equilibrium point whereby the amount of each product produced and consumed is both on the production possibilities frontier and on a consumer utility curve that maximizes consumer satisfaction (utility), given what consumers can afford. A tangent line drawn through the point where these two curves 'kiss' each other will both be a feasible point, budget-wise, and will determine the relative prices of the two products. Specifically, the slope of this budget line will be the price ratio.

If we cast Figure 8.15 in terms of the dual view we have seen previously, absolute prices of the two products will be determined at an equilibrium point and ratios of the output quantities will be determined from a corresponding budget line. But the equilibrium point itself is the same point, whether viewed from the primal or dual side. So the equilibrium point is complete in specifying the quantities and prices of the two products. Extending the analysis to more than two products is a straightforward mathematical generalization to higher dimensions, and gives results that the reader might correctly guess to be fundamentally no different from the two-products case.

The equilibrium point so determined leads us at long last to the insights about energy consumption that we are seeking. Hearkening back to our depiction of the single output situation, we see that for each product we have determined a quantity of output that will be produced given consumer preferences. Thus we have implicitly determined the amount of energy input each product requires (glance back at Figure 8.1). The important point is this: even if, as will generally be the case, each product requires a different amount of energy input to produce that specific quantity of output (that is, each has a different E/Y ratio), the total energy used in this two-product 'economy' will be the sum of the two. And it has now by this methodology been determined, given full consideration of multiple products and consumer preferences.

The purpose of going through all this pain can now be made apparent. That is, we can now show how changes in consumer preferences can affect energy use and rebound. We can also show the effects, as before, of an energy price increase and an increase in energy efficiency.

Shifting consumer preferences

A change in consumer preferences is illustrated in Figure 8.16. We see that a shift in the consumers' utility curve shifts the equilibrium point (and also changes the relative price ratio). We could imagine this change occurring because consumers on the whole suddenly would rather, say, spend their budgets on more vacation travel than larger televisions. It is important to note that the shift reflects an underlying change in inherent preferences, not simply a response to changed prices of the products – response to price changes is already reflected in any fixed utility curve.

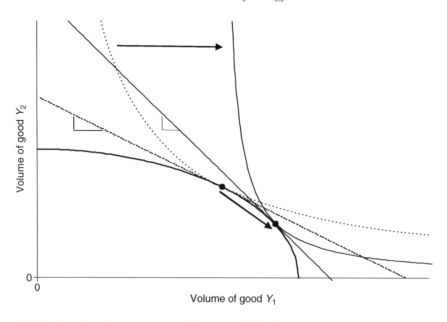

Figure 8.16   Producer/consumer equilibrium with shifting preferences

From the fact that the new equilibrium point has a different ratio of products produced and consumed, we can see that energy used in the production of those products will likely change also. Note that such a shift in consumer preferences can cause energy use to either increase or decrease since different products will in general require different quantities of energy to produce.

All of this affects rebound phenomena, as will become more apparent below.

A final clarifying note: to tie this back to the discussion of neoclassical growth theory, it needs to be understood that 'consumption' as we have used the term in this section is actually a combination of consumption and investment. The output produced is to be used not only for consumption by consumers, but also for investment to create new means of production. Consumers, in their utility curves, will want to take some of this output and deploy goods and services (indirectly by their savings that go to ownership as shareholders in firms – about which more later in Section 8) toward this end. So the utility curves reflect their 'proxy' consumption of goods and services for this investment end.

Energy price increase
The effect of an increase in energy price is illustrated in Figure 8.17. If consumer preferences stay the same but energy price rises, the space of profitable production possibilities shrinks. This can be seen by looking back at Figure 8.1, where the slope of the curve must match the real energy price: points on the curve to the right of the point where the slope equals the prevailing energy price represent unprofitable production; if energy price increases, maximum profitable output shifts leftward. In fact, looking back to Figure 8.13 we see both production and consumption shrink. In Figure 8.13, consumption is reduced because real income is reduced (although nominal income is fixed, it buys less real output

Figure 8.17   Producer/consumer equilibrium with increased energy price

since the price of that output has gone up). This means that the overall consumer budget is lower, so in Figure 8.17 consumers can achieve a lower utility. The new equilibrium point, we see, corresponds to lower levels of output and consumption of both products.

But the energy price increase may not affect output of the products equally. As illustrated, the space of profitable production possibilities for product Y_2 may be reduced more than for product Y_1. Recalling Figure 8.1, this depends in large measure on the ease with which producers can substitute other inputs for energy. The equilibrium point will be determined by these newly restricted production possibilities when combined with consumer preferences. (Note that in contrast to the shifting preferences case of Figure 8.16, consumers' underlying preferences have not changed here even though they select a new combination of products; they are simply responding to new price signals triggered when an energy price rise differentially affects the output prices of the two products.)

At this new equilibrium, energy use will go down, but how much depends on how much of each product is produced/consumed and on each product's energy intensity at that equilibrium point.

To summarize: with unchanged consumer preferences an energy price increase will reduce energy consumption (and economic activity), but the magnitude of this energy use reduction will depend on the relative input substitution potentials available to producers of different goods and services, and also on the exact structure of consumer preferences among those goods and services.

Energy efficiency gain
We are now in a position to take all of this and integrate it into the rebound story. The effect of an increase in energy efficiency is illustrated in Figure 8.18. If consumer preferences stay the same but energy efficiency increases, the space of profitable production

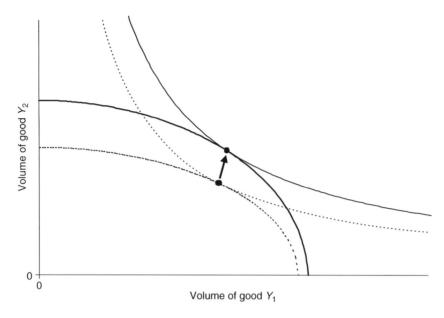

Figure 8.18   Producer/consumer equilibrium with energy efficiency gain

possibilities increases, as we saw in Figure 8.3. Further, looking back at Figure 8.14 we see that both production and consumption are expanded.

With two products, an energy efficiency gain may affect the products differently. Figure 8.18 illustrates the case where energy efficiency gains differentially favor product Y_2 in terms of production possibilities, but we can see that it could go either way. The resulting energy use, which is what we care about, will depend on how the output and intensity effects of the efficiency gain play out for each product. On the production side, this is determined in large part by the input substitution potential available in the production of each product, as we have seen (see Figures 8.3 and 8.4 and associated discussion).

So what we have is this: the degree of energy consumption rebound due to energy efficiency gains for different products (or we can think of different sectors) will depend on the size of the efficiency gain for each, the degree to which their associated production processes permit substitution of other inputs for energy, and the nature of consumer preferences for each product. Further, rebound can change if underlying consumer preferences change. Understanding or predicting the net result requires knowledge of all these features. (However, strong intuition can be gained by adopting some simplifying assumptions – see Box 8.2)

8   General Equilibrium

We can now dispose of the final assumptions that the astute reader will have found to be troublesome and disturbingly simplistic. In the 'comparative statics' sections, we have invoked assumptions about the supply of inputs to production that clearly do not obtain in reality. Specifically, we have in these sections assumed the supply of non-energy inputs, R, to be fixed. While in the 'time dynamics' sections that rely on neoclassical

BOX 8.2   SIMPLIFYING ASSUMPTIONS THAT AID
INTERPRETATION OF FIGURE 8.18

If one is willing to adopt a simple, but often useful picture of consumer preferences and production possibilities, it becomes surprisingly straightforward to
predict or at least visualize rebound results in the multiple-product world we
have presented. Specifically, on the production side, we assume 'constant
returns to scale' production. This simply means that if one doubles all the
inputs to this type of function, output also doubles. With this type of function any
improvement in efficiency has the same effect on output as it does on output
price – if the efficiency gain increases output by x percent, the output price will
decrease by x percent.

On the consumption side, there is a widely used description of consumer
preferences called a Cobb–Douglas utility function, described mathematically
as:

$$u = y_1^{\alpha 1} \, y_2^{\alpha 2} \cdots y_i^{\alpha i} \cdots y_n^{\alpha n},$$

where the y_i are the quantities of products consumed that delivers a total
utility u to consumers (we can see many combinations of the various y_i can
lead to the same utility u). In this description of consumer preferences, it can
be shown that if the price of product y_i is reduced by x percent, the quantity of that product demanded by consumers will increase by x percent. So
this description of consumer preferences exactly matches the price/quantity
dynamic on the production side. That is, one can assume any size efficiency
gain in the production of any of the products/sectors and the resulting pro-
ducer/consumer equilibrium will shift in a highly predictable way – each
product/sector's output/consumption will increase exactly the same amount
as if it were considered in isolation from other products/sectors. This means
that one can, with these assumptions, consider each product/sector's production function independently as regards energy efficiency gains, without
worrying that consumer preferences will shift demand toward or away from it.
Practitioners can invoke this mental model to understand the source of sectoral shifts that depart from this behavior either in real-world data or in models
they create. Of course, they will have to relax these assumptions to get the
true picture of reality. But reality will be much easier to comprehend against
this background.

growth theory these assumptions have been somewhat relaxed, we have gingerly glossed
over the fact that in reality the inputs to production themselves will be strongly subject
to competitive market forces and will hardly be fixed.

Ideally, we would like a framework that simultaneously considers market forces
that efficiently allocate inputs to production, treats the outputs from that production

according to a logical set of production possibilities, and accommodates the preferences of consumers for choosing which outputs they would like to consume given their budgets.

Fortunately, economic theory provides us with such a framework. In perhaps what is the most substantial accomplishment in the theory of economics in the past many decades (which earned its main developer, Gerard Debreu, the Nobel Prize), this goal has been achieved.

This framework is called 'general equilibrium theory'. The theory rests entirely on a set of assumptions that most would deem common sense, and the theory conclusively demonstrates that the result of honoring these assumptions will always be an equilibrium condition where consumers maximize their satisfaction (utility) and competitive producers maximize their profits, leading to what is called maximum 'economic welfare' for the economy.

This condition corresponds to a situation where individuals freely choose the amount of labor they will contribute as against their desire for leisure time. Accordingly, like neoclassical growth theory, the primary driver of economic equilibrium is labor supply.

But beyond this, in general equilibrium theory, individuals contribute both labor and *capital* to the production of economic output. It is important to realize that general equilibrium theory rests on the notion of a 'private ownership' economy, also called an 'Arrow–Debreu' economy in recognition of the contributions to the theory made by Kenneth Arrow (also a Nobel Prize winner). Individuals not only have command over the labor they contribute to the economy but, via their savings/investments, own the means of production. Remarkably, this leads naturally to a situation of maximum economic welfare.

To tie this to what has gone before and to set the stage for discussing rebound in this most general of economic settings, we first note that consumers' utility functions will now include preferences regarding another 'good', namely leisure. (Note also that consumers will treat some energy consumed as end-use 'goods', as in automobile transportation and home heating.) The trade-off that consumers make between leisure and other goods determines the supply of labor. For any producer, inputs to production are this labor and outputs from other producers. Additionally, the theory allows producers to 'store' outputs from other producers rather than consume them, most particularly in the form of physical capital – plant and equipment – used for production. This depiction of inputs is what fundamentally 'closes' the system and obviates the need to assume fixed supplies of inputs to production, such as we have done in previous sections.

For rebound theory, this has certain consequences. To visualize what happens when new energy efficiency technology is introduced, one must simultaneously consider all the effects we have so far discussed and changes that may affect the use of inputs in the production of any product. One change we have not discussed is what happens to the prices of the inputs we have lumped together in the variable R. As in the time dynamics section, it is adequate for the discussion here to split this into two inputs, capital K and labor L.

In general, an increase in energy efficiency will increase the marginal productivity (the amount of output gained by increasing the input a little bit) of both these inputs. As we have seen with energy, producers maximize profits when this marginal productivity equals the price of the input. If we for the moment consider a product/sector in isolation and assume that the economy-wide input prices stay fixed, this increase in marginal productivity will draw in more of both these inputs until marginal productivity is reduced to its previous level (look at Figure 8.1 and think of the *x*-axis as capital or labor input instead of energy). As this happens, output will also go up; and as output goes up, as we have seen, it drags energy use up. So in this world of an isolated product/sector, allowing inputs to not be fixed would seem to increase rebound.

It is of course subtler than this in reality. Producers of different products/(in different sectors) will compete for these inputs, and the supply of them will be limited. Those with greater potential to use them profitably will have an advantage. These will be producers for whom an energy efficiency gain most increases marginal productivity (prior to reestablishing balance). The consequences for rebound will therefore depend on whether these advantaged products/sectors have greater or lesser rebound propensity, based on the analysis we have seen before.

So the situation is this: the degree of energy consumption rebound due to energy efficiency gains for different products/sectors will depend on the size of the efficiency gain for each, the degree to which their associated production processes permit substitution of other inputs for energy, the nature of consumer preferences for each product, and now, the degree to which increases in inputs create profitable opportunities for producers of each product/in each sector.

This is too much for the average person to keep in their head. So researchers fall back on quantitative models. Practitioners use so-called 'computable general equilibrium' (CGE) models to take account of all these various forces and to calculate economic equilibria. For the application to real-world economies they will ideally use measured production/cost functions and measured consumer utility functions (or demand functions derived from these). This measurement issue is our final topic and we turn to it now.

In a world where the 'swing' supply of energy is in the hands of non-competitive oil producers, account must be taken of energy pricing that deviates from that which would be seen under perfect competition. This additional challenge needs to be considered when we are seeking to understand rebound effects qualitatively.

Further reading on this section
The theoretical foundations of general equilibrium are found in Debreu (1952, 1959) and Arrow and Hahn (1971). Applications of general equilibrium theory to the study of rebound are Doufournaud et al. (1993), Grepperud and Rassmussen (2004), Washida (2004) and Glomsrød and Wei (2005). Hanley et al. (2006). provide an analysis that highlights what they call the 'open economy' rebound effect, which arises when an economy's energy consumption accounts for the production of goods and services for export. Wei (2006) shows how theoretical predictions of rebound are altered when general equilibrium considerations are introduced.

9 Measuring Rebound

To be of practical value, the theory of rebound must allow and indeed enable both prediction and the understanding of historical evidence. This requires measurement. Measurement of rebound is still in its infancy. Sorrell, in Chapter 9 in this volume, speaks to the evidence for rebound in the real world. As will be seen there, it is not presently known the degree to which rebound occurs in reality or can be expected to in the

194 International handbook on the economics of energy

future. But learning this presents an urgent task for economists. Accordingly, we here outline some of what will be required to effectively link theory to measurement.

As will be evident to the long-suffering reader who has endured our painfully vague and abstract definitions of the functions f and g, actual functional forms will have to be invoked if real measurement is to take place.

Economists have many candidates for these functions. Such functions must, in the eyes of the economist, satisfy certain so-called 'regularity conditions', such as if you put more input into it the function should produce more output. And as you try to favor one input over others, the harder and harder it should become to produce gains in output. There are other such conditions, but it is possible to produce many functions that behave according to all the common-sense requirements of the economist.

In fact, not all these functional forms are suitable for analyzing rebound, being not 'rebound flexible'. But there are a few, and a particular breed of economist, called econometricians, is developing the means to measure these from historical data. One challenge in this is finding forms that are both rebound flexible and readily accommodate sensible depictions of energy efficiency gains that are easily measurable. But the task is engaged, and economists will find elegant ways to do this.

A comparable task is to find suitable functional forms on the consumer side. Again, such forms must, for the economist, satisfy certain common-sense conditions and be readily measurable.

A further challenge will be the data. For some economies the necessary data are readily available; for others they are not. Since global warming is, after all, global, paucity of data for large energy-consuming economies poses a serious problem. Initiatives to gather such data will be critical to developing sound policy that takes account of rebound phenomena.

In the end, it will be general equilibrium modelers, knowledgeable about growth dynamics and in possession of measured production/cost and consumer demand functions based on solid data, who will give us what is needed to understand what the past can tell us and develop sound policy for the future. A number of researchers are already well on the way to this goal.

Further reading on this section
For more on finding rebound-flexible production/cost functions, see Saunders (2008a). For how to specify efficiency gains for inputs beyond just energy, see Saunders (2008b). Saunders (2005) gives a method for predicting rebound, given measured production/cost functions.

10   Cautions and Limitations

Lest any reader be misled into thinking that the theoretical framework presented in this chapter is in any sense complete, we offer the following cautions and limitations:

- We have adopted the standard assumptions of theoretical economists; it is entirely possible to challenge these as descriptors of the real-world economy.
- We have considered only an idealized economy operating under perfectly competitive conditions with no inefficiencies. We have not considered non-competitive agents (for example, OPEC – Organization of the Petroleum Exporting Countries),

nor have we considered any inefficiencies. Some researchers make a strong case that there is much to be gained, energy reduction-wise, by the simple elimination of wastage (activities and behaviors that add no value to anyone).

- We have considered the global economy as a whole – a single, 'closed' economy – and have ignored the effects of trade. Some researchers make the case that rebound for any individual economy can be greatly exaggerated when imports and exports are considered.
- We have considered only energy efficiency gains that are specific to energy. Efficiency technologies that affect other inputs, even if they are targeted at energy, typically will increase rebound.
- We have considered only three inputs to production, capital, labor, and energy. In reality there are others (such as materials).
- We have not considered governments as economic agents. Governments are both producers of goods and services and consumers of them. Furthermore, by their ability to tax, set monetary policy, and affect exchange rates, they have the power to alter the behavior of agents in an otherwise competitive private economy.
- We have treated 'economic welfare' as equivalent to the total output of goods and services without consideration of so-called 'externalities'. Externalities are those things not explicitly priced in the economy. Such externalities might include environmental deterioration or social displacements.
- We have construed 'economic welfare' in a narrow sense that ignores the future economic costs that could arise if, say, global warming brings costs that destroy productive assets or otherwise reduce the potential of the economy to produce output.
- We have not considered any human values related to the distribution of wealth.
- We have not explicitly considered new goods or sectors not imagined today (although once seen, they can be included).

11 Economic Conclusions from the Theory of Rebound

We summarize below the conclusions developed in this chapter based on the economic theory of rebound.

- A reduction in energy input to an economy will reduce economic output/income (economic activity), but not in a one-for-one fashion.
- The reduction in economic output/income from a decrease in energy input depends largely on the ease with which other inputs to production can be substituted for energy: if this substitution is easy, the impact of a reduction in energy input on economic activity will be small; but if it is hard, the impact will be large.
- An energy price increase (such as due to a carbon tax) reduces economic activity (economic welfare, construed narrowly) and reduces energy use.
- An increase in energy efficiency increases economic activity.
- Whether an improvement in energy efficiency reduces or increases energy use, and the degree to which it does so, depends largely on the ease with which other inputs to production can be substituted for energy: if substitution is easy, energy use will be reduced less (rebound) and may even increase (backfire); if substitution is hard, energy use will be reduced more.

- These effects will evolve over time according to the rapidity with which the capital stock is turned over.
- A one-time increase in energy price (as with a one-time carbon tax) does not alter the underlying growth rate of energy use, or of economic activity.
- Accordingly, continual energy price increases (as through continual increases in a carbon tax) are required to alter the growth rate of energy use, but these will reduce the growth rate of economic activity.
- A one-time improvement in energy efficiency does not alter the underlying growth rate of energy use, or of economic activity.
- Whether a one-time improvement in energy efficiency reduces or increases the level of energy use (not its growth rate) depends largely on the ease with which other inputs to production can be substituted for energy.
- Accordingly, if substitution is hard, continual energy efficiency improvements will be needed to restrain energy use; if substitution is easy, continual energy efficiency improvements will make restraining energy use more difficult, since it makes energy use greater than it would have been with hard substitution. If substitution is exceptionally easy (leading to 'backfire'), continual energy efficiency improvements will actually increase the growth rate of energy use.
- In a multi-product (or multi-sector) economy, an increase in energy price can change energy use depending on the change in relative economic production volumes of different products, which depends on a combination of how the production possibilities are affected and on consumer preferences for those products.
- In a multi-product (or multi-sector) economy, an increase in energy efficiency can change energy use in a way depending on the rebound propensity of the production possibilities for each product and on consumer preferences.
- Changes in consumer preferences can change rebound in either direction.
- General equilibrium considerations matter. Inputs to production are themselves subject to competitive forces and this can alter rebound effects. In a general equilibrium world, rebound is determined by the following: the size of the efficiency gain for each good/sector, the degree to which their associated production processes permit substitution of other inputs for energy, the nature of consumer preferences for each good, and the degree to which increases in inputs create profitable opportunities for producers of each good/in each sector.
- Measurement of rebound is in its infancy. But it is a critical task for economists seeking to inform policy decisions.

12   Policy Implications Summarized

The policy implications we here summarize are largely aimed at demand-side global warming remedies. But they also apply to policy initiatives aimed at reducing environmental impacts in general as well as initiatives aimed at reducing dependency on energy imports:

- A carbon tax (or equivalently, a carbon emissions cap) will reduce economic activity and accordingly, economic welfare, narrowly construed.

- The degree of economic impact from such a policy depends largely on the ease with which other inputs can be substituted for energy.
- The effectiveness of a carbon tax in reducing energy use will likewise depend on the ease of substitution.
- A one-time carbon tax will not alter the underlying growth rate of energy use.
- Research and development initiatives aimed at energy efficiency can either reduce or increase energy use, again depending on the ease of substitution among inputs.
- Changes in consumer preferences can alter energy consumption rebound in either direction.
- A uniform carbon tax (or uniformly applied emissions cap) can adversely affect those sectors with greater energy efficiency potential more than those with less. Furthermore, overall economic welfare will likely be harmed more than necessary by a uniform carbon tax if the goal is a specific reduction in energy use.
- Energy consumption rebound will depend on complex interactions among sectors related to their ability to profitably use inputs to production.
- Sound policy must take account of all these considerations.

13 Conclusion

While it is not presently known the degree to which rebound occurs in reality, its potential impact on policy is such that the stakes are significant. In the end, economic theory must always bow to the exacting taskmaster of real-world data. For the current state of empirical research, see Chapter 9 in this handbook. But economic theory is a powerful tool for informing judgment, and the economic forces it purports to describe are powerful as well. It is hoped that this chapter gives the reader a beginning but solid foundation for logically deconstructing and dispassionately judging the issues at stake, which appear to be exceptionally consequential in the case of the global warming debate.

Further reading on this section
An authoritative general reference on production, consumption and general equilibrium is Luenberger (1995).

Note

1. Technically $GDP = Y - p_E E$, where E is energy input and p_E is energy price. This reflects the idea that *GDP* is a value-added measure: by convention, the net value added to the economy by production excludes the cost of natural resource inputs.

References

Arrow, K. and F. Hahn (1971), *General Competitive Analysis*, San Francisco, CA: Holden-Day.
Broadstock, D., L.C. Hunt and S. Sorrell (2007), *Review of Evidence for the Rebound Effect: Technical Report 2 – Elasticity of Substitution Studies*, London: UK Energy Research Centre.
Debreu, G. (1952), 'A social equilibrium existence theorem', *Proceedings of the National Academy of Sciences*, **38**, 886–93.
Debreu, G. (1959), *Theory of Value*, New York: John Wiley & Sons.
Diewert, W. (1982), 'Duality approaches to microeconomic theory', in K. Arrow and M. Intriligator (eds), *Handbook of Mathematical Economics*, vol. II, Amsterdam: North-Holland, pp. 285–330.
Dufournaud, C., J. Quinn and J. Harrington (1993), 'An applied general equilibrium (AGE) analysis of a

policy designed to reduce household consumption of wood in the Sudan', *Resource and Energy Economics*, **16**, 67–90.

Glomsrød, S. and T. Wei (2005), 'Coal cleaning: a viable strategy for reduced carbon emissions and improved environment in China?', *Energy Policy*, **33**, 525–42.

Grepperud, S. and I. Rassmussen (2004), 'A general equilibrium assessment of rebound effects', *Energy Economics*, **26**, 261–82.

Hanley, N., P. McGregor, J. Swales and K. Turner (2006), 'The impact of a stimulus to energy efficiency on the economy and the environment: a regional computable general equilibrium analysis', *Renewable Energy*, **31**, 161–71.

Herring, H. and S. Sorrell (eds) (2008), *Energy Efficiency and Sustainable Consumption: Dealing with the Rebound Effect*, London: Palgrave Macmillan.

Hogan, W. and A. Manne (1977), 'Energy–economy interaction: the fable of the elephant and the rabbit?', in *Energy and the Economy, EMF Report 1 of the Energy Modeling Forum* (Stanford University), available at: http://www.stanford.edu/group/EMF/publications/index.htm (accessed 22 February 2009).

Luenberger, D. (1995), *Microeconomic Theory*, San Francisco, CA: McGraw-Hill.

Saunders, H. (1984a), 'The macrodynamics of energy shocks, short- and long-run', *Energy Economics*, **6** (4), 23–34.

Saunders, H. (1984b), 'On the inevitable return of higher oil prices', *Energy Policy*, **12** (3), 310–20.

Saunders, H. (1992), 'The Khazzoom–Brookes postulate and neoclassical growth', *The Energy Journal*, **13** (4), 131–48.

Saunders, H. (2005), 'A calculator for energy consumption changes arising from new technologies', *Topics in Economic Analysis and Policy*, **5** (1), Article 15, available at: http://www.bepress.com/bejap/topics/vol5/iss1/art15.

Saunders, H. (2008a), 'Fuel conserving (and using) production functions', *Energy Economics*, **30** (5), September, 2184–235.

Saunders, H. (2008b), 'Specifying technology for analyzing rebound', in H. Herring and S. Sorrell (eds), *Energy Efficiency and Sustainable Consumption: Dealing with the Rebound Effect*, London: Palgrave Macmillan.

Schipper, L. (ed.) (2000), *On the Rebound: The Interaction of Energy Efficiency, Energy Use and Economic Activity*, Special Issue of *Energy Policy*, **28** (6–7).

Solow, R. (1956), 'A contribution to the theory of economic growth', *Quarterly Journal of Economics*, **70**, 65–94.

Sorrell, S. (2007), *Review of Evidence for the Rebound Effect: Summary Report*, London: UK Energy Research Centre.

Sorrell, S. and J. Dimitropoulos (2007), *Review of Evidence for the Rebound Effect: Technical Report 5 – Energy Productivity and Economic Growth Studies*, London: UK Energy Research Centre.

Washida, T. (2004), 'Economy-wide model of rebound effect for environmental policy', paper presented at International Workshop on Sustainable Consumption, University of Leeds, 5–6 March 2004.

Wei, T. (2006), 'Impact of energy efficiency gains on output and energy use with Cobb–Douglas production function', *Energy Policy*, **35**, 2023–30.

9 The rebound effect: definition and estimation
*Steve Sorrell**

1 Introduction

To achieve reductions in carbon emissions, most governments are seeking ways to improve energy efficiency throughout the economy. It is generally assumed that such improvements will reduce overall energy consumption, at least compared to a scenario in which such improvements are not made. But a range of mechanisms, commonly grouped under the heading of 'rebound effects' may reduce the size of the 'energy savings' achieved. Indeed, there is some evidence to suggest that the introduction of certain types of energy-efficient technology in the past has contributed to an overall *increase* in energy demand – an outcome that has been termed 'backfire'. This applies in particular to pervasive new technologies, such as steam engines in the nineteenth century, that significantly raise overall economic productivity as well as improving energy efficiency (Alcott, 2005).

These rebound effects could have far-reaching implications for energy and climate policy. While cost-effective improvements in energy efficiency should improve welfare and benefit the economy, they could in some cases provide an ineffective or even a counterproductive means of tackling climate change. However, it does not necessarily follow that *all* improvements in energy efficiency will increase overall energy consumption or in particular that the improvements induced by policy measures will do so.

The nature, operation and importance of rebound effects are the focus of a long-running debate within energy economics. On the micro level, the question is whether improvements in the technical efficiency of energy use can be expected to reduce energy consumption by the amount predicted by simple engineering calculations. For example, will a 20 per cent improvement in the fuel efficiency of passenger cars lead to a corresponding 20 per cent reduction in motor-fuel consumption for personal automotive travel? Simple economic theory suggests that it will not. Since energy efficiency improvements reduce the marginal cost of energy services such as travel, the consumption of those services may be expected to increase. For example, since the cost per kilometre of driving is cheaper, consumers may choose to drive further and/or more often. This increased consumption of energy services may be expected to offset some of the predicted reduction in energy consumption.

This so-called 'direct rebound effect' was first identified by Khazzoom (1980) and has since been the focus of several empirical studies (Greening et al., 2000). But even if there is no direct rebound effect for a particular energy service (even if consumers choose not to drive any further in their fuel-efficient car), there are a number of other reasons why the economy-wide reduction in energy consumption may be less than simple calculations suggest. For example, the money saved on motor-fuel consumption may be spent on other goods and services that also require energy to provide. These so-called 'indirect rebound effects' can take a number of forms that are briefly outlined in Box 9.1. Both

---

BOX 9.1   INDIRECT REBOUND EFFECTS

- The equipment used to improve energy efficiency (for example, thermal insulation) will itself require energy to manufacture and install and this 'embodied' energy consumption will offset some of the energy savings achieved.
- Consumers may use the cost savings from energy efficiency improvements to purchase other goods and services which themselves require energy to provide. For example, the cost savings from a more energy-efficient central heating system may be put towards an overseas holiday.
- Producers may use the cost savings from energy efficiency improvements to increase output, thereby increasing consumption of capital, labour and materials inputs which themselves require energy to provide. If the energy efficiency improvements are sector-wide, they may lead to lower product prices, increased consumption of the relevant products and further increases in energy consumption.
- Cost-effective energy efficiency improvements will increase the overall productivity of the economy, thereby encouraging economic growth. The increased consumption of goods and services may in turn drive up energy consumption.
- Large-scale reductions in energy demand may translate into lower energy prices which will encourage energy consumption to increase. The reduction in energy prices will also increase real income, thereby encouraging investment and generating an extra stimulus to aggregate output and energy use.
- Both the energy efficiency improvements and the associated reductions in energy prices will reduce the cost of energy-intensive goods and services to a greater extent than non-energy-intensive goods and services, thereby encouraging consumer demand to shift towards the former.

---

direct and indirect rebound effects apply equally to energy efficiency improvements by consumers, such as the purchase of a more fuel-efficient car (Figure 9.1), and energy efficiency improvements by producers, such as the adoption of energy-efficient process technology (Figure 9.2).

As shown in Box 9.2, the *overall* or *economy-wide* rebound effect from an energy efficiency improvement represents the sum of these direct and indirect effects. It is normally expressed as a percentage of the *expected* energy savings from an energy efficiency improvement. Hence, a rebound effect of 100 per cent means that the expected energy savings are entirely offset, leading to zero net savings.[1] Backfire means that rebound effects exceed 100 per cent.

Rebound effects need to be defined in relation to a particular *timeframe* (short, medium or long term) and *system boundary* for the relevant energy consumption (household, firm, sector, national economy). The economy-wide effect is normally defined in relation to a national economy, but there may also be effects in other countries through

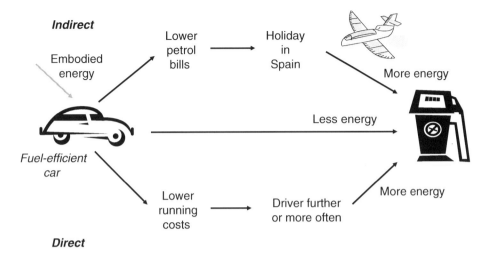

Figure 9.1   Illustration of rebound effects for consumers

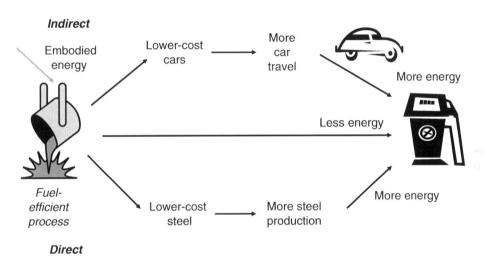

Figure 9.2   Illustration of rebound effects for producers

changes in trade patterns and international energy prices. Rebound effects may also be expected to increase in importance over time as markets, technology and behaviour adjust.

Rebound effects tend to be almost universally ignored in official analyses of the potential energy savings from energy efficiency improvements. A rare exception is UK policy to improve the thermal insulation of housing, where it is expected that some of the benefits will be taken as higher internal temperatures rather than reduced energy consumption (DEFRA, 2007). But the direct rebound effects for other energy efficiency measures are generally ignored, as are the potential indirect effects for all measures. Much the same applies to energy modelling studies and to independent estimates of energy efficiency

BOX 9.2   CLASSIFYING REBOUND EFFECTS

The economy-wide rebound effect represents the sum of the direct and indirect effects. For energy efficiency improvements by consumers, it is helpful to decompose the direct rebound effect into:

a)   a *substitution effect*, whereby consumption of the (cheaper) energy service substitutes for the consumption of other goods and services while maintaining a constant level of 'utility', or consumer satisfaction; and

b)   an *income effect*, whereby the increase in real income achieved by the energy efficiency improvement allows a higher level of utility to be achieved by increasing consumption of all goods and services, including the energy service.

Similarly, the direct rebound effect for producers may be decomposed into:

a)   a *substitution effect*, whereby the cheaper energy service substitutes for the use of capital, labour and materials in producing a constant level of output; and

b)   an *output effect*, whereby the cost savings from the energy efficiency improvement allows a higher level of output to be produced – thereby increasing consumption of all inputs, including the energy service.

It is also helpful to decompose the indirect rebound effect into:

a)   the *embodied energy*, or indirect energy consumption required to *achieve* the energy efficiency improvement, such as the energy required to produce and install thermal insulation; and

b)   the *secondary effects* that result as a *consequence* of the energy efficiency improvement, which include the mechanisms listed in Box 9.1.

A diagrammatic representation of this classification scheme is provided above. The relative size of each effect may vary widely from one circumstance to another and in some cases individual components of the rebound effect may be negative. For example, if an energy service is an 'inferior good', the income effect for consumers may lead to reduced consumption of that service, rather than increased consumption.

potentials. For example, the Stern Review of the economics of climate change overlooks rebound effects altogether (Stern, 2006), while the Fourth Assessment Report from the Intergovernmental Panel on Climate Change simply notes that the literature is divided on the magnitude of the effect (IPCC, 2007).

While energy economists recognise that rebound effects may reduce the energy savings from energy efficiency improvements, there is dispute over how important these effects are. Some argue that rebound effects are of minor importance for most energy services, largely because the demand for those services appears to be inelastic in most cases and because energy typically forms a small share of the total costs of those services (Lovins et al., 1988; Lovins, 1998; Schipper and Grubb, 2000). Others argue that they are sufficiently important to completely offset the energy savings from improved energy efficiency (Brookes, 2000; Herring, 2006). The dispute has a number of origins, including competing definitions of the relevant independent variable for the rebound effect (energy efficiency) and the sparse and ambiguous nature of the empirical evidence (Sorrell, 2007).

The objective of this chapter is to summarise the *quantitative estimates* of direct, indirect and economy-wide rebound effects that are available from a number of sources. The chapter does not discuss the various theoretical and 'indirect' sources of evidence for economy-wide rebound effects, although these form a key component of the arguments in favour of backfire (Brookes, 1984, 1990, 2000, 2004; Saunders, 1992, 2000, 2007; Alcott, 2005). Readers interested in a review of these broader issues should refer instead to Sorrell and Dimitropoulos (2007c) and also to Chapter 8 in the current volume. The chapter is based upon a comprehensive literature review of rebound effects, conducted by the UK Energy Research Centre (Sorrell, 2007). This review sought in particular to clarify the definitional and methodological issues associated with quantifying such effects – an emphasis that is reflected in what follows.

The chapter is structured as follows. Section 2 describes the choices available for the independent and dependent variables for the rebound effect and the possible implications of these choices. Section 3 describes the nature and operation of direct rebound effects, summarises the quantitative estimates that are available from a number of studies and highlights some potential sources of bias. Section 4 describes the nature and operation of indirect and economy-wide rebound effects, summarises the quantitative estimates available from energy modelling studies and highlights some potential methodological weaknesses. Section 5 concludes.

2   Definitional Issues

Energy efficiency improvements are generally assumed to reduce energy consumption below where it would have been without those improvements. Rebound effects reduce the size of these energy savings. However, estimating the size of any 'energy savings' is far from straightforward, since:

- real-world economies do not permit controlled experiments, so the relationship between a change in energy efficiency and a subsequent change in energy consumption is likely to be mediated by a host of confounding variables;
- we cannot observe what energy consumption 'would have been' without the energy efficiency improvement, so the estimated 'savings' will always be uncertain; and
- energy efficiency is not controlled externally by an experimenter and may be influenced by a variety of technical, economic and policy variables. In particular, the direction of causality may run in reverse – with changes in energy consumption (whatever their cause) leading to changes in different measures of energy efficiency.

Energy efficiency may be defined as the ratio of useful outputs to energy inputs for a system. The system in question may be an individual energy conversion device (for example, a boiler), a building, an industrial process, a firm, a sector or an entire economy. In all cases, the measure of energy efficiency will depend upon how 'useful' is defined and how inputs and outputs are measured. The options include:

- *thermodynamic measures*: where the outputs are defined in terms of heat content or the capacity to perform useful work;
- *physical measures*: where the outputs are defined in physical terms, such as vehicle-kilometres or tonnes of steel; or
- *economic measures*: where the outputs are defined in economic terms, such as value added or GDP (economic measures of energy efficiency are frequently referred to as 'energy productivity').

The choice of measures for inputs and outputs, the appropriate system boundaries and the timeframe under consideration can vary widely from one study to another. The conclusions drawn regarding the magnitude and importance of rebound effects will depend upon the particular choices that are made.

Economists are primarily interested in energy efficiency improvements that are consistent with the best use of all economic resources. These are conventionally divided into two categories: those that are associated with improvements in overall, or 'total factor' productivity ('technical change'), and those that are not ('substitution'). The former are usually assumed to occur independently of changes in relative prices, while the latter are assumed to occur in response to such changes. The consequences of technical change are of particular interest, since this contributes to the growth in economic output. However, distinguishing empirically between the two can be challenging.[2]

Many commentators assume that the relevant independent variable for the rebound effect is improvements in the thermodynamic efficiency of individual conversion devices or industrial processes. But such improvements will only translate into comparable improvements in different measures of energy efficiency, or measures of energy efficiency applicable to wider system boundaries, if several of the mechanisms responsible for the rebound effect fail to come into play. For example, improvements in the number of litres used per vehicle-kilometre will only translate into improvements in the number of litres used per passenger-kilometre if there are no associated changes in average vehicle load factors.

Rebound effects may be expected to increase over time and with the widening of the system boundary for the dependent variable (energy consumption). Hence, to capture the full range of rebound effects, the system boundary for the independent variable (energy efficiency) should be relatively narrow, while the system boundary for the dependent variable should be as wide as possible. However, estimating the economy-wide effects of micro-level improvements in the thermodynamic efficiency is, at best, challenging. Partly for this reason, the independent variable for many theoretical and empirical studies of rebound effects is a physical or economic measure of energy efficiency that is applicable to relatively wide system boundaries – such as the energy efficiency of an industrial sector. But such studies may overlook the 'lower-level' rebound effects resulting from improvements in physical or thermodynamic measures of energy efficiency appropriate to narrower system boundaries (for example, the diffusion of energy-efficient motors within the sector).[3] Also, improvements in aggregate measures of energy efficiency are unlikely to be caused solely (or even mainly) by the diffusion of more thermodynamically efficient conversion devices.

Aggregate measures of energy efficiency will also depend upon how different types of energy input are combined. While it is common practice to aggregate different energy types on the basis of their heat content, this neglects the 'thermodynamic quality' of each energy type, or its ability to perform useful work.[4] The latter, in turn, is only one of several factors that determine the economic productivity of different energy types, with others including cleanliness, amenability to storage, safety, flexibility and the use to which the energy is put (Cleveland et al., 2000).[5] In general, when the 'quality' of energy inputs is accounted for, aggregate measures of energy efficiency are found to be improving more slowly than is commonly supposed (Hong, 1983; Zarnikau, 1999; Cleveland et al., 2000).[6]

Improvements in any measure of energy efficiency rarely occur in isolation but are typically associated with broader improvements in the productivity of other inputs. As illustrated in Box 9.3, this may be the case even when the primary objective of the relevant investment or behavioural change is to reduce energy costs. Importantly, if the total cost savings exceed the saving in energy costs, then any rebound effects may be amplified.

3 The Evidence for Direct Rebound Effects

This section summarises the empirical evidence for direct rebound effects, focusing in particular on energy services in the household sector, since this is where the bulk of evidence lies.

Direct rebound effects relate to individual energy services, such as heating, lighting and refrigeration and are confined to the energy required to provide that service. Such services are provided through a combination of capital equipment, labour, materials and energy. An

---

BOX 9.3   EXAMPLES OF THE LINK BETWEEN IMPROVED ENERGY EFFICIENCY AND IMPROVED TOTAL FACTOR PRODUCTIVITY

- Lovins and Lovins (1997) used case studies to argue that better visual, acoustic and thermal comfort in well-designed, energy-efficient buildings can improve labour productivity by as much as 16 per cent. Since labour costs in commercial buildings are typically 25 times greater than energy costs, the resulting cost savings can potentially dwarf those from reduced energy consumption.
- Pye and McKane (1998) showed how the installation of energy-efficient motors reduced wear and tear, extended the lifetime of system components and achieved savings in capital and labour costs that exceeded the reduction in energy costs.
- Worrell et al. (2003) analysed the cost savings from 52 energy efficiency projects, including motor replacements, fans/duct/pipe insulation, improved controls and heat recovery in a range of industrial sectors. The average payback period from energy savings alone was 4.2 years, but this fell to 1.9 years when the non-energy benefits were taken into account.
- Using plant-level data, Boyd and Pang (2000) estimated fuel and electricity intensity in the glass industry as a function of energy prices, cumulative output, a time trend, capacity utilisation and overall productivity. Their results show that the most productive plants are also most energy efficient and that a 1 per cent improvement in overall productivity results in a more than 1 per cent improvement in energy efficiency.

---

essential feature of an energy service is the *useful work* obtained – with the term being used here to refer to both thermodynamic and physical measures of the useful outputs obtained from energy conversion devices. Energy services may also have broader attributes that may be combined with useful work in a variety of ways. For example, all cars deliver passenger-kilometres, but they may vary widely in terms of speed, comfort, acceleration and prestige. Consumers and producers may therefore make trade-offs between useful work and other attributes of an energy service; between energy, capital and other market goods in the production of an energy service; and between different types of energy service.

By reducing the marginal cost of useful work, energy efficiency improvements may, over time, lead to an increase in the number of energy conversion devices, their average size, their average utilisation and/or their average load factor. For example, people may buy more cars, buy larger cars, drive them further and/or share them less. The relative importance of these variables may be expected to vary widely between different energy services and over time. Over the very long term, the lower cost of energy services may contribute to fundamental changes in technologies, infrastructures and lifestyles – such as a shift towards car-based commuting and increasing distances between residential, workplace and retail locations. But as the time horizon extends, the effect of such changes on the demand for the energy service becomes increasingly difficult to separate from the effect of income growth and other factors.

The estimated size of the direct rebound effect will depend upon how useful work and hence energy efficiency is defined. For example, the majority of estimates of the direct rebound effect for personal automotive transport measure useful work in terms of vehicle-kilometres, which is sometimes decomposed into the product of the number of vehicles and the mean distance travelled per vehicle per year. Energy efficiency is then defined as vehicle-kilometres per litre of fuel and direct rebound effects are measured as increases in distance driven. But this overlooks any changes in mean vehicle size and weight as a result of energy efficiency improvements (for example, more SUVs: sport-utility vehicles), as well as any decrease in average vehicle load factor (for example, less car sharing).[7]

The magnitude of direct rebound effects may be expected to be proportional to the share of energy in the total cost of energy services,[8] as well as the extent to which those costs are 'visible'. But as the consumption of a particular energy service increases, saturation effects (technically, declining marginal utility) should reduce the size of any direct rebound effect. This suggests that direct rebound effects will be higher among low-income groups, since these are further from satiation in their consumption of many energy services (Milne and Boardman, 2000).

Increases in demand for an energy service may derive from existing consumers of the service, or from consumers who were previously unable or unwilling to purchase that service. For example, improvements in the energy efficiency of home air-conditioners may encourage consumers to purchase portable air-conditioners for the first time. The abundance of such 'marginal consumers' (Wirl, 1997) in developing countries points to the possibility of large direct rebound effects in these contexts, offset to only a limited extent by saturation effects among existing consumers (Roy, 2000).

While energy efficiency improvements reduce the energy cost of useful work, the size of the direct rebound effect will depend upon how other costs are affected. For example, direct rebound effects may be smaller if energy-efficient equipment is more expensive than less-efficient alternatives, because the availability of such equipment should not encourage an increase in the number and capacity of the relevant conversion devices. However, once purchased, such equipment may be expected to have a higher utilisation. In practice, many types of equipment appear to have both improved in energy efficiency over time and fallen in total cost relative to income.

Even if energy efficiency improvements are not associated with changes in capital or other costs, certain types of direct rebound effect may be constrained by the real or opportunity costs associated with increasing demand. Two examples are the opportunity cost of space (for example, increasing refrigerator size may not be the best use of available space) and the opportunity cost of time (for example, driving longer distances may not be the best use of available time). However, space constraints may become less important if technological improvements reduce the average size of conversion devices or if rising incomes lead to an increase in average living space (Wilson and Boehland, 2005). In contrast, the opportunity cost of time should increase with income.

Approaches to estimating direct rebound effects

There are two broad approaches to estimating direct rebound effects: namely quasi-experimental and econometric.

The Quasi-experimental Approach

One approach relies on measuring the demand for useful work before and after an energy efficiency improvement: for example, measuring the change in heat output following the installation of a fuel-efficient boiler. The demand for useful work before the energy efficiency improvement could be taken as an estimate for what demand 'would have been' in the absence of the improvement. However, various other factors may also have changed the demand for useful work which need to be controlled for (Meyer, 1995; Frondel and Schmidt, 2005).

Since it can be very difficult to measure useful work for many energy services, an alternative approach is to measure the change in energy consumption for that service. But to estimate direct rebound effects, this needs to be compared with a counterfactual estimate of energy consumption that has at least two sources of error, namely: (i) the energy consumption that would have occurred without the energy efficiency improvement; and (ii) the energy consumption that would have occurred following the energy efficiency improvement had there been no behavioural change. The first of these gives an estimate of the energy savings from the energy efficiency improvement, while the second isolates the direct rebound effect. Estimates for the latter can be derived from engineering models, but these frequently require data on the circumstances of individual installations and are prone to error.

Both of these approaches are rare, owing in part to measurement difficulties. There are relatively few published studies and nearly all of these focus on household heating (Sommerville and Sorrell, 2007). The methodological quality of most of these studies is relatively poor, with the majority using simple before and after comparisons, without the use of a control group or explicitly controlling for confounding variables. This is the weakest methodological strategy and prone to bias (Meyer, 1995; Frondel and Schmidt, 2005). Also, several studies are vulnerable to selection bias, since households choose to participate rather being randomly assigned (Hartman, 1988). Other weaknesses include small sample sizes, high variance in results and monitoring periods that are too short to capture long-term changes. There is also confusion between:

- *shortfall*, the difference between actual savings in energy consumption and those expected on the basis of engineering estimates;
- *temperature take-back*, the change in mean internal temperatures following the energy efficiency improvement; and
- *behavioural change*, the proportion of the change in internal temperature that derives from adjustments of heating controls and other variables by the user (for example, opening windows).

Typically, only a portion of temperature take-back is due to behavioural change, with the remainder being due to physical and other factors (Sanders and Phillipson, 2006).[9] Similarly, only a portion of shortfall is due to temperature take-back, with the remainder being due to poor engineering estimates of potential savings, inadequate performance of equipment, deficiencies in installation and so on. Hence, behavioural change is one, but not the only (or necessarily the most important) explanation of temperature take-back and the latter is one, but not the only explanation of shortfall. Direct rebound effects are normally interpreted as behavioural change, but it may be misleading to interpret this solely as a rational response to lower heating costs, partly because energy efficiency improvements may change other variables (for example, airflow) that also encourage behavioural responses. Also, measures of temperature take-back may be difficult to translate into estimates of shortfall because of a nonlinear and household-specific relationship between energy consumption and internal temperature. Isolating rebound effects from such studies can therefore be challenging.

The Econometric Approach
A more common approach to estimating direct rebound effects is through the econometric analysis of secondary data sources that include information on the demand for energy, useful work and/or energy efficiency. This data can take a number of forms (for example, cross-sectional, time series) and apply to different levels of aggregation (for example, household, region, country). Such studies typically estimate *elasticities*, meaning the percentage change in one variable following a percentage change in another, holding other variables constant. If time-series data are available, an estimate can be made of short-run elasticities, where the stock of conversion devices is assumed to be fixed, as well as long-run elasticities where it is variable. Cross-sectional data are usually assumed to provide estimates of long-run elasticities.

Depending upon data availability, the direct rebound effect may be estimated from one of two *energy efficiency* elasticities:[10]

- $\eta_\varepsilon(E)$: the elasticity of demand for energy (E) with respect to energy efficiency (ε), and
- $\eta_\varepsilon(S)$: the elasticity of demand for useful work (S) with respect to energy efficiency (where $S = \varepsilon E$).

$\eta_\varepsilon(S)$ is generally taken as a direct measure of the rebound effect. Under certain assumptions, it can be shown that: $\eta_\varepsilon(E) = \eta_\varepsilon(S) - 1$ (Sorrell and Dimitropoulos, 2007a). Hence, the actual saving in energy consumption will only equal the predicted saving from engineering calculations when the demand for useful work remains unchanged following an energy efficiency improvement (that is, when $\eta_\varepsilon(S) = 0$).[11]

Instead of using $\eta_\varepsilon(E)$ or $\eta_\varepsilon(S)$, most studies estimate the rebound effect from one of three *price* elasticities:

- $\eta_{P_S}(S)$: the elasticity of demand for useful work with respect to the energy cost of useful work (P_S),
- $\eta_{P_E}(S)$: the elasticity of demand for useful work with respect to the price of energy, and
- $\eta_{P_E}(E)$: the elasticity of demand for energy with respect to the price of energy,

where $P_S = P_E/\varepsilon$. Under certain assumptions, the negative of $\eta_{P_S}(S)$, $\eta_{P_E}(S)$ or $\eta_{P_E}(E)$ can be taken as an approximation to $\eta_\varepsilon(S)$ and hence may be used as a measure of the direct rebound effect (ibid.). The use of price elasticities in this way implicitly equates the direct rebound effect to a behavioural response to the lower cost of energy services. It therefore ignores any other reasons why the demand for useful work may change following an improvement in energy efficiency.

The choice of the appropriate elasticity measure will depend in part upon data availability. Generally, data on energy consumption (E) and energy prices (P_E) is both more available and more accurate than data on useful work (S) and energy efficiency (ε). Also, even if data on energy efficiency are available, the amount of variation is typically limited, with the result that estimates of either $\eta_\varepsilon(E)$ or $\eta_\varepsilon(S)$ can have a large variance. In contrast, estimates of $\eta_{P_S}(S)$ may have less variance owing to significantly greater variation in the independent variable. This is because the energy cost of useful work depends upon the ratio of energy prices to energy efficiency ($P_S = P_E/\varepsilon$) and most datasets include considerable cross-sectional or longitudinal variation in energy prices. In principle, rational consumers should respond in the same way to a decrease in energy prices as they do to an improvement in energy efficiency (and vice versa), since these should have an identical effect on the energy cost of useful work (P_S). However, there may be a number of reasons why this 'symmetry' assumption does not hold. If so, estimates of the direct rebound effect that are based upon $\eta_{P_S}(S)$ could be biased.

Estimates of $\eta_{P_S}(S)$ are largely confined to personal automotive transportation, household heating and space cooling, where proxy measures of useful work are most readily available. These energy services form a significant component of household energy demand in Organisation for Economic Co-operation and Development (OECD) countries and may be expected to be relatively price elastic. There are very few estimates of $\eta_{P_S}(S)$ for other consumer energy services and practically none for producers. Furthermore, the great majority of studies refer to the United States.

In many cases, data on energy efficiency are either unavailable or inaccurate. In these circumstances, the direct rebound effect may be estimated from $\eta_{P_E}(S)$ and $\eta_{P_E}(E)$. But this is only valid if: first, consumers respond in the same way to a decrease in energy prices as they do to an improvement in energy efficiency (and vice versa); and second, energy efficiency is unaffected by changes in energy prices. Both these assumptions are likely to be flawed, but the extent to which this leads to biased estimates of the direct rebound effect may vary widely from one energy service to another and between the short and long terms.

Under certain assumptions, the own-price elasticity of energy demand ($\eta_{P_E}(E)$) for a particular energy service can be shown to provide an *upper bound* for the direct rebound effect (Dahl and Sterner, 1991; Dahl, 1993, 1994; Barker et al., 1995; Espey, 1998; Graham and Glaister, 2002; Hanley et al., 2002; Espey and Espey, 2004). Reviews of the extensive literature on this topic generally suggest that energy demand is inelastic in the majority of sectors in OECD countries (that is, $|\eta_{P_E}(E)| < 1$) (Barker et al., 1995). The implication is that the direct rebound effect alone is unlikely to lead to backfire in these circumstances – although there are undoubtedly exceptions.

For the purpose of estimating rebound effects, estimates of $\eta_{P_E}(E)$ are most useful when the energy demand in question relates to a single energy service, such as refrigeration. They are less useful when (as is more common) the measured demand derives from a collection of energy services, such household fuel or electricity consumption. In this case, a large value for $\eta_{P_E}(E)$ may suggest that improvements in the 'overall' efficiency of fuel or electricity use will lead to large direct rebound effects (and vice versa), or that the direct rebound effect for the energy services that dominate fuel or electricity consumption may be large. However, a small value for $\eta_{P_E}(E)$ would not rule out the possibility of large direct rebound effects for individual energy services.

Whatever their scope and origin, estimates of price elasticities should be treated with caution. Aside from the difficulties of estimation, behavioural responses are contingent upon technical, institutional, policy and demographic factors that vary widely between different groups and over time. Demand responses are known to vary with the level of prices, the origin of price changes (for example, exogenous versus policy induced), expectations of future prices, government fiscal policy (for example, recycling of carbon tax revenues), saturation effects and other factors (Sorrell and Dimitropoulos, 2007b). The past is not necessarily a good guide to the future in this area, and it is possible that the very long-run response to price changes may exceed those found in empirical studies that rely upon data from relatively short time periods.

Estimates of direct rebound effects

By far the best-studied area for the direct rebound effect is personal automotive transport. Most studies refer to the US, which is important since fuel prices, fuel efficiencies and residential densities are lower than in Europe, car ownership levels are higher and there is less scope for switching to alternative transport modes.

Studies estimating $\eta_\varepsilon(E)$, $\eta_\varepsilon(S)$ or $\eta_{P_S}(S)$ for personal transport vary considerably in terms of the data used and specifications employed. Most studies use aggregate data which can capture long-term effects on demand such as fuel efficiency standards, while household survey data can better describe individual behaviour at the micro level. Aggregate studies face numerous measurement difficulties, however (Schipper et al., 1993), while disaggregate studies produce results that are more difficult to generalise. The measures chosen for useful work vary between total distance travelled, distance travelled per capita, distance travelled per licensed driver, distance travelled per household and distance travelled per vehicle (Sorrell and Dimitropoulos, 2007b).

Following a review of 17 econometric studies of personal automotive transport, Sorrell and Dimitropoulos (ibid.) conclude that the long-run direct rebound effect for this energy service lies somewhere between 10 and 30 per cent. The most reliable estimates come from studies using aggregate panel data, owing to the greater number of observations. For example, Johansson and Schipper's (1997) cross-country study gives a best guess for the long-run direct rebound effect of 30 per cent, while both Haughton and Sarkar (1996) and Small and van Dender (2005) converge on a long-run value of 22 per cent for the US (see Box 9.4). Most studies assume that the response to a change in fuel prices is equal in size to the response to a change in fuel efficiency, but opposite in sign. However, few studies test this assumption explicitly and those that do are either unable to reject the hypothesis that the two elasticities are equal, or find that the fuel efficiency elasticity is *less* than the fuel cost per kilometer-elasticity. The implication is that the direct rebound effect may lie towards the lower end of the above range.

A number of studies suggest that the direct rebound effect for personal automotive travel declines with income, as theory predicts (Greene et al., 1999; Small and van Dender, 2005). The evidence is insufficient to determine whether direct rebound effects are larger or smaller in Europe, but it is notable that the meta-analysis by Espey (1998) found no significant difference in long-run own-price elasticities of gasoline demand. Overall, Sorrell and Dimitropoulos (2007b) conclude that direct rebound effects in this sector have not obviated the benefits of technical improvements in vehicle fuel efficiency. Between 70 and 100 per cent of the potential benefits of such improvements appear to have been realised in reduced consumption of motor fuels.

BOX 9.4   THE DECLINING DIRECT REBOUND EFFECT

Small and van Dender (2005) provide one of the most methodologically rigorous estimates of the direct rebound effect for personal automotive transport. They estimate an econometric model explaining the amount of travel by passenger cars as a function of the cost per mile and other variables. By employing simultaneous equations for vehicle numbers, average fuel efficiency and vehicle-miles travelled, they are able allow for the fact that fuel efficiency is endogenous: that is, more-fuel-efficient cars may encourage more driving, while the expectation of more driving may encourage the purchase of more-fuel-efficient cars. Their results show that failing to allow for this can lead to the direct rebound effect being overestimated.

Small and van Dender use aggregate data on vehicle numbers, fuel efficiency, gasoline consumption, vehicle-miles travelled and other variables for 50 US states and the District of Columbia covering the period from 1961 to 2001. This approach provides considerably more observations than conventional aggregate time-series data, while at the same time providing more information on effects that are of interest to policy makers than do studies using household survey data. The effect of the CAFE (corporate automobile fleet efficiency) standards on vehicle fuel efficiency are estimated by incorporating a variable representing the gap between the fuel efficiency standard and an estimate of the efficiency that would have been chosen in the absence of the standards, giving prevailing fuel prices.

Small and Van Dender estimate the short-run direct rebound effect for the US as a whole to be 4.5 per cent and the long-run effect to be 22 per cent. The former is lower than most of the estimates in the literature, while the latter is close to the consensus. However, they estimate that a 10 per cent increase in income reduces the short-run direct rebound effect by 0.58 per cent. Using US average values of income, urbanisation and fuel prices over the 1997–2001 period, they find a direct rebound effect of only 2.2 per cent in the short term and 10.7 per cent in the long term – approximately half the values estimated from the full dataset. If this result is robust, it has some important implications. However, two-fifths of the estimated reduction in the rebound effect derives from the assumption that the magnitude of this effect depends upon the absolute level of fuel costs per kilometre. But since the relevant coefficient is not statistically significant, this claim is questionable.

Although methodologically sophisticated, the study is not without its problems. Despite covering 50 states over a period of 36 years, the data provide relatively little variation in vehicle fuel efficiency, making it difficult to determine its effect separately from that of fuel prices. Direct estimates of $\eta_\varepsilon(S)$ are small and statistically insignificant, which could be interpreted as implying that the direct rebound effect is approximately zero, but since this specification performs rather poorly overall, estimates based upon $\eta_{P_S}(S)$ are preferred. Also, the model leads to the unlikely result that the direct rebound effect is negative some states (Harrison et al., 2005). This raises questions about the use of the model for projecting declining rebound effects in the future, since increasing incomes could make the estimated direct rebound effect negative in many states (ibid.).

The next best studied area for direct rebound effects is household heating. Sommerville and Sorrell (2007) review 15 quasi-experimental studies of this energy service and conclude that standard engineering models may overestimate energy savings by up to one half – and potentially by more than this for low-income households. Temperature take-back appears to average between ~0.4°C and 0.8°C, of which approximately half was estimated to be accounted for by the physical characteristics of the house and the remainder by behavioural change. On the basis of this evidence, Sommerville and Sorrell conclude that direct rebound effects for household heating should typically be less than 30 per cent and may be expected to decrease over time as average internal temperatures increase.

Relatively few econometric studies estimate $\eta_\varepsilon(E)$, $\eta_\varepsilon(S)$ or $\eta_{P_S}(S)$ for household heating and even fewer investigate rebound effects. Most studies rely upon detailed household survey data and exhibit considerable diversity in terms of the variables measured and the methodologies adopted. Sorrell and Dimitropoulos (2007b) review nine estimates and find values in the range of 10 to 58 per cent for the short run and 1.4 to 60 per cent for the long run. As with the quasi-experimental studies, the definition of the direct rebound effect is not consistent between studies and the behavioural response appears to vary widely between different households. Nevertheless, for the purpose of policy evaluation, a figure of 30 per cent would appear a reasonable assumption.

Sorrell and Dimitropoulos (ibid.) found only two studies of direct rebound effects for household cooling and these provided estimates comparable to those for household heating (that is, 1 to 26 per cent). However, these were relatively old studies, conducted during period of rising energy prices and using small sample sizes. Their results may not be transferable to other geographical areas, owing to differences in house types and climatological conditions. Also, both studies focused solely upon changes in equipment utilisation. To the extent that ownership of cooling technology is rapidly increasing in many countries, demand from 'marginal consumers' may be an important consideration, together with increases in system capacity among existing users.

Sorrell and Dimitropoulos (ibid.) find that the evidence for water heating is even more limited, although Guertin et al. (2003) provide estimates in the range of 34 to 38 per cent, which is significantly larger than the results from quasi-experimental studies reported by Nadel (1993). A methodologically rigorous study of direct rebound effects for clothes washing (Box 9.5) suggests that direct rebound effects for 'minor' energy services should be relatively small – as theory suggests. However, this study confines attention to households that already have automatic washing machines and therefore excludes rebound effects from marginal consumers.

Table 9.1 summarises the results of Sorrell and Dimitropoulos's survey of econometric estimates of the direct rebound effect. Despite the methodological diversity, the results for individual energy services are broadly comparable, suggesting that the evidence is

BOX 9.5   DIRECT REBOUND EFFECTS FOR CLOTHES
WASHING

Davis (2007) provides a unique example of an estimate of direct rebound
effects for household clothes washing – which together with clothes drying
accounts for around one-tenth of US household energy consumption. The
estimate is based upon a government-sponsored field trial of high-efficiency
washing machines involving 98 participants. These machines use 48 per cent
less energy per wash than standard machines and 41 per cent less water.

While participation in the trial was voluntary, both the utilisation of existing
machines and the associated consumption of energy and water were monitored
for a period of two months prior to the installation of the new machine. This
allowed household specific variations in utilisation patterns to be controlled for
and permitted unbiased estimates to be made of the price elasticity of machine
utilisation.

The monitoring allowed the marginal cost of clothes washing for each household to be estimated. This was then used as the primary independent variable
in an equation for the demand for clean clothes in kg/day (useful work). Davis
found that the demand for clean clothes increased by 5.6 per cent after receiving the new washers, largely as a result of increases in the weight of clothes
washed per cycle rather than the number of cycles. While this could be used as
an estimate of the direct rebound effect, it results in part from savings in water
and detergent costs. If the estimate was based solely on the savings in energy
costs, the estimated effect would be smaller. This suggests that only a small
portion of the gains from energy-efficient washing machines will be offset by
increased utilisation.

Davis estimates that time costs form 80–90 per cent of the total cost of
washing clothes. The results therefore support the theoretical prediction that,
for time-intensive activities, even relatively large changes in energy efficiency
should have little impact on demand. Similar conclusions should therefore apply
to other time-intensive energy services that are both produced and consumed
by households, including those provided by dishwashers, vacuum cleaners,
televisions, power tools, computers and printers.

relatively robust to different datasets and methodologies. Also, consideration of the
potential sources of bias (Box 9.6) suggests that direct rebound effects are more likely to
lie towards the lower end of the range indicated here. The results suggest that the mean
long-run direct rebound effect for personal automotive transport, household heating
and household cooling in OECD countries is likely to be 30 per cent or less and may
be expected to decline in the future as demand saturates and income increases. Both
theoretical considerations and the limited empirical evidence suggest that direct rebound
effects are significantly smaller for other consumer energy services. However, the same
conclusion may not follow for energy efficiency improvements by producers or for low-
income households in developing countries. Moreover, the evidence base is sparse and

Table 9.1   Estimates of the long-run direct rebound effect for consumer energy services in the OECD

End-use	Range of values in evidence base (%)	'Best guess' (%)	No. of studies	Degree of confidence
Personal automotive transport	3–87	10–30	17	High
Space heating	0.6–60	10–30	9	Medium
Space cooling	1–26	1–26	2	Low
Other consumer energy services	0–41	<20	3	Low

has a number of important limitations, including the neglect of marginal consumers, the relatively limited time periods over which the effects have been studied and the restricted definitions of 'useful work' that have been employed. For these and other reasons, it would be inappropriate to draw conclusions about rebound effects 'as a whole' from this evidence.

4   The Evidence for Indirect and Economy-wide Rebound Effects

This section summarises the results of a limited number of studies that provide quantitative estimates of indirect and economy-wide rebound effects.

Indirect rebound effects derive from two sources: the energy required to produce and install the measures that improve energy efficiency, such as thermal insulation, and the indirect energy consumption that results from such improvements. The first of these ('embodied energy') relates to energy consumption that occurs prior to the energy efficiency improvement, while the second ('secondary effects') relates to energy consumption that follows the improvement.

Many improvements in energy efficiency can be understood as the 'substitution' of capital for energy within a particular system boundary. For example, thermal insulation (capital) may be substituted for fuel to maintain the internal temperature of a building at a particular level. It is these possibilities that form the basis of estimated 'energy-saving' potentials in different sectors. However, estimates of energy savings typically neglect the energy consumption that is required to produce and maintain the relevant capital – frequently referred to as 'embodied energy'. For example, energy is required to produce and install home insulation materials and energy-efficient motors. Substituting capital for energy therefore shifts energy use from the sector in which it is used to sectors of the economy that produce that capital. As a result, energy use may increase elsewhere in the economy (Kaufmann and Azary-Lee, 1990).[12]

In contrast to other sources of the economy-wide rebound effect, the contribution from 'embodied energy' may be expected to be smaller in the long term than in the short term. This is because the embodied energy associated with capital equipment is analogous to a capital cost and hence diminishes in importance relative to ongoing energy savings as the lifetime of the investment increases. An assessment of the embodied energy associated

BOX 9.6   POTENTIAL SOURCES OF BIAS IN ESTIMATES OF THE DIRECT REBOUND EFFECT

Most estimates of the direct rebound effect assume that changes in energy prices have an opposite effect to changes in energy efficiency and that the latter are 'exogenous'. In practice, both of these assumptions may be incorrect.

First, while changes in energy prices are generally not correlated with changes in other input costs, changes in energy efficiency may be. In particular, higher energy efficiency may only be achieved through the purchase of new equipment with higher capital costs than less efficient models. Hence, estimates of the direct rebound effect that rely primarily upon historical and/or cross-sectional variations in energy prices could overestimate the direct rebound effect, since the additional capital costs required to improve energy efficiency will not be taken into account (Henly et al., 1988).

Second, energy price elasticities tend to be higher for periods with rising prices than for those with falling prices (Gately, 1992, 1993; Dargay and Gately, 1994, 1995; Haas and Schipper, 1998). For example, Dargay (1992) found that the reduction in UK energy demand following the price rises of the late 1970s was five times greater than the increase in demand following the price collapse of the mid-1980s. An explanation may be that higher energy prices induce technological improvements in energy efficiency, which may also become embodied in regulations (Grubb, 1995). Also, investment in measures such as thermal insulation is largely irreversible over the short to medium term. But the appropriate proxy for improvements in energy efficiency is *reductions* in energy prices. Since many studies based upon time-series data incorporate periods of rising energy prices, the estimated price elasticities may overestimate the response to falling energy prices. As a result, such studies could overestimate the direct rebound effect.

Third, while improved energy efficiency may increase the demand for useful work (for example, you could drive further after purchasing an energy-efficient car), it is also possible that the anticipated high demand for useful work may increase the demand for energy efficiency (for example, you purchase an energy-efficient car because you expect to drive further). In these circumstances, the demand for useful work depends on the energy cost of useful work, which depends upon energy efficiency, which depends upon the demand for useful work (Small and van Dender, 2005). Hence, the direct rebound effect would not be the only explanation for any measured correlation between energy efficiency and the demand for useful work. This so-called 'endogeneity' can be addressed through the use of simultaneous equation models, but these are relatively uncommon owing to their greater data requirements. If, instead, studies include the 'endogenous' variable(s) within a single equation and do not use appropriate techniques to estimate this equation, the resulting estimates could be biased. Several studies of direct rebound effects could be flawed for this reason.

with a particular energy efficiency improvement should also take into account the relevant alternatives. For example, a mandatory requirement to replace existing refrigerators with more-energy-efficient models may either increase or decrease aggregate energy consumption over a particular period, depending upon the age of the existing stock, the lifetime of the new stock, and the direct and indirect energy consumption associated with different models of refrigerator. In practice, however, such estimates are rare.

Unlike embodied energy, 'secondary effects' follow the energy efficiency improvement and result from the induced changes in demand for other goods and services. For example, the diffusion of more-fuel-efficient cars may reduce demand for public transport, but at the same time increase demand for leisure activities that can only be accessed with a private car. Each of these goods and services will have an indirect energy consumption associated with it and the changed pattern of demand may act to either increase overall energy consumption or reduce it.

Very similar effects will result from energy efficiency improvements by producers. For example, energy efficiency improvements in steel production should reduce the cost of steel and (assuming that these cost reductions are passed on in lower product prices) reduce the input costs of manufacturers that use steel. This in turn should reduce the cost of steel products and increase demand for those products. Such improvements could, for example, lower the cost of passenger cars, increase the demand for car travel and thereby increase demand for motor fuel.

This example demonstrates how energy efficiency improvements could lead to a series of adjustments in the prices and quantities of goods and services supplied throughout an economy. If the energy efficiency improvements are widespread, the price of energy-intensive goods and services may fall to a greater extent than that of non-energy-intensive goods and services, thereby encouraging consumer demand to shift towards the former. If energy demand is reduced, the resulting fall in energy prices will encourage greater energy consumption by producers and consumers and will feed through into lower product prices, thereby encouraging further shifts towards energy-intensive commodities. Reductions in both energy prices and product prices will increase consumers' real income, thereby increasing demand for products, encouraging investment, stimulating economic growth and further stimulating the demand for energy. In some circumstances, such improvements could also change trade patterns and international energy prices and therefore impact on energy consumption in other countries.

A number of analysts have claimed that the secondary effects from energy efficiency improvements in consumer technologies are relatively small (Lovins et al., 1988; Greening and Greene, 1998; Schipper and Grubb, 2000). This is because energy makes up a small share of total consumer expenditure and the energy content of most other goods and services is also small.[13] Analogous arguments apply to the secondary effects for producers: since energy forms a small share of total production costs for most firms and sectors (typically <3 per cent) and since intermediate goods form a small share of the total costs of most final products, the product of these suggests an indirect effect that is much smaller than the direct effect (Greening and Greene, 1998). However, while plausible, these arguments are not supported by the results of several of the energy modelling studies reviewed below. In addition, they assume that the only effect of the energy efficiency improvement is to reduce expenditure on energy. But improvements in the energy efficiency of production processes are frequently associated with improvements in the productivity of capital and labour as well, and therefore lead to cost savings that exceed the savings in energy costs alone. In some cases, similar arguments may apply to energy efficiency improvements by consumers: for example, a shift from car travel to cycling could save on depreciation and maintenance costs for vehicles as well as motor-fuel costs (Alfredsson, 2004). In these circumstances, the secondary effects that result from the adoption of a particular technology could be substantial.

Estimates of indirect and economy-wide rebound effects

There are two broad approaches to estimating indirect and economy-wide rebound effects: namely, embodied energy estimates and energy modelling.

Embodied Energy Estimates
Some indication of the importance of embodied energy may be obtained from estimates of the own-price elasticity of *aggregate* primary, secondary or final energy demand in a national economy. In principle, this measures the scope for substituting capital, labour and materials for energy, while holding output constant. Most energy price elasticities are estimated at the level of individual sectors and therefore do not reflect all the embodied energy associated with capital, labour and materials inputs. Since the own-price elasticity of aggregate energy reflects this indirect energy consumption, it should in principle be smaller than a weighted average of energy demand elasticities within each sector. However, the aggregate elasticity may also reflect price-induced changes in economic structure and product mix which in principle could make it larger than the average of sectoral elasticities (Sweeney, 1984). These two mechanisms could therefore act in opposition.

Based in part upon modelling studies, Sweeney puts the long-run elasticity of demand for primary energy in the range –0.25 to –0.6. In contrast, Kaufmann (1992) uses econometric analysis to propose a range from –0.05 to –0.39, while Hong (1983) estimates a value of –0.05 for the US economy. A low value for this elasticity may indicate a limited scope for substitution and hence the potential for large indirect rebound effects.[14] But this interpretation is not straightforward, since both direct rebound effects and changes in trade patterns may contribute to the behaviour being measured. Also, measures of the quantity and price of 'aggregate energy' are sensitive to the methods chosen for aggregating the prices and quantities of individual energy carriers, while the price elasticity will also depend upon the particular composition of price changes (for example, increases in oil prices relative to gas) (EMF 4 Working Group, 1981). In particular, when different energy types are weighted by their relative marginal productivity, the estimated elasticities tend to be lower (Hong, 1983) As a result, the available estimates of aggregate price elasticities may be insufficiently precise to provide much indication of the magnitude of indirect rebound effects.

Relatively few empirical studies have estimated the embodied energy associated with specific energy efficiency improvements, and those that have appear to focus disproportionately upon domestic buildings. In a rare study of energy efficiency improvements by producers, Kaufmann and Azary Lee (1990) estimate that, in the US forest products industry from 1954 to 1984, the embodied energy associated with capital equipment offset the direct energy savings from that equipment by as much as 83 per cent (Box 9.7). But since their methodology is crude and the results specific to the US context, this study provides little indication of the magnitude of these effects more generally.

BOX 9.7   LIMITS TO SUBSTITUTION FOR PRODUCERS

Kaufmann and Azary Lee (1990) examined the embodied energy associated with energy efficiency improvements in the US forest products industry from 1954 to 1984. First, they estimated a production function for the output of this industry and used this to derive the 'marginal rate of technical substitution' (MRTS) between capital and energy in a given year – in other words, the amount of gross fixed capital that was used to substitute for a thermal unit of energy in that year. Second, they approximated the embodied energy associated with that capital by means of the aggregate energy/GDP ratio for the US economy in that year – hence ignoring the particular type of capital used, as well as the difference between the energy intensity of the capital-producing sectors and that of the economy as a whole. The product of these two variables gave an estimate of the indirect energy consumption associated with the gross capital stock used to substitute for a unit of energy. This was then multiplied by a depreciation rate to give the energy associated with the capital services used to substitute for a unit of energy.

Finally, they compared the estimated indirect energy consumption with the direct energy savings in the forest products sector in each year. Their results showed that the indirect energy consumption of capital offset the direct savings by between 18 and 83 per cent over the period in question, with the net energy savings generally decreasing over time. The primary source of the variation was the increase in the MRTS over time, implying that an increasing amount of capital was being used to substitute for a unit of energy. However, the results were also influenced by the high energy/GDP ratio of the US economy, which is approximately twice that of many European countries. Overall, the calculations suggest that the substitution reduced aggregate US energy consumption, but by much less than a sector-based analysis would suggest. Also, their approach did not take into account any secondary effects resulting from the energy efficiency improvements.

The simplicity of this approach suggests the scope for further development and wider application. Accuracy could be considerably improved by the use of more-flexible production functions and more-precise estimates for the indirect energy consumption associated with specific types and vintages of capital goods. However, to date no other authors appear to have applied this approach to particular industrial sectors or to have related it to the broader debate on the rebound effect.

Estimates of the embodied energy of different categories of goods and services can be obtained from input–output analysis, life-cycle analysis (LCA) or a combination of the two (Chapman, 1974; Herendeen and Tanak, 1976; Kok et al., 2006). A full LCA is time consuming to conduct and must address problems of 'truncation' (that is, uncertainty over the appropriate system boundary)[15] and joint production (that is, how to attribute energy consumption to two or more products from a single sector) (Leach, 1975; Lenzen and Dey, 2000). Hence, many studies combine standard economic input–output tables with additional information on the energy consumption of individual sectors, to give a comprehensive and reasonably accurate representation of the direct and indirect energy required to produce rather aggregate categories of goods and services. More detailed, LCA-based estimates are available for individual products such as building materials, but results vary widely from one context to another depending upon factors such as the fuel mix for primary energy supply (Sartori and Hestnes, 2007).

As an illustration, Sartori and Hestnes reviewed 60 case studies of buildings, and found that the share of embodied energy in life-cycle energy consumption ranged between 9 and 46 per cent for low-energy buildings and between 2 and 38 per cent for conventional buildings – with the wide range reflecting different building types, material choices and climatic conditions. Two studies that controlled for these variables found that low-energy designs could achieve substantial reductions in operating energy consumption with relatively small increases in embodied energy, leading to 'payback periods' for energy saving of as little as one year (Feist, 1996; Winther and Hestnes, 1999; Royal Commission on Environmental Pollution, 2007). However, Casals (2006) shows how the embodied energy of such buildings could offset operational energy savings, even with an assumed 100-year lifetime. Such calculations typically neglect differences in energy quality and the results are sensitive to context, design and building type. Moreover, similar estimates have not been developed in a systematic fashion for other types of energy efficiency improvement.

By combining estimates of the embodied energy associated with different categories of goods and services with survey data on household consumption patterns, it is possible to estimate the total (direct plus indirect) energy consumption of different types of household, together with the indirect energy consumption associated with particular categories of expenditure (Kok et al., 2006). If these data are available at a sufficiently disaggregated level, they could also be used to estimate the secondary effects associated with energy efficiency improvements by households – provided that additional information is available on either the cross-price elasticity between different product and service categories, or the marginal propensity to spend[16] of different income groups. By combining the estimates of embodied energy and secondary effects, an estimate of the total indirect rebound effect may be obtained. Such approaches are 'static' in that they do not capture the full range of price and quantity adjustments, but could nevertheless be informative. However, of the 19 studies in this area reviewed by Kok et al., only three were considered to have sufficient detail to allow the investigation of such micro-level changes.

A rare example of this approach is Brännlund et al. (2007), who examine the effect of a 20 per cent improvement in the energy efficiency of personal transport (all modes) and space heating in Sweden. They estimate an econometric model of aggregate household expenditure, in which the share of total expenditure for 13 types of good or service is expressed as a function of the total budget, the price of each good or service and an overall price index. This allows the own-price, cross-price and income elasticities of each good or service to be estimated.[17] By combining estimated changes in demand patterns with CO_2 emission coefficients for each category of good and service (based upon estimates of direct and indirect energy consumption) Brännlund et al. estimate that energy efficiency improvements in transport and heating lead to economy-wide rebound effects (in carbon terms) of 120 and 170 per cent, respectively. These results contradict the econometric evidence on direct rebound effects reviewed above, since carbon emissions for heating and transport are estimated to increase. The study also lacks transparency and employs an iterative estimation procedure that is truncated at the first estimation step. A comparable study by Mizobuchi (2007) overcomes some of these weaknesses, but nevertheless estimates broadly comparable rebound effects for Japanese households.

In summary, while techniques based upon embodied energy estimates provide a promising approach to quantifying indirect and economy-wide rebound effects, the application of these approaches remains in its infancy.

Energy Modelling Estimates
Embodied energy estimates are less useful for quantifying rebound effects from energy efficiency improvements by producers. In this case, a more suitable approach is to use energy-economic models of the macro economy (Grepperud and Rasmussen, 2004). Such models are widely used within energy studies (Bhattacharyya, 1996) but have only recently been applied to estimate rebound effects. The literature is therefore extremely sparse, but now includes two insightful studies commissioned by the UK government (Allan et al., 2006; Barker and Foxon, 2006). A key distinction is between computable general equilibrium (CGE) models of the macro economy and those based upon econometrics.

CGE models are widely used in energy studies, partly as a consequence of the ready availability of modelling frameworks and the associated benchmark data. This approach is informed by neoclassical economic theory, but can deal with circumstances that are too complex for analytical solutions. CGE models are calibrated to reflect the structural and behavioural characteristics of particular economies and in principle can indicate the approximate order of magnitude of direct and indirect rebound effects from specific energy efficiency improvements. A CGE model should allow the impacts of such improvements to be isolated, since the counterfactual is simply a model run without any changes in energy efficiency, as well as allowing the rebound effect to be decomposed into its constituent components, such as substitution and output effects (see Box 9.1). In principle, CGE models also provide scope for sensitivity analysis, although in practice this appears to be rare.

CGE models have a number of important limitations that have led many authors to question their realism and policy relevance (Barker, 2005). While developments in CGE methodology are beginning to overcome some of these weaknesses, most remain. Also, the predictive power of such models is rarely tested and different models appear to produce widely varying results for similar policy questions (Conrad, 1999). Hence, while CGE models may provide valuable insights, the quantitative results of such models should be interpreted with caution.

Allan et al. (2007) identify and review eight CGE modelling studies of economy-wide rebound effects (Table 9.2). The models vary considerably in terms of the production functions used, the manner in which different inputs are combined (the 'nesting' structure), the assumed scope for substitution between different inputs, the treatment of labour supply, the manner in which government savings are recycled and other key parameters. All the studies simulate energy efficiency improvements as 'energy-augmenting technical change',[18] but some introduce an across-the-board improvement while others introduce a specific improvement in an individual sector, or combination of sectors. This diversity,

Table 9.2 Summary of CGE studies of rebound effects

Author/date	Country or region	Nesting structure	ESUB with energy	Assumed energy efficiency improvements	Estimated rebound effect	Comments
Semboja (1994)	Kenya	Elec, fuel, *K, L*	1.0	Two scenarios: an improvement of energy production efficiency and an improvement in energy-use efficiency.	>100%	Intuitive presentation, no sensitivity tests, lack of transparency
Dufournaud et al. (1994)	Sudan	Utility functions	0.2 and 0.4	100%, 150% and 200% improvement in efficiency of wood-burning stoves	47–77%	Models efficiency improvements in domestic stoves. Wide range of sensitivity tests and good explanation of the factors at work
Vikstrom (2005)	Sweden	*(KE)L*	Values range from 0.07 to 0.87	15% increase in energy efficiency in non-energy sectors and 12% increase in energy sectors	50–60%	Applies to 1957–62 period in which known changes in energy efficiency productivity and structure are combined in turn. Results apply only to energy efficiency component
Washida (2004)	Japan	*(KL)E*	0.5	1% in all sectors modelled as change in efficiency factor for use of energy in production	53% in central scenario	Presentation unclear, although there is some sensitivity analysis, including varying elasticity of substitution from 0.3 to 0.7 jointly with other parameters. Rebound effect increases as energy/value added, labour/capital and level of energy composite substitution elasticities increase
Grepperud and Rasmussen (2004)	Norway	*(KE)L*	Between 0 and 1	Doubling of growth rates of energy productivity. Four sectors have electricity efficiency doubled, and two have oil efficiency doubled	Small for oil but >100% for electricity	Model is simulated dynamically with a counterfactual case in which projections of world economic growth, labour force growth, technological progress and net foreign debt are assumed until 2050

Study	Region	Nesting structure	ESUB	Scenario	Result	Comments
Glomsrød and Wei (2005)	China	Elec, fuel, K, L	1.0	Business-as-usual scenario compared to case where costless investments generate increased investments and productivity in coal cleaning – lowering price and increasing supply	>100%	Coal-intensive sectors benefit, as does whole economy due to high use of coal in primary energy consumption. Also examines cases where coal use is subject to emissions tax
Hanley et al. (2005)	Scotland	(KL)(EM)	0.3	5% improvement in efficiency of energy use across all production sectors	>100%	Region is significant electricity exporter and result depends in part on increased electricity exports
Allan et al. (2006)	UK	(KL)(EM)	0.3	5% improvement in efficiency of energy use across all production sectors (including energy sectors)	37% in central scenario	See Box 9.10

Note: The production functions combine inputs into pairs, or 'nests'. For example, a nested production function with capital (K), labour (L) and energy (E) inputs, could take one of three forms, namely: $K(LE)$; $(KL)E$; $(KE)L$. ESUB means the elasticity of substitution between energy and other inputs. Interpretation depends upon the nesting structure. For example, for $K(LE)$ ESUB refers to the elasticity of substitution between L and E, while for $(KL)E$ it refers to elasticity of substitution between (KL) and E.

combined with the limited number of studies available makes it difficult to draw any general conclusions.

The most notable result is that all of the studies find economy-wide rebound effects to be greater than 37 per cent and most studies show either large rebounds (>50 per cent) or backfire. The latter was found in two studies of economies in which energy forms an important export and import commodity, suggesting that this is a potentially important and hitherto neglected variable. Allan et al. (2006) find a long-term rebound effect of 37 per cent from across-the-board improvements in the energy efficiency of UK production sectors, including primary energy supply. This study is summarised in Box 9.8.

All but one of the models explore the implications of energy efficiency improvements in production sectors and the CGE literature offers relatively little insight into the implications of energy efficiency improvements in consumer goods. Since there are differences across income groups, this would require a much greater detail on the demand side of the CGE models than is commonly the case. Also, most of these studies assume that energy efficiency improvements are costless. Only Allan et al. (2006) consider the implications of additional costs associated with energy efficiency improvements and they find that rebound effects are correspondingly reduced.

One final approach to estimating economy-wide rebound effects is through the use of macro-econometric models of national economies. These can overcome several of the weaknesses of CGE modelling while at the same time providing a greater level of disaggregation that permits the investigation of specific government policies. In contrast to their CGE counterparts, macro-econometric models do not rely upon restrictive assumptions such as constant returns to scale and perfect competition and replace the somewhat ad hoc use of parameter estimates with econometric equations estimated for individual sectors. However, this greater realism is achieved at the expense of greater complexity and more onerous data requirements.

At the time of writing (2008), Barker and Foxon (2006) provide the only example of the application of such models to economy-wide rebound effects. The MDM-E3 model was used to simulate the macroeconomic impact of a number of UK energy efficiency policies from 2000 to 2010. The study combined exogenous estimates of 'gross' energy savings and direct rebound effects with modelling of indirect effects. The direct rebound effects were estimated to reduce overall energy savings by 15 per cent, while the indirect effects reduced savings by a further 11 per cent – leading to an estimated economy-wide rebound effect of 26 per cent in 2010. The indirect effects were higher in the energy-intensive industries (25 per cent) and lower for households and transport (7 per cent). The primary source of the indirect effects was substitution between energy and other goods by households, together with increases in output by (particularly energy-intensive) industry, which in turn led to increased demand for both energy and energy-intensive intermediate goods. Increases in consumers' real income contributed relatively small rebound effects (0.2 per cent).

However, there are a number of reasons why this study may have underestimated the economy-wide effects. First, while output effects were estimated, the substitution between (cheaper) energy services and other inputs was ignored. Second, the modelling implicitly assumed 'pure' energy efficiency improvements, with no associated improvements in the productivity of other inputs. But if energy-efficient technologies are commonly associated with such improvements, rebound effects could be larger. Third, the model did not

BOX 9.8 CGE ESTIMATES OF ECONOMY-WIDE REBOUND EFFECTS FOR THE UK

Allan et al. (2006) estimate economy-wide rebound effects for the UK following a 5 per cent across-the-board improvement in the efficiency of energy use in all production sectors. Since their model allows for the gradual updating of capital stocks, they are able to estimate a short-run rebound effect of 50 per cent and a long-run effect of 37 per cent.

The energy efficiency improvements increase long-run GDP by 0.17 per cent and employment by 0.21 per cent. They have a proportionally greater impact on the competitiveness of energy-intensive sectors which is passed through in lower product prices despite a 0.3 per cent increase in real wages. Output is increased in all sectors, with the iron and steel and pulp and paper sectors benefiting the most with long-run increases of 0.67 per cent and 0.46 per cent, respectively. In contrast, the output of the oil-refining and electricity industries (that is, oil and electricity demand) is reduced, with the price of conventional electricity falling by 24 per cent in the long run. This fall in energy prices contributes a significant proportion of the overall rebound effect and results from both cost reductions in energy production – due to the energy efficiency improvements – and reduced energy demand.

In practice, a 5 per cent improvement in energy efficiency may not be feasible for an industry such as electricity generation which is operating close to thermodynamic limits. It would also require major new investment and take time to be achieved. Allan et al.'s results suggest that the rebound effect would be smaller if energy efficiency improvements were confined to energy users, but the importance of this cannot be quantified. Moreover, the results demonstrate that energy efficiency improvements in the energy supply industry may be associated with large rebound effects.

A notable feature of this study is the use of sensitivity tests. Varying the assumed elasticity of substitution between energy and non-energy inputs between 0.1 and 0.7 (compared to a baseline value of 0.3) had only a small impact on economic output (from 0.16 per cent in the low elasticity case to 0.10 per cent in the high case), but a major impact on the rebound effect. This varied from 7 per cent in the low case to 60 per cent in the high case. Grepperud and Rasmussen (2004) report similar results, which highlights the importance of this parameter for CGE simulations. Unfortunately, the empirical basis for the assumed parameter values in CGE models is extremely weak, while the common assumption that such parameters are constant is flawed (Broadstock et al., 2007).

Varying the elasticity of demand for exports was found to have only a small impact on GDP and energy demand, suggesting that the energy efficiency improvements had only a small impact on the international competitiveness of the relevant industries. However, different treatments of the additional tax revenue were found to be important.

reflect the indirect energy consumption embodied within the energy-efficient technologies themselves. Finally, the study confined attention to national energy use and ignored the indirect energy consumption associated with increased imports and tourism. This omission could be significant from a climate change perspective, since this corresponds to approximately ~40 per cent of the extra domestic output.[19]

In summary, given the small number of studies available, the diversity of approaches and the methodological weaknesses associated with each, it is not possible to draw any general conclusions regarding the size of the economy-wide rebound effect from either embodied energy or energy modelling studies. Indeed, the most important insight is that the economy-wide rebound effect varies greatly from one circumstance to another, so general statements on the size of such effects are misleading. It is notable, however, that the available studies suggest that economy-wide effects are frequently large (that is, >50 per cent) and that the potential for backfire cannot be ruled out. Moreover, these estimates derive from pure energy efficiency improvements and therefore do not rely upon simultaneous improvements in the productivity of capital and labour inputs.

5   Conclusions

This chapter has clarified the definition of direct, indirect and economy-wide rebound effects, highlighted the methodological challenges associated with quantifying such effects and summarised the estimates that are currently available. The main conclusions are as follows:

1. *Rebound effects are significant, but they need not make energy efficiency policies ineffective in reducing energy demand*   Rebound effects vary widely between different technologies, sectors and income groups and in most cases cannot be quantified with much confidence. However the evidence does not suggest that improvements in energy efficiency routinely lead to economy-wide increases in energy consumption, as some commentators have suggested. At the same time the evidence does not suggest that economy-wide rebound effects are generally small (for example, <10 per cent) as many analysts and policy makers assume.
2. *For most consumer energy services in OECD countries, direct rebound effects are unlikely to exceed 30 per cent*   Improvements in energy efficiency should achieve 70 per cent or more of the expected reduction in energy consumption for those services – though the existence of indirect effects means that the economy-wide reduction in energy consumption will be less. However, these conclusions cannot be extended to producers or to households in developing countries. These conclusions are also subject to a number of important qualifications, including the neglect of 'marginal consumers' and the relatively limited time period over which the effects have been studied
3. *There are relatively few quantitative estimates of indirect and economy-wide rebound effects, but several studies suggest that the economy-wide effect may frequently exceed 50 per cent*   The magnitude of economy-wide effects depends very much upon the sector where the energy efficiency improvement takes place, and is sensitive to a number of variables. A handful of modelling studies estimate

economy-wide rebound effects of 26 per cent or more, with half of the studies predicting backfire. These effects derive from 'pure' energy efficiency improvements by producers (not consumers) and therefore do not reflect the effect of simultaneous improvements in the productivity of other inputs, which would tend to amplify the rebound effect. However, the small number of studies available, the diversity of approaches used and the variety of methodological weaknesses associated with the CGE approach all suggest the need for caution when interpreting these results.

Given the potential importance of rebound effects, the evidence base is remarkably weak. While this is partly a consequence of the inherent difficulty of estimating such effects, there is considerable scope for improving knowledge in a number of areas. For example, econometric studies need to address several potential sources of bias, while quasi-experimental studies need to improve in rigour. Data permitting, both approaches need to be extended to a greater range of countries, sectors and energy services. Systematic estimates need to be developed of the embodied energy associated with various types of energy efficiency improvement. Such estimates may be usefully combined with models of consumer behaviour to estimate secondary effects. Both CGE and macro-econometric models offer considerable potential for exploring economy-wide rebound effects, but require systematic and informed sensitivity analysis and more careful attention to methodological weaknesses.

While the precise quantification of rebound effects may be an elusive goal, it should be possible to gain a much better understanding of the determinants of these effects than we have at present – including the conditions under which they are more or less likely to be large. This understanding has been inhibited in the past by confusion over basic definitions, an excessive focus upon theoretical arguments and an overly polarised debate around the likelihood of 'backfire'.[20] The size and importance of rebound effects from different types of energy efficiency improvement should be treated instead as an empirical question, amenable to investigation through a variety of means.

Notes

* This chapter is based upon evidence of rebound effects, conducted by the UK Energy Research Centre (Sorrell, 2007). The financial support of the UK Research Councils is gratefully acknowledged. It draws upon the work of the full Project Team for the UKERC study, namely: John Dimitropoulos (Sussex Energy Group); Lester C. Hunt and David C. Broadstock (Surrey Energy Economics Centre, SEEC, University of Surrey); Grant Allan, Michelle Gilmartin, Peter McGregor, Kim Swales and Karen Turner (Fraser of Allander Institute and Department of Economics, University of Strathclyde); and Matt Sommerville and Dennis Anderson (ICEPT, Imperial College).

  The author is grateful for the comments received from Harry Saunders, Manuel Frondel, Karsten Neuhoff, Jake Chapman, Nick Eyre, Serban Scrieciu, Blake Alcott, Len Brookes, John Feather, Gordon Mackerron, Horace Herring, Lester Hunt and Paolo Agnolucci. Thanks also to Jim Skea, Rob Gross and Phil Heptonstall for guidance, comments, patience and moral support. A debt is also owed to Lorna Greening and David Greene for their previous synthesis of empirical work in this area. The usual disclaimers apply.

1. This may be expressed as $REB = [(DIR + IND)/ENG] * 100\%$, where ENG represents the expected energy savings from a particular energy efficiency improvement without taking rebound effects into account; DIR represents the increase in energy consumption resulting from the direct rebound effect; and IND represents the increase in energy consumption resulting from the indirect rebound effects.

2. Technical change is said to be 'neutral' if it reduces the use of all inputs by an equal amount and 'biased',

if it reduces the use of some inputs more than others. 'Energy-saving' technical change reduces the share of energy in the value of output by proportionately more than the share of other inputs, while 'energy-using' technical change does the reverse. This bias in technical change is closely related to (but not the same as) the rate of growth of energy efficiency over time, holding relative prices constant. This so-called 'autonomous energy efficiency improvement' (AEEI) is an important parameter in many energy-economic models (Löschel, 2002).

3. For example, improvements in the energy efficiency of electric motors in the engineering sector may lead to rebound effects within that sector, with the result that the energy intensity of that sector is reduced by less than it would be in the absence of such effects. But if the energy intensity of the sector is taken as the independent variable, these lower-level rebound effects will be overlooked.

4. A common measure of the ability to perform useful work is 'exergy', defined as the maximum amount of work obtainable from a system as it comes (reversibly) to equilibrium with a reference environment (Wall, 2004). Exergy is only non-zero when the system under consideration is distinguishable from its environment through differences in relative motion, gravitational potential, electromagnetic potential, pressure, temperature or chemical composition. Unlike energy, exergy is 'consumed' in conversion processes, and is mostly lost in the form of low temperature heat. A heat unit of electricity, for example, will be ranked higher on an exergy basis than a heat unit of oil or natural gas, since the former can do more useful work.

5. The marginal product of an energy input into a production process is the marginal increase in the value of output produced by the use of one additional heat unit of energy input. In the absence of significant market distortions, the relative price per kilowatt hour of different energy carriers can provide a broad indication of their relative marginal productivities (Kaufmann, 1994).

6. For example, on a thermal input basis, per capita energy consumption in the US residential sector decreased by 20 per cent over the period 1970 to 1991, but when adjustments are made for changes in energy quality (notably the increasing use of electricity), per capita energy consumption is found to have increased by 7 per cent (Zarnikau et al., 1996). This difference demonstrates that technical progress in energy use is not confined to improvements in thermodynamic efficiency, but also includes the substitution of low-quality fuels by high-quality fuels (notably electricity), thereby increasing the amount of utility or economic output obtained from the same heat content of input (Kaufmann, 1992).

7. If energy efficiency was measured instead as tonne-kilometres per litre of fuel, rebound effects would show up as an increase in tonne-kilometres driven, which may be decomposed into the product of the number of vehicles, the mean vehicle weight and the mean distance travelled per vehicle per year. To the extent that vehicle weight provides a proxy for factors such as comfort, safety and carrying capacity, this approach effectively incorporates some features normally classified as attributes of the energy service into the measure of useful work. It also moves closer to a thermodynamic measure of energy efficiency, by focusing upon the movement of mass rather than the movement of people.

8. For example, if energy accounts for 50 per cent of the total cost of an energy service, doubling energy efficiency will reduce the total costs of the energy service by 25 per cent. But if energy accounts for only 10 per cent of total costs, doubling energy efficiency will reduce total cost by only 5 per cent. In practice, improvements in energy efficiency may themselves be costly.

9. For example, daily average household temperatures will generally increase following improvements in thermal insulation, even if the heating controls remain unchanged. This is because insulation contributes to a more even distribution of warmth around the house, reduces the rate at which a house cools down when the heating is off and delays the time at which it needs to be switched back on (Milne and Boardman, 2000).

10. The rationale for the use of these elasticities, and the relationship between them, is explained in detail in Sorrell and Dimitropoulos (2007a). In the case of personal automotive transport, they could correspond to: $\eta_\varepsilon(E)$, the elasticity of the demand for motor fuel (for passenger cars) with respect to kilometres per litre; $\eta_\varepsilon(S)$ the elasticity of the demand for vehicle-kilometres with respect to kilometres per litre; $\eta_{P_S}(S)$ the elasticity of the demand for vehicle-kilometres with respect to the cost per kilometre; $\eta_{P_E}(S)$ the elasticity of the demand for vehicle-kilometres with respect to the price of motor fuel; and $\eta_{P_E}(E)$ the elasticity of the demand for motor fuel with respect to the price of motor fuel.

11. Under these circumstances: $\eta_\varepsilon(E) = -1$. A positive rebound effect implies that $\eta_\varepsilon(S) > 0$ and $0 > \eta_\varepsilon(S) > -1$, while backfire implies that $\eta_\varepsilon(S) > 1$ and $\eta_\varepsilon(E) > 0$.

12. Some authors argue that similar conclusions apply to the substitution of labour for energy, since energy is also required to feed and house workers and thereby keep them economically productive (Kaufmann, 1992). However, there is some dispute over whether and how to account for the 'energy cost of labour' (Costanza, 1980). Similarly, while economists conventionally distinguish between substitution and technical change (Box 9.4), the latter is also associated with indirect energy consumption since it is embodied in capital goods and skilled workers (Stern and Cleveland, 2004).

13 For example, suppose that energy efficiency improvements reduce natural gas consumption per unit of

space heated by 10 per cent. If there is no direct rebound effect, consumers will reduce expenditure on natural gas for space heating by 10 per cent. If natural gas for heating accounts for 5 per cent of total consumer expenditure, consumers will experience a 0.5 per cent increase in their real disposable income. If *all* of this were spent on motor fuel for additional car travel, the net energy savings (in kWh thermal content) will depend upon the ratio of natural gas prices to motor-fuel prices, and could in principle be more or less than one. In practice, however, motor fuel accounts for only a portion of the total cost of car travel and car travel accounts for only a portion of total consumer expenditure. For the great majority of goods and services, input–output data suggest that the effective expenditure on energy should be less than 15 per cent of the total expenditure. Hence, by this logic, the secondary effect should be only around one-tenth of the direct effect (Greening and Greene, 1998).

14. This is in contrast to the own-price elasticity of energy demand for an individual energy service, where high values may indicate the potential for large direct rebound effects.
15. For example, should the indirect energy costs of a building also include the energy used to make the structural steel and mine the iron ore used to make the girders? This is referred to as the 'truncation problem' because there is no standard procedure for determining when energy costs become small enough to neglect.
16. Defined as the change in expenditure on a particular product or service, divided by the change in total expenditure. The marginal propensity to spend on different goods and services varies with income and it is an empirical question as to whether the associated indirect energy consumption is larger or smaller at higher levels of income. However, the greater use of energy-intensive travel options by high-income groups (notably flying) could be significant in some cases.
17. Brännlund et al. employ the almost ideal demand (AID) model, which has been shown to have a number of advantages over other models of consumer demand (Deaton and Muellbauer, 1980; Xiao et al., 2007). The model relies on the assumption of 'staged budgeting': for example, consumers are assumed to first decide on the proportion of their budget to spend on transport, and then decide how to allocate their transport budget between different modes. While analytically convenient, this assumption is likely to be flawed.
18. CGE models are based upon neoclassical production functions for individual sectors, which represent output (Y) as a function of capital (K) labour (L) energy (E) and materials (M) inputs: $Y = f(K, L, E, M)$. Energy-augmenting technical change is represented by a multiplier on energy inputs (kE), which implies that the economic productivity of energy inputs has increased. This means that the same output (Y) can now be obtained with fewer energy inputs, or alternatively that more output can be obtained from the same quantity of energy inputs. The product kE is commonly referred to as 'effective' energy and the multiplier (k) is frequently assumed to be an exponential function of time.
19. Also, any similarity between this result and that of Allan et al. (2006) is spurious, since they use different approaches to model different types of rebound effect from different types and size of energy-efficiency improvement in different sectors.
20. Arguments in favour of backfire have been formalised by Saunders (1992) as the 'Khazzoom–Brookes postulate', which states: 'with fixed real energy prices, energy efficiency gains will *increase* energy consumption above what it would be without those gains' (added emphasis). The term 'postulate' implies a starting assumption for which other statements are logically derived and which does not have to be either self-evident or supported by empirical evidence. A preferable approach would be to treat the statement as a hypothesis and seek out testable implications.

References

Alcott, B. (2005), 'Jevons' paradox', *Ecological Economics*, **54**(1), 9–21.
Alfredsson, E.C. (2004), '"Green" consumption – no solution for climate change', *Energy*, **29**, 513–24.
Allan, G., M. Gilmartin, P.G. McGregor, K. Swales and K. Turner (2007), 'UKERC Review of Evidence for the Rebound Effect: Technical Report 4: Energy-economic Modelling Studies', UK Energy Research Centre, London.
Allan, G., N. Hanley, P.G. McGregor, J. Kim Swales and K. Turner (2006), 'The macroeconomic rebound effect and the UK economy', Final report to the Department of Environment Food and Rural Affairs, Department of Economics, University of Strathclyde, Strathclyde.
Barker, T. (2005), 'The transition to sustainability: a comparison of general equilibrium and space–time economics approaches', Working Paper 62, Tyndall Centre for Climate Change Research, Norwich, UK.
Barker, T., P. Ekins and N. Johnstone (1995), *Global Warming and Energy Demand*, Routledge, London.
Barker, T. and T. Foxon (2006), 'The macroeconomic rebound effect and the UK economy', Report to the Department of the Environment, Food and Rural Affairs, 4CMR, Cambridge.

Bhattacharyya, S.C. (1996), 'Applied general equilibrium models for energy studies: a survey', *Energy Economics*, **18**, 145–64.

Boyd, G.A. and J.X. Pang (2000), 'Estimating the linkage between energy efficiency and productivity', *Energy Policy*, **28**, 289–96.

Brännlund, R., T. Ghalwash and J. Nordstrom (2007), 'Increased energy efficiency and the rebound effect: effects on consumption and emissions', *Energy Economics*, **29**(1), 1–17.

Broadstock, D., L.C. Hunt and S. Sorrell (2007), 'UKERC Review of Evidence for the Rebound Effect: Technical Report 3: Elasticity of Substitution Studies', UK Energy Research Centre, London.

Brookes, L.G. (1984), 'Long-term equilibrium effects of constraints in energy supply', in L. Brookes and H. Motamen (eds), *The Economics of Nuclear Energy*, Chapman & Hall, London, pp. 381–403.

Brookes, L.G. (1990), 'The greenhouse effect: the fallacies in the energy efficiency solution', *Energy Policy*, **18**(2), 199–201.

Brookes, L.G. (2000), 'Energy efficiency fallacies revisited', *Energy Policy*, **28**(6–7), 355–66.

Brookes, L. (2004), 'Energy efficiency fallacies—a postscript', *Energy Policy*, **32**(8), 945–7.

Casals, X.G. (2006), 'Analysis of building energy regulation and certification in Europe: their role, limitations and differences', *Energy and Buildings*, **38**, 381–92.

Chapman, P. (1974), 'Energy costs: a review of methods', *Energy Policy*, **2**(2), 91–103.

Cleveland, C.J., R.K. Kaufmann and D.I. Stern (2000), 'Aggregation and the role of energy in the economy', *Ecological Economics*, **32**, 301–17.

Conrad, K. (1999), 'Computable general equilibrium models for environmental economics and policy analysis', in J.C.J.M van den Bergh (ed.), *Handbook of Environmental and Resource Economics*, Edward Elgar, Cheltenham, UK and Northampton, MA, USA, pp. 1060–98.

Costanza, R. (1980), 'Embodied energy and economic valuation', *Science*, **210**, 1219–24.

Dahl, C. (1993), 'A survey of energy demand elasticities in support of the development of the NEMS', Prepared for US Department of Energy, Contract No. De-AP01-93EI23499, Department of Mineral Economics, Colorado School of Mines, Golden, CO.

Dahl, C. (1994), 'Demand for transportation fuels: a survey of demand elasticities and their components', *Journal of Energy Literature*, **1**(2), 3–27.

Dahl, C. and T. Sterner (1991), 'Analyzing gasoline demand elasticities – a survey', *Energy Economics*, **13**(3), 203–10.

Dargay, J.M. (1992), *Are Price and Income Elasticities of Demand Constant? The UK Experience*, Oxford Institute for Energy Studies, Oxford.

Dargay, J.M. and D. Gately (1994), 'Oil demand in the industrialised countries', *The Energy Journal*, **15**(Special Issue), 39–67.

Dargay, J.M. and D. Gately (1995), 'The imperfect price irreversibility of non-transportation of all demand in the OECD', *Energy Economics*, **17**(1), 59–71.

Davis, L.W. (2007), 'Durable goods and residential demand for energy and water: evidence from a field trial', Working Paper, Department of Economics, University of Michigan.

Deaton, A. and J. Muellbauer (1980), 'An almost ideal demand system', *American Economic Review*, **70**, 312–26.

DEFRA (2007), 'Consultation document: energy, cost and carbon savings for the draft EEC 2008-11 illustrative mix', Department of Environment, Food and Rural Affairs, London.

Dufournaud, C.M., J.T. Quinn and J.J. Harrington (1994), 'An applied general equilibrium (AGE) analysis of a policy designed to reduce the household consumption of wood in the Sudan', *Resource and Energy Economics*, **16**(1), 67–90.

EMF 4 Working Group (1981), 'Aggregate elasticity of energy demand', *The Energy Journal*, **2**(2), 37–75.

Espey, J.A. and M. Espey (2004), 'Turning on the lights: a meta-analysis of residential electricity demand elasticities', *Journal of Agricultural and Applied Economics*, **36**(1), 65–81.

Espey, M. (1998), 'Gasoline demand revisited: an international meta-analysis of elasticities', *Energy Economics*, **20**, 273–95.

Feist, W. (1996), *Life-cycle Energy Balances Compared: Low Energy House, Passive House, Self-sufficient House*, Proceedings of the International Symposium of CIB W67, Vienna, Austria.

Frondel, M. and C.M. Schmidt (2005), 'Evaluating environmental programs: the perspective of modern evaluation research', *Ecological Economics*, **55**(4), 515–26.

Gately, D. (1992), 'Imperfect price-reversibility of U.S. gasoline demand: asymmetric responses to price increases and declines', *The Energy Journal*, **13**(4), 179–207.

Gately, D. (1993), 'The imperfect price reversibility of world oil demand', *The Energy Journal*, **14**(4), 163–82.

Glomsrød, S. and T.Y. Wei (2005), 'Coal cleaning: a viable strategy for reduced carbon emissions and improved environment in China?', *Energy Policy*, **33**(4), 525–42.

Graham, D.J. and S. Glaister (2002), 'The demand for automobile fuel: a survey of elasticities', *Journal of Transport Economics and Policy*, **36**(1), 1–26.

Greene, D.L., J.R. Kahn and R.C. Gibson (1999), 'Fuel economy rebound effect for US household vehicles', *The Energy Journal*, **20**(3), 1–31.

Greening, L.A. and D.L. Greene (1998), 'Energy use, technical efficiency, and the rebound effect: a review of the literature', Report to the US Department of Energy, Hagler Bailly & Co., Denver, CO.

Greening, L.A., D.L. Greene and C. Difiglio (2000), 'Energy efficiency and consumption – the rebound effect: a survey', *Energy Policy*, **28**(6–7), 389–401.

Grepperud, S. and I. Rasmussen (2004), 'A general equilibrium assessment of rebound effects', *Energy Economics*, **26**(2), 261–82.

Grubb, M.J. (1995), 'Asymmetrical price elasticities of energy demand', in T. Barker, P. Ekins and N. Johnstone (eds), *Global Warming and Energy Demand*, Routledge, London and New York, pp. 305–13.

Guertin, C., S. Kumbhakar and A. Duraiappah (2003), 'Determining demand for energy services: investigating income-driven behaviours', International Institute for Sustainable Development, Guertin, Manitoba.

Haas, R. and L. Schipper (1998), 'Residential energy demand in OECD-countries and the role of irreversible efficiency improvements', *Energy Economics*, **20**(4), 421–42.

Hanley, M., J.M. Dargay and P.B. Goodwin (2002), 'Review of income and price elasticities in the demand for road traffic', Final report to the DTLR under Contract number PPAD 9/65/93, ESRC Transport Studies Unit, University College London, London.

Hanley, N., P.G. McGregor, J.K. Swales and K. Turner (2005), 'Do increases in resource productivity improve environmental quality? Theory and evidence on rebound and backfire effects from an energy–economy–environment regional computable general equilibrium model of Scotland', Department of Economics, University of Strathclyde, Strathclyde.

Harrison, D., G. Leonard, B. Reddy, D. Radov, P. Klevnäs, J. Patchett and P. Reschke (2005), 'Reviews of studies evaluating the impacts of motor vehicle greenhouse gas emissions regulations in California', National Economic Research Associates, Boston, MA.

Hartman, R.S. (1988), 'Self-selection bias in the evaluation of voluntary energy conservation programs', *Review of Economics and Statistics*, **70**(3), 448–58.

Haughton, J. and S. Sarkar (1996), 'Gasoline tax as a corrective tax: estimates for the United States, 1970–1991', *The Energy Journal*, **17**(2), 103–26.

Henly, J., H. Ruderman and M.D. Levine (1988), 'Energy savings resulting from the adoption of more efficient appliances: a follow-up', *The Energy Journal*, **9**(2), 163–70.

Herendeen, R. and J. Tanak (1976), 'The energy cost of living', *Energy*, **1**(2), 165–78.

Herring, H. (2006), 'Energy efficiency – a critical view', *Energy*, **31**(1), 10–20.

Hong, N.V. (1983), 'Two measures of aggregate energy production elasticities', *The Energy Journal*, **4**(2), 172–7.

IPCC (2007), 'Climate Change 2007: Mitigation of Climate Change', Working Group III contribution to the IPCC Fourth Assessment Report, Intergovernmental Panel on Climate Change, Geneva.

Johansson, O. and L. Schipper (1997), 'Measuring long-run automobile fuel demand: separate estimations of vehicle stock, mean fuel intensity, and mean annual driving distance', *Journal of Transport Economics and Policy*, **31**(3), 277–92.

Kaufmann, R.K. (1992), 'A biophysical analysis of the energy/real GDP ratio: implications for substitution and technical change', *Ecological Economics*, **6**(1), 35–56.

Kaufmann, R.K. (1994), 'The relation between marginal product and price in US energy markets: implications for climate change policy', *Energy Economics*, **16**(2), 145–58.

Kaufmann, R.K. and I.G. Azary-Lee (1990), *A Biophysical Analysis of Substitution: Does Substitution Save Energy in the US Forest Products Industry?*, Ecological economics: its implications for forest management and research, Proceedings of a Workshop held in St Paul, Minnesota, 2–6 April.

Khazzoom, J.D. (1980), 'Economic implications of mandated efficiency in standards for household appliances', *The Energy Journal*, **1**(4), 21–40.

Kok, R., R.M.J. Benders and H.C. Moll (2006), 'Measuring the environmental load of household consumption using some methods based on input–output energy analysis: a comparison of methods and a discussion of results', *Energy Policy*, **34**(17), 2744–61.

Leach, G. (1975), 'Net energy analysis – is it any use?', *Energy Policy*, **3**(4), 332–44.

Lenzen, M. and C. Dey (2000), 'Truncation error in embodied energy analyses of basic iron and steel products', *Energy*, **25**(6), 577–85.

Löschel, A. (2002), 'Technological change in economic models of environmental policy: a survey', *Ecological Economics*, **43**(2–3), 105–26.

Lovins, A.B. (1998), 'Further comments on Red Herrings', Letter to *New Scientist*, No. 2152, 18 September.

Lovins, A.B., J. Henly, H. Ruderman and M.D. Levine (1988), 'Energy saving resulting from the adoption of more efficient appliances: another view; a follow-up', *The Energy Journal*, **9**(2), 1–44.

Lovins, A.B. and L.H. Lovins (1997), 'Climate: making sense and making money', Rocky Mountain Institute, Old Snowmass, CO.

Meyer, B. (1995), 'Natural and quasi experiments in economics', *Journal of Business and Economic Statistics*, **13**(2), 151–60.

Milne, G. and B. Boardman (2000), 'Making cold homes warmer: the effect of energy efficiency improvements in low-income homes', *Energy Policy*, **28**, 411–24.

Mizobuchi, K.I. (2007), 'An empirical evidence of the rebound effect considering capital costs', Working Paper, Graduate School of Economics, Kobe University, Kobe, Japan.

Nadel, S. (1993), 'The take-back effect – fact or fiction', U933, ACEEE, Washington, DC.

Pye, M. and A. McKane (1998), *Enhancing Shareholder Value: Making a More Compelling Energy Efficiency Case to Industry by Quantifying Non-energy Benefits*, Proceedings 1999 Summer Study on Energy Efficiency in Industry, Washington, DC.

Roy, J. (2000), 'The rebound effect: some empirical evidence from India', *Energy Policy*, **28**(6–7), 433–8.

Royal Commission on Environmental Pollution (2007), 'The Urban Environment', London.

Sanders, M. and M. Phillipson (2006), 'Review of differences between measured and theoretical energy savings for insulation measures', Centre for Research on Indoor Climate and Health, Glasgow Caledonian University, Glasgow.

Sartori, I. and A.G. Hestnes (2007), 'Energy use in the life-cycle of conventional and low-energy buildings: a review article', *Energy and Buildings*, **39**, 249–57.

Saunders, H.D. (1992), 'The Khazzoom–Brookes postulate and neoclassical growth', *The Energy Journal*, **13**(4), 131–48.

Saunders, H.D. (2000), 'A view from the macro side: rebound, backfire, and Khazzoom–Brookes', *Energy Policy*, **28**(6–7), 439–49.

Saunders, H.D. (2007), 'Fuel conserving (and using) production function', Working Paper, Decision Processes Inc., Danville, CA.

Schipper, L. and M. Grubb (2000), 'On the rebound? Feedback between energy intensities and energy uses in IEA countries', *Energy Policy*, **28**(6–7), 367–88.

Schipper, L., M. Josefina, L.P. Figueroa and M. Espey (1993), 'Mind the gap: the vicious circle of measuring automobile fuel use', *Energy Policy*, **21**(12), 1173–90.

Semboja, H.H.H., (1994), 'The effects of an increase in energy efficiency on the Kenyan economy', *Energy Policy*, **22**(3), 217–25.

Small, K.A. and K. van Dender (2005), 'A study to evaluate the effect of reduced greenhouse gas emissions on vehicle miles travelled', Prepared for the State of California Air Resources Board, the California Environment Protection Agency and the California Energy Commission, Final Report ARB Contract Number 02-336, Department of Economics, University of California, Irvine, CA.

Sommerville, M. and S. Sorrell (2007), 'UKERC Review of Evidence for the Rebound Effect: Technical Report 1: Evaluation Studies', UK Energy Research Centre, London.

Sorrell, S. (2007), 'The rebound effect: an assessment of the evidence for economy-wide energy savings from improved energy efficiency', UK Energy Research Centre, London.

Sorrell, S. and J. Dimitropoulos (2007a), 'The rebound effect: microeconomic definitions, limitations and extensions', *Ecological Economics*, **65**(3), 636–49.

Sorrell, S. and J. Dimitropoulos (2007b), 'UKERC Review of Evidence for the Rebound Effect: Technical Report 3: Econometric Studies', UK Energy Research Centre, London.

Sorrell, S. and J. Dimitropoulos (2007c), 'UKERC Review of Evidence for the Rebound Effect: Technical Report 5: Energy, Productivity and Economic Growth Studies', UK Energy Research Centre, London.

Stern, D.I. and C.J. Cleveland (2004), 'Energy and economic growth', Rensselaer Working Paper in Economics, No. 0410, Rensselaer Polytechnic Institute, Troy, NY.

Stern, N. (2006), *Stern Review on the Economics of Climate Change*, HM Treasury, London, www.hm.treasury.gov.uk/sternreview_index.htm.

Sweeney, J.L. (1984), 'The response of energy demand to higher prices: what have we learned?', *American Economic Review*, **74**(2), 31–7.

Vikstrom, P. (2005), 'Energy efficiency and energy demand: a historical CGE investigation of the rebound effect in the Swedish economy', Department of Economic History, Umeå University, Umeå.

Wall, G. (2004), 'Exergy', in C.J. Cleveland (ed.), *Encyclopaedia of Energy: Volume 2*, Elsevier Academic Publishers, Amsterdam and New York, pp. 593–606.

Washida, T. (2004), 'Economy-wide model of rebound effect for environmental efficiency', International Workshop on Sustainable Consumption, University of Leeds, Leeds.

Wilson, A. and J. Boehland (2005), 'Small is beautiful: U.S. house size, resource use, and the environment', *Journal of Industrial Ecology*, **9**(1–2), 277–87.

Winther, B.N. and A.G. Hestnes (1999), 'Solar versus green: the analysis of a Norwegian row house', *Solar Energy*, **66**(6), 387–93.

Wirl, F. (1997), *The Economics of Conservation Programs*, Kluwer, Dordrecht.

Worrell, J.A., M. Ruth, H.E. Finman and J.A. Laitner (2003), 'Productivity benefits of industrial energy efficiency measures', *Energy*, **28**(11), 1081–98.

Xiao, N., J. Zarnikau and P. Damien (2007), 'Testing functional forms in energy modeling: an application of the Bayesian approach to U.S. electricity demand', *Energy Economics*, **29**(2), 158–66.

Zarnikau, J. (1999), 'Will tomorrow's energy efficiency indices prove useful in economic studies?', *The Energy Journal*, **20**(3), 139–45.

Zarnikau, J., S. Guermouches and P. Schmidt (1996), 'Can different energy resources be added or compared?', *Energy*, **21**(6), 483–91.

10 Modelling energy savings and environmental benefits from energy policies and new technologies
*David L. Ryan and Denise Young**

1 Introduction

Technological change, especially when it involves improvements in energy efficiency, is often viewed as a harbinger of good news as far as efforts to improve environmental quality are concerned. This view underlies many policy initiatives that target the adoption of new technologies in the residential, commercial/industrial and transportation sectors. For example, as part of their overall plan to reduce primary energy consumption by 20 per cent, the top two priorities of the Action Plan for Energy Efficiency of the Commission of the European Communities focus on (i) labelling and minimum energy performance standards for a variety of appliances ranging from boilers, water heaters, televisions, street lighting and appliances; and (ii) requirements for energy performance standards in new and renovated buildings (Commission of European Communities, 2006).

In this chapter, we discuss several issues related to the evaluation of the potential effectiveness of policies that focus on the adoption of new technologies. Although we draw primarily on examples from the residential sector, the general arguments and approaches apply to all sectors.

The initial evaluation of the potential for a new technology (such as compact fluorescent light bulbs, energy-efficient household appliances, or programmable thermostats, for example) to save energy, and thereby put fewer stressors on the environment, is generally based primarily on engineering calculations. These engineering calculations often provide an upper limit on the potential benefits from widespread adoption of these technologies. In practice, however, these upper limits are unlikely to be reached. This is due to the fact that behavioural decisions made by individual economic agents ultimately determine how and when these new technologies are used, as discussed in previous chapters.

In order to design policies and evaluate their effectiveness, it is therefore necessary to take into account the economic incentives faced by individual agents. The purpose of this chapter is to examine how (empirical) microeconomic modelling approaches can be used to help evaluate the expected outcomes of policies targeting the widespread adoption of new technologies as a means of reducing energy demand and/or improving environmental quality.

The structure of the chapter is as follows. In Section 2 we examine various ways in which expected energy savings from new technologies might be calculated from a mainly engineering perspective. Section 3 presents latent variable and hazard model approaches to modelling the adoption of new technologies by consumers. This is followed, in Section 4, with an examination of issues pertaining to gauging the extent of aggregate energy savings and environmental benefits that can be expected from the adoption of new technologies. These issues include rebound effects, synergies, and the roles of prices and income. Section 5 concludes with an overview of the strengths and weaknesses of the various approaches to calculating expected energy and environmental benefits from the introduction of new technologies into the marketplace.

2 'Engineering-based' Approaches to Evaluating New Technologies

As discussed in Chapters 8 and 9 of this handbook, the energy-saving potential of a new technology depends not only on the 'engineering savings' but also any change in behaviour by consumers. A study of 98 households by Davis (2008), indicates that the demand for clean clothes increased by 5.6 per cent after the acquisition of a high-efficiency washer. Most, but not all of this increase came through an increase in the average load size. In this particular case, an engineering-based evaluation may be reasonably accurate. However, this will not necessarily be the case for all technologies, as discussed in previous chapters. Additional examples are discussed in Sorrell and Dimitropoulos (2008).

In situations where consumers have an option of whether or not to adopt a new technology, a typical engineering-based approach combines information on energy-use characteristics with energy price estimates and capital costs or cost differentials in order to determine whether or not it makes economic sense for the technology to be purchased by the typical consumer. If the technology is economically viable, then the energy-use characteristics of the new technology are used to forecast the impacts of widespread adoption on energy demand and the environment.

The life-cycle cost approach

One commonly used approach that is used to determine whether or not consumers will purchase a new technology is to calculate the life-cycle costs (LCC) associated with installing and using the new appliance or product. The general formula for the LCC associated with the purchase of any given product model j with an expected lifetime T_j, where the household faces a discount rate of r, is given by:

$$LCC_j = (Purchase\ and\ Installation\ Costs)_j + \sum_{t=0}^{T_j} \frac{(Operating\ Costs)_{jt}}{(1 + r)^t}.$$

The LCC associated with a new technology comprises two components. There are the fixed costs related to the purchase and installation of the technology and the variable costs associated with its operation. Purchase and installation costs will vary widely across applications. For example, if a household opts to switch to the use of compact fluorescent light bulbs, this requires much smaller financial and time commitments than those associated with the replacement of an old low-efficiency furnace with a new high-efficiency model.[1]

Unlike purchase and installation costs, operating costs accrue over time. These costs will depend on a variety of factors. The most obvious factor is the cost of the energy used in the operation of the appliance or product. Expected energy costs are calculated based on the engineering specifications of the product (that is, how much energy is used in its 'typical' operation) and the expected prices of energy. In the case where the new technology is replacing an older technology that provides the same type of service (such as light or heat or refrigeration, for example), it is generally assumed that these variable costs can be calculated based on the same intensity of use that was typical for the previous technology. A typical LCC evaluation for a high-efficiency furnace, for example, will apply forecast electricity and natural gas prices over the expected lifetime of the furnace, assuming that the thermostat is set at the same temperature regardless of the efficiency of the furnace, in order to calculate the (expected) present value of the operating costs. Thus, all savings result from the (present value of the) reduced energy use (electricity, natural gas, and so on) by the new furnace relative to its previous counterpart, less the difference in capital costs. Similarly, a typical LCC calculation for fluorescent light ballasts will assume that the lights will be operated for the same number of hours per year as when magnetic ballasts were used.

Real-world decisions, however, are often more complicated. Some households will replace a furnace due to the fact that the current furnace breaks down. If the breakdown occurs during a period of inclement weather and the furnace needs to be replaced immediately, a household will not likely be able to search across various models and make a perfectly informed decision regarding which model performs best according to LCC criteria. Even the worst new model on the market will likely use less energy than the furnace that is being replaced. That is, regardless of the new model selected, energy savings will be achieved if temperature settings remain the same. Other households may replace a currently working furnace with a new more energy-efficient model. These households will be better able to search over competing models.

Other operating costs that may be relevant for a particular technology include those associated with maintenance and repair and with any 'hands-on' time required when using the product. Once all of the purchase, installation and operating costs have been accounted for, and an appropriate discount rate has been selected, the LCC for the new technology can be compared to those for other options. If competing technologies have different lifetimes and different replacement costs, these features must be taken into consideration in the calculation of LCC values for these different technologies.

Table 10.1 provides an example of LCC analysis that was undertaken by Natural Resources Canada (NRCan) to examine the potential benefits of switching from magnetic to electronic ballasts for fluorescent lighting in Canada (Canada, 2003). The final column contains the differences in the LCC for the two technologies under their base-case scenario of a 7 per cent discount rate, average Canadian electricity prices (measured in constant 2001 Cdn dollars) and an expected lifetime for ballasts of 50 000 hours. Other assumptions in the calculations include (i) ballasts are used for 3600 hours per year in commercial establishments and 4000 hours per year in industrial establishments; (ii) a heating/cooling factor of 0.78 which is applied to the net gains due to the fact that a change in ballast type will have an impact on heating, ventilation and air conditioning (HVAC) requirements, given the differences in waste heat across the two technologies; (iii) a useful life of fluorescent lamps that depends on the model used (19 000 hours for F40T12 lamps and 11 000 hours for F96T12 and F96T12HO lamps); and (iv) specific differences in energy usage characteristics across ballasts designed for inputs of 120 versus 347 volts.

From Table 10.1 we see that in most applications considered, the differences in the LCC values for the two technologies indicate that there are net financial savings to be

Table 10.1   LCC analysis of switch to electronic from magnetic ballasts in Canada

Ballast for the operation of:	Voltage	Annual energy savings (kWh/ year/unit)	NPV of benefits (2001 Cdn$)
1 × F40T12 lamp (4 ft; 1.5 inch diameter)	120V	39	13.74
	347V	28	−6.67
2 × F40T12 lamps (4 ft; 1.5 inch diameter)	120V	44	14.81
	347V	35	9.50
2 × F96T12 lamps (8 ft; 1.5 inch diameter)	120V	49	7.96
	347V	49	−0.04
2 × F96T12HO lamps (8 ft; 1.5 inch diameter)	120V	119	24.23
	347V	119	10.23

Source: Canada (2003).

achieved from a switch from magnetic to electronic light ballasts. For all applications using 120V inputs, the LCC cost for the electronic ballasts are lower than for the magnetic ballasts. For the case of 347V inputs, the electronic ballasts have a lower or virtually identical LCC for three of the four situations considered. While these results would seem to suggest that in most applications a switch from a magnetic to an electronic ballast is an obvious decision to make, before reaching such a conclusion it is necessary to take into account the extent to which the assumptions that underlie these calculations are likely to hold. We discuss how this uncertainty might be dealt with in a subsequent subsection.

Payback period
When making a selection among available technologies, the additional costs associated with the purchase of a more energy-efficient product must be weighed against the associated savings in energy costs. In many instances, the incremental capital costs are substantial when compared to the short-term energy savings. The payback period is a measure of the length of time until the purchaser of the technology recoups the initial investment. It is measured as the ratio of the incremental capital cost to the annual energy savings. As is the case for computing the LCC, the calculation of energy savings to determine the payback period relies on engineering information on energy-usage characteristics of the product, predictions of future energy prices, and an assumption that the new technology will be used with the same intensity as the one that it is replacing. Implicit in both the LCC and payback period calculations, as typically performed, is the assumption that all technologies are equally reliable and have similar repair costs in the case of a malfunction.

Dealing with uncertainty in LCC calculations
When evaluating a specific new technology, values must be specified for a variety of key variables such as energy prices, discount rates, and the expected lifetime of the product. None of these values is known with certainty. Furthermore, some key variables may vary across regions and individuals. In many jurisdictions, energy prices vary across regions,

238 International handbook on the economics of energy

while expected lifetimes of some products, such as heating and air-conditioning equipment, may be affected by local climatic conditions. Discount rates are known to vary widely across individual consumers.

This uncertainty plays a greater role in LCC calculations than it does in payback period calculations. Payback period calculations are used to determine the amount of time required for the initial purchase and installation costs to be offset by the energy savings from a new technology. Since such calculations do not require the analyst to specify a discount rate or the expected lifetime of the product, fewer 'key variables' are used. Furthermore, forecasts of future energy prices do not have to be extended as far into the future. Given that uncertainty plays a much larger role in the case of LCC calculations, we shall limit our discussion to methods of dealing with uncertainty in LCC analysis.

Uncertainty with respect to key variables can be dealt with in a rudimentary way by checking for robustness of LCC results as the values of forecast prices, discount rates and appliance lifetimes are altered. This can be done via discrete sensitivity analysis where one key variable is changed at a time or via scenario analysis where more than one key variable changes across the cases considered (Brent, 1996; Campbell and Brown, 2003). If the LCC for a new energy-efficient technology is lower than that for alternative technologies over what is considered to be a reasonable range of values for prices, discount rates and expected lifetimes, then the new technology would be considered to be economically viable. Two drawbacks to these methodologies are: (i) only a limited set of combinations of key variables can feasibly be considered through the specification of discrete scenarios; and (ii) if the new technology has a lower LCC in some scenarios and a higher LCC in others, then the evaluation of the technology in terms of its economic viability becomes somewhat problematic.

One way to deal with both the limited scope of scenarios that can be considered and the problem of potentially uncertain outcomes that may result from a standard scenario analysis framework is to frame the problem in such a way so that an unfavourable outcome in a relatively 'likely' scenario is weighted differently from an unfavourable outcome in a relatively 'unlikely' scenario. This can be done by assigning (subjective) probability distributions to the sample spaces of key variables in order to perform continuous sensitivity analysis. This approach results in a probability distribution for LCC values, allowing for a more precise measurement of the risks associated with the introduction of new technologies.

Software such as Crystal Ball (an add-on to Microsoft Excel) can be used to perform continuous sensitivity analysis.[2] Specifications regarding the distributions of the key variables and their correlations are used as an input into Monte Carlo simulations that are used in turn to generate probability distributions for the LCC associated with a particular technology. Some recent examples of continuous sensitivity analysis can be found in applications from Canada and the US (Lockerbie and Ryan, 2005; USDOE, 2000a, 2007). The USDOE studies use continuous sensitivity analysis in their assessment of water heater technologies and more recently in their LCC evaluations of dishwashers, dehumidifiers, cooktops, ovens, microwave ovens and commercial clothes washers. In a Canadian context, this approach has been used to examine the minimum efficiency performance standards associated with fluorescent light ballasts (Lockerbie and Ryan, 2005).

Table 10.2   Specifications for continuous sensitivity analysis for fluorescent light ballasts

Assumption	Distribution	Parameters
Discount rate	Triangular	min = 5%; max = 10%; most likely = 7%
Annual usage	Normal	mean = 3600; std dev = 360
Life of ballast	Normal	mean = 50 000; std dev = 5000
Lamp life	Normal	mean = 11 000; std dev = 550

Table 10.3   Summary NPV results using assumptions in Table 10.2

Summary statistic	Average prices (Canada)	High prices (Saskatchewan)	Low prices (Manitoba)
Mean NPV	Cdn$6.29	Cdn$12.78	–Cdn$1.10
Minimum NPV	–Cdn$2.43	Cdn$1.90	–Cdn$7.37
Maximum NPV	Cdn$15.94	Cdn$24.80	Cdn$5.83
Standard deviation NPV	Cdn$2.53	Cdn$3.16	Cdn$1.82
% of NPV values > 0	99.6%	100.0%	26.44%

Table 10.2 provides information on one set of distributions considered by Lockerbie and Ryan for the case of a switch from a magnetic to an electronic fluorescent light ballast using two F96T12 lamps and an input of 120 volts. These distributions are applied to a variety of pricing assumptions based on differences in electricity prices across regions in Canada. Summary statistics for this continuous sensitivity analysis are provided in Table 10.3 for Canada as a whole as well as for two of its provinces. The results illustrate the impact of changes in the values of key parameters on the results of LCC analysis. The results show that whether or not it will make economic sense for individuals to adopt a new technology can be very sensitive to the underlying assumptions regarding key parameters. In this particular case, while the sensitivity analysis indicates that the net present value (NPV) is always positive in regions with high electricity prices, in areas of the country facing lower electricity prices, there is a good chance that the NPV for the switch from magnetic to electronic light ballasts will be negative.

Aggregate energy savings from new technologies
LCC and/or payback period calculations are often used as building blocks in aggregate models of energy demand in order to determine whether new technologies are expected to achieve widespread adoption given current and expected prices, and if so, the implications for aggregate energy use and environmental impacts. The LCC or payback period calculations provide useful information for the prediction of market shares for new technologies. If these calculations indicate that there are significant economic benefits to switching technologies, then these results can be combined with information on how often individuals replace various sorts of technologies in order to forecast how quickly technologies will enter into widespread use. Once these market shares have been predicted, future energy consumption predictions are made. These energy consumption predictions are also based on engineering figures. Although the details of the aggregate modelling process are beyond the scope of this chapter, LCC calculations form a portion

of the underlying basis for analyzing the impacts of new technologies on energy use in a variety of studies.

As a simplified example, consider the estimation of future aggregate residential energy demand due to the use of a particular appliance, such as a dishwasher. As new households purchase energy-efficient models and other households replace older models that break down with the new models, the 'vintage' mix of dishwashers shifts over time. Given a 'typical' intensity of use for the appliance, the portion of aggregate energy demand attributable to any given appliance type k, such as dishwashers, where there are $j = 1, \ldots, J$ models/vintages of dishwashers in use at any point in time, can be calculated as:

$$TEU_{kt} = \sum_{j=1}^{J} EPU_{kj} \cdot UNIT_{kjt},$$

where:

> TEU_{kt} = total energy use attributable to appliance k at time t;
> EPU_{kj} = energy use per unit of models of appliance k of vintage j;
> $UNIT_{kjt}$ = number of units of vintage j of appliance k in use at time t.

Detailed explanations of how these aggregate models are structured can be found in various publications such as Interlaboratory Working Group (2000) and USDOE (2007).

Other issues

In practice, LCC calculations tend to ignore all costs except for the purchase price and the energy costs associated with the 'typical' operation of a product. This can have implications for the analysis of the energy-use impacts of technologies. If the omitted portions of the installation and operating costs differ across technologies, relative LCC figures will be distorted. In such cases, results that indicate that a new technology will (will not) be widely adopted may be misleading.

Several other uncertainties beyond the 'key variables' considered in discrete and continuous sensitivity analysis, as well as many real-world complications, are not dealt with in basic engineering approaches that are used to evaluate the energy-savings potential of new technologies. Although sensitivity analysis may be used to check for robustness across prices, discount rates and expected lifetimes, there are other sources of uncertainty that remain uncaptured by these approaches. These include expected product reliability (in terms of frequency and complexity of repairs, for example) and the possibility that a new energy-efficient technology will quickly become obsolete. For example, in many countries there is currently a push for consumers to replace incandescent light bulbs with compact fluorescent lamps (CFLs). Although the capital cost of a CFL is considerably greater than for an incandescent bulb, industry and government studies have shown that this will be more than offset by the energy savings over the life of the CFL (which greatly exceeds the life of an incandescent bulb). Meanwhile, the next expected change in light bulb technology appears to be to light emitting diodes (LEDs). For example, one project being conducted under the California Energy Commission's Public Interest Energy Research (PIER) Program entitled Lighting California's Future is working towards creating commercially viable LED 'downlighting' systems in a residential (kitchen lighting) context (Graeber, 2007). However, it may be expected that consumers who have recently switched to CFLs will be reluctant to change again to LEDs, especially if they have stockpiled CFLs (which have a longer life than incandescent bulbs anyway). Alternatively, consumers who are aware that LEDs are more efficient than CFLs and are expected to be available soon, may be reluctant to embrace the CFL technology if they have a reasonable expectation that it will soon be obsolete.

Perceptions of reliability also matter when making a capital investment in a new technology. The more risk averse agents are, the less likely they will be to invest in a technology that does not yet have a track record of proven reliability. Risk-averse agents may be willing to trade off the higher energy costs of an older technology that has proven to be reliable against the expected costs (based on their subjective assessment) associated with breakdowns of a newer technology. For example, unlike older models, newer high-efficiency furnaces have integrated ignition control systems for their electronic ignition systems. Extra components found on the high-efficiency models, such as the control board, increase the number of possible parts that can fail on the furnace, providing additional perceived risk for some agents, especially when many of these components are very expensive. These perceived risks are likely to be higher when the technology is relatively new, possibly leading purchasers to view the lifetime of the furnace as being closer to the warranty period than to the stated furnace specifications. Such views would be likely to materially affect LCC and payback period calculations, and may translate into a reluctance to embrace new technologies. As mentioned above in the context of CFLs, another risk facing agents is that a new technology that they invest in may become obsolete. Given observed advances in technologies, some agents may delay investing in a more efficient product in the hope that something even better may come along.

Other factors that may come into play include increased complexity of use (for programmable thermostats, for example) and differences in non-tangibles (such as harsher light from CFL bulbs). For large appliances, the costs of installation (which may vary according to the complexity of the technology embodied in the appliance) as well as disposal of the current appliance will also be included in any calculation of the benefits and costs of changing technologies.

Even if all costs could be accurately captured, engineering-based calculations will never be able to properly capture the true differences in either LCC or payback periods across technologies. This is because individuals respond to prices and other aspects of the economic environment not only by deciding whether to purchase energy-efficient technologies but also by determining the intensity of use of appliances and products. As a household's energy bill falls after installing a more efficient furnace or air-conditioner, the household may use the extra disposable income that results in order to increase 'thermal comfort'. A high-income household may decide to purchase a new energy-efficient refrigerator and continue to use an older less efficient refrigerator as a 'beer fridge'. A low-income household may decide to repair an older energy-inefficient washing machine, while a high-income household in the same circumstances may elect to purchase a new energy-efficient model. Furthermore, the combination of technologies that is used matters. The installation of a programmable thermostat that does not function properly with a high-efficiency furnace, for example, will not lead to any energy savings for a household. In the next section we examine ways in which decisions to replace/purchase new technologies can be modelled.

3   Modelling the Adoption of New Technologies by Consumers

Whether an individual agent will adopt a particular new technology depends on a variety of factors. Among these factors are the expected remaining life of the currently installed technology, replacement costs, expected energy cost savings, perceived risks with respect to reliability and repair costs, and the speed at which technology is evolving. At one end of the spectrum, there are energy-efficient alternatives, such as CFL bulbs, for which the required financial outlay is relatively small and the technology that is being replaced (incandescent bulbs) does not represent a significant previous investment. Furthermore, a consumer can easily assess the reliability of the technology and the desirability of using it on a widespread basis by trying it out (for example, by using one or two CFL bulbs) before switching technologies completely.

At the other end of the spectrum there are technologies that are costly to evaluate and install. A new furnace, for example, requires an initial time investment in order to obtain information about which available models and features may be appropriate for any particular building. Price information is relatively difficult to obtain, as typically quotes must be gathered via visits from representatives of specialized firms that do not have retail outlets. Installation is costly in terms of time and inconvenience. And there may be uncertainty as to whether other related pieces of equipment (such as programmable thermostats) will function properly with a particular new model. Some households may replace a furnace that is still functioning properly due to the perceived energy savings that can be obtained. However, given the initial investment cost of the currently used model, many households will wait until the useful life of the current appliance is deemed to be over.

A particular household's assessment of the desirability of adopting a new technology will likely depend on a variety of socioeconomic factors. Standard demand theory predicts that as household income increases and access to credit markets improves, earlier adoption of relatively expensive energy-savings technologies such as new furnaces becomes more likely. The demand for energy-saving technologies is also expected to be inversely related to the purchase price of the technology and positively related to the prices of the required energy inputs such as electricity and/or natural gas. As family size increases, the demand for services such as refrigeration, clean clothes and lighting is likely to increase. With more people in a household and more-intensive use of technologies there will likely be an increase in the number of lighting fixtures in use at any given time, for example. Furthermore, appliances may break down earlier and therefore require earlier replacement. In summary, household income, prices, family size and composition and other factors, including building characteristics, are liable to affect the decision regarding whether (and when) to adopt a new technology. An understanding of how these factors play into the decision-making process, both qualitatively and quantitatively, can be useful to policy makers who are interested in increasing the uptake of these technologies.

An understanding of these factors is useful for aggregate models of residential energy consumption that rely on estimates of the rate at which technology will be adopted. Given that initial LCC or payback period analyses indicate that new technologies are economically viable, assumptions about the rates at which such technologies can be expected to be adopted are often based on (i) 'survival' or 'retirement' curves that are used to model how quickly or slowly households tend to replace old technologies with new ones; and/or (ii) latent variable models of the technology replacement decisions made by households. In this section we shall examine ways in which detailed microeconomic data can be used to examine the issue of appliance replacement, with a focus on the potential impacts of household socioeconomic characteristics on the decision to retire an old appliance and replace it with a newer more energy-efficient model.

Appliance retirement and hazard models

In analyzing appliance purchase decisions, it is useful to distinguish between 'new' households that are purchasing a particular appliance for the first time, and 'existing' households, that is, those households that already have an existing model of the appliance in question, although possibly one that does not embody recent technological or energy efficiency improvements that are incorporated in new models. Whereas 'new' households have a relatively straightforward choice regarding which products to purchase, the decisions made by 'existing' households are more complex. The former group can simply look at LCC or payback periods, for example, when selecting among technologies, and though these calculations will vary across households because of differences in key variables such as price expectations, discount rates, and even credit constraints, their decision is relatively simple – select the technology with the most favourable LCC or payback period. For 'existing' households, the decision is more complex since they must also decide 'when/if' to purchase a new appliance to replace the one already in use.

Appliance retirement rates (the proportion of the current stock of appliances in the economy that will be replaced by new appliances) can be estimated somewhat crudely on the basis of information on aggregate appliance shipments and available information on expected product lifetimes.[3] While calculations of this type provide a rough estimate of *what* is happening in terms of appliance replacement, they do not provide any information about *why* it is happening, and therefore whether this rate might be expected to persist, or how it might be influenced by various socioeconomic factors. This can have important implications for assessing the rate and extent to which new technology will be dispersed, and energy efficiencies realized. For example, suppose that shipment and product lifetime information suggests that 20 per cent of a particular type of appliance is replaced each year. This might be viewed as indicating that a new model embodying energy efficiency characteristics would completely replace the stock of existing models within 5 years. However, a household's decision to replace (or retire) existing appliances depends on income as well as a variety of other socioeconomic factors, and ignoring this information is likely to result in completely unreliable estimates. To incorporate the effects of these and other factors, a different type of approach is needed.

Hazard models, also referred to as 'duration' or 'survival' models, can be useful for exploring how factors such as income and household size affect the decision of when to replace an appliance. In these models, the length of time a piece of equipment (such as an appliance or a furnace) is kept by a household, which in most cases also represents the length of time that will elapse before any new technology may potentially be adopted by that household, can be modelled as a function of the household's socioeconomic characteristics. These hazard models obviously have greater data requirements than the method described earlier. Specifically, in addition to information on the socioeconomic characteristics of households, detailed individual household-level data are also required on (i) the length of ownership of previous appliances that have been replaced, and (ii) the length of ownership of appliances that are still in use. Applications of hazard models to household survey data include examinations of replacement of space heating and central air-conditioning units in the US (Fernandez, 2001) and for a variety of household appliances in Canada (Young, 2008a).

The basic set-up of these models is quite straightforward. The length of time that an appliance is used by a household before it is 'retired', denoted as t, is considered to be a random variable with a corresponding 'survival function', $S(t)$. This survival function defines the probability that an appliance will be used for at least t years before it is retired (either due to failure or to a decision by a household to 'retire' a still-functioning appliance). Generally, the survival function is expressed in terms of a cumulative distribution function (CDF) for t, denoted $F(t)$. By definition, $F(t)$ indicates the probability that the appliance will be retired before time t. Since an appliance can only be used for at least t years if it was not retired before time t, it must be the case that: $S(t) = 1 - F(t)$.

These models can also be expressed in terms of what are referred to as 'hazard rates'. The hazard rate provides a measure of the likelihood that an appliance will be retired at age t, given that it has survived to an age of at least t. The hazard rate, $h(t)$, is defined as $f(t)/[1 - F(t)]$, where $f(t)$ is the probability density function (PDF) corresponding to $F(t)$. Given the relationship between $S(t)$, $f(t)$, $F(t)$, and $h(t)$, the specification of any one of these functions is sufficient. The choice is often made based on the desired shape of the hazard function.

Studies based on household-level data in the US and Canada indicate that, for most appliances, empirical hazard functions are upward sloping, or exhibit positive duration dependence (Fernandez, 2001; Young, 2008a).[4] That is, conditional on having 'survived' up to age t, the likelihood that an appliance will be retired at age t, increases with t. In these instances, a 'Weibull' specification can be used since it always generates a hazard function that changes monotonically with t (Greene, 2008). Occasionally, empirical hazards for appliances have other shapes. Such is the case for dishwashers in Canada, for example, where the empirical hazard is hill-shaped. In these cases, a log-normal or a log-logistic specification will be more appropriate, since their hazard functions are hill-shaped. Figures 10.1 and 10.2 depict the empirical hazards for dishwashers and clothes washers for Canada based on the 2003 Survey of Household Energy Use (SHEU03).

Mathematically, the Weibull, log-normal and log-logisitic specifications are most compactly expressed in terms of their survival functions (Greene, 2008):

Weibull: $S(t) = \exp[(-\lambda t)^p]$;
log-normal: $S(t) = \Phi[-p\ln(\lambda t)]$ where Φ represents the standard normal CDF;
log-logistic: $S(t) = 1/[1 + (\lambda t)^p]$.

For any of these specifications, the survival function depends on two basic parameters. One is a scale parameter (p) and the other is a location parameter (λ). The impacts of household characteristics are introduced by allowing the location parameter for household i, λ_i, to be a function of a vector of characteristics corresponding to that household (x_i): $\lambda_i = \exp[-x_i'\beta]$.[5]

Results from Canadian household-level data examined in Young (2008a) indicate that the impact of various socioeconomic factors on appliance replacement varies

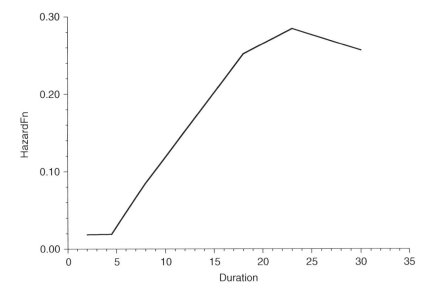

Source: Young (2008a).

Figure 10.1 Empirical (Kaplan–Meier) hazard function for dishwashers

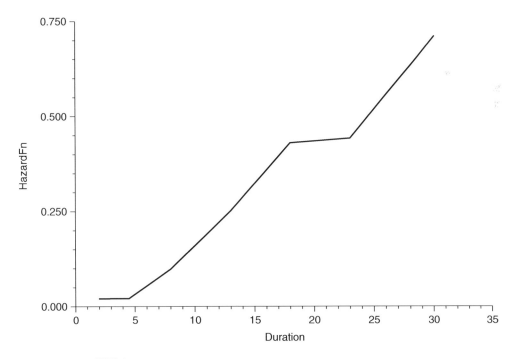

Source: Young (2008a).

Figure 10.2 Empirical (Kaplan–Meier) hazard function for clothes washers

Table 10.4   Significant factors in parametric survival models

Appliance	Significant covariates
Refrigerator	Residence is owner occupied (+)
Freezer	Residence is a mobile home (−), residence is in an urban area (+), number of individuals in the household (−), number of children in the household (+)
Dishwasher	Residence is owner occupied (−), number of individuals in the household (−)
Clothes washer	Income (−), residence is in an urban area urban (+), number of individuals in the household (−), number of children in the household (+)
Dryer	Residence has somebody at home during the day (+), number of individuals in the household (−)

Source: Young (2008a).

across appliance types. While household size (and often the number of children in the household), which might be expected to affect the intensity of use for certain appliances, matters for most appliances considered (freezers, dishwashers, clothes washers and clothes dryers), the only appliance that had replacement rates which were income sensitive were clothes washers. Table 10.4 summarizes the results in this study. The +/− signs indicate the direction of the impact of a particular factor on the length of time that an appliance remains in household use. For example, income (which was incorporated into the models via a set of dummy variables for various income ranges) shows a significant negative relationship with the length of time that a household will keep a clothes washer. This means that higher-income families will tend to replace clothes washers earlier than those in lower-income brackets.

It is interesting to note that in the SHEU03 dataset used in this study, survey respondents were asked whether an appliance was still in working condition when replaced. Although many refrigerators were still in working order when replaced, this was not the case for clothes washers. The fact that clothes washer replacement rates are income sensitive may be due to the subjective nature of appliance 'failure'. When deciding whether to replace a broken-down appliance, agents will take into account the cost of repair to correct the apparent 'failure'. While a high-income household may opt to replace a failed but repairable appliance, a lower-income household may prefer to pay a repair bill that requires a smaller cash outlay than would be required for a replacement purchase. The fact that replacement rates for other appliances were not income sensitive in the Canadian duration models may be due to the fact many factors vary across appliances, including the costs and feasibility of repairs, the retail price of the appliance, and the expected post-repair lifetime of the appliance.

Latent variable models: logit/probit analysis
Another approach to modelling appliance replacement is to examine the factors that determine whether a household will purchase a particular technology. It is assumed that the decision to purchase a clothes washer, for example, will depend on a variety of factors including the age of any appliance currently in use, market conditions, socioeconomic characteristics of individual households and the attributes/features of new appliances (some of which are considered in standard LCC or payback period analysis).

A common approach to modelling this type of decision from an applied microeconomic perspective is to consider a latent or unobserved variable model having the form:

$$Y_i^* = x_i'\beta + \varepsilon_i,$$

where:

$$Y_i = \begin{cases} 1 & \text{if } Y_i^* > 0 \\ 0 & \text{if } Y_i^* \leq 0. \end{cases}$$

In this formulation, Y_i^* is an unobservable (latent) measure of the 'desirability' of purchasing a new energy-efficient technology for the ith household. This unobserved 'desirability' will, in general, be a function of the characteristics of the new technology (relative to other available options) and the socioeconomic characteristics of the household, as measured by variables contained in the vector x_i. Once this 'desirability' reaches a certain threshold, the household will purchase the technology. Although the latent variable is unobservable, the outcome of the decision of whether to purchase a new technology is observed. This decision is captured empirically through the binary variable Y_i which takes a value of 1 in the case where a household purchases the technology and 0 otherwise. For symmetric distributions of the random error term (ε), this model can be rewritten as:

$$E(Y|x_i) = \text{Prob }(Y_i = 1|x_i) = \text{Prob}(Y_i^* > 0|x_i) = \text{Prob}(x_i'\beta + \varepsilon_i > 0|x_i)$$

$$= \text{Prob}(\varepsilon_i > -x_i'\beta|x_i) = 1 - \text{Prob}(\varepsilon_i < -x_i'\beta|x_i) = 1 - F(-x_i'\beta),$$

where $F(\cdot)$ is the CDF of ε. In practice, either a normal or logistic CDF is generally used, resulting in either a 'probit' or a 'logit' model.

One recent example of the use of a latent variable approach to the adoption of new energy-efficient technologies can be found in USDOE (2000b). This particular study examines clothes-washer ownership and replacements in the US. At any point in time, a household that owns a washing machine may find itself in one of three situations: (i) the current appliance is functioning properly; (ii) the current appliance is in need of repair; or (iii) the current appliance has failed and is beyond repair. In the first case, with the introduction of new energy-efficient technologies, a household that owns a functioning washing machine faces the decision of whether to replace its current appliance. In the second case, the household must decide whether to repair, purchase a new appliance or purchase a used appliance. In the third case, the household must decide whether to replace the failed appliance with a new or used model. In this study, the decisions are modelled as a function of the relative prices of the various options, features of the appliances, income and interest rates. The logit results indicate that appliance price is a major driving force behind the purchase decision. Another recent application, discussed in detail in Section 4 below, uses a probit specification to examine the determinants of a household's decision to install and use a programmable thermostat.

Logit and probit models were also used in a recent study of the factors associated with the decision by many households to keep a secondary 'beer' fridge in the home in Canada (Young, 2008b). This phenomenon can lead to an increase in energy use instead of a decrease as many households purchase a new energy-efficient refrigerator and then continue to use an older inefficient model, thereby creating an increase in refrigeration capacity for the household. Controlling for a variety of socioeconomic characteristics of the household and for the type of residence, income was found to be a significant driver behind this decision. Compared with the base group of households with annual incomes below $20 000 (Cdn), those in the ($20 000 to $39 999) and ($40 000 to $59 000) ranges had about 10 per cent higher probability of using a secondary refrigerator, while households with annual incomes of $80 000 or more had about a 15 per cent higher probability.

Other ways in which the economic behaviour of individuals can affect the energy savings available from the introduction of new technologies are discussed in the next section.

4   Aggregate Energy Savings Potential and Economic Behaviour

Once a new energy-efficient technology has been purchased, its impact on energy use and the environment depends on how it is used. Engineering studies show that both control strategies and the features of the physical environment in which a technology are used can be important considerations. For example, 'exergy-efficient' space-heating technologies (such as embedded coils in floors) require a well-insulated building shell if they are going to be capable of providing sufficient heat in a living or work space (Ala-Juusela, 2003).[6] The importance of well-insulated building materials is also relevant for other heating and cooling technologies. Indoor climate control effectiveness will be affected by a variety of factors including the location of the building, the level of comfort required, the number of occupants and the periods of occupancy, the physical characteristics of the building (such as roof and wall types), and the activities undertaken in the building (Monts and Blisset, 1981). The fact that some technologies will provide energy savings only in the presence of other physical features of a building illustrates that 'synergies' matter; that is, in many cases, a combination of factors is necessary for energy efficiency gains to be realized.

For given technologies and 'building envelope' configurations, engineering studies show that variations in operational strategies can lead to substantial differences in energy use. For example, Becker and Paciuk (2002) examine pre-cooling and ventilation strategies for office buildings in a warm climate. They find that altering strategies can have significant impacts on peak-load energy demand, with the appropriate strategy depending on the specific features of a building. In another recent study, Canbay et al. (2004) explain how altering control schemes can be a cost-effective method of reducing energy use for a given HVAC system. These authors demonstrate that a 22 per cent energy saving could be achieved in a shopping center in Turkey through an adjustment in HVAC control strategies.

While these engineering studies could be viewed as indicating that human factors play at least some role in determining realized energy savings associated with energy-efficient technologies, in general these types of study do not tend to consider the specific role, or generally the importance, of human behaviour in affecting realized energy savings. Similarly, the roles of economic (and possibly other) considerations in affecting human behaviour, and hence realized energy savings, are also typically not examined in any detail, if at all. In such circumstances, the expected energy savings associated with a new energy-efficient technology may often appear to be overstated, or at least may not be fully realized in the periods following its adoption. Yet in many cases, by modelling the adoption decision and energy use to take account of human behaviour, it may be possible to indicate the extent to which this non-realization of energy savings is likely to occur, and perhaps more importantly, to identify the factors associated with this so that policies can be adopted that might mitigate these effects.

Consider, for example, the situation where a new technology, Technology B, becomes available, where Technology B uses 20 per cent less energy than Technology A. Based on this information, it might be argued that if all individuals using Technology A could only be convinced/required to switch to Technology B, aggregate energy savings amounting to 20 per cent of energy usage by those currently using Technology A could be achieved (see, for example, Sekhar and Toon, 1998, p. 315). Of course there are a number of reasons why this might not occur and indeed, even if it did occur, might not be desirable. First, as in this scenario, and as is often the case, there is no mention of the cost of switching technologies; that is, no NPV or LCC calculation, or payback period – even assuming no change in behaviour by those who switch from Technology A to Technology B. Second, as is discussed elsewhere in this volume, there may often be a change in behaviour associated with the adoption of new technology, resulting in rebound effects. To use a simple example, the installation of new energy-efficient windows or increased insulation in a house might mean that energy use in that house actually increases as rooms that were previously too cold to be used effectively, and in which space heating was not utilized because it was found to be ineffective, may now be heated effectively and utilized to a greater extent. Third, the technology may not be utilized correctly, or at least effectively, so that even abstracting from changes in behaviour, expected energy savings are not realized. Finally, there may be particular characteristics of those who adopt the new technology, or at least possibly among the early adopters, that result in energy savings being less than what would be expected. For example, suppose that a particular technology – such as energy-efficient lighting – is only adopted by those who could be considered to be 'energy aware'. Thus, this group includes people who turn lights off when rooms are unoccupied, and who used the previously most energy-efficient technology. As a result, realized energy savings associated with the adoption of the new lighting technology might prove to be much smaller than expected. In the following, based on Ryan and Cherniwchan (2007), we provide an empirical illustration of these last two effects in the context of Canadian households, some of whom use programmable thermostats (PTs) to control their space-heating requirements.

A PT is a temperature-sensitive switch that controls a furnace (and/or air-conditioner) by adjusting the temperature setting to preset levels for prescribed periods, such as when the home is unoccupied during working hours, or when a lower (higher) ambient temperature is less of a comfort concern, such as during the night (day). Estimates of the savings that can be obtained by using the features of a PT vary, but are generally quite large. Claims of the amount of estimated savings that can result from using such a device range from as much as 2 per cent of the home heating bill for each degree Celsius (1.8 degrees Fahrenheit) that the thermostat is set lower at night[7] to approximately US$150 of annual energy costs assuming a typical, single-family home with an 8-hour daytime setback and a 10-hour nighttime setback of 8°F in winter and 4°F in summer.[8] Further, these claimed savings apparently can be achieved quite inexpensively. According to cost and savings information provided on the US home energy saver website, an Energy Star PT has an incremental cost of US$107 and generates annual bill savings of US$29, so that the simple payback period is just 3.7 years.[9] In Canada, PTs are readily available at an even lower cost, and in view of the greater space-heating requirements in Canada, the payback period would be considerably less. According to the US home energy saver website, the annual rate of return after-tax for such a device is calculated at 30 per cent, rating it fourth best out of 10 energy efficiency measures that were considered, and well in excess of the 16 per cent average rate of return on investment for all 10 measures.

In view of their low purchase and retrofit cost, and the apparently large energy savings that they are claimed to be able to generate, it might be expected that programmable thermostats would have been widely adopted in the Canadian residential sector. In fact, since per capita residential end-use energy consumption in Canada, influenced by such factors as climate, efficiencies of space- and hot water heating equipment, and housing characteristics, is primarily (57 per cent) required for space-heating purposes,[10] this would appear to be an ideal setting for PT use. Yet, such is not the case. In the 2003 Canadian Survey of Household Energy Use (SHEU03), only 28.6 per cent of households had a PT, an increase from 14.6 per cent in 1997, and this percentage varied quite noticeably across different regions. Of course, one possible explanation for the relatively low uptake of PTs is that the claimed energy savings are not typically realized. To assess whether there is empirical evidence that installing and using a programmable thermostat actually reduces energy consumption, we combine the latent variable modelling approach presented in the previous section with an energy demand model in which the endogeneity of the decision to utilize a PT is incorporated.

Estimation of a simple energy demand equation for 1496 households in SHEU03 that use natural gas for their primary form of space heating – households for which a PT is likely to be most effective – controlling for prices of natural gas and electricity, region, income, education, household size, house age, yields a coefficient estimate of –6.6 (which is significant at a 5 per cent level) on a binary (dummy) variable reflecting the presence of a PT. This indicates that a household that has a PT will, holding these other factors constant, have a total energy consumption that is lower by 6.6 gigajoules, which represents approximately 4 per cent of energy consumption for these households. While at first glance this estimate appears to confirm the energy-saving claims for a PT, a problem with this approach is that it has not taken account of the fact that homeowners choose whether to have a PT, and indeed – as we discuss later – whether to use it effectively. Failure to take account of this endogeneity of the dummy variable results in a biased estimator. This problem has been considered widely in the so-called 'treatment effect' literature, and a variety of approaches for dealing with this have been considered (see, for example, Greene, 2008). Here we focus on a two-step procedure analogous to a sample-selectivity type correction that might be used if we were to focus only on an endogenously selected subsample.

Here we represent the energy demand equation as:

$$C_i = x_i'\beta + \delta PT_i + \varepsilon_i,$$

where C_i refers to energy consumption, x_i is a vector of explanatory variables for the ith household, PT_i is a dummy variable that equals 1 if household i has a PT and equals zero otherwise, and the coefficient δ on this dummy variable is the parameter of interest. Since PT_i is endogenous it can be modelled in terms of a latent or unobserved variable where:

$$PT_i^* = z_i'\beta + e_i,$$

where:

$$PT_i = \begin{cases} 1 \text{ if } PT_i^* > 0 \\ 0 \text{ if } PT_i^* \leq 0. \end{cases}$$

Here PT_i^* is an unobservable (latent) measure of the 'desirability' of having a PT for the ith household which depends on z_i, a vector of characteristics pertaining to the ith house and household. As shown by Greene (2008), among others, under the assumption that the error terms are normally distributed,

$$E(C_i|PT_i = 1) = x_i'\beta + \gamma + a IMR_i$$

$$E(C_i|PT_i = 0) = x_i'\beta + a IMR_i,$$

where

$$IMR_i = \begin{cases} \phi(z_i'\gamma)/\Phi(z_i'\gamma) & \text{if } PT_i = 1 \\ \phi(-z_i'\gamma)/[1 - \Phi(z_i'\gamma)] & \text{if } PT_i = 0, \end{cases}$$

and where $\phi(\cdot)$ is the standard normal PDF and $\Phi(\cdot)$ is the standard normal CDF.

Thus, estimation of the originally specified energy demand equation can be viewed as resulting in a biased estimator because the IMR_i variable is omitted. This can be resolved by including IMR_i as an additional explanatory variable in the energy demand equation, that is, by estimating:

$$C_i = x_i'\beta + \gamma PT_i + a IMR_i + \varepsilon_i.$$

Of course, IMR_i is unknown since it depends on the parameter vector γ. Hence the two-step procedure involves first estimating a probit model of the decision to have a PT and using the estimated parameters to calculate an estimated IMR_i variable, and then including this estimated variable in the energy demand equation. In addition, the standard errors of this final model need to be adjusted to take account of the generated regressor, IMR_i, that has been included.

Estimation of the probit model as the first-step of this two-step process using the SHEU03 data reveals that the probability of having a PT is significantly increased for those with higher education, higher income, a forced air furnace, central air conditioning, recently replaced windows, or one or more energy efficiency improvements in the last two years, while it is significantly decreased for those with older houses. Overall, the probit model correctly predicts the presence or absence of a PT in 67 per cent of the 1496 households that use natural gas for their primary form of space heating. Inclusion of the generated IMR from this estimation in the energy demand equation results in a coefficient estimate on the PT dummy variable of –0.6, which is no longer significant even at a 10 per cent level of significance. Thus, once the endogeneity of the decision to have a PT is taken into account, it is seen that having this device does not significantly reduce energy consumption. A similar result is obtained if, as outlined in Greene (2002), instead of including the *IMR* variable, the predicted probabilities from the probit model are used as an instrument for the *PT* variable.

There are several possible explanations for this result. First, it may be the case that households that install PTs are the same ones that in the absence of a PT would manually turn the thermostat down at night, up in the morning when they rise, down when they leave for work, and up again when they return home from work in the evening. In such cases, the presence of a PT makes it easier to control the temperature in different periods to reduce energy consumption but it does not actually result in a reduction in energy consumption relative to the level that would be achieved anyway.

A second explanation may be that the households that have a PT do not use it properly, or at least not effectively. In such cases, knowing that a household possesses a PT might simply mean that the thermostat that is present in the household *could* be programmed, but that it is simply being used in place of a regular thermostat in exactly the same way – as an on/off switch that maintains the internal temperature of the house at a specified level throughout each day. In such cases, little – if any – energy savings would be expected to be attributable to the household having a PT. The extent to which this might be the case can be examined in the SHEU03 dataset as respondents who had a PT were also asked if they programmed it. Of those with PTs, 26.8 per cent stated that they did not program it. On this basis, although 28.6 per cent of survey respondents possessed PTs, only 21 per cent possessed a PT *and* claimed to utilize its features by actually programming it.

Of course, claiming to program a thermostat is not actually the same as programming it effectively, in the sense of having different settings on the thermostat at different times of the day. To elicit this information, SHEU03 respondents were also asked what temperature setting they use for different periods – day, evening, and night – during the heating season. In many cases, the settings are the same in two or even three of these periods. Almost 38 per cent of all households (over 20 per cent of whom have a PT) had the same temperature setting for all three periods, while only 23.5 per cent either had different settings for all three periods or at least different settings for the daytime and evening periods. Of course there can be many explanations for this result, including the presence of someone in the home during the day – for example, in households in SHEU03 that set the daytime and evening temperatures the same, over 70 per cent had the house occupied during daytime hours, while in 75 per cent of houses with the same daytime and nighttime temperature setting, no-one was at home during the day. Anecdotal evidence suggests that the decision to maintain the same temperature setting throughout the day even when nobody is at home may also be due to a desire to keep pets warm while their owners are away.

There are, of course, a number of other possible explanations, including the possibility of rebound effects if automation of the process of changing temperature in different periods via a PT might mean that the temperature is set higher during some periods than would otherwise be the case, as householders no longer have to worry about the extra energy consumed in a subsequent period if they forget to reset the thermostat manually. Regardless of the particular explanation, the key finding from this analysis is that the energy savings that are expected from technology may not be achieved once human behaviour is taken into account.

5   Strengths and Weaknesses of Various Approaches

Commonly held expectations that improvements in the energy efficiency properties of widely used technologies will lead to a lower demand for energy may not always be borne out in practice. Simply looking at engineering features when predicting the expected impacts of the introduction of new technologies can be misleading. This is because the decisions made by the (potential) users of these technologies are affected by a variety of factors such as income, prices, the age of any currently installed technology, and so on. As a result, although engineering studies play an important role in the evaluation of new technologies, they need to be supplemented by studies of the decision-making processes of households and firms.

In practice, many models of aggregate energy demand, such as those used in Europe and North America, make attempts to incorporate human behaviour and the impacts of socioeconomic factors when they examine the impacts of energy-saving technological improvements on overall energy demand. In the absence of household-level data on which to model decisions related to the uptake and intensity of use for these new technologies, attempts to accurately capture behavioural decisions can take a variety of forms. For instance, in their models of energy demand in the European Union, Mantzos et al. (2003) use a much higher discount rate for the investment decisions of households (17.5 per cent) than for other agents in the economy (12 per cent for industry and 8 per cent for utilities). One rationale for the higher discount rate is simply that it reflects differences in access to credit markets across households and firms. On a practical level, use of a higher discount rate for households may simply help to 'track' the energy-use behaviour of households in that it slows down their adoption of new technologies within the model, resulting in better overall tracking of historical residential energy demand. Other factors that enter into play in the European Union model of Mantzos et al. include the size and number of households, the size of homes, income levels, and 'climatic and cultural' conditions.

Unfortunately, human behaviour is neither as easy to model nor as easy to observe as the engineering characteristics of technologies embodied in durable goods such as household appliances or transportation equipment. As a result, there is a tendency to focus on NPV and payback period analysis since this is much easier to implement once the necessary data related to energy use and prices are obtained. Furthermore, all of the required calculations for these types of analyses can be performed on a spreadsheet. However, these approaches tend to ignore all costs except for the purchase price and energy costs associated with the 'typical' operation of the product. In addition, although there are methods available for dealing with some of the uncertainties associated with the key variables used in these analyses, other sources of uncertainty, particularly those associated with human perceptions and behaviour, cannot readily be taken into account. Further, the fact that individuals ultimately determine the intensity of use of appliances and products, and respond to prices and other aspects of their economic environment in making these decisions, means that the final energy savings associated with any product or appliance embodying a more energy-efficient technology are unlikely to match predictions based on engineering specifications. Consequently, standard NPV and LCC calculations are unlikely to accurately reflect the true costs and benefits of these products or appliances.

While these drawbacks of the NPV and LCC analyses can be rectified to some extent using the micro-econometric modelling approaches outlined in Sections 3 and 4, these methods require extensive individual-level data if they are to be implemented. Survival or duration models, for example, require detailed individual household-level data. Information on the period of ownership of previous appliances that have been replaced, and on the period of ownership of appliances that are still in use, needs to be combined with details regarding the socioeconomic characteristics of households in order to explore the factors that determine how long a household keeps an appliance before considering the purchase of a new more energy-efficient model. Appropriate datasets are not collected on a frequent basis, and may not be sufficiently detailed in any case, or sufficiently accurate – depending on how the information is collected, and results from any given country or time period are not necessarily representative of what may occur in another jurisdiction at another time.

In terms of modelling and analysis of the adoption decision for products or appliances embodying energy-efficient technologies, similar data requirements apply. In this case, as well as characteristics pertaining to the house and household for both adopters and non-adopters, necessary information includes energy consumption for these two types of households, ideally with enough information to account for those factors that, even in the absence of the technology adoption, would cause energy consumption to differ for different household. For this type of analysis it is necessary to model the decision to adopt as well as the relationship between energy consumption and the adoption choice that was made. As the results reported here for programmable thermostats demonstrate, the apparent energy savings from the new technology are not necessarily realized once the endogeneity of the decision to adopt is taken into account in the estimation procedure. Of course, different results will be obtained in different circumstances, so it is not possible to generalize and claim that the anticipated energy savings from new technology will never be (fully) realized. Rather, the message is that it is not obvious from a cursory examination of the data, or even from a simple regression analysis, that more energy-efficient products actually result in a reduction in energy consumption. What is clear, however, is that the energy savings that could hypothetically be achieved from new technologies are, in general, unlikely to be fully realized once human behaviour is taken into account. Thus, while advances in technology have the potential to have an impact on the demand for primary energy, policy makers in particular need to be aware of the role of human decision making when assessing the extent to which energy efficiency programs or policies that are introduced are likely to achieve their objectives.

Finally, it is worth noting that in this chapter we have focused on the demand side of energy-efficient technologies, and have discussed how consumer reactions to prices, and so on, may limit the extent of energy efficiency gains that are achieved from new technology. An implicit assumption here is that if there are more energy-efficient products that can be produced, they will be produced and made available for purchase to consumers. However, even if mandated minimum efficiency performance standards are imposed on production, this does not guarantee that the products embodying such standards will actually be produced and marketed. Manufacturers have to be able to recover standards-induced costs through higher prices, and already concerns have been raised that such is apparently not necessarily the case, particularly for appliances such as dishwashers and dehumidifiers (see USDOE, 2007, ch. 12). Indeed, if the increases in costs associated with energy-efficient products are too high, an option for consumers in such situations is to repair rather than replace existing appliances. Although this aspect of consumer choice was considered here, the interaction between this choice and production decisions, which is also likely to affect the extent to which energy-efficient technologies penetrate the marketplace, remains as an interesting area for further research.

Notes

*   We are grateful to Mark Maxson for research assistance and to Natural Resources Canada for funding provided through the Canadian Building Energy End-Use Data and Analysis Centre (CBEEDAC).
1.   In North America, the term 'furnace', when used in a household context, refers to a central device used for heating homes. In the UK a similar appliance would generally be referred to as a boiler or heater.
2.   See documentation at http://download.oracle.com/docs/cd/E12825_01/epm.111/cb_user_manual.pdf.
3.   For detailed information on how shipment information can be used to estimate rates of replacement of appliances in the residential sector see, for example, USDOE (2007).
4.   An empirical hazard is based on 'actuarial' life tables constructed from the data and does not include the impacts of any socioeconomic factors. See, for example, Greene (2002).
5.   Given that the socioeconomic characteristics enter into the model via the location parameter, the effects of individual characteristics on the expected length of time that an appliance will remain in use are not given directly by the parameters (β). Rather, as shown by Greene (2008), for a Weibull hazard $E[t|x_i] = \exp(x_i'\beta)\, \Gamma\,[(1/p) + 1]$, where $\Gamma\,[\,\cdot\,]$ is the gamma function. For a log-logistic or log-normal hazard: $E[\ln(t)|x_i] = x_i'\beta\ E[\ln(t)|x_i] = x_i'\beta$.
6.   Exergy is defined as a combination of energy quantity (which is conserved according to the first law of thermodynamics) and energy quality (which is consumed according to the second law of thermodynamics). See Ala-Juusela (2003) for further details on exergy efficiency.
7.   Natural Resources Canada, 'Heating with Electricity', available at: http://www.oee.nrcan.gc.ca/publications/infosource/pub/home/heating_with_electricity_chapter3.cfm?text=N&printview=N (accessed 16 February 2009).
8.   US Department of Energy, 'Programmable Thermostats – Proper Use Guidelines', available at: http://www.energystar.gov/index.cfm?c=thermostats.pr_thermostats_guidelines (accessed 16 February 2009).
9.   See http://hes.lbl.gov/hes/profitable_dat.html (accessed 16 February 2009).
10.   Natural Resources Canada, 'Energy Efficiency Trends in Canada, 1990 to 2004', available at: http://oee.nrcan.gc.ca/Publications/statistics/trends06/index.cfm (accessed 16 February 2009).

References

Ala-Juusela, M. (ed.) (2003), *Heating and Cooling with Focus on Increased Energy Efficiency and Improved Comfort: Guidebook to IEA ECBCS Annex 37 Low Energy Systems for Heating and Cooling Buildings*, Espoo, Finland: VTT Technical Research Centre of Finland.
Becker, R. and M. Paciuk (2002), 'Inter-related effects of cooling strategies and building features on energy performance of office buildings', *Energy and Buildings*, **34**, 24–31.
Brent, R.J. (1996), *Applied Cost–Benefit Analysis*, Cheltenham, UK and Brookfield, VT, USA: Edward Elgar.
Campbell, H. and R. Brown (2003), *Benefit–Cost Analysis: Financial and Economic Appraisal using Spreadsheets*, Cambridge: Cambridge University Press.
Canada, Government of (2003), 'Energy Efficiency Act: Regulations Amending the Energy Efficiency Regulations', *Canada Gazette*, P.C. 2003-511, Ottawa, April 10.
Canbay, C.S., A. Hepbasli and G. Gokcen (2004), 'Evaluating performance indices of a shopping centre and implementing HVAC control principles to minimize energy use', *Energy and Buildings*, **36**, 587–98.
Commission of European Communities (2006), *Action Plan for Energy Efficiency: Realising the Potential*, Brussels.
Davis, L.W. (2008), 'Durable goods and residential demand for energy and water: evidence from a field trial', *Rand Journal of Economics*, **39**, 530–46.
Fernandez, V. (2001), 'Observable and unobservable determinants of replacement of home appliances', *Energy Economics*, **23**, 305–23.
Graeber, K. (2007), 'PROJECT 7 – Advanced LED Downlighting Systems', California Energy Commission Public Interest Energy Research Program (Architectural Energy Corporation), available at: http://www.

archenergy.com/lcf/documents/7-PIER-LCF-Presentation-LED-downlight-s.pdf (accessed 16 February 2009).

Greene, W. (2002), *LIMDEP Version 8.0 Econometric Modeling Guide*, Vol. 2, Plainview, NY: Econometric Software Inc.

Greene, W. (2008), *Econometric Analysis*, 6th edn, Upper Saddle River, NJ: Pearson Prentice-Hall.

Interlaboratory Working Group (2000), 'Scenarios for a Clean Energy Future', ORLN/CON-476 and LBNL-44029, Oak Ridge, TN, Oak Ridge National Laboratory and Berkeley, CA, Lawrence Berkeley National Laboratory.

Lockerbie, M. and D.L. Ryan (2005), 'Minimum Energy Performance Standards', Canadian Building Energy End-Use Data and Analysis Centre Research Report CBEEDAC 2005–RP-3, Edmonton.

Mantzos, L., P. Capros, N. Kouvaritakis and M. Zeka-Paschou (2003), *EU-15 Energy and Transport Outlook to 2030*, Luxembourg: Office for Official Publications of the European Communities.

Monts, J.K. and M. Blisset (1981) 'Assessing energy efficiency and energy conservation potential among commercial buildings: a statistical approach', *Energy*, 7, 861–9.

Ryan, D.L. and J. Cherniwchan (2007), 'Ownership and Use of Programmable Thermostats in Canada in 2003', Canadian Building Energy End-Use Data and Analysis Centre Research Report CBEEDAC 2007-RP-9, Edmonton.

Sekhar, S.C. and K.L.C. Toon (1998), 'On the study of energy performance and life cycle cost of smart window', *Energy and Buildings*, **28**, 307–16.

Sorrell, S. and J. Dimitropoulos (2008), 'The rebound effect: microeconomic definitions, limitations and extensions', *Ecological Economics*, **65**, 636–49.

United States Department of Energy (USDOE) – Office of Energy Efficiency and Renewable Energy (2000a), 'Technical Support Document: Energy Efficiency Standards for Consumer Products: Residential Water Heaters, Including: Regulatory Impact Analysis', Washington, DC.

United States Department of Energy (USDOE) – Office of Building Research and Standards (2000b), 'Final Rule Technical Support Document (TSD): Energy Efficiency Standards for Consumer Products: Clothes Washers', US DOE Report No. LBNL-47462, Washington, DC.

United States Department of Energy (USDOE) – Office of Energy Efficiency and Renewable Energy (2007), 'Technical Support Document: Energy Efficiency Program for Consumer Products and Commercial and Industrial Equipment, Residential Dishwashers, Dehumidifiers and Cooking Products, and Commercial Clothes Washers', Washington, DC, available at: http://www.eere.energy.gov/buildings/appliance_standards/residential/home_appl_tsd.html (accessed 16 February 2009).

Young, D. (2008a), 'When do energy efficient appliances generate energy savings? Some evidence from Canada', *Energy Policy*, **36**, 34–46.

Young, D. (2008b), 'Who pays for the "beer fridge"? Evidence from Canada', *Energy Policy*, **36**, 553–60.

11 Bottom-up models of energy: across the spectrum
Lorna A. Greening and Chris Bataille

1 Introduction

For most genres of economic models, standard practice denominates all inputs, outputs, and other measures in a monetary currency. However, analysis of energy and environmental policy requires technological explicitness; the same end-use service can be provided by many different technologies using different fuels and having completely different emissions profiles, and yet cost roughly the same. To meet this requirement, a class of technology-oriented models, collectively known as 'bottom-up' models, developed in the 1970s. Since their inception, ongoing issues continue to drive development (Hoffman and Wood 1976; Hoffman and Jorgenson 1977; Manne et al. 1979):

- the inadequacy of standard money-denominated macroeconomic models, which do not usually differentiate technology stocks within overall invested capital, and eventual recognition of the need for models that explicitly represent the energy-using technology stock;
- technology data collection and availability and, in the early days at least, computing power;
- the challenge of finding methods to 'run' or 'drive' technology selection (capital investment) in a way that is useful and defensible to policy makers and consistent with economic theory; and
- the need to include dynamics to represent macroeconomic adjustments, specifically demand for end-use services that use energy.

'Bottom-up' modeling began with simple, single-sector accounting tools and has gradually evolved into an increasingly complex and dynamic set of optimization and simulation frameworks with varying scopes (from local to worldwide). More recent models, so called 'hybrid' frameworks, include greater levels of economic detail and the dynamic characteristics of 'top-down' models, thus, prompting speculation as to whether a reconciliation of bottom up and top down is possible. This could occur by addition of increasingly sophisticated economic dynamics to 'bottom-up' models, or by increasing technological detail in macroeconometric or computable general equilibrium (CGE) frameworks. At present the majority of hybrid models are modified CGE models; however, other methods have also been employed, with no clear direction towards harmonization. Figure 11.1 provides a schematic of these diverse trajectories of development and where a reconciled model would sit in terms of its technological explicitness, behavioral realism and its macroeconomic completeness. This chapter focuses on efforts to embed economic dynamics in bottom-up models (that is, to increase their behavioral realism and macroeconomic completeness), and the possibility of including sufficiently large amounts of technological detail in existing macroeconometric or CGE frameworks.

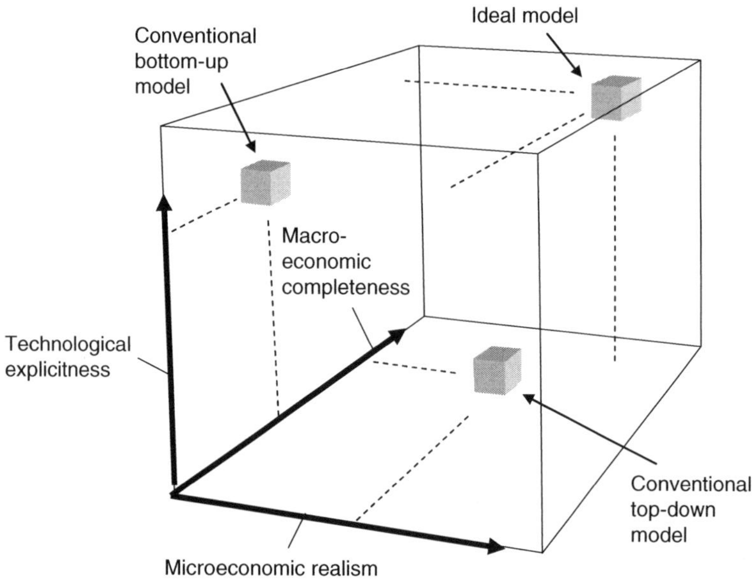

Source: Hourcade et al. (2006). This figure copyrighted and reprinted by permission from the International Association for Energy Economics. The figure first appeared in *The Energy Journal* (Volume 27, Special Issue on Hybrid Modeling of Energy–Environment Policies: Reconciling Bottom-up and Top-down, 2006).

Figure 11.1   Three-dimensional assessment of energy–economy models

Energy system models have been referred to as 'techno-economic' models. Some of them track energy and emissions from cradle to grave for a specific sector. Others are more comprehensive, and include the entire economy (Hoffman and Wood 1976). They have been applied in any number of settings, including:

- regulatory planning (for example, Neubauer et al. 1997);
- tactical planning by energy companies (for example, Deam et al. 1973);
- oil shocks of 1973 and 1980;
- energy supply analysis, for example, for world liquefied natural gas (LNG) markets (for example, EMF 23);
- research and development planning (for example, Kypreos 1996; Sato et al. 1998; Seebregts et al. 2000; Gielen et al. 2001; Difiglio and Gielen 2007); and
- national, regional and global greenhouse gas (GHG) and air emissions forecast and policy analysis (for example, Connor-Lajambe 1988; Zhang and Folmer 1998; Kanudia and Loulou 1999; Jaccard et al. 2003; Labriet and Loulou 2003; Bataille et al. 2006).

The purpose of the analysis determines the level of detail (Hoffman and Wood 1976). A model of the electricity sector used in regulatory planning will have a great deal of technological detail for a specific area (for example, types of generation technologies available to meet base-load requirements, at various capacity factors). A global model, on the other hand, may only use gross characterizations of technologies, but include more technology types and possibly more economic interactions. No matter the scope, all of these models explicitly define a technology by fuel or energy carrier use, efficiency and type, fixed and variable costs, and more recently emissions. The remainder of this chapter provides an overview of some of the more common or longer-lived models in this class of models. Simulation models are discussed in Section 3. Bottom-up models and macroeconomic hybridization are discussed in Section 4, while the hybridization of top-down models with bottom-up characteristics is discussed in Section 5. Section 6 concludes. We proceed with a discussion of optimization models in Section 2.

2 Optimization Models

Optimization techniques were some of the first to be applied in the area of energy system modeling. These models as a class identify the 'best', 'least-cost' or 'optimal' technology, based on costs and constraints defined by technology characteristics. The majority of these models use linear programming for ease of solution. But in so doing, critical characteristics of energy systems, such as economies of scale, cannot be modeled, or only with great difficulty or abstraction. Further, the process of linearizing parameters requires a number of simplifying assumptions and key economic behaviors that are often not represented.

For this discussion, five models were selected as representative (in terms of longevity, level of development, and characteristics of interest) of optimization frameworks: ETA, MERGE, MARKAL, TIMES and MESSAGE. Each is discussed in turn.

Energy Technology Assessment (ETA)

ETA was one of the first 'energy system' models to appear during the early to mid-1970s. The original framework of ETA focused on oil, gas, and uranium resource exhaustion, and was used to evaluate the benefits of the US nuclear energy program (Hafele and Manne 1975; Manne 1976; Manne and Richels 1978; Lejtman and Weyant 1981). ETA is unique among 'energy system models' in that the framework was specified as a partial equilibrium, non-linear programming problem. The objective function maximized the sum of consumers' and producers' surplus; as a result, demand was price responsive. Energy demands were divided into two broad categories of secondary energy forms consisting of 'electric' and 'non-electric' with imperfect substitution.

The representation of supply and demand in ETA used two different approaches. Supply was handled with conventional linear programming techniques where specific technologies and resources were depicted. However, the demand side was based upon a hybrid of econometrics and process analysis. Demand curves were not directly specified; demand was instead viewed as a function of the US economy, maximizing welfare by allocating expenditures between two categories, energy and other requirements. Embedded in this approach is the assumption that expenditures on energy are so small as to not affect the marginal utility of consumers' expenditures on items other than energy. Substitution possibilities between the two categories were assumed to be unitary, with consumption maximized subject to a budgetary constraint.

Run as a medium-sized nonlinear program, the model had a number of positive traits.

The framework could be run for 75 years (which allowed a better evaluation of nuclear options) and the model could handle both inter-fuel substitution and conservation (or energy efficiency) options, and still produce plausible results. However, the technological detail in the model was limited to energy supplies, and then only 16 technologies were depicted. The partial equilibrium specification allowed ETA and MACRO, a two-sector growth model (Manne 1979), to be linked, resulting in a fuller representation of economic behaviors in a 'bottom-up' framework. MERGE and MARKAL–MACRO stemmed from these models as do 'hybrid' modeling frameworks.

MERGE

The bottom-up framework of ETA has over time been folded into an integrated assessment framework. The primary application of MERGE has been to evaluate the implications of carbon mitigation policies rather than energy policy. MERGE is a multi-regional, global model that grew from the linkage between ETA and MACRO and now includes a bottom-up representation of the energy system coupled with macroeconomic, atmospheric carbon concentration and damage assessment modules (Manne and Richels 1990a, 1990b, 1995, 1999; Manne et al. 1995). In the current version, MERGE 4.5, the bottom-up component has received little development beyond that found in ETA. Like ETA, only two energy supply sectors are defined, and linear optimization is used to choose between energy technologies. With a global view and a carbon mitigation perspective, the number of technologies in the choice set has increased to include low-carbon options such as renewable energy. Technological change was originally addressed utilizing 'back-stop' technologies. However, in the most recent version, a nonlinear 'learning-by-doing' function has been included (Bahn and Kypreos 2003; Manne and Barreto 2004; Manne and Richels 2004; Kypreos 2005). Costs are assumed to decline with cumulative experience globally, and as a result, experience in one region benefits other regions.

From a modeling perspective, the linkage of the various components of MERGE into a single cohesive framework is the interesting feature and the strong theoretic foundation has much to recommend the framework.

MARKAL family

MARKAL (MARKet ALlocation model) is actually a family of bottom-up energy system models with a number of different variants (Goldstein and Greening 1999). Although a number of similar optimization frameworks developed during the late 1970s, MARKAL is the most popular with over 70 current user groups and there is continued development under the auspices of the Energy Technology Systems Analysis Programme of the International Energy Agency (http://www.etsap.org).

The original and simplest variant of this family of models is MARKAL, which is a bottom-up, dynamic linear programming model (Fishbone and Abilock 1981; Johnsson and Wene 1993). In MARKAL, all energy supplies and demands for energy services are depicted, and these are matched to energy service demands on the basis of technology costs and technical characteristics. Technologies within the modeling framework are described by initial investment, operating and maintenance (fixed and variable) costs, capacity utilization or availability depending upon the technology type, and the efficiency of fuel use. As is typical of energy system models, energy flows are conserved, all demands are satisfied, previous investments in technologies are preserved, peak-load electricity requirements are honored, and capacity limits are observed. Technologies are selected by comparison of life-cycle costs of alternative investments with the goal of minimizing total system costs while satisfying demands for a given energy service.

Coverage and degree of aggregation in the framework are determined largely by the data available, and the intended purpose of a specific MARKAL model. Although there are a few models with extensive detail, such as one built for the US with over 4000 technologies depicted, the majority of MARKAL models are restricted to much smaller technology choice sets (Greening and Schneider 2003a, 2003b; Greening 2007). This is due to the labour intensity of building a dataset, and often the lack of appropriate data for all of the required parameters. Further, most of these models are limited to a single geographic area, normally a country, state or municipality (for example, Fragniere and Haurie 1996a; Josefsson et al. 1996; Sato et al. 1998). The advent of the regional version of MARKAL has eliminated this limitation and as a result, evaluation of energy commodity trading and of environmental policies such as global and regional carbon mitigation or permit trading have been undertaken (for example, Bahn et al. 1996; Loulou et al. 1996; Labriet and Loulou 2003; Labriet et al. 2004; Difiglio and Gielen 2007; Gielen and Taylor 2007; Rafaj and Kypreos 2007). The development of the TIMES framework and its supporting facilities has made implementation of a regional model far more feasible than under the older MARKAL framework (Loulou et al. 2005; Loulou and Labriet 2007).

In the basic linear programming form, MARKAL has a number of limitations stemming from the assumptions underlying the framework. Perhaps one of the most limiting is the assumption of perfect foresight over the forecast horizon. This assumption results in 'optimistic' solutions based on the underlying assumption of perfect knowledge by firms and consumers of not only current but future energy prices as well as technology and technological change. Generally, this implies that total costs of energy efficiency or pollution reduction targets could be much lower if these uncertainties did not exist. These uncertainties are usually explored through the implementation of multiple deterministic scenarios in the base version of MARKAL. In addition to the issue of modeling uncertainties, various other key assumptions must be exogenously defined by the user. For example, demands for energy services over time are defined outside of the framework, and do not update in response to changes in the price of the service. Nor are other fundamental drivers represented, such as impacts of GDP or income growth on energy consumption. Therefore, within the basic framework, key economic behaviors are not linked to energy service consumption.

In order to address some of these shortcomings, developers of MARKAL have implemented several variants which extend MARKAL. The first extension was MARKAL–MACRO (Hamilton et al. 1992; Goldstein 1995). This framework links a nonlinear, top-down macroeconomic growth model to the basic bottom-up MARKAL framework. As a result of this extension, an endogenous update of energy service demands is allowed in response to changes in energy prices, and the resulting change in consumer utility.

Although a useful extension, MARKAL–MACRO maintains the limitations inherent with nonlinear frameworks, specifically the size of problem that can be solved and the linkage of multiple MARKAL models. Also, the model can only roughly capture changes in energy demand resulting from changes in economic structure and other sources, such as changes in consumer preferences or income. Finally, MACRO assumes a balanced growth path, which limits investigation of disequilibrium conditions stemming from economic or political conditions.

To address economic behaviors more fully, MARKAL has been extended to a partial equilibrium framework (Loulou and Lavigne 1996; Goldstein and Greening 1999). Exogenously defined demands with no response to changes in prices have been replaced by demand functions which relate levels of demand to price. These functions satisfy the usual conditions of continuity, differentiability, a negative slope, and the constraints imposed by cross-price elasticities. Two approaches to the depiction of demand have been implemented: (i) MARKAL-MICRO (MICRO); and (ii) MARKAL-ELASTIC-DEMAND (MARKAL-ED). For both frameworks, the MARKAL objective function has been altered to maximize the sum of consumer and producer surplus which allows for the determination of equilibrium prices. MICRO is a nonlinear framework, and has the limitation that price response is assumed to be symmetric. By ignoring the asymmetry of demand due to capital turnover and technological innovation, MICRO tends to overestimate levels of demand increase in response to price declines. MARKAL-ED uses a stepwise linear approximation of demand, and as a result, does allow for the asymmetry of demand response and income elasticities. Because of the linear approach, this version of MARKAL has been used for the first global MARKAL model, and has been translated into TIMES, the next generation of the MARKAL family.

Several other variants of the MARKAL family have been developed to address specific analytical problems. To examine the relationship between energy and materials, the basic structure of MARKAL has been extended to include material flows (Gielen et al. 1998, 2001). Materials are tracked from cradle to grave with provisions for recovery using the same flow structure as that used for energy. The integrated energy and materials approach allows for the evaluation of the influence of one system on the other, for example, the potential impacts of recycling. However, the addition of materials increases the data-intensity requirements for a model, limiting use of this variant (Greening 2007).

Another variant of the MARKAL family, MARKAL-ETL (MARKAL-Endogenous Technology Learning) allows for the endogenous representation of technology learning (Seebregts et al. 2000; Barreto and Kypreos 2002). Using the observed relationship between the sales of a technology and investment costs, a logistic representation of 'learning by doing' has been implemented in a mixed integer programming (MIP) framework. This implementation assumes that technologies will undergo a steady and stable future development, and as a result, provides a greatly simplified representation of the process. However, no single economic theory adequately explains the innovation and diffusion processes of technological change; as a result, the assumptions in ETL limit full exploration of the process.

MARKAL Stochastic allows for explicit characterization of uncertainty (Fragniere and Haurie 1996b; Loulou and Kanudia 1999; Condevaux-Lanloy and Fragniere 2000). Unlike traditional scenario analysis, this version allows for the identification of a range of possible futures. The user may assume a set of possible futures which are solved to produce a single view with consideration of a number of trajectories for reaching that future. As a result, this variant has been used to explore 'hedging' strategies. Unfortunately, this version has been limited to two stages in its publicly distributed form, and is not yet completely developed as envisaged by its designers (for example, lags associated with nuclear energy are not modeled in Stochastic). This has resulted in limited application of the variant.

MARKAL's longevity and ad hoc development means the framework is not totally cohesive; the user needs to select a variant, which may not necessarily draw on the benefits of other variants. Further, the MARKAL framework has not transitioned into an implementation that uses modern programming techniques, thus restricting its usefulness.

The integrated MARKAL–EFOM system (TIMES)

The next generation of optimization model, TIMES, combines aspects of both MARKAL and EFOM (Loulou et al. 2005; Loulou and Labriet 2007). Development was initiated in 1999 and TIMES was formally made public in June 2007. This framework continues the tradition of the detailed bottom-up framework, but extends MARKAL in a number of critical directions:

- The framework is scaleable from local to global, but has been mainly applied to date as a global or multi-country model.
- TIMES was designed from the beginning as a multi-region framework.
- Unlike MARKAL, TIMES does allow for vintaging of technologies. This feature significantly reduces the size of the technology database required and allows for the decay of technologies (for example, energy efficiency) with time.
- TIMES allows for flexible time slices improving representation of daily load curves for electricity generation and consumption.
- Variable lengths of the time periods over the forecast horizon allow for increasing uncertainty about technologies or other conditions in the future over the forecast horizon.
- Unlike MARKAL, a distinction can be made between service life and economic life of technologies.
- TIMES continues to use the Reference Energy System concept developed in MARKAL. However, the representation of different types of technologies has been given greater flexibility and simplified.

TIMES may be run in one of two modes. Continuing the MARKAL tradition, the model may be run as a simple cost-minimizing framework with technology-related decision variables. As an alternative, the framework includes the aspects of flow-related variables found in Energy Flow Optimization Model (EFOM) where the objective function is expressed as the discounted sum of sum of annual costs minus revenues. As such, users may represent investment as a stream of annual incremental payments. This allows for a more sophisticated modeling of capital investment and provides for decommissioning or dismantling costs with appropriate time lags.

The developers of TIMES have also included partial equilibrium properties in the framework such that total surplus is maximized. An energy consumer's price responsiveness can be included, and demands are endogenously determined. However, other economy-wide behaviors, such as capital formation and labour markets, have not been addressed. Thus, TIMES is still an 'energy only' framework and is still in the early stages of testing (Blesl et al. 2007).

While the TIMES framework is a significant advance over MARKAL, especially in terms of its enhanced capacity for the depiction of critical economic behaviors, it remains to be seen if these developments will be sufficient for the needs of the modeling community. Developments in the hybridization of other models may very well continue to impede wider adoption of the framework.

MESSAGE

MESSAGE is another technology-rich dynamic systems engineering model. Developed at the International Institute for Applied Systems Analysis (IIASA), this framework has also gone through a long period of evolution, but not the wide dissemination of MARKAL. MESSAGE has been used to analyze a number of different energy and environmental problems (for example, Dayo and Adegbulugbe 1988; Chae et al. 1995, Lee and Lee 2007). Most notably, the framework has been used by the World Energy Council to study energy development and the role of technology. As with MARKAL, MESSAGE utilizes a reference energy system to track flows of energy through the system, and utilizes constraints to balance supplies and demands. Demands are exogenously defined at the level of useful energy. This global model is disaggregated into 11 regions with trade of energy commodities linking the regions.

As with MARKAL, MESSAGE has a number of different variants. Developers have linked MESSAGE to MACRO (Wene 1996). However, this is 'soft linked', and the model is solved iteratively (Messner and Schrattenholzer 2000; Klaassen and Riahi 2007). Also, 'endogenous technology learning' has been implemented in the framework using a mixed integer approach where investment costs decline as a function of cumulative experience with a technology (Gritsevskyi and Nakicenovic 2000). Using this feature, a number of energy and environmental, particularly carbon mitigation, issues have been evaluated (for example, Riahi and Roehlr 2000; Riahi et al. 2004a, 2004b; Keppo and Rao 2006; Rao et al. 2006). Also, a stochastic version has been implemented (Messner et al. 1996). Unlike the publicly distributed version of MARKAL Stochastic which only allows for two stages, MESSAGE Stochastic provides for multiple stages and more complicated problems. Finally, MESSAGE has proven to be a robust and flexible tool, because the IIASA early on adopted the strategy of a modular approach using object-oriented programming. Both of these innovations are being increasingly used by the rest of the modeling community.

3   Simulation Models

Bottom-up simulation models are designed to represent the economic and technological dynamics of the energy–economic system as realistically as possible. Made possible by advances in programming languages that allow for abstract entities and their dynamics, the primary purpose of this family of models is provision of probable, not least-cost, responses to policy shocks or other events. Because of energy policy or strategy motivations, these models have often focused on the representation of regional differences in energy systems. As there are many simulation models in existence, we have selected four example models, ENPEP/BALANCE, NEMS, POLES 4, and CIMS, which are representative of the spectrum of sophistication discussed in the literature.

ENPEP/BALANCE

ENPEP was developed by the Centre for Energy, Environmental and Economic Systems Analysis at Argonne National Laboratory, for use in integrated energy/electricity system planning and evaluation of potential policies. It is distributed free in a relatively easy to use Windows platform that makes extensive use of graphic dynamic relationships, and is especially popular in developing and transition countries. By 2000, the framework was used by 80 different organizations or institutions (for example, Christov et al. 1997; Molnár 1997; Argonne National Laboratory 2001; Jaber et al. 2001; CEEESA 2002; Mirasgedis et al. 2004a, 2004b).

ENPEP's basic module, BALANCE, is used to trace the flow of energy through the entire energy system from resource extraction, via processing and conversion, to demands for useful energy (for example heating, transportation, and electrical appliances). ENPEP employs a nonlinear market-based equilibrium simulation approach to project future energy supply/demand balances. It is based on the concept that the energy sector consists of autonomous energy producers and consumers that carry out production and consumption activities with different objectives. This last characteristic is what differentiates most simulation models from optimization models, which generally operate from the perspective of a single optimizing decision maker.

ENPEP is based on the fundamental assumption that producers and consumers of energy are responsive to price. ENPEP, which is myopic from period to period, seeks to find the intersection of the supply and demand curves for all energy forms and uses depicted. Equilibrium is defined by a set of prices and quantities that satisfy all relevant equations and constraints. Market share and total quantity demanded of an energy form is defined by its relative price in a group of substitutable energy forms and end-use demands.

ENPEP uses a sequential iterative simulation process to find an equilibrium set of prices and demands; a practise common with simulation models. During simulation, prices are changed as a result of the application of policy, demands adjust in response to prices, and the simulation is rerun if the price changes are more than a preset amount. The process is repeated until a new equilibrium is found. If the model is well-calibrated and deterministic, this process is highly likely to lead to a new equilibrium within a few iterations.

Data necessary to calibrate ENPEP for a base year as well as to project future energy needs can be divided into the following categories, which are similar for most simulation models:

- macroeconomic data, including demographics, national and sectoral output, wage rates and the rental cost of capital;
- structure of energy consumption in the base year and structure of activity variables (production, dwellings, passenger-kilometers, and so on); and
- technical–economic performance data for energy-using technologies (for example, capital cost, unit efficiency, variable costs, lifetime, and similar characteristics).

Regional energy systems are represented in ENPEP by subsystems and sectors that cover the main economic and energy activities, including energy supply, conversion and consumption, a differentiation generic to most simulation models:

- Energy supply is disaggregated by primary energy form, including hydropower and other renewables, and whether the fuel is imported or domestically produced.
- Energy conversion is disaggregated into refineries (based on the total installed capacity), and electricity generation from fossil fuels.
- Final demand includes five main sectors (agriculture, industry, transport, tertiary and residential), which are further decomposed into subsectors and then into specific energy end-uses (for example, space heating, air conditioning, process energy, and so on). Seventy energy uses and 300 alternative technologies are represented in a typical ENPEP model. Technologies consume final energy, and convert this to useful energy to provide a specific energy service.

ENPEP outcomes are highly sensitive to the technologies and dynamics included in a given version, especially in the transition from base case to the first iteration of the model. These issues are typical of the concerns of other simulation modelers, and are endemic to the method. A typical technology that can completely change the results of a simulation model in the case of GHG policy analysis is the inclusion of carbon capture and storage. This caveat also applies to other potential 'backstop' technologies (for example, solar photovoltaics).

National Energy Modeling System (NEMS)
NEMS is a large, technology-rich, regionally disaggregated simulation model of US energy markets, with a forecasting horizon to 2030. The primary purpose of NEMS is to forecast US energy demand and to analyze the energy-related consequences of alternative energy policies or energy market shocks (Gabriel et al. 2001; Hadley and Short 2001; Koomey et al. 2001; Morris et al. 2002; Kydes 2007). Developed by the Energy Information Administration (EIA), an independent statistical and analytical agency within the US Department of Energy, NEMS is supplied free of charge to interested parties; versions have been used by various US non-governmental agencies, and a version of NEMS has been converted for use by Natural Resources Canada. As the EIA is required, by US law, to provide extensive documentation for the NEMS model (available at www.eia.doe.gov), the framework is a benchmark against which many other modeling systems are measured. Finally, during design, development and update, the EIA has solicited the input from the broader energy analysis community and peer groups.

Key features of NEMS include: (a) regional outputs of energy supply and consumption, economic activity and environmental emissions for the US; (b) use of a modular modeling structure to facilitate and enable the model builders to work with particular aspects of the model independently; (c) integration of engineering and economic approaches to represent actual producer and consumer behavior; (d) use of a projection period spanning 20 to 25 years; and, (e) endogenous technology learning.

The policy questions of interest to the EIA and to those whom the agency is responsible have determined the level of detail depicted within the structure of NEMS. Accordingly, the electrical generation technologies depicted in NEMS are focused on analysis of national carbon mitigation policies and air quality issues. NEMS also contains sufficient detail in the transportation sector to project use of alternative or reformulated fuels, and the potential impact of energy efficiency policies. As such, the NEMS design accounts for existing government regulations and energy policy (for example, electricity restructuring), the effects of research and development of new energy-related technologies, the increased use of renewable sources of energy (especially intermittent technologies), and the potential for demand-side management, conservation, and increases in the efficiency of energy use. On the supply side, due to security and resource depletion concerns raised during several oil-price shocks and from a steady increase in energy imports, all of the fossil-fuel sectors have extensive detail. The representation of energy markets in NEMS therefore focuses on four important relationships:

- interactions among the energy supply, conversion and consumption sectors;
- interactions between the domestic energy system and the general domestic economy;
- interactions between the US energy system and world energy markets; and
- interaction between current production and consumption decisions and expectations about the future.

Using a market-based approach, NEMS balances the supply and demand for energy for each fuel and consuming sector, taking into account the economic competition between energy sources. The NEMS system consists of four supply modules (oil and gas, natural gas transmission and distribution, coal, and renewable fuels), two conversion modules (electricity and petroleum refineries), four demand modules (residential, commercial, transportation and industrial sectors), one module to simulate energy/economy interactions (macroeconomic activity), one to simulate world or international energy/domestic energy interactions, and one module to provide the mechanism to achieve a general market equilibrium among all the modules (the integrating module). The primary flows between the NEMS modules are the delivered prices of energy and the energy quantities consumed by product, region, and sector based on total costs of an energy service (that is, initial investment, annual fixed and variable costs). The delivered prices of fuels incorporate all activities necessary to produce, import, transport and convert fuels into final energy.

The various NEMS modules are coordinated from an integrating module, and, to facilitate modularity, the components do not pass information to each other directly but communicate through a central data file. This modular design provides the capability to execute modules individually or to substitute alternative modules, thus allowing decentralized development of the system, and independent analysis and testing of alternative modules. This modularity also allows the flexibility to use the methodology and level of detail most appropriate for each energy sector.

The individual components of NEMS are solved iteratively by applying the Gauss–Seidel convergence method with successive over-relaxation. Each fuel supply, conversion, or end-use demand module is called in sequence by the integrating module and solved, assuming all other variables in the other energy markets are fixed. For example, when solving for the quantities of fuels demanded in the residential sector for an input set of energy product prices, all other sectors of the economy are held fixed. The modules are iteratively called until end-use prices and quantities remain constant within a specified tolerance. This equilibration is conducted annually until 2030.

Projections using NEMS depend on uncertain assumptions, including the estimated size of the economically recoverable resource base of fossil fuels, changes in world energy supply and demand, the rate at which new energy technologies are developed and the rate and extent of their adoption and penetration. As a result, the EIA produces a number of cases based on differing assumptions in addition to the base case.

POLES 4

The POLES 4 simulation model was designed for the development and analysis of regionally disaggregated, long-term (2030) world energy supply and demand scenarios (Criqui 2001; Ghersi and Hourcade 2006). As such, POLES 4 is different from previously discussed simulation models because of its global scope. The model is designed to identify strategic areas for emission control policies (including development and diffusion of key energy technologies), simulation of potential CO_2 abatement targets with and without emissions trading systems of varying scope, and the impacts on international energy markets.

The model structure is a system of connected modules: international energy markets, regional energy balances, national energy demands, new technologies, electricity production, primary energy production systems and CO_2 sectoral emissions. The main exogenous input variables are GDP and population for each country/region, and the initial price of energy (which is later adjusted in the international energy market modules). The development of POLES 4 was made possible by the availability of a complete International Energy Balance database (from 1971) provided by ENERDATA. Techno-economic data was gathered and organized at the Institute of Energy Policy and Economics at the University of Grenoble; and, key macroeconomic variables were provided by the CHELEM–CEPII database.

In the current version of the model, the world is divided into 14 regions:

- North America, Central America, South America;
- European Community (15), Rest of Western Europe;
- Former Soviet Union, Central Europe;
- North Africa, Middle East, Africa South of Sahara;
- South Asia, South East Asia; and
- Continental Asia, Pacific OECD.

In most of these regions, energy demands for the larger countries are explicitly identified and treated. In the current version of POLES 4, these countries are the G7 countries plus the countries of the rest of the European Union, and five key developing countries: Mexico, Brazil, India, South Korea and China. The countries forming the rest of the regions are dealt with as collections of homogeneous economies.

For each region, the model articulates four modules dealing with:

- final energy demand by main sectors;
- new and renewable energy technologies;
- electricity production and oil and gas refining; and
- primary energy supply.

Simulation of regional energy balances allows for the calculation of import demand and export capacities by region. Global integration is managed by the energy markets module, whose main inputs are import demands and export capacities for the different regions. Due to differing cost, market and engineering structures, only one world market is considered for crude oil, while three regional markets (America, Europe, and Asia) are distinguished for coal and natural gas. Using iterative recursive simulation, import and export capacities for each market allow for the determination of the price for the following period. Combined with the different lag structure of demand and supply in the regional modules, this allows for the simulation of market disequilibrium, with the possibility of price shocks or counter-shocks similar to those that occurred in oil markets in the 1970s and 1980s.

While indicative of the class of simulation models with a very wide scope, development of POLES was made possible only by its association with ENERDATA, the University of Grenoble and the CHELEM–CEPH database. Simulation models of any reasonable scope require enormous amounts of data, which so far has been possible only in association with institutions capable of undertaking specialized data-gathering projects.

CIMS

CIMS was initiated originally as a single sector model, the Inter Sectoral Technology Use Model (ISTUM) (Jaccard et al. 1996, 2003).[1] Development into a national simulation model was done by the Energy and Materials Research Group at Simon Fraser University in Vancouver, Canada. CIMS Canada is the most highly developed version and is used for national and regional policy analysis. Versions for the US, North America and China have also been developed, and in 2008, researchers developed CIMS Global, a version covering the world in six blocks. Besides being technologically disaggregated and designed to mimic the energy system like other simulation modeling systems, CIMS is unique from the perspective of its technology competition and end-use service demand adjustment algorithms. The technology competition algorithms use discrete choice methods (Horne et al. 2005; Rivers and Jaccard 2005) and the end-use services use components, parameters and data from existing CGE models (Bataille et al. 2006).

CIMS simulates the technological evolution of fixed capital stocks (including process equipment, buildings and rolling stock) and the resulting effect on capital, labour, material and energy costs, energy use, emissions, and other material flows. The stock of capital is tracked in terms of energy service provided (for example, freight or personal kilometers traveled or m² of lighting or space heating) or units of physical product (for example, metric tons of pulp or steel). New capital stocks are acquired as a result of time-dependent retirement of existing stocks and growth in stock demand. Market shares of technologies competing to meet new stock demands are determined by a combination of standard financial factors as well as behavioral parameters from empirical research on consumer preferences and firm technology choices.

Like other simulation models, CIMS is divided into three modules – energy supply, energy demand, and the macro economy – which can be simulated as an integrated model or individually. The model is disaggregated into end-uses as indicated on Table 11.1.

A model simulation comprises the following basic steps:

1. A base-case macroeconomic forecast initiates model runs. If the forecast output is in monetary units, these must be translated into forecasts of physical product and energy services.

Table 11.1   CIMS subsectors

Sector models	End-uses or products of the sector models*
Commercial/institutional (m²)	Space heating/cooling, refrigeration, cooking, hot water, and plug load
Transportation (km)	Freight (marine, road, rail and rail), personal (intercity and urban, split into single and high-occupancy vehicles, public transit and walking and cycling) and off-road
Residential (m²)	Space heating/cooling , refrigeration, dishwashers, freezers, ranges, clothes washers and dryers, and other
Iron and steel (tonnes)	Slabs, blooms and billets
Pulp and paper (tonnes)	Newsprint, linerboard, uncoated and coated paper, tissue and market pulp
Metal smelting (tonnes)	Lead, copper, nickel, titanium, magnesium, zinc and aluminium
Chemical production (tonnes)	Chlor-alkali, sodium chlorate, hydrogen peroxide, ammonia, methanol, and polymers
Mining (tonnes)	Open-pit, underground and potash
Industrial minerals (tonnes)	Cement, lime, glass and bricks
Other manufacturing ($GDP)	Food, tobacco, beverages, rubber, plastics, leather, textiles, clothing, wood products, furniture, printing, machinery, transportation equipment, electrical and electronic equipment
Petroleum refining (GJ)	Gasoline, diesel, kerosene, naptha, aviation fuel, and petroleum coke
Electricity production (GJ)	Electricity
Natural gas production (GJ)	Natural gas and natural gas liquids
Coal mining (GJ)	Lignite, sub-bituminous, bituminous and anthracite coal
Crude oil production (GJ)	Light/medium and heavy crude oil, bitumen and synthetic crude oil

Note: * Includes space heating and cooling, pumping, compression, conveyance, hot water, steam, air displacement, and motor drive as applicable.

2. In each time period, some portion of existing capital stock is retired according to stock lifespan data. Retirement is time dependent, but sectoral decline can also trigger retirement of some stocks before the end of their natural life span. The output of the remaining capital stock is subtracted from the forecast energy service or product demand to determine the demand for new capital stock in each time period.

3. Prospective technologies compete for new capital stock requirements based on financial considerations (capital cost, operating cost), technological considerations (fuel consumption, life span), and consumer preferences (perception of risk, status, comfort). Market shares are a probabilistic consequence of these various attributes.

4. A competition also occurs to determine whether technologies will be retrofitted or prematurely retired. This is based on the same types of considerations as the competition for new technologies.

5. The model iterates between the macro economy, energy supply and energy demand modules in each time period until equilibrium is attained. Once the final stocks are

determined, the model sums energy use, changes in costs, emissions, capital stocks and other relevant outputs.

The key market-share competition in CIMS can be modified by changing various assumptions about key drivers. Technologies can be included or excluded at different time periods. Minimum and maximum market shares can be set. The financial costs of new technologies can decline as a function of market penetration, reflecting economies from learning. Intangible factors in consumer preferences for new technologies can change to reflect growing familiarity and lower risks as a function of market penetration.

CIMS' technology data is collected and reviewed in collaboration with the Canadian Industrial Energy End Use Data Analysis Centre (CIEEDAC), an independent data collection and analysis agency co-funded by the Canadian federal government and industry associations, and the other residential, commercial and transportation sectors DACs across Canada. CIMS' technology competition behavior parameters are researched and established in cooperation with the Energy and Material Research Group of Simon Fraser University; the key parameters in CIMS are set using revealed and stated preference discrete choice studies, and literature review where necessary.

The association of CIMS with CIEEDAC highlights a critical issue with the creation and maintenance of a simulation model, or bottom-up models in general. Because they are so detailed and technologically disaggregated, their appetite for data is voracious. Datasets of sufficient disaggregation and quality are rare. Often the building and maintenance of these datasets becomes an activity unto itself, with funding provided by government and public access specifications.

CIMS is notable in that its developers have been working for many years to advance the model on two fronts, including making its simulation dynamics realistic at the investment/technology competition level and by adding macroeconomic feedbacks to simulate change in end-use demand. These goals are indicative of weaknesses in the current state of the bottom-up modeling art. CIMS is one of the few modeling approaches that have met the first challenge head on, but the second challenge, that of the need for more general macroeconomic feedbacks, is more commonly acknowledged and has seen more development.

4 Bottom-up Models and Macroeconomic Hybridization

Bottom-up models, and simulation models in particular, are generally designed with energy policy modeling as a primary objective. They are supposed to represent as closely as possible the dynamics of the real world, including the possibility that an energy policy shock may affect final demand for a given energy service. This possibility can be plausibly ignored for analysis of small shocks and when analysts look at small parts of the energy system. But, analysis of potentially larger energy price shocks, such as might be associated with a system-wide carbon price regime, requires the capability for the adjustment of output and changes in economic structure. These effects require macroeconomic hybridization of bottom-up models.

An energy model most useful for policy analysis would be technologically explicit (including an ability to assess how policies can promote technology commercialization and diffusion), behaviorally realistic (including an ability to assess how policies to increase market share might affect the future intangible costs of acquiring new technologies), and have feedbacks linking the production cost of final and intermediate input goods and services to their supply and demand, as well as more general macroeconomic feedbacks, including long-term balancing of the government budget and labour and investment market equilibrium (Jaccard 2005; Hourcade et al. 2006).

Here we describe a set of 'bottom-up' models incorporating various levels of macroeconomic feedbacks including efforts with the MARKAL optimization modeling system, other experiments with Manne's MACRO model and a sequence of bottom-up models (ETA–MACRO/Green/Global 2100 models), the NEMS model of the US EIA, and the CIMS model.

Bottom-up model linkages to MACRO
MACRO is a simple long-term optimal growth model that lends itself to combination with technology models (Manne 1979). MACRO has been paired with several models with various amounts of energy technology detail: ETA (later Global 2100, now MERGE 4.5) (Manne and Richels 1992), MARKAL (Manne and Wene 1992) and IIASA's MESSAGE (Messner and Schrattenholzer 2000).

MACRO has gone through several permutations, with a common basic structure. A single consumer maximizes the discounted value of their consumption over time, calculated as income (production) minus capital investment and energy consumption. Income is generated through a simple nested constant elasticity of substitution (CES) structure for production; capital and labour are nested against an energy composite, which is usually the sum of energy demands, modified for efficiency, brought together with capital and labour to produce output. Capital grows and depreciates linearly, while labour grows linearly. Equation (11.1) describes MACRO's CES production function:

$$Y_t = \left[\gamma K_t^{\rho\alpha} L_t^{\rho(1-\alpha)} + \sum_{dm} b_{dm}(D_{dm,t})^\rho \right]^{1/\rho},$$ (11.1)

where:

α = share parameter for capital;
ρ = 1–1/ESUB (where ESUB is the elasticity of substitution between energy and the value added aggregates);
γ = coefficient determined through the base year calibration;
K_t = capital (grows and depreciates linearly with time);
L_t = labour (grows linearly with time);
Y_t = income or production;
$D_{dm,t}$ = demand for useful energy (or service), dm, before adjustment for autonomous energy efficiency improvements (output by ETA, MARKAL, or MESSAGE); and
b_{dm} = efficiency adjustment parameter for each energy service (AEEI, DDF, and so on).

$D_{dm,t}$ is a specific energy service demand that comes from the detailed technology models. These demands are modified by the efficiency parameter, b_{dm}, a single autonomous energy efficiency index (AEEI) in the case of ETA–MACRO and a sector-specific demand-decoupling factor (DDF) in the case of MARKAL–MACRO. Capital for energy elasticity of substitution (ESUB) and AEEI must be exogenously specified. Because the entire economy in a given region has only one producer and consumer, no structural change at this level is possible, unless it occurs through the AEEI. ESUB does not update or change as it does in some CGE frameworks.

MERGE 4.5 is multi-region version of the ETA–MACRO model, each region having its own representative producer/consumer. ETA is a technologically detailed resource supply model. It describes the primary energy supply of fossil fuels, and secondary energy supply of electricity. The rest of the linkage between primary energy supply and final consumption by demand sectors is supplied by a constant AEEI. Supply and demand are equilibrated within each individual time period, but there are 'look-ahead' features that allow for interactions between periods. It operates using a 'putty-clay' system – older capital stocks are viewed as hard-baked 'clay', and subsequent investments are malleable 'putty' which then become 'clay' themselves in following periods. New vintages are chosen using a CES production function, while the mix of inputs for older vintages is fixed using a Leontief functional form. This mix of fixed and flexible capital means that price responsiveness is lower in the short run than in the long run.

Energy for capital substitution is modeled through a single ESUB parameter. When energy costs are a small fraction of total output, the ESUB parameter is approximately equal to the absolute value of the price elasticity of demand. In ETA–MACRO/Global 2100/MERGE, this parameter is measured at the point of secondary energy production: electricity at the bus bar, crude oil, and synthetic fuels at the refinery gate. For the Organisation for Economic Co-operation and Development (OECD) countries, the standard assumption is that ESUB is 0.4; that is, a 1 percent price increase will lead to a decline of 0.40 percent in the demand for energy. All non-priced induced energy efficiency changes are bundled into a single AEEI. For the OECD countries an annual AEEI of 0.5 percent annually is used.

Although MACRO is simple and founded in economic theory the modeling output is extremely sensitive to the required exogenous assumptions for ESUB and AEEI. Good estimates of these are difficult to calculate, especially for future periods, and subjective values are often used for these parameters (Bataille et al. 2006). Depending upon the implementation, those assumed values are held constant over the forecast period. From a practical standpoint, MACRO is nonlinear and requires a nonlinear solver for optimization purposes. Early commercial nonlinear solvers had limited capabilities in terms of the level of detail that could be embedded in the energy system component of the model; this limited the number of technologies and energy service demands that could be represented for a model such as MARKAL.

NEMS' macroeconomic module

The macroeconomic module in NEMS, or MAM, represents another approach to inserting or linking broader macroeconomic behaviors to a 'bottom-up' energy system model (the development of MAM is available from the US DOE NEMS documentation, www.eia.doe.gov/oiaf/aeo/overview/overview.html). The original form of MAM operated as a 'response surface' model, and was generated using output from DRI's (Data Resources Incorporated) macroeconomic model for the United States. This form represented a matrix of possible responses to energy price changes. The original MAM interacted with the rest of NEMS by adjusting sector output using elasticity values which resulted in percentage changes in demand for given changes in prices and quantities. No allowance was made for a rebound in overall demand associated with structural readjustment to new prices, for example, the movement to less energy-intense capital investment and economic recovery after an oil-price shock. In 1999, kernel regressions were substituted for the single elasticity responses in the response surface. This enhancement incorporated direct price responses and allowed for some structural changes.

In the current representation of MAM, the bottom-up side of NEMS iterates with a macroeconomic modeling system of the US economy (currently the Global Insight Models of the US economy, industry and employment, and the EIA regional models). To start the process this modeling system is fed an initial set of energy prices, demands and domestic energy output from an initial simulation of NEMS. After the appropriate NEMS variables have been extracted, the three sets of models – macroeconomic, industry and employment, and regional – are run in sequence. A modified set of macroeconomic drivers are then passed back to the supply, demand, and conversion modules of NEMS. NEMS is then rerun with these new values and the resulting energy prices and quantities are passed back to MAM. Iteration continues until convergence of all parts of the system is achieved, and is repeated on an annual basis to the end of the forecast horizon.

The revised MAM framework is more responsive to changes in the economy than previously, but is not completely satisfactory. The major components of the macroeconomic model are demand driven with a focus on the short run, thus providing a somewhat myopic and simplified view of investment. Given that investment is also the vehicle for the penetration of energy efficiency, fuel switching, direct emissions reduction technologies (for example, SO_x scrubbers, carbon capture and storage), and other policy-induced technological change (for example, 'learning by doing'), subtle but significant changes may not be apparent in model output. These shortcomings are offset by a link to a Ramsey growth model, where investment is a factor, and by solving on an annual basis. This process, however, is computationally intensive, and could potentially fail to reach a solution under certain conditions such as an oil-price shock.

CIMS' macroeconomic module

CIMS uses another approach to embedding economic dynamics into a bottom-up simulation model by moving towards a general equilibrium framework similar to that found in CGE models (Bataille et al. 2006). The framework estimates the effect of a policy by comparing a business-as-usual market equilibrium with one generated by a policy. The model operates by iteration of two sequential phases in each five-year period, with as many iterations as necessary to arrive at equilibrium in each period. The scope of a policy can range from one that affects a single technology, such as a subsidy to a specific technology, to a technology competition, where one might apply an efficiency standard to a single market, all the way up to an economy-wide carbon tax or emissions permit trading system.

The first phase, equilibrium of energy supply and demand, is described schematically in Figure 11.2. In this first phase, the models representing the final goods and services producing sectors of the economy are run (the transportation, residential, commercial and industrial models on the left side of the figure). The firms and consumers in these sectors choose capital stocks based on CIMS' technological choice algorithms, which

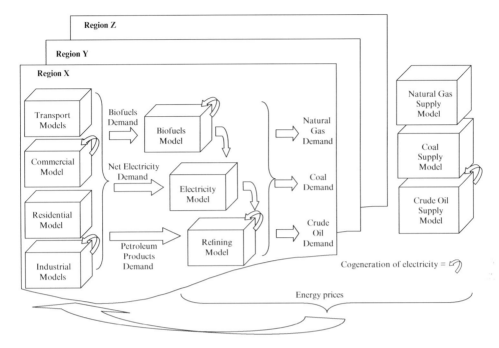

Figure 11.2   CIMS' energy supply and demand flow model

minimize financial and intangible expenditure on capital, labour, energy and emissions charges are based on an initial set of input prices. The model then calculates the demand and cost of delivery for various energy forms, including any policy effects (the middle and right side of the figure). If the cost of producing any of these commodities has changed by a threshold amount (normally 5 percent) from the business-as-usual case, the model is considered to be in disequilibrium and is rerun based on prices calculated from the new production costs. Prices are adjusted using multipliers of the base-case absolute values. The model will iterate until a new equilibrium set of energy prices and demands is reached, that which usually occurs within three iterations.

In the second phase, once a new equilibrium set of energy prices has been reached, the model then calculates the degree to which the costs of producing traded goods and services have changed; assuming perfectly competitive markets, these changes translate directly into prices. These new prices are used to adjust demand for internationally traded goods using price elasticities which follow the Armington specification, where a demand response blends domestic and international demand of a good. Demand for freight transportation is linked to the combined value added of the industrial sectors, while personal transportation is adjusted using an own-price personal kilometres traveled elasticity. If demand for any good or service has shifted more than a threshold amount, the model is considered to be in disequilibrium and reruns both the energy supply and final demand phases using the last set of prices and the new demands. The model continues reiterating until supply and demand for all goods and services comes to a new equilibrium, and repeats this convergence procedure every five years until the end of the forecast horizon, which can last from 5 to 50 years.

The key dynamics lacking in CIMS are capital, wage and currency markets, as well as balancing of government finances. Each of these weaknesses is a strength of the CGE approach, hence efforts to alleviate them have focused on use of CGE models and methods. Three approaches are being used to tackle these issues: CIMS is used to parameterize an existing CGE model, more CGE dynamics can be added to CIMS, or CIMS can be used to directly replace the production functions in an existing CGE framework. In the first case, CIMS has been used to calculate long-term elasticities of substitution between capital and energy and between fuels under a range of energy prices (Bataille et al. 2006); these elasticities have since been installed in a CGE model of Canada for use in policy analysis. Experiments are also proceeding to add capital and wage markets to CIMS, and to directly link CIMS to an existing CGE system as replacement for the standard CES production functions.

5   Is Bottom Up's Future Top Down? Hybridization of Top-down Models with Bottom up Characteristics

> Been top down for so long it looks like bottom up to me.
>
> (Huntington 1994, p. 833)

The goal of combining technological explicitness, microeconomic realism and macroeconomic feedbacks in the same policy modeling system is not confined to bottom-up modeling. In fact, because of the existence of many more top-down than bottom-up modeling teams, especially those using CGE models, the majority of researchers have been trying to solve the problem from the opposite direction, via the addition of technological explicitness to an existing CGE or macroeconometric model.

Historically, two key parameters have been used to describe the capacity for technological change in top-down models: ESUBs and the AEEI. ESUBs indicate the substitutability between any two pairs of aggregate inputs (capital, labour, energy, materials), and between the different forms of final energy as relative prices change. The higher the capital-for-energy and inter-fuel ESUBs, the lower will be the cost of policies to reduce energy use or GHG emissions. AEEI indicates the rate at which price-independent technological evolution improves energy productivity, and is a function of changes in technology and capital stock turnover. The higher AEEI is, the faster the economy is becoming more efficient at using energy (and by implication reducing GHG intensity). When analyzing any type of policy that involves long-run technological adjustment, it is critical that both types of parameter accurately reflect the underlying system dynamics (Bataille et al. 2006).

Policy makers are interested in the extent to which their policies might influence the characteristics and financial costs of future technologies, and the likely willingness of consumers and businesses to adopt these. If the ESUB and AEEI are estimated from aggregate, historical data, there is no guarantee that these parameter values will remain valid into the future under different policies for environmental improvement (Grubb et al. 2002). The emergence of hybrid gasoline–electric vehicles, for example, will probably increase the transportation sector's AEEI, because it allows for improved energy efficiency, and increased ESUB, because it will enhance the consumer's ability to choose between capital and energy in response to their relative input prices. On a larger scale, until recently there was little incentive to design and commercialize technologies with zero or near-zero GHG emissions; today, such technologies are under development worldwide. As GHG policy develops and firms build it into their expectations and investment, the estimated cost of GHG abatement is likely to decrease, but the ESUB and AEEI approaches to modeling technology in top-down models will have difficulty with this dynamic. Increasingly concerned with these long-term parameterization problems, ways of treating technological change endogenously are being explored. However, there has been little success in linking real-world evidence to the estimation of aggregate parameters of technological change in these models (Löschel 2002).

Policy makers are also pushed towards technology-specific policies in the form of tax credits, subsidies, regulations and information programs, especially in the case where emission charges may need to be high to achieve a given environmental improvement. This encourages policy makers to apply a mix of policies whose incidence is targeted to minimize the public reaction that significant energy price increases may trigger. Because conventional top-down models represent technological change as an abstract, aggregate phenomenon – characterized by ESUB and AEEI parameter values – this approach helps policy makers assess only economy-wide policy instruments such as taxes and tradable permits. A more useful model should be able to assess the combined effect of economy-wide, price-based policies with technology-focused policies, which requires the explicit representation of individual technologies that top-down models lack (Jaccard 2005).

Several different methods have been developed to hybridize top-down models with technological explicitness:

- the use of mixed complementarity problem-solving routines to simulate discrete and limited technology choices (Böhringer 1998; Böhringer and Rutherford 2008);
- the use of fixed input ratio Leontief functions to represent technologies, and simulation-style competitions between the technologies based on life-cycle cost (Sands 2004, and Schumacher and Sands 2007 using the SGM model; Babiker et al. 2001, McFarland et al. 2004, and Sue Wing 2008 using the MIT–EPPA model);
- the calibration of standard CES functions to represent discrete technology substitution (Hanson and Laitner 2004, Laitner and Hanson 2006 using the AMIGA model);
- the use of envelope functions calculated from a bottom-up model to proxy technological response in a CGE model (Ghersi and Hourcade 2006 using POLES and IMACLIM-S);
- active passing of variables between a top-down model and a bottom-up transportation model (for example, Shaefer and Jacoby 2005 and 2006 using the MIT–EPPA model); and
- incorporating of sufficient equations in a macroeconometric framework (Köhler et al. 2006 using the E3ME model).

This work is generally confined to electricity generation or highly energy-intensive industry with significantly different technology options (for example, Schumacher and Sands 2007 used it for the iron and steel sector). Other authors in this area include: Jacobsen

1998, Koopmans and te Velde 2001, Morris et al. 2002, Frei et al. 2003, and Bosetti et al. 2006.

These developments have been necessary for CGE and macroeconometric models so that these models may realistically model large energy policy shocks, specifically those to do with high carbon prices. There appear, however, to be serious impediments to adding substantial technological detail to top-down models, preventing them from providing all the analysis services of the bottom-up models. In terms of CGE modeling, which represents most of the top-down efforts because of its desirability for long-term modeling over estimated macroeconometric models, the most important issue is the initial calibration of a social accounting matrix. The addition of every new technology (if modeled as a producing sector) tends to add a whole new dimension of relationships with other existing variables. Modelers using the MIT–EPPA model (for example, Sue Wing 2008) have possibly made the most progress in establishing a standardized method for adding technological disaggregation. While it is possible to add a number of new sectors, beyond a certain number, calibration of the social accounting matrix may become impossible with current practices. Also, it is currently beyond possibility to duplicate the thousands of energy demand and supply technologies seen in sophisticated bottom-up frameworks. Future generations of CGE frameworks may overcome this limitation.

A question remains, however, as to how much technological detail is really necessary and realistic. Those of the top-down modeling community have argued that forecasts of technology characteristics are highly uncertain, and are representative only for limited periods of time. Those of the bottom-up persuasion instead insist that there are a broad set of 'absolutely necessary' technological details, including at a minimum fuel switching and energy efficiency competitions at the sectoral level, potential new technologies, and the ability to apply regulations to subsets of technologies. Arguments by both groups represent the end-points of a trade-off that must be made while building a model.

To simplify calibration, CGE models tend to use CES functions to represent production. While this may be sufficient for sectors where inputs are smoothly substitutable for each other over a wide range of input combinations (like between capital and labour in services) in many sectors capital, labour and energy are not smoothly substitutable; they are instead substitutable in discrete 'lumps'. CES functions have difficulty representing discrete, lumpy or discontinuous technology choice. Laitner and Hanson (2006) tackle this directly by trying to calibrate CES functions to existing data, while Ghersi and Hourcade (2006) instead use an envelope function to represent components of the POLES 4 model in the IMACLIM-S CGE. Another option was offered by McKitrick (1998), who argued for generalized functional forms, such as the translog, normalized quadratic or generalized Leontief, as alternatives to a CES. These other forms can take the shape of any possible production function. While there are other adherents to this proposition (for example, McKibbin and Wilcoxen 1999, running the G-cubed model), the sheer difficulty of estimating the parameters for CGE models, and finding data to do so, has precluded most from using them in the place of calibrated models.

In sum, while both bottom-up and top-down modelers have actively worked to add macroeconomic feedbacks in the first case, and technological explicitness in the second case, neither has completely succeeded, and both approaches will likely be applied as most appropriate for the foreseeable future.

6 Summary and Future Developments

> . . . all models are wrong, but some are more useful.
>
> (Box 1979, p. 202)

The driving force behind bottom-up continues to be the need to describe the energy economy, or components of it, at a much higher level of technology and process detail than available from alternatives. The genre began with single-sector models, designed to explicitly account for inflows and outflows of energy forms from processes or the energy economy system in general. This approach to analyzing energy use encouraged a movement towards technological disaggregation, a move 'pulled' by the increasing need for policy tools that could distinguish between technologies that could cost virtually the same and provide the same service, but have radically different energy and emission profiles. Once it became commonplace to model technology sets, modeling firms' and consumers' decisions between technological options was the next challenge. The use of cost minimization, also referred to as optimization in certain contexts, combined with the need to model an increasingly wider scope of the economy, eventually allowed and encouraged the development of highly sophisticated forecasting models of the entire energy system, of which the various versions of MARKAL are the exemplary development.

Technological developments in computing have also allowed bottom-up models to more realistically simulate the structure of the energy system (for example, the flow of petroleum products from wells to batteries, to refineries and processors, to distributors and retailers, and finally to the end-use consumer), eventually leading to the 'simulation' family of models. These have become more realistic in structure, with models emerging that depict the flow of the entire energy system for individual energy types from primary sources, through energy conversion, distribution and retaining industries, to various heterogeneous consumers. This drive to a realistic structure has encouraged a parallel if less immediately successful drive to more realistically simulate the dynamics of technology choice, be it firm investment behavior or consumer consumption behavior.

Beyond microeconomic realism, 'bottom-up' modelers have gradually recognized the necessity of including economic behaviors beyond the energy system. This has led to the inclusion of more sophisticated feedbacks in this class of model. The technologically explicit nature of these models means that these feedbacks have focused on adjusting the demand for energy using goods and services in response to changes in cost of their delivery, generally using own-price demand elasticities and basic macroeconometric equations, or simulacrums of full macroeconomic models. However, it is generally acknowledged that these methods account for only the direct adjustment effects of the economy to energy price changes, and not what happens to overall effects on wages, cost of capital, exchange rates, and government budgets. These 'secondary macroeconomic effects' have long been a primary concern of the more common macroeconometric and CGE approaches. At the same time, macroeconometric and CGE modelers, especially when modeling significant GHG reduction policies, have recognized the technological deficiency of their methods, and have striven to improve this.

The two fundamentally different approaches of bottom up and top down to the same policy analysis goals raise the question of whether there is the possibility of harmonization on one approach to modeling the energy system. Any new modeling paradigm would need to include all the following characteristics:

1.   Monetary and physical flows would be explicitly represented and accounted for.
2.   Distinct representative agents for consumers, firms, government and the rest of the world would be depicted so that behavior could be assigned explicitly to an economic decision maker in question.
3.   A full end-to-end representation of energy end-use, conversion, supply, and import and export activities would be provided and embedded in the relevant greater economic context.
4.   The framework would be completely constructed on a generic, robust and flexible software architecture that allows, through the endogenous calculation of market-clearing prices, for the balancing of all market inputs or as close to general equilibrium as possible.
5.   Such a framework would have integrated and callable bottom-up sectoral components, with sufficiently discrete and disaggregated technology subcomponents, for all necessary energy demand and supply processes.
6.   Finally, the framework should be scalable, allowing for simple and more complex models as necessary, but with interchangeable subcomponents.

   In summary, bottom-up models have become increasingly detailed and more sophisticated in their handling of technology choice, and increasingly representative of the dynamics of the energy system. At the same time, capabilities have been added for simulating the relationships between the physical stock and the greater economy. Finally, the energy policy requirements that drove all of these trends remain unchanged and will continue to drive development.

Note

1.   As is often the case, energy system models for the entire economy evolve from single-sector models. Several frameworks use ISTUM as a starting point including NEMS and a version of MARKAL (Greening, 2007). ISTUM was developed at Pacific Northwest Laboratory under the auspices of the US Department of Energy.

References

Argonne National Laboratory (2001), *Greenhouse Gas Mitigation Analysis Using ENPEP: A Modeling Guide*, Vienna: International Atomic Energy Agency.
Babiker, M., J. Reilly, M. Mayer, R. Eckaus, I. Wing and R. Hyman (2001), *The MIT Emissions Prediction and Policy Analysis Model: Revisions, Sensitivities, and Comparisons of Results*, Cambridge, MA: MIT Joint Program on the Science and Policy of Global Change, Massachusetts Institute of Technology.
Bahn, O., A. Haurie, S. Kypreos and J.-P. Vial (1996), 'A decomposition approach to multiregional environmental planning: a numerical study', in C. Carraro and A. Haurie (eds), *Operations Research and Environmental Management*, Dordrecht: Kluwer Academic, pp. 119–32.
Bahn, O. and S. Kypreos (2003), 'Incorporating different endogenous learning formulations in MERGE', *Energy*, **19**(4), 333–58.
Barreto, L. and S. Kypreos (2002), 'Multi-regional technological learning in the energy-systems MARKAL model', *Global Energy Issues*, **17**(3), 189–213.
Bataille, C., M. Jaccard, J. Nyboer and N. Rivers (2006), 'Towards general equilibrium in a technology-rich model with empirically estimated behavioral parameters', *The Energy Journal*, 27 (Special Issue on Hybrid Modeling of Energy–Environment Policies: Reconciling Bottom-up and Top-down), 93–112.

Blesl, M., A. Das, U. Fahl and U. Remme (2007), 'Role of energy efficiency standards in reducing CO$_2$ emissions in Germany: an assessment with TIMES', *Energy Policy*, **35**(2), 772–85.
Böhringer, C. (1998), 'The synthesis of bottom-up and top-down in energy policy modeling', *Energy Economics*, **20**(3), 233–48.
Böhringer, C. and T. Rutherford (2008), 'Combining bottom-up and top-down', *Energy Economics*, **30**(2), 574–96.
Bosetti, V., C. Carraro, M. Galeotti, E. Massetti and M. Tavoni (2006), 'WITCH: a world induced technical change hybrid model', *The Energy Journal*, **27** (Special Issue on Hybrid Modeling of Energy–Environment Policies: Reconciling Bottom-up and Top-down), 13–38.
Box, G. (1979), 'Robustness in the strategy of scientific model building', in R.L. Launer and G.N. Wilkinson (eds), *Robustness in Statistics*, New York: Academic Press, pp. 201–36.
Center for Energy, Environment, and Economic Systems Analysis (CEEESA) (2002), *Energy and Power Evaluation Program (ENPEP): Model Overview*, Argonne, IL: Argonne National Laboratory.
Chae, K.N., D.G. Lee, C.Y. Lim and B.W. Lee (1995), 'The role of nuclear energy system for Korean long-term energy supply strategy', *Progress in Nuclear Energy*, **29**(Supplement 1), 71–8.
Christov, C., K. Simeonova, S. Todorova and V. Krastev (1997), 'Assessment of mitigation options for the energy system in Bulgaria', *Applied Energy*, **56**(3–4), 299–308.
Condevaux-Lanloy, C. and E. Fragniere (2000), 'An approach to deal with uncertainty in energy and environmental planning: the MARKAL case', *Environmental Modeling and Assessment*, **5**(3), 145–55.
Connor-Lajambe, H. (1988), 'Renewable energy and long-term energy planning', *The Energy Journal*, **9**(3), 143–51.
Criqui, P. (2001), 'POLES: prospective outlook on long-term energy systems', Institut d'Économie et de Politique de l'Énergie, Grenoble, France, available at: http://www.upmf-grenoble.fr/iepe/textes/POLES8p_01.pdf (accessed August 2006).
Dayo, F.B. and A.O. Adegbulugbe (1988), 'Utilization of Nigerian natural gas resources: potentials and opportunities', *Energy Policy*, **16**(2), 122–30.
Deam, R.J., M.A. Laughton, J.G. Hale, J.R. Isaac, J. Leather, F.M. O'Carroll and P.C. Ward (1973), 'World energy modelling: the development of western European oil prices', *Energy Policy*, **1**(1), 21–34.
Difiglio, C. and D. Gielen (2007), 'Hydrogen and transportation: alternative scenarios', *Mitigation and Adaptation Strategies for Global Change*, **12**(3), 387–405.
Fishbone, L.G. and H. Abilock (1981), 'MARKAL, a linear-programming model for energy systems analysis: technical description of the BNL version', *Energy Research*, **5**(4), 353–75.
Fragniere, E. and A. Haurie (1996a), 'MARKAL–Geneva: a model to assess energy–environment choices for a Swiss canton', in C. Carraro and A. Haurie (eds), *Operations Research and Environmental Management*, Dordrecht: Kluwer Academic, pp. 41–68.
Fragniere, E. and A. Haurie (1996b), 'A stochastic programming model for energy/environment choices under uncertainty', *International Journal of Environment and Pollution*, **6**(4–6), 587–603.
Frei, C., P. Haldi and G. Sarlos (2003), 'Dynamic formulation of a top-down and bottom-up merging energy policy model', *Energy Policy*, **31**(10), 1017–31.
Gabriel, S.A., A.S. Kydes and P. Whitman (2001), 'The National Energy Modeling System: a large-scale energy–economic equilibrium model', *Operations Research*, **49**(1), 14–25.
Ghersi, F. and J.C. Hourcade (2006), 'Macroeconomic consistency issues in E3 modeling: the continued fable of the elephant and the rabbit', *The Energy Journal*, **27** (Special Issue on Hybrid Modeling: New Answers to Old Challenges), 39–62.
Gielen, D.J., M.A.P.C. de Feber, A.J.M. Bos and T. Gerlagh (2001), 'Biomass for energy or materials? A Western European systems engineering perspective', *Energy Policy*, **29**(4), 291–302.
Gielen, D.J., T. Gerlagh and A.J.M. Bos (1998), *Matter 1.0: A Markal Energy and Materials System Model Characterisation*, Petten: Netherlands Energy Research Foundation (ECN).
Gielen, D. and M. Taylor (2007), 'Modeling industrial energy use: the IEA's energy technology perspectives', *Energy Economics*, **29**(4) (Special Issue on the Modeling of Industrial Energy Consumption), 889–912.
Goldstein, G.A. (1995), *MARKAL–MACRO: A Methodology for Informed Energy, Economy and Environmental Decision Making*, Brookhaven, NY: Brookhaven National Laboratory.
Goldstein, G.A. and L.A. Greening (1999), 'Energy planning and the development of carbon mitigation strategies: using the MARKAL family of models', available at: http://www.ecn.nl/unit_bs/etsap/ (accessed June 6, 2001).
Greening, L.A. (2007), 'Industrial energy consumption forecasting: the things that matter', in L. Kavanagh and K. Kissock (eds), *Improving Industrial Competitiveness: Adapting to Volatile Energy Markets, Globalization, and Environmental Constraints*, Washington, DC: American Council for an Energy Efficient Economy.
Greening, L.A. and E. Schneider (2003a), 'Economic implications of the US spent nuclear fuel legacy', paper presented at the Western Economic Association 78th Annual Conference, Denver, CO, June 15.

Greening, L.A. and E. Schneider (2003b), 'The US spent nuclear fuel legacy and the sustainability of nuclear power', *IAEE Newsletter*, **12**(4), 12–19.

Gritsevskyi, A. and N. Nakicenovic (2000), 'Modeling uncertainty of induced technological change', *Energy Policy*, **28**(13), 907–21.

Grubb, M., I. Köhler and D. Anderson (2002), 'Induced technical change in energy and environmental modeling: analytical approaches and policy implications', *Annual Review of Energy and the Environment*, **27**, 271–308.

Hadley, S.W. and W. Short (2001), 'Electricity sector analysis in the Clean Energy Futures Study', *Energy Policy*, **29**(14), 1285–98.

Hafele, W. and A.S. Manne (1975), 'Strategies for a transition from fossil to nuclear fuels', *Energy Policy*, **3**(1), 3–23.

Hamilton, L.D., G.A. Goldstein, J. Lee, A.S. Manne, W. Marcuse, S.C. Morris and C.O. Wene (1992), *MARKAL–MACRO: An Overview*, Brookhaven, NY: Brookhaven National Laboratory.

Hanson, D. and J.A.S. Laitner (2004), 'An integrated analysis of policies that increase investments in advanced energy-efficient/low-carbon technologies', *Energy Economics*, **26**(4), 739–55.

Hoffman, K.C. and D.W. Jorgenson (1977), 'Economic and technological models for evaluation of energy policy', *Bell Journal of Economics*, **8**(2), 444–66.

Hoffman, K.C. and D.O. Wood (1976), 'Energy system modeling and forecasting', *Annual Review of Energy and the Environment*, **1**, 423–53.

Horne, M., M. Jaccard and K. Tiedemann (2005), 'Improving behavioral realism in hybrid energy–economy models using discrete choice studies of personal transportation decisions', *Energy Economics*, **27**(1), 59–77.

Hourcade, J.-C., M. Jaccard, C. Bataille and F. Ghersi (2006), 'Hybrid modeling: new answers to old challenges', Introduction to the special issue *The Energy Journal*, **27** (Special Issue on Hybrid Modeling of Energy–Environment Policies: Reconciling Bottom-up and Top-down), 1–12.

Huntington, H. (1994), 'Been top-down so long looks like bottom-up to me', *Energy Policy*, **22**(10), 833–39.

Jaber, J., M. Mohsen, S. Probert and M. Alees (2001), 'Future electricity-demands and greenhouse-gas emissions in Jordan', *Applied Energy*, **69**(1), 1–18.

Jaccard, M. (2005), 'Hybrid energy–economy models and endogenous technological change', in R. Loulou, J.-P.Waaub and G. Zaccour (eds), *Energy and Environment*, New York: Springer, pp. 81–110.

Jaccard, M., A. Bailie and J. Nyboer (1996), 'CO_2 emission reduction costs in the residential sector: behavioral parameters in a bottom-up simulation model', *The Energy Journal*, **17**(4), 107–34.

Jaccard, M., J. Nyboer, C. Bataille and B. Sadownik (2003), 'Modeling the cost of climate policy: distinguishing between alternative cost definitions and long run cost dynamics', *The Energy Journal*, **24**(1), 49–73.

Jacobsen, H. (1998), 'Integrating the bottom-up and top-down approach to energy–economy modeling: the case of Denmark', *Energy Economics*, **20**(4), 443–61.

Johnsson, B.R. and C.O. Wene (1993), 'CHP production in integrated energy systems: examples from five Swedish communities', *Energy Policy*, **21**(2), 176–90.

Josefsson, A., J. Johnsson and C.O. Wene (1996), 'Community-based regional energy–environment planning', in C. Carraro and A. Haurie (eds), *Operations Research and Environmental Management*, Dordrecht: Kluwer Academic, pp. 3–24.

Kanudia, A. and R. Loulou (1999), 'Advanced bottom-up modeling for national and regional energy planning in response to climate change', *International Journal of Environment and Pollution*, **12**(2/3), 191–216.

Keppo, I. and S. Rao (2006), 'International climate regimes: effects of delayed participation', *Technological Forecasting and Social Change*, **74**(7), 962–79.

Klaassen, G. and K. Riahi (2007), 'Internalizing externalities of electricity generation: an analysis with MESSAGE–MACRO', *Energy Policy*, **35**(2), 815–27.

Köhler, J., T. Barker, D. Anderson and H. Pan (2006), 'Combining energy technology dynamics and macro-econometrics: the E3MG model', *The Energy Journal*, **27** (Special Issue on Hybrid Modeling of Energy–Environment Policies: Reconciling Bottom-up and Top-down), 113–34.

Koomey, J.G., R.C. Richey, J.A. Laitner, R.J. Markel and C. Marnay (2001), 'Technology and greenhouse gas emissions: an integrated scenario analysis using the LBNL–NEMS model', *Advances in the Economics of Environmental Resources*, **3**, 175–219.

Koopmans, C.C. and D.W. te Velde (2001), 'Bridging the energy efficiency gap: using bottom-up information in a top-down energy demand model', *Energy Economics*, **23**(1), 57–75.

Kydes, A.S. (2007), 'Impacts of a renewable portfolio generation standard on US energy markets', *Energy Policy*, **35**(2), 809–14.

Kypreos, S. (1996), 'Allocation of carbon tax revenues to national and international mitigation options', in C. Carraro and A. Haurie (eds), *Operations Research and Environmental Management*, Dordrecht: Kluwer Academic, pp. 133–52.

Kypreos, S. (2005), 'Modeling experience curves in MERGE (Model for Evaluating Regional and Global Effects)', *Energy*, **30**(14), 2721–35.

Labriet, M. and R. Loulou (2003), 'Coupling climate damages and GHG abatement costs in a linear programming framework', *Environmental Modeling and Assessment*, **8**(3), 261–74.
Labriet, M., R. Loulou and A. Kanudia (2004), 'Global energy and CO$_2$ emission scenarios – analysis with a 15 region world MARKAL model', in A. Haurie and L. Viguier (eds) *The Coupling of Climate and Economic Dynamics*, Boston/Dordrecht/London: Kluwer Academic, pp. 205–35.
Laitner, J.A.S. and D. Hanson (2006), 'Modeling detailed energy-efficiency technologies and technology policies within a CGE framework', *The Energy Journal*, **27** (Special Issue on Hybrid Modeling of Energy–Environment Policies: Reconciling Bottom-up and Top-down), 151–69.
Lee, C.M. and K.J. Lee (2007), 'A study on operation time periods of spent fuel interim storage facilities in South Korea', *Progress in Nuclear Energy*, **49**(4), 303–12.
Lejtman, T.M. and J.P. Weyant (1981), 'Managing an oil bonanza, an analysis of alternative Mexican export policies', *Energy Policy*, **9**(3), 186–96.
Löschel, A. (2002), 'Technological change in economic models of environmental policy: a survey', *Ecological Economics*, **43**(2/3), 105–26.
Loulou, R. and A. Kanudia (1999), 'Minimax regret strategies for greenhouse gas abatement: methodology and application', *Operations Research Letters*, **25**(5), 219–30.
Loulou, R., A. Kanudia and D. Lavigne (1996), 'GHG abatement in central Canada with interprovincial cooperation', *Energy Studies Review*, **8**(2), 120–29.
Loulou, R. and M. Labriet (2007), 'ETSAP-TIAM: TIMES integrated assessment model part 1: model structure', *Computational Management Science*, **24**(1), 7–40.
Loulou, R. and D. Lavigne (1996), 'MARKAL model with elastic demands: application to greenhouse gas emission control', in C. Carraro and A. Haurie (eds), *Operations Research and Environmental Management*, Dordrecht: Kluwer Academic, pp. 201–20.
Loulou, R., U. Remne, A. Kanudia, A. Lehtila and G. Goldstein (2005), 'Documentation for the TIMES model', Energy Technology Systems Analysis Programme, available at: http://www.etsap.org/tools.htm (accessed 25 June 2007).
Manne, A. (1976), 'ETA: a model for energy technology assessment', *Bell Journal of Economics*, **7**(2), 379–406.
Manne, A. (1979), 'ETA–MACRO: a model for energy–economy interactions', in R. Pindyck (ed.), *Advances in the Economics of Energy and Resources*, vol. 2, Greenwich, CT: JAI Press, pp. 205–34.
Manne, A. and L. Barreto (2004), 'Learning-by-doing and carbon dioxide abatement', *Energy Economics*, **26**(4), 621–33.
Manne, A.S., R. Mendelsohn and R. Richels (1995), 'MERGE: a model for evaluating regional and global effects of GHG reduction policies', *Energy Policy*, **23**(1), 17–34.
Manne, A. and R. Richels (1978), 'A decision analysis of the US breeder reactor program', *Energy*, **3**(6), 747–67.
Manne, A. and R. Richels (1990a), 'CO$_2$ emission limits: an economic cost analysis for the USA', *The Energy Journal*, **11**(2), 51–74.
Manne, A.S. and R.G. Richels (1990b), 'The costs of reducing US CO$_2$ emissions – further sensitivity analyses', *The Energy Journal*, **11**(4), 69–78.
Manne, A. and R.G. Richels (1992), *Buying Greenhouse Gas Insurance: The Economic Costs of CO$_2$ Emission Limits*, Cambridge, MA: MIT Press.
Manne, A. and R. Richels (1995), 'The greenhouse debate: economic efficiency, burden sharing and hedging strategies', *The Energy Journal*, **16**(4), 1–37.
Manne, A. and R. Richels (1999), 'The Kyoto Protocol: a cost-effective strategy for meeting environmental objectives?', *The Energy Journal*, **20** (Special Issue on The Costs of the Kyoto Protocol: A Multi-model Evaluation), 1–23.
Manne, A. and R. Richels (2004), 'The impact of learning-by-doing on the timing and costs of CO$_2$ abatement', *Energy Economics*, **26**(4), 603–19.
Manne, A., R.G. Richels, and J.P. Weyant (1979), 'Energy policy modeling: a survey', *Operations Research*, **27**(1), 1–36.
Manne, A. and C.O. Wene (1992), 'MARKAL–MACRO: a linked model for energy–economy analysis', Brookhaven, NY: Brookhaven National Laboratory.
McFarland, J., J. Reilly and H. Herzog (2004), 'Representing energy technologies in top-down economic models using bottom-up information', *Energy Economics*, **26**(4), 685–707.
McKibbin, W. and P. Wilcoxen (1999), 'The theoretical and empirical structure of the G-cubed model', *Economic Modeling*, **16**(1), 123–48.
McKitrick, R. (1998), 'The econometric critique of computable general equilibrium modeling: the role of functional forms', *Economic Modeling*, **15**(4), 543–73.
Messner, S., A. Golodnikov and A. Gritsevskii (1996), 'A stochastic version of the dynamic linear programming model MESSAGE III', *Energy*, **21**(9), 775–84.

Messner, S. and L. Schrattenholzer (2000), 'MESSAGE–MACRO: linking an energy supply model with a macroeconomic module and solving it iteratively', *Energy*, **25**(3), 267–82.

Mirasgedis, S., G. Conzelmann, E. Georgopoulou, V. Koritarov and Y. Sarafidis (2004a), 'Long-term GHG emissions outlook for Greece: results of a detailed bottom-up energy system simulation', paper presented at the 6th IAEE European Conference on 'Modeling in Energy Economics and Policy', Zurich, Switzerland, September 2–3.

Mirasgedis, S., Y. Sarafidis, E. Georgopoulou, D.P. Lalas and C. Papastavros (2004b), 'Mitigation policies for energy related greenhouse gas emissions in Cyprus: the potential role of natural gas imports', *Energy Policy*, **32**(8), 1001–11.

Molnár, S. (1997), 'Assessment of mitigation measures and programs in Hungary', *Applied Energy*, **56**(3–4), 325–39.

Morris, S., G. Goldstein and V. Fthenakis (2002), 'NEMS and MARKAL–MACRO models for energy–environmental–economic analysis: a comparison of the electricity and carbon reduction projections', *Environmental Modeling and Assessment*, **17**(3), 207–16.

Neubauer, F., E. Westman and A. Ford (1997), 'Applying planning models to study new competition: analysis for the Bonneville Power Administration', *Energy Policy*, **25**(3), 273–80.

Rafaj, P. and S. Kypreos (2007), 'Internalisation of external cost in the power generation sector: analysis with global multi-regional MARKAL model', *Energy Policy*, **35**(2), 828–43.

Rao, S., K. Ilkka and R. Keywan (2006), 'Importance of technological change and spillovers in long-term climate policy', *The Energy Journal*, **27** (Special Issue on Endogenous Technological Change and the Economics of Atmospheric Stabilization), 123–39.

Riahi, K. and R.A. Roehlr (2000), 'Greenhouse gas emissions in a dynamics-as-usual scenario of economic and energy development', *Technological Forecasting and Social Change*, **63**(2–3), 175–205.

Riahi, K., E.S. Rubin and L. Schrattenholzer (2004a), 'Prospects for carbon capture and sequestration technologies assuming their technological learning', *Energy*, **29**(9–10), 1309–18.

Riahi, K., E. Rubin, M. Taylor, L. Schrattenholzer and D. Hounshell (2004b), 'Technological learning for carbon capture and sequestration technologies', *Energy Economics*, **26**(4), 539–64.

Rivers, N. and M. Jaccard (2005), 'Combining top-down and bottom-up approaches to energy–economy modeling using discrete choice methods', *The Energy Journal*, **26**(1), 83–106.

Sands, R. (2004), 'Dynamics of carbon abatement in the second generation model', *Energy Economics*, **26**(4), 721–38.

Sato, O., K. Tatematsu and T. Hasegawa (1998), 'Reducing future CO_2 emissions – the role of nuclear energy', *Progress in Nuclear Energy*, **32**(3/4), 323–30.

Schaefer, A. and H. Jacoby (2005), 'Technology detail in a multisector CGE model:transport under climate policy', *Energy Economics*, **27**(1), 1–24.

Schaefer, A. and H. Jacoby (2006), 'Experiments with a hybrid CGE–MARKAL model', *The Energy Journal*, **27** (Special Issue on Hybrid Modeling of Energy–Environment Policies: Reconciling Bottom-up and Top-down), 171–7.

Schumacher, K. and R.D. Sands (2007), 'Where are the industrial technologies in energy–economy models? An innovative CGE approach for steel production in Germany', *Energy Economics*, **29**(4), (Special Issue on Industrial Energy Consumption), 799–825.

Seebregts, A., T. Kram, G.J. Schaeffer and A. Bos (2000), 'Endogenous learning and technology clustering: analysis with MARKAL model of the Western European energy system', *International Journal of Global Energy Issues*, **14**(1), 289–320.

Sue Wing, I. (2008), 'The synthesis of bottom-up and top-down approaches to climate policy modeling: electric power technology detail in a social accounting framework', *Energy Economics*, **30**(2), 547–753.

Wene, C.O. (1996), 'Energy–economy analysis: linking the macroeconomic and systems engineering approaches', *Energy*, **21**(9), 809–24.

Zhang, Z. and H. Folmer (1998), 'Economic modelling approaches to cost estimates for the control of carbon dioxide emissions', *Energy Economics*, **20**(1), 101–20.

12 The structure and use of the UK MARKAL model
Ramachandran Kannan, Paul Ekins and Neil Strachan*

1 Introduction

The previous chapter introduced and reviewed the widely applied bottom-up, dynamic, linear programming optimisation model known as the MARKAL model. Developed in the late 1970s, MARKAL has been continually supported by the International Energy Agency (IEA) via the Energy Technology and Systems Analysis Program (ETSAP) and has contributed to numerous and wide-ranging energy policy studies; for example, the IEA Energy Technology Perspectives (ETP) project (IEA, 2006). This chapter illustrates the use of the model in more depth, reporting on the development and initial use of the United Kingdom (UK) MARKAL model.[1] Section 2 describes the general structure and methodological process of the MARKAL model. Section 3 elucidates the development of the UK MARKAL with respect to its input data assumptions, validation and calibration processes. More detailed information on the development of the UK MARKAL model is given in Strachan et al. (2006, 2008a). Section 4 provides indicative results[2] from the model to demonstrate its analytical strength, range of outputs, and how it deals with uncertainties. Section 5 concludes.

2 MARKAL Model Description

The MARKAL energy system model is a data-driven, technology-rich bottom-up cost-optimisation modelling framework. The optimised quantity is the total energy system cost, with the decision variables the investment and operation of all the interconnected system elements. The model is energy-service driven and encompasses the entire energy system from imports and domestic production of fuel resources, through fuel processing and representation of infrastructures, conversion to secondary energy carriers and end-use technologies.

Reference Energy System
MARKAL's Reference Energy System (RES) is a network description of energy flows with a precise description of all technologies that are involved (or potentially involved) in the production, transformation and use of various energy forms. To satisfy energy *service* demands (also known as 'useful energy') required by economic activities, demand devices/technologies that transform energy carriers into useful demands are used. For example, energy service demands in the residential sector include space heating, hot-water, lighting, cooking and so on. Storable energy carriers such as gasoline and diesel are produced by process technologies, while non-storable energy forms such as electricity and heat are generated by conversion technologies. The process and conversion technologies use primary energy forms obtained from energy resource technologies. A highly simplified RES – focusing on the electricity component of the full model – illustrates this

model structure and is given as Figure 12.1. Resource technologies refer to the means by which energy enters (or leaves) the energy system other than by end-use consumption. They include mining/extraction, renewables, imports and so on of energy resources. Process technologies refer to technologies that convert or transport one energy carrier into another, for example, oil refineries, nuclear fuel enrichment facilities, pipeline infrastructure and so on. Conversion technologies refer to technologies that convert an energy carrier to electricity and/or heat, for example, power plants and combined heat and power generation (CHP) technologies. Demand technologies refer to technologies that consume an energy carrier to deliver end-use energy service demands, that is useful energy.

The models may have constraints designed to replicate the physical, regulatory and policy aspects of the energy system being modelled. These are designed such that the optimisation occurs under a realistic engineering and economic framework of the deployment of new infrastructures, fuels and technologies. It should be noted that MARKAL is a cost-driven model and delivers an economy-wide solution of cost-optimal energy market development under a range of input assumptions. As a perfect foresight model, all market participants are assumed to have perfect intertemporal knowledge of future policy and economic developments. Further detailed information on the MARKAL modelling system, including the economic rationale of this partial equilibrium model, an explanation of the linearisation process for energy supply and

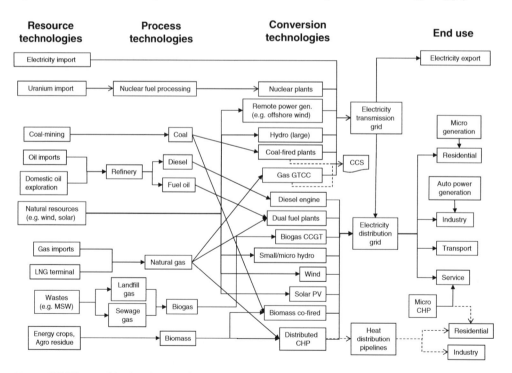

Note: CCGT = combined cycle gas turbine (same as GTCC – gas turbine combined cycle).

Figure 12.1   Highly aggregated example of a MARKAL reference energy system

demand as well as the precise mathematical structure of the optimisation set is given in Loulou et al. (2004a).

Model inputs and outputs

It is important to note that a 'technology' in MARKAL refers to the entire range of variables in the model, including energy resource supply, pipeline, refineries, power plants, end-use technologies and conservation measures. Energy carriers connect these technologies.

A key input to the model is energy service demands and their corresponding supply and end-use technologies. The model may have thousands of technologies each with a range of time-stepped or time-independent parameters. Therefore another key input to the model is a realistic representation of technologies. Typically, energy service demands are expressed in peta-joules (PJ) or billion vehicle-kilometres (bvkm). Input parameters for a technology include technical efficiency, lifetime, capital and operational costs, and so on. The emission component of the model encompasses the environmental impacts of the energy system. Emission carriers are used to track emissions at energy resource and technology levels. Figure 12.2 illustrates typical input parameters required to represent a technology.

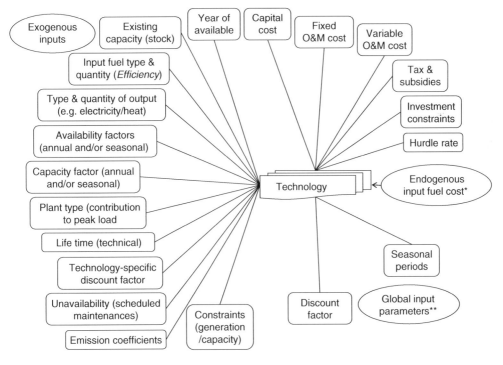

Notes:
* Takes into account the necessary infrastructure to deliver the fuel.
** Applied to all technologies and energy carriers.
O&M = operation and maintenance.

Figure 12.2   Typical input parameters for electricity generation technology

To meet a given energy service demand, MARKAL generates a detailed set of cost-optimal outputs to characterise the evolution of the energy system. Key outputs include energy system costs, imports, exports and domestic production of resources, use of pipelines and refineries, fuel and technology mixes, electricity generation and capacity investments, marginal costs of fuels including seasonal/diurnal detail of electricity and heat, environmental emission levels and emission shadow prices (see Section 4). Furthermore, when the model is run in MACRO mode (see below), resultant demand levels are a key model variable. Furthermore the MACRO variant generates detail on GDP, investment, and consumption at the economy level.

Consideration of uncertainty
A key strength of the MARKAL optimisation approach is a systematic approach to uncertainty. This is achieved through a 'what-if' analysis that seeks to quantify sensitivities and tipping-points of moving between technology categories and energy pathways. This is enabled through a range of sensitivity scenarios. The alternative results briefly discussed elsewhere in this chapter are an example of how the complexity of insights as generated from a large energy model should be interpreted and viewed. The generation of alternative scenarios comes from the input technology data (that is, a core part of the model's assumptions) being varied both parametrically and according to assessed technology ranges of fixed cost, variable cost and efficiency. These ranges are normally determined through an assessment of established energy data sources, including through a detailed literature review and comparison (for example, see Smith, 2007). In addition, data may be validated through stakeholder consultation and bilateral expert reviews of specific energy chains.

Model strengths and weaknesses
Like all energy models, MARKAL has strengths and weaknesses, and partial solutions to these weaknesses. MARKAL is a widely used, proven and continually evolving model for assessing a wide range of energy and environmental planning and policy issues. It has a coherent, open-source and transparent modelling framework, where the data assumptions are open and each result may be traced to its technological cause. Its well understood analytic framework (least-cost equilibrium computation in efficient or regulated markets) is well suited for assessing the role of technology in achieving environmental and policy goals. It encompasses the entire energy system to ensure a comprehensive assessment of interdependencies between sectors as they compete for limited resources (energy and fiscal), as well as the co-benefit arising from actions.

MARKAL's weaknesses include its data intensiveness, including the characterisation of technologies and the reference energy system. Like all models, results are dependent on the quality of input technology data and other parameter values, and can be sensitive to small changes in data assumptions. However, stepped supply curves, and market share algorithms can partially remedy this, while extensive sensitivity analysis may be used to explore thresholds and tipping-points between alternative energy technology pathways. MARKAL has a limited ability to model behaviour, such as hidden costs of technology switching. However, growth constraints, damping costs, 'hurdle' rates (higher or lower than normal discount rates), and (in certain model versions) demand elasticities partially remedy this. Finally, MARKAL has a limited representation of the economic impact of energy policy, either through linkage to a simple neoclassical MACRO module, or through use of the elastic demand version of the model.

MARKAL–MACRO

MARKAL–MACRO (M–M) hard-links a detailed energy systems model (MARKAL) with a simple neoclassical growth model. Hence M–M combines MARKAL's rich technological characterisation of an energy system with a dynamic intertemporal general equilibrium model. Using this approach, M–M allows a subsectoral demand-side response to supplement supply-side technology pathway optimisation, as well as allowing direct analysis of the impacts of various energy and environmental policies on the growth of the economy. The M–M maximises the discounted utility function subject to a national budget constraint. In M–M there are three other economic agents in addition to suppliers and consumers of energy (the energy market), as in MARKAL. These additional economic agents are producers, which supply other goods and services, consumers and a generic capital market. All these markets are assumed to operate in a single sector with perfect foresight. Demand changes respond to one single price elasticity and are asymmetric with price. However subsectoral demands will react differently dependent on the overall economic implications of their reductions (expressed via demand marginals). The precise mathematical equations of the M–M are given in Loulou et al. (2004b).

M–M has the following four major features:

- an explicit calculation of GDP and other macro variables (consumption, investment);
- demand response due to changes in energy prices. In this formulation, although all subsectoral demands have the same price elasticity, they will respond differently depending on the total cost implications of altering demands for energy services. *All other things being equal, this additional system response and flexibility should produce lower policy costs*;
- autonomous demand changes (for example, with respect to increased aviation travel) allow the M–M model to undertake scenario analysis where energy demands are decoupled from economic growth; and
- technological change and energy system interactions within MARKAL as before.

The basic input factors of production are capital, labour and energy service demands. The economy's outputs are used for investment, consumption and inter-industry payments for the cost of energy. Investment is used to build up the stock of (depreciating) capital, while labour is exogenous. M–M has been implemented for the UK (see Strachan et al., 2008a for a detailed description and results from the MARKAL–MACRO model).

3 Development of the New UK MARKAL Model

The new UK model described in this chapter was substantially extended and improved from an earlier (2003) version of the model, which was used in the preparation of the 2003 UK Energy White Paper (DTI, 2003). To construct the new model, the specific characteristics of the UK energy system were mapped into the model, including a highly detailed and validated set of resource, process, conversion and end-use technologies, disaggregated energy service demands, and constraints based on physical, regulatory and policy aspects. Substantial enhancements to this version of the MARKAL model include:

- complete update of technology parameters;
- inclusion of domestic and imported resource supply curves;
- specification of energy processes including a refining sector, hydrogen pathways (production, distribution and storage), and a full nuclear fuel cycle;
- detailed technological specification of end-use sectors notably industry, transport, residential and service (commercial) sectors;
- explicit depiction of all fuel infrastructures, also allowing sectoral fuel and emissions tracking;
- explicit depiction of alternative electricity grid configurations including micro and remote grids; and
- inclusion of a MACRO module to allow demand responses, and calculation of GDP and consumption effects.

To construct the UK model, the specific characteristics of the UK energy system, including resource supplies, energy conversion technologies, energy service demands, and the technologies used to satisfy these energy service demands were defined. This is based on a rich technology dataset, stemming from a pre-existing model (FES, 2003), supplemented by stakeholder workshops and a wide range of peer-reviewed data sources (see Smith, 2007 and Strachan et al., 2008a for details). Inputs into the model include base levels for global energy prices (DTI, 2006b), and detailed energy service demands in units of useful energy.

The UK model has some hundreds of constraints designed to replicate the physical, regulatory and policy aspects of the whole UK energy system. The model is calibrated in its base year (2000) to within 1 per cent of actual resource supplies, energy consumption, electricity output and installed technology capacity, as published in national statistics including relevant published chapters and internet-only foreign trade (Annex G) (DUKES, 2006). This entails a corresponding definition of residual technology capacities and use, and characterises when these plants would be retired and hence allows investment in new technologies as the model moves in 5-year time steps through to 2070. Until the date of retirement, the total costs of new technologies must compete with the marginal costs of paid-off plants.

In addition to calibration, considerable attention has been given to near-term (2005–10) convergence of sectoral energy demands and carbon emissions with the econometric output of the DTI energy model. The UK MARKAL model of the UK energy system is therefore consistent with standard government projections, as well as the implementation of major current environmental and economic policies – in essence all legislated policies as of 2007 are included. In its projections, MARKAL solves in 5-year time steps for an optimal evolution of energy pathways and technology deployment and use. Indicative outputs from long-term carbon reduction scenarios are detailed and discussed in Section 4.

Key assumptions

As noted above, a range of key inputs and systems parameters are required for MARKAL, including exogenous guidance on upstream energy prices. In this updated version of MARKAL, domestic fossil and renewable resources, and fossil imports are depicted via supply curves rather than discrete values. Table 12.1 lists the range of fossil-fuel import prices in £2000 (DTI, 2006b). Multipliers calibrated from baseline relative prices are used to translate these into prices for both higher-priced supply steps as well as imported refined fuels. Additional systematic sensitivity analysis may be carried out on these input prices.

A similar exogenous depiction is used for energy service or 'useful' energy demands, in physical units (for example, billion vehicle-kilometres for transport modes). Energy service demands are further broken down into specific end uses. For example, in the residential sector this includes cooking, lighting, space heating, water heating and air conditioning. Future energy service demands were calculated from a range of literatures including projections of the number of households and other variables from Building Research Establishment (BRE) studies (see www.bre.co.uk; Shorrock et al., 2005; Pout and MacKenzie, 2006), the final energy forecast from the DTI (2006b) energy model, the DfT (2005) transport model and so on. Figure 12.3 illustrates sample energy service demands for selected modes in the transport sector. Note that only domestic transportation (for shipping and aviation) is included in model runs in line with national emissions accounting.

A range of system parameters also need to be defined for the MARKAL model. These include the diurnal and seasonal variation of energy service demands, electricity reserve margins (to account for instantaneous daily peaks plus reserve capacity), and a range of emission factors for CO_2 and SO_2 which are tracked based on input fuels. Sectoral emissions are also tracked (agriculture, electricity, industry, residential, services (commercial), transport, and upstream processes (oil/gas extraction and refineries)).

Finally, a key system parameter is the discount rate for intertemporal trade-offs. The

Table 12.1 Exogenous imported fossil fuel prices (£2000)

Year	Baseline			High prices			Low prices		
	Oil $/bbl	Gas p/therm	Coal $/GJ	Oil $/bbl	Gas p/therm	Coal $/GJ	Oil $/bbl	Gas p/therm	Coal $/GJ
2005	55.0	41.0	2.4	55.0	41.0	2.4	55.0	41.0	2.4
2010	40.0	33.5	1.9	67.0	49.9	2.4	20.0	18.0	1.4
2015	42.5	35.0	1.9	69.5	51.4	2.6	20.0	19.5	1.2
2020	45.0	36.5	1.8	72.0	53.0	2.6	20.0	21.0	1.0
2025	47.5	38.1	1.9	77.0	56.0	2.6	22.5	22.5	1.1
2030	50.0	39.6	2.0	82.0	59.0	2.8	25.0	24.0	1.2
2035	52.5	41.1	2.1	82.0	59.0	3.0	27.5	25.5	1.3
2040	55.0	42.6	2.2	82.0	59.0	3.0	30.0	27.0	1.3
2045	55.0	42.6	2.2	82.0	59.0	3.0	32.5	28.5	1.4
2050	55.0	42.6	2.2	82.0	59.0	3.0	35.0	30.0	1.5

Note: bbl = barrel; GJ = giga-joule.

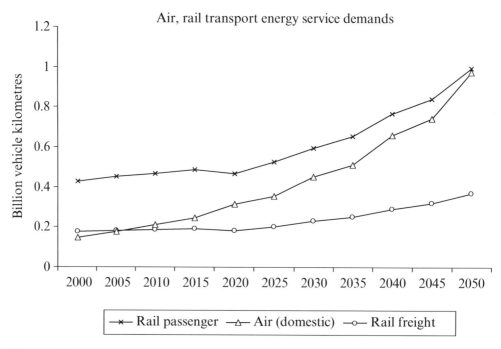

Figure 12.3   Transportation energy service demands by selected mode

global model parameter is the social time preference which accounts for time preference (both pure time preference and the element of possible catastrophe that wipes out return from investment), plus a value related to future income growth and hence declining marginal utility of future returns. The UK government uses a discount rate of 3.5 per cent (HMT, 2006). However, in the UK MARKAL, technologies are specified with a higher technology-specific discount or hurdle rate to account for market risks and consumer preferences. Electricity and other conversion technology investments use a rate of 10 per cent to reflect current market instability, while new and advanced end-use technology options must overcome a 25 per cent hurdle rate to reflect documented barriers of risk or non-economic factors such as information availability (see Train, 1985). Discount rates are another metric that sensitivity analysis can be applied to.

A key methodological issue is the treatment of energy conservation. In addition to the 25 per cent hurdle rate, further standardisation of the uptake of energy conservation options in MARKAL's cost-optimal framework is required. This is to ensure that in the business-as-usual base case at least, historical rates of conservation uptake are continued. The model is then given complete long-term freedom in carbon-constrained runs to select accelerated energy conservation measures if it is cost optimal to do so. It is important to note the three types of energy efficiency in the model:

- *energy-efficient technologies*: devices that produce energy carriers or meet energy service demands at lowered levels of input fuel (for example, condensing boilers, hybrid cars), which are bundled into the overall MARKAL energy pathways;

- *energy conservation*: devices that reduce demand for energy services (for example, loft insulation), which are labelled 'conservation' in the model; and
- *behavioural change*: responses to delivered energy prices (for example, lowering home thermostat temperatures), which is only considered using the MACRO variant.

Technology database

A key input into the model is a realistic representation of future technology costs – which are enabled through data covering capital and operating costs, efficiency, availability, operating lifetime, and diurnal or seasonal characteristics (see Figure 12.2). Fossil extraction, energy processes (for example, refineries), infrastructures, nuclear technologies, end-use vehicles, buildings, industrial and many electricity technologies utilise vintages to represent improvements through time, while less mature renewable electricity and hydrogen technologies have exogenously calculated learning rates based on the published literature (McDonald and Schrattenholzer, 2002) together with global technology uptake forecasts (European Commission, 2005). The underlying principles guiding this process are as follows:

- technologies were assumed to be developed globally and to benefit from advances in design, engineering and production;
- costs and performance data were set to be representative of commercially deployed technologies enjoying the benefits of volume production, and of good installation and operation practices; and
- energy taxation and other financial mechanisms are incorporated explicitly at the appropriate point in the energy chain.

Detailed documentation on the model input parameters and key assumptions is also available (Kannan et al., 2007). As noted above, the technology data used in the model went through an extensive validation and quality assurance process (see Strachan et al., 2008a for details).

Model validation and calibration

The UK MARKAL model is a publicly available model, designed to have its assumptions, data sources and workings as transparent as possible. In addition to having the model literature placed on the UK Energy Research Centre (UKERC) website (www.ukerc.ac.uk), a range of specific model validation and calibration exercises have been undertaken, including data workshops for road transportation and electricity generation, a number of bilateral sectoral reviews (on the nuclear, hydrogen, biomass, carbon capture and storage (CCS) pathways), and a model peer review by an expert from the Energy Centre of the Netherlands (ECN), which resulted in a number of model improvements.

In terms of calibration, MARKAL is exactly calibrated to the DUKES (2006) figures for the base year (2000) for final energy demand (by sector), electricity demand and CO_2 emissions. MARKAL's year 2000 energy consumption is 6158 PJ (= 10^{15} joules), which when including international air transport (469 PJ) and non-energy fossil-fuel use (514 PJ), matches to actual total energy consumption of 170.56 million tonnes of oil

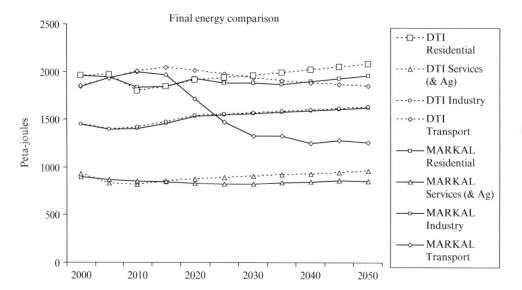

Figure 12.4   MARKAL–DTI model final energy convergence

equivalent (mtoe) or 7141 PJ. In future time periods, the MARKAL model generates its own trends for these and all other metrics.

Despite major differences between the models, the MARKAL outputs are also closely matched to the short-term energy forecast from the DTI energy model. MARKAL's final energy demand (a model output based on energy service demands) is compared with aggregated sectoral energy demand projections in actual energy units from DTI (2006b). Energy demands are verified using additional sources including BRE buildings data (Shorrock et al., 2005; Pout and MacKenzie, 2006) and Department for Transport projections (DfT, 2005; FES, 2006). Figure 12.4 illustrates the comparison of final energy between MARKAL and the DTI energy model. The models converge within 0.3 per cent in 2005 and 0.9 per cent in 2010 for total final energy demand. In future years (post-2010) MARKAL gives a lower level of energy demand due to accelerated technological change (for example, penetration of hybrid cars). MARKAL energy demands already take into account legislated programmes (for example, the energy efficiency commitment (EEC) phase 1 and 2, renewables obligation) through to 2020 (DEFRA, 2005a).

Focusing on total CO_2 emissions, Figure 12.5 illustrates the comparison between MARKAL and the DTI energy model. MARKAL generates an exact match to 2000 (DEFRA, 2005b) of 544.8 million tonnes of CO_2 (mtCO_2) or 148.6 million tonnes of carbon (mtC). MARKAL emissions in 2005 are higher than the 2000 levels, but 1.5 per cent lower than DTI (and actual 2005 emissions). Note that MARKAL converges with the DTI's earlier (April) projections (DTI, 2006a) for 2005 emissions. The discrepancy is likely due to short-term drivers, for example, high natural gas prices leading to a shift to coal for electricity generation and industrial use. MARKAL and DTI emissions converge to within 0.5 per cent in 2010. Again in future years MARKAL gives lower carbon emissions due to accelerated technological change (higher efficiency and fuel substitution). Future year emissions coincide with the projections including measures identified

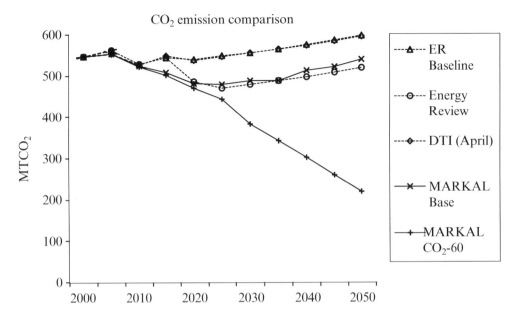

Figure 12.5   MARKAL–DTI model CO₂ emissions convergence

under the Energy Review (ER, DTI, 2006c). This does not mean that MARKAL selects the same measures as identified in the Review, but it does appear logical that a model which selects the cost-optimal solution (provided that non-cost barriers are addressed, and technologies fulfil their mitigation potential) provides baseline projections that are in agreement with the case where government policies seek to achieve this. Note that sectoral CO_2 emissions in the two models are difficult to compare owing to allocation of electricity, hydrogen, upstream and agricultural emissions.

4   Indicative Findings

This section presents and discusses indicative runs based on the standard version (partial equilibrium) of the new UK MARKAL model. As noted in the introduction, further results (which include macroeconomic interactions and aggregated demand responses) are given in Strachan et al. (2008a) and Strachan and Kannan (2007, 2008). Care should be exercised when viewing any one set of results under a certain set of technology and other assumptions from such a complex modelling exercise. A detailed set of core model results using reviewed data is followed by alternative runs under equally plausible data assumptions, which represent an initial step in characterising uncertainty in model results as well as robust insights. This section details an integrated set of UK MARKAL results for two separate runs:

- *Base case*: projected baseline emissions (including legislated policy measures).
- *CO₂-60 case*: as above but with an economy-wide CO_2 constraint applied at 30 per cent below the 2000 level in 2030 and declining linearly to 60 per cent below the 2000

level in 2050. This is consistent with the long-term CO_2 targets outlined in RCEP (2000) and adopted as a government target in the Energy White Paper (DTI, 2007).

Table 12.2 summarises key elements of these model runs, many of which are discussed in more detail elsewhere in this chapter. One point to stress is that in the base case, uptake of energy conservation measures are coded to near-term projections (DEFRA, 2005a) and restricted to a linear extrapolation of these projections to represent historical

Table 12.2   Summary description of indicative core input parameters

Parameter	Value/source
Timeframe	2000–2070 in 5-year time steps (reporting only to 2050)
Sectoral coverage	Entire energy system from energy resource production to end use through fuel processing, representation of infrastructures, conversion to secondary energy carriers (including electricity, heat and hydrogen)
	End-use sectors include industry, services, residential, transport and agriculture
Input parameters	Energy service demands: estimated from a range of literature (for example, household forecast) and government energy demand forecasts
	Details of energy technology and resources (see Figure 12.2)
	Fuel price: DTI (2006b) base import level; import and domestic stepped supply curves (see Table 12.1)
Discount rate	Global 10 per cent (market investment rate)
	25 per cent for new and advanced end-use technologies, including conservations to represent increased payback period requirements
Treatment of energy efficiency and future technology	Vintages for process, electricity, industrial, transport, residential and commercial technologies
	Exogenous learning curves for less matured renewable energy technologies
	Historical rates of conservation uptake are continued in the base case and then given long-term (post-2020) freedom in the CO_2-constrained cases
Taxation and policy measures	Included: climate change levy (CCL), hydrocarbon duty, transport fuel duty, large combustion plant (LCP) directive, renewables obligation (electricity & road transport), energy efficiency commitments (EEC). European Union emission trading scheme (EUETS) is not yet included
Emissions	System-wide CO_2 and SO_2. CO_2 is additionally tracked by end-use, electricity and upstream sectors and hydrogen production process
Calibration	Base year 2000 to DUKES (2006): final energy, primary energy, CO_2 emissions, electricity generation, fuel resources: aggregate (within 1 per cent) and sectoral disaggregation (within 2 per cent)
	Short term to DTI (2006b) energy model: sectoral energy and CO_2 emissions, within 1 per cent in 2005 and 2 per cent in 2010
Emissions cap	CO_2-60: 30 per cent reduction by 2030; linear trend to 60 per cent reduction by 2050

levels of energy conservation uptake. In the CO_2-60 constraint case the model has longer-term freedom to choose energy conservation up to its technical potential if it is cost effective to do so.

Figure 12.5 illustrates the difference between the two runs in terms of economy-wide CO_2 emissions with and without an emissions cap. Total CO_2 abatement becomes very significant as the 60 per cent target is reached, amounting to a reduction of 320 $mtCO_2$ or 87 mtC in 2050. To convert between the two, multiply carbon values by 44/12 for equivalent CO_2 values.

Primary energy demands
Figure 12.6 illustrates economy-wide primary energy consumption. Declining primary energy is partially driven through upstream and downstream efficiency improvements including conservation options. The overall efficiency improvement is somewhat greater in the CO_2-60 constraint case. In 2050, rising primary energy indicates the shift to less energy-efficient but lower carbon energy supply as the model struggles to decarbonise to meet a tightening CO_2 target.

Figure 12.7 compares shares of primary energy by fuel in the base and CO_2 constraint cases. In the base case, coal use increases largely due to increased electricity generation, while the share of natural gas holds steady at around one-third largely due to direct use in the residential, service and industrial sectors. Oil use shows a relative decline due to greater efficiency in the transport sector and later movement to hydrogen in some modes. Nuclear energy drops out of the UK energy mix. In the CO_2-60 constrained case, natural gas retains its primary energy share at around 45 per cent, due to relatively low emissions

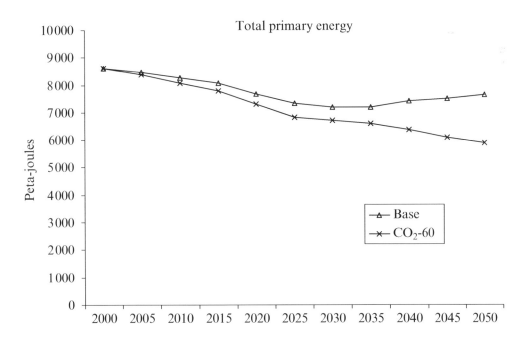

Figure 12.6   Economy-wide primary energy demands

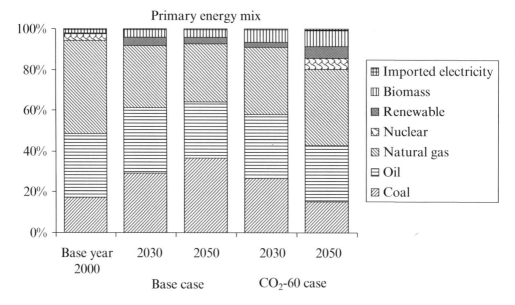

Figure 12.7   Primary energy mix in base and CO_2 constraint cases

and efficient use. Coal is restricted to electricity generation using the UK's finite carbon storage potential. Nuclear remains at low levels, before experiencing strong growth towards 2050. Oil use declines due to efficiency gains followed by an accelerated transition to hydrogen. Renewable energy sources including biomass show a steady growth.

   UK MARKAL has a full resource sector tracking imports, exports, and domestic production of all fuels, including description of key enabling technologies including natural gas inter-connectors and liquefied natural gas (LNG) terminals, and the refining sector. Figure 12.8 illustrates the demise of domestic production of fossil fuels, notably natural gas and oil. However, with gradually rising oil prices previously marginal fields become economic in 2030–45. Domestic coal production remains, albeit at a low level, and less than steam and coking coal imports. Figure 12.9 shows the corresponding base-case growth in energy imports. Oil imports interchange with later domestic production (note that fossil energy exports are run down by 2015 and cease in 2030 with the exception of refined products from the refining stock). Natural gas imports remain strong, with first Norwegian fields and then gas through the EU pipeline following the construction of increments of inter-connector capacity. LNG imports using existing or to-be commissioned facilities remain steady.

Electricity generation mix
Figure 12.10 shows the electricity generation mix in 2030 and 2050 in the absence of and with an imposed CO_2 constraint. Note that total electricity generation varies due to interchanges with electric boilers and other end-use options. In the base case, new vintages of coal generation ensure its dominance for electricity generation. Tight natural gas supplies and infrastructure ensure that gas is predominantly directly used in high-efficiency end-use applications. Nuclear capacity is run down with no reinvestment. However,

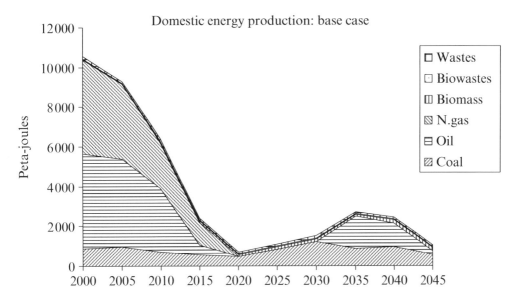

Figure 12.8   Domestic production of fossil fuels and harvested renewables

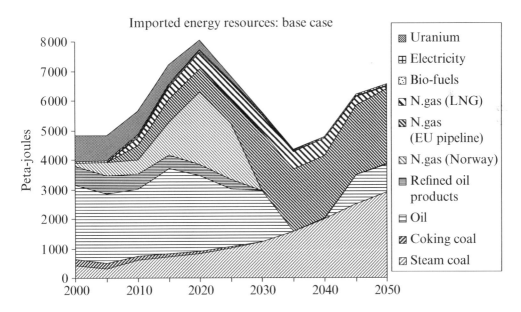

Figure 12.9   Imports of fossil fuels, uranium and bio-fuels

natural gas retains its 37 per cent electricity market share through 2020 (and continues at a lower level after this), and nuclear life-extended plants operate through to 2020 (advanced gas-cooled reactor: AGR) and to 2030 (pressurised water reactor: PWR).

In the CO_2-60 constrained case, electricity generation illustrates a shift through coal

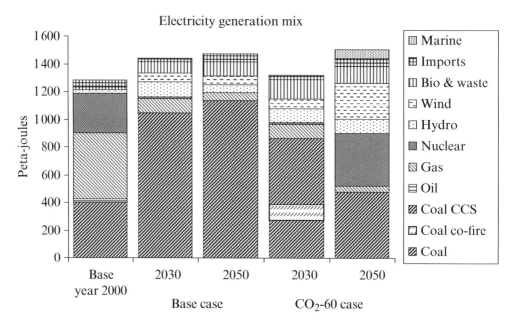

Figure 12.10   Electricity generation mix in base and CO₂ constraint cases

co-firing, coal CCS which is limited by economic UK CCS capacity, biomass, wind, nuclear and finally marine technologies in 2050. Although coal CCS is deployed before new nuclear plant, by 2050 nuclear's share (at 25.5 per cent) is comparable to coal CCS (at 31.5 per cent). The growth in 2050 in electricity production in the constraint case illustrates the difficulty of the 60 per cent target, as switching to (decarbonised) electricity in key end-use technologies (and hydrogen electrolysis) become the marginal mitigation options.

As illustrated in Figure 12.11, renewable electricity's share meets the renewables obligation (RO) and is held above the 15 per cent RO threshold even in the base case. In the constraint case, renewables push to a combined electricity share of 37 per cent in 2045 before relatively falling back slightly due to the growth of new nuclear.

Sectoral insights

Looking beyond the electricity sector, MARKAL finds a wide range of mitigation opportunities across end-use sectors, and technologies. Figure 12.12 details the share of sectoral energy that conservation measures (energy-saving devices – for example, loft insulation) reduce demand by. Note that this does *not* include more efficient devices or demand technologies or behavioural changes. Conservation measures in the base case are tuned to DEFRA (2005a) estimates of near-term potential and longer-term uptake is relatively modest. In the CO₂ constraint case, with greater access to the technical potential of conservation measure plus the induced impact of the carbon price signal, the role of pure conservation expands significantly, with up to 17 per cent of service sector energy demand being saved by 2050.

Finally focusing on the transport sector, Figures 12.13 and 12.14 detail technology

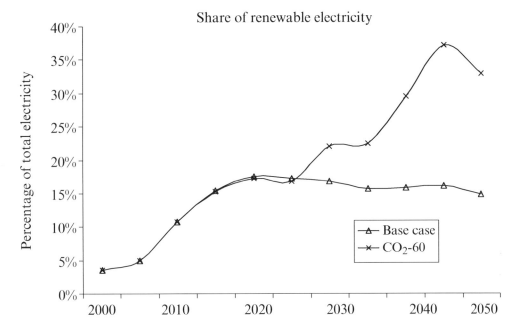

Figure 12.11   Share of renewable-based electricity generation

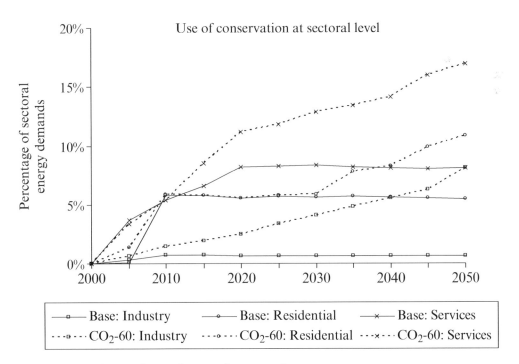

Figure 12.12   Sectoral contribution of conservation measures

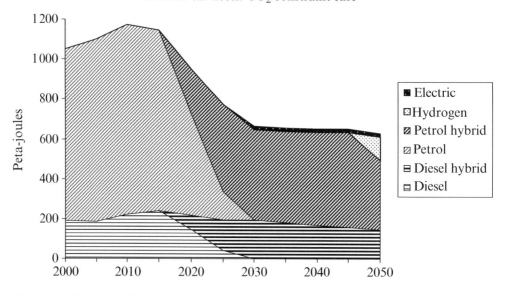

Figure 12.13   *Technology transitions in private car transport*

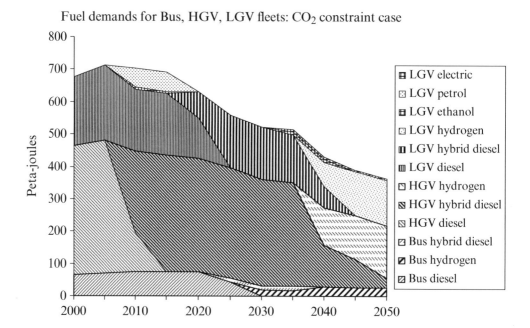

Figure 12.14   *Technology transitions in bus, LGV and HGV transport modes*

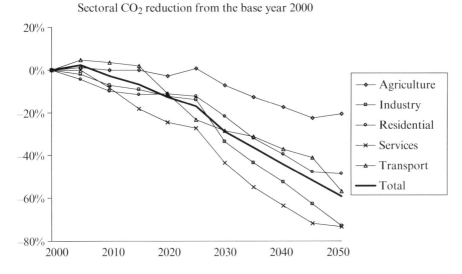

Sectoral CO$_2$ reduction from the base year 2000

Figure 12.15   Percentage of sectoral decarbonisation

transitions in private cars and in buses, light goods vehicles (LGVs), and heavy goods vehicles (HGVs) under the CO$_2$ constraint case. Significant oil product reductions are seen, largely due to efficient (conventional hybrid vehicles) and latterly the shift to hydrogen. Note that diesel includes a small mandated percentage of bio-diesel under the renewable transport fuels obligation. HGV, car, and LGV transitions to hybrids (both petrol and diesel) occur from 2010 through 2030. The uptake of efficient hybrids also occurs in the base case due to the interplay between rising oil prices and falling incremental hybrid engine costs. Niche markets for electric and ethanol vehicles (especially in the interim period in LGVs) occur before being limited by resource availability and infrastructure requirements. Buses are then the first mode to transition to hydrogen from 2025 to 2040, largely due to the fact that they require the simplest new refuelling infrastructure. This is followed by LGV, HGV and private car vehicles as the hydrogen infrastructure expands. Last, although not shown here, aviation as a sector sees very little abatement due to the lack of technological alternatives.

Comparing CO$_2$ abatement across end-use sectors (with electricity and hydrogen emissions assigned to relevant demands) Figure 12.15 details sectoral decarbonisation as a percentage of sectors' base year 2000 emission levels. If all sectors were to contribute equally to meet the 60 per cent emission reduction targets, then they would all reach 60 per cent by 2050. Instead, the service and industrial sectors decarbonise further due to use of decarbonised electricity, fuel switching to (higher efficiency) natural gas, and take-up of conservation measures. Early penetration of cost-effective conservation in the residential sector occurs although that sector's overall contribution is relatively less. Transport is the last major sector to decarbonise (noting the significant technological change already embodied in the base case). Later periods' CO$_2$ reduction in transport illustrate higher-cost mitigation options requiring significant infrastructure deployment (hydrogen or bio-fuels).

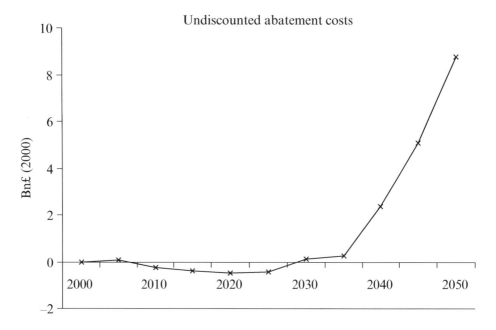

Figure 12.16   Economy-wide CO₂ abatement costs

Abatement costs

Turning to the overall economy, Figure 12.16 shows abatement costs for the 60 per cent reduction in CO_2 emissions. Following near-term economic gains due to advanced penetration of conservation measures, the CO_2 constrained case requires a rapid rise in abatement costs to decarbonise the energy sector by 60 per cent – this reaches an undiscounted level of around £8.8 billion per year. This is in comparison to the total energy system costs (encompassing every aspect of the energy system from cost of imported and domestically mined fuel resources, refineries, power plants, transmission and distribution infrastructures, and end-use technologies including vehicles and appliances) which rise to an (undiscounted) value of £325 billion. This is relative to current UK GDP of just over £1 trillion although of course UK GDP in 2050 would be expected to be 3.4 to 4.4 times larger (using an annual growth rate of 2.5–3.0 per cent).

The stringent carbon reduction target is illustrated in high CO_2 shadow prices, with Figure 12.17 giving marginal and average prices. Marginal carbon prices by 2050 rise to £136/tCO_2 (or £500/tC). Average abatement prices however are significantly less than the simple mean of prices at the margin, with 2050 average abatement prices at £27/tCO_2 (or £100/tC). This shows that the mitigation cost curve is not normally distributed, but rather is skewed towards cheaper abatement options with relatively fewer expensive options required when the emissions reduction target is stretched to 60 per cent. Note that access to cost-effective conservation options in the carbon reduction case leads to a net benefit in the early years of the carbon reduction policy. Finally, additional flexibility mechanisms (for example, international emissions trading, or behavioural change) would be expected to moderate these emission prices.

CO₂ abatement price

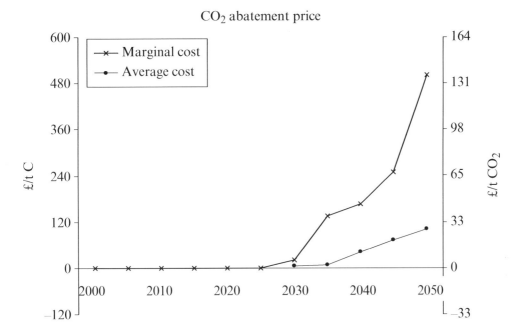

Figure 12.17   Marginal and average CO₂ prices

Uncertainty analysis

The base and CO_2 constrained runs result from a plausible set of assumptions related to energy service demands, resource costs, technology characteristics and so on. However, the strength of an integrated approach such as MARKAL is to look at other plausible assumptions, and investigate trade-offs and tipping-points between alternative energy pathways. This subsection elucidates just one such alternative pathway, with reduced nuclear costs. The uncertainties surrounding nuclear cost assessments may be one of the most opaque and problematic issues in the entire energy technology field (see SDC, 2006 for a further discussion on the difficulties in defining nuclear costs).

The three sensitivities presented below are the results of a series of diagnostic runs with UK MARKAL and represent tipping-points between differing technology pathways. The first alternative run (Nu-1) merely assumes that the uranium resource curve supply is flat and held at 2010 prices. Thus in this case it is assumed that the expansion of uranium mining keeps pace with any expansion of global demands. The second run (Nu-2) includes flat uranium supply plus a 30 per cent decrease in enrichment costs. The third run (Nu-3) includes the flat uranium supply, the 30 per cent decrease in enrichment costs, plus a 30 per cent decrease in capital costs. This last improvement takes nuclear generation investment costs down to the most optimistic industry estimates (WNA, 2005).

Figure 12.18 illustrates the changing electricity mix under these cumulative improvements in the economics of nuclear electricity. With only the alteration of uranium resource assumptions, nuclear generation dominates coal CCS as the carbon-free base-load generation in 2050. Moving to an additional improvement in nuclear enrichment costs ensures nuclear generation in the interim period (2020–50) also dominates coal

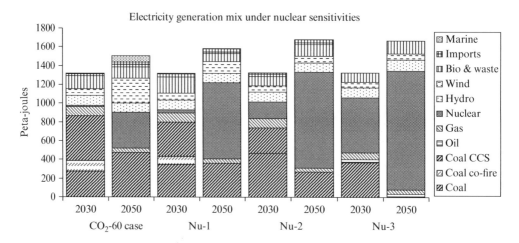

Figure 12.18   Electricity generation mix under nuclear chain improvements

CCS, while the additional improvement in nuclear capital costs ensures that coal CCS is never chosen as a mitigation option. Thus the trade-off between nuclear generation and coal CCS is well within the plausible range of uncertainty of these two technology classes and hence it is impossible to draw any conclusions on which is superior on cost grounds. Note also that nuclear economics is in reality an even more complex issue. Although not displayed here, MARKAL can investigate additional issues such as forced 'lumpy invest-ments' (for example, commissioning a fleet of 10 stations) or forced upfront payments for disposal and decommissioning.

Finally, improving the nuclear costs assumption also means that the renewables market share is eroded. This is particularly true of technologies that require economies of learning before they can compete on cost grounds. This includes marine and wind technologies, and essentially they do not improve fast enough to compete with improved nuclear plants. Last, electricity imports are also restricted alleviating the need to build new inter-connector capacity with the French network.

Figure 12.19 illustrates the marginal and average CO_2 price reductions from the improved nuclear technology cost assumptions. Reductions in both metrics are both significant, and illustrate the feasible policy cost reductions from improvements in just one key technology.

As a final illustration of the considerable uncertainty permeating technology costs, Figure 12.20 shows a 'best-case' scenario, with total abatement costs under improved technology assumptions for a range of key technology classes: conservation, nuclear, coal CCS, remote renewables, grid-connected renewables, and distributed generation (fossil and renewable). In year 2050, undiscounted economy-wide costs have declined from £8.8 billion to only around £2 billion.

Finally, note that assumptions producing costs on the upper side of the core runs could just have easily been displayed and would illustrate that the uncertainty surround-ing higher cost-inducing assumptions is just as great. Such scenarios might include those with restrictions on technology classes (for example, no nuclear or CCS) or scenarios with reduced innovation.

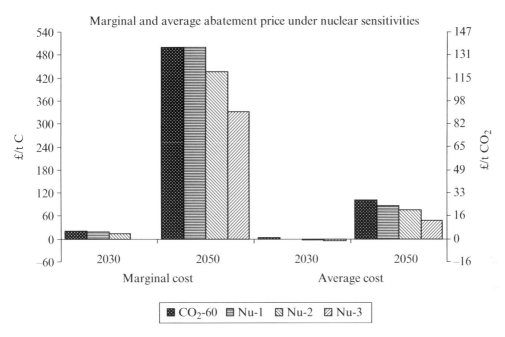

Figure 12.19   Marginal and average carbon prices under improved nuclear supply chain

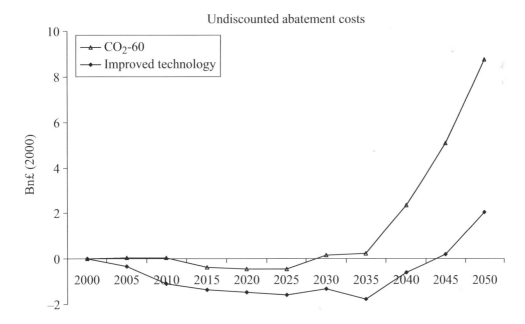

Figure 12.20   Total abatement costs with all technological improvements

5   Concluding Remarks

This chapter has detailed the development of a new UK MARKAL energy systems model. This development was enabled through the energy systems modelling theme of the UK Energy Research Centre, and facilitated by a project commissioned by DTI and DEFRA for substantive analytical input to the 2007 Energy White Paper.

Discussion of the new UK MARKAL model has covered its complete rebuild with a range of enhancements to improve its functionality and analytical sophistication. As part of this development a detailed data update and stakeholder validation process was carried out, with key input assumptions summarised here. In addition, a model calibration exercise was concluded with the DTI's econometric energy model for short- and mid-term agreement in core-case forecasts.

Indicative results from the new standard model are presented. These focus on characterising uncertainties between alternative energy pathways under scenarios of long-term carbon reductions. The UK overall primary energy demand declines due to energy efficiency improvements at supply and demand sides. In terms of its primary mix in the base case, coal is dominating due to coal-based electricity generation while natural gas holds steady at around one-third for direct applications in end-use sectors. Oil use declines due to greater efficiency gains in the transport sector. Nuclear energy drops out of the UK energy mix. However, in the low carbon case (that is, 60 per cent emission reduction by 2050) nuclear reappears to meet carbon constraints and gas retains its share due to relatively low emissions.

In the power sector, coal-based electricity generation dominates in the base case driven by new vintages of coal-generation technologies, and cheaper cost. In the CO_2 constrained case, coal-based electricity generation shifts to coal CCS, biomass co-firing, nuclear and finally marine technologies as the carbon constraint tightens. Renewables-based electricity share reaches 37 per cent in 2045 before falling back due to the growth of new nuclear.

In terms of mitigation, MARKAL finds a wide range of mitigation opportunities across end-use sectors. All sectors are not equally decarbonised to meet the 60 per cent emission reduction – instead the power sector is extremely decarbonised. The transport sector is the last major sector to decarbonise through the shift in private cars towards hybrid cars and latterly to hydrogen and biofuels. The uptake of efficient hybrids also occurs in the base case due to the interplay between rising oil prices and falling incremental hybrid engine costs.

In terms of abatement costs for the 60 per cent reduction in CO_2 emissions, near-term economic gains due to advanced penetration of conservation measures reach an undiscounted level of around £8.8 billion per year. The marginal carbon price by 2050 rises to £136/tCO_2 (or £500/tC). Average abatement prices, however, are significantly less than the simple mean of prices at the margin, with 2050 average abatement prices at £27/tCO_2 (or £100/tC). This shows that the mitigation cost curve is not normally distributed, but rather is skewed towards cheaper abatement options with relatively fewer expensive options required when the emission target stretches to a 60 per cent cut. Note that access to cost-effective conservation options in the carbon reduction case leads to a net benefit in the early years of the carbon reduction policy. Finally, additional flexibility mechanisms (for example, international emissions trading, or behavioural change) would be expected to moderate these emission prices.

Care should be exercised when viewing any one set of results under a certain set of technology and other assumptions from such a complex modelling exercise. For example, the uncertainties surrounding nuclear and CCS cost assessments may be one of the most opaque and problematic issues in the entire energy technology field. With only the alteration of uranium resource assumptions, nuclear generation dominates coal CCS as the carbon-free base-load generation in 2050. Moving to an additional improvement in nuclear enrichment costs ensures that nuclear generation in the interim period (2020–50) also dominates coal CCS, while the additional improvement in nuclear capital costs ensures that coal CCS is never chosen as a mitigation option. Thus the trade-off between nuclear generation and coal CCS is well within the plausible range of uncertainty of these two technology classes and hence it is impossible to draw any conclusions on which is superior on cost grounds. This shows an initial step in characterising uncertainty in model results as well as robust insights.

Notes

*   This research was conducted under the auspices of the UK Energy Research Centre (UKERC) which is funded by the Natural Environment Research Council, the Engineering and Physical Sciences Research Council and the Economic and Social Research Council. Any views expressed are those of the authors alone and do not necessarily represent the view of UKERC or the Research Councils. We are grateful to the Research Councils for their support. The authors would like to acknowledge the contributions of Nazmiye Balta-Ozkan from the Policy Studies Institute, and Steve Pye and Peter Taylor from AEA Energy and Environment during the development of this MARKAL energy system model.
1.   This development was carried out as part of the work programme of the energy systems modelling theme of the UK Energy Research Centre (UKERC), supplemented by a project commissioned by Department of Trade and Industry (DTI) and Department for Environment Food and Rural Affairs (DEFRA) to provide substantive analytical input into the 2007 UK Energy White Paper (DTI, 2007).
2.   The development of a new energy systems model is an iterative process, and UK MARKAL will be progressively updated and run in a variety of applications over the next few years. Ongoing policy and academic outputs from the model, including the development of a general equilibrium MARKAL–MACRO (M–M) model are given in Strachan et al. (2008a, 2008b); Strachan and Kannan (2007, 2008). For further papers including extensions and detailed analysis of key energy pathways, see Strachan et al. (2007a); Kannan and Strachan (2009).

References

DEFRA (2005a), *The Energy Efficiency Innovation Review*, Department for Environment, Food and Rural Affairs and HM Treasury, London, available at: http://www.hm-treasury.gov.uk/d/pbr05_energy_675.pdf (accessed 17 February 2009).
DEFRA (2005b), *UK Carbon Emissions*, Department for Environment, Food and Rural Affairs, London, available at: http://www.defra.gov.uk/environment/statistics/globatmos/index.htm (accessed 17 February 2009).
DfT (2005), *National Transport Model (NTM)*, Department for Transport, London, available at: www.dft.gov.uk/pgr/economics/htm (accessed 17 February 2009).
DTI (2003), *Our Energy Future – Creating a Low Carbon Economy*, Energy White Paper, Department of Trade and Industry, London, February.
DTI (2006a), *Updated Energy Projections* (updated from EP-68), Department of Trade and Industry, London, April.
DTI (2006b), *Updated Energy Projections* (updated from EP-68), Department of Trade and Industry, London, July.
DTI (2006c), *The Energy Challenge*, Energy Review, Department of Trade and Industry, London, July.
DTI (2007), *Meeting the Energy Challenge*, Energy White Paper, Department of Trade and Industry, London, May.
DUKES (2006), *Digest of United Kingdom Energy Statistics*, Department of Trade and Industry, London.
European Commission (2005), *World Energy Technology Outlook – 2050 (WETO–H2)*, DG Research (Energy), available at: http://ec.europa.eu/research/energy/gp/gp_pu/article_1257_en.htm (accessed April 2007).

FES (2003), *Options for a Low Carbon Future – Phase 2*, a report produced for the Department of Trade and Industry, Future Energy Solutions, London.

FES (2006), *UK Energy Review: Transport Sector Projections to 2050*, report to the Department for Transport, Future Energy Solutions, London, June.

HMT (2006), 'The Green Book: appraisal and evaluation in Central Government', The HM Treasury, London, www.hm-treasury.gov.uk/data_greenbook_index.htm (accessed 17 November 2008).

IEA (2006), *Energy Technology Perspectives: Scenarios and Strategies to 2050*, International Energy Agency, Paris.

Kannan, R. and N. Strachan (2009), 'Modelling the UK residential energy sector under long-term decarbonisation scenarios: comparison between energy systems and sectoral modelling approaches', *Applied Energy*, **86**(4), 416–28.

Kannan, R., N. Strachan, N. Balta-Ozkan and S. Pye (2007), 'UK MARKAL model documentation', UK Energy Research Centre (UKERC) working paper, available at: http://www.ukerc.ac.uk/ResearchProgrammes/EnergySystemsandModelling/ESMMARKALDocs08.aspx (accessed 17 February 2007).

Loulou, R., G. Goldstein and K. Noble (2004a), *Documentation for the MARKAL Family of Models: Part I – Standard MARKAL*, Energy Technology Systems Analysis Programme, www.etsap.org/MrKLDoc-I_StdMARKAL.pdf (accessed 17 February 2009).

Loulou, R., G. Goldstein and K. Noble (2004b), *Documentation for the MARKAL Family of Models: Part II – MARKAL–MACRO*, Energy Technology Systems Analysis Programme, www.etsap.org/MrKLDoc-I_StdMARKAL.pdf (accessed 17 February 2009).

McDonald, A. and L. Schrattenholzer (2002), 'Learning curves and technology assessment', *International Journal of Technology Management*, **23** (7/8), 718–45.

Pout, C. and F. MacKenzie (2006), *Reducing Carbon Emissions from Commercial and Public Sector Buildings in the UK*, Building Report Establishment (BRE) Client Report for Global Atmosphere Division, DEFRA, www.bre.co.uk.

RCEP (2000), *Energy – The Changing Climate*, Royal Commission on Environmental Pollution, London.

Sustainable Development Commission (SDC) (2006), *The Role of Nuclear Power in a Low Carbon Economy*, Sustainable Development Commission position paper, London, www.sd-commission.org.uk/publications/downloads/SDC-NuclearPosition-2006.pdf.

Shorrock L.D., J. Henderson and J.I. Utley (2005), *Reducing Carbon Emissions from the UK Housing Stock*, Building Research Establishment (BRE) Press, Watford, UK.

Smith, D. (2007), 'Comparative cost information – supporting the development of the MARKAL–MACRO model', report to the Ashden Trust, mimeo, Policy Studies Institute, London.

Strachan, N. and R. Kannan (2007), 'Quantifying technological and economic implications of long term carbon reduction scenarios for the UK', paper presented at the 9th International Association for Energy Economics (IAEE) European Conference, Florence, June.

Strachan, N. and R. Kannan (2008), 'Hybrid modelling of long-term carbon reduction scenarios for the UK', *Energy Economics*, **30** (6), 2947–63.

Strachan, N., N. Balta-Ozkan, R. Kannan, N. Hughes, K. McGeevor and D. Joffe (2007a), *State-of-the-art Modelling of Hydrogen Infrastructure Development for the UK: Geographical, Temporal and Technological Optimisation Modelling*, Final Report on Modelling Methodology and Modelling Outputs for Department for Transport, London

Strachan, N., R. Kannan, N. Balta-Ozkan, S. Pye and P. Taylor (2006), *Development of the UK MARKAL Energy Systems Model*, 2nd Interim Report, Report for DTI/DEFRA, London.

Strachan, N., R. Kannan and S. Pye (2008a), *Scenarios and Sensitivities on Long-term UK Carbon Reductions using the UK MARKAL and MARKAL–MACRO Energy System Models*, Research Report, UK Energy Research Centre (UKERC) London, available at: www.ukerc.ac.uk/Downloads/PDF/S/ Scenariosreport.pdf (accessed 17 February 2009).

Strachan, N., S. Pye and N. Hughes (2008b), 'International drivers of a UK evolution to a low carbon society', *Climate Policy*, **8**, S17–S29.

Train, K. (1985), 'Discount rates in consumers' energy-related decisions', *Energy: The International Journal*, **10** (12), 1243–53.

WNA (2005), *The New Economics of Nuclear Power*, World Nuclear Association, London.

13 Combining top down and bottom up in energy economy models
Mark Jaccard

1 Introduction: Designing Induced Technological Change Models and Estimating Their Parameters

Many environmental concerns, including the risk of human-induced climate change, motivate public policy efforts to influence the direction of technological evolution – what is known as 'induced technological change' (ITC). Since technological change is a long-run phenomenon that occurs as society's capital stock grows and is renewed, the likely outcome of alternative policies is inevitably uncertain, and more so the further one projects into the future. But even though future technological evolution and the behavior of consumers and businesses are uncertain, this is no excuse to engage in unsupported speculation about the future adoption of new technologies. A speculative or wishful scenario of the future, with negligible connection to real-world evidence, is ultimately unhelpful to policy makers and may lead to ITC policies that are ineffective or have unintended consequences.

The appropriate policy modelling response to this challenge has at least two major tasks. The first is to characterize the necessary attributes of an energy–economy model for assessing ITC policies. Some of these attributes are generic. Future technological potential, future responsiveness of consumers and businesses to policy signals, and future economy-wide feedbacks must be characterized under any modelling of ITC. Other model attributes, however, depend on the specific policy objective and scope. Thus, a model for determining greenhouse gas (GHG) reduction targets for groups of countries within a global framework will differ in degree of resolution and structure from a model for assessing a specific policy program for GHG reduction in an individual country.

The second major modelling task is to populate the policy model with technology-specific data and parameter values in which policy makers can have some degree of confidence, even though uncertainty about the future is of course unavoidable. Models that are technologically explicit require reliable data for the stocks of technologies – their market shares, capital costs, operating costs, energy use, emissions. These and all other models also require realistic, empirically based parameters for simulating technological evolution under different policies. This is an enormous challenge for modelling ITC. The quantities and operating characteristics of current capital stocks are incompletely known. The future costs and operating characteristics of emerging technologies, not to mention future innovations, can only be guessed at, hopefully with reliable guidance from experts. Finally, the response of businesses and consumers to policies intended to influence their preferences for these emerging technologies and future innovations can be estimated approximately from current sources in one of two ways: either from market decisions taken under historical conditions ('revealed preferences'), or from hypothetical market choices when these economic agents are surveyed about their preferences for technologies under future market and policy conditions ('stated preferences').

There is a considerable literature devoted to characterizing the ideal attributes of a model for simulating ITC policies. Many analysts have been engaged in the effort to design comprehensible and consistent energy–economy policy models. With the second task, however, the literature is much thinner. For while there are many modelling exercises that feed into international and national processes to develop energy–environment targets and policies, most of these are vague on the empirical research that supports the key parameters in the model. Often, the reviewer of this work is uncertain as to the importance of various parameters and the extent to which such parameters are based on revealed or stated preferences of real-world businesses and households.

This chapter explores both of these tasks, especially the latter. First, it outlines the ideal attributes of ITC policy models, noting the deficiencies and strengths of conventional approaches before explaining some recent modelling innovations that attempt to combine the best qualities of competing conventional models. It then focuses on the second task of parameter estimation in some detail. To ground the discussion, a specific ITC model is examined. While this model is not particularly unique, its method of simulating technological change provides a concrete example of the challenges of providing a real-world empirical basis for estimating how businesses and consumers are likely to respond to a slate of ITC policies in a given country or group of countries.

2   Ideal Attributes for ITC Policy Models

Although recent modelling innovations have made the distinction less clear, it is pedagogically helpful to contrast top-down and bottom-up models as the major alternative approaches to modelling ITC policies for energy–environment objectives (Carraro and Hourcade, 1998). Bottom-up analysis, applied frequently by engineers, physicists and environmental advocates, estimates how changes in energy efficiency, fuel, emission control equipment, and infrastructure might influence energy use and thus environmental impacts. Technologies that provide the same energy service are generally assumed to be perfect substitutes except for differences in their anticipated financial costs and emissions. When their financial costs in different time periods are converted into present value using a social discount rate, many emerging technologies available for abating emissions appear to be profitable or just slightly more expensive relative to existing equipment and buildings. This is especially the case for energy-efficient technologies in comparison to their more conventional substitutes. Bottom-up models often show, therefore, that environmental improvement from energy efficiency can be profitable or low cost if these low-emission technologies were to achieve market dominance.

Many economists criticize this approach, however, for its assumption that a single, anticipated estimate of financial cost indicates the full social cost of technological change (Sutherland, 1991; Jaffe and Stavins, 1994; Jaffe et al., 1999). New technologies present greater risks, as do the longer paybacks associated with investments such as energy efficiency. Some low-cost, low-emission technologies are not perfect substitutes in the eyes of the businesses or consumers expected to adopt them. To the extent that they ignore some of these costs, bottom-up models may inadvertently suggest the wrong technological and policy options for policy makers. Ironically, with their simplistic portrayal of consumers as financial cost minimizers, some bottom-up modellers may be more susceptible than many economists to the critique of applying a 'rational-economic-man' view of the world.

The alternative, top-down analysis, usually applied by economists, estimates aggregate relationships between the relative costs and market shares of energy and other inputs to the economy, and links these to sectoral and total economic output in a broader equilibrium framework. Elasticities of substitution (ESUB) indicate the substitutability between any two pairs of aggregate inputs (capital, labor, energy, materials), and between the different forms of primary energy (coal, oil, natural gas, renewables) or secondary energy (electricity, processed natural gas, gasoline, diesel, methanol, ethanol, hydrogen) as their relative prices change. Another key parameter in top-down models, the autonomous energy efficiency index (AEEI), indicates the rate at which price-independent technological evolution improves energy productivity. At their most basic, these conventional top-down models represent the economy through a series of simultaneous equations linking economic outputs and inputs (especially energy), whose parameters are estimated econometrically from time-series data. Models that link all of the major macroeconomic feedbacks in a full equilibrium framework are referred to as computable general equilibrium (CGE) models.

High parameter values for energy-related ESUB (a high degree of substitutability between energy and capital, and between different forms of energy) imply that technological change for environmental improvement may occur at relatively low cost. If this parameter is estimated from past market data, as energy prices and consumption changed historically, it is assumed to reveal the actual preferences of consumers and businesses. With AEEI and ESUB estimated, economists then simulate the economy's response to a financial signal (an emissions tax, an emissions permit price) that increases the relative cost of emission-intensive technologies and energy forms. The magnitude of the financial signal necessary to achieve a given emission-reduction target indicates its implicit cost, including the less tangible costs related to the special risks of new technologies, the risks of long payback technologies, and specific preferences of consumers and businesses for the attributes of one technology over its competitor.

A significant challenge for top-down models, however, is the estimation of statistically significant top-down parameters from real-world experience. Often there is insufficient variability in the historical record for confident parameter estimation, and therefore most CGE modellers set the key ESUB parameters in their models judgmentally (Loschel, 2002). The top-down approach is also vulnerable to the criticism of being unhelpful to policy makers. In the pursuit of substantial technological change for environmental objectives, policy makers need to know the extent to which their policies might influence the characteristics and financial costs of future technologies, and the likely willingness of consumers and businesses to adopt these. If the critical top-down parameters for portraying technological change – ESUB and AEEI – are estimated from aggregate, historical data, there is no guarantee that these parameter values will remain valid into a future under substantially different policies, different energy prices and with different technological options for environmental improvement (Grubb et al., 2002; DeCanio, 2003; Laitner et al., 2003). For example, until recently, there was little motivation to design and commercialize technologies with zero or near-zero GHG emissions. Today, such technologies are under development worldwide, providing households and firms with new choices. ESUB values in future may be different. AEEI may also evolve differently. Oil prices are well above historical highs. As this process unfolds, the estimated cost of GHG abatement may decrease, but top-down models are unable to help policy makers assess this dynamic. Increasingly concerned with this problem, some top-down modellers are exploring ways of treating technological change endogenously, but again the question becomes whether their parameters have any real-world empirical basis and, if so, the extent to which these are likely to be useful indicators of behavior under future, much different, regulatory and price conditions.

Another difficulty with the top-down approach is that policy makers often prefer, for political acceptability, policies that focus on individual technologies in the form of technology- and building-specific tax credits, subsidies, penalties, regulations and information programs. This is especially the case where emission charges would need to be high in order to overcome significant costs of environmental improvement, which would trigger politically unacceptable reactions from consumers and businesses. Because conventional top-down models represent technological change as an abstract, aggregate phenomenon – characterized by ESUB and AEEI parameter values – this approach helps policy makers assess only economy-wide policy instruments such as taxes and tradable permits. At national and subnational levels, a model would be more useful if it could assess the combined effect of these economy-wide, price-based policies along with technology-focused policies, but this requires the explicit representation of individual technologies that conventional top-down models lack.

Because they incorporate to some extent the transitional costs and risks of technological change, top-down cost estimates for ITC are almost always higher than bottom-up cost estimates. Analyses of the costs of achieving the US Kyoto Protocol commitments provide an example. After signing the Kyoto Protocol in 1997, the US government commissioned studies on the potential costs of meeting its Kyoto obligations by five national research laboratories. These studies used a bottom-up modelling approach and found that a 30 percent reduction in GHG emissions from business-as-usual levels could be achieved at no net cost to the economy (Brown et al., 1998). They suggested that this level of reduction could be achieved domestically through a tax on carbon emissions of no more than 25/tC as well as a host of other policies.

In contrast, top-down analyses have come to different estimates of the potential cost to the US of reducing its emissions. Weyant and Hill (1999) summarized the results of a multi-model comparison of the costs of meeting the US Kyoto Protocol commitments; most of the models in their study were of the CGE (top-down) variety. Of the 11 participating models, eight found that a tax of at least US$150/tC would be required to meet Kyoto commitments and, of these, four required a tax of at least US$250/tC. GDP impacts ranged from modest levels to the loss of over 3 percent of economic output.

Policy makers see results from both of these types of study and are understandably perplexed – not sure whom to believe, and what policies to apply. On the one hand, conventional bottom-up models indicate that environmental goals can be reached at low cost, suggesting that only mild policies are required, such as subsidies and information programs. On the other hand, conventional top-down models indicate that achieving environmental goals is costly, and that more-stringent policies such as emissions taxes, emissions cap and trade regulations, or technology- and fuel-specific regulations are required. The reality is likely to be somewhere between these two extremes. Policy makers are likely to acquire more reliable information from a modelling approach that combined the critical elements of these two conventional approaches.

Ideally, then, policy makers need models that can evaluate the effect of economy-wide policies working in concert with technology- and fuel-specific measures, and that incorporate regulations as well as market-based policies. Such models would need to satisfy at least three criteria: explicit representation of the potential for technological change, microeconomic realism in accounting for how businesses and firms will decide among future technology options, and macroeconomic feedbacks in reflecting how changes in production costs and preferences will change the structure of the economy and the growth rate of total output.

The cube in Figure 13.1 depicts how different modelling approaches perform against these three criteria. Conventional bottom-up models do well in terms of technological explicitness, but less well in terms of the other two attributes. Conventional top-down models appear to do well in terms of microeconomic realism (if their parameters have a real-world empirical basis as opposed to being guesstimates), and may do well in terms of macroeconomic feedbacks if they are general equilibrium models. However, they lack technological explicitness, making them ineffective for assessing the full range of policies that policy makers wish to consider.

As the figure suggests, an ideal technology policy model would be situated at the right, top rear corner of the cube. It would be technologically explicit, including an assessment

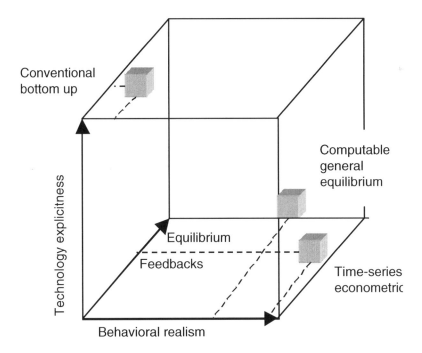

Source: Jaccard et al. (2003).

Figure 13.1   Criteria for comparing energy–economy models

of how policies to promote technology commercialization and diffusion might affect the future financial costs of acquiring new technologies. It would be behaviorally realistic, including an assessment of how policies to increase market share might affect the future intangible costs of acquiring new technologies. And it would have equilibrium feedbacks, linking energy supply and demand, and both of these together with structural change and total economic output. This equilibrium dimension might include feedback between countries in cases where the environmental challenge is one that requires a global effort, such as with GHG abatement.

Modellers refer to such an ideal model as a 'hybrid' or 'top-down/bottom-up' model in that it would incorporate key features of both top-down and bottom-up models. Efforts toward hybrid modelling usually involve either incorporation of technological detail into a top-down framework (Bohringer, 1998; Jacobsen, 1998; Koopmans and te Velde, 2001; Frei et al., 2003) or incorporation of behavioral realism and/or macroeconomic feedbacks into a bottom-up framework (Jaccard et al., 1996; Nystrom and Wene, 1999; Sanstad et al., 2001; Morris et al., 2002; Bataille et al., 2006). Hourcade et al. (2006) provide an overview of recent hybrid modelling efforts.

The past decade has seen significant advances in the development of hybrid modelling approaches. Increasingly, such models applied to assessing policies to induce technological change include at least some degree of technological explicitness, microeconomic behavioral realism and macroeconomic feedbacks.

In terms of technological explicitness, there are several critical pieces of information that hybrid models should include. They need to indicate the cost and physical potential of major zero-emission technology and energy supply options. In the case of GHG abatement options – a multi-decade effort – this would include the next generation of nuclear power technologies, renewable energy technologies that include some form of energy storage to overcome intermittency, and fossil-fuel conversion technologies that include carbon capture and storage. They also need to indicate how new technology costs would decline with greater production and diffusion. Technology modellers refer to 'learning curves' or 'experience curves', nonlinear functions that show how capital and operating costs fall, especially in the early phases of a technology's development and penetration of the market. Another important technology characteristic is the AEEI trend. This indicates how energy intensity is likely to change even in the absence of climate policies. Without some confidence in this trend, policy makers will be uncertain if their policies are having an effect on energy intensity levels in the economy – assuming that reduced energy intensity is a policy goal.

In terms of behavioral realism, hybrid models need to include the key factors affecting technology and fuel choices by consumers and businesses. Two technologies may appear to provide the same service, such as the number of lumens from a light bulb. But a new light bulb is likely to have a greater risk of premature failure, an expensive light bulb has risks because of the long payback period of the extra investment in efficiency, and a new bulb may not be a perfect substitute because of its shape, the hue of its light, its ability to operate with other devices (such as dimmer switches) or the time it takes to reach full intensity. Hybrid models can incorporate these factors by having parameters for time preference and the intangible costs related to differential risks between technologies and consumers' preferences. To reflect the heterogeneity of markets, such models should also have some way of accounting for the different costs faced by different consumers and the diversity of their preferences.

Finally, in terms of macroeconomic feedbacks, hybrid models may need to track the structural and output effects of ITC policies. However, this necessity depends on the intensity of policies that are pursued. Most policy makers will be unwilling to apply policies that significantly increase some prices in their jurisdiction alone, while other jurisdictions fail to act, and will provide policy exemptions for economic sectors that are vulnerable to external competition. The emissions tax policies in European countries thus far have protected to some extent the more vulnerable industries. In such cases, macroeconomic implications are unlikely to be substantial. Nonetheless, governments are under pressure to demonstrate to skeptics that their initially modest energy–environment policies will not have adverse consequences for specific industries, so this alone provides a rationale for the inclusion of macroeconomic feedbacks in a hybrid model. In the case of GHG emissions, the more likely outcome is the near-simultaneous application of emissions policies by many countries. Again, governments will need to demonstrate that they have tried to estimate the economic consequences, at a fairly disaggregated industry level within their own country, of a multinational effort to reduce GHG emissions substantially over a long period.

Today, there is a fairly broad agreement as to the importance of these attributes for an ideal model. As a consequence, the past decade has witnessed the development of numerous hybrid models for assessing ITC policies. However, this advance in model design has not been accompanied by an equivalent advance in developing the empirical foundation for such models. Indeed, as models get more complex, the task of empirically estimating their parameter values becomes increasingly difficult.

Jaccard et al. (2003) and Bataille et al. (2006) establish the means of empirically estimating the parameters of a hybrid model so that policy makers might achieve some understanding of what these parameters are based on, of how uncertain they are, and of how significant this uncertainty is for predicting the likely effect of a given policy or package of policies. The next section provides a brief description of this particular modelling approach in order to explain in some detail the empirical efforts to estimate key parameters.

3 Efforts to Empirically Estimate the Parameters of a Hybrid Energy–Economy ITC Policy Model

Model design

The hybrid model, called CIMS, is an integrated, energy–economy equilibrium model that simulates the interaction of energy supply–demand and the macroeconomic performance of key sectors of the economy, including trade effects.[1] Unlike most CGE models, however, the current version of CIMS does not equilibrate government budgets and the markets for employment and investment. Also, its representation of the economy's inputs and outputs is skewed toward energy supply activities, energy-intensive industries, and key energy end uses in the residential, commercial/institutional and transportation sectors.

CIMS simulates the evolution of capital stocks over time through retirements, retrofits, and new purchases, in which consumers and businesses make sequential acquisitions with limited foresight (Jaccard et al., 2003). The model calculates energy costs (and emissions) at each energy service demand node in the economy, such as heated commercial floor space or person-kilometers traveled. In each time period, capital stocks are retired according to an age-dependent function (although retrofit of unretired stocks is possible if warranted by changing economic conditions), and demand for new stocks grows or declines depending on the initial exogenous forecast of economic output, and then the subsequent interplay of energy supply–demand with the macroeconomic module. A model simulation iterates between energy supply–demand and the macroeconomic module until energy price changes fall below a threshold value, and repeats this convergence procedure in each subsequent five-year period of a complete run, which usually extends for 30–50 years but could continue indefinitely.

CIMS simulates the competition of technologies at each energy service node in the economy based on a comparison of their life-cycle cost (LCC) mediated by some technology-specific controls, such as a maximum market share limit in the cases where a technology is constrained by physical, technical or regulatory means from capturing all of a market. Instead of basing its simulation of technology choices only on financial costs and social discount rates, CIMS applies a formula for LCC that allows for divergence from that of conventional bottom-up analysis by including intangible costs that reflect revealed and stated consumer and business preferences with respect to specific technologies and time. Equation (13.1) presents how CIMS simulates technology market shares for new capital stocks:

$$
MS_j = \frac{\left[CC_j^* \dfrac{r}{1 - (1 + r)^{-n_j}} + MC_j + EC_j + i_j \right]^{-v}}{\displaystyle\sum_{k=1}^{K} \left\{ \left[CC_k^* \dfrac{r}{1 - (1 + r)^{-n_k}} + MC_k + EC_k + i_k \right]^{-v} \right\}},
\qquad (13.1)
$$

where MS_j is the market share of technology j, CC_j is its capital cost, MC_j is its maintenance and operation cost, n_j is the average lifespan of the technology, EC_j is its energy cost, which depends on energy prices and energy consumption per unit of energy service output – producing a ton of steel, heating one square meter of a residence, transporting a person or tonne of cargo one kilometer. The r parameter represents the weighted average time preference of decision makers for a given energy service demand; it is the same for all technologies competing to provide a given energy service, but can differ between different energy services according to empirical evidence. The i_j parameter represents all intangible costs and benefits that consumers and businesses perceive, additional to the simple financial cost values used in most bottom-up analyses, for technology j as compared to all other technologies k at a given energy service node. For example, public transit and single-occupancy vehicles compete to provide the service of personal transportation. Empirical evidence suggests that some consumers place an intangible, non-financial cost on public transportation to reflect their perceptions of its lower convenience, status, and comfort relative to the personal vehicle. These costs are captured in CIMS using the i_j parameter.

The v parameter represents the heterogeneity in the market, whereby different consumers and businesses experience different LCCs, perhaps as a result of divergent preferences, perhaps as a result of real financial costs being different for different customers. It determines the shape of the inverse power function that allocates market share to technology *j*. A high value of *v* means that the technology with the lowest LCC captures almost the entire new market share. A low value for *v* means that the market shares of new equipment are distributed fairly evenly, even if their LCCs differ significantly. At *v* = 10, when technology A becomes 15 percent more expensive than B, B captures 85 percent of the market. At *v* = 1, when technology A becomes 15 percent more expensive than technology B, B only captures 55 percent of the market. This second case implies a more heterogeneous market, and the first case a more homogeneous market. A conventional bottom-up optimization model, with no market share constraints, operates as if *v* = ∞, equivalent to a step function where the cheapest technology captures 100 percent of the market – a completely homogeneous market.

Thus, CIMS is technologically explicit and incorporates microeconomic behavior in portraying the selection of technologies by businesses and consumers. It also incorporates substantial feedbacks, although not yet to the full extent of CGE models. CIMS would be depicted toward the top right rear corner of Figure 13.1, albeit still a considerable distance from the corner. This suggests that in an ideal sense, it should be a useful model to policy makers in pursuit of ITC. However, its usefulness depends on the extent to which its parameters have a meaningful empirical foundation.

Most of the key parameters in CIMS are found in equation (13.1) above, and can be categorized as technological and behavioral. The following subsections describe estimation of these technological and behavioral parameters.

Estimating technological parameters
Equipment manufacturers, trade journals, marketers, government ministries, and international agencies provide information on the capital costs (CC) and operating characteristics (MC and EC) of many energy-using and energy-producing technologies. There is usually not a great variation in these estimates, suggesting that policy makers can have confidence in the values provided for technologies competing in the near future to satisfy the demand for new capital stocks.

There is less confidence, however, in the market shares and operating characteristics of currently installed capital equipment. The longer that equipment and buildings have been in service, the greater the chance that their operating characteristics (efficiency, operating cost) have changed since initial installation. Also, the more numerous and less expensive a type of capital equipment, the less the chance that sound data are available on its current market penetration. In the residential sector, for example, information is incomplete on the current capital stocks and operating characteristics of installed compact fluorescent light bulbs. While there are sales data for these light bulbs, there is scant information on their operating lifespan when uncertain factors such as rate of accidental breakage, rate of premature malfunction, frequency of use and instances of non-installation (leaving the bulb in a drawer) are considered.

Surveys focused on larger industrial equipment (major process equipment, boilers, motors) are more reliable. This is especially so for capital stocks of energy production, conversion and distribution as these technologies are often under the control of major energy companies, and in the electricity and natural gas sectors these companies are required to provide detailed information to utility regulators, with much information in the public domain.

As the period of policy interest extends further into the future, models that explicitly track technologies – namely bottom-up models and hybrids – face additional challenges as various uncertainties are amplified. One challenge is to anticipate the direction and shape of innovation and new product or technology commercialization. Some researchers focus their surveys and analysis on the potential for energy efficiency through new technologies and improvements to existing capital equipment (Worrell et al., 2004). While this type of analysis and modelling can provide useful information to policy makers, it can also be misleading if it omits an assessment of those emerging technologies that will conversely lead to increased energy use. In transportation, for example, this would be tantamount to assessing in 1985 the potential for cars to become more efficient within their conventional size categories (compact, sedan, van, sport utility vehicle) without anticipating the shift from smaller to larger vehicles and from lower to higher horsepower. In the residential sector, this would be equivalent to assessing the potential for greater efficiency in fridges, stoves and other appliances without anticipating the rapid development in wealthy countries of new energy-using technologies such as home spas, outdoor patio heaters, decorative lighting, wine coolers, home business and communications equipment, and decorative natural gas fireplaces. If technologically explicit models are to be useful in helping policy makers understand the impact of policies to induce technological change, they need to also account for trends in innovation that might work against the focus of their research.

Finally, another issue is the long-run cost evolution of new and emerging technologies. New technologies of all types (more and less energy intensive) experience a financial cost decline as firms gain experience in manufacturing and operating them. This occurs especially because of economies of scale and economies of learning in production, installation and operation with new technologies. The CIMS model has a declining capital cost function which links a technology's financial cost in future periods to its cumulative production, as in equation (13.2). In this formulation – sometimes referred to as a learning curve – $C(t)$ is the financial cost of a technology at time t, $N(t)$ is the cumulative production of a technology at time t, and PR is the progress ratio, defined as the percentage reduction in cost associated with a doubling in cumulative production of a technology:

$$C(t) = C(0)\left[\frac{N(t)}{N(0)}\right]^{\log_2(PR)}. \tag{13.2}$$

Considerable effort has been made to estimate learning curves from the market experience of various technologies. Researchers have found empirical evidence of this relationship for energy-related technologies, with PR values typically ranging from 75 to 95 percent depending on the maturity of the technology and any special characteristics such as scale, modularity, thermodynamic limits, and special material requirements (Argote and Epple, 1990; Neij, 1997; McDonald and Schrattenholzer, 2001). This research provides the basis for most of the technology parameter values in CIMS, given that the energy technologies available in the global market do not exhibit great variation from one jurisdiction to another.

Estimating behavioral parameters for consumers and businesses

Estimation of behavioral parameters is more challenging. In previous applications of CIMS, the three key behavioral parameters in equation (13.1) (i, r and v) were estimated through a combination of literature review, judgment, and meta-analysis. However, the available literature usually provides only separate estimates for the three parameters, often using the discount rate to account for several factors, such as time preference and risk aversion to new technologies. This creates problems for predicting the costs and effects of policies that attempt to influence only one of these factors.

More recent efforts to estimate these three behavioral parameters involve the use of discrete choice surveys for estimating models whose parameters can be transposed into the i, r and v parameters in CIMS (Rivers and Jaccard, 2005). The data for a discrete choice model can be acquired from the revealed preferences in actual market transactions or from the stated preferences in a discrete choice survey. In the latter case, a sample of consumers or business managers are presented with hypothetical choice sets and asked to choose the alternative that they prefer the most.

CIMS is made up of over 1000 technologies competing for market share at hundreds of nodes throughout the economy. Gathering information on consumer and firm choices at each of these nodes is an impossible task, so discrete choice research has been focused on several critical nodes for policies to influence energy-related technology choices in the energy supply, residential, transportation and industrial sectors. Evidence from this research is used to inform the setting of parameters at other decision nodes.

Recent applications of discrete choice research for estimating CIMS' parameters have used stated preference surveys. There are several reasons for this choice. First, the explanatory variables in revealed preference data are often highly collinear and exhibit little variability in the marketplace, which can make estimating a model based on this kind of data difficult. Second, revealed preference data may have less plausibility in analyzing the impact of policies designed to move the economic system beyond its current technological context. Stated preference experiments are designed by the analyst and so avoid most of these problems.

However, stated preference data can be biased because when answering a survey, consumers do not face real-world budgetary or information constraints. Also, biases may arise if consumers do not understand the survey properly or if they answer strategically (Louviere et al., 2000; Train, 2002). Consumers, for example, often demonstrate a higher affinity for energy-efficient technologies, such as fuel-efficient vehicles, on stated preference surveys than they do in reality (Urban et al., 1996). Therefore, while stated preference surveys are likely to continue to dominate parameter estimation where dramatically new technologies are involved, there is an interest in combining this with some revealed preference research where feasible (Train and Atherton, 1995).

The discrete choice model used for estimating parameters in CIMS is a linear-in-parameters utility function, as in equation (13.3):

$$U_j = \beta_j + \sum_{k=1}^{K}\beta_k x_{jk} + e_j, \tag{13.3}$$

where U_j is the utility of technology j, β_j is the alternative specific constant, β_k is a vector of coefficients representing the importance of attribute k, x_{jk} is a vector of the k attributes of technology j, and e_j is the unobservable error term. In its generic form for discrete choice surveys, equation (13.3) can be represented as equation (13.4), where OC is non-energy operating cost, EC is energy cost and $OTHER$ is non-financial preferences:

$$U_j = \beta_j + \beta_{CC}CC + \beta_{OC}OC + \beta_{EC}EC + \beta_{OTHER}OTHER + e_j. \qquad (13.4)$$

By assuming that the unobserved error terms (e_j) are independent and identically distributed, it is possible to generate a model of the probability of a firm choosing technology j from the available set of technologies, K. This is called the multinomial logit model (Train, 2002), as shown in equation (13.5), where U'_j is simply the observable portion of utility, and $U'_j = U_j - e_j$:[2]

$$\Pr(j) = \frac{e^{U'_j}}{\sum_{k=1}^{K} e^{U'_k}}. \qquad (13.5)$$

A maximum likelihood routine is then used to find the β parameters that most closely match the left-hand side to the right-hand side of equation (13.4) for the set of observations. This produces the set of parameters for the discrete choice model that best matches the actual choices that respondents indicated in their survey answers.

The estimated parameters of the discrete choice model can be used to provide estimates for the three key CIMS behavioral parameters (Rivers and Jaccard, 2005). The weighted average implicit discount rate applied by decision makers at a node can be determined by the ratio of the capital cost parameter to the annual cost parameters, as long as the capital stock lifespan is expected to be greater than about 15 years (Train, 1985, 2002).[3] In equation (13.6), β_{AC} is a parameter weighting all annual costs parameters together – the non-energy and energy operating costs in the case of equation (13.3):

$$r = \frac{\beta_{CC}}{\beta_{AC}}. \qquad (13.6)$$

Similarly, the (annual) intangible cost parameter can be calculated by comparing non-cost parameters to the parameter weighting the annual cost parameters as in equation (13.7). This parameter shows the annual monetary estimate of the intangible (non-financial) qualities of a given technology. For example, on average, consumers might be willing to pay \$400/year extra to drive a car, and avoid the (real or perceived) discomfort of riding a bus. If required in CIMS, the annual cost can be converted to a single up-front cost for inclusion with the capital cost in the calculation of LCC:

$$i_j = \frac{\beta_j}{\beta_{AC}}. \qquad (13.7)$$

The final CIMS behavioral parameter (v), representing the degree of heterogeneity in the market, is roughly equivalent to the 'scale' of the multinomial logit model (Train, 2002). If the error terms (e_j) are comparable in magnitude to the parameter (β_j and β_k*x_{jk}) values, the model shows a more heterogeneous market where the error term plays a dominant role in predicting technology choices. Since the error term is not known, even where one technology appears to have a clear advantage over others, the presence of a large error term can lead to the other technologies capturing a significant portion of the market. In contrast, if the error terms are much smaller than the parameter values, the model shows a much more homogeneous market, where predictions of technology choices are strongly dependent on the relative attributes of the technologies. Unfortunately, although both the CIMS and discrete choice models (such as the multi-nomial logit model) show similar logistic curves of technology adoption, they are different enough that it is not possible to directly estimate the CIMS heterogeneity factor from the scale of the discrete choice model. It is possible, however, to use ordinary least squares to find the value of v for which predictions from CIMS are consistent with predictions from the multinomial logit model over a broad range of energy, capital cost and non-energy cost conditions.

From this combination of discrete choice surveys and literature review, the behavioral parameters in CIMS cover a range of values depending on the decision maker whose technology acquisition behavior is being simulated. In general, industry and electricity generation sectors have lower discount rates, lower and in some cases zero intangible values, and less market heterogeneity compared to household energy consumption, personal transportation and some commercial energy uses.

Recent empirical research for estimating CIMS' parameters has thus focused on stated preference studies for key energy-related technology choices:

- consumers' choices of vehicle types and response to changes in road pricing, parking pricing, vehicle costs, fuel costs, access to express lanes, access to appropriate filling stations, preferences for lower emissions, and preferences for more power;
- consumers' choice of commuting modes and response to changes in travel time, weekly commuting cost, number of public transit transfers, frequency of public transit service, amount of walking required for public transit, and presence or absence of dedicated cycling lanes;
- consumers' choice of residential renovation and response to changes in capital cost, fuel cost, air quality, and the presence of a subsidy to encourage energy-efficient home retrofits;
- consumers' choice of home heating system and response to changes in capital cost, operating cost, heating response time, and presence or absence of a subsidy to encourage energy-efficient heating systems;
- industrial firms' choice of steam generation system and response to changes in capital cost, operating cost, fuel cost, and electricity offset through the use of a combined heat and power system.

For recent applications to the Canadian economy, surveys were completed by 800–1200 final respondents for each of the household surveys (residential and transportation) and about 300 final respondents for the industrial survey. Some surveys were conducted using a combined telephone–mail method and some using an on-line questionnaire method. The surveys had response rates ranging from 17 percent for the industrial survey to 84 percent for one of the transportation surveys. Analysis of survey results was conducted using a multinomial logit method, and resulted in statistically significant models with all estimated parameters taking on the expected signs.

Table 13.1 shows the discount rate (r parameter in CIMS) calculated from the studies described above. For most of the experiments reported, the implicit discount rate is

Table 13.1   Discount rates from discrete choice studies

Technology node in CIMS	Source	Derived r
Gasoline vehicle	Horne et al. (2005)	0.226
Alternative fuel vehicle	Horne et al. (2005)	0.226
Hybrid electric vehicle	Horne et al. (2005)	0.226
Hydrogen vehicle	Horne et al. (2005)	0.226
Hydrogen fuel cell vehicle	Mau et al. (working paper)	0.276
Hybrid gas–electric vehicle	Mau et al. (working paper)	0.2184
Standard efficiency boiler	Rivers and Jaccard (2005)	0.347
High efficiency boiler	Rivers and Jaccard (2005)	0.347
Cogenerator	Rivers and Jaccard (2005)	0.347
Home construction retrofit	Jaccard and Dennis (2005)	0.20–0.26
Home heating	Jaccard and Dennis (2005)	0.09

significantly higher than that used in conventional bottom-up analyses. The higher values in this research are slightly lower than the implicit discount rates in many revealed preference studies, possibly because the survey seeks to separate pure time preference from other technology-specific attributes that might be correlated with this. Train (1985) summarizes several studies on implicit discount rates and finds results ranging from 15 to 70 percent in the residential and transportation sectors. The low value of 9 percent for home heating systems is suspect and has led to additional research. Other values from the empirical research have led to the adjustment of the CIMS parameter values.

Intangible costs (i parameter in CIMS) were also calculated from the regression results to reflect technology-specific, non-financial preferences in the choices made by consumers. A table similar to that for discount rates could be produced from these. Again they have led to changes in the values used in the model. Finally, each of the discrete choice surveys also led to estimates of the degree of market heterogeneity (the v parameter in CIMS) at individual decision nodes in the model. Empirical estimates for the v parameter reveal that there is significant preference and behavior heterogeneity in the market, so basing model predictions on an 'average' consumer or producer may lead to misleading results.

Another important consideration for ITC modellers is to provide policy makers with some sense of how their policies might shift the preferences of businesses and consumers over time. Various types of policies – subsidies, information programs, technology forcing regulations – are aimed at encouraging early adoption of certain technologies and then the transition to widespread dissemination. Research in the marketing industry is replete with studies on how successful technologies negotiate these phases of market development. Concepts such as the 'neighbor effect' link threshold levels of market penetration with declining intangible costs (lack of information, skepticism) for new technologies. In effect, these imply that the ESUB values, resulting from energy technology choices, are able to rise – implying in turn that an environmental objective such as GHG emission reduction could get easier.

There are, of course, many potential explanations for changes in consumer preferences, some predictable and some seemingly random to the analyst. While not all can be captured in an energy–economy model, market research literature suggests that the neighbor effect is particularly important in assessing the potential for new technologies to achieve significant market penetration (Hautsch and Klotz, 2002). Recent empirical research with CIMS involves, again, the discrete choice framework, to estimate empirically how intangible costs – the i parameter – change in response to change in the surrounding environment, notably in the decisions by other agents in the economy.

CIMS has a declining intangible cost function which links the intangible costs of a technology in a given period with its market share in the previous period, reflecting improved availability of information and decreased perceptions of risk as new technologies penetrate the market. Attraction to a new technology can increase as its market share increases and information about its performance becomes more available (Arthur, 1989; Banerjee, 1992).[4] Intangible costs for technologies decline according to equation (13.8), where $i(t)$ is the intangible cost of a technology at time t, MS_{t-1} is the market share of the technology at time $t-1$, and A and k are estimated parameters reflecting the rate of decline of the intangible cost in response to increases in the market share of the technology:

$$i(t) = \frac{i(0)}{1 + Ae^{k*MS_{t-1}}}.$$ (13.8)

A series of recent discrete choice surveys have estimated the changes in preferences for alternative vehicle types as information and use of these becomes diffused through the economy (Axsen et al., 2009; Mau et al., 2008). This information includes changes over time in key attributes such as range and fuel availability, but also market penetration.

With its emphasis on technological richness, the behavioral focus in CIMS is on providing an empirical foundation for simulating how consumers and businesses will respond to technological options that may differ significantly in the future in part because of policy initiatives. However, as already noted above, this depiction at the microeconomic level explains only part of the adjustment that may occur to policies intended to induce technological change. A further adjustment may occur in the demands for final and intermediate goods and services as their relative costs change, leading to structural change in the economy and changes in total activity levels. A rising cost for domestic steel production may lead to a decrease in domestic demand and a declining competitive position for domestic producers relative to foreign producers in domestic and export markets. A rising cost for mobility in personal vehicles may lead to a decline in the demand for mobility as well as modal shifts to public transit.

To include these broader equilibrium feedback effects, the energy supply–demand component of CIMS interacts with its macroeconomic module via demand functions whose elasticities represent the long-run demand response to a change in the cost of providing a good or service. These Armington elasticities were econometrically estimated from historical data (Wirjanto, 1999). They may or may not be valid in depicting the future response to changes in the costs of providing goods and services, but there is as yet no alternative empirical way of assessing how future demands might change as a result of production cost changes. One consolation in the face of this uncertainty is that most policies currently contemplated, even those focused on GHG emissions, do not result in enormous changes in the costs of providing most goods and services covered by the Armington elasticities, so past responses may provide a reliable basis for simulating future responses. In specific cases where a significant response is anticipated, one that is outside the range of historical experience, additional empirical analysis that estimates likely changes in relative production costs between competing jurisdictions is advisable. An example would be the case in which an aggressive carbon tax in one country pushed the production cost of its cement industry beyond the historical cost differentials with its international competitors.

4　Some Sample Applications

With these parameters estimated and integrated into the model, CIMS has been used to simulate portfolios of technology-specific and economy-wide instruments. The examples in this section focus on climate-motivated ITC policies.

Representing forecast uncertainty for policy makers

The empirical efforts to estimate the behavioral parameters of a hybrid model such as CIMS generates information about uncertainty that might be useful to policy makers. In particular, the parameters estimated in the discrete choice surveys are only the single most likely estimates of the model parameters from the data. To represent what this uncertainty means for the model results requires the construction of multidimensional joint probability density functions for the model parameters using equation (13.9):

$$LL(\beta) = \sum_{n=1}^{N} \frac{\ln[P_{n,j}(\beta)]}{N}, \tag{13.9}$$

where $LL(\beta)$ is the log of the likelihood for the parameters β, N is the number of observations in the dataset, and $P_{n,j}(\beta)$ is the probability that the model assigns to the choice j that was actually made by the respondent at observation n with the particular combination of β parameters being tested. $P_{n,j}(\beta)$ is calculated using the multinomial logit model (equation (13.5)). Uniform sampling from this probability density function provides the discrete choice model parameters in equation (13.4) (each discrete choice model will have different parameters). Each point on the probability density function is characterized by the discrete choice model's parameter values and a probability, and from these one can construct marginal probability density functions for each of the CIMS parameters. The uncertainty in the parameter values can then be propagated to the results of the CIMS model through a simplified sampling procedure.

Figure 13.2 shows the results of this exercise for a policy tested in the industrial sector – a 20 percent capital cost subsidy on cogeneration technologies. While the simulation results using the maximum likelihood estimation (MLE) parameters predict an increase in cogeneration market share of about 20–25 percent over business as usual, the 95 percent confidence intervals show that one could expect an increase of anywhere from about 12–36 percent over the 30-year simulation period. Clearly, a policy analysis based only on the MLE parameters does not fully reflect uncertainty in the dataset.

Finally, it is important to note that the uncertainty portrayed in Figure 13.2 does not fully represent the uncertainty associated with this modelling exercise. It represents the uncertainty associated with the behavioral parameter estimates only if the dataset is a perfect representation of firm behavior. It may not be for the many reasons mentioned earlier, particularly the challenges for stated preference research in revealing the likely

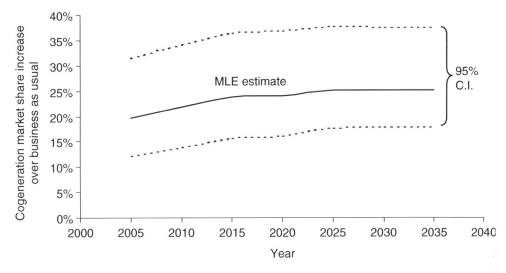

Figure 13.2   Uncertainty in CIMS-generated simulation of 20 percent capital subsidy for industrial cogeneration

behavior of agents in the economy when faced with real-world instead of hypothetical decisions.

Estimating long-run ESUB and AEEI values for CGE modelling

The earlier discussion of conventional top-down models noted their challenges for modelling ITC policies. In particular, if their critical parameters for technological change, ESUB and AEEI, are estimated from historical data, these values may not apply to future conditions in which technology options and expectations have changed dramatically. Even top-down modellers who are concerned with this have no empirical means of estimating alternative future values for ESUB and AEEI when their models lack technological explicitness and behavioral realism at the technology selection level of consumers and businesses. By how much might the emergence of plug-in hybrid and biofuel vehicles change the interfuel ESUB value related to personal vehicles for transportation? By how much might carbon capture and storage technologies change the interfuel ESUB value related to electricity generation as GHG taxes rise?

With its detailed representation of how consumers and businesses might respond to new technologies and changing costs, a hybrid model can generate ESUB and AEEI values that reflect future technological conditions and shifting preferences of businesses and consumers, and these can be used to guide the setting of these parameters in top-down CGE models that assess policies for ITC. In recent research, CIMS was applied to this end by price-shocking the model with a strongly contrasted range of energy prices (Bataille et al., 2006). The CIMS outputs (pseudo-data) from this exercise can provide the standard data (changes in costs and inputs of capital and individual forms of energy) used to estimate the parameters of production function models such as the Cobb–Douglas, the constant elasticity of substitution, and the translog. Used to estimate ESUB values with the translog production function, the CIMS pseudo data generated a long-run capital for energy ESUB value for Canada of 0.27 and interfuel ESUB values in the range of 0.8–2.0. The values differed widely between sectors, suggesting that structural change in future will also change aggregate ESUB values. A long-run simulation of CIMS with all prices held constant also produced an AEEI estimate of 0.4–0.6 depending on the sector. This compares to 0.25–0.5 percent for top-down estimates in the literature, and 0.75–1.5 percent for bottom-up estimates about the future AEEI rate.

Forecasting a portfolio of climate-related ITC policies
In 2007, the Canadian federal government presented a portfolio of climate policies that it claimed would reduce domestic GHG emissions by 20 percent (from 2006 levels) by 2020 and put the country on a path for its target of 65 percent reductions by 2050. The policy portfolio included an intensity-based emissions cap applying to major industrial emitters (including electricity generators) in conjunction with several focused regulations, subsidies and information programs for non-industrial emitters. The policy did not have a cap or tax on non-industrial emissions, but allowed industrial emitters the option of meeting all of their intensity cap obligations by subsidizing reductions in other producing and consuming sectors of the economy.

With its technology detail and empirically estimated behavioral parameters, a hybrid model such as CIMS provides an opportunity to assess the likelihood of such claims by government. An assessment like this may be an important check on government policy claims, given that the Canadian government has set three different targets since 1988 for GHG emission reductions and launched six different policy initiatives that it claimed would achieve the targets. In every case, the policies have failed to achieve the targets and emissions have continued to rise over the past two decades.

Thus, unlike conventional bottom-up models, a hybrid model such as CIMS, with its empirically estimated behavioral parameters, can be used to forecast the response of consumers and businesses to such a portfolio of regulatory and fiscal policies, as shown in Figure 13.3 (Jaccard and Rivers, 2007). Parameter uncertainty in the model is shown in the figure with 90 percent confidence intervals around the forecast of the policy's effect. The results suggest that once again the Canadian government's policies will fail to achieve its claims for them.

5 Conclusion

The shift to technologies that reduce the impacts and risks of the energy system faces substantial transitional challenges because of the high initial cost of many of these technologies and the healthy skepticism of those called upon to acquire them. To assess policies for overcoming these high transitional costs, policy makers need evaluation tools that combine technological explicitness with behavioral realism to estimate how actors in the economy will respond to alternative policies. These tools should also show how such microeconomic decisions would affect the overall macroeconomic evolution of the economy in terms of its structure and total output, as these will be important considerations in garnering policy acceptance.

The conventional top-down and bottom-up energy–economy models offered to policy makers are deficient in terms of at least one of these three attributes and thus are less useful than they could be. This explains the recent drive for ITC policy modelling,

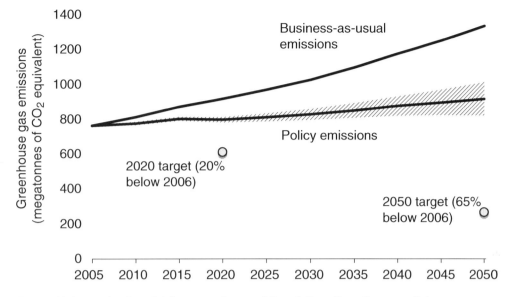

Figure 13.3 Hybrid model forecast of a portfolio of Canadian climate policies

involving the design and application of hybrid models that are technologically explicit, behaviorally realistic and provide macroeconomic equilibrium feedbacks. A special challenge with such models is the empirical estimation of their behavioral parameters in order to provide policy makers with some confidence in the forecast response to their ITC policies. Recent research with discrete choice surveys offers one promising approach for addressing this challenge, but considerable uncertainty about the future response of consumers and businesses to ITC policies remains.

Notes

1. CIMS is a proper name, not an acronym.
2. Discrete choice literature usually denotes the observable portion of utility as V_j. It is presented as U'_j here to avoid confusion with the CIMS' v parameter.
3. For shorter-lived technologies, r is replaced by $r/[1-(1+r)^{-n}]$.
4. This application of CIMS has some similarities to what is referred to as agent-based modelling in that it establishes a basic set of assumptions about initial behavior and then simulates behavioral dynamics as key conditions change – financial cost of a new technology, proportion of neighbors, family and friends who have acquired it.

References

Argote, L. and D. Epple (1990), 'Learning curves in manufacturing', *Science*, **247**(1), 920–24.
Arthur, B. (1989), 'Competing technologies, increasing returns, and lock-in by historical events', *Economic Journal*, **99**(394), 116–31.
Axsen, J., D. Mountain and M. Jaccard (2009), 'Combining stated and revealed choice research to simulate preference dynamics: the case of hybrid electric vehicles', *Resource and Energy Economics*, **31**(3), 221–38.
Banerjee, A. (1992), 'A simple model of herd behavior', *Quarterly Journal of Economics*, **107**(3), 797–817.
Bataille, C., M. Jaccard, J. Nyboer and N. Rivers (2006), 'Towards general equilibrium in a technology-rich

model with empirically estimated behavioural parameters', *The Energy Journal*, Special Issue on Hybrid Modeling of Energy–Environment Policies: Reconciling Bottom-up and Top-down, 93–112.

Bohringer, C. (1998), 'The synthesis of bottom-up and top-down in energy policy modelling', *Energy Economics*, **20**(3), 233–48.

Brown, M., M. Levine, J. Romm, A. Rosenfeld and J. Koomey (1998), 'Engineering–economic studies of energy technologies to reduce greenhouse gas emissions: opportunities and challenges', *Annual Review of Energy and the Environment*, **23**, 287–385.

Carraro, C. and J.-C. Hourcade (1998), 'Climate modelling and policy strategies: the role of technical change and uncertainty', *Energy Economics*, **20**(5–6), 463–71.

DeCanio, S. (2003), *Economic Models of Climate Change: A Critique*, New York: Palgrave Macmillan.

Frei, C., P.-A. Haldi and G. Sarlos (2003), 'Dynamic formulation of a top-down and bottom-up merging energy policy model', *Energy Policy*, **31**, 1017–31.

Grubb, M., I. Kohler and D. Anderson (2002), 'Induced technical change in energy and environmental modelling: analytical approaches and policy implications', *Annual Review of Energy and the Environment*, **27**, 271–308.

Hautcsh, N. and S. Klotz (2002), 'Estimating the neighborhood influence on decision makers: theory and an application on the analysis of innovation decisions', *Journal of Economic Behavior and Organization*, **52**(1), 97–113.

Horne, M., M. Jaccard and K. Tiedemann (2005), 'Improving behavioral realism in hybrid energy–economy models using discrete choice studies of personal transportation decisions', *Energy Economics*, **27**, 59–77.

Hourcade, J.-C., M. Jaccard, C. Bataille and F. Ghersi (2006), 'Hybrid modelling: new answers to old challenges', *The Energy Journal*, Special Issue on Hybrid Modelling of Energy–Environment Policies: Reconciling Bottom-up and Top-down, 1–12.

Jaccard, M., A. Bailie and J. Nyboer (1996), 'CO$_2$ emission reduction costs in the residential sector: behavioral parameters in a bottom-up simulation model', *The Energy Journal*, **17**(4), 107–34.

Jaccard, M. and M. Dennis (2005), 'Estimating home energy decision parameters for a hybrid energy–economy policy model', *Environmental Modelling and Assessment*, **11**(2), 1–10.

Jaccard, M., J. Nyboer, C. Bataille and B. Sadownik (2003), 'Modelling the cost of climate policy: distinguishing between alternative cost definitions and long-run cost dynamics', *The Energy Journal*, **24**(1), 49–73.

Jaccard, M. and N. Rivers (2007), 'Estimating the effect of the Canadian government's 2006–2007 greenhouse gas policies', CD Howe Institute, Toronto.

Jacobsen, H.K. (1998), 'Integrating the bottom-up and top-down approach to energy–economy modelling: the case of Denmark', *Energy Economics*, **20**(4), 443–61.

Jaffe, A., R. Newell and R. Stavins (1999), 'Energy-efficient technologies and climate change policies: issues and evidence', Resources for the Future, Washington, DC.

Jaffe, A. and R. Stavins (1994), 'The energy efficiency gap: what does it mean?', *Energy Policy*, **22**(10), 804–10.

Koopmans, C.C. and D.W. te Velde (2001), 'Bridging the energy efficiency gap: using bottom-up information in a top-down energy demand model', *Energy Economics*, **23**(1), 57–75.

Laitner, J., S. DeCanio, J. Koomey and A. Sanstad (2003), 'Room for improvement: increasing the value of energy modelling for policy analysis', *Utilities Policy*, **11**, 87–94.

Loschel, A. (2002), 'Technological change in economic models of environmental policy: a survey', *Ecological Economics*, **43**, 105–26.

Louviere, J., D. Hensher and J. Swait (2000), *Stated Choice Methods*, Cambridge: Cambridge University Press.

Mau, P., J. Eyzaguirre, M. Jaccard, C. Collins-Dodd and K. Tiedemann (2008), 'The neighbour effect: simulating dynamics in consumer preferences for new vehicle technologies', *Ecological Economics*, **68**, 504–16.

McDonald, A. and L. Shrattenholzer (2001), 'Learning rates for energy technologies', *Energy Policy*, **29**, 255–61.

Morris, S., G. Goldstein and V. Fthenakis (2002), 'NEMS and MARKAL–MACRO models for energy–environmental–economic analysis: a comparison of the electricity and carbon reduction projections', *Environmental Modelling and Assessment*, **17**, 207–16.

Neij, L. (1997), 'The use of experience curves to analyse the prospects for diffusion and adoption of renewable energy technology', *Energy Policy*, **23**(13), 1099–107.

Nystrom, I. and C.-O. Wene (1999), 'Energy–economy linking in MARKAL–MACRO: interplay of nuclear, conservation and CO$_2$ policies in Sweden', *International Journal of Environment and Pollution*, **12**(2–3), 323–42.

Rivers, N. and M. Jaccard (2005), 'Combining top-down and bottom-up approaches to energy–economy modelling using discrete choice methods', *The Energy Journal*, **26**(1), 83–106.

Sanstad, A., S. DeCanio, G. Boyd and J. Koomey (2001), 'Estimating bounds on the economy-wide effects of the CEF policy scenarios', *Energy Policy*, **29**, 1299–311.

Sutherland, R. (1991), 'Market barriers to energy efficiency investments', *The Energy Journal*, **12**(3), 15–34.

Train, K. (1985), 'Discount rates in consumers' energy related decisions: a review of the literature', *Energy: The International Journal*, **10**(12), 1243–53.

Train, K. (2002), *Discrete Choice Methods with Simulation*, Cambridge: Cambridge University Press.

Train, K. and T. Atherton (1995), 'Rebates, loans, and customers' choice of appliance efficiency level: combining stated- and revealed-preference data', *The Energy Journal*, **16**(1), 55–69.

Urban, G., B. Wienberg and J. Hauser (1996), 'Premarket forecasting of really-new products', *Journal of Marketing*, **60**(January), 47–60.

Weyant, J. and J. Hill (1999), 'Introduction and overview', *The Energy Journal*, Special Issue on the Costs of the Kyoto Protocol: A Multi-Model Evaluation.

Wirjanto, T. (1999), *Estimation of Import and Export Elasticities: A Report Prepared for the Economic and Fiscal Policy Branch at the Department of Finance*, Department of Economics, University of Waterloo, Ontario.

Worrell, E., S. Ramesohl and G. Boyd (2004), 'Advances in energy forecasting models based on engineering economics', *Annual Review of Environment and Resources*, **29**, 345–81.

14 Computable general equilibrium models for the analysis of energy and climate policies
Ian Sue Wing*

1 Introduction

This chapter is a simple, rigorous, practically oriented exposition of computable general equilibrium (CGE) modeling. The general algebraic framework of a CGE model is developed from microeconomic fundamentals, and employed to illustrate how a model may be calibrated using the economic data in a social accounting matrix, how the resulting system of numerical equations may be solved for the equilibrium values of economic variables, and how computing the perturbations to this equilibrium that result from introducing price or quantity distortions facilitates analysis of the economy-wide impacts of energy and climate policies.

Walrasian general equilibrium prevails when supply and demand are equalized across all of the interconnected markets in the economy. CGE models are simulations that combine the abstract Arrow–Debreu general equilibrium structure with realistic economic data to solve numerically for the quantities and prices of reproducible commodities and non-reproducible factors that support equilibrium across a specified set of markets.

CGE models have emerged as a standard pseudo-empirical tool for policy evaluation. Their strength lies in their ability to prospectively elucidate the character and magnitude of the economic impacts of energy and environmental policies. Perhaps the most important of these applications is the analysis of measures to reduce greenhouse gas (GHG) emissions – principally carbon dioxide (CO_2) from the combustion of fossil fuels. The decade since the survey by Bhattacharyya (1996) has seen an explosion of work in this area, with more than 150 articles in edited volumes and peer-reviewed journals, and an even larger grey literature. GHG mitigation policies can incorporate a number of instruments ranging from taxes and subsidies to income transfer schemes to quotas on the carbon content of energy goods. Carbon-rich fossil fuels are the principal source of energy, which in turn serves an input to virtually every type of economic activity. Coupled with the limited possibilities for using substitute commodities in place of energy, the implication is that these policies' effects will ripple through multiple markets, with far larger consequences than fossil fuels' small share of national income might suggest. This phenomenon is the central motivation for the general equilibrium approach.

But, notwithstanding their popularity, CGE models continue to be viewed in some quarters (for example, Panagariya and Duttagupta, 2001) as a 'black box', whose complex internal workings obfuscate the linkages between their outputs and features of their input data, algebraic structure, or method of solution, and worse, allow questionable assumptions to be hidden within them that end up driving their results. Such criticisms behove CGE modelers to open up the black box to scrutiny, and the present chapter aims to do precisely this by elucidating the algebraic framework shared by all CGE models (regardless of their size or apparent complexity), the key features of their data base and numerical calibration, and the techniques used to solve the resulting mathematical programming problem.

To accomplish all this it will be necessary to move beyond a traditional survey of the modeling literature, which is necessarily broad, and of which examples abound (for example, Conrad, 1999, 2001; Bergman, 2005). Taking a cue from earlier reviews which build on the microeconomic foundations of consumer and producer theory (Shoven and Whalley, 1984; Kehoe and Kehoe, 1995; Kehoe, 1998a; Böhringer et al., 2003; Paltsev, 2004), the chapter develops an algebraic framework capable of representing a CGE model of arbitrary size and dimension. The framework is then used to demonstrate how a social accounting matrix may be used to calibrate the coefficients of the model equations, how the resulting system of numerical equations is solved, and how the equilibrium thus solved for may be perturbed and the results used to analyze the economic effects of various types of energy policies. The result is a transparent and systematic, yet also theoretically coherent and reasonably comprehensive, introduction to the subject of CGE modeling.

The plan of the chapter is as follows. Section 2 introduces the circular flow of the economy, and demonstrates how it serves as the fundamental conceptual starting point for Walrasian equilibrium theory that underlies a CGE model. Section 3 presents a social accounting matrix and illustrates how the algebra of its accounting rules reflects the conditions of general equilibrium. Section 4 develops these relationships into a workable CGE model using the device of the constant elasticity of substitution (CES) economy in which households have CES preferences and firms have CES production technology. Section 5 uses the CES economy to illustrate how models are numerically calibrated and discusses the issues which commonly arise in solving CGE models. Section 6 explains how CGE models are used to analyze energy and climate policies. An application is presented in Section 7, where the foregoing ideas are brought together to analyze the consequences of limiting the CO_2 emitted by the US economy. Section 8 offers a brief summary and concluding remarks.

2 Foundations: The Circular Flow and Walrasian Equilibrium

The fundamental conceptual starting point for a CGE model is the familiar circular flow of commodities in a closed economy, shown in Figure 14.1. Households own the factors of production and are the final consumers of produced commodities, while firms rent the factors of production to produce goods and services that the households then consume. Many CGE models also explicitly represent the government, but its role in the circular flow is often passive: to collect taxes and disburse these revenues to firms and households as subsidies and lump-sum transfers, subject to rules of budgetary balance that are specified by the analyst.

Equilibrium in the economic flows in Figure 14.1 results in the conservation of both product and value. Conservation of product holds even when the economy is not in equilibrium. It reflects the physical principle of material balance that the quantity of a factor with which households are endowed, or of a commodity produced by firms, must

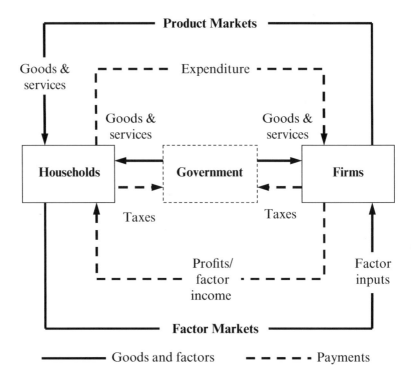

Figure 14.1   The circular flow

be completely absorbed by firms or households (respectively) in the rest of the economy. Conservation of value (that is, price × quantity) reflects the accounting principle of budgetary balance. Firms' expenditures on inputs must be balanced by the value of the revenue generated by the sale of the resulting product, households' expenditures on goods must be balanced by their income, and each unit of expenditure has to purchase some amount of some type of commodity or factor. Thus, product and value can never simply appear or disappear: a change in generalized purchasing power can only come about through a transfer of some positive amount of some produced good or primary factor service, and vice versa.

These accounting rules are the cornerstones of Walrasian general equilibrium. Conservation of product is an expression of the principle of no free disposability, and ensures that firms' outputs are fully consumed by households, and that households' endowment of primary factors is in turn fully employed by firms. Thus, for a given commodity the quantity produced must equal the sum of the quantities that are demanded by the other firms and households in the economy. Analogously, for a given factor the quantities demanded by firms must completely exhaust the aggregate supply endowed to the households. This is the familiar condition of 'market clearance'.

Conservation of value implies that the sum total of revenue from the production of goods must be allocated to households as receipts for primary factors rentals, or to other industries as payments for intermediate inputs, or to the government as taxes. The value of a unit of each commodity in the economy must then equal the sum of the values of all the inputs used to produce it: the cost of the inputs of intermediate materials as well as the payments to the primary factors employed in its production. The principle simultaneously reflects constancy of returns to scale in production and perfectly competitive markets for produced commodities, which ensure that in equilibrium producers make *zero profit*.

Lastly, the returns to households' endowments of primary factors, which are the value of their factor rentals to producers, constitute income which the households exhaust on goods purchases. The fact that households' factor endowments are fully employed, so that no amount of any factor is left idle, and that households exhaust their income, purchasing some amount of commodities – even for the purpose of storage or saving, reflects the principle of balanced-budget accounting known as 'income balance'. One can also think of this principle as a zero-profit condition on the production of a 'utility good', whose quantity is given by the aggregate value of households' expenditures on commodities, and whose price is the marginal utility of aggregate consumption, or the unit expenditure index.

CGE models employ the conditions of market clearance, zero profit and income balance to solve for the set of prices and the allocation of goods and factors (the solid lines in Figure 14.1) that support general equilibrium. Because the compensating financial transfers may be deduced from the price and quantity allocation, it suffices to represent equilibrium in terms of barter trade in commodities and factors, without the need to explicitly keep track of money as a commodity. But by the same token, the relative values of the different commodities and factors must be denominated in terms of some common unit of account. This is accomplished by expressing the simulated flows in units of a single commodity (the so-called 'numeraire good') whose price is fixed. For this reason, CGE models solve only for relative prices, a point about which more will be said in Section 4.

3 The Algebra of Equilibrium and the Social Accounting Matrix

The next step in understanding a CGE model is to develop an algebraic expression of the circular flow. Consider a hypothetical closed economy made up of N industries, each of which produces its own type of commodity, and an unspecified number of households that jointly own an endowment of F different types of primary factors. Three key assumptions about this economy simplify the analysis which follows. First, there are no tax or subsidy distortions, or quantitative restrictions on transactions. Second, the households act collectively as a single representative agent who rents out the factors to the industries in exchange for income. Households then spend the latter to purchase the N commodities for the purpose of satisfying D types of demands (for example, demands for goods for the purposes of consumption and investment). Third, each industry behaves as a representative firm that hires inputs of the F primary factors and uses quantities of the N commodities as intermediate inputs to produce a quantity y of its own type of output.

I use the indices $i = \{1, \ldots, N\}$ to indicate the set of commodities, $j = \{1, \ldots, N\}$ to indicate the set of industry sectors, $f = \{1, \ldots, F\}$ to indicate the set of primary factors, and $d = \{1, \ldots, D\}$ to indicate the set of final demands. The circular flow of the economy can be completely characterized by three data matrices: an $N \times N$ input–output matrix of industries' uses of commodities as intermediate inputs, $\overline{X}$, an $F \times N$ matrix of primary factor inputs to industries, $\overline{V}$, and an $\mathcal{N} \times \mathcal{D}$ matrix of commodity uses by final demand activities, $\overline{G}$.

It is straightforward to establish how the elements of the three matrices may be arranged to reflect the logic of the circular flow. First, commodity market clearance implies that the value of gross output of industry i, which is the value of the aggregate supply of the ith commodity $(\overline{y}_i)$ must equal the sum of the values of the j intermediate uses $(\overline{x}_{i,j})$ and the d final demands $(\overline{g}_{i,d})$ which absorb that commodity:

$$\overline{y}_i = \sum_{j=1}^{\mathcal{N}} \overline{x}_{i,j} + \sum_{d=1}^{\mathcal{D}} \overline{g}_{i,d} \tag{14.1}$$

Similarly, factor market clearance implies that the sum of firms' individual uses of each primary factor $(\overline{v}_{f,j})$ fully utilize the representative agent's corresponding endowment $(\overline{V}_f)$:

$$\overline{V}_f = \sum_{j=1}^{\mathcal{N}} \overline{v}_{f,j}. \tag{14.2}$$

Second, the fact that industries make zero profit implies that the value of gross output of the jth sector $(\overline{y}_j)$ must equal the sum of the benchmark values of inputs of the i intermediate goods, $\overline{x}_{i,j}$, and f primary factors, $\overline{v}_{f,j}$, employed by that industry's production process:

$$\overline{y}_j = \sum_{i=1}^{\mathcal{N}} \overline{x}_{i,j} + \sum_{f=1}^{\mathcal{F}} \overline{v}_{f,j}. \tag{14.3}$$

Third, the representative agent's income, $\overline{\mathcal{I}}$, is made up of the receipts from the rental of primary factors – all of which are assumed to be fully employed. The resulting income must balance the agent's gross expenditure on satisfaction of commodity demands. Together, these conditions imply that income is equivalent to the sum of the elements of $\overline{V}$, which in turn must equal the sum of the elements of $\overline{G}$. Thus, by equation (14.2),

$$\overline{\mathcal{I}} = \sum_{f=1}^{\mathcal{F}} \overline{V}_f = \sum_{i=1}^{\mathcal{N}} \sum_{d=1}^{\mathcal{D}} \overline{g}_{i,d}. \tag{14.4}$$

The accounting relationships in equations (14.1)–(14.4) jointly imply that, in order to reflect the logic of the circular flow, the matrices $\overline{X}$, $\overline{V}$ and $\overline{G}$ should be arranged according to Figure 14.2. This diagram is a cash-flow statement known as a social accounting matrix (SAM), which is a snapshot of the inter-industry and inter-activity flows of value within an economy at equilibrium in a particular benchmark period. The SAM is an array of input–output accounts that are denominated in the units of value of the period for which the flows in the economy are recorded, typically the currency of the benchmark year. Each account is represented by a row and a column, and the cell elements record the payment from the account of a column to the account of a row. Thus, an account's components of income of (that is, the value of receipts from the sale of a commodity) appear along its row, and the components of its expenditure (that is, the values of the

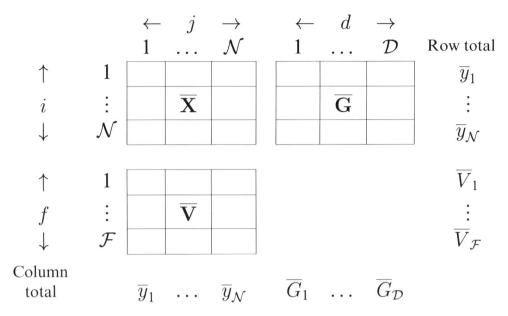

Figure 14.2   A social accounting matrix

inputs to a demand activity or the production of a good) appear down its column (King, 1985).

The structure the SAM reflects the principle of double-entry book-keeping, which requires that for each account, total revenue (the row total) must equal total expenditure (the column total). This is apparent from Figure 14.2, where the sum across any row in the upper quadrants $\overline{X}$ and $\overline{G}$ is equivalent to the expression for goods market clearance from equation (14.1), and the sum across any row in the southwest quadrant $\overline{V}$ is equivalent to the expressions for factor market clearance from equation (14.2). Likewise, the sum down any column of the left-hand quadrants $\overline{X}$ and $\overline{V}$ is equivalent to the expression for zero-profit in industries from equation (14.3). Furthermore, once these conditions hold, the sums of the elements of the northeast and southwest quadrants ($\overline{G}$ and $\overline{V}$, respectively) should equal one another, which is equivalent to the income balance relationship from equation (14.4). The latter simply reflects the intuition that in a closed economy GDP (the aggregate of the components of expenditure) is equal to value added (the aggregate of the components of income). These properties make the SAM an ideal data base from which to construct a CGE model.

4   From a SAM to a CGE Model: The CES Economy

CGE models' algebraic framework results from the imposition of the axioms of producer and consumer maximization on the accounting framework of the SAM. The pedagogic device of a CES economy is used to illustrate the relevant procedures. Throughout, households will be treated as a representative agent with CES preferences, while industry sectors will be modeled as representative producers with CES production technologies. Note that the algebra thus far has all been developed in terms of flows of value. In the subsequent analysis it will be necessary to distinguish between the prices and quantities of goods and factors. Accordingly, let the variables p_i and w_f denote the prices of commodities and factors, respectively, and $x_{i,j}$, $v_{f,j}$ and $g_{i,d}$ (that is, without bars) indicate the quantity components of the previously defined value variables.

Households
The objective of the representative agent is to maximize utility (u) by choosing levels of goods consumption ($g_{i,C}$), subject to ruling commodity prices (p_i) and the agent's budget constraint. The agent may also demand goods and services for purposes other than consumption (C). In the present example it is assumed that $d = \{C, O\}$, where O indicates other final demands (for example, saving/investment) which are given by the exogenous vector $g_{i,O}$. Using equation (14.4), the agent's disposable income (μ) is then:

$$\mu = \sum_{f=1}^{\mathcal{F}} w_f V_f - \sum_{i=1}^{\mathcal{N}} p_i g_{i,O}, \tag{14.5}$$

which allows us to specify the agent's problem as:

$$\max_{g_{i,C}} u[g_{1,C}, \ldots, g_{N,C}] \text{ s.t. } \mu = \sum_{i=1}^{\mathcal{N}} p_i g_{i,C}. \tag{14.6}$$

We assume that the representative agent has CES preferences, so that his/her utility function is:

$$u = \left[\sum_{i=1}^{\mathcal{N}} \alpha_i g_{i,C}^{(\omega-1)/\omega} \right]^{\omega/(\omega-1)},$$

where the α_is are the technical coefficients of the utility function, and ω is the elasticity of substitution.

Rather than solve (14.6) directly, it will prove useful to solve the dual expenditure minimization problem. The agent therefore seeks to minimize his/her expenditure to gain a unit of utility (θ), subject to the constraint of his/her utility function by choosing the levels of unit commodity demands, ($\hat{g}_{i,C}$):

$$\min_{\hat{g}_{i,C}} \theta = \sum_{i=1}^{\mathcal{N}} p_i \hat{g}_{i,C} \text{ s.t. } 1 = \left[\sum_{i=1}^{\mathcal{N}} \alpha_i \hat{g}_{i,C}^{(\omega-1)/\omega} \right]^{\omega/(\omega-1)}. \tag{14.6'}$$

The variable θ is known as the unit expenditure index, and can be interpreted as the marginal utility of aggregate consumption. The solution to this problem is the vector of unit demands for the consumption of commodities ($\hat{g}_{i,C} = \alpha_i^\omega \theta^\omega p_i^{-\omega}$), which implies the conditional final demands:

$$g_{i,C} = \hat{g}_{i,C} u = \alpha_i^\omega \theta^\omega p_i^{-\omega} u, \tag{14.7}$$

where u indicates the representative agent's level of activity.

Producers

Each producer maximizes profit (π_j) by choosing levels of intermediate inputs ($x_{i,j}$) and primary factors ($v_{f,j}$) to produce output (y_j), subject to the ruling prices of output (p_j) intermediate inputs (p_i), factors (w_f) and the constraint of its production technology (ϖ_j). The jth producer's problem is thus:

$$\max_{x_{i,j}, v_{f,j}} \pi_j = p_j y_j - \sum_{i=1}^{N} p_i x_{i,j} + \sum_{f=1}^{F} w_f v_{f,j} \text{ s.t.}$$

$$y_j = \varpi_j[x_{1,j}, \ldots, x_{N,j}; v_{1,j}, \ldots, v_{F,j}]. \tag{14.8}$$

Producers have CES technology, so that the production function ϑ_j takes the form

$$y_j = \left[\sum_{i=1}^{N} \beta_{i,j} x_{i,j}^{(\sigma_j - 1)/\sigma_j} + \sum_{f=1}^{F} \gamma_{f,j} v_{f,j}^{(\sigma_j - 1)/\sigma_j} \right]^{\sigma_j/(\sigma_j - 1)},$$

where, $\beta_{i,j}$ and $\gamma_{i,j}$ are the technical coefficients on intermediate commodities and primary factors respectively, while σ_j denotes each industry's elasticity of substitution.

It is customary to solve the dual cost minimization problem in place of (14.8). Firm j seeks to minimize its unit cost subject to the constraint of its production technology by choosing the levels of the unit input demands for commodities ($\hat{x}_{i,j}$) and the primary factor ($\hat{v}_{f,j}$):

$$\min_{\hat{x}_{i,j}, \hat{v}_{f,j}} p_j = \sum_{i=1}^{N} p_i \hat{x}_{i,j} + \sum_{f=1}^{F} w_f \hat{v}_{f,j} \text{ s.t.}$$

$$1 = \left[\sum_{i=1}^{N} \beta_{i,j} \hat{x}_{i,j}^{(\sigma_j - 1)/\sigma_j} + \sum_{f=1}^{F} \gamma_{f,j} \hat{v}_{f,j}^{(\sigma_j - 1)/\sigma_j} \right]^{\sigma_j/(\sigma_j - 1)} \tag{14.8'}$$

The solution to this problem yields the unit demands for inputs of intermediate commodities and primary factors ($\hat{x}_{i,j} = \beta_{i,j}^{\sigma} p_j^{\sigma} p_i^{-\sigma_j}$ and $\hat{v}_{h,j} = \gamma_{f,j}^{\sigma} p_j^{\sigma} w_f^{-\sigma_j}$), which imply the conditional input demands:

$$x_{i,j} = \hat{x}_{i,j} y_j = \beta_{i,j}^{\sigma} p_j^{\sigma} p_i^{-\sigma_j} y_j, \tag{14.9}$$

$$v_{f,j} = \hat{v}_{f,j} y_j = \gamma_{f,j}^{\sigma} p_j^{\sigma} w_f^{-\sigma_j} y_j, \tag{14.10}$$

where y_j indicates producers' activity levels.

General equilibrium

To formulate the algebraic structure of a CGE model it is necessary to develop analogues of the three general equilibrium conditions in Section 3, into which the demands derived above may be incorporated. To begin, note that for (14.7), (14.9) and (14.10) to be consistent with the flows in the SAM, it must be the case that $\bar{x}_{i,j} = p_i x_{i,j}$, $\bar{v}_{f,j} = w_f v_{f,j}$, $\bar{g}_{i,d} = p_i g_{i,d}$, $\bar{y}_i = p_i y_i$ and $\bar{V}_f = w_f V_f$. Using this result, equations (14.1)–(14.4) may be expanded to resolve prices and quantities, yielding the conditions of market clearance for goods and factors, zero profit for industries, and income balance for the representative agent:

$$p_i y_i = p_i \left(\sum_{j=1}^{N} x_{i,j} + g_{i,C} + g_{i,O} \right),$$ (14.1′)

$$w V_f = w \sum_{j=1}^{N} v_{f,j},$$ (14.2′)

$$p_j y_j = \sum_{i=1}^{N} p_i \hat{x}_{i,j} y_j + \sum_{f=1}^{\mathcal{F}} w_f \hat{v}_{f,j} y_j,$$ (14.3′)

$$\mu = \sum_{f=1}^{\mathcal{F}} w_f V_f - \sum_{i=1}^{N} p_i g_{i,O} = \sum_{i=1}^{N} p_i \hat{g}_{i,C} u = \theta u.$$ (14.4′)

A crucial insight, due to Mathiesen (1985a,b), is that equations (14.1′)–(14.4′) are analogous to the Karush–Kuhn–Tucker conditions for the optimal allocation of commodities and factors and the distribution of activities in the economy. In particular, the variable which is the common factor in each of the foregoing equations exhibits complementary slackness with respect to the corresponding residual primal or dual constraint. Far from being a mere technical detail, this characteristic is what has revolutionized the formulation and solution of CGE models.

The economic intuition behind complementary slackness is straightforward (see Paltsev, 2004). In (14.3′), any producer earning negative profit will shut down with an output of zero; accordingly, the expression for unit profit is complementary to the relevant producer's level of activity (y_j). The constraint qualification may therefore be written:

$$p_j < \sum_{i=1}^{N} p_i \hat{x}_{i,j} + \sum_{f=1}^{\mathcal{F}} w_f \hat{v}_{f,j}, \, y_j = 0 \text{ or } p_j = \sum_{i=1}^{N} p_i \hat{x}_{i,j} + \sum_{f=1}^{\mathcal{F}} w_f \hat{v}_{f,j}, \, y_j > 0.$$ (14.11)

An additional insight is that similar logic applies to the representative agent, whose optimal consumption decision can be thought of as zero profit in the 'production' of utility: if the cost of the goods necessary to generate a unit of final consumption exceeds the latter's marginal utility, then there will be no consumption activity. The extreme right-hand equality in (14.4′) therefore implies:

$$\theta < \sum_{i=1}^{N} p_i g_{i,C}, u = 0 \text{ or } \theta = \sum_{i=1}^{N} p_i g_{i,C}, u > 0.$$ (14.12)

In (14.1′) and (14.2′), any commodity or factor which is in excess supply will have a price of zero; therefore the balance between supply and demand for each of these inputs is complementary to the corresponding price level (p_j and w_f, respectively):

$$y_i > \sum_{j=1}^{N} x_{i,j} + g_{i,C} + g_{i,O}, p_i = 0 \text{ or } y_i = \sum_{j=1}^{N} x_{i,j} + g_{i,C} + g_{i,O}, p_i > 0,$$ (14.13)

$$V_f > \sum_{j=1}^{N} v_{f,j}, w_f = 0 \text{ or } V_f = \sum_{j=1}^{N} v_{f,j}, w_f > 0.$$ (14.14)

The incorporation of utility as a good within the equilibrium framework permits the specification of a market clearance condition for u, which states that a supply of utility in excess of that provided by consumption results in zero unit expenditure:

$$u > \mu/\theta, \theta = 0, \text{ or } u = \mu/\theta, \theta \geq 0. \tag{14.15}$$

Finally, it is worth noting that the definition of disposable income, which is restated as the extreme left-hand equality in (14.4′), does not exhibit complementary slackness with respect to any of its constituent variables, and moreover is made redundant by (14.15). In the specification of general equilibrium it plays the simple role of an accounting identity. One way to make this role explicit is to designate the unit expenditure index as the numeraire price by fixing $\theta = 1$. This automatically drops equation (14.15) by fixing $\mu = u$.

The CGE model in a complementarity format

The specification of a CGE model in a complementarity format involves pairing each of the expressions (14.11)–(14.15) with the associated complementary variable so as to make complementarity explicit (Rutherford, 1995). Using (14.7), (14.9) and (14.10) to make the appropriate substitutions yields the algebraic system (14.16a)–(14.16f) shown in Table 14.1. These equations are what is referred to as 'a CGE model'.

This system is simply a mathematical statement of Walras's Law (see, for example, Varian, 1992, p. 343), which defines the pseudo-excess demand correspondence of the economy:

$$\Xi(\mathbf{z}) \geq 0, \quad \mathbf{z} \geq 0, \quad \mathbf{z}'\Xi(\mathbf{z}) = 0, \tag{14.16}$$

where $\Xi = \{\mathbf{p}, \theta, \mathbf{y}, V, u, \mu\}'$ is the stacked vector of $2\mathcal{N} + \mathcal{F} + 3$ equations and $\mathbf{z} = \{\mathbf{y}, u, \mathbf{p}, \mathbf{w}, \theta, \mu\}$ is the $2\mathcal{N} + \mathcal{F} + 3$ vector of unknowns:

1. $\mathcal{N} + 1$ zero profit inequalities $\{\mathbf{p}, \theta\}$ in as many unknowns $\{\mathbf{y}, u\}$,
2. $\mathcal{N} + \mathcal{F} + 1$ market clearance inequalities $\{\mathbf{y}, V, u\}$ as many unknowns $\{\mathbf{p}, \mathbf{w}, \theta\}$, and
3. a single income definition equation (μ) in a single unknown (μ).

Henceforth the shorthand notation '$\perp$' is used to denote the complementary slackness relationship exhibited by the model's equations and its associated variables, writing (14.16) compactly as:

$$\Xi(\mathbf{z}) \geq 0 \perp \mathbf{z}.$$

Note that in equilibrium the equations in the leftmost column of Table 14.1 will all be satisfied with equality, while the variables in the middle column will all be positive.

5   Numerical Calibration and Solution

The problem in equation (14.16) is highly nonlinear, with the result that a closed-form solution for $\mathbf{z}$ does not exist. This is the reason for the 'C' in CGE models: to find the

Table 14.1   The equations of the CGE model

Zero profit

$$p_j \leq \left(\sum_{i=1}^{N} \beta_{i,j}^{\sigma_j} p_i^{1-\sigma_j} + \sum_{f=1}^{F} \gamma_{f,j}^{\sigma_j} w_f^{1-\sigma_j} \right)^{1/(1-\sigma_j)}, \quad y_j \geq 0, \quad y_j \left[p_j - \left(\sum_{i=1}^{N} \beta_{i,j}^{\sigma_j} p_i^{1-\sigma_j} + \sum_{f=1}^{F} \gamma_{f,j}^{\sigma_j} w_f^{1-\sigma_j} \right)^{1/(1-\sigma_j)} \right] = 0 \quad \forall j \qquad (14.16\text{a})$$

$$\theta \leq \left(\sum_{i=1}^{N} \alpha_i^{\omega} p_i^{1-\omega} \right)^{1/(1-\omega)}, \quad u \geq 0, \quad u \left[\theta - \left(\sum_{i=1}^{N} \alpha_i^{\omega} p_i^{1-\omega} \right)^{1/(1-\omega)} \right] = 0 \qquad (14.16\text{b})$$

Market clearance

$$y_i \geq \sum_{j=1}^{N} \beta_{i,j}^{\sigma_j} p_j^{\sigma_j} p_i^{-\sigma_j} y_j + \alpha_i^{\omega} \theta^{\omega} p_i^{-\omega} u + g_{i,o}, \quad p_i \geq 0, \quad p_i \left(y_i - \sum_{j=1}^{N} \beta_{i,j}^{\sigma_j} p_j^{\sigma_j} p_i^{-\sigma_j} y_j - \alpha_i^{\omega} \theta^{\omega} p_i^{-\omega} u - g_{i,o} \right) = 0 \quad \forall i \qquad (14.16\text{c})$$

$$V_f \geq \sum_{j=1}^{N} \gamma_{f,j}^{\sigma_j} p_j^{\sigma_j} w_f^{-\sigma_j} y_j, \quad w_f \geq 0, \quad w_f \left(V_f - \sum_{j=1}^{N} \gamma_{f,j}^{\sigma_j} p_j^{\sigma_j} w_f^{-\sigma_j} y_j \right) = 0 \quad \forall f \qquad (14.16\text{d})$$

$$u \geq \mu/\theta, \quad \theta \geq 0, \quad \theta(u - \mu/\theta) = 0 \qquad (14.16\text{e})$$

Income balance

$$\mu = \sum_{f=1}^{F} w_f V_f - \sum_{i=1}^{N} p_i g_{i,o}, \quad \mu \geq 0, \quad \mu \left[\mu - \left(\sum_{f=1}^{F} w_f V_f - \sum_{i=1}^{N} p_i g_{i,o} \right) \right] = 0 \qquad (14.16\text{f})$$

general equilibrium of an economy with realistic utility and production functions, the corresponding system of equations must be calibrated on a SAM introduced in Section 3 to generate a numerical problem that can be solved using optimization techniques.

Calibration

To numerically calibrate our example CES economy, it is necessary to establish equivalence between equations (14.1)–(14.4) and (14.1')–(14.4'). There are different ways of doing this, depending on what kind of information is available in addition to the SAM. Kehoe (1998a) describes a procedure when data exist on benchmark prices, however, far more often they are lacking. In the latter situation the simplest method to 'fit' equation (14.16) to the benchmark equilibrium in the SAM is to treat the price variables as indices with benchmark values of unity: $p_i = w_f = \theta = 1$, and treat the activity and income variables as real values which are set equal to the row and column totals in the SAM: $x_{i,j} = \bar{x}_{i,j}, v_{f,j} = \bar{v}_{f,j}, g_{i,d} = \bar{g}_{i,d}, y_i = \bar{y}_i, V_f = \bar{V}_f, u = \mu = \bar{G}_C$. Then, the technical coefficients of the cost and expenditure equations may be computed by substituting these conditions into the demand functions (14.7), (14.9) and (14.10):

$$\alpha_{i,C} = (\bar{g}_{i,C}/\bar{G}_C)^{1/\omega}, \ \beta_{i,j} = (\bar{x}_{i,j}/\bar{y}_j)^{1/\sigma_j} \text{ and } \gamma_{f,j} = (\bar{v}_{f,j}/\bar{y}_j)^{1/\sigma_j}. \quad (14.17)$$

This result is essentially the same as the 'calibrated share form' of CES function (see, for example, Böhringer et al., 2003).

Inserting the foregoing calibrated parameters into the expressions in Table 14.1, along with values for the elasticities of substitution σ and ω specified by the analyst, generates a system of numerical inequalities in which constitutes the actual CGE model. It is particularly important to realize that to satisfy the resulting expressions with equality, one simply has to set the price variables equal to unity and the quantity variables equal to the corresponding values in the SAM. This procedure, known as '*benchmark replication*', permits the analyst to verify that the calibration is correct. The intuition is that since a balanced SAM represents the initial equilibrium of the model, plugging the values in the SAM back into the calibrated numerical pseudo-excess demand correspondence should yield an equilibrium.

Note that (14.17) allows us to replace the terms $\alpha_{i,C}^\omega, \beta_{i,j}^{\sigma_j}$ and $\gamma_{f,j}^{\sigma_j}$ in equation (14.16) with coefficients given by the ratio of the relevant cells of the SAM and the corresponding column totals. The key implication is that the values of the substitution elasticities have no practical impact on the benchmark equilibrium, which makes intuitive sense because the model's initial equilibrium is determined by SAM, and is therefore consistent with an infinite number of potential values for σ and ω. The corollary is that the substitution possibilities in the economy – that is, the degree of adjustment of economic quantities in response to changes in prices, both within and between sectors – are fundamentally determined by the SAM.

A simple example clarifies this point. Figure 14.3 illustrates the intra-industry margin of substitution for a hypothetical industry that produces output, Y, from inputs of energy, E, and materials, M. Benchmark data on the values of the inputs ($\bar{E}$ and $\bar{M}$) and output ($\bar{Y} = \bar{E} + \bar{M}$), together with the assumption of unitary prices (given by the $-45°$ line PP), define a unique calibration point: A. An infinite number of potential isoquants pass through this point, so to pin down the industry's specific technology it

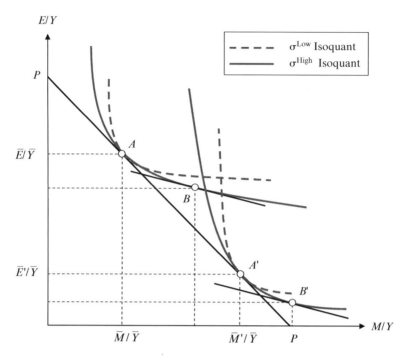

Figure 14.3   Calibration, the elasticity of substitution, and adjustment to price changes

is necessary to make an assumption about the elasticity of substitution (σ). A low or a high value for this parameter (σ^{Low} or σ^{High}) makes the isoquant more or less highly curved, thus admitting a smaller or larger adjustment in input intensities in response to a given rotation of the relative price line, $A \rightarrow B$. The locus of the calibration point is equally important for this process: starting from another benchmark input distribution, A' (where $\overline{Y} = \overline{E}' + \overline{M}'$), the difference between the new pattern of adjustment ($A' \rightarrow B'$) and the original is easily as large as the shift induced by a change in σ.

This discussion raises the question of how precisely to determine the elasticity of substitution, which turns out to be a thorny issue. In our simple CES economy there are more free parameters than there are model equations or observations of benchmark data, which makes (14.17) an underdetermined mathematical problem. This difficulty is magnified in real-world CGE models, in which it has become popular to specify industries' cost and consumers' expenditure functions using hierarchical CES functions, each of which has multiple elasticities of substitution.

The nested production and cost functions in the Goulder (1995) model are shown in Figure 14.4, in which each node of the tree denotes the output of a CES function and the branches denote the relevant inputs. In each industry, the substitution possibilities among capital (K), labor (L), energy (E) and materials (M) are controlled by five elasticity parameters: substitution between primary factors (KL) and intermediate goods (EM) by σ^O, capital–labor substitution by σ^{KL}, energy–material substitution by σ^{EM}, inter-fuel substitution by σ^E, and substitution among non-energy intermediate inputs by σ^M.

It is not possible to either estimate or compute the values of these elasticities without a

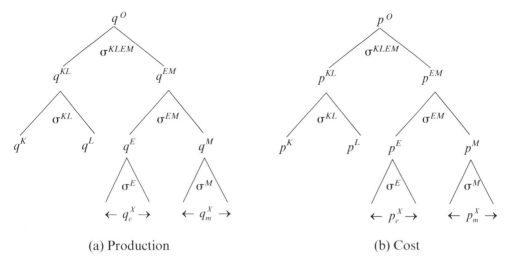

(a) Production   (b) Cost

Note: p^O, q^O = price and quantity of output; $\mathbf{P} = \{p^K, p^L, p^E, p^M\}$, $\mathbf{Q} = \{q^K, q^L, q^E, q^M\}$ = price and quantity of capital, labor, energy and materials; p_e^X, q_e^X = price and quantity of intermediate energy commodities; p_m^X, q_m^X = price and quantity of intermediate material commodities; p^{KL}, q^{KL} = price and quantity of value-added composite; p^{EM}, p^{EM} = price and quantity of energy–materials composite.

Figure 14.4   Goulder (1995) KLEM production structure

host of auxiliary information.[1] Faced with this data constraint, modelers frequently resort to selecting values for these parameters from the empirical literature based on judgment and assumptions. The ad hoc nature of this process has been criticized by mainstream empirical economists (for example, Jorgenson, 1984; McKitrick, 1998), who advocate an econometric approach to CGE modeling in which the pseudo-excess demand correspondence is built up from statistically estimated cost and expenditure functions.

The econometric approach remedies the problematic inconsistency between the nested CES functional forms employed in models and the flexible power series approximations of arbitrary cost or expenditure functions employed by empirical studies, which estimate the pairwise Allen–Uzawa elasticities of substitution (AUES) among the various inputs to production and consumption. For example, the translog form of the cost function in Figure 14.4 might specify the logarithm of the output price as a quadratic function of the logarithms of the input prices (**P**) and time (t):

$$\log p^O = \delta_0 + \boldsymbol{\delta}_P \log \mathbf{P}' + \delta_T t + \tfrac{1}{2}\log \mathbf{P}\boldsymbol{\delta}_{PP}' \log \mathbf{P} + \boldsymbol{\delta}_{PT}\log \mathbf{P}'t + \tfrac{1}{2}\delta_{TT}t^2, \quad (14.18)$$

where δ_0, δ_T, δ_{TT}, $\boldsymbol{\delta}_P$, $\boldsymbol{\delta}_{PP}$, and $\boldsymbol{\delta}_{PT}$ are vectors of parameters to be estimated. By Shephard's lemma, the derivative of this expression with respect to the logarithms of the input prices yields a vector of input cost shares, $\mathbf{s} = \{s^K, s^L, s^E, s^M\}$:

$$\frac{\partial \log p^O}{\partial \log \mathbf{P}'} = \frac{\text{diag}(\mathbf{PQ}')}{p^O q^O} = \mathbf{s}' = \boldsymbol{\delta}_P' + \log \mathbf{P}\boldsymbol{\delta}_{PP} + \boldsymbol{\delta}_{PT}'t, \quad (14.19)$$

where **Q** is the vector of input quantities.

Estimating (14.18) and (14.19) as a system yields a vector of numerically calibrated linear equations which may be used in our example model in place of equation (14.17). This alternative would entail using (14.18) in place of the CES cost function (14.16a), and substituting commodity and factor demands derived from (14.19) into the market clearance conditions (14.16c) and (14.16d). Substitution possibilities would then be determined by the AUES between each pair of inputs k and l: $\zeta_{kl} = 1 + \delta_{kl}/(\underline{s}^k \underline{s}^l)$, where $\underline{s}$ indicates the mean value of each input's share of total cost in the data sample. Note that our original assumption of CES technology implies that $\zeta_{KL,j} = \zeta_{KE,j} = \zeta_{KM,j} = \zeta_{LE,j} = \zeta_{LM,j} = \zeta_{EM,j} = \sigma_j$, which is a stringent restriction on the estimated parameters. Dawkins et al. (2001) provide an excellent survey of these issues.

Despite its rigor, the econometric approach is not without drawbacks. First and foremost, it is data intensive, requiring time-series observations of prices and quantities of the inputs and outputs for every industry represented in the CGE model. Often such data are simply not available, which has restricted its application to comparatively few models (for example, Jorgenson, 1984; McKibbin and Wilcoxen, 1998; McKitrick, 1998; Fisher-Vanden and Ho, 2007). A second, more subtle shortcoming involves flexible functional forms themselves. For the general equilibrium condition of no free disposability to be satisfied, the simulated cost shares must be strictly positive at all prices. But it has long been known (for example, Lutton and LeBlanc, 1984) that large and negative estimated values of δ^{PP} can give rise to cost shares which are negative! For this reason, Perroni and Rutherford (1998) argue that flexible functional forms lack *global regularity*, in the sense that (14.18) or (14.19) are not guaranteed to map an arbitrary vector of positive prices into $\Re^+$. In practice, it is not possible to predict a priori when such problems will arise, and in any case, modelers have come up with ad hoc countermeasures.[2] Nevertheless, this remains an important issue for energy and climate policy simulations, as the imposition of a sufficiently high tax on energy (say) may cause p^E to increase outside of the historical range of values, with the result that $s^E < 0$ if the own- or cross-price energy elasticities are sufficiently large.

Computation of equilibrium
The calibration procedure transforms (14.16) into a square system of numerical inequalities known as a mixed complementarity problem or MCP (Ferris and Pang, 1997), which may be solved using algorithms that are now routinely embodied in modern, commercially available software systems for optimization. The basic approach, described by Mathiesen (1985a,b) and Rutherford (1987), is a Newton-type algorithm which iteratively solves a sequence of linear complementarity problems or LCPs (Cottle et al., 1992), each of which is a first-order Taylor series expansion of the non-linear function Ξ. The LCP solved at each iteration is thus one of finding:

$$\mathbf{z} \geq 0 \text{ s.t. } \boldsymbol{\xi}_1 + \boldsymbol{\xi}_2 \mathbf{z} \geq 0, \mathbf{z}^T(\boldsymbol{\xi}_1 + \boldsymbol{\xi}_2 \mathbf{z}) = 0, \tag{14.20}$$

where, linearizing Ξ around $\mathbf{z}_{\{\iota\}}$, the state vector of prices, activity levels and income at iteration ι, $\boldsymbol{\xi}_1[\mathbf{z}_{\{\iota\}}] = \nabla\Xi[\mathbf{z}_{\{\iota\}}]\mathbf{z}_{\{\iota\}} - \Xi[\mathbf{z}_{\{\iota\}}]$ and $\boldsymbol{\xi}_2[\mathbf{z}_{\{\iota\}}] = \nabla\Xi[\mathbf{z}_{\{\iota\}}]$. The value of $\mathbf{z}$ that solves the sub-problem (14.20) at the ιth iteration is $\mathbf{z}^*_{\{\iota\}}$. Then, starting from an initial point, $\mathbf{z}_{\{0\}}$, the algorithm generates a sequence of vectors $\mathbf{z}$ which is propagated according to the linesearch:

$$\mathbf{z}_{\{t+1\}} = \lambda_{\{t\}} \mathbf{z}^*_{\{t\}} + (1 - \lambda_{\{t\}}) \mathbf{z}_{\{t-1\}}, \tag{14.21}$$

where the parameter $\lambda_{\{t\}}$ controls the length of the forward step at each iteration. The convergence criterion for the algorithm made up of equations (14.20) and (14.21) is $\|\Xi(\mathbf{z}^*)\| < \varphi$, the maximum level of excess demand, profit or income at which the economy is deemed by the analyst to have attained equilibrium.

The operations research literature now contains numerous refinements to this approach, based on path-following homotopy methods outlined theoretically in Garcia and Zangwill (1981), and described in application by Kehoe (1991, pp. 2061–5) and Eaves and Schmedders (1999). Dirkse and Ferris (1995), Ferris et al. (2000) and Ferris and Kanzow (2002) provide details of the algorithms and discussions of their convergence properties. In modern software implementations, φ is routinely six orders of magnitude smaller than the value of aggregate income.

The foregoing exposition raises the question of how good CGE models are at finding an equilibrium. Experience with the routine solution of CGE models calibrated on real-world economic data and containing a variety of price and quantity distortions suggests that the procedures outlined above are robust. However, a definitive answer to this question is both involved and elusive, as it hinges on the existence, uniqueness, and stability of the simulated general equilibrium. Lack of space precludes discussion of these issues, but suffice it to say that tests of the multiplicity of equilibria in real-world CGE models are rare, with the vast majority of studies proceeding on the assumption that their models' solutions are unique and stable. For details, the reader is referred to the excellent surveys by Kehoe (1991, 1998b) and an assessment of this literature by the author (Sue Wing, 2004).

6 Modeling Energy and Climate Policies

Policy variables in CGE models most often take the form of parameters that are exogenously specified by the analyst, and are either price based – that is, taxes and subsidies, or quantity based – that is, constraints on demand and/or supply. Beginning with the initial equilibrium represented in the SAM, a change in one or more of these parameters perturbs the vector of prices and activity levels, causing the economy to converge to a new equilibrium. To evaluate the effect of the policy represented by this change, the analyst compares the pre- and post-change equilibrium vectors of prices, activity levels, and income levels, subject to the caveats of the accuracy and realism of the model's assumptions.

This approach has the advantage of measuring policies' ultimate impact on consumers' aggregate well-being in a theoretically consistent way, by quantifying the changes in the income and consumption of the representative agent that result from the myriad supply–demand interactions among the markets in the economy. Ironically, this functionality is at the root of the 'black box' criticism articulated in the introduction, as policy makers may be tempted to treat CGE models as a sort of economic crystal ball. By contrast, CGE models' usefulness as tool for policy analysis owes less to their predictive accuracy, and more to their ability to shed light on the mechanisms responsible for the transmission of price and quantity adjustments among markets. Therefore, CGE models should properly be regarded as computational laboratories within which to analyze the dynamics of the economic interactions from which policies derive their impacts.

The remainder of the chapter focuses its attention on production in the energy sectors and the uses of energy commodities in the economy. It bears emphasizing that energy commodities are reproducible, created by combining inputs of natural resources (that is non-reproducible, primary energy reserves) with labor, capital and intermediate goods. Accordingly, the vectors of commodities and industries are partitioned into subsets of $\mathcal{E}$ energy goods/sectors, indexed by e, and $\mathcal{M}$ non-energy material goods/sectors, indexed by m.

Price instruments
It is easiest to illustrate the impact on equilibrium of price instruments such as taxes and subsidies. Within CGE models, taxes are typically specified in an ad valorem fashion, whereby a tax at a given rate determines the fractional increase in the price level of the taxed commodity. For example, an ad valorem tax at rate τ on the output of industry e drives a wedge between the producer price of output, p_e, and the consumer price, $(1 + \tau)$ p_e, in the process generating revenue from the y_e units of output in the amount of $\tau p_e y_e$. A subsidy which lowers the price may also be incorporated in this way, by specifying $\tau < 0$.

Conceptually, there are three types of markets in the economy in which basic energy taxes or subsidies can be levied: the markets for the output of energy sectors (indicated by the superscript Y), the market for consumption of energy (indicated by the superscript C), and the markets for energy inputs to production in each industry (indicated by the superscript X). Let the tax or subsidy rates that correspond to each of these markets be denoted by τ_e^Y, τ_e^C and $\tau_{e,j}^X$, respectively. These ad valorem rates are easily integrated into our CES economy by treating them as exogenous policy parameters. The representative agent's problem becomes:

$$\min_{\hat{g}_{i,C}} \theta = \sum_{e=1}^{\mathcal{E}} (1 + \tau_e^C)(1 + \tau_e^Y)p_e \hat{g}_{e,C} + \sum_{m=1}^{\mathcal{M}} p_m \hat{g}_{m,C}$$

$$\text{s.t. } 1 = \left[\sum_{i=1}^{N} \alpha_i \hat{g}_{i,C}^{(\omega - 1)/\omega} \right]^{\omega/(\omega - 1)}, \tag{14.6''}$$

while the producer's problem becomes:

$$\min_{\hat{x}_{i,j}, \hat{v}_{f,j}} p_j = \sum_{e=1}^{\mathcal{E}} (1 + \tau_{e,j}^X)(1 + \tau_e^Y)p_e \hat{x}_{e,j} + \sum_{m=1}^{\mathcal{M}} p_m \hat{x}_{m,j} + \sum_{f=1}^{\mathcal{F}} w_f \hat{v}_{f,j}$$

$$\text{s.t. } 1 = \left[\sum_{i=1}^{N} \beta_{i,j} \hat{x}_{i,j}^{(\sigma_j - 1)/\sigma_j} + \sum_{f=1}^{\mathcal{F}} \gamma_{f,j} \hat{v}_{f,j}^{(\sigma_j - 1)/\sigma_j} \right]^{\sigma_j/(\sigma_j - 1)}, \tag{14.8''}$$

giving rise to new final and intermediate demands for energy commodities:

$$g_{e,C} = \alpha_e^\omega \theta^\omega [(1 + \tau_e^C)(1 + \tau_e^Y)p_e]^{-\omega} u, \tag{14.22}$$

$$x_{e,j} = \beta_{e,j}^{\sigma_j} p_j^{\sigma_j} [(1 + \tau_{e,j}^X)(1 + \tau_e^Y)p_e]^{-\sigma_j} y_j. \tag{14.23}$$

Every tax (subsidy) generates a positive (negative) revenue stream that increases (reduces) the income of some consumer while negatively (positively) affecting the production and absorption of the commodity in question. In representative–agent models, the simplest way to represent this phenomenon is to treat the government as a passive entity that collects tax revenue and immediately recycles it to the single household as a lump-sum supplement to the income from factor returns. This approach circumvents the need to represent the government as an explicit sector within the model; taxes and subsidies may be specified simply as transfers of purchasing power to and from the representative agent. In this situation, the demand functions (14.22) and (14.23), as well as the necessary adjustments to income lead to the transformation of (14.16) into the new pseudo-excess demand correspondence (14.24):

$$p_j \leq \left\{ \sum_{e=1}^{\mathcal{E}} \beta_{e,j}^{\sigma_j} [(1 + \tau_{e,j}^X)(1 + \tau_e^Y)p_e]^{1-\sigma_j} \right.$$

$$\left. + \sum_{m=1}^{\mathcal{M}} \beta_{m,j}^{\sigma_j} p_m^{1-\sigma_j} + \sum_{f=1}^{\mathcal{F}} \gamma_{f,j}^{\sigma_j} w_f^{1-\sigma_j} \right\}^{1/(1-\sigma_j)} \quad \perp y_j \qquad (14.24a)$$

$$\theta \leq \left\{ \sum_{e=1}^{\mathcal{E}} \alpha_e^{\omega} [(1 + \tau_e^C)(1 + \tau_e^Y)p_e]^{1-\omega} + \sum_{m=1}^{\mathcal{M}} \alpha_m^{\omega} p_m^{1-\omega} \right\}^{1/(1-\omega)} \quad \perp u \quad (14.24b)$$

$$y_e \geq \sum_{j=1}^{\mathcal{N}} \beta_{e,j}^{\sigma_j} p_j^{\sigma_j} [(1 + \tau_{e,j}^X)(1 + \tau_e^Y)p_e]^{-\sigma_j} y_j$$

$$+ \alpha_e^{\omega} \theta^{\omega} [(1 + \tau_e^C)(1 + \tau_e^Y)p_e]^{-\omega} u + g_{e,O} \quad \perp p_e \qquad (14.24c')$$

$$y_m \geq \sum_{j=1}^{\mathcal{N}} \beta_{m,j}^{\sigma_j} p_j^{\sigma_j} p_m^{-\sigma_j} y_j + \alpha_m^{\omega} \theta^{\omega} p_m^{-\omega} u + g_{m,O} \quad \perp p_m \qquad (14.24c'')$$

$$V_f \geq \sum_{j=1}^{\mathcal{N}} \gamma_{f,j}^{\sigma_j} p_j^{\sigma_j} w_f^{-\sigma_j} y_j \quad \perp w_f \qquad (14.24d)$$

$$u \geq \mu/\theta, \quad \perp \theta \qquad (14.24e)$$

$$\mu = \sum_{f=1}^{\mathcal{F}} w_f V_f - \sum_{i=1}^{\mathcal{N}} p_i g_{i,O} + \sum_{e=1}^{\mathcal{E}} \tau_e^Y p_e y_e$$

$$+ \sum_{e=1}^{\mathcal{E}} \tau_e^C (1 + \tau_e^C)^{-\omega} [(1 + \tau_e^Y)p_e]^{1-\omega} \alpha_e^{\omega} \theta^{\omega} u$$

$$+ \sum_{e=1}^{\mathcal{E}} \sum_{j=1}^{\mathcal{N}} \tau_{e,j}^X (1 + \tau_{e,j}^X)^{-\sigma_j} [(1 + \tau_e^Y)p_e]^{1-\sigma_j} \beta_{e,j}^{\sigma_j} p_j^{\sigma_j} y_j \quad \perp \mu. \qquad (14.24f)$$

The foregoing system of equations may be solved for a new, tariff-ridden equilibrium, whose price and quantity allocation may be compared with that of the original benchmark equilibrium without taxes. The measure of the taxes' aggregate impact on economic well-being is equivalent variation. This is approximated by the change in the representative agent's consumption (*u*) with respect to the initial equilibrium, which is the loss of household's real purchasing power induced by the distortion in relative prices. It is noteworthy that the most significant adjustments to the original pseudo-excess demand correspondence are the additional terms in the income definition equation (14.24f). The implication is that the welfare effect of a single tax or subsidy depends on the interactions among a myriad of factors: the level of the tax and the distribution of other taxes and subsidies across all markets in the economy, the characteristics of the particular market in which the tax is levied, the linkages between this market and the others in the economy, and the values of the vectors of calibrated parameters α, β and γ.

The ability to rigorously account for the income consequences of inter-market price and quantity adjustments is what sets the current approach apart from partial equilibrium analysis. But it also highlights a kernel of truth to the black box criticism. The nonlinearity and dimensionality of the pseudo-excess demand correspondence make it difficult to intuit the net impact of adding or removing a single distortion, even in models with only a modest number of sectors and/or households. Moreover, to sort through and understand the web of interactions that give rise to the post-tax equilibrium often requires the analyst to undertake a significant amount *ex post* analysis and testing.

Quantity instruments

In comparison with taxes, quantity instruments vary widely in their characteristics and methods of application. It is useful to draw a distinction between the instrument itself, which is represented by one or more exogenous quantity parameters, and its effect on supply or demand in a particular market or set of markets, which must be expressed using one or more auxiliary equations. Although quantity instruments may be simple to parameterize, capturing the subtle characteristics of their economic effects through proper formulation of the auxiliary equations can sometimes be a challenge. Modeling quantity constraints within the complementarity framework necessitates the introduction of an additional (dual) variable with which the (primal) auxiliary equation can be paired. Intuitively, the quantity distortion defined by this equation generates a complementary price distortion which has the same effect as a tax or a subsidy. Thus, while in the previous section the price distortion was an exogenous parameter, here it is a shadow price – an endogenous variable that exhibits complementary slackness with respect to the quantity instrument. Furthermore, as with taxes, quantity distortions generate a stream of rents that must be allocated somewhere in the economy.

The auxiliary equation is often specified as a rationing constraint in which the quantity instrument sets an upper or lower bound on the supply and/or use of one or more energy commodities. Such constraints may be direct, where the energy good in question itself is the subject of restriction, or indirect, where some attribute of the good (for example, its CO_2 content) is being limited. They may also be expressed in absolute or relative terms, with the former corresponding to an exogenous limit on energy or its attributes, and the latter tying these quantities to other variables in the economy.

Figure 14.5 summarizes these considerations and provides examples. Production and/ or consumption of an energy commodity may be rationed directly, a situation which corresponds to a curtailment of energy supply, or the sorts of direct government intervention in markets seen in times of crisis. As well, policies such as the renewable portfolio standard (RPS), which has emerged as a popular means to promote alternative sources of electricity supply, act as a relative rationing constraint by imposing a lower bound on the production of renewable energy that is indexed to the sales of conventional energy. In contrast to such direct measures, policies such as climate change mitigation limit the

	Relative	Absolute
Direct	Renewable portfolio standard	Rationing/supply curtailment
Indirect	GHG intensity cap	GHG emission cap

Figure 14.5   Quantity instruments: taxonomy and examples

emissions from a portfolio of fossil fuels, which ends up indirectly and endogenously curtailing demand for the most CO_2-intensive fuels. Finally, emission caps may be posed in a relative form such as the intensity target discussed by Ellerman and Sue Wing (2003). By judiciously choosing the level of such a target, the *ex ante* impact on GHG emissions and the supply and demand for energy can be the same as its absolute counterpart under certainty. However, the introduction of *ex post* uncertainty (for example, by simulating the CGE model with different elasticity parameters) will lead to the targets denominated in absolute and intensity terms having different economic effects.[3]

The case of pure rationing is straightforward. Returning to the no-tariff world of equation (14.16), assume that there is a particular energy commodity (say, e') whose supply faces a binding quantity limit $q_{e'}$. The simplest way to model this constraint to apply an endogenous ad-valorem tariff, $\tau_{e'}^Y$, to the output of e'. Note that $\tau_{e'}^Y$ is not a parameter but an auxiliary variable which is dual to the quota: by increasing the tax-inclusive price $p_{e'}$ the tariff attenuates aggregate demand for e' to the point where the limit is just satisfied. The new pseudo-excess demand correspondence, equation (14.25), is made up of equations (14.16b)–(14.16e), a new zero-profit condition incorporating the endogenous output tariff:

$$p_{e'} \leq (1 + \tau_{e'}^Y)\left(\sum_{i=1}^{N} \beta_{i,j}^{\sigma_j} p_m^{1-\sigma_j} + \sum_{f=1}^{\mathcal{F}} \gamma_{f,j}^{\sigma_j} w_f^{1-\sigma_j} \right)^{1/(1-\sigma_j)} \qquad \perp y_{e'} \qquad (14.25a')$$

$$p_j \leq \left(\sum_{i=1}^{N} \beta_{i,j}^{\sigma_j} p_m^{1-\sigma_j} + \sum_{f=1}^{\mathcal{F}} \gamma_{f,j}^{\sigma_j} w_f^{1-\sigma_j} \right)^{1/(1-\sigma_j)} \qquad \perp y_j \ j \neq e', \qquad (14.25a'')$$

the rationing constraint with the dual tariff:

$$y_{e'} \leq q_{e'} \qquad \perp \tau_{e'}^Y, \qquad (14.25g)$$

and a new income definition equation incorporating the pure rent from constraining supply, which is assumed to redound to the representative agent:

$$\mu = \sum_{f=1}^{\mathcal{F}} w_f V_f - \sum_{i=1}^{N} p_i g_{i,0} + \tau_{e'}^Y q_{e'} \qquad \perp \mu. \qquad (14.25f)$$

It is possible to make alternative assumptions about where to allocate this stream of revenue. For example, we could model the rents as accruing to a particular industry (say, j'), by defining an endogenous ad valorem subsidy to that sector's output ($\tau_{j'}^Y < 0$) in which the value of the subsidy revenue was constrained to equal the value of the rent: $\tau_{e'}^Y q_{e'} = \tau_{j'}^Y p_{j'} y_{j'}$. This constraint would constitute an additional auxiliary equation, to which $\tau_{j'}^Y$ would be the complementary variable. Moreover, it would be necessary to re-specify the zero profit condition for j' in a manner similar to equation (14.24a′) to account for the distortionary effects of the subsidy on relative prices.

The second example is an RPS policy in which the government mandates that a proportion of the aggregate energy supply ($\rho \in (0, 1)$) must come from renewable sources. Let the set of energy industries be partitioned into conventional and renewable sources, indicated by $\mathcal{E}^C$ and $\mathcal{E}^R$, respectively, and suppose that each unit of activity in these sectors, y_e, generates ε_e physical units of energy. Then the RPS can be expressed by the rationing constraint $\Sigma_{e \in \mathcal{E}^R} \varepsilon_e y_e \geq \rho \Sigma_{e=1}^{\mathcal{E}} \varepsilon_e y_e$. To comply with the standard, energy suppliers must collectively tax themselves to finance the production of ρ units of renewable energy for every unit of energy produced systemwide. The marginal financing charge per unit of aggregate energy supplied can be thought of as an endogenous tax, τ^{RPS}, whose proceeds are recycled to renewable energy producers. Every energy firm therefore pays an additional cost $\rho \tau^{RPS}$ per unit of energy produced, while renewable suppliers as a group receive the full τ^{RPS} per unit of energy they produce.[4]

An intuitive way of understanding this result is to think of the RPS as a tradable renewable energy credit scheme (see, for example, Baron and Serret, 2002). A unit of energy supplied by a renewable producer generates one credit which may be sold, whereas a unit of energy produced – regardless of its origin – requires the purchase of ρ credits as a renewable financing charge. An important implication is that, in contrast to the rationing example, the RPS does not create pure rents – it merely redistributes revenue from conventional to renewable energy producers, with indirect impact on aggregate income which operates through the prices of energy commodities. Accordingly, in the new excess demand correspondence, (14.26), all the action occurs in the zero profit condition for industries:

$$p_j \leq \left(\sum_{i=1}^{N} \beta_{i,j}^{\sigma_j} p_m^{1-\sigma_j} + \sum_{f=1}^{\mathcal{F}} \gamma_{f,j}^{\sigma_j} w_f^{1-\sigma_j} \right)^{1/(1-\sigma_j)} \qquad \perp y_j \ \ j \in \mathcal{M} \qquad (14.26a')$$

$$p_j \leq \left(\sum_{i=1}^{N} \beta_{i,j}^{\sigma_j} p_m^{1-\sigma_j} + \sum_{f=1}^{\mathcal{F}} \gamma_{f,j}^{\sigma_j} w_f^{1-\sigma_j} \right)^{1/(1-\sigma_j)} + \rho\tau^{RPS} \qquad \perp y_j \ \ j \in \mathcal{E}^C \qquad (14.26a'')$$

$$p_j + \tau^{RPS} \leq \left(\sum_{i=1}^{N} \beta_{i,j}^{\sigma_j} p_m^{1-\sigma_j} + \sum_{f=1}^{\mathcal{F}} \gamma_{f,j}^{\sigma_j} w_f^{1-\sigma_j} \right)^{1/(1-\sigma_j)} + \rho\tau^{RPS} \qquad \perp y_j \ \ j \in \mathcal{E}^R, \qquad (14.26a''')$$

while the rationing constraint merely determines the value of the auxiliary financing charge:

$$\sum_{e \in \mathcal{E}^R} \varepsilon_e y_e \geq \rho \sum_{e=1}^{\mathcal{E}} \varepsilon_e y_e \qquad \perp \tau^{RPS}, \qquad (14.26g)$$

and the remaining equations are unchanged, given by (14.16b)–(14.16f).

The final policy which this chapter examines is a cap on aggregate emissions of CO_2. It is necessary to establish the relationship between the levels of production and demand activities and the quantity of emissions. The simplest way to proceed is to assume a fixed stoichiometric relationship between the quantity of emissions in the benchmark year and the value of aggregate demand for the fossil-fuel commodities which generate them, expressed as a set of commodity-specific emission coefficients (φ_e). A tax on emissions (τ^{CO_2}) therefore creates a set of commodity taxes that are differentiated according to the carbon contents of energy goods, adding a mark-up to the price of each fossil fuel in the amount of $\tau^{CO_2}\phi_e$.

Let Q^{CO_2} denote a quantitative CO_2 target which sets an upper bound on the emissions from aggregate fossil-fuel use. The shadow price on this constraint is the tax τ^{CO_2}, which can be thought of as the endogenous market-clearing price of emission allowances in an economy-wide cap-and-trade scheme. Interestingly, in the present setting the two main methods for allocating allowances – auctioning and grandfathering to firms – are modeled in the same way and generate identical welfare impacts. Grandfathering allowances is equivalent to defining a new factor of production that increases the profitability of firms but at the same time is also owned by the households, so that the returns to permits accrue as income to the representative agent. Likewise, auctioning allowances generates additional government revenue which is then immediately recycled to the representative agent in a lump sum.

As in (14.24a–14.24f), the price distortion simultaneously affects the zero profit and market clearance and income balance conditions. The relevant pseudo-excess demand correspondence, equation (14.27), is thus made up of (14.24d) and (14.24e) along with:

$$p_j \leq \left[\sum_{e=1}^{\mathcal{E}} \beta_{e,j}^{\sigma_j}(p_e + \tau^{CO_2}\phi_e)^{1-\sigma_j} \right.$$
$$\left. + \sum_{m=1}^{\mathcal{M}} \beta_{m,j}^{\sigma_j} p_m^{1-\sigma_j} + \sum_{f=1}^{\mathcal{F}} \gamma_{f,j}^{\sigma_j} w_f^{1-\sigma_j} \right]^{1/(1-\sigma_j)} \quad \perp y_j \qquad (14.27a)$$

$$\theta \leq \left[\sum_{e=1}^{\mathcal{E}} \alpha_e^{\omega}(p_e + \tau^{CO_2}\phi_e)^{1-\omega} + \sum_{m=1}^{\mathcal{M}} \alpha_m^{\omega} p_m^{1-\omega} \right]^{1/(1-\omega)} \quad \perp u \qquad (14.27b)$$

$$y_e \geq \sum_{j=1}^{N} \beta_{e,j}^{\sigma_j} p_j^{\sigma_j}(p_e + \tau^{CO_2}\phi_e)^{-\sigma_j} y_j$$
$$+ \alpha_e^{\omega}\theta^{\omega}(p_e + \tau^{CO_2}\phi_e)^{-\omega} u + g_{e,O} \quad \perp p_e \qquad (14.27c')$$

$$y_m \geq \sum_{j=1}^{N} \beta_{m,j}^{\sigma_j} p_j^{\sigma_j} p_m^{-\sigma_j} y_j + \alpha_m^{\omega}\theta^{\omega} p_m^{-\omega} u + g_{m,O} \quad \perp p_m \qquad (14.27c'')$$

$$\mu = \sum_{f=1}^{\mathcal{F}} w_f V_f - \left[\sum_{e=1}^{\mathcal{E}} (p_e + \tau^{CO_2}\phi_e) g_{e,O} + \sum_{m=1}^{\mathcal{M}} p_m g_{m,O} \right]$$
$$+ \tau^{CO_2} Q^{CO_2} \quad \perp \mu \qquad (14.27f)$$

and a rationing constraint which is denominated in terms of the emission content of intermediate and final demands for fossil energy:

$$Q^{CO_2} \geq \sum_{e=1}^{\mathcal{E}} \phi_e \left[\sum_{j=1}^{N} \beta_{e,j}^{\sigma_j} p_j^{\sigma_j}(p_e + \tau^{CO_2}\phi_e)^{-\sigma_j} y_j \right.$$
$$\left. + \alpha_e^{\omega}\theta^{\omega}(p_e + \tau^{CO_2}\phi_e)^{-\omega} u + g_{e,O} \right] \quad \perp \tau^{CO_2}. \qquad (14.27g)$$

Note that in the present closed-economy model the rationing constraint could have been expressed simply as $Q^{CO_2} \geq \Sigma_{e=1}^{\mathcal{E}} \phi_e y_e$. However, in an open-economy model where trade in energy goods creates a divergence between the production and consumption of fossil fuels, the real source of emissions is consumption, as specified in equation (14.27g).

One final point deserves mention. With either a price or a quantity instrument, the direct effect of a policy on the welfare of the representative agent operates through two channels: the substitution effect in consumption induced by changes commodity prices, and the income effect of changes in factor remuneration induced by shifts in factor prices. The latter is indicated by the change in the magnitude of the first term on the right-hand side of the income definition equation, and can be thought of as a summary measure of the policy's primary economic burden in terms of its factor incidence. But it bears emphasizing that neither this quantity, nor GDP, nor even the 'Harberger triangle' welfare approximation (which in the case of output taxes τ_j^Y that induce changes in production Δy_j is given by $\frac{1}{2} \Sigma_j \tau_j^Y \Delta y_j$ – see Hines, 1999) is sufficient to capture the full range of general equilibrium impacts on consumers' utility. The theoretically correct summary welfare measure is the quantity of aggregate consumption indicated by the activity level u. The implication is that the choice of numeraire influences the measurement of policies' welfare effects (for example, Hosoe, 2000): designating θ as the numeraire price equates utility with the expression for disposable income.

7   A Realistic Worked Example: The Impacts of Abating Fossil-fuel CO_2 Emissions in the US

This section undertakes a simple yet realistic application of the CES economy developed above. The goal is to shed light on the costs and economy-wide impacts of reducing emissions of CO_2 from the combustion of fossil fuels in the US economy.

Model structure
The simulation is an extension of the CES economy developed in the previous sections. The structure of the economy is summarized in Figure 14.6(a). Firms are classified into eight broad sectoral groupings: coal mining, crude oil and gas mining, natural gas distribution, refined petroleum, electric power, energy-intensive manufacturing (an amalgam of the chemical, ferrous and non-ferrous metal, pulp and paper, and stone, clay and glass industries), purchased transportation, and a composite of the remaining manufacturing, service, and primary extractive industries in the economy. Households are modeled as a representative agent, who is endowed with fixed quantities of three primary factors: labor, capital, and primary energy resources. While the first two of these can be re-allocated among industries in response to intersectoral shifts in factor demand, energy resources play the role of sector-specific fixed factors, of which there is one type in coal mining, another in crude oil and gas and a third in electricity.

An important feature of the model is the presence of pre-existing distortions. Real-world GHG mitigation policies will generate interactions between the distortionary effects of quantitative limits or Pigovian fees on emissions and the preexisting tax system, particularly taxes on labor, capital and fossil fuels. The simplest way of accounting for these impacts is to introduce pre-existing ad valorem taxes on production and imports $(\bar{\tau}_j^Y)$, which are assumed to be levied on the output of each industry. As before (see

Energy (e)	Non-energy (m)	Final demands
1. Coal mining	6. Energy-intensive industries	C Private consumption
2. Crude oil and gas	7. Transportation	O Other (Investment
3. Gas works and distribution	8. Other industries	+ Government + Net Exports)
4. Refined petroleum	Primary factors (f)	
5. Electric power	L Labor	
(a) Fossil fuel generation	K Capital	
(b) Carbon-free generation	R Primary energy resources	

(a) Sectoral structure

	1	2	3	4	5(a)	5(b)	6	7	8	C	O	Total
1	0.207	0.000	0.000	0.001	2.748	0.000	0.216	0.002	0.277	0.008	0.514	3.973
2	0.006	2.181	5.501	19.417	0.000	0.000	0.591	0.533	1.491	0.000	15.072	14.648
3	0.000	0.018	0.105	0.294	3.343	0.000	0.408	0.059	1.956	4.287	0.023	10.494
4	0.093	0.153	0.104	4.369	0.513	0.000	2.375	4.858	15.241	8.871	2.084	34.492
5	0.034	0.133	0.013	0.220	0.021	0.000	1.195	0.288	13.740	14.392	-0.035	30.002
6	0.063	0.312	0.023	0.692	0.179	0.071	16.679	0.348	48.898	21.713	-6.456	82.521
7	0.141	0.150	0.808	1.069	0.966	0.383	3.071	6.477	27.023	15.565	7.770	63.422
8	0.646	4.098	0.525	3.989	2.613	1.037	25.696	19.972	684.784	755.850	405.703	1904.913
L	1.009	1.078	0.823	0.968	2.908	1.154	15.897	20.179	667.040			711.058
K	0.972	3.168	2.160	3.320	7.248	2.875	15.484	9.081	365.512			409.819
R	0.648	2.592	0.000	0.000	0.000	0.533	0.000	0.000	0.000			3.773
ψ	0.154	0.765	0.430	0.151	3.413		0.908	1.626	78.952			86.399
Total	3.973	14.648	10.494	34.492	30.002		82.521	63.422	1904.913	820.685	390.363	3355.512
q^{CO_2}	2094		1170	2487								5751
ϕ_e	0.053		0.011	0.007								

(b) Benchmark social accounts for the year 2005

Notes:
Monetary flows: 10^{10} 2004 dollars, CO_2 emissions ($\bar{q}^{CO_2}$): 10^6 tons, emission coefficients (φ): tons CO_2 per dollar.
ψ Payments of state and federal taxes on production and imports net of subsidies.
GDP: $12.1 trillion, Gross output: $33.6 trillion.

Figure 14.6   Model sectoral structure and database

equation (14.27f)), the assumption is that the revenue raised by both these taxes and the auctioning or grandfathering of emission allowances is recycled to the representative agent in a lump sum. However, a key result from the large literature on the impacts of environmental policies in the presence of prior tax distortions (see, for example, Goulder, 2002) is that the alternative use of permit revenues to finance a revenue-neutral reduction in $\bar{\tau}_j^Y$ has the potential to significantly lower the welfare cost of the emission constraint.

Industries' outputs are produced by combining inputs of intermediate energy and non-energy goods with primary factors. A signal characteristic of climate change mitigation policies is that higher fossil-fuel prices induce an expansion of carbon-free sources of energy supply, the bulk of which occur in the electric power sector. Accordingly, the single-level CES function of the previous sections is employed to model production in every sector except electric power (sector 5), where a bi-level nested CES function is used to capture the substitution between fossil-fuel electric generation (5(a)) and carbon-free primary electricity (5(b) – a composite of nuclear, hydro and renewables). In turn, each type of generation is represented by the CES functions used in other industries. To distinguish between the generation subsectors it is assumed that all fossil-fuel inputs to electric power are used by 5(a), while 5(b) is entirely responsible for the sector's demand for primary energy resources.

However, even this simple structure significantly complicates the specification of the pseudo-excess demand correspondence. It is necessary to introduce new activity variables for the fossil and renewable subsectors $y_{5(a)}$ and $y_{5(b)}$, as well as complementary dual variables $p_{5(a)}$ and $p_{5(b)}$ to track the marginal costs of these activities. Then, incorporating the electricity subsectors into the set of activities as $j = \{1, \ldots, 5(a), 5(b), \ldots, 8\}$ while keeping electricity as a homogeneous commodity with $i = \{1, \ldots, 5, \ldots, 8\}$, the resulting model is:

$$p_j \leq \left\{ \sum_e \beta_{e,j}^{\sigma_j}[(1 + \bar{\tau}_e^Y)p_e + \tau^{CO_2}\phi_e]^{1-\sigma_j} \right.$$

$$+ \sum_m \beta_{m,j}^{\sigma_j}[(1 + \bar{\tau}_m^Y)p_m]^{1-\sigma_j}$$

$$\left. + \sum_{f=L,K} \gamma_{f,j}^{\sigma_j}w_f^{1-\sigma_j} + \gamma_{R,j}^{\sigma_j}w_{R,j}^{1-\sigma_j} \right\}^{1/(1-\sigma_j)} \qquad \perp y_j \qquad (14.28a')$$

$$p_5 \leq (\eta_{5(a),5}^\vartheta p_{5(a)}^{1-\vartheta} + \eta_{5(b),5}^\vartheta p_{5(b)}^{1-\vartheta})^{1/(1-\vartheta)} \qquad \perp y_5 \qquad (14.28a'')$$

$$\theta \leq \left\{ \sum_e \alpha_e^\omega[(1 + \bar{\tau}_e^Y)p_e + \tau^{CO_2}\phi_e]^{1-\omega} \right.$$

$$\left. + \sum_m \alpha_m^\omega[(1 + \bar{\tau}_m^Y)p_m]^{1-\omega} \right\}^{1/(1-\omega)} \qquad \perp u \qquad (14.28b'')$$

$$y_e \geq \sum_j \beta_{e,j}^{\sigma_j}p_j^{\sigma_j}[(1 + \bar{\tau}_e^Y)p_e + \tau^{CO_2}\phi_e]^{-\sigma_j}y_j$$

$$+ \alpha_e^\omega\theta^\omega[(1 + \bar{\tau}_e^Y)p_e + \tau^{CO_2}\phi_e]^{-\omega}u + g_{e,O} \qquad \perp p_e \qquad (14.28c')$$

$$y_m \geq \sum_j \beta_{m,j}^{\sigma_j}p_j^{\sigma_j}[(1 + \bar{\tau}_m^Y)p_m]^{-\sigma_j}y_j$$

$$+ \alpha_m^\omega\theta^\omega[(1 + \bar{\tau}_m^Y)p_m]^{-\omega}u + g_{m,O} \qquad \perp p_m \qquad (14.28c'')$$

$$y_i \geq \eta_{i,5}^\vartheta p_5^\vartheta p_i^{-\vartheta}y_5 \qquad \perp p_i, \ i = 5(a), 5(b) \qquad (14.28c''')$$

$$V_f \geq \sum_j \gamma_{f,j}^{\sigma_j}p_j^{\sigma_j}w_f^{-\sigma_j}y_j \qquad \perp w_f, \ f = K, L \qquad (14.28d')$$

$$V_{R,j} \geq \gamma_{R,j}^{\sigma_j}p_j^{\sigma_j}w_{R,j}^{-\sigma_j}y_j \qquad \perp w_{R,j} \qquad (14.28d'')$$

$$u \geq \mu/\theta, \qquad \perp \theta = 1 \qquad (14.28e)$$

$$\mu = \sum_{f=K,L} w_f V_f + \sum_j w_{R,j}V_{R,j}$$

$$- \sum_e [(1 + \bar{\tau}_e^Y)p_e + \tau^{CO_2}\phi_e)g_{e,O}$$

$$- \sum_m [(1 + \bar{\tau}_m^Y)p_m]g_{m,O}$$

$$+ \tau^{CO_2}Q^{CO_2} + \sum_i \bar{\tau}_i^Y p_i y_i \quad \perp \mu \qquad (14.28f)$$

$$Q^{CO_2} \geq \sum_e \phi_e \left\{ \sum_j \beta_{e,j}^{\sigma_j} p_j^{\sigma_j}[(1 + \bar{\tau}_e^Y)p_e + \tau^{CO_2}\phi_e]^{-\sigma_j} y_j \right.$$

$$\left. + \alpha_e^\omega \theta^\omega [(1 + \bar{\tau}_e^Y)p_e + \tau^{CO_2}\phi_e]^{-\omega} u + g_{e,O} \right\} \quad \perp \tau^{CO_2}. \qquad (14.28g)$$

The final term on the right-hand side of (14.28f) represents the revenue from preexisting taxes recycled to the representative agent. Interactions between Q^{CO_2} and $\bar{\tau}_j^Y$ occur through the effect of the former on industries' output prices and activity levels. We shall see that, apart from its direct impact on factor remuneration, the indirect effect of an emission limit is to provide additional income from recycled CO_2 permit-cum-tax revenues while at the same time attenuating the revenue from pre-existing taxes through its distortionary impact on commodity prices. With θ selected as the numeraire, the sum of these three effects determines the policy's aggregate welfare impact.

Data and calibration
The SAM used to calibrate the model in (14.28a)–(14.28g) is constructed from the Bureau of Labor Statistics' 200-sector nominal make and use tables for the year 2004, using the industry technology assumption.[5] The components of value added are disaggregated using data on industries' shares of labor, capital, taxes and subsidies in GDP from the Bureau of Economic Analysis GDP by Industry accounts. The resulting benchmark flow table is aggregated to eight sectoral groupings outlined above, and scaled to approximate the US economy in the year 2005 using the growth rate of real GDP. Adjustments were made to the intermediate transactions matrix to match Energy Information Administration (EIA) statistics on fossil-fuel use, especially in the electric power sector, and to the factor supply matrix to disaggregate natural resource inputs from the returns to capital, following Sue Wing (2001). Finally, since 28.4 percent of the electricity generated in 2005 was supplied by carbon-free primary energy (nuclear, hydro and renewables), the electric power sector was split to disaggregate these sources of supply from fossil fuels.[6]

The final SAM is shown in Figure 14.6(b). While its structure is similar to Figure 14.2, it disaggregates the fossil-fuel and carbon-free electricity subsectors, and includes an additional vector of benchmark payments of net taxes on production and imports in each industry (Ψ). These distortions affect the benchmark equilibrium, and therefore need to be taken into account in calibrating the model. As these flows are assumed to represent payments of taxes on industries' outputs, it is a simple matter to find the ad valorem net tax rates implied by the SAM ($\bar{\tau}_j^Y = \bar{\psi}_j/\bar{y}_j$) and employ the result to compute the technical coefficients along the lines of equation (14.17): $\alpha_{i,C} = (\bar{g}_{i,C}/\bar{G}_C)^{1/\omega}$, and for the non-electric sectors, $\beta_{i,j} = (\bar{x}_{i,j}/\bar{y}_j)^{1/\sigma_j}(1 + \bar{\tau}_j^Y)^{-1/\sigma_j}$ and $\gamma_{f,j} = (\bar{v}_{f,j}/\bar{y}_j)^{1/\sigma_j}(1 - \bar{\tau}_j^Y)^{-1/\sigma_j}$.

To calibrate the electric power cost function we need to deal with the fact that the tax payments recorded in the SAM are not apportioned between the subsector activities.

Indexing the subsectors by $k = 5(a)$, $5(b)$, a simple solution is to define the gross-of-tax level of activity of the aggregate electric power sector as $\bar{y}_5 = \Sigma_k \bar{y}_k + \bar{\psi}_5$, where $\bar{y}_k = \Sigma_i \bar{x}_{i,k} + \Sigma_j \bar{v}_{f,k}$ denotes the net-of-tax levels of activity of the subsectors. The technical coefficients may then be computed on a gross-of-tax basis as $\eta_k = (\bar{y}_k/\bar{y}_5)^{1/\vartheta}(1 + \bar{\tau}_5^Y)^{-1/\vartheta}$ at the upper level of the production hierarchy, and on a net-of-tax basis as $\beta_{i,k} = (\bar{x}_{i,k}/\bar{y}_k)^{1/\sigma_k}$ and $\gamma_{f,k} = (\bar{v}_{f,k}/\bar{y}_k)^{1/\sigma_k}$ at the lower level.

The final parameters necessary to calibrate the model are the substitution elasticities. In the absence of specific empirical estimates for these parameters, values are assumed which lie within the range observed in other modeling studies (see McKibbin and Wilcoxen, 1998). For simplicity, commodity inputs to consumption are assumed to be inelastic substitutes, which is reflected by setting $\omega = 0.5$. Substitution among inputs to production is also treated as being uniformly inelastic, and to keep things simple the corresponding elasticities values are assumed to be the same all sectors: $\sigma_j = 0.8 \; \forall j$. The top-level elasticity in the electric power sector is different, however, because of the fossil-fuel and carbon-free generation subsectors are near-perfect substitutes for one another in the production electricity. This is captured by setting $\vartheta = 10$.

Substituting the parameter values and the relevant flows from the SAM into the foregoing calibration equations and simulating the resulting model replicates the initial distorted equilibrium in Figure 14.6(b). The model was algebraically specified, numerically calibrated, and expressed as an MCP using the MPSGE subsystem (Rutherford, 1999) for GAMS (Brooke et al., 1998), and was solved using the PATH solver (Dirkse and Ferris, 1995; Ferris et al., 2000; Ferris and Munson, 2000).

Policy analysis

The policy under consideration is a limit on aggregate CO_2 emissions in the year 2012, which may be analyzed using a three-step procedure. The first step is to establish the link between emissions and the demands for the various fossil fuels solved by the model in monetary terms. For this purpose, we use US EPA (2007) data on the CO_2 emissions associated with the aggregate use of each fuel in 2005, indicated by $\bar{q}_e^{CO_2}$ in Figure 14.6(b). The emission coefficients are computed by dividing this quantity by the aggregate demand for each fossil fuel in the SAM ($\phi_e = \bar{q}_e^{CO_2}/\bar{y}_e$), which enables the calibration run of the model to replicate aggregate CO_2 emissions.

The second step is to project the future baseline emission level in 2012, by simulating the future expansion of the economy and the decline in its CO_2 intensity. Economic growth is modeled by scaling the benchmark endowments of primary factors upward at the average annual growth rate of GDP observed over the 1999–2006 period in the national income and product accounts (2.6 percent). This results in simulated GDP growth of approximately 15 percent from 2005 to 2012. To model the decline in aggregate emission intensity, the coefficients on energy in the model's cost and expenditure functions (α_e and $\beta_{e,j}$) are scaled downward at the average annual rate of decline in the CO_2–GDP ratio over the 1999–2005 period tabulated by EIA (–1.7 percent). This procedure is the equivalent of introducing into the model an index of autonomous energy efficiency improvement (AEEI), which is a popular device for capturing the non-price induced secular decline in the aggregate energy or emissions intensity observed in many economies (see Sue Wing and Eckaus, 2007). Here, its effect is to reduce the simulated aggregate CO_2 intensity by just under 8 percent from 2005 to 2012.

Table 14.2(a) summarizes the characteristics of the no-policy 'business-as-usual' (BAU) economy in 2012. Projected emissions from fossil fuels are 6183 million tons (mt) of CO_2, some 7 percent above 2005 levels, which represents a slightly faster growth of emissions than has been observed since 1999. The bulk of CO_2 emanates from the fossil-fuel electric subsector where the majority of the nation's coal is burned. The other significant contributions to aggregate emissions are made by the 'rest-of-economy' sector, which is responsible for the bulk of petroleum demand, and household consumption, which uses substantial amounts of both petroleum and natural gas.

The third step is to solve the model with a quantity restriction on CO_2 emission as a counterfactual policy scenario. The emission target is loosely based on the proposed Climate Stewardship and Innovation Act of 2007 (S.280/H.R. 620), which seeks to limit annual emissions of a basket of six GHGs to 6,130 mt over the 2012–19 period. As non-CO_2 GHGs are not accounted for within the model, an assumption needs to be made regarding the policy's impact on CO_2. It is simplest to assume that CO_2 emitted from fossil-fuel combustion is limited in the same proportion that fossil CO_2 contributes to aggregate GHG emissions in 2005: 79 percent of the 7260 mt of total GHG emissions on a carbon-equivalent basis (US EPA, 2007). The result is a CO_2 target of 4856 mt, approximately 16 percent below the 2005 emission level and 22 percent below the BAU scenario.

The impacts of the policy are shown in Table 14.2(b). The emission limit induces significantly higher fossil-fuel prices, which are recorded on a gross-of-CO_2 mark-up basis. (Net-of-mark-up fossil-fuel prices decline sharply as a consequence of shrinking demand.) The increase is especially large for coal, whose consumer price almost doubles. Electricity's consumer price rises as well, but only by 9 percent, reflecting both power generators' ability to substitute non-energy intermediate goods and labor and capital for fossil fuels, and the ability of carbon-free electric generators to expand supply. Thus, on a percentage basis the electricity price increase is smaller than the rise in the marginal cost of fossil generation, but is twice as large as the rise in the marginal cost of carbon-free power. Prices of non-energy commodities exhibit a negligible response, while the price of crude oil and gas mining falls with the demand for that sector's output.

Overall, the output of the energy sectors is sharply curtailed. At one extreme, coal production declines by 41 percent, with double-digit declines in the demand for this fuel in every sector. At the other extreme, the generation of electric power declines by a mere 6 percent, with reductions in demand of a similar magnitude in non-energy sectors and three to eight times that in the energy sectors. However, this aggregate picture belies the fact that the fossil-fuel subsector declines by 19 percent, while the carbon-free subsector experiences a massive expansion in its output, which increases by nearly 50 percent. As before, the impact on production in non-energy sectors is very slight, with slight declines in output of less than 1 percent.

The most vigorous CO_2 abatement occurs in coal mining and fossil-fuel electricity generation, while the largest quantities of emissions are reduced by the fossil power and rest-of-economy sectors, with household consumption, transportation, coal mining and petroleum accounting for most of the remaining cuts. For the most part, these reductions have a negative impact on the revenue raised by pre-existing taxes, especially in energy industries. The important exception is electric power, whose output is increased and price is moderated by the expansion of carbon-free generation, but the overall effect

Table 14.2 *The economic impacts of a CO$_2$ emission target*

(a) The no-policy 'business-as-usual' scenario for 2012

	1	2	3	4	5	5(a)	5(b)	6	7	8	Hhold	Total
Prices[a]	0.96	0.95	0.97	0.95	0.96	0.95	0.98	1.00	0.99	1.01	–	–
Activity levels[b]	4.18	15.14	11.25	37.89	33.03	23.61	5.67	100.18	76.54	2293.14	992.61	1386.00[e]
Consumption[b]	0.01	0.00	4.68	9.78	15.78			26.35	18.93	913.36	–	–
Energy demand[b]												
Coal	0.20	0.00	0.00	0.00	2.88	2.88	–	0.24	0.00	0.31	0.01	4.18
Petroleum	0.09	0.14	0.10	4.32	0.54	0.54	–	2.67	5.42	17.04	9.78	37.89
Natural gas	0.00	0.02	0.10	0.29	3.48	3.48	–	0.45	0.07	2.15	4.68	11.25
Electricity	0.03	0.12	0.01	0.22	0.02	0.02	–	1.33	0.32	15.23	15.78	33.03
Tax revenue[b]	0.16	0.75	0.45	0.16	3.62	–	–	1.10	1.95	95.57	–	103.75
Pre-existing	0.16	0.75	0.45	0.16	3.62	–	–	1.10	1.95	95.57	–	103.75
CO$_2$ permits	–											
Emissions[c]	109.39	12.13	18.47	343.88	1945.44	1945.44	–	369.68	399.47	1630.64	1231.74	6183.82

(b) Policy impacts: changes from business-as-usual values (%, unless indicated otherwise)

	1	2	3	4	5	5(a)	5(b)	6	7	8	Hhold	Total
Prices	87.66	-5.78	16.85	11.11	9.19	10.84	4.26	0.25	0.34	-0.35		-0.14[e]
Activity levels	-40.77	-15.92	-13.83	-9.65	-6.06	-19.18	49.16	-0.75	-0.91	-0.10	-0.16	–
Consumption	-27.12	0.00	-7.64	-5.29	-4.46	–	–	-0.29	-0.33	0.01	–	–
Energy demand												
Coal	-66.51	-51.55	-49.24	-46.31	-46.96	-46.96	–	-39.89	-39.95	-39.80	-27.12	-40.77
Oil	-49.06	-26.31	-22.80	-18.35	-19.34	-19.34		-8.59	-8.67	-8.44	-5.29	-9.65
Gas	-51.07	-29.22	-25.85	-21.58	-22.52	-22.52		-12.20	-12.28	-12.06	-7.64	-13.83
Electricity	-48.35	-25.28	-21.71	-17.20	-18.20	-18.20		-7.30	-7.39	-7.15	-4.46	-6.06
Tax revenue	-3.15	-18.73	-11.13	297.52	57.43	57.43		46.56	32.06	2.16	2.01	7.50
Pre-existing	-45.50	-20.78	-16.54	-11.55	2.57			-0.50	-0.57	-0.46	–	-0.66
CO$_2$ permits[d]	42.34	2.05	5.42	309.07	54.86	54.86		47.06	32.63	2.62	2.01f	8.16
Emissions[c]	-65.49	-27.06	-24.65	-18.70	-41.54	-41.54		-19.84	-8.82	-12.08	-6.37	-21.60
Abatement[c]	-71.64	-3.28	-4.55	-64.30	-808.13	-808.13		-73.34	-35.24	-197.00	-78.44	-1335.92

Note: [a] Index: year 2005 = 1.00; [b] 10^{10} 2004 dollars; [c] Million tons CO$_2$; [d] Calculated as a percentage of revenues raised by pre-existing taxes; [e] Aggregate activity level proxied for by GDP; [f] Value of allowance purchases by the representative agent in 10^{10} 2004 dollars (there is no revenue from pre-existing taxes from which a percentage may be calculated).

of the emission target on revenue from benchmark taxes is less than 1 percent. This outcome is in contrast to the recycled revenues from CO_2 allowances, which account for an 8 percent increase in tax revenue over the BAU scenario, and mostly emanate from the electric power, rest-of-economy and final consumption sectors.

Finally, looking at the impact on the economy as a whole, the shadow price on the emission target is modest: $17.50 per ton, GDP falls by 0.14 percent relative to its BAU level, while the decline in aggregate consumption is slightly larger: 0.16 percent, all of which suggest that the near-term macroeconomic costs of the emission target are small. However, both the price of CO_2 and the attendant welfare losses are much smaller than those computed by Paltsev et al. (2007) using the MIT–EPPA model, a large-scale multi-regional simulation that resolves emissions of non-CO_2 GHGs and their abatement possibilities in addition to representing the frictions associated with the 'putty-clay' character of capital adjustments (Paltsev et al., 2005). Exploring these and other sources of divergence helps to shed light on the limitations of the modeling approach pursued thus far, as well as initiate discussion of methods for addressing them which fall under the rubric of advanced topics that space constraints prevent me from dealing with here.

Caveats, and potential remedies

Returning to the black-box critique, it is useful to note that underlying the results in Table 14.2 are several driving forces whose precise effects on the macroeconomic costs of the policy shock have not been explicitly quantified. On one hand, decomposition analysis is a structured method for undertaking this kind of investigation which is gaining popularity because of its ability to accommodate simulations with large numbers of sectors, regions and exogenous parameters (see, for example, Harrison et al., 2000; Paltsev, 2001; Böhringer and Rutherford, 2002). On the other hand, constructing highly stylized maquette models with a simplified structure and few sectors can also go a long way toward making the constituent economic interactions transparent. But this also implies that the present results should be taken with a grain of salt: simplified models such as the CES economy inevitably gloss over important real-world features of the economy that have potentially important implications for the effects of the policy under consideration. Several of these caveats are discussed below.

The first limitation is that consumption is the only price-responsive category of final uses. The constant 'other final demand' vector implies that the economy's net export position and level of investment are both invariant to the emission limit, which is highly unrealistic. Addressing this shortcoming requires the modeler to disaggregate both gross trade flows and investment and model them as endogenous variables, with imports and exports specified as functions of the joint effects of changes in aggregate income and the level of gross-of-carbon-tax domestic prices in relation to world prices, and investment responding to the forward-looking behavior of households and the adjustment of saving and investment behavior to the policy shock. The model can then be re-cast in the format of a small open economy (for example, Harrison et al., 1997), with imports and exports linked by a balance-of-payments constraint, and commodity inputs to production and final uses represented as Armington (1969) composites of imported and domestically produced varieties.

Specifying and calibrating a fully forward-looking CGE model in the complementarity format of equilibrium is too complex an undertaking discuss here, and in any case Lau et al. (2002) provide an excellent introduction to the fundamentals. Recursive dynamic CGE models, which solve for a sequence of static equilibria chained together by intertemporal equations that update the economy's primary factor endowments and adjust the values of key time-varying parameters, have proven far more popular due to their comparative simplicity. The core of these models' dynamic process is an investment equation that uses the values of current-period variables to approximate the theoretically correct intertemporal demand for new capital formation. The realism of the present model could be markedly improved by enabling aggregate investment to adjust endogenously through the incorporation of a similar investment demand scheme.

A second limitation is the model's neglect of the important influences of capital malleability (the ability to adjust the factor proportions of production processes which employ extant capital) and intersectoral capital mobility on the short-run costs of emission constraints (Jacoby and Sue Wing, 1999). At issue is the treatment of capital as a homogeneous factor which is capable of being frictionlessly reallocated as relative prices change, which causes production to exhibit complete reversibility. But in reality, changes in production activity of the magnitude seen in Table 14.2 would likely necessitate the scrapping and retrofit of energy-using capital on a massive scale, incurring substantial costs of adjustment. Such frictions may be captured by designating a portion of each sector's capital input as extant capital which is responsible for the production of output using a fixed input proportions technology. The likely consequence will be a substantial reduction in the mobility of – and returns to – capital, especially in declining sectors, with concomitantly larger abatement costs and reductions in welfare.

A third limitation is that, like capital, labor is modeled as being in inelastic supply. This, combined with the full employment assumption typical of many CGE models, implies that the reduction in the labor demanded by declining fossil-fuel and energy-using sectors cannot result in unemployment. Instead, the wage falls, allowing the labor market to clear and surplus labor to move to other sectors, where it is re-absorbed. But in reality labor is likely to be far less mobile, implying that these types of price and quantity adjustments will occur more slowly, with the appearance of frictional unemployment in the interim. This phenomenon is easily simulated by introducing a labor supply curve into the model, through which the fall in the wage reduces the representative agent's endowment of labor (see, for example, Balistreri, 2002). Depending on the value of the labor supply elasticity the distorted equilibrium may exhibit significant unemployment, but general equilibrium interactions make it difficult to predict whether the welfare loss from an emission limit will be larger or smaller than in the inelastic labor supply case.

Lastly, perhaps the biggest deficiency of the current model is the CES assumption itself. Real-world policy analysis models routinely represent consumers' and producers' substitution possibilities using nested CES functions whose substitution elasticities vary simultaneously among levels of the nesting structure and across sectors. The present model therefore underestimates the degree of intersectoral heterogeneity in substitution possibilities, implying that the results in Table 14.2 are subject to a range of biases in different directions. When faced with these sorts of issues, analysts typically undertake a sensitivity analysis to compare the results of simulations with different combinations of values for the various parameters in their models. However, the application of structured uncertainty analysis techniques that employ empirically derived probability distributions over input parameters (for example, Webster and Cho, 2006) has the potential to dramatically enhance our understanding of the scope and consequences of uncertainties in CGE models' structure and assumptions, and thereby generate robust insights into policies' economic impacts.

8 Summary

This chapter has provided a lucid, rigorous and practically oriented introduction to the fundamentals of computable general equilibrium modeling. The objective has been to demystify CGE models and their use in analyzing energy and climate policies by developing a simple, transparent and comprehensive framework within which to conceptualize their structural underpinnings, numerical parameterization, mechanisms of solution and techniques of application. Beginning with the circular flow of the economy, the logic and rules of social accounting matrices were developed, and it was demonstrated how imposing the axioms of producer and consumer maximization on this framework made it possible to construct a synthetic economy that could then be calibrated on these data. There followed a description of the techniques of numerical calibration and solution techniques, and a discussion of their implications for the uniqueness and stability of the simulated equilibria. The focus then shifted to techniques of application, introducing the kinds of structural modifications that allow CGE models to analyze the economy-wide impacts of various price and quantity distortions that arise in energy and environmental policy, which culminated in a practical demonstration using a realistic numerical example.

Despite the broad swath of territory covered by this survey, space constraints have precluded discussion of many of the methodological tricks of the trade that are standard in CGE analyses of energy and climate policy. In particular, this chapter's closed-economy focus has paid scant attention to important issues of trade closure rules, model calibration in the presence of pre-existing import tariffs and/or export levies, or the specification and calibration of multi-region models which combine SAMs for individual economies with data on interregional trade flows. Hopefully, the base of practical and theoretical knowledge developed here can lay the groundwork for the reader to study these and other advanced topics in applied general equilibrium analysis.

Notes

* This research was supported by the U.S. Department of Energy Office of Science (BER) grants DE-FG02-02ER63484 and DE-FG02-06ER64204, and has benefited from valuable insights by Tom Rutherford.
1. See Arndt et al. (2002), who develop a maximum-entropy data assimilation technique for calibrating substitution elasticities based on auxiliary information on prices and subjective bounds on parameter values.
2. See, for example, Wilcoxen (1988, p. 127, especially footnote 2).
3. Section 5's discussion of the invariance of models' benchmark replication to the values of their substitution parameters figures prominently here. Imagine two static models, each with different substitution elasticities, calibrated so as to reproduce the same benchmark SAM in the absence of policy-induced distortions. An absolute emission limit can be imposed on the first model, and the value of GDP in the resulting distorted equilibrium used to compute an *ex ante* equivalent intensity target. Imposing this target on the first model will yield the same distorted equilibrium, but constraining the second model with this target will have different impacts as a result of the alternative parameterization's effect on GDP.
4. Observe that the revenue raised from all producers is $\sum_{e=1}^{\mathcal{E}} \rho \tau^{RPS} \varepsilon_e y_e$, while that received by renewable producers is $\sum_{e \in \mathcal{E}^R} \tau^{RPS} \varepsilon_e y_e$. Equating these expressions and canceling τ^{RPS} on both sides of the resulting expression yields the rationing constraint in the text. The implication is that the marginal financing charge exhibits complementary slackness with respect to the RPS constraint: the latter is either binding and $\tau^{RPS} > 0$, or it is non-binding and $\tau^{RPS} = 0$.

5. For details see, for example, Reinert and Roland-Holst (1992). Gabriel Medeiros of the Bureau of Economic Analysis provided sterling assistance with the procedure.
6. The column disaggregation of the sector was performed very simply: 28.4 percent of labor, capital and non-energy intermediate inputs, as well as all of the primary energy resource inputs, were allocated to carbon-free electricity generation, while the remaining inputs of intermediate goods and primary factors were allocated to fossil-fuel electricity generation. Sue Wing (2008) develops a more sophisticated method of disaggregating individual technologies from an aggregate economic sector.

References

Armington, P.S. (1969), 'A theory of demand for products distinguished by place of production', IMF Staff Papers, **16** (1), 170–201.
Arndt, C., S. Robinson and F. Tarp (2002), 'Parameter estimation for a computable general equilibrium model: a maximum entropy approach', *Economic Modelling*, **19** (3), 375–98.
Balistreri, E.J. (2002), 'Operationalizing equilibrium unemployment: a general equilibrium external economies approach', *Journal of Economic Dynamics and Control*, **26**, 347–74.
Baron, R. and Y. Serret (2002), 'Renewable energy certificates: trading instruments for the promotion of renewable energy', in *Implementing Domestic Tradeable Permits: Recent Developments and Future Challenges*, OECD Proceedings, Paris: OECD, pp. 105–40.
Bergman, L. (2005), 'CGE modeling of environmental policy and resource management', in K.-G. Maler and J.R. Vincent (eds), *Handbook of Environmental Economics*, Vol. 3, Amsterdam: Elsevier, pp. 1273–306.
Bhattacharyya, S.C. (1996), 'Applied general equilibrium models for energy studies: a survey', *Energy Economics*, **18**, 145–64.
Böhringer, C. and T.F. Rutherford (2002), 'Carbon abatement and international spillovers', *Environmental and Resource Economics*, **22** (3), 391–417.
Böhringer, C., T.F. Rutherford and W. Wiegard (2003), 'Computable general equilibrium analysis: opening a black box', Discussion Paper No. 03-56, ZEW, Mannheim, Germany.
Brooke, A., D. Kendrick, A. Meeraus and R. Raman (1998), *GAMS: A User's Guide*, Washington, DC: GAMS Development Corp.
Conrad, K. (1999), 'Computable general equilibrium models for environmental economics and policy analysis', in J. van den Bergh (ed.), *Handbook of Environmental and Resource Economics*, Cheltenham, UK and Northampton, MA, USA: Edward Elgar, pp. 1061–87.
Conrad, K. (2001), 'Computable general equilibrium models in environmental and resource economics', in T. Tietenberg and H. Folmer (eds), *The International Yearbook of Environmental and Resource Economics 2002/2003*, Cheltenham, UK and Northampton, MA, USA: Edward Elgar, pp. 66–114.
Cottle, R.W., J.-S. Pang and R.E. Stone (1992), *The Linear Complementarity Problem*, Boston, MA: Academic Press.
Dawkins, C., T. Srinivasan and J. Whalley (2001), 'Calibration', in J. Heckman and E. Leamer (eds), *Handbook of Econometrics*, Vol. 5, Amsterdam: Elsevier Science, pp. 3653–703.
Dirkse, S.P. and M.C. Ferris (1995), 'The PATH solver: a non-monotone stabilization scheme for mixed complementarity problems', *Optimization Methods and Software*, **5**, 123–56.
Eaves, B.C. and K. Schmedders (1999), 'General equilibrium models and homotopy methods', *Journal of Economic Dynamics and Control*, **23**, 1249–79.
Ellerman, A.D. and I. Sue Wing (2003), 'Absolute vs. intensity-based emission caps', *Climate Policy*, **3** (Supplement 2), S7–S20.
Ferris, M.C. and C. Kanzow (2002), 'Complementarity and related problems', in P. Pardalos and M. Resende (eds), *Handbook of Applied Optimization*, New York: Oxford University Press, pp. 514–30.
Ferris, M.C. and T.S. Munson (2000), 'Complementarity problems in GAMS and the PATH solver', *Journal of Economic Dynamics and Control*, **24**, 165–88.
Ferris, M.C., T.S. Munson and D. Ralph (2000), 'A homotopy method for mixed complementarity problems based on the PATH solver', in D. Griffiths and G. Watson (eds), *Numerical Analysis 1999*, London: Chapman & Hall, pp. 143–67.
Ferris, M.C. and J.-S. Pang (1997), 'Engineering and economic applications of complementarity problems', *SIAM Review*, **39** (4), 669–713.
Fisher-Vanden, K. and M.S. Ho (2007), 'How do market reforms affect China's responsiveness to environmental policy?', *Journal of Development Economics*, **82** (1), 200–233.
Garcia, C. and W.I. Zangwill (1981), *Pathways to Solutions, Fixed Points, and Equilibria*, Englewood Cliffs, NJ: Prentice-Hall.
Goulder, L.H. (1995), 'Effects of carbon taxes in an economy with prior tax distortions: an intertemporal general equilibrium analysis', *Journal of Environmental Economics and Management*, **29**, 271–97.

Goulder, L.H. (ed.) (2002), *Environmental Policy Making in Economies with Prior Tax Distortions*, Cheltenham, UK and Northampton, MA, USA: Edward Elgar.

Harrison, W.J., J.M. Horridge and K. Pearson (2000), 'Decomposing simulation results with respect to exogenous shocks', *Computational Economics*, **15**, 227–49.

Harrison, G.W., T.F. Rutherford and D.G. Tarr (1997), 'Quantifying the Uruguay round', *Economic Journal*, **107**, 1405–30.

Hines, J.R. (1999), 'Three sides of Harberger triangles', *Journal of Economic Perspectives*, **13**, 167–88.

Hosoe, N. (2000), 'Dependency of simulation results on the choice of numeraire', *Applied Economics Letters*, **7**, 475–77.

Jacoby, H.D. and I. Sue Wing (1999), 'Adjustment time, capital malleability, and policy cost', *The Energy Journal Special Issue: The Costs of the Kyoto Protocol: A Multi-Model Evaluation*, 73–92.

Jorgenson, D.W. (1984), 'Econometric methods for applied general equilibrium analysis', in H. Scarf and J.B. Shoven (eds), *Applied General Equilibrium Analysis*, Cambridge: Cambridge University Press, pp. 139–207.

Kehoe, P.J. and T.J. Kehoe (1995), 'A primer on static applied general equilibrium models', in Kehoe and Kehoe (eds), *Modeling North American Economic Integration*, Boston, MA: Kluwer Academic, pp. 1–31.

Kehoe, T.J. (1991), 'Computation and multiplicity of equilibria', in W. Hildenbrand and H. Sonnenschein (eds), *Handbook of Mathematical Economics*, Vol. IV, Amsterdam: North-Holland, pp. 2049–143.

Kehoe, T.J. (1998a), 'Social accounting matrices and applied general equilibrium models', in I. Begg and S. Henry (eds), *Applied Economics and Public Policy*, Cambridge: Cambridge University Press, pp. 59–87.

Kehoe, T.J. (1998b), 'Uniqueness and stability', in A.P. Kirman (ed.), *Elements of General Equilibrium Analysis*, Oxford: Basil Blackwell, pp. 38–87.

King, B. (1985), 'What is a SAM?', in J. Pyatt and J. Round (eds), *Social Accounting Matrices: A Basis for Planning*, Washington, DC: World Bank, pp. 1–15.

Lau, M., A. Pahlke and T. Rutherford (2002), 'Approximating infinite-horizon models in a complementarity format: a primer in dynamic general equilibrium analysis', *Journal of Economic Dynamics and Control*, **26**, 577–609.

Lutton, T. and M. LeBlanc (1984), 'A comparison of multivariate logit and translog models for energy and nonenergy input cost share analysis', *The Energy Journal*, **5** (4), 45–54.

Mathiesen, L. (1985a), 'Computation of economic equilibria by a sequence of linear complementarity problems', *Mathematical Programming Study*, **23**, 144–62.

Mathiesen, L. (1985b), 'Computational experience in solving equilibrium models by a sequence of linear complementarity problems', *Operations Research*, **33**, 1225–50.

McKibbin, W. and P.J. Wilcoxen (1998), 'The theoretical and empirical structure of the G-cubed model', *Economic Modelling*, **16** (1), 123–48.

McKitrick, R.R. (1998), 'The econometric critique of applied general equilibrium modelling: the role of functional forms', *Economic Modelling*, **15**, 543–73.

Paltsev, S. (2001), 'The Kyoto Protocol: regional and sectoral contributions to the carbon leakage', *The Energy Journal*, **22**, 53–79.

Paltsev, S. (2004), 'Moving from static to dynamic general equilibrium economic models (notes for a beginner in MPSGE)', Technical Note No. 4, MIT Joint Program on the Science and Policy of Global Change, Cambridge, MA.

Paltsev, S., J. Reilly, H. Jacoby, R. Eckaus, J. McFarland, M. Sarofim, M. Asadoorian and M. Babiker (2005), 'The MIT emissions prediction and policy analysis (EPPA) model: Version 4', Report No. 125, MIT Joint Program on the Science and Policy of Global Change, Cambridge, MA.

Paltsev, S., J.M. Reilly, H.D. Jacoby, A.C. Gurgel, G.E. Metcalf, A.P. Sokolov and J.F. Holak (2007), 'Assessment of U.S. cap-and-trade proposals', Working Paper No. 13176, National Bureau of Economic Research, Cambridge, MA.

Panagariya, A. and R. Duttagupta (2001), 'The "gains" from preferential trade liberalization in the CGE models: where do they come from?', in S. Lahiri (ed.), *Regionalism and Globalization: Theory and Practice*, London: Routledge, pp. 39–60.

Perroni, C. and T.F. Rutherford (1998), 'A comparison of the performance of flexible functional forms for use in applied general equilibrium modelling', *Computational Economics*, **11** (3), 245–63.

Reinert, K.A. and D.W. Roland-Holst (1992), 'A detailed social accounting matrix for the USA, 1988', *Economic Systems Research*, **4**, 173–87.

Rutherford, T.F. (1987), 'Implementational issues and computational performance solving applied general equilibrium models with SLCP', Cowles Foundation Discussion Paper No. 837, Yale University, New Haven, CT.

Rutherford, T.F. (1995), 'Extensions of GAMS for complementarity problems arising in applied economic analysis', *Journal of Economic Dynamics and Control*, **19**, 1299–324.

Rutherford, T.F. (1999), 'Applied general equilibrium modeling with MPSGE as a GAMS subsystem: an overview of the modeling framework and syntax', *Computational Economics*, **14**, 1–46.

Shoven, J.B. and J.L. Whalley (1984), 'Applied general equilibrium models of taxation and international trade: an introduction and survey', *Journal of Economic Literature*, **22**, 1007–51.
Sue Wing, I. (2001), 'Induced Technical Change in CGE Models for Climate Policy Analysis', PhD thesis, Massachusetts Institute of Technology, Cambridge, MA.
Sue Wing, I. (2004), 'Computable general equilibrium models and their use in economy-wide policy analysis', Technical Note No. 6, MIT Joint Program on the Science and Policy of Global Change, Cambridge, MA.
Sue Wing, I. (2008), 'The synthesis of bottom-up and top-down approaches to climate policy modeling: electric power technology detail in a social accounting framework', *Energy Economics*, **30**, 547–73.
Sue Wing, I. and R.S. Eckaus (2007), 'The decline in U.S. energy intensity: its origins and implications for long-run CO_2 emission projections', *Energy Policy*, **35**, 5267–86.
US EPA (2007), *Inventory of U.S. Greenhouse Gas Emissions and Sinks: 1990–2005*, Washington, DC: Government Printing Office.
Varian, H.R. (1992), *Microeconomic Analysis*, New York: Norton.
Webster, M. and C.-H. Cho (2006), 'Analysis of variability and correlation in long-term economic growth rates', *Energy Economics*, **28**, 653–66.
Wilcoxen, P.J. (1988), 'The Effects of Environmental Regulation and Energy Prices on U.S. Economic Performance', PhD thesis, Harvard University, Cambridge MA.

15 Energy–economy–environment modelling: a survey
Claudia Kemfert and Truong Truong

1 Introduction

Concern about fossil-fuel resource depletion in the early 1970s has led to the development of theoretical and applied economic models of energy–economy linkages with a detailed representation of the energy market. Pioneering energy–economy modelling efforts focused primarily on the representation of scarce resources such as oil and its impact on world economies. More recently, not only the scarcity of energy resources, but also other natural resources in the environment played a major role in economic modelling. The complexity of models has increased considerably, especially in areas relating to global environmental issues such as acid rain, ozone depletion and climate change. Take the issue of climate change as an example. Here, it is generally agreed (or assumed) that one of the important cause of this likely phenomenon is anthropogenic greenhouse gas (GHG) emissions which originate mainly from fossil-fuel consumption. To prevent or mitigate against this likely event, integrated energy–environmental strategies and policies are required which need to take into account the complex interactions between climate, ecological and economic systems. Such integrated policies and strategies are often studied within the framework of the so-called integrated assessment modelling (IAM) approach.[1] Existing literature on IAM focuses mainly on a comparison of modelling results.[2] The aim of this chapter is to provide an overview of the theoretical backgrounds, the methodologies and model designs. Section 2 explains the theories and general methodologies of different models, and Section 3 looks at applied models. Section 4 considers some specific issues such as energy substitutability and the role of energy and environment resources in economic models, as well as providing a brief survey of existing major energy–economy–environment models, and Section 5 concludes.

2 Economic Theories

Economists usually distinguish between two major economic theories: *neoclassical* and *neo-Keynesian*. Neoclassical economic theory covers the microeconomic decisions of individuals and investigates the distribution and allocation of scarce resources towards alternative objectives under the assumption of fixed resource constraints and market clearance. Consumers maximise their utilities subject to budget constraints and firms maximise their profits under costs constraints. At equilibrium, the marginal utilities of consumption or marginal products of factors are equal to their relative prices. Substitution processes are induced by changes in relative prices. Clearance in all markets is reached by the adjustment of market prices. This is the theory of general equilibrium where the primary focus is on the microeconomic allocation of scarce resources among alternative uses so as to maximise social welfare. There are generally four different markets in which the theory seeks to explain their equilibrium positions: goods market, labour market, capital market and money market. In the labour market, it is assumed that both labour supply and demand are influenced by real wages. Full employment is then reached when the real wage adjusts so as to balance supply and demand. The capital market is governed by investment decisions of firms, and savings decisions of households. The capital market clears when the rate of interest – which influences investment and savings decisions of firms and households – adjusts so as to balance supply (savings) and demand (investment). Finally, equilibrium in the money market is also achieved via the adjustment of the market rate of interest which influences money demand, and given a particular level of money supply which is often assumed to be determined exogenously by the monetary authority. General equilibrium is then defined as the situation when all markets clear. Without government intervention, general equilibrium can be achieved if we assume the working of the so-called 'invisible hands of the markets'. In contrast, in neo-Keynesian theory, it is believed that general market equilibrium cannot always be achieved because of the 'inflexibility' or 'stickiness' of money wages (in the downward direction) in the labour market. This also makes real wages inflexible, and labour demand, therefore, cannot always adjust to the level of labour supply. Unemployment (dis-equilibrium) therefore can exist in the labour market. To represent this dis-equilibrium situation in a 'general equilibrium' model, a 'slack' variable is introduced, which takes on a non-zero value whenever there exists such a dis-equilibrium gap between supply and demand.

Most general equilibrium models are based on neoclassical theory. In some cases, however, elements of neo-Keynesian theory can also be introduced into a general equilibrium model via the use of 'slack' variables as mentioned above. Robinson (2006) describes the mixture of theories used in computable general equilibrium (CGE) models under three headings: (i) the Fundamentalist school, (ii) the Bahá'i school, and (iii) the Ecumenical school. Under the Fundamentalist school, strict neoclassical (or Walrasian) economic theory applies, this means that equilibrium is assumed for the goods, labour, and capital markets. The money market is often not specified in a Walrasian model, which is concerned only with physical flows and relative prices. To determine the money market equilibrium and the absolute level of prices, one has to resort to a separate macroeconomic model. This macroeconomic model specifies the money market variables and their relation to other macroeconomic variables such as aggregate consumption, investment, savings, government spending and taxation. There is the issue of how to relate the levels of these macroeconomic variables to the levels of the microeconomic variables specified in the Walrasian model. Under the Fundamentalist school, this issue does not seem to be addressed. Under the Bahá'i school, the issue is avoided to some extent by the insertion of certain elements of the Keynesian (or other types of) macroeconomic model directly into the Walrasian equilibrium model itself. This, however, decreases the transparency or purity of the Walrasian model. Finally, under the Ecumenical school, where the maxim is 'Render unto Walras the things which are Walras, and unto Keynes the things which are Keynes', a (neoclassical) CGE model can be kept separate and distinct from a Keynesian (or other types of) macroeconomic financial model. An attempt is then made to 'link' the two models together, for example, by allowing for some variables to be specified as exogenous in one model but endogenous in the other (see, for example,

Powell 1981; Tyson and Robinson 1983). According to Robinson, in the past decade, the influence of the Fundamentalist school has declined, while that of the Bahá'i school and the Ecumenical school has grown.

General equilibrium models are often static or only 'recursively' dynamic (static results of one time period are fed into the database of the next time period while the behaviours of individual decision makers remain 'myopic'). Intertemporal or truly dynamic general equilibrium models are built only for small models with a limited number of sectors, regions, and/or time periods because of the extra computational burden associated with intertemporal decision. Typically, CGE models assume an infinitely lived consumer (or social planner) who optimises an intertemporal utility (or social welfare) function subject to some resource constraints (such as population growth, energy supply), and under conditions of certainty, competitive markets, and constant returns to scale in production (for example, Ramsey infinite-horizon optimisation model). The model often employs an aggregate production function that includes only a few inputs such as labour, capital and perhaps a natural resource input such as energy. In contrast, there are overlapping generation (OLG) models that allow for different consumers of different generations who have finite lifetimes (see, for example, Stephan et al. 1997; Howarth 1998; Gerlagh and van der Zwaan 2001). Different generations in different time periods can then trade with each other. The results of OLG models do not often coincide with those of the Ramsey models, which also means that Pareto optimality (which is achievable in a Ramsey model) may not necessarily be achieved in an OLG model.

3 Applied Models

Applied models can be classified according to the purpose for which they are constructed. For example, there is a distinction between *forecasting* and *evaluation* (or *simulation*) models. Forecasting models are often built around econometric studies that use historical data and are employed to extrapolate historical trends into the future. Simulation models, on the other hand, are used to address the 'what if' policy question. To do this, a 'business as usual' or reference scenario is first constructed with certain assumptions about major economic variables such as population growth, physical resources growth, substitution elasticities, and rates of technical progress. Next, a particular policy scenario is constructed which allows for certain key economic variables to be varied. The results from both the policy and the reference scenarios are then compared which will help to shed light on the effects of the changes in the key economic variables.

Applied models can also be classified according the geographic or time scale of analysis. For example, global models are those that include information on many regions or nations and used to analyse the economic relations or reactions among them at a highly aggregate level. Regional models focus primarily on a specific region such as Europe or Asia, while national models look at economic relations within particular countries. Many applied models concentrate the analysis on one or only a few sectors within an economy, while others cover many sectors. Single-sector models (or models with a few sectors) are used to analyse macroeconomic issues such as optimal growth or optimal resource extraction while multi-sector models are used for the analysis of microeconomic issues such as structural change or distributional impacts of trade and tax reforms. On the time scale, global climate impact models often cover a long time horizon (at least 50 years), while other economic structural change models cover a medium term of 5 to 10 years. Short-term impact or forecasting models cover a period of 1 to 5 years.

Finally, applied models are also classified according to the level of aggregation and the theoretical approaches being used. For example, 'top-down' models look at the aggregate energy–economy–environmental linkages from the perspective of at the national, regional, or global economy as a whole. In contrast, 'bottom-up' models look at the issues from the perspective of a specific sector (such as transport, or electricity generation) and contain more details on various activities or technologies being used in this sector than top-down models. Bottom-up models often use the mathematical techniques of linear or nonlinear programming for their analysis, whereas top-down models often employ a highly aggregate production function approach. Different approaches or methods of analysis can lead to quite different results (Hourcade et al. 1996). For example, in relation to the issue of energy efficiency and substitution, top-down models tend to produce results which are less optimistic than those from bottom-up models. This can be partly explained by the fact that top-down models often include *general* equilibrium feedbacks (which implies that indirect costs are taken into account) whereas bottom-up models do not (Grubb et al. 1993). The 'partial equilibrium' nature of bottom-up models also constitutes one of their inherent weaknesses, and therefore, to overcome this, bottom-up models are often linked to a top-down model in so-called 'hybrid' approaches. One technique for linking the two types of model is to allow for certain variables to be defined as exogenous in one model but then endogenously determined within the other. The passing of information from one model to the other can be carried out either sequentially and iteratively until some criteria of 'convergence' is achieved within both models (this is called a 'soft link'), or simultaneously – perhaps by 'embedding' the bottom-up model within the top-down model itself (see, for example, Böhringer and Löschel 2006) (which is called a 'hard link'). The hard-link approach has the advantage of guaranteeing full consistency between the results of both models, but it also presents greater difficulty in terms of theory development as well as computational techniques. Hence the technique is not very often employed, especially when the models are large. In practice, modellers are content with just some 'soft links', or even using the results of one model (bottom up) to generate information that is then used to estimate certain key parameters (such as the elasticities of substitution) which will be employed in the other (top-down) model.

Depending on the type of model being constructed, the data used are also different. Forecasting models often employ time-series data, whereas impact studies models use input–output data with parameters (such as elasticities of substitution) estimated from either cross-sectional and/or time-series data. Data reliability and consistency is an important issue for large-scale models. For example, with global economic models requiring data (input–output, trade data) coming from different countries, there is a need to harmonise and reconcile these different databases into a consistent set (see, for example, Hertel 1999). Increasingly, energy–economy–environment modelling also requires the compilation of 'physical flows' information (such as energy usage and emissions data in physical units) in parallel with traditional economic (value flow) data (such as input–output or national account data). The harmonisation and reconciliation of physical (material-balanced) data with economic (value-balanced) data presents a more difficult challenge, conceptually as well as empirically, than does the harmonisation and reconciliation of different databases from different regions but of the same type, that is, either physical, or economic, data.

4 The Role of Energy and the Environment in Economic Models

Traditional energy–economy linkage approach

Mainstream neoclassical economics looks at energy and the environment as 'inputs' into consumption or production activities. Energy is an input produced from natural resources (such as fossil fuels), and the environment is also considered as an 'input' in the sense that it can act as a 'sink' for production activity wastes. The limited supply and non-renewable nature of some of the energy resources can put a limit on the capacity of the economy to sustain growth in the long term. The natural environment also has a limited capacity to absorb 'wastes' from economic activities and therefore this can act as a constraint on long-term sustainable economic growth. One of the objectives of energy–economy–environment modelling is to find out the limits (if any) to economic growth in the long term, stemming from limited energy and environmental resources.

Consider the following aggregate production function typically used in a neoclassical top-down model:

$$X = f(K, L, M, E, N);\tag{15.1}$$

where X is gross output, K is capital, L is labour, M is non-energy intermediate inputs ('materials'), E indicates fuel or energy inputs, and N is the environment input. In most cases E is an aggregate of various fossil and non-fossil fuels. A typical top-down model may also consist of many sectors with each being represented by a production function of the type described by (15.1). For simplicity, we assume here that there is only one sector; hence X can be considered as the gross national output of the economy. To simplify the production function (15.1) further in order to concentrate on the critical issues, we assume that capital, labour, and non-energy material inputs can be combined into a single aggregate factor so that (15.1) is simplified into:

$$X = f(K, E, N; A),\tag{15.2}$$

where K stands for the composite capital–labour–material input, and A is the technological change parameter.

Assume that output X is used for consumption and also for investment. Consumption generates welfare whereas investment is used to add to the stock of human-made capital K (investment for growth) and/or to 'induce' technological change (a change to the parameter A). For simplicity, we consider here only investment for growth,[3] that is,

$$\dot{K}(t) = X(t) - C(t).\tag{15.3}$$

Here, $C(t)$ is consumption, and a dot ($\cdot$) over a variable denotes the rate of change over time, that is, $\dot{K}(t) = dK/dt$. Constraint on resource extraction is described by the following equations:

$$\dot{R}(t) = -E(t), R(0) = R_0; \ R(t) \geq 0,$$ (15.4)

with R being the energy resource stock, which is non-renewable and in fixed supply of R_0 at time $t = 0$. The rate of extraction of the energy resource, that is, $-\dot{R}(t)$, is determined by the rate of energy usage in production activities, that is, $E(t)$.

In the 'traditional' energy–economy (E^2) linkage approach, the environment variable N is not considered explicitly, or equivalently; it is assumed to be a 'free' resource, that is, one with zero cost, hence its presence in the production function (15.2) can in fact be ignored. The objective of the economy then is simply to maximise the following inter-temporal welfare function:

$$W = \int_0^\infty \left[\frac{1}{1 - 1/\sigma} C(t)^{1 - 1/\sigma} \right] e^{-\rho t} dt,$$ (15.5)

subject to the production function (15.2) and the constraints (15.3)–(15.4). The parameter σ in equation (15.5) stands for the inter-temporal elasticity of utility substitution, and ρ is the discount rate. In this standard approach, the focus of attention is on the division of output X between consumption and investment activities so as to maximise welfare W. The main issue here is the optimal rate of (energy) resource depletion, to sustain economic growth and consumption in the long term. It turns out that one of the crucial parameters that will determine the answer to this question of sustainable growth for the economy is the elasticity of substitution between K and E. If this substitution elasticity is greater than or equal to one, then sustainable economic growth and consumption is achievable even if the energy resource is in fixed supply. This can be explained as follows: if human-made capital K can be made to replace the use of natural resource E and the process can continue without limit and also without diminishing returns, then so long as part of the current production output is put aside to build up the capital stock K, this can then be used in the future to 'substitute' for part of the natural energy resource stock which is now being depleted. Future economic growth and consumption therefore can be sustained even if the supply of energy resource is limited. When the substitution elasticity is less than one, this implies that there are diminishing returns in the process of substitution of human-made capital K for natural resource E. In this case, sustainable economic growth may still be achievable if technological progress can be made to 'compensate' for the effect of diminishing returns. If, however, both the elasticity of K–E substitution is less than one (diminishing returns) and technological progress is not sufficient to compensate for this effect, then long-term economic growth and consumption will not be sustainable due to the limited supply of E.

Empirical estimation of the K–E substitution elasticity

Empirical evidence on the value of the K–E substitution elasticity has been rather mixed (Berndt and Wood 1979; Apostolakis 1990). Estimated values of this parameter have tended to depend not only on the level of aggregation, but also on the type of data used and the specification of the empirical production function. First, on the issue of aggregation, it is now recognised that the estimated value of the K–E substitution elasticity can be highly dependent on the level of aggregation used (for example, whether we look at sectoral or national data). This is partly explained by the fact that the potential for energy substitution is less at the aggregate level of the national economy than at the microeconomic level of a household or a sector. At the microeconomic level, estimation of the potential for energy savings and substitution often does not take into account the 'indirect costs'. For example, home insulation at the household level may directly substitute for heating fuel, but this also involves some indirect (energy) costs (associated with the manufacturing of the insulation materials themselves). These indirect costs are taken into account only at the aggregate national economy level (Stern 1997; Stern and Cleveland 2004). Furthermore, general equilibrium feedback effects (also called the 'rebound' effects; see, for example, Allan et al. 2007; Sorrell 2007) are often not taken into consideration at the microeconomic level. People who save energy in one activity (home insulation) may end up spending the savings on another activity (for example, increased travel) due to the income as well as substitution effects, and these effects are considered only at the aggregate sectoral or national economy levels. In some cases, the rebound effects may even be greater than the initial savings in energy consumption. This is called a 'backfire' which results in a *net increase* in total energy usage rather than a decrease (Khazzoom 1980; Brookes 1990; Allan et al. 2007). To take into account the problem of the variability of the estimated *K–E* substitution elasticity with the level of aggregation, therefore, one solution is to estimate this parameter at a microeconomic level and then use such parameters also at a microeconomic level in a multi-sector general equilibrium model in which important inter-sectoral linkages can be adequately taken account of. This is preferable to the estimation of such elasticities at a highly disaggregate level and then using it in a highly aggregate model, or vice versa.

The next issue is the variability of the empirically estimated *K–E* elasticity of substitution with the type of data used (times series or cross-section). Originally, this was thought to imply that capital and energy are substitutes in the long run (cross-section data) and complements in the short run (time-series data). However, in view of the recent literature on cointegration, this interpretation – that time-series regressions in levels represent short-run results – is now no longer considered to be valid. The empirical estimation method therefore needs to be revaluated and the interpretation of the estimated parameters also needs to be re-examined (Stern and Cleveland 2004).

A third issue is the variability of the empirically estimated elasticity of substitution between *K* and *E* with the form and specification of the production function used (in particular, the question of whether non-energy material is included in the production function as a separate factor or not; see Berndt and Wood 1979; Frondel and Schmidt 2002). From a theoretical as well as empirical viewpoint, it seems that non-energy material needs to be included in any estimation function because it is an important input in most economic activities, and also because it is often explicitly considered in most applied energy–economy models.

A final issue which is more difficult to resolve from both a theoretical as well as empirical viewpoint, is the fact that it is now well recognised that there are not one but several different concepts of 'substitution elasticities' which can be used to refer to the 'ease of substitution' (or otherwise) between a human-made factor of production (*K*) and a natural resource (*E*) (see, for example, Blackorby and Russell 1989; Stern 2004). Theoretically, this issue goes beyond the problem of mere definition and can involve a fundamental debate about the appropriate role of the energy in economic activities (see the discussion on the ecological approach, below). Empirically, this means that the estimated elasticity needs to be clearly defined and accurately identified. An exhaustive study on this issue (Stern 2004, p. 29) has in fact come to the conclusion that 'capital and energy are at best weak substitutes and possibly are complements'. This statement implies that, using the neoclassical approach, sustainable economic growth in the long term for an economy which is dependent on energy as an important input in its activities is at best achievable but only with substantial technological progress regarding energy efficiency and energy substitution.

The addition of an environmental resource constraint

In contrast to the traditional energy–economy linkage approach, where the role of the environment variable N in economic activities is not explicitly taken into account, in more recent energy–economy–environment (E^3) linkage approaches, the role of this variable is now taken explicitly into consideration and given an importance equal to that of the energy resource variable E. The fact that this environmental resource is also in fixed supply is recognised by adding an additional constraint to the list of constraints (previously considered under equation (15.4)):

$$N(t) = eE(t); \dot{S}(t) = N(t); S(T) \leq \bar{S}, \tag{15.6}$$

where e is the pollution or environmental usage coefficient (for example, GHG emission coefficient per unit of energy used), S is the accumulated stock of pollution, that is, of the environmental resource (clean air) used up, and $\bar{S}$ is some kind of limit to the depletion of this environmental resource at some future time $t = T$ so as to avoid irreversible damage to this environment. For simplicity, we have assumed that the environment variable (the flow variable $N(t)$ or the stock variable $S(t)$), does not enter into the welfare function W directly but acts only as a constraint on economic activities. This allows us to ignore the *direct* environmental impacts on human welfare (for example, direct impacts of air pollution or climate change on human health and human properties) and consider only the indirect effects (that is, losses in production activities such as indicated by a slowdown in economic growth, or increased production costs such as due to increased abatement activities). The use of this simplified approach also implies that the problem considered here is not a full benefit–cost analysis (BCA),[4] but only a 'cost-effectiveness' study of the least cost method for achieving a particular environmental objective (such as that represented by the constraint $S(T) \leq \bar{S}$ in equation (15.6) above).[5]

Endogenous (or induced)[6] technological change

So far, the issue of investment is considered only in relation to the question of capital accumulation, and this accumulation is viewed in the neoclassical context of the use of a human-made capital to 'substitute' for the depletion of a natural capital, such as the energy stock. As there may be diminishing returns in this process of substitution, and unless there is sufficient technological improvement to compensate for this effect, long-term economic growth and consumption may not be sustainable (see the traditional linkage approach, above). To 'induce' technological improvement, part of the investment expenditure may be devoted towards the objective of research and development (R&D) to increase the 'stock of human knowledge' H, rather than the stock of physical capital K. This stock of human knowledge can then be utilised to improve on the technology of production (that is, on productivity) which is represented by the parameter A in equation (15.2). For simplicity of exposition, we have described 'technological change' as though it can be captured by a single parameter A. In actual fact, there may be more than one type of technological change. For example, there can be a *Hicks-neutral* technological change that affects the use of all inputs without bias. There can also be an *energy-specific* (or energy-augmented) technological change that affects (improves upon) the use of E only; and finally, there can also be an *environment-specific* technological change that improves upon the use of the environment resource N. Each of these technological change components can be induced by a different 'type' of investment, and therefore, to distinguish between these different types of technological changes and different components of investments relating to these changes, we use a subscript 'i' where $i = \{H, E, N\}$ to indicate the types of technological changes (Hicks-neutral, energy-specific and environment-specific) as well as the types of investment relating to (or 'inducing') these technological changes. Equation (15.3) can now be modified to:

$$\dot{K}(t) = X(t) - C(t) - \sum_{i=\{H,E,N\}} I_i(t). \tag{15.3'}$$

The 'induced technological change' equations can then in general be described as:

$$A_i(t) = f_i[I_i(t)] \quad i = \{H, E, N\}, \tag{15.7}$$

that is, the technological change or 'productivity' parameter A_i is a function $f_i(\cdot)$ of the investment level I_i. For example, if we consider only an energy-augmented (or energy-efficiency) technological improvement, we can assume an 'induced technological change' equation as follows:[7]

$$A_E(t) = E(t)/X(t)$$

$$\dot{A}_E(t)/A_E(t) = \alpha[I_E(t)/E(t)]^\gamma. \tag{15.8}$$

Here, the technology parameter A_E stands for the energy intensity of production. The rate of change of this intensity, that is $\dot{A}_E(t)/A_E(t)$, is seen to be related to the level of energy-specific investment I_E (relative to the total level of energy usage E). The parameters α and γ are to be calibrated so that the function (15.8) can fit with empirical data.

Another type of induced technological change can be described as 'learning by doing' (Arrow 1962). The 'doing' here is measured, for example, by the cumulative volume of production, and the technological change is measured in terms of the reduction in unit cost $c(t)$ at time t relative to initial unit cost $c(0)$:

$$c(t)/c(0) = \left[\sum_{t=0}^{t} X(t)/X(0) \right]^\beta. \tag{15.9}$$

The parameter β indicates how fast unit cost will decrease as the 'volume' of learning indicated through the cumulative volume of production increases. Typically, the value of β is estimated from empirical studies, and it has been found that the value of 2^β (also called the 'progress ratio' because it indicates how much the unit cost will be reduced when the volume of cumulative production is doubled) is in the range of 0.75–0.95, with the smaller value (faster cost reductions) being associated with relatively immature technologies, and larger value with more mature technologies (see Boston Consulting Group 1968; Rivers and Jaccard 2006).

Other more sophisticated approaches to the specification of 'induced technological change' function can also be used. For example, Sue Wing (2006), and Sue Wing and Popp (2006), use the investment I_E to accumulate the stock of human capital H and then use the service of H to induce technological change via a production process where H can be used as an input, just like any other economic inputs. This means that human capital (knowledge) H can be used to replace (that is, substitute for) other *physical* economic or natural inputs, and this implies a reduction in physical inputs per unit of output (that is, improvement in efficiency).

Brief survey of models using induced technological change for climate policy studies
Induced technological change is an important factor in studies that look at the impacts and the cost-effectiveness of climate policy. Given this importance, in this subsection we give a brief survey of the many models that include the use of induced technological change in their studies of climate policy. The survey is not exhaustive as the objective is simply to give a broad overview of the types of models used and their results.

We start with econometric models. These include models such as E3ME (Lee et al. 1990) or WARM (Carraro and Galeotti 1997) which incorporate simple approaches of induced technological change. IAMs such as ICAM3 (Dowlatabadi 1998) use more sophisticated approaches of modelling induced technological changes. Macroeconomic and general equilibrium models such as DICE (R&DICE, ENTICE) (Nordhaus 1999; Popp 2004) and WIAGEM (Kemfert 2002, 2005) also encompass induced technological change that can affect the use of carbon energy. Finally, energy system models such as the newer versions of POLES (Kouvaritakis et al. 2000), MARKAL (Barreto and Kypreos 2000), and MESSAGE (Grübler and Messner 1998) also contain induced technological changes in their approaches, with MESSAGE incorporating some form of learning-by-doing functions into its energy system framework.

In general, it can be said that the exclusion of endogenously determined technological change can lead to results which tend to overestimate the compliance costs of climate policy (Löschel 2002; Sue Wing and Popp 2006). As initial installation of technological innovations is very often expensive, models with a learning-by-doing function can specify how this initial cost will decline over time with increasing experience (Dowlatabadi 1998; Azar and Dowlatabadi 1999; Grübler et al. 1999; Gerlagh and van der Zwaan 2001). The decline in costs over time will help to explain how an early introduction of climate policy can have an overall positive economic impact because it helps to reduce the costs of compliance over time.

One negative aspect of induced technological change is the fact that increased investment for R&D will compete with other types of investment and hence can lead to crowding-out effects which increase the overall opportunity cost of investment funds and can lead to a decrease in overall output (Goulder and Schneider 1999). Nordhaus (2002), Buonanno et al. (2003) and Popp (2004), also find that although induced technological change can lead to significant welfare gains, its climate impacts tend to be small in the long run.

The ecological approach to the role of energy in economic activities

The neoclassical assumption that energy is merely an 'intermediate input' in production activities which can be substituted by human-made capital is challenged by ecological or evolutionary economists[8] who regard energy mostly as a 'necessary' or 'essential' input into economic activities. This essential input is used to produce 'work'[9] an integral part of many economic activities. Seen from this perspective, energy is more of a 'complement' to capital (machineries) rather than a substitute (see, for example, Ayres and Ayres 1996; van den Bergh 1999).

At one level, this difference in perspectives between neoclassical and evolutionary economists can be said to arise from the difference in the level of aggregation used in their respective analyses and hence also in the different concepts of 'capital'. For an ecological economist who looks at the issues from a disaggregate or bottom-up perspective of individual technologies, capital (that is, machinery) and energy are complements rather than substitutes. On the other hand, for a neoclassical economist who views the problem from the top-down perspective of the economy as a whole, capital indicates the aggregate of all technologies and hence the 'substitution' of capital for energy indicates the use of 'more' (that is, more energy efficient and hence more costly) capital to save on energy. Thus, van den Bergh (1999) and Stern and Cleveland (2004) make a distinction between *direct* substitution (or 'replacement') of one factor by another – such as the use of capital (machinery) in place of labour, and *indirect* substitution (or 'saving') of one factor by the use of another, which applies to the case of energy saving by the use of a more fuel-efficient machinery. Müller (2000) also refers to this latter process as the substitution of better-*quality* capital for energy. Here quality of capital is defined in terms of energy efficiency. To take into account this heterogeneous characteristic of capital within the traditional neoclassical framework, Müller suggested that first, an energy 'conservation supply curve' (CSC) can be constructed using engineering data, which shows how increasingly greater amounts of energy can be saved by using increasingly more energy-efficient (and hence more expensive) capital. The curve is upward sloping and can be interpreted as the reverse of the capital–energy substitution isoquant in a traditional neoclassical production function approach. The isoquant is then used to calibrate the substitution elasticity between capital (quality) and energy. Presumably, this substitution applies only to *new* capital where the decision to trade off between higher-quality capital and (saved) energy can only be made at the time of the investment decision. Once the decision has been made, the quality of capital is then fixed, and subsequently (*old*) capital and energy are seen to be complements rather than substitutes. This putty–clay approach therefore requires a capital-vintage method, with at least two types of capital: old and new. Old capital is 'clay', and cannot be changed in its energy efficiency (hence, it is a complement with energy). New capital, on the other hand, is 'putty', that is, its exact energy efficiency level can be decided at the time of investment and this is based on a trade-off between expenditure on capital quality and (expected future) energy running cost. This trade-off is based on relative prices of capital and (future) energy inputs. The heterogeneous treatment of the capital stock is typical of many bottom-up or technology-based approaches (see, for example, Jaccard et al. 2003; Jaccard 2005). However, the ecological approach perhaps goes even further than this simple distinction between top-down and bottom-up approaches and the heterogeneous characteristics of capital. It makes a distinction between energy as an 'intermediate' input (as viewed from the neoclassical approach) and energy as a 'primary' input (as viewed from the ecological perspective). Energy as an intermediate input means that it can be 'created during the production period under consideration' and is 'used up entirely in production', while if it is a 'primary' input, it must exist 'at the beginning of the period under consideration' and is 'not directly used up in production' (but perhaps only 'degraded') (Stern and Cleveland 2004, p. 5). The fact that energy is *not used up* in the production process is consistent with the First Law of thermodynamics which says that energy (and matter) must be conserved. The 'degradation' of the (quality) of energy is then related to the Second Law of thermodynamics which says that for a closed system (such as within the human economic system), the 'ability to do work' – as measured by the so-called 'exergy',[10] or 'quality' of the energy volume contained within this economic system – must decrease rather than increase as more work has been 'extracted' from that volume (during economic activities).

If we consider only the human economic system as a closed system, then the provision of energy primary inputs into this system must come from the available energy resource *stock* which, in each period, is determined *exogenously* of the human economic system (for example, by the geological constraints which fix the rate of energy extraction, see, for example, Gever et al. 1986). The ecological approach then goes further and proposes that energy is the *only* primary factor while capital and labour inputs are in fact 'flows' rather than stocks, which can be measured in terms of the energy 'embodied' or being associated with them, and the entire value added in the economy must then be regarded as rent accruing only to this primary (energy) factor (Costanza 1980; Hall et al. 1986; Gever et al. 1986; or Kaufmann 1987). Energy surplus or rent is then distributed to the owners of fuels, labour, capital, and land, with the actual distribution depending on the relative bargaining power of the different social classes and the suppliers of fuel (Kaufmann 1987; Stern and Cleveland 2004). The implication of this 'energy theory of value' as proposed in this 'fundamentalist' version of ecological economics is that energy is now seen as the only crucial factor determining the growth of production activities in the economy, and any attempt at 'decoupling' energy from economic growth – as attempted in the neoclassical approach via concepts such as substitution elasticity and 'autonomous energy efficiency improvement' (AEEI) (the reduction of energy usage per unit economic activity via exogenous technological progress), is deemed to be theoretically unfounded.

5   Conclusion

In this chapter, we have given a brief survey and overview of the types of models used in the analysis of energy–economy–environment linkages, their theoretical background as well as practical model constructions. Mainstream neoclassical and the more recent ecological approaches to the treatment of energy and environment in economic models are described and contrasted. Although it can be said that perhaps in general, neoclassical approaches tend to be more optimistic than the ecological approaches regarding the issue of whether and how economic activities can be 'decoupled' from energy and environmental exploitation, this also depends to some extent on how energy is specified and modelled within each approach. For example, top-down aggregate neoclassical models tend to be more pessimistic than bottom-up technology-based models regarding the possibility of substituting human-made capital for energy. On the other hand, a bottom-up approach which starts from a position that considers energy as a kind of 'primary' factor, or an 'essential' input into most economic activities (using the ecological approach which tends to view energy from a thermodynamic perspective rather than an economic perspective) will tend to consider the possibility of substituting a human-made factor for energy input as almost impossible. Different theoretical approaches and different model constructions therefore can lead to significantly different results regarding the role of energy and the environment in economic activities. It is the objective of the brief survey in this chapter to give a description of the many components and characteristics of different approaches, so that the results from each can be more clearly understood.

Notes

1. See, for example, Dowlatabadi and Granger (1993), Toth (1995), Rotmans and Dowlatabadi (1998) and Edmonds (1998) for reviews on these models.
2. See Weyant et al. (1996), Bosello et al. (1998), Springer (2003) and Hourcade and Ghersi (2001). Grubb et al. (1993) and Hourcade et al. (1996) give a summary representation of some modelling approaches and classifications.
3. The issue of investment for (induced) technological change will be considered in Section 4 below.
4. Full BCA has to come up with methods for tackling difficult issues such as the quantification of the physical damages caused by the direct environmental impacts (loss of lives, loss of property caused by climate change, for example) and also a valuation of these damages in economic terms (how much value to put on a human life).
5. An example of this environmental target is the limitations on the level of GHG emissions to satisfy the Kyoto Protocol agreements.
6. We use the terms 'endogenous' or 'induced' technological change interchangeably. Endogenous because it is determined within the model, and 'induced' because it is caused by some form of action such as R&D investment or learning by doing.
7. See for example, Edenhofer et al. (2006). For other more comprehensive approaches see, for example, Smulders (2005).
8. It can be said that the ecological approach to environmental economics is concerned with the basic question of 'material (and energy) balance' (conservation of matter, and of energy, as determined by the laws of thermodynamics), in contrast to the neoclassical approach where the issue is 'value balance' (value theory). The ecological approach can perhaps be said to date back to Georgescu-Roegen (1971). For a modern exposition, see, for example, Ayres (1978), Cleveland and Ruth (1997) and van den Bergh (1999).
9. An input is 'necessary' if without it, output also falls to zero. It is furthermore 'essential' if, as in the case of a non-renewable resource, consumption will fall to zero in the long run when this (natural resource) input is completely exhausted. 'Work' implies a higher-quality form of energy, which manifests in the form of mechanical motion. Thus, electricity, for example, is a higher-quality form of energy as it can be used to run electric motors. In contrast, the burning of wood is a lower-quality form of energy because it can be used only to produce heat.
10. For a definition of 'exergy' see, for example, Wall (1977), Cleveland et al. (1984), Ayres (2005), Sciubba and Wall (2007) and Cleveland and Budikova (2007).

References

Allan, G.J., M. Gilmartin, K.R. Turner, P.G. McGregor and J.K. Swales (2007), 'Technical Report 4: Computable general equilibrium modeling studies', UKERC Review of Evidence for the Rebound Effect, UK Energy Research Centre, London, October.
Apostolakis, B.E. (1990), 'Energy–capital substitutability/complementarily: the dichotomy', *Energy Economics*, **12**, 48–58.
Arrow, K. (1962), 'The economic implications of learning by doing', *Review of Economic Studies*, **29**, 155–73.
Ayres, R.U. (1978), *Resources, Environment and Economics: Applications of the Materials/Energy Balance Principle*, New York: Wiley-Interscience.
Ayres, R.U. (2005), *Mass, Exergy, Efficiency in the US Economy*, Interim Report IR-05-034, International Institute for Applied Systems Analysis, Laxenburg, Austria.
Ayres, R.U. and L.W. Ayres (1996), *Industrial Ecology: Closing the Materials Cycle*, Cheltenham, UK, and Brookfield, VT, USA: Edward Elgar.

Azar, C. and H. Dowlatabadi (1999), 'A review of the treatment of technological change in energy economic models', *Annual Review of Energy and the Environment*, **24**, 513–44.

Barreto, L. and S. Kypreos (2000), 'Multi-regional technological learning: some experiences with the MARKEL model', Energy Modelling Group, Villigen, Switzerland.

Berndt, E.R. and D.O. Wood (1979), 'Engineering and econometric interpretations of energy capital complementarity', *American Economic Review*, **69**, 342–54.

Blackorby, C. and R.R. Russell (1989), 'Will the real elasticity of substitution please stand up? (A comparison of the Allen/Uzawa and Morishima elasticities)', *American Economic Review*, **79**(4), 882–8.

Böhringer, C. and A. Löschel (2006), 'Promoting renewable energy in Europe: a hybrid computable general equilibrium approach', *The Energy Journal*, Special Issue on Hybrid Modeling of Energy–Environment Policies: Reconciling Bottom-up and Top-down, 135–50.

Bosello, F., C. Carraro and C. Kemfert (1998), 'Advances of climate modelling for policy analysis', *Nota di Lavoro*, 82/98.

Boston Consulting Group (1968), *Perspectives on Experience*, Boston, MA: Boston Consulting Group, Inc.

Brookes, L. (1990), 'The greenhouse effect: the fallacies in the energy efficiency solution', *Energy Policy*, **18**, 199–201.

Buonanno, P., C. Carraro and M. Galeotti (2003), 'Endogenous induced technical change and the costs of Kyoto', *Resource and Energy Economics*, **25**, 11–34.

Carraro, C. and M. Galeotti (1997), 'Economic growth, international competetiveness and environmental protection, R&D and innovation strategies with the WARM model', *Energy Economics*, **19**(1), 2–28.

Cleveland, C.J. (Lead Author) and D. Budikova (Topic Editor) (2007), 'Energy quality', in C.J. Cleveland (ed.), *Encyclopedia of Earth*, Cleveland, Washington, DC: Environmental Information Coalition, National Council for Science and the Environment. First published in *Encyclopedia of Earth* February 22, 2007; last revised February 23, 2007; available at: http://www.eoearth.org/article/Energy_quality (accessed April 29, 2008).

Cleveland, C.J., R. Costanza, C.A.S. Hall and R.K. Kaufmann (1984), 'Energy and the U.S. economy: a biophysical perspective', *Science*, **225**, 890–97.

Cleveland, C.J. and M. Ruth (1997), 'When, where and by how much do biophysical limits constrain the economic process? A survey of Nicholas Georgescu-Roegen's contribution to ecological economics', *Ecological Economics*, **22**(3), 203–24.

Costanza, R. (1980), 'Embodied energy and economic valuation', *Science*, **210**, 1219–24.

Dowlatabadi, H. (1998), 'Sensitivity of climate change mitigation estimates to assumptions about technical change,' *Energy Economics*, **20** (5–6), 473–93.

Dowlatabadi, H. and M.M. Granger (1993), 'Integrated assessment of climate change', *Science*, **259** (26 March), 1813–932.

Edenhofer, O., K. Lessmann and N. Bauer (2006), 'Mitigation strategies and costs of climate protection: the effects of ETC in the hybrid model MIND', *The Energy Journal*, Special Issue on Endogenous Technological Change and the Economics of Atmospheric Stabilization, 206–22.

Edmonds, J. (1998), 'Climate change economic modelling: background analysis for the Kyoto Protocol', OECD Workshop, Paris.

Frondel, M. and C.M. Schmidt (2002), 'The capital–energy controversy: an artifact of cost shares?', *The Energy Journal*, **23**(3), 53–79.

Georgescu-Roegen, N. (1971), *The Entropy Law and the Economic Process*, Cambridge, MA: Harvard University Press.

Gerlagh, R. and B. van der Zwaan (2001), 'The effects of aging and an environmental trust fund in an overlapping generations model on carbon emission reductions', *Ecological Economics*, **36**, 311–26.

Gever J., R.K. Kaufmann, D. Skole and C. Vörösmarty (1986), *Beyond Oil: The Threat to Food and Fuel in the Coming Decades*, Cambridge, MA: Ballinger.

Goulder, L. and S. Schneider (1999), 'Induced technological change and the attractiveness of CO_2 abatement policies', *Resource and Energy Economics*, **21**, 211–53.

Grubb, M., J. Edmonds, P. ten Brink and M. Morrison (1993), 'The costs of limiting fossil fuel CO_2 emissions: a survey and analysis', *Annual Review of Energy and the Environment*, **18**, 397–478.

Grübler, A. and S. Messner (1998), 'Technological change and the timing of mitigation measures', *Energy Economics*, **20**, 495–512.

Grübler, A., N. Nakicenovic and D.G. Victor (1999), 'Modeling technological change: implications for global environment', *Annual Review of Energy and the Environment*, **24**, 545–69.

Hall, C.A.S., C.J. Cleveland and R.K. Kaufmann (1986), *Energy and Resource Quality: The Ecology of the Economic Process*, New York: Wiley Interscience.

Hertel, T. (ed.) (1999), *Global Trade Analysis: Modelling and Applications*, Cambridge: Cambridge University Press.

Hourcade, J.-C. and F. Ghersi (2001), 'The economics of a lost deal', Discussion Paper 01-48, Resources for the Future, Washington, DC.

Hourcade, J.-C., R. Richels, J. Robinson and L. Schrattenholzer (1996), 'Estimating the costs of mitigating greenhouse gases', in J.P. Bruce, H. Lee and E. Haites (eds), *Climate Change 1995: Economic and Social Dimensions of Climate Change*, Contribution of Working Group III to the Second Assessment Report of the IPCC, Cambridge: Cambridge University Press, pp. 267–96.
Howarth, R.B. (1998), 'An overlapping generations model of climate–economy interactions', *Scandinavian Journal of Economics*, **100**, 575–91.
Jaccard, M. (2005), 'Hybrid energy–economy models and endogenous technological change', Chapter 1 in R. Loulou, J.-P. Waaub and G. Zaccour (eds), *Energy and Environment*, New York: Springer.
Jaccard, M., J. Nyboer, C. Bataille and B. Sadownik (2003), 'Modeling the cost of climate policy: distinguishing between alternative cost definitions and long-run cost dynamics', *The Energy Journal*, **24**(1), 49–73.
Kaufmann, R.K. (1987), 'Biophysical and Marxist economics: learning from each other', *Ecological Modelling*, **38**, 91–105.
Kemfert, C. (2002), 'An integrated assessment model of economy–energy–climate – the model WIAGEM', *Integrated Assessment*, **3**(4), 281–99.
Kemfert, C. (2005), 'Induced technological change in a multi-regional, multi-sectoral trade model', Special Issue of *Ecological Economics*, **54**, 293–305.
Khazzoom, D.J. (1980), 'Economic implications of mandated efficiency standards for household appliances', *The Energy Journal*, **1**(4), 21–39.
Kouvaritakis, N., A. Soria, S. Isoard and C. Thonet (2000), 'Endogenous learning in world post-Kyoto scenarios: application of the POLES model under adaptive expectations', *International Journal of Global Energy Issues*, **14**(1–4), 222–48.
Lee, K., M.H. Pesaran and R. Pierce (1990), 'Labour demand equations for the UK economy', in T. Barker and M.H Pesaran (eds), *Disaggregation in Econometric Modelling*, London and New York: Routledge, pp. 404–26.
Löschel, A. (2002), 'Technological change in economic models of environmental policy – a survey', *Ecological Economics*, **43**(2–3), 105–26.
Müller, T. (2000), 'Integrating bottom-up and top-down models for energy policy analysis: a dynamic framework', Working paper 00.02, Centre universitaire d'étude des problèmes de l'énergie, Université de Genève.
Nordhaus, W. (1999), 'Modelling induced innovation in climate change policy', in A. Grubler, N. Nakićenović and W.D. Nordhaus, *Induced Innovation and Climate Change: Collected Essays*, Washington, DC: Resources for the Future Press, pp. 259–89.
Nordhaus, W. (2002), 'Modelling induced innovation in climate change policy', in A. Grübler, N. Nakicenovic and W. Nordhaus (eds), *Technological Change and the Environment*, Washington, DC: Resources for the Future, pp. 97–127.
Popp, D. (2004), 'ENTICE: endogenous technological change in the DICE model of global warming', *Journal of Environmental Economics and Management*, **48**, 742–68.
Powell, A. (1981), 'The major stream of economy-wide modelling: is rapprochement possible?', in J. Kmenta and J. Ramsey (eds), *Large Scale Econometric Models: Theory and Practice*, Amsterdam: North-Holland, pp. 47–67.
Rivers, N. and M. Jaccard (2006), 'Choice of environmental policy in the presence of learning by doing', *Energy Economics*, **28**, 223–42.
Robinson, S. (2006), 'Macro models and multipliers: Leontief, Stone, Keynes, and CGE models', in A. de Janvry and R. Kanbur (eds), *Poverty, Inequality and Development: Essays in Honor of Erik Thorbecke*, New York: Springer, pp. 205–32.
Rotmans, J. and H. Dowlatabadi (1998), 'Integrated assessment of climate change: evaluation of models and other methods', in S. Rayner and E. Malone (eds), *Human Choice and Climate Change: An International Social Science Assessment*, Columbus, OH: Battelle Press, pp. 85–102.
Sciubba, E. and G. Wall (2007), 'A brief history of exergy from the beginnings to 2004', *International Journal of Thermodynamics*, **10**(1), 1–26.
Smulders, S. (2005), 'Endogenous technical change, natural resources and growth', Chapter 8 in R.D. Simpson, M.A. Toman and R.U. Ayres (eds), *Scarcity and Growth Revisited*, Washington, DC: Resources for the Future, pp. 46–69.
Sorrell, S. (2007), 'The rebound effect: an assessment of the evidence for economy-wide energy savings from improved energy efficiency', Report produced by the Sussex Energy Group for the Technology and Policy Assessment function of the UK Energy Research Centre.
Springer, U. (2003), 'The market for GHG permits under the Kyoto Protocol: a survey of model studies', *Energy Economics*, **25**(5), 527–51.
Stephan, G., G. Müller-Fürstenberger and P. Previdoli (1997), 'Overlapping generations or infinitely-lived agents. Intergenerational altruism and the economics of global warming', *Environmental and Resource Economics*, **10**, 27–40.

Stern, D.I. (1997), 'Limits to substitution and irreversibility in production and consumption: a neoclassical interpretation of ecological economics', *Ecological Economics*, **21**, 197–215.

Stern, D.I. (2004), 'Elasticities of substitution and complementarity', Rensselaer Working Papers in Economics, No. 0403, Department of Economics, Rensselaer Polytechnic Institute, Troy, NY.

Stern, D.I. and C.J. Cleveland (2004), 'Energy and economic growth', Rensselaer Working Papers in Economics, No. 0410, Department of Economics, Rensselaer Polytechnic Institute, Troy, NY.

Sue Wing, I. (2006), 'Representing induced technological change in models for climate policy analysis', *Energy Economics*, **28**(5–6), 539–62.

Sue Wing, I. and D.C. Popp (2006), 'Representing endogenous technological change in models for climate policy analysis: theoretical and empirical considerations', Chapter 7 in M. Hannemann and A. Farrell (eds), *Managing Greenhouse Gas Emissions in California*, Report by the California Climate Change Center at UC Berkeley.

Toth, F. (1995), 'Practice and progress in integrated assessment of climate change: a workshop overview', *Energy Policy*, **23**(4/5), 253–68.

Tyson, L.D. and S. Robinson (1983), 'Modeling structural adjustment: micro and macro elements in a general equilibrium framework', in H. Scarf and J. Shoven (eds), *Applied General Equilibrium Analysis*, Cambridge: Cambridge University Press, pp. 127–42.

van den Bergh, J.C.J.M. (1999), 'Materials, capital, direct/indirect substitution, and materials balance production functions', *Land Economics*, **75**(4), 547–61.

Wall, G. (1977), 'Exergy – a useful concept within resource accounting', report no. 77-42, Institute of Theoretical Physics, Göteborg.

Weyant, J.P., O. Davidson, H. Dowlatabadi, J.A. Edmonds, M. Grubb, E.A. Parson, R. Richels, J. Rotmans, P.R. Shukla, R.S.J. Tol, W.R. Cline and S. Fankhauser (1996), 'Integrated assessment of climate change: an overview and comparison of approaches and results', in J.P. Bruce, H. Lee and E.F. Haites (eds), *Climate Change 1995: Economic and Social Dimensions – Contribution of Working Group III to the Second Assessment Report of the Intergovernmental Panel on Climate Change*, Cambridge: Cambridge University Press, pp. 371–96.

16 The oil security problem

Hillard G. Huntington[*]

1 Introduction

Oil trading was suddenly curtailed after the nationalization of the Suez Canal in July 1956 and the subsequent invasion of Egypt by Israel, France and Britain. During the first three months of 1957, US oil prices rose at a quarterly rate of 7.6 percent (more than 30 percent on an annual basis) at a time when the Texas Railroad Commission effectively fixed oil prices. An economic recession ensued. Since that event, Middle Eastern oil has played a critical role in the military strategies, foreign affairs and the economies of many Western nations for more than five decades. The fundamental economic problem has been how to balance the large gains from free and open trade with oil security policies that may limit dependence upon Persian Gulf energy supplies.

This chapter brings together several important recent strands in the energy security literature and evaluates their contributions. Although these studies emphasize the US oil security problem, the methodologies and basic principles apply to many European and Asian countries, too. The chapter does not survey the literature, because Bohi and Toman (1993, 1996) and Toman (1993) have already provided excellent reviews and raised important reservations about how governments implement the security principle. Improving oil security in this chapter will refer to reducing an oil-importing country's reliance on insecure sources of foreign oil.

Section 2 discusses when private markets may fail to provide appropriate signals for economic efficiency and public policy might be considered. Section 3 reviews a recent effort to estimate the benefits of limiting US oil imports, based upon the externalities discussed in the previous section. Section 4 presents the key results from an effort to estimate the risks of another oil disruption over the next 10 years. This study uses risk analysis techniques to elicit probabilities from leading geopolitical and oil security experts. Finally, Section 5 discusses why recent oil price trends are unlikely to create the same economic dislocations experienced by Western economies in the past. Concluding comments are summarized in a sixth and final section.

2 Oil Security as an Externality

When buyers and sellers negotiate an oil price in the private market, they may not incorporate all of the oil security costs associated with increased oil use or imports. The oil import premium should represent the difference between the societal and private costs of purchasing one more barrel of imported oil. Some policy makers think of the premium as 'hidden costs' because buyers and sellers do not directly see them.

Although this issue is fundamental to energy security analysis, it does not represent all of the issues that energy policy makers must address. Below are three fundamental decisions:

1.   How much should the government spend to abate energy security costs?
2.   Should policy makers use a particular policy for offsetting the impacts of price shocks, such as tariffs, fuel efficiency standards, renewable portfolio standards, oil stockpiling reserves, monetary policy, or fiscal policy?
3.   Is the oil security premium substitutable for the oil environmental premium or are the two premia complementary?

The premium addresses the first issue. Its estimation is important, because a small or non-existent value will make the other two questions moot. Estimating the premium (the first question), however, reveals nothing about the second question (the appropriate trade-off between energy policies, monetary policies, or military expenditures to make oil less risky) or the third question (how to combine the oil security and environmental premia).

Market failures
This discussion will focus on the security but not the environmental premium. There are potentially three important market failures that might create hidden security costs.

First, oil producers might charge a price that exceeds their marginal costs. Governments owning oil resources and wanting to stay in power often exploit their resources more slowly than private companies. The resulting higher oil prices allow these governments to provide a range of public services that reinforce their control of the country's political process. Without effective competition from private companies in developing these resources, governments have some leeway to depart from pricing strategies that achieve economic efficiency. Moreover, explicit or informal cooperation among oil-producing countries enhance the opportunities to overprice oil resources relative to competitive conditions. Although monopolistic conditions may expand or contract over time as market conditions change, many experts view the Organization for Petroleum Exporting Countries (OPEC) as a clumsy cartel that still exerts some upward pressure on oil prices (Adelman 1980). Empirical estimates of the oil import premium incorporate this market failure somewhat imprecisely as the market (or monopsony) power component, estimated as the ability of the oil-importing society (organized as one buying unit rather than as individual consumers) to reduce the monopoly price charged by OPEC.[1]

Second, oil suppliers and consumers may not understand the actual risks of another oil disruption caused by political unrest in overseas areas. Typically, Organisation for Economic Co-operation and Development (OECD) governments spend enormous resources to develop information about political trends overseas and they do not share what they learn with the private sector. Although the government might overestimate the risks of oil disruptions under some conditions, it seems just as likely that the private sector may underestimate these risks. For example, the best analysis of private oil stockpiling within the OECD nations implies that it takes a reduction of eight or nine barrels of public stockpiles to encourage one more barrel of private crude oil stockpiles (Aldy 2007). This 8:1 ratio represents a very low 'crowding out' between private and public stockpiles, much lower than for many other public expenditures.

Empirical estimates of the oil import premium include this market failure as the import cost disruption component. It equals the real income lost during a disruption by importing more expensive petroleum. This component will depend upon assumptions about how much oil producers and consumers correctly anticipate the risks of another disruption. Bhagwati and Srinivasin (1976) and Mayer (1977) argue that when an unanticipated disruption occurs, adjustment costs prevent producing firms from providing the lost good except at a very high price. Appropriate policy would be a subsidy to encourage more domestic production prior to a disruption because producers are undervaluing the commodity during normal times. Tolley and Willman (1977) expand this concept to include energy consumers with rigid capital stocks and longstanding habits. Since both consumers and producers of the embargoed commodity are undervaluing it, an oil tariff rather than a production subsidy is preferred. If firms and consumers correctly internalize the effects of future disruptions, however, their current private decisions will value the embargoed commodity properly (Srinivasan 1987).

Third, firms and workers may make pricing and output decisions that harm other sectors of the economy in the form of increased unemployment and idle capacity. These effects might be considered macroeconomic externalities. Unlike the security costs in the second point above that are incurred by the decision maker who lacks sufficient information, these costs are external to the ones making the decisions. Since these interdependencies operate through the market system, these macroeconomic externalities should be viewed as pecuniary rather than technical externalities. If the oil-using economy comprises many competitive sectors, these pecuniary externalities can be ignored, because they do not influence welfare (Folkerts-Landau 1984). Many macroeconomic and industrial organization economists, however, think that monopolistic competition may be a better representation than perfect competition for modern economies (Bresnahan 1989). Under such a market environment, pecuniary externalities cannot be ignored because they do influence welfare (Romer 1996, p. 114). Using such a framework, Huntington (2003) shows that the risk-adjusted macroeconomic externalities might produce welfare losses that are comparable to the market or monopolistic power component.

OPEC taxes and terrorism
Other suggested components for the oil import premium are either subsets of the above market failures or do not belong in the estimate. For example, some public commentary calls today's higher oil price an oil tax imposed by governments owning oil resources. Although oil taxes on a single commodity are economically inefficient, the market or monopsony power component already incorporates this effect.

Alternatively, the revenue received by oil-exporting countries may finance terrorism, belligerent dictators controlling oil resources and other activities that are particularly distasteful to the OECD nations.[2] Essentially, this issue means that a dollar sent overseas to an oil-producing country represents a cost that exceeds that dollar. Cost–benefit analysis can place different values on the market power component to reflect our distaste for revenues collected by these governments and recirculated to harmful groups, but this approach would be an adjustment to the market power component rather than a new component. Generally, estimates of the oil import premium exclude this issue, because it is very difficult to determine a monetary value.

Military expenditures
Empirical premium estimates correctly exclude military expenditures to maintain peace and property rights in oil-producing countries. The premium measures what governments

should spend to reduce a set of damages. Actual military expenditures indicate what the government *does* spend. What the government does spend may have nothing to do with the damages incurred by countries that depend too much on oil imports (Bohi and Toman 1993). These expenditures describe the costs of a policy choice rather than the societal damages caused by the oil import level. The latter have already been captured by the market failures identified above. If you add military costs to the premium, you are essentially double counting damages or costs.

To elaborate further, suppose that you know that greenhouse gas emissions cost society $25 per ton-equivalent of carbon in terms of the damages on health, seacoast preservation and other socioeconomic impacts. The government responds by implementing a greenhouse gas emission fee of $25 per ton-equivalent of carbon. Adding the cost of the program (the greenhouse gas emission fee) to the damages that you are trying to avoid is similar to combining military expenditures with the premium. This procedure inflates the premium estimate to the point that it now has no meaning as a policy benchmark. In short, premiums should refer to damages caused by climate change or oil insecurity rather than the costs of implementing policies in response to those damages. In all likelihood, the government may spend too little on emissions reductions or too much on military protection to be good indicators of the true costs to society.

On the other hand, the premium computed previously may be useful for judging actual military expenditures that can be clearly identified with the US oil interests. According to the director of the US Congressional Budget Office, annual US military expenditures in Iraq are about US$113 billion (2007). If costs are spread over 5 billion barrels imported by the United States, the cost is approximately US$23 per barrel. This simple calculation suggests that the United States is spending too much if its military commitment was due solely to reaping societal oil benefits (estimated to be about US$13 per barrel, as reported in Table 16.1 below). In addition to excluding other reasons for its military commitment in Iraq, this simple calculation also ignores the wider social costs associated with additional deaths and permanent injuries.

Strategic petroleum reserve expenditures
The costs of maintaining the strategic petroleum reserve (SPR) should not be included in the premium estimates for the same reasons that military expenditures should be excluded. They are not damages caused by too much dependence upon oil imports but rather are policy options for reducing those damages. On the other hand, policy makers should use the oil premium estimates to decide whether to build additional public oil stockpiles.

3   A Recent Estimate of the Oil Import Premium

The most widely cited empirical estimate of the oil import premium is Leiby et al. (1997), which has been updated recently by Leiby (2007). These ambitious efforts have done much to clarify the oil import premium estimate and to provide policy makers with some useful benchmarks for evaluating policies. They use a probabilistic simulation framework to estimate the premium for the United States that incorporates many different perspectives on market behavior, including the assumption that US actions may have very little impact on oil prices under some circumstances. Given the intensity of beliefs between those who believe in energy security market failures and those who do not, this eclectic approach serves a very useful purpose.

Oil market conditions and premium estimates

The newer Leiby estimates show that the oil import premium increases when baseline oil prices are higher than they were 10 years ago. The critical assumption is that the oil price elasticities for demand inside and outside of the United States and for supply inside and outside of the oil-exporting cartels are unchanged between the two time periods. This assumption appears justified by available empirical estimates for oil demand, for example, see Goodwin et al. (2004), Graham and Glaister (2004), and Dargay et al. (2007). Combined with the assumption that the share of the US imports in the total market is not dramatically different between the two periods, these conditions imply that the percentage change in the premium should be approximately the same. But if the baseline oil price *levels* are higher, the premium *level* will also increase proportionately. (Leiby provides a useful mathematical exposition of this point.)

These premium estimates are based upon a single oil market projection for the US Energy Information Administration's reference case. This procedure is consistent with how the study's disruption probabilities were developed, which will be discussed in Section 4. It should be recognized, however, that this sole projection for world oil market conditions might bias the results towards higher oil premia. Gately (2007) criticizes these EIA projections as being much too bullish about OPEC's willingness to supply oil in future markets. Disruptions in any region will have a larger impact on the world oil price if that region is providing a larger share of the total market.

The estimates

The new and previous estimates are compared in Table 16.1. The median monopsony power premium increases from US$2.57 per barrel in the 1997 study to US$8.90 per barrel in the 2006 study (all prices are in 2004 US dollars). When the macroeconomic premium is added to the first component, the median full premium increases from US$3.59 per barrel to US$13.58 per barrel between the 1997 and 2006 estimates.

Aggregating the two components implies that the total import premium should include the market power component when there is a disruption. The market power

Table 16.1   Mean estimate of oil import premium

Effect/Study	1997 Study (2004$/BBL)	2006 Study (2004$/BBL)
Monopsony component	$2.57	$8.90
	($1.54–$3.59)	($2.91–$18.40)
Macroeconomic disruption/Adjustment costs	$1.03	$4.68
	($1.03–$2.05)	($2.18–$7.81)
Total mid-point	$3.59	$13.58
	($2.57–$5.64)	($6.71–$23.25)

Note: Ranges are reported in parentheses below the mean estimate.

Sources: Leiby et al. (1997) and Leiby (2007).

premium, however, usually applies to stable market conditions rather than to disruptions.[3] If importing countries do not earn market power benefits during disruptions, these estimates may be overstated.

Leiby recognizes that the macroeconomic externalities may derive more from the total consumption of an unstable energy source than from oil imports alone. But he also argues that oil imports increase the exposure to disruptions in the Middle East and cause disrupted prices to be higher than otherwise; hence, his justification for including the macroeconomic component for US oil imports. If one believes, on the other hand, that there is little direct link between oil imports and the macroeconomic externalities of an oil price shock, one may prefer to focus exclusively on the market power component of the premium shown in Table 16.1. Although greater domestic ethanol or Arctic National Wildlife Refuge (ANWR) production may reduce imports, this development does not protect the economy from future oil price shocks. GDP effects may still apply for US oil consumption when world oil market supplies are unstable, but that result suggests that there may be an oil *consumption* rather than an oil *import* premium component for macroeconomic externalities.

This estimate of the premium computes the damages attributable to macroeconomic externalities in terms of reduced real output as measured by GDP, the principal activity variable analyzed by macroeconomists. GDP is not the preferred measure for cost–benefit analysis because output changes do not necessarily reflect lost opportunities or welfare. It is unclear whether the use of real GDP overstates or understates the welfare lost from an economic recession. Those who argue that GDP losses and rising unemployment overstate the welfare losses usually argue that workers and firms anticipate and cope with many market frictions in an efficient manner (Bohi and Toman 1996). Those who argue that recession-induced welfare losses often exceed the decline in GDP usually focus on the deadweight triangular losses from producing less than optimal output (Gertler et al. 2007). As output departs further from the full-employment level, welfare declines more than proportionately.

4   Oil Disruption Risks

The probability of the size and duration of another oil disruption is critical to the estimated oil import premium. Leiby and Bowman (2003) show that various estimates of the risk of comparable disruptions during the 1990s varied by as much as a factor of five depending upon the approach and assumptions. In response to the need for credible estimates of these disruption probabilities, in 2006 the Energy Modeling Forum at Stanford University organized a working group of leading geopolitical and oil market experts. This group developed a risk assessment framework and evaluated the likelihood of at least one foreign oil disruption over the next 10 years (Beccue and Huntington, 2005). The study had three objectives:

- to develop a risk assessment framework and utilize expert judgment to develop the overall probability of a major oil disruption;
- to characterize the likelihood, effective magnitude, and duration of potential supply disruptions; and
- to clearly document the logic and assumptions driving the risk analyses.

Formal probabilistic risk assessments have been widely used to analyze a range of topics where:

- uncertainty is paramount;
- many interrelated factors cause significant complexity;
- information is available from many sources; and
- policy makers want a quantitative, logical, and defensible analysis of the associated risks.

The most detailed, thorough and structured approach for evaluating these risks lies in elicitation of the views of an expert panel, such as that previously conducted by the Stanford Energy Modeling Forum (EMF) in 1996 (Huntington et al. 1997). This approach, drawing on the tools and principles of decision analysis (Clemen 1996), is based upon structured modeling where specific events are identified and their probabilities are evaluated. Critically, the approach allows interdependencies to exist between events, thereby providing a richer evaluation of the underlying risks of disruptions. The assessment incorporates expert judgment to provide an explicit quantification of the magnitude, duration and likelihood of oil supply events that could cause significant upward deviations in world oil prices.

The EMF conducted a series of three workshops between December 2004 and July 2005. These meetings focused on incorporating expert judgment in the explicit quantification of the magnitude and likelihood of oil disruptions. The panel consisted of leading geopolitical, military and oil market experts, who provided their perspective on the probability of different events occurring and their corresponding link to major disruptions in key oil market regions. Special attention was made to differentiate disruptions by their magnitude, duration and likelihood of occurrence. Panel members represented a wide range of institutional/organizational backgrounds and were asked to reflect their individual judgments and to avoid technical or policy positions taken by their organizations. The participants are recorded in the more recent report (Beccue and Huntington 2005).

Shortfalls and supply regions
For the oil risk assessment, a disruption or shortfall is defined as:

> A sudden shortfall in oil production from a world supplier that results in at least 2 MMBD unavailable within 1 month of the beginning of the disruption. After the period, world production recovers to the same level prior to the shortfall. The disruption occurs at least one time during the 10-yr period 2005–2014. (Beccue and Huntington 2005, p. 6)

This definition provides an explicit event for experts to evaluate the probability of an oil disruption. More than one disruption can occur during the 10-year timeframe 2005–14. In these evaluations, a shortfall is not defined in terms of a specific movement in prices.

The evaluations focused on possible disruptions in four major oil supply regions: (i) Saudi Arabia, (ii) Other Persian Gulf countries, (iii) West of Suez, and (iv) Russia and Caspian states. The Other Persian Gulf group included Iran, Iraq, Kuwait, Qatar, United Arab Emirates, and Oman. The West of Suez countries included Algeria, Angola, Libya, Mexico, Nigeria, and Venezuela. The analysis treated each set of countries within

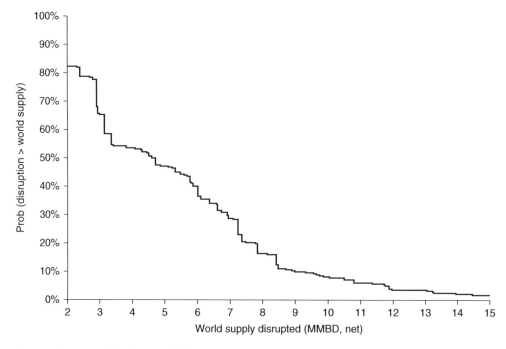

Source: Beccue and Huntington (2005).

Figure 16.1   Probability of an oil disruption lasting 1–6 months

a region as a group. The production capacities from the International Energy Outlook (IEO) Reference Case for 2010 were nearly identical across regions, ranging from 13.2 million barrels per day (MMBD) for Saudi Arabia and Russia and the Caspian States to 15.7 MMBD for the heterogeneous West of Suez grouping.

The group estimated net disruptions after allowing offsets from undisrupted regions. Major offsets to the gross disruptions consist of excess capacity primarily located in Saudi Arabia, and to a lesser extent, the Other Persian Gulf sources. The US SPR is not included as an offset, because the analysis estimates net disruptions arising from a lack of policy intervention by the US government.

This information was entered into DPL software, a state-of-the-art decision and risk analysis package (Syncopation Software 2003). To obtain summary information, the model calculated the disruption size for all combinations of event states (over 20 million scenarios) and weighted each scenario by its likelihood of occurrence.

The scenario-probability pairs are succinctly summarized and displayed in Figure 16.1 for all disruptions. The curve plots along the vertical axis the probability that a disruption will occur in the next 10 years of at least *x*, for each value of *x* (in MMBD, net of offsets) on the horizontal axis. The graph focuses on magnitudes of 2 MMBD and greater, because smaller disruptions are unlikely to have significant price impacts. These smaller disruptions are also difficult to identify and attribute to specific events. This figure shows that the data point at 5 MMBD and 45 percent can be described as a 45 percent chance that a 5 MMBD disruption or larger will occur at least once in the

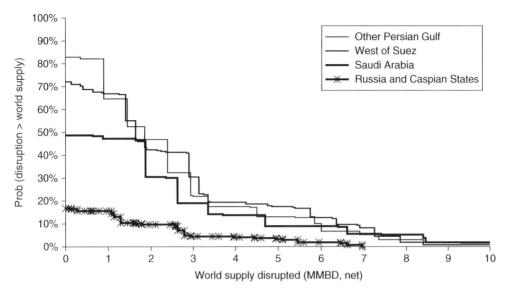

Source: Beccue and Huntington (2005).

Figure 16.2   Comparison of short-duration disruptions by region

10-year timeframe 2005–14. It is very likely that a net (of offsets) disruption of 2 MMBD or more and lasting at least 1 month will occur (over 80 percent).[4] The chance of a 3 MMBD net disruption or more lasting at least 1 month is 65 percent; the chance of 5 MMBD or more is about 50 percent. However, it is unlikely that disruptions greater than 15 MMBD will occur (less than 1 percent).

This curve allows one to easily identify the likelihood of disruption sizes within a range. For example, the probability of a disruption between 5 and 10 MMBD is 37 percent (probability of >5 is 45 percent, probability of >10 is 8 percent, difference is 45 percent – 8 percent = 37 percent). Figure 16.1 shows a larger weighting for 3 MMBD and 8 MMBD by the steep drop in the curve in these regions. The reader should be extremely cautious in making conclusions for these specific magnitudes, because they reflect approximations underlying the assessment method.

The distribution in Figure 16.1 is a combination of events in each of four regions. The approach can show the contribution of each region to the summary distribution by eliminating disruptions in other regions (assuming no disruption occurs) and showing the results for a region independently. Figure 16.2 shows each region independently on the same probability graph. Other Persian Gulf and West of Suez regions have the larger probabilities of disruption (for any given disruptions size) than Saudi or Russian and Caspian States.[5] The probability of any disruption lasting more than a month is higher in the other Persian Gulf countries (83 percent) or in the West of Suez region (72 percent) than in Saudi Arabia (49 percent). The comparable probability for Russia and the Caspian States (17 percent) is lower than the Saudi Arabian estimate.

Offsets from the use of excess capacity outside the disrupted region reduce the size of

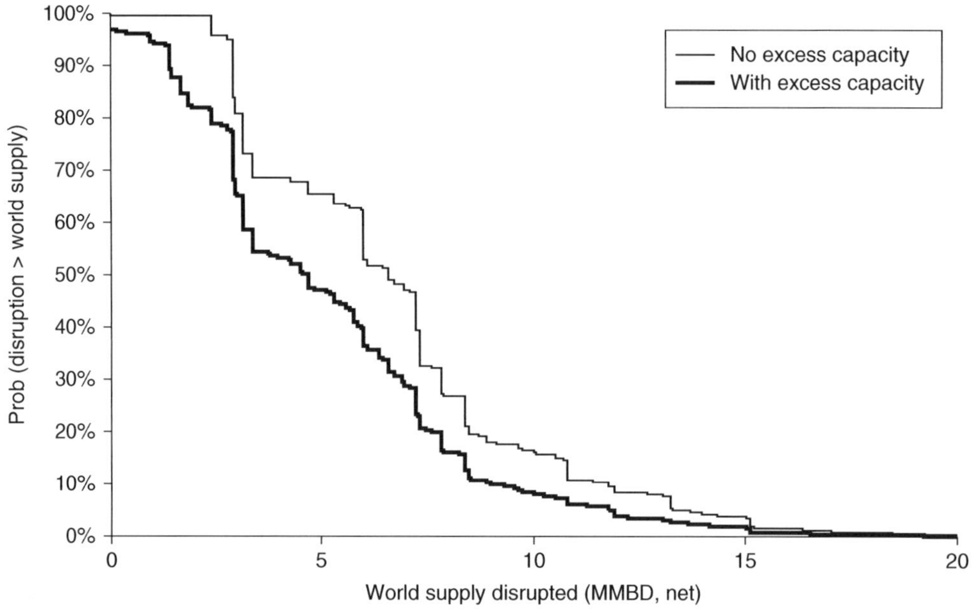

Source: Beccue and Huntington (2005).

Figure 16.3   Sensitivity to removing excess capacity

the disruption. Without the availability of this excess capacity, a flat region appears in Figure 16.3 between 0 and 3 MMBD, representing a near certainty that a disruption of this magnitude will occur in the next 10 years. The effect of eliminating any excess capacity tends to shift the distribution to the right by roughly 1 MMBD, indicating that net disruptions are larger without this excess capacity. The figure reveals that offsets reduce the probability that the net disruption reaches any given size by approximately 5–15 percent.

A key influence on these disruption risks are the possible events in the West of Suez region, which was excluded from the analysis conducted 10 years ago. If this region were assumed to be stable in the most recent analysis, the probability of a disruption is 5 percent lower for sizes less than 3 MMBD, and 15 percent in the range of 3–7 MMBD, as shown in Figure 16.4.

Middle East conflict was a critical, underlying event jointly affecting disruption risks in multiple regions. Figure 16.5 contrasts the base case assumptions with two extreme conditions in the Middle East: stable conditions with no conflicts, and extended or active war in the region. At 5 MMBD or greater, the probability varied from 34 to 60 percent, confirming the notion that Middle East events and their linkages to the regional shortfall risks are an important element of the oil risk assessment.

Relative to a similar EMF risk assessment in 1996, these updated estimates indicate an increased likelihood of disruptions equal to or below 10 MMBD, but a similar likelihood of disruptions that exceed 10 MMBD (7–8 percent or lower). The current assessment covers four regions of the world instead of two regions, has updated probabilities

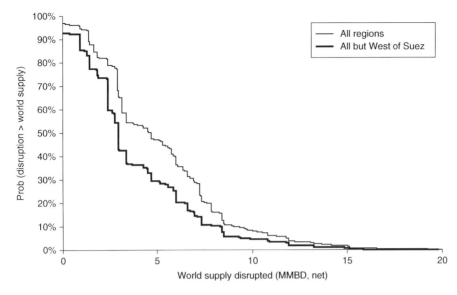

Source: Beccue and Huntington (2005).

Figure 16.4   Sensitivity to removing West of Suez region

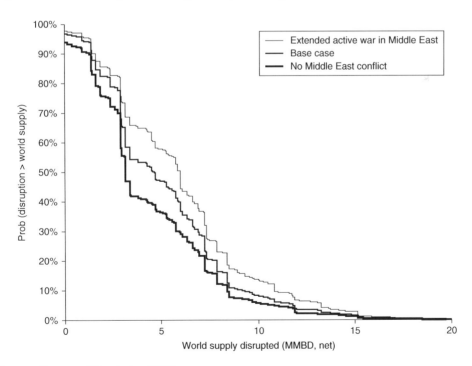

Source: Beccue and Huntington (2005).

Figure 16.5   Sensitivity to war in the Middle East

to reflect current world conditions, and has modified excess capacity and oil supply forecasts.

5   Oil Disruption Impacts

High world oil prices have transferred enormous wealth from oil-importing to oil-exporting countries in recent years, but they have not derailed world economic growth. Since most countries report their economic activity in terms of GDP (an indicator of real output), this loss in real income is often disguised by official statistics (Huntington 2007). Nevertheless, the absence of declining real output when oil prices are high has been somewhat of a puzzle for many observers. The oil price movements over the last few years have received recent attention from several macroeconomists (for example, see Blanchard and Gali 2007, and Nordhaus 2007).

Two frequent explanations emphasize the declining oil intensity in the economy and the demand-side origins of recent price increases. Declining oil intensity in the economy will reduce the direct impacts, but the substitution towards the relatively price-insensitive, transportation applications for petroleum may offset this effect. Demand-oriented oil price increases may be more gradual than oil price shocks from supply disruptions. They may also have different international trade effects than supply disruptions, because all economies are growing rather than stagnating.

Oil prices and prior economic conditions

Huntington (2005) emphasizes two important differences between recent oil price increases and the 1970s' experience. Prices have searched for higher ground gradually over many months rather than being surprise shocks. In addition, these price increases have occurred in economies that have been relatively free from inflationary pressures. Both developments have made the economy relatively invulnerable to oil prices.

Figure 16.6 shows the oil price path over several critical periods in the last three decades. In each case, the line shows the oil price relative to its level in the beginning period for each of the following 17 months. Thus, the October 1973 oil price shock was 15 percent higher after one month but more than 120 percent higher by the third month. The 1990 line also displays a shock, while the 1979 path, while rising quickly, tends to increase more gradually than the 1973 and 1991 shocks. In contrast, the experience that began at the end of 2004 represented a more gradual elevation in the price level. It was high enough to outrage drivers at the gasoline stations, but it seems very different from the 1973 and 1990 price shocks.

Table 16.2 considers four scenarios that highlight the different influences attributable to the type of oil price increase and the underlying macroeconomic conditions prior to the oil price change. 'Higher oil price' conditions in the upper row on the far left reflect a situation much like today when market conditions are pushing prices along a steady upward or elevated path to restore demand and supply imbalances. Since oil prices are inherently volatile, this elevated path will not be smooth but it will avoid any major surprise events. These conditions are fundamentally different from those represented in the second row for the 'oil price shock' conditions, where sudden supply or demand changes induce rapid price increases that scare people and firms and create such wide-spread uncertainty that firms and households delay major investments. Such price events

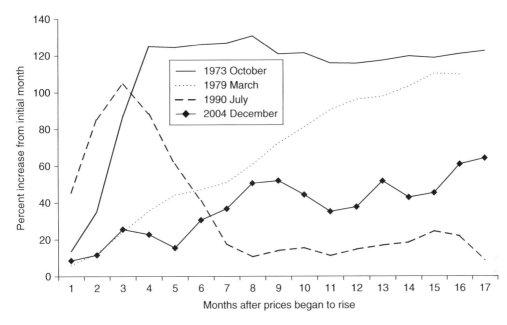

Figure 16.6   Oil price path for four different price increases

Table 16.2   Oil price and prior economic conditions

		Low Inflationary Expectations and Interest Rates Prior to Oil Price Change	High Inflationary Expectations and Interest Rates Prior to Oil Price Change
		Monetary policy can be accommodating	Monetary policy can not be accommodating
Higher Oil Price	Oil prices move steadily higher but not rapidly over consecutive months.	Policy Fix	?
Oil Price Shock	Oil prices move rapidly upward over consecutive months.	?	Possible Recession

Source: Huntington (2005).

appear more representative of the 1970s than recent price volatility. Although many energy economists treat these two conditions the same, they should be considered as very distinct events.

Both of these price events can happen at a time when economic conditions either prevent or allow an effective monetary policy response as an offset to the disruption. During the 1970s, policy makers were faced with high interest rates and high inflationary expectations. Many professional economists at that time were pessimistic that the central bank could intervene successfully to offset output reductions without accelerating inflation. Since then, inflation rates have been tamed and interest rates are relatively low. Armed with a policy rule that adjusts monetary policy to expected output growth and inflation rates (the Taylor rule), many economists are more confident about what they can achieve.

This confidence can be misleading for several reasons. First, monetary authorities throughout the world are very concerned about keeping inflation rates and expectations under control. Small mistakes in managing a nation's money supply can quickly worsen the situation. And second, the world is tiptoeing around the problem of terrorism, belligerent dictators and war in the major oil-producing regions. Small perturbations in very tight oil markets can become the catalyst for very rapid oil price shocks. If inflationary expectations should worsen just prior to an oil price shock, the world would be faced with a very different set of problems.

The box in the southeast corner of the table summarizes the 'perfect storm' conditions, where oil shocks are rapid, unexpected and very scary to firms in the economy and where macroeconomic conditions prevent the central bank from mounting an effective offset. As with the California electricity restructuring fiasco, another 'perfect storm', economists knew that the state was managing its electricity restructuring poorly, but they could not convince the policy makers to make the necessary changes before disaster struck.

Completely opposed to these conditions are those in the northwest box carrying the label 'policy fix'. At the end of 2007, oil prices are moving steadily higher but firms and households understand the trends. They know that some arbitrage to protect themselves from higher prices in the future can help them adjust to the new conditions. As a result, the central bank does not need to make major adjustments in their monetary policy to keep the economy's path from veering. And when they do adjust their rules, economic conditions are favorable to their success.

The other two boxes are more difficult to characterize. An economy with low inflationary expectations could survive a surprise shock, just as an economy with high inflationary expectations may be able to absorb oil prices that gradually move higher. Without more experiences to draw from, it is not possible to generalize about these alternatives.

Sudden and gradual price increments

Sudden price increases scare people and create widespread uncertainty about deciding the appropriate production techniques, purchasing new equipment or consumer durable goods such as automobiles, and negotiating wages and prices. As firms and households adjust to the new conditions, some plant and equipment will remain idle and some workers will be temporarily unemployed. In contrast to a gradual oil price increase, the economy may no longer be operating along its long-run production-possibility frontier.

An important characteristic of a price shock is that the price change should be large relative to recent price changes. The price shocks during the Suez Canal crisis and the 1970s were immediately preceded by very stable oil prices that neither increased nor decreased much between months. After oil prices crumbled in 1986, oil price volatility became much more pronounced. With increased price volatility, market participants began to expect price oscillations and started to diversify their price risks through oil futures markets. Despite being pressured by steadily rising oil prices in the last several years, the economy has been relatively free of surprise oil price shocks in the last two decades, except for the events leading up to the first Persian Gulf War in 1990.

Economic impact estimates

Macroeconomists have estimated that a 10 percent increase in crude oil prices will cause the GDP *level* to be between 0.2 and 0.5 percent lower than otherwise after six quarters.[6] This range, however, reflects the use of two very different methodologies. At the lower end are estimates from large macroeconomic models that do not distinguish current high oil prices from events where oil supplies are explicitly disrupted. At the high end are estimates from smaller research econometric studies focusing explicitly on oil shocks.

The advantage of the large macroeconomic model is that new conditions and policies may be represented more comprehensively than in the smaller research studies. This greater detail, however, requires a number of important assumptions to control for these factors, about which there may be some critical differences of opinion. Moreover, their lower economic impact estimates may reflect their assumption that the economic response to oil price shocks are no different from the response to gradual oil price increases as well as price decreases.

A number of empirical studies have used reduced-form, time-series analyses relating economic growth and oil price changes, although they sometimes include several other variables. These empirical studies have shown that oil price shocks must be considered separately from other oil price changes. Gradual oil price increases as well as price declines fail to contribute to real aggregate output (GDP) changes. The principal concern about these statistical studies is that they may fail to control for key macroeconomic variables and relationships that influence how the economy responds to oil price changes.

After reviewing a number of different economic impact estimates, Huntington (2005) concludes that recent estimates from large macroeconomic models might be appropriate when inflationary fears are low and monetary authorities are more confident that they can accommodate oil price shocks. These frameworks usually simulate conditions similar to today's economic trends and often assume that monetary authorities will offset much of the output lost to disruptions. After six quarters in these simulations, the *level* of real GDP is approximately 2 percent lower for a rapidly doubling of crude oil prices.

If inflationary expectations become considerably higher in the future, Huntington (2005) concludes that the estimates from the reduced-form, statistical approach may be more applicable, because the estimates will be incorporating the responses during periods of higher inflationary expectations. Under these conditions, the level of real GDP is approximately 5 percent lower for a doubling of crude oil prices. If there were a 40 percent chance that the economy could return to an environment of high inflationary expectations, the expected GDP loss after six quarters across both high and low inflationary expectation states would be 3.2 percent (= 0.4 × 5 percent + 0.6 × 2 percent) from a disruption that doubled the price of crude oil.

6   Summary

Many countries are facing a twin-headed energy challenge over the next several decades. The 'coal' problem relates to the perceived threat from global climate change if we continue to rely upon coal and other fossil fuels to propel our future power needs and economies. The 'oil' problem results from our reliance upon petroleum supplies as the principal source for mobility at a time when oil supplies are probably more vulnerable than in our recent past. Policy must balance both concerns if robust strategies are to be developed.

After identifying possible externalities, this chapter has selectively reviewed three economic issues that are central to the discussion of the oil security problem. The oil import premium measures the value of intervening in oil market conditions to make the economy less vulnerable to an oil-exporting cartel and to sudden oil price disruptions. The premium says nothing about which oil-reduction policy should be adopted. Recent estimates for the United States suggest that the monopsony premium, the most widely adopted measure, ranges from approximately $3 to $18 per barrel, with a median estimate of almost $9 per barrel. If oil prices should continue to rise over the next few years, these estimates should increase, more or less proportionately.

A second issue in this chapter concerns the risks of another oil supply interruption. A principal difference over the last 10 years has been the spread of risks beyond the Persian Gulf region. An EMF study on oil disruptions done in 1996 focused on Saudi Arabia and the neighboring Persian Gulf states. More recent estimates have expanded the coverage to Russia and the Caspian states as well as to a set of countries bordering up and down the Atlantic Ocean (principally, Nigeria, Angola, Venezuela and Mexico). Each of these countries could potentially experience political problems that would make its oil supplies vulnerable. An evaluation of top geopolitical and Middle Eastern experts in 2006 concluded that there was an 80 percent chance that a significant oil disruption could happen at some point over the next 10 years.

A third and final issue focuses upon the vulnerability of the economy to an oil disruption. If we could lock today's inflation-free economy into the future, there would be less urgency to resolve the turmoil in the Middle East or to accommodate other leaders of oil-rich states, although an oil disruption may still be quite harmful. If countries want to cushion the impact of future disruptions, their energy policies will need to focus upon oil consumption reductions more than oil import limitations.

Notes

*   The author acknowledges the significant contributions of Phillip Beccue in conducting the risk analysis and Paul Leiby for providing thorough comments on the Energy Modeling Forum (EMF) studies. In addition, many useful comments were received from participants at the EMF workshops on oil risk disruption analysis and on the macroeconomic impact of energy price shocks as well as seminars at the US Energy Information Administration, Stanford University and the University of Southern California. The views expressed are the author's.
1. A large oil importer can reduce the price set by an oil-exporting cartel that consistently maximizes net profits. Retaliation by the exporting cartel would require that it deviate from its wealth-maximization position.
2. It may be that these activities detract from and make more costly other public goods provided by oil-importing countries, such as international negotiations in politically sensitive regions where oil production dominates the economy. In these situations, the oil weapon may be used to thwart foreign affairs conducted by oil-importing countries. None of the premium estimates includes such a cost.
3. See, for example, the premium estimates developed in Energy Modeling Forum (1982).
4. Under stylized assumptions, this 10-year probability (80 percent) converts to approximately a 15 percent annual probability. The latter equals $1 - (1 - 0.80)^{(1/10)}$.
5. Minor exception at 8 MMBD.

6. This range applies for the United States as summarized by Brown and Yücel (2002), Brown et al. (2004) and Jones et al. (2004), but it also seems consistent with international studies (Jimenez-Rodriguez and Sanchez, 2005).

References

Adelman, M.A. (1980), 'The clumsy cartel', *The Energy Journal*, **1** (1), 43–53.
Aldy, Joseph E. (2007), 'The economic impacts of publicly-held emergency oil stocks', presentation at the International Energy Workshop, Stanford University, Stanford, CA, June 25.
Beccue, Phillip and Hillard G. Huntington (2005), *Oil Disruption Risk Assessment*, Energy Modeling Forum Special Report 8, Stanford University, Stanford, CA, August.
Bhagwati, Jagdish N. and T.N. Srinivasan (1976), 'Optimal trade policy and compensation under endogenous uncertainty: the phenomenon of market disruption', *Journal of International Economics*, **6**, 317–36.
Blanchard, Olivier J. and Jordi Gali (2007), 'The macroeconomic effects of oil shocks: why are the 2000s so different from the 1970s?', NBER Working Paper No. 13368, National Bureau of Economic Research, September.
Bohi, Douglas R. and Michael A. Toman (1993), 'Energy security: externalities and policies', *Energy Policy*, **21** (11), 1093–109.
Bohi, Douglas R. and Michael A. Toman (1996), *The Economics of Energy Security*, Norwell, MA: Kluwer Academic.
Bresnahan, Timothy (1989), 'Empirical methods for industries with market power', in Richard Schmalensee and Robert Willig (eds), *Handbook of Industrial Organization*, Vol. II, Amsterdam: Elsevier Science Publishers B.V., ch. 17.
Brown, Stephen P.A. and Mine K. Yücel (2002), 'Energy prices and aggregate economic activity: an interpretative survey', *Quarterly Review of Economics and Finance*, **42**, 193–208.
Brown, Stephen P.A., Mine K. Yücel and John Thompson (2004), 'Business cycles: the role of energy prices', in Cutler J. Cleveland (ed.), *Encyclopedia of Energy*, Amsterdam: Academic Press, Elsevier.
Clemen, R.T. (1996), *Making Hard Decisions: An Introduction to Decision Analysis*, 2nd edn, Belmont, CA: Duxbury Press.
Dargay, Joyce M., Dermot Gately and Hillard Huntington (2007), 'Price and income responsiveness of world oil demand, by product', Energy Modeling Forum Occasional Paper EMF OP 61, Stanford University, Stanford, CA, August.
Energy Modeling Forum (1982), *World Oil*, EMF Report 6, Stanford University, Stanford, CA.
Folkerts-Landau, Elena (1984), 'The social cost of imported oil', *The Energy Journal*, **5** (3), 41–58.
Gately, Dermot (2007), 'What oil export levels should we expect from OPEC?', *The Energy Journal*, **28** (2), 151–73.
Gertler, Mark, Jordi Gali and David Lopes-Salido (2007), 'Markups, gaps and the welfare costs of business cycles', *Review of Economics and Statistics*, **89** (1), February, 44–59.
Goodwin, P., J. Dargay and M. Hanly (2004), 'Elasticities of road traffic and fuel consumption with respect to price and income: a review', *Transport Reviews*, **24** (3), 275–92.
Graham, D. and S. Glaister (2004), 'Road traffic demand elasticity estimates: a review', *Transport Reviews*, **24** (3), 261–74.
Huntington, Hillard (2003), 'Energy disruptions, interfirm price effects and the aggregate economy', *Energy Economics*, **25** (2), 119–36.
Huntington, Hillard G. (2005), 'Macroeconomic Consequences of Higher Oil Prices', Energy Modeling Forum Special Report 9, Stanford University, Stanford, CA, August.
Huntington, Hillard G. (2007), 'Oil shocks and real U.S. income', *The Energy Journal*, **28** (4), 31–46.
Huntington, H., J. Weyant, A. Kann and P. Beccue (1997), 'Quantifying Oil Disruption Risks Through Expert Judgment', Energy Modeling Forum Special Report 7, Stanford University, Stanford, CA, April.
Jimenez-Rodriguez, Rebecca and Marcelo Sanchez (2005), 'Oil price shocks and real GDP growth: empirical evidence for some OECD countries', *Applied Economics*, **37** (2), 201–28.
Jones, Donald W., Paul N. Leiby and Inja K. Paik (2004), 'Oil price shocks and the macroeconomy: what has been learned since 1996', *The Energy Journal*, **25** (2), 1–32.
Leiby, Paul N. (2007), *Estimating the Energy Security Benefits of Reduced U.S. Oil Imports*, Oak Ridge National Laboratory ORNL/TM-2007/028, Oak Ridge, TN, Revised July.
Leiby, P. and D. Bowman (2003), 'Oil Market Disruption Risk Assessment: Alternatives and Suggested Approach', Oak Ridge National Laboratory internal report, Oak Ridge, TN.
Leiby, Paul N., Donald W. Jones, T. Randall Curlee and Russell Lee (1997), *Oil Imports: An Assessment of Benefits and Costs*, ORNL-6851, Oak Ridge National Laboratory, Oak Ridge, TN, November.

Mayer, Wolfgang (1977), 'The National Defense Tariff argument reconsidered', *Journal of International Economics*, **7**, 363–77.

Nordhaus, William (2007), 'Who's afraid of a big bad oil shock?', Prepared for the Brookings Panel on Economic Activity, Washington, DC, Fall 2007.

Romer, David (1996), *Advanced Macroeconomics*, New York: McGraw-Hill.

Srinivasan, T.N. (1987), 'The National Defense argument for government intervention in foreign trade', in Robert M. Stern (ed.), *U.S. Trade Policies in a Changing World Economy*, Cambridge, MA: MIT Press, pp. 337–63.

Syncopation Software (2003), *DPL 6.0 Professional Getting Started Guide*, Syncopation Software, Inc., Concord, MA.

Tolley, George S. and John D. Willman (1977), 'The foreign dependence question', *Journal of Political Economy*, **85**, 323–47.

Toman, Michael A. (1993), 'The economics of energy security: theory, evidence, policy', in A.V. Kneese and J.L. Sweeney (eds), *Handbook of Natural Resource and Energy Economics*, vol. III, ch. 25, New York: Elsevier Science Publishers B.V.

17 Petroleum taxation
Carole Nakhle

The art of taxation consists in so plucking the goose as to obtain the largest amount of feathers with the least possible amount of hissing.

(Jean-Baptiste Colbert, French Finance Minister to Louis XIV, Crawson, 2004, p.12)

1 Background: Plucking the Oil Industry Goose

Petroleum taxation is the instrument of choice for sharing hydrocarbon wealth between host governments and international oil companies. For all parties, the Colbert adage holds. The concept of taxing oil companies is simple, but the detail is complex and is an art as it requires fine judgement.

Compared to the taxation of other sectors and industries, petroleum taxation has some particular features arising from the oil industry's special characteristics, the central contribution the oil and gas sectors make to all advanced economies, the volatility of oil prices, the large operating and development costs, the high uncertainty associated with petroleum geology, the specific characteristics of individual oilfields and the possibility of re-investment. The costs of petroleum projects tend to be incurred up-front and the time lags between the discovery of oil or gas reserves to the time of first production can be significant. This adds to the challenge of designing and implementing an appropriate petroleum tax system aimed at achieving a balance between both government and industry interests.

There are two fundamental objectives of petroleum taxation; to ensure a fair share of the wealth accruing from the extraction of the petroleum resource while also providing sufficient incentives to encourage investment and optimal economic recovery of the hydrocarbon resources. These two objectives compete. They are not complementary. Then there is the added difficulty of defining what is 'fair'; a fair share at US$30 per barrel may be seen unfair at US$60 per barrel. Since there is no objective yardstick for sharing economic wealth between the various parties involved in the petroleum activity, controversy will always exist between investors and the host government. Yet, a trade-off should be found, since in the end both government and oil companies want to maximise their own rewards. Tax rates that are set too low can leave the government or the nation, the owner of the resource, a small and inequitable portion. Such a situation is unlikely to endure under political pressures. But, if tax rates are too high, investment can be discouraged in both new projects and in sustaining the capital investment required to maximise future value added from existing operations.

Those considering investment consider basin competitiveness as determined by the basin prospectivity and the chance of finding oil or gas, the volumetric potential and how large the discoveries are, the basin cost structure (overall finding, development and operating costs per billion of oil equivalent), the access to infrastructure and opportunities, and the fiscal regime – its evolution, complexity and stability. For instance, an increase in the crude oil price is often regarded as an increase in oil companies' profits. But higher oil prices can encourage greater activity and because there is a limited pool of rigs available worldwide, when demand for rigs increases, the cost of hiring those rigs will increase as well. Soaring oil prices are not always the bonanza which the tax policy makers assume. While other factors go beyond government control, taxation lies squarely within government jurisdiction (Nakhle, 2007).

The design of different fiscal regimes, and how they compare, can be a critical factor in shaping perceptions of basin competitiveness. All round the world many countries are seeing their production aspirations undermined, and in some cases production declining, because their fiscal terms are poorly designed for the character and features of the province in question. The right choice of fiscal regime can improve the trade-off between the government and oil companies' interests. Policy makers also need to consider that what works in one country may not necessarily work in another. Petroleum fiscal regimes are applied under specific circumstances and there is no one ideal fiscal regime suitable for all petroleum projects in all countries. Due to the significant differences in geological prospect and economic environment between various countries, a fiscal package that is appropriate for one country may prove to be inappropriate for another. This chapter proceeds with an examination of the specific characteristics of the oil industry in Section 2. Section 3 studies the theoretical background to petroleum taxation. Section 4 analyses the principal fiscal packages that have been applied around the world. Section 5 offers concluding remarks.

2   Oil: A Complex Industry

There are six phases in the life of an oilfield; namely the acquisition of the licence, exploration, appraisal, development, production and abandonment phases.

1. *The acquisition of the license or concession*   The search for oil begins when the government announces its intention to offer oil companies the right to explore in a part of its territories.
2. *Exploration*   At this phase, seismic surveys are carried out to identify the prospect. If the conditions are suitable to continue with the project, drilling an exploration well follows. If the well proves to be dry, the exploration costs of the dry hole are written off, whereas if oil is found, the company proceeds to the testing phase. The exploration phase can cost tens or hundreds of millions of dollars. It also involves high risk. Until a hole is drilled, the existence of oil or gas is theoretical; 'dry' holes are common even in established production areas and even with modern technologies. To be commercially viable, a well must be able to produce enough oil or gas to justify the costs of drilling and placing it on production.

Appraisal, development and production phases follow successful exploration.

3. *Appraisal*   If exploratory wells confirm the presence of producible quantities of oil or gas, development wells are drilled to define the size and extent of the field. In development drilling the odds for success are higher: perhaps six or seven successful wells for every 10 drilled. But risk is still present: there may not be enough oil or

gas to be commercially attractive; or the technology required to produce oil or gas may be too expensive. Once data have been obtained and interpreted, the decision to develop the discovery is taken. This decision depends on several factors, including an estimate of the future oil price at the time the project would be expected to come on-stream.

4. *Development* If the field is commercially feasible, the next stage is the development phase. A decision is taken with respect to the development technology to be employed in exploiting the reserves of the field in the most efficient way. In many countries, a detailed development plan has to be submitted to the government for approval before construction progresses.

5. *Production* Once the first production wells are drilled, the production phase begins and the project comes 'on-stream'. The natural pressure within the reservoirs pushes the oil up the wellbore, allowing it to be delivered to an offshore production facility on the sea surface or to a production facility onshore. It is only when production starts that both operating revenues and operating costs occur. The costs occurring before the production stage are generally regarded as capital expenditures.

6. *Abandonment* This is the final stage in the cycle, where the field is no longer profitable and is decommissioned. Economic cut-off is the point at which production levels fall to a level which ceases to cover operating costs. Abandonment or decommissioning costs are the cost associated with abandoning a well or production facility; they can amount to tens of billions of dollars. Decommissioning of oil and gas production facilities at the end of their producing lives, particularly in an offshore environment, represents perhaps the second most financially material event in the exploration and production business cycle, after installation of the facilities themselves.

Decisions in the petroleum industry factor in uncertainties which occur at each stage of a project's life cycle, long time horizons, various alternatives, and complex value issues into the decision. Risks can be political, exploration (chance of failure), technical (reserves and cost estimation), economic (oil and gas prices), or commercial (fiscal risk). Oil and gas projects are by nature long term, with much of the investment and costs being incurred upfront. The exploration and appraisal stages, in particular, can last many years. There is also a significant time lag, often of many years, from the initial discovery of oil or gas reserves to the time of first production. The oil industry is also capital intensive. Substantial amounts must be spent annually on exploration to discover sufficient oil to replace the oil that is currently consumed. But unlike other businesses, an oil project has a finite life because its reserves are depletable. This means that the company has a limited number of years over which to realise a competitive rate of return on its investment.

Governments have therefore to take fully into account the special complexity of oil and gas activity and the costs and risks related to this industry when structuring fiscal regimes. An internationally competitive petroleum tax regime is one which recognises and is tailored to the special characteristics of the oil industry.

3 The Main Functions of Petroleum Taxation

Taxes are the principal source of revenue that governments use to finance public expenditures. Petroleum taxation, in particular, has traditionally generated substantial revenues for government. In the UK, more than £215 billion or approximately US$430 billion (2005 money terms) has flowed to the Treasury between 1968 and 2006 thereby contributing to healthcare, education and various other services funded by government (Oil & Gas UK, 2007). Much bigger sums have flowed into the coffers of major Middle East oil producer governments and other major oil-producing nations such as the Russian Federation.

Since natural resources are frequently owned or controlled by governments, petroleum taxation can also be considered as the owner's claim to net resource value, defined as the net value of revenues received from the sale of the recovered product less all claimed production costs. It is, at least in theory, the means that divides rewards between the investor and the government.

By changing tax rates, a government can encourage, or discourage, economic activity. Taxation can be used to mitigate certain economic problems such as the so-called 'Dutch disease', where the petroleum industry can adversely impact upon the international competitiveness of the non-oil sector.[1] Taxation can also be applied to moderate the pace of exploration and exploitation of petroleum and at the same time to reduce the depletion rate. In other cases where, for instance, there is chronic balance of payments problem, the government can use taxation to accelerate the development of export-oriented natural resources, as occurred in the UK in the late 1970s.

Tax instruments are also used to address energy-related environmental issues. Pollution or 'green' taxes such as those on CO_2 emissions are designed to reduce pollution and other adverse effects on the environment.

The principles of taxation

The theory of taxation identifies the principles of an ideal tax. These constitute the basic criteria, against which any tax can be initially assessed. The most important of these attributes are outlined below:

1. *Efficiency*   The efficiency principle refers to the impact of a tax on the allocation of resources in the economy, as determined by the tastes and preferences of individuals. It is often referred to as the 'social optimal position'. The allocative efficiency concept has been the main point of departure for the economic theory of optimal taxation.[2] Reduced efficiency implies reduced output and lower standard of living, when as a consequence of a tax being imposed investments are not placed where the productivity of capital is highest. An efficient tax neither reduces the productive capacity of an economy, nor does it create distortions in the allocation of resources by favouring one industry or investment at the expense of others. The concept of efficiency is often combined with the neutrality principle (see below).
2. *Neutrality*   The neutrality principle refers to whether the tax system intervenes with investment and operational decisions in such a way as to cause them to deviate from what is the social optimum. A non-neutral, distortionary tax affects the decision-making process, so that individuals make inferior choices to those that would have been made in the absence of the tax. As such, resources are not allocated efficiently. In the petroleum sector, a neutral tax does not deter exploitation of a range of field sizes, or alter project rankings or interfere with production decisions.
3. *Equity*   The concept of horizontal equity implies that taxpayers with equal ability to pay should pay the same amount of tax. Also, firms in the same economic conditions

or oilfields with the same characteristics, including similar cost structures, should be taxed in the same way if a degree of 'horizontal' equity is to be achieved. By contrast, 'vertical' equity requires that taxpayers with a greater ability to pay should pay more tax. It also refers to the equivalent treatment of companies or resources with different characteristics. A progressive tax is more likely to meet this principle. Firms that exploit more valuable resources have a greater ability to pay and so their tax liabilities can be greater. Similarly, fields with high profitability can be taxed more heavily than those with low profitability. The size of an oilfield is not necessarily an indicator of its profitability. Some large fields can be less profitable than smaller fields if they have a higher cost structure. Intergenerational equity requires an equitable tax that ensures future generations get a fair share of the resources or compensation for those that are depleted. The creation of a petroleum fund is intended to contribute to intergenerational equity however defining 'fair' with predictions about future circumstances is difficult.

4. *Risk sharing*   The attitude of an investor depends not only on the level of tax, but also on the extent to which the government shares the project's risks. Companies have the means to diversify certain levels of risks through, for instance, a large, worldwide portfolio, but they also try to avoid those situations where the potential rewards are outweighed by the perceived risks. There is also the matter of fiscal risk (see below).

5. *Stability*   Stability of a fiscal regime directly affects the confidence of investors in government policy, particularly in the case of petroleum extraction activity where long-term projects are the norm. If a tax system changes frequently and in an unpredictable way, it can seriously affect future development projects. A tax system subject to continuous tinkering can increase political risk and reduce the value placed by investors on future income streams. By the same token, a tax system should have some level of predictability to enable governments to know how much revenue will be collected and when. As such, tax revenues should not rely on volatile exogenous factors such as short-term variations in crude oil price otherwise this can undermine Budget arithmetic creating the need for tax rises elsewhere in the economy if revenue forecasts prove to be overoptimistic.

6. *Clarity and simplicity*   These principles are relevant to the administration and monitoring of the tax system, also referred to as 'administrative efficiency'. An ideal tax is simple to understand and inexpensive to administer. It is levied on a well-defined tax base that is simple and easy to collect. The simpler a tax base is, the lower the administrative costs are, for both administrations and the taxpaying businesses. A simple tax system makes it easier for taxpayers to judge the tax consequences of their actions. Transparency is equally important; it allows taxpayers to know the true cost of transactions.

Meeting the criteria

As in most areas of taxation there are inevitable compromises in satisfying all the basic principles of an ideal tax.

Neutrality and Simplicity

Several studies[3] have questioned the suitability of neutrality as a major characteristic of tax systems. A major disadvantage with neutral taxes is their complicated administration, especially in the case of petroleum extraction, recognising the individual characteristics of oilfields (including size, location and quality). To maintain neutrality, the government is required to evaluate different levels of rent (see below) and expected yields in order to value each individual field properly, subsequently imposing what would be called a fully differentiated tax. Such a task is impractical since it can be significantly complicated to administer.

Neutrality and Revenue Generation

A neutral tax system provides incentives for companies to exploit marginal fields. However, because marginal fields do not generate resource rent, they do not generate revenues for the government. Authors such as Mommer (1999) argue that under a neutral tax regime the company can exploit the resource without paying any tax.

Equity, Simplicity and Efficiency

Governments often try to incorporate tax allowances and reliefs to reduce the tax burden on marginal fields as a means of ensuring equity. Such allocations, however, can impose additional administrative costs, thereby making the tax system complicated. Also, these allowances can generate misallocation of resources, thereby creating inefficiencies. Furthermore, the concept of fairness is subjective. Some view an income tax as fair if it represents a higher percentage of a high-income taxpayer's income relative to a lower-income taxpayer (that is, the system is progressive). Others view an income tax as fair if everyone pays the same rate.

Stability and Fiscal Risk

Although stability of the tax regime is desirable, in reality it cannot be fully achieved. A certain degree of flexibility should be allowed in any tax system if it is to respond to differing conditions and to evolve as a result of major structural changes in the external environment, such as the evolution of the production, oil and gas prices, cost structure, profile and basin competitiveness. But all this can increase the sense of risk associated with any particular project or investment. What looks a profitable investment at the outset, with attractive rates of return, can be turned bitter by unanticipated changes in tax arrangements which, to the government, may look entirely reasonable.

Risk Sharing

Risk sharing between government and investors may not be as essential when companies have a portfolio of activities and are able to diversify certain forms of risk.

Competing objectives and interests of government and the private investor imply that compromise is necessary when designing and implementing a practical tax system. In general, a tax based on economic rent is likely to be an ideal tax.[4] However, compromise means that the principal tax instruments suggested in the literature fail to satisfy all the criteria of optimal taxation.

Economic rent

Economic rent represents 'the surplus return above the value of the capital, labour and other factors of production employed to exploit the resource. It is the surplus revenue of the resource after accounting for the costs of all capital and labour inputs' (Banfi et al., 2003, p. 2). In addition to the capital and labour inputs referred to, further inputs in respect of entrepreneurial reward and risk taking are usually incorporated.

There are three main types of economic rent:

1. *Scarcity rent* Scarcity rent results from the natural scarcity of the resource, which limits the output available. It represents the forgone future profits as a result of extraction today. Hotelling (1931) observed that a mining firm with a given stock of reserves will behave differently from other firms. Competitive firms continue to increase their output until the cost of producing the next unit – the marginal cost – equals the market price it receives. But a mining operation, in addition to its production costs, must also consider the opportunity cost associated with producing one more unit of output during the current period, because reserves exploited today are not available in the future. This cost, which is also referred to as 'scarcity rent' or 'user cost', equals the net present value of the loss in future profits associated with producing one more unit of output today. It can also be expressed as 'the difference between marginal revenue and marginal production cost that can only come about as a result of the natural or policy induced scarcity of the resource' (Kooten and Bulte, 2001, p. 65). If the market price is not high enough to cover both the production and user costs, a firm is better off keeping the reserves in the ground for use in the future.

2. *Differential or Ricardian rent* Ricardo (1951) argued that arable land could be divided into different classes according to its fertility. Increasingly greater levels of rent accrue to land of increasing productivity, with land at the margin receiving no rent. This is illustrated in Figure 17.1. AC and MC, respectively, represent the average costs and marginal cost of food production. Land A enjoys the largest rent as it can produce food at the lowest cost. The next best land, B, has higher costs, but still earns rent as its unit production cost is lower than the market price. The marginal land, C, does not since its AC is too great and is equal to the unit price. The rent accruing to A and B is determined in comparison to C, as they benefit from greater productivity or better soil quality as compared with C. That is why such rent is referred to as 'differential' or 'quality' rent; it normally arises because extraction

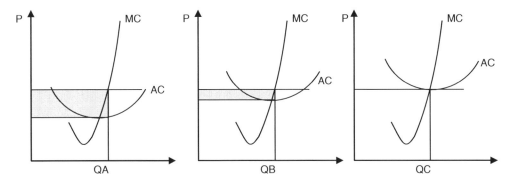

Source: Adapted from Kooten and Bulte (2001).

Figure 17.1 Ricardian rent

costs depend on differences in the quality of the resource and location. This is analogous to the returns accruing to oilfields. Fields with unit costs below market prices – because of efficiencies or favourable physical properties – enjoy Ricardian rent, reflecting greater profitability. The marginal field is the field with a unit cost equal to the market price; it has no rent (Watkins, 2001).

3. *Quasi-rent*   The third type of rent represents the returns that accrue to firms from past investment and innovative practice or as a result of changes in the market. Such rents only occur in the short run before they are competed away. They are earnings over and above that required to maintain a firm in business in the short run. Short-run rent, then, is the difference between the market price and the supply prices of variable inputs (labour, power and the like). Normally, short-run rents can be expected to exceed long-run rents.

Economic rent: a desirable but complex tax base

Because economic rent is considered as a financial return not required to induce desired economic behaviour, there is a general assumption that a tax based on economic rent is optimal since it meets the tax criteria.[5] It is often argued that if taxes are only levied on economic rent, there will be no effect on the incentive of firms to undertake any activity since rent is not required by the firm to continue or initiate operations. Additionally, if the tax seeks to capture economic rent, then the tax-take falls when economic rent decreases and rises when it increases. As such, the tax base responds in the right direction to variations in costs and crude oil prices. A tax, aimed at absorbing economic rent, is considered neutral and stable, and it allows for risk sharing between government and investor.

The exploitation of exhaustible natural resources can generate significant economic rent. Oil, in particular, is not only an exhaustible resource but also a commodity which for most of the oil industry's recorded lifetime has had no perfect substitute (although this could be changing). This implies that the extraction of oil can earn substantial amounts of economic rent, and that has become the widely held assumption in the minds of petroleum tax policy makers.

However, many complications, including distinguishing between various types of rent, arise when trying to estimate economic rent (Nakhle, 2008). The distinction between scarcity and differential rent is rather artificial, since any rent could be understood to be generated by either scarcity or differential effects alone and governments find it difficult to distinguish between the two types of rent. The resource rent (scarcity rent and differential rent) is an appropriate tax base since taxation of this rent does not affect the behaviour of the firm. This is not the case with quasi-rent. Although quasi-rent is part of economic rent, it only occurs in the short run. The capture of quasi-rent can alter the long-run efficiency behaviour of firms, often causing them to reduce investment and therefore the social optimum level of output. Any firm strives to retain the quasi-rent generated by its more efficient behaviour in comparison to other firms. But it will be competed away in the long run since competitors will learn from the firm generating quasi-rent. Accordingly, quasi-rent is not to be included in the tax base but the question is how to identify or quantify that rent and distinguish it from other types.

A second complication is the difficulty governments have in determining acceptable rates of return for all companies as they do not normally reveal directly their required rate of return on investment. The question therefore arises as to how the rent element is to be sensibly judged as between different enterprises which may well have varying views about what constitutes an acceptable rate of return.

Third, measuring economic rent requires knowledge of the differing costs of the individual factors of production and their opportunity costs. But this is by itself a very complex task as the size of a given discovery and its related exploitation costs can vary substantially, and economic rent will vary from field to field. Although this problem can be partly overcome by a progressive tax system, it is difficult to make fiscal systems sufficiently flexible and focused on resource rent across a wide range of variables such as price and different cost structures.

Finally, rents are found in many sectors. If mining rents are to be taxed, should not the same apply for all rents? Economic rent capture is not quite so straightforward.

Tax instruments
A variety of tax instruments have been used in the literature on energy taxation in an attempt to capture the economic rent from oil activity. Four tax instruments are selected namely gross royalty, Brown tax, resource rent tax (RRT) and income tax. Royalty is an output-based tax because it is levied on the unit or the value of production, whereas the other three instruments are profit-based or cash-flow taxes, because they are imposed on net profit or operating income after capital investment. A description of each of these instruments follows.

Gross Royalty
A royalty is 'a payment made for the right to use another's property for purposes of gain' (Stiegeler, 1985, p. 376). It can be a per unit tax, which is a uniform fixed charge levied on a specified level of output (volume of production) or an ad valorem tax, which is a fixed charge levied on the value of the output (gross revenues).

Imposed on the amount or the value of the output royalty is a simple tax. It also ensures a share of revenue for the government as soon as production starts, in contrast to profit-based taxes where the government obtains its first tranche of revenues only when the net cash flow starts to turn positive.

But since a royalty tax is imposed on gross revenues (or the amount of output), it ignores costs and profits associated with the project hence it is not targeted on economic rent. There is a general agreement in the literature that royalty is a regressive tax, which can render profitable projects unattractive on a post-tax basis and can also deter marginal investment as they are not profit based. This explains why in many mature basins such as the UK and Norway, royalty has been abolished.

Royalty is a non-neutral tax as it is imposed as soon as production starts irrespective of the size of the field and so it is equivalent to an increase in the resource extraction cost, affecting the depletion decision of the investor (Hotelling, 1931), and possibly leading a premature abandonment of the field. Royalty pushes more of the commercial risk onto the investor with little protection arising from cost increases or reduced oil prices. At low prices, royalty taxes have the potential to cause the investor to incur a loss.

Sliding-scale royalty may be less distortionary. In China, different royalty rates are charged based on production or oil price; when production or oil price are low so too is the royalty, thereby decreasing the possibility of negative cash flows. Thus although the administrative complexity has increased, the generation of early revenues as is the case with a normal royalty, is combined with a progressive aspect in contrast to the impact of a fixed rate.

Brown Tax[6]

The Brown tax is the oldest type of neutral tax imposed on extractive industries. It is levied as a fixed proportion of a project's net cash flow in each period. When net cash flow is positive, firms have to pay the tax but when the net cash flow is negative, firms receive a rebate. In other words, the Brown tax involves the payment of a proportional subsidy or tax credits on annual cash losses and an equivalent tax on annual cash profits. The Brown tax is a tax on net cash flow – with full contribution by the government where the net cash flows are negative. It is financially equivalent to the government having contributed equity in an oilfield (Garnaut and Clunies-Ross, 1983).

Because the Brown tax is a cash-flow tax it incorporates the different costs that an investor incurs in each period. It is based on economic rent and satisfies principally the criteria of neutrality and risk sharing. But in practice, the Brown tax is an unpopular option, not least because it imposes an unacceptable level of risk on the government. Its biggest problem is the requirement for the government as owner to contribute capital up-front. Furthermore, since companies know that in the case of unsuccessful exploration the government will subsidise their investment, they have less incentive to reduce costs and improve efficiency.

Resource Rent Tax (RRT)

The RRT (Garnaut and Clunies-Ross, 1975) was developed primarily for application in less-developed countries, mainly those that rely on external sources of capital investment. It is a modified version of the Brown tax but instead of paying tax credits in years with negative cash flows, the government allows such negative amounts to be carried forward and deducted from positive cash flows in later periods. However, the negative net cash flows are uplifted by a minimum rate of return requirement (the floor level – also called the 'threshold rate') and added to the next year's net cash flow. The accumulation process is continued until a positive net cash flow is generated. No tax is payable until the firm has recovered its costs inclusive of a threshold rate of return which is compounded from year to year. As such, the RRT involves carrying forward losses, whereas the Brown tax provides a rebate for losses. With RRT, the government makes no direct contribution to a project's capital's cost; tax kicks in only when positive cash flows emerge, the project investment is recovered and a threshold return on the investment is made.

RRT is designed to capture economic rent and therefore considered to be a neutral tax.[7] It is based on estimated profitability after allowance for a threshold rate of return representing normal profits. It is a progressive tax that responds automatically to a variety of outcomes. As with any tax based on profits, RRT tends to share risk with the government; if costs rise or oil prices fall, taxable profits change in sympathy, as does the tax burden. Furthermore, as a company only pays tax when a profit is made, the payback period of the investment will be shorter than if a royalty tax is applied.

There are some problems with RRT. The tax can give rise on occasion to overinvestment, hence affecting the rate of resource depletion. It is also difficult to raise large amounts of revenue and preserve neutrality, especially in view of the difficulties related to determining economic rent. In fact, problems result from the determination of the threshold at which RRT should be levied. The threshold represents the rate of return that investors require to undertake a project. Not all companies are motivated by the prospect of normal profit. Watkins (2001) argues that it is relevant that RRT is levied on a project basis rather than on aggregate company income. Theory has the appropriate threshold rate varying across projects; however, a uniform threshold rate often applies in practice.

RRT implies that revenues are delayed until several years after first production, because the threshold rate has to be achieved before RRT becomes payable. Consequently, some authors argue that RRT is politically unacceptable since it may delay tax payments and can only be imposed in conjunction with corporate tax.

Income Tax

Income tax, a corporation tax or tax on corporate net income is levied at a corporate rather than oilfield or project level. Income tax in most countries allows current expenses, interest expense and historic cost depreciation to be deducted. All forms of income tax allow relief for capital expenditure, but extra reliefs are sometimes given to provide incentives to develop high-cost 'marginal' projects and are called 'uplift' allowances on capital expenditure.

As a profit-based tax with full and immediate loss offsets, income tax is neutral because when profits are zero, income tax revenues are also zero (Musgrave, 1982). This is unlike royalty, where if profits are zero the tax revenue is still positive. A proportional income tax can leave undistorted the choice among projects of different economic lives and time-line profiles (Samuelson, 1986).

However, large tax reliefs lead to a gold-plating effect whereby the investment in capital equipment may result in tax relief exceeding the original investment. Immediate deductibility of costs is a point of contention. In practice, income tax does allow for the deduction of capital costs but usually over a period of time using depreciation, which can apply over the life of the project. In contrast to the Brown tax and RRT, with income tax, investors usually do not recover their costs immediately, and this can result in early payments of revenues to the government. Thus for the investor the pattern of cost recovery relates to the economic life of the asset.

No Magic Bullet

In an attempt to capture the economic rent and minimise distortions in the investment decision, oil-producing countries, including Australia and the UK[8] have found it necessary to adopt a combination of two or more tax instruments. The most appropriate tax instrument is one which creates the least distortion, and the more a tax is targeted towards economic rent, the less the distortion created. Although a tax instrument can create distortions, this is no ground to rule it out. In selecting the combination of fiscal arrangements, the government needs to be careful when determining the relative weights given to different elements in the system's structure.

4 International Petroleum Fiscal Regimes

In the case of minerals in the ground, and petroleum in particular, governments see themselves as fully entitled to collect a revenue stream from what they own. But oil activity requires significant financial resources that can exceed the capability of most of oil-producing countries, especially as deeper and more remote wells are drilled. The ever higher risks involved, as a result of geology and oil price volatility, make a purely national approach to the exploitation of petroleum increasingly outdated. It follows that exploration and exploitation activities present delicate legal, technical, financial and political problems and any solution requires a balancing act between the respective interests of the producing countries and the oil companies.

In the case of petroleum, local influences, both external and internal to the industry itself, such as province maturity, field size, self-sufficiency, security of supply considerations and specific characteristics can still be decisive in shaping the tax regime and in turn influencing the overall attractiveness of the province, which explains the variety of fiscal regimes and packages which exist around the world. Johnston (1998, p. 5) has observed that 'there are more petroleum fiscal regimes in the word than there are countries', for example in Canada, provincial variations in the management and taxation of resources occur and differing patterns co-exist (Nakhle, 2008).

Two basic categories of agreement have developed – concessionary systems and contractual agreements. The concessionary system originated at the very beginning of the petroleum industry (1850s), while the contractual system emerged a century later (1950s). Mommer (2001) describes the two categories of fiscal regime as liberal and proprietary, respectively. In liberal regimes, oil companies are in a much stronger position compared with the proprietary systems, where the government exercises a stronger control over the exploitation and production of the natural resource. But the reality which has emerged behind these different approaches is one of ideology and political fashion.

Concessionary regime: basic features

A concession is an agreement between a government and a company that grants the company the exclusive right to prospect for, develop, produce, transport and market the petroleum resource at its own risk and expense within a fixed area for a specific amount of time (Blinn et al., 1986). The degree of 'concession' can vary. Under one type of concessionary arrangement, resources in the ground (or seabed) remain the property of the state or crown, while oil companies take title to produced oil at the wellhead and then pay the appropriate royalties and taxes. The company is entitled to ownership of the production and can freely dispose of it, subject to the obligation to supply to the local market. A broader type of concession, as in the United States, assigns rights of ownership to the actual reserves in the ground to the discoverer of those reserves. However in other OECD countries, the concessionaire acquires the ownership of the production only at the wellhead, while the minerals remain the property of the state until produced.

One of the earliest concessions granted by the Persian monarchy in 1901 covered the entire national territory for between 60 and 75 years. Similar 'long-lease' concessions were granted (sometimes up to 99 years in Kuwait), providing exclusive ownership to the international oil company (IOC) of the reserves found in the area covered by the concession. The financial benefits accruing to the host government were limited and consisted chiefly of payments based on volume of production labelled royalties at a flat rate. The concessionaire retained control over nearly all aspects of the operations, including the rate of exploration, the decision to bring new fields into exploitation, and the determination of production levels, among others. This type of early concessionary agreement did not provide for any possibility of renegotiation of the terms and conditions of the agreement, should a change of circumstances warrant it. It did not enable the government to participate in the ownership of the petroleum produced.

After the Second World War, a second generation of concessionary agreements was developed, providing for a more active role for the host government and a corresponding decrease in the rights of the IOCs. The concessionary areas were limited to blocks, and the awarding of concession was restricted to a limited number of blocks. Modern concessionary agreements also include provisions for the surrender of most of the original area and the duration of the concession tends to be far more tightly limited. They also include bonuses payable on agreement, on discovery of a petroleum field and on reaching various levels of production.

As a consequence of the 1970s' oil crisis, more-complex tax regimes have been devised. Special taxes enable host governments to increase their take in relation to the profitability of petroleum operations. Host governments, where there has not been outright reversion to state ownership, have nevertheless assigned to themselves the authority to exercise increasingly intrusive monitoring and control over the private sector's decisions, for example, by requiring minimum exploration work programmes, participation in the decision-making process and approval of the exploration costs and expenses.

There are about 55 countries applying a concessionary system to petroleum activity (Johnston, 2001). The usual way of taxing oil companies in a concessionary regime involves a combination of income tax, special petroleum tax and royalty. Thus concessionary regimes are commonly known as 'royalty/tax systems' (R&T).

Royalties are typically either specific levies or ad valorem. Royalty rates are generally set at a level close to 12.5 per cent of production. Some countries have introduced a profit element via a sliding scale royalty, by having royalties depend on the level of production.

Income tax is generally the most frequently deployed instrument used in oil-producing countries of the world. Income tax systems usually consist of a basic single rate structure (plus provisions for deduction of certain items from the tax base, supplementary levies and tax incentives). The overall corporate income tax rate in several countries lies in the range 30 to 35 per cent. Various countries provide an incentive for exploration and development by allowing exploration costs to be recovered immediately and allowing accelerated recovery of development costs (tax depreciation), for example, over five years. In addition to tax deductions, losses carried forward and/or back are commonly allowed tax incentives (Sarma and Naresh, 2001). Invariably the income tax regime for oil and gas companies is the same regime that applies to all corporate activities for all industries in the country in question.

In addition to income tax, most oil-producing countries impose a special petroleum tax in order to capture a larger share of economic rent from oil production. The special tax is normally based on cash flow but is imposed only when cumulative cash flow is positive.

Other payments can also be made to the government. These include bonuses, which are lump-sum payments made to the government. They can be a 'signature bonus', payable upon signing the agreement with the government, a 'discovery bonus' payable when a commercial discovery is made or a 'production bonus', payable at an agreed amount upon the achievement of a stated level of daily production. Production bonuses are normally on a sliding scale of production, therefore if daily production reaches a certain level the government takes a fixed sum, which increases if daily production reaches higher levels. Depending on the tax regime, bonuses may be deductible for income tax purposes. In most cases, discovery and production bonuses have little effect on the profitability of a field. Signature bonuses would appear to have a negative effect; while they are not taxes in the strict sense, they recover the economic rent up-front. The sums can be very large (circa US$1 billion per block); they comprise a material proportion of overall government take and of course are paid before discoveries are made.

Some countries ring-fence their oil and gas activities while others ring-fence individual projects (Sunley et al., 2002). Ring-fencing imposes a limitation on deductions for tax purposes across different activities or projects undertaken by the same taxpayer. These rules matter for two main reasons. First, the absence of ring-fencing can delay government tax receipts because a company that undertakes a series of projects is able to deduct exploration and development costs from each new project against the income of projects that are already generating taxable income. Second, as an oil and gas area matures, the absence of ring-fencing may discriminate against new entrants that have no income against which to subtract exploration or development expenditures.

Contractual regimes: basic features

Under the typical contractual-based systems, the oil company is appointed by the government as a contractor on a certain area. The government retains ownership of production while the IOC operates at its own risk expense and is under the control of the government.

The two parties agree that the contractor will meet the exploration and development costs in return for a share of production or a fee for this service, if production is successful. If the company receives a share of production (after the deduction of government share), the system is known as a 'production sharing contract' (PSC) or a 'production sharing agreement' (PSA), and in this case the oil company takes title to its share of petroleum extracted. If it is paid a fee (often subject to taxes) for conducting successful exploration and production operations, the system is known as a 'service contract', also called a 'risk-service agreement'. The latter is so-called because in a service contract, the host government (or its national oil company) hires the services of an international oil company and in the case of commercial production out of the contractual area, the oil company is paid in cash for its services without taking title to any petroleum extracted.

Contractual regimes were first applied in Indonesia in the 1960s. There are 64 countries adopting a PSC system to their petroleum activities and only 12 countries following a service contract (Johnston, 1998).

In contractual regimes, the oil company bears all the costs and risks of exploration and development. It has no right to be paid in the event that discovery and development do not occur. However, if there is a discovery, 'cost recovery' or 'cost oil' allows the company to recover the costs it has incurred.

Cost recovery is similar in outcome to cost deductions under the concessionary systems. It includes mainly unrecovered costs carried over from previous years, operating expenditures, capital expenditures, abandonment costs and some investment incentives. Financing cost or interest expense is generally not a recoverable cost. Normally, a predetermined percentage of production is allocated on a yearly basis for cost recovery.

However, in general there is a limit for cost recovery that on average ranges between 30 and 60 per cent of gross revenue. In other words, for any given period the maximum level of costs recovered is 60 per cent of revenue, although contracts with unlimited cost recovery are also in existence (see Indonesia, Bahrain and Algeria, for instance). Many PSCs either specify annual cost oil allowances on a sliding scale or state that this variable is biddable or negotiable up to a certain maximum value. Full cost recovery occasionally comes with a time limit attached to it. The share of production set aside for cost oil will decline after, say, five years. In this sense it works similar to a tax holiday. Unrecovered costs in any year can be carried forward to subsequent years. Also, some contracts allow these costs to be uplifted by an interest factor to compensate for the delay in cost recovery. Investment credits or uplift may also be provided to allow the contractor to recover an additional percentage of capital costs through cost recovery. The more generous the cost recovery limit, the longer it takes for the government to realise its take. There is usually a ring-fence on petroleum activities, hence all costs associated with a particular block or licence must be recovered from revenues generated within that block.

Royalties can also feature in PSC regimes but many will argue that the same economic impact can be secured by adjusting cost oil limits which also ensure an early flow of revenues to the state. Royalty is paid to the government before the remaining production is split. Nevertheless, an alternative to a royalty is to have a limit on cost oil, to ensure that there is 'profit oil' as soon as production commences. Such a limit on cost recovery has a similar economic impact to a royalty, with the government receiving revenue – its share of profit oil – as soon as production commences.

The principle of cost recovery applies to both a PSC and in risk-service agreement. However, the basis of the contractor's remuneration after it has recovered its cost differs in type.

In a PSC, the remaining oil after the oil company recovered the costs of the project (cost oil) is termed 'profit oil' or 'production split' and is divided between the host government and the company according to a predetermined percentage negotiated in the contract. The split can be a fixed profit-oil split, linked to production rates or a progressive split linked to project profitability, that is, to rate of return – ROR – or R-factors. Under the ROR systems, the effective government take increases as the project ROR increases. The government is guaranteed early revenues due to the operation of the cost oil ceiling which ensures that there is always a minimum quantity of profit oil to be shared between the investor and the state in each year. The elements determining the R-factor vary from one country to the other, but normally both revenue and cost are included in the equation. As such, the R-factor can be broadly defined as the ratio of cumulative net earnings to cumulative total expenditures. The R-factor is calculated in each accounting period and once a threshold is reached, a new tax rate will apply in the next accounting period. The objective of the ROR and the R-factor is to link the sharing between the government and the contractor to profitability. Profit oil is usually, but not always taxed.

In some countries, like in Indonesia, the government has the option to purchase a certain portion of the contractor's share of production at a price lower than the market price. This is called 'domestic market obligation' (DMO). There can also be an additional government take in form of bonus payments, whether signature or production bonuses. Most PSAs allow for bonuses to be tax deductible but they are not allowable for cost recovery.

Royalties, cost oil, profit oil and production bonuses can be levied either as fixed shares of production or on the basis of sliding scales. The latter method is becoming standard procedure. The two most common ways of calculating payments using sliding scales are based on either average daily production or R-factors.

Over time, PSAs have changed substantially and today they take many different forms. One cannot refer to, say, a typical Asian or a typical Eastern European contract. Terms vary between one country and the other. But in its most basic form a PSA has four main properties. The international oil company pays a royalty on gross production to the government, if applicable. After the royalty is deducted, the company is entitled to a predetermined share of production for cost recovery. The remainder of the production, so-called profit oil, is then shared between the government and the international oil company at a prespecified share. The contractor then has to pay income tax on its share of profit oil.

In a service agreement, the government allows the contractor to recover the costs associated with exploration and development of the hydrocarbon resources, through sale of the oil and gas. Additionally, the government pays the contractor a fee based on a percentage of the remaining revenue. All production belongs to the government. Since the contractor does not receive a share of production, terms such as 'production sharing' and 'profit oil' are not appropriate even though the arithmetic will often carve out a share of revenue in the same fashion as a PSA shares production. The fixed fee remuneration – service fee – of the contractor can be subject to tax. It is analogous to taxable income in a concessionary system and profit oil in a PSA.

The remuneration fee under a risk service contract is usually determined using profitability indicators, such as the project's ROR or ratios such as the R-factor, discussed above.

Concessionary and contractual regimes: further comparison

The contractual regime is often seen as an alternative to the concessionary regime – the main difference being of a legal nature, namely the title to production ownership. In concessionary regimes, the government can maintain some of its entitlement to production through the national oil company but that entitlement is relatively limited. In theory, contractual regimes enable governments to exercise more control over both petroleum operations and the ownership of production. In practice, this is less so.

In a concessionary system, the oil company receives the net income after costs, tax and royalty. Under a PSC, the company gets cost recovery and a share of the remaining profit, while under a service contract it receives the cost recovery and a profit fee or remuneration until handover date – the predetermined date where the project is handed over to the national oil company. Although the principles are the same under a PSC and a service contract, such a difference in remuneration generates a further distinction in terms of duration of contract, cost-reduction incentives and impact of changes in oil price and reservoir characteristics. PSCs can be long term in nature, but in service agreements the contractor involvement depends on the handover date, which in turn is affected mainly by the capital expenditure and oil revenue. Generally, service agreements are short term, usually nine years, while PSCs last up to 30 years. Under a PSC, the contractor receives profit throughout the life of the contract, which is normally the life of the field, whereas under a service agreement the contractor cost recovery and profit remuneration end at the handover date.

As a consequence of the limit on cost recovery, contractors are normally encouraged to reduce their capital cost. However, a limit of the service contract is that the contractor has no incentive to reduce the long-term costs, since the field is likely to be under the control of the government. Therefore, service agreements are more suited to low-risk, short-term projects, rather than to marginal oilfields.

The contractor is largely exposed to reservoir and oil price risks with both types of contractual agreement. In the case of unsuccessful exploration, the contractor does not receive any compensation. If the oil price declines, then the share of revenue allowed for cost recovery decreases too. The predetermined remuneration fee of the service contract, unlike the PSC means that the contractor does not benefit from any upturn in reservoir or oil price.

5 Final Comment

Government and oil companies are the principal players in the upstream sector of petroleum industry; the level of competition varies from basin to basin. Governments normally seek to generate high levels of take from oil-related activity while oil companies want to ensure an appropriate, predictable and sufficient level of profitability in their operations. Taxation removes a considerable slice of the producers' profits, therefore oil companies prefer fiscal systems that result in a low overall tax level thereby allowing high post-tax returns. The challenge is therefore to design a fiscal regime that meets two competing objectives, and in doing so cut a way through the complications associated with petroleum taxation given the structure of the oil extraction industry.

There are no uniform solutions to the challenges of petroleum taxation. Variety, flexibility and a readiness to adapt and evolve are the key requirements. Multifaceted geological, technical, and market factors together with unstable and unpredictable political influences shape the petroleum fiscal regime employed. Natural resources, such as petroleum, have special characteristics that complicate the design of an optimal tax system. Oil is an exhaustible resource, with an uncertain level of reserves before any investment takes place. It is both a raw material input as well as a final product with no obvious close substitutes (so far).

None of the tax instruments put forward in previous studies offers an optimal tax. The main tax instruments often suggested are royalty, Brown tax, RRT and income tax. Each tax has both advantages and limitations. But, although a tax instrument can create distortions, it cannot be ruled out solely for this reason. The most appropriate tax instrument is one which creates the least distortion, and the more a tax is targeted towards economic rent, the less the distortion created. The concept of an ideal tax is a useful paradigm against which to test actual or proposed fiscal systems.

Across the oil-producing world, widely varied systems and techniques whereby governments acquire their share of national oil proceeds have developed, underpinned by a large variety of fiscal packages. The key determinants have been local conditions, especially those relating to the chosen style of relationship between the governing authorities and the oil-extracting enterprises concerned. These in turn tend to be determined by the general state of political maturity of the state in question and by prevailing ideologies and political fashions. Although one might expect to find tougher terms on contractual arrangements, this is not necessarily the case. Concessionary arrangements can be just as tough and while two concessionary regimes may have similar structures, the tax rates applied within them can lead to major differences in outcome as evidenced in the UK and Norway.

The tax rate gives a poor guide to the underlying fiscal regimes, its strengths and effectiveness; fiscal reliefs and the way the tax base is calculated, lead to major differences between fiscal packages.

Notes

1. The discovery of natural gas in the Netherlands in the 1960s had adverse effects on the Dutch manufacturing sector, mainly through the appreciation of the real exchange rate. By the end of the 1970s, when the high gas income from the gas resources fell, the traditional industries could not compensate for the loss of revenues from the energy sector and as a consequence unemployment rose. The negative consequence for traditional industries of a natural resource discovery has commonly been referred to as the Dutch disease.
2. The theory of optimal taxation concentrates primarily on personal income taxes and focuses on the effects of taxation on households rather than producers. A detailed discussion of optimal taxation theory can be found in Ramsey (1927), Diamond and Mirrlees (1971a, b), Dasgupta and Stiglitz (1971), Samuelson (1986), and Heady (1993). Altay (2000) presents a detailed summary of the different studies on optimal tax theory.
3. Detailed study is done by Raja (1999); also see Bond et al. (1987) and Smith (1999).
4. See, for instance, Garnaut and Clunies-Ross (1979), Swan (1984), Rowland and Hann (1986) and Kemp et al. (1997).
5. Kemp et al. (1997).
6. After its proposer Brown (1948), as referred to in Watkins (2001).
7. See Garnaut and Clunies-Ross (1975), Devereux and Morris (1983), Kemp and Stephens (1997).
8. The UK petroleum fiscal regime has included (over time) a royalty, petroleum revenue tax (similar to RRT) and corporation tax (income tax).

References

Altay, A. (2000), 'The theory of optimal taxation and new approaches: a survey', available at: http://www.sbe. deu.edu.tr/SBEWEB/dergi/dergi05/altay.htm (accessed Spring 2002).

Banfi, S., M. Filippini and A. Mueller (2003), 'Rent of hydropower generation in Switzerland in a liberalised market', Working Paper, Centre for Energy Policy and Economics (CEPE), Federal Institute of Technology, Zurich.

Blinn, K., C. Duval and H. Leuch (1986), 'International Petroleum Exploration & Exploitation Agreements – Legal, Economic and Policy Aspects', Report, Barrows Company Inc., New York.

Bond S., M. Devereux and M. Sunders (1987), 'North Sea Taxation for the 1990's', Report, Institute for Fiscal Studies, London.

Brown, E. (1948), 'Business income taxation and investment incentives', in L.A. Metzler (ed.), *Employment and Public Policy, Essays in Honour of A.H. Hansen*, New York: Norton, pp. 300–316.

Crawson, P. (2004), *Astride Mining: Issues and Policies for the Minerals Industry*, Mining Journal Books Ltd.

Dasgputa, P. and J. Stiglitz (1971), 'Differential taxation, public production and economic efficiency', *Review of Economic Studies*, **38**, 151–74.

Devereux, M. and C. Morris (1983), 'North Sea oil tax revenues: a disaggregated model', Institute for Fiscal Studies Working Paper No. 40.

Diamond, P. and J. Mirrlees (1971a), 'Optimal taxation and public production I: production efficiency', *American Economic Review*, **61**, 8–27.

Diamond, P. and J. Mirrlees (1971b), 'Optimal taxation and public production II: tax rules', *American Economic Review*, **41**, 277–96.

Garnaut, R. and A. Clunies-Ross (1975), 'Uncertainty, risk aversion and the taxing of natural resource projects', *Economic Journal*, **85**, 272–87.

Garnaut, R. and A. Clunies-Ross (1979), 'The neutrality of the resource rent tax', *Economic Record*, **55**, 193–201.

Garnaut, R. and A. Clunies-Ross (1983), *Taxation of Mineral Rents*, Oxford and New York: Oxford University Press.

Heady, C. (1993), 'Optimal taxation as a guide to tax policy: a survey', *Fiscal Studies*, **14**, 15–41.

Hotelling, H. (1931), 'The economics of exhaustible resources', *Journal of Political Economy*, **39**, 111–19.

Johnston, D. (1998), *International Petroleum Fiscal Systems and Production Sharing Contracts*, Tulsa, OK: PennWell Books.

Johnston, D. (2001), *International Production Sharing Contract Cash Flow Model*, Hancock, NH: Daniel Johnston & Co., Inc.

Kemp, A. and L. Stephens (1997), 'The UK petroleum fiscal system in retrospect', Working Paper, University of Aberdeen, Scotland.

Kemp, A., L. Stephens and K. Masson (1997), 'A reassessment of petroleum taxation in the UKCS', Working Paper, University of Aberdeen, Scotland.

Kooten, C. and E. Bulte (2001), *The Economics of Nature: Managing Biological Assets*, Oxford: Blackwell.

Mommer, B. (1997), 'Oil price and fiscal regimes', Oxford Institute for Energy Studies, WPM 24.

Mommer, B. (2001), 'Fiscal regimes and oil revenues in the UK, Alaska and Venezuela', Oxford Institute for Energy Studies, WPM 27.

Musgrave, R. (1982), 'A brief history of fiscal doctrine', in A. Auberbach and M. Feldstein (eds), *Handbook of Public Economics*, vol. 1, Amsterdam: Elsevier Science, pp. 1–59.

Nakhle, C. (2007), 'Do high oil prices justify an increase in taxation in a mature oil province? The case of the UK continental shelf', *Energy Policy*, **35**, 4305–18.

Nakhle, C. (2008), *Petroleum Taxation: Sharing the Oil Wealth*, London: Routledge.

Oil & Gas UK (2007), 'The 2007 economic report', www.ukooa.co.uk/issues/economic/index.cfm.

Raja, A. (1999), 'Should neutrality be the major objective in the decision-making process of the government and the firm', available at: www.dundee.ac.uk/cepmlp/main/html/car_article2.htm (accessed December 2000).

Ramsey, F. (1927), 'A contribution to the theory of taxation', *Economic Journal*, **37**, 47–61.

Ricardo, D. (1951), *The Principles of Economy and Taxation*, Vol. 1: *Works and Correspondence*, edited by P. Sraffa and M.H. Dobb, Cambridge: Cambridge University Press, as referred to by Watkins (2001).

Rowland, C. and D. Hann (1986), 'UK oil taxation: failings and reform', Discussion Paper, SEEDS No. 32, Surrey Energy Economics Centre, University of Surrey, Guildford.

Samuelson, P. (1986), 'Theory of optimal taxation', *Journal of Public Economics*, **30**, 137–43.

Sarma, J. and G. Naresh (2001), 'Mineral taxation around the world: trends and issues', *Asia-Pacific Tax Bulletin*, January, 2–10.

Smith, B. (1999), 'The impossibility of a neutral resource rent tax', Working Paper no. 380, Faculty of Economics and Commerce, Australian National University, Canberra.

Stiegeler, S. (ed.) (1985), *Dictionary of Economics and Business*, 2nd edn, Aldershot: Gower.

Sunley, E., T. Baunsgaard and D. Simard (2002), 'Revenue from the oil and gas sector: issues and country experience', IMF Conference Proceedings on Fiscal Policy Formulation and Implementation in Oil Producing Countries, Washington, DC, June 5–6.

Swan, P. (1984), 'Resource rent tax', *Economic Papers*, **3**, 1–11.

Watkins, C. (2001), 'Atlantic Petroleum Royalties: fair deal or raw deal', The AIMS Oil and Gas Papers, Atlantic Institute for Market Studies, Halifax, Nova Scotia.

18 The behavior of petroleum markets: fundamentals and psychologicals in price discovery and formation
Dalton Garis

Nature obeys laws that operate independently of whether they are understood or not; the only way man can bend nature to his will is by understanding and applying these laws. That is why alchemy failed and natural science reigns supreme.

But social phenomena are different: they have thinking participants. Events do not obey laws that operate independently of what anybody thinks. On the contrary, the participants' thinking is an integral part of the subject matter. This creates an opening for alchemy that was absent in the sphere of natural science. Operational success can be achieved without attaining scientific knowledge. By the same token, [the] scientific method is rendered just as ineffectual in dealing with social events as alchemy was in altering the character of natural sciences.

(Soros, 2003, p. 311)

1 Introduction

Soros (2003) captures the difficulty of modeling the behavior of markets including commodity futures markets such as oil, gas and petroleum products. These energy futures markets are more complex as they are the obligation to buy or sell some amount of the good at a previously specified price within a specified time period.

More behavioral complexity is created by the use of equity markets, including hedge funds. The result has been price runs leading to increased irrationality of petroleum markets. Market instability is set to continue as petroleum markets have undergone a fundamental change, limiting some of the usefulness and applicability of fundamental supply–demand analysis for price discovery and expectations.

The fundamentals of supply and demand typically form the central discussion of petroleum price formation; however, this chapter is concerned with those circumstances that lead traders to reject fundamental supply–demand analysis in petroleum markets, in favor of psychological characteristics. In this chapter we present a behavior analysis of petroleum markets to demonstrate how petroleum market prices behave under various scenarios. Of particular interest is the reason why the fundamentals of supply and demand are ignored in some instances while at other times they form the guiding analysis. Such an understanding will facilitate time-valued cost–benefit analyses. The chapter proceeds with a discussion of benchmarking crude oil prices, the role of the futures market in price discovery and market participant behavior.

On 10th July, 2008, the crude oil benchmark on the New York Mercantile Exchange, the West Texas Intermediate nearby futures contract, reached an all-time price spike of US$147.27/bbl. At the same time the Dubai Mercantile Exchange's Oman futures nearby contract, the benchmark for Gulf Middle East heavy sour crude, reached US$143.20/bbl. These prices subsequently plummeted as markets were unable to absorb the exponential price increases. By the end of February 2009, crude in New York sold for US$44.12/bbl, with Dubai Mercantile Exchange's Oman heavy sour being sold for US$45.39/bbl. This pattern of crude oil prices contributed to the 2008/09 troubles in the world economy. The exponentially increasing crude prices translated into exponentially increasing gasoline, heating oil, diesel, and jet fuel prices. Significant increases in these fuel costs had significant implications for consumers' expenditure as they contribute as much as 40 percent of food and transportation costs. Behavioural market analysis is used to explain why prices rose so high so quickly, why they fell in even less time, and how market participants can gauge the next big price movement in order to protect commercial activities.

2   The Markets for Crude

The International Crude Oil Market Handbook, 2007 (Energy Intelligence, 2007) lists and discusses 187 different crude oils that are produced and utilized by the world's energy users. However, only a tiny fraction of this production is sold directly to the market. Practically all of the world's production is traded from producer to consumer directly, without going through the terminal market intermediary, where open outcry and posted bid and ask prices are there for all to see.[1] The result is that the actual selling price of most of the world's crude production is observed only indirectly over one or more trading cycles.

Posted prices from the major oil exchanges, such as the New York Mercantile Exchange (NYMEX), the Dubai Mercantile Exchange (DME), or the Intercontinental Exchange (ICE), are, however, used as the price against which the price of all these other crudes is established. This 'establishing' is done through a combination of administrated pricing and comparing against prices such as NYMEX West Texas Intermediate, ICE Brent, or the new DME Oman sour. Crudes will be offered at a discount, or at a premium, to the benchmark being the closest in characteristics to the exchanged crude in question.

Thus, the world's crude oil is priced more or less against one of the existing marketed benchmark crudes. How, then, are the prices of these benchmarks established? What elements are involved in their pricing? What does a crude benchmark price really represent, and to what extent is it a reflection of the actual marginal cost in production?

3   Benchmark Crude Oils and Their Pricing

Pricing
The role of marker or benchmark crude oils in world oil markets is to discover the *willingness to pay* a given price per barrel for the next barrel of crude and equate it with the *willingness to supply* the next barrel of crude when the market offers a specified price per barrel (bbl) sold. In the non-Middle East–North Africa (MENA) region, oil production is not being replaced by new finds.[2] And it can be argued that at least for Middle East crudes the price of around US$89.00/bbl for West Texas Intermediate sold on the NYMEX (first week of December 2007) does not reflect the actual marginal cost of production – which could be as low as US$6.00/bbl for some Gulf state producing fields, it does indeed reflect the cost of *additional* production from those same wells and reservoirs.

First principles of economics dictate that the price for an exchanged good or service is where the marginal cost in its production for the supplier is equated to its marginal value in use for the demander. But this is not entirely true for oil. If true, then as for other commodities, oil produced at the cheapest cost would sell first, followed by more expensive production oil. Rather, some of the most expensively produced oil is sold next to cheaper production oil in the same market at a price commensurate with the marginal cost of the most expensive production oil, with the producers having lower-cost schedules banking the difference. Therefore, in a time of markets for scarce commodities becoming ever more globalized, and adjusting for qualitative differences and transaction costs, crude oil would seem to sell at approximately its highest marginal cost of production rather than its lowest.

In fact, oil is sold at a price reflecting more or less its *value in use* rather than its marginal cost of production. This explains why something that is relatively cheap to produce in large quantities in some parts of the world sells for far more than its cost of production. It is because consumers are competing for the world's supply of crude oil at unprecedented levels, forcing demand schedules ever outward. Supply–demand relationships and their current effect on crude prices is discussed in more detail in Section 10.

In the Arabian Gulf region, reservoirs are becoming more complex. They are mostly carbonates and experience large amounts of water intrusion, or water cut. While MENA wells generally contain more oil, their flow is not as high as in other world oil provinces. Much of the onshore and offshore infrastructure is becoming old, over 35 years in age, and is in need of upgrading. And this is at a time when such upgrades are expected to cost far more than prices obtaining just three years ago, due to competition with China and other growing economies for basic resources, such as steel. Costs of steel and other building materials have increased as China's rise to economic prominence empties the world's shelves of available commodities for its infrastructural expansion, and consumption for its multiplying middle class.

To these ordinary costs, shared by all other oil provinces seeking production expansion, must be added the additional costs associated with the Middle East's own brand of political risks. This risk premium is estimated to be adding as much as US$18.00–$24.00 to the current price of crude, according to the author's own estimates for 2006–07. Therefore, the world's benchmark crudes, were US$89.00/bbl on 5 December 2007 acting as a close approximation to the cost of obtaining an additional barrel of oil.

Benchmark uses
Benchmark crudes are used almost exclusively as *price insurance* in their capacity to track oil price changes expected during the transaction period of the physically traded crude stream of interest. As discussed in detail below, hedgers and speculators use benchmark crude prices as a proxy in tracking price changes for their own physical crude sales and deliveries. Even though the benchmark crudes are dissimilar from them in terms of their physical characteristics, the essential quality is that the benchmarks track price changes in tandem with the physical crude for which they serve as a price proxy. It is this characteristic which allows them to offer price insurance against untoward price movements for oil industry participants. The trade in benchmark crudes bought and sold in futures markets is approximately 20-fold greater than their existing available physical quantities,[3] almost none of which ends in actual physical delivery, as explained below.[4] Toward the end of the contract period as the purchase or sale of the actual crude stream they

handle gets closer, the purpose of holding the benchmark contracts as price insurance having been accomplished, traders exercise a 'round turn' to dissolve their futures contract positions for the benchmark.

The world's main benchmarks associated with the particular market where their primary sales occur as of 2008 are as follows:

1. *West Texas Intermediate (WTI)*   WTI is marketed on the NYMEX. It is a light, sweet crude, a blend of crude streams from West Texas and Eastern New Mexico in the United States. Its physical production is approximately 750 000 barrels per day (bpd). It is a landlocked crude almost never physically sold outside the United States. However, due to its association with the largest single oil-consuming market in the world, it has found popularity and abiding support as a benchmark crude, due to its accurately mirroring changes in American consumption demand.

    WTI is under pressure from falling production, however, which threatens its role as a benchmark. It currently benchmarks about 18 percent of the world's total crude oil trade of 83 mbd (million barrels per day). In order for a benchmark to be effective there must be sufficient physical sales to provide a good measure of market sentiment; otherwise its price can experience wild price swings from being a thinly traded entity. It is also a light sweet crude, very dissimilar to most of the world's physical production, which tends to be heavier and more sour. However, there is no move afoot to replace WTI with another benchmark, as it is well understood by market participants and is therefore a trusted marker crude.

2. *ICE Brent*   This is a time-blended and physically blended crude benchmark which marks most of the world's crude oil sales at present (Energy Intelligence, 2007). It is another light sweet blend, and also under pressure from falling production. However, due to its trade flexibility and structural versatility it has been utilized most particularly by Middle East producers to price their crudes, only one of which is for sale on any spot market.

3. *DME Oman*   This is the newest crude benchmark and in the opinion of this author, is destined to dominate the other benchmarks over time. It is sold exclusively in the Dubai Mercantile Exchange, a 50 percent–50 percent partnership with the NYMEX, which cross-lists its products. Physical production is around 700 000 bpd. DME Oman is a heavy sour, as is becoming most of the world's crude production. It is also produced in the Middle East, where its marginal production costs better reflect Middle East production realities. And finally, as other oil provinces outside the MENA regions become depleted, the intensity of Middle East crudes as a percentage of the world's total conventional crude production must increase, strengthening demand for a Middle East heavy sour marker crude to track prices for physical crude sales. Already, the Kingdom of Oman uses the daily closing price of the DME Oman futures contract to set its official selling price (OSP) for its crude sales. The other Gulf States are likely to follow suit before much longer.

Benchmark crude trade in practice

While much of the world's crude is quantified in terms of metric tonnes, benchmark crude oil is a contract to deliver or take delivery at a specified future date of a standardized lot of 1000 barrels, each barrel being 42 US gallons, specified as to specific gravity and sulfur content. No other characteristics of the crude are generally accounted for in the benchmark contract.[5] As just mentioned, these contracts are bought and sold in order for market participants to hedge the price risk inherent in being in the physical market for oil on either the buying or the selling side. A producer who has oil to sell is 'long' in oil, in the market to sell it. The fear is that the price will fall before the physical transaction is completed, resulting in a loss of revenue. A speculator agrees to purchase the production today, at a mutually agreeable price, in the hope of reselling it at a higher price in future. Thus, the producer receives the revenue needed, and the speculator, on the chance of reaping a profit, assumes all the price risk the producer chooses to avoid.

The benchmark crude oil market is actually a *market for price risk insurance*, wherein risk is bought and sold. On any given day, WTI's 750 000 barrels have contracts outstanding equaling 15 000 000 barrels. Very few of these traded contracts are actually delivered against. Rather, they act as surrogates in tracking the prices of the oil the buyers or sellers actually market. Buyers and sellers 'close out' these contracts by purchasing their opposite in what is called a 'round turn' and thereby being net zero in the benchmark market. It is not important that the benchmark has the same price as the physical crude whose price is being hedged; only that its price move and react to market conditions in tandem with the physical crude being hedged.

Benchmark crudes, being exchanged in open outcry or electronic bid-and-ask market arenas, are bought and sold, utilizing brokers to actually execute trades. Buyers and sellers also may avail themselves of any market intelligence that could possibly enhance their understanding of what prices are expected to do in future. A prime source of such intelligence is from the traders and brokerage firms themselves, those actually in the trading pits experiencing the ebb and flow of buy and sell orders as they occur, and who have some idea about the relative strength of market upside or downside potential at any moment. But understanding oil futures markets and benchmark trades as really being risk markets, where price risk is exchanged between buyers and sellers, makes clear what might otherwise seem puzzling behavior when observed using another contextual lens.

4   The Importance of the Futures Market in Discovering Cash Prices: Hedging and Speculating

The importance of the crude oil futures markets is in their dominance in determining cash prices, because it is the *expected future price* which is used to price things in the present. Even the local fruit vendor must price his or her stock based upon the expected replacement cost for whatever is sold at present. Crude oil is treated exactly the same.

The futures markets for crude are the largest futures commodity markets there are in terms of exchanged volume.[6] They have also developed a complexity and sophistication enabling market users a broad spectrum of positions to exchange risk with ease and transparency.

In these markets are the hedgers, who are in the market to offset their price risks, and their partners, the speculators, who seek risk in order to profit from it. Hedgers are physical users of crude oil or its products in one form or another, either buyers or sellers. They may be refiners who buy oil as a feedstock, or sellers to refineries, or distributors. The important point is that being an owner of crude or a buyer of crude exposes you to price risk, the chance that the price will move against you, and you pay too much or receive

Table 18.1   Gains and losses with futures market hedging for 1000 bbl

	Cash market	Futures market
Today	$97.00	Buy 1 @ $88.00/bbl
In six months	$88.00	Sell 1 @ $97.00/bbl
Loss or gain	($9.00)/bbl	$9.00

too little. Therefore, it is in your best financial interest to attempt to insure against such losses if at all possible. Since the price for crude cannot be controlled, the next best thing is to attempt to pre-buy or pre-sell a surrogate oil at an acceptable price today, to insure against financial loss in the physical market. Then it is someone else who will worry about changing prices, but not you.

Using a simplistic example, imagine that you own crude oil and sell it to a refinery on a delivery schedule over 12-month period. Your fear is that over the intervening months the price of oil might drop, hurting your revenues. You are 'long' crude oil in the physical market, owning it for resale in future. You seek to hedge against its losing value before it is time to sell. You go onto the futures exchange and 'sell' the oil today for future delivery, locking in a price that covers your expenses. When it is time to sell the physical crude, you 'buy back' the crude previously sold on the futures market. Because of the opposing positions taken for physical and futures contracts, a loss in one is offset by a gain in the other.

As Table 18.1 illustrates, the losses in the cash market experienced from selling at a lower price than its purchase price are exactly offset by the gains in the futures market position. Thus, the hedger takes the opposite position in the futures market than what obtains in the physical market. This serves as a rough insurance against price moves eroding the producer's revenues over time. The process is easily reversed for a refinery that must buy crude on a regular basis for its operations. In that case, it 'buys' the crude today on the futures market, then 'sells' it back to the market on or before taking delivery of the physical crude. Again, gains and losses between the two markets are offset.

The hedger has oil business from which s/he attempts to profit, and for which buying or selling oil, whose price fluctuates with each piece of news, is not part of the business plan. The hedger's revenues are in adding value to oil and gas products and not in riding the price of oil.

Speculators accept price risk from the hedgers and attempt to make a profit from price moves in oil. No wealth is created in the economic sense of adding value. Rather, the speculator acts as a *facilitator* of economic wealth creation, by taking the price risk, so that the hedger can perform the function of turning lower-valued resources into higher-valued finished goods.

Where futures markets are lacking or dysfunctional true values are difficult to ascertain, the economy makes costly mistakes of both over- and underproduction.

Futures markets now include all manner of industrial and mining commodities, financials, swaps, and numerous other entities, where price insurance through hedging can be quantified, unitized and standardized into saleable and exchangeable contracts.

Of the many regional and over-the-counter crude markers, such as the Platts Dubai traded in Singapore, only these three benchmarks have been discussed due to their dominance in – or promise to dominate – benchmark crude trading. Understanding how crude benchmarks are utilized by oil market participants in a general way, we can now discuss crude oil price behavior and the behavior of their participants under two distinct scenarios: (i) when market circumstances encourage price discovery based on the fundamentals of supply and demand, and (ii) when markets switch to a fear-and-greed analytical mindset.

5   How Floor Traders' Attributes Affect the Formation of Crude Oil Prices

External shocks and internal changes in the trader's psychological complexion over time impact on market behavior and render models of market and price behavior useless.

Pricing models back-tested using daily closing prices as a test procedure fail dismally under real-time circumstances, where prices are the result of split-second decisions and competitive behavior between buyers and sellers for any possible trading edge.

Market agents, in their opinions, biases, herding behavior, imitative practices, their fears and greed, do not act like atoms in space and time, where results are independent of those thoughts and proclivities. It is as if the atoms and molecules in space were able to decide for themselves if $PV = nRT$, or if it is a good thing to follow $F = ma$ right now. In nature, the subjective thoughts and impressions of the players in space matter not at all in terms of results. The laws are unaffected by beliefs, and results are not subject to them.

Prices are formed and maintained by market participants. That is why certain price patterns, having no independently verifiable predictive power, do, in fact, predict prices, because it is *believed* that a certain observed pattern results in an associated price behavior. It is the *belief* that caused the result, rather than the result forming independent and verifiable data, in a circular feedback process of a self-fulfilling prediction.

Economics recognizes that certain parameters change the positioning of demand and supply functions in economic space, including the number of demanders and technology sets. Suppliers and demanders – producers and consumers – are influenced by market and price expectations as to future realities, which cause their own behavior to change. Add to this that while individuals ordinarily act rationally and do not normally repeat errors systematically, groups of these rational individuals routinely and repeatedly commit systematic errors in judgment. That is, individuals are usually rational; groups rarely are.

Thus, the trading process occurs by rational individuals acting in quasi-rational groups, wherein expectations influence behavior, and predictions, based on subjective emotional constructions, may be self-fulfilling. These characteristics form the nexus of the price formation process in crude oil markets.

Traders operate under various strong and weak rules of behavior among themselves, causing them to trade so as to maximize profits. These characteristics of quasi-individual rational behavior within group restrictions add another layer of psychological factors to an already complex price discovery process. 'Behavioral finance', discussed by Montier (2003), suggests that the behavior of traders in economic space includes:

1.   *Herding behavior*   Here it is defined as a person retaining his/her individuality and autonomy, who nonetheless, follows the leadership exhibited by a well-respected group member (Fenton-O'Creevy et al., 2005). It is usually present when the trader

lacks certainty about his or her trading strategy, so looks towards a leader to clear up the darkness.

2. *Anchoring* This is letting initial thinking rule when the context in which it existed has changed, and the thinking should be updated, but is not. Outside of the trading floor the colloquial expression is 'stubbornness'. This can lead to disaster, especially when the price regime has suddenly shifted with new information, but the trading strategy has not kept pace. Such behavior is responsible for some of the most devastating losses in market trading, including LTCM, Enron Trading, and the collapse of Amaranth Advisors, LLC.

3. *Reputation* In the absence of certainty about a trade, it is best to follow what those with good reputations on Wall Street are doing. In the spring of 2006, Goldman Sachs released a study predicting that oil prices would reach US$105.00/bbl within a few years (Shenk, 2007). There was nothing new or even unexpected in this report; however, upon its release crude futures markets rose about US$2.45/bbl for the nearby contract, and retain that gain for days; at a time when crude prices usually sag as North America switches from refining for middle distillates to gasoline.

4. *Conventions bias* In times of severe uncertainty, do the conventional thing. The saying is 'No one got fired for shorting heating oil in April', meaning, making the status quo bet, the safe bet, is a good strategy when reasons to do otherwise are not convincing.

5. *Imitation* Again, when in doubt and trades must be made, imitating others is at least a possible strategy. It is not surprising, therefore, that markets reacted as they did with the release of the Goldman Sachs research report just mentioned. Since it was a bullish report by a respected Trading House, then naturally, traders would bid crude up in response. Since this was anticipated, even those traders who would have preferred to ignore the report as 'nothing new', were unable to do so. All of them had to get in to purchase crude needed for immediate use, which only made the price rise even higher.

Market participants know that uncertainty in the price discovery process means that 90 percent of all traders will be losers and only 10 percent winners. Most traders have a life cycle of about five to eight years of high success, followed by a move into management, increasing failure in trading, or complete burnout. Only a few are capable of bridging this life cycle to achieve successful lifelong trading careers.

Expectations concerning future prices influence cash or spot market prices for oil, even if based solely upon expectations of other traders' reactions to exogenous stimuli, and on the nature of the stimuli themselves. For example, a news item reports that temperatures are expected to fall this winter in the US Northeast and in Europe, the primary consumers of heating oil. The expected response for crude prices is for prices to rise in anticipation of increasing demand for heating fuel in those markets due to the trader attributive reasons just covered.

But even if stocks are already adequate for the expected freeze, prices will likely rise. Because traders, anticipating that such news would increase demand and therefore prices, must buy now, before prices rise too much, since they know that waiting will result in paying higher prices later. Thus, even if supplies are more than adequate – even if in surplus – prices will rise, and not because of actual physical demand increases but rather because of the buying behavior of the traders themselves. And since each knows that all others will buy on bullish news and sell on bearish news, they must themselves act before the rest do, in order to lock in the best price for their client.

Not only does this result in economic reality conforming to emotional beliefs, it also results in an *acceleration* of crude price moves in response to exogenous stimuli. This is a scenario for price volatility and price instability.[7]

6   The Market Participants

Market participants in crude oil futures markets can be divided into 'commercials' and 'non-commercials'.

First, a *commercial* trader is 'An entity involved in the production, processing, or merchandising of a commodity' (CFTC Glossary, 2008). They include oil producers, processors, wholesale sellers and buyers, and retail sellers of petroleum products. These businesses profit from their services in the petroleum industry, and not from changes in oil prices and have physical quantities of crude oil to be price hedged.

Second, *non-commercials* have no business directly with buying or selling physical quantities of petroleum from which they profit, but they may have indirect linkages and exposure to price risks in that a sudden fall or rise in crude prices could impact on their businesses. These may be:

1.   drilling and service companies in the oil industry, oil rig construction companies;
2.   catalyst suppliers to refineries;
3.   distribution, transportation, transshipment and storage companies who do not actually take ownership of the product;
4.   oil and petroleum banks having a large proportion of their loan funds tied up in the petroleum industry; or
5.   funds, comprising a very price-influencing group of large, non-commercial players. They are financial enterprises whose responsibility is to increase their value for their investors. They are usually run by a board of directors or an oversight committee who in turn hire a manager to take ultimate responsibility for their trading decisions and strategies. They may have trading floors or rooms replete with dozens of traders, young guns trading with millions of dollars per trade. They are speculators, attempting to profit from oil price changes.

Unlike the commercials, who own quantities of crude oil for which price hedging is sought, and whose owned physicals act as collateral against their futures positions, non-commercials have no actual physical stock of oil to collateralize their futures positions. They are required to follow a slightly different set of trading and disclosure rules in order to maintain market orderliness and protect market participants against reckless behavior that could destabilize markets to the detriment of all. For example, they must announce a 'large' buy or sell position before execution of the trade.

The largest players in the non-commercial group are the hedge funds. Most of these funds are new and relatively inexperienced in the ways of physical commodity futures markets. This inexperience can cause trouble for the markets and make their use by experienced parties relying on these markets to hedge their inherent petroleum business risk far more dangerous.

There are a number of funds categories:

1. *Hedge funds*   Take very large positions and use borrowed capital to leverage these already large positions to massive size. They are largely unregulated, but this is changing since the Amaranth Hedge Fund bankruptcy (late September 2006), when one of its traders accumulated a massive position in natural gas that moved against him.
2. *Pension funds*   These are large funds that invest member capital for the sake of growing value necessary to pay out pensions and annuities to retired workers or subscribers in perpetuity.
3. *Mutual funds*   These are usually open-ended funds that buy, hold, and sell in markets in order to increase the share value of their fund for their subscribers.
4. *Funds of funds*   These come in all types and are often very large and influential, sometimes being able to alter the trading strategy of those funds in which they are heavily invested.

These are the main non-commercial participants in petroleum market futures trading. They have differing objectives but in the long run, realize the mutually obtainable advantages of having a well-ordered and functioning cash and futures market.

Of primary importance to the futures and cash market regulators is the distinction between *price takers* and *price makers*. Price makers, especially if non-commercial, are so characterized due to their giant speculative positions. In the case of the commercials, they usually have physical assets to offset their large futures positions. But the non-commercial speculators, such as a hedge fund, can acquire a massive, non-hedged and highly leveraged position, which, if it turns against the fund and must be liquidated, could upset market prices. They can affect prices by getting in or getting out of the market unannounced. Regulations, therefore, require them to duly notify the market in advance of any expected purchase or liquidation of an existing position, in order to avoid even the appearance of market manipulation.

Price takers, on the other hand are mere mortals in these markets, who strive not to get crushed by the big players. Their entry or exit has no effect on market prices because their positions are deemed too small. It is the regulators' responsibility to ensure that this risk highway, populated simultaneously by giant earth-shaking trucks and scooters, tricycles and bicycles, functions in the best interest of all involved.

The real difficulty for commercials using futures and options markets is the number of large-position inexperienced players who increase market instability and volatility. They create inefficiencies in the market by failing to discover the 'correct' price, and if a large player, take a lot of other traders with them when the 'actual' price is later discovered. As discussed below, there really is no practical way to protect one's self against their costly mistakes.

7   Price Behavior in Futures Markets

Since cash, or spot, pricing has replaced long-term contracting for the large majority of crude selling,[8] and futures market prices dominate cash price formation, then how futures prices behave is the starting point in any serious analysis of world oil markets. Presented here is a description of the main forces affecting oil futures pricing. Making the analysis complex is that there is not a single regime for crude price behavior. The regime changes with the circumstances of the daily oil balance and expectations of the extent to which surplus production capacity can be readied to supply the market as needed. If the market believes that there is sufficient surplus supply capacity for any expected set of eventualities, then the fundamentals of supply and demand dominate; but if excess production capacity has fallen below some perceived tipping point, then markets abandon supply–demand analysis and fall back on fear-and-greed analysis. At that point, psychologicals completely rule price behavior in crude markets.

The numerous funds, and funds of funds, referred to above, which before the recent crude oil price rise were largely anchored in the equities and bond markets, have brought a level of chaos into commodity futures markets due to their inexperience.

With transaction costs falling, making it possible for vast sums of money to be put in or pulled out of various trades and investments at a moment's notice, all markets have become less stable as real long-term investing, often the result of the high transaction costs in getting in or out of a market position, has given way to real speculation, with 'hot money' chasing the best trade, and large dedicated computers finding these trades and making them automatically as soon as certain criteria are sensed by the trading program. Such program trading is becoming the norm in all markets. Managers are less trusting of a trader's hunch than a sophisticated quantitative trading program when it comes to risking millions of dollars on a trade's outcome.

But program trading has exacerbated market instability. Assume that there are hundreds of such trading programs written and used by hundreds or even thousands of traders. Now, rather than a market where some thousands of trades occur somewhat randomly, huge trading positions accumulate on one side of a trade due to the correlation of the computer trading programs, causing massive liquidity holes and instability. This was shown by the stock market crash in the United States on 19 October 1987. As the evidence would show, the presence of so-called 'portfolio insurance' and financial engineering exacerbated the price collapse because all the computer programs were correlated in the extreme of market tendencies, automatically executing the 'sell' orders as market characteristics deteriorated. Sell orders piled up in a down market, causing lower prices and even more sell orders. There ensued a classic 'run on the bank', or simply a price run, a cascading or domino effect, caused by positions becoming highly correlated, with Chicago stock futures hard wired to New York cash market trading floors.

Price runs are more likely in 'thin' markets, where there are few traders, thereby increasing the likelihood of highly correlated positions. In this case the market 'thinness' was caused by the hundreds of thousands of traders subscribing to relatively few computer trading programs. So, instead of an atomistic market we have a very thin market in terms of the distribution of trade reactions to the stimuli of market news.

By itself, this situation increases market price sensitivity to news and makes it harder to play these markets due to increasing instability, as distinct from market price volatility, which is easier to manage. But making the situation worse is the presence of novice hedge fund players whose experiences in equity and bond markets leave them ill prepared for trading in commodities markets. Because of their naivety and inexperience with commodities markets in general and crude oil markets in particular, their presence in oil markets is upsetting. Experienced industry users on the hedging and speculating side get blind-sided by market prices acting erratically and unexpectedly due to the presence of these neophytes. In time, they will obtain the requisite experience to play oil markets with the old hands, but in the meantime, and with every new such wave of neophytes, market behavior experiences chaos, with numerous and large trading mistakes being made which lead the market toward inefficiencies. The 'correct' relative value is not discovered because too many players do not understand the market's characteristics and flow, and just guess wrong about its expected future direction.

Finally, the tendency of the new actors in the crude oil markets, the hedge funds and funds of funds in particular, to use *excessive leverage* in taking their positions adds even more price instability to crude oil futures markets by shortening the 'patience' that can be exercised when prices turn against the position taken. With most of the position being held using borrowed funds, a losing position must be quickly abandoned, lest it ruin the trading firm. This obviously reduces market price stability as it has a tendency toward generating price runs.

The 2006 collapse of the hedge fund Amaranth Advisors, LLC, is instructive. Amaranth, a multi-strategy hedge fund, made its living in convertible arbitrage and had assets in excess of US$9.2 billion. Witnessing the commodity market boom, it moved into commodity futures after profitable trades in its main line became more difficult to find. (Winners attract imitators; and with no barriers to entry and exit, the winnings, or *rents*, are bid away to the level of ordinary market returns not worth the riskiness of the trades.) Amaranth began to bet on the future price of natural gas. The fund abruptly collapsed after one of its traders bet on natural gas futures and lost the company US$6 billion in a week, causing a run on the bank by investors redeeming their funds, and consequently the bank's demise. According to a Senate report, Amaranth had engaged in natural gas calendar-spread trading on a vast scale in which the fund was long winter-delivery contracts and short non-winter-month contracts in the 2006 through at least 2010 maturities (Till, 2007).

This is not to condemn all commodity and energy hedge funds. Indeed, the hedge fund of experienced oil men like T. Boone Pickens and Michael Farmer, BP Capital Commodity Energy Fund, performed well, correctly predicting the anticipated direction of oil. The presence in the oil futures markets of such an experienced and profitable player directs market participants to discover the 'actual' value of the commodity in future time. With this information the market functions efficiently.

The characteristics of market traders, crude market behavior and price formation results in the following attributes.

First, crude oil price aggregated time-series distributions are heteroskedastic. For a given aggregated time series, generally no single probability distribution can adequately represent it (Mandelbrot, 2004). There may be several distributions operating simultaneously, with part of the series coming from an extreme-valued distribution, such as a Weibul, a gamma or Cauchy, and other parts intermingling, looking more like a fat-tailed Gaussian distribution, all with non-stable variances. While true that the central limit theorem (CLT) can normalize all the various mean values, we must ask how useful such a statistic would be in describing underlying behavior.

Second, critical events in crude oil price time series, which are predicted to occur extremely rarely, happen more often than predicted by standard models. The result is that extreme-valued price behavior is *not* unusual and must be prepared for by market participants (ibid.). Commodity markets, due to their liberal use of leverage and their

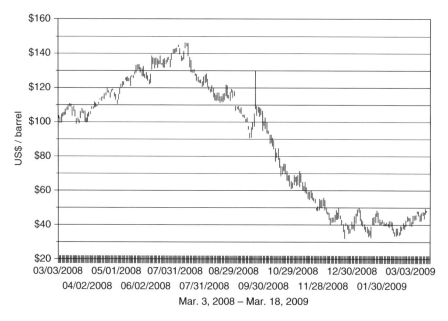

Source: WTRG Economics ©2009. www.wtrg.com. (479) 293-4081.

Figure 18.1   NYMEX crude oil futures high–low (front month)

short time horizon, are highly news sensitive and are already known for their tendency to do the unexpected, but may be far more dangerous than thought.

Third, critical events occur in swift succession, with one extreme-valued event presaging another. Then, markets experience relative calm for a relatively long period until exogenous forces again result in unstable and extreme-valued price behavior. The practical implication is in making market entrance and exit to protect assets very difficult or impossible at the very moment it is most needed. Consider the price time series as shown in Figure 18.1.

In this series, each bar represents one day of trading. Observe how the price plummeted toward the end of 2008. Now imagine the difficulty of getting a 'sell' order executed during that time. Few were buying and most were selling. The trading pits were filled with traders, their hands palm-out, indicating a sell, and almost no one with the hand palm-in, indicating a buy. So, the price continued to slide until at last it had fallen far enough to interest someone on the buying side. And so it would go on, day after day. No matter how the trader might have attempted to protect his or her position with 'stop-loss' sell orders, these could not have been executed anywhere near the specified price, and the trader would have seen his or her position continue to lose money.

Fourth, periods of calm in oil market price behavior are generally associated with low relative prices and the presence of large quantities of surplus oil production in reserve which can be placed on the market within a few weeks or months. Such calm periods, being the result of readily available surplus production capacity, are capable in themselves of inducing lowered commodity prices, since the danger of undersupply at current prices has been otherwise diminished.

Fifth, market prices are more often unstable rather than volatile; unstable in the sense of exhibiting 'price runs' – when prices move rapidly and continuously in one direction before stabilizing or reversing.[9] Volatility, prices changing direction rapidly and repeatedly, is of less concern to industry futures market users than price instability because it is the price runs that can force them out of the market at the very time when the price risk insurance that the markets provide is most sorely needed.

Sixth, market behavior has memory. It remembers what events occurred previously, what the market reaction was and what the result was, and tends thereby to 'fight the last war', or tends to utilize the same set of procedures learned from the last similar event (Fenton-O'Creevy et al., 2005). This may lead even seasoned experts to fail to adjust to a changing price behavior regime causing losses until the lesson is re-learned. The saying in the trading pits is that the next price bubble will come when most of those who lived through the last bubble are gone.

Seventh, crude oil prices, being the record of traders' actions and proclivities, are biased, causing prices to become at times either rigid down – refusing to fall – or rigid up – refusing to rise. Often the market disposition discounts any bad news which would ordinarily cause oil prices to fall, while reacting to any news indicating a rise in prices by bidding oil prices higher. Then, after a time, the market 'changes its mind' and any bad news causes a downward price move while any good news is largely ignored. This aspect of crude oil market behavior offers a wealth of interesting research questions. Among them: (a) What causes a bull market to suddenly reverse direction and become a bear? (b) Is there a quantifiable half-life for the influence of news? Could a *novelty index* or elasticity be calculated, to model when the market is likely to lose interest in some bit of news and when it fastens onto it as of great moment?

Eighth, the tendency toward bull or bear biasing exacerbates the phenomenon known in economics as the 'fallacy of composition'. This is when individuals, acting rationally in response to market signals, cause markets to become unstable as all take the same action for the same or a similar reason. For example, if you become convinced that oil prices will rise in the next few days due to a sharp change in weather and Organization of Petroleum Exporting Countries (OPEC) pronouncements that the market 'is well supplied with oil at present', your rational decision is to buy oil today before prices rise. But all others are reacting to the same information stream and all think the same way. The result is that prices go up farther and faster than otherwise – overshooting – because of the behavior of the traders' themselves in response to information streams they all share.

Ninth, the fallacy of composition generates self-fulfilling expectations. It is a self-fulfilling expectation when, because traders think that prices will head upwards, then trade in anticipation of the rise, and by acting cause the rise, then believe themselves to be vindicated in their market thinking concerning the expected movement of prices. It was their own actions which ensured that the price rise would occur, thus creating the self-fulfillment of the expectation. This also works on the downside.[10]

Tenth, self-fulfilling expectations explain the success of backward-looking market trading tools such as price charting, Fibonacci numbers and other similar analyses. Because traders *believe* that a 'head-and-shoulders' top on a graph indicated a market price top, they begin to sell off their long positions. And prices do indeed fall, just as expected. This is why even traders who reject the actual predictive content of such technical analyses nonetheless must not ignore it, because they know others will act upon its signals, and therefore prices will likely move as the chart predicts. The common saying among commodity traders is, 'Use the fundamentals of supply and demand to determine whether you should be long or short (a buyer or seller), but use the technical analysis to time your trades'.[11] Consider the example of technical chart analysis for oil, as depicted in Figure 18.2. If past behavior is indicative of future patterns of behavior then this chart will be useful for predicting future market outcomes. But this can only be true if enough of the participating market traders act upon its predictions. This is a classical example of the *post hoc ergo propter hoc*, or 'after this, therefore because of this' fallacy.

Eleventh, price instability – the tendency for prices to run – is far more dangerous for hedgers and speculators alike than is price volatility. Instability can make markets for risk too dangerous to utilize with futures contract hedging, while volatility is far easier for market players to manage on either the speculating or hedging side. (This situation has improved somewhat due to the new tools of *options on futures*, whereby the total risk associated with the futures side of a hedged position is limited to no more than the option premium.)

These are the 11 attributes of futures markets for crude oil. Note how they are dominated by psychological characteristics rather than supply and demand analytics. Does this mean that fundamental analysis has no place in the tool bag of the energy economist? Certainly not; but what it does mean is that it is no longer possible for practicing energy economists and engineers to ignore psychologicals when pricing energy revenues and calculating payout times for projects, especially mega-projects, and offers another variable which, if understood, can provide the economist with greater pricing prediction facility.

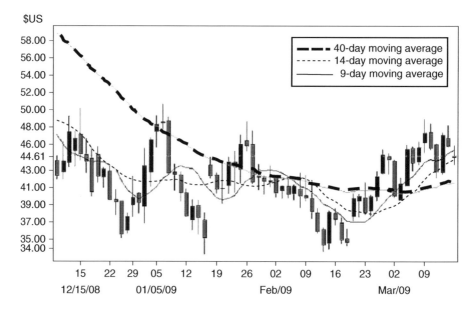

Figure 18.2   Technical analysis of oil price time series

8   Fundamentals, or Fear and Greed: Which and When?

When available surplus crude oil production in the daily oil balance falls below some psychologically important level in light of geopolitical and economic risks, then fundamental analysis gives way to fear-and-greed analysis and psychological reaction functions become paramount. The fundamental and geopolitical conditions of December 2007 suggest that when available surplus production capacity falls below 2 mbd, markets change from using fundamentals to using psychologicals in gauging expected price behavior. In 1979, OPEC had cut supplies to some Western consuming nations for a brief period. The market behavior reflected the perception that oil might be in short supply. Prices rose accordingly. However in 2004, the price move was demand driven. But the world never really became short of oil, only oil at older and lower prices.

In each case the market perceived that there might be a shortage of oil and buying behavior bid up the oil price. Figure 18.3 shows that during the intervening years, prices moderated and did not experience any significant spikes.

Trading is a competitive enterprise where reaction functions, fear and greed hold sway at any instant. Key to understanding price behavior is knowing which market regime is presently ascendant – bullish tendencies or bearishness – particularly during times when expectations are the governing tendencies. In the long run, fundamentals matter most; but in the short run psychologicals tend to dominate. The difficulty is that for traders themselves the long run is usually a few moments or even seconds, with a few days being an eternity.

The oil price series in Figure 18.4 is for the nearby futures contract for WTI crude

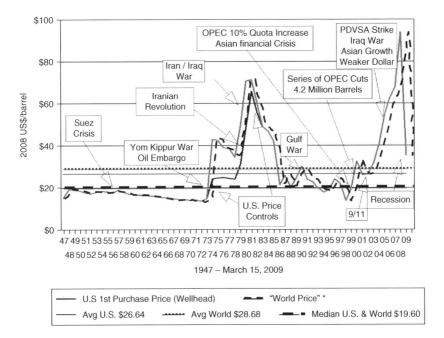

Source: WTRG Economics ©1998–2009. www.wtrg.com. (479) 293-4081.

Figure 18.3   Crude oil prices 2008 dollars

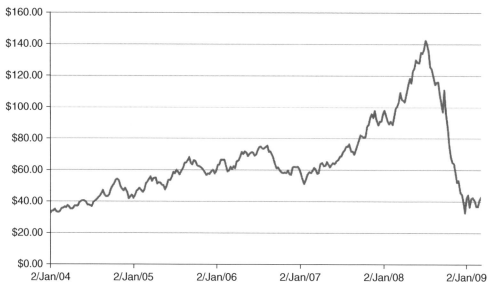

Source: www.WTRG.com.

Figure 18.4   New York crude oil front month prices 2004–2009

marketed on the NYMEX. It is one of the three most important benchmark crudes. Even at nearly US$100.00/bbl, buyers were capable of pushing the price up over US$140.00 – an all-time high for a barrel of crude. The reason was that a US$100.00/bbl purchase is better than a US$140.00 purchase, so buy now, before it rises even higher. But the very act of buying at US$100.00/bbl forced the price up over US$140.00 as the number of demanders forced the demand curve ever rightwards and along the short-run fixed supply curve.

9   The Structure of Fundamental Analysis

Fundamental analysis of supply and demand represents the starting point for any price theory of oil pricing. Such analysis reveals information to all market participants; of interest is the relative rather than the absolute value of the goods traded. The efficient market hypothesis holds that markets are efficient and that all costs and resource returns are reflected in the market price.

Oil supply and oil demand data are reported by such public agencies as the Energy Information Administration (EIA) of the US Department of Energy, the International Energy Agency in Paris, France, and by the business press. Every Wednesday at 10:00 AM Eastern Time, the EIA reports oil, gas and petroleum product inventory and stock levels for the United States. The market has the power to radically and quickly move prices. These data establish expected price fluctuations based on the difference between the quantity which can be supplied and the quantity demanded in the market period. It enables psychologically based reaction functions to recalibrate their status quo ante

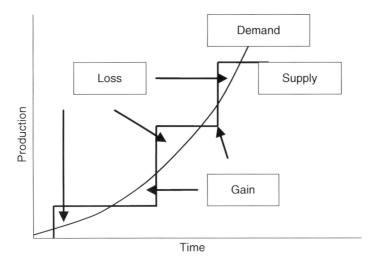

Figure 18.5   Relationship between production supply and production demand

positions and thus to 'guesstimate' what markets are likely to do in response to new bearish or bullish information streams.

10   Supply, Demand and the Current Oil Price: A Brief Discussion

Supply limitations in the presence of increasing demand: what are the dangers?
In 2006, after crude oil prices had increased twofold, the majors, the international and national oil companies ramped up exploration and production and refinery production (Garis, 2005; *Oil & Gas Journal*, 2006; MEES, 2006). The structural shift was thought to be another price cycle in crude oil. International oil company profits were increasing at an increasing rate and some, such as ExxonMobil and Royal Dutch/Shell, preferred to use the money to buy back their own stocks rather than dedicate these additional funds to increasing E & P activities.

Oil production, distribution and refining taken as a single venture is a cyclical industry. When prices for crude are low, there is little incentive to increase investment and infrastructural expansion; but when prices rise, such expansion will take five years, causing prices to spike. The result is for there to be either too little production capacity to meet demand at moderate prices or too much capacity to maintain prices that are capable of making such infrastructural investments profitable. Figure 18.5 shows that over time, demand is continuously increasing function while production supply is discontinuous with discrete increases. This causes producers to experience times of profit, when the quantity demanded is greater than supply at current prices, followed by times of loss, when the quantity supplied is greater than demand at current prices.

Demand increasing faster than supply
Since 2001, China has significantly increased its demand of commodities from the world at a rate of acceleration of unprecedented scale. The demand is not only for oil, but also includes cement, steel, copper, aluminum, coal, both thermal and metallurgical (coking),

lead and iron ore. By 2006, the daily rental rate for an off-shore exploratory drilling rig has surpassed US$650 000/day. Steel is in such short supply that it is pushing up the development and production costs of oil (and gas) projects. It now takes two years to deliver an oil tanker ordered from a shipyard. Even highway bridges and other steel-intensive projects are delayed, with associated cost increases.

China's 2007 demand was mostly for infrastructure expansion and investment; with only about 25 percent consumer driven, demand is less sensitive to price increases than otherwise. India's demand has also risen significantly. Sub-Saharan Africa is likely to be the next region to undergo explosive energy demand growth.

This will increase crude oil demand faster than it can be supplied at current prices. Indeed, it is not clear that oil production can be increased much beyond current levels in the short run. No significant new oil discoveries are scheduled to ease the supply–demand situation in the short run. Therefore prices are likely to remain above US$85–90.00/bbl, because this reflects the marginal value in use and likely is very close to the marginal cost of new oil production. Outside the MENA region, in sub-Saharan Africa, the Pacific Rim, the Atlantic Basin and the Arctic, there has been no large (in excess of five billion barrels) field of crude discovered. The oil majors, the international oil company giants such as ExxonMobil, Shell and BP, have not been able to replace their production in spite of spending billions of dollars. It appears that oil production outside the MENA regions is shrinking, notwithstanding some significant finds in Brazil and the yet to be exploited Caspian Basin, regions of Libya and Iran.

Even in the MENA region, where over 60 percent of the world's conventional crude reserves are located, and where fields can produce hundreds of thousands of barrels per day, increased production is difficult. According to petroleum engineering sources at the Petroleum Institute, an Abu Dhabi National Oil Company (ADNOC) affiliate engineering college, gathered over several years of personal conversations, the low-cost production oil is already being pumped out and is spoken for. Any production capacity increases from this point onwards will require expensive technology and complex drilling patterns in order to achieve meaningful production additions.

The real danger for conventional crude oil producers, therefore, would seem to be in falling behind accelerating demand increases, forcing crude prices to rise to a level that will sustain the viable commercialization of non-conventional crude production, most particularly for transport fuel, which makes up 70 percent of total crude oil demand. By assuming that the recent price increases in crude resulted from an ordinary cyclical process, and failing to understand that there would be a structural change in demand from the rise in world economic prominence of China and India, oil majors have not yet received the economic signal to increase investment.

11   Summary: The Dominance of Behavioral Analysis in Market Pricing

Traders operated within a short-run context. In the short run, fundamentals are ordinarily drowned out by psychological noise and concerns; trader behavioral characteristics including herding, imitation, anchoring and leadership tendencies dominate. The result is that crude markets experience an array of challenges in discovering a crude price reflecting its relative value in the economy. At times when the daily oil balance is slack, that is, when available supply production is capable of addressing a geopolitically created reduction in the world's current oil supply, prices tend to revert to reflecting actual supply–demand relationships. When available surplus daily production falls below 2 mbd, markets abandon fundamentals and turn to the more atavistic motivators of fear and greed. Each time this production is available, which was not the case in 2006/07, markets recalibrate their expectations somewhat, so that more time is needed during which the available surplus production falls below 2 mbd to again divorce prices from the realities of the fundamentals. Fear and greed will take over from supply–demand analysis as soon as available surplus production is deemed inadequate to redress a supply shortfall in some part of the world's long crude oil supply chain.

The overwhelming role of expectations in crude price behavior mostly explains why oil prices have continued to rise in the presence of seemingly adequate world supply, together with the realization that the next barrel of crude produced will not come as easily – and therefore as cheaply – as current production. Crude oil sells at a market price that reflects less its marginal cost of production and more its marginal value in use.

Accelerating trend expectations occurs whenever prices of crude oil increase solely due to some piece of news about future expectations but have no relevance to current supply–demand relationships, causing price increases to take on a life of their own and making crude markets dynamically unstable, in addition to – or rather than – being simply volatile. Momentum trading, herding and the fallacy of composition, backward-looking and self-fulfilling expectational charting analysis – all these elements are attempts by traders to gain even the least possible edge in the competitive world of trading for oil, as they know only too well the likelihood that 90 percent of a year's trades will be wrong.

The irrationality of crude markets is also on display when we see under- and overshooting in price discovery as prices attempt to adjust to new realities for demand or supply in a process of translation and divining from terse and cryptic news.

The risk premium for MENA crude explains why it sells for a price equal to high-cost production areas, such as deepwater offshore Atlantic Basin production.[12] It is fairly easy to predict that were the geopolitical risks in the Arabian Gulf threatening crude supplies and transportation (60 percent of Asian imports travel through the Strait of Hormuz), oil prices could fall back by as much as US$18.00/bbl. Indeed, OPEC is unlikely to be sanguine about crude prices in excess of US$70.00/bbl as it hastens the day that non-conventional crudes begin replacing Middle East conventional crudes in transport fuel and energy generation, and therefore threatens maximum monetization of their conventional crude reserves.

A research line of possible utility is an analysis of the half-life of the ability of a piece of news to move crude market prices. It is observed that after a time, additional bad news from one of the oil provinces fails to move prices as previously. The market reaches a point of 'news fatigue' concerning that item, completely 'discounting' the news as being already fully incorporated into current prices. The timeline of this discounting is of interest for predicting price activity where regularities could be discovered.

Notes

1. See www.nymex.com.
2. 'Energy Intelligence survey shows world oil reserves are not being fully replaced', 16 April 2007, available at: www.energyintel.com (accessed 2006).
3. See www.nymex.com.

4. See www.nymex.com.
5. Contract specifications are readily available from www.nymex.com.
6. See www.nymex.com.
7. This is based on as yet unpublished research by the author.
8. See www.nymex.com.
9. From unpublished research by the author.
10. Unpublished research by the author.
11. As heard by the author from numerous pit traders on the NYMEX and the CME whose names are long forgotten.
12. However, current prices above US$88.00 (December 2007) are allowing the making of economic profits. Thus, the risk premium in some parts of the world is supplying the entire industry with economic rents in the current market period (2006 only). However, when these profits are spread over the entire life cycle of a cyclical industry, it is likely that the rents will disappear.

References

CFTC Glossary (2008), 'A guide to the language of the future industry', Washington, DC, Commodities Futures Trading Commission of the United States, available at: www.cftc.gov/educationcenter/glossary/index.htm (accessed 28 February 2009).
Energy Intelligence (2007), *The International Crude Oil Market Handbook*, *2007*, New York: Energy Intelligence Group, available at: www.energyintel.com.
Fenton-O'Creevy, Mark, Nigel Nicholson, Emma Soane and Paul Willman (2005), *Traders: Risks, Decisions, and Management in Financial Markets*, Oxford: Oxford University Press.
Garis, Dalton (2005), 'Fighting the last War: What do Rig Counts Say?', *OGN: Oil & Gas News*, May 2–8.
Mandelbrot, Benoit (2004), *The (Mis)Behavior of Markets: A Fractal View of Risk, Ruin, and Reward*, New York: Basic Books, Chs VII, XII.
Middle East Economic Survey (MEES) (2006), Nicosia, Cyprus: Middle East Petroleum & Economic Publications (Cyprus) Ltd, available at: www.mees.com.
Montier, James (2003), *Behavioral Finance: Insights into Irrational Minds and Markets*, Chichester: John Wiley.
Oil & Gas Journal (2006), Pennwell Petroleum Group, Tulsa, OK, available at: www.ogj.com.
Shenk, M. (2007), '$100 Oil Price May Be Months Away, Say CIBC, Goldman I (Update 1)', Bloomberg.com, update 23 July.
Soros, George (2003), *The Alchemy of Finance*, rev. edn, Chichester: John Wiley.
Till, Hillary (2007), 'The Amaranth Collapse: What Happened and What Have We Learned Thus Far?' École De Hautes Études Commerciales du Nord Business School, Risk and Asset Management Research Centre, Paris, Nice, Lille, August.

Further reading
The following are some useful texts on the subjects covered in this chapter. Outside of doctoral dissertations most of the research into the behavior of markets has concentrated on financial and foreign exchange markets, with little – except for Mandelbrot – on commodity time-series data.

Beutel, Peter C. (2005), *Surviving Energy Prices*, Tulsa, OK: Pennwell Corporation. (A good introduction to petroleum futures, options and options on futures.)
Kaufman, Perry J. (2003), *A Short Course in Technical Trading*, Hoboken, NJ: John Wiley. (A good introduction to most aspects of technical trading currently employed by commodity traders.)
Kindleberger, Charles P. and Robert Aliber (2005), *Manias, Panics, and Crashes: A History of Financial Crises*, 5th edn, Hoboken, NJ: John Wiley. (The definitive text on price bubbles.)
Schleifer, Andrei (2000), *Inefficient Markets: An Introduction to Behavioral Finance*, New York: Oxford University Press. (An accessible economic analysis of behavioral anomalies and their effects on markets and prices.)
Sornette, Didier (2004), *Why Stock Markets Crash: Critical Events in Complex Financial Systems*, Princeton, NJ: Princeton University Press. (A survey of current dynamic modeling techniques for market behaviors in times of crises. Technical but accessible to the numerate non-professional.)

19 The prospects for coal in the twenty-first century[1]
Richard L. Gordon

1 Introduction

During the twentieth century, coal moved from the principal general-use fuel to one whose use increasingly was concentrated in generation of electricity. In addition, many historically heavily coal-dependent countries reduced total coal consumption. This transition naturally appalled the industry and its supporters. Much expensive and futile effort was devoted to stemming these changes. A key theme is that the ample availability of coal should lead to far greater use. A final less impressive development is the rise of a new world seaborne coal trade dominated by a few relative newcomers to both coal production and export.

This discussion begins with an explanation of the defects of assertions made about vast coal supplies, the misunderstanding of available resource-availability data, and the neglect of the underlying economics. In Section 3, attention turns to the problems of producing, transporting, transforming, and consuming coal. Formidable problems prevail even if environmental impacts were ignored. Then the history of coal production is reviewed, as is the substantial reorganization of the industry. Coal trade patterns are examined in Section 4. US policies on mine safety and coal leasing are then reviewed in Section 5. The discussion concludes with a view of the prospects in Section 6.

2 Coal, Investment Myopia, and the End of Oil: The Theory and Practice of Energy Transition

It is often argued that a decline in oil production is impending and private investors are not correctly anticipating this development. These assertions inevitably link back to Hubbert's much-cited but little-read[2] prediction of the decline of US oil based on a statistical appraisal of the physical availability of oil in the United States.

In practice, economic limits kick in well before these technological limits are reached as was the case with oil. US oil declined, not because of depletion, but because a superior alternative – Middle Eastern oil – arose. The peak was reached *later* than desirable because of the resistance to imports. Thus, it was coincidence that the pattern of decline determined by changing energy policy matched what Hubbert expected due to physical limits.

Private investors and the free market are better able to anticipate future trends than government (see Cohen and Noll 1991) and therefore produce efficient levels of investment.

Importantly, better anticipation is not identical to slowing the decline of oil. Economic analysis beginning with that of Gray (1914) and including Hotelling (1931) provides an extensive literature on exhaustible-resource management. Gordon (1966, 1967),

Herfindahl (1967), Scott (1967), and particularly Cummings (1969)[3] made the critical contribution producing the essence of the theory of Hotelling's earlier observations.[4]

Hotelling's theory explains the optimal behavior of production of a good available in an amount fixed by nature. A critical tacit assumption is that the demand for that good will persist long enough that if the good is sold at a price equal to its marginal cost of production, later generations will get none of a good that they desire. Gordon (1967), Herfindahl (1967), and Koopmans (1974) noted that should the critical time of unsatisfied demand be nonexistent or simply at a sufficiently distant date, efficient current behavior would ignore the eventual depletion. When depletion comes nearer, resource owners respond by restricting output to provide for later generations. However, contrary to some treatments of Hotelling, this would not produce a simple, readily observable impact on *prices*. Hotelling's analysis started with a simpler, better-developed case that tacitly dealt with extraction of homogeneous resources producible at constant costs.[5] In that case, what Hotelling termed the 'net price' (the average *profit* per unit of output) would rise at r, the market rate of interest, percent per year. With pure competition in mineral rights, these rents would be paid as royalties. However, since production incurs costs, the market price would necessarily grow at a slower rate than profits since price exceeds profits and thus a given amount of increase is a smaller percentage of market price than of profit.

Exhaustible-resource economics involved numerous independent discoveries, often many years apart. Among these was that in the general case, two other rewards to hoarding occur. The simpler is due to increasing costs as output rises in any time period. A further benefit of reducing output over time is declining marginal costs (Gray 1914).

In addition, if resources are heterogeneous, the additional benefit of reduced output is delaying the increasing costs of cumulative production. The benefits of delaying depletion of better resources were simply the sum of the present values of the resulting cost savings.[6]

The cases usually considered produce rising prices and falling output. These outcomes are not inevitable. Rapid but decelerating shifts in demand could require rising output to offset an excess profit rise from constant output; rapid downwards *shifts* in costs could require price decreases again to reduce the profit rise to the required level.[7]

Thus, in general, the r percent rule degenerates into the general proposition that something is valuable, and thus an asset, only if some combination of immediate payments and capital gains gives an overall yield of at least r percent. Critically, exhaustibility introduces no new market failures. If the assumptions for pure competition prevail, response to exhaustion is efficient. To make matters worse, the impacts of market failure differ. Monopoly still usually produces inefficiently low output; detrimental externalities still lead to excess output. Imperfect capital markets, if interpreted narrowly, might imply excessive output. However, in general this is not true.

The economic interpretation of inadequate concern for the future is the use of too high a rate of interest to evaluate the true present worth of future incomes to current investors. If inefficiently high interest rates are reduced, oil production may indeed be slowed because of increased incentives not to produce. However, this can be counteracted by the increased incentives to invest in and operate new producing capacity. In a simple exhaustible-resource model, concern for the future inspires through rising prices over time hoarding of supply for future generations of consumers.[8] A too high rate of interest has the direct effect of making hoarding less attractive. However, an indirect effect of raising the cost of utilizing equipment discourages investment in and utilization of producing capacity. Neither effect will always outweigh the other. For producers hoarding so much that prices are well above current production costs, the reduced attractiveness of hoarding is critical. Where costs are closer to price, the investment-disincentive effect dominates (see Gordon 1966). Theory indicates what would happen if demand for a physically limited material lasts forever. Some would say that the theory provides indicators of what happens when exhaustion is a pressing problem.

Contrary to assertions early in the years of price rises, oil-exporter behavior is better explained by theories of cartelization than of exhaustion. An exhaustion theory implies that decisions be consistent and that unilateral action is, if anything, preferable. The opportunity to hoard exists whatever other producers do and indeed the less others hoard the more the actual hoarders benefit. In contrast, cartelization does require coordination. Consistent behavior also is preferable to those hoping to cartelize, but the theory and practice of cartelization indicates that differences among potential participants often leads to breakdowns. The fitful path of oil prices since 1971 is clear evidence that unstable cartelization is the most likely situation.

There are implications for procurement of information on resource endowment. Adelman (1990) notes the critical distinction between exploration and development. (Exploration is the initial, far less costly step of locating potentially valuable mineral occurrences. Development is the much more expensive step of constructing the facilities needed to extract the minerals.) Exploration is undertaken steadily to build up a backlog of sites that potentially are worth developing. Then as justified, the area is developed. Such development can continue for decades, and indeed even centuries, as conditions dictate. Exploration is an ongoing activity driven, not by fear of depletion, but by recognition that good opportunities to reduce costs may exist. Exploration and development are limited to serving immediate opportunities to produce.

The actual endowment of most minerals is unknown; what is known is the amount of 'proved' reserves – the amount in developed occurrences. Neglect of this fundamental point perennially produces unfounded concern. A second front on resource availability has opened that admits resources are ample but decries their use on environmental grounds (Holdren 2002).

Indicators exist on the vast physical availability of several alternatives to oil and natural gas including coal, oil shale, tar sands, uranium supplies as extended by breeder reactors, hydrogen, wind, and solar. The broad prediction that ultimately the world economy will move to one or more of these alternatives is probably correct, but the lack of knowledge of the optimum outcome is still a hindrance. The preferred options and the timing of the transition cannot be known, and concern among oil companies about depletion has not left the public-relations realm. Two broad classes of scenarios emerge. In one case, moving through coal and perhaps shale and tar sand is undertaken before moving to one or more non-fossil alternatives. Others would skip the first stage. Clearly, the differences lie in views of the overall economics of the alternatives and whether the direct costs of the fossil alternatives are low enough to outweigh the perceived high environmental costs. In sum, the theory and practice of depletion strongly indicate that a market solution is vastly superior to intervention.

3   Problems of Coal

A solid fuel competing against a liquid or a gas faces profound problems. Every step of the chain from extraction to waste disposal is more problematic. Coal, of course, is part of the broader field of energy. The sector, in turn, is defined to include only inanimate energy sources, and usually not all of them. Five types of sources – coal, oil, gas, uranium, and water power – are invariably covered. Depending upon their importance in a country and the interests of the observer, such substitutes as wood, animal wastes, other sources of biological origin, wind, and solar energy also are treated. These alternatives receive limited attention in studies of industrialized countries.

Each of the first three fossil-fuel sources is actually a collection of heterogeneous occurrences. They differ within as well as among deposits in such key characteristics as amount and form of the fuel contained, the extent of contamination by other material, and the ease of extraction. Solid fuels range from the very hard (anthracite) to the boggy (peat). While classifications differ among countries, coals extend at most to the softer, more ash-laden forms called lignites or brown coals. Often, lignite is treated as being distinct from the harder coals – anthracite, bituminous, and subbituminous – and even subdivided into better and worse qualities. Thus, the Germans distinguish between *braunkohle* and *pechkohle*.

The work done by these fuels primarily involves providing heating, lighting, and cooling to residential, commercial, and industrial buildings, powering industrial processes, and fueling automobiles and other forms of transportation. With the rise of electric power in the late nineteenth century, a tendency has arisen increasingly to consume fuels to produce electricity.

The obvious physical characteristics of each fuel are a major influence on their production, transportation, processing, and utilization economics and on the information we have about them. Coals are solid fuels that are more readily found than oil, gas, or uranium; otherwise this solid state is an economic drawback. Extraction, transportation, and use are more difficult than oil and gas. In particular, while oil can be fairly cheaply transformed physically and chemically, coals are expensive to transform. The expense has been such that only an economy such as South Africa with a strong desire for self-sufficiency heavily engages in coal transformation.

With the prevailing scarcity pattern, the role of coal is to fill niches, for example, in large boilers. Such energy use on a larger scale produces economies of scale; however, where they are exhausted is unclear. It is at a level much smaller than the total electric power market but apparently much larger than that maintained by most manufacturing plants. These scale economies narrow, but do not eliminate, the cost disadvantages of using coal. If large cheap enough coal supplies exist, savings on fuel costs will justify the endurance of higher costs in other areas and lead to more coal use by electric utilities.

Environmental impacts of burning coal are a further problem. Devices that capture particulates (the solid matter emitted when burning coal) have made invisible the classic impacts of coal use. Sulfur oxide emissions from combustion of the sulfur in coal and nitrogen oxides are also a concern. Nitrogen-oxide control requires changes in combustion practices and control devices. These and switching to coals lower in sulfur content are ways to control sulfur oxides. Combinations of these alternatives are in use in countries with strong pollution-control policies. Carbon dioxide as a greenhouse gas is believed to be causing rising temperatures around the world due to human release of such greenhouse gases. Reductions in discharges as well as radical changes in fuel-use patterns to energy sources that do not involve combustion (solar, wind, and nuclear) are possible solutions. All these alternatives have problems of their own. Opponents of nuclear power are concerned about the radiation hazards at various stages of the cycle from mining to waste storage. Solar and wind do not provide the steady flows of energy needed by modern electric-power systems. These alternatives are uneconomic in the short term without some intervention such as large taxes on greenhouse gas emissions.

Other alternatives include shifting towards fuels such as natural gas that produce less greenhouse gas, which in turn might be captured and stored.

The locus of coal production, 1800–2006

Among the important aspects of coal economics is the limited and much changed geographic scope of the industry. A national-level database starting in 1800 (but with 1900 as the earliest year for which a world total is available) was employed. It includes data covering several small producers in Western Europe in addition to the leading producers – 16 countries in total. By adding the coal production of Indonesia to that of these 16 countries, over 90 percent of world coal production is accounted for in all but one year since 1900.[9]

Quite disparate situations prevail among the 17 countries. At one extreme, China has surged, particularly after World War II, from a trivial producer to by far the world's largest producer of coal. The United States established itself as a major producer in the last decades of the nineteenth century and maintains that role. In the years immediately after World War II, US coal use became increasingly concentrated in electricity generation as other markets shrank. Most dramatically, railroads totally replaced coal, predominantly with diesel-electric engines. Residential and commercial use nearly vanished; use in industrial boilers also dropped sharply. For many years, the specialized use of coal for coking for pig-iron blast furnaces persisted, but it collapsed in the 1980s. Growth in electricity use persists. By 1960, other markets had become so small that losses were greatly offset by electricity gains. The US coal industry embarked on an expansion that has continued.

Several countries including India, Australia, South Africa, and Indonesia embarked on expansions that turned them into the leading middle-rank producers. India produces for internal use. South Africa uses the majority of its coal internally but is a major exporter. Australia exports the majority of its output. Indonesia developed its coal output largely for export markets.

The former Soviet Union was a major producer, but substantial oil and natural gas discoveries led to coal declines before the Soviet break-up. Subsequent reforms have not reversed the situation. Poland had moved into the middle ranks of producers, but since the fall of communism, Polish coal output has declined.

In contrast, despite large infusions of assistance, the seven Western European producers have undergone massive decreases in output. Indeed, France, Belgium, the Netherlands, and Italy have ceased coal production while Great Britain, Germany, and Spain produce significantly lower levels. These countries, which accounted for 51 percent of 1900 output, provided less than 1 percent of the 2006 and 2007 production. Japan has also ceased production. Canada developed coal mines in its western provinces to serve export markets, but since 1998, difficulties in competing have caused declining output. As a result, the seven largest producers of 2006 – namely China, the United States, India, the Russian Federation, Australia, and South Africa – accounted for 96 percent of 2006 and 93 percent of 2007 production in contrast to only 60 percent in 1946. This is the net of lower shares for the United States and Russia and sharp rises elsewhere. Critically, a few countries account for almost all of the world coal output, which is used mainly within the producing countries. The US pattern of increasing reliance on electric power as a market is emerging in the other main coal-producing countries.

The coal companies
There were profound changes in ownership patterns. The most radical changes were those away from socialism in the former Soviet Union, Poland, and the United Kingdom. More convoluted adjustments arose in the United States, Australia, South Africa, and Colombia. Among the key alterations was the entry and exit of the major oil companies (Exxon, Shell, BP, Chevron, Arco, Continental, Sun, Kerr-McGee, and Occidental) and some other large companies. A mixture of acquisitions of existing companies and creation of new companies prevailed.

The largest acquisition in the United States was in 1966 when Continental Oil acquired an Appalachian-based company, Consolidation Coal. Continental Oil in turn was acquired by Dupont in 1981, spun off in 1998, and merged with Phillips in 2002. In 1990, Dupont sold half of Consolidation to Rheinbraun, a wholly owned subsidiary of the German electric utility RWE. In 1999, Rheinbraun bought out Dupont, undertook a public offering of part, and retained 73.7 percent. Occidental, which bought Island Creek in 1968, resold it to Consolidation in 1993.

Standard Oil of Ohio (now absorbed in BP) purchased Old Ben Coal, a middle western company that later became one of several purchases by Ziegler, a small long-extant coal company. The resulting company failed and went through several reorganizations. Chevron entered the coal business by acquiring Gulf Oil in 1984. Gulf had acquired Spencer Chemical and its Pittsburg and Midway coal division in 1964. This operation is still owned by Chevron. Shell participated by both creating a new coal company and buying half of an established one; these were combined and later sold to Zeigler in 1992.

Arco, Ashland, Exxon, Sun, and Kerr-McGee entered the US industry as newcomers, stressing development of western coal resources. All largely exited by selling their mines; Exxon sold all its western operation but retains one in the middle West.

Some established companies became increasingly important and new companies emerged. Peabody Coal became the largest producer. Acquisitions included the Wyoming operations of Exxon. Peabody had a convoluted ownership history, particularly after the 1977 court decision that its 1968 purchase by Kennecott restricted competition (because Kennecott was a potential de novo entrant). A consortium of firms then acquired Peabody. This ended when Hanson, a British conglomerate, secured full ownership in 1990. In 1998, Hanson decided to separate its parts. In a complex deal, Lehman Merchant Bank secured a 57 percent share and sold the rest in a public offering.

Another company with an increased role was Arch; its half ownership by Ashland was divested. Kennecott, by then a subsidiary of the British mineral giant Rio Tinto (now renamed Rio Tinto Energy America), emerged as a new force in the 1990s. In 1993, it secured the western coal operations of Sun and the electric utility Pacificorp. In 1998, it bought a Wyoming mine from Kerr-McGee.

RAG, the company that presided over the demise of the German coal industry, acquired the western operations of Cyprus-Amax Coal in 1999. Cyprus-Amax Coal was a division of a diversified mining company in the process of being acquired by Phelps Dodge. In 2004, RAG sold its holdings to a US-owned private-equity company.

In Australia, South Africa, and Colombia, there was an increased role of four mineral giants: BHP Billiton, Anglo-American, Rio Tinto, and Xstrata via numerous purchases and divestitures. All but Rio Tinto are in both Australia and South Africa. The most important step was that what is now BHP Billiton (as BHP merged with Billiton in 2000) became Australia's leading coal producer by purchase of a controlling share in Utah International in 1984. Utah International was a US-based company which was the largest producer in Queensland. In 1984, Utah International was owned by the US General Electric Company, whose interest presumably lay in Utah's role as the leading US uranium producer and thus a potential source of fuel for GE's reactors. Other acquisitions also contributed to its importance. Rio Tinto's Australian position combines a straightforward development of large mines in Queensland and a complex series of deals in New South Wales that made it strong. The Anglo-American story is much simpler: in 2000, it acquired the operations of Shell in both New South Wales and Queensland. Xstrata arose in 2002 from another newly created company called Glencore that had holdings in coal and other minerals in South Africa. Glencore then started in Australia in 1998 with the acquisition of about 10 mines in New South Wales and in 2003 Xstrata completed a total takeover of MIM, a mining company with coal interests in Queensland.

In South Africa, Anglo remains the leading coal producer. Billiton acquired the coal interests of two other South African conglomerates, and these became part of BHP-Billiton. Xstrata also has coal interests. A joint venture between Exxon and the Colombian government was acquired by BHP-Billiton, Anglo American, and Xstrata in 2002.

4   World Trade

World coal trade has also profoundly changed. In 1913, inter-European coal trade dominated.[10] About 155 million tonnes of coal were traded with almost 75 million tonnes from the UK and 35 million tonnes from Germany. This trade largely stayed in Europe. The next most important exporter was the United States, exporting 23 million tonnes; 14 million tonnes of which went to Canada. The total amount of coal exported in 1929 was 147 million tonnes. All three of the 1913 leaders exported less than in 1913 but to the same countries. The UK coal exports fell to 46 million tonnes; Germany, 24 million tonnes; the USA, 17 million tonnes. Poland, which regained its independence, became the number four exporter because the territory granted included coal-producing regions formerly in Germany.

By 1952, world trade was down to 105 million metric tonnes. The United States with 47 million tonnes was by far the largest exporter; Canada remained the largest market, but Europe and Japan together purchased almost as much. The other three main exporters of 1929 were the next highest. Poland had risen to 25 million tonnes; the UK had fallen to 12 million tonnes; Germany to 16 million tonnes.

The world level in 1959 was only 93 million tonnes with the USA 35 million tonnes, Poland 16 million tonnes, and Germany 18 million tonnes. By 1973, flows had hit 190 million tonnes.

In 2006, the International Energy Agency (IEA) reported 815 million tonnes of coal flows. Australia accounted for 231 million tonnes of this; Indonesia, 129 million tones; Russia, 92 million tonnes; South Africa, 69 million tonnes; China, 63 million tonnes; Colombia, 60 million tonnes, and the USA, 45 million tonnes. As would be expected, Australia, Indonesia, and China sold the majority of their exports in Asia. Australia sent 106 million tonnes to Japan and 78 million tonnes elsewhere in Asia; Indonesia, 32 million tonnes and 104 million tonnes; China, 19 million tonnes and 37 million tonnes. Fifty-five million tonnes went from South Africa to OECD Europe; Russia shipped 58 million tonnes to OECD Europe.

Of these flows, steam coal was 593 million tonnes; coking, 222 million tonnes. Australia accounted for over half the coking coal (121 million tonnes), which was just over half Australian exports. For the United States, coking coal was 25 million tonnes of exports. Canada had almost the same coking coal level out of a total of 27 million tonnes. Japan (73 million tonnes) was the largest coking coal importer; other Asia accounted for 60 million tonnes; OECD Europe 55 million tonnes. Australia was the dominant supplier to the first two areas – 45 and 35 million tonnes, respectively, and at 22 million tonnes the largest coking coal supplier to OECD Europe.

5   Coal-mine Health and Safety in the US

A severe mine disaster in the US in 1968 caused increased attention to worker safety. US regulation was revised in the Coal Mine Health and Safety Act of 1969 (CMHSA). Control was made more stringent including addition of regulations of health effects. Administration was transferred from the US Bureau of Mines of the Department of the Interior (DOI) to a newly created Mine Safety and Health and Safety Administration (MSHA), which was initially in the DOI but transferred in 1977 to the Department of Labor.

Regulation has involved both setting rules for operating mines and federal inspection of the mines. The 1969 act both tightened the rules and increased the frequency of inspection. New rules included requirements that no mine work occur under unsupported roof, an improvements in ventilation, use of curtains and watering to ensure reduction of 'respirable dust' levels, an increase in the flow of air to the 'face' where mining was occurring, and increases in the monitoring of the mine to determine levels of methane, dust, and other dangerous material. Inspections increased greatly.

In the years immediately following the enforcement of the act, underground coal-mining productivity declined from a peak of 1.95 short tons per worker hour in 1969 to a low of 1.04 short tons in 1978. At that point, a trend toward improved productivity began and has continued.

Much effort was devoted to determining the role of the act in the initial productivity declines. However, multiple, interrelated influences, on which data were unavailable, prevailed. In particular, the passage of the act coincided with an influx of inexperienced miners. The act appears to have required more labor use in mines. The need to increase inspections contributed to the need for new workers because experienced miners were recruited as inspectors. Thus, the various studies of the causes of productivity decline differed markedly in their appraisal of the causes of the decline and in their estimates of the health and safety benefits created by the act.

The drawbacks of coal health and safety regulation are substantial because no externality is involved. To justify the intervention to protect people from unsafe transactions, two tests have to be met. First, it must be true that government aid is the cheapest way to provide such protection. Second, regulation of practices must be the cheapest form of government action. The validity of these arguments is particularly suspect in coal labor in which powerful experienced unions operate. It would be a serious indictment of trade unionism to claim that it could not protect its members better than a government agency.

Land disturbance practice

Land disturbance is a universal policy concern. However, it is unclear whether control is worth its cost and, if control is viable, what level of government should handle regulation. Individual states in the United States gradually introduced laws requiring surface mine reclamation, and thus the need for federal regulation was unclear. The often-cited rationale is that competition among the states stresses attractiveness to industry and leads to weaker than desirable rules. The counterargument is that the competition stresses total attractiveness and to attract people and industries other than coal mining, rules will be made as stringent as possible.

A national law, the US Surface Mining Control and Reclamation Act of 1977 (SMCRA), set up an Office of Surface Mining (OSM) in DOI and set principles for guiding reclamation. OSM was to supervise the development of state programs to implement the law or if the state chose not to develop a program, regulate mines in that state. The law covered reclamation of both active and abandoned coal mines. Taxes were levied on surface and underground coal mines to finance reclamation of abandoned mines. Section 403 of the law stated that the order of the six general objectives indicated the assigned priority. The first goal of SMCRA was 'the protection of public health, safety, and property from extreme danger of adverse effects of coal mining practices'. The second was the first with 'from extreme danger' omitted. The third was 'restoration of land and water resources and the environment'. The fourth was research on reclamation methods; the fifth action on public works affected by mining; and the sixth, development of publicly owned land affected by mining.

For operating mines, the law required the establishment of permitting systems under which the right to mine was granted only when extensive data including the mining and reclamation plans and information on the impacts of mining were submitted. Mine inspections were also mandatory.

The law made complex provisions prohibiting or discouraging surface mining on certain types of land including 'prime agricultural land'. More than 10 pages of principles of reclamation were listed, including restoration to the 'approximate original contour', restoration of the land to support its prior use or better ones, and segregation of topsoil so it could be replaced.

SMCRA also contained a provision that increased the rights of many surface owners. Those who resided on the land or used it for farming or ranching had to give written permission before the coal could be leased. Thus, the law was complex, vague, and establishment of universal rules without justification.

Coal leasing and the fear of windfall profits
Concern over excess profits is also a major influence on US federal land management[11] whose land ownership pattern is one of the most complex. US land ownership is divided between the public and private sectors. Ownership can range from complete private ownership of the land and subsurface to complete government ownership and operation. All levels of government own land. The energy experience is part of a broader development involving the nearly total reversal in US public-land policy.[12] The US government is a major landowner as historically the states ceded to the federal government unoccupied portions of the lands the British crown had granted to individual colonies. Annexations, starting with the Louisiana Purchase, added more land. Stress has shifted over time from seeking disposal as occurred east of the Mississippi to retention in the western lands that presently dominate the holdings.

Important federal holdings include oil and gas resources offshore and on federal land and much of the coal west of the Mississippi. Coal leasing produced more problems than oil and gas. Oil and gas auctions worked so well as to produce little opposition on rent-collecting grounds (see Mead et al. 1984, 1985). The great dispute remains over how much offshore oil and gas should be closed to development on environmental grounds. However, establishing a coal-leasing program was more controversial.

In the traditional coal-producing regions east of the Mississippi, private ownership is predominant. In the western areas in which production has increased sharply since the early 1970s, federal government ownership of land or at least the coal under it is the main pattern. In particular, it is the dominant owner of coal in such western states as Wyoming, Montana, Colorado, Utah, North Dakota, and New Mexico.

Pre-1920 outright grants of coal-bearing land, extensively leasing, and severing coal from surface ownership necessitating accords with surface owners produced fragmentation of property rights. An important element was the construction incentive given to railroads by granting large amounts of land surrounding areas where new lines were built. Other public land was dedicated to non-mining use, often with transfer of the surface to private ownership.

Until the late 1960s, the DOI proceeded under rarely changed laws. Under the 1872 Mining Act, mineral-bearing land could be claimed and owned outright by anyone who could prove that valuable minerals occurred on the land (see Leshy 1987). Subsequently, some minerals, particularly oil, gas, and coal, were removed from the system by the 1920 Mineral Leasing Act. Leases could be acquired but not the land.

Coal-leasing law and its administration remained virtually unchanged from 1920 to 1971. Leases were freely granted under the provisions of the 1920 Mineral Leasing Act. These policies allowed satisfaction of most industry desires for leases. Coal leasing proceeded modestly until the late 1960s, when it spurted. In anticipation of growth, those interested in producing coal vigorously leased rights to extract US government-owned coal, mostly in western states.

Since the late 1960s, Congress has made profound changes in the legislation governing federal-land management. The 1969 National Environmental Policy Act (NEPA) had significant influence. The act required preparation of an environmental impact statement (EIS) when the federal government undertook 'major' actions.

Resolving questions about the meaning of this requirement inspired extensive litigation. The courts imposed broad definitions of what constituted a major decision and also required extensive inquiries about impacts and how to mitigate them. Anderson (1973) provides an overview of the early history of NEPA.

SMCRA applies to federal coal. The Federal Land Policy and Management Act 1976 (FLPMA) established provisions for land-use planning on all public lands. FLPMA also made retention of public lands the preferred policy goal. Another clause made environmental preservation, recreation, and 'human occupancy and use' the primary goals.

The Coal Leasing Amendment Act of 1976 radically altered coal-leasing policy in the US. This legislation required that competitive bidding prevail on all federal coal leases and that these bids lead to receipt of 'fair market value', a concept essentially identical to the economic concept of a competitive price. Proof that fair market value is attained becomes impossible when, as was true in coal leasing, extensive, publicized markets do not exist, and federal leasing was unlikely to create them. Further requirements included a minimum 12.5 percent royalty on surface-mined production.

These basic principles were supplemented by 21 further requirements. These involved among other things increasing to 50 percent the state share in gross revenues to the DOI from all forms of payments (royalties and whatever was initially paid for the lease) made by leaseholders, limits on leaseholding size and duration, reserving leases for governmental bodies and electric cooperatives, land-use, environmental and economic assessments for each lease, and impact studies by the DOI, the Department of Justice, and the Office of Technology Assessment (a now defunct advisory arm of the US Congress). President Ford vetoed the act, but the veto was overridden.

These amendments illustrate typical errors about the theory and practice of public policy. The core analytic misstep is belief that an optimum time for leasing exists. If markets are efficient, leasing delays can only be inefficient. Any private firm making a lease or purchase before it is efficient to utilize the property will wait until the socially most desirable exploitation date. It is possible to lease too late. Resources may not be made available to a qualified operator until after the most desirable time for exploitation.

Concerns about adequate payments due to premature sale arise from failure to realize that the competitive market value is determined by the existence of the mineral, not its ownership. The land sale or lease transfers control without altering supply. With sufficient rationality among potential operators and the expectation that land will be made available on a timely basis, the existence of the land affects markets independently of when the transfers are made and where resource ownership is concentrated, as by federal mineral holdings, greater selling or leasing can increase efficiency. The excess profits the federal government could obtain by restricting supply are prevented. Restriction is again by definition the failure to lease all properties that could be profitably exploited. The federal government would be inadvertently collecting monopoly profits by reducing production below its socially best level.

No cure exists for violation of any of the requirements for efficiency. By assumption, the inadequacy is persistent and will adversely affect bidding whenever it occurs. Delaying bidding can offset this only if some improvement in competition can be effected.

Timing requirements are similarly undesirable. Four outcomes are possible with a diligence requirement on lease timing. Two are innocuous, but two are harmful. The optimum starting date may be before the expiration of the diligence deadline; the redundancy of the requirement then renders it harmless. Similarly, if the requirement is not met, the lease is forfeited, and if the DOI reissues the lease soon enough for development to occur at the optimal time, no harm will occur. Injury is produced when premature development is more profitable than surrender or when reissue by the DOI of a surrendered lease is delayed past the optimum time for starting to mine. It is unrealistic to believe that leasing can be controlled to avoid these defects.

Diligence requirements also have undesirable effects on competition in bidding and on prevention of mining when superior private uses exist. If lease lengths were unlimited, the leaseholder could refrain forever from mining the land. Someone who believed that other uses were more profitable than mining could prevent mining by buying the lease and not mining it. This would eliminate the resort to land-use planning to intervene in choosing the best private uses. The limited term of the lease lowers the willingness to pay of someone wishing to obtain the land for other purposes. Only the present value of the income obtained from another use over the term of the lease can be paid. Lease-length limits prevent increasing bids to reflect additional revenues from continuing the other activity after the expiration of the lease. Similarly, the risk of loss to diligence requirements lessens the willingness of arbitrageurs to participate.

Royalties or production taxes inefficiently reduce the amount of a mineral that can be produced profitably. The tax causes a disincentive to produce because not all of the funds paid by buyers are available to compensate producers for their efforts. A pure sales tax is unrelated to any real resource costs of production. Thus, the costs as seen by the firm are raised above resource costs. These resource costs measure the actual sacrifices made to secure the increased output and are thus the only ones that should influence output. The universal tendency to use distorting royalties or production taxes removes the classic theoretic justification for taxes on land use, that the charges can be levied in a nondistorting fashion. Once this advantage is lost, the desirability of mineral taxes over other methods of raising revenue or transferring economic rents in minerals becomes questionable.

Congressional posturing about the vigor of competition is also problematic. The various restrictions on leaseholdings, based on holding size, are so designed that they are unrelated to any meaningful economic indicator of the vigor of competition. The concerns fly in the face of a lack of evidence of monopoly problems in coal including an inability of the Justice Department to find problems that caused termination of its annual reviews. In fact, all the restrictions do is lessen the ability to attract more bidders for leases by limiting the role of the largest companies. The difficulties of providing conclusive proof force caution in leasing.

The US government's caution about how much to lease may restrict supply more than would be appropriate for exploiting monopoly power. Curtailment below the monopoly level necessarily keeps leases below the even higher efficient competitive market level of leasing. The principal corrective was that substantial amounts of coal were leased before the excessive fears of giveaways.

The effects of these laws interacted with pre-existing pressures to cause the virtual disappearance of federal coal leasing. In 1971, the DOI became concerned by an acceleration of leasing without a concomitant increase in output. By the time the DOI realized that western development was occurring, the agency faced first new environmental requirements and then new legislation affecting leasing procedures. The result was that coal leasing between 1971 and 1981 ceased, only to resume briefly in 1981 and be stopped again in 1983 for a time before slowly reappearing. Leasing stopped in 1971 largely due to concerns as to the adequacy of the environmental-protection procedures in the coal-leasing program. Law suits were directed at the 1975 EIS prepared for the coal-leasing program. By the time that the critical District Court decision on NEPA compliance of the EIS had been made in 1977, the Carter administration decided not to appeal the decision, preferring instead to reshape the program in a new EIS. This took so long that the leasing did not resume until the Reagan administration.

The prevailing approach seems unworkable. Securing optimum payments in a less burdensome fashion, stimulating vigorous competition for leases, and being able to rely on bonus bidding would be preferable. Analysis and experience strongly vindicate the preference among natural resource economists for leasing or sale by competitive bid with all payments made as a lease bonus.

6 Conclusions: The Prospects for Coal

A wide range of possibilities for coal are postulated in the literature. The peak-oil advocates see a need for switches to alternatives that might include coal while those concerned about global warming in varying degrees want to discourage coal use. Without either pressure, coal use would continue increasingly to be concentrated in the electric-power industries of a few countries, most of which are coal producers.

Notes

1. This draws heavily on much prior work. In addition to that cited below, see Gordon (1970, 1973a, 1973b, 1974a, 1974b, 1975, 1976, 1978a, 1978b, 1978c, 1978d, 1978e 1981b, 1987b, and 1987c).
2. In particular, I have never read any of his writings and here epitomize the many reports on him. Since the next-to-last submission of the manuscript of this chapter, I discovered the site Hubbertpeak.com from which his writings can be downloaded. A skimming indicates that the critics correctly convey the mindlessness of Hubbert's approach. (For the first of his articles see Hubbert, 1949).
3. Cummings (1969) showed that Hotelling's general case could be developed to show that hoarding had a second benefit of the cumulative cost saving from delaying the depletion of higher-quality resources; many others subsequently independently developed the case. Levhari and Liviatan (1977) show that the more advanced mathematics employed by Cummings were not needed to derive the proof. Two widely spaced efforts showed that a discrete-time approach greatly simplified the derivations: Baumol and Oates (1975) and Modiano and Shapiro (1980).
4. Numerous surveys of the literature are available. Baumol and Oates's text on environmental economics included a good survey of exhaustion theory but only in its first edition. Gordon (1981a) is another simpler survey. Dasgupta and Heal (1979) produced the fullest available review, but it is unnecessarily complex.
5. Hotelling does not make this clear; Herfindahl stated and Gordon (1967) proves this case. The simplicity of the case causes its frequent use, but the more general model must be used in practice.
6. This is the case sketched by Hotelling that Cummings and the others previously noted later developed.
7. Gordon (1981a) discusses this case. Perpetual rapid growth in exhaustible resources is subject to the paradox discussed in the general literature on investment that it is more profitable to trade the asset than to use it. However, in the exhaustible-resource case, where demand initially grows rapidly but then slows down, optimal behavior is to start before the demand growth slowdown and exhaust during the slow growth period. The criterion of rapidity is a growth of more than r percent of the marginal profitability of the optimum output at any time.
8. To simplify, assume no effects of saving high-quality resources.
9. Three sources were used. A Swiss research institute published a compendium of energy-production data from 1800 to 1985 (Etemad and Luciani 1991). A German trade association (Unternehmensverband Ruhrbergbau 1955 and 1961) published a few compendiums of coal data, and the German coal-data-reporting service (Statistik der Kohlenwirtschaft e. V. annual b) annually reports on production from selected countries.
10. German sources (Statistik der Kohlenwirtschaft e. V. annual a) were used for the earlier years. For more recent years, these German data were combined with those from the International Energy Agency (annual). It gives a steam-coal-coking coal breakdown but generates totals larger than the German

source. For the latest year both reported, 2005, the bulk of the 84 million excess of IEA over Statistik der Kohlenwirschaft (SdK) was 33 million for the former Soviet Union and the balancing item. The IEA shows a total of 36.6 million tonnes from all non-OECD exporters; the closest correspondence from SdK is its other country figure of minus 7.3 million tonnes.

11. The author was heavily involved in advising the US government, Resources for the Future, and energy producers about coal-leasing problems, serving in 1983–84 as a member of the US Commission on Fair Market Value Policy for Federal Coal Leasing (1984). This section draws heavily upon Gordon (1981c, 1985, 1987a, and 1988).

12. See Clawson (1983) for a thoughtful balanced discussion. A companion volume of essays edited by Brubaker (1984) is a useful supplement. Leshy (1987) reviews the history of efforts to overcome the deficiencies of US law for exploiting minerals on federal land; he feels mining was excessively encouraged but may be arguing too far in the other direction. Libertarian groups have a literature too vast to cover here on the defects of this policy. The Pacific Institute pioneered the effort; more recently the Political Economy Research Center has assumed the lead.

References

Adelman, M.A. (1990), 'Mineral depletion, with special reference to petroleum', *Review of Economics and Statistics*, **72**(1), February, 1–10.

Anderson, Frederick R. (1973), *NEPA in the Courts: A Legal Analysis of the National Environmental Policy Act*, Baltimore, MD: Johns Hopkins University Press for Resources for the Future.

Baumol, William J. and Wallace E. Oates (1975), *The Theory of Environmental Policy: Externalities, Public Outlays, and the Quality of Life*, Englewood Cliffs, NJ: Prentice-Hall.

Brubaker, Sterling (ed.) (1984), *Rethinking the Federal Lands*, Washington, DC: Resources for the Future.

Clawson, Marion (1983), *The Federal Lands Revisited*, Baltimore, MD: Resources for the Future.

Cohen, Linda and Roger Noll (1991), *The Technology Pork Barrel*, Washington, DC: Brookings Institution.

Cummings, Ronald G. (1969), 'Some extensions of the economic theory of exhaustible resources', *Western Economic Journal*, **7**(3), September, 201–10.

Dasgupta, Partha and G.M. Heal (1979), *Economic Theory and Exhaustible Resources*, Cambridge: Cambridge University Press.

Etemad, Bouda and Jean Luciani (under the direction of Paul Bairoch and Jean-Claude Toutain) (1991), *World Energy Production 1800–1985 (Production Mondiale d'Energie)*, Geneva: Librairie Droz.

Gordon, Richard L. (1966), 'Conservation and the theory of exhaustible resources', *Canadian Journal of Economics and Political Science*, **32**(3), August, 319–26.

Gordon, Richard L. (1967), 'A reinterpretation of the pure theory of exhaustion', *Journal of Political Economy*, **75**(3), June, 274–86.

Gordon, Richard L. (1970), *The Evolution of Energy Policy in Western Europe: The Reluctant Retreat from Coal*, New York: Praeger Special Studies in International Economics and Development.

Gordon, Richard L. (1973a), 'Alternatives to oil and natural gas', *The National Energy Problem; Proceedings of the Academy of Political Science*, **31**(2), December, 74–86.

Gordon, Richard L. (1973b), 'Coal's role in a national materials policy', in Samuel Ellison, Jr (ed.), *Towards a National Policy on Energy Resources and Mineral Plant Foods*, Austin, TX: University of Texas Bureau of Economic Geology, 84–98.

Gordon, Richard L. (1974a), 'Coal: our limited vast resource', in E.W. Erickson and L. Waverman (eds), *The Energy Question*, vol. 2, Toronto: University of Toronto Press, 49–75.

Gordon, Richard L. (1974b), 'Coal's role in the age of environmental concern', in Michael S. Macrakas (ed.), *Energy: Demand, Conservation, and Institutional Problems*, Proceedings of MIT Conference (February 1973), Cambridge, MA: MIT Press, 225–35.

Gordon, Richard L. (1975), *U.S. Coal and the Electric Power Industry*, Baltimore, MD: Johns Hopkins University Press for Resources for the Future.

Gordon, Richard L. (1976), 'Coal – the swing fuel', in Robert J. Kalter and William A. Vogely (eds), *Energy Supply and Government Policy*, Ithaca, NY: Cornell University Press, 193–215.

Gordon, Richard L. (1978a), *Coal in the U.S. Energy Market: History and Prospects*, Lexington, MA and Toronto: Lexington Books, D.C. Heath.

Gordon, Richard L. (1978b), 'Coal schizophrenia, or be sure who makes the magic potion', in Bernhard J. Abrahamsson (ed.), *Conservation and the Changing Direction of Economic Growth*, Boulder, CO: Westview Press, 99–116.

Gordon, Richard L. (1978c), 'Coal supply prospects in the United States – an appraisal of current knowledge', in International Energy Agency, *Workshops on Energy Supply and Demand*, Paris: Organisation for Economic Co-operation and Development, 29–74.

Gordon, Richard L. (1978d), 'The hobbling of coal: policy and regulatory uncertainties', *Science*, **200** (14 April), 153–8. Reprinted in Philip H. Abelson and Allen L. Hammond (eds), *Energy II: Use Conservation and Supply*, a special *Science* compendium, Washington, DC: American Association for the Advancement of Science, 1978.

Gordon, Richard L. (1978e), 'Hobbling coal – or how to serve two masters poorly', *Regulation*, **2**(4), July/ August, 36–45.

Gordon, Richard L. (1981a), *An Economic Analysis of World Energy Problems*, Cambridge, MA: MIT Press.

Gordon, Richard L. (1981b), 'Prospects for U.S. coal', *Energy Policy*, **9**(4), December, 279–88.

Gordon, Richard L. (1981c), *Federal Coal Leasing Policy, Competition in the Energy Industries*, Washington, DC: American Enterprise Institute for Public Policy Research.

Gordon, Richard L. (1985), 'Levies on U.S. coal production', *The Energy Journal*, **6**, Special Tax Issue, 241–54.

Gordon, Richard L. (1987a), 'Coal in U.S. land policy', in John Byrne and Daniel Rich (eds), *Planning for Changing Energy Conditions*, New Brunswick, NJ: Transaction Books, 139–72.

Gordon, Richard L. (1987b), 'Coal policy in perspective', in Richard L. Gordon, Henry D. Jacoby and Martin B. Zimmerman (eds), *Energy: Markets and Regulation*, Cambridge, MA: MIT Press, 59–82.

Gordon, Richard L. (1987c), *World Coal: Economics, Policies and Prospects*, Cambridge: Cambridge University Press.

Gordon, Richard L. (1988), 'Federal coal leasing: an analysis of the economic issues', Discussion Paper EM88-01, Washington, DC: Energy and Materials Division, Resources for the Future, July.

Gray, Lewis C. (1914), 'Rent under the assumption of exhaustibility', *Quarterly Journal of Economics*, **28**(2), May, 466–89. Reprinted in Mason Gaffney (ed.) (1967), *Extractive Resources and Taxation*, Madison, WI: University of Wisconsin Press, 423–46.

Herfindahl, Orris C. (1967), 'Depletion and economic theory', in Mason Gaffney (ed.), *Extractive Resources and Taxation*, Madison, WI: University of Wisconsin Press, 63–90.

Holdren, John P. (2002), 'Energy: asking the wrong question', *Scientific American* (January), 65–7.

Hotelling, Harold (1931), 'The economics of exhaustible resources', *Journal of Political Economy*, **39**(2), April, 137–75.

Hubbert, M. King (1949), 'Energy from fossil fuels', *Science*, **109**(2823), 103–9.

International Energy Agency (IEA) (annual), *Coal Information*, Paris: Organisation for Economic Co-operation and Development.

Koopmans, Tjalling C. (1974), 'Ways of looking at future economic growth, resource and energy use', in Michael S. Macrakis (ed.), *Energy: Demand, Conservation, and Institutional Problems*, Cambridge, MA: MIT Press, 3–15.

Leshy, John D. (1987), *The Mining Law: A Study in Perpetual Motion*, Washington, DC: Resources for the Future.

Levhari, David and Nissan Liviatan (1977), 'Notes on Hotelling's economics of exhaustible resources', *Canadian Journal of Economics*, **10**(2), May, 177–92.

Mead, Walter J., Asbjorn Moseidjord, Dennis D. Muraoka and Philip E. Sorensen (1985), *Offshore Lands: Oil and Gas Leasing and Conservation on the Outer Continental Shelf*, San Francisco, CA: Pacific Institute for Public Policy Research.

Mead, Walter J., Asbjorn Moseidjord and Philip E. Sorensen (1984), 'Competitive bidding under asymmetrical information: behavior and performance in Gulf of Mexico drainage lease sales, 1959–69', *Review of Economics and Statistics*, **61**(3), August, 505–8.

Modiano, Eduardo M. and Jeremy F. Shapiro (1980), 'A dynamic optimization model of depletable resources', *Bell Journal of Economics*, **11**(1), Spring, 212–36.

Scott, Anthony (1967), 'The theory of the mine under conditions of certainty', in Mason Gaffney (ed.), *Extractive Resources and Taxation*, Madison, WI: University of Wisconsin Press, 25–62.

Statistik der Kohlenwirtschaft e. V. (annual a), *Der Kohlenbergbau in der Energiewirtschaft der Bundesrepublik Deutschland*, Essen: Statistik der Kohlenwirtschaft.

Statistik der Kohlenwirtschaft e. V. (annual b), *Zahlen zür Kohlenwirtschaft*, Essen: Statistik der Kohlenwirtschaft.

US Commission on Fair Market Value Policy for Federal Coal Leasing (1984), *Report of the Commission*, Washington, DC: US Government Printing Office.

Unternehmensverband Ruhrbergbau (1955), *Die Kohlenwirtschaft der Welt in Zahlen*, Essen: Verlag Glückauf.

Unternehmensverband Ruhrbergbau (1961), *Die Kohlenwirtschaft der Welt in Zahlen*, Essen: Verlag Glückauf.

20 Natural gas and electricity markets
W.D. Walls

1 Introduction

The natural gas and electric power industries – once the classic examples of natural monopoly – are increasingly being open to market forces instead of public service commissions. The emergence of markets in the North American natural gas industry in the mid-1980s resulted largely from the failure of regulation, and a consequence of this regulatory failure was the separation of the energy commodity from its transportation. This simple change in the organization – where the energy commodity was unbundled from its transmission – provides the basis for restructuring natural gas and electricity markets. The natural gas and electricity industries are being transformed so that they more closely resemble a commodity market than a public utility in the move toward market-oriented allocation mechanisms for production, transmission, and distribution.

2 The Emergence of Markets

Competitive markets for natural gas in the US emerged in the 1980s; since that time the natural gas and electric power industries in numerous countries around the globe have been transformed from a regulated structure to one based on markets, including those in Argentina, Australia, Canada, New Zealand, the US, and the United Kingdom among others. In the European Union (EU), a directive on opening up markets was adopted in 1998; however, nearly 10 years later, numerous countries – including France, Germany, Austria, Bulgaria, Cyprus, Greece, Luxembourg, Latvia and Slovakia – remain resistant to the full unbundling of energy production and transmission.[1] In contrast to the energy market reforms being imposed on EU member states, the initial emergence of markets in the US natural gas industry was not part of a conscious design to restructure an industry long held to be the classic example of a natural monopoly. Instead, it was an expedient way of correcting a long succession of regulatory mistakes.[2] Markets developed rapidly where permitted and within a few years dozens of spot markets for natural gas were in operation.[3] New market institutions were developed by industry participants for trading gas since there were no such institutions under the old system.[4] In North America, gas trading is decentralized in over-the-counter markets that span a large geography. Prices are now discovered in markets, not in regulatory proceedings.

Throughout most of the twentieth century the natural gas industry has adapted to an environment determined by government regulation. Markets were suppressed and were not part of the industry's basic institutions or ways of doing business. Everything turned on questions of regulatory approval and procedure. The industry functioned poorly, especially in the US (MacAvoy and Pindyck, 1975; Tussing and Barlow, 1984; De Vany and Walls, 1995). By the late 1970s, natural gas was the worst regulated industry in the

US. Shortages and curtailments there were common and disastrous. Industries were shut down or their gas use was rationed. Gas reserves reached a historic low relative to consumption. Regulation had not only lost control, it was causing the damage, and no hearing or resolution of a technical regulatory issue could restore the integrity of the gas supply system.

The long-term contracts which had organized the natural gas industry were unsustainable. Price shocks and price regulation together caused the contractual relations to unravel. Regulators attempted to alleviate the shortages they caused, but this led to further problems. The slow collapse of the industry and the potential for very serious gas shortages forced Congress to increase the industry's reliance on markets and diminish the scope and harm of regulation. But changes in the patchwork of regulation that had been built up over the 50–70-year history of government control of industry structure and operation began to pull the whole fabric apart.[5] Once the existing contracts and regulation became unsustainable in 1983, some of the major pipelines were on the verge of bankruptcy from their contractual purchase obligations. They had to sell gas, and to do that they had to transport it to the customer. That was the beginning of contract or what has become known as 'open access' transportation. The accumulated constraints of merchant carriage and onerous regulation became unsustainable and adjustments had to be made everywhere. This could not be accomplished by augmenting existing regulation. The industry reconstructed itself in the wake of the final crisis. What were the tools of this reconstruction? They were contesting markets, intermediaries and brokers, futures contracts and markets, storage programs, tariff discounting, interconnects, arbitrage, lower prices, well-behaved prices, prices that contain valuable information (not the mix of ancient and stale rate hearing history), prices that guide decisions, hubs, and the emergence of a strongly connected interstate pipeline grid.

In contrast to the natural gas industry, the emergence of comprehensive markets in the electricity industry was a more centrally designed process. Of course, decentralized markets isomorphic to those that emerged in the natural gas industry had existed in the US for many years. In these markets, electric utilities would trade wholesale power across their transmission networks, sometimes 'wheeling' the power across their network from one utility to another (Joskow and Schmalensee, 1983). In the US, the Energy Policy Act of 1992 provided non-utility entities with access to the transmission network and this supported increased wholesale trade in power and this increased competition for wholesale power in an industry structured as vertically integrated monopolies (De Vany and Walls, 1999b). Like customers located behind the city gate of a gas distributor, customers located inside an electrical utility's service area could not purchase power unless they could get access to wheel power through the local grid. Equally, the point applies to a power transaction that involves utilities located on opposite sides of an intervening utility's territory. To transact, they must be able to wheel the power through the intervening utility's grid. With pooling and wheeling, the US industry began to dissolve the territorial boundaries erected under the Public Utility Holding Company Act and subsequent regulation by federal and state authorities who carved territories into jurisdictional protectorates. As in the gas industry, access began to promote a more integrated power grid.

While natural gas markets emerged in a spontaneous way in the US, the first totally restructured electric power market – where the vertically integrated monopoly structure was dissolved – was located in England and Wales. While natural gas deregulation occurred in response to a series of regulatory crises in the industry, the motivation for electricity deregulation came from policy circles combined with the introduction of market rules that opened up the power transmission network. While the market rules opening up the transmission system were at a national level in the US, individual states have the authority to regulate the electric utilities within their geographic boundaries. As a result, individual states embarked on deregulation programs in the US and these programs typically included the vertical disintegration of generation, transmission, and distribution. Restructured power markets did not begin to operate in the US until the end of the 1990s.[6] Power market restructuring is still under way in Europe, though opening up the power transmission system is a thorny issue (Serralles, 2006). Electricity markets are also being restructured in a number of other countries. For example, power markets are being restructured in Indonesia (Pintz and Korn, 2005), Taiwan (Hsu and Chen, 1997; Wang, 2006), Thailand (Chirarattananon and Nirukkanaporn, 2006; Mulugettaa et al., 2007; Nakawiro and Bhattacharyya, 2007), Japan (Asano, 2006), Singapore (Chang and Tay, 2006), Russia (Pittman, 2007), India (Balachandra, 2006; Singh, 2006), China (Xu and Chen, 2006), Israel (Tishler et al., 2006), and others.

3   Markets versus Regulation

The natural gas and electric power industries were considered to be natural monopolies and they were regulated as the theory prescribes (Scherer, 1980; Kahn, 1988). The conclusion that these industries were monopolies was based on economies of scale in firm size and output, that duplicating infrastructure would be wasteful, and that there was a need to plan the installation of infrastructure and coordinate its operation to achieve the economies that are inherent in a network. Proponents of regulation argued that decisions and actions were best made by a single organization and the regulated monopoly is the institutional embodiment of this argument. In this context, the state is the central coordinator and planner and the regulated monopoly is its agent; the hybrid organization combining state and monopoly is thought to provide the optimal span of control to solve the coordination problem and the right size of the production unit to realize economies of scale. The other half of the argument for regulation is that competition, with its decentralized and individualistic actors, could not effectively coordinate all the required decisions.

Decentralized competitive markets seem to provide no central place to collect the information required for coordination, and no mechanism for integrating it to plan and operate the system. It is said that there would be too much competition and wasteful duplication of facilities in the absence of an agent to serve as a central planner; as a result there would be inefficient coordination, excessive entry and exit, and volatile prices. Transmission was considered to be a natural monopoly because there are economies of scale in construction and operation up to a limit which is sufficient to serve the largest markets. Costs are sub-additive and one firm is enough to serve the market at least cost if its average cost is declining at an output sufficient to fill demand at a price that exceeds average cost. Two or more firms having the same costs would raise total cost by duplicating facilities. They would also reduce each other's output, which would raise average cost. Increasing returns to scale is a justification for regulation on two grounds, according to the theory: to avoid or control monopoly power and to prevent duplication of capital and a loss of scale economies. To accomplish these ends, it is said that price must be regulated to prevent monopoly pricing and inefficient output. Moreover, entry must be prevented to prevent duplication and a division of output that loses economies of scale.

Regulation was also thought to improve coordination in an industry where there are externalities. A network industry, such as gas and power transmission, could fail to realize the economies of coordination if each transmission link is independently owned and operated. Competition, the theory says, cannot achieve the coordination needed to operate the network efficiently, because each firm controls only a small part of it and cannot internalize the gains of coordination over the portion of the network where they occur. Full coordination might require that all the segments be owned and operated by a single firm, so that all the externalities are internalized inside the firm. Since this would mean that the firm would be a monopoly, the theory prescribes regulation to prevent inefficient monopoly pricing. The implication is that planning the network configuration is best accomplished by a single entity, be that a company or a regulator.

Commitment and opportunism are also important elements in the normative theory of regulation. A pipeline, for example, is a fixed asset; so is the collection system feeding gas to it from producing wells, and so is the distribution system that sends gas from the pipeline to users. No part of the system can operate without the other and the value of the assets in each part depends on what every part does. Since these assets are specialized and have little value independent of the other components, there is a potential for each to hold up the others. If, after all the assets are in the ground, one segment opportunistically seizes on an unanticipated event or an ambiguity in the agreements to hold up the others, they cannot move their assets to another use. It may not be possible to write a contract that prevents all the possibilities for opportunistic actions. To prevent opportunism, the components could be merged, but that would give the merged firm too much power, according to this theory.

By supplying a tribunal for adjudicating these disputes and specifying rules of behavior, regulation might avoid the opportunism to which private contracting is susceptible. The theory asserts that regulation can supply a more secure and broader form of contracting than markets. By reducing the scope for opportunistic behavior, regulation can lower the required rate of return for specialized assets and permit a socially valuable project to go ahead. However, since the regulator holds no equity in the regulated firm, it bears no cost for taking opportunistic actions against it. The constraint that would bind is if the firm goes out of business. The contract theory would make more sense if the regulator had something at stake to limit its own opportunism.

The simple theory of economies of scale neglects important features of the industry. Producers and users are diverse. Their uses vary by type of transmission, by time, by season, and by location. Supply sources also are diverse and variable. Uncertainty and diversity can alter the simple picture given by the theory of scale economies, where output, cost, and demand are assumed to be known and certain. In this case, a more dispersed pattern of transmission lines and energy sources can be more efficient than a single, large source of supply. A network of smaller lines can connect to more points of supply and use to pool their variations and load patterns. A network can provide more paths between points and make it possible to alter routes to avoid capacity bottlenecks.

Centralized control is not clearly more effective than decentralized control once the system becomes large and complex. There is a confusion in the natural monopoly argument between coordination and allocation. To grant the authority to coordinate transportation on a pipeline does not grant the authority to allocate transportation among users. The two functions are separable. A good example is the procedure that pipelines and their customers use to coordinate the monthly transportation volumes. The pipeline customers – the shippers – nominate the volumes they intend to transport through the pipeline. They must inject and withdraw gas according to the rules of operation of the pipeline and in accordance with their nominations. This achieves coordination of shipments and pipeline operations.

The case for economic regulation rests on the particular organizational structure that the theory of natural monopoly assumes of the firm. Regulation encouraged or even required centralized ownership and control of the pipeline. It discouraged vertical integration of the pipeline with gas producers and distributors. In the US, federal legislation, in the Public Utility Holding Company Act, barred holding companies. These companies integrated horizontal segments of the pipeline grid and spanned wide geographic areas. They also were effective competitors to locally franchised gas utilities. The same legislation balkanized the US electric power industry and may have caused a great deal of inefficiency in the process (Schrade and Walls, 2006).

The monopoly problem is an organizational problem, the consequence of combining and centralizing the authority to coordinate and allocate output in the hands of one agent. When the firm holds all of its transportation capacity, it considers the impact of each marginal unit of output on the price it receives for all units of output. It is this centralization of the output decision that causes the inefficiency usually attributed to monopoly. But, when units of capacity are owned by separate individuals, they compete with one another to supply transportation. The decentralized ownership structure that results from separate ownership eliminates the monopoly problem because each owner does not consider how his or her actions affect the prices received by other holders of capacity.

Another claim made for regulated natural monopoly is that, as an organization, it is a superior planner to competition. This would say that the natural monopoly is guided by the regulator, who approves all projects and pricing. Since the regulator looks over all projects, he or she may be able to plan the system in a way that is superior to unregulated monopoly or competition. Planning means that the impact on the entire network is considered and that the future plays a part in approving projects. This theory does not stand up to the facts. The pipeline network never took form until deregulation and the emerging gas market transformed it. Before that, pipelines were separate and segmented because regulation blocked the formation of a connected network. As to the superior foresight of regulators, one need only point to the chaos and crises that drove the move to deregulate wellhead prices and which is moving through every segment of the industry from the wellhead to users.

Another claim made for regulation is that it prevents wasteful duplication. The ironic aspect of this argument is how far from realizing the supposed benefits of preventing duplication we are under the present system of regulation. Intra- and interstate pipelines duplicate one another to a significant degree as do power lines. This is partly the fault of the artificial jurisdictional boundaries that carve regions into isolated protectorates.

In nearly every local distribution area, there are private distribution systems operating in parallel with the public utility distribution company. One reason they do this is to get better terms and reliability than the local distributor can give them. Another is to cover parts of the region that the distributor's system does not. Yet another is to augment the coverage where the distributor's coverage is inadequate.

Given a complex system and a dynamic world, regulation can build a system of prices and services that becomes unsustainable. We have seen this several times in natural gas. Agreements and contracts had to be undone, price regulation went through five regimes, and regulation spread from the user all the way back to the producers and then came apart. As in any sustainable coalition that achieves political control of an industry, the combined claims of the members, which reflect what they can get outside the coalition, must not exceed the total value of resources available to the coalition. When they do, the system must collapse. It then can only be rebuilt on a new, and reduced, set of claims and, maybe, with different members. By blocking exit and altering constraints, the system can be made to work for a time, but the complexity of the interlocking constraints means that they must frequently be violated. Then a fix is required, as in the many changes of regulatory regime that have been made to natural gas. However, do regulators understand what they are doing? In this complex problem, regulation is just a blind search for a sustainable coalition and not for efficiency.

4 Markets in Operation

It will become evident in this section that the evidence on the performance of markets in natural gas and electric power is mixed. Where markets succeeded, it is largely because open access transportation gave them the scope to operate. Where markets failed, it is usually due to the imposition of an inflexible and centralized market design that misaligned incentives. The institutions separating the merchant and transportation functions allowed new kinds of traders into the market, and gave these traders the means to trade over wide areas. When the market design works, open access and transportation trading make it possible to create a more connected grid with flexible routings, and this more connected network topology expands the power of arbitrage to discipline prices across the locations of energy supply and use.

In the US, the unbundling of gas transportation from the commodity completely changed the way the industry works. Pipelines coordinate their customers' transmission demands during what is called 'bidweek'.[7] During the bidweek, usually the third week of each month, pipeline customers nominate the gas volumes they plan to ship during the following month. These nominations specify the injection point, the withdrawal point, and the volume of gas to be shipped. Customers may nominate volumes only up to the amount of their firm transmission rights. Those pipeline customers who transfer their transmission capacity to third parties are responsible for nominating and paying for it. The simultaneity of gas and interruptible transportation markets during the bidweek coordinates the purchase of gas and transportation. The spot contracts are for volumes to be delivered to specific injection points on the pipeline system. From the injection point, the gas flows through the interruptible transmission right that is purchased in the bulletin board market to the downstream destination.

Holders of firm transportation contracts may trade with one another or transfer their rights to brokers and other parties; however the federal regulator has not permitted transportation to become a fully transferable property right.[8] Unused firm transmission capacity reverts to the pipeline, which sells it as interruptible transportation. Brokers buy and sell gas throughout the pipeline network, even though they do not have uninterruptible transmission rights of their own. They aggregate the supplies of producers and the demands of gas users. By purchasing interruptible transmission from the pipeline, they can ship gas from the producers to the users. Essentially, brokers hold a portfolio of gas market transactions which they match. Some brokers act as the purchasing agent for downstream local distribution companies. These brokers use the customer's transmission capacity to deliver the gas which they sell to the customer. Pipeline mergers have created extended networks. The technology for interconnecting pipelines quickly developed after 1985, so that it is now possible to interconnect lines with different pressures and to change the flow between them.[9] Markets quickly came forth as pipelines chose open access status. A few years after the initial institutionalization of open access by the federal regulator, the gas industry publication *Gas Daily* was reporting spot prices at over 50 market locations.

By 1989 almost all the major US pipelines had open access and by 1991 more than 65 percent of the regional markets had become integrated (De Vany and Walls, 1993). These findings have been echoed by other researchers who found an increase in the geographical extent of the market after 1985 and concluded that open access created a national competitive natural gas market (Doane and Spulber, 1994). Kleit (1998), using an arbitrage cost approach, also found less strong evidence of market integration. Cuc and King (1996) also found an increasing degree of market integration in the North American natural gas market, but indicated the presence of an east–west split in North American natural gas markets; however, Serletis (1997) finds on further examination, that markets are integrated and that there is no east–west split. The strong market integration at the field level was not completely reflected at the downstream city markets (Walls, 1994).

The benefits from open access may not be large when the pipeline network is not very dense since pipelines lack an incentive to price their interruptible capacity efficiently (Lawrey, 1998). In the absence of an established pipeline network, which is the case in many markets, pipelines may have little incentive to price their excess capacity efficiently. In this case, attempts to promote an efficient allocative outcome through privatization and open access are unlikely to be as successful as they have been in North America. This view is consistent with recent theoretical work which finds that building excess transmission capacity leads to increased market integration through the mitigation of local market power (Cremer and Laffont, 2002).

In recent years, natural gas utilities have faced increasing demand, slower growth of production and pipeline capacity and several episodes of sharp spot price increases, in the two most recent cases, lasting many months. Most of the gas sold to residential customers is done so under terms that simply pass through the commodity costs of acquiring the gas. Further, there are few effective options for these consumers to observe changing gas spot prices in real time or to switch to alternative fuels in the short to mid-term. Recent survey evidence indicates a great deal of disparity in the practices of regulated utilities with regard to hedging their purchases of natural gas. This disparity in utility purchasing practices appears to indicate a systemic problem, with the regulatory environment not conducive to regulators accepting the appropriate use of the hedging tools (Ludwigson et al., 2006).

The restructuring of natural gas in the UK took shape with the privatization of British Gas and the creation of a new regulator, Ofgas, in 1986. Due to the highly centralized structure of the industry and the dominance of British Gas, active spot markets did not evolve until the 1990s (Asche et al., 2006). The restructuring of the European natural gas industry, while centrally directed by the EU, has not been implemented with the same rapidity that characterized deregulation in the US and UK (Heren, 1999; Percebois, 1999; Radetzki, 1999). Lee et al. (1999) study the market performance of gas utilities across countries with different regulatory structures and conclude that the North American market, with its decentralized market structure and intense competition, does not guarantee a more desirable market outcome than the European centralized and highly regulated structure. While different approaches to regulatory reform in natural gas markets have been applied, the price evidence indicates convergence toward a single market: Asche et al. (2002, 2006) and Siliverstovs et al. (2005) find evidence of market integration in European natural gas markets.

In the US gas industry, the institutions and practices took some time to emerge and evolve to a level of refinement that let markets operate well. Several years were required to get smooth operation in gas markets even after open access was a completed property of the pipeline network. Unlike gas pipelines, the concept of shared transmission capacity has been used in electricity for some time.[10] Because power pools, wheeling, and energy trading have a long history in the electricity industry, the necessary institutions and practices were in place for increased wholesale trade once the transmission network began to open up. Before comprehensive introduction of market restructuring in electricity, decentralized wholesale power trading did lead to an increased integration of markets though the scope in trade was limited (De Vany and Walls, 1999a, 1999b). The advantages of an interconnected power grid are many. Generating resources could be pooled; load variations could be smoothed over the many markets and users on the grid; diverse customers could be combined into portfolios that balance loads by time and direction of flow; and power could flow from low-cost generators to replace high-cost generators. An active network of markets, which makes prices daily or by the hour, supplies the information needed to direct energy flows over the network of resources and users so as to minimize the total cost of electricity. As in the gas industry, access means that buyers and sellers could deal directly.[11] It also means that they can search over the network for the best price. This ability to search puts competitive pressure on the local utility to supply cheaper power.

The balancing of supply and demand for electricity is much more complex than for any other commodity. Due to the absence of much cost-effective storage, and the fact that equipment that runs on electricity is quite sensitive to changes in voltage and frequency, the supply of and demand for electricity must at all times be maintained in almost precise and instantaneous balance. This is further complicated by the fact that consumers of electricity, by virtue of custom and the state of installed technology, cannot effectively be excluded from consuming electricity, and therefore, there must always be enough power on the grid at all times to meet whatever demand is placed on it. Among other things, this requires some centralized control over the operation of the entire electricity grid. The grid operator must have enough control over the operation of generators to make instantaneous adjustments to the supply in response to unscheduled changes in demand. Superimposing competitive markets for wholesale electricity on this system has proven to be a challenge (Joskow and Tirole, 2005).

Results from an analysis of wholesale electricity spot prices on the western US electricity transmission system from 1994 to 1996 find a high degree of market integration (De Vany and Walls, 1999a, 1999b); at this time, electricity markets had not yet been comprehensively restructured but instead there was decentralized trade in wholesale power along the same lines in which open access transmission had been introduced to gas pipelines. The restructuring process in the electricity industry developed slowly, and wholesale trade in electric power was the logical way for the industry to evolve. But because there was no single national entity responsible for the power network in the US, different states and regions have restructured their industries differently. However, in each jurisdiction a centralized market mechanism has been implemented to account for the complexity of balancing of supply and demand for electricity in a way that is consistent with the physics of the transmission network. Numerous different models have been employed, the main difference between gas and electricity markets being the decentralization of the former and the centralization of the latter. In power markets there is typically an auction institution for power in combination with centralized dispatch of power that accounts for the constraints of the transmission system.[12]

The performance of electricity markets that have been comprehensively restructured is mixed. Most markets are working in a sustainable way, though some markets that experienced problems – such as Ontario and California – have essentially halted their restructuring programs. The disaster in the California power market and the exercise of market power in that state's wholesale power market has been well documented and merits a short discussion here.[13] California restructured its electricity industry in the mid-1990s. The intention was to increase wholesale competition and then to gradually introduce retail competition. There were two principal flaws in the design of California's electricity markets that began operation in April 1998. The first was that the rate structure for the state's three investor-owned utilities (IOUs) all but precluded the development of retail competition that might have introduced some measure of demand response to the market. Rates for the three utilities' customers were reduced by 10 percent and frozen, which simultaneously reduced the margin that might have encouraged retail competition and removed the option of increasing rates in the event that wholesale prices rose. Second, the same three IOUs were encouraged (some argue required) to divest themselves of their fossil-fuel generating facilities without signing any long-term contracts to buy back the power from these or other generators. As a result, the IOUs were in a position of buying a large proportion of the power to serve their load in the day-ahead and hour-ahead markets operated by the California Power Exchange. It is generally agreed that at the time the divestments were made, there was a surplus of power in the region and long-term contracts for power could have been purchased quite cheaply. In fact, for two years, the surplus capacity in the region kept wholesale market prices very low relative to the previous rate-regulated cost of electricity, and by design, the frozen rates of the IOU customers meant that the IOUs were recovering large amounts of their negotiated stranded costs.

The design of the California market implemented institutions and rules that were almost guaranteed to create market power in the event of tight supply conditions. The power exchange was set up to operate day-ahead and hour-ahead markets and the three IOUs were encouraged (required), after divesting much of their generating capacity, to buy all their power in these markets. Other suppliers of electricity were not similarly constrained. The root cause of the 2000–01 crisis was a tight supply caused by static thermal generating capacity over a number of years coupled with rising demand and reduced hydro power as a result of a dry year. The resulting scarcity in the spring and early summer of 2000 caused prices to rise and allowed isolated exercise of market power by individual suppliers. However, the response by the system operator of (indirectly) capping prices in the day-ahead and hour-ahead markets had the effect of driving suppliers out of those markets. These suppliers either sold power out of state – exports and imports of power rose during this period – or waited to sell directly to the system operator closer to real time. In the latter case, the transmission system operator lacked the political will to credibly commit to shedding load if prices rose too high and so they were in a position of engaging in multiple bilateral negotiations under tremendous time pressure and where their bargaining opponents knew the system operator would have to blink first.[14] The problem worsened when the cap was lowered because it drove even more of the suppliers out of the day-ahead and hour-ahead markets and closer to real time. As the system operator was forced to buy increasing amounts of energy close to real time, their ability to negotiate and to seek alternatives to high price offers became even more constrained. As the price caps were reduced, the imbalance between demand – the entire load of the three IOUs – and supply – the remaining capacity (nuclear and hydro) plus power from those suppliers who did not flee to real time – became greater. As a result, prices rose toward the cap in more and more hours as the cap was reduced, causing average prices in these markets to rise.

Another important and specific issue is the way in which power industry restructuring has changed the incentives to provide additional generation capacity. One key feature of restructuring has been a move away from centralized planning where utilities planned for development of new generating capacity and transmission upgrades in order to meet expected increases in future demand. In its place, a decentralized process of development and investment decisions – largely by non-utility companies – is evolving. Unlike the rate-regulated regime of the past, the development and investment plans of these companies are not subject to approval of public utilities commissions or centrally coordinated. Even under a market organization, government entities influence investments through licensing and permitting processes, through the terms of transmission interconnection agreements. There is considerable variation across locations in the administration of the development process and thereby in the costs that developers must incur to gain the approval of governmental entities. In addition to the development costs associated with acquiring regulatory approval, new power plants must be interconnected with the transmission grid, frequently requiring costly upgrades to the system to maintain reliability.

A study of US power plant investment found that the addition of new power plants is much more prevalent in states that have either restructured their retail electricity markets or signaled an initial intent to do so than in states that have taken no restructuring actions (Walls et al., 2007). Such development is also more prevalent in areas of the country with a robust wholesale market infrastructure. Non-utility companies accounted for most new power plants in states taking restructuring actions, while utilities maintained a dominant role in states that have not restructured. States that implement retail competition have more investment in new power plants. These patterns indicate that regulatory actions are an important determinant of how well overall restructuring will ultimately work. The bulk of the potential benefits of restructuring the industry will come from improvements in efficiency of wholesale generation and sale of electricity, and this depends critically on the ability of new companies to enter and exit. However, non-utility companies are far less likely to make the investments necessary to achieve these benefits in jurisdictions not committed to developing a competitive environment.

5   Moving Forward

Open access transportation has given us a glimpse of what market competition really looks like in natural gas, the first such view that can actually inform us as to how markets would work in this industry. What we have seen is very different from what the theory of regulated monopoly says should have happened. According to this theory, competition is unsuited to natural gas; it would lead to wasteful duplication, would not efficiently coordinate the use of the pipeline network, and would produce erratic price behavior. The evidence in North America – where open access transportation has been adopted – indicates that competition led to gas price convergence over the network, eliminating pockets of non-responsive and possibly monopolistic prices, and integrating markets. The gas market is functionally competitive. The move toward market-based allocation in power has been more problematic.

What does functional competitiveness imply about the validity of the structural measures of monopoly and competition that market monitors and regulators apply? Interconnections and paths in the transmission network are the fundamental structural elements in the determination of prices. Open access and flexible transmission create the functional paths on this structure and they are assembled in response to prices and arbitrage opportunities. The market is functionally competitive if it produces competitive prices, whatever its physical structure. The market is competitive if the spatial distribution of prices over the network exhibits the right kind of convergence and dynamics.[15] Price evidence is functional and far more compelling than structural evidence, though there may be allowances for how easy it is to connect to a nearby, presently unconnected, transmission line and other such factors.

Any structural organization of the energy market that can deliver competitive prices is functionally competitive, no matter how it is structured. The ideal of perfect competition is wholly structural in content and not a model of function. The conditions that the model assumes are neither necessary nor sufficient for competitive pricing. North American gas markets show this clearly, since virtually none of these conditions is met and yet the gas market is functionally competitive, based on the price evidence. What is called perfect competition, and held up to be the ideal that regulation should strive to emulate, is a very poor market structure. It is maladaptive to changing circumstances. It does not deliver products with the kind of variety that is required to serve diverse customers. It is non-innovating; in fact, it just assumes that there is a product that customers want without ever telling how it is discovered. It does not capture the noise and chaos which any adaptive market must possess and which any real market exhibits.

Far from perfection, perfectly competitive markets do not function well because they share certain characteristics with planning. In planning, all the equations of the system are solved by the planning bureau, who then calls out allocations or prices to managers whose behavioral rules tell them to set marginal cost equal to price. The model of perfect competition is similar in that in it markets solve the problem of computing a price vector, and profit-maximizing managers do the rest. Neither task is doable and the solutions they would obtain, if they could find them, are inept and narrow. It is time to stop apologizing for competition on the grounds that it is not perfect; perfect competition, like any homogeneous and noiseless process, is incapable of evolving and its structural perfection is its greatest weakness.

Prices that are made daily or hourly or even by 10-minute intervals in spot markets scattered over the grid can supply the information needed to guide the flow of electricity through the network, producing it at the lowest-cost generators and sending it to the markets where its value is highest. With prices made continuously in a network of markets, the flow of energy can take place nearly in real time. Moreover, prices reflect the state of the network at each trading interval and they can supply state information to guide flows through the network. The signal that the process is working is the convergence of prices over the network, just as we have seen in the gas industry. Therefore, we should be looking at prices – spot, contract, and utility retail prices – over the power grid for evidence of competitiveness. Structural features such as the number of lines into or out of a territory are important only if prices are out of line. Yet it is the price evidence that is decisive. Prices are likely to track the competitive arbitrage band, as we saw in US natural gas markets, if the power grid is open and competitive market institutions are in place.

6 Conclusion

In the move toward market-oriented allocation mechanisms, the natural gas and electric power industries are increasingly being regulated by market forces so that they more closely resemble a commodity market than a regulated public utility. The separation of the energy commodity from its transportation has provided the basis for restructuring natural gas and electricity markets. Competition in gas and power markets has been more like evolution than like solving a well-defined mathematical problem. Evolution is robust and opportunistic; it searches a broad landscape and promotes diversity. Selection eliminates weak solutions and random innovations present new alternatives for selection to affect. This is precisely what we have seen in the gas and electricity markets as they have evolved over the past two decades of relaxed regulation. Markets succeeded under open access to gas transmission because participants built effective institutions to govern their trade in gas and transportation. Under these institutions, markets have achieved a high degree of coordination between commodity trading and transportation. The transition from planned industry to markets in natural gas was easier in the US than one might have thought. A believer in what the theory of regulation claims would not have prepared for what happened. Market participants created the institutions that were required to support competitive exchange in gas across the transmission grid. Access to transmission opened paths in the network and let arbitrage force gas prices to converge to a spatial distribution that is competitive. None of the dire predictions of the theory of regulated natural monopoly about competition and markets came true. However, due to the complexity of balancing of supply and demand for electricity, the introduction of market-based allocation mechanisms has proven to be far more difficult for electric power than was the case for natural gas; in these cases, regulatory failures in design have resulted when the mandated rules and institutions did not appropriately reflect the constraints and incentives of the regulated market. Nowhere has this been more evident than in restructured electricity markets.

Notes

1. 'Breaking up is hard to do: attempts to reform Europe's energy markets are losing out to protectionism', *The Economist*, 13 September 2007.
2. See, for example, MacAvoy and Pindyck (1975) and Tussing and Barlow (1984) for historical and economic analysis of natural gas price regulation. Brief accounts are contained in Michaels (1993) and in De Vany and Walls (1995).
3. Prior to this time nearly all gas was sold under long-term contracts that have been analyzed thoroughly in the economics literature. See, for example, Masten and Crocker (1985), Mulherin (1986a, 1986b), Hubbard and Weiner (1986, 1991), Masten (1988), and De Canio and Frech (1993).
4. The system of tradable property rights proposed in Smith et al. (1988) is an example of the type of institution that can be created by industry participants, in this case an association of natural gas suppliers.
5. See US Energy Information Administration (1989), Cramer (1991), and De Vany and Walls (1994a, 1994b) for more details on the transition from merchant carriage to contract carriage.
6. Although comprehensive restructuring did not occur in practice until the late 1990s, economic models of spatial spot pricing that incorporated the physics of alternating current were developed much earlier. See, for example, Schweppe et al. (1988) and the numerous references to the work of Schweppe and associates referenced therein.
7. The discussion of the market institutions follows closely De Vany and Walls (1994a).
8. See Smith et al. (1988, 1990), Alger and Toman (1990) and De Vany and Walls (1994a) for a more detailed discussion of gas pipeline regulatory reform.
9. See *Oil & Gas Journal* (1990, pp. 41–8).
10. See, for example, the discussion in Joskow and Schmalensee (1983).
11. Although the power market is typically an auction institution, this does not foreclose other transactions. See the many examples contained in Stoft (2002).
12. The different implemented architectures and discussed in depth in Stoft (2002). Wilson (2002) provides a more theoretical discussion of the incentive properties of various architectures for power market design.
13. See, for example, the papers of Faruqui et al. (2001), Borenstein et al. (2002), Joskow and Kahn (2002), Wolak (2003), US General Accounting Office (2002a, 2002b), and many others. A discussion of the Ontario electricity market is contained in Trebilcock and Hrab (2005).
14. Under the design of California's electricity market, the system operator did not have broad authority to mitigate market power as did system operators in other restructured markets. On numerous occasions the system operator did request such authority from the Federal Energy Regulatory Commission (FERC) and also requested that FERC step in to mitigate prices that appeared to be far in excess of generation costs. FERC declined to act in the early stages of the crisis and the only tool the California Independent System Operator (CAISO) had at its disposal was price caps.
15. Some electric power markets are even characterized as being informationally efficient; see, for example, Serletis and Bianchi's (2007) analysis of Alberta electricity spot prices.

References

Alger, D. and Toman, M. (1990), 'Market-based regulation of natural gas pipelines', *Journal of Regulatory Economics*, **2**(3): 262–80.
Asano, H. (2006), 'Regulatory reform of the electricity industry in Japan: what is the next step of deregulation?', *Energy Policy*, **34**(16): 2491–7.
Asche, F., Osmundsen, P. and Sandsmark, M. (2006), 'The UK market for natural gas, oil and electricity: are the prices decoupled?', *The Energy Journal*, **27**: 27–40.
Asche, F., Osmundsen, P. and Tveteras, R. (2002), 'European market integration for gas? Volume flexibility and political risk', *Energy Economics*, **24**: 249–65.
Balachandra, P. (2006), 'Implications of private sector participation in power generation – a case study from India', *Energy Policy*, **34**(16): 2466–79.
Borenstein, S., Bushnell, J. and Wolak, F. (2002), 'Measuring market inefficiencies in California's restructured wholesale electricity market', *American Economic Review*, **92**(5): 1376–405.
Chang, Y. and Tay, T.H. (2006), 'Efficiency and deregulation of the electricity market in Singapore', *Energy Policy*, **34**(16): 2498–508.

Chirarattananon, S. and Nirukkanaporn, S. (2006), 'Deregulation of ESI and privatization of state electric utilities in Thailand', *Energy Policy*, **34**(16): 2521–31.

Cramer, C. (1991), 'The economic effects of unbundled transportation services in the natural gas pipeline industry', *Transportation Journal*, **31**(2): 24–32.

Cremer, H. and Laffont, J.J. (2002), 'Competition in gas markets', *European Economic Review*, **46**: 928–35.

Cuc, M. and King, M. (1996), 'Price convergence in North American natural gas spot markets', *The Energy Journal*, **17**(2): 17–42.

De Canio, S.J. and Frech, H.E. (1993), 'Vertical contracts: a natural experiment in gas pipeline regulation', *Journal of Institutional and Theoretical Economics*, **149**(2): 370–72.

De Vany, A.S. and Walls, W.D. (1993), 'Pipeline access and market integration in the natural gas industry: evidence from cointegration tests', *The Energy Journal*, **14**(4): 1–19.

De Vany, A.S. and Walls, W.D. (1994a), 'Natural gas industry transformation, competitive institutions and the role of regulation: lessons from open access in U.S. natural gas markets', *Energy Policy*, **22**(9): 755–63.

De Vany, A.S. and Walls, W.D. (1994b), 'Open access and the emergence of a competitive natural gas market', *Contemporary Economic Policy*, **12**(2): 77–96.

De Vany, A.S. and Walls, W.D. (1995), *The Emerging New Order in Natural Gas: Markets versus Regulation*, Quorum Books, Westport, CT.

De Vany, A.S. and Walls, W.D. (1999a), 'Cointegration analysis of spot electricity prices: insights on transmission efficiency in the western US', *Energy Economics*, **21**(5): 435–48.

De Vany, A.S. and Walls, W.D. (1999b), 'Price dynamics in a network of decentralized power markets', *Journal of Regulatory Economics*, **15**(2): 123–40.

Doane, M.J. and Spulber, D.F. (1994), 'Open access and the evolution of the U.S. spot market for gas', *Journal of Law and Economics*, **37**: 477–515.

Faruqui, A., Chao, H.P., Niemeyer, V., Platt, J. and Stahlkopf, K. (2001), 'Analyzing California's power crisis', *The Energy Journal*, **22**: 29–52.

Heren, P. (1999), 'Removing the government from European gas', *Energy Policy*, **27**: 3–8.

Hsu, G.J.Y. and Chen, T.Y. (1997), 'The reform of the electric power industry in Taiwan', *Energy Policy*, **25**: 951–7.

Hubbard, R.G. and Weiner, R.J. (1986), 'Regulation and long-term contracting in the U.S. natural gas market', *Journal of Industrial Economics*, **35**: 71–9.

Hubbard, R.G. and Weiner, R.J. (1991), 'Efficient contracting and market power: evidence from the U.S. natural gas industry', *Journal of Law and Economics*, **34**: 25–68.

Joskow, P.L. and Kahn, E. (2002), 'A quantitative analysis of pricing behaviour in California's wholesale electricity market during summer 2000', *The Energy Journal*, **23**(4): 1–35.

Joskow, P.L. and Schmalensee, R. (1983), *Markets for Power: An Analysis of Electric Utility Deregulation*, MIT Press, Cambridge, MA.

Joskow, P. and Tirole, J. (2005), 'Merchant transmission investment', *Journal of Industrial Economics*, **53**: 233–64.

Kahn, A. (1988), *The Economics of Regulation*, MIT Press, Cambridge, MA.

Kleit, A. (1998), 'Did open access integrate natural gas markets? An arbitrage cost approach', *Journal of Regulatory Economics*, **14**: 19–33.

Lawrey, R. (1998), 'Pricing and access under national competition policy: the case of the natural gas pipeline sector', *Australian Economic Review*, **31**: 91–106.

Lee, J.D., Park, S.B. and Kim, T.Y. (1999), 'Profit, productivity, and price differential: an international performance comparison of the natural gas transportation industry', *Energy Policy*, **27**: 679–89.

Ludwigson, J., Rusco, F.W. and Walls, W.D. (2006), 'A case for integrating the regulation for natural gas utilities', in *Proceedings of the 26th Annual IAEE North American Conference*, International Association for Energy Economics, Cleveland, OH, pp. 1–7.

MacAvoy, P.A. and Pindyck, R.S. (1975), *The Economics of the Natural Gas Shortage (1960–1980)*, North-Holland, Amsterdam and New York.

Masten, S.E. (1988), 'Minimum bill contracts: theory and policy', *Journal of Industrial Economics*, **37**: 85–97.

Masten, S.E. and Crocker, K.J. (1985), 'Efficient adaptation in long term contracts: take or pay for natural gas', *American Economic Review*, **75**(5): 1083–93.

Michaels, R.J. (1993), 'The new age of natural gas: how regulators brought competition', *Regulation*, **16**(1): 68–79.

Mulherin, J. (1986a), 'Complexity in long term natural gas contracts: an analysis of natural gas contractual provisions', *Journal of Law and Economic Organization*, **2**: 105–17.

Mulherin, J. (1986b), 'Specialized assets, governmental regulation, and organizational structure in the natural gas industry', *Journal of Institutional and Theoretical Economics*, **142**: 528–41.

Mulugettaa, Y., Mantajitb, N. and Jackson, T. (2007), 'Power sector scenarios for Thailand: an exploratory analysis 2002–2022', *Energy Policy*, **35**: 3256–69.

Nakawiro, T. and Bhattacharyya, S.C. (2007), 'High gas dependence for power generation in Thailand: the vulnerability analysis', *Energy Policy*, **35**: 3335–46.

Oil & Gas Journal (1990), August 6 edition, 41–8.

Percebois, J. (1999), 'The gas deregulation process in Europe: economic and political approach', *Energy Policy*, **27**: 9–15.

Pintz, P. and Korn, A. (2005), 'Development of a competitive electricity market in Indonesia', *Energy Studies Review*, **13**: 56–70.

Pittman, R. (2007), 'Restructuring the Russian electricity sector: re-creating California?', *Energy Policy*, **35**: 1872–83.

Radetzki, M. (1999), 'European natural gas: market forces will bring about competition in any case', *Energy Policy*, **27**: 17–24.

Scherer, F.M. (1980), *Industrial Market Structure and Economic Performance*, 2nd edn, Houghton Mifflin, Boston, MA.

Schrade, W.R. and Walls, W.D. (2006), 'Holding companies, market liquidity, and the development of the electric power industry', *Journal of Energy and Development*, **32**(1): 1–18.

Schweppe, F.C., Caramanis, M.C., Tabors, R.D. and Bohn, R.E. (1988), *Spot Pricing of Electricity*, International Series in Engineering and Computer Science, Kluwer, Boston, MA.

Serletis, A. (1997), 'Is there an east–west split in North American natural gas markets?', *The Energy Journal*, **18**: 47–62.

Serletis, A. and Bianchi, M. (2007), 'Informational efficiency and interchange transactions in Alberta's electricity market', *The Energy Journal*, **28**: 121–43.

Serralles, R.J. (2006), 'Electric energy restructuring in the European Union: integration, subsidiarity and the challenge of harmonization', *Energy Policy*, **34**: 2542–51.

Siliverstovs, B., L'Hegaret, G., Neumann, A. and von Hirschhausen, C. (2005), 'International market integration for natural gas? A cointegration analysis of prices in Europe, North America and Japan', *Energy Economics*, **27**: 603–15.

Singh, A. (2006), 'Power sector reform in India: current issues and prospects', *Energy Policy*, **34**(16): 2480–90.

Smith, R.T., De Vany, A.S. and Michaels, R.J. (1988), 'An open access rights system for natural gas pipelines', in *Interstate Natural Gas Pipeline Rate Design Studies*, Natural Gas Supply Association, Washington, DC, pp. 155–225.

Smith, R.T., De Vany, A.S. and Michaels, R.J. (1990), 'Defining a right of access to interstate natural gas pipelines', *Contemporary Policy Issues*, **8**: 142–58.

Stoft, S. (2002), *Power System Economics: Designing Markets for Electricity*, IEEE/Wiley Press, Piscataway, NJ.

Tishler, A., Newman, J., Spekterman, I. and Woo, C. (2006), 'Cost–benefit analysis of reforming Israel's electricity industry', *Energy Policy*, **34**(16): 2442–54.

Trebilcock, M.J. and Hrab, R. (2005), 'Electricity restructuring in Ontario', *The Energy Journal*, **26**(1): 123–46.

Tussing, A.R. and Barlow, C.C. (1984), *The Natural Gas Industry: Evolution, Structure and Economics*, Ballinger, Cambridge, MA.

US Energy Information Administration (1989), *Growth in Unbundled Natural Gas Transportation Services: 1982–1987*, US GPO, Washington, DC.

US General Accounting Office (2002a), 'Lessons learned from restructuring: transition to competitive markets underway, but full benefits will take time and effort to achieve', Technical Report GAO-03-271, GAO, Washington, DC.

US General Accounting Office (2002b), 'Restructured electricity markets: California market design enabled exercise of market power', Technical Report GAO-02-828, GAO, Washington, DC.

Walls, W.D. (1994), 'Price convergence across natural gas production fields and city markets', *The Energy Journal*, **15**(4): 37–48.

Walls, W.D., Rusco, F.W. and Ludwigson, J. (2007), 'Power plant investment in restructured markets', *ENERGY – The International Journal*, **8**: 1403–13.

Wang, K.M. (2006), 'The deregulation of Taiwan electricity supply industry', *Energy Policy*, **34**(16): 2509–20.

Wilson, R. (2002), 'Architecture of power markets', *Econometrica*, **70**: 1299–340.

Wolak, F. (2003), 'Measuring unilateral market power in wholesale electricity markets: the California market 1998 to 2000', *American Economic Review (Papers and Proceedings)*, **93**(2): 425–30.

Xu, S. and Chen, W. (2006), 'The reform of electricity power sector in the PR of China', *Energy Policy*, **34**(16): 2455–65.

21 Incentive regulation of energy networks
Thomas Weyman-Jones

1 Introduction

Incentive regulation commonly based on price or revenue capping has become widely used by European, US, Latin American and Australian network regulators as part of their regulatory regimes. This has gone hand in hand with the wide adoption of comparative efficiency and productivity analysis, more commonly known as 'benchmarking'. Another regulatory tool is that of sliding scale regulation; which is used when the regulator is not only unable to observe effort, but is also unsure of the firm's productive potential. This chapter sets out the key regulatory principles and tools employed when regulating energy networks. Section 3 discusses the virtues of competition and regulation. Regulatory models and their implementation are set out in Sections 4 to 9. Section 10 presents partial and general equilibrium analysis, while Section 11 concludes. The chapter proceeds with an outline of the characteristics of regulated energy networks in Section 2.

2 Characteristics of Regulated Energy Networks

Regulatory issues in energy network industries, for example, electricity and gas, are illustrated in Table 21.1, showing the types of firm or organisation which may be involved in the overall supply of the fuel product and the associated customer services.

In network industries the two principal activities are *production* and *delivery* through the network of wires or pipes. In electricity, for example, production is represented by *generation*, and electricity is delivered through a *transmission* (high-voltage) network and

Table 21.1   Network industry structures

Model 1: Not liberalised POU or IOU, single company	Model 2: Partly liberalised competitive companies & regulated IOUs without access	Model 3: Completely liberalised competitive companies & regulated IOUs with access
Production: many plants, one company, no entry	*Production*: several competitive companies, free entry	*Production*: many competitive companies, free entry
Transmission: integrated with production monopoly	*Transmission*: regulated single monopoly	*Transmission*: regulated single monopoly
Distribution: integrated with production monopoly	*Distribution*: regulated single monopoly or regional/local monopolies	*Distribution*: regulated single or regional/local monopolies
Supply: coincides with distribution	*Supply*: coincides with distribution, regulated single or regional/local monopolies	*Supply*: competitive entry with access charges for use of distribution pipes and wires

then a *distribution* (low-voltage) network. In natural gas, production is represented by exploration, drilling and extraction, and the natural gas fuel is delivered through a transmission system at high pressure (which may also be used as storage) and a distribution system at low pressure for customer appliances. In both industries, there may also be an additional activity, *supply*, which is metering and billing the delivered product. Reading down the table any or all of these activities may be carried out by a publicly owned utility (POU, owned by government) or an investor-owned utility (IOU). Therefore ownership is one issue in the regulatory debate, but the modern literature on regulation takes the IOU as the typical organisational structure. Arriving at the nature of ownership may be the result of a decision to privatise a state-owned utility which in turn raises the issue of the degree of entry to the market that will be permitted by the government or competition authority in the economy concerned. Consequently reading across the table, the different degrees of liberalisation can be identified.

Model 1 represents a single vertically integrated industry, which could be a POU or an IOU. Model 2 shows that the production activity has been separated and opened to competition. The natural monopoly areas of transmission and distribution may be privately owned but regulated. In model 3, a further degree of separation has been adopted. Customers may buy supply from one company but have it delivered to them by another. The supply company may be specialised in billing, or it may be another distribution company, or it may be a production company. Transmission and distribution may still be regulated, but production may be competitive (though with a small number of firms in some cases), while supply may be contestable. A producer needs a production facility, plus a contract to sell electricity or gas either to consumers or to a distribution company. A distribution company needs a network of pipes or wires connecting customers, plus a contract to buy electricity, while a supply company needs only a list of customers, a contract to buy electricity, and a contract allowing it *access* to a distribution company's network of pipes or wires. Each company is involved in buying or selling both a network activity and a non-network activity, but only the companies selling network activities may need to be regulated on grounds of being natural monopolies with market power arising from the scale of operations; the type of regulation mechanism chosen by the economic policy authorities is the major concern of this chapter, but it can be seen that the considerations of privatisation, liberalisation and regulation are strongly interdependent.

Figure 21.1 shows the structure of a typical mature liberalised energy supply network similar to model 3 in Table 21.1. Many networks around the world are in transition from model 1 through to model 3. In 2007 for example, the European Union established fully liberalised competitive conditions in supply among member states, but many individual country members still maintained characteristics of models 1 and 2 in the other activities of the industry. In Figure 21.1, regulated entities are shown enclosed in boxes. There are a number of independent and competitive producers, for example, electricity generators or gas production facilities. These feed energy flows directly into a high-level grid, which typically is under the management of a single privately owned but regulated grid company. The grid operates over long distances at high voltage or high pressures, and feeds into a number of local distribution companies. Typically these will be regulated and some will be investor owned while others may be municipally or publicly owned. These local distribution entities distribute energy flows to individual customers, that is,

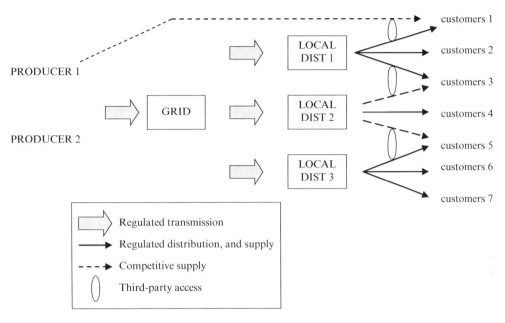

Figure 21.1   Energy network structures after liberalisation

households and firms, and also act as the supply entity through the billing and metering process. However, customers can also be supplied by other entities than their local
distributor, for example taking energy directly from a producer, or from another distribution company. In Figure 21.1, customer group 1 has the choice of competitive supply
services from either local distributor 1 or producer 1. In the case of the supply from producer 1, the distribution service is still operated by the network of distribution company
1 but managed by a network access contract with producer 1. Similarly, customer groups
3 and 5 have the choice of competitive supply from different local distribution companies
through other network access agreements. In this way production and supply services
can be potentially competitive or at least contestable, while the natural monopoly (cost
sub-additive) transmission and distribution services are provided by non-competitive
but regulated entities, some or all of which may be privately owned, or owned by municipalities or regional public bodies. Ownership structures can become complex. Under
different jurisdictions, it may be possible for the grid company, or a producer, or a local
distribution company to own, through a holding company structure, other producers or
other local distribution companies. This has an impact on the potential for regulation
by yardstick competition, since the number of apparently comparable companies in a
yardstick competition benchmarking exercise may be larger than the number of separate
management and ownership teams involved.

3   Competition versus Regulation

Traditionally, the explanation for preferring regulation to unfettered competition is that
there may be increasing returns to scale, especially in transmission and distribution,

which will confer market power on the incumbent utility. A measure of returns to scale is the elasticity of scale:[1]

$$S = AC/MC = C/qMC$$

where C, AC, and MC are total, average, and marginal cost, respectively, and q is output. Then, $S > 1$ means that there are increasing returns to scale, $S = 1$ means constant returns to scale, and $S < 1$ means decreasing returns to scale. S is the reciprocal of the elasticity of total cost with respect to output:

$$S = 1/E_{Cq}.$$

When there is more than one product, new concepts are needed. To begin with there is no concept of average cost for the firm producing $R > 1$ outputs, since it may not be possible to define $\sum_{r=1}^{R} q_r$. Define instead

$$S = \frac{C}{\sum_{r=1}^{R} q_r MC_r}$$

and then the same criteria for returns to scale apply.

However, S is affected by more than the individual outputs, because the ability to produce both products together may allow cost to be lower than if they were produced separately. This is called economies of scope, and a two-product example is:

$$S_c = \frac{C(q_1, 0) + C(0, q_2) - C(q_1, q_2)}{C(q_1, q_2)}.$$

This concept measures by how much the costs of separate production proportionally exceed the costs of joint production: $S_c > 0$ means that there are economies of scope. When this occurs the possibility of natural monopoly may become more likely in an industry. The key to whether size is a desirable attribute of a utility is therefore cost sub-additivity, and this can be illustrated simply by a diagram in input space (Färe et al., 1994), as shown in Figure 21.2.

There are two producers, a and b, using two inputs: x_1 and x_2 to produce output q. The input requirements set for each individual producer is $I(q)$, and its boundary is the firm's isoquant. The aggregate of the individual producers' outputs has input requirements: $I(q^a) + I(q^b)$, and for given input prices, $\mathbf{w} = (w_1, w_2)$, the aggregate cost of output is $C(q^a, \mathbf{w}) + C(q^b, \mathbf{w})$. Cost sub-additivity will (weakly) justify a merger into a single utility if the merged cost is not more than the aggregate individual cost:

$$C(q^a + q^b, \mathbf{w}) \leq C(q^a, \mathbf{w}) + C(q^b, \mathbf{w}).$$

This is illustrated in Figure 21.2 where the merged cost is represented by the isocost line passing through the point: $(x_1^a + x_1^b), (x_2^a + x_2^b)$, and tangential to the isoquant

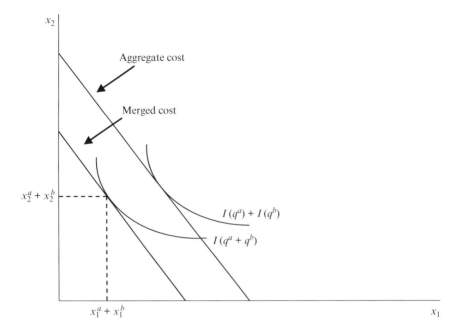

Figure 21.2   Cost sub-additivity and input requirements super-additivity

boundary of the merged input requirements set: $I(q^a + q^b)$. From the figure we can see that cost sub-additivity is therefore equivalent by duality to super-additivity of the input requirements sets:

$$I(q^a + q^b) \subseteq I(q^a) + I(q^b).$$

This follows because the aggregated input requirement to produce at the minimum cost along $I(q^a) + I(q^b)$ clearly exceeds $(x_1^a + x_1^b)$, $(x_2^a + x_2^b)$ as shown in Figure 21.2. Consequently, allowing large-scale firms to own and operate a network as a monopoly may yield efficiency gains. To offset the consequent market power will then require some form of regulation that does not destroy the firm's ability to benefit from these efficiency gains. This is an important objective of incentive regulation.

The first-best world described above provides the traditional case for regulation. In this situation the regulator would know, with certainty, the required efficient level of costs and demand for quality of service at all periods in time. However, preservation of scale efficiency despite market power is not the only reason for regulation of utilities; an equally if not more important problem is the question of asymmetric information. Such a situation requires that the interaction between a regulator and the regulated utility is modelled as a principal–agent game.

4   Regulatory Models

Two types of information asymmetry are modelled in the theoretical literature on principal–agent regulation: *hidden information*, or adverse selection, and *hidden action*, or moral hazard. In the first case the regulator does not know the firm's type: it could be a highly productive efficient firm, or an unproductive, inefficient firm. In this case, the type of firm is a random variable chosen by nature before the regulatory game begins. Therefore, the regulator is compelled to consider the spectrum of high-powered, intermediate and low-powered contracts, and the extent to which managers are expected to be risk averse will influence the options available to the regulator for trading off incentives and insurance. The second case arises when the regulator's only problem is that the firm's effort in taking cost-reducing action is unobservable. Now the regulator is primarily interested in high-powered contracts only. The number of companies in the industry will determine the feasibility of using mechanisms that are based on comparative analysis. The legal and institutional framework of the regulatory regime will also influence the choices that can be made, for example, the regulator's ability to commit to particular mechanisms may be determined by the law, and the extent to which the regulator is independent from policy makers may influence the way in which the potentially conflicting objectives of technical efficiency, allocative efficiency and distribution objectives are balanced. In recent years, forward-looking incentive regulation often based on price or revenue capping has become widely used by European, US, Latin American and Australian network regulators as part of their regulatory regimes. This has gone hand in hand with the wide adoption of comparative efficiency and productivity analysis, more commonly known as 'benchmarking'. The European Union Electricity Directive of 2003 requires that *ex ante* regulation will become the norm throughout the European Union, leading to wider use of efficiency and productivity analysis as noted by Filippini et al. (2005). Such regulation involves the setting of a regulatory contract for subsequent years usually with a price or revenue cap and a supporting comparative efficiency analysis.

In the theoretical literature, a great deal of work has been devoted to the hidden information game, notably by Laffont and Tirole (1993) and Armstrong and Sappington (2006) (the latter also contains an excellent survey of the whole field of regulation). The prime motivation is the revelation of information by the regulated company as part of the process of choosing from a menu of regulatory contracts. A simple review of the main models with some practical applications is Burns et al. (2006). However, in practice with real-world regulated energy networks, more regulatory attention has been directed towards the hidden action game than to the hidden information game, notably since the pioneering work by Littlechild (1983) that set in motion the UK's privatisation programme. To set out the theoretical background to the hidden action game, it is useful to adopt a standard framework and this is provided by Armstrong et al. (1994), which is very similar in spirit to the treatments of Schmalensee (1989), Bogetoft (1997), Gasmi et al. (1994) and Joskow (2005).

The regulator seeks to set a price (or revenue) control by relating the regulated price, P to the observed cost, c, without observing managerial effort, e. The basis of the regulated control P can represent either average or total revenue, and c can represent either average or total cost. A linear regulatory contract model is:

$$P = \overline{P} + (1 - \rho)c, \rho \in [0, 1],$$

where $\overline{P}$ is the fixed element of the price control, and the parameter ρ is called the incentive power of the control. The higher the value of ρ the weaker the relationship between

STAGE 1
Regulator chooses parameters of a linear regulatory contract $(\bar{P}, \rho)$ to minimise the price of output and induce participation in the game

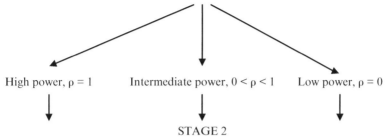

| High power, $\rho = 1$ | Intermediate power, $0 < \rho < 1$ | Low power, $\rho = 0$ |

STAGE 2
Firm chooses optimal effort $e^*(\rho)$ to maximise expected utility using the common knowledge probability distribution of the production conditions and the power of the regulatory contract
Or, depending on its reservation utility U_0, firm rejects the price control on offer

RESOLUTION
Nature randomly draws the production conditions, effort is applied and cost is observed; the actual price is set at: $P = \bar{P} + (1-\rho)\,c$, while the firm collects its actual profit and utility

Figure 21.3   Extensive form of a two-stage regulation game

the price or revenue cap and the firm's observed cost, and consequently the more high powered is the regulatory contract.

In the case of a single regulated firm, the regulator chooses $(\bar{P}, \rho)$ to minimise the level of the price or revenue cap to the firm, taking effort, e, as given by the firm's choice, The firm chooses effort, e, to maximise its utility taking $(\bar{P}, \rho)$ as given by the regulator's choice. Assume that the disutility of effort function is known to the regulator; this enables the regulator to take this function into account when designing a price control. Although the regulator cannot observe effort, he or she knows that cost, which can be verified, depends on both effort and a random variable that is outside the firm's control. Assume that marginal extra effort reduces cost by £1, $\Delta c/\Delta e = 1$. The probability distribution of the random element in cost is common knowledge (or subjectively shared by all parties to the regulatory contract). The regulation problem is that there is not a perfect correlation between the firm's effort or productive efficiency and its observed cost because the random element in observed cost introduces noise into the inference of effort. The firm's profit or rent is revenue[2] minus production cost and the monetary disutility cost of effort, but the firm's utility function indicates that it enjoys economic rent but dislikes its variability, consequently there is a known degree of risk aversion in the regulated firm. Will the firm accept the contract and participate in the game? This will depend on its reservation utility, U_0, which is the amount of utility (in monetary terms) that it could gain in an alternative economic activity.

The extensive form of the game is illustrated in Figure 21.3. It can be seen that this is a two-stage game, with the regulator choosing the price control parameters, $(\bar{P}, \rho)$, first, then the firm choosing the effort level when it knows these parameters and if it accepts the regulatory contract, by operating on the basis of expectations about the random variable that will affect production conditions. Solution is by backward induction as usual.

Begin with the firm's sub-game in stage 2, taking the regulator's choice of $(\overline{P}, \rho)$ in stage 1 as given. The utility-maximising firm chooses effort to reflect the incentive power of the regulatory contract by setting the marginal disutility of effort to whatever value of ρ the regulator has chosen. The reasoning is simple: since the parameters $(\overline{P}, \rho)$ are determined by the regulator, the firm's profit can only be altered by varying its marginal cost through additional effort. Any change in cost impacts on profit through the regulatory power parameter, ρ, since $P = \overline{P} + (1 - \rho)c$, so that the marginal benefit of extra effort is $\rho(\Delta c/\Delta e) = \rho$ and this is equated to the marginal disutility of effort. Solving for the firm's optimal effort from this condition and then substituting this value $e^* = e^*(\rho)$ into its utility function,[3] the firm's equilibrium expected utility level from participating in the game therefore is seen to depend on the regulator's price control formula, the known mean and variance (risk) parameters of the random variable representing production conditions, and the owners' (or manager's if incentivised) risk-aversion coefficient:

$$U^* = U(\overline{P}, \rho; \text{risk parameters}).$$

The regulator's subgame has the following solution: choose $\overline{P}$, ρ given $e^* = e^*(\rho)$ and U^*, and ensuring that the participation constraint will be satisfied: $U^* \geq U_0$.

The solution is the pair of optimal linear regulatory contract parameters, $\overline{P}^*$, ρ^*:

$$\overline{P}^* = \overline{P}^*(U_0; \text{risk parameters})$$

and

$$\rho^* = \rho^*(\text{risk parameters}).$$

Interpret this as follows. The variable part of the price control ρ depends on the amount of risk represented by the variance of the random variable affecting production conditions and the coefficient of risk aversion. The fixed part $\overline{P}$ depends on three factors: the reservation utility that must be covered to induce participation in the game U_0, the mean of the random variable representing the expected value of production conditions, and the variable incentive power part of the price control ρ. If the principal chooses the value of ρ suboptimally, say by opting for a high-powered contract $\rho = 1$ when the agent is risk averse and therefore an intermediate power contract, $0 < \rho < 1$, is indicated, then all that happens is that the expected utility of the agent will be reduced, $\partial U^*/\partial \rho < 0$, and non-participation, that is, rejection of the regulator's contract becomes more likely.[4] If the agent does participate nevertheless, effort will be higher than in the case of optimal choice of ρ. In summary, the effect of choosing a suboptimally high-powered contract is:[5]

$$\rho' > \rho^* \Rightarrow U' < U^*, \text{ but } e' > e^*.$$

For IOUs, the shareholders can reject a regulatory contract by selling their equity in the firm to other participants who will take on the regulator's contract at a reduced share

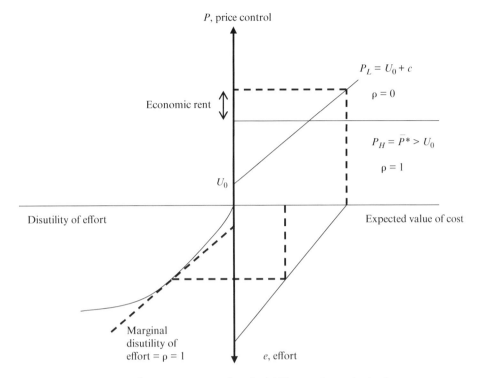

Figure 21.4   Linear regulatory contracts for the hidden action principal–agent game

price. This possibility is closed off when the regulated firms are local municipal networks as is often the case in European regulatory jurisdictions.

The high-powered contract gives the firm the greatest reward but exposes it to the highest risk. It chooses the maximal effort and the outcome price is entirely independent of the firm's marginal cost. The low-powered contract confiscates all of the firm's profit, leaving only the reservation level (normal profit), but results in the least effort ($e = 0$) and the highest price. An intermediate power contract would relate part of the price to the firm's reported cost but would not cover all of the cost risk. The firm would choose some effort to lower marginal cost. These conclusions are illustrated in Figure 21.4.

In the figure, begin with the lower left quadrant which shows the outcome of the regulated firm's (that is, the agent's) subgame. Effort is chosen to equate the marginal disutility of effort to the coefficient measuring the power of the regulatory contract, ρ. This effort level will determine the expected cost of production when account is taken of the common knowledge probability distribution of cost. In turn this will determine the utility level of the regulated firm and the actual price control that is implemented according to the regulatory contract. Figure 21.4 illustrates two possible contracts. A low-powered contract covers the firm's observed cost which embodies zero effort, and uses the fixed part of the linear contract to leave the firm with just the reservation utility level. It is the polar case of a cost-plus contract:

$$\overline{P}_L = U_0, \rho = 0 \Rightarrow P_L = U_0 + c.$$

A high-powered contract completely decouples the firm's allowed price or revenue from its observed cost, so that price (or revenue) is exogenously capped and is therefore independent of the expected value of cost, but the cap is generous enough to allow the firm to retain an informational rent in excess of reservation utility:

$$\overline{P}_H > U_0, \rho = 1 \Rightarrow P_H = \overline{P}_H.$$

This represents the other extreme of a fixed-price contract. An intermediate power contract (not shown in Figure 21.4), for example, $P_I = U_1 + 0.5c$, $U_0 < U_1 < \overline{P}_H$, will embody some non-zero effort in cost reduction but will also cover a proportion of the firm's cost when production conditions are adverse. Note that the high-powered contract results in the lowest level of price: $P_H < P_I < P_L$ and the highest reward to the firm: $U_0 < U_1 < \overline{P}_H$. However this does not mean that a high-powered contract is necessarily the optimal outcome of this Bayesian principal–agent game, a point first made most clearly by Schmalensee (1989) and reiterated in many other papers in the literature, such as Bogetoft (1997) and Joskow (2005). The optimal outcome is one that takes account of the agent's preferences, and consequently reflects the regulated firm's degree of risk aversion together with the parametric variance of the firm's profit which is conditional on the properties of the probability distribution of the random element in costs, whose realisation is determined in the game by nature after the contract has been adopted, as is characteristic of hidden action games. For example, in the Armstrong et al. (1994) version of this game, the optimal contract in general has incentive power given by:

$$\rho = \frac{1}{(1 + \gamma\sigma^2)},$$

where γ is the agent's (that is, regulated firm's) coefficient of risk aversion, and σ^2 is the variance of the random element in cost conditions, so that the variance of the firm's profit is: $\mathrm{var}\pi = \rho^2\sigma^2$. Schmalensee (1989) and Joskow (2005) report a similar conclusion.

As noted above, the consequences of suboptimal choice of the (P, ρ) parameters results in inefficient participation in the regulatory game, leading in practice to capital leaving the industry and reallocating to activities with a more preferred risk–return trade-off. It will be seen later in the survey that the problem of retaining capital in the regulated industry to maintain the integrity and quality of the networks is a real preoccupation for regulators who are operating with high-powered contracts, as many governments have chosen to do throughout the world.[6]

The model can extend to regulation by yardstick competition (Shleifer, 1985); examples are the regulation of several regional water supply companies, or several regional gas or electricity distribution monopolies.

Armstrong et al. (1994) suggest a regulatory price formula that takes the form:

$$P_i = \overline{P} + (1 - \rho)c_i + \rho(kc_j).$$

Here the price control for firm i contains a fixed element, plus a weighted average of its own observed marginal cost and a proportion ($k > 0$) of the observed marginal cost of another comparable firm j. The regulator is engaged in two simultaneous two-stage games with each company. How does this change the solution? Imagine a model with two regulated regional utilities. Begin by thinking of the relationship between the costs of the firms. A simplification is to assume that the variance of the random variable is the same for both firms, and to write: $\text{cov}(c_i, c_j) = r\sigma^2$, where r is the correlation coefficient between the random variables representing productive conditions in each of the two firms. Each firm independently sets the marginal disutility of effort equal to the regulator's choice of the cost pass through parameter. Consequently, the regulator expects each firm to adopt the same effort level or productive efficiency level in equilibrium – unless each has very different preferences about the disutility of effort. The regulator has three variables to consider: k is the proportion of the other company's observed cost which is weighted in with each regulated company's marginal cost; and $\overline{P}, \rho$ are the fixed part of the price control and the incentive power of the optimal contract, as before. The optimal solution for k is very simple: $k = r$, the proportion of the other firm's cost which is counted is equal to the correlation coefficient between the random variables determining the production conditions. The major impact lies in the correlation between the random variables representing production conditions. If $r = 0$, then the optimal contract reduces to the single agent case. If $r = 1$, then the optimal contract reduces to:

$$\overline{P} > U_0; \rho = 1; P_i = \overline{P} + c_j.$$

The firm has the highest incentive power because $\rho = 1$ and it keeps all of the cost savings it makes from reducing its own costs. This is the maximum incentive power even if the firm is risk averse and faces highly variable costs whatever its effort level. It is, however, *fully insured* because it can pass on the full level of costs observed from its competitor in the yardstick mechanism, and it receives the same revenue whatever the state of the world, and the level of its own marginal cost.[7] Consequently, with perfectly correlated random elements in cost, the high-powered contract is optimal in yardstick competition.[8] This gives yardstick competition a very powerful basis for application in practice with regional or local monopoly networks such as those which characterise many parts of the international gas and electricity distribution industries. Armstrong and Sappington (2006: 344–5) draw attention to this fact: 'yardstick competition can provide strong incentives for efficient performance by all monopolists when they are known to operate in similar settings . . . relative performance comparisons can help to discipline and motivate monopoly suppliers'.

In practice, however, efficiency and productivity analysis plays a major role in both the single and multiple firm cases. The model treats the regulator's sub-game as an analytical optimisation exercise, but this does not generalise to reality. In the real world, each regulator needs a numerical algorithm to determine the level of the price or revenue control that meets the regulatory objective of minimising the capture of economic rent from consumers by the regulated firm, subject to the financial viability of the participating firms that accept the contract. Since an analytical solution is not available in reality, the numerical algorithm must focus on the participation constraint; for example, in the multiple firm case this is:

$$U^*(\overline{P}, \rho, k) - U_0 \geq 0.$$

Treating U_0 as the money metric required for financial viability, efficiency and productivity analysis can be used to determine a numerical approximation to the feasible level of $[U* - U_0]$, that is, the amount of economic rent or slack that can be feasibly trans-ferred from financially viable regulated firms if each locates on the efficient frontier. This efficiency change is conditional on the power of the regulatory contract that is in place. Regulatory benchmarking is needed, therefore, to determine a feasible numerical solu-tion to the regulator's problem of determining the optimal transfer of economic rent. In summary, efficiency and productivity analysis becomes a device for capturing economic rent. Drawing on this theoretical framework, there are three types of regulatory mecha-nism that are used in practice in real-world energy networks. These are price-capping, revenue-capping and sliding scale regulation. Each has its own issues and problems to be analysed. The practical implementation of a fourth mechanism: yardstick competi-tion is treated in detail in Chapter 25 on efficiency measurement in the electricity and gas distribution sectors.

5   Price-capping Regulation

Figure 21.5 represents a single product monopoly facing a price cap. The usual demand, that is, average revenue, and marginal revenue curves are shown, but at the level of the price cap, the average revenue and marginal revenue are both constant and equal, and

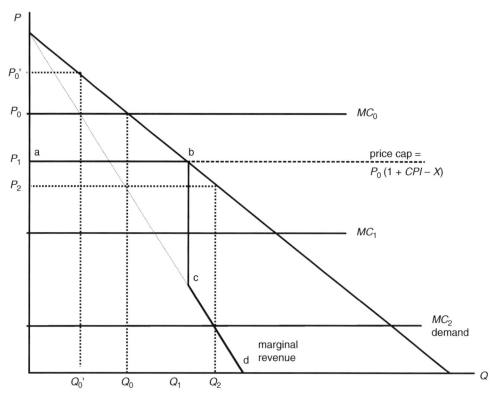

Note: With price cap at [ab], profit-maximising output depends on new *MC*.

Figure 21.5   Equilibrium with price capping

the price cap corresponds to the horizontal demand curve facing a competitive firm. The whole average revenue curve has a kink at the price cap, and the marginal revenue curve is horizontal along the segment [ab] up to the point of the kink, vertical over the range [bc] at the kink, and downward sloping over the range [cd] when average revenue lies below the price cap.

The monopoly has no market power beyond the price cap, consequently it is often argued that price-capping regulation is an attempt to mimic the discipline of a competitive market. The monopoly could choose to set price below the price cap. In that case the downward-sloping market demand curve becomes operative with the corresponding downward-sloping marginal revenue curve. The equilibrium depends on the position of the marginal cost curve when price-capping regulation is imposed. MC_0 represents the marginal cost of an inefficient firm, for example, the position under state ownership with no incentive to reduce cost through additional effort.[9] It could also represent a privately owned (that is, investor-owned) but X-inefficient firm where the managers have no incentive to minimise cost. Let us examine several alternative equilibrium positions. After privatisation (or liberalisation or de-regulation), it may be assumed that the firm has an incentive to improve cost-reducing effort, and that marginal cost falls to MC_1 for an efficient firm or even to MC_2 for a super-efficient firm. The analysis presumes that the management of the regulated company is able to respond to incentives from the owners.[10]

Here is a simple model of cost and cost-reducing effort. The firm's output is Q, and total cost is: $C = F + (\beta - e)Q$ where F is fixed cost and $(\beta - e)$ is marginal cost. Effort is symbolised by e and so higher effort reduces marginal cost. However, managers dislike using effort to reduce cost; their disutility of effort is $D(e)$, and this rises more than proportionately as effort rises. Marginal disutility of effort is positive and rising, but is zero if effort is zero:

$$D'(e) > 0;\ D''(e) > 0;\ D(0) = 0;\ D'(0) = 0.$$

Note that in this simple model the marginal benefit of additional effort is the marginal cost saved and this is just equal to the number of units of output produced, $-\Delta C/\Delta e = Q$.

Now consider two situations: in the first the firm's managers are paid a fixed salary irrespective of the profits, while in the second the firm's managers keep all or a share of the profits. When managers are paid a fixed salary, S, their objective is:

$$\max_e S - D(e).$$

First- and second-order conditions are:

$$-D'(e) = 0 \Rightarrow e = 0,$$

$$-D''(e) < 0.$$

Here the managers choose zero effort to minimise their disutility:

marginal cost is: β,
total cost is: $C = F + \beta Q$.

On the other hand, when managers keep the profits, while the firm's owners wish to maximise profit, π, then the managers' objective is the same as the owners' minus the disutility of effort: the managers' objective is:

$$\max \pi = P(Q)Q - [F + (\beta - e)Q] - D(e).$$

First-order conditions are:

$$\partial\pi/\partial Q = MR - MC = P(Q) + QP'(Q) - (\beta - e) = 0,$$

$$\partial\pi/\partial e = Q - D'(e) = 0.$$

Second-order conditions are:

$$\partial^2\pi/\partial Q^2 = \partial(MR - MC)/\partial Q = 2P'(Q) + QP''(Q) < 0,$$

$$\partial^2\pi/\partial e^2 = -D''(e) < 0,$$

$$(\partial^2\pi/\partial Q^2)(\partial^2\pi/\partial e^2) - (\partial^2\pi/\partial Q\partial e)^2 = 2[P'(Q) + QP''(Q)][- D''(e)] - 1 > 0.$$

Interpret the first-order conditions as follows:

1. marginal revenue = marginal cost, implying a positive amount of output Q^*,
2. marginal disutility = the positive output Q^*, implying positive effort e^*.

Consequently when managers can keep all or a share of the profits there will be positive effort to reduce marginal cost:

1. marginal cost is: $\beta - e^* < \beta$,
2. total cost is: $C = F + (\beta - e^*)Q$.

Consider now four different outcomes of the change to price-capping regulation in Figure 21.5, labelled 1–4:

1. (Q_0', P_0'),
2. (Q_0, P_0),
3. (Q_1, P_1),
4. (Q_2, P_2).

In each case there are two rules to determine the outcome:

- To determine *output*, set the marginal benefit of one more unit of output equal to the marginal cost.
- To determine which *marginal cost curve* will operate, set the marginal benefit of cost-reducing effort equal to the marginal private cost of more effort.

Equilibrium 1 (Q_0', P_0') is the outcome with an X-inefficient firm[11] in unregulated monopoly. It is also inefficient in the allocative sense because price exceeds marginal cost. There is a potential allocative efficiency gain of $[\frac{1}{2}(P_0' - MC_0)(Q_0 - Q_0')]$ from imposing marginal cost pricing, for example, through state ownership or price control. The marginal private benefit of output is MR, but the marginal social benefit of output is P. The marginal benefit of more effort is zero (there is no incentive) so zero effort is used.

Equilibrium 2 (Q_0, P_0) is the outcome under state ownership with marginal-cost pricing but X-inefficient management who have no incentive to lower cost through extra effort. There is a potential gain from improving X-efficiency, even if most or all of it is kept by the owners of the firm. The marginal benefit of more effort is still zero (there is no incentive) so zero effort will be used. One consequence of the lack of incentives for good performance for managers could be a tendency towards strong trade union membership to capture additional benefits for managers, irrespective of performance. This has been characteristically observed in state-owned public services, and was especially prevalent in UK publicly owned energy industries prior to the privatisation programmes of the 1980s and 1990s.

Equilibrium 3 (Q_1, P_1) is the outcome if the firm is privatised, and then subject to price-cap regulation. The firm keeps any profit made by cutting cost below the cap (revenue is (Q_1, P_1)). The owners can pass on the incentive to reduce cost to managers who engage in more cost-reducing effort. Now managers set the marginal benefit of cost-reducing effort equal to the marginal cost of more effort, and since there is a positive benefit to reducing cost there will be positive effort by the managers, and marginal cost will fall to MC_1. The price cap has been set at the pre-privatisation price adjusted for inflation in the consumer price index, CPI,[12] but with a productivity offset or X-factor that lowers the inflation-adjusted price over time:

$$P_1 = P_0(1 + CPI - X).$$

How will the firm determine its output? It is price capped but chooses its own output rule. It sets marginal private benefit of output equal to marginal cost, and chooses the output where MC_1 intersects the MR curve. This is at Q_1 below the vertical segment of the MR curve. Compared with equilibrium 2, there has been consumer surplus gain of $[\frac{1}{2}(P_0 - P_1)(Q_1 - Q_0)]$, and producer surplus gain of $[(Q_1 - Q_0)(P_1 - MC_1)]$.

Equilibrium 4 (Q_2, P_2) corresponds to the performance of a super-efficient firm. The incentive to reduce cost has been so powerful that marginal cost has fallen to MC_2. Output is now determined at Q_2, below the point where MC_2 intersects the downward-sloping part of the MR curve. The firm sets a price below the price cap at P_2. Consumer surplus gain is: $[\frac{1}{2}(P_0 - P_2)(Q_2 - Q_0)]$, producer surplus gain is: $[(Q_2 - Q_0)(P_2 - MC_2)]$.

In both of the price-cap equilibrium positions, 3 and 4, there is still allocative inefficiency. For example in equilibrium 3 it is given by $[\frac{1}{2}(P_1 - MC_1)(Q_1^* - Q_1)]$, where Q_1^* is the output (not shown) where MC_1 intersects the demand curve. To capture this for consumers by profit regulation would remove the strong incentive to the firm to engage in cost-reducing effort, consequently this allocative inefficiency is the price to be paid for securing the X-efficiency gain from reduced marginal cost. This emphasises a dilemma for the regulator in price-capping regulation. By using a high-powered regulatory contract, maximum productivity and efficiency gains have been secured, but at the expense of leaving economic rent with the regulated company. The regulator may prefer to trade off some of this productivity gain in exchange for securing some allocative efficiency improvement. This is another reflection of the fact that the optimal regulatory contract may require intermediate- rather than high-power incentives. This issue is examined further in sliding scale regulation in Section 7.

Over time, X-efficiency gains are transferred to consumers through the X-factor or productivity offset. Every five years or so, regulators may decide to review the price cap. This takes two forms:

- review the X-factor or productivity offset; and
- review the P_0 price ('P-nought') from which the process started.

For example, after five years, the regulator may change the cap to: $P_1(1 + CPI - X')$. This transfers some of the future producer surplus gain $[(Q_1 - Q_0)(P_1 - MC_1)]$ from the original price-cap incentive to consumers from that point onwards, and adjusts the X-factor as well. On the other hand, if marginal cost rises for exogenous reasons outside the firm's control, the price cap will only apply to the component of the price which is under the firm's control. If cost rises exogenously, part or all of P_0 can be adjusted upwards to reflect this.

Where does the regulator get information on X? This has to come from studies of the future productivity potential of the industry. If X is underestimated, consumers do not gain as much benefit as they could, but if it is overestimated, the firm could go out of business, and the service to consumers might disappear. This problem is taken up later in the chapter, but first it is necessary to consider other forms of price control.

6 Revenue-capping Regulation

Revenue-capping regulation is frequently adopted as an alternative to price-capping regulation. However, under revenue-capping regulation the firm has an incentive to reduce output relative to the unregulated profit-maximising level, and consequently an amended or hybrid revenue cap may be recommended. An example of such a hybrid revenue cap calibrated on a productivity offset applied to a benchmarked level of total cost appears in the Federal Energy Network Regulations for electricity and gas in Germany (Bundesnetzagentur, 2006), and in discussion of the regulation of the proposed privatised electricity networks in Turkey in the preparation for application to the European Union accession programme (Bagdadioglu et al., 2007). Bundesnetzagentur states three reasons for its preference for a revenue cap:

1. *practical advantages*: it believed that much less information may be needed to operate a revenue cap than a price cap;

2. *institutional fit*: it was argued that a revenue cap had a better fit with the German Energy Law and ordinances on networks; and
3. *conservation incentives*: it was felt that a revenue cap does not give an incentive for increasing loads/volumes and therefore was in the spirit of the environmental objective of the energy law.

The simple algebraic analysis is shown below. The demand curve is $p(q)$ and total cost is increasing in output and decreasing in effort; this is a generalisation of the simple cost function used above:

$$C = C(q, e); \; C_q = \partial C/\partial q > 0; \; C_e = \partial C/\partial e < 0.$$

Kuhn–Tucker nonlinear programming analysis is used to determine equilibrium behaviour by the managers who prefer more profit to less but also prefer less effort to more. Their behaviour is constrained by a cap on total revenue, as shown in the statement of the problem and the corresponding Lagrangean function:

$$\max \pi = R - C = qp(q) - C(q, e) - D(e) \; \text{s.t.} \; R \le \bar{R},$$

$$L = qp(q) - C(q, e) - D(e) + \lambda[\bar{R} - qp(q)].$$

The necessary Kuhn–Tucker conditions are:

$$\partial L/\partial q = (1 - \lambda)[p + qp'(q)] - C_q \le 0, \; q\partial L/\partial q = 0;$$

$$\partial L/\partial e = -C_e - D'(e) \le 0, \; e\partial L/\partial e = 0;$$

$$\partial L/\partial \lambda = [\bar{R} - qp(q)] \ge 0, \; \lambda\partial L/\partial \lambda = 0.$$

Assuming an interior optimum: $e > 0, \lambda > 0, q > 0$, the first-order conditions translate as follows. To choose effort, the same separate incentive to optimise effort remains as under the price cap; the marginal benefit of cost-reducing effort, which is the cost saved, is set equal to the marginal private disutility cost of more effort, $-C_e = D'(e)$.

To choose output, the revenue-capped firm sets marginal revenue in excess of marginal cost, because revenue is a constrained variable due to the revenue-capping mechanism: $MR = MC/(1 - \lambda)$. Since, by the envelope theorem, the shadow price on the revenue constraint can be interpreted as: $\lambda = \partial \pi/\partial R \approx (MR - MC)/MR$, it can be argued that $\lambda \in (0, 1)$. Then output is restricted until marginal revenue exceeds marginal cost to ensure maximum distance between the revenue cap and total cost. This outcome is illustrated in Figure 21.6, where q_M is the unregulated profit-maximising output and q_R is the profit-maximising output under the revenue cap.

How does a revenue cap operate? The first decision by the regulator is the size of the revenue cap, and a standard solution (for example, Bundesnetzagentur, 2006) is to set the revenue cap at the current level of cost just prior to privatisation or regulatory review adjusted by a productivity offset or X-factor. The initial cost base is either observed from the regulatory accounts or benchmarked by efficiency and productivity analysis.

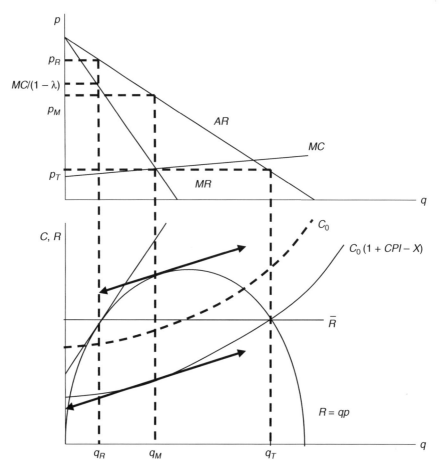

Figure 21.6   Revenue-capping regulation and the output effect

In the bottom half of Figure 21.6, this is the revenue cap which is illustrated, based on a projection of the revenue corresponding to the target zero profit output, q_T, after adjusting the current cost level by the productivity offset:

$$C_0(1 + CPI - X) = q_T p(q_T) = \overline{R}.$$

The unregulated profit-maximising output and price: (q_M, p_M) would be determined in the usual manner by equating marginal revenue and marginal cost, and are shown for comparison. However, the regulated firm is free to choose the quantity and price combination that meets the revenue cap, and consequently can seek the equilibrium shown by (q_R, p_R). This is in fact the constrained profit-maximising optimum since it corresponds to the necessary condition equality:

$$(1 - \lambda)[p + qp'(q)] - C_q = 0.$$

A severe drawback of revenue capping therefore is the incentive to meet the cap by restricting output and raising price. In the top half of Figure 21.6, the constrained profit-maximising equilibrium (q_R, p_R) is shown by the output and price combination at which $MR = MC/(1 - \lambda)$. There are corresponding respective intersection and tangency points for (q_R, p_R) and (q_M, p_M) in both parts of the figure. Because of this incentive to distort the resource allocation away from (q_T, p_T) towards (q_R, p_R), it may become essential for the regulator to signal an incentive to the regulated company to expand rather than contract output when subject to a revenue cap.

In that case, a hybrid revenue cap whereby the cap is lifted when output rises, may be adopted:

$$\overline{R} = C_0(1 + CPI - X)(1 + \Delta \log q).$$

In this case a positive growth rate in output,[13] $\Delta \log q$, permits the revenue cap to be raised if positive growth in output is recorded, so that the incentive is for the firm to move away from (q_R, p_R) in the direction of raising output and lowering price. In the case of the Federal Network Agency in Germany in 2006, such a hybrid revenue cap was the one adopted (Bundesnetzagentur, 2006).

7 Sliding Scale Regulation

Both price- and revenue-capping regulation represent a commitment to a high-powered regulatory contract, but it was apparent from the different theoretical agency models of optimal regulation examined earlier, that an intermediate power regulatory contract may in general be optimal when the regulated company's owners and managers exhibit risk aversion. This finding can be made much more general. A long-established intermediate power regulatory contract dating from the nineteenth century is known as 'sliding scale regulation' (see Joskow and Schmalensee, 1986). This has been reconsidered more recently by, among others, Laffont and Tirole (1993), Burns et al. (1998) and Hawdon et al. (2007). These authors consider a hidden information game in which the regulator is not only unable to observe effort, but is also unsure of the firm's productive potential. The firm's productivity type is a random variable ranging from efficient to inefficient; the realisation of this intrinsic productivity is known to the firm before the regulator draws up the contract, but is not known by the regulator. This introduces an additional dimension of uncertainty which makes the regulatory problem one of hidden information as well as hidden action. The regulator proposes a menu of contracts – this is a standard response to a hidden information game. Each contract on the menu differs according to the observed or reported marginal cost, c, for the firm. If the firm chooses the contract contingent on a low report of cost, designed for an efficient producer, the regulated price in this preferred contract hardly varies with the reported cost, and consequently any cost savings are retained intact by the firm; however, if it chooses a very high-cost contract designed for an inefficient firm, the regulated price varies strongly with the cost report so that any cost savings are immediately passed on intact to the consumer. A firm which knows it is efficient and that it will be able to contain cost can opt for the contract designed for an efficient firm with the price largely decoupled from reported marginal cost, and thereby reveal its productivity type. In order to minimise the incentive reward needed to elicit this information from a firm with information monopoly, the inefficient firm is permitted to achieve second-best cost saving effort and therefore an inefficiently high level of marginal cost. The regulator trades off this inefficiency for the opportunity to limit the rent achievable by the efficient firm as reward when it reveals its type by its choice of contract.

Imagine two estimates of the utility's unit costs: the first, $\bar{c}$, is the regulator's exogenous estimate of a ceiling on unit cost embodied in the price cap that will ensure the continued viability of the utility, and the second, c, is the utility's own report of its unit cost. The incentive mechanism is designed to encourage the utility to keep $c \leq \bar{c}$, and price capping is designed to provide an incentive to beat the regulator's guess, $\bar{c} > c$. The regulated price, P can then be written as:[14]

$$P = \rho\bar{c} + (1 - \rho)c = c + \rho(\bar{c} - c).$$

Here $\rho = 0$ represents cost-plus regulation with zero incentive power because the utility keeps none of its rent (its share of rent is zero), while $\rho = 1$ represents high-powered price-cap regulation in which the utility keeps all of its rent from beating the price cap (its share is 1), and $0 < \rho < 1$ represents intermediate power profit-sharing regulation. In other words the incentive power, ρ, is also the share of profits from lower costs retained by the utility. In this context, the following expression represents an example of sliding scale regulation:

$$0 < \rho < 1; \rho'(P) < 0.$$

In this simple framework, the parameter, ρ, is varied between zero and unity to characterise the move from one regulatory system to another. Sliding scale requires that the sharing parameter, ρ, is a decreasing function of the regulated price, $d\rho/dP < 0$.

This sliding scale pricing rule can be shown to implement a model of optimal linear price regulation in the universal service principal–agent game due to Laffont and Tirole (1993). To meet the requirements outlined above in which the incentive power sharing parameter ρ is inversely related to the regulated price allowed to the firm, this sharing parameter ρ should rise as the firm accepts a contract that embodies a lower regulated price. This will cause the optimal price rule to be an increasing and convex function of reported marginal cost. To see this, totally differentiate the price rule:

$$dP = dc + \rho(P)(d\bar{c} - dc) + (\bar{c} - c)\rho'(P)dP.$$

By definition, $d\bar{c} = 0$, and therefore, the conditions : $0 < \rho < 1; \rho'(P) < 0$ ensure that for $\bar{c} > c$:

$$\frac{dP}{dc} = \left[\frac{1 - \rho(P)}{1 - (\bar{c} - c)\rho'(P)}\right] > 0,$$

$$\frac{d^2P}{dc^2} = \frac{-\rho'(P)[1 - \rho(P)]}{[1 + (\bar{c} - c)\rho'(P)]^2} > 0.$$

How will this be implemented?

A number of contracts are offered with different intercepts and slopes, each of which is tangential to the price control. The firm responds by choosing one from among these N different contracts:

$$P = a_i + b_i c; i = 1, \ldots, N,$$

and therefore reveals whether it believes itself to be a producer capable of containing cost to a low level. Figure 21.7 illustrates this solution. It shows three different contracts each of which is tangent to the optimal price rule, and the choice of high-, intermediate- or low-power contract that reveals whether or not the firm believes it is good at containing costs.

The most striking aspect of Figure 21.7 is that it is very similar to the top-right quadrant in Figure 21.4, which illustrated the choice between a high- and a low-powered contract in the hidden action game. In Figure 21.4, the regulated price is a function of the utility's expected cost based on the common knowledge probability distribution of the random element in cost. The regulator chose one of these contracts, with the optimal choice being dependent on the risk parameters affecting the firm; in practice the regulator's choice is often for a high-powered price cap, but this need not be optimal. It will induce the best performance but generally fails to extract rent from the firm, because as shown in Figure 21.5, price capping will still lead to allocative inefficiency and fail to maximise the consumer surplus available. Now in Figure 21.7, the regulator does not choose a single contract, but offers a range from which the firm makes its own choice.

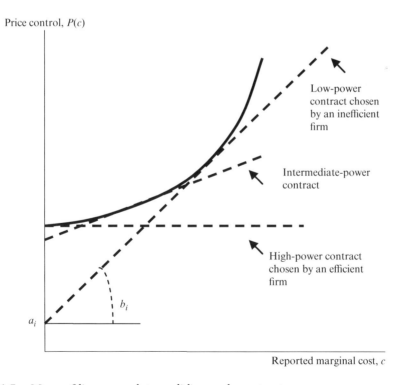

Figure 21.7   Menu of linear regulatory sliding scale contracts

Each contract plots the regulated price against observed or reported marginal cost. The intercept decreases and the slope increases as the menu moves from high- to low-powered contracts in order to ensure that the highly productive firm type has no incentive to pretend to be a high-cost producer. The least-efficient firm type is allowed to report high marginal cost (the result of low effort as well as its productive potential) in order to limit the rent that goes to the efficient firm.

8   Implementation of Incentive Regulation

The analysis has identified three types of regulatory contract: low-powered cost of service regulation, intermediate-powered sliding scale regulation, and high-powered price or revenue-capping regulation. In practice, each can be implemented through the operation of a price index formula for the regulated utility. This raises separate measurement issues, especially when the utility produces multiple products, for example, peak and off-peak energy deliveries, as is often the case. A suggestion by Burns et al. (1998) expresses the mechanism in terms of an index of the utility's product prices, using weights corresponding to past consumption levels.

The multiproduct price index is:

$$P_t = \frac{\sum_{i=1}^{R} q_{it-1} p_{it}}{\sum_{i=1}^{R} q_{it-1} p_{it-1}},$$

and this is used to contrast the three different contract types after adjusting for the rate of change of consumer prices, *CPI*:

- *Cost of service* (low-incentive power regulation) extracts the utility's profits or rents π:

$$\frac{P_t}{P_{t-1}} = 1 + CPI - \frac{\pi_{t-1}}{\sum_i p_{it} q_{it-1}}.$$

  Profits and rents are fully confiscated by offsetting the *CPI* adjustment by the rate of profit over turnover, and consequently there is no incentive to use unobserved effort.

- *Price or revenue cap* (high-incentive power regulation) extracts no rent but maximises the incentive to be efficient:

$$\frac{P_t}{P_{t-1}} = 1 + CPI - X.$$

  The utility keeps all of the profits or rents and there is no trade-off against productivity. However, although high-powered regulation produces the best performance by the utility, it may not be optimal because of the failure to extract rent and maximise the sum of consumer and producer surplus. The productivity offset X-factor is set exogenously.

- *Sliding scale* (intermediate-power incentive regulation) does trade off rent extraction and productivity, is often optimal for the hidden action game, and if expressed as a menu or spectrum of contracts is optimal for the hidden information game.

$$\frac{P_t}{P_{t-1}} \leq 1 + CPI - X^*.$$

The utility keeps a share of profits which rises as X^* rises, and the regulated firm itself chooses the X-factor rate of decline of prices to maximise its utility; it does this by choosing in advance of its production an X-factor from a range: $X \in [0, X^*]$. The closer that its chosen X-factor is to X^*, the greater is the share of its economic profit that it can retain. Implementation of both cost of service and sliding scale regulation requires that the regulator estimates the firm's economic profit and monitors this on an ongoing basis, but sliding scale regulation maintains a productivity-enhancing incentive.

In these regulatory adjustment processes, the regulator takes no interest in the precise balance among the different product prices in the index, other than to require that the weights in the index reflect previous output levels and hence are exogenous to the firm at the time of calculation of the index. This non-intervention ensures that the firm itself is able to pursue price discrimination in a form that will converge to the optimal Ramsey prices over time (Vogelsang and Finsinger, 1979).

9 Setting the X-factor in CPI-X Incentive Regulation

Consider now the implementation of price- and revenue-capping ideas in practice, in particular the choice of the productivity offset X for the frontier-efficient company. Since the rate of change of variables over time plays a central role in the analysis, it is necessary to have a standard expression for proportional rates of change.

In continuous time, the rate of change of a time-dependent variable, $Z(t)$ is:

$$\dot{Z} = [1/Z(t)][dZ(t)/dt] = d \log Z/dt,$$

and the discrete approximation to this is:

$$\frac{(Z_t - Z_{t-1})}{Z_{t-1}} \equiv \Delta \log Z.$$

In CPI-X regulation in practice, a corporate finance model of the regulated network utility is frequently adopted. For example in price capping, the model targets an average revenue figure for each year of the control period, and sets the rate of change of regulated prices:

$$P_t = P_0(1 + CPI - X)^t \Rightarrow \frac{P_t - P_{t-1}}{P_{t-1}} \equiv \Delta \log P = CPI - X.$$

Two key ingredients of the model are the regulatory asset base and the P-nought (P_0) initial price. The regulatory asset base (RAB_t) is determined by adding the capital expenditure flow (*CAPEX*) and subtracting the depreciation flow (*D*) during the period to adjust the starting stock value:

$$RAB_t = RAB_{t-1} + CAPEX_t - D_t.$$

The regulator calculates the companies' weighted average cost of capital (*wacc*) and determines an estimate of the company's regulatory asset base (*RAB*). The return on capital allowed in the cost projections is: (*wacc* × *RAB*). Consequently, in this financial model of regulatory economic value added, the company's costs are treated as falling into three categories: operating expenditures (*OPEX*), depreciation (*D*) and the return on capital, that is, *OPEX* + *D* + (*wacc*)*RAB*. The key ingredients in the financial model have become the P_0 settlement:[15] this is the initial price which is to form the basis for the future revenue flows of the company from the start of the new control period, and the X-factor implied in the projection of costs. Usually *X* is fixed to achieve those cost savings over the control period that reflect the shift in the frontier efficiency of the companies. The initial price correction can be solved as a present value (*PV*) calculation conditional on a given set of demand forecasts (*Q*):

$$P_0 = \frac{PV[OPEX + D + (wacc)RAB]}{PV[(1 + CPI - X)Q]}.$$

To determine P_0, the X-factor has been taken as fixed in advance by the regulator. This X-factor can be related to expected productivity growth, and the X-factor in CPI-X regulation can be embedded in either a partial or a general equilibrium framework.

10   What Does the X-factor Mean?

In a partial equilibrium setting, the X-factor is given by:[16]

$$X = CPI - \Delta \log w^R + \Delta TFP^R - \Delta \log \mu^R.$$

The regulated utility sector is denoted by the superscript *R*, and *w* is the vector of input prices, *TFP* is the rate of growth in total factor productivity, and μ is the rate of profit, that is, the mark-up of revenue over cost. If this is assumed not to change (in expectation) then $\Delta \log \mu^R$ is zero. Bernstein and Sappington (1999) developed a wider general equilibrium framework by introducing both a competitive, unregulated sector, and a regulated industry.

In the competitive sector of the economy, denoted by the superscript *G*, assuming that all input prices have been properly accounted for including the return on capital for shareholders, profit will be at the zero level in long-run equilibrium. Then:

$$\pi^G \equiv p^G y^G - w^G x^G = 0 \Rightarrow p^G y^G / w^G x^G = [1 + (\pi^G / w^G x^G)] = \mu^G = 1.$$

This in turn provides the result:

$$\Delta \log p^G - \Delta \log w^G + \Delta \log y^G - \Delta \log x^G = \Delta \log p^G - \Delta \log w^G + \Delta TFP^G = 0.$$

However, unless the regulated sector is very large relative to the whole economy, it will be the case that the rate of output price change in the competitive, unregulated sector will define, or be very close to, the general rate of output price inflation, *CPI*:

$$\Delta \log p^G \equiv CPI.$$

The results for both sectors can now be shown together to contrast and compare:

regulated sector: $X = CPI - \Delta \log w^R + \Delta TFP^R - \Delta \log \mu^R$,
competitive sector: $0 = CPI - \Delta \log w^G + \Delta TFP^G$.

It is immediately clear that the results differ in the predicted rate of change of prices between the two sectors. From Bernstein and Sappington (1999) we see that under either of the conditions: constant profitability (regulated sector) or zero profit level (competitive sector), a stronger re-distributive requirement is imposed on the regulated sector than on the competitive sector.

$$\Delta \log p^R = CPI - X; \; X \geq 0,$$

$$\Delta \log p^G = CPI.$$

The general equilibrium result from Bernstein and Sappington can be expressed below:

$$X = (\Delta \log w^G - \Delta TFP^G) - (\Delta \log w^R - \Delta TFP^R) - \Delta \log \mu^R.$$

Therefore, it is clear that the forward-looking X-factor reflects the expectations of the ratio of the rate of change of input prices relative to productivity for the regulated business relative to the same ratio in the rest of the economy. However, these results appear to refer to the short run only, because they predict a systematic difference between the rate of price evolution between the whole economy and one sector of it. If this result were in fact a long-run equilibrium outcome, it would imply that the regulated sector was always on a different steady-state path from the competitive remainder of the economy. This could arise if the incentive regulation mechanism were expected to systematically fail to deliver the efficient outcome that it was designed to achieve. We note that this finding is not a consequence of a higher price level in the regulated sector; the X-factor is the compound rate of change of regulated sector prices after allowing for productivity and input price changes. If these are zero, then the difference between X and *CPI* is the assumed rate of change of the profit mark-up, and if this is positive then the implication is that market power distortions are becoming worse rather than better over time and therefore justify a positive X-factor. The persistence of positive X-factor determinations by regulators decades after deregulation and privatisation suggests that there is an underlying dynamic mechanism that has not been investigated. Consequently, in order to justify systematically different rates of output price inflation between the regulated and the competitive sectors, it would be necessary to explain why systematic differences in the productivity rates of regulated businesses and the rest of the economy were not captured by similar systematic differences in input prices. Or, to put it another way, if X is positive, why are the owners of the inputs in regulated businesses apparently systematically unable to obtain the same rewards from greater productivity performance than they are able to do in the rest of the economy, as a simple rearrangement illustrates:

$$\Delta \log w^R - CPI = \Delta TFP^R - X,$$

$$\Delta \log w^G - CPI = \Delta TFP^G.$$

In the short run, there are a number of reasons why the X-factor could either be positive or negative:

1. *Agency hidden information* Regulated utilities have monopoly rents (including informational rent) which must be captured and continually recaptured for the consumer (in advance) by providing the businesses with profit incentives to reveal that information.
2. *Agency hidden action* Without competition, regulated companies will have costs that exceed the efficient frontier level and need an incentive to reduce these costs.
3. *Input price inflation (relative to the input's productivity)* This is both different from the rest of the economy and which relates to an input to which the regulated business is more exposed than businesses in the rest of the economy.
4. *The existence of measured slack in the activity of the regulated firm* This is the inefficiency that is treated as a potential source of catch-up cost savings, and that can be assumed to tend to zero if the regulatory mechanism is effective in providing a profit incentive to the firm which it can retain. This factor signals to owners of the firm that their incentives to managers are deficient.

In the longer term, as the informational rent dissipates and the pre-reform inefficiency is removed, the first two motivations for a positive X-factor disappear. In fact, the risk of persisting with a positive X-factor for longer is that the regulator is in danger of violating the input owner's participation constraint, forcing labour and capital out of the regulated sector and into the rest of the economy where rewards relative to productivity are greater.

The question posed here is why should the X in CPI-X be different from zero in the long run? This question is a reflection of a point made by Crew and Kleindorfer (2002) and Crew and Parker (2006) to the effect that a major driver in the economics of regulation has been the issue of rent seeking and rent re-distribution. Crew and Kleindorfer in particular draw attention to the issue of regulatory commitment failure as a key drawback of incentive-based regulation. It is clear from the analysis above that the assumption that the X-factor must always be a positive number is critically related to this idea of a regulator's inability to commit to the incentive mechanism imposed at an earlier stage on the regulated business.

11   Conclusion

This chapter has presented a summary of some of the current ideas in incentive regulation of energy networks. However, nothing has been said about the structure of individual prices for different products and services, although many regulators still take a detailed interest in such topics even in a liberalised industry where it could be argued that such decisions are optimally left to the individual competitive or contestable suppliers. Dynamic issues have not been explored as deeply as they might but much regulatory discussion has remained static in scope. The issues arising in repeated game encounters between the regulated companies and the authorities have a dynamic impact and generate their own problems. A major omission is the issue of quality of supply regulation, which is naturally a dimension of interest to regulators when firms are given incentives to cut costs under price capping.

Notes

1. Strictly S is the elasticity of size computed for cost-minimising input ratios and coincides with the elasticity of scale computed for constant input ratios only in the case of homothetic production functions (Chambers, 1988).
2. Armstrong et al. (1994) fix the level of output at unity, and assume a zero elasticity of demand, at least for the range of price variability that is to be modelled. This allows the model to be applied equally to price- or revenue-capping situations.
3. Effort, e, is increasing in the power of the contract, ρ, if the agent's disutility of effort function is increasing and convex in effort.
4. In the sense that with suboptimal ρ, the range of values of $\overline{P}$ for which the contract will be rejected expands.
5. See note 4, above.
6. This is the converse of the well-known Averch–Johnson (1962) problem of inefficiently high capital to labour ratio that arises under cost-plus regulation.
7. Note that each firm is assumed to have the same reservation level of utility determined by the capital market.
8. With less than perfectly correlated cost, an intermediate power contract is optimal, with the regulated price related both to the firm's own observed cost and to that of the yardstick competitor. Put another way, with less than perfectly correlated cost, the adoption of a high-powered contract is suboptimal.
9. Total cost is the area under the marginal cost curve. Therefore, the analysis does not include fixed cost. Either this is covered by a separate charge, or it comes out of the producer surplus captured by the firm.
10. This assumption that owners incentivise their managers to implement the regulator's incentives is implicit throughout the regulatory economics literature.
11. Equilibrium positions 1 and 2 below are the classic case of the lack of constraint concern described by Leibenstein (1966) in the seminal paper on the subject of X-efficiency.
12. In the UK case this is RPI, the retail price index.
13. See below for precise definitions of growth rates.
14. This price mechanism could include an intercept, α, to cover the reservation utility necessary for participation in the industry, but nothing is lost by arbitrarily setting $\alpha = 0$.
15. In the case of revenue capping, the critical figure is the initial total cost base, C_0.
16. This section is based on Burns and Weyman-Jones (2008).

References

Armstrong, M., S. Cowan and J. Vickers (1994), *Regulatory Reform: Economics Analysis and British Experience*, Cambridge, MA: MIT Press.

Armstrong, M. and D. Sappington (2006), 'Regulation competition and liberalization', *Journal of Economic Literature*, **44**, June, 325–66.

Averch, H. and L.L. Johnson (1962), 'Behavior of the firm under regulatory constraint', *American Economic Review*, **52**(5), December, 1052–69.

Bagdadioglu, N., C. Waddams Price and T. Weyman-Jones (2007), 'Measuring potential gains from mergers among electricity distribution companies in Turkey using a non-parametric model', *The Energy Journal*, **28**(2), 83–110.

Bernstein, J.I. and D.E.M. Sappington (1999), 'Setting the X factor in price-cap regulation plans', *Journal of Regulatory Economics*, **16**(1), July, 5–25.

Bogetoft, Peter (1997), 'DEA-based yardstick competition: the optimality of best practice regulation', *Annals of Operations Research*, **73**, 277–98.

Bundesnetzagentur (2006), *Incentive Regulation in the German Electricity and Gas Sector: efficiency and reliability to set the yardstick*, International Scientific Conference of the Bundesnetzagentur (Federal Network Agency), Bonn, Bad Godesberg, April 25–26.

Burns, P., C. Jenkins and T. Weyman-Jones (2006), 'Information revelation and incentives', in M. Crew and D. Parker (eds), *International Handbook of Economic Regulation*, Cheltenham, UK and Northampton, MA, USA: Edward Elgar, pp. 164–87.

Burns, P., R. Turvey and T. Weyman-Jones (1998), 'The behaviour of the firm under alternative regulatory constraints', *Scottish Journal of Political Economy*, May, 133–57.

Burns, Philip and Thomas Weyman-Jones (2008), 'The long-run level of X in RPI-X – Bernstein and Sappington revisited', Working Paper, Frontier Economics Ltd, 11 July.

Chambers, R.G. (1988), *Applied Production Analysis: A Dual Approach*, Cambridge: Cambridge University Press.

Crew, Michael and David Parker (2006), 'Development in the theory and practice of regulatory economics', in Michael Crew and David Parker (eds), *International Handbook on Economic Regulation*, Cheltenham, UK and Northampton, MA, USA: Edward Elgar, pp. 1–33.

Crew, Michael and Paul Kleindorfer (2002), 'Regulatory economics: twenty years of progress', *Journal of Regulatory Economics*, **21**(1), 5–22.

Färe, R., S. Grosskopf and C.A. Knox Lovell (1994), *Production Frontiers*, Cambridge: Cambridge University Press.

Filippini, M., M. Farsi and A. Fetz (2005), 'Benchmarking analysis in electricity distribution', CEPE Working Paper 39, Centre for Energy Policy and Economics, Swiss Federal Institutes of Technology, Zurich, March.

Gasmi, F., M. Ivaldi and J.J. Laffont (1994), 'Rent extraction and incentives for efficiency in recent regulatory proposals', *Journal of Regulatory Economics*, **6**, 151–76.

Hawdon, D., L.C. Hunt, P. Levine and N. Rickman (2007), 'Optimal sliding scale regulation: an application to regional electricity distribution in England and Wales', *Oxford Economic Papers*, **59**(3), July, 458–85.

Joskow, P. (2005), 'Incentive regulation in theory and practice: electricity distribution and transmission networks', paper presented at National Bureau of Economic Research Conference on Economic Regulation, Washington, DC, September 9–10.

Joskow, P. and R. Schmalensee (1986), 'Incentive regulation for electric utilities', *Yale Journal on Regulation*, **4**, Fall, 1–49.

Laffont, J.-J. and J. Tirole (1993), *A Theory of Incentives in Procurement and Regulation*, Cambridge, MA: MIT Press.

Leibenstein, H. (1966), 'Allocative efficiency vs. "X-efficiency"', *American Economic Review*, **56**(3), June, 392–415.

Littlechild, S. (1983), *Regulation of British Telecommunications' profitability: report to the Secretary of State*, February, London: Department of Industry.

Schmalensee, R. (1989), 'Good regulatory regimes', *Rand Journal of Economics*, **20**(3), Autumn, 417–36.

Shleifer, A. (1985), 'A theory of yardstick competition', *Rand Journal of Economics*, **16**(3), Autumn, 319–27.

Vogelsang, I. and J. Finsinger (1979), 'A regulatory adjustment process for optimal pricing by multiproduct firms', *Bell Journal of Economics*, **10**, 157–71.

22 The economics and regulation of power transmission and distribution: the developed world case
Lullit Getachew and Mark N. Lowry

1 Introduction

In this chapter we focus on the economics and regulation of power transmission and distribution (T&D) in the developed world. These wires businesses are natural monopolies. Both involve large fixed costs to transmit and distribute power, a commodity that cannot be stored. Once set up, the T&D assets provide power using variable inputs and exhibit declining average costs indicating the presence of scale economies over a large range of outputs. Thus, it is not economic to have two companies providing 'wires' services to customers in the same area. Traditionally, this situation has led to provision of a 'wires' license to a business over a defined service territory.

To prevent monopoly abuses, countries have historically set up mechanisms to regulate their rates and service provisions and/or have placed them under state ownership. Regulation of T&D utilities has evolved remarkably in the last two decades. Statistical research on the cost of T&D services plays an increasingly prominent role in the regulatory process.

The licensing agreements under which T&D utilities operate compel them to provide service to all customers in their service territories. The number of customers connected to their systems is one important 'driver' of cost as firms must plan for and invest to accommodate the number of connections. Their planning also takes into consideration the maximum amount of power they expect to wheel or deliver through their systems. The volume of energy delivered, often measured in megawatt hours (MWh), is another important cost driver.

Obviously the prices of the various inputs that go into building and operating the systems also affect cost. The large fixed costs needed to build and run T&D networks means that capital price is an especially important cost driver and factors that influence the cost of capital affect T&D cost significantly. Labor and material input prices also affect cost as do various other important conditions in the operating environment.

One of the main aims of this chapter is to identify and study the cost structure of the power T&D businesses. We use US data to do so. These data reveal the extent of scale economies possible, which is very informative because the US power industry is considered 'mature'.

As already indicated, such scale economies indicate why it has been historically necessary to regulate the industry. We explore the various regulatory mechanisms used in countries of the developed world and trace the trend in the use of incentive-based regulatory schemes in the recent past.

The geographical coverage of the study of the regulatory system is fairly comprehensive.

In particular, we have chosen to focus on the nature of regulation in the industries of North America, covering the US and Canada; Europe, consisting of some of the original European Union (EU) member states and Norway; and the Pacific Region, including the industries in Australia, New Zealand and Japan.

We examine the regulatory mechanisms under which the industries in these countries operate in Section 3. Before turning to this topic, however, we focus on the economics of the two industries in Section 2. We provide concluding comments in Section 4.

2   Economics of Power Line Businesses

Transmission

There is a general lack of studies on the cost structure of transmission.[1] This is due in large measure to the general lack of standardized data on power transmission operations. To remedy this gap, we focus on the cost structure of power transmission in this section. Such a study helps us identify important cost drivers that determine the underlying technology of the industry, including the nature of scale economies in the sector. This sort of study can also be used to benchmark the performance of transmission companies, which has an important role in the regulation and management of power transmission.

The power transmission business

Power transmission is the long-distance transportation of electricity over stationary conducting lines. These lines are usually elevated above the ground by poles or towers but are sometimes routed through underground conduits. Transmission is conducted at higher voltages than those at which power is generated or consumed. This reduces line losses and, by increasing the speed of power flows, reduces the size of required conductors and supporting structures. Voltage transformation occurs at substations where voltage is raised in preparation for transmission or lowered in preparation for distribution. The boundaries of the transmission system are conventionally demarcated by these stations. Points of voltage transformation also permit a distinction to be drawn between the extra high voltage (EHV) grid used for longer-distance transport and the lower voltage transmission lines that often connect this grid to locations of generation and distribution. Power flows must be managed carefully to preserve system integrity. The quantity of power received from generating stations and other transmission systems must be matched almost exactly by the quantity of deliveries at each instant. Flows at each point in the system cannot exceed transfer capacity. The coordination of deliveries and receipts requires switching equipment and benefits from sophisticated information technology (IT). The complexity of the task increases with the number of power shippers. Many transmission providers also provide various ancillary services, such as load balancing, to customers.

The cost of providing transmission service depends on the peak load that must be handled, the distance transmitted, and the voltage at which receipts and deliveries are made. Changing voltage involves the use of costly transformers and other substation facilities. Substation services account for roughly a quarter of the cost of transmission for a typical utility.

The substation services that are provided by transmission utilities, or classified as transmission in vertically integrated utilities, vary considerably around the world. The step down of voltage to distribution levels is a transmission function in some countries but not in others. Some large-volume industrial customers take delivery directly from the grid and own their own substations. Utilities for which this is most likely to matter are those with large industrial loads.

Systems also vary in the degree to which reporting utilities gather power from generating stations. In some countries, step-up transformers are typically owned by power generators. In those where transmission utilities provide this service, the extensiveness of the service can vary widely.

Some companies have substantially urban service territories where extensive generation has historically been impractical due to considerations of environmental damage, water availability, and/or site costs. Some companies have territories where there is plenty of room for base-load units but it is more economical to rely on supplies originating in other transmission systems. Other companies have service territories with unusual concentrations of generation and do a disproportionate amount of power gathering.

Power transmission cost also depends greatly on the prices of transmission system inputs. The major categories of inputs are capital, labor, and other operation and maintenance (O&M) inputs. Of these, capital is by far the most important, accounting for over three-quarters of the total cost for a typical utility. The price of transmission capital inputs depends on their rate of depreciation, the installed cost of plant, the cost of funds, and the rate of depreciation.

Below we present an econometric model of transmission cost to identify important cost drivers that can be used to benchmark performance and examine scale economies using sample data from the US power transmission industry. We first discuss the data, and then we present the cost model and estimation method that we employ, followed by the results of the model and a discussion of the implications that emerge from these results.

US power transmission data
Data on US power transmission companies have a number of advantages in cost function estimation. More than 100 utilities provide transmission service. Transmission is regulated by the Federal Energy Regulatory Commission (FERC), and all investor-owned companies providing transmission services are required to report extensive data on their operations. Reports are standardized using FERC reporting guidelines called the Uniform System of Accounts.

There is considerable variety in the business conditions facing US transmission companies. The variety is especially great in the size of transmission operations. The input prices faced by transmission utilities also vary considerably, due principally to variations in the price of labor that affects transmission cost both directly and indirectly, through the cost of constructing transmission plant.

While the numerous advantages of data on American transmission operations recommend their use in cost function estimation, it is important to understand some of their idiosyncrasies. We briefly summarize some of the main ones in the balance of this section.

Vertical Integration
The great bulk of US transmission services are provided by utilities that are also engaged in the distribution of power; many are also involved in generation. These companies

incur administrative and general costs that are substantially common to the provision of services of all three kinds. These costs must, as a practical matter, be allocated between the services using somewhat arbitrary allocation factors.

Peak Load
Peak load is well known to be an important driver of the cost of transmission. Unfortunately, US investor-owned utilities (IOUs) report peak-load data only for the subset of their total power deliveries that cover their sales to final customers and requirements sales for resale. Excluded from the peak-load numbers are quantities resulting from non-requirements sales for resale and wheeling. Non-requirements sales for resale are sales of economy energy. These will frequently be curtailed when use of the transmission system is at a peak. Wheeling is the transmission of power that is not owned by the transmission utility. Data are reported by transmission IOUs on the total quantity of power they deliver. We have used these in our model in place of peak load.

Distance Carried
There are no data readily available on the distance that US transmission companies carry power. The best available proxy data are those on the circuit miles of transmission capacity. These data are sorted into classes on the basis of their kilovolt (kV) rating. Lines with a higher kilovolt rating can carry more power. It is then sensible to weight circuit miles by their kilovolt rating if our goal is to proxy distance carried.

Voltage of Receipts and Deliveries
Quality data are not available on the voltage at which power is received or delivered by reporting transmission IOUs. We do have data on amounts obtained from company-owned generation and purchases from independent power producers. However, some company-owned generation is located on the transmission systems of other utilities. As for independent power producer (IPP) purchases, data on which IPPs own their own step-up transformers are generally unavailable.

Regarding power deliveries, it can generally be assumed that sales for resale and wheeling deliveries are made at high voltage. However, there are considerable variations in the quantity of sales to ultimate customers that are delivered by reported transmission facilities at medium voltage.

Categorization of Transmission and Distribution Facilities
US IOUs are not entirely consistent in the way that they assign their power delivery facilities to T&D for purposes of cost accounting. The guidelines for classifying power delivery costs in the FERC's Uniform System of Accounts are somewhat vague. Transmission facilities are clearly intended to include transformers that step up voltage to transmission levels at generating sites, substations at interconnections with other transmission systems, facilities moving power from supply sources to 'distribution centers', and facilities that 'augment, integrate, or tie together sources of power supply' even if these are located in a distribution center. Transmission facilities clearly exclude substations that reduce voltage to distribution levels. However, the definition of distribution level voltage is not always clear.

These guidelines clearly sanction the classification of subtransmission, for instance

69 kV, lines and the substations that feed them as transmission facilities when they do not pass through distribution centers, do not connect to generating stations, and are primarily used to transport power to distant end users. Subtransmission lines make sense in areas of low-load density because the higher cost of substations and supporting structures for higher-voltage cable offsets the savings on the costs of line losses and cable when the volume delivered is low. However, some utilities might consider an area of low-load density to be a distribution center and arbitrarily categorize all lower-voltage lines as distribution, especially those that are of radial character.

As for lines in urban centers, there is some flexibility in classification due to uncertainty as to what constitutes the entrance to a distribution center. Some companies may define a distribution center as a low-voltage delivery system and its entry as a distribution substation and thus classify subtransmission lines traversing urban areas as transmission. This interpretation would be especially plausible where distribution networks are not connected, so that a line may be said to carry power to distant centers. Others may define a distribution center as an urban area served by numerous low-voltage systems. In that event, subtransmission, or even higher-voltage lines may be classified as distribution facilities even if they carry power well beyond individual distribution networks.

It is standard practice for US transmission IOUs to treat medium-voltage lines and associated step-down facilities as distribution facilities in urban areas and as transmission facilities in rural areas. Highly urban utilities may then have comparatively small transmission services. Highly rural utilities are apt to have comparatively large transmission services.

It is often difficult to identify companies with unusual 'T versus D' accounting procedures since most reporting companies serve a mix of urban, suburban, and rural areas. It is possible that middle-voltage lines reported as transmission are used only in rural areas where they really do play a transmission role. One suspicious case is when a utility with a highly urbanized service territory reports appreciable medium-voltage transmission line miles and few middle-voltage distribution line miles. Another suspicious case is that of a utility with a highly rural service territory that reports few medium-voltage transmission line miles and extensive medium-voltage distribution line miles.

In conclusion, there appear to be fairly extensive irregularities in the classification of power delivery facilities as transmission or distribution in the FERC Form 1. However, there are enough observations to make appraisals for 'normal' utilities. The problem can be made manageable by excluding companies whose data reveal significant classification irregularities. We have excluded several companies from the sample on these grounds.

Other Sources of Variation in the Provision of Substation Services
In 1998, transmission substations accounted for 42 percent of gross transmission plant value and 21 percent of transmission O&M expenses for major US electric IOUs. Substation ownership, operation, and maintenance thus accounts for a large share of the cost of the US power transmission business.

Arbitrary classification of transmission facilities as distribution facilities creates substation service modeling problems. Suppose, by way of example, that a utility arbitrarily classifies medium-voltage rural lines as distribution lines. They will then classify the associated bulk power substations as distribution facilities. This can have an appreciable impact on reported transmission cost of a utility that makes a high percentage of deliveries to rural customers.

We have dealt with the sources of variation in substation services in two ways. One has been to exclude companies from the sample that seem to have unusual substation activities. Another has been to consider explanatory variables tied to the nature of power receipts. These have generated inconclusive results. One possible reason is that the effect on transmission cost of receipts from certain classes of customers may depend on the additional control challenges that they pose as well as the voltages that they require.

Data for Cost Model

Cost model parameters were estimated using data from a sizable sample of US electric IOUs covering the three-year period from 1998 to 2000. The primary source of the data was FERC Form 1. This form is filed annually by all companies classified as major electric IOUs, along with certain non-utility entities that are also jurisdictional to the FERC.[2] Selected Form 1 data have been published annually by the Utility Data Institute (UDI) in a series of commercially available files.

All major electric IOUs in the US that filed the FERC Form 1 electronically in 1997 and that have reported the necessary data continuously since they achieved a 'major' designation were considered for inclusion in the sample. Forty-three companies met these standards and were used in the econometric work. As a result, the number of observations in the dataset is 129. The included companies are listed in Table 22.1.

Publicly available data from other sources were also used. Data on the cost of funds and the general trend in economy-wide inflation were obtained from various issues of the *Survey of Current Business* of the Bureau of Economic Analysis (BEA) of the US Department of Commerce. Data on intertemporal trends in the regional cost of constructing US power transmission plant were obtained from the *Handy–Whitman Index of Public Utility Construction Costs*. This is a publication of Whitman, Requardt, & Associates (1993). Additionally, we used 1998 data from an RS Means & Company publication, *Heavy Construction Cost Data, 13th Annual Edition* (1999), to capture regional differences in the cost of construction.

Defining Cost

Definition of power transmission cost

The measure of power transmission cost used in this study was the sum of O&M expenses allocated to transmission in the FERC Form 1, assigned capital cost based, chiefly, on the reported value of transmission plant, and share of administrative and general (A&G) expenses and the cost of general plant. The A&G expenses reported by utilities on Form 1 consist mainly of pensions and other benefits and costs resulting from injuries and damages for all employees, of the salaries of personnel not assigned to power transmission and other 'line' positions, and expenses for office supplies and outside services. General plant consists mainly of structures and improvements not allocated to specific functions, communications equipment, office furniture and equipment, and transportation equipment. The portion of these costs assigned to power transmission was for each

Table 22.1   List of companies in the power transmission econometric sample

Company	Company
Alabama Power	Montana Power
AmerenUE	Montana-Dakota Utilities
Appalachian Power	Nevada Power
Bangor Hydro-Electric	Northern Indiana Public Service
Carolina Power & Light	Ohio Power
Central Hudson Gas & Electric	Orange and Rockland Utilities
Central Illinois Light	Otter Tail Power
Cleco	Portland General Electric
Columbus Southern Power	Potomac Electric Power
Empire District Electric	Public Service Co of Colorado
Entergy Arkansas	Public Service Co of New Hampshire
Entergy Louisiana	Public Service Co of New Mexico
Florida Power	Public Service Co of Oklahoma
Georgia Power	Puget Sound Energy
Gulf Power	Rochester Gas and Electric
Interstate Power	South Carolina Electric & Gas
Kansas City Power & Light	Virginia Electric and Power
Kentucky Utilities	Western Resources
Louisville Gas and Electric	Wisconsin Electric Power
Madison Gas and Electric	Wisconsin Power and Light
Mississippi Power	Wisconsin Public Service
Monongahela Power	

Note: Number of companies in sample: 43.

utility its share of non-A&G salaries and wages. The salary and wage data were drawn from FERC Form 1.

Capital cost
We used a service price approach to capital costing, which posits that capital cost in each period t is the product of a capital service price index and an index of the quantity of capital in place at the end of the prior period. The formula may be stated formally as $CK_t = WKS_t \cdot XK_{t-1}$ where, in each period t, CK_t is the cost of capital, WKS_t is the capital service price index, and XK_{t-1} is the capital quantity index value at the start of the period. The capital quantity index is constructed using inflation-adjusted data on the value of net utility plant in a benchmark year, on gross plant additions in subsequent years, and an assumption about service lives.

The service price approach to developing capital prices has a solid basis in economic theory.[3] It controls in a precise and standardized fashion for differences between utilities in the age of plant additions. The service price approach also has ample precedent in cost research. It is used by the Bureau of Labor Statistics (BLS) of the US Department of Labor in computing multi-factor productivity indexes for the US private business sector and for several subsectors, including the utility services industry.

Under the service price approach employed in this study, capital cost has four components: taxes paid, opportunity cost, depreciation, and capital gains. The capital service price index is given by the formula:

$$WKS_t = \frac{\text{Taxes}_t}{XK_{t-1}} + r_t \cdot WKA_{t-1} + d_t \cdot WKA_t - (WKA_t - WKA_{t-1})$$

Here, r_t is the user cost of capital for the US economy.[4] This is the return to capital implicit in the National Income and Product Accounts (NIPA) produced by the Department of Commerce. The parameter d_t is the economic depreciation rate that is calculated as a weighted average of the depreciation rates for the structures and equipment used in the applicable industry. For each category of capital this was obtained from the BEA of the US Department of Commerce, which prepares data on the stocks and service lives of the capital of local distribution companies. The weights were based on net stock value data drawn from the same source. WKA_t is an index of the price of capital assets used in power transmission. We compute this index using data on differences in the cost of constructing utility plant between regions, and within regions over time. In particular, we use the Handy–Whitman indexes for total power transmission plant and reinforced concrete building construction, which vary over time but not across region. We determine the relative levels of utility plant asset prices, for 1998, using the city cost indexes for electrical work in RS Means's *Heavy Construction Cost Data* (1999). These indexes measure differences among cities in the cost of labor needed to install electrical equipment as well as differences in equipment prices. The construction service categories covered are raceways; conductors and grounding; boxes and wiring devices; motors, starters, boards, and switches; transformers and bus ducts; lighting; electric utilities; and power transmission and distribution. The level of the asset price index for each utility was the simple average of the RS Means index values for cities in the service territory.

Business Condition Variables

Output quantity variables
There are two output quantity variables in our model. These are the total transmission delivery volume of the utility and the kV circuit miles of transmission lines it owns. Data for both output quantity variables are drawn from FERC *Form 1*.

The kV circuit miles variable is calculated by summing the product of circuit miles for transmission lines in five voltage ranges and the typical kilovolts of lines in each range. It is intended as a measure of the distance and quantity of power being transmitted. Because it is a measure of capacity rather than quantities transmitted, it does not control for differences between utilities' excess line capacity.

Input prices
In this model we have specified input price variables for capital, labor, and other O&M inputs. The other O&M category includes materials, rentals, and outside labor services. This breakdown of production inputs has been widely used in cost function research.[5]

Our computation of a service price index for capital was described above. The price of labor for each utility was calculated as salaries and wages paid by the utility per full-time equivalent employee. Salaries and wages and the number of employees were reported by US transmission IOUs on FERC Form 1 during the sample period. Prices for other

O&M inputs are assumed to be the same in a given year for all companies. They are escalated by the chain-weighted price index for gross domestic product (GDPPI).

Other business conditions

Several other variables were considered in our study and ultimately excluded due to data quality problems or the lack of statistical significance of their parameter estimates. These included peak load; load factor; the square miles of service territory served; a revenue-share weighted customer index; cooling degree days as a measure of hot weather severity; heating degree days as a measure of cold weather severity; precipitation, which is a proxy for O&M spending associated with tree trimming; substation capacity; and the percentage of power receipts from self-generation and purchases from independent generators.

In the end we included three additional business condition variables: the percent of power transmission plant in electric and gas transmission and distribution plant, the percent of transmission overhead miles in total transmission miles, and substation work effort.[6] Providing gas and power distribution services in addition to power transmission may allow firms to enjoy economies of scope. Firms often realize scope economies by sharing inputs across different production processes. If significant scope economies exist between gas and power delivery, the parameter of this variable should be positive. Underground lines are typically more expensive to construct. Accordingly, a company with a higher percentage of overhead lines should have lower total cost, all else equal. Our measure of substation activity was computed through a three-step process. First, we divided the gross value of substation plant by MWh receipts. Next, we divided the gross value of line plant by miles of transmission line. Finally, we took the ratio of these quotients, with the substation measure as the numerator. A greater value for this variable indicates that the utility is providing greater substation services *vis-à-vis* line services. This is expected to raise costs, so we expect this variable to have a positive coefficient.

We provide summary statistics of the data used in our study in Table 22.2.

Model specification and estimation

A translog function was selected for the cost model. Its general form, after suppressing time and firm subscripts, is given as:

$$\ln C = \alpha_o + \sum_i \alpha_i \ln Y_i + \sum_j \beta_j \ln W_j + \sum_h \gamma_h \ln Z_h$$
$$+ \frac{1}{2}\left(\sum_i \sum_k \alpha_{ik} \ln Y_i \ln Y_k + \sum_j \sum_n \beta_{jn} \ln W_j \ln W_n \right)$$
$$+ \sum_i \sum_j \alpha_{ij} \ln Y_i \ln W_j + \alpha_t t + \varepsilon.$$

Here the Ys quantify output, the Ws input prices, and the Zs other business conditions. This form has been widely used in cost function research.[7] A major advantage is its flexibility, which permits it to provide a good approximation for the wide range of functional forms that the data can reflect. The assumption of a well-behaved production technology permits us to impose some restrictions on model parameters. The restrictions include linear homogeneity in input prices and symmetry in the parameters of the price interaction terms.

Table 22.2 Summary statistics of variables in the econometric cost model: power transmission

Variable	Units	Average	S.D.	Minimum	Maximum
Power transmission total cost	US dollars	98447691	91516284	11900485	474240102
Deliveries (retail + bulk power + wheeling delivered)	MWh	26500300	21642165	1923242	89377704
Circuit miles (kV)	KVCM	535272	427948	32413	1699889
Price of capital services	Index number	13.38	1.39	10.56	16.44
Price of labor services	Dollars per employee	32737	2695	27480	40114
Price of materials	Index number	104.97	1.59	103.20	107.04
Percent of electric Tx plant in value of electric and gas T&D plant	Percent	24.7%	8.6%	7.9%	42.7%
Percent of Tx line miles that are overhead	Percent	97.6%	7.4%	64.0%	100.0%
Substation/line plant unit cost ratio	Ratio	0.135	0.126	0.032	0.808

Using Shephard's lemma we derive cost share equations that we estimated jointly with the cost function. The general form of the cost share equation for input *j* is given by:

$$S_j = \beta_j + \sum_i \alpha_{ij} \ln Y_i + \sum_n \beta_{jn} \ln W_n + \upsilon_j.$$

Since contemporaneous correlation exists between the errors in a system of regressions, more efficient estimates can be obtained using a feasible generalized least squares (FGLS) procedure. We used an iterative FGLS procedure[8] that estimates the unknown disturbance matrix consistently.[9] The estimates we compute are equivalent to maximum likelihood estimates (MLEs).[10] Our estimates thus possess all the desirable properties of MLEs, which include consistency and efficiency. Since the cost share equations by definition must sum to one at every observation, one cost share equation is redundant and is dropped. This does not pose a problem since yet another property of the MLE procedure is that it is invariant to any such reparameterization. Hence, the choice of which equation to drop will not affect the resulting estimates.

Results

Estimates of the parameters of the transmission cost model are reported in Table 22.3. Because mean-scaled data are used in the estimation process, the parameters of the first-order terms are elasticities at sample mean values of the business conditions. We find that the key parameter estimates in all cases are plausible and have high statistical significance. The estimated elasticities of cost with respect to input prices for the sample mean firm are positively signed, as expected. The estimates reveal that transmission cost was much more sensitive to a change in the price of capital services than to changes in the prices of labor or other inputs. This makes sense since capital services accounted for by far the largest share of applicable total cost. The parameter estimates for the other business condition variables also have the expected sign and are statistically significant; that for the percent of electric transmission plant in total electric and gas T&D plant is positive, that for the percent of overhead transmission miles is negative and that for the measure of substation work is positive.

The estimated sample mean elasticities of cost with respect to the delivery volume and kV circuit miles, 0.78 and 0.16, respectively, are both positive and statistically significant. The sum of these two estimates, 0.94, indicates the existence of incremental scale economies under sample mean business conditions. Using total cost computed based on the cost model's elasticities, we calculate and then plot mean-scaled average cost, presented in Figure 22.1, over the entire output range. As this figure indicates, scale economies exist for companies with output values below the mean, where average cost declines, and no incremental scale economies or diseconomies for the larger firms, where the average cost curve is rather flat for large portions of the output range. Based on this, we cannot rule out the natural monopoly character of the power transmission business.

Power distribution

Local delivery companies (LDCs) receive power in bulk near points on high-voltage transmission grids and deliver it to consumers. Receipt commonly occurs at substations, where voltage is reduced from transmission to distribution levels. Power is in most cases delivered to end users at the voltage at which it is consumed.[11] Many power distributors

Table 22.3   Econometric cost model for power transmission

Variable	Coefficient	t-statistic
Constant	13.868	384.487
L	0.063	34.734
LL	0.037	1.296
LK	0.078	4.142
LY	−0.002	−0.684
LKV	−0.009	−3.38
K	0.849	174.958
KK	−0.041	−0.903
KY	0.002	0.239
KKV	0.035	4.324
Y	0.778	13.952
YY	−0.333	−3.258
YKV	0.471	5.297
KV	0.157	3.73
KVKV	−0.375	−4.553
T	0.413	8.624
OH	−2.175	−13.711
S	0.204	4.59
Trend	−0.016	−1.377
Other results		
System R bar-squared		0.911
Sample period		1998–2000
Number of observations		129

Variable key:
L = labor price.
K = capital price.
Y = total deliveries.
KV = kV circuit miles.
T = percent of transmission plant in value of electric plus gas T&D plant.
OH = percent of transmission line miles that are overhead.
S = substation/line plant unit cost ratio.

also provide metering, billing and information services to their customers. These services can account for a sizable share of O&M expenses.

Continuous use of electric power is essential to the functioning of modern homes and businesses. Power storage, self-generation and self-delivery from the grid are generally not cost competitive with power produced in bulk and delivered by a network. It follows from these demand attributes that the vast majority of residences and business establishments want local delivery capability available continuously. The technology for providing continuous deliveries requires a system that is physically connected to the premises of end users. Delivery is achieved via a network of conductors that are usually held above ground but pass underground in some areas through conduits. Important facilities used in distribution include conductors, line transformers, station equipment, poles and conduits, meters, vehicles, storage facilities, office buildings, and IT inputs such as computer

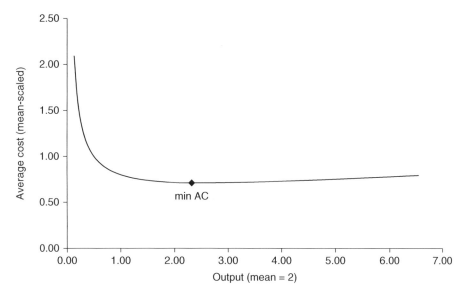

Figure 22.1   Power transmission average cost curve

hardware and software. LDCs commonly construct, operate, and maintain such facilities but may outsource certain functions.

The character of power demand is such that interruptions in power delivery are costly to customers. LDCs are, therefore, expected to deliver power reliably and to establish service quickly for new customers. Systems with overhead lines are subject to disruption from wind and ice storms. These conditions are unpredictable. When disruptions occur, LDCs are expected to restore service promptly. End-use electrical equipment is also designed to operate within a narrow range of voltage levels. The stability of power voltage is thus another important dimension of distribution service quality.

The workload of an LDC has several dimensions. Econometric cost research around the world has suggested that the list of potentially relevant output variables includes the number of customers served, peak demand, delivery volume, various reliability measures, and the distance transported. This research includes the studies by Neuberg (1977), Hjalmarsson and Veiderpass (1992), Salvanes and Tjøtta (1994), Yatchew (2001), Jamasb and Pollitt (2003), Farsi and Filippini (2004), and Lowry et al. (2005).

Cost research has also identified a wide range of additional business conditions that may affect local delivery cost. These include the customer mix that distributors serve, the extent of forestation, system undergrounding, and the provision of a gas distribution service. The last is one of several variables that can shed light on the presence of scope economies. Such economies along with scale economies, and sometimes vertical economies, have important implications for the structure of the power distribution industry.

Econometric research using US data suggests that scale economies can generally be realized up to an operating scale of sample mean size. The mean number of customers in our current sample is around 700 000. Some relevant work in this area include Sing (1987), Filippini (1996), Yatchew (2000), Ida and Kuwahara (2004), and Kwoka (2005). It is important to note, however, that research to date has not attempted to distinguish between the scale economies available from the growth of a service territory and the economies available from the amalgamation of service territories.

We structure our presentation of the empirical work for power distribution in the same way that we did power transmission. We first discuss the data, second the cost model and estimation approach, and finally we present the results and some discussion.

Power distributor data
We use data from the US power distribution sector to undertake new econometric research for this chapter on the cost structure of power distribution. As in the transmission case, data on US power distribution companies have a number of advantages in cost function estimation. Although power distribution is under the jurisdiction of state regulators, the major IOUs in the US are legally obligated to provide data on their distribution and customer service operations on FERC Form 1. These must also conform to the Uniform System of Accounts. There are good data for many distributors going back over several decades. The large size of the resultant dataset, as well as the wide variation in business conditions, facilitates the development of a flexible cost model with many business condition variables. Last, but maybe most importantly, the dataset contains good capital data covering several decades. This facilitates the calculation of accurate capital cost, which is always a challenging undertaking even in the best of circumstances.

Data for Cost Model
As already mentioned, the primary source of the cost and quantity data used in the econometric work was the FERC Form 1. Major electric IOUs in the United States are required by law to file this form annually. Data reported on Form 1 must conform to the FERC's Uniform System of Accounts. Details of these accounts can be found in Title 18 of the Code of Federal Regulations.

Data were considered for inclusion in the sample from all major US IOUs that filed Form 1 electronically in 2004 and distributed power during the sample period. To be included in the study the data also had to be plausible. Data from 66 companies were used in the econometric work. These companies are listed in Table 22.4. The sample period was 1991–2004. The resultant dataset has 922 observations on each model variable.[12]

Other sources of data were also accessed in the research. As in the study involving power transmission cost, these were used primarily to measure input prices. The supplemental data sources included the BEA of the US Department of Commerce; the 1998 *National Compensation Survey* of the BLS of the US Department of Labor; Form 861 of the US Energy Information Administration (EIA); RS Means & Associates; and Whitman, Requardt & Associates.

Defining Cost

Definition of power distribution cost
The applicable total cost of power distribution was calculated as assigned O&M expenses and assigned capital costs. For both of these cost categories we assigned all costs reported by the utility for power distribution, customer accounts, sales, and customer service and information but excluded any costs of power procurement.[13] Many power distributors in the sample are vertically integrated in the sense that they also provide other utility

Table 22.4   List of companies in the power distribution econometric sample

Company	Company
Alabama Power	Northern Indiana Public Service
Ameren UE	Northern States Power
Arizona Public Service	Ohio Power
Appalachian Power	Oklahoma Gas and Electric
Atlantic City Electric	Orange and Rockland Utilities
Avista	Otter Tail Power
Baltimore Gas and Electric	Pacific Gas and Electric
Bangor Hydro Electric	PacificCorp
Boston Edison	Potomac Edison
Carolina Power and Light	Potomac Electric Power
Central Hudson Gas and Electric	Public Service of Colorado
Central Illinois Light	Public Service of New Hampshire
Central Maine Power	Public Service of Oklahoma
Central Vermont PSC	PSI Energy
Cincinnati Gas and Electric	Public Service Electric & Gas
Central Louisiana Electric	Rochester Gas and Electric
Columbus Southern Power	San Diego Gas and Electric
Duke Energy Corp	South Carolina Electric & Gas
Edison Sault Electric	Southern California Edison
El Paso Electric	Southern Indiana Gas
Empire District Electric	Southwestern Electric
Florida Power	Tampa Electric
Florida Power & Light	Texas-New Mexico Power
Green Mountain Power	Toledo Edison
Idaho Power	Tucson Electric Power Co
Kansas City Power & Light	Union Light Heat & Power
Kentucky Power	United Illuminating
Kentucky Utilities Co	Virginia Electric
Kingsport Power	West Penn Power
Louisville Gas and Electric	Western Massachusetts Electric
Madison Gas and Electric	Wisconsin Electric Power
Maine Public Service	Wisconsin Power and Light
Mississippi Power	Wisconsin Public Service

Note: Number of companies in sample: 66.

services such as transmission and generation. Certain common costs arising from such vertical integration are reported as administrative and general O&M expenses or as general plant. We assigned sensible portions of these costs to the total cost of distribution. The gross O&M expenses considered did not include the costs of franchise fees or pensions and other benefits.

Capital cost
The measurement of capital cost follows the method outlined for power transmission. Thus, we give only a brief outline here and refer the reader to the relevant section in

power transmission for the details. As in the transmission case, we used a service price approach to measure the cost of plant ownership. In constructing the capital quantity indexes we took 1964 as the benchmark or starting year for power distribution.

The cost of capital calculation normally includes tax expenses. However, tax expenses were unusually volatile for many electric utilities during the study period chiefly due to electric power industry restructuring. Restructuring has made their allocation between distribution and other utility functions especially difficult. As a result, we excluded tax expenses from the computation of the power distribution capital cost.

Business Condition Variables

Output quantity variables
There are three output quantity variables in our distribution cost model: the number of retail customers, the power delivery volume, and the miles of distribution line.[14] Data for the first two variables are drawn from FERC Form 1 and Form EIA 861. Line miles are the best available proxy of the distances over which local deliveries are made.[15] The source of our line miles data is a directory that is currently entitled *Directory of Electric Power Producers and Distributors*. This is an annual publication of McGraw-Hill. We expect the cost to be higher the higher are the values of each of these workload measures.

Input prices
There are input prices in the power distribution model for capital, labor, and other O&M inputs. These are sourced and measured in the same way as in the input prices for power transmission. The price of labor calculation is, however, supplemented by data from the BLS.

Other business conditions
Four other business condition variables are included in the cost model. One is the percentage of the reported value of distribution plant that is not underground. This variable is calculated from FERC Form 1 data. We use it to measure the extent of system undergrounding. Underground plant provides a higher-quality service than overhead plant but involves markedly higher capital costs that tend to be only partially offset by lower operating costs. The extent of undergrounding varies greatly across America's distribution systems. Generally speaking, undergrounding is greater in urban areas and where state and local governments encourage it.

A second business condition variable added to the model is the number of customers that the utility provides with natural gas distribution services. This variable was calculated chiefly from FERC Form 2 data. It is intended to capture the extent to which an LDC has diversified into gas distribution. Such diversification will typically lower the total cost of power distribution due to the realization of scope economies.

A third business condition variable added to the model is a measure of service territory forestation. We would expect this variable to have a positive relationship to total cost. The forestation measure was calculated using US Forest Service data.

A fourth business condition that has been added to the model is the percentage of power deliveries that are made to residential and commercial customers. These customers typically have more peaked loads and rely on the distributor for more services than do the larger-volume customers. We therefore expect the relationship between cost and this variable to be positive. This variable was calculated using FERC Form 1 data and Form EIA 861.

The model also contains a trend variable. This permits predicted cost to shift over time. It captures the net effect on cost of diverse conditions such as technological change. We expect total cost to shift downward over time.

We provide summary statistics of the data used in our study in Table 22.5.

Model specification and estimation
The cost model form used, the translog, is the same as that used in the power transmission study. In addition, the cost model was part of a system of equations, where the other equations are cost shares derived using Shepherd's lemma. The estimation method is also largely the same and will not be discussed further here.

Results
Estimates of the parameters of the distribution cost model of the first-order terms are presented in Table 22.6. Again, since the data is mean-scaled, the parameter values are elasticities for the sample mean firm. The signs and magnitudes of the parameter estimates are plausible. We find that a 1 percent increase in the price of capital raises cost by 0.59 percent. This is more than three times the estimated elasticity of the price of labor reflecting the capital intensiveness of the power distribution business.

At the sample mean, 1 percent increases in the number of customers, delivery volumes and lines miles are estimated to raise cost by 0.47 percent, by 0.33 and 0.17 percent, respectively. We find that the incremental scale economies available to the sample mean firm are close to zero. This suggests that for the combination of output that the utilities serve, the average firm is close to the minimum efficient scale. In order to fully explore the nature of scale economies, once again we provide a plot of average cost against the full range of output provided by the firms in the sample in Figure 22.2. As the figure indicates, the average cost curve is flat, and in fact, declining at a very slow rate, at larger levels of output. Based on this, we can again surmise that power distribution is a natural monopoly business.

The parameter estimates for the additional business condition variables were also sensible. Total distribution cost is lower the greater is the extent of system overheading and the higher is the number of gas distribution customers served. Total distribution cost is higher the higher the extent of service territory forested and the percentage of total retail deliveries made to residential and smaller-volume business customers. The estimate of the trend variable parameter indicates a downward shift over time in total distribution cost, which some researchers find to be an indication of technical progress.

3   Regulation

Since transmission and distribution are natural monopolies, they have historically been subject to regulation. Regulation affects the terms of service provision, such as rates, reliability, other technical requirements, and the universality of service.

One of the most widely used forms of rate regulation is cost of service regulation (COSR). Under this system, the rates approved by a regulator are expected to recover a company's prudently incurred cost of providing regulated services. This cost includes

Table 22.5 Summary statistics of variables in the econometric cost model: power distribution

Variable	Units	Average	S.D.	Minimum	Maximum
Power distribution total cost	US dollars	392 717 924	476 444 344	8 352 089	3 116 110 661
Retail customers	Customer numbers	735 839	890 881	19 724	4 985 193
Retail deliveries	MWh	18 827 673	19 422 590	109 596	99 339 144
Distribution line miles	Miles	21 427	22 750	1 110	110 049
Price of capital services	Index number	12 880	2 898	3 937	36 510
Price of labor services	Dollars per employee	36 277	5 989	23 867	55 132
Price of materials	Index number	96.24	7.32	84.46	109.46
Percent overhead plant in total Dx plant	Percent	82.5%	10.5%	52.9%	99.7%
Number of gas customers	Customer numbers	168 373	510 014	0	3 954 720
Percent service territory forested	Percent	44.1%	24.9%	0.4%	91.3%
Percent residential & commercial deliveries	Percent	66.1%	12.9%	33.2%	95.9%

516

Table 22.6   Econometric cost model for power distribution

Variable	Coefficient	t-statistic
Constant	15.137	1482.737
L	0.150	115.314
LL	−0.044	−3.522
LK	−0.025	−3.736
LN	0.014	2.996
LV	−0.039	−9.177
LM	0.008	2.145
K	0.592	249.881
KK	0.087	6.978
KN	−0.040	−4.745
KV	0.082	10.653
KM	−0.022	−3.869
N	0.474	18.261
NN	−0.483	−5.150
NV	0.410	3.752
NM	0.058	1.117
V	0.330	13.947
VV	0.571	6.495
VM	−0.033	−0.636
M	0.169	9.753
MM	−0.089	−1.528
OH	−0.587	−11.533
G	−0.006	−6.383
F	0.019	2.927
RC	0.258	7.587
Trend	−0.016	−12.724
Other results		
System Rbar-squared		0.986
Sample period:		1991–2004
Number of observations		922

Variable key:
L = labor price.
K = capital price.
N = number retail customers.
V = retail deliveries.
M = distribution line miles.
OH = percent of distribution plant that is overhead.
G = number of gas distribution customers.
F = forestation.
RC = percent retail deliveries that are residential and commercial.

a return on capital.[16] Rate cases are held periodically to estimate the prudent cost of capital, labor, and other inputs used to provide regulated services. This becomes the base-rate revenue requirement.[17]

Once the revenue requirement is determined, it must be allocated for recovery from the various regulated services offered. The rate for each service recovers its assigned cost

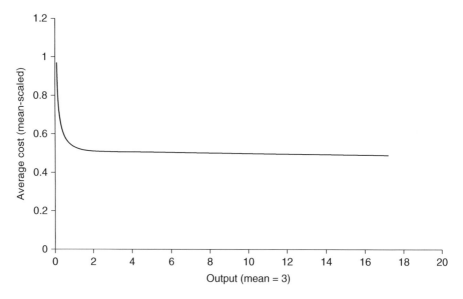

Figure 22.2   Power distribution average cost curve

given estimates of delivery volumes and other billing determinants. The regulated service offerings and rate designs require regulator approval. These terms are reviewed occasionally at the insistence of either the utility or the regulatory agency. The determination of the revenue requirement and its allocation among customer groups are both complicated by common costs in cases where a utility is a multi-service provider. These are costs that are incurred jointly in the provision of various services, including in many cases non-core services. The inherently arbitrary nature of common cost allocations makes them a source of controversy in COSR.

In the last two decades there has been growing use of alternatives to COSR in T&D regulation. Most notable among these alternatives have been those that fall under the heading of incentive regulation, also called performance-based regulation (PBR) and price control regulation.[18] Most approved PBR plans involve multi-year caps on the growth of utility rates or revenues.

The mechanisms for limiting rate or revenue growth are diverse but all have the attribute of being largely external to the company's operation during the plan years. The simplest approach is to hold rates constant for the plan duration. This approach is called a 'rate freeze' or 'rate case moratorium'. A simple variant of the rate freeze is a set of pre-scheduled rate adjustments, called 'stair step', which may be increases or decreases.

Escalation in rates or revenues is also commonly capped using indexes. Under a rate cap, for instance, growth in baskets of the utility's prices may be measured using actual price indexes (APIs). Growth in each API is limited using a price cap index (PCI),[19] such that growth API ≤ growth PCI. PCI growth is commonly determined by a formula that includes the growth in an inflation measure less an X-factor. The formulas for revenue cap indexes often include, additionally, a term for output growth.

One common approach to rate indexing, first used on a large scale in North America, makes extensive use of index research. Under this approach a PCI is calibrated to track the industry unit cost trend. In practice, this is generally achieved by using a price infla-tion index that tracks short-term input price fluctuations and an X-factor that reflects the long-run historical productivity trend of the industry. The price inflation index may be an industry-specific input price index but is also commonly a familiar macroeco-nomic inflation measure such as the consumer price index (CPI). In the latter event, the X-factor typically reflects a productivity differential between the productivity trends of the industry and the economy, and an input price differential between the input price trends of the economy and the industry.

A stretch factor is often added to X that reflects a company's potential for accelerated productivity growth under the rate plan. The stretch factor is typically the same for all companies in North America but can in principle vary between companies based on the results of benchmarking research.

In addition to the North American approach there is a British approach to the design of rate and revenue cap indexes. This approach originated in Britain and is still widely used there.[20] Under this approach, rate cases are typically held every five years in which five-year cost and output forecasts are considered. The principal 'building blocks' of the total cost forecast are the forecasts of the value of the current capital stock and of capital spending, depreciation, the rate of return on capital, and O&M spending. A macroeconomic inflation index such as the retail price index (RPI), the equivalent of the CPI, is used as the inflation measure of the PCI. Given the forecasts of growth in total cost, billing determinants, and the RPI, it is possible to choose a combination of initial rates and an X-factor such that the expected net present value of forecast revenue equals forecast cost. Alternatively, rates can be adjusted in a predetermined stair-step fashion.

The British approach has a greater ability to tailor the rate adjustment mechanism to the capital spending needs of a utility. This is an important advantage in applications to busi-nesses such as power transmission which often do not have steady capital spending pat-terns. A notable downside of the British approach is the difficulty of establishing consensus on multi-year cost forecasts. In Britain, regulators have been driven by this challenge to retain independent engineering consultants to appraise capital spending forecasts.

Statistical benchmarking can provide valuable information to both approaches of index design. Benchmarking methods used around the world include data envelopment analysis (DEA), econometric modeling, and productivity indexes. All of these methods require quality standardized data for accuracy. The popularity of the econometric approach is greater where sizable datasets are available for model estimation.

Power transmission regulation
The regulation of the rates for power transmission, based on one of the methods dis-cussed above, has taken diverse paths in the developed world, reflecting the specific insti-tutional settings under which the industry has operated. We discuss these developments in North America, Europe and the Pacific Region in the sections that follow.

North America

United States
The chief responsibility of the FERC and its predecessor agency, the Federal Power Commission (FPC), has traditionally been to regulate the interstate commerce of US

energy utilities including power transmission services. Most such US energy utilities are investor owned and have been subject to COSR for decades by the FERC or FPC.[21] The FERC and the FPC have over the years been involved in some of the classic court decisions that have shaped the development of COSR in the US.[22] The FERC can thus draw on many years of COSR experience in deciding how to regulate power transmission today.

The FERC and the FPC have experimented with alternatives to COSR over the years. FERC Order 2000 discussed the need for miscellaneous ratemaking innovations.[23] The term 'innovative ratemaking' in this order was intended to encompass PBR and various other ratemaking measures. As a result, PBR ideas were discussed in the Order 2000 compliance filings of several transmission owner (TO) groups. Most of these proposals were non-specific. In 2000, the FERC conditionally approved a PBR plan for International Transmission.[24] This plan involved a four-year rate moratorium.[25] However, delays in the spin-off of International Transmission and in its participation in a regional transmission organization (RTO)[26] subsequently postponed the start of the plan and significantly shortened its term.

In 2001 the FERC issued three decisions that clarified the nature of acceptable PBR proposals for TOs. In a decision involving Southern Company, it found that PBR incentives are acceptable that 'motivate the grid *operator* to perform in response to the market and to improve grid operation' (italics added).[27] Incentives are not acceptable that 'would flow to the transmission owners who, because they are proposed to be passive owners of the RTO . . . cannot respond to a price signal' (ibid.). Thus, the Southern Company filing was deemed unacceptable on this ground, as well as others, and was rejected.

In a 2001 decision involving RTO West, the Commission addressed a PBR proposal by TransConnect, a planned subordinate Transco in the Pacific Northwest. It noted that under Order 2000 the RTO, as the sole administrator of the transmission tariff for the region, has the exclusive authority to file the rates for service under that tariff. TOs are entitled only to make Section 205 filings with the FERC to recover the costs that they incur under RTO operation. When a TO is *independent* of market participants but is not the RTO, it can include in such revenue requirement filings a request for PBR and other incentive-oriented rate-recovery mechanisms. Such incentive provisions, however, 'must reward or penalize the transmission owners for actions that they (instead of RTO West) control (*e.g.* incentives to reduce operating and maintenance costs or incentives to expand the grid)'.[28] The FERC later addressed the PBR provisions of a TransConnect rate filing, accepting some and rejecting others.[29] TransConnect, however, never became an operational utility.

In a 2001 order provisionally granting RTO status to PJM (Pennsylvania–New Jersey–Maryland),[30] the FERC rejected a PBR proposal by PJM TOs on the grounds that most of these companies lacked the requisite independence characteristics. A request for rehearing was denied.[31]

In 2002, the FERC conditionally approved a PBR proposal of Michigan Electric Transmission Company (METC). The conditionally approved plan froze the company's currently effective rates for approximately three years. Additionally, the company was allowed to recover, on a deferred basis over five years beginning at the end of the plan, the annual cost, depreciation and return on investment, of any new transmission facilities incurred from January 1, 2001 through December 31, 2005. METC had noted in its filing the need for substantial capital spending.[32]

Legislative authorization to pursue innovative ratemaking was strengthened by the Energy Policy Act of 2005 (EPAct). Section 219 of the EPAct gave the FERC one year to establish, by rule, performance-based and other 'incentive-based rate treatments' for power transmission that promote capital investment and the deployment of new transmission technologies. Pursuant to this directive, the FERC issued a final rulemaking on the promotion of transmission investment through pricing reform in Order 679.[33]

Order 679 provided extensive discussion of innovative pricing. It made provisions for 'incentive-based' return on equities (ROEs) for new investments in transmission facilities that were approved. It also authorized several policies that can accelerate the recovery of the cost of new investments where utilities can demonstrate the need for such measures. Approved measures include the expensing of prudently incurred pre-commercial costs and the inclusion of 100 percent of prudently incurred transmission-related construction work in progress (CWIP) in the rate base. The Order also encouraged the use of formula rates, sanctioned the use of accelerated depreciation, and indicated that a service life for conventional assets as short as 15 years would be considered.[34]

Since the passage of the 2005 EPAct, the FERC has issued declaratory orders for several investment projects that are consistent with the pricing reform policies contained in Order 679. One order approves an incentive rate treatment for a large transmission investment by Allegheny Power that is part of the PJM's Regional Transmission Expansion (RTEP) process.[35] Another approves an incentive rate treatment for a large project of American Electric Power in the event that it is included as a part of the PJM RTEP.[36] Both approved treatments include the options to obtain timely recovery of the return on CWIP and to expense and recover on a current basis certain costs incurred in the pre-construction and pre-operation period.

The FERC also permits utilities to operate under formula rates. A formula rate is a ratemaking mechanism that automatically adjusts rates periodically to reflect a utility's changing cost of service. Most commonly, rates for a given year are adjusted to reflect the pro forma cost of service in the previous year. The formulas sometimes reflect estimates of construction costs during the applicable year, subject to later true-up, and/or a return on CWIP. Formula rates were reportedly popular in the early 1980s when unit cost pressures due to major plant additions and brisk input price inflation drove utilities to file rate cases frequently under COSR. The special appeal of this ratemaking treatment in a power transmission application arises from special conditions that include a situation in which an acute need for new investments in some localities coincides with an unusual level of investment risk; and the economies afforded in the regulatory process by formula rates for a regulator that, like the FERC, has jurisdiction over dozens of utilities.[37]

Some salient precedents for the use of formula rates to regulate passive TOs include formula rates approved for Boston Edison that accelerated the commencement of new investment cost recovery in 2000 and 2004;[38] formula rate for San Diego Gas & Electric in 2003;[39] formula rate for Northeast Utilities that was designed to accelerate the recovery of new investment costs in 2004;[40] and a formula rate option for PJM TOs to facilitate their recovery of costs incurred under the PJM's RTEP process in 2005.[41]

Canada

Power transmission service in Canada is provided chiefly by provincially owned utilities. The regulation of these utilities occurs chiefly at the provincial level. The National

Energy Board plays a much smaller role in power transmission regulation than its US counterpart. The provinces have moved to make their publicly owned utilities operate more like IOUs. IOUs own most transmission assets in Alberta, Nova Scotia, and Prince Edward Island and all are provincially regulated.

Alberta[42]   Transmission utilities are regulated in Alberta by the Alberta Utilities Commission, which was previously called the Energy Utilities Board. This Commission must approve the transmission facility owner tariffs that TOs file with the transmission administrator. These are essentially revenue requirement applications.

British Columbia   Energy utilities in BC are subject to the jurisdiction of the BC Utilities Commission. The rates of BC Hydro were legislatively frozen in 1996. COSR however, resumed in 2003. British Columbia Transmission Corporation, the system operator, has during its brief history been subject to COSR. The revenue requirement approved includes BC Hydro's compensation for ownership of the transmission system.

Manitoba   Manitoba Hydro is regulated by the Manitoba Public Utilities Board. The Board uses a cost of service (COS) approach to regulation. Manitoba Hydro, however, has operated for extended periods without rate increases. An interim rate case was concluded in March 2007 that resulted in a 2.25 percent rate increase.

New Brunswick   The New Brunswick Board of Commissioners of Public Utilities has traditionally used COSR to regulate electric utilities. Its regulation of New Brunswick Power Transmission does involve one PBR-style innovation, an ROE range.

Newfoundland and Labrador   Newfoundland and Labrador Hydro and Newfoundland Power are regulated by the Newfoundland and Labrador Board of Commissioners of Public Utilities. The Board uses a largely traditional COS approach to regulation. Rate cases were recently concluded for both transmission service providers (TSPs) in the province. One innovation with a PBR flavor was the use of an annual adjustment formula for the rate of return which uses bond yields in Canadian capital markets.

Nova Scotia   The Nova Scotia Utility and Review Board regulates Nova Scotia Power Inc. (NSPI) using COSR. The Board's most recent rate case for NSPI was completed on February 5, 2007.

Ontario   The Ontario Energy Board regulates the transmission operations of Hydro One, the province's main transmission company, and of two other small companies involved in transmission in the province. The Board has to date regulated these operations using COSR.

Quebec   Hydro Quebec's TransEnergie, the transmission subsidiary, has operated for several years under the jurisdiction of the Regie de l'Energie, which uses COSR. It has expressed an interest in PBR for TransEnergie but the company has resisted this move, favoring instead a near-term focus on the development and monitoring of a set of performance indicators.

Prince Edward Island Maritime Electric is regulated by the Prince Edward Island Regulatory and Appeals Commission. The company operated for several years under a PBR plan that set rates for bundled power service at 110 percent of the equivalent rates that New Brunswick Power charged in its service territory. In December 2003, the Government of Prince Edward Island passed legislation returning Maritime Electric to traditional cost of service regulation.

Saskatchewan Rate proposals of SaskPower are reviewed by the Saskatchewan Rate Review Panel and must ultimately be approved by the provincial cabinet. The Rate Review Panel uses a COS approach to regulate SaskPower. The most recent rate case was held in 2007.

Synopsis COSR has been used almost exclusively to date in the regulation of Canadian power transmission. Possible reasons for this include the absence of any type of PBR to date in any electric utility application in some provinces. In addition, the transmission systems in Alberta, Ontario, and New Brunswick are now operated by independent, non-profit entities whereas the TSPs in most other Canadian provinces are not independent of market participants. Thus, PBR cannot be used to facilitate better transmission service promotion in these provinces. The short-term performance gains that are possible in transmission cost management are also generally modest due to its capital-intensive character. Further, major investments are expected in the transmission systems of several provinces, such as in Alberta and Quebec, in the next few years. These can be difficult to accommodate under forms of comprehensive PBR that are popular in North America while British-style PBR is not well known in Canada. Finally, most provincial regulators have jurisdiction over only one or two transmission utilities. This sharply reduces the potential regulatory cost savings from PBR. Moreover, most provincial regulators have considerable experience and comfort with COSR.

Europe

Transmission ratemaking in Western Europe complies with the second European Commission Directive's requirement for regulated third-party access (TPA), discussed in detail in the next chapter. There has been a move to regulatory mechanisms with stronger cost containment incentives in recent years. Countries, including Belgium and Finland, that use COSR have set rates with explicit lengthy regulatory terms or lags. Some countries have moved to PBR in the form of price caps with a British-style building block approach. Norway uses PBR in the form of a revenue cap, where the X-factor is based on benchmarking, which has the effect of externalizing rates. PBR is thought to provide stronger efficiency and cost-reducing incentives. France and Germany are also considering the use of PBR to set future transmission rates.

Austria

The Energy Regulatory Authorities Act (E-RBG) passed in 2000 created two regulatory bodies: Energie-Control Kommission (E-Control Commission) and Energie-Control GmbH (E-Control). The former is in charge of approving terms and conditions of network access; determining network tariffs; resolving network access related disputes; and hearing appeals of decisions made by E-Control. The latter is charged with monitoring market unbundling, competition and cross-border trade; publishing prices; and proposing market and technical operation rules.[43] Energie-Control Kommission regulates transmission rates using COSR (Energie-Control Kommission, 2007).

Belgium

A 1999 law changed the existing regulator, the Commission for Regulation of Electricity, to the Federal Gas and Electricity Regulatory Commission. This regulatory body is in charge of, among other things, setting the tariffs for transmission and distribution. The law required it to set these annually on the basis of COSR. In 2005, the law was changed requiring rates to be set for four-year terms in order to improve efficiency incentives. There are also regional regulators: VREG in Flanders, CWaPE in Wallonia and IBGE-BIM in Brussels. These agencies do not have rate-setting authority but monitor and give advice on regional market developments (IEA, 2005).

Denmark

There are two energy regulators in Denmark; the Danish Energy Regulatory Authority (DERA) and the Danish Energy Authority (DEA). DERA's responsibilities are to regulate the prices of the network utilities and fair access to the networks. It has enforcement powers, which involves levying fees for non-compliance with its regulatory decisions. DEA is in charge of issuing operating licenses and monitoring compliances with conditions set out in the licensing agreements. The tariffs of the high voltage transmission operator are regulated by the Act Governing Energinet.dk. The Act provides for a COSR regulatory scheme (DERA, 2007).

Finland

The Electricity Market Act of 1995 founded the Electricity Market Authority (EMA) as the industry regulator. The EMA regulates the tariffs of the transmission and distribution grids. Until 2005, it regulated the tariffs of these grids on an *ex post* basis. Under this system, the grid operators set their own tariffs and the regulator simply examined them for reasonableness after the fact. This system proved unsuitable and failed to meet the EU directives for TPA. Thus, the regulatory method was reformed and a new tariff-setting approach was instituted starting in 2005. The first term was set for three years, covering 2005 through 2007, as part of a transitional process. Subsequent regulatory terms will be four years starting in 2008 (Energy Market Authority, 2007).

The new regulatory mechanism is based on COSR. The regulatory process involves an initial stage where the regulator sets out the method that the network owner should use to calculate its prices. This method will detail suitable capital valuation approaches for a network industry, the reasonable rate of return for this capital, principles for calculating network operations income and expenses, and the efficiency goal of these operations. At the end of each year, the regulator will calculate and inform the company of its findings on the rate of return. This step is just for information purposes; the regulator decides the appropriateness of the rate of return as a whole only at the end of the regulatory period. If it finds that a utility has earned more (less) than a reasonable amount it instructs it to reduce (increase) its prices by the amount overearned (underearned) in the next regulatory period.[44]

France

The '2000 Law' created a regulator for the energy sector, which was named the Commission de régulation de l'énergie (CRE). CRE was charged with monitoring public access to the utility networks, and regulating the market. To regulate network tariffs, CRE has historically used COSR. It draws up tariffs for the networks, based on its cost assessments of expenses needed to cover grid development and replacement, or investment, and grid maintenance and operations. It submits the proposals to the ministers of economy and energy, who can either accept or reject them without modification. Application of this methodology is prospective, based on future cost projections, starting in 2006. CRE, however, has expressed an interest in incentive regulation in general, and price caps in particular, to set network tariffs in its 2007 annual report[45] (Commission de régulation de l'énergie, 2007).

Germany

The Energy Industry Act of 2005 created the Federal Network Agency for Electricity, Gas, Telecommunications, Posts and Railway, or Bundesnetzagentur (BNetzA) in German. The Act assigned the BNetzA with regulating TPA to the grid, and assigned the regulation of small local networks serving less than 100 000 customers to state regulators (OECD, 2006).

Until 2006, the BNetzA used COSR to set electricity grid tariffs. It is currently working to introduce incentive-based regulation in 2009 based on revenue caps with increasing X-factors, which reflect expected productivity gains. In future years X will also reflect the results of statistical benchmarking of operating efficiency that is currently underway[46] (IEA, 2007).

Ireland

The 1999 Electricity Regulation Act created an independent regulator, the Commission for Energy Regulation (CER). Regulation of revenues earned by Electricity Supply Board (ESB), both in transmission and distribution, are conducted every five years.[47] The first regulatory period was 2000–05 and the second is 2006–10. The CER determines appropriate revenues through the use of a building block type of revenue cap. Towards this, it considers the regulated asset base, and efficient operating cost and capital expenditures. The X-factor used in the CPI-X formulation is set so as to recover the revenue requirement. The CER also regulates access conditions and prices so that they are fair and transparent (Commission for Energy Regulation, 2005a, 2005b and 2007).

Italy

The Autorità per l'Energia Electtrica e il Gas (AEEG), established by law 481 in 1995, started operations in 1997. It regulates tariffs, service quality, and access conditions in the electricity and gas sectors. It formulates regulatory requirements in accordance with relevant government policy and EU guidelines.[48] AEEG instituted a new tariff system on January 1, 2000, which started the first regulatory period. Under this system, it set tariffs for captive customers directly and placed two price-cap levels on tariffs that utilities can charge customers. The first capped charges made on any single customer and the second capped prices that can be charged for each user group type, of which there were nine (IEA, 2003a).

Since then, the regulator has adopted price-cap regulation with four-year terms. The second regulatory period was 2004–07, and the third began in 2008 and is set to end in 2011. To set the second period's price cap, operating costs were determined by carrying forward efficient and inflation-adjusted 2001 operating costs to 2004. These were then adjusted for a target X-factor of 3 percent for transmission over the four-year period. The return on invested capital was also set using the weighted cost of capital (WACC), and was reviewed annually to take account of actual invested capital and the capital price deflator as published by the National Statistics Office (AEEG, 2007). Thus, the regulator uses a building block-based price cap.

The Netherlands

The 1998 Electricity Act established DTe (Directie Toezicht Energie), which became part of the Netherlands Competition Authority NMA (Nederlandse Mededingingsautoriteit) in 2005. Together with the board of directors of the NMA, DTe's enforcement unit has the power to make an assessment of compliance with the Act, levy penalties for non-compliance, and settle disputes. It sets all *ex ante* regulatory rules through its Network Companies Unit for all energy network owners and operators.

DTe sets the tariff of TenneT, the stand-alone transmission company using a CPI-X revenue cap, where X is based on the building-block approach. It set the X-factor of the first regulatory period, 2001–03, at 8 percent,[49] and that of the second period, 2004–06, at 7.2 percent.[50] The X-factor for the third regulatory period, 2007–10, was set at 1.4 percent. Transmission X-factors reflect TenneT's efficient capital costs determined by the WACC and depreciation. The X-factor is also based on TenneT's efficient operating costs obtained by benchmarking these costs relative to Austrian, Danish and Norwegian transmission grid operating costs (Office of Energy Regulation (DTE), 2005).

Norway

The 1990 Energy Act appointed the Norwegian Water Resources and Energy Directorate, NVE, as the regulator. Prior to 1997, NVE set rates annually using COSR. Starting in 1997, it began using incentive regulation with rate periods of five years. There have been two rate periods since then, for the years 1997–2001 and 2002–07, and the third one, for 2008–11, is underway (Rothwell and Gomez, 2003).

During the first two regulatory periods, revenue caps based on benchmarking were used to set rates. The general formula was $R_t = R_{t-1} * \Delta CPI * (1 - X) * (1 + \varepsilon_F \Delta F)$, where R_t is revenue in year t, ΔCPI is the consumer price inflation, X is the efficiency in year t, ΔF is grid expansion proxied by load growth, and ε_F is its scale factor. Thus, revenue was adjusted for inflation, measured efficiency and network expansion. Efficiency benchmarking was based on DEA in both periods, using 1994–95 data for the first period and 1996–99 data for the second period. Statnett's performance both as a system owner and operator was benchmarked relative to Sweden's transmission owner and operator, Svenska Kraftnat. The NVE also used an earnings-sharing mechanism. Maximum allowed profit was set at 15 and 20 percent of invested capital in the first and second periods, respectively. A 2 percent minimum rate of return (ROR) was also in place (ibid.).

For the third period, the NVE has altered the revenue cap such that 40 percent of allowed revenue is based on prudent costs and 60 percent on efficient cost determined through benchmarking. The formula is $R_t = 0.4*C_{t-2} + 0.6*C^E_{t-2}$ where revenue in year t is determined using prudent costs incurred in year $t - 2$ and efficient costs in year $t - 2$ as determined through yardstick competition. Benchmarking for yardstick competition is based on a set of international systems (NVE, 2007). It is evident then that NVE has adopted a hybrid regulatory system incorporating elements of ROR and incentive regulation. It plans to evaluate this approach at the end of 2011.

Portugal

Law number 187 created the independent National Regulatory Authority, Entidade Reguladora dos Servicos Energeticos (ERSE) in 1995. ERSE regulates the rates of all the network companies in the public electricity system of Portugal.[51] It uses COSR to set the tariffs of the transmission system[52] (Energy Services Regulatory Authority, 2007).

Spain

The Hydrocarbons Act of 1998 established the regulator of the energy sector, Comision Nacional de Energia (CNE), and empowered it to supervise all of the activities of the newly reorganized electricity industry.[53] CNE uses a revenue cap to set the tariff of the transmission system. This revenue cap was introduced in 1998 and has three components, two of which are updated annually using $RPI - X$. The first part corresponds to the cost of installed equipment, the second corresponds to cumulative investment expenses, and the third is incentive revenue paid as a reward for system availability. The formula for the revenue cap for utility i in period t is $R_{it} = O_{it} + I_{it} + N_{it}$ where O_{it} is the cost of installed equipment that has been updated by the RPI-X formula; I_{it} is cumulative investment expenses between 1998 and $t - 1$ also updated by RPI-X; and N_{it} is incentive revenue given for system availability in year $t - 1$. The X-factor was set to 1 percent from 1998 to 2002[54] and to 0.6 percent from 2003 to 2006 (Crampes and Fabra, 2005).

Sweden

The energy regulator was legally established and operational in 1998. Its legal basis was amended in 2005 establishing the Energy Markets Inspectorate within the Swedish Energy Agency.[55] Tariffs are regulated on an *ex post* basis where the national transmission owner Svenska Kraftnat sets its own tariffs and the regulator intervenes only if it deems these unreasonable. The regulator determines the reasonableness of the tariffs based on a reference network created using annual information on the activities of the company. This method is referred to as the performance assessment model. Currently, studies are underway to determine how the regulator can best set transmission tariffs rather than allowing the company to set its own rates (Energy Markets Inspectorate, 2007).

Pacific Region

Australia

Most transmission companies in Australia are subject to the jurisdiction of the Australia Competition and Consumer Commission (ACCC). The ACCC has used British-style revenue-cap indexes to set markedly different X-factors for the companies that reflect differences in their expected investments. In Queensland, New South Wales, and Victoria regulators have explicitly recognized the need for increased investments and have set negative X-factors, such that revenues are determined by CPI plus X rather than by CPI minus X. Such increases were mostly provided during the first regulatory periods of the utilities.

New Zealand
With the enactment of the Electricity Industry Bill in 2001, the Commerce Commission was charged with regulating the price or revenue of the electricity line businesses that breach thresholds set by it. This regulatory oversight applies to the price that Transpower charges. To set the thresholds that apply for the regulatory period beginning in 2004, the Commission used the CPI-X mechanism. Since the Commission did not have sufficient international data against which to compare Transpower's efficiency, its X-factor was only based on an economy and industry-wide productivity differential called the B-factor. Lacking sufficient data to compute transmission sector productivity, the Commission used the distribution sector's total factor productivity (TFP) for this purpose (Commerce Commission, 2003).

In 2005, the Commission initiated a 'declaration of control' after Transpower announced tariff increases that breached its thresholds. In response, Transpower decided to suspend its price increases and proposed a building block-based regulatory mechanism to regulate transmission tariffs going forward. The Commission passed a draft decision accepting Transpower's proposals in October 2007. A final decision approving this is expected, which would change Transpower's price-cap mechanism from a North American- to a British-based approach. New Zealand transmission regulation then seems to be following the path of its Australian counterparts (Commerce Commission, 2007).

Japan
Although there is no independent power industry regulator in Japan, the Ministry of Economy, Trade and Industry (METI) sets power tariffs using US-style COSR. Rates are based on generation, transmission and distribution costs and a fair rate of return. It appears that prudence reviews used to include some benchmarking, where costs of the three categories of service of each company were compared to those of others in the industry and fully allowed for recovery if they were in the top tercile of the group reflecting highest efficiency. Those in the other tiers were allowed to recover 99 and 98 percent of their costs, respectively (IEA, 2003b).

Table 22.7 presents a summary of the rate making mechanisms in effect in the developed countries covered above.

Power distribution

North America

United States
Most state public utility commissions (PUCs) regulate the rates for the distribution services of vertically integrated utilities (VIUs) using COSR.[56] Regulation of unbundled

Table 22.7 Rate regulation mechanisms of transmission service providers (TSPs)

Jurisdiction	Regulator	Company	Regulatory mechanism	Term	Rate setting method
US					
US	Federal	All[1]	COSR	Irregular	Prudence reviews & fair ROR
US	Federal	International Transmission	PBR	2000–03	Rate freeze
US	Federal	Michigan Electric Transmission	PBR	2002–04	Rate freeze
US	Federal	Allegheny Power	PBR[2]	2004	Rapid recovery of investments[3]
US	Federal	American Electric Power	PBR[2]	2006	Rapid recovery of investments[3]
US	Federal	Boston Edison	COSR	2000, 2004	Formula rate
US	Federal	San Diego Gas & Electric	COSR	2003	Formula rate
US	Federal	Northeast Utilities	COSR	2004	Formula rate
US	Federal	PJM Transmission Owners	COSR	2005	Formula rate
Canada					
Canada	Provincial	All	COSR	Irregular	Prudence reviews & fair ROR
Europe					
Austria	Federal	All	COSR	Annual	Prudence reviews & fair ROR
Belgium	Federal	All	COSR	Four Years	Prudence reviews & fair ROR
Denmark	Federal	All	COSR	Irregular	Prudence reviews & fair ROR
Finland	Federal	All	COSR	Four Years	Prudence reviews & fair ROR
France	Federal	All	COSR[4]	Irregular	Prudence reviews & fair ROR
Germany	Federal	All	COSR[4]	Irregular	Prudence reviews & fair ROR
Ireland	Federal	All	PBR	Five Years	Revenue caps – building block approach
Italy	Federal	All	PBR	Four Years	Price caps – building block approach
The Netherlands	Federal	All	PBR	Four Years	Revenue caps – building block approach
Norway	Federal	All	PBR	Five Years	Hybrid approach – price caps & COSR
Portugal	Federal	All	COSR	Irregular	Prudence reviews & fair ROR
Spain	Federal	All	PBR	Annual	Revenue caps[5]
Sweden	Federal	All	None	Irregular	*Ex post* network reference models

Table 22.7 (continued)

Jurisdiction	Regulator	Company	Regulatory mechanism	Term	Rate setting method
Australia					
Australia	Federal	All	PBR	Five years	Price caps – building block approach
New Zealand					
New Zealand	Federal	All	PBR	One year	Price thresholds – benchmarks
Japan					
Japan	Federal	All	COSR	Irregular	Prudence reviews & fair ROR

Notes:
1. In some cases 'All' refers to one company as there is only one transmission company provider in the service territory.
2. For pre-construction and construction work in progress involving large investments.
3. Pre-construction costs expensed and CWIP recovered immediately before investment comes online.
4. PBR under consideration.
5. X-factor setting method unkown.

power distribution services has not yet displayed a clear pattern, since many utilities operated for several recent years under transitional rate freezes designed in part to recover stranded generation costs. Some jurisdictions have, however, used PBR to regulate distribution rates.

The first PBR plan based on rate indexing approved for a US electric utility was that for the bundled power services of PacifiCorp (CA). Since then, plans have been approved for the bundled power service of Central Maine Power (ME) and the power distribution services of Bangor Hydro Electric (ME), National Grid (MA), San Diego Gas and Electric (SDG&E) and Southern California Edison (CA). Most of these plans have featured X-factors based on TFP trend research. The plan for SDG&E featured an industry-specific input price index.

Canada

In Canada, a rate indexing plan was approved for the power distribution services of EPCOR of Alberta in 2000. A rate indexing plan was approved for the power distribution services of Ontario utilities in 2000 and later suspended.[57] The price-cap index in this plan featured an industry-specific inflation measure and an X-factor based on TFP trend research. The Ontario utilities have been operating under a transitional plan involving a price-cap index that was chosen to reflect North American precedents. In 2007, the Ontario Energy Board initiated a third incentive regulation mechanism (IRM3) to set rates for power distributors, which number over 90. After a lengthy period of consultation with stakeholders, the board issued a decision on an incentive rate mechanism to apply from 2009–2014 based on a North American price-cap index, where the X-factor reflects industry TFP and stretch factors are set using a benchmarking study.[58]

Europe

The regulatory mechanisms used to set rates by some European regulators are the same for the distribution and transmission networks, which were discussed in the previous section. In what follows, we discuss those mechanisms that have been exclusively designed for power distribution rates. We note that where incentive regulation is used to set rates in these Western European countries, there has been extensive use of statistical benchmarking.

Austria

The regulator switched from COSR to incentive regulation to set the tariffs of electricity distributors in 2005. The new mechanism uses a revenue cap where cost is annually adjusted for inflation, efficiency, and output changes. The regulatory term is four years, with the current one covering the years 2006–09. Adjustment for efficiency is made using 'cost adjustment factors', which are essentially X-factors. These are composed of a common frontier shift or technical change of 1.95 percent and firm-specific efficiency measures. The regulator determined the technical change value based on international precedents and studies of technical change for the industry, which it found to be 1.5 percent. It added a value of 0.45 percent to this amount since the revenue cap would not require earnings-sharing. Individual firm inefficiency levels were calculated using DEA and econometric models, the maximum amount of which was 3.5 percent. Thus, the X-factors range from 1.95 to 5.45 percent per year for the first regulatory period (Energie-Control GmbH, 2005).

Denmark
Starting in 2004, agreement was reached to place the tariffs of distribution companies under a 'price cap' until 2008 by freezing rates at their 2004 levels. Companies may apply for exemption from this cap if they can demonstrate a need for extra investment to meet security of supply requirements. Starting in 2008, DERA plans to apply revenue caps and has been working on appropriate benchmarking models to use for that purpose (DERA, 2007).

Norway
The method used to regulate power distribution companies by the Norwegian regulator is the same as that used for power transmission: the regulator uses revenue caps. The companies' revenues are updated using CPI-X and, as of the second regulatory period, load growth.[59] The X-factors are set by benchmarking the relative performance of the power distributors in the country. DEA is used for this purpose.

The Netherlands
Starting in 2000, DTe has used a price cap to set tariffs, where aggregate and not individual tariff elements are capped using a CPI-X formula. Each year's prices are set by adjusting the previous period's price for inflation, as measured by CPI, and a productivity offset or X-factor. The first regulatory period's price cap, for 2001–03, was challenged in court by distributors for using DEA to help set firm-specific X-factors. The DTe had opted for first eliminating existing cost inefficiencies that differ across companies in order to 'level the playing field' by setting X-factors that ranged from +2 percent to –8 percent. Its decision was overturned on the grounds that the law only authorized a common X-factor and not because of the methodology used. Thus, DTe was forced to use a common productivity-based X-factor of 3.2 percent.

The law was subsequently amended to allow individual X-factors, which require each firm to catch up to the efficient frontier by reducing its inefficiency relative to it over time.[60] This approach was used by DTe in the second regulatory period of 2004–06 (van Dame, 2005). DTe set X-factors that ranged from +6.3 percent to –3.6 percent for this second period. In 2005 DTe added a Q-factor to the price-cap formula to incentivize distributors to take account of service quality in their service provision. The second period's price cap was thus modified to CPI-X-Q, whereby tariff charges were adjusted according to quality of service provided. Currently the price cap of the third regulatory period, covering 2007–09, is in effect. The price cap is still based on the familiar CPI-X-Q formula. During this period, however, DTe has determined that there is a 'level playing field' and, hence, has set a common X-factor. This was calculated using average annual productivity growth of all distributors over 2003–05 and was set at 1.3 percent.

Portugal
The regulator ERSE uses incentive regulation in the form of a PCI to set distribution rates. The regulatory period is set to three years. During the first regulatory period of

1999–2001, the X-factor was set at 5 percent and during the second regulatory period of 2002–04, it was set at 7 percent.[61] In the third regulatory period of 2006–08 it has been set to 4 percent (SEC, 2006) The formula used to set the price cap is $P_F * (RPI - X_F) + P_V * (RPI - X_V)$, where the first term is the price of fixed inputs adjusted by consumer price inflation and efficiency gains in fixed inputs. The second term is the price of variable inputs adjusted for consumer price inflation and efficiency gains in variable inputs. The efficiency gains are determined using benchmarking. ERSE used stochastic frontier models to set the efficiency gains in the current period (Energy Services Regulatory Authority, 2007).

Spain

The tariff of the distribution system is regulated through a revenue cap. The formula used for this purpose is a traditional one and is given by $R_{it} = R_{it-1} * \{[1 + (RPI_t - X)]/100\} * [1 + (\Delta DR_{it} * Eff)]$ where revenue is updated annually for inflation less an X-factor, and incremental increase in output adjusted for efficiency. The first term in brackets is the RPI inflation less the X-factor term, and the second term is the increase in volume delivered from the previous year, which is set to zero if there is a decrease, times an efficiency factor capped at 0.4 (Rothwell and Gomez, 2003).

In its latest annual report to the European Commission, the CNE has indicated that it is developing a regulatory mechanism based on a reference network model to regulate the tariffs charged by the network companies (CNE, 2007).

Pacific Region

Australia

PBR is also common in Australian distribution regulation. Rates or revenues for energy distributors in the states of Queensland, New South Wales and Victoria are subject to indexing. The indexing approach used in Australia, however, differs from those used in North America. The British approach to PCI design is the norm. The state of Victoria, though, has used a hybrid approach to set rates where it used the British approach to establish the revenue requirement for capital but used a North American-style index to establish revenue requirements for operation, maintenance and administrative (OM&A) expenses.

New Zealand

Rate regulation of power distribution is also under the Commerce Commission oversight. The Commission sets a price path threshold for the average rates that distributors can charge. The threshold is set using the CPI-X framework. A TFP index was used to set a common X-factor component, which we indicated was the B-component earlier, for the current 'control period' of 2004–09. The common X-factor was adjusted by stretch factors determined using TFP-level indexes, which determined the C or relative efficiency components. Distributors deemed to have inferior cost performance were granted no price escalation or zero stretch factors (Commerce Commission, 2003). This use of benchmarking in regulation can be explained by New Zealand's very limited experience with cost of service regulation of electric utilities, which made the regulator receptive to PBR using benchmarking. The Commission is currently working to establish distribution price thresholds that will apply for the control period of 2009–14.

Japan

As stated earlier, Japan has historically used COSR to set rates for the power industry. The government body for rate 'regulation,' METI reviews the cost of the ten IOUs and determines their appropriate cost levels and a fair rate of return. Since the IOUs are vertically integrated, the rate setting methodology is the same as that described in the power transmission sector.

We present a summary of the regulatory methodologies used to set power distribution rates in Table 22.8 for the countries covered above.

4   Concluding Remarks

Power transmission and distribution are natural monopoly activities, characterized by the existence of scale economies. We have demonstrated the importance of scale economies with econometric models developed using US data from publicly available sources. These models can also be used in benchmarking and shed light on business conditions that should be considered in a good benchmarking study. Although US T&D business arrangements have some unique features, due to the different historical setting under which they evolved, they provide ample evidence of the factors that affect the industry in the developed world.

These factors have not only shaped the operation of the companies in the industry, but have also had strong implications for the regulatory institutions and methods that have been developed to oversee their activities, including their rates. In particular, the natural monopoly character of the businesses has necessitated that regulation on the conditions of service, service territory designation, and rates be instituted.

The countries of the developed world have responded in different ways to this requirement. Generally, countries with a long history of private ownership in the power industry have chosen to continue with the COS approach to regulation which was developed decades ago for this purpose. The US and Japan are prime examples of this. PBR, often aided by statistical benchmarking, is more common where regulation is relatively new and regulators confront a large number of regulated entities. However, several North American jurisdictions were early innovators in using productivity research to fashion price-cap indexes. The extensive data available in the US has also encouraged the use of econometric benchmarking.

PBR in the form of index-based regulation lends itself particularly well to power distribution regulation because of the relatively steady or smoother patterns of investment that the businesses in the industry undertake. These firms invest to expand capacity to accommodate customer connections to the grid, which generally grows at steady and predictable rates every year. Transmission investment, on the other hand, is lumpy as the system must be expanded to meet additional capacity requirements over greater time intervals. As a result, greater rate increases may be needed at various intervals to accommodate such expansions than is made available by index-based PBR. The power distribution industry has also prompted the use of benchmarking in regulation. The relatively large number of operators with standardized data has made it possible

Table 22.8 Power distribution and rate regulation mechanisms

Jurisdiction	Regulator	Regulatory mechanism	Rate setting method
US			
US	State	Mostly COSR	Prudence reviews & fair ROR
US	State	Some PBR	Mostly rate freeze, rate indexing, ROE bands
Canada			
Canada	Provincial	Mostly COSR	Prudence reviews & fair ROR
Canada	Provincial	Some PBR	Mostly rate freeze, rate indexing, ROE bands
Europe			
Austria	Federal	PBR	Revenue caps – benchmarking to set X-factor
Belgium	Federal	COSR	Prudence reviews & fair ROR
Denmark	Federal	PBR[1]	Rate freeze
Finland	Federal	COSR	Prudence reviews & fair ROR
France	Federal	COSR[2]	Prudence reviews & fair ROR
Germany	Federal	COSR[2]	Prudence reviews & fair ROR
Ireland	Federal	PBR	Price caps – building block approach
Italy	Federal	PBR	Price caps – building block approach
The Netherlands	Federal	PBR	Price caps – benchmarking to set X-factor
Norway	Federal	PBR	Hybrid approach – price caps & COSR
Portugal	Federal	PBR	Price caps – benchmarking to set X-factor
Spain	Federal	PBR	Revenue caps3, 4
Sweden	Federal	None	*Ex Post* network reference models
Australia			
Australia	State/Federal as of 2008	PBR	Price caps – building block approach
New Zealand			
New Zealand	Federal	PBR	Price thresholds – benchmarks
Japan			
Japan	Federal	COSR	Prudence reviews & fair ROR

Notes:
1. Revenue caps planned starting in 2008.
2. PBR under consideration.
3. A reference network model under development.
4. X-factor setting method unknown.

to benchmark their performance, and use the results in the rate-setting process. This explains partly the popularity of benchmarking in the European power distribution industry.

Notes

1. One study that deals with the cost of transmission is Baldick and Khan (1993). In general though, studies on the power transmission sector have largely focused on transmission pricing and investment. Vogelsang (2006) provides an example of a study on transmission pricing policy under an incentive-based regulatory mechanism. Studies on transmission investment include one by the EEI (2005), which details needed investments in the US transmission sector, and Joskow (2005), which provides a general discussion of the patterns of transmission investment. The transmission company structure most conducive for system expansion is the subject of a number of studies. Graves and Clapp (2001), Hogan and Chandley (2002), Morey (2003), and Morey and Hurst (2003), favor the for-profit transmission model regulated by an incentive-based mechanism as an ideal tool for eliciting much needed transmission investment.
2. The selection criteria used in determining the major IOU classification is detailed in EIA (1993, p. 2).
3. See Hall and Jorgensen (1967) for a seminal discussion of the use of service price methods for measuring capital cost.
4. The US economy user cost of capital is not directly observable, but it can be measured by applying two economic relationships. The first economic relationship pertains to the National Income and Product Accounts (NIPA) definitions of gross domestic product (GDP) and the cost of inputs used by the US economy. In the NIPA, the total cost of the US economy inputs is equal to GDP. At the economy-wide level there are two inputs: labor and capital. Therefore the total cost of capital is equal to GDP less labor compensation (CL), or $CK = GDP - CL$ where CK represents the total cost of capital. The second relationship is between the total cost of capital and the components of the capital price equation. The total cost of capital is equal to the product of the quantity of capital input and the price of capital input, or $CK = P_k \cdot K$ where P_k represents the price and K the quantity of capital input. The price of capital can be decomposed into the price index for new plant and equipment (J), the opportunity cost of capital (r), the rate of depreciation (d), the inflation rate for new plant and equipment (l), and the rate of taxation on capital (t), $P_k = J \cdot (r + d - l + t)$. Combining the second and third equations, we obtain the relationship $CK = J \cdot (r + d - l + t) \cdot K = r \cdot J \cdot K + d \cdot J \cdot K - l \cdot J \cdot K + t \cdot J \cdot K$, which gives $CK = r \cdot VK + D - l \cdot VK + T$, where D represents the total cost of depreciation, T total indirect business taxes and corporate profits taxes, and VK the current cost of plant and equipment net stock. Combining the above with the first equation, one can derive the following equation for the opportunity cost of capital: $r = (GDP - CL - D - T + l \cdot VK)/(VK)$. GDP, labor compensation, depreciation, and taxes are reported annually in the NIPA. The current cost of plant and equipment net stock and the inflation rate for plant and equipment are not reported in the NIPA, but are reported in *Fixed Reproducible Tangible Wealth in the United States* (BEA, various issues b).
5. The materials price does not appear in the estimated parameter tables due to the imposition of the linear homogeneity restriction predicted by economic theory.
6. Some sampled utilities owned gas distribution systems.
7. In their Monte Carlo studies of functional forms' performance, Gagne and Ouellette (1998) use the translog as a benchmark because 'it is the most widely used' functional form.
8. See Zellner (1962).
9. That is, we iterate the procedure until the determinant of the difference between any two consecutive estimated disturbance matrices is approximately zero.
10. See Dhrymes (1971), Oberhofer and Kmenta (1974) and Magnus (1978).
11. Voltage levels are higher for many industrial customers than for residential users.
12. Some observations for companies in the sample were excluded due to data problems.
13. Utilities that are subject to retail competition typically sell or transfer their generation assets but continue to provide retail services.
14. Data on the peak load of the sampled distributors were unavailable.
15. Due to missing values of line miles over time, we have used one cross-sectional value for each utility.
16. This characterization of cost of service regulation is, of course, stylized. The terminology and precise procedure for setting rates varies considerably across regulated industries and regulatory jurisdictions. For a seminal presentation of COSR, see Kahn (1998).
17. The volatility of energy prices has prompted some regulators to provide for a shorter lag between the purchase of energy inputs and the addition of these costs to the revenue requirement.
18. For a comprehensive discussion of incentive ratemaking or PBR, see Lowry and Kaufmann (2002).

Additional discussion can be found in Bell (2002), Jamasb and Pollitt (2001, 2003), and Lowry and Kaufmann (2006).
19. The useful abbreviations API and PCI appear to have developed in US Federal Communications Commission proceedings.
20. The decision to use rate indexing in British utility regulation was strongly influenced by the recommendations of Littlechild (1983) to adjust British Telecom's rates using an index with a growth rate formula of RPI-X.
21. Publicly owned utilities, such as the Bonneville Power Administration, Tennessee Valley Authority, and the Western Area Power Administration, have been established chiefly to produce and transport power from federally controlled hydropower sites.
22. See, for example, the landmark Supreme Court decision, *Federal Power Commission et al. vs. Hope Natural Gas Co.* 320 US 591 (1943).
23. 89 FERC 61,285 (1999).
24. 92 FERC 61,276 (2000).
25. The company also requested some operating flexibility during the moratorium period. Specifically, it reserved the right to introduce new, innovative, and optional transmission products and services on a pilot program basis, and to pursue market-based transmission projects.
26. RTOs are like ISOs (independent system operators) but differ in the larger transmission service area that they administer and in always being under FERC jurisdiction. Some ISOs like ERCOT of Texas do not cross state lines and are not subject to FERC oversight.
27. 94 FERC 61,271 (2001).
28. Avista Corporation et al., 95 FERC 61,114 (2001).
29. 100 FERC 61,297 (2002).
30. PJM Interconnection, L.L.C. et al., 96 FERC 61,061 (2001).
31. 101 FERC 61,345 (2002).
32. In addition, PBR ideas advanced by Entergy in its Order 2000 compliance filing were not addressed by the FERC when it rejected the filing for other reasons in 2001. Entergy's 2004 proposal to contract with an Independent Coordinator of Transmission had no PBR content. 96 FERC 61,062 (2001).
33. Docket No. RM06-4-000, July 20 2006.
34. In 2003, the FERC had approved the expensing of pre-commercialization costs and the inclusion of 100 percent of CWIP in rate base by American Transmission. American Transmission Company, L.L.C 105 FERC 61,388 (2003).
35. 116 FERC 61, 058 (2004).
36. 116 FERC 61, 059 (2006).
37. Formula rates are also common for the recovery of the costs of ISOs. While formula rates are possible, some ISOs are known to operate under stated rates. The Electric Reliability Council of Texas (ERCOT) is an ISO subject to the jurisdiction of the Public Utility Commission of Texas. It operates under a stated rate per MWh, which is set annually.
38. 91 FERC 61,198 (2000) and 109 FERC 61,300 (2004).
39. 105 FERC 61,301 (2003).
40. 108 FERC 61,240 (2004).
41. 111 FERC 61,308 (2005).
42. The discussion on transmission rate regulation for Canada is based either on the authors' personal knowledge or on information from the provincial regulators' websites.
43. Note, however, that the provincial governments are in charge of licensing the electric utilities. This review must, in principle, consider the regulation of passive TOs where applicable.
44. See http://www.emvi.fi/.
45. In its 2007 *Activity Report*, it states that 'Increasingly specific knowledge of operator costs, along with experience acquired from application of the various tariffs proposed by CRE since its founding, now makes it possible to set up increasingly incentive-based regulation', p. 50.
46. This plan is subject to parliamentary approval, which is pending.
47. CER also undertakes annual price control reviews for ESB's generation and supply businesses.
48. See http://www.autorita.energia.it/inglese/about/eng_index.htm.
49. Frontier Economics (2000).
50. See http://www.dte.nl/engels/electricity/decisions_electricity/factor.asp.
51. There are two electricity markets in Portugal: the public electricity system (PES) and the independent electricity system (IES). The former is the regulated market where the price of power is fixed and energy is supplied through purchasing power agreements between REN, the transmission operator, and generators. The latter is 'the free market' where power is supplied by non-binding contracts between generators and eligible customers able to choose their suppliers (IEA, 2004).
52. This method is also used to set the tariffs of the transmission and distribution networks, run by

Electricidade dos Acores, S.A. (EDA), in the Azores Islands, and those of the Madeira Islands, run by Empresa de Electricidade de Madeira, S.A. (EEM). The marketing activities of the distribution company are also subject to ROR.
53. See http://www.cne.es/cne/.
54. Rothwell and Gomez (2003).
55. See http://www.energimarknadsinspektionen.se/.
56. VIUs do, however, often operate for extended periods under base rate freezes.
57. Decision with Reason. RP-1999-0034. In the matter of a proceeding under sections 19(4), 57, 70, and 78 of the Ontario Energy Board Act, 1998 S.O. 1998, c. 15, Schedule B to determine certain matters relating to the Proposed Electric Distribution Rate Handbook for licensed electricity distributors.
58. The details of the proceedings, including the board's decisions can be found at http://www.oeb.gov. on.ca/OEB/Industry + Relations/OEB + Key + Initiatives/3rd + Generation + Incentive + Regulation/ (accessed February 2009).
59. In the second regulatory period, customer additions were also included in calculating grid expansion. During this period a general 'X-factor' of 1.5 percent was set while individual 'X-factors' varied from 0 to 5.2 percent. These had been 1.5 percent and 0 to 3 percent, respectively, during the first regulatory period (NVE, 2002 and Grasto, 1997).
60. See http://www.dte.nl/engels/electricity/decisions_electricity/factor.asp.
61. No X-factor was set for the one-year regulatory period of 2005.

References

Autorità per l'Energia Elettrica e il Gas (AEEG) (2007), *Annual Report to the European Commission on Regulatory Activities and the State of the Services of the Electricity and Gas Sectors – Italy*, European Regulators' Group for Electricity and Gas, Italy.
Baldick, Ross and Edward Khan (1993), 'Network costs and the regulation of wholesale competition in electric power', *Journal of Regulatory Economics*, **5**, 367–84.
Bell, Matthew (2002), 'Performance-based regulation: a view from the other side of the Pond', *Electricity Journal*, January/February, 67–73.
Bureau of Economic Analysis (BEA) (various issues a), *Survey of Current Business*, US Department of Commerce, Washington, DC.
Bureau of Economic Analysis (BEA) (various issues b), *Fixed Reproducible Tangible Wealth in the United States*, US Department of Commerce, Washington, DC.
Bureau of Economic Analysis (BEA), Unpublished data on the stocks and service lives of the capital of Local Distribution Companies, US Department of Commerce, Washington, DC.
Bureau of Labor Statistics (BLS) (1998), *National Compensation Survey*, US Department of Labor, Washington, DC.
Comision Nacional de Energia (CNE) (2007), *Spanish Regulator's Annual Report to the European Commission*, European Regulators' Group for Electricity and Gas.
Commerce Commission (2003), *Regulation Electricity Lines Businesses – Targeted Control Regime Threshold Decisions* (regulatory period beginning 2004), available at: www.comcom.govt.nz (accessed January 2004).
Commerce Commission (2007), *Regulation of Electricity Lines Businesses Targeted Control Regime: Draft Decisions and Reasons for Not Declaring Control and Draft Decision on Resetting Transpower's Thresholds*, available at: www.comcom.govt.nz (accessed February 2008).
Commission de régulation de l'énergie (2007), *Activity Report, France*, available at: http://www.cre.fr/en/documents/publications/rapports_annuels (accessed October 2007).
Commission for Energy Regulation (2005a), *2006–2010 Transmission Price Control Review Transmission Asset Owner (TAO) and Transmission System Operator (TSO)*, September 9, available at: http://www.cer.ie/en/electricity-transmission-network-decision-documents.aspx (accessed October 2007).
Commission for Energy Regulation (2005b), *Decision Paper on Distribution System Operator Revenues*, September 9, available at: http://www.cer.ie/en/electricity-distribution-network-decision-documents.aspx (accessed October 2007).
Commission for Energy Regulation (2007), *Regulators' Annual Report to the European Commission – Ireland*, European Regulators' Group for Electricity and Gas.
Crampes, Claude and Natalia Fabra (2005), 'The Spanish Electricity Industry: Plus ça change', *The Energy Journal*, European Energy Liberalization Special Issue, 127–53.
Danish Energy Regulatory Authority (DERA) (2007), *Regulators' Annual Report to the European Commission – Denmark*, European Regulators' Group for Electricity and Gas.
Dhrymes, P.J. (1971), 'Equivalence of iterative Aitkin and maximum likelihood estimators for a system of regression equations', *Australian Economic Papers*, **10**, 20–24.

EEI (2005), *EEI Survey of Transmission Investment: Historical and Planned Capital Expenditures (1999–2008)*, Edison Electric Institute, Washington, DC.

Energie-Control Kommission (2005), *Annual Report*, available at: http://www.e-control.at (accessed October 2007).

Energie-Control Kommission (2007), *National Report to the European Commission – Austria*, European Regulators' Group for Electricity and Gas.

Energy Information Administration (EIA) (1993), *Financial Statistics of Major U.S. Investor-owned Electric Utilities*, US Department of Energy, Washington, DC.

Energy Information Administration (EIA) (various issues), *Form 861*, US Department of Energy, Washington, DC.

Energy Market Authority (2007), *Annual Report to the European Commission – Finland*, European Regulators' Group for Electricity and Gas.

Energy Markets Inspectorate (2007), *The Swedish Energy Markets Inspectorate's Report in Accordance with the EC Directives for the Internal Markets for Electricity and Natural Gas*, European Regulators' Group for Electricity and Gas.

Energy Services Regulatory Authority (2007), *Annual Report to the European Commission – Portugal*, European Regulators' Group for Electricity and Gas.

Farsi, Mehdi and Massimo Filippini (2004), 'Regulation and measuring cost-efficiency with panel data models: application to electricity distribution utilities', *Review of Industrial Organization*, **25**, 1–19.

Federal Energy Regulatory Commission (FERC) (various years), *FERC Form 1*, Washington, DC.

Federal Energy Regulatory Commission (FERC) (various years), *FERC Form 2*, Washington, DC.

Filippini, Massimo (1996), 'Economies of scale and utilization in the Swiss electric power distribution industry', *Applied Economics*, **28** (5), 543–50.

Frontier Economics (2000), *The Efficiency of the Dutch Network and Supply Companies*, Report prepared for DTe, London.

Gagne, Robert and Pierre Ouellette (1998), 'On the choice of functional forms: summary of a Monte Carlo experiment', *Journal of Business and Economics Statistics*, **16** (1), 118–24.

Grasto, Ketil (1997), *Incentive-based Regulation of Electricity Monopolies in Norway. Norwegian Water Resources and Energy Directorate*, available at: http://webb2.nve.no/FileArchive/185/paperonregulalation.pdf (accessed April 2004).

Graves, Joseph S. and John D. Clapp (2001), 'The future of electric transmission', *Electricity Journal*, November, 11–22.

Hall, R. and D.W. Jorgensen (1967), 'Tax policy and investment behavior', *American Economic Review*, **57**, 391–414.

Hjalmarsson, L. and A. Veiderpass (1992), 'Efficiency and ownership in Swedish electricity retail distribution', *Journal of Productivity Analysis*, **3**, 7–23.

Hogan, William W. and John D. Chandley (2002), *Independent Transmission Companies in a Regional Transmission Organization*, Center for Business and Government, John F. Kennedy School of Government, Harvard University, Cambridge, MA.

Ida, Takanori and Tetsuya Kuwahara (2004), 'Yardstick cost comparison and economies of scale and scope in Japan's electric power industry', *Asian Economic Journal*, **18** (4), 423–38.

International Energy Agency (IEA) (2003a), *Energy Policies of IEA Countries: Italy*, 2003 Review, IEA, Washington, DC.

International Energy Agency (IEA) (2003b), *Energy Policies of IEA Countries: Japan*, 2003 Review, IEA, Washington, DC.

International Energy Agency (IEA) (2004), *Energy Policies of IEA Countries: Portugal*, 2004 Review, IEA, Washington, DC.

International Energy Agency (IEA) (2005), *Energy Policies of IEA Countries: Belgium*, 2005 Review, IEA, Washington, DC.

International Energy Agency (IEA) (2007), *Energy Policies of IEA Countries: Germany*, 2007 Review, IEA, Washington, DC.

Jamasb, T. and M. Pollitt (2001), 'Benchmarking and regulation: international electricity experience', *Utilities Policy*, **9**, 107–30.

Jamasb, Tooraj and Michael Pollitt (2003), 'International benchmarking and regulation: an application to European electricity distribution utilities', *Energy Policy*, **31**, 1609–22.

Joskow, Paul L. (2005), *Patterns of Transmission Investment*, Harvard Electricity Policy Group, John F. Kennedy School of Government, Harvard University, Cambridge, MA.

Kahn, Alfred E. (1998), *The Economics of Regulation: Principles and Institutions*, Cambridge, MA: MIT Press.

Kwoka, John E. (2005), 'Electric power distribution: economies of scale, mergers, and restructuring', *Applied Economics*, **37**, 2373–86.

Littlechild, Stephen (1983), *Regulation of British Telecommunications' Profitability*, Report to the Secretary of State, Department of Industry, London.

Lowry, Mark N., Lullit Getachew and David Hovde (2005), 'Econometric benchmarking of cost performance: the case of US power distributors', *The Energy Journal*, **26** (3), 75–92.

Lowry, Mark N. and Lawrence Kaufmann (2002), 'Performance-based regulation of utilities', *Energy Law Journal*, **23**, 399–457.

Lowry, Mark N. and Lawrence Kaufmann (2006), 'Alternative regulation for North American electric utilities', *Electricity Journal*, **19** (5), 15–26.

Magnus, J.R. (1978), 'Maximum likelihood estimation of the GLS model with unknown parameters in the disturbance covariance matrix', *Journal of Econometrics*, **7**, 281–312.

McGraw-Hill (various years), *Directory of Electric Power Producers and Distributors*, New York.

Morey, Matthew J. (2003), 'Performance-based regulation for independent transmission companies: delivering the promise of standard market design', *Electricity Journal*, June, 35–51.

Morey, Matthew J. and Eric Hurst (2003), 'The role of the independent transmission company in standardized wholesale electricity markets', *Electricity Journal*, May, 31–45.

Neuberg, L. (1977), 'Two issue in municipal ownership of electric power distribution systems', *Bell Journal of Economics*, **8**, 302–23.

Norwegian Water Resources and Energy Directorate (NVE) (2002), *Economic Regulation of Electricity Monopolies*, available at: http://www.nve.no/ (accessed April 2004).

Norwegian Water Resources and Energy Directorate (NVE) (2007), *Report on Regulation and the Electricity Market – Norway*, European Regulators' Group for Electricity and Gas.

Oberhofer, W. and J. Kmenta (1974), 'A general procedure for obtaining maximum likelihood estimates in generalized regression models', *Econometrica*, **42**, 579–90.

Office of Energy Regulation (DTE) (2005), *Annex A to the decision approving the method for determining the price cap to promote the efficient operation of the manager of the national high-voltage grid, pursuant to section 41 (4) of the Electricity Act of 1998*, Number: 101155–44.

Organisation for Economic Co-operation and Development (OECD) (2006), *Economic Survey of Germany 2006: Sustained Competition is Absent in Energy Markets*, available at: www.oecd.org/eco/surveys/germany (accessed October 2007).

Rothwell, Geoffrey and Tomas Gomez (eds) (2003), *Electricity Economics: Regulation and Deregulation*, Hoboken, NJ: John Wiley.

RS Means (1999), *Heavy Construction Cost Data, 13th Annual Edition*, Kingston, MA.

Salvanes, K. and S. Tjøtta (1994), 'Productivity differences in multiple output industries', *Journal of Productivity Analysis*, **5**, 23–43.

Securities Exchange Commission (SEC) (2006), *Form 20-F Filing–Annual and Transition Report of Foreign Private Issuers–EDP S.A.*, available at: http://www.sec.gov/ (accessed October 2007).

Sing, Merrile (1987), 'Are combination gas and electric utilities multiproduct natural monopolies?', *Review of Economics and Statistics*, **69** (3), 392–8.

van Dame, Eric (2005), 'Liberalizing the Dutch electricity market: 1998–2004', *The Energy Journal*, European Energy Liberalization Special Issue, 155–79.

Vogelsang, Ingo (2006), 'Electricity transmission pricing and performance-based regulation', *The Energy Journal*, **27** (4), 97–126.

Whitman, Requardt, and Associates (1993), *Handy–Whitman Index of Public Utility Construction Costs*, Baltimore, MD.

Yatchew, A. (2000), 'Scale economies in electricity distribution: a semiparametric analysis', *Journal of Applied Econometrics*, **15**, 187–210.

Yatchew, A. (2001), 'Incentive regulation of distributing utilities using yardstick competition', *Electricity Journal*, January/February, 56–60.

Zellner, Arnold (1962), 'An efficient method of estimating seemingly unrelated regressions and tests of aggregation bias', *Journal of the American Statistical Association*, **57**, 348–68.

23 The market structure of the power transmission and distribution industry in the developed world
Lullit Getachew

1 Introduction

Power industries of developed countries have been undergoing tremendous changes in the last 30 years. Institutional, market and technological developments have rendered the once natural monopoly activities of generation and retailing, or supply as it is called in some jurisdictions, competitive. As a result, policy makers have been quite keen on restructuring the industry by separating the monopoly activities of distribution and transmission from the competitive sectors.

The former remain regulated but have undergone changes due to the structural transformation of the industries in which they operate. Although the pace of restructuring has proceeded at different rates and in different ways, in developed countries, there is a widely held view that some sort of separation between transmission and generation, and distribution and retailing is needed in order to foster competition in the power market. We study the various ways in which such separations have been instituted in the same developed economies that we focused on in the previous chapter; namely, the US, Canada, Western European countries, Japan, Australia and New Zealand. There is consensus that access to the wires of these businesses ought to be on an equal, transparent and fair basis. We also discuss arrangements that have been provided to accommodate this.

As we shall see in Section 2, the transmission sector's restructuring has resulted in fairly varied providers. These range from stand-alone transmission companies to those that still are part of the vertically integrated utility (VIU) model. We also explore the variation and evolution of the ownership of transmission businesses. In Section 3, we examine the current condition of the power distribution business. As in the transmission case, we focus on the extent of unbundling, access arrangements, and ownership status of distribution businesses. We provide concluding remarks in Section 4.

2 Power Transmission

Industry structure
Transmission services are provided by a variety of industry structures around the world. In the developed world, due to massive restructuring in the power industry since the early 1990s intended to change the power supply business, bold experiments are underway in transmission market designs. To understand the changes it is helpful to consider the traditional organization of the power industry, in which utilities held monopolies on the supply and delivery of power to retail customers. Conventionally, the local utility supplied most of its power from on-system generation. Thus, the traditional structure for the electric

utility industry consisted of VIUs that owned and operated the system.[1] Power supply and transmission were planned jointly to contain, if not minimize, their combined cost.

In an effort to foster bulk power market competition, in recent years policy makers have mandated the provision of unbundled transmission services to market participants, such as power wholesalers.[2] Other restructuring initiatives such as retail competition have broadened the demand for these services. Many transmission systems are now operated by agents who are independent of system ownership.

The call for independent transmission operation arose from policy makers' concerns that transmission service providers (TSPs) might use their market power to favor their generation affiliates. Various initiatives have resulted in different types of independent transmission providers (ITPs) that provide objective transport services in the developed world. We can classify ITPs that have emerged through these efforts in one of four categories. In some jurisdictions, such as England and Norway, specialized independent transmission companies (ITCs) or 'transcos' own and operate the system and are independent of market participants.[3] These are stand-alone transmission, mostly private, for-profit companies and constitute one type of ITP. In much of North America today, an alternative structure prevails in which the power business is divided between relatively passive transmission asset owners (TOs) and independent system operators (ISOs).[4] The ISOs, which constitute the second type of ITP, are the point of contact with system users and administer tariffs that include compensation to the TOs for their ownership of assets and any other services that they provide. ISOs typically own only control center facilities and purchase many operation, maintenance and administrative (OM&A) services from the TOs. ISOs are often public agencies. Some system operators provide their services on a for-profit basis. We shall call such companies 'gridcos', which are the third type of ITPs. These function in much the same way as ISOs by being neutral transmission service coordinators, independent of any market participants. Due to the ongoing transformation of the power industry, a fourth ITP, which is hybrid in nature, has also come into existence. This form of ITP is still affiliated with a VIU or a market player, but is functionally independent of its market partner or parent company. It can be characterized as an affiliate or subsidiary, and is required by law or regulation to conduct its business independently of the other energy businesses with which it is associated. We call this the functionally independent operator (FIO). It can be considered an intermediate case between the ITC model and the VIU. Table 23.1 summarizes the types of TSP that exist currently.

Given these general classifications, we detail below the structures, ownerships and related characteristics of transmission services that have emerged and are still evolving in various jurisdictions of developed countries. In particular, we provide an overview of the systems in North America, encompassing the US and Canadian power markets; Europe, focusing on the systems that have developed in most of the original European Union (EU) member countries and Norway;[5] and the Pacific region by spotlighting the systems of Japan, Australia and New Zealand.

North America

United States
Most power transmission services of US electric utilities are under the jurisdiction of the Federal Energy Regulatory Commission (FERC) in Washington.[6] Like other

Table 23.1 Classification of transmission service providers (TSPs)

TSP type	Independent from market participants	Own transmission system	Operate transmission system	Operate as a for-profit or non-profit
Vertically integrated utilities (VIUs)	No	Yes	Yes	For-profit[1]
Independent transmission companies (ITCs)/Transcos	Yes	Yes	Yes	For-profit[1]
Independent system operators (ISOs)	Yes	No	Yes	Non-profit
Gridcos	Yes	No	Yes	For-profit
Functionally independent company (FIO)	Yes[2]	Yes	Yes	For-profit[1]

Notes:
1. Most major VIUs and ITCs in the developed world are investor owned or corporatized public companies.
2. This is the case in theory; in practice it is an empirical question.

Washington regulatory agencies, the FERC has devoted a great deal of time and effort in the last 20 years to the promotion of competition in segments of its jurisdictional industries where competition is feasible.[7]

In 1992, the US Congress passed the National Energy Act. Since a continuation of vertical integration was deemed to be an obstacle to the development of competitive bulk power markets, Title VII of the Act required open access to the interstate power transmission system. The FERC, as the chief regulator of US power transmission, was charged with implementing this. However, it encountered many challenges in its efforts since it has limited legal authority to compel vertically integrated investor-owned utilities (IOUs) to restructure in ways that would create ITCs.

Faced with a situation where utilities unwilling to restructure could deviate from good transmission operating practices in pursuit of power market advantages,[8] the FERC designed alternative arrangements that did not require radical restructuring. It used the federal government's Public Utility Regulatory Policies Act (PURPA)[9] to encourage vertically integrated utilities to purchase more power from independent producers. In the 1996 decision Order No. 888,[10] it required transmission utilities to offer unbundled transmission service pursuant to a standard open access transmission tariff (OATT) and to provide transmission service under the same terms that they offer to their own generators. The FERC has since revised Order 888 to strengthen open access to transmission networks under Order 890, which became effective in mid-2007.[11]

Structural separations between generation and transmission could, in principle, have been urged by some of the 50 state governments and the District of Columbia. Most states, however, have not encouraged any type of unbundling. Many states that have prompted retail competition have not required separation. In these states, which include Connecticut, Illinois, Ohio, Maryland, Michigan, New Jersey, Pennsylvania, and Texas, utilities have typically transferred their generating plants to unregulated affiliates. Only two transcos have yet been established. It follows from this history that most owners of US transmission facilities are still extensively involved in power generation.

Independence is by no means the only complication the FERC has encountered in its efforts to unbundle power transmission. For instance, the service territories of most US utility companies have traditionally been limited to parts of just one state.[12] While some consolidation of the industry has occurred in recent years – most notably, the merger of American Electric Power and Central & Southwest – ownership of the US power transmission grid is still highly balkanized. Long-distance shipments of power can then potentially involve serious coordination problems for affected utilities and sizable transaction costs for shippers. Long-distance shippers in the early days of open access sometimes paid charges to multiple TOs along the contract path, a phenomenon called 'rate pancaking'.

The traditional balkanization of service territories has also meant that the US transmission system was not designed to support large-volume, long-distance power flows. The capacity to deliver power between regions is in some cases limited, and this can accentuate regional bulk power price disparities. Bulk power prices can be especially high in certain load 'pockets' in which the power generation industry is not competitively structured and the ability of power trade to provide price relief is limited.

In 1999, FERC Order 2000[13] responded to this challenge by encouraging utilities to place their transmission assets under the control of regional transmission organizations

(RTOs) that would be independent of power market participants. RTOs would be responsible for both the day-to-day operation and the longer-term investment decisions of the transmission systems in their region. They would establish the terms of transmission service and serve as the point of contact between the utility and other shippers.

The FERC did not mandate a particular approach to RTO organization. In fact, it explicitly indicated openness to a range of organizational structures that included ISOs, transcos, and 'hybrid' structures in which one or more subordinate transcos operated under the direction of an ISO. Proposals to establish RTOs were approved for the Midwest Independent Transmission System Operator (MISO) in 2001, the PJM Interconnection in 2002, ISO New England in 2004, and the Southwest Power Pool in 2005. All of these organizations are non-profit ISOs. Such ISOs are also operating with FERC blessing in California, New York, and Texas. The FERC has, additionally, sanctioned the establishment within ISOs of for-profit Transcos that lack the scale and scope to be RTOs. Such companies have been allowed to perform certain functions that the RTO would otherwise perform.

While non-profit ISOs are ubiquitous, the Commission has retained some interest in for-profit system operators. In 2001, for example, it conditionally approved the establishment of GridSouth, a gridco that would operate transmission systems in the Carolinas.[14] In 2002, the FERC conditionally approved the establishment of Grid Florida, a company that would operate the transmission systems of some Florida TOs and acquire and operate the systems of others in exchange for a passive ownership interest. These initiatives faltered after the general idea of an RTO performing the functions expected by the FERC, including the management of power markets, proved unpopular in the southeast.

Since the FERC has not mandated RTO participation, the transmission systems in several areas of the United States are still operated by TOs subject to the guidelines in FERC Order 888, now revised under Order 890. The affected regions are the southeastern, southwestern, Rocky Mountain, and northwestern states, as well as Alaska and Hawaii. Virtually all of the TOs in these states have continued their extensive involvement in generation. We can thus conclude that most transmission service in the US is provided by VIUs while some transmission service is provided by ISOs.

Canada

Unlike the case in the United States, regulation of Canada's electric transmission utilities occurs chiefly at the provincial level. In addition, power transmission service in Canada is provided chiefly by provincially owned utilities, except in Alberta, Nova Scotia and Prince Edward Island where IOUs own most transmission assets. The former provinces, however, have moved to make these utilities operate more like IOUs. The resultant corporatized utilities have been subject to increasingly close oversight by provincial regulators.

Policy makers in most Canadian provinces have in recent years required TSPs to offer unbundled transmission services. These efforts have been motivated in part by a desire to promote power market competition and in part by a desire to facilitate exports to the US by conforming to FERC guidelines for transmission utilities laid forth in Order 888 and other decisions. Prior to these unbundling initiatives, all of the larger TSPs were also extensively involved in power generation, which has inevitably led to concerns about independence. The provinces have pursued different solutions to this challenge.

Alberta   Transmission services in Alberta were for many years provided by a trio of vertically integrated IOUs. After a provincial initiative to promote power market competition, all three of these companies continued to own and operate generating plants in the province. However, one company spun off its sizable transmission system and thus created an independent transmission utility, AltaLink, in 2002 (Alberta Energy and Utilities Board, 2002). Another company established a specialized transmission subsidiary, EPCOR Transmission. The province established a power pool and engaged a for-profit entity, ESBI, for several years to be Alberta's 'transmission administrator'. Both functions have since been provided by a non-profit ISO, the Alberta Electric System Operator. The TOs are thus passive but continue to perform many OM&A functions (Alberta Energy, 2003).

British Columbia   Transmission service in British Columbia was provided by the vertically integrated crown corporation BC Hydro for many years. In 2003, British Columbia Transmission Corporation (BCTC) was established as an independent and provincially owned company to provide transmission services. It was also set up to operate, maintain, plan, and direct any needed expansion of BC Hydro's high-voltage grid. While BCTC owns control centers and certain other system operation assets, BC Hydro owns the grid (BCTC, 2003).

Manitoba   In Manitoba, generation and transmission service has for many years been provided by a vertically integrated crown corporation, Manitoba Hydro. An unbundled transmission tariff was first established in 1997. Currently, Manitoba Hydro offers service under an OATT administered by the Midwest ISO (MISO) (Manitoba Hydro, 2008).

New Brunswick   In New Brunswick, transmission services were for many years provided by a vertically integrated crown corporation, New Brunswick Power. An OATT was approved for the company in 2003. The transmission assets have since been transferred to a specialized subsidiary, New Brunswick Power Transmission. This company performs many OM&A functions, but tariff design and implementation are now undertaken by a new non-profit ISO called the New Brunswick System Operator, which came into existence in 2004 (New Brunswick System Operator, 2004).

Newfoundland and Labrador   Power transmission service in Newfoundland and Labrador is provided chiefly by two VIUs: Newfoundland and Labrador Hydro, a crown corporation, and Newfoundland Power, an IOU. These companies do not trade with the United States and power transmission is not separately regulated (Newfoundland and Labrador Board of Commissioners of Public Utilities, 2007).

Nova Scotia   In Nova Scotia, power transmission services are still provided by a vertically integrated IOU, Nova Scotia Power Inc. An OATT was approved for the company in 2005. The company operates the grid and administers the tariff (Nova Scotia Utility and Review Board, 2007).

Ontario   In Ontario a crown corporation, Ontario Hydro, provided most of the generation and transmission services in the province for many years. The province undertook a radical restructuring in late 1998. Subsequently, it placed power transmission operations in a provincially owned power delivery utility, Hydro One Networks in 2000. Hydro One is a large power distributor but is unaffiliated with any generating company. However, the province, which owns 100 percent of Hydro One, still owns extensive generation capacity in Ontario. Hydro One owns 97 percent of the province's transmission system and one-third of its distribution system[15] (Hydro One Networks, 2007). The Ontario power grid is now operated by a non-profit ISO called the Independent Market Operator (Independent Electricity System Operators, 2007).

Quebec In Quebec, transmission service was for many years provided by a vertically integrated crown corporation, Hydro-Quebec. In 1997, transmission assets were transferred to an affiliated company, Hydro-Quebec TransEnergie (Hydro-Québec TransÉnergie, 2007). This company provides unbundled transmission services under an OATT.[16]

Prince Edward Island Transmission service on Prince Edward Island is provided by Maritime Electric, a vertically integrated IOU (Island Regulatory and Appeals Commission, 2005).

Saskatchewan In Saskatchewan, transmission services have for many years been provided by SaskPower, a vertically integrated crown corporation. In 2001, the province introduced wholesale power competition and SaskPower began to provide transmission services to wholesale suppliers. The company now provides unbundled power transmission services under an OATT (SaskPower, 2007).

Table 23.2 shows the current status of the power transmission industry in Canada.

Europe

To examine power market developments in Western European countries, we discuss efforts they have undertaken through internal initiatives and EU-mandated programs. The latter, aimed at reforming national markets and expanding interstate trade, have had a profound effect on electricity market structures in Europe. EU mandates have been motivated by the wish to ensure efficiency and lower energy prices, and by the objective of establishing a single European power market. The European Commission has adopted two major directives thus far, and is currently preparing a third and final directive.

The first EU directive, 96/92/EC, sought among other things to unbundle the competitive segments of electricity production and retailing from the monopoly businesses of transmission and distribution. In particular, it required accounting unbundling whereby a utility had to keep separate accounts on all its activities including generation, transmission, distribution, and retailing to prevent cross-subsidization and promote wholesale competition. It also required access to both the transmission and distribution networks to be non-discriminatory. Network access regimes based on negotiated third-party access (TPA)[17] or regulated TPA were required to meet this provision. Under the former, consumers and suppliers must negotiate access to the network with the system operator. Under the latter, on the other hand, the network operator had an obligation to provide access based on published tariffs without any sort of bilateral arrangements. Member countries had to adopt these provisions by passing enabling legislation.[18]

Table 23.2 Summary of Canadian transmission service providers (TSPs)

Province	Number of TSPs	Ownership	Utility owner type	System operator
Alberta	3	IOUs	1 ITC, 2 VIUs	ISO
British Columbia	1	Provincial	Gridco	Gridco
Manitoba	1	Provincial	VIU	ISO
New Brunswick	1	Provincial	ISO	ISO
Newfoundland and Labrador	2	IOU & Provincial	VIUs	VIUs
Nova Scotia	1	IOU	VIUs	VIU
Ontario	1	Provincial	T&D[1]	ISO
Quebec	1	Provincial	FIO[2]	FIO[2]
Prince Edwards Island	1	IOU	VIU	VIU
Saskatchewan	1	Provincial	VIU	VIU[3]

Notes:
1. T&D = Transmission and distribution company.
2. FIO = Functionally independent transmission operator.
3. Provides unbundled TX service.

548

The second EU directive, 2003/54/EC,[19] had similar goals but required stronger unbundling commitments and TPA to networks, independent regulators, and measures to strength market integration. In particular, it required legal as well as accounting unbundling of transmission from generation. The additional requirement of legal unbundling called for a *separate* network company for the grid in order to strengthen non-discriminatory access. The same requirement was set out for distribution so that the network company becomes legally independent and able to make decisions uninfluenced by affiliated competitive business interests. Exemptions from legal unbundling were provided for small distributors. TPA rules to the networks were fortified by requiring systems for network access to be non-discriminatory and applicable to all customers. Member countries had to comply with these provisions by July 2007 at the latest. During this round, the Commission also implemented the binding EC Regulation No. 1228/2003, which provided rules of interconnection access and tariffs to promote cross-country trade and interconnection expansion.

The third EU effort is still being finalized as of June 2009 but seeks to strengthen security of supply and 'fair' consumer prices.[20] Towards these ends, it proposes to require not just legal or functional unbundling of network assets but also ownership unbundling. Alternatively, if a utility chooses not to divest its grid, then the Commission proposes to transfer the operation of the grid to an independent transmission system operator (ISO). All investors will need to comply with this requirement. To ensure that the goal of a single market is realized, it also proposes to set up a European Network for Transmission System Operators that will develop common commercial and technical codes and security standards. Further, to strength TPA and increase market transparency, it proposes to make information on network operation and supply accessible to all on an equal basis. It also proposes to establish an Agency for the Cooperation of National Energy Regulators, empowered to make binding decisions on cross-border trade to facilitate the development of a single European market. Related to this, it plans to propose measures that will assure independence of all national regulators.

Using this backdrop, next we examine developments in the transmission industry of individual countries. We look at acts and legislations that have been passed either in response to or in anticipation of the EU directives as well as the transmission systems that have resulted from them.

Austria

Directive 96/92/EC was implemented in 1998 by the Electricity Industry and Organization Act (EIWOG). The EIWOG has been amended several times since 1998. One of its main stipulations was the reorganization and authorization of three existing transmission areas, East Austria, Tirol and Voralberg provinces, by defining the responsibilities of 'control area managers' for each. Three majority publicly owned power companies, Verbund, TIWAG and VKW, were set up as transmission system operators of the three areas. Since EIWOG and its amendments have adopted both EU directives, the transmission systems have been both accounting and legally unbundled (European Commission Directorate-General for Energy and Transport, 2005).

The Austrian transmission system is mainly under public ownership.[21] The system does not strictly fit the ISO model since the system operators are not market neutral public entities; they can, however, be classified as FIOs. The type of unbundling under which they operate can be considered as an intermediate step to creating an ITC that is publicly owned; when and if the third EU directive succeeds in effecting ownership unbundling from market participants, the system can be considered to be run by public ITCs. At present, the system is supposed to run on a neutral basis.[22] The EIWOG has been updated to adopt regulated TPA and regulated access to interconnectors (Energie-Control GmbH, 2007).

Belgium

A federal law passed in 1999 adopted EU Directive 96/92/EC. The law set conditions to ensure non-discriminatory regulated TPA. In order to implement the unbundling requirement in the directive, the law also called for an appointment of a transmission system operator (TSO). Initially the law required that the TSO be a major market participant with a market share of at least 75 percent covering at least two-thirds of the three regions of Flanders, the Brussels-Capital Region and Wallonia. The major generation operator, Electrabel, was the only one qualified and thus appointed as a TSO under the new name of Elia.[23] At the time, Electrabel had a 64 percent share in Elia, the second biggest generator SPE had a 7 percent share, and the remaining 30 percent were owned by municipal utilities. In order to ensure the independence of the TSO, so that it fulfills the objective of providing non-discriminatory TPA, Electrabel and SPE were obligated to reduce their shares in the transmission system. After some delay due to unfavorable market conditions, the two companies sold their shares in 2005 so that their combined ownership was reduced to 30 percent. Private investors acquired 40 percent of the shares and the municipal utilities kept 30 percent (IEA, 2005).

As a result, Belgium went further than required by the first directive by instituting both accounting and legal unbundling of transmission from market participants. Belgium adopted the second EU directive by passing another energy law in 2005. This law strengthened the independence of the TSO by requiring that its board of directors be non-executives of the transmission company and that half of them hold no management function within it or any of its subsidiaries. Since Belgium had already initiated legal unbundling and instituted regulated and strong non-discriminatory TPA following the first EU directive, it had already met most of the provisions led out under the second EU directive (European Commission Directorate-General for Energy and Transport, 2005).

In order to comply with both the 2003 EU directive and regulation on fair and transparent interconnector allocation, the regulators of Belgium and France have formulated both explicit and implicit auction methods to provide access to cross-border interconnection capacity. Under their scheme, monthly and annual allocations will be based on direct auctions, whereas daily allocations will be based on implicit allocation; implicit allocation prices capacity based on the difference of power prices on each side of the border. Belgian regulators intend to adopt this form of implicit auction to allocate interconnection capacity for trade with Dutch utilities as well (IEA, 2005).

Denmark

The Danish government implemented the 1996 EU directive by passing the Act on Supply of Electricity in 1999. This act required legal unbundling of the networks from market players, which went beyond the requirement of accounting unbundling set out by the 1996 directive and, in fact, fulfilled the provisions for this set out in the 2003 directive.

The government amended this law in 2004 to strengthen functional unbundling. It set rules prohibiting managers of network operators, particularly executives, from playing any role in companies directly or indirectly affiliated with any generation or retailing activities. In order to meet the conditions of non-discriminatory TPA, the law also required the network companies to prepare programs on how to achieve this (European Commission Directorate-General for Energy and Transport, 2005). Currently, TPA is regulated rather than provided by negotiation.

At the time of the 2004 amendment there were 11 transmission companies, two of which ran the high-voltage grids of 400 kV in Denmark and nine of which ran regional networks with 132/150 kV and 60 kV. Because of calls for functional unbundling, the two high-voltage grids, Eltra amba and Elkraft Transmission, merged to form the publicly owned Energinet.dk.[24] This high-voltage network has further been ownership unbundled. The regional transmission operators meet the legal and functional unbundling required by the 2004 law (ibid.). They are also largely owned by, and thus can be classified as, distribution network companies (International Energy Regulation Network, 2006). Based on ownership unbundling, the high-voltage Danish transmission fits the transco/ITC model.

Interconnection capacities are managed by Energinet.dk along with other Nordic and German transmission operators in line with EU regulation on cross-border trade.[25] Congestion is managed using market-based instruments, mainly implicit and explicit auctions (Danish Energy Regulatory Authority, 2007).

Finland

Market reforms were initiated in 1995 before the 1996 EU directive came into effect. The reforms resulted in the legal unbundling of transmission from generation in 1997. The Finnish transmission network is owned and operated by Fingrid, which is 88 percent privately owned and 12 percent state owned (European Commission Directorate-General for Energy and Transport, 2005). In addition, there are 13 regional transmission companies required to comply with legal unbundling, which are owned by both the private sector and municipalities (International Energy Regulation Network, 2007a). As in the Danish case, these can largely be viewed as distribution companies. Currently, Fingrid has no generation or retail affiliates and is only engaged in the business of transmission. Thus, the Finnish transmission system is ownership separated and fits the transco/ITC model.

Even though such a market neutral transmission system has been set up, the electricity regulator has set out guidelines so that grid owners and operators comply with non-discriminatory access to the network by third parties. The guidelines standardize the non-discriminatory actions to be taken by the networks. The standards include the separation of the management of the grid from the management of any market participating affiliate; equitable customer treatment through consistent contracts, metering, accurate invoicing, and providing access to the grid in return for service payment; appropriate and safe customer data handling; and annual reporting of compliance measures taken (Energy Market Authority, 2006).

The rules for interconnection set out in the second EU directive and EU Regulation 1228/2003 were enacted by the amendments to the Electricity Market Act. Based on these, the Electricity Market Regulator was put in charge of overseeing compliance with access and tariff setting for interconnection. Finland further amended congestion management rules for cross-border trade in 2006 based on the EU guidelines. The implicit auction used by the transmission owner for trade in the Nord Pool was deemed to satisfy the coordination of market operations and fair allocation rules set out in the 2006 amendments (Energy Market Authority, 2007).

France

Law 2000-108, the '2000 Law', split the management of the transmission system of the state owned vertically integrated utility Electricité de France (EDF) from those of generation and retailing in order to meet the mandate of the 1996 EU directive[26] (European Commission Directorate-General for Energy and Transport, 2005). It also stated that internal accounts of transmission activities must be kept distinct to prevent cross-subsidization of competitive activities using revenues earned from captive customers.[27]

Since 2000, France has passed several pieces of legislation to further liberalize the electricity market. In 2004 it passed Law 2004-803, the '2004 Law', which adopted the 2003 EU directive. Specifically, it created a separate entity, Réseau de transport de l'électricité (RTE) to run the transmission system of EDF and thereby met the provision for legal unbundling. In their article on the effect of the reform of the French electricity sector, Glachant and Finon (2005) characterize the successive French laws passed in 2000, 2003, and 2004 to implement the EU directives as 'a typical case of reform without industrial restructuring of the dominant operator' (p. 181). They indicate, however, that RTE, which operates as an internal department of EDF, is guaranteed independence in its investment and pricing by the regulator. To ensure independence, RTE must prepare and submit to the regulator a compliance report on measures it adopts to prevent discriminatory access (European Commission Directorate-General for Energy and Transport, 2005). The French transmission system, thus, typifies an FIO model.

EDF is the largest power exporter in Europe. This is facilitated by the absence of any or very limited congestion on RTE's interconnections (Glachant and Finon, 2005). The IEA's 2004 report on the French energy industry indicates that the interconnection capacities of RTE with its neighbors range from 1300 MW with Spain to 4300 MW with Germany. RTE is also interconnected with Belgian, Italian, Swiss, and UK transmission systems. It determined the allocation and prices of interconnection with the UK's National Grid through an explicit auction, with Italy's GRTN based on negotiated agreements, with Belgium's Elia based on a 'priority list', and with Germany's and Spain's grid operators based on implicit auctions (IEA, 2004). The interconnection arrangements with Belgium have been remedied since 2005; capacity and prices are now allocated through auctions. In addition, explicit auctions are in effect on the interconnector with Germany since 2005 and with Spain since 2006 (Commission de Régulation de l'Énergie, 2006).

Germany

To implement EU Directive 96/92/EC, Germany passed the Energy Act of 1998. This initiated the liberalization of the German electricity industry by requiring retail choice for all customers, accounting unbundling, and negotiated TPA. Accounting unbundling was aimed at increasing system transparency and reducing the extent of vertical integration in order to foster competitive markets. The German provision for this stipulation was, however, ineffectively administered and did not really restrict vertical integration (Brunekreeft and Twelemann, 2005).

At the time of the 1998 Energy Act, the German electricity sector was two-tiered. The first tier consisted of a small number of VIUs (*Verbundunternehmen*), which owned and operated the transmission network and most of the country's generation.[28] The second tier was composed of about 950 small municipally owned distribution utilities (*Stadtwerke*). Following the Energy Act of 1998 vertical integration and horizontal concentration increased. The *Verbundunternehmen* acquired distributors and merged their operations with the parent utility to form large vertically integrated utilities (OECD, 2006).

One outcome of this degree of vertical integration has been high transmission charges and possible 'cross-subsidization' of competitive businesses. The low margins of the generation and retailing activities of the *Verbundunternehmen*, where prices for these activities might have been kept low to deter entrance, relative to transmission activities can be cited as evidence (Brunekreeft and Twelemann, 2005).

The Energy Act also instituted negotiated and not regulated TPA, which were to be arranged on the basis of 'association agreements'. The Federal Cartel Office was placed in charge of overseeing that these agreements did not result in discriminatory access arrangements on an *ex post* basis. It was to use the competition laws to examine compliance with equitable access, but these laws were weak and did not ensure effective TPA (OECD, 2006).

Following the EU Directive 2003/54/EC, Germany modified the Energy Act in 2004. The modified version came into effect in 2005[29] with the aim of correcting the weaknesses noted in the earlier version of the law. In keeping with the 2003 EU directive, the revision requires legal and operational, or functional, unbundling for transmission. All VIUs, regardless of the number of customers they serve, must ensure that their transmission systems are run independently of their generation and retail businesses (ibid.).

Lessons from the previous round had made it obvious that accounting unbundling did not prevent vertical integration, cross-subsidization and discriminatory access (Brunekreeft and Twelemann, 2005). The IEA report on Germany's energy policy in 2007 indicates that the ineffective and complex negotiated TPA regime has been replaced with a regulated one. In addition, the legal unbundling of all transmission operation has been finalized (IEA, 2007a). Currently, the four large utilities, E.ON Netz, RWE Transportnetz, EnBW Tranportnetze and Vattenfall Europe Transmission, run the transmission system over four control areas. They are mostly owned by private interests, although the federal states and local governments hold some stake in them (International Energy Regulation Network, 2008a). Since the high-voltage network is operated by entities that have been unbundled, legally and in accounting terms, the German transmission system most closely fits the FIO model.

Germany's transmission grid is interconnected with those of its neighbors.[30] Currently, there is 15 to 17 GW of interconnection capacity that represents about 16 percent of total grid capacity. This exceeds the EU's recommended level of 10 percent cross-border capacity. Despite this excess, the interconnection capacity is congested most of the time with Denmark, the Netherlands and the Czech Republic but not with Austria. Since there is almost no congestion internally, the cross-border tight capacity probably reflects congestion that is pushed to the borders. Congestion charges are market based and thus meet the EU's guideline on fair interconnection access. Access is allocated to users on all borders based on an explicit auction on a use-it-or-lose-it basis (IEA, 2007a).

Ireland

The passage of the Electricity Regulation Act in 1999 initiated electricity market liberalization in Ireland. Ireland then passed the European Communities (Internal Market in Electricity) Regulations in 2000 to implement the 1996 EU directive. These regulations ordered that the management of transmission and distribution become independent from generation and retail management. They put the regulator in charge of monitoring this unbundling and the implementation of Codes of Good Conduct by the newly unbundled transmission and distribution networks[31] (European Commission Directorate-General for Energy and Transport, 2005).

At the time of the adoption of the first EU directive, Ireland had one public electric utility, the Electricity Supply Board (ESB), which owned the entire transmission and distribution grids. It was also the dominant generator and supplier. Per the 2000 Regulations, the transmission grid was accounting and management unbundled, and was put under a ring-fenced unit of ESB, ESB National Grid. Following legal unbundling, initiated in 2001 and fully completed in 2006, EirGrid took over the running of the transmission grid; ESB is the transmission asset owner while EirGrid, a state-owned entity, became the transmission system operator[32] (IEA, 2007b). To ensure its independence, EirGrid had to execute an 'Infrastructure Agreement' with ESB and was explicitly prohibited from providing cross-subsidies under its licensing agreement (European Commission Directorate-General for Energy and Transport, 2005). Therefore, the transmission system of Ireland most closely fits the FIO model with an ISO.

The Republic of Ireland has interconnectors with Northern Ireland, which has a capacity of 330 MW. Capacity on this interconnection is allocated through auctions supervised by the Commission for Energy Regulation (CER) in Ireland. With the planned all-island expansion of the power market to include Northern Ireland, under the Single Electricity Market, the construction of another interconnection between the two areas has been approved. In addition, there are plans to build interconnection with Britain (Commission for Energy Regulation, 2007).

Italy

The first EU directive was implemented through Decree 79/1999 (the electricity decrees), which required accounting and administrative unbundling of each activity that a utility engaged in. To ensure that such unbundling was carried out, companies were required to submit detailed data on each activity to the Regulator, Autorità per l'Energia Electtrica e il Gas (AEEG). Part of the motivation for this sort of unbundling was to avoid cross-subsidization[33] (European Commission Directorate-General for Energy and Transport, 2005).

The 1999 electricity decrees also required the legal unbundling of generation, transmission, and retail activities of the major Italian utility, ENEL. Thus transmission was legally unbundled in addition to being accounting unbundled. Its operations were placed under the state-owned entity GRTN (Gestore della Rete di Trasmissione Nazionale) while it was owned by TERNA SPA, a subsidiary of the ENEL group; this is the ISO model. Based on a decree in 2003, the ownership and operation of the national transmission system was unified when TERNA SPA and GRTN merged in 2005; this is the FIO model.[34] As of 2007, private entities that take a stake in TERNA are not allowed to have more than 20 percent of the company's share if they have any direct or indirect connection to generation and retail activities[35] (ibid.).

Following the unbundling of transmission, the AEEG established guidelines for TPA access to the grid under a Grid Code, which set out conditions for non-discriminatory access to ensure impartial transmission and dispatching services to all users. In addition, TERNA SPA was required to adopt a compliance program that details internal guidelines for its personnel so that they do not engage in discriminatory behaviors. The company was also prohibited from providing more than 5 percent voting rights to any stakeholder who is a market participant (ibid.).

Italy's transmission system is interconnected with those of France, Switzerland, Austria and Slovenia. Italy imports more power from these countries than it exports. The total interconnection capacity with these countries, 90 percent of which was with France and Switzerland, was 6000 MWs in 2000 and reached almost 10 percent of the minimum interconnection capacity recommended by the European Commission. Since there was congestion on the cross-border links, AEEG set capacity allocation on a pro rata basis; the proportion of capacity made available was fixed based on an operator's capacity not exceeding 10 percent of total available capacity. Unused capacity was then sold through tenders, or offers to supply (IEA, 2003a).

Since 2003 the Ministry of Productive Activities (MAP) has been entrusted with designing methods to allocate interconnection capacity. In 2005, MAP established the implicit auction method as a means of allocating such capacity. In keeping with the provisions of EU Regulation 1228/2003, the implicit auction method enables interconnection capacity to be allocated using non-discriminatory market- rather than transaction-based standards. It also provides economic signals both to interconnection users and transmission system operators (AEEG, 2005 and 2007).

The Netherlands

The Netherlands passed the Electricity Act of 1998 in order to adopt EU Directive 96/55/EC. The 1998 Act went beyond the requirement of account unbundling and implemented legal unbundling of the networks by compelling the owners of networks to set up independent network units or companies[36] (van Dame, 2005).

To comply with legal unbundling, the owners of the national transmission network, the Association of Electricity Producing Companies (SEP), established TenneT in 1998 as the independent network operator. Initially, the state acquired 51 percent ownership in TenneT. The Office of Energy Regulation (DTe) had the responsibility of ensuring non-discriminatory access to all the network grids. Concerns that SEP was abusing its dominant position by providing discriminatory access to the grid eventually led the state to fully acquire TenneT in 2001. TenneT then became the state-owned and -regulated transmission operator (ibid.). It was prohibited from providing services or taking ownership interests that compromise non-discriminatory TPA (European Commission Directorate-General for Energy and Transport, 2005). In 2006, TenneT acquired the shares of the transmission grid from the Dutch government and assumed the legal ownership of the national transmission grid (TenneT, 2006).

At the time TenneT was established, the Dutch system was interconnected with

Belgium, with a capacity of 1150 MW, and Germany, with a capacity of 2200 MW. The Netherlands tends to import more from Germany than it exports to it, while electricity flows with Belgium are more balanced. Capacity for such exchanges is made available through explicit auctions for year-ahead and month-ahead transactions (Office of Energy Regulation, 2006).[37] These market-based allocations have thus enabled the Netherlands to meet non-discriminatory cross-border access provisions set out in EU Regulation 1228/2003.[38]

Norway

The Energy Act of 1990 initiated electricity sector reforms long before the EU directives for internal energy market restructuring were formulated. The act separated grid operations from competitive activities by instituting separate financial reporting for each activity. The goals for such unbundling included cost reductions in energy provision through competition, elimination of cross-subsidization among consumer groups, and inducement of efficient investment in the industry. Its consequences have included ownership unbundling of transmission, account unbundling of distribution from retail, the institution of non-discriminatory TPA to all the network grids in the country, and the establishment of a Norwegian power pool that later became Nord Pool (Rothwell and Gomez, 2003).

At the time of the act, Norway's generation, transmission and distribution were under state, county and municipal ownership. The major state-owned energy company, Statkraft, owned the country's high-voltage transmission assets. When the act came into effect in 1991, Statkraft divested the transmission assets. These came under the ownership of a separate state company, Statnett SF. Statnett remains a state-owned transmission system owner and operator. It owns 80 percent of the nation's transmission assets while regional grid companies own the rest. In its capacity as the system operator, Statnett rents additional capacity from the regional grid companies and is responsible for system dispatch, ancillary services and grid interconnection management. The act set up system operation guidelines that detailed grid users' rights to receive and Statnett's obligation to provide non-discriminatory access to the grid based on tariffs established by NVE (ibid.). The transmissions system of Norway thus falls under the ITC model that is publicly owned.

Based on the rules set out in the Energy Act, interconnection capacity is allocated through implicit auctions. Statnett determines maximum capacity that is available for cross-border day-ahead trade and provides that information for publication at the Nord Pool (ibid.). Border tariffs among countries in the Nord Pool have been eliminated, but cross-border transmission capacity constraints remain. While there is considerable need for investment in this and other types of transmission capacity in the Nord Pool area, reluctance among regulators and ineffective interconnection capacity coordination by the TSOs have limited such investment (von der Fehr et al., 2005). Therefore, Statnett's provision of adequate cross-border interconnection capacity at Norwegian borders, as envisaged by EU Regulation 1228/2003, is still important for market integration.

Portugal

Following the first EU directive, the Portuguese government adopted a new legal framework for the energy sector, which did not institute any type of unbundling. Entidade

Riguladora dos Servicos Energeticos (ERSE), the energy regulator, however, adopted regulatory codes that introduced accounting unbundling. In particular, ERSE Codes on Tariffs and Commercial Relations established accounting unbundling and required integrated utilities to set up codes of conduct to ensure independence of managers of different activities (European Commission Directorate-General for Energy and Transport, 2005).

The government subsequently passed a new law, number 29, in 2006 to adopt the second EU directive (Energy Services Regulatory Authority, 2006). Going beyond this law's requirement, the transmission system was ownership separated from the Energias de Portugal Group, the dominant generation company in Portugal, and became the system operator under the name of Rede Electrica Nacional (REN). The state owns 20 percent of its shares and other private players own the rest (International Energy Regulation Network, 2007d). The Portuguese transmission system is thus a classic transco/ITC.

ERSE has a separate code, Regulation on the Access to the Networks and Interconnection, to ensure fair treatment of all market participants. Since both the transmission and distribution network companies must abide by this code, the regulator has effectively put regulated TPA in place (European Commission Directorate-General for Energy and Transport, 2005).

The Portuguese transmission system is interconnected with the Spanish system. In 2006, the interconnection capacity between the two countries averaged around 1100 MW.[39] Until mid-2007, the transmission system operator, REN, managed interconnection congestion on a pro rata basis, whereby a reduction factor was applied to cross-border flow based on the ratio of the flow relative to available capacity. Since July 2007, an increasing amount of the interconnection capacity between Portugal and Spain has been allocated through explicit auctions based on the principles of EU Regulation 1228/2003[40] (Energy Services Regulatory Authority, 2006).

Spain

The laws governing the electricity sector were overhauled when Spain passed the Electricity Law of 1997. This law adopted the provisions of accounting unbundling and fair TPA called for by the first EU directive. It mandated both the accounting and legal separation of monopoly activities from competitive ones immediately (Rothwell and Gomez, 2003).

The main Spanish transmission system owner and operator, Red Electrica de Espana (REE), has been in existence since 1984. Created by the Spanish government, initially it was under state ownership, but the government has since divested a large part of its stake in the company. At present, about 30 percent of the firm's shares are owned by a public company, about 10 percent are owned by the four large Spanish generating companies, and about 60 percent are traded on the Spanish stock market. REE owns 98 percent of the 400 kV high-voltage grid and most of the 220 kV medium-voltage grid (Crampes and Fabra, 2005). REE has been ownership unbundled since its inception and thus the unbundling provisions of the 1997 law do not apply to it.[41] The law, however, made it the official system operator of the grid and revoked its role as a market operator (Rothwell and Gomez, 2003).

A 1998 version of the law guaranteed non-discriminatory access to the networks by all companies. It obligated all grid operators to provide access to the networks in an objective and transparent manner. As a result, access to all the grids, including the distribution networks, is subject to regulated TPA (European Commission Directorate-General for Energy and Transport, 2005). In addition, decrees passed in 2000 and 2001 further outlined procedures to enforce access to the transmission grid; it is thus subject to regulated TPA (Crampes and Fabra, 2005).

Historically, interconnection capacity between Spain and its neighbors was mainly built for security of supply. Thus, interconnection capacity is limited, reflecting this fact. Ever since the establishment of the Spanish electricity market in 1998, however, interconnections have played an increasing role in the electricity trade. The interconnection capacity between Spain and France, Portugal, and Morocco was 2.5 percent, 1.7 percent, and 0.8 percent of installed capacity in the early 2000s, respectively[42] (ibid.). Interconnection capacity is allocated through implicit auctions for the day-ahead market and explicit auctions for longer-term bilateral transactions. The interconnection with France is allocated based on a mechanism that the regulators of the two countries set up in 2005. The mechanism provides for explicit auction for day-ahead capacity rights which can be either exercised by the holder of the right or 'sold' to other market participants. This was set up to replace the 'use-it-or-lose-it' mechanism by the 'use-it-or-get-paid-for-it' system. It is more than fully compliant with EU Regulation 1228/2003 (Comision Nacional de Energia, 2007). As of July 2007, interconnection capacity between Spain and Portugal is also allocated based on explicit auctions.

Sweden
Reform efforts in the electricity industry started before the enactment of the first EU directive. In 1992 the government separated generation and retail from network operations at the national level by creating the state-owned transmission company Svenska Kraftnat. The ownership unbundled transmission company was also appointed as the system operator of the national grid[43] (European Commission Directorate-General for Energy and Transport, 2005). It owns and operates the 400 kV and 220 kV power lines. The Swedish transmission system can be classified as an ITC where the transmission owner is the state.

The Swedish electricity system is interconnected with the systems of all the Nordic countries, Germany, and Poland. Interconnection capacity in this highly integrated system is allocated by a market-based mechanism known as 'market splitting'. When cross-border trade flow exceeds capacity, the market is split in eight potential price zones. Capacity is then allocated based on the price difference between the exporting and importing areas.[44] Thus, interconnection capacity allocation meets the rules put forth by EU Regulation 1228/2003 (Energy Markets Inspectorate, 2007).

Synopsis
The most typical transmission system in the EU countries examined above is the ITC, with half under public and half under private ownership. One-third of the transmission systems are FIOs and these are also about half state and half privately owned. Most of the countries also have a single transmission operator or owner, which is not surprising given the natural monopoly nature of the business and the size of the service territories they serve. The presence of four transmission companies in Germany may partly be

explained by its relatively large size, but as in Austria, it is also the artifact of history. Almost all the transmission systems also provide regulated access and allocate interconnection using market-based systems. Table 23.3 presents the current status of the TSPs of these countries. Given the European Commission's desire to create a single internal power market, the next phase of transmission development in these countries is likely to lead to greater integration of these national systems.

Pacific Region

Australia
In the wake of reforms undertaken by various government bodies and commissions, Australia's transmission system has been operating as a national grid. The national character of the grid must be qualified to indicate that it covers the most densely settled eastern and southern parts of the country, including Tasmania;[45] Western Australia and the Northern Territories are not part of the eastern grid since the great distances of their service territories from this grid makes interconnection with it uneconomic.

While the current ownership of the grid is a mix of private and public, prior to the reforms started in the 1990s all transmission assets were owned and operated by the state governments. Save for a few interconnections to ensure reliability, the various systems did not operate on a national basis. All capacity planning, extension and system operation were conducted at the state level. The reference to systems, in addition, indicates that the transmission lines were part of a vertically integrated public electricity grid (ERIG, 2007).

Reforms that have produced the current national grid took place at both the national and state levels, and as a result, the restructuring of the industry has proceeded along different lines. There is currently a process underway to harmonize the system so that it expands, operates and is regulated in a standard fashion. The process was initiated in early 2006, by the Council of Australian Governments (COAG),[46] which established the Energy Reform Implementation Group (ERIG) for this purpose (ibid.).

Developments at the national level   In mid-1991, the heads of the federal and state governments of Australia agreed to set up a National Grid Management Council (NGMC) to examine the status of the electricity grid and plan changes to encourage an 'economically efficient' and 'environmentally sound' electricity industry[47] (Outhred, 1998).

The NGMC prepared a draft proposal, partly based on earlier work of a federal statutory commission, which outlined the restructuring of the industry and laid the foundation for the current structure of electricity transmission.[48] After revisions, the draft proposal was used to develop rules codifying the recommended changes. The result was the National Electricity Code,[49] which was proposed to the Australian Competition and Consumer Commission[50] in 1996 and approved in 1997 (EIA, 1997).

The legal basis for the restructured industry including the National Electricity Code was provided by the National Electricity (South Australia) Act of 1996; it was later revised as the National Electricity Rules of 2005[51] (Outhred, 2007).

At the time of the initial phase of the transition, in the mid-1990s, the states had minimal transmission interconnections; the only interconnections that existed were between New South Wales and Victoria, the Snowy–Victoria interlink with a 1500 MW

Table 23.3 *Current status of European transmission service providers (TSPs)*

Country	Number of main TSPs	Ownership	Extent of unbundling	System operator	TPA access	Interconnection access & tariffs
Austria	3	Public	accounting, legal	FIO	regulated	regulated
Belgium	1	Private	accounting, legal	FIO	regulated	market based
Denmark	1	Public	ownership	ITC	regulated	market based
Finland	1	Private	ownership	ITC	regulated	market based
France	1	Public	accounting, legal	FIO	regulated	market based
Germany	4	Private	accounting, legal	FIO	regulated	market based
Ireland	1	Public	accounting, legal	ISO	regulated	market based
Italy	1	Private	ownership	FIO	regulated	market based
The Netherlands	1	Public	ownership	ITC	regulated	market based
Norway	1	Public	ownership	ITC	regulated	market based
Portugal	1	Private	ownership	ITC	regulated	market based[1]
Spain	1	Private	ownership	ITC	regulated	market based
Sweden	1	Public	ownership	ITC	regulated	market based

Note: 1. Portuguese interconnection capacity allocation is increasingly, though not yet entirely, market based.

capacity;[52] and between South Australia and Victoria, the Heywood interlink, with a 500 MW capacity.[53] In 1993, a 500 MW subsea link, Basslink, was approved between Victoria and Tasmania,[54] but was completed and under operation only in 2006.

There were also plans to establish an interlink between New South Wales and Queensland, and South Australia and New South Wales. The interlink between the first two, QNI with a 1000 MW capacity, was built in 2001. The interconnector between South Australia and New South Wales that was proposed by the government-owned Transgrid was initially approved by the National Electricity Market Management Company (NEMMCO) and the National Electricity Tribunal, where the privately owned Murraylink interconnector had applied for a review of NEMMCO's decision. The approval was finally overturned when the Victoria Supreme Court, siding with Murraylink on some points of the company's appeal, remanded the decision back to the National Electricity Tribunal, which ruled against the project.[55] Currently, the privately owned Murraylink operates as a regulated interconnector between the systems of these two states.

There is another privately owned underground interconnector, Directlink, which connects New South Wales and Queensland. It was built in 2000 and has a 180 MW power rating. It has recently been acquired by Australia's biggest gas pipeline owner and operator, Australian Pipeline Trust (*The Australian*, 2006).

Developments at the state level   In addition to the different paces at which the interconnections needed to advance the development of the national grid were built, the unbundling of the industry and related reforms proceeded at different rates and means in the eastern and southern 'national' market states.

Victoria unbundled the state-owned electricity utility, the State Electricity Commission of Victoria, in 1993 and started privatizing the various segments of the newly restructured utility in 1995. Initially it divided the transmission sector into PowerNet Victoria, which owned the grid, and Victoria Power Exchange, which operated it (EIA, 1997). The state privatized the transmission grid in 1997 when GPU, a US utility, bought it, and in 2000 it became SPI Networks when Singapore Power acquired it (Thomas, 2006). It has been operating as SP AusNet Transmission since 2005.[56] In addition, there is a non-profit shared network transmission services provider in the state called VENCorp. However, it neither owns nor operates any transmission networks.

New South Wales initiated the reform of the state-owned Electricity Commission of New South Wales in 1991, which it renamed Pacific Power. At the time, it restructured Pacific Power into six smaller business entities. In 1995, it unbundled the transmission network and formed a separate state-owned corporation called Trans Grid. This business is still under state ownership (EIA, 1997 and Thomas, 2006).

Queensland initiated the reform of the state-owned Queensland Electricity Commission in 1995 by separating it into generation, AUSTA Electric, network segments, Queensland Transmission and Supply Corporation (QTSC) and the transmission network, called Powerlink. Powerlink is still the state-owned corporation that maintains and operates the grid (EIA, 1997).

South Australia restructured and corporatized the state-owned vertically integrated utility, Electric Trust of South Australia, in 1995. At the time it created four subsidiaries each in charge of power generation, transmission, distribution and marketing, and gas trading. The transmission corporation was called ETSA transmission and was responsible for system operation and planning (ibid.). In 1998, the parent utility split the company into ETSA utilities, the distribution piece; ETSA Power, the retailer; and ElectraNet SA, the transmission business, in preparation for privatization. ElectraNet was privatized in 2003, and manages and plans the state's transmission network (Thomas, 2006).

Under the Tasmania Electricity Code of 1998, the vertically integrated Hydro-electric Commission of Tasmania was unbundled into distribution, transmission and generation segments. The transmission owner and operator became Transend, which remains state owned along with the generator Hydro Tasmania.[57]

Australian transmission networks can then be classified into two general models: state-owned and privately owned ITCs. The transmission networks of New South Wales, Queensland, and Tasmania fall under the former, while those of Victoria and South Australia are of the latter type.

New Zealand

Prior to the deregulation of the electricity sector, which began in 1987, New Zealand's main generation and transmission assets were owned by a state monopoly. During that year this monopoly was corporatized and renamed the Electricity Corporation of New Zealand (ECNZ). It remained vertically integrated, however, until 1994 when the transmission system was separated from ECNZ. The transmission enterprise, Transpower, remains the current stand-alone system operator but is still state owned (Lee, 2004).

When the transmission assets were separated to form Transpower, the Treasury encumbered it with the debt of ECNZ to raise the market price of the generation business. To counter the resulting high debt–equity ratio, Transpower's assets were revalued to reflect replacement cost and the grid charge was raised. It took Transpower 10 years following separation to pay down its legacy debt, but it was able to sustain the high grid charge due to the 'light-handed' approach to regulation the government employed. Since then, competition from distributed generation that is directly connected to the distribution system has kept the grid price it charges somewhat in check (Bertram, 2006).

Japan

The Japanese electricity industry, like that of the US, has historically been dominated by private VIUs or IOUs. The restructuring process that the Japanese government initiated in 1995, due to its concern about high power prices compared to all other OECD countries,[58] has had some impact on the 'wires' segments of the industry. At the time of the reform there were 10 IOUs, which were monopoly suppliers with designated service territories.[59] The 1995 law opened the generation and wholesale markets to independent power producers (IPPs)[60] (Takahashi, 2002).

There have been two amendments to the 1995 law. During the first round of amendments, there was recognition of the need for impartial TPA to the grid to ensure effective competition. Therefore, the amendment made provisions for wheeling service rules that govern access to the transmission networks (IEA, 2003b). The result was the introduction of cross-area wheeling service contracts, which required equitable service provision and detailed the charges that a utility can levy for the use of its grid (Wada, 2006). The wheeling rules promoted TPA to some extent but created a problem of pancaked rates, as in the US, whereby each utility was allowed to charge a transmission service fee for wheeling power through its system that was destined for another service territory (IEA, 2003b).

The third amendment to the electricity law in 2003 abolished the pancaking of transmission rates by revising wheeling service rules. These rules replaced the existing cross-system transmission charges by uniform connection charges. To ensure fair TPA, the Electric Power System Council of Japan (ESCJ) was also created. ESCJ oversees and makes rules for system operation and grid access and also oversees dispute resolution and arbitration.[61] To further promote TPA, rules were set up prohibiting the cross-subsidization of competitive operations, using revenues from regulated segments, and any discriminatory treatment.[62]

The 2003 amendments also mandated the unbundling of regulated and non-regulated segments. In particular, they required IOUs to unbundle the accounts of their transmission networks from other activities and put in place information firewalls to separate the 'wires' businesses from competitive segments.[63] Accounting unbundling involved the separation and disclosure of revenues and expenditures of grid activities. Informational firewalls ensure that the management of the grid is shielded from that of the competitive businesses such that network-owning utilities have the same information on transmission systems as IPPs, other generators and retailers.

Aside from the requirements for account unbundling and informational firewalls, the Japanese transmission system largely remains part of VIUs. None of the transmission grids is run by independent third parties. Thus, the system operators of the transmission grids are VIUs.

As already noted, Japan's electricity system was designed such that utilities supply power to customers in their designated service territories. This system meant that each utility had to be self-sufficient in generating power to serve its customers. While the grid system within each territory was developed extensively to achieve this goal, there has been limited interconnection with inadequate capacity mostly set up to meet reliability requirements (Asia Pacific Energy Research Center, 2004). This limitation is evident when the interconnection capacity is compared to the generation capacity between three of Japan's largest utilities, TEPCO, Kansai and Chubu. The relative capacity of interconnection to generation between TEPCO and Chubu[64] was 1.1 percent for TEPCO and 3.6 percent for Chubu in 1999, and declined slightly in 2006 since generation capacity increased but interconnection capacity did not. In addition, the relative capacity of interconnection to generation between Kansai and Chubu was 10 percent for Chubu both in 1999 and 2006, and it was 9 and 8 percent for Kansai in 1999 and 2006, respectively.[65]

Table 23.4 presents the structure of the Pacific region's transmission systems.

3 Power Distribution

Industry structure
Before the start of restructuring, power distributors carried out all retailing functions, which included power procurement for retail customers, metering, billing, customer care and demand-side management services. With the implementation of customer choice and restructuring, retailing has been unbundled from distribution in some parts of the developed world. Retailers are unregulated as they provide services on a competitive

Table 23.4 Transmission service providers (TSPs): Pacific region

Service territory	Transmission company	Ownership	Extent of unbundling	System operator	TPA access
Australia					
Victoria	SP AusNet	Private	ownership	ITC	regulated
New South Wales	TransGrid	Public	ownership	ITC	regulated
Queensland	Powerlink	Public	ownership	ITC	regulated
South Australia	ElectraNet	Private	ownership	ITC	regulated
Tasmania	Transend	Public	ownership	ITC	regulated
New Zealand	Transpower	Public	ownership	ITC	regulated
Japan					
Hokkaido region	Hokkaido EP Co.	Private	accounting	VIU	regulated
Tohoku region	Tohoku EP Co.	Private	accounting	VIU	regulated
Kanto region	Tokyo EP Co.	Private	accounting	VIU	regulated
Chubu region	Chubu EP Co.	Private	accounting	VIU	regulated
Chubu region	Hokuriku EP Co.	Private	accounting	VIU	regulated
Kansai region	Kansai EP Co.	Private	accounting	VIU	regulated
Chugoku region	Chugoku EP Co.	Private	accounting	VIU	regulated
Shikoku region	Shikoku EP Co.	Private	accounting	VIU	regulated
Kyushu region	Kyushu EP Co.	Private	accounting	VIU	regulated
Okinawa region	Okinawa EP Co.	Private	accounting	VIU	regulated

basis. These services include financial arrangements to procure power from wholesalers, which they sell to end-use residential, commercial and industrial customers. They may also provide metering, billing and customer care services; outsource these to third parties; or rely on distributors to provide them. Distributors continue to provide regulated retail services on a default or standard offer basis to customers who do not contract to receive retailing from independent providers.

The extent of retailing activities carried out by distributors, retailers and other third-party providers varies in the jurisdictions where there is retail unbundling from distribution. The separation between distribution and retailing is not always clear. As a result, the industry is characterized by entities that have varying degrees of independence from distributors. We now turn to a discussion of the situation in the three regions featured in the transmission section.

North America

United States
In the US, the state governments have jurisdiction over structural changes in the power distribution industry. In addition, most IOUs have evolved to serve service territories mostly confined to the states in which they operate. The state regulators, which are commonly called public utility commissions, decide whether to implement retail power market competition. More than half of the 50 states have, in fact, chosen not to pursue retail competition at all. Most states that have implemented retail competition have not induced a complete separation. Thus for the typical US IOU, distribution and retailing are jointly provided and competitive marketers pay a fee for retail services such as metering and billing. In addition, there may not be further reforms following recent experiences with high power prices in states that have undertaken power restructuring: some have blamed restructuring in general for these woes. Recent notable cases of this are Maryland (Platts, 2007a) and Illinois (Platts, 2007b), where power prices surged following the end of rate freezes that were in place when restructuring first got underway; the coincidence of high fuel prices did not help matters much.[66] Moreover, there have been some retreats from restructuring by states, such as Virginia (Platts, 2007c) and Montana (Platts, 2007d), which have recently taken steps to reverse the process.

Canada
In Canada, provincial governments and regulators only in Alberta and Ontario instituted retail and distribution separation when they restructured their power industries and introduced retail competition. Alberta began restructuring its power industry in 1996 by passing the Electric Utilities Act (EUA) of 1995, which led to the establishment of a power pool. At the time of the restructuring, three main utilities – Edmonton Power, now EPCOR; TransAlta; and ATCO Electric – produced, transmitted and, to some extent, distributed the province's power; EPCOR is owned by the city of Edmonton while the other two are IOUs. In addition, municipal utilities distributed power to local customers and the City of Calgary Electric System, now ENMAX, distributed power to Calgary. Following the passage of EUA, the province introduced retail competition in 2001, which allowed new retailers to enter the market and allowed power distributors, including EPCOR, ATCO Electric and ENMAX, to compete for and sell power to

customers outside their service territories. Consumers can buy power from their regulated distributors under a regulated rate option[67] or from unregulated retailers (National Energy Board, 2001). Currently, there are four distributors including FortisAlberta, which bought the distribution system of TransAlta, in the province.

A new EUA in 2003 places a 'limitation on functions performed by electric distribution system owners' whereby 'an owner of an electric distribution system shall not carry out any function required or permitted by this Act . . . to be carried out by a retailer except' if a retailer, after obtaining a customer's consent, asks it to do so or the distributor provides such service under a regulated rate tariff.[68] Essentially, this creates legal separation of retailing from distribution services in the province. For example, EPCOR Energy Alberta Inc. is the energy services subsidiary of EPCOR.[69]

Similar provisions have also been placed on such separation in Ontario. The province introduced power market restructuring by passing the Energy Competition Act and the Electricity Act in 1998. Before restructuring, most of the province's power was distributed by over 300 municipal utilities. Ontario Hydro, the provincially owned generation and transmission company, distributed power to rural customers. Following restructuring, distribution companies were required to separate the 'wires' business from their other energy businesses to prevent cross-subsidization. The Ontario Energy Board Act of 1998 sets out the provision for this separation by requiring that 'a transmitter or distributor shall not, except through one or more affiliates, carry on any business activity other than transmitting or distributing electricity',[70] and that 'every distributor shall keep its financial records associated with distributing electricity separate from its financial records associated with other activities'.[71] The former led to functional unbundling and the latter to accounting unbundling between distribution and retailing (National Energy Board, 2001). Following subsequent consolidation, including purchases by Hydro One, there are about 90 power distributors in the province at the present time.[72]

Distributors, like transmission companies, were also required to make their system available on a transparent and non-discriminatory basis. The Electricity Act of 1998 requires that 'a transmitter or distributor shall provide generators, retailers and consumers with non-discriminatory access to its transmission or distribution systems in Ontario in accordance with its license'.[73]

Europe
The distribution industry of Europe has been strongly shaped by EU directives. Some countries, such as Norway, however, restructured the industry before these directives were passed. The following briefly details the developments in the EU countries featured in this chapter.

Austria
Provincial and municipal distribution utilities own some generation. In addition, there is substantial cross-ownership among provincial utilities, and between federal and provincial electric utilities (IEA, 2002). A report prepared for the European Commission indicates that Austria has 132 electricity distributors 122 of which serve less than 100 000 customers.[74] Distribution and retailing functions are accounting and functionally unbundled in compliance with the second EU requirements. Despite this, the 2007 regulator report to the European Commission indicates that competition is restricted

by distributors that provide services on favorable terms to their own retailers (Energie-Control GmbH, 2007).

Belgium
The legal unbundling of the distribution companies from retail market participants was handled at the regional level. At the time of unbundling, Flanders had 15 distributors, Wallonia 14, and Brussels one. The total number of distributors was 27 as some served more than one region.[75] Distributors were wholly or partly owned by the municipalities that they served. Fifteen of the municipalities operate their system in cooperation with Electrabel, which has an ownership interest in them. Electrabel's ownership interest in these utilities is to decrease overtime until it divests all of its holdings by 2018 (European Commission Directorate-General for Energy and Transport, 2005).

Denmark
The 2004 law that set out legal and functional unbundling rules for transmission applied to the distribution sector as well but it adopted the exemptions from functional unbundling made for distributors serving less than 100 000 customers. At the time, Denmark had 115 distribution companies, 107 of which served fewer than 100 000 customers. According to the latest statistics provided by the Danish Energy Association,[76] there are currently 112 distribution companies of which 103 are municipal companies and cooperatives and nine are private. The requirements for TPA access programs and compliance reports are applicable to distribution operators as well.

Finland
The 1995 Act was amended to comply with the second EU directive, which mandated legal unbundling for all network companies by 2007. This affected the 91 distribution companies operating in Finland, which are municipally owned and generally involved both in generation and retailing. The amendment allowed an exemption for utilities that distributed 200 GWh/year or less for the previous three calendar years and had fewer than 50 000 customers. Fifty-nine of the 91 distributors, or nearly two-thirds of the total that provide power to only 15 percent of Finnish customers, qualified for this exemption. Of the remaining one-third of utilities, only 10 percent have fulfilled the legal unbundling requirement by 2004. By 2006, a total of 16 distribution companies have been legally separated, bringing the unbundling compliance to 50 percent (Energy Market Authority, 2007).

France
Neither the '2000 Law' nor the '2004 Law' instituted the unbundling requirement set forth by the EU directives on French distributors. While EDF owns and operates 95 percent of the country's distribution networks, there are also 170 distributors, most of which were publicly held. The 2004 legislation, however, required all distributors, including EDF, to create separate internal units for distribution services that are not involved in managing any generation or retailing activities. It also specified rules that adopt the exemption for utilities serving fewer than 100 000 customers from the unbundling requirement. As a result, only six distributors were faced with the internal partitioning rule (European Commission Directorate-General for Energy and Transport, 2005). In 2006, France passed a law that required all distributors serving more than 100 000

customers to implement legal unbundling of their generation or retail activities by July 2007 (Commission de Régulation de l'Énergie, 2007).

The proviso on independence of a distributor so that it provides unbiased TPA is also applicable for this sector. The terms for independence include a code of good conduct, ensuring the confidentiality of sensitive customer information, prohibiting personnel overlap, and physical separation of the business sites of distribution from those of generation and retailing (European Commission Directorate-General for Energy and Transport, 2005).

Germany
The implementation of legal unbundling was delayed to 2007 for distributors with more than 100000 customers. However, accounting unbundling is in effect for all but very small isolated utilities (IEA, 2007a). At present, there are about 876 distribution companies, which are largely private (International Energy Regulation Network, 2008a).

Ireland
The distribution business, ESB Networks, like the transmission network was ring-fenced in 2001, whereby its operations were accounting and functionally unbundled from production and supply. CER enforces this separation through the license conditions of the utility and business separation compliance programs. Unlike the transmission operator, the distribution business is owned and operated by ESB and has some shared-service business units with the parent company (Commission for Energy Regulation, 2007).

Italy
Municipally operated electricity distributors that served more than 300000 customers were subjected to 'functional unbundling' in 1999.[77] The Marzano Law of 2004 further required legal unbundling for these large distribution companies. This law has since been amended and legal unbundling is not in force. Distributors must still comply with accounting and administrative unbundling. In addition, they are required to provide non-discriminatory TPA based on the tariffs set out by AEEG (European Commission Directorate-General for Energy and Transport, 2005).

In January 2007, the regulator modified the requirement of functional and accounting unbundling so that it follows that of the second EU directive. The modifications strengthen the neutral provisions of distribution services, improve cost transparency, and rationalize information required to conduct effective tariff and related regulations (AEEG, 2007).

The Netherlands
The Electricity Act of 1998 necessitated the legal unbundling of all distribution networks from other activities including retailing. At the time, there were 23 distribution companies owned by municipalities and provinces[78] (van Dame, 2005). Currently, there are 10 distribution companies, which are still publicly owned and subject to legal unbundling (International Energy Regulation Network, 2008b). Legal unbundling requires each distributor, even those serving fewer than 100000 customers, to appoint an independent distribution grid manager with no affiliation to retailers or other market participants. The manager is to work with a board whose members are also not connected to any

trading, retailing or production activities. The distribution management is also to draw up provisions detailing fair TPA to the grid. Due to strict oversight by the regulator, these provisions have been met successfully (European Commission Directorate-General for Energy and Transport, 2005).

Norway

The distribution system comprises two grid levels: regional and local. At the present time, there are 152 regional and local distribution companies, 17 of which operate the regional grid and 76 of which operate the local grid, while the rest operate both (International Energy Regulation Network, 2007c). Ninety percent of grid operators are publicly owned, although there are varying amounts of private interest in 40 percent of them, and 10 percent are privately owned (NVE, 2007).

Distribution companies are required to provide fair TPA based on tariffs set by NVE. Therefore, they provide regulated rather than negotiated TPA. Following EU Regulation 1228/2003 and EU Directive II, Norway required that all grid operators serving more than 100 000 customers be legally unbundled from retailing, starting in July 2007. This applied only to six distribution operators with more than 100 000 customers. It is, however, up to NVE and the Ministry to require legal unbundling for those serving any number of customers (ibid.).

Portugal

The one major distribution company, as part of the EDP Group, is vertically integrated with affiliates in generation and retailing. It operates under the name of EDP Distribuicao-Energia, S.A,[79] and is subject to accounting and legal unbundling. Under this arrangement, the distributor's employees work exclusively for it, and follow an ethics code that prohibits them from disclosing commercially sensitive information of competitors to the parent or any other company. The company also has the necessary power to manage, operate, maintain and develop the network. The parent company, however, is permitted to exercise influence over the distribution company and directs major decisions on investment and debt. In addition, it provides some common services such as accountancy and office building maintenance (European Commission Directorate-General for Energy and Transport, 2005).

Spain

Legal unbundling of distribution from retailing was completed by the end of 2000. Since the resulting distribution model included the procurement of electricity at regulated prices, this legal unbundling was only partial (ibid.). Since then, Spain has passed the Electricity Law of 2007, overhauling the 1997 law and mandating complete legal unbundling of retailing and distribution (Comision Nacional de Energia, 2007).

Distribution in Spain is mainly carried out by the subsidiaries of the main private VIUs; the five most prominent are Endesa, Iberdrola, Union Fenosa, EDP/Hidrocantabrico, and Viesgo-Enel.[80] Until the passage of the Electricity Law of 2007, the only safeguard against unfair TPA to the distribution grid was the requirement for neutral access to the grids, the provision of transparent information on grid availability and the regulator's ability to settle conflicts in cases of disputes over access (European Commission Directorate-General for Energy and Transport, 2005).

Sweden
Electricity Law 1997 modernized the existing 1902 electricity law and formalized the reforms that the government had developed since 1992. In 1998, this law was amended to adopt the provisions of the first EU directive. Distribution businesses had to undertake accounting unbundling. They also had to legally unbundle from all other businesses, as entities engaged in generation and retail were no longer allowed to engage in distribution (ibid.).

The law was further amended to adopt the second EU directive in 2005. Among other things, the amendment instituted functional unbundling which prohibited the management of distribution businesses from participating in the management of competitive undertakings. Distribution businesses that serve fewer than 100 000 customers were exempted from this requirement. All distributors were required to introduce a compliance program to ensure that they would not favor affiliates. The required procedures for objective service to all third parties thus launched regulated TPA.

Sweden has about 175 distribution companies that had to establish compliance guidelines. The six largest distribution companies among these serve about 60 percent of all customers (ibid.). Some of the distribution companies are publicly owned regional networks and the rest are local networks under both private and public ownership (Energy Markets Inspectorate, 2007).

Pacific Region
As in Europe, developments of the distribution industry in the Pacific region have been largely affected by restructuring efforts undertaken by policy makers and regulators. We look at the situation in Australia, New Zealand, and Japan in turn.

Australia
At the time of the initial restructuring, Victoria's electric distributors were consolidated into five companies and were subsequently all privatized in 1995. Currently, the five electric distributors in the state are Alinta, CitiPower, United Energy, SP AusNet and Powercor.[81] Retail competition was introduced in 2001, and although the Essential Services Commission does not require ownership separation between distribution and retailing, it has instituted accounting and operational, or functional, separation between the two activities. Operational separation requires separate organizational units, separate work areas, and separate staff for the two lines of business. The ring-fencing guidelines also require non-discrimination in that a distribution company must provide the same level of service and information to all retailers (Essential Services Commission, 2004).

In 1991, New South Wales consolidated the distribution segment into six publicly owned businesses and corporatized them in the following year. Currently there are three distribution utilities in the state that are still under state ownership: Country Energy, EnergyAustralia, and Integral Energy.[82] New South Wales introduced retail competition in 2002, and, as in Victoria, has ring-fencing requirements between distribution service provision and retailing. Distributors are required to have accounting and functional divisions between their distribution and retailing businesses through financial, physical office, information, and staff separations. The access requirements of the ring-fencing guidelines also oblige a distributor to provide service and information to all retailers on the same basis as those it provides to its own retail business (IPART, 2003).

The network segment of Queensland's QTSC included seven regional distribution companies following the restructuring. In 1999, six of the seven regional distributors were merged into a single company, Ergon Energy, to improve reliability and governance. Currently there are two state-owned distributors, Ergon Energy and Energex.[83] Queensland introduced retail competition progressively starting in 1998 with the institution of full retail competition in 2007. At the time it introduced full competition, the Queensland government sold the retailing businesses of the electricity distributors in order to enhance competition. Therefore, retailing is ownership unbundled from distribution as of 2007, and retailers are privately owned (Queensland Government Department of Mines and Energy, 2007).

The state utility of South Australia that provides distribution services, ETSA Utilities, was privatized in 1999. ETSA Utilities remains the sole power distributor in the state. Its only function is to distribute power in the state of South Australia.[84] Thus, there is complete ownership separation between distribution and retailing in the state.

Following the 1998 restructuring of the vertically integrated utility of Tasmania, the distribution business is owned and operated by the state-owned Aurora Energy. Retail competition was initiated in 2006 and will be completed in 2010. Some retailers supply contestable customers, but Aurora provides retail services to customers that are not eligible to choose their own retailer.[85]

New Zealand

Before deregulation, 61 electric supply authorities (ESAs), run by state power boards and municipal electric departments, owned and operated the distribution systems and provided retail services in New Zealand. Some ESAs had limited generation assets. Following the Energy Companies Act of 1992, these entities were corporatized and some privatized. In fact, the privatization of the distribution sector had begun in 1990, in anticipation of the Energy Companies Act (Electricity Group Resources and Networks Branch, 2005). As a result of this process, there has been considerable consolidation in this sector (Scully, 1999). At present, there are 28 distribution businesses in New Zealand, some of which are small cooperatives and community trusts. All electricity distributors are prohibited from retail supply activities by the Electricity Industry Reform Act of 1998, which explicitly prohibits cross-ownership between the wires and supply businesses, including retailing and generation, in the power industry.

Japan

Although the Japanese distribution networks are owned by VIUs, they are subject to accounting unbundling to ensure the transparency of the network operations.[86] The nature of accounting unbundling is the same as that which applies to the transmission system discussed in the previous section.

Table 23.5 summarizes the power distribution industry's structure in the developed countries discussed.

4   Concluding Remarks

The transformation of the power industry discussed in this chapter has resulted in a variety of transmission service arrangements in developed countries. In North America,

Table 23.5 Power distribution industry structure: the developed world

Jurisdiction	Retail unbundling	Utility structure	Ownership
US	Mostly Bundled	VIU	Private
Canada			
Alberta	Unbundled	D	Mixed
British Columbia	Bundled	VIU	Public
Manitoba	Bundled	VIU	Public
New Brunswick	Bundled	D	Public
Newfoundland and Labrador	Bundled	VIU	Private
Nova Scotia	Bundled	VIU	Private
Ontario	Unbundled	D	Public
Quebec	Bundled	VIU	Public
Prince Edwards Island	Bundled	VIU	Private
Saskatchewan	Bundled	VIU	Public
Europe			
Austria	Unbundled	FID	Public
Belgium	Unbundled	FID	Mixed
Denmark	Unbundled	FID	Mixed
Finland	Unbundled	FID	Public
France	Partially unbundled	VIU, D	Public
Germany	Partially unbundled	D	Mixed
Ireland	Unbundled	FID	Public
Italy	Unbundled	FID	Private
The Netherlands	Unbundled	FID	Public
Norway	Unbundled	FID	Mixed
Portugal	Unbundled	FID	Private
Spain	Unbundled	FID	Private
Sweden	Unbundled	FID	Public

Australia			
Victoria	Unbundled	FID	Private
New South Wales	Unbundled	FID	Mixed
Queensland	Unbundled	D	Public
South Australia	Unbundled	D	Private
Tasmania	Unbundled	D	Public
New Zealand	Unbundled	D	Mixed
Japan	Unbundled (accounting)	VIU	Private

Notes:
FID = Functionally independent distributor.
VIU = Vertically integrated utility.
D = Distribution company.

the predominant change has been the transfer of transmission operations to non-profit system operators. In some regions, US power companies have embraced the ISO model actively advanced by the FERC; the FERC advocates open access transmission to promote competitive wholesale power markets. Despite the transfer of transmission service operation to ISOs, the majority of US power utilities remain vertically integrated. The same is the case in Canada, even though more of the country's transmission service is provided by independent system operators: nearly two-thirds of this service is under ISO, gridco or FIO oversight. Independent transmission service provision in Canada has largely developed to meet FERC's eligibility requirements to sell power in the US. As in the US, most of Canada's power industry is, nevertheless, vertically integrated.

The majority of power transmission systems in Europe and the Pacific region, on the other hand, have generally experienced complete or ownership unbundling. Japan is one notable exception as its transmission is still part of VIUs. Most transmission systems in these two regions are stand-alone companies and operate as ITCs/transcos.

Similar motivations have also caused structural changes in the distribution sector of the power industry. These changes have mainly focused on the unbundling of retailing activities from distribution. Nevertheless, about half of North American utilities are still part of traditional VIUs. Where retail competition exists, most companies still provide default procurement services and many have generation affiliations. The integration of retailing and distribution in Japan is even more pronounced, where the only form of retail unbundling that exists is for accounting. This is so despite the fact that in Japan, power reform activity has primarily focused on introducing generation and retailing competition. By contrast, Australia, New Zealand and Western Europe have instituted the most retail unbundling from distribution seen in the developed world to date.

Market structure developments in some ways have been a reflection of the ownership status of power utilities. For instance, the market design similarities between Japan and the US are partly due to the private ownership of most major power utilities in the two countries. On the other hand, most Canadian utilities are public enterprises, although they have been transformed into crown corporations and operate as for-profit businesses.

The ownership picture in Europe is mixed since some utilities have been privatized following the initiation of restructuring. The same is evident in Australia and New Zealand, where some utilities have been privatized while others remain under public ownership.

The evolution of the power industry is far from finished. There have been some retreats from restructuring in response to unprecedented power price increases and some reliability problems. It will be interesting to observe the changes that will occur in the coming decade.

Notes

1. Though the industry was characterized by such self-contained systems, there existed limited trade among utilities. For instance, in the US inter-utility trade occurred mainly where some utilities had a major generation cost advantage, an example of which is the Bonneville Power Administration. Such trade also occurred where adjacent regions had complementary seasonal peaks, for example between upstate and downstate New York, which encouraged economy energy exchanges.
2. It is believed that overall cost savings and efficiencies are higher from competition in generation and retailing than the loss in vertical economies resulting from unbundling. For discussions on economies from the integration of grid operation with generation and retailing, see Kaserman and Mayo (1991), Gilsdorf (1994), Kwoka (2002), Nemoto and Goto (2004), Jara-Díaz et al. (2004), and Arocena (2005).

3. For a discussion on this form of TSP, see Graves and Clapp (2001), Hogan and Chandley (2002), Morey (2003), and Morey and Hurst (2003).
4. The TOs may or may not own or be affiliated with companies that own extensive generation assets.
5. We do not discuss developments in the UK because there is a separate chapter devoted to the topic. We do not focus on the Greek market because its system is mostly interconnected with the Eastern European systems. Developments in Luxembourg mirror those of its neighboring countries and since its market is relatively small we have chosen not to include it in the discussion. On the other hand, we give attention to the Norwegian system because Norway was one of the earliest innovators in market restructuring and its system is highly integrated with its neighboring countries.
6. The FERC also regulates US bulk power markets and interstate oil and natural gas transmission. It does not have jurisdiction over power or natural gas retail sales or distribution.
7. For a recent discussion of US transmission policy, see Joskow (2005).
8. For example, they might offer transmission services to competitors in the bulk power market, which compared to the terms on which they use their transmission system to make power sales, might involve higher charges and/or inferior quality.
9. PURPA was passed by the US Congress as part of the National Energy Act of 1978. The act appears in US Code Title 16 – Conservation, Chapter 12 – Federal Regulation and Development of Power, Subchapter II – Regulation of Electric Utility Companies Engaged in Interstate Commerce, available at: http://uscode.house.gov/download/pls/16C12.txt (accessed December 2007).
10. FERC, *Promoting Wholesale Competition Through Open Access Non-discriminatory Transmission Services by Public Utilities and Recovery of Stranded Costs by Public Utilities and Transmitting Utilities*, Order No. 888 61 FERC 21540 (May 1996).
11. FERC, *Preventing Undue Discrimination and Preference in Transmission Service*, Order No. 890 (RM05-17-000, 002 and RM05-25-000) (February 16, 2007).
12. Notable exceptions have included the multi-state transmission systems of Allegheny Power, American Electric Power, Central and Southwest, Northeast Utilities, Pacificorp, and the Southern Company.
13. FERC, *Regional Transmission Organizations*, Order No. 2000 (RM99-2-00) (December 1999).
14. The FERC conditionally approved a similar arrangement for SeTrans Grid Company in 1992.
15. Great Lakes Power and Canadian Niagara Power, two smaller transmission systems, provide limited and local transmission services.
16. Hydro-Quebec Open Access Transmission Tariff (Decisions D-2007-08 and D-2007-34), available at: http://www.hydroquebec.com/transenergie/oasis/en/pdf/tarifs.pdf (accessed November 2007).
17. Third parties are those who neither own nor operate the networks.
18. Due to the principle of subsidiarity, EU member states are able to use their own strategies to implement EU-mandated rules on electricity restructuring (Serralles, 2006).
19. The legislation for both the 1996 and 2003 directives can be found on the European Commission website: http://ec.europa.eu/energy/index_en.html.
20. See the Commission's September 2007 proposal on the European Commission website: http://ec.europa.eu/energy/energy_policy/doc/09_internal-gas-and-electricity-market_en.pdf (accessed February 2009).
21. Austrian law mandates at least 51 percent public ownership of utilities with generating capacity of more than 200 KW or with supply that is more than twice the amount they generate. Thus, the large utility, Verbund, operating at the national level, nine at the provincial level, and the rest at the municipal level that fall under this criteria are owned by the federal, provincial and municipal governments, respectively. Verbund, is the largest power generator and owns most of the transmission lines; the provincial utilities own the rest (European Commission Directorate-General for Energy and Transport, 2005).
22. Although the systems have largely complied with legal unbundling, there is evidence that suggests that the legislation has had limited effect. First, the utilities have responded by setting up subsidiaries to fulfill the requirement of legal unbundling. Under this arrangement their network subsidiaries provide service that favors the parent company. Second, the parent companies sometimes accept terms for service that suggest the existence of cross-subsidization, and they report the fees paid for network services as 'other operating income', circumventing transparency. This is especially unhelpful in terms of meeting the provision of non-discriminatory TPA access for transmission services (European Commission Directorate-General for Energy and Transport, 2005).
23. Unlike most transmission operators, Elia operates the grid from 380 kV to 30 kV.
24. This company also owns and operates the major gas pipeline, Gastransmission.dk A/S, available at: http://www.energinet.dk/en/menu/About+us/Profile/Profile.htm (accessed October 2007).
25. The Danish electricity system is divided into east and west with no interconnection between the two. West Denmark is connected with continental Europe while East Denmark is connected with the Scandinavian countries. Recently, there has been a plan for a link between the two systems, with construction to start in 2010 (Danish Energy Regulatory Authority, 2005).

26. EDF owned and continues to own 100 percent interest in RTE (International Energy Regulation Network, 2007b).
27. Captive customers are ones that cannot purchase power from any supplier other than the local utility.
28. The 2006 OECD survey on Germany's economy reports that there were nine such utilities and that they owned 80 percent of generation capacity.
29. Germany passed a new Energy Industry Act (Energiewirtschaftsgesetz, EnWG) and associated legislation, which came into effect in July 2005, governing grid access and pricing.
30. It coordinates its operations based on the guidelines of the Union for the Co-ordination of Transmission of Electricity (UCTE), an association of Central and Western European grid operators.
31. The European Communities (Internal Market in Electricity) Regulations 2005 implemented EU Directive 2003/54/EC. Mainly, these set up conditions for consumer protection and Provider of Last Resort.
32. Furthermore, CER indicates that the government is preparing to transfer ownership of the transmission asset from ESB to EirGrid (Commission for Energy Regulation, 2007).
33. Italy had initiated changes in its electricity sector with laws 9/1991 and 10/1991, which permitted the generation of power from renewable sources, and with law 333/1992, which transformed the state-owned power monopoly ENEL into a joint stock company (European Commission Directorate-General for Energy and Transport, 2005).
34. The switch to this model arose due to inefficiencies and difficulties in the operation and coordination of transmission services between the operator and owner (AEEG, 2006).
35. In 2006, TERNA owned 90 percent of the transmission assets in the country (European Commission Directorate-General for Energy and Transport, 2005).
36. The Netherlands amended the Electricity Act of 1998 in 2004 in order to adopt the second EU directive into law. Since most of its provisions had already been met, the 2004 amendment merely tightened conditions under which the network grids are managed (van Dame, 2005).
37. For the day-ahead interconnection with Germany there is an explicit auction, while there is a trilateral implicit auction for day-ahead interconnection with Belgium and France.
38. TenneT and the Norwegian grid operator, Statnett, got approval from DTe to build a 700 MW interconnector to connect their respective power markets in 2004. One condition for the approval of the project was that capacity be made available through auctions. This interconnector came into operation on May 6, 2008, and capacity is made available through auctions. This update is reported by TenneT at http://www.tennet.org/english/tennet/new/langste_onderzeese_hoogspanningskabel_ter_wereld_geopend.aspx (accessed February 2009).
39. Note that the Portuguese electricity system comprises three subsystems that are not interconnected. The mainland system is interconnected with Spain, while there are two island systems, serving the autonomous regions of the Azores and Madeira.
40. A regional electricity market between the two countries, the Iberian Electricity Market (MIBEL), is in its initial stages of operation. The market-based auction for interconnection capacity is also a means of facilitating the development of this market.
41. It was the first exclusive transmission owner and operator in the world (European Commission Directorate-General for Energy and Transport, 2005). Thus, we can consider it the first model of a transco/ITC.
42. These percentages have not increased much by 2007 since interconnection capacity between Portugal and Spain is about the same as it was in the early 2000s.
43. The company administers a generation company whose sole purpose is to ensure security in the system by providing power in cases of emergency. Since it does not participate in the market, the transmission owner is considered as a stand-alone transmission company.
44. If there is no congestion, the whole market forms one price area.
45. The others include South Australia, Victoria, New South Wales, the Australian Capital Territory, and Queensland.
46. COAG is an association of federal, state and local governments of Australia that coordinates activities among them.
47. This proposal was given further impetus by the Hilmer Commission Report of 1993, which recommended appropriate reforms to induce competition in many industries including electricity that would benefit the whole economy significantly (EIA, 1997).
48. The Federal Commission, called the Industry Commission, had proposed the corporatization, privatization, unbundling into generation, transmission and distribution of the industry, and the creation of a national grid whose sole function would be the transport of electricity (EIA, 1997).
49. This code also set out the rules under which market participants operated in the National Electricity Market (NEM), and the market mechanism under which electricity is traded and whose full operations began in 1998 under the management of the National Electricity Market Management Company (NEMMCO) (Lee, 2004).

50. This a federal body in charge of administrating the 1974 Trade Practices Act of the Commonwealth.
51. Various versions of these rules can be found on the website of the Australian Energy Market Commission: http://www.aemc.gov.au/electricity.php.
52. This was upgraded to 1900 MW in 2002 (Electricity Supply Industry Planning Council, 2003).
53. Roarty (2003).
54. Tasmania Department of Premier and Cabinet (2002).
55. Victoria Supreme Court (2003).
56. See http://www.sp-ausnet.com.au/.
57. There have since been entry into the retail and generation industries entry by private utilities. See http://www.energyregulator.tas.gov.au/domino/otter.nsf.
58. A study by the OECD reports that Japan's electricity prices were the highest in the OECD. Some of the reasons for this include lack of domestic energy resources for generation and thus high fuel costs; high generation capital costs for nuclear and other plants as a result of stringent safety requirements including earthquake resistance, scarcity of land, and payments to local communities; high distribution and transmission costs because of high land costs, remote generation station citing, very high construction standards to withstand earthquake and typhoon risks, and high operating standards; and regulatory costs particularly due to strict environmental regulations to limit pollutant emissions (OECD, 1999).
59. In addition, at the time of the initial reform undertaking Japan had two main public generating companies, the Electric Power Development Corporation (EPDC) and the Japanese Atomic Power Corporation (JAPC). There were also 34 small public enterprises owned and operated by local governments. All three sold power to the private utilities for resale to final consumers. Large industrial plants also produced power mostly for self-consumption (OECD, 1999).
60. The law was further amended in 1999 to allow retail competition such that large power consumers, with annual peak demand greater than 2 MW, can choose their own suppliers. In addition, the 10 private utilities were granted permission to supply power to large customers outside their service territories (OECD, 1999).
61. The ESCJ began its operations in 2005 (Wada, 2006).
62. As Goto and Yajima (2006) indicate, the rules set up by the ESCJ are not enforceable but adhered to on a voluntary basis. But the *ex post* role played by the Ministry of Economy, Trade and Industry (METI), whereby it can sanction a utility found to have engaged in discriminatory manner and create public embarrassment for the utility, act as powerful deterrents to such violations. However, it is still too early to assess the effect of the various TPA promoting mechanisms discussed above.
63. ANRE, http://www.enecho.meti.go.jp/english/policy/index.html.
64. In addition, the two utilities operated in regions with different delivery frequency. TEPCO is part of northern Japan's 50 Hz system, while Chubu was part of Japan's western 60 Hz system. Kansai is like Chubu part of the western frequency system.
65. Calculation made based on system and interconnection capacity figures from Hartley (2000) and Nanahara et al. (2007).
66. The California energy crisis also encouraged retreats from reform. For a thorough discussion of the California energy crisis, see Cicchetti et al. (2004).
67. This is currently in effect until 2010.
68. Electric Utilities Act 2003, Chapter E-5.1, Section 106.
69. See http://www.epcor.ca.
70. Ontario Energy Board Act 1998, Chapter 15, Schedule B, Section 71 (1).
71. Ontario Energy Board Act 1998, Chapter 15, Schedule B, Section 72.
72. At the time it initiated restructuring, the government of Ontario also announced that retail access would become available in November 2000. Retail market opening was postponed, however, until May 2002 because market participants were not ready. When retail competition began in May 2002 consumers in Ontario were allowed to buy power from distributors at regulated default rates or from retailers at market rates. Due to 'unexpected' power price spikes, however, a retail price freeze was put in place in December 2002; a large number of retailers were forced to exit the retail market as a result. A new government elected in 2003 found this freeze unsustainable and introduced price increases in 2004 and 2005. Consumers wishing not to participate in the new price structures were free to sign fixed-price contracts with retailers or buy power on the spot market (Trebilcock and Hrab, 2005).
73. Electricity Act 1998, Chapter 15, Schedule A, Section 26 (1).
74. European Commission Directorate-General for Energy and Transport (2005).
75. There has been some consolidation since then so that there are currently 26 distributors and the one serving the Brussels area is now private (Commission de Regulation de l'Électricité et du Gas, 2007).
76. See http://www.danishenergyassociation.com/Statistics.aspx.
77. Distribution licenses are granted by the Ministry for Productive Affairs (MAP). Following the 1999 Electricity Decrees, each municipality was granted only one license by MAP, until 2030, and was allowed to acquire ENEL's distribution assets in areas where it served more than 100 000 customers. Although

this created 38 such distributors, there are only three distributors that serve more than 300 000 customers. As a result of this ongoing process of consolidation, the number of distributors has fallen from 200 in 2000 to 169 in 2006 (AEEG, 2006).

78. The municipal and provincial owners of these companies had favored privatization. Despite the legal separation safeguards concerns that private distribution companies might discriminate against retailers and engage in cross-subsidization kept distribution companies under public ownership. Ownership unbundling was proposed by the Minister of Economics in 2004 (van Dame, 2005). A recent bill passed by Parliament requires economic or ownership unbundling of all network grids from retailing by 2011 (Office of Energy Regulation (DTe), 2006).

79. In addition, there are 10 small distribution companies created to serve small industries.

80. In addition, there are approximately 326 small distribution outfits serving local areas (International Energy Regulation Network, 2007e).

81. See http://www.esc.vic.gov.au/public/Energy/Links.htm.

82. See http://www.ipart.nsw.gov.au/electricity/electricity.asp.

83. See http://www.dme.qld.gov.au/Energy/electricity_in_queensland.cfm.

84. See http://www.etsautilities.com.au/.

85. See http://www.energyregulator.tas.gov.au/.

86. Note that as in the US, the Japanese private utilities cannot be compelled to vertically separate their competitive businesses from the monopoly segments. Thus, these rules do not call for vertical ownership disintegration but only for functional and accounting unbundling.

References

Alberta Energy (2003), Transmission *Development – The Right Path for Alberta – A Policy Paper*, available at: http://www.energy.gov.ab.ca/Electricity/pdfs/transmissionPolicy.pdf (accessed November 2007).
Alberta Energy and Utilities Board (2002), *Sale of Transalta Transmission Assets and Business to Altalink*, Decision 2002–038.
Arocena, Pablo (2005), 'The measurement of scope, sale and diversification economies: how (in)efficient is electricity restructuring and unbundling?', Working Paper No. 2005/1: Institut d'Economia de Barcelona.
Asia Pacific Energy Research Center (2004), *Electric Power Grid Interconnections in the APEC Region*, Tokyo, Japan.
Autorità per l'Energia Elettrica e il Gas (AEEG) (2005), *Annual Report to the European Commission on the State of the Services and on the Regulation of the Electricity and Gas Sectors – Italy*, European Regulators' Group for Electricity and Gas.
Autorità per l'Energia Elettrica e il Gas (AEEG) (2006), *Annual Report to the European Commission on the State of the Services and on the Regulation of the Electricity and Gas Sectors – Italy*, European Regulators' Group for Electricity and Gas.
Autorità per l'Energia Elettrica e il Gas (AEEG) (2007), *Annual Report to the European Commission on Regulatory Activities and the State of the Services of the Electricity and Gas Sectors – Italy*, European Regulators' Group for Electricity and Gas.
Bertram, Geoff (2006), 'Restructuring the New Zealand electricity sector 1984–2005', in Fereidoon P. Sioshansi, and Wolfgang Pfaffenberger (eds), *Electricity Market Reform: An International Perspective*, Oxford: Elsevier, pp. 203–34.
British Columbia Transmission Corporation (BCTC) (2003), *Transmission Corporation Act*, available at: http://www.bctc.com (accessed November 2007).
Brunekreeft, Gert and Sven Twelemann (2005), 'Regulation, competition and investment in the German electricity market: RegTP or REGTP', *The Energy Journal*, European Energy Liberalization Special Issue, 99–126.
Cicchetti, Charles J., Jeffrey A. Dubin and Colin Long (2004), *The California Electricity Crisis: What, Why and What's Next*, Dordrecht: Kluwer Academic.
Comision Nacional de Energia (2007), *Spanish Regulator's Annual Report to the European Commission*, European Regulators' Group for Electricity and Gas.
Commission de Régulation de l'Électricité et du Gas (2007), *Rapport Annuel 2006 à la Commission Européenne – Belgique*, European Regulators' Group for Electricity and Gas.
Commission de Régulation de l'Énergie (2006), *Activity Report – France*, available at: http://www.cre.fr/en/documents/publications/rapports_annuels (accessed October 2007).
Commission de Régulation de l'Énergie (2007), *Activity Report – France*, available at: http://www.cre.fr/en/documents/publications/rapports_annuels (accessed October 2007).
Commission for Energy Regulation (2007), *Regulators' Annual Report to the European Commission – Ireland*, European Regulators' Group for Electricity and Gas.

Crampes, Claude and Natalia Fabra (2005), 'The Spanish electricity industry: plus ça change', *The Energy Journal*, European Energy Liberalization Special Issue, **26**, 127–53.

Danish Energy Regulatory Authority (2005), *Regulators' Annual Report to the European Commission – Denmark*, European Regulators' Group for Electricity and Gas.

Danish Energy Regulatory Authority (2007), *Regulators' 2007 National Report to the European Commission – Denmark*, European Regulators' Group for Electricity and Gas.

Directive 96/92/EC Concerning Common Rules of the Internal Market in Electricity (1996), available at: http://ec.europa.eu/energy/electricity/legislation/legislation_en.htm (accessed October 2007).

Directive 2003/54/EC of the European Parliament and of the Council of 26 June 2003 Concerning Common Rules for the Internal Market in Electricity and Repealing Directive 96/92/EC (2003), available at: http://ec.europa.eu/energy/electricity/legislation/legislation_en.htm (accessed October 2007).

Electricity Group Resources and Networks Branch (2005), *Chronology of New Zealand Electricity Reform*, Ministry of Economic Development.

Electricity Supply Industry Planning Council (2003), *The South Australian Annual Planning Report*, available at: http://www.esipc.sa.gov.au/webdata/resources/files/2003_Exec_Summary.pdf (accessed September 2007).

Energie-Control GmbH (2007), *National Report to the European Commission – Austria*, European Regulators' Group for Electricity and Gas.

Energy Information Administration (EIA) (1997), 'Electricity reform and privatization in Australia', in *Electricity Reform Abroad and U.S. Investment*, available at: http://www.eia.doe.gov/emeu/pgem/electric/ch3.html (accessed September 2007).

Energy Market Authority (2006), *For a Scheme of Measures Ensuring Electricity System Operator's Compliance with Nondiscrimination Provisions and for Related Reporting*, Finland.

Energy Market Authority (2007), *Annual Report to the European Commission – Finland*, European Regulators' Group for Electricity and Gas.

Energy Markets Inspectorate (2007), *The Swedish Energy Markets Inspectorate's Report in Accordance with the EC Directives for the Internal Markets for Electricity and Natural Gas*, European Regulators' Group for Electricity and Gas.

Energy Reform Implementation Group (ERIG) (2007), *Energy Reform: The Way Forward for Australia*, available at: http://www.erig.gov.au/ (accessed September 2007).

Energy Services Regulatory Authority (2006), *Annual Report to the European Commission – Portugal*, European Regulators' Group for Electricity and Gas.

Essential Services Commission (2004), *Final Decision: Ring-Fencing in the Victorian Electricity Industry*, available at: www.esc.vic.gov.au (accessed October 2007).

European Commission Directorate-General for Energy and Transport (2005), *Study on Unbundling of Electricity and Gas Transmission and Distribution System Operators: Annexes – Country Overview*, available at: http://ec.europa.eu/energy/electricity/publications/doc/2006_03_08_annexes.pdf (accessed October 2007).

Gilsdorf, Keith (1994), 'Vertical integration efficiencies and electric utilities: a cost complementarity perspective', *Quarterly Review of Economics and Finance*, **34** (3), 261–82.

Glachant, Jean-Michel and Dominique Finon (2005), 'A competitive fringe in the shadow of a state owned incumbent: the case of France', *The Energy Journal*, European Energy Liberalization Special Issue, 181–204.

Goto, Mika and Masayuki Yajima (2006), 'A new stage of electricity liberalization in Japan: issues and expectations', in Fereidoon P. Sioshansi and Wolfgang Pfaffenberger (eds), *Electricity Market Reform: An International Perspective*, Oxford: Elsevier, pp. 617–44.

Graves, Joseph S. and John D. Clapp (2001), 'The future of electric transmission', *Electricity Journal*, November, 11–22.

Hartley, Peter (2000), *Reform of the Electricity Supply Industry in Japan*, Prepared in Conjunction with an Energy Study Sponsored by the Center for International Political Economy and the James A. Baker III Institute for Public Policy, Rice University, Houston, TX.

Hogan, William W. and John D. Chandley (2002), *Independent Transmission Companies in a Regional Transmission Organization*, Cambridge, MA: Center for Business and Government, John F. Kennedy School of Government, Harvard University.

Hydro One Networks (2007), *About Hydro One Networks*, available at: http://www.hydroonenetworks.com/en/ (accessed November 2007).

Hydro-Québec TransÉnergie (2007), *Discover Hydro-Québec TransÉnergie and Its System*, available at: http://www.hydroquebec.com/transenergie/en/index.html (accessed November 2007).

Independent Electricity System Operators (2007), *The Power Grid*, available at: http://www.ieso.ca/imoweb/powerGrid/powergrid.asp (accessed November 2007).

Independent Pricing and Regulatory Tribunal of New South Wales (IPART) (2003), *Distribution Ring Fencing Guidelines*, available at: http://www.ipart.nsw.gov.au (accessed October 2007).

International Energy Agency (IEA) (2002), *Energy Policies of IEA Countries: Austria*, 2002 Review.
International Energy Agency (IEA) (2003a), *Energy Policies of IEA Countries: Italy*, 2003 Review.
International Energy Agency (IEA) (2003b), *Energy Policies of IEA Countries: Japan*, 2003 Review.
International Energy Agency (IEA) (2004), *Energy Policies of IEA Countries: France*, 2004 Review.
International Energy Agency (IEA) (2005), *Energy Policies of IEA Countries: Belgium*, 2005 Review.
International Energy Agency (IEA) (2007a), *Energy Policies of IEA Countries: Germany*, 2007 Review.
International Energy Agency (IEA) (2007b), *Energy Policies of IEA Countries: Ireland*, 2007 Review.
International Energy Regulation Network (2006), *Denmark*, available at: http://www.iern.net/country_factsheets/market-denmark.htm (accessed October 2007).
International Energy Regulation Network (2007a), *Finland*, available at: http://www.iern.net/country_factsheets/market-finland.htm (accessed October 2007).
International Energy Regulation Network (2007b), *France*, available at: http://www.iern.net/country_factsheets/market-france.htm (accessed October 2007).
International Energy Regulation Network (2007c), *Norway*, available at: http://www.iern.net/country_factsheets/market-norway.htm (accessed November 2007).
International Energy Regulation Network (2007d), *Portugal*, available at: http://www.iern.net/country_factsheets/market-portugal.htm (accessed November 2007).
International Energy Regulation Network (2007e), *Spain*, available at: http://www.iern.net/country_factsheets/market-spain.htm (accessed November 2007).
International Energy Regulation Network (2008a), *Germany*, available at: http://www.iern.net/country_factsheets/market-germany.htm (accessed February 2008).
International Energy Regulation Network (2008b), *The Netherlands*, available at: http://www.iern.net/country_factsheets/market-netherlands.htm (accessed February 2008).
Island Regulatory and Appeals Commission (2005), *Electric Power Act*, available at: http://www.irac.pe.ca/utilities/ (accessed November 2007).
Jara-Diaz S., J. Ramos-Real and E. Martínez-Budría (2004), 'Economies of integration in the Spanish electricity industry using a multistage cost function', *Energy Economics*, **26**, 995–1013.
Joskow, Paul L. (2005), 'Transmission policy in the United States', *Utilities Policy*, **13**, 95–115.
Kaserman, David L. and John W. Mayo (1991), 'The measurement of vertical economies and the efficient structure of the electric utility industry', *Journal of Industrial Economics*, **39** (5), 483–502.
Kwoka, John E. (2002), 'Vertical economies in electric power: evidence on integration and its alternatives', *International Journal of Industrial Organization*, **20**, 653–71.
Lee, Dong-Wook (2004), *Intermediary Report on Comparative Analysis of Electricity Reform in OECD Pacific Countries*, International Energy Agency, available at: http://www.iea.org/textbase/papers/2004/ele_reform.pdf (accessed September 2007).
Manitoba Hydro (2008), *Open Access Transmission Tariff Business Practices*, available at: http://oasis.midwestiso.org/OASIS/MHEB (accessed February 2008).
Morey, Matthew J. (2003), 'Performance-based regulation for independent transmission companies: delivering the promise of standard market design', *Electricity Journal*, June, 35–51.
Morey, Matthew J. and Eric Hurst (2003), 'The role of the independent transmission company in standardized wholesale electricity markets', *Electricity Journal*, May, 31–45.
Nanahara, Toshiya, Yasuto Akiyama and Satoshi Morozumi (2007), *Japanese Perspectives and Related R&D in Japan*, available at: http://www.iea.org/textbase/work/2007/grids/Nanahara.pdf (accessed September 2007).
National Energy Board (2001), *Canadian Electricity Trends and Issues: An Energy Market Assessment*, Calgary, Alberta.
Nemoto J. and M. Goto (2004), 'Technological externalities and economies of vertical integration in the electric utility industry', *International Journal of Industrial Organization*, **22** (1), 67–81.
New Brunswick System Operator (2004), *New Brunswick Electricity Act*, available at: http://www.gnb.ca/acts/acts/e-04-6.htm (accessed December 2007).
Newfoundland and Labrador Board of Commissioners of Public Utilities (2007), *Newfoundland Electric Utilities*, available at: http://www.pub.nf.ca/links.htm#canutil (accessed November 2007).
Norwegian Water Resources and Energy Directorate (NVE) (2007), *Report on Regulation and the Electricity Market – Norway*, European Regulators' Group for Electricity and Gas.
Nova Scotia Utility and Review Board (2007), *Electricity*, available at: http://www.nsuarb.ca/functions/regulatory/electricity/index.html (accessed November 2007).
Office of Energy Regulation (DTe) (2004), *DTe Approves Cable to Norway Subject to Conditions*, available at: http://www.nma-dte.nl (accessed December 2007).
Office of Energy Regulation (DTe) (2006), *Annual Report by the Office of Energy Regulation (DTe) to the European Commission – The Netherlands*, European Regulators' Group for Electricity and Gas.
Organisation for Economic Co-operation and Development (OECD) (1999), *Regulatory Reform in Japan: Regulatory Reform in the Electricity Industry*, Paris: OECD.

Organisation for Economic Co-operation and Development (OECD) (2006), *Economic Survey of Germany 2006: Sustained Competition is Absent in Energy Markets*, available at: www.oecd.org/eco/surveys/germany (accessed October 2007).
Outhred, Hugh (1998), 'A review of electric industry restructuring in Australia', *Energy Power Systems Research*, **44**, 15–25.
Outhred, Hugh (2007), 'Electricity Industry Restructuring in Australia: Underlying Principles and Experience to Date', *Proceedings of the 40th Hawaii International Conference on System Sciences*, January, 1–19.
Platts (2007a), 'Maryland PSC Chair, linked to rate hikes, resigns under pressure from new Governor', *Electric Utility Week*, February 5.
Platts (2007b), 'Illinois legislators continue to push for Ameren, ComEd rate rollback', *Electric Utility Week*, March 5.
Platts (2007c), 'Virginia OKs "Re-Regulation" Bill: ends existing rate cap', *Electric Utility Week*, February 26.
Platts (2007d), 'Montana OKs Bill to repeal "Restructuring" allowing NorthWestern to own generation', *Electric Utility Week*, April 23.
Queensland Government Department of Mines and Energy (2007), *Sale of the Queensland Government's Energy Retail Businesses*, available at: http://www.dme.qld.gov.au (accessed November 2007).
Regulation (EC) No 1228/2003 of the European Parliament and of the Council of 26 June 2003 on Conditions for Access to the Network for Cross-Border Exchanges in Electricity (2003), available at: http://ec.europa.eu/energy/electricity/legislation/legislation_en.htm (accessed October 2007).
Roarty, Mike (2003), *Electricity Deregulation Outside the New South Wales and Victorian Markets*, Science, Technology, Environment and Resources Group: Research Note no. 40 2002–03, available at: http://www.aph.gov.au/library/pubs/rn/2002-03/03rn40.htm (accessed September 2007).
Rothwell, Geoffrey and Tomas Gomez (eds) (2003), *Electricity Economics: Regulation and Deregulation*, Hoboken, NJ: John Wiley.
SaskPower (2007), *Open Transmission Access*, available at: http://www.saskpower.com/poweringyourfuture/opportunities/oatt.shtml (accessed November 2007).
Scully, Gerald W. (1999), 'Reform and efficiency gains in the New Zealand electrical supply industry', *Journal of Productivity Analysis*, **11**, 133–47.
Serralles, Roberto J. (2006), 'Electric energy restructuring in the European Union: integration, subsidiarity and the challenge to harmonization', *Energy Policy*, **34**, 2542–51.
Takahashi, Minoru (2002), 'The current status of electric power industry deregulation in Japan and the influence of the California crisis', *Japan and the World Economy*, **14**, 341–5.
Tasmania Department of Premier and Cabinet (2002), *Order Enabling Basslink Project of State Significance to Proceed, State Policies and Projects Act 1993 Section 26 (6)*, available at: http://www.dpac.tas.gov.au/divisions/policy/documents/basslinkorder.pdf (accessed September 2007).
TenneT (2006), *Annual Report 2006*, TenneT Holding B.V.: The Netherlands.
The Australian (2006), 'States', power connector sold for $170m', December 6, available at: http://www.theaustralian.news.com.au/story/0,20867,20956773-31037,00.html (accessed September 2007).
Thomas, Steve (2006), *Electricity Reform Experiences in Asia, Pacific Region, GATS and Privatisation of the Industry*, Public Services International Research Unit (PSIRU), Business School, University of Greenwich.
Trebilcock, Michael J. and Roy Hrab (2005), 'Electricity restructuring in Ontario', *The Energy Journal*, **26** (1), 123–46.
van Dame, Eric (2005), 'Liberalizing the Dutch electricity market: 1998–2004', *The Energy Journal*, European Energy Liberalization Special Issue, 155–79.
Victoria Supreme Court (2003), *Murraylink Transmission Company Pty Ltd v National Electricity Market Management Company Ltd [2003] VSC 265 (24 July 2003)*, available at: http://austlii.law.uts.edu.au/au/cases/vic/VSC/2003/265.html (accessed September 2007).
von der Fehr, Nils-Henrik M., Eirik S. Amundsen and Lars Bergman (2005), 'The Nordic market: signs of stress?', *The Energy Journal*, European Energy Liberalization Special Issue, 71–98.
Wada, Kenichi (2006), *Electricity Liberalization and Reliability Assurance*, Institute of Energy Economics Japan (IEEJ).

24 Mechanisms for the optimal expansion of electricity transmission networks
Juan Rosellón*

1 Introduction

Electricity transmission grid expansion and pricing have received increasing attention in recent years.[1] Transmission networks provide the fundamental support upon which competitive electricity markets depend. Congestion of transmission networks might increase market power in certain regions, impose entry barriers on potential competitors in the generation business, and in general reduce the span of competitive effects. A well-functioning transmission network is a critical component of wholesale and retail markets for electricity.

The formal analysis of adequate incentives for network expansion in the electricity industry is complicated due to externalities generated by the physical characteristics of electricity itself as well as due to cost sub-additivity and economies-of-scale features of the grid (Vogelsang, 2006). Externalities in electricity transmission are mainly due to 'loop flows',[2] which arise from interactions in the transmission network (Joskow and Tirole, 2000; Léautier, 2001). The effects of loop flows imply that transmission opportunity costs and pricing critically depend on the marginal costs of power at every location. Energy and transmission costs are not independent since they are determined simultaneously in the electricity dispatch and the spot market. Thus, certain transmission investments in a particular link might have negative externalities on the capacity of other transmission links.

The analysis of incentives for transmission investment is further complicated since equilibria in forward electricity transmission markets have to be coordinated with equilibria in other markets such as the energy spot market, the forward energy market, and the generation capacity-reserves market (Wilson 2002). Likewise, electricity pricing is a complex issue since electricity is not storable, and because it has to simultaneously guide long-term investment decisions by transmission companies as well as to ration demands in the short run due to congestion. Furthermore, the effects of an increase in transmission capacity are uncertain. For instance, the net welfare outcome of an expansion in the transmission grid depends on the weight in the welfare preferences of the generators' profits relative to the consumers' weight (Léautier, 2001). Generation revenue gains, due to improved access to increased transmission charges and new markets, might be overcome by the loss of local market power.

The institutional structure of the system operator, and its relationship with the transmission network, are also key components that define the alternatives that might attract new investment to the grid. There are three possible structures for a system operator (Wilson 2002). The first is an independent system operator (ISO) – different from the company that owns the transmission grid – that is *decentralized* and intrudes to the least possible extent in the markets. The second is a *centralized* ISO that controls and coordinates the markets. The third is an integrated company, the transmission company (*transco*), which combines ownership of the transmission network with system operation.[3]

The economic analysis of electricity markets has typically concentrated on short-term issues such as short-run congestion management, and nodal pricing. However, investment in transmission capacity is long run in nature as well as stochastic. In the short run, the difference of electricity prices between two nodes in a power-flow model defines the price of congestion (Hogan 2002b). Nevertheless, an 'optimal' way to attract investment for the long-term expansion of the transmission network is still an open question both formally, and in practice (Vogelsang, 2006).

There are two main disparate (*non-Bayesian*) analytical approaches to transmission investment:[4] one employs the theory based on long-term financial transmission rights (LTFTRs) (merchant approach), while the other is based on the incentive-regulation hypothesis (performance-based-regulation (PBR) approach).[5] Hence, practical approaches to transmission expansion have to a large extent been designed according to particular criteria as opposed to being based on general economic theory, or on the more specific regulatory economics literature. In this chapter, Sections 2 and 3 review recently developed approaches for PBR and merchant mechanisms. Section 4 provides insights so as to build a comprehensive approach that combines both mechanisms in a setting of price-taking electricity generators and loads. Section 5 concludes.

2   The Incentive-regulation Approach to Transmission Expansion

The PBR approach to transmission expansion relies on incentive-compatible regulatory mechanisms for a transco. Such mechanisms provide the firm with incentives to make efficient investment decisions as well as to earn enough revenues to recover capital and operating costs (Grande and Wangesteen, 2000; Léautier, 2000; Vogelsang, 2001; Joskow and Tirole, 2005). In the international practice, PBR schemes for transmission expansion have basically been applied in England, Wales and Norway to guide the expansion of the transmission network. In the case of the two first countries, transmission pricing has been typically separated from energy pricing. A regulatory mechanism based on an 'out-turn' has been used there. The out-turn is the difference between the price actually paid to generators and the price that would have been paid in the absence of congestion. An 'uplift management rule' is then applied to the transco responsible for the full cost of the out-turn, plus any transmission losses. In Australia, a combination of regulatory mechanisms and merchant incentives has been implemented (Littlechild, 2003). Argentina has also relied on a combined regulatory-merchant approach under an ISO regime with nodal pricing (Littlechild and Skerk, 2004a, 2004b).

The formal analyses of PBR mechanisms for transmission expansion basically rely on comparing a transco's performance with a measure of welfare (Gans and King, 1999; Grande and Wangesteen, 2000; Léautier 2000; Joskow and Tirole, 2002). The transco is penalized for increasing congestion costs in the network, and is responsible for the costs of congestion it creates and the needed investment to relieve it. For instance, Joskow and Tirole (2002) propose a simple surplus-based mechanism to provide the transco with enough incentives to expand the transmission network. The idea is to reward the transco according to the redispatch costs avoided by the expansion, so that the transco faces the entire social cost of congestion. Such a mechanism would presumably eliminate the problems associated with lumpiness and loop flows, but it could still be subject to manipulation of bids in the energy market by a transco that is vertically integrated with generation. Even with no vertical integration, generators might invest no more than what is needed to match existing transmission capacity.

An alternative PBR approach is to explicitly study the nature of transmission cost and demand functions (Vogelsang, 2001). The monopolistic nature of a for-profit transco that owns the complete transmission network is isolated. This scheme might also be applied in a combined institutional structure where a (centralized) ISO takes care of the short-run market, and an independent transmission company handles investment issues. Regulation of transmission must then solve the duality of incentives for the transmission firm both in the short run (congestion), and in the long run (investment in network expansion). Conditions for optimal capacity expansion have been studied by the peak-load pricing literature: the per unit marginal cost of new capacity must be equal to the expected congestion cost of not adding an additional unit of capacity (Crew et al., 1995). However, there is still the question on how price regulation can provide incentives to reach such a stage. Price-cap mechanisms deal with regulation of 'price level' and regulation of 'price structure' (Brown et al., 1991). Price-level regulation refers to the long-run distribution of rents and risks between consumers and the regulated firm. Applied alternatives for level regulation typically include cost-of-service, price-cap, and yardstick regulations. Price structure regulation refers to the short-run allocation of benefits and costs among distinct types of consumers. Alternatives for regulation of price structure include price bands, flexible price structures as well as fixed or non-fixed weight regulation (Vogelsang, 1999). As in other network industries, electricity transmission price-level regulation is applied together with inflation (RPI) and efficiency factors (X), and a cost-of-service check every five years.

Price structure regulation is used by Vogelsang (2001) to solve transmission congestion, in the short run, as well as capital costs and investment issues in the long run. In a two-part tariff regulatory model with a variable (or usage) charge, and a fixed (or capacity) charge, the variable charge is mainly based on nodal prices and relieves congestion. Recuperation of long-term capital costs is achieved through the fixed charge that can be interpreted as the price for the right to use the transmission network. The fixed charge can also provide incentives for productive efficiency and, if it does not affect the number of transmission consumers, allocative efficiency – that is, convergence to the Ramsey price structure – can be intertemporally achieved.[6] The basic model proposed in Vogelsang (2001) is:

$$\max \pi^t = p^t q^t + F^t N - C(q^t, K^t) \qquad (24.1)$$

subject to:

$$F^t \leq F^{t-1} + (p^{t-1} - p^t) q^w / N, \quad q^t < K^t,$$

where:

F_t = fixed fee in period t;
p_t = variable fee in period t;
q_t = real oriented energy flow in period t (in kWh);
K_t = available transmission capacity in period t;
w = type of weight; and
N = number of consumers.

The transmission cost function $c(q, K)$ reflects the sunk cost nature of transmission investment and has the following form:

$$C(q^t, K^{t-1}) = C(q^{t-1}, K^{t-1}), \forall q^t, q^{t-1} \leq K^{t-1},$$

$$C(q^t, K^t) = C(q^t, K^{t-1}) + f(K^{t-1}, I^t), \text{for } q^t > K^{t-1},$$

where investment I_t is such that:

$$I^t = K^t - K^{t-1}.$$

Assuming that constraints are binding, and that μ^t is the Lagrange multiplier of the capacity constraint, the first-order condition with respect to p_t is:

$$\left(\frac{\partial q^t}{\partial p^t}\right)\left(p^t + \mu^t - \frac{\partial C}{\partial q^t}\right) = q^w - q^t.$$

For the optimal level of investment, $q^* = K^*$ it is true that $\mu^t = 0$, so that the first-order condition yields the (equilibrium) Ramsey rule:

$$\left(p^t - \frac{\partial C}{\partial q^t}\right) = -\left(\frac{q^w}{q^t - 1}\right)/\varepsilon,$$

where ε is the price elasticity of demand.

The proper incentives for efficient investment in the expansion of the network in the Vogelsang model are reached by the rebalancing of fixed and variable charges. Likewise, incentives for investment crucially depend on the type of weights used. For instance, a Laspeyres index uses the quantity of the previous period as weight for the price so that the transco will intertemporally invest until its transmission tariffs converge to Ramsey prices. However, this will not occur automatically since the firm faces a tension between short-run gains from congestion, and increases in capacity investment. These results are true only if it is assumed that cost and demand functions are stable, and that the transco does not use strategic conduct in setting its prices (see Vogelsang, 1999, pp. 28–31). In the case of changing cost and demand functions, or non-myopic profit maximization, convergence to Ramsey prices under the Laspeyres index cannot be guaranteed (see Ramírez and Rosellón, 2002). Thus, when there is congestion in capacity the transco will expand the network because its profits increase with network expansion when congestion variable charges are marginally larger than the marginal costs of expanding capacity. On the contrary, in times of excess capacity, the variable charge of the two-part tariff will be reduced, causing an increase in consumption. The fixed charge, in turn, increases so that total income augments despite the decrease in the variable charge. As a consequence, the transco ceases to invest in capacity expansion, and net profits expand since costs do not increase.

The pure price-cap approach in Vogelsang (2001), however, relies on simplifying assumptions that are rarely met in practice. Transmission demand functions are assumed differentiable and downward sloping, while transmission marginal costs curves are supposed to cut demand only once. These assumptions are generally invalid since, under loop flows, an expansion in a certain transmission link can result in decreases of other network links leading to discontinuities in the marginal-cost function (Hogan, 2002a). Likewise, transmission activity is considered as a physical output (or throughput) process as opposed to a transmission output defined in terms of point-to-point transactions.[7] This task is impossible since the physical flow through a meshed transmission network cannot be traced (Bushnell and Stoft, 1997; Hogan, 2002b, 2002c).[8]

One of the main problems of PBR mechanisms is their inconsistency with timing issues of transmission networks. Vogelsang (2006) then proposes a framework based on the distinction of ultra-short periods, short periods and long periods. The ultra-short period is motivated by real-time pricing of point-to-point transmission services, and there are no possibilities within this period for cost reductions. So, the main allocative-efficiency problem is price rationing of congested inputs. The short period coincides with the application of RPI-X factors, and is also the period for the calculation of fixed fees. The long period is given by the regulatory lag of the PBR mechanisms; that is, the time between (cost-of-service) tariff revisions (of typically five years). The long period crucially depends on the regulatory commitment so as to avoid ratcheting.

In the Vogelsang (2001) mechanism, investment in the grid occurs at the beginning of each period while fixed fees are calculated at the end of the period. Therefore, this mechanism implicitly lumps together the short and the long periods, and assumes that investments do not occur beyond such a period. The Vogelsang (2006) mechanism on the contrary combines the ultra-short, short and long periods and allows for the possibility of no investment for several short periods or even for times beyond a long period. This mechanism then depends on previous price performance of the mechanism in the past as well as on the long-run certainty provided by revisions based on rate-of-return regulation.

The combined approach for all types of periods in Vogelsang (2006) relies on a combination of Vogelsang (2001) and the incremental surplus subsidy scheme (ISS) (Sappington and Sibley, 1988; Gans and King, 1999). According to the ISS, the firm receives a subsidy in each period equal to the difference between the last period's profit and the current period's consumer-surplus increase. In Vogelsang (2006), the subsidy is financed through the fixed fee of a two-part tariff and consumer surplus is calculated with a verifiable approximation. The Vogelsang (2001) price-cap constraint is then used in Vogelsang (2006) for pricing in the ultra-short and short periods, together with an RPI-X adjustment for short periods and a profit adjustment at the end of long periods. Prices would then be average revenues from ultra-short periods. The RPI-X adjustments would affect only the fixed fees, and partially counteract any consumer-surplus increases handed to the transco.

3   Merchant Transmission Investment

The merchant approach to transmission expansion is based on auctions of financial transmission rights (FTRs) that seek to attract voluntary participation by potential investors. Incremental FTRs provide market-based transmission pricing that attracts transmission investment since it implicitly defines property rights. FTR auctions are carried out within a bid-based security-constrained economic dispatch with nodal pricing (which includes a short-run spot market for energy and ancillary services) of an ISO. The ISO runs a power-flow model that provides nodal prices derived from shadow prices of the model's constraints.[9] FTRs are subsequently derived from nodal price differences. Due to the long-run nature of electricity transmission, the ISO allocates long-term (LT) FTRs through an auction so as to protect the holders from future unexpected changes in congestion costs. Therefore, LTFTR auctions work in parallel with LT generation contracts.[10] The long-run concept is important for transmission expansion projects for investors. They usually have a useful life of approximately 30 years, so that auctions allocate FTRs with durations of several years. An FTR can in practice materialize in an obligation, a flowgate right or an option. 'Point-to-point' (PTP) forward obligations are in practice the most feasible instruments, while PTP options and flowgate rights are of limited applicability.[11] PTP-FTR obligations can be either 'balanced' or 'unbalanced'. Through a balanced PTP-FTR a perfect hedge is achieved, while an unbalanced PTP-FTR obligation is a forward sale of energy.

An example of an FTR auction is the New York ISO's allocation of transmission congestion contracts as a hedge for congestion costs, both in the short and long runs (Pope, 2002). Incremental FTRs are allocated to parties that pay for the expansion only if the new FTRs are made possible by the expansion. FTR awards are mainly derived from investors' choices but the ISO might also identify some needed incremental FTRs. When investors choose new FTRs for transmission expansion, simultaneous feasibility[12] of both the already existing FTRs and the new FTRs must be satisfied, because both flows and amount of transferred power among nodes are modified by the expansion. The ISO also temporarily reserves some feasible FTRs prior to the expansion project. Auctions are carried out both for short-term FTRs (six months) and LTFTRs (20 years). LTFTRs are allocated before short-term FTRs through auctioned and unauctioned mechanisms. The unauctioned mechanism simply reserves capacity for sales in later auctions, while in an LTFTR auction, investors reveal their preferences for expansion FTRs by assigning to each one a certain positive weight. Investors' preferences are maximized preserving simultaneous feasibility together with all pre-expansion FTRs. Losses are included in the dispatch and only balanced PTP-FTRs are defined to provide payments for congestion costs but not for losses.[13]

A mixture of planning and auctions of long-term transmission rights has also been applied in Pennsylvania–New Jersey–Maryland (PJM). The centralized PJM-ISO applies an LTFTR approach within a DC-load (direct current) dispatch model where locational prices differ according to congestion. PTP-FTRs are thus defined for congestion-cost payments. Revenues from FTRs are returned to owners of the transmission capacity in order to defray capital, operation and maintenance costs. Secondary FTR markets have also developed in several regions of the Northeast of the USA. FTR secondary markets are generally imbedded in the ISO's dispatch process so that their revenue adequacy is met.[14] Whenever there is need for an FTR between any two nodes, it is usually possible to derive it from nodal-price differences. Likewise, FTRs can be traded within various time frameworks (such as weeks, months and years). Nonetheless, no restructured electricity sector in the world has adopted a pure merchant approach to transmission expansion. The auction-planning combination has also being considered in New Zealand and Central America, while in Australia a combined merchant–regulatory approach has been attempted (Littlechild, 2003).

The formal analyses of FTR auctions can be subdivided into long- and short-term models. The short-run FTR models provide efficiency results only under strong assumptions of perfect competition, such as: absence of market power and sunk costs, an ISO without an internal preference on effective transmission capacity, complete future markets, lack of uncertainty over congestion rents, nodal prices that internalize network externalities and that reflect consumers' willingness to pay, as well as non-increasing returns to scale (Joskow and Tirole, 2005). The lifting of these assumptions would imply inefficient results on the use of FTRs. For instance, whenever market power exists, prices will not reflect the marginal cost of production. Generators in constrained regions will withdraw capacity (increasing generation prices), which would overestimate the cost-saving gains from investments in transmission. Likewise, market power in the FTR market by a generator provides an incentive to curtail output so as to make FTRs more valuable (Joskow and Tirole, 2000; Léautier, 2001; Gilbert et al., 2002).

Furthermore, increasing returns and lumpiness in transmission investment imply that social surplus created by transmission investments will be greater than the value paid to investors through FTRs. This is why investors in transmission expansion projects would prefer LT contracts, and exclusive property rights (at least temporarily) in the use of increased capacity. To this, it must be added that existing transmission and incremental capacities cannot be well defined since they are of a stochastic nature. Even in a radial line, realized capacity could be less than expected capacity so that the revenue-adequacy condition is not met. Stochastic changes in supply and demand conditions imply uncertain nodal prices as well.

More importantly, for meshed networks with loop flows an addition in transmission capacity in a link of the network might result in an actual reduction of capacity of other links. This, combined with asymmetry of information among the different agents in the electricity industry (generators, ISO, and transmission owners), might result in negative social value (Hogan, 2002a; Kristiansen and Rosellón, 2006).

All these insights are deemed as relevant by the LTFTR model. LTFTR auctions grant efficient outcomes under lack of market power and non-lumpy marginal expansions of the transmission network (Hogan, 2003). Regulation thus has an important role in large and lumpy projects in order to mitigate market power and let LTFTR auctions efficiently attract investors. In particular, market-power alleviation in the FTR market could be fostered by keeping transmission-owner buyers and sellers of LTFTRs under strict enforcement of open access to their grid facilities.

Furthermore, contingency and stochastic concerns are mainly taken care of by a security-constrained dispatch of a meshed network with loops and parallel paths (Hogan, 2002b). Likewise, agency problems and information asymmetries are indeed part of an institutional structure of an electricity industry where the ISO is separated from transmission ownership, and where market players are decentralized. However, the boundary between merchant and regulated expansion projects can hardly be affected by asymmetry of information. The need for regulation is therefore acknowledged in LTFTR auction mechanisms, and complete reliance on market incentives for transmission investment is thus undesirable. Rather, merchant and regulated transmission LTFTR mechanisms could be combined so that regulated transmission is used for projects that are lumpy (where only a single project makes sense as opposed to many small projects), and large (relative to the market size) (Hogan, 1999, 2003).

The implications of loop flows on transmission investment have also received detailed consideration by the LTFTR literature. A first seminal idea is to require the agent making an expansion to 'pay back' for the possible loss of property rights of other agents (Bushnell and Stoft, 1997). A new transmission link creates in turn a new feasible set that requires a redispatch of the net loads at each node. Loads and associated FTRs that were not previously feasible (pre-investment) become feasible (post-investment), while other pairs of loads (and associated FTRs) that were feasible might become infeasible. In this process, the expansion link might reduce social welfare when it is a binding constraint on low-cost generation schedules. Thus, to restore feasibility, the investor in the new link must buy back sufficient rights from initial holders.

Further, LTFTR auctions designed for small-scale networks subject to relatively marginal expansions, might rely on several axioms in order to solve the loop-flow dilemma (Hogan, 2002a; Kristiansen and Rosellón, 2006). The LTFTR auction should maximize the investors' objective function, both for decreases and for increases in grid capacity. More importantly, under an initial condition of incomplete allocation of FTRs the transmission energy balance and capacity constraints, as well as the power-flow equations, must be satisfied for the existing and incremental FTRs. Simultaneous feasibility should also prevail given that certain currently unallocated rights – or 'proxy awards' – are preserved. Under these assumptions, and when FTRs are simply defined as PTP obligations, LTFTR auctions will not reduce social welfare of the *hedged* agents.

Furthermore, proxy awards are to be defined according to the *best* use of the current grid along the same direction that the incremental FTRs were awarded. 'Best' is defined in terms of preset proxy references so that proxy awards maximize the value of such references. Given a proxy rule, the auction is carried out in order to maximize the investor's preferences to award the needed FTRs in the direction of the expansion, subject to the simultaneously feasibility conditions and the 'best' rule. Kristiansen and Rosellón (2006) develop a bi-level programming model for allocation of LTFTRs according to the best rule, and apply it to different network topologies.

When the preset proxy rule is used, Kristiansen and Rosellón (ibid.) derive prices that maximize the investor preference $\beta(a\delta)$ for an award of a MW of FTRs in direction δ:

$$\max_{a,\hat{\imath},\delta} \beta(a\delta),$$

subject to:

$K^+(T + a\delta) \leq 0;$
$K^+(T + \hat{\imath}\delta + a\delta) \leq 0;$
$\hat{\imath} \in \text{argmax}_{t}\{tp\delta|K(T + t\delta) \leq 0\};$
$\|\delta\| = 1;$ and
$a \geq 0,$

where $K^+(T + a\delta) \leq 0$ and $K^+(T + \hat{\imath}\delta + a\delta) \leq 0\delta$ are the feasibility constraints for 'existing plus incremental FTRs $(T + a\delta)$' and 'existing plus proxy plus incremental FTRs $(T + \hat{\imath}\delta + a\delta)$', respectively. This is a nonlinear and non-convex problem, and its solution depends on the parameter values, the current partial allocation (T), and the topology of the network prior to and after the expansion.[15] Simultaneous technical feasibility is shown to crucially depend on the investor- and the proxy-preference parameters. Likewise, the larger the current capacity the greater the need to reserve some FTRs for possible negative externalities generated by the expansion changes.

However, as previously argued, the described LTFTR mechanism implies that future investments in the grid cannot decrease the welfare of FTR *holders* only. FTRs cannot provide perfect hedges *ex post* for all possible transactions. The FTR feasibility rule always preserves the property that the incidence of any welfare reductions falls to those whose transaction were not selected *ex ante* to be hedged by FTRs. The special case of FTRs matching dispatch is consistent with welfare maximization, but in the case where there is not a full allocation of the existing grid, the likely result is that there would be more scope for welfare-reducing investments. The need for regulatory oversight would then not be eliminated with FTR auctions, but the intent is that the scope of the regulatory intervention would typically be reduced.

In an applied European transmission-market context, Brunekreeft et al. (2005) argue that unregulated merchant investment should also be complemented with a light-handed regulatory approach so as to increase welfare. In the welfare–competition trade-off, welfare should be more relevant so that third-party access and must-offer provisions are not necessary in the European Union regulations that promote unregulated merchant investments in electricity transmission (see also Brunekreeft and Newbery, 2006).

Likewise, cross-border transmission issues are relevant in the European case. Market-coupling mechanisms with voluntary participation are necessary due to the politically infeasibility of implementing a location-marginal-pricing mechanisms. Kristiansen and Rosellón (2007) carry out an application of the merchant FTR model for transmission expansion to the trilateral market coupling (TLC) border arrangements in Europe (such as the TLC among Netherlands, Belgium and France). The potential introduction of FTRs to the TLC is part of a wider interest in Europe for hedging products for cross-border trade, and congestion management by several regulatory bodies at the European continental level as well as at the national levels (for example, Spain, France, and Italy). The model of an ISO that reserves some proxy FTR awards and resolves the negative externalities derived from transmission expansion is simulated for the interconnector between France and Belgium. Such a project is shown to be feasible under the proposed FTR auction system. Other likely projects – such as an interconnector that invests in parallel to an existing line, or a third interconnector that links to the TLC arrangement thus forming a three-node network (such as an undersea cable from France to the Netherlands, or the links with Nord Pool or Germany) – are possible. These examples show that FTR-supported expansion projects in Europe could be technically and financially feasible. However, the actual employment of FTRs in TLC arrangements would also require clear definitions of the roles of system operators and power exchanges, daily settlements in implicit auctions between power exchanges, as well as the identification and provision of appropriate risk-sharing and regulatory incentives (see also Brunekreeft et al., 2005).

4   The Combined Merchant–Regulatory Approach

As seen in the previous sections, there is not yet in theory or in practice a single system that guarantees an optimal long-term expansion of all types of electricity transmission networks. This is especially true for non-Bayesian mechanisms, which are usually designed for allocative and productive efficiency improvements in the short run. However, the distinct study efforts suggest a second-best standard that combines the merchant and PBR transmission models so as to reconcile the dual short-run incentives to congest the grid, and the long-run incentives to invest in expanding the network.[16] The merchant mechanisms are easiest to understand for incrementally small expansions in meshed networks under an ISO environment. The price-cap method seeks to regulate a monopoly transco. Thus, 'small' transmission expansion projects might rely on the merchant approach while 'large and lumpy' projects could be developed through PBR incentive regulation, combining price-level and price-structure regulation so as to reconcile short- and long-run incentives.[17] More specifically, LTFTR auctions could be used within regions with meshed transmission networks regions of the country for marginal expansions,[18] while price-cap methodology – which also takes care of the loop-flow issue – could be applied to develop the large lumpy links among such regions. In this section, I analyze the basic elements needed to construct a coherent framework for the latter issue.

As previously discussed, the basic PBR model on a regulatory approach to transmission expansion postulates cost and demand functions with fairly general smooth properties, and then adapts some known regulatory adjustment processes to the electricity transmission problem. A concern with this approach is that the properties of transmission cost and demand functions are scarcely known and suspected to differ from usual functional forms. The assumed well-behaved cost and demand properties may actually not hold for a transmission firm. Loop flows imply that certain investments in transmission upgrades might cause negative network effects on other transmission links, so that capacity is multidimensional. Thus, the transmission capacity cost function can be discontinuous.

There have been some recent developments that tackle the issue of defining a price-cap model for transmission expansion within a power-flow model, so as to define a system that is coherent under loop flows. One such attempt, Tanaka (2007), derives optimal transmission capacity from the effects of capacity expansion on flows and welfare. A welfare function is maximized with respect to capacity subject to the transco's budget constraint, which is further defined as the difference between capacity cost and congestion rents. Various incentive mechanisms are then analyzed since the transco alone would prefer to maximize the difference between congestion rents and costs, rather than social welfare. A Laspeyres-type price cap on nodal prices is shown to converge to optimal transmission capacity over time under its budget constraint. A second mechanism is a two-part tariff cap also based on Laspeyres weights. Finally, another mechanism based on an incremental surplus subsidy, where the regulator observes the actual cost but not the complete cost function, is analyzed. These last two mechanisms are also shown to achieve optimal transmission capacity over time but without a budget constraint. However, Tanaka still relies on the big assumption of a well-behaved capacity cost functions for electricity transmission.

Another recent model, Hogan et al. (2007) (HRV), combines the merchant and regulatory approaches in an environment of price-taking generators and loads. A crucial aspect is to redefine the transmission output in terms of incremental LTFTRs in order to apply the basic price-cap mechanism in Vogelsang (2001) to large and lumpy meshed networks, and within a power-flow model. Very importantly, the HRV model does not make any previous assumption on the behavior of cost and demand transmission functions. In this model, the transco intertemporally maximizes profits subject to a cap on its two-part tariff, so that choice variables are the fixed and the variable fees. The fixed part of the tariff plays the role of a complementary charge that recovers fixed costs, while the variable part is the price of the FTR output, and is then based on nodal prices.

In the HRV model there is a sequence of auctions at each period t where participants buy and sell LTFTRs. LTFTRs are assumed to be PTP balanced FTR obligations. The transco maximizes expected profits at each auction subject to simultaneous feasibility constraints, and a two-part-tariff cap constraint. The transmission outputs are the incremental LTFTRs between consecutive periods. The model first defines the least-cost solution for the network configuration that meets a given demand. Over the domain where ι^t $q = 0$ (that is, no losses):

$$c^*(q, K^{t-1}, H^{t-1}) = \min_{K^t \in K, H^t \in H} \{c(K^t, K^{t-1}, H^t, H^{t-1}) | H^t q \le K^t\},$$

where:

q^t = the net injections in period t

$$\text{FTRs are derived from: } \sum_j \tau_j^t = q^t; \tau_j^t = \begin{pmatrix} -x \\ 0 \\ 0 \\ . \\ . \\ +x \\ 0 \end{pmatrix};$$

K^t = available transmission capacity in period t;
H^t = transfer admittance matrix at period t;
ι^t = a vector of ones; and
$c(K^t, K^{t-1}, H^t, H^{t-1})$ is the cost of going from one configuration to the next.

For a DC load approximation model, the transco's profit-maximization problem is then given by:

$$\max_{t^t, F^t} \pi^t = \tau^t[q(\tau^t) - q^{t-1}] + F^t N^t - c(K^t, K^{t-1}, H^t, H^{t-1}),$$

subject to:

$$\tau^t Q^w + F^t N^t \le \tau^{t-1} Q^w + F^{t-1} N^t,$$

where:

τ^t = vector of transmission prices between locations in period t;
F^t = fixed fee in period t;
N^t = number of consumers in period t;
$Q^w = (q^t - q^{t-1})^w$; and
w = type of weight.

The price-cap index is defined on two-part tariffs: a variable fee τ^t and a fixed fee F where the output is incremental LTFTRs. The weighted number of consumers N^t is assumed to be determined exogenously. When the demand and optimized cost functions are differentiable the first-order optimality conditions yield:

$$\nabla q(\tau - \nabla_q c^*) = Q^w - [q(\tau) - q^{t-1}].$$

The results of this model then show convergence to marginal-cost pricing (and to Ramsey pricing) under idealized weights, while under Laspeyres weights there is evidence of such a convergence under more restrictive conditions.[19] Likewise, transmission cost functions are shown to have typical economic properties under a variety of circumstances. This holds, in particular, if the topology of all nodes and links is given and only the capacity of lines can be changed, which implies that unusually behaved cost functions require modification of the network topology.

The HRV mechanism is further tested for different network topologies in Rosellón and Weigt (2007). First, the behavior of cost functions (in terms of FTRs) for distinct network topologies is studied. Second, the HRV regulatory model is incorporated in a mathematical program with equilibrium constraints (MPEC) problem and tested for three-node networks. Finally, the HRV mechanism is applied to Northwestern Europe. The results of the cost function analysis in Rosellón and Weigt show how, due to loop flows, rather simplistic extension functions can lead to mathematical problematic global cost function behavior. Furthermore, the linkage between capacity extension and line reactances, and thus the flow patterns, leads to complex results that are highly sensitive to the underlying grid structure. However, for modeling purposes the logarithmic cost form leads to nonlinearities with non-smooth behavior, thus making it demanding with respect to calculation effort and solver capability. Quadratic cost functions show a generally continuous behavior that makes them suitable for modeling purposes. In an overall analysis, the piecewise linear nature of the resulting global cost functions makes the derivation of global optima feasible. Hence, the testing of HRV regulatory model as an MPEC problem in Rosellón and Weigt results in a transco expanding the network so that prices develop in the direction of marginal costs. These results are confirmed when the MPEC approach is tested using a simplified grid of Northwestern Europe with a realistic generation structure. The nodal prices that were subject to a high level of congestion converge to a common marginal price level.

These results show then that the HRV mechanism has the potential to foster investment in congested networks in an overall desirable direction, satisfying the simultaneous-feasibility and revenue-adequacy constraints. However, further analysis is needed to estimate impacts of externalities such as the generation implications on the transco's behavior. Furthermore, the extension functions and restrictions have to be adjusted for a better representation of real-world conditions, particularly with regard to the lumpiness of investments as well as property-right issues, and existing long-term transaction contracts.

5   Concluding Remarks

Network expansions are relevant in many parts of the world such as in the European electricity market. Due to the liberalization processes initiated in the late 1990s, former national electricity networks with only limited cross-border capacities should now build the infrastructure for emerging wide energy markets. However, in Europe 10 years after the first liberalization efforts, the extended network is still segmented into several regional and national subnetworks with little expansion incentives between countries. Other regions in the world face similar problems too. Deeper understanding of the factors that determine a reliable framework for the investment in transmission networks is therefore of utmost importance.

In this chapter, I addressed the developments in the literature regarding merchant and PBR non-Bayesian mechanisms, as well as their combination, for non-vertically integrated firms. A combined merchant–regulatory mechanism to expand electricity transmission was analyzed. The merchant mechanism in Kristiansen and Rosellón (2006) for marginal increments in small links of severely meshed networks is such that internalization of possible negative externalities caused by potential expansion is possible according to the proxy rule: allocation of FTRs before (proxy FTRs) and after (incremental FTRs) the expansion is in the same direction and according to the feasibility rule. For large and lumpy networks, the HRV mechanism redefines transmission output in terms of incremental LTFTRs in order to solve the loop-flow issue. Constructing the output measure and property rights model in terms of FTRs provides the regulatory model with a connection to the merchant investment theory, and adapts the known regulatory adjustment processes in the network economics literature to the electricity transmission problem.

Of course much future research effort would be of value. Although some progress has been made (as in Rosellón and Weigt, 2007), the HRV model needs to characterize in detail piecewise cost functions when changes in topology are incorporated, as well as to address global rather than local optimality properties of incentives. Likewise, since proxy award mechanisms are in use and more are under development, further analytical investigation of the private incentives, welfare effects and regulatory implications would be very useful. Finally, formal research on the relationship between FTR auctions and social welfare is needed. Such analysis would require a new model that from its origin provides an FTR mechanism that simultaneously addresses the expansion problem, and that maximizes social preferences as well.

Notes

*   Support from the Programa Interinstitucional de Estudios sobre la Región de América del Norte (PIERAN) at El Colegio de México, the Alexander von Humboldt Foundation and Conacyt (p. 60334) is gratefully acknowledged.
1.   Problems related to coordination and capacity to the transmission network partly caused power outages

in the northeast of the US during 2003, which affected more than 20 million consumers and six control areas (Ontario, Quebec, Midwest, PJM, New England, and New York), and shut down 61 000 MW of generation capacity. Similar recent events in other parts of the world such as the UK, Italy, Sweden, Brazil, Argentina, Chile New Zealand, and Germany (incidence of E.ON Netz that blacked out large chunks of Europe in 2006) also awakened the interest in the factors that ensure reliability of transmission grids.

2. Loop flow is the characteristic of electricity that takes it through all available routes (path of least resistance) to get from one point to another. For instance, if a second line becomes available that is identical to a first line, the electricity that had been flowing over the first line will 'divide' so that half of it will remain flowing through the first line and the other half will flow over the second (see Brennan et al., 1996).

3. In practice, the ISO model has been used in Argentina and Australia. System operation is carried out by the ISO and transmission ownership is carried out by another independent company, the gridco. ISOs also exist in California, New England, New York, Pennsylvania–New Jersey–Maryland (PJM), and Texas. ISO practical experiences and proposals have been centralized. The transco model has been typically used in practice in the UK, Spain and the Scandinavian countries.

4. A third alternative method for transmission expansion seeks to derive optimal transmission expansion from the power-market structure of electricity generation, and considers conjectures made by each generator on other generators' marginal costs due to the expansion (Wolak, 2000). This method uses a real-option analysis to derive the net present value of both transmission and generation projects through the calculation of their joint probability. Transmission expansion only yields benefits until it is large enough compared to a given generation market structure. Likewise, many small upgrades are preferable to a large greenfield project.

5. Vogelsang (2006) differentiates between 'Bayesian' and 'non-Bayesian' mechanisms for transmission expansion. The Bayesian approach derives from the merger of the principal–agent theory and the optimal-pricing approach, and implies a theoretical framework supported by the '*revelation principle*' but that does not in general translate into rules that regulators can apply directly. According to the canonical model of regulation, under asymmetric information the need for prices to provide incentives arises when transfers from the regulator are not possible (Laffont, 1994). Non-Bayesian mechanisms arise from more practical reasons so as to improve inadequacies associated with rate-of-return regulation. Then PBR regulation, including price caps and yardsticks, were developed as non-Bayesian instruments to promote cost minimization. However, the application of PBR to network industries has been scarce, mainly due to the lumpy and long-term nature of networks, such as the electricity grid.

6. Baldick et al. (2007), provide practical guidelines for allocation among consumers of the costs of transmission expansion.

7. See Hogan et al. (2007) for a redefinition of transmission outputs in terms of point-to-point financial transmission rights (FTRs).

8. An application of the Vogelsang (2001) PBR model is carried out in Rosellón (2007) for the electricity transmission system in Mexico, under stable demand growth for electricity. Three scenarios are studied: (a) a single transco providing transmission services nationally, which applies postage-stamp tariffs; (b) several regional companies that operate separately in each of the areas of the national transmission system, which charge different prices; and (c) a single transco owns all the regional systems in the nation but charges different prices in each region. Achieved capacity and network increases are highest under the first scenario, while higher profits are implied by the second approach. These results are found to critically depend on two basic effects; namely, the 'economies-of-scale effect' and the 'discriminatory effect'. The economies-of-scale effect produces greater capacity and network expansion whereas the discriminatory effect increases profit.

9. The typical power-flow model framework is that of a centralized ISO that maximizes social welfare subject to transmission-loss and flow-feasibility constraints in a spot market. In practice, this model has been applied in Argentina, Australia, and several regions in the United States (PJM, New York, Texas, California). The economic dispatch model can also be understood within a static competitive equilibrium model. The producing entity is an ISO that provides transmission services, receives and delivers power, and coordinates the spot market. Meanwhile, consumers inject power into the grid at some nodes and remove power out at other points (see Hogan, 2002b).

10. FTRs give their holders a share of the congestion surpluses collected by the ISO under a binding constraint. The quantity of FTRs is normally fixed *ex ante* and allocated to holders. This reflects the capacity of the network. The difference between allocated FTRs and actual transmission capacity provides congestion revenues for the ISO. FTRs are defined in terms of the difference in nodal prices (see Joskow and Tirole, 2002).

11. Flowgate rights are defined in terms of the constraints implied from limits in the selling of capacity (Hogan, 2000).

12. A set of FTRs is simultaneously feasible if the associated set of net loads satisfies the energy balance and transmission capacity constraints, as well as the power-flow equations.

13. Other LTFTR allocation practical mechanisms are provided by Harvey (2002), and Gribik et al. (2002).

14. Revenue adequacy is the financial counterpart of the physical concept of availability of transmission

capacity. FTRs meet the revenue-adequacy condition when they are also simultaneously feasible (Hogan, 1992).

15. A general solution method utilizing Kuhn–Tucker conditions would check which of the constraints are binding. One way to identify the binding inequality constraints is the active set method. Kristiansen and Rosellón (2006) solve the problem in detail with simulations for different network topologies, including a radial line and three-node networks.

16. This would be an alternative approach to the previously seen model in Vogelsang (2006). A main difference would be that the combined merchant–regulatory approach mainly focuses in generalizing the price-cap constraints for electricity transmission (as in Vogelsang, 2006) within a power-flow model. Likewise, this combined model aims to redefine the output of transmission in terms of PTP transactions (or incremental FTRs) as well as to seriously tackle the 'heroic' assumption of smooth well-behaved transmission cost functions of the models in Vogelsang (2001, 2006) and Tanaka (2007).

17. Of course, this includes RPI-X adjustments together with cost-of-service tariff reviews at the end of each regulatory lag.

18. The Kristiansen and Rosellón (2006) model is an example of a concrete merchant mechanism designed for small line increments in meshed transmission networks.

19. Under Laspeyres weights – and assuming that cross-derivatives have the same sign – if goods are complements and if prices are initially above marginal costs, prices will intertemporally converge to marginal costs. When goods are substitutes, this effect is obtained only if the cross-effects are smaller than the direct effects. If prices are below marginal costs the opposite results are obtained.

References

Baldick, R., A. Brown, J. Bushnell, S. Tierney and T. Winter (2007), 'A National Perspective on Allocating the Costs of New Transmission Investment: Practice and Principles', White Paper prepared by the Blue Ribbon Panel on cost allocation for WIRES (Working Group for Investment in Reliable and Economic Electric Systems), September, available from: http://www.ksg.harvard.edu/hepg/Papers/Rapp_5-07_v4.pdf (accessed January 2007).

Brennan, T.J., K.L. Palmer, R.J. Kopp, A.J. Krupnick, V. Stagliano and D. Burtraw (1996), *A Shock to the System: Restructuring America's Electricity Industry*, Baltimore, MD: Johns Hopkins University Press for Resources for the Future.

Brown L., M.A. Einhorn and I. Vogelsang (1991), 'Toward improved and practical incentive regulation', *Journal of Regulatory Economics*, **3**: 313–38.

Brunekreeft, G., K. Neuhoff and D. Newbery (2005), 'Electricity transmission: an overview of the current debate', *Utilities Policy*, **13** (2): 73–93.

Brunekreeft, G. and D. Newbery (2006), 'Should merchant transmission investment be subject to a must-offer provision', *Journal of Regulatory Economics*, **30**: 233–60.

Bushnell, J.B. and S.E. Stoft (1997), 'Improving private incentives for electric grid investment', *Resource and Energy Economics*, **19**: 85–108.

Crew, M.A., C.S. Fernando and P.R. Kleindorfer (1995), 'The theory of peak-load pricing: a survey', *Journal of Regulatory Economics*, **8**: 215–48.

Gans, J.S. and S.P. King (1999), 'Options for electricity transmission regulation in Australia', Working Paper, University of Melbourne, September 10.

Gilbert, R., K. Neuhoff and D. Newbery (2002), 'Mediating market power in electricity networks', mimeo, Center for Competition Policy Working Paper No. CPC02-32, University of California, Berkeley.

Grande, O.S. and I. Wangesteen (2000), 'Alternative models for congestion management and pricing impact on network planning and physical operation', *CIGRE 37-203-2000*, Paris, August/September.

Gribik, P.R., J.S. Graves, D. Shirmohammadi and G. Kritikson (2002), 'Long term rights for transmission expansion', mimeo, P.A. Consulting Group, London.

Harvey, S.M. (2002), 'TCC expansion awards for controllable devices: initial discussion', mimeo, Law and Economics Consulting Group (LECG).

Hogan, W. (1992), 'Contract networks for electric power transmission', *Journal of Regulatory Economics*, **4**: 211–42.

Hogan, W. (1999), 'Restructuring the electricity market: coordination for competition', mimeo, JFK School of Government, Harvard Electricity Policy Group, Harvard University, available at: http://www.ksg.harvard.edu/people/whogan (accessed August 2007).

Hogan, W. (2000), 'Flowgate rights and wrongs', mimeo, JFK School of Government, Harvard Electricity Policy Group, Harvard University, available at: http://www.ksg.harvard.edu/people/whogan (accessed August 2007).

Hogan, W. (2002a), 'Financial transmission right incentives: applications beyond hedging', Presentation to

Harvard Electricity Policy Group Twenty-Eighth Plenary Sessions, May 31, available at http://www.ksg. harvard.edu/people/whogan (accessed August 2007).

Hogan, W. (2002b), 'Financial transmission right formulations', mimeo, JFK School of Government, Harvard Electricity Policy Group, Harvard University, http://www.ksg.harvard.edu/people/whogan (accessed August 2007).

Hogan, W. (2002c), 'Electricity market restructuring: reform of reforms', *Journal of Regulatory Economics*, **21**: 103–32.

Hogan, W. (2003), 'Transmission market design', mimeo, JFK School of Government, Harvard Electricity Policy Group, Harvard University, available at: http://www.ksg.harvard.edu/people/whogan (accessed August 2007).

Hogan, W., J. Rosellón and I. Vogelsang (2007), 'Toward a combined merchant–regulatory mechanism for electricity transmission expansion', Conference Proceedings, 9th International Association for Energy Economics (IAEE) European Energy Conference, Florence, Italy, June 10–13.

Joskow, P. and J. Tirole (2000), 'Transmission rights and market power on electric power networks', *RAND Journal of Economics*, **31**: 450–87.

Joskow, P. and J. Tirole (2002), 'Transmission investment: alternative institutional frameworks', mimeo, IDEI (Industrial Economic Institute), Toulouse, France, http://idei.fr/doc/conf/wme/tirole.pdf (accessed August 2007).

Joskow, P. and J. Tirole (2005), 'Merchant transmission investment', *Journal of Industrial Economics*, **53** (2), June: 233–64.

Kristiansen, T. and J. Rosellón (2006), 'A merchant mechanism for electricity transmission expansion', *Journal of Regulatory Economics*, **29** (2), March, 167–93.

Kristiansen, T. and J. Rosellón (2007), 'Merchant mechanism electricity transmission expansion: a European case study', Conference Proceedings, 9th International Association for Energy Economics (IAEE) European Energy Conference, Florence, Italy, June 10–13.

Laffont, J.-J. (1994), 'The new economics of regulation ten years after', *Econometrica*, **62** (3): 507–37.

Léautier, T.-O. (2000), 'Regulation of an electric power transmission company', *The Energy Journal*, **21**: 61–92.

Léautier, T.-O. (2001), 'Transmission constraints and imperfect markets for power', *Journal of Regulatory Economics*, **19**: 27–54.

Littlechild, S. (2003), 'Transmission regulation, merchant investment, and the experience of SNI and Murraylink in the Australian national electricity market', mimeo, Electricity Policy Research Group, University of Cambridge, http://www.eprg.group.cam.ac.uk/wp-content/uploads/2008/11/littlechildtransmission.pdf (accessed August 2007).

Littlechild, S. and C.J. Skerk (2004a), 'Regulation of transmission expansion in Argentina. Part I: State ownership, reform and the Fourth Line', Cambridge Working Papers in Economics CWPE 0464.

Littlechild, S. and C.J. Skerk (2004b), 'Regulation of transmission expansion in Argentina. Part II: Developments since the Fourth Line', Cambridge Working Papers in Economics CWPE 0465.

Pope, S. (2002), 'TCC Awards for Transmission Expansions', mimeo, Law and Economics Consulting Group (LECG), March 20, available at: www.nyiso.com (accessed August 2007).

Ramírez, J.C. and J. Rosellón (2002), 'Pricing natural gas distribution in Mexico', *Energy Economics*, **24** (3): 231–48.

Rosellón, J. (2007), 'A regulatory mechanism for electricity transmission in Mexico', *Energy Policy*, **35** (5), May: 3003–14.

Rosellón, J. and H. Weigt (2007), 'A combined merchant–regulatory mechanism for electricity transmission expansion in Europe', Conference Proceedings, 9th International Association for Energy Economics (IAEE) European Energy Conference, Florence, Italy, June 10–13.

Sappington, D. and D. Sibley (1988), 'Regulating without COST information: the incremental surplus subsidy scheme', *International Economic Review*, **29**: 297–306.

Tanaka, M. (2007), 'Extended price cap mechanism for efficicient transmission expansion under nodal pricing', *Network and Spatial Economics*, **7**: 257–75.

Vogelsang, I. (1999), 'Optimal price regulation for natural and legal monopolies', *Economía Mexicana. Nueva Época*, **8** (1): 5–43.

Vogelsang, I. (2001), 'Price regulation for independent transmission companies', *Journal of Regulatory Economics*, **20** (2): 141–65.

Vogelsang, I. (2006), 'Electricity transmission pricing and performance-based regulation', *The Energy Journal*, **27** (4): 97–126.

Wilson, R. (2002), 'Architecture of power markets', *Econometrica*, **70** (4): 1299–340.

Wolak, F.A. (2000), 'An empirical model of the impact of hedge contract on bidding behavior in a competitive electricity market', *International Economic Journal*, Summer: 1–40.

25 Efficiency measurement in the electricity and gas distribution sectors

Mehdi Farsi and Massimo Filippini

1 Introduction

In the last two decades the electricity and gas distribution sectors have witnessed a wave of regulatory reforms aimed at improving the economic efficiency. In the design of these reforms the information on several efficiency concepts, including scale efficiency, scope efficiency, and cost efficiency has become very important. The first two concepts are directly related to the economies of scale and scope, which are characteristics of the production technology, whereas the concept of cost efficiency is mainly a firm's characteristic related to its economic performance facing market and technological conditions.

Scale efficiency addresses the question of whether, for instance, an electricity distribution company is operating at the minimum of its long-run average cost curve. Any deviation from this level of production could result in inefficiency in terms of scale of operation. Thus, scale efficiency arises when the company cannot lower average costs by changing its output levels. For multiproduct energy companies, that is, a company distributing electricity and gas, scope efficiency focuses on the relative cost of joint production to the cost of producing the same total output in multiple companies. Scope inefficiency exists if the costs can be lowered by changing the output mixes across companies. The concepts of scale and scope efficiency rely on the assumption that the market structure, particularly outputs, can be adjusted to provide the companies with the greatest possibility of exploiting synergies. Cost efficiency measures the ability of energy distribution companies to minimize costs, given specific demand and market conditions. Cost inefficiency, also called 'X-inefficiency', occurs when the company fails to produce with full efficiency at the cost frontier. The performance of a company in minimizing costs can be decomposed into two types of efficiency. The first one is technical efficiency; the extent to which the energy distribution companies could reduce inputs for a given level of outputs (input orientation) or expand outputs for given levels of inputs (output orientation). The distance to an optimal production frontier measures technical efficiency. The second component of cost efficiency is allocative efficiency; that is, the possible reduction in costs by using the different inputs in optimal proportions or equivalently, by operating on the least-cost expansion path.

Due to the economic importance of the regulatory reforms in the electricity and gas distribution sectors, it seems essential that the design of these reforms be based on a clear empirical understanding of the cost structure and efficiency level of the electricity and gas distribution companies. For instance, this understanding is relevant to several regulatory as well as business decision issues. First, it provides information about the validity of the natural monopoly argument in the distribution of gas and electricity. Second, it contributes to an evaluation of the definition of the optimal size of service areas. Third, it gives information on the importance of the potential synergies through 'horizontal' integration, which allows local multi-utility companies to save on costs by exploiting the economies of scope. This information is very important in the assessment of a policy for unbundling multi-utilities.

Finally, performance indicators such as cost efficiency are used to monitor the companies' economic performance by comparing companies with the most-efficient practices. The regulators increasingly use such benchmarking practices in various incentive regulation schemes. For instance, one of the most widely used methods in electricity and gas networks is price-cap regulation (RPI-X). This method sets the maximum rate of increase for the regulated prices equal to the inflation rate of the retail price index (RPI) minus a productivity growth offset referred to as 'X-factors'.[1] In relatively new regulatory regimes (mostly adopted by European regulators), X-factors are set equal to the annual target change in cost efficiency for each individual company. Therefore, the regulator can set differentiated price caps based on the companies' efficiency performance estimated from an empirical analysis. However, the increasing use of efficiency analysis in the electricity industry has raised serious concerns among regulators and companies regarding the reliability of efficiency estimates.[2] In fact the empirical evidence suggests that the estimates are sensitive to the adopted efficiency measurement approach.[3] This implies that the choice of the approach can have important effects on the financial situation of the companies. There are, however, alternative strategies that can be used to improve efficiency measurement methodology regarding the sensitivity issues that we shall shortly discuss in this chapter.

The main goal of this chapter is to present and discuss the empirical measurement of the productive efficiency in the distribution of electricity and gas so as to draw recommendations for regulatory practice as well as business strategic decisions at the company level. An adequate analysis of productive efficiency should consider all the efficiency aspects, including those related to the scale and scope of the distribution networks. From a policy standpoint it is important to distinguish between the three concepts of efficiency. While allowing the companies to exploit the potential economies of scale and scope to the greatest possible extent, the regulators should introduce incentive measures to ensure cost efficiency. However, the measures of firms' cost efficiency should consider the different limitations that various companies face in exploiting the potential synergies, mainly due to their different levels of output, as well as the unobserved heterogeneity in external factors across companies.

The rest of the chapter proceeds as follows. Section 2 reviews some elements of the production theory. Section 3 provides a general overview of the concepts of scale, scope and cost efficiency. Section 4 illustrates the different econometric approaches that can be used to measure the level of efficiency of the companies. A selection of relevant empirical studies of scale, scope and cost efficiency in the electricity and gas distribution sectors are reviewed separately in Sections 5, 6 and 7. Section 8 provides a brief discussion of benchmarking practice in the regulation of electricity distribution networks along with a simple case study from Switzerland's utilities. Section 9 concludes the chapter with a final discussion and policy recommendations.

2   Review of Traditional Production Theory

The microeconomic theory of production is extensively documented in the literature (for example, Shephard, 1953; Chambers, 1988; Jehle and Reny, 1998; Varian, 1992) and will not be repeated here. Instead, this section focuses on some elements of the micro-economic theory of production that are relevant for understanding the measurement of productive and scale efficiency in the electricity and gas distribution industry.

Generally, the empirical studies model the production of firms in an industry which use g inputs $\mathbf{x} = (x_1, x_2, \ldots, x_g)$ to produce m outputs $\mathbf{y} = (y_1, y_2, \ldots, y_m)$. A reasonable way to represent the firm's technology of turning inputs into output in the long run is to specify a transformation function, $T(x_1, \ldots, x_g, y_1, \ldots, y_m) = 0$, in the multiple-output case or as a production function, $y = f(x_1, x_2, \ldots, x_g)$ in the single-output case. These functions represent the border of a set that includes all the production possibilities.

If the firm faces competitive input markets and chooses input bundles to minimize costs in the long run, then the cost-minimizing process can be represented as:

$$\min_x C = \sum_{j=1}^{g} w_j x_j, \text{s.t.} \ f(\mathbf{x}) \geq \mathbf{y}, \tag{25.1}$$

where C represents long-run total cost, w_j is the price of input x_j, and f is the production function relating the vector of inputs $\mathbf{x}$ to the output vector $\mathbf{y}$. The solution to (25.1) is of the form $C(\mathbf{y}, \mathbf{w})$, where $\mathbf{y} = (y_1, y_2, \ldots, y_m)$ and $\mathbf{w} = (w_1, w_2, \ldots, w_g)$.

Provided that the transformation function $T(x_1, \ldots, x_g, y_1, \ldots, y_m) = 0$ borders a strictly convex set, McFadden (1978) has shown that the cost function, $C(\mathbf{y}, \mathbf{w})$ has the following properties (regularity conditions):

1. $C(\mathbf{y}, \mathbf{w}) > 0$ for $\mathbf{w} > 0$ and $\mathbf{y} > 0$ (non-negativity);
2.   if $\mathbf{w}' > \mathbf{w}$, then $C(\mathbf{y}, \mathbf{w}') \geq C(\mathbf{y}, \mathbf{w})$ (non-decreasing in $\mathbf{w}$);
3. $C(\mathbf{y}, \mathbf{w})$ is concave and continuous in $\mathbf{w}$;
4. $C(\mathbf{y}, \mathbf{w})$ is homogeneous of degree one in input prices: $C(\mathbf{y}, t\mathbf{w}) = t\,C(\mathbf{y}, \mathbf{w})$ for $t > 0$;
5.   if $\mathbf{y} > \mathbf{y}'$, then $C(\mathbf{y}, \mathbf{w}) \geq C(\mathbf{y}', \mathbf{w})$ (non-decreasing in $\mathbf{y}$); and
6. $C(0, \mathbf{w}) = 0$ (no fixed costs).

Furthermore, according to Shephard's lemma, the cost-minimizing input demand functions are derivable from the cost functions. If the cost function is differentiable in input prices at the point $(\mathbf{y}^*, \mathbf{w}^*)$ then the following property holds:

7.   Shephard's lemma: $\mathbf{x}(\mathbf{y}, \mathbf{w}) = \nabla_w C(\mathbf{y}^*, \mathbf{w}^*)$, where $\mathbf{x}$ denotes the cost-minimizing vector of inputs required to produce the vector $\mathbf{y}^*$ of outputs given input prices $\mathbf{w}^*$.

The long-run total cost methodology shares the stringent behavioral assumption that all inputs are employed at their long-run cost-minimizing level. Some empirical studies present an alternative model where, in the short run, some inputs available to the firms are assumed to be fixed, implying that firms attempt to minimize cost conditional on given quasi-fixed inputs.

There is a dual relationship between the cost function and the transformation function presented above. This implies that if we define a production function and derive its cost function, we can take that cost function to generate a production function. Further, any cost function satisfying properties 1–7 implies some technology for which it represents the minimum costs. Therefore, according to Shephard's (1953) duality theorem, all structural characteristics of production possibilities are contained in the functional specification of the cost function satisfying properties 1–7.

In econometric applications, working with a cost function has many advantages over its dual transformation or production function. For instance, cost functions in comparison to transformation and production functions focus more on economic relationships than on technological relationships, thus facilitating the discussion of economic relationships. Moreover, in production functions typically high correlation between the input variables can result in a multicollinearity problem, which might preclude the estimation of the model or lead to an imprecise interpretation of the estimated coefficients. This problem is less pronounced when a cost function approach is employed. However, two assumptions are required for the cost function to be a valid dual representation of production technology. First, firms should face exogenous input prices and outputs. Second, firms are assumed to adjust input levels to minimize costs. Of course, in certain cases this assumption may be considered too restrictive. It can happen that the firms' optimization strategies do not fully correspond to a perfectly minimal cost function. In such cases, the functions based on cost optimization may still be used as 'behavioral' cost functions and can be helpful in studying the behavior and cost structure of such firms (Bös, 1986, p. 343).

3 Scale, Scope and Cost Efficiency

A large part of the cost estimation literature focuses on the estimation of the returns to scale. Chambers (1988) defines the returns to scale as the proportional change in output as an input bundle is changed by a scalar. If a proportional increase in all inputs results in a higher output increase, then the production function is said to demonstrate increasing returns to scale. If a proportional increase in all inputs results in a lower output increase, then the production function is said to show decreasing returns to scale. If a proportional increase in all inputs results in an output increase in the same proportion, then the production function is said to have constant returns to scale. Whether a production technology exhibits constant, decreasing, or increasing returns to scale has implications for determining the most efficient structure of the industry. In particular, if an industry were characterized by a single-output production technology with increasing returns to scale for a given output range, the efficient industry structure would entail a natural monopoly within that range.

Returns to scale are usually defined in terms of the relative increase in output resulting from a proportional increase in all inputs. In general, returns to scale need to be defined along a specific input-mix ray that is chosen arbitrarily. Considering this problem, Hanoch (1975) noted that it is more relevant to measure returns to scale by the relationship between total cost and output along the expansion path.

To translate the definition of returns to scale in terms of the cost function, Chambers (1988) proposed the concept of 'cost flexibility' that can be measured with the ratio of marginal cost to average cost, or with the cost elasticity of size. The degree of cost flexibility e_{cy} can then be measured using the following expression:

$$e_{cy} = \sum_{k=1}^{m} \frac{\partial \ln C}{\partial \ln y_k} = \sum_{k=1}^{m} \left(\frac{\partial C}{\partial y_k} \Big/ \frac{C}{y_k} \right), \qquad (25.2)$$

with m different outputs y_k.

The reciprocal of the cost elasticity of size is then defined as the economies of size or economies of scale (ES):

$$ES = 1 \Big/ \left(\sum_{k=1}^{m} \frac{\partial \ln C}{\partial \ln y_k} \right). \qquad (25.3)$$

There are economies of scale if ES is greater than 1, and conversely, there are diseconomies of scale if ES is below 1. In the case of $RS = 1$ we do not have economies or diseconomies of scale. Chambers shows that the definition of economies of scale is equivalent to the definition derived from production technology if and only if the production technology is homothetic. Generally, the empirical studies on the estimation of cost functions for electricity and gas distribution companies do not impose such an assumption and, therefore, use the concept of economies of scale.[4] From this discussion it follows that the presence of economies of scale shows that the companies have scale inefficiency.

In neoclassical production and cost theory, all output units are homogeneous. Hence, production of any one unit of output is indistinguishable from the next, and can be interchanged without any impact on costs. In energy distribution, however, an industry is characterized not only by the total output produced but also by the structure of the network served. The motivation for this complex characterization arises from the fact that costs in network industries are influenced not only by the total output produced but also by the network structure and area size. Therefore, for network industries such as gas and electricity distribution, the classical definition of economies of scale can be modified, in order to take into account, for instance, that different service areas and/or network structures have different impacts on the costs.

For these reasons, applied economists have suggested including several output characteristics in the cost model specification for network industries. These characteristics should capture the heterogeneity of the outputs, along with aggregated outputs. For example, in the following cost function, some output characteristics variables are included,

$$C = f(\mathbf{y}, \mathbf{w}, \mathbf{q}_{h+k}), \qquad (25.4)$$

where C is total cost, $\mathbf{y}$ is a vector of outputs, $\mathbf{w}$ is a vector of input prices, and $\mathbf{q}_{h+k}$ is a vector of variables reflecting output characteristics. The load factor, the number of customers and the size of the electric utility service area are examples of output characteristic variables for the electric industry.

The inclusion in a cost function of the number of customers and/or the size of the service area allows for the distinction of economies of output density, economies of customer density and economies of scale.

Following Roberts (1986), for the single output electricity and gas distribution companies it is possible to define economies of output density (EOD) as the proportional increase in total costs brought about by a proportional increase in output (y), holding all input prices, and the output characteristic variables such as the number of customers

(*CU*) and the size of the service territory (*AS*) fixed. This is equivalent to the inverse of the elasticity of total cost with respect to output:

$$EOD = 1\left/\left(\frac{\partial \ln C}{\partial \ln y}\right)\right..$$

(25.5)

The economies of output density exist if *EOD* is greater than 1, and the presence of diseconomies of output density is indicated if *EOD* is below 1. In the case of *EOD* = 1, no economies or diseconomies of output density exist. Economies of output density exist if the average costs of an electricity distribution utility decrease as the volume of electricity sold to a fixed number of customers in a service territory of a given size increases. This measure is relevant to decide whether side-by-side competition or local monopoly is the most efficient form in the electricity distribution industry.

Economies of customer density (*ECD*) are defined as the proportional increase in total costs brought about by a proportional increase in output and the number of customers, holding all input prices, and the other output characteristics fixed. *ECD* can thus be defined as:

$$ECD = 1\left/\left(\frac{\partial \ln C}{\partial \ln y} + \frac{\partial \ln C}{\partial \ln CU}\right)\right..$$

(25.6)

Similarly, the economies of customer density are not fully exploited if *ECD* is greater than 1, and conversely, diseconomies of scale are present if *ECD* is below 1. In the case of *ECD* = 1, no economies or diseconomies of customer density exist. This measure is relevant for analyzing the cost of distributing more electricity to a fixed service area as it becomes more densely populated.

Finally, the economies of scale (*ES*) are defined as the proportional increase in total costs brought about by a proportional increase in output, the number of customers and the size of the service area, holding all input prices fixed. *ES* can thus be defined as:

$$ES = 1\left/\left(\frac{\partial \ln C}{\partial \ln y} + \frac{\partial \ln C}{\partial \ln CU} + \frac{\partial \ln C}{\partial \ln AS}\right)\right..$$

(25.7)

The presence of the economies of scale corresponds to *ES* values greater than 1, while values smaller than 1 indicate diseconomies of scale. In the case of *ES* = 1, no economies or diseconomies of scale exist. This measure is relevant for analyzing the impact on cost of merging two adjacent electricity or gas distribution companies.

In the energy sector, there is a certain tendency that local utility companies operate in both electricity and gas distribution. Generally, this horizontal integration strategy allows the local multi-utility companies to save on costs by exploiting the economies of scope and to provide customers with an integrated set of services. Baumol et al. (1982) highlight that the economies of scope can result from sharing or joint utilization of inputs such as labor and capital. Economies of scope are present when costs can be reduced by joint production of multiple outputs. Following Baumol et al., the degree of global economies of scope (*ESCO*) across two outputs is defined as the ratio of excess costs of separate production relative to the costs of joint production of all outputs:

$$ESCO = \frac{C(y_1, 0) + C(0, y_2) - C(y_1, y_2)}{C(y_1, y_2)}. \tag{25.8}$$

A positive (negative) value for the above expression implies the existence of global economies (diseconomies) of scope.

A common measure of the technical inefficiency (*TIN*) of the firm which produces output, *y*, with inputs, *x*, is given by:

$$TIN = \frac{y}{y^*}, \tag{25.9}$$

where y^* is the frontier output associated with the level of input x. This measure does not include allocative inefficiency, namely, the potential savings by reallocating input factors. Cost inefficiency is an input-oriented measure overall inefficiency, which is defined as the distance from the cost frontier.[5] A measure of the cost inefficiency (*CIN*) of the firm which produces output, *y*, with cost, *C*, is given by:

$$CIN = \frac{C}{C^*}, \tag{25.10}$$

where C^* is the frontier cost associated with the level of output *y*. Each of the above-mentioned measures has their respective advantages and drawbacks. A major advantage of *TIN* is that it does not require any data on costs and prices. These data are usually difficult to obtain but are required for estimating *CIN*. However, *TIN* does not provide any information on the cost minimization process, which is more interesting from an economic standpoint. The cost-inefficiency measure includes both allocative and technical inefficiencies but does not provide an easy way to separate these two components.[6] Another important feature of the cost efficiency approach is that it treats the output as given. This is a realistic assumption in most regulated industries where the level of output is set by the regulator or determined by the demand factors.

4   Econometric Approaches to Efficiency Measurement

Measurement of efficiency in the electricity and gas distribution sectors is done by both cost and production functions in the empirical literature. The discussion that follows, while focusing mainly on cost-based methods, applies equally well to methods based on production function. There are two streams of this empirical literature. First, there are studies that estimate a cost function using, for instance, ordinary least squares (OLS) (or more elaborate econometric methods) without a stochastic component for inefficiency where all the companies are assumed to operate on the cost frontier (so no cost inefficiency is observed). From the estimation of this cost function it is possible to calculate the level of scale and scope inefficiency of the companies. Another group of empirical studies adopt the frontier approach assuming that the full cost efficiency is limited to those companies that are identified as the best-practice producers. All other companies are assumed to operate above the cost frontier, hence just non-zero inefficiency. In this case the econometric estimation of the best-practice cost frontier allows the calculation of the companies' level of cost inefficiency in addition to their scale and scope efficiency. Here we refer to the former approaches as 'non-frontier' methods, in which the estimated cost function is based on average performance, as opposed to 'frontier' analysis based on the best observed practice(s).

The estimation of the cost function in line with the non-frontier approach can be based on the OLS estimation of a parametric cost function, usually expressed in logarithms:

$$\ln C_i = f(\mathbf{y}_i, \mathbf{w}_i) + \varepsilon_i, \tag{25.11}$$

where C is total cost incurred by company i, $f(\cdot)$ is the cost function, $\mathbf{y}$ is a vector of outputs, $\mathbf{w}$ is a vector of input prices, and ε_i is the stochastic error term. The efficiency of parameter estimates can be improved by combining the cost function with the factor share equations implied by Shephard's lemma. According to cost-minimization theory, certain parameters in the cost function are identical to certain parameters in the share equations. Therefore, additional degrees of freedom are gained without the need to estimate any additional parameters. The input share equations take the following form:

$$S_{ji} = g(\mathbf{y}_i, \mathbf{w}_i) + \varepsilon_{iji}, \tag{25.12}$$

where S_{ji} is share cost incurred by company i for input j, $g(\cdot)$ is the input share function, $\mathbf{y}$ is a vector of outputs, $\mathbf{w}$ is a vector of input prices, and ε_{ji} is the stochastic error term. The cost system is usually estimated using the iterative Zellner technique (Zellner, 1962) for seemingly unrelated regressions (SUR). This allows for the possibility of correlation between the disturbance terms of the cost and share equations for each observation, while assuming independence across observations within a given equation. As the share equations sum to one, an equation must be omitted from the system to implement SUR. However, using the iterative Zellner technique, the resulting estimates are equivalent to maximum likelihood estimates (MLEs) (Kmenta and Gilbert, 1968), and they are invariant to which share equation is deleted (Barten, 1969).

The frontier analysis approach is well developed with a wide variety of parametric methods. More generally, the estimation of production or cost frontier can also be performed using non-parametric approaches. These approaches, such as data envelopment analysis (DEA) and free disposal hull, use linear programming to determine a company's efficiency frontier. In these approaches, the cost frontier is considered as a deterministic function of the observed variables. These methods are non-parametric in that they do not impose any specific functional form or distribution assumption. Thanks to their relative simplicity and availability, such methods, particularly DEA, are quite popular among both researchers and regulators in energy distribution networks – the advantages and drawbacks have been extensively discussed elsewhere.[7] In this chapter, the focus is upon the econometric approaches with a parametric specification. In Section 8 a brief illustration of the DEA method is given through a simple example.

Figure 25.1 presents a general classification of efficiency measurement approaches base on econometric methods. Apart from a few exceptions, all parametric methods have a stochastic element in their frontier function. Thus, this group of methods is also called 'stochastic frontier analysis' (SFA). The main exception with a deterministic frontier is the COLS method. In this approach the inefficiencies are defined through a constant shift of the OLS residuals (see Greene, 1980). As the entire stochastic term is considered as inefficiency, the frontier remains deterministic.

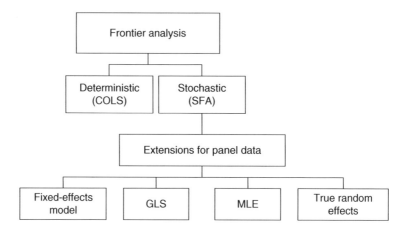

Figure 25.1   Efficiency measurement using econometric methods

The COLS approach is based on the OLS estimation of a parametric cost function, usually expressed in logarithms:

$$\ln C_i = f(\mathbf{y}_i, \mathbf{w}_i) + \varepsilon_i, \tag{25.13}$$

where the parameters are defined above. After correcting the stochastic error term ε_i, by shifting the intercept such that all residuals are positive, the COLS model can be written as:

$$\ln C_i = f(\mathbf{y}_i, \mathbf{w}_i) + \min(\varepsilon_i) + u_i, \text{ with } u_i = \varepsilon_i - \min(\varepsilon_i) \geq 0, \tag{25.14}$$

where u_i is a non-negative term representing the firm's inefficiency. The cost efficiency of firm i is thus given by: $Eff_i = \exp(u_i)$.

The main shortcoming of this method is that it confounds inefficiency with statistical noise: the entire residual is classified as inefficiency. In the stochastic frontier model the error term is divided into two uncorrelated parts: u_i is a one-sided non-negative disturbance reflecting the effect of inefficiency, and v_i is a symmetric disturbance capturing the random noise. Usually the statistical noise is assumed to be normally distributed, while the inefficiency term u_i is assumed to follow a half-normal distribution.[8] A basic SFA model can be written as:

$$\ln C_i = f(\mathbf{y}_i, \mathbf{w}_i) + u_i + v_i. \tag{25.15}$$

This model with a normal-half-normal composite error term can be estimated using the MLE method. Similarly the cost efficiency of firm i is given by: $Eff_i = \exp(u_i)$.

SFA models allow for a random unobserved heterogeneity among different firms (as represented by v_i) but need to specify a functional form for the cost or production function. The main advantage of such methods over deterministic approaches is the separation of the inefficiency effect from the statistical noise due to data errors and omitted variables.

Within the econometric approaches, as represented in Figure 25.1, there exist several models that can be used, and the choice of model is not usually straightforward. Several studies have reported discrepancies in efficiency estimates between different approaches and model specifications. For instance, using a cross-section of 63 power distribution utilities in Europe, Jamasb and Pollitt (2003) show that there are substantial variations in estimated efficiency scores and rank orders across different approaches (parametric and non-parametric) and among different econometric models. Similarly, using data from South America, Estache et al. (2004) provide evidence of 'weak consistency' between parametric and non-parametric methods.[9] These results are supported by two other studies (Farsi and Filippini, 2004, 2005), which show that the efficiency ranking of the companies can differ significantly across econometric models and across different approaches. Such discrepancies are partly due to methodological sensitivity in the estimation of individual efficiency scores and are not limited to a specific network industry.[10] The regulated companies operate in different regions with various environmental and network characteristics that are only partially observed. Given that the unobserved factors are considered differently in each method,[11] the resulting estimates can vary across methods. The magnitude of variation depends on the importance of the unobserved factors, which might change from one case to another.

In most cases, there is no clear criterion for the choice of the model and approach. Thus, it is assumed that the results are valid if they are independently obtained from several models. For instance, Bauer et al. (1998) have proposed a series of criteria that can be used to evaluate if the efficiency estimates from different methods are mutually 'consistent', that is, lead to comparable scores and ranks. However, the empirical results suggest that these criteria are not satisfied in many cases in network industries. The significant uncertainties in efficiency estimates could have important undesired consequences, especially because in many cases the estimated efficiency scores are directly used to reward/punish individual companies through regulation schemes such as price-cap formulas. Given these problems, it is not surprising that the benchmarking models used in electricity and gas networks have frequently been criticized (see, for instance, Irastorza, 2003; Shuttleworth, 2003). The stochastic frontier literature has provided a variety of panel data models that can be used to overcome some of these shortcomings and provide more attractive instruments to use in regulation.[12] In particular, these models can better control for the firm- or network-specific unobserved heterogeneity, which is a source of discrepancy across different benchmarking methods. The use of panel data models is especially interesting as data for several years have become available to an increasing number of regulators in many countries.[13]

The frontier model in (25.13) can be rewritten for panel data using subscripts i and t, respectively, representing the firm and the operation year:

$$\ln C_{it} = f(\mathbf{y}_{it}, \mathbf{w}_{it}) + u_{it} + v_{it}. \tag{25.16}$$

Typically, it is assumed that the heterogeneity term v_{it} is normally distributed and that the inefficiency term u_{it} has a half-normal distribution that is, a normal distribution truncated at zero:

$$u_{it} \sim |N(0, \sigma_u^2)|, \; v_{it} \sim N(0, \sigma_v^2). \tag{25.17}$$

This model is based on the original cost frontier model proposed by Aigner et al. (1977). The firm's inefficiency is estimated using the conditional mean of the inefficiency term as proposed by Jondrow et al. (1982) that is: $E[u_{it}|\hat{\varepsilon}_{it}]$, where $\varepsilon_{it} = u_{it} + v_{it}$.

The first use of panel data models in stochastic frontier models was by Pitt and Lee (1981), who assumed that the inefficiency term u_{it} is constant over time, that is: $u_i \sim |N(0, \sigma_u^2)|$. Pitt and Lee's model is different from the conventional random-effect model in that the individual-specific effects are assumed to follow a half-normal distribution. Important variations of this model were presented by Schmidt and Sickles (1984) who relaxed the distribution assumption and used the generalized least squares (GLS) estimator, and by Battese and Coelli (1988) who assumed a truncated normal distribution. In cases where the individual firm effects (u_i) are correlated with the explanatory variables, the estimated parameters may be biased. Schmidt and Sickles proposed a fixed-effects approach to avoid such biases.

The main restriction of these models is that the unobserved factors are random over time and across firms, which implies that the unobserved network and environmental characteristics that are usually time invariant are not considered as heterogeneity. Moreover, with a few recent exceptions such as Sickles (2005), the variation of efficiency over time is deterministic and/or follows the same functional form for all firms. Given that sources of inefficiency depend on technology shocks and other variations in the input markets as well as the managers' abilities to cope with them, it can be argued that inefficiencies are random over time.[14]

The 'true' panel models extend the original stochastic frontier model to panel data by adding an individual time-invariant effect. These models (Kumbhakar, 1991; Polachek and Yoon, 1996; and more recently Greene, 2005a) include two stochastic terms for unobserved heterogeneity, one for the time-variant factors and one for the firm-specific constant characteristics. Assuming that network and environmental characteristics and their effects on production do not vary considerably over time and that the inefficiency is time variant, these models help separate these unobserved effects from efficiency estimates.

Some of these models have been successfully used in electricity distribution networks (Farsi et al., 2006a), as well as other public service sectors (see Farsi et al., 2005, 2006b). The models can be written by adding a firm-specific stochastic term (α_i) in the right-hand side of equation (25.14):

$$\ln C_{it} = f(\mathbf{y}_{it}, \mathbf{w}_{it}) + \alpha_i + u_{it} + v_{it}. \tag{25.18}$$

The term α_i is an iid random component in a random-effects (RE) framework, or a constant parameter in a fixed-effects (FE) approach. The inefficiency term is assumed to be an iid random variable with half-normal distribution. This implies that the inefficiency is not persistent and each period brings about new idiosyncratic elements, thus new sources of inefficiency. This is a reasonable assumption particularly in industries that are constantly facing new technologies. Such models have an important advantage in that they allow for time-variant inefficiency while controlling for firm-level unobserved heterogeneity through fixed or random effects. The main difficulty of these models is that they are numerically cumbersome.

Another problem arises when the firm-specific effects are correlated with the explanatory variables. In such cases, the RE estimators are affected by heterogeneity bias,[15] but the FE model while being consistent regarding the cost-frontier slopes, usually overestimates efficiency variations. Moreover, there is an important practical problem with the FE model in that it requires the estimation of a large number of parameters, which limits its application to reasonably long panels with sufficient within-firm variation. Generally, in short panels the fixed effects are subject to considerable estimation biases, which directly reflect in the inefficiency scores.[16]

When panel data are available, regulators also have the possibility of using panel data parametric methods for the prediction of intervals for companies' costs. The predicted intervals can be used in the application of yardstick competition (Schleifer, 1985) among companies or to assess if the costs reported by the companies and used, for instance in rate-of-return regulation, are reasonable. In these cases, the regulated companies are required to contain the costs within the interval imposed by the regulator, or have to justify any costs beyond the predicted range. A similar approach has been used in Italian water supply regulation (see Antonioli and Filippini, 2001, for more details). In principle this approach is also possible with cross-sectional data; in panel data, the repeated observations of the same companies are used to identify part of their unobserved time-invariant characteristics and adjust the predictions accordingly. Farsi and Filippini (2004) show in an example that panel data frontier models allow a reasonably low prediction error.

To date the use of panel data parametric methods has been limited to academic research. However, despite the sensitivity problems, these methods can provide the regulators with useful information. As the availability of panel data increases, so too should the application of these methods in regulatory practice.

The choice of functional form $f(\cdot)$ is another important aspect of the parametric estimation of cost frontiers. A variety of functional forms have been employed to estimate cost functions in the literature.[17] The main distinction is between traditional and flexible functional forms. Traditional functional forms are first-order approximations to an arbitrary continuous and twice differentiable function, whereas the flexible functional forms provide a second-order approximation.[18] The most important difference between traditional and flexible functional forms is that the former impose restrictions on the values of the first and second partial derivatives whereas the latter do not. Traditional functional forms such as the Cobb–Douglas and the constant elasticity of substitution impose a priori restrictions on technology. For example, the Cobb–Douglas form imposes the restriction of a unitary elasticity of substitution and a value of economies of scale that does not vary with output. Whereas flexible functional forms such as the translog or quadratic forms allow for values of economies of scale, and input price and substitution elasticities to vary with output. Further, flexible functional forms allow the possibility of testing for several technological characteristics, such as homothetical production technology. Moreover, the quadratic functional form has been considered as one of the most relevant options for estimating scope economies because unlike logarithmic forms, it accommodates zero values for outputs thus, allowing a straightforward identification of scope economies.

The first empirical studies focused on the simple relationships between output and costs (see, for example, Nordin, 1947; Johnston, 1952; Huettner and Landon, 1974). These studies employed uncomplicated cost models assumed to be linear or polynomial in output. Later, cost function models were based on the application of duality theory to neoclassical production theory utilizing more elaborate functional forms. Nerlove's (1963) pioneering study on the cost structure of US electric utilities employed the traditional Cobb–Douglas specification. Christensen et al. (1971)'s paper on translog functional form made a significant impact on the empirical literature in applied production analysis. Most of the analyses of cost structures of electric and gas distribution utilities published in the last two decades use either the Cobb–Douglas or the translog functional form. Starting, for example, from the following long-run cost function:

$$C = C(y_1, w_1, w_2), \tag{25.19}$$

where C is total cost, w_1, w_2 are the input prices and y_1 is the output, the following Cobb–Douglas, translog and quadratic cost functions can be written as:

$$\ln C = \alpha_0 + \alpha_{w_1} \ln w_1 + \alpha_{w_2} \ln w_2 + \alpha_{y_1} \ln y_1 \quad \text{(COBB–DOUGLAS)}$$

$$\ln C = \alpha_0 + \alpha_{w_1} \ln w_1 + \alpha_{w_2} \ln w_2 + \alpha_{y_1} \ln y_1 + \frac{1}{2} \alpha_{w_1 w_1} (\ln w_1)^2 + \frac{1}{2} \alpha_{w_2 w_2} (\ln w_2)^2$$

$$+ \frac{1}{2} \alpha_{y_1 y_1} (\ln y_1)^2 + \alpha_{w_1 w_2} (\ln w_1)(\ln w_2) + \alpha_{w_1 y_1} (\ln w_1)(\ln y_1) + \alpha_{w_2 y_1} (\ln y_1)(\ln w_2)$$

$$\text{(TRANSLOG)}$$

$$C = \alpha_0 + \alpha_{w_1} w_1 + \alpha_{w_2} w_2 + \alpha_{y_1} y_1 + \frac{1}{2} \alpha_{w_1 w_1} (w_1)^2 + \frac{1}{2} \alpha_{w_2 w_2} (w_2)^2 + \frac{1}{2} \alpha_{y_1 y_1} (y_1)^2$$

$$+ \alpha_{w_1 w_2} (w_1)(w_2) + \alpha_{w_1 y_1} (w_1)(y_1) + \alpha_{w_2 y_1} (y_1)(w_2) \quad \text{(QUADRATIC)}$$

5   Empirical Studies on the Scale and Cost Efficiency in the Distribution of Gas

Farsi et al. (2007c) review the limited literature on econometric estimation of cost or production functions in gas distribution companies. A few studies that use a cost function approach to analyze the economies of scale and density and/or the level of cost efficiency in a sample of gas distribution companies are presented here.

Kim and Lee (1996) highlight the importance of accounting for output characteristics in estimating a translog cost function for gas distributors. The following cost model specification was adopted:

$$TC = f(y, q_1, q_2, q_3, \mathbf{P}),$$

where TC indicates the total cost of gas distribution, y is the volume of gas served, q_1, q_2, and q_3 are, respectively, the customer density, the average 'customer size' measured as average consumption and the 'supply rate' measured as the number of total customers relative to the number of total potential customers. $\mathbf{P}$ is a vector of input prices (labor price and the unit price of pipeline). In the estimation of the cost function, a translog functional form was employed to estimate the cost function of seven companies between 1987 and 1992. Almost all the firms were found to be exhausting their scale economies, and the average cost trend can be expressed as a function of output quantity and spatial characteristics.

Fabbri et al. (2000) estimated a total distribution translog cost function for 31 Italian companies observed during two years. Using the long-term cost function:

$$TC = f(V, C, \mathbf{H}, \mathbf{P}, T, O),$$

where TC indicates the total cost of gas distribution, V is the volume of delivered gas, C is the number of customers, $\mathbf{H}$ is a vector of territorial variables, $\mathbf{P}$ is a vector of input prices, T is a time-shift variable and O is a shift variable for private firms. The yearly average cost per employee is used as labor price, the book value of equipment divided by the length of the distribution network is used as capital price and the price of material and services is calculated as the residual expenses divided by network length. Output is measured as the volume of delivered gas and the number of customers. The specification also includes the ratio of network length to the number of customers, share of urban population, the average altitude of the service area, and dummy variables for owner-ship differences and time effects. The results suggest more cost-efficient production in private firms; however, the economies of scale are not significant at the output levels yet economies of density appear to be considerable. These results are in line with most of the findings reported in other studies.

Farsi et al. (2007c) study the cost structure of gas distribution utilities in Switzerland. Three stochastic frontier models are applied to a panel of 26 companies operating from 1996 to 2000. Efficiency is assumed to be constant over time. The output is measured as total volume of natural gas delivered. Input factors consist mainly of the gas purchased from a transmission company, labor and capital. The cost function is specified as:

$$TC = f(Y, P_C, P_L, P_E, LF, TB, CUD, ASIZE),$$

where TC represents total costs; Y is the energy value of the delivered gas measured in MWh; and P_C, P_L and P_E are, respectively, the prices of capital, labor and purchase price of natural gas. In addition to these variables, the load factor LF, the number of terminal blocks TB, the customer density CUD and the area size $ASIZE$ have been introduced in the model as output characteristics variables. Given the small size of the sample and the large number of parameters[19] in the translog model, a Cobb–Douglas form is used.

The analysis highlights the importance of output characteristics such as customer density and network size. The application of three cost frontier models suggests an average inefficiency of about 7 percent in the sector. This result is robust across all the models. The individual efficiency scores and ranks estimated from different models show a strong correlation. However, the companies identified as 'best' and 'worst' practices change across models. Therefore, the individual efficiency estimates cannot be directly used as X-factors in the price-cap formulas. As for the scale and density economies, the results are more or less consistent with the findings of studies performed in other coun-tries, in that they provide evidence of considerable density economies but insignificant or weak scale economies. This implies that distributors could decrease their average costs by increasing the output as long as they use the same network, but the extension of net-works does not result in any significant economies.

The empirical evidence reported suggests that franchised monopolies, rather than side-by-side competition, is the most efficient form of production organization in the gas distribution industry. Further, consolidation of small utilities whose service territories are adjacent is likely to reduce costs. However, for large and medium-sized companies consolidation would not bring about large savings.

6   Empirical Studies on the Scale and Cost Efficiency in the Distribution of Electricity

The literature on econometric estimation of cost functions in electricity distribution companies is relatively large. In this section we present a selection of studies that have used a cost function approach. The emphasis has been placed on the studies that analyze the economies of scale and density and/or the level of cost efficiency.[20]

Roberts (1986) was the first attempt to estimate a cost function for electricity production and distribution using the duality theory and a flexible functional form. Previous cost studies on electricity production and distribution had focused on simpler relationships between cost, output and service area characteristics. The specified cost model assumes that firms follow a two-stage production optimization process. In the first stage they make decisions regarding electricity generation, while in the second they make decisions concerning electricity distribution. Thus, in the second stage, firms are viewed as buyers of electricity either from their own plants or from other suppliers.

A cross-section of 65 privately owned vertically integrated electric utilities in 1978 is considered by Roberts. The electricity generation activity of these utilities was very high. Approximately 80 percent of kWh input was self-generated, while the remaining 20 percent was purchased from other electric generation utilities. The cost structure of this vertically integrated industry is specified in the following total cost function:

$$TC = g(Y_L, Y_H, AS, CU, P_L, P_E, P_C),$$

where TC is the total cost, P_L, P_C and P_E are input prices of labor, capital and purchased electricity. Y_L, Y_H are, respectively, the low- and high-voltage deliveries. To control for other determinants of production and delivery costs, the services area, AS, and the total number of customers, CU, were also included. Therefore, Roberts tried to capture the heterogeneous nature of kWh deliveries by including two outputs as well as two variables characterizing these outputs, as explanatory variables in the cost function. In this way, the economies of density, customer density, and size may be distinguished from each other. The empirical results showed the existence of substantial economies of density and slight economies of customers and size in the production and distribution of electricity; indicating no strong evidence that larger service areas result in any economies of power delivery.

Salvanes and Tjøtta's (1994) made the first attempt to estimate a cost function only for distribution companies using a cross-section of 100 Norwegian public electricity distribution utilities in 1988. These companies behave as local natural monopolies, whose activities include transportation of electricity to end users, installation and maintenance of equipment and administration. The following short-run cost function is used to analyze the cost structure:

$$VC = g(Y, N, P_L, P_E, F),$$

where *VC* is the variable cost specified as a translog functional form, and P_L and P_E are input prices of labor and purchased electricity. The wage rate is defined as the annual labor expenses divided by the total labor force. The aggregate measure of output is given by *Y*. To control for other determinants of delivery cost, the total number of customers, *N*, and the length of the distribution lines *F* were also included.

Like Roberts (1986), Salvanes and Tjøtta distinguish between economies of density and economies of scale and identify considerable economies of density but only moderate economies of scale. The coefficient of the capital stock variable is positive, implying variable costs are increasing in fixed input (capital), violating the non-increasing regularity condition at the median of the data.

Filippini (1998) is the first paper with a total cost function only for distribution companies. The firm's total cost of distributing electricity has been represented by a translog cost function:

$$TC = C(y, P_c, P_p, P_l, LF, CU, ST, T),$$

where *TC* represents total cost and *y* is the output represented by the total number of kWh delivered, and *Pc*, *Pp* and *Pl* are the prices of capital, kWh input and labor, respectively. *LF* is the load factor, *ST* the size of the service territory of the distribution utility measured in squares kilometers and *CU* the number of customers. These variables are introduced in the model as output characteristics. The load factor has been included in order to capture the impact on cost of the intensity of use of the plant. *T* is a time variable which captures the shift in technology representing change in technical efficiency. The cost model has been estimated for cross-sectional samples of publicly owned electricity distribution utilities operating in Swiss cities. The dataset is composed of a sample of 39 city electricity distribution utilities observed for four years, from 1988 to 1991. The results indicate the existence of economies of output and customer density as well as economies of scale for most output levels.

The cost efficiency of a sample of Swiss electricity distribution utilities is estimated by Farsi et al. (2006a) using three alternative frontier models to estimate the firm's total cost function:

$$C = C(Y, P_K, P_L, P_P, LF, CU, AS, HGRID, DOT, DW, T),$$

where *C* represents total cost; *Y* is the output in kWh; P_K, P_L and P_P are, respectively, the prices of capital, labor and input power; and *T* is a time variable representing the linear trend in technological progress.

Also included in a cost function model are the six output (and network) characteristics: *LF* is the 'load factor' defined as the ratio of utility's average load on its peak load; *AS* the size of the service area served by the distribution utility; *CU* is the number of customers; *HGRID* is a binary indicator to distinguish the utilities that operate a high-voltage transmission network in addition to their distribution network; *DOT* is a dummy variable representing the utilities whose share of auxiliary revenues is more than 25 percent of total revenues; and *DW* is an indicator for the cases in which more than 40 percent of the service area is covered by forests to capture the relatively high maintenance costs and risk of damage to power lines in forests.

Table 25.1   Efficiency scores of Swiss distribution utilities

	GLS	MLE	TRE
Average	0.868	0.887	0.957
Minimum	0.723	0.735	0.861
Maximum	1	0.993	0.996
Correlation coefficients			
with GLS	1	0.970	0.042
with MLE	0.970	1	0.055

Source: Farsi et al. (2006a).

A Cobb–Douglas functional form has been adopted. The authors excluded the trans-log form to avoid the potential risk of multicollinearity among second-order terms due to strong correlation between output and the larger number of characteristics variables. An unbalanced panel of 59 Swiss distribution utilities over a nine-year period (1988 to 1996) included 380 observations with a minimum of four observations per company. Three cost-frontier models, namely GLS (Schmidt and Sickles, 1984), MLE (Pitt and Lee, 1981), and the true random effects (TRE) model (Greene, 2005a) were estimated. A descriptive summary of the efficiency estimates from different models and their correlation matrix is presented in Table 25.1. While GLS and MLE models give similar results (12 to 15 percent excess costs), the TRE model predicts a much higher average efficiency rate, implying only about 4 percent excess in costs. There is a high correlation between GLS and MLE estimates whereas the TRE estimates show a weak correlation with the conventional models. These results generally confirm the existence of discrepancies in efficiency estimates between different cost-frontier models.

The TRE model assumes a time-variant inefficiency term and a separate stochastic term for firm-specific unobserved heterogeneity the results suggest that the other models might overestimate the inefficiency. This conclusion is valid to the extent that inefficiencies do not remain constant over time and unobserved network effects remain constant.[21] Unfortunately these relatively new models can only give a partial solution to the sensitivity problems.

In general, the empirical evidence reported in these outlined studies suggests that franchised monopolies, rather than side-by-side competition, is the most efficient form of production organization in the electricity distribution industry. Further, consolidation of small utilities whose service areas are adjacent is likely to reduce costs. However, similar large and medium-sized gas distribution companies, a consolidation would not imply large savings. The concept of small, medium and large companies is relative to the size of the companies included in each sample.

7   Empirical Studies on the Scale and Scope Efficiency in the Distribution of Electricity and Gas

There are only a few studies on the economies of scope in multi-utilities: Mayo (1984) and Sing (1987) in electricity and gas distribution, and Fraquelli et al. (2004) and Farsi et al. (2007a) in the electricity, gas and water sectors. Mayo (1984) estimates a quadratic cost function for two cross-sectional data sets from the US electricity and gas distribution sectors and reports scope economies only for small companies. Sing (1987), also using a cross-sectional dataset including electricity and gas distributors, estimates a generalized translog cost function with a Box–Cox transformation for outputs. In addition to the factor prices of labor, capital and fuel, the customer density is included as an output characteristic. While reporting diseconomies of scope for the sample mean, Sing finds scope synergies for certain output combinations, without any clear pattern regarding the outputs magnitude.

Fraquelli et al. (2004) use data from 90 Italian electricity, gas and water distributors over three years. However, the data are pooled across the years and no panel data models are applied. They compare different functional forms such as the translog cost function with a small value transformation, the generalized translog, the separable quadratic and the composite cost function introduced by Pulley and Braunstein (1992). They conclude that economies of scope exist but their statistical significance can only be asserted over small outputs.

Farsi et al. (2007a) analyzed the cost structure of a panel dataset from 87 electricity, gas and water utilities in Switzerland. Assuming firms minimized cost and used a quadratic cost function specified as:

$$C = C(q^{(1)}, q^{(2)}, q^{(3)}, w^{(1)}, w^{(2)}, w^{(3)}, w^{(4)}, r, \tau^{(1)}, \tau^{(2)}, \tau^{(3)}),$$

where C represents total costs; $q^{(1)}$, $q^{(2)}$ and $q^{(3)}$ are, respectively, the distributed electricity, gas and water during the year, $w^{(1)}$, $w^{(2)}$, $w^{(3)}$ and $w^{(4)}$ are, respectively, the input factor prices for labor and capital services and the purchased electricity and gas; r is the customer density measured by the number of customers divided by the size of the service area measured in square kilometers; and the sector-specific linear trends are represented by $\tau^{(1)}$, $\tau^{(2)}$ and $\tau^{(3)}$, respectively, for the electricity, gas and network sectors.

The econometric analysis based on a random effect GLS model and a random coefficient specification uses an unbalanced panel dataset containing financial and technical information from 87 companies observed during the nine-year period between 1997 and 2005. The results suggest the presence of scope and scale economies at most output levels with a well-behaved variation of the synergies, output indicated a fall (rise) in both scale and scope economies as outputs increase (decrease).

8   Case Study: Benchmarking and Regulation in the Electricity Distribution Sector

The use of benchmarking in the regulation of electricity distribution operators is a prominent example of a direct policy application of efficiency measurement methods. In many countries regulatory reforms are relatively advanced in the electricity industry. A characterizing feature of these reforms is that the introduction of competition in the generation and retail sectors is often combined with the implementation of an incentive regulation scheme, and increasingly benchmarking practices, in the distribution sector. The use of parametric methods in the estimation of efficiency is however limited to a few cases.[22] An interesting example is the application of COLS by the UK electricity regulator (Ofgem) in setting the prices based on individual X-factors estimated from a sample of 14 observations (Pollitt, 2005). The validity of the adopted approach can be questioned mainly because of the limited size of the sample and the deterministic nature of the frontier that does not distinguish between inefficiency and statistical noise. The robustness of the efficiency estimates could be improved using panel data and a stochastic frontier approach.

In this section we study a similar example of benchmarking of power distribution utilities to illustrate the potential differences across models and the resulting sensitivity problems in estimating efficiency, encountered by the regulators. These problems are particularly important in cases such as Ofgem, in which the benchmarking analysis is based on cross-sectional data (CEPA, 2003). Here, the example has been chosen from the Swiss power distribution sector. The sample consists of 52 utilities operating in 1994. The cost efficiency of these companies has been analyzed using two parametric approaches (COLS and SFA) and one non-parametric method (DEA). This choice provides the opportunity for comparing the results among different approaches to draw conclusions for the regulators.

A three-input single-output production function has been considered. The output is measured as the total delivered electricity in kWh, and the three input factors are capital, labor and the input power purchased from the generator. Capital price is measured as the ratio of capital expenses (depreciation plus interest) to the total installed capacity of the utility's transformers in kVA (kilo volt-ampere). The capital costs are approximated by the residual costs that is, total costs minus labor and purchased power costs. Labor price is defined as the average annual salary of the firm's employees.

The costs of distribution utilities consist of two main parts: the costs of the purchased power and the network costs including labor and capital costs. There are therefore two alternatives for measuring cost efficiency: total costs approach and network costs approach. The network costs approach has a practical advantage in that the estimated average costs can be directly used in a price-cap formula.[23] However, this approach neglects the potential inefficiencies in the choice of the generator and also in the possibility of substitution between capital and input energy. In this example we use the first approach based on the total costs.

In addition to input prices and output, three output characteristics are included. The resulting specification of the cost function can be written as:

$$C = C(Y, PK, PL, PP, LF, CU, AS), \tag{25.20}$$

where C represents total cost; Y is the output in kWh; P_K, P_L and P_P are, respectively, the prices of capital, labor and input power; LF is the 'load factor' defined as the ratio of utility's average load on its peak load; CU is the number of customers; and AS the size of the service area served by the distribution utility.

For the parametric models we have chosen a Cobb–Douglas functional form. The condition of linear homogeneity in input prices is imposed by dividing the input prices by the price of purchased electricity. The cost function can therefore be formulated as:

$$\ln\left(\frac{C}{P_P}\right)_i = \beta_0 + \beta_Y \ln Y_{it} + \beta_K \ln\left(\frac{P_K}{P_P}\right)_i + \beta_L \ln\left(\frac{P_L}{P_P}\right)_i$$
$$+ \gamma_1 \ln LF_i + \gamma_2 \ln AS_i + \gamma_3 \ln CU_i + r_i, \tag{25.21}$$

with $i = 1, 2, \ldots, N$, where r_i represents the residuals, namely, a mean-zero iid error term for COLS and a composite normal-half-normal iid term for the SFA model.

The specification given in (25.20) can be readily used in the DEA method. In this method there is no need to specify any functional form. In a sample of N companies with a k-input–m-output production function with variable returns to scale (VRS), the measurement of cost efficiency using DEA method reduces to the following minimization problem:

$$\min_{\lambda, x_i} w_i' x_i$$

$$\text{s.t.: } - y_i + Y\lambda \geq 0, \, x_i - X\lambda \geq 0, \, \mathbf{N}'\lambda = 1, \, \lambda \geq 0, \tag{25.22}$$

where w_i and x_i are $k \times 1$ vectors, respectively, representing input prices and quantities for firm i ($i = 1, 2, \ldots, N$); y_i is an $m \times 1$ vector representing the given output bundle; X and Y are, respectively, input and output matrices namely, a $k \times N$ and an $m \times N$ matrix consisting of the observed input and output bundles for all the companies in the sample; $\mathbf{N}$ is an $N \times 1$ vector of ones; and λ is an $N \times 1$ vector of non-negative constants to be estimated. The VRS property is satisfied through the convexity constraint ($\mathbf{N}\lambda = 1$) that ensures companies are benchmarked against companies with similar size.

The minimization problem given in (25.22) can be solved by linear programming (LP) methods. The LP algorithm finds a piece-wise linear isoquant in the input space, which corresponds to the minimum costs of producing the given output at any given point. The solution gives the minimum feasible costs for each company namely, $w_i' x_i^*$, where x_i^* is the optimal input bundle for firm i. The cost efficiency of each production plan is then estimated as its distance to the envelope. Namely, firm i's cost efficiency is therefore obtained by: $Eff_i = (w_i' x_i^*)/(w_i' x_i^o)$ where x_i^o is the observed input bundle used by company i.

The quantities of labor, capital stock and the amount of input energy are considered as input. Labor and capital inputs are, respectively, measured as the number of full-time equivalent employees and the installed capacity of the transformers.[24] The output (Y) and the three output characteristics are consiered as output. With the exception of the load factor (LF) all these characteristics take resources, thus can be considered as an output. As for the load factor, since a higher LF implies a smoother demand, thus lower costs, the corresponding output characteristics in the DEA model is defined as the inverse of LF. Therefore, the DEA model can be considered as a production with three inputs and four outputs. We assume VRS for the DEA model.[25]

The three models have been applied to the cross-sectional data (from 52 companies in 1994). Summary statistics of the estimated efficiency scores are given in Table 25.2. The efficiency scores are normalized to a scale between 0 and 1, where the highest value (1) implies a perfectly efficient company and the difference with 1 approximates the percentage of the total costs that the company can potentially save. The results in Table 25.2 suggest the companies are on average about 86 to 92 percent efficient. The COLS efficiency scores are lower than the other models by an average of 6 percent. COLS and DEA methods are similar in that neither accounts for stochastic variation in the frontier. However, the DEA model has a non-parametric frontier, which allows certain flexibility for a better adjustment with different companies. The average efficiency estimate is quite

Table 25.2   Efficiency scores of Swiss distribution utilities (52 utilities in 1994)

	DEA	SFA	COLS
Average	0.917	0.920	0.858
Minimum	0.734	0.819	0.727
Maximum	1	0.977	1
Correlation coefficients			
with DEA	1	0.563	0.603
with SFA	0.563	1	0.961

similar between the SFA and DEA models, suggesting that a rigid model like COLS can underestimate the efficiency. These results also suggest that in our example, allowing for stochastic variation or removing parametric restrictions have, at least on average, a similar effect on efficiency estimates.

The correlation coefficients between the efficiency scores obtained from different models are also listed in Table 25.2. Although the COLS and SFA estimates show quite a high correlation, their correlation with the DEA estimates is relatively low. These results suggest that the efficiency ranking of the companies could change considerably, depending on the adopted model.

In order to see the differences in ranking individual companies, the rank status of the 10 most-efficient and least-efficient companies according to the SFA method is considered. Table 25.3 lists the efficiency ranks of these 20 companies based on the two other models. The results indicate a similar ranking across the two parametric methods (SFA and COLS), which is considerably different from that of DEA. However, the differences are less important for the first 10 companies. In fact, the DEA model predicts a higher than 98 percent efficiency for all these companies. According to this model, 19 companies are perfectly efficient and 24 companies have an efficiency of higher than 95 percent. But for the 10 companies at the bottom of the list, the differences are quite considerable. For instance, two of these companies are evaluated as perfectly efficient by the DEA model. Ten of the 19 companies evaluated as 100 percent efficient by DEA are less than 95 percent efficient, and three are less than 90 percent efficient.

Overall, our comparison shows that the DEA model predicts perfect efficiency more often than SFA. This might be due to the fact this model has no parametric restriction, thus provides more flexibility to account for unobserved differences among companies. However, such perfect efficiency scores might be due to the sensitivity of the DEA model to outlier values and/or to the 'curse of dimensionality', a general problem in non-parametric methods with a large number of variables.[26] Unfortunately, there is no simple method to identify the extent of such problems, especially for individual companies.

This example illustrates a main problem in benchmarking analysis that is, the discrepancy of the results across different methods. In some cases, the sensitivity of individual efficiency estimates is so high that a slight change in the model's assumptions or including an additional variable might change the results considerably. Given the extremely large variety of models and specifications, this problem does not appear to have a clear solution. However, as our example suggests, the sensitivity problems are less severe if the efficiency is estimated at the sector level rather than for individual companies.

Table 25.3   Efficiency ranks for the 'best' and 'worst' practices (1994)

Companies ordered according to SFA	DEA*	COLS
1	22	1
2	1–19	2
3	1–19	4
4	1–19	3
5	1–19	5
6	1–19	6
7	20	7
8	1–19	8
9	1–19	9
10	1–19	10
.	.	.
.	.	.
.	.	.
43	1–19	43
44	47	44
45	41	46
46	39	45
47	45	47
48	46	49
49	1–19	48
50	34	50
51	52	51
52	38	52

Note: * According to DEA method, 19 companies are 100% efficient.

9   Concluding Remarks

We presented an overview of the different methods of efficiency measurement in the electricity and gas distribution sectors. Asserting that the productive efficiency should be considered in the design and organization of the sector as well as in the incentive regulation of individual companies, we presented the efficiency concept with regard to three aspects: scale, scope and cost efficiency. The scale and scope efficiency are mainly related to the market structure, particularly the company's output level and mix, whereas cost efficiency is mainly due to the specific company's economic performance facing the external market conditions. An effective regulatory reform should consider all the dimensions of productive inefficiency and its patterns across companies. An adequate understanding of these patterns requires a clear distinction between the three aspects of efficiency.

Among these three concepts, the estimation of inefficiencies related to the scale and scope of the distribution utilities is relatively straightforward. In fact technological characteristics such as the economies of scale and scope can be estimated using the coefficients of a cost function. These estimates help determine the optimal size and scope of the production and the extent of natural monopoly in gas and electricity distribution.

Regulatory reforms should aim at an optimal organization of the distribution networks that allows companies the greatest possibility of using various synergies to reduce their costs. In many cases the empirical evidence reported in the literature suggests that an optimal organization might require relatively large distribution utilities that operate in both the gas and the electricity sectors.

Moreover, the empirical findings generally confirm the natural monopoly characteristic of energy distribution networks favoring local monopoly on side-by-side competition models. In such situations, an effective incentive regulation system is especially important because of the absence of direct competition among companies. Hence, the measurement of companies' economic performance in terms of cost efficiency or similar indicators has an essential role in ensuring the productive efficiency as well as restricting the monopolists' market power.

This chapter illustrates the measurement of cost efficiency to be the contentious issue that it is, especially if the performance of the individual companies is of interest. We argue that an effective regulation system requires appropriate models for the measurement of cost efficiency. Such models need to account for unobserved heterogeneity across companies, which can be provided by certain panel data models. Moreover, since different models posit various assumptions on the variation of efficiency across companies and over time, it is important that these assumptions are clearly specified and the efficiency estimates are interpreted accordingly. In many cases, it is important to view the efficiency from several angles, which requires the application of several models with different assumptions.

Notes

1. In addition to inflation, the changes beyond companies' control may include changes in input factor prices and exogenous changes in demand and network characteristics, generally referred to as 'Z-factors'.
2. Shuttleworth (2005) provides a critical overview of the use of benchmarking in the regulation of electricity networks.
3. See Jamasb and Pollitt (2003), Estache et al. (2004) and Farsi and Filippini (2004) for examples.
4. In the literature on the cost structure of electricity distributors, some authors have estimated a variable cost function. In this case it is possible to calculate a measure of utilization economies. For instance, Caves and Christensen (1988) define economies of utilization as unity divided by a proportional increase in variable cost resulting from a proportional increase in output holding the capital stock constant. For an empirical analysis on the electricity distribution sector, see Filippini (1996).
5. 'Production frontier' represents the maximum output produced by a given set of inputs, whereas 'cost frontier' defines the minimum costs of producing an output level with given input prices.
6. The only way to disentangle allocative and technical inefficiencies in a cost-frontier framework is through input factor demand equations. Because of the complexity of the resulting error structure, a satisfactory econometric solution remains to be developed (Greene, 1997; Kumbhakar and Lovell, 2000).
7. See for instance, Murillo-Zamorano (2004) for a general presentation of different methodologies and Coelli et al. (2003) for more details on DEA.
8. Other extensions of the basic frontier model have also considered exponential and truncated normal distributions for the inefficiency term. See, for instance, Battese and Coelli (1992).
9. Other authors such as Horrace and Schmidt (1996), Jensen (2000) and Street (2003) reported substantial errors and inconsistency problems in the estimation of individual efficiency scores in cross-sectional data.
10. Horrace and Schmidt (1996), Jensen (2000) and Street (2003) reported substantial errors and inconsistency problems in the estimation of individual efficiency scores in cross-sectional data. The first paper shows that such problems persist in a panel dataset with six periods.
11. While the econometric approach uses additive stochastic terms, the linear programming method allows heterogeneity in production by relaxing the restrictions imposed by a specific functional form.
12. Some of these alternative models have been used in a few recent studies (Alvarez et al., 2004; Greene, 2005a; Farsi and Filippini, 2004; Farsi et al., 2006a).
13. Panel datasets are characterized by repeated observations for a sample of units over several periods.

14. Alvarez et al. (2004) show that even in cases where inefficiency is due to time-invariant factors such as constant managers' capability, the resulting inefficiencies can vary over time because it depends on a host of time-variant factors that have an interacting effect with the manager's skills.
15. The term 'heterogeneity bias' has been used by Chamberlain (1982) to refer to the bias induced by the correlation between individual effects and explanatory variables in a general RE model.
16. See Greene (2005b) for more details. This author considers a panel of 5 years as a short panel.
17. Griffin et al. (1987) and Chambers (1988) provide insightful overviews of various functional forms in applied production analysis.
18. Within a group of flexible functional forms we can differentiate those functional forms derived from second-order Taylor series approximations, such as the translog, the generalized Leontief and the quadratic or the functional forms derived from Fourier or Laurent series approximations. The former are characterized by local flexibility, which implies a perfect approximation for an arbitrary function and its first two derivatives at a particular point. The latter are distinguished by their global flexibility. In applied work, however, the global approximation in Fourier or Laurent form is not commonly used, mainly because they usually need a considerably higher number of parameters than are required for a functional form derived from second-order Taylor approximations.
19. The number of coefficients in a translog model would have been 36, which results in a relatively small number of degrees of freedom in a sample of 26 companies with 129 observations.
20. For a review of a larger number of studies, see Ramos-Real (2005).
21. If instead it is assumed that inefficiencies are persistent and do not change considerably over time, then the results obtained from conventional panel models provide better estimates of the inefficiencies.
22. See Jamasb and Pollitt (2001) and Farsi et al. (2007b) for surveys of different regulation practices in electricity markets around the world.
23. Price cap is generally applied to the network access.
24. The measurement unit of input factors is not relevant, as long as the prices are defined such that the resulting costs have the same unit.
25. The alternative assumption would be constant returns to scale. This assumption is too restrictive because it implies that all companies operate at the optimal scale. See Coelli et al. (2005) for more details.
26. See Simar and Wilson (2000) for a discussion of 'curse of dimensionality' and Simar (2003) for the outliers issue.

References

Aigner, D., C.A.K. Lovell and P. Schmidt (1977), 'Formulation and estimation of stochastic frontier production function models', *Journal of Econometrics*, **6**, 21–37.
Alvarez, A., C. Arias and W.H. Greene (2004), 'Accounting for unobservables in production models: management and inefficiency', Working Paper E2004/72, Centro de Estudios Andaluces, Seville, Spain.
Antonioli, B. and M. Filippini (2001), 'The use of a variable cost function in the regulation of the Italian water industry', *Utilities Policy*, **10** (3–4), 181–7.
Barten, A.P. (1969), 'Maximum likelihood estimation of a complete system of demand equations', *European Economic Review*, **1**, 25–9.
Battese, G.E. and T.J. Coelli (1988), 'Prediction of firm-level technical efficiencies with a generalized frontier production function and panel data', *Journal of Econometrics*, **38**, 387–99.
Battese, G.E. and T. Coelli (1992), 'Frontier production functions, technical efficiency and panel data: with application to paddy farmers in India', *Journal of Productivity Analysis*, **3**, 153–69.
Bauer, P.W., A.N. Berger, G.D. Ferrier and D.B. Humphrey (1998), 'Consistency conditions for regulatory analysis of financial institutions: a comparison of frontier efficiency methods', *Journal of Economics and Business*, **50**, 85–114.
Baumol, W.J., J.C. Panzar and R.D. Willig (1982), *Contestable Markets and the Theory of Industry Structure*, New York: Harcourt Brace Jovanovich.
Bös, D. (1986), *Public Enterprise Economics*, Amsterdam: North-Holland.
Caves, D.W. and L.R. Christensen (1988), 'The importance of economies of scale, capacity utilization, and density in explaining interindustry differences in productivity growth', *Logistics and Transportation Review*, **24**, 3–31.
CEPA (2003), *Background to work on assessing efficiency for the 2005 distribution price control review*, Scoping study, Final report, Prepared for the UK Office of Gas and Electricity Markets (Ofgem), Cambridge Economic Policy Associates, available at: www.ofgem.gov.uk (accessed 16 February 2009).
Chamberlain, G. (1982), 'Multivariate regression models for panel data', *Journal of Econometrics*, **18**, 5–46.
Chambers, R.G. (1988), *Applied Production Analysis: A Dual Approach*, Cambridge: Cambridge University Press.
Christensen, L.R., D. Jorgenson and L.J. Lau (1971), 'Trascendental logarithmic production frontiers', *Review of Economics and Statistics*, **55**, 28–45.

Coelli, T., A. Estache, S. Perelman and L. Trujillo (2003), *A Primer on Efficiency Measurement for Utilities and Transport Regulators*, World Bank Institute of Development Studies, Washington, DC: World Bank.

Coelli, T., D.S.P. Rao and G.E. Battese (2005), *An Introduction to Efficiency and Productivity Analysis*, 2nd edn, New York: Springer Verlag.

Estache, A., M.A. Rossi and C.A. Ruzzier (2004), 'The case for international coordination of electricity regulation: evidence from the measurement of efficiency in South America', *Journal of Regulatory Economics*, **25** (3), 271–95.

Fabbri, P., G. Fraquelli and R. Giandrone (2000), 'Costs, technology and ownership of gas distribution in Italy', *Managerial and Decision Economics*, **21**, 71–81.

Farsi, M., A. Fetz and M. Filippini (2007a), 'Economies of scale and scope in the Swiss multi-utilities sector', CEPE Working Paper 59, Centre for Energy Policy and Economics, ETH Zurich, September.

Farsi, M., A. Fetz and M. Filippini (2007b), 'Benchmarking and regulation in the electricity distribution sector', in M. Marrelli, F. Padovano and I. Rizzo (eds), *Servizi Pubblici: Nuovo tendenze nella regolametazione nella produzione et nel finanziamento*, Milano: Franco Angeli, pp. 159–76.

Farsi, M. and M. Filippini (2004), 'Regulation and measuring cost efficiency with panel data models: application to electricity distribution utilities', *Review of Industrial Organization*, **25** (1), 1–19.

Farsi, M. and M. Filippini (2005), 'A benchmarking analysis of electricity distribution utilities in Switzerland', Working Paper No. 43, Centre for Energy Policy and Economics, Swiss Federal Institute of Technology, Zurich, Switzerland.

Farsi, M., M. Filippini and W.H. Greene (2005), 'Efficiency measurement in network industries: application to the Swiss railway companies', *Journal of Regulatory Economics*, **28** (1), 69–90.

Farsi, M., M. Filippini and M. Kuenzle (2007c), 'Cost efficiency in the Swiss gas distribution sector', *Energy Economics*, **29** (1), 64–78.

Farsi, M., M. Filippini and W.H. Greene (2006a), 'Application of panel data models in benchmarking analysis of the electricity distribution sector', *Annals of Public and Cooperative Economics*, **77** (3), 271–90.

Farsi, M., M. Filippini and M. Kuenzle (2006b), 'Cost efficiency in regional bus companies: an application of new stochastic frontier models', *Journal of Transport Economics and Policy*, **40** (1), 95–118.

Filippini, M. (1996), 'Economies of scale and utilization in the Swiss electric power distribution industry', *Applied Economics*, **28**, 543–50.

Filippini, M. (1998), 'Are municipal electricity distribution utilities natural monopolies?', *Annals of Public and Cooperative Economics*, **2**, 157–74.

Fraquelli, G., M. Piacenza and D. Vannoni (2004), 'Scope and scale economies in multi-utilities: evidence from gas, water and electricity combinations', *Applied Economics*, **36** (18), 2045–57.

Greene, W.H. (1997), 'Frontier production functions', in M.H. Pesaran and P. Schmidt (eds), *Handbook of Applied Econometrics, Vol. II: Microeconomics*, Oxford: Blackwell, ch. 3, pp. 81–166.

Greene, W.H. (1980), 'Maximum likelihood estimation of econometric frontier functions', *Journal of Econometrics*, **13**, 27–56.

Greene, W.H. (2005a), 'Reconsidering heterogeneity in panel data estimators of the stochastic frontier model', *Journal of Econometrics*, **126** (2), 269–303.

Greene, W.H. (2005b), 'Fixed and random effects in stochastic frontier models', *Journal of Productivity Analysis*, **23** (1), 7–32.

Griffin, R.C., J.M. Montgomery and M.E. Rister (1987), 'Selecting functional form in production function analysis', *Western Journal of Agricultural Economics*, December, 216–27.

Hanoch, G. (1975), 'The elasticity of scale and the shape of average costs', *American Economic Review*, **65**, 956–65.

Horrace, W.C. and P. Schmidt (1996), 'Confidence statements for efficiency estimates from stochastic frontier models', *Journal of Productivity Analysis*, **7**, 257–82.

Huettner, D.A. and J.H. Landon (1974), 'Electric utilities: economies and diseconomies of scale', Working Paper No. 55, Research Program in Industrial Economics, Case Western Reserve University, Cleveland, OH.

Irastorza, V. (2003), 'Benchmarking for distribution utilities: a problematic approach to defining efficiency', *Electricity Journal*, **16** (10), 30–38.

Jamasb, T. and M. Pollitt (2001), 'Benchmarking and regulation: international electricity experience', *Utilities Policy*, **9** (3), 107–30.

Jamasb, T. and M. Pollitt (2003), 'International benchmarking and regulation: an application to European electricity distribution utilities', *Energy Policy*, **31**, 1609–22.

Jehle, G.A. and Ph.J. Reny (1998), *Advanced Microeconomic Theory*, Englewood Cliffs, NJ: Prentice-Hall International.

Jensen, U. (2000), 'Is it efficient to analyse efficiency rankings?', *Empirical Economics*, **25**, 189–208.

Johnston, J. (1952), 'Statistical cost functions in electricity supply', *Oxford Economic Papers*, **7**, 68–105.

Jondrow, J., I. Materov, K. Lovell and P. Schmidt (1982), 'On the estimation of technical inefficiency in the stochastic frontier production function model', *Journal of Econometrics*, **19** (2/3), August, 233–8.

Kim, T.-Y. and J.-D. Lee (1996), 'Cost analysis of gas distribution industry with spatial variables', *Journal of Energy and Development*, **20** (2), 247–67.

Kmenta, J. and R.F. Gilbert (1968), 'Small sample properties of alternative estimators of seemingly unrelated regressions', *Journal of the American Statistical Association*, **63**, 1180–200.

Kumbhakar, S.C. (1991), 'Estimation of technical inefficiency in panel data models with firm- and time-specific effects', *Economics Letters*, **36**, 43–8.

Kumbhakar, S.C. and C.A.K. Lovell (2000), *Stochastic Frontier Analysis*, Cambridge: Cambridge University Press.

Mayo, J.W. (1984), 'Multiproduct monopoly, regulation, and firm costs', *Southern Economic Journal*, **51** (1), 208–18.

McFadden, D. (1978), 'Cost, revenue, and profit functions', in Melvyn Fuss and Daniel L. McFadden (eds), *Production Economics: A Dual Approach to Theory and Applications Volume I: The Theory of Production*, Amsterdam: North-Holland, pp. 3–109.

Murillo-Zamorano, L.R. (2004), 'Economic efficiency and frontier techniques', *Journal of Economic Surveys*, **18** (1), 33–77.

Nerlove, M. (1963), 'Return to scale in electricity supply', in C.F. Christ (ed.), *Measurement in Economic Studies in Honor of Yehuda Grunfeld*, Stanford, CA: Stanford University Press, pp. 167–98.

Nordin, J. (1947), 'Note on a light plant's cost curves', *Econometrica*, **15**, 321–35.

Pitt, M. and L. Lee (1981), 'The measurement and sources of technical inefficiency in the Indonesian weaving industry', *Journal of Development Economics*, **9**, 43–64.

Polachek, S. and B. Yoon (1996), 'Panel estimates of a two-tiered earnings frontier', *Journal of Applied Econometrics*, **11**, 169–78.

Pollitt, M. (2005), 'The role of efficiency estimates in regulatory price reviews: Ofgem's approach to benchmarking electricity networks', *Utilities Policy*, **13**, 279–88.

Pulley, L.B. and Y.M. Braunstein (1992), 'A composite cost function for multiproduct firms with an application to economies of scope in banking', *Review of Economics and Statistics*, **74** (2), 221–30.

Ramos-Real, F.J. (2005), 'Cost functions and the electric utility industry: a contribution to the debate on deregulation', *Energy Policy*, **33** (1), 69–87.

Roberts, M.J. (1986), 'Economies of density and size in the transmission and distribution of electric power', *Land Economics*, **62**, 378–87.

Salvanes, K.G. and S. Tjøtta (1994), 'Productivity differences in multiple output industries: an empirical application to electricity distribution', *Journal of Productivity Analysis*, **5**, 23–43.

Schleifer, A. (1985), 'A theory of yardstick competition', *Rand Journal of Economics*, **16** (3), 319–27.

Schmidt, P. and R.E. Sickles (1984), 'Production frontiers and panel data', *Journal of Business and Economic Statistics*, **2**, 367–74.

Shephard, R.W. (1953), *Cost and Production Functions*, Princeton, NJ: Princeton University Press.

Shuttleworth, G. (2003), 'Firm-specific productive efficiency: a response', *Electricity Journal*, **16** (3), 42–50.

Shuttleworth, G. (2005), 'Benchmarking of electricity networks: practical problems with its use for regulation', *Utilities Policy*, **13**, 310–17.

Sickles, R. (2005), 'Panel estimators and the identification of firm-specific efficiency levels in parametric, semi-parametric and nonparametric settings', *Journal of Econometrics*, **126** (2), 305–34.

Simar, L. (2003), 'Detecting outliers in frontier models: a simple approach', *Journal of Productivity Analysis*, **20**, 391–424.

Simar, L. and P.W. Wilson (2000), 'Statistical inference in nonparametric frontier models: the state of the art', *Journal of Productivity Analysis*, **13**, 49–78.

Sing, M. (1987), 'Are combination gas and electric utilities multiproduct natural monopolies?', *Review of Economics and Statistics*, **69** (3), 392–8.

Street, A. (2003), 'How much confidence should we place in efficiency estimates?', *Health Economics*, **12** (11), 895–907.

Varian, H.R. (1992), *Microeconomic Analysis*, New York: Norton.

Zellner, A. (1962), 'An efficient method of estimating seemingly unrelated regressions and test for aggregation bias', *Journal of the American Statistical Association*, **58**, 348–68.

26 Wholesale electricity markets and generators' incentives: an international review
*Dmitri Perekhodtsev and Seth Blumsack**

1 Introduction

Under regulation both short-run decisions regarding the operation of power plants and long-run decisions on investment in generating capacity were made by vertically integrated utilities, either regulated or owned by the state. Generating units were remunerated on an average-cost basis through rates determined by the regulatory process.

The transition to a deregulated environment in the US, Europe, and other parts of the world, has dramatically changed the short- and long-run incentives faced by private generating companies.

This chapter reviews critical properties of electricity markets and elements of market design applied in wholesale electricity markets around the world that affect generators' incentives for pricing and operation, as well as for investment in generating capacity. Case studies from various electricity markets have been used to illustrate the law of unintended consequences. Flaws in electricity market design that allow generators to engage in market manipulation have often resulted in a very speedy and significant transfer of wealth from customers to producers, as happened during the power crisis in California in 2000 (Borenstein et al. 2002; Sweeney 2002). Flaws in certain elements of market design aimed at aligning investment incentives may promptly result in over- or underinvestment in generating capacity.

The critical design elements include the organization of wholesale markets for electric energy. What we think of as the 'electricity market' is actually a number of submarkets in energy (both spot and forward), operating reserves, transmission congestion management, and other ancillary services, coupled with some form of generator unit commitment. In organizing electricity markets, careful attention must be paid to persistent arbitrage opportunities and adverse incentives that may be created by market rules even in the case of perfect competition. We review several examples of these market rules from electricity markets in the US and in Europe.

Due to a series of physical properties of electricity, markets for electricity are more susceptible to the exercise of market power than markets for other products. We review the findings on generators' exercise of market power in the US, Europe and elsewhere. We also review methods used for measuring market power in electricity markets and market power backstop elements of electricity market designs.

Market power issues suggest that generators might earn supra-competitive profits. However, an equally serious problem might be that generators, in particular peaking units and units that are required for reliability reserve, might earn too little to be profitable in the long run, or to encourage new investment. This is particularly true in those markets where price-limiting mechanisms are in place keeping energy market prices close to the marginal operating cost. We review studies on mechanisms adopted internationally to ensure the generation resource adequacy, and discuss the effectiveness of these 'capacity' mechanisms.

To perform an independent continuous surveillance of electricity markets, market monitors have generally been established in US electricity markets. They identify elements of market design that can potentially create adverse incentives, and process enormous amounts of data generated by these markets every day to gauge their efficiency and competitiveness. In cooperation with market participants and industry regulators, they suggest ways in which the efficiency of market design might be improved. The institution of independent market monitors is less developed in other parts of the world, in particular, in European countries. However, this does not mean that these markets are less susceptible to manipulation and other issues than their US counterparts. Rather, this may mean that critical flaws in these markets have not (yet) made themselves apparent.

The remainder of the chapter is structured as follows. Section 2 outlines some of the critical elements of electricity market design and presents examples of flaws in such elements from the international experience. Section 3 presents the problem of market power in electricity markets and the difficulties involved in measuring and controlling it. Section 4 describes mechanisms developed in electricity markets internationally to ensure the amount of generating capacity necessary for reliability. Section 5 discusses the role of market monitoring in the development of well-functioning and competitive market designs. Finally, Section 6 concludes.

2   Elements and Flaws of Wholesale Electricity Market Designs

Why do electricity markets need to be organized?

Before describing the critical issues of electricity market design, we review why wholesale electricity markets need to be carefully and deliberately designed in the first place. Most conventional markets do not require any special organization. Buyers and sellers find each other with no or little centralized coordination. In electricity markets, organization is necessary to ensure that supply matches demand with high precision at any given moment. This 'real-time' balancing is necessary because electricity cannot be economically stored in large quantities. Thus, demand variations within a day, hour or even minute must be matched by the supply side.[1] Mismatches between supply and demand of electricity can be very costly, sometimes resulting in wide-ranging blackouts many orders of magnitude larger than the original imbalance.

At the precise moment of operation there is no time to schedule generation on the market base to match the demand; only small last-moment alignment can be ensured by engineering equipment with little to no involvement of market forces. However, forward trades can and do take place hours and minutes before the operation to pre-schedule the generating resources to meet the demand. Forward markets for delivery on the following day are of particular importance and are organized in many jurisdictions. These 'day-ahead' markets signal system operators as to which set of generating units should be scheduled and dispatched to meet demand in every hour of the following day in the most economic way.

Existing day-ahead electricity markets involve different degrees of centralized coordination. The range of design elements presented in electricity markets around the globe, as well as the potential impact of these design elements on generators' incentives are discussed below.

Principal organization schemes: bilateral markets, exchanges and pools

Much of the debate surrounding restructuring in the 1990s focused on how the day-ahead electricity market ought to be organized. The organization schemes that have received the most attention can be grouped into three broad categories in order of increasing centralization: bilateral markets, exchanges and pools.

In a bilateral electricity market, buyers and sellers trade directly with minimal intervention of a coordinator. The transmission operator collects trade data from market participants to ensure that the resulting physical dispatch will not overload any transmission lines or other equipment on the system.

A power exchange is a step towards centralization. An exchange is an entity that collects simple price–quantity demand bids and supply offers during each hour of the following day. It further intersects these supply and demand curves to determine the market-clearing quantity. Exchanges usually calculate a single market-clearing price found at the intersection of supply and demand curves. This price is then paid by all cleared bids to all cleared offers.

Pools are similar to exchanges but accept more complex bids from generators. In addition to the bid price, such bids may include start-up costs, no-load costs, ramp rates, and minimum run times. The pool schedules generation to meet the system demand so as to minimize the total as-bid cost, setting the price at the last accepted bid price. The clearing price may not always be enough to cover the start-up and no-load costs of some units, which means that some generators could be scheduled in a way that will yield negative profit for the owner of units that are nevertheless scheduled to run. In these cases the pool provides side payments to ensure that scheduled generation receives an economic profit. Such payments are sometimes called 'bid production cost guarantees', or 'uplift payments'.

Each of these general design schemes has advantages and disadvantages. Proponents of the bilateral model of electricity market organization argue that only bilateral markets give market participants the ability to tailor the terms and the price of a contract according to individual needs. The variety of contract prices and terms provides for product differentiation that (among other things) makes implicit price collusion more difficult for generators. However, pools and exchanges do not oblige participants to perform all trades at the spot prices. Bilateral trades can be and are made alongside centrally organized pool or exchange using so-called contracts for differences (CfD) (Hogan 1992). In fact, a large volume of bilateral trades employing CfDs have been documented in the pools of England and Wales, and in Pennsylvania–New Jersey–Maryland (PJM) (Green 1998; Apt et al. 2007).

A pure bilateral electricity market has a significant disadvantage in efficiently solving generation scheduling and unit-commitment problems, as well as management of transmission constraints. These functions require coordination among a large number of parties. Efficiently solving both problems is best achieved by a coordinator that simultaneously observes all power schedules, unit commitment costs of all generators, and available transmission capacity. This type of coordination is usually performed by power pools. In practice, bilateral electricity markets (such as the Western US prior to

California's restructuring) have resembled loosely organized power pools, with one or more large transmission-owning utilities acting as centralized 'scheduling coordinators'.

Being placed between pools and fully bilateral markets in terms of centralized coordination, power exchanges share some benefits and drawbacks of both of these market organization schemes. Some elements of explicit transmission congestion management can be seen in power exchanges.

Most markets in the US are structured as pools.[2] Markets in Spain, Australia, and New Zealand also share features of a pool. The original market of England and Wales was also operated as a pool until 2001 when it was replaced by a bilateral market known as the New Electricity Trading Arrangements (NETA). In 2005 the NETA was expanded to include Scotland and became known as the British Electricity Transmission and Trading Arrangements (BETTA). Most European markets, however, run power exchanges. These include France, Germany, Italy, the Netherlands, and the Nordic countries. The original electricity market of California also featured a power exchange, though California is in the process of revamping its market design so that it more closely resembles the power pools of the Eastern US markets.

Further details of electricity markets

Understanding market design issues requires some more details on how electricity markets are organized and what submarkets they include. These details include relationships between day-ahead and real-time balancing markets, mechanisms of ancillary services provision, and transmission congestion management.

Day-ahead and Real-time Balancing Markets

In day-ahead markets, power plants are committed and scheduled to meet the forecast load on the following day. However, closer to real time (one hour to several minutes before delivery), actual demand and the generators' availability may change and adjustments to the day-ahead schedules may be required. These adjustments are made in the real-time or balancing markets by changing the dispatch of generators committed in the day-ahead market. In most jurisdictions, day-ahead schedules are settled at day-ahead prices while all real-time imbalances are settled at real-time prices. Exceptions are the markets of Australia and New Zealand where all the schedules, day ahead and real time are settled at the *ex post* real-time prices.

Most power pools and power exchanges in the US, Australia, New Zealand, Spain, Italy, the UK, and in other countries operate real-time balancing markets to complement the day-ahead scheduling. In the US both markets are performed by independent system operators (ISOs). In European countries the real-time balancing market is usually operated by the transmission system operator (TSO) while the day-ahead power exchange is operated by a different entity.

Ancillary Services

In addition to providing energy, generators perform certain services to counter the minute to minute fluctuations in electricity consumption (regulation or frequency control) and to offset possible forced outages of generating or transmission facilities (operating reserves). Regulation is provided by partially loaded generating units (operating above the minimum operating limit but below maximum capacity) able to respond to frequent signals from the system operator to increase or decrease output. Operating reserves are provided by partially loaded generators able to increase output in case of an outage of generation or transmission capacity (Kranz et al. 2003). In European electricity markets, regulation and operating reserves are sometimes referred to as secondary and tertiary reserves respectively.

In some jurisdictions (for example, in the US markets, Australia, New Zealand, Italy, and Spain) ancillary services are allocated to generators in explicit markets. In other jurisdictions ancillary services are provided by generators under a long-term contract with the system operator.

Transmission Congestion Management
Transmission congestion occurs when generation and demand schedules cleared in a uniform-price market result in an infeasible set of power flows due to the constraints on the transmission system. When this happens, the congestion is alleviated by setting some generators to produce more and some generators to produce less than they would at a single unconstrained market price; a practice known as 're-dispatch'. Electricity markets vary in the way they manage this re-dispatch.

Markets organized as pools often manage the transmission congestion simultaneously with clearing the energy markets. They minimize the as-bid cost of generating enough power to serve the demand in the system while respecting the entire set of transmission constraints (including contingency constraints). As a result, in the presence of congestion, each location may be cleared at a different price, reflecting the cost of meeting the incremental energy demand at that location or node (Hogan 1992). This nodal pricing method of transmission congestion management has been adopted in many US electricity markets, such as PJM, New York, New England and the Midwest. The New Zealand pool has also adopted the nodal pricing method.

A step away from nodal pricing is the zonal pricing or market splitting. When congestion occurs, this method splits the larger market into segment markets ('zones') and clears the demand and supply bids separately in each zone. Zonal markets can usually approximate a relatively simple radial transmission grid topology. Zonal congestion management has been adopted in the Nordic and Italian markets. In the US, both California and Texas originally featured zonal congestion management; both markets are currently transitioning to a nodal model. The Australian electricity market can also be considered as an example of zonal market.

Finally, congestion in single-price markets or within each zone of zonal markets is managed through re-dispatch payments. The TSO re-dispatches generation capacity in order to resolve transmission constraints, paying generators for deviations from their planned output level at the market-wide or zonal-clearing price. If, due to system constraints, a plant is not dispatched, it is paid its theoretical lost profit equal to the market price less its own bid. Conversely, if a plant is uneconomic at the market-clearing price but is still dispatched to relieve congestion, it is paid the price of its energy offer.

In most electricity markets in Europe, such as the UK, France, the Netherlands, Sweden, Spain and Germany, congestion within each national market is not expected to occur often. Therefore, these markets are cleared at a single national price. If congestion still occurs, it is cleared by a re-dispatch usually performed by the TSO during real-time balancing.

Market design flaws: arbitrage opportunities

Even if an electricity market is perfectly competitive, market design issues may potentially create problems and become costly for customers. One important group of such issues involves the creation of artificial arbitrage opportunities for generators.

Generators often have a choice between offering their power in forward, day-ahead, or real-time markets. They may also have the option of selling power in their own location or (by acquiring the necessary transmission rights) at a different location. In an ideal world, market forces would make all these possibilities equally profitable for market participants and would not create any consistent temporal or locational arbitrage opportunities. In reality, market rules may impose certain restrictions that allow arbitrage opportunities to persist. These opportunities may induce market participants to shift the bulk of market operations towards the most profitable submarket and away from other submarkets. Such a shift in volumes across submarkets may create serious problems. As more market participants flee from one submarket to chase the arbitrage opportunities in others, the market operator increasingly has to resort to administrative means to match supply and demand. These damage control interventions can be very costly and may result in decreased reliability of electricity supply.

Two examples from PJM and California are presented below to illustrate these types of market design issues.

Example: Congestion Management in the PJM Market

The Pennsylvania–New Jersey–Maryland Interconnection (PJM) began market operations as a restructured pool in 1997. Market designers did not originally expect much congestion, so the design of the pool used a strict single-price structure. That is, all loads paid the market-clearing price for the power they consumed and all generators were paid the clearing price for provided power. If congestion occurred, the system operator would pay the generators the value of their (incremental) bids for the additional power needed. One particularly interesting feature of the original market design was that nothing was paid to the generators for the reduction of the output needed to alleviate congestion, the thought being that paying generators for not running might create perverse incentive effects.

In June 1997, when congestion did arise in the PJM system, this market design created adverse incentives, which required a number of command-and-control interventions on the part of PJM. The problem was in the arbitrage opportunity created by the system. Generators in export-constrained areas that expected to be turned off (due to the congestion) quickly arranged bilateral trades alongside the pool. Since their generating cost was lower than the clearing price, these bilateral contracts were more attractive to loads than buying at the clearing price.

However, these bilateral schedules simply acted to restore the congestion and PJM had to turn to other controllable generators to reduce output. These generators in turn followed suit and moved their supply into the bilateral market. PJM quickly ran out of controllable generators and had to restrict bilateral transactions and to resort to administrative measures for congestion management. The situation in the summer of 1997 showed that the single-price market mechanism originally used in PJM could not work in the presence of congestion; even small amounts of congestion could create adverse price incentives. PJM switched to the locational pricing system shortly thereafter in April 1998 (Hogan 1998, 1999).

Example: Enron Gaming Schemes in the California Market

The original design of California's electricity market provided a large number of opportunities for price arbitrage once it went live in 1998. Many of them were actively exploited (or 'gamed') by the energy trading company Enron during the California crisis of 2000–01. Enron's manipulations of California markets have been widely documented; some of the more flagrant instances included outright violations of antitrust laws and moral norms, including agreements with power companies to take plants off-line during strategic times. These actions contributed to price increases and, possibly, to rolling blackouts in California during the crisis. It is important to realize, however, that many of Enron's more famous trading strategies did not violate any US laws or regulations and were simply an example (however extreme) of a firm taking advantage of arbitrage opportunities. This applies to the strategies nicknamed 'Fat Boy', 'Death Star', 'Ricochet', 'Load Shift' and others.

Some of these strategies took advantage of arbitrage between the day-ahead and real-time markets, for example, 'Get Shorty' and 'Fat Boy'. They allowed Enron to go around artificial market rules which limited such arbitrage trades, creating inconsistencies between the day-ahead and real-time markets.

Another strategy took advantage of the fact that California prices were capped at \$250/MWh while imports from other states were not subject to the price caps. This allowed Enron to sell power out of California and then sell it back above the cap ('Export of California power', or perhaps more colourfully as it became known, 'megawatt laundering'). Here the arbitrage opportunity was created by the rules setting caps differently for exported power and power sourced internally.

Other strategies used locational arbitrage created by inefficient transmission congestion management. This allowed Enron to simultaneously schedule one transaction from South to North through California and another transaction from North to South through neighbouring states ('Death Star'). In a physical system, the two transactions effectively cancel each other and would bring no money in a well-designed market. Yet, the way congestion was managed in California could make such a transaction profitable (Falk 2002).

Market design flaws: opportunity costs and incentive compatibility

Another set of issues that may be presented by market design deals with the creation of opportunity costs by rules that are not incentive compatible. In the general sense, such opportunity costs arise whenever generators believe that if they offer their capacity in a market at variable cost and are dispatched based on competitive bidding, they would wish they had bid differently upon observing the market outcome. A similar situation arises when a generator dispatched based on bidding at variable costs does not recover all costs associated with generation. In these cases, when submitting bids for energy generation in spot markets, generators incorporate the opportunity costs into their energy bids in addition to the variable cost of energy generation.

The opportunity costs created by market rules generally result in both short- and long-run inefficiency of electricity markets. Unlike the direct cost of energy, opportunity costs are often uncertain and generators can only incorporate their best expectation of these costs in their bids. Energy bids that are based on under- or overestimated opportunity costs result in inefficient dispatch and an increase of the overall cost of energy provision.

Prices that are based on opportunity-cost bidding do not reflect the marginal cost of energy and therefore, may provide inefficient long-term investment signals.

Opportunity-cost bidding is often confused with the exercise of market power, which is discussed at length in Section 3, although the two phenomena have little in common. Opportunity-cost bidding does not have the purpose of profitably increasing or otherwise influencing market price. Even a very small generator that has no market power at all may be stimulated by the market rules to bid based on opportunity cost rather than variable cost to maximize profits. An important relationship between the exercise of market power and opportunity-cost bidding is that the latter substantially complicates the detection of market power exercise, as explained in more detail in Section 3 (Harvey and Hogan 2001). Opportunity-cost bidding also makes it hard to form a basis for market-power mitigation procedures (such as cost-based bid caps).

We now present some examples of how bidding may be influenced by market designs featuring single-price or zonal transmission congestion management, sequential pricing of ancillary services or inexplicit treatment of unit commitment costs.

Example: Transmission Congestion Management in Single-price Markets
European national electricity markets are mostly organized as single-price or zonal markets, in which clearing occurs, assuming that no congestion exists within the market or within a zone. Similar designs were used in early US markets, such as PJM, New England and California. In these designs the system operator re-dispatches generating capacity in order to resolve transmission constraints, providing generators with payments for deviations from the optimal dispatch at the market-wide or zonal clearing price.

When a plant cannot be dispatched because of constraints, it is paid its theoretical lost profit equal to the market price less its own bid; when a plant is turned on to relieve congestion, it would be paid its energy offer even though it is above the market price. Essentially, transmission congestion management in the single-price markets or within the zones of zonal markets is done on a pay-as-bid basis rather than on the uniform-price basis.

As a result, generators that expect to be constrained on or off to relieve the congestion do not have incentives to bid their true variable energy cost, since by doing so they may forgo the possibility of obtaining larger profits from the re-dispatch payments. The profit-maximizing behaviour of such generators would be to bid at the marginal cost of the most expensive unit that the generator expects to be actually dispatched in its location.

This type of bidding was identified in the original English electricity pool by the electricity regulator in 1992. Similar bidding behaviour was observed more recently in the UK (Ofgem 2008, 2009) and in Spain (Crampes and Fabra 2005). In all these cases bidding behaviour was investigated as anti-competitive.

This problem does not exist in markets with nodal pricing, where the energy market is cleared simultaneously with transmission congestion management, as it is done in US markets and in the New Zealand market. In these markets the price in each location is set at the as-bid cost of serving an incremental unit of demand at this location. This pricing mechanism does not create opportunity costs within the energy market; a competitive generator (without market power) maximizes its profit by bidding its true variable cost of energy.

Example: Sequential Clearing of Ancillary Services

Markets for ancillary services may present another source of opportunity costs when these markets are cleared independently from the energy markets. In this case, generators bidding their true variable cost into the energy market may forgo possible profits that they may earn offering the same capacity in the ancillary services markets, if the ancillary services market clears after the energy market. The expectation of possible ancillary services profits will then constitute the opportunity cost of bidding competitively in the energy market and will naturally be factored into the energy bids.

Another type of inefficiency of design of ancillary services markets creating opportunity costs arises when several ancillary services are cleared one after the other.

The California independent system operator procures four types of ancillary services: regulation (RG), spinning reserves (SR) that are synchronized and available within 10 minutes, non-spinning reserves (NS), that are not synchronized but can be made available within 10 minutes and replacement reserves (RS) that can be made available within 60 minutes. These products are hierarchically substitutable. RG resources can also provide SR, NS, and RS. Spinning reserves can provide NS and RS whereas non-spinning reserves can provide RS. There exists thus a hierarchical nature that allows substitution of a high-quality reserve for a lower-quality one.

In the initial market design, the auction for the four ancillary services was conducted sequentially from the highest to the lowest quality. Generators were allowed to rebid resources that were not accepted in a round into a next round (possibly at a different price). Such market clearing was found to be inefficient since it created price reversals, that is, situations when lower-quality reserves cleared at higher price than higher-quality reserves (Brien 1999).

Price reversals pose serious incentive compatibility problems since even competitive generators anticipating such a reversal may be induced to understate their capability in a high-quality reserve market, in order to wait for a later round of the market that is expected to yield higher prices. A similar problem has also been observed in the early design of the New England electricity market (Oren 2001).

All these situations can be avoided if markets for energy and all ancillary services are simultaneously cleared. The New York market is one example of such markets (Kranz et al. 2003). Simultaneous clearing ensures that the capacity is allocated to the submarket in which it is most needed and where it would earn the most profit. Thus, no opportunity cost issue would arise.

Example: Unit Commitment Cost Pricing

A similar issue is presented by unit commitment costs that are not explicitly addressed in some markets. For instance, power exchanges often accept bids in simple quantity–price pairs and do not explicitly deal with unit commitment costs and constraints, such as start-up costs, minimum load costs, minimum run-time constraints and ramping constraints. Generators bidding into a power exchange may expect that if they are dispatched based solely on their energy bid, the market-clearing price of energy will not be sufficient to cover their energy and unit commitment costs. Then, to ensure that they do not start up only to lose money, they may incorporate some of the unit commitment costs into their energy bids in addition to the energy variable costs (Harvey and Hogan 2001, 2002; Borenstein et al. 2002). Incorporation of the commitment costs into the energy costs involves making predictions regarding energy prices over the following day. The probability of guessing incorrectly, resulting in an inefficient dispatch, is high.

This issue does not exist in power pools that accept complicated bids including start-up costs, no-load costs, ramp rates and minimum run times. The pool then schedules the generation to meet the load minimizing the total as-bid cost and setting the price at the last accepted bid price. When the clearing price still does not cover the energy and unit commitment costs of a dispatched generator, pools provide uplift payments to ensure that generators do not lose money.

3 Generators' Market Power

Market power in electricity markets

Since the beginning of the liberalization process in the electricity industry, horizontal market power of generators has been of much more concern than in any other market.[3] The main reasons are certain properties of demand and supply of electricity.

On the demand side, the demand for electricity is reasonably inelastic in the short run; consumption does not significantly decrease in response to price increases. On the supply side, generators cannot increase their output beyond their capacity limits and the power from remote generators often cannot be imported due to transmission constraints. In other markets, such short-run production capacity constraints and demand inelasticity could be smoothed out using inventories. In electricity markets this option is not economic with current technology, or is very limited at best.

These features of electricity markets may endow generators with market power under conditions that would not create competition concerns in other markets. For instance, if demand in an electric system cannot be met without dispatching the capacity of a given generator, that generator essentially has infinite market power. Since the capacity of the generator is indispensable in such hours, the generator can sell at as high a price as market rules allow. At the same time, such a 'pivotal' generator may represent only a small share of the market, say 10 or 15 per cent, which would not be considered a problem under regular competition policy (Borenstein et al. 1999; Blumsack et al. 2002).

As in other markets, generators may exercise market power by restricting output in order to derive additional profits from selling a reduced quantity at a higher price. Electricity markets are most often subject to two types of output restriction: physical and economic capacity withholding. Physical withholding involves reducing the physical availability of generating capacity in the market by de-rating the capacity limits or declaring unit outages. Economic withholding involves bidding higher than a competitive price for a unit, effectively pricing this generator out of the market. While the two types of withholding involve different mechanisms, the end result in both cases is a steeper bid supply curve than the market would have seen if firms behaved competitively.

In addition, electricity markets have many properties that are believed to simplify coordinated practices (both tacit and explicit). Electricity is a homogeneous product traded in rather transparent markets that usually do not exhibit much growth or many long-term cycles. Generating companies have similar cost structures and interact frequently. These features suggest that the electricity markets may be prone not only to unilateral market power but also to collective dominance (Ivaldi et al. 2003).

Finally, it should be noted that market power is not limited to markets for energy; it may be manifest in other submarkets of the electricity market, such as markets for ancillary services, capacity markets and markets for transmission congestion contracts.

Locational market power

The market power problem in electricity markets is further exacerbated by the presence of transmission constraints. Binding transmission constraints within a single coordinated market result in fragmented geographic submarkets, in which market concentration (the degree to which suppliers can be pivotal) is often higher than at the broader market level. For instance, when transmission constraints are binding in the direction of a large load centre, this centre becomes a separate relevant market, or a 'load pocket'. A generator from outside of the load pocket may not exert any competitive pressure on the generators within the pocket and as a result, the market concentration in these load pockets is often much higher than over the entire market.

In fact, constraints do not even have to be binding for locational market power to become an issue. The mere possibility of transmission constraints becoming binding, in the event of a price increase by a generator located inside a load pocket, may itself trigger the exercise of locational market power (Borenstein et al. 2000).

The nature of electricity flows over transmission lines makes locational market power an even more complex issue, giving rise to more-elaborate strategies than simple capacity withholding. For instance, in some cases generators can exercise locational market power simultaneously using two sets of generating plants that have opposing and disproportionate effects on a transmission constraint. The power output of one set is increased to create congestion on the line, while the output of the other set is restrained to exercise the locational market power resulting from this artificially created congestion (Cardell et al. 1997).

It is important to realize that the ability of generators to exercise locational market power does not depend much on how congestion is managed in a given market; it primarily depends on the topology of the transmission network and the locations of load centres and generators within the network.

In markets where congestion pricing is integrated within energy markets through locational marginal prices, local market power can be exercised through increasing the locational price. Although it is impossible to do this in single-price or zonal energy markets, it does not mean that these types of market design are any less prone to the exercise of local market power than are nodal markets. Generators that possess locational market power in single-price or zonal markets can generally exercise their market power by manipulating incremental/decremental congestion payments received from the system operator for the re-dispatch necessary to relieve congestion. In fact, it is likely that designs that separate energy markets from transmission congestion management, such as single-price and zonal markets, create additional opportunities for locational market power (Harvey and Hogan 2000).

Examples of alleged exercises of local market power in single-price markets have been documented in the UK (Offer 1992; Ofgem 2008, 2009) and in Spain (Crampes and Fabra 2005).

Regional electricity markets in the US, such as PJM, New York and the Midwest, are generally large enough to make the system-wide exercise of market power difficult for any single generating firm. However, the existing transmission topology of these markets does not always allow generators to compete freely across the entire territory. Load pockets with high market concentration often occur in these markets, giving rise to the possibility of exercising locational market power.

If, in future, the national electricity markets in continental Europe are integrated through market coupling, the existing capacity of cross-border transmission corridors will be used more efficiently. However, this capacity is unlikely to be sufficient for generators to compete freely across Europe. National load pockets are likely to remain, each of which may be susceptible to locational market power (Perekhodtsev 2008).

Methods and problems of measuring generators' market power

Although there is a clear risk of market power being exercised in electricity markets, the issues of how market power ought to be measured and detected are much less clear. We now turn to a discussion of these two issues.

Structural Measures

Structural measures of market power are used to assess the *ex ante* potential of exercise of market power (that is, before a generator actually attempts to exercise market power). This type of analysis is common in assessing the competitive effects of mergers, of market deregulation, or even of transmission upgrades that may change the boundaries of relevant geographic markets.

Soon after the first deregulated electricity markets became operational it became clear that many conventional measures of market structure, based on market shares of participants, are misleading when applied to electricity markets. General competition policy applies a Herfindahl–Hirschman index (HHI) to assess market concentration in a variety of markets. This index is calculated as the sum of squared market shares of participants. A simple model of oligopoly predicts that the market price will be proportional to the HHI and inversely proportional to the price elasticity of demand. However, when applied to electricity markets, the index fails to provide meaningful results due to the nearly zero demand elasticity (Borenstein et al. 1999).

Structural measures that are more relevant for electricity markets are generally based on some measure of the residual demand faced by particular generators. These measures focus on the potential of a particular supplier to make an impact on the market price, assuming that other suppliers bid competitively. Residual demand may be explicitly estimated based on the available bid data (Wolak 2000, 2003; Baselice 2007). However, in most cases only stylized measures of the residual demand can be assessed. Such stylized measures include the indicator of pivotal supplier index (PSI) and the residual supply index (RSI). The former is a binary indicator of whether the demand can or cannot be met without the capacity of a given generator, that is, whether the generator is 'pivotal' in meeting the demand in a given hour, as discussed above (Borenstein et al. 1999). The latter is a continuous measure of the degree of 'pivotality' of particular generators. The RSI is calculated as the ratio of the available generating and import capacity, excluding the capacity of a given generator, to demand (Sheffrin 2001). A pivotal generator thus has an RSI less than 1; the smaller the value of the RSI, the more market power a generator has.

In many electricity markets, particularly the wide-area US regional markets in PJM, New York, New England, California, Texas, and the Midwest, locational rather than system-wide market power presents the most concern. Some of these markets apply automatic processes to screen the effect of generators' bids on transmission constraints and measure how 'pivotal' generators are in causing congestion. This is done in PJM and similar methods are planned to be implemented in the new market designs of California and Texas (Casey 2006; Reitzes et al. 2007).

It is important to realize that the *ex ante* structural measures of concentration can only measure the *potential* of the generators to exercise market power. Whether generators really would choose to exercise their market power depends on a large number of factors and incentives that are not accounted for in simple structural indices.

For instance, generators may be selling their capacity under long-term contracts or may be relying on their capacity to serve own load at a predetermined price. Such contractual obligations may significantly reduce the amount of capacity available to generators in the spot market for the exercise of their 'pivotality' (Bushnell et al. 2008). Even when a generator possesses market power, it may choose not to behave opportunistically to avoid being scrutinized and penalized by the competition authorities.

Behavioural Measures
Structural measures are insufficient to identify whether market power has in fact been exercised. Although various behavioural measures have been devised for detecting the actual exercise of market power, few of them are compelling enough to firmly establish market manipulation or the effects of any manipulation.

Cases of the exercise of market power or, in the language of competition authorities, abuse of dominant position with excessive pricing, are rarely investigated in markets for regular products. It is usually very hard to find a credible approach to estimate prices that would have prevailed in the absence of the assumed abusive practices. Even under the most basic assumptions that competitive prices should be set at variable production costs, these costs are often very hard to measure and the data requirements are all but insurmountable.

Electricity markets may seem to be less affected by this problem. The technological data on heat rates and capacity of generating plants are often available. Fuel costs, which represent the bulk of variable production costs, can be assessed from price series available publicly or from private reporting services. In the US, actual fuel costs at the generator level are required to be reported to the Federal Energy Regulatory Commission (FERC) each quarter. Thus, estimating costs of electricity generation may seem to be more straightforward and precise than in other industries.

Many studies analysing generators' behaviour compare actual prices with the estimates of competitive prices based on variable production costs, for instance calculating a Lerner index.[4] Costs of generators assessed from average heat rates and fuel prices are used together with generators' capacity to construct a short-run market marginal cost curve by stacking generators from least to most expensive. This curve represents the supply curve that should prevail under competition. The estimates of hourly competitive prices are further obtained by intersecting these supply curves with hourly demand. To add realism to this modelling, some studies also account for import supply, requirements for operation reserves and the probability of unit outages (Borenstein et al. 2002; Joskow and Kahn 2002; Mansur 2008).

These simulation models still fail to account for a large number of complexities of electricity markets, resulting in significant underestimation of generation costs. Simple simulation models are usually static and do not account for intertemporal constraints faced by the generating plants, such as ramp rates and minimum-run time constraints, and for the unit commitment costs, such as start-up costs and minimum load costs. These simulation models often assume that the market is single priced and ignore the effect of transmission constraints on marginal costs. More details on this issue of simple simulation models are given in Harvey and Hogan (2001, 2002), Rajamaran and Alvarado (2003), Smeers (2005), and Mansur (2008).

All these details impose significant restrictions on the combined production possibility frontier of generators in a given market. Actual marginal costs may be much higher than the costs estimated without taking these restrictions into account. A further problem is that simple cost estimations tend to yield the most inaccurate results when demand is high and approaches the system capacity constraint. Coincidentally, in these conditions, generators are more likely to become pivotal and the exercise of market power gives rise to the greatest concern. Thus, the simplified models may yield a large number of 'false positive' results, making them an unreliable tool in detecting market power exercise (Harvey and Hogan 2002).

Many of the issues described above can be avoided when detecting market power using the data on bids submitted by generators. The bids of generators that are suspected of market power exercise can be compared with similar bids that are known a priori to be competitive. For example, bids submitted by a large generating company that is (statistically, anyway) pivotal in a large number of hours can be compared with bids from power plants with identical or similar characteristics submitted by small generators having little to no market power.

Alternatively, bids submitted by a large generator during hours of high demand, when the potential for the exercise of market power is the highest, can be compared with bids submitted by the same generator for the same plants during the hours of low demand, when potential for the exercise of market power is low (Peredkhodtsev and Baselice 2008).

Publicly available bid data have often been used to assess the competitive structure of markets and conduct of generators. Several studies measure the elasticity of residual demand and assess potential market power in California, Australia and Italy (Wolak 2000, 2003; Baselice 2007). Other studies have performed behavioural tests using the bid data from the electricity markets of the UK, California and Texas (Wolfram 1998; Barmack 2003; Hortacsu and Puller 2007).

International evidence of generators' market power

Many existing electricity markets in the US, in Europe and elsewhere have experienced price spikes which could have been attributed to the exercise of market power. Numerous studies have been carried out to establish whether the market power was indeed exercised in these markets.

Shortly after the opening of the power pool of England and Wales in 1991, Green and Newbery (1992) showed that the market equilibrium with only two dominant firms should have resulted in prices well above the marginal costs. A similar conclusion was made by Wolfram (1999). In a different study, Wolfram (1998) has shown that generators engaged in strategic bidding in the pool of England and Wales. The subsequent divestitures of power companies has reduced concentration and removed most of the general market power concerns (Green 1998). Yet, the locational market power has likely remained. The operation of the expanded British wholesale market BETTA, which now includes England, Wales and Scotland, has shown that locational market power problems could exist in Scotland (Ofgem 2008).

The California crisis of 2000–01 gave rise to a very large number of studies of market power. Summer 2000 brought an unusual combination of conditions in California. Dry and hot weather increased demand while reducing the amount of available hydropower; the power supply was also limited by an outage at a large nuclear station and a natural-gas pipeline explosion. The increase of prices of natural gas and emission permits (NOx) naturally led to increased costs at many Californian gas-fired power plants. Yet, according to studies by Borenstein et al. (2002) and Joskow and Kahn (2002), the level of electricity prices exceeded the most conservative estimate of electricity marginal cost by a large margin, suggesting that prices were manipulated by the five dominant players. Harvey and Hogan (2001) have criticized these results, suggesting that high prices may simply reflect the high opportunity costs faced by generators in California's markets and thus, cost estimates based on prevailing fuel and emission prices were irrelevant. Wolak (2003) has used the bid data from the California market to conclude, based on the estimated elasticity of residual demand, that large generating companies possessed significant structural market power during the crisis. Based on similar data, Barmack (2003) showed that bidding patterns of large generators may suggest non-competitive behaviour.

Although other US markets have not experienced such long and extraordinary episodes of high electricity prices, several studies have suggested that market power has been exercised in these markets as well. For instance, Mansur (2001) finds that during the first years of PJM operations, market prices were often exceeding the estimated marginal costs. Analysing the bids from the Texas balancing market in 2000–01, Hortascu and Puller (2008) conclude that large generating firms often bid strategically, maximizing their unilateral profits, whereas small generators did not act in the same way.

Continental Europe an markets have also shown some evidence of the exercise of market power and strategic behaviour. In the Spanish market the four largest companies were found to have bid strategically in 1998 (Fabra and Toro 2005). More recently, there have been five cases opened by the competition authorities in Spain regarding the abuse of locational market power. Different firms have been involved in these cases over the years: Endesa, Unión Fenosa, Gas Natural, Enel Viesgo, and Iberdrola. The Spanish Competition Court imposed the maximum fine on generating companies Endesa, Iberdrola and Unión Fenosa for abuse of local dominant position in November 2001. The Court argued that those firms had made use of their local market power by bidding higher prices when the transmission lines were congested (Crampes and Fabra 2005).

During 2005 and 2006, the Italian antitrust authority (AGCM) investigated a possible abuse of dominant position by Enel.[5] Using the bidding data from the Italian market, Baselice (2007) has found that the dominant generator, Enel, has a significant structural market power during most of the hours of the year. Perekhodtsev and Baselice (2008) have also shown, based on the bidding data, that Enel has on average submitted significantly higher bids to the wholesale market than it would have if it were competitive. These bids have been shown to have a significant impact on prices.

In the Nord Pool, a wholesale spot market involving Norway, Sweden, Finland, and Denmark, the potential abuse of the locational market power by a Danish operator

Elsam has been investigated by the Danish Competition Authority (DCA) (Christenseny et al. 2007).

In Germany, the comparison of energy prices observed in the national power exchange with estimates of marginal costs also suggested an exercise of market power (Weigt and von Hirschhausen 2007).

Market power mitigation

In general competition policy and antitrust practice, horizontal market power is mainly dealt with by not allowing markets to become too concentrated (that is, through merger control). All further investigations of market power abuse practices and their mitigations are often carried out by competition authorities *ex post* upon receiving complaints from market participants or customer groups.

This approach may be too light-handed for electricity markets, since they are highly susceptible to market power abuse. Market concentration and market competitiveness may need to be assessed on a continuous basis. California's experience has shown that mitigation measures need to be prompt, or the costs to consumers will accumulate.

In electricity markets of the US, the UK, Australia and the Nordic countries, market surveillance is often performed by market monitors that are either a part of the energy regulator or independent (Reitzes et al. 2007). Market power mitigation in the UK, the Nordic countries and Australia is still done *ex post*: regulatory intervention happens after the possible abuse is detected by the market monitors.

In addition to such *ex post* measures, electricity markets (mostly in the US) also apply *ex ante* mitigation procedures aimed at limiting the ability of market participants to exercise their market power by increasing prices or capacity withholding.

Ex ante price-control mitigation measures, in particular, should be devised with care. Overly strict controls may suppress prices and cause some generators to exit, perhaps prematurely (early retirement), while providing few incentives for entry by new generators. Price caps are an example of this type of mitigation. A less-restrictive measure would be a selective mitigation of generator bids that are believed to reflect the exercise of market power. This concept is used in the automatic market power mitigation procedures applied in the pool markets of New York, New England, and the Midwest. These markets perform screening and mitigation of bids during the market-clearing process. The bids are mitigated (reduced to their respective reference bid level) only when it is established that they are both sufficiently high and may considerably affect the market price. This method minimizes the probability of applying mitigation measures prematurely (ibid.).

4 Resource Adequacy and Capacity Mechanisms

While market power and market design inefficiencies may result in supra-competitive profits of generators at the expense of customers, the revenues earned by generators in energy markets in the absence of market power may be too low. In fact, these revenues might even be insufficient for generators to invest and to maintain the amount of capacity necessary for meeting peak demand and maintaining the capacity margins for reliability purposes.

The generators' revenues are restrained by the combination of administrative procedures put in place to mitigate market power and the lack of demand response. Spot prices often cannot be set by responsive demand and are mainly determined by the highest generator bid, which can then be subject to bid caps and bid mitigation. As a result, high-cost generators that run only during a handful of hours per year may be receiving little to no profit in the energy markets and may not be able to recover their fixed capacity costs (the so-called 'missing money' problem). Generating capacity additions needed to ensure reliability may not be built if economic profits cannot be earned in the energy market alone.

The missing money problem would be less serious if energy spot prices were allowed to fully reflect scarcity rents, that is, to significantly exceed generators' bids during times of shortage. However, scarcity pricing is often politically infeasible, partly due to the difficulties in distinguishing between market power abuse and true scarcity rents.

To ensure that enough generating capacity is in place to meet the peak load and to maintain reliability reserve, a revenue stream has to be arranged to complement the revenues from energy markets. Mechanisms providing such revenue streams are referred to as 'resource adequacy mechanisms' or 'capacity mechanisms' (Cramton and Stoft 2005; Harvey 2005; Hogan 2005).

Revenues earned by generators through capacity mechanisms are sometimes considered as a means to mitigate the risk of price volatility that would be expected if energy spot prices were allowed to fully reflect scarcity rents. Capacity mechanisms are often thought of as a transitory measure pending the development of price responsive demand and true scarcity pricing.

The international experience in electricity markets has seen many different capacity mechanisms. The most common are capacity payments, capacity markets and energy-only market designs. There also exist intermediate mechanisms such as reliability contracts of various sorts. These mechanisms are discussed in more detail below. However, most of the current European markets do not have explicit capacity mechanisms.

Capacity payments
Perhaps the most straightforward way to ensure a revenue stream for generating capacity complementary to the revenues from energy markets is simply to give a per-MW payment to all generators whose capacity is available. Examples of capacity payments created with this idea in mind could be found in Argentina, the UK, Spain and Italy. Many of these capacity mechanisms, however, have been found not to be efficient. Some of them have created incentives to use energy bids to manipulate the capacity payments, further aggravating the missing money problem.

Example: England and Wales
The electricity pool that was in place in England and Wales from 1990 to March 2001 had a capacity payments system. The payment was calculated every half-hour based on the difference between the value of the lost load (VOLL) and the system marginal price (SMP), scaled down by the loss of load probability (LOLP).[6] The VOLL was originally set at £2000 in 1990 and was indexed in the subsequent years. The LOLP was estimated in each half-hour interval depending on capacity availability and demand. Generating units received the capacity payment when they were available for generation, but the payment was not contingent on actual generation (Green 1998).

The LOLP was an extremely complex function of demand and available capacity. This created opportunity for gaming by dominant generators. They could announce as unavailable the capacity that was not economic to generate at a given hour. This would increase the LOLP and inflate the capacity payment for the remaining available capacity (Bower 2002).

This capacity payment scheme was abandoned after the comprehensive market design changes and the introduction of NETA in 2001.

Example: Argentina
The electricity market of Argentina administered by CAMMESA has included a capacity payment since 1994. Originally, the capacity payment was set at $10/MWh and was given to generators who offered electricity to the spot market (EIA 1997; IDFC 1998; Nuñez-Luna and Woodhouse 2005).

The eligibility for capacity payment, however, was directly linked to the dispatch. This induced generators to bid below marginal cost so as to increase production and capacity payment revenues. As a result, energy prices were actually lower than economically efficient levels, necessitating even larger capacity payments (Oren 2000).

The value of the capacity payment was increased to US$12/MWh in 2003. At that time, the structure of the capacity payment was also changed. Generators now are paid based on the forecast dispatch rather than on actual dispatch (Luchilo 2003).

Example: Spain
Starting from its inception in 1998 the Spanish electricity pool has been paying a capacity payment to generators that were available to provide energy. The capacity price was originally set at 0.78 c€/kWh but was subsequently reduced to 0.67 c€/kWh and then to 0.48 c€/kWh in spite of a shrinking capacity margin. To be eligible to receive the capacity payment two requirements were imposed on generators. First, generators must bid their generation in the day-ahead market. Second, the eligibility for capacity payment depends on the amount of energy generated by plants over the preceding year (Fraser and Lo Passo 2003; Crampes and Fabra 2005).

Spain's particular requirements for capacity payments introduced adverse incentives. The first requirement may discourage generators from participating in bilateral sales outside of the pool. The second may distort economic dispatch by making the peaking units offer their generation at below-cost prices in order to become eligible for the capacity payment (a similar problem as in Argentina's capacity market).

Example: Italy
The blackouts in Italy in 2003 have clearly indicated that the country has inadequate generating capacity. Following these events the Italian government decided to put in place a competitive design system to remunerate generation capacity. Both capacity mechanisms based on capacity obligations and capacity payments were considered (Fraser and Lo Paso 2003).

Currently, a capacity payment is paid *ex post* to all generation units that were offered in the balancing market, as long as these generators were actually available to produce during the peak days in previous years. The capacity payment varies according to the type of hours, that is, peak and off-peak (CEER 2006).

In parallel, the Italian energy regulator (AEEG) has considered introducing a centralized capacity market where the TSO would be required to buy a prescribed volume of reliability contracts from generators on behalf of the demand side.

Comment

Although the capacity payments may seem to be straightforward, they have many shortcomings. For instance, an administratively set capacity payment may seem to represent a steady revenue stream for generating capacity. However, small errors in establishing the capacity price may result in a large error in capacity investment, relative to the efficient amount (Oren 2000). As a result, the regulator might re-examine the capacity rate to correct the investment incentives. The changes in the capacity price set in the electricity markets of Argentina and Spain are examples of this situation.

Thus, capacity payments may be unable to ensure the necessary amount of capacity on the one hand and cannot be considered as a reliable source of revenues by generating plants on the other.

Finally, the examples of Spain and Argentina also show that adverse incentives may be created when available capacity is determined based on the past or current dispatch. This reduces the energy price and thus contributes to the 'missing money' problem that the capacity payment is supposed to solve.

Capacity markets

Early Capacity Markets

Instead of setting a capacity payment, an alternative is to directly set a fixed capacity reliability requirement, usually in terms of a percentage of the peak load. The market then determines the equilibrium capacity payment based on the capacity requirement. Many centralized markets in the US, such as PJM, New York and New England originally adopted this approach. The capacity markets were also considered as an option for Italy in 2003 (Fraser and Lo Paso 2003).

In these systems, load-serving entities were required to own or contract with generators for a prescribed level of reserve capacity above their peak load within a certain timeframe. A capacity credit market was also established to allow the load-serving entities to exchange the capacity 'credits' between each other and with independent generators to ensure that the load-serving entities meet their capacity obligation at the least cost. The reserve requirements and the capacity credit markets provide generators with the opportunity to collect extra revenue for their peaking and reserve generation capacity and introduce incentives for investment in such capacity as the load grows.

Problems of the Early Capacity Markets

While it is unclear whether these capacity markets have resolved problems they were meant to resolve, they have clearly created many new ones.

First, the administratively set vertical capacity requirement has resulted in significant volatility of capacity credits prices. The price dropped to zero whenever the available capacity exceeded the requirement and the price would jump to the level of the penalty for capacity non-compliance when there was a short-term capacity shortage. The inelastic demand for capacity matched with a rather inelastic short-run capacity supply has also created market power problems (Cramton and Stoft 2005).

Second, a common problem of simple capacity markets, and to some extent, of markets with capacity payments, is the measurement of supply. Generators are supposed to receive capacity payments in exchange for being available to provide power when needed for reliability. However, it is not always clear that the capacity that claims to be available would indeed be available when needed. In the early US capacity markets, payments were made based on generators' historic measure of frequency of forced outages (EFOR'd). This measure is convenient, but may be misleading in assessing a plant's contribution to reliability. According to EFOR'd, a generator may have a high availability simply because it almost never gets to generate, which does not necessarily mean that this plant contributes significantly to reliability. Thus, the very definition of the 'quantity' of the product sold in capacity markets creates possibilities for gaming (ibid.).

Finally, most of the early capacity markets in the US were originally designed to produce a single capacity price for the entire region. This presents a clear problem in failing to acknowledge the locational nature of capacity requirements. Due to limited transfer capabilities within a single regional market, local reliability requirements must be met by local capacity and thus, capacity should be valued differently depending on its location. This created problems in the early capacity markets in PJM and New England.

In PJM, generation additions were predominantly built in the west of the system, while some units needed for reliability in the import-constrained eastern zones of PJM were retired in 2005 for economic reasons (Chandley 2005; PJM 2007).

In New England, generators needed for local reliability in import-constrained zones also did not appear to receive enough revenue to cover their fixed costs. Instead of selling power and capacity in the markets, an increasing number of generators have been opting to offer their capacity through reliability-must-run contracts signed with the New England ISO in 2003. Under these contracts the generators are paid fixed and variable costs in exchange for the obligation to serve whenever they are needed by the ISO. The problem is that plants operating under these contracts are often removed from consideration when clearing the spot energy markets, and thus do not participate in price determination. This tends to suppress energy prices in the import-constrained areas even more, exacerbating the 'missing money' problem for the remaining generators (Hogan 2005).

Advanced Capacity Markets
To address some of these problems, the ISOs of New England and PJM have been undertaking serious reorganizations of their original capacity markets. Their new proposed capacity markets feature locational capacity requirements accounting for local deliverability problems, and administratively set 'capacity demand curves' to reduce price volatility and mitigate market power.

These redesigned capacity markets also hope to reduce price volatility and encourage generation investment by extending the time horizon of the market going several years forward. This allows new capacity (not yet online) to compete with existing capacity (LaCasse et al. 2003; Oren 2005; Cramton and Stoft 2006). In addition, PJM's redesigned capacity market, known as the reliability pricing model, also allows curtailable load and demand response to participate in forward capacity markets (in effect, customers receive payments for obligation offers to curtail demand in some future period).

Although the capacity market of New York has long featured a locational capacity requirement and decreasing demand curves, this market is also currently under revision.

Energy-only Markets

Capacity mechanisms are devised to treat the problem of 'missing money' for existing generators, and to encourage the construction of new generation. To the extent that these mechanisms are overly simplistic, such as capacity payments or the early capacity markets, they may create new problems rather than solve old ones. The new features of the more 'advanced' capacity markets of PJM and the New England ISOs have made the new designs increasingly complex, almost as complex as the energy markets with locational marginal prices. In addition, the modified capacity market proposals increase the number of variables that must be set administratively, rather than through market mechanisms.

Given the never-ending stream of complexities and problems that seem to arise from the most well-intentioned and well-thought-out capacity markets, there is an obvious appeal in returning to a market design focused solely on the energy market. Such an 'energy-only' market can only work (that is, provide incentives for existing generators to offer their power, and for investment in new plants) if price spikes are allowed under actual capacity shortage conditions while controlling for the possible exercise of generator market power.

Extreme shortage conditions when energy demand reaches total available capacity are rare. More often, shortages may be observed when energy demand exceeds the available capacity after accounting for capacity needed to provide operating reserves (that is, spare generating capacity to be available at all times). Operating reserves are needed so that the system could withstand an outage of a large generation or transmission facility. The requirement for operating reserves is usually fixed by regulators based on engineering assessments. However, nothing indicates that the amount of operating reserves cannot be reduced when the system is under stress.

Thus, a workable model of an 'energy-only' market may be based on an administratively set decreasing (but steep) demand for operating reserves and joint clearing of markets of energy and operating reserves (Hogan 2005). Since the markets clear simultaneously, the high price of reserves during the shortage will also result in a high energy price, reflecting arbitrage between production of energy and providing operating reserves. The shortage price is set by the reserves demand curve and not by generators' bids, meaning that the 'missing money' problem can be solved even if certain generators' bids are capped to mitigate market power.[7]

Similarly to the demand curves for *capacity* reserves administratively set in the capacity markets, this type of energy-only market requires an administratively set demand for *operating* reserves. The important difference is that in the energy-only market, the clearing price for operating reserves transforms into an energy price and pays on the basis of production rather than on the basis of capacity. If energy markets are locational, then the energy-only market design naturally solves the locational 'missing money' problems. However, the investment incentives created by energy-only markets depend on the shape of the administratively set demand curve for operating reserves.

Scarcity pricing mechanisms are in place in different stages in New York and PJM, in addition to their capacity markets. Electricity markets in Texas (ERCOT), the US Midwest (MISO) and Alberta (Canada) rely exclusively on an energy-only design similar to that briefly described here and in more detail in Hogan (2005).

To some extent, shortage pricing can be arranged even when reserves markets do not exist or are not simultaneously cleared with energy. For instance, the National Electricity Market (NEM) in Australia features an energy-only market design imposing a high shortage price cap of A$10 000/MWh.

5   The Role of Market Monitoring

The fact that electricity markets are so susceptible to the creation of unexpected pricing incentives, price manipulation, and insufficient investment incentives means that the organization and operation of wholesale electricity markets should be closely monitored. Most countries where energy markets have been liberalized have set up economic regulators for the energy industry. However, the mandate of these regulators is quite broad, and often does not extend beyond general oversight of market development. In particular, the energy regulators generally do not perform regular detailed screening and monitoring of the massive flows of data generated by electricity markets. Particularly in many US electricity markets, special market monitors have been created for that role.

The main role of market monitors is to act preventively by continuously detecting and correcting incentives that may exist for generators to exercise market power. Thus, a primary function of the market monitor is to head off market manipulation before any abuses actually occur. Market monitors also analyse and correct flaws in market rules that may cause efficiency losses unrelated to market power, such as those discussed in Section 2. In collaboration with market participants, the system operator, and industry regulators, market monitors are tasked with adjusting the market rules so as to promote a well-functioning competitive wholesale electricity market producing efficient signals for long-term development. Independence of the market monitor is critical, in order for its analysis not to be distorted in favour of any of the stakeholders and market participants (Wolak 2004).

In US electricity markets, the market monitoring units have historically existed as an internal division of the system operator. However, it is a general practice among the system operators in the US to delegate many if not all market monitoring functions to outside consultants. The pioneer in this institutional structure appears to be California, which set up an independent Market Monitoring Committee following its power crisis in 2000–01. Currently, electricity markets in Texas, New England and the Midwest have external independent market monitors; these monitors are normally made up of a team of industry experts from consulting and academia. US system operators that do not have external independent market monitors are generally in the process of forming these bodies.

Market monitoring has also been increasingly introduced outside of the US. In the UK, Australia and New Zealand the role of market monitors has increased dramatically in recent years (ibid.). In Europe (outside of the UK) some but not all market monitor functions are usually performed by national energy regulators. One of the few

European examples of an independent market monitor is the one established in 2000 in the Nord Pool to monitor the physical and financial markets of the Nordic Power Exchange (Twomey et al. 2004). In the Netherlands, the office of Energy Regulation (DTe) and the competition authority, Netherlands Competition Authority (NMa) set up, in 2001, a joint body, the Market Surveillance Committee to monitor the developments in the Dutch electricity markets. More recently, French energy regulator, Commission for Energy Regulation (CRE), has started producing market monitoring reports on wholesale electricity and gas markets (CRE 2009). Development of an independent market monitoring practice may help to create viable and competitive national markets in Europe and to ensure a smooth transition to an integrated European electricity market.

6   Conclusion

This chapter has reviewed elements of wholesale electricity market designs around the world, and how these elements affect generators' incentives for pricing, operation and investment. The chapter focuses on the three primary design elements: market design rules linking all of the submarkets of the electricity market; issues of market power, its detection and mitigation; and resource adequacy and capacity mechanisms. Due to the unique properties of electricity, poor design of these market elements may substantially increase the cost of serving electricity to customers.

The electricity markets internationally vary greatly in the way they address these market design elements. Nearly every market has a history of failures on certain design elements and their subsequent modifications. Yet, none of them (to our knowledge) has overcome every potential problem described in this chapter. The US electricity markets have come a long way, but still certain problems remain to be resolved (capacity markets are among the most contentious).

Independent market monitors testing elements of market design that can potentially create adverse incentives, and performing a continuous surveillance of the competitiveness of electricity markets, may and do help create functional and competitive electricity markets.

Notes

*   The views presented in this chapter are those of the authors and do not necessarily reflect those of LECG (Law and Economics Consulting Group) or the Pennsylvania State University.
1.   Although demand-side participation is becoming increasingly important, it still remains very limited.
2.   Prior to restructuring, US utilities often engaged in bilateral trading; the most organized of these markets was in the Western US. Apart from California, most of the Western US still operates bilaterally.
3.   Vertical market power issues were usually handled through divestiture or unbundling of the transmission utility business from generation and retail business and a requirement to transmission owners to provide open and non-discriminatory access to their facilities.
4.   The Lerner index is calculated as the price–cost mark-up relative to the price, $LI = (p - c)/p$.
5.   See Case A366 AGCM, Avvio istruttoria 14,174, *Comportamenti restrittivi sulla borsa elettrica*.
6.   LLOP*(VOLL – SMP).
7.   Physical withholding still remains a means of price gauging. Thus, physical withholding has to be closely monitored under shortage pricing.

References

Apt, J., S. Blumsack and L. Lave (2007), 'Competitive Energy Options for Pennsylvania', report to the Team Pennsylvania Foundation, Electricity Industry Center, Carnegie Mellon University, Pittsburgh, PA.

Barmack, M. (2003), 'What do the ISO's public bid data reveal about the California market?', *Electricity Journal*, **24**, 63–73.

Baselice, R. (2007), 'Italian power exchange and unilateral market power in Italian wholesale electricity market', *Economia delle Fonti di Energia e dell'Ambiente*, no. 1.

Blumsack, S., D. Perekhodtsev and L. Lave (2002), 'Market power in deregulated electricity markets: issues in measurement and the cost of mitigation', *Electricity Journal*, **15** (9), 1–24.

Borenstein, S., J. Bushnell and C. Knittel (1999), 'Market power in electricity markets: beyond concentration measures', *The Energy Journal*, **20** (4), 65–88.

Borenstein, S., J. Bushnell and S. Stoft (2000), 'The competitive effects of transmission capacity in a deregulated electricity industry', *RAND Journal of Economics*, **3** (2), 294–325.

Borenstein, S., J. Bushnel and F. Wolak (2002), 'Measuring market inefficiencies in California's restructured wholesale electricity market', *American Economic Review*, **92** (5), 1376–405.

Bower, J. (2002), 'Why did electricity prices fall in England and Wales? Market mechanism or market structure?', Oxford Institute for Energy Studies Working Paper EL 02.

Brien, L. (1999), 'Why the ancillary services markets in California don't work and what to do about it', *Electricity Journal*, **12** (5), 38–49.

Bushnell, J., E. Mansur and C. Saravia (2008), 'Vertical arrangements, market structure, and competition: an analysis of restructured U.S. electricity markets', *American Economic Review*, **98**(1), 237–66.

Cardell, J., C. Hitt and W. Hogan (1997), 'Market power and strategic interaction in electricity networks', *Resource and Energy Economics*, **19** (1), 109–37.

Casey, K. (2006), Prepared direct testimony. Docket No. ER06-615-000, before the Federal Energy Regulatory Commission (FERC), Washington, DC.

Chandley, J. (2005), 'ICAP reform proposals in New England and PJM', LECG, LLC, Cambridge, MA.

Christenseny, B.J., R.E. Jensen and R. Nølgaard (2007), 'Market power in power markets: evidence from forward prices of electricity', CREATES Research Paper 2007-30, Center for Research in Econometric Analysis of Time Series, Aarhus, Denmark.

Commission de Régulation de l'Energie (CRE) (2009), 'Rapport de surveillance: Le fonctionnement des marches, de gros français de l'eletricité et du gaz naturel en 2007', CRE, Paris.

Council of European Energy Regulators (CEER) (2006), 'Survey of capacity support mechanisms in the energy community', 8th Athens Forum, Athens, Greece.

Crampes, C. and N. Fabra (2005), 'The Spanish electricity industry: Plus ça change', *The Energy Journal*, **26**, 127–53.

Cramton, P. and S. Stoft (2005), 'A capacity market that makes sense', *Electricity Journal*, **18** (7), 43–54.

Cramton, P. and S. Stoft (2006), 'The convergence of market designs for adequate generating capacity', White Paper for California Electricity Oversight Board.

Energy Information Agency (EIA) (1997), 'Electricity Reform Abroad and U.S. Investment', US Department of Energy.

Fabra, N. and J. Toro (2005), 'Price wars and collusion in the Spanish electricity market', *International Journal of Industrial Organization*, **23** (3–4), 155–81.

Falk, J. (2002), 'Substituting outrage for thought: the Enron "smoking gun" memos', *Electricity Journal*, **15** (7), 13–22.

Fraser, H. and F. Lo Paso (2003), 'Developing a capacity payment mechanism in Italy', *Electricity Journal*, **16** (9), 54–8.

Green, R. (1998), 'Draining the pool: the reform of electricity trading in England and Wales', *Energy Policy*, **27** (9), 515–25.

Green, R.J. and D.M. Newbery (1992), 'Competition in the British electricity spot market', *Journal of Political Economy*, **100** (5), 929–53.

Harvey, S. (2005), 'ICAP systems in the Northeast: trends and lessons', LECG, LLC, Cambridge, MA.

Harvey, S. and W. Hogan (2000), 'Nodal and zonal congestion management and the exercise of market power', working paper, LECG, LLC, Cambridge, MA.

Harvey, S. and W. Hogan (2001), 'Identifying the exercise of market power in California', LECG, LLC, Cambridge, MA.

Harvey, S. and W. Hogan (2002), 'Market power and market simulations', LECG, LLC, Cambridge, MA.

Hogan, W. (1992), 'Contract networks for electric power transmission', *Journal of Regulatory Economics*, **4** (3), 211–42.

Hogan, W. (1998), 'Getting the prices right in PJM: what the data teaches us', *Electricity Journal*, **11** (7), 61–7.

Hogan, W. (1999), 'Getting the prices right in PJM: analysis and summary: April 1998 through March 1999, the first anniversary of full locational pricing', Working Paper, John F. Kennedy School of Government, Harvard University, Cambridge, MA.

Hogan, W. (2005), 'On an "energy only" electricity market design for resource adequacy', Working Paper, John F. Kennedy School of Government, Harvard University, Cambridge, MA.

Hortascu, A. and S. Puller (2008), 'Understanding strategic bidding in multi-unit auctions: a case study of the Texas electricity spot market', *Rand Journal of Economics*, **39** (1), 86–114.

Infrastructure Development Finance Company Ltd (IDFC) (1998), 'Power Sector Reform In Argentina: A Summary Description', report, Chennai, India.

Ivaldi, M., B. Jullien, P. Rey, P. Seabright and J. Tirole (2003), 'The economics of tacit collusion', Report for DG Competition, European Commission, Institut d'Économie Industrielle (IDEI) Toulouse.

Joskow, P. and E. Kahn (2002), 'A quantitative analysis of pricing behaviour in California's wholesale electricity market during summer 2000', *The Energy Journal*, **23** (4), 1–35.

Kranz, B., R. Pike and E. Hirst (2003), 'Integrated electricity markets in New York', *Electricity Journal*, **15** (2), 64–5.

LaCasse, C., P. Kalmus and B. Neenan (2003), 'Central resource adequacy markets for PJM, NY-ISO and NE-ISO', NERA Economic Consulting, New York.

Luchilo, J. (2003), 'Argentine Power Sector', paper presented at APEX Conference, Cartagena, CO, October.

Mansur, E. (2001), 'Pricing behavior in the initial summer of the restructured PJM wholesale electricity market', PWP-083, POWER Working Paper, University of California Energy Institute (UCEI), USA.

Mansur, E. (2008), 'Measuring welfare in restructured electricity markets', *Review of Economics and Statistics*, **90** (2), May, 369–86.

Nuñez-Luna, A. and E. Woodhouse (2005), 'The IPP investment experience in Argentina', Program on Energy and Sustainable Development (PESD) Working Paper 44, Stanford University, Stanford, CA.

Office of Electricity Regulation (Offer) (1992), 'Report on Constrained-On Plant, Birmingham', Office of Electricity Regulation, United Kingdom.

Office of Gas and Electricity Markets (Ofgem) (2008), 'Ofgem Launches Competition Act Investigation into Scottish Power Limited and Scottish and Southern Energy Plc', Office of Gas and Electricity Markets, United Kingdom.

Office of Gas and Electricity Markets (Ofgem) (2009), 'Competition Act investigation into Scottish Power and Scottish and Southern Energy', Office of Gas and Electricity Markets, United Kingdom.

Oren, S. (2000), 'Capacity payments and supply adequacy in competitive', VIIth Symposium of Specialists in Electric Operational and Expansion Planning, Curitiba, Brazil, May.

Oren, S. (2001), 'Design of ancillary services markets', Proceedings of the 34th Annual Hawaii International Conference on System Sciences, Maui, HI, January.

Oren, S. (2005), 'Generation adequacy via call options obligations: safe passage to the promised land', *Electricity Journal*, **18** (9), 28–42.

Perekhodtsev, D. (2008), 'Measuring market concentration in European power exchanges "coupled" over a meshed cross-border network', Proceedings of the 5th International Conference on the European Electricity Market, Lisbon, Portugal, May.

Peredkhodtsev, D. and R. Baselice (2008), 'Measuring competitive behaviour in the Italian power exchange', 31st International Association for Energy Economics (IAEE) International Conference, Istanbul, Turkey, June.

PJM (Pennsylvania–New Jersey–Maryland) (2007), '2006 State of the Market Report', Market Monitoring Unit, PJM LLC.

Rajaraman, R. and F. Alvarado (2003), '(Dis)Proving market power', Power Systems Engineering Research Center (PSERC) Working Paper, University of Wisconsin, Madison, WI.

Reitzes, J., J. Pfeifenberger, P. Fox-Penner, G.N. Basheda, J.A. García, S.A. Newell and A.C. Schumacher (2007), 'Review of PJM's market power mitigation practices in comparison to other organized electricity markets', Brattle Group, Cambridge, MA.

Sheffrin, A. (2001), 'Empirical evidence of strategic bidding in the California ISO real time market', Department of Market Analysis, California ISO, Folsom, CA.

Smeers, Y. (2005), 'How well can one measure market power in restructured electricity systems?', Center for Operation Research and Econometrics (CORE) Discussion Paper 2005/50, Catholic University of Louvain, Belgium.

Sweeney, J. (2002), *The California Electricity Crisis*, Stanford, CA: Hoover Institution Press.

Twomey, P., R. Green, K. Neuhoff and D. Newbery (2004), 'A review of the monitoring of market power: the possible roles of TSOs in monitoring for market power issues in congested transmission systems', Cambridge Working Papers in Economics CWPE 0504, University of Cambridge, UK.

Weigt, H. and C. von Hirschhausen (2007), 'Price formation and market power in the German electricity wholesale market – is big really beautiful?', Dresden University of Technology, Electricity Markets Working Papers WP-EM-16, Dresden.

Wolak, F. (2000), 'An empirical analysis of the impact of hedge contracts on bidding behaviour in a competitive electricity market', *International Economic Journal*, **14** (2), 1–40.

Wolak, F. (2003), 'Measuring unilateral market power in wholesale electricity markets: the California market, 1998–2000', *American Economic Review*, **93** (2), 425–30.

Wolak, F. (2004), 'Lessons from international experience with electricity market monitoring', Center for the Study of Energy Markets (CSEM) Working Paper 134, University of California, Berkeley, CA.

Wolfram, C. (1998), 'Strategic bidding in a multiunit auction: an empirical analysis of bids to supply electricity in England and Wales', *RAND Journal of Economics*, **29** (4), 703–25.

Wolfram, C. (1999), 'Measuring duopoly power in the British electricity spot market', *American Economic Review*, **89** (4), 805–26.

27 Security of supply in large hydropower systems: the Brazilian case

Luciano Losekann, Adilson de Oliveira and Getúlio Borges da Silveira

1 Background

Security of supply is a key aspect in any power sector reform. Different mechanisms are used to secure supply in a competitive environment (Turvey, 2003; Cramton and Stoft, 2006). Based on US experience, Joskow (2006) argues that wholesale power markets do not stimulate investments in new capacity, as they are not fully remunerated.

A fully competitive electricity market has two general states of nature which are set out in Figure 27.1. In the first state, which characterizes the usual operation of power systems, power generation is lower than installed capacity, moving energy price to the operational costs of the most expensive power plant dispatched. Cheaper power plants earn an infra-marginal rent, the difference between the system price and their marginal cost.

In the second state of nature, which takes place in only a few hours of the average year, the system operates at full capacity (K_{max}) to meet demand and the energy price moves to the value of lost load (VOLL). In this situation, two kinds of rent are generated. The usual infra-marginal rent and a scarcity rent, measured by the difference between the system price and the marginal cost of the most expensive power plant.

Infra-marginal and scarcity rents are both essential to pay for the capital costs of the power plants. However, price caps (institutional constraints) are usually used to limit the escalation of the energy price, limiting the amount of the scarcity rent that power plants can capture. As a result, the power plants cannot fully recover their capital costs.

Underpricing when the system is under stress generates the 'missing money' problem identified in the US by Joskow (2006). This problem is a strong deterrent to potential investors in generating capacity, and the lack of generating capacity is the main source of insecurity for the supply of power.

Capacity payments have long been used to ensure that power systems meet the stresses which periodically present themselves. However, hydropower systems' security of supply is contingent on more than just sufficient capacity. In Section 2, the missing money problem is discussed, and then the Brazilian electricity system is outlined in Section 3. The simulation results presented in Section 4 suggest that while the probability of water shortages is low, when such shortages do occur they are persistent and are ultimately likely to result in power rationing as has been observed in Brazil. In spite of measures taken by the Brazilian government to ensure minimum reserve levels, water shortages are still not fully incorporated into the energy price, sending inaccurate signals to the market participants. Section 5 concludes.

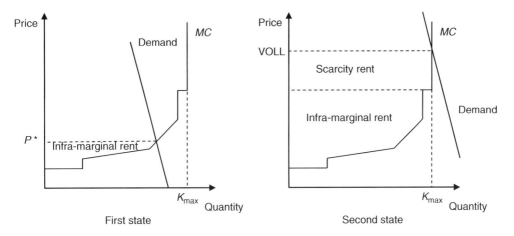

Source: Joskow (2006).

Figure 27.1   States of nature of thermopower systems

2   The Missing Money Problem in Large Hydropower Systems

Power systems that largely rely on hydropower plants do not suffer from the problem of lack of capacity to supply peak demand. Hydropower plants have installed capacity to accommodate different levels of energy flow and they use energy stored in their reservoirs in the off-peak periods to be dispatched during the peak periods. In spite of these characteristics, large hydropower systems do experience the missing money problem.

Hydropower generation is highly dependent on volatile energy flows. Figure 27.2 shows the monthly distribution of the natural energy flow (NEF) to the hydropower plants of the Brazilian Southeast and Midwest since 1931 (76 years). Typically, in a favorable hydrological year, energy flows are around three times higher than in an unfavorable year. Moreover, the average energy flow varies seasonally.

In the 'dry' period, the energy stored in reservoirs during the 'wet' period is used to meet demand as the NEF cannot meet demand. Water depletion of all reservoirs generates scarcity of energy.

The economic value of the energy stored in the reservoirs is small when they are full but it rapidly increases as the energy supply drops (Figure 27.3). Reservoir depletion is the main source of insecurity of energy supply in large hydropower systems. From the economic point of view, the crucial decision to be made when considering security of supply is whether to use the energy stored in the reservoirs.

There are also two states of nature in large hydropower systems. During favorable hydrological years, reservoirs are full; the marginal cost of the system (economic value of the energy) is low and it is unable to meet the full cost of a new hydropower plant's supply (Figure 27.4). The second state of nature occurs during bad hydrological periods when the energy available in hydro reservoirs is scarce, causing the price to reach the VOLL.

This second state of nature is infrequent in large hydropower systems but in contrast

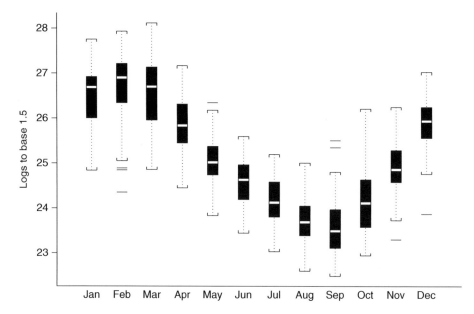

Notes: (i) Vertical unitary displacements correspond to 50% change; (ii) Inner boxes: Heights for white mark and extremes equal the 3 quartiles.

Source: Elaborated by the authors based on ONS data.

Figure 27.2   Monthly distribution of natural energy flow: Brazilian Southeast/Midwest subsystem, 1931–2006

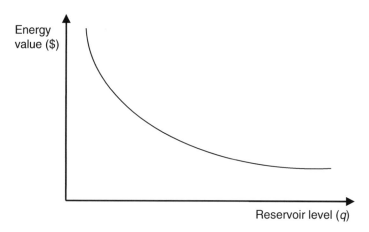

Source: Author.

Figure 27.3   Value of the energy stored in hydroreservoirs

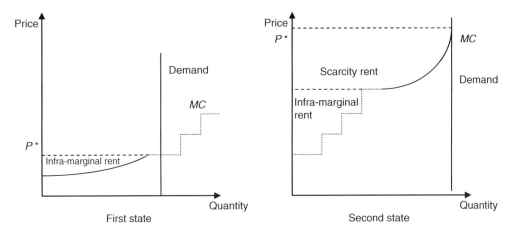

Note: Dotted line corresponds to thermoelectric supply and continued line corresponds to hydroelectric supply.

Source: Author.

Figure 27.4   States of nature of large hydropower systems

to thermal power systems, when it happens, it can last for an extended period (several months). Price caps are usually introduced to avoid the uncomfortable economic and social impacts, and in so doing the scarcity rent that the power plants can recover in dry years is diminished. The hydro reservoir owner has no financial incentive to store energy to use when the NEF becomes critically low.[1]

The lack of incentives to keep *a certain amount* of energy unavailable in the hydro reservoir until the critical period arrives is the 'missing money' of large hydropower systems. This situation has significant implications for the security of supply of hydropower systems.

Thermal power plants provide the energy that the hydropower plants lack in the critical periods to alleviate this problem, subject to limits on fuel supply.

3   Electricity Generation in Brazil

Hydropower plants account for almost 80 percent of the Brazilian power installed capacity (Figure 27.5), meeting 90 percent of the demand in wet years. The power capacity is substantially higher than the peak demand (64.3 GW).[2] The hydro reservoirs can store energy to supply roughly half of the annual electricity consumption. They are used on a pluriannual depletion scheme[3] to save fossil-fuel consumption while thermal power plants are used to moderate the hydro reservoirs' depletion rate.

Until the mid-1990s, the system was state owned and operated monopolistically. A cost-plus regime was used to determine energy prices and the system had sufficient excess capacity to meet demand during a critical period. However, whenever the system was unable to meet demand, rationing of power was used to balance the market.

In the mid-1990s, liberalization and privatization radically changed the Brazilian power market (de Oliveira, 2006). A wholesale power market to determine energy prices was organized into four submarkets (South; Southeast and Mid-West; North; and

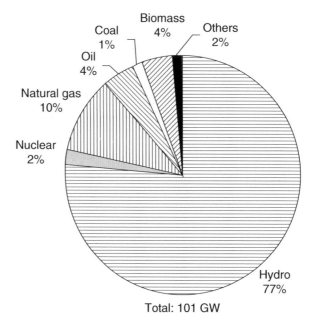

Total: 101 GW

Source: ANEEL (2008).

Figure 27.5   Brazil's installed capacity (March 2008)

Northeast) due to transmission restrictions. However, the decision to use the energy stored in the hydro reservoirs remained centrally managed by the system operator and the key criteria for the depletion of the hydro reservoirs did not change. Thermal power plants were expected to remain idle most of the time in order to minimize the use of fossil fuels. A set of computer models, previously used for the merit order dispatch, was rearranged to fix the system energy price.

This arrangement proved unsustainable. The prices produced by the computer models were unable to cover the full costs of new generating capacity and the missing money problem described by Joskow meant that power projects crucial for balancing the market were postponed, implying that stored energy intended for the periods of critical imbalance were gradually depleted by the system operator to avoid power shortage. Such a strategy led to the unavoidable consequence of power rationing (Figure 27.6) to avoid hydro reservoirs being further depleted, forcing the government to take urgent measures and launch an emergency plan (Losekann, 2003).

In 2004, a second wave of power sector reform was initiated primarily to secure supply. The new regulatory framework drastically transformed the wholesale market (Losekann, 2008).

Two trade environments were created for the wholesale market. The regulated environment is destined to supply power to captive consumers of distribution companies (discos) and the free market to supply free consumers.[4] It is expected that all energy trade will be carried out using long-term contracts. The spot price should be used by generators and consumers to correct small, outstanding contractual unbalances.

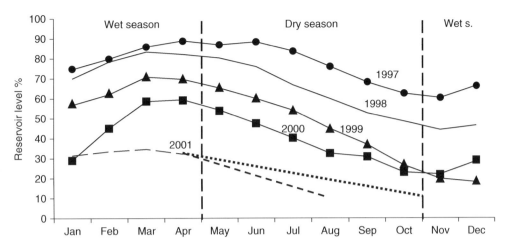

Note: The dashed line represents estimated evolution if the rationing measures were not adopted. The dotted line represents the evolution intended by the rationing measures, even with poor hydrology.

Source: Author / ONS data.

Figure 27.6   Reservoir depletion and estimated rationing impact (reservoir level in SE/ MW subsystem (%): January 1997–April 2001)

Power is sold in the regulated market in public auctions organized by the regulator under rules fixed by the government. Free consumers are required to purchase their power from generators using bilateral contracts but they can buy power in the spot market, after making a penalty payment for not having a power supply contract. A price cap for the spot market was introduced to limit the exposure of market players to the value of loss of load.

Monthly minimum levels for the hydro reservoirs were imposed by the government to avoid the risk of the reservoir depletion to crisis levels. The system operator has the responsibility of maintaining reservoir levels monitored by a committee (Monitoring Committee of the Electricity Sector) comprising government representatives. At the end of 2007 the committee used its powers to implement modifications in the dispatch rules to ensure that the water depletion was at a 'desirable' rate.

Hydropower and thermal power plants compete to supply on slightly different terms. The former offer prices for their energy supply, while the latter offer prices for their capacity availability. When dispatched, thermal power plants' fuel costs are passed on to consumers.

4   Securing Supply: Simulations

To analyze the security of supply problem in Brazil, we estimated a model that simulates the monthly equilibrium between supply and demand in the four (regional) submarkets that comprise the integrated Brazilian system.

Energy demand for each of the four subsystems is driven by GDP, population and regional measures of industrial activity.[5] In our simulation exercises we considered a GDP annual growth rate of 5.1 percent. Future population movements were taken from

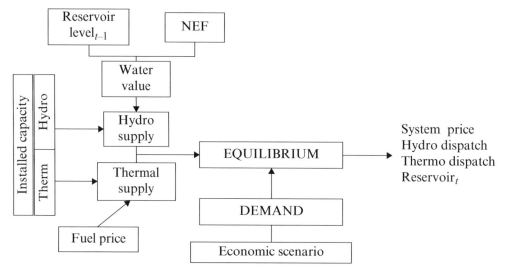

Source: Author.

Figure 27.7   Schematic description of the simulation model

the Brazilian Institute of Geography and Statistics (IBGE), the Brazilian agency for population (among others) issues. Industrial activity figures were obtained as regional responses to GDP movements by means of simple econometric models.

Supply has hydrology as its main ruler. Flexible models for the regional NEF series were estimated based on the observations of the 76 years, from 1931 to 2006. Based on the estimated models, 2000 hydrological series were generated using Monte Carlo simulation. Issues of uncertainty, including probabilities of dispatch, about future NEF developments are all based on the 2000 series generated. The water value is determined as a function of reservoir levels adjusted seasonally, as Figure 27.3 illustrates.[6] Figure 27.7 presents our model in a schematic fashion.

The focus here is on the Southeast, which is the main Brazilian subsystem. The thermopower plants were grouped according to their current declared prices. Starting in March 2008, we simulated power dispatch through to February 2012 using the 2000 generated series.

Figures 27.8 and 27.9 present the supply curve of the Southeast subsystem in the two different states of nature. The first state in Figure 27.8 reflects a situation where water is abundant cheap and no thermopower plant is dispatched. By contrast, the second state when water is scarce and expensive is illustrated in the situation results presented in Figure 27.9; in this scenario, all the thermopower plants are operating.

The first state of nature (Figure 27.8), is the usual operation of the Southeast subsystem. Over the four years (2008–12), the simulation results suggest that the average probability of this situation is 63 percent (Figure 27.10).

The second state of nature, where water is scarce and therefore expensive, is very infrequent. The estimated dispatch probability of all thermal capacity available at the same time is close to 1 percent (Figure 27.11). However, when this second state of nature

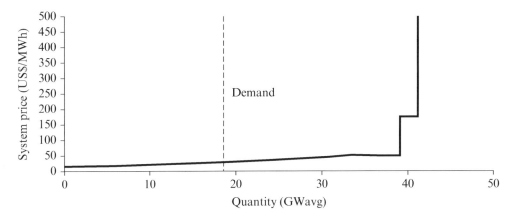

Note: Reservoirs are set in 50% of their seasonal adjusted capacity. Demand corresponds to total demand minus out of merit supply. We used the 2007 average exchange rate (US$1.00 = R$ 1.94).

Source: Author.

Figure 27.8   Supply curve in Southeast subsystem during first state of nature

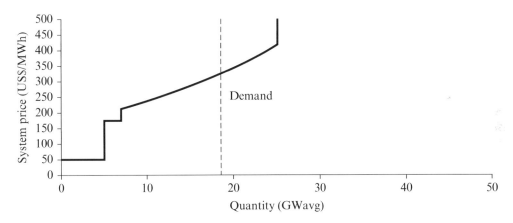

Note: Reservoirs are set in 10% of their seasonal adjusted capacity. Demand corresponds to total demand minus out of merit supply. US$1.00 = R$1.94.

Source: Author.

Figure 27.9   Supply curve in Southeast subsystem during second state of nature

occurs it tends to persist. In more than 70 percent of water scarcity occurrences, the problem persists for three or more months and ultimately results in a power rationing.

In spite of the Brazilian government's required minimum reservoir levels, the missing money problem still occurs as water shortages are not fully incorporated into the energy price. Consequently, the economic signal does not direct market participants' behavior to avoid draining reservoirs to dangerously low levels. Instead, the market

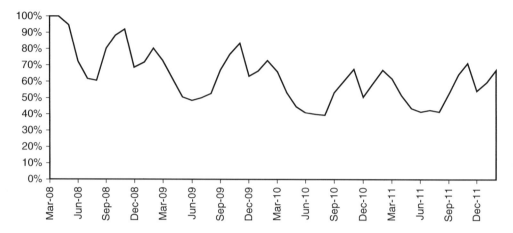

Source: Author.

Figure 27.10   Probability of first state of nature

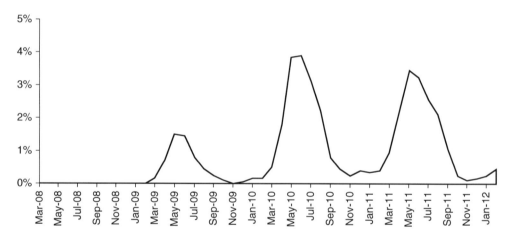

Source: Author.

Figure 27.11   Probability of second state of nature

price is artificially lower than it otherwise would be, had the water shortages been fully incorporated into the energy prices, and there is excess supply and consumption of this artificially cheap energy.

We estimated the effect on prices of alternative dispatch schemes designed to keep more or less water in hydro reservoirs, one of which reflects the current rule. The estimates presented in Table 27.1 show that the higher the level of hydro reservoirs, the more frequent is the dispatch of intermediary thermal plants including natural gas. Therefore, spot prices and operational costs are higher. The situation that imposes a reservoir level 15 per cent above the current scheme increases average prices by US$13/MWh.[7]

Table 27.1   *Average expected energy prices by alternatives dispatch schemes*

Dispatch scheme	Average price (US$/MWh)
Current*	48
Plus 10%	54
Plus 15%	61
Less 4%	44

Note: * The current situation represents the expected price with regard to the present dispatch scheme. The alternatives were designed to keep more or less water in hydro reservoirs.

Table 27.2   *New energy auctions results*

		Starting year	Contracts length (years)	Average price (US$/MWh)*	Quantity (MWavg**)
1st Auction (A – 5)	Hydro	2008	30	49.74	71
	Thermo	2008	15	61.52	561
	Hydro	2009	30	53.15	46
	Thermo	2009	15	60.12	855
	Hydro	2010	30	53.51	889
	Thermo	2010	15	56.66	862
2nd Auction	Hydro	2009	30	58.96	1028
(A – 3)	Thermo	2009	15	61.58	654
3rd Auction (A – 5)	Hydro	2011	30	56.22	569
	Thermo	2011	15	63.93	535
4th Auction (A – 3)	Thermo	2010	15	62.64	1304
5th Auction (A – 5)	Hydro	2012	30	60.07	715
	Thermo	2012	15	59.71	1597
Sto. Antônio	Hydro	2013	30	36.68	1468

Notes:
* The average price of the thermopower plants is calculated on the basis of the dispatch and fuel prices expectations made by EPE (Energy Research Company).
** 1 MW average = 8760 MWh/year.
   US$1.00 = R$ 1.94.

Source: CCEE (2008).

New generating capacity

The new energy auctions promoted the expansion of Brazilian generating capacity. Between December 2005 and March 2008, five new energy auctions took place, the results of which are presented in Table 27.2. In December 2007, an auction specifically to license a large (3150 MW of installed capacity) hydropower plant in the Amazonian Forest known as Santo Antônio[8] was successfully undertaken.

Figure 27.12 shows the generating mix following the new energy auctions, including Santo Antônio's auction. The auctions provided for 12.4 GW of new generation capacity to be installed over the five-year period, 2008–13. Hydropower plants represent 55

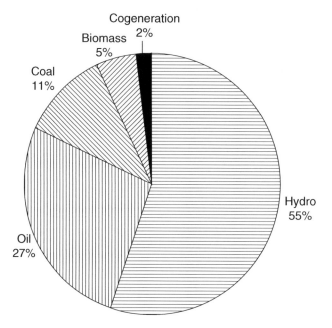

Source: Authors. CCEE Data.

Figure 27.12   Structure of generating capacity expansion

percent of the total. However, only 0.6 GW will start operation before 2011.[9] Until 2010, 63 percent of the expansion will be oil-fueled power plants.

Although the government has chosen capacity payments to stimulate investments in thermopower plants, capacity payments will not solve the missing money problem in large hydro systems. This is because during critical periods it is not the generating capacity that is scarce but the energy source, that is, water in the reservoirs.

Also the capacity payment does not remunerate the infrastructure to supply fuel to power plants. This is particularly relevant for natural gas-fueled plants, for which transport infrastructure is very expensive. Figure 27.10 shows that the Brazilian power system operates most of the time without the dispatch of natural gas-fueled power plants. Therefore another example of the missing money problem in large hydro systems is that the gas infrastructure is under-remunerated.

The very low rate of dispatch of gas power plants after the rationing led Petrobras, the company controlling the natural gas industry, to divert the fuel into industry and the transport markets. In March 2008, only 30 percent of existing natural gas generating capacity has available fuel to operate.[10]

The oil-fueled power plants that dominated the new energy auctions are not adequate to solve the energy security problem in Brazil. Dispatch from thermoelectric plants is intense during adverse hydrology periods and their relatively high operational cost would be prohibitively expensive. Given the generation mix of plants selected in the auctions, the estimated annual cost will reach US$2 billion, resulting in a 10 percent increase in energy tariffs.

A pricing procedure that creates an incentive to keep water in reservoirs also induces an adequate remuneration of natural gas infrastructure. It generates a more frequent dispatch from gas plants and therefore the infrastructure owners are not tempted to direct gas to alternative uses.

5 Conclusion

Despite substantial differences in the nature of security of supply issues in hydro-dominated electricity systems, there are similar problems to those experienced by thermopower systems. The missing money problem of the hydro generators is due to under-remuneration of energy stored in reservoirs, not a lack of generation capacity (as generating capacity is abundant in the system), and is enhanced by uncertainty.

In spite of the measures that the Brazilian government has taken to enhance security of supply, the missing money problem still holds as the price signals are not inducive to keeping energy reserved in reservoirs to meet demand when the electricity generation system is under stress. It also results in under-remuneration of gas infrastructure. As a result, the system is still vulnerable to adverse hydrologic conditions, and generating mix expansion is inadequate. Although the analysis presented here is of the Brazilian electricity generation market, the underlying principles are also applicable to other electricity generation systems with similar generation profiles and market features.

Notes

1. The NEF can be considered critical when the rainfall is close to the worst year ever recorded. In the Southeast of Brazil, it was in 1955.
2. The average capacity factor of the hydropower plants is close to 55 percent.
3. Water can be stored to respond to demands of over a year ahead.
4. Only consumers with demand greater than or equal to 3 MW are free to buy power in this market.
5. Remaining seasonal effects are modeled using seasonal dummies.
6. The stochastic model that sets system price and electricity dispatch in Brazil (Newave) considers other variables to determine the value of water including the expected water inflow, expected demand and VOLL. The function used in this exercise was estimated based on the observed reservoir level and system price.
7. With regard to the total consumption in the Southeast, it would amount to a bill of US$3.5 billion.
8. After long debate this project was approved by the environment agency (IBAMA) following some adjustments to mitigate the project's impact in this very sensitive environmental area.
9. The government decided to auction only the hydropower sites that already had environmental licenses to operate so as to reduce investors' risk. However, the government faced many difficulties when licensing, extending the process beyond the period anticipated.
10. This fuel limit was not considered on our simulations presented earlier.

References

Agência Nacional de Energia Elétrica (ANEEL) (2008), *Banco de Informações de Geração*, Brasília, ANEEL, available at: http://www.aneel.gov.br (accessed 1 April 2008).

Câmara de Comercialização de Energia Elétrica (CCEE) (2008), 'Leilão de Energia Nova – Resultados', Brasília, CCEE, available at: http://www.ccee.org.br (accessed 15 January 2008).

Cramton, P. and S. Stoft (2006), 'The Convergence of Markets Designs for Adequate Generating Capacity with Special Attention to the CAISO's Resource Adequacy Problem', White Paper for the Electricity Oversight Board, available at: http://stoft.com/p/50.html (accessed 22 June 2007).

de Oliveira, A. (2006), 'The political economy of the Brazilian power industry reform', in D. Victor and T. Heller (eds), *The Political Economy of Power Sector Reform: The Experiences of Five Major Developing Countries*, Cambridge: Cambridge University Press, pp. 31–75.

Joskow, P. (2006), 'Competitive electricity markets and investment in new generating capacity', draft paper, available at: econ-www.mit.edu/faculty/download_pdf.php?id=1348 (accessed 20 March 2008).
Losekann, L. (2003), 'Reestruturação do Setor Elétrico Brasileiro: Coordenação e Concorrência', PhD thesis, Rio de Janeiro, IE/UFRJ.
Losekann, L. (2008), 'The second reform of the Brazilian electricity sector', *International Journal of Global Energy Issues*, **29** (1/2): 75–87.
Turvey, R. (2003), 'Ensuring adequate generation capacity', *Utilities Policy*, **11**: 95–102.

28 Electricity retail competition and pricing: an international review
Seth Blumsack and Dmitri Perekhodtsev

1 Introduction

Historically there has been a strong link between the electricity industry performance and the actions taken by its regulators. Until modern restructuring began in the 1990s in the UK, the US, and elsewhere in the world, most consumers of electric power had never experienced anything other than either their local or regional regulated and vertically integrated or publicly owned national utility company.

During the regulated era, prices faced by consumers were set at a level which would allow the utility to recover its capital, operating, and maintenance costs, plus an acceptable level of profit. In the US, rates were generally set through a series of hearings before state regulatory bodies known as public utility commissions.[1] Rate-of-return ratemaking seemed to serve customers and the industry well throughout much of the twentieth century. The low risk involved in utility capital projects made the industry quite attractive to investors, and technological change was rapid as money was easily available to build ever-bigger power stations and expand local transmission systems. Regulation also allowed governments to promote social programs such as rural electrification (Morgan et al. 2005).

Price regulation in electricity was not without its problems. Electric rates to different customer classes were influenced by social or economic development policy and not by any notion of cost imposed on the system. In particular, large industrial customers enjoyed lower-than-average rates, cross-subsidized by higher rates for commercial and residential customers. In addition, the essentially risk-free investment environment enjoyed by utilities gave them incentives to overinvest, a phenomenon referred to as the 'Averch–Johnson effect' (Averch and Johnson 1962). Finally, having flat-rate or declining-block pricing (where the marginal rate would decline with additional consumption) offered no incentives for conserving power.

The low cost and technological advances in power generation rendered these inefficiencies largely unnoticeable until the 1970s. Rising energy prices, due to oil conflicts, coupled with disastrous attempts in the US to build thousand-megawatt nuclear power plants, forced regulators to raise electricity prices to the point where consumers (particularly large industrial consumers) and politicians demanded change.

Modern electricity restructuring in many countries has brought with it a set of reasonably vibrant wholesale electricity markets. With some notable exceptions such as California's power crisis in 2000–01, these markets have generally produced competitive prices with the aid of vigilant and proactive market monitors. In the US and many other countries, wholesale market liberalization was coupled with retail market liberalization, which allowed individual consumers to choose their electricity supplier. There were hopes that robust competition would also erupt among retail providers for all classes of customers. However, with a few notable exceptions, it would be a stretch to call retail electric competition a complete success.

Our aim in this chapter is to address the transition from regulated monopoly pricing to retail competition in electricity, and the associated introduction of new pricing structures, regulations, and institutions. We begin the chapter with a detailed description of rate-of-return ratemaking in electricity, with a discussion of the inherent economic inefficiencies. We then review the major retail electricity market designs from several countries and US states, as well as the successes and failures of these markets. Despite a decade or more of experience, there is still no widely accepted model of how to design a market for retail electric competition. Comparing market designs to records of success and failure, we can start to develop this missing model for how an industrialized nation might design a market to transition away from the monopoly utility and towards active and beneficial retail competition.

2   Ratemaking under Regulation

Regulatory regimes
The primary factor in determining electric rates was raising sufficient revenue for the electric utility. Regulators set a price for each customer class that would allow utilities to recover operating and maintenance costs, as well as capital costs into the future. This method of regulatory price-setting is referred to as 'rate-of-return' regulation, and was dominant in the US for many years.

One of the alternatives to the rate-of-return regulation is known as 'price-cap' or 'revenue-cap' regulation, sometimes called CPI-X in the US and RPI-X in the UK (Kahn 1988). Under revenue-cap regulation, prices are adjusted annually for the rate of inflation (hence the use of the CPI in the US and RPI in the UK), with an adjustment factor taken off the rates to account for efficiency gains that regulators would expect from the utility. Regulating revenues rather than profits, revenue-cap regulation provides utilities the incentives to reduce costs. Since the X-factor would typically be reviewed only every few years, revenue-cap regulation also gave utilities incentives to improve efficiency beyond the X-factor, since these gains could be returned to shareholders rather than customers.

In practice, the distinction between rate-of-return and revenue-cap regulation is sometimes blurry. Both reduced risk to the utility, making it easy for the utility to raise capital for system assets that increased reliability for customers. In some sense, raising capital became *too* easy for the regulated utility. Since the utility's profits were regulated and largely guaranteed, this gave utilities incentives to invest in higher amounts of capital than a profit-maximizing firm might have; this phenomenon is known as the Averch–Johnson effect (Averch and Johnson 1962), and has been verified empirically for US electric utilities by Spann (1974). An oversimplification of the Averch–Johnson effect is to assume that a utility can earn a guaranteed rate of return on all capital projects in which it invests, thus giving the utility incentives to undertake as many investments as the regulator will allow.

Structure of regulated rates

In the simplest cases, regulated rates for each customer class were fixed, and did not change with the hour of the day or with the time of year. Retail rates reflected average costs and not marginal costs. Thus, at some times customers would effectively be over-paying for electricity (relative to what it cost the utility to generate or purchase it) and at some times customers would effectively be underpaying.

Many consumers benefited from having flat rates that often would not change for years at a time. Taylor (1975), Kahn (1988), and Kiesling (2006) discuss a number of economic inefficiencies engendered in the rate structure, the effects of which were not fully felt until some countries started down the path of restructuring.

Mismatch of Retail Prices and Costs

The first problem with regulated rates concerns the difference between average and marginal costs and prices. As mentioned above, the rates set by regulators were based on average costs, which differed from marginal costs (depending on the season and time of day). In particular, the cost to the utility of serving peak demand levels was normally many times larger than the average rate faced by the customer.

Data from modern deregulated wholesale markets allow us to illustrate this mismatch between energy costs and retail rates, which (particularly for households) remain largely flat in these markets. Figure 28.1 shows the energy price duration curve for the PJM (Pennsylvania–New Jersey–Maryland) Interconnection (the largest system operator in

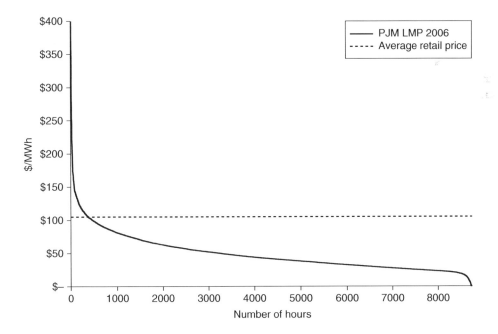

Source: PJM and Edison Electric Institute.

Figure 28.1 *Price duration curve in the PJM wholesale market and the average retail price within the PJM footprint*

the US) with the average residential energy tariff rate within the PJM footprint. The sharp increase in the energy prices with peak demand is costly both for the utility and the system, but consumers generally do not see these costs.

This wedge between the wholesale market with its fluctuating prices and the retail market, where prices remain more or less fixed, is a common feature of electricity restructuring, particularly in the US where political pressure to keep consumer prices low has been quite intense. During the California energy crisis of 2000–01, the differential between average wholesale and retail prices grew so large that one utility, Pacific Gas & Electric, was forced to declare bankruptcy, and the state's other investor-owned utilities came close to following suit (Sweeney 2002).

Time-of-use and Peak-load Pricing

Some utilities have dealt with the peak-load problem by creating a two-part tariff, with the customary energy charge (the average rate for electricity use) plus a charge based on the consumer's peak energy demand during a given billing period (normally one month). Other utilities have experimented with time-of-use pricing (Caves et al. 1984), where customers are charged one average rate for a defined peak period and a lower average rate for an off-peak period. Imposition of demand charges or time-of-use pricing represents a particularly simple attempt by utilities to engage in peak-load pricing (Steiner 1957). Under a more general peak-load pricing system, the utility two-part tariff features one energy charge for the peak period during a given day and a lower energy charge during the rest of the day.

Economists have generally concluded that time-differentiated pricing has the capacity to leave consumers better off, relative to a single average rate. Bergstrom and Mackie-Mason (1991) show that the introduction of peak-load pricing can reduce prices in both the peak and off-peak periods if consumers can substitute easily between peak and off-peak consumption. Simulation analyses of real-time pricing by Borenstein (2005) and Spees and Lave (2007) would seem to confirm this finding. Analysis of a pricing experiment by Caves et al. (1984), however, finds very low elasticity of demand substitution among consumers. Wolak (2006) studies a peak-load pricing experiment in California and finds that residential consumers reduce peak demand by as much as 12 percent, and that peak demands are highly sensitive to large peak prices.

Taylor (1975) pays special attention to the declining-block pricing used by many utilities under revenue-cap or rate-of-return regulation. Under such a tariff, consumers face flat average rates, but those rates decline as the consumer uses more electricity.

Cross-subsidization

Another economic problem with electric rates under regulation was the rampant cross-subsidization that occurred between customer classes. In particular, rates charged to the commercial and residential classes were inflated in order to lower rates for industrial customers. These large customers were given favorable treatment since they represented a large revenue source for the utility and provided a large number of jobs (Apt et al. 2007). Borenstein (2005) finds that moving to time-sensitive pricing reduces this cross-subsidization considerably. This creates economic welfare gains, but may also cause political problems, since rates for large customers would rise substantially.

3 Development of Competitive Retail Pricing

Attempts to introduce competitive retail electricity markets for all customer classes arose from the desire of large industrial customers in the US, starting in the 1970s, to have the option of leaving the monopoly utility to purchase electricity services from a third party (Lave et al. 2007). Despite this, retail competition actually emerged in other countries far before the first restructuring experiments in the US began in California and Pennsylvania in 1998.

Chile began experimenting with retail competition in 1980 (Bergara and Spiller 1996). Norway introduced retail competition 10 years later, in 1990. By the late 1990s, a large number of (mostly) industrialized countries, including the US (1998, for California and Pennsylvania), the UK (1990), New Zealand (1993), Finland (1995), Spain (1998) and Australia (1994, for Victoria) had instituted some form of retail choice for one or more customer classes (Beato and Fuente 1999).

The European Community mandated a gradual opening of the retail market for its member states starting in 1999, when the largest customers (those with annual loads of 40 GWh and more) became eligible to choose their retail provider. The full market opening to retail competition was to be completed in July 2007. Several European countries, such as the UK, Germany, and the Nordic countries fully opened their retail markets long before 2007 (Boisseleau and Hakvoort 2003).

There has not been a single common motivation for opening retail electricity markets to competition. Based on Beato and Fuente (1999) and de Vries (2006), we identify five principal factors that have led some US states and countries to implement retail competition in electricity.

The first, and perhaps most important, is a perception that electricity prices were too high under regulation. It is easy to see why costs would have been on the minds of many customers. In the US, for example, the turbulence in world oil markets and the rise of the environmental movement led to two related but unfortunate events (unfortunate for electricity consumers). The first was that a slowing economy led to a fundamental change in the nature of the growth of electricity demand. For the first eight decades of the industry's history, demand for electricity grew at an exponential rate of around 3 percent per year. Beginning in the 1970s, there was an abrupt shift to a linear growth rate, as shown in Figure 28.2 (Hirsh 1999). Expecting previous growth rates to continue in the future, utilities had sought and been granted permission to pass the costs of large new generation stations (particularly nuclear power) on to customers. An era of rising costs and falling demand thus produced higher average prices. The forces of competition were expected to lower these prices.

Second, retail competition emerged in many countries as a part of general liberalization in the electric sector. In countries where a state-owned electric utility dominated the market for many years, the introduction of retail competition and reforms on retail pricing were viewed as measures necessary to break up the state electricity monopoly. The US is somewhat unusual among highly industrialized countries in that it has never really had a state-owned electricity generation or distribution enterprise, in contrast with the UK, many European countries, and much of South America (Belgium and Germany are two European examples where electricity has not been dominated by a state-owned enterprise).

The third reason for the move towards retail competition was political pressure to

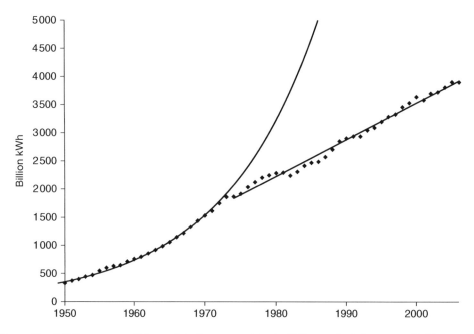

Note: The shift from exponential growth to linear growth in the 1970s can clearly be seen and is illustrated by the two trend lines.

Sources: Hirsh (1999); Morgan et al. (2005).

Figure 28.2   US electricity demand, 1950–2003

reduce or end cross-subsidization. Partly for political reasons, and partly to keep customers from abandoning the utility for other alternatives (such as shifting production to other regions or rolling out distributed generation), rates for commercial and residential customers were often inflated in order to offer lower rates to large industrial customers. An admittedly crude but informative metric of cross-subsidization is the ratio of electric rates between different customer classes.[2] The ratio of industrial rates to residential rates for several US states is shown in Figure 28.3.

Fourth, retail competition was seen as a way to give customers the opportunity to pay a premium to purchase renewable energy. During the 1970s, some US utilities signed a large number of high-priced contracts with alternative generation sources (due to a US regulation known as the Public Utilities Regulatory Policy Act). These contracts were successful in raising prices for consumers, but were not successful in adding much capacity to the US system as a whole. For much of the following 20 years, regulators in the US were hesitant to encourage utilities to invest in costly generation sources.

Finally, two technology advances hold promise for changing basic utility economics. The first is the emergence of small generation units. The conventional view has long been that wholesale competition in generation is possible (given a sufficiently robust transmission system and market monitors), but the wires side of the electricity business (transmission and particularly distribution) was likely to remain a natural monopoly (Joskow and Schmalensee 1983). However, the emergence of small, highly portable generating

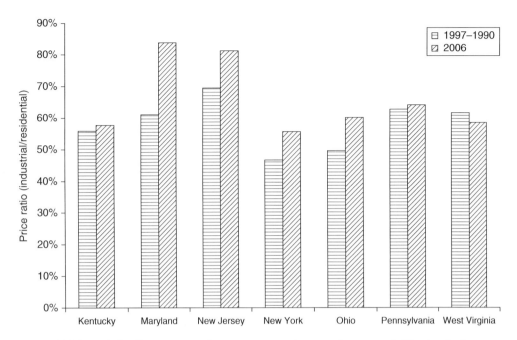

Note: A higher ratio implies greater equality among rates and suggests less cross-subsidization. In the figure, Kentucky and West Virginia have retained traditional regulation, while the other states have opened their markets to retail competition.

Source: Author calculations, based on data from the US Energy Information Administration.

Figure 28.3 *The ratio of industrial electric rates to residential electric rates in several US states*

units suggests that in some areas not historically conducive to competition (such as load pockets in traditional utility systems), the possibility exists of establishing at least a contestable market, if not outright competition. The second technological change is in metering technologies, lowering the costs of administering time-differentiated rate schedules (Faruqui and Hledik 2007).

4   Design Elements of Retail Competition

In addition to liquid wholesale markets and open-access regulations for transmission (as in Orders 888, 889, and 890 issued by the US Federal Energy Regulatory Commission, or FERC), a few additional regulations or market institutions have generally been created in order to promote retail competition in electric generation.

Before getting into each of these design elements, we emphasize again that retail competition affects only the portion of a customer's retail electricity bill related to generation, and sometimes metering and billing. Individual consumers can choose to purchase generation services from a third-party supplier who may own or contract for generation to supply customers or buy generation from the market. The third-party supplier may also provide competitive metering and billing services.

However, the actual electricity is still delivered via transmission and distribution wires owned by the transmission and distribution companies that remain regulated. These distribution services are not affected by customers' retail choice.

Specific pricing policies under retail competition chosen by individual countries and US states vary widely. However, all retail competition programs share several important features. These features include rules related to the appointment of a default service provider, and regulation and pricing of its services; institution of a transition period and regulatory restrictions imposed during this period; and regulations restricting and phasing in customer choice.

Regulation and pricing of default service

One particular company is chosen as the 'default' generation service provider for customers who do not express a preference for any particular supplier or in places where there has been no entry of third-party suppliers.[3] Normally this responsibility falls to the historic distribution utility. In countries formerly dominated by state-owned monopolies, the state distribution utility has been broken up into a number of smaller companies, which are given (or bid for, in the case of the UK) licenses to serve as the default utility. Default service goes by a number of different names throughout the world. Common in the US is the term 'provider of last resort' as well as 'standard offer' service. The UK uses the term 'first-tier supplier' to describe a seller of electricity services who also owns the local distribution wires. For the purpose of standardization, we shall use the term 'default service' to describe the generation company assigned to customers who do not express a preference over suppliers, as well as the tariffs and rates for these customers.

An important issue is deciding how the default service utility procures generation services for its default customers or those who explicitly choose the default utility. This mechanism is normally chosen by regulators, and can be more complex if the default utility has also engaged (by rule or voluntarily) in vertical disintegration and divestiture of generation assets.

One dominant model of default service involves direct rate-setting by public utility regulators. These default service rates are determined in a proceeding similar to a rate case for a regulated utility, and are generally based on the utility's generation costs (if it remained vertically integrated) or expected power purchase costs (long-term contracts and spot markets). Although regulated default service tariffs appear to have been more common in Europe than in the US, this method of determining default rates has been used in parts of Pennsylvania, for example (Blumsack et al. 2007).

Another often-used model is to hold an auction, where independent generators bid to provide power to the default utility. This is generally a better way of integrating default service prices with market prices (since the auction rather than the regulator determines the default service rate), but can be open to political manipulation if regulators or politicians are unhappy with the results. This has occurred in several US states, for example (see Apt et al. 2007 for a discussion of default rates in Maryland and Illinois).

Default rates can be set quite high in an attempt to drive customers away from the default utility to the competitive suppliers. Setting default prices at high levels for the purpose of enticing competitive suppliers to enter the market, and enticing consumers to leave the default utility in favor of those suppliers, has earned the nickname 'ugly' default service in the US. This has been the approach favored in Texas, for example, and has been considered in some US states as a way to promote competition in the post-transition period (ibid.).

Restrictions are generally placed on the types of product that the default service utility can offer. Some US regulators, for example, have restricted the default utility from offering long-term contracts to customers (ibid.).

Transition period
Most countries moving forward with electricity restructuring have instituted a 'transition period' to full retail competition for all customers. Accompanying this transition period, regulators have often imposed rate caps or rate freezes (or both, in the case of California) on the default service utility. The level and duration of these caps have been determined variously at either the state or country level, or the utility level.

There is a twofold logic behind the rate caps. The first is to provide the default utility with a time line and benchmarks for retiring stranded costs. A common assumption at the time of restructuring was that competition would cause prices to fall, much as they had fallen in markets for crude oil and natural gas. This meant that the price caps imposed on the default service providers would be increasingly high relative to the market, but the utilities would be allowed to retire stranded costs based on the difference between the market price and the artificially frozen retail price.

The second purpose for freezing the price for the default utility was to keep the utility from using its dominant market position and financial resources to keep potential entrants out of the retail electricity market. The frozen default rate essentially sets a benchmark 'price to beat' for potential competitive suppliers.

In addition to using retail-market revenues to retire stranded costs, some utilities were allowed explicit customer surcharges for stranded-cost recovery. In the US, these so-called 'competitive transition charges' vary widely across utilities, and even across time for a single utility. The variation through time in US competitive transition charges is shown in Figure 28.4. While the average stranded-cost recovery charge in the US has been around one cent per kilowatt-hour (roughly 10 percent of the average residential customer's total bill), some utilities have been allowed stranded-cost surcharges of more than three cents per kWh (Edison Electric Institute, various years).

Regulation of retail access
Regulators have set guidelines specifying which customer classes can search for competitive electricity suppliers, and how often these customers can switch without penalty. In many European countries, regulators have also set explicit fees for switching, although some countries are trying to reduce or eliminate these fees (Andersson 2005).

Most US states are either at the point where 100 percent of customers in all rate classes are eligible to switch to a competitive third-party supplier, or are in a transition period to this point (some states, such as New York, initially allowed retail access only for large customers, phasing smaller customers into the market gradually).

The European Commission has taken the approach of phasing in customer classes eligible for retail choice. The phase-in has generally been according to customer size, starting with the largest customers. According to the directive of the European Commission, customers with annual demands of 40 GWh and larger became eligible by

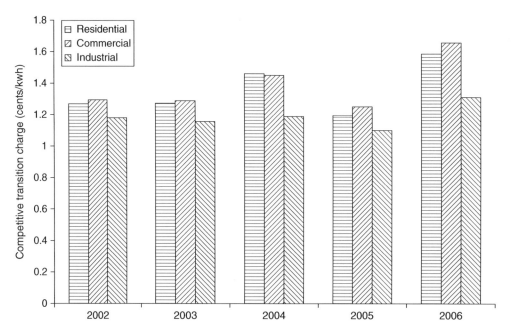

Source: Edison Electric Institute.

*Figure 28.4   US average competitive transition charges for three customer classes,
2002–2006*

1999, customers consuming over 20 GWh per year became eligible in 2000 and customers consuming over 9 GWh followed in 2003. By July 2007, 100 percent of customers
in EU Member States were required to become eligible for retail choice. Several countries, however, have opened their retail markets ahead of the schedule set by the EC
(Boisseleau and Hakvoort 2003).

Rules regarding switching providers are highly variable. In some cases (Pennsylvania,
for example), customers are given great latitude to switch electricity suppliers nearly as
often as they would like, without any penalty. This amount of latitude is highly beneficial
to consumers who are active switchers, but since electric systems must still be centrally
planned to some extent (for example, default service utilities must plan to purchase, or in
some cases build, generation in anticipation of future default service load), active costless
switching imposes some costs on the default service utilities and on default customers
who are not switching generation providers actively.

The actual policy decisions made by countries and US states have been fairly diverse.
Table 28.1 provides an overview of the preferred policies chosen by several countries and
US states. The table suggests a wide variety of different approaches to designing retail
electricity markets, both internationally and within the US. The table also indicates (as
we discuss in Section 5 below) that there is no economic model of retail electricity competition that has been universally agreed upon by economists or regulators.

Retail competition has emerged at a somewhat uneven pace, as shown by the first
few columns in Table 28.1. Generally speaking, Europe began experimenting with retail

Table 28.1 Retail competition policies for several countries and US states

State/country	First year of implementation	Full retail access	Stranded cost allowance?	Default ratemaking process	Rates capped/ frozen during transition period
US states					
Connecticut	January 2000	July 2000	Yes	Regulation	1996–2006
District of Columbia	January 2001	January 2001	Yes	Auction	1999–2007
Illinois	October 1999	January 2007*	Yes	Auction*	1998–2007*
Maine	March 2000	March 2000	Yes	Auction	None mandated
Maryland	July 2000	July 2000	Yes	Auction	1999–2006**
Massachusetts	March 1998	March 1998	Yes	Market-based rates	1999–2005
New Jersey	November 1999	November 1999	Yes	Auction	1999–2003
New York	January 2001	January 2001	Yes	Marked-based rates	None mandated***
Ohio	January 2001	January 2001	Yes	Regulation	1999–2008**
Pennsylvania	January 1999	January 2000	Yes	Regulation	1999–2010**
Texas	January 2002	January 2002	Yes	Market-based rates	1999–2007
European countries					
Denmark	2002	2002	Yes	Regulation	N/A
Finland	1995	1997	Yes	Market-based rates	None mandated
France	2004	2007	Yes	Regulation	N/A
Germany	1998	1999	Yes	Regulation	N/A
Netherlands	1998	2001	Yes	Regulation	N/A
Norway	1991	1991	N/A	Regulation	N/A
Spain	1998	2003	Yes	Regulation	N/A
Sweden	1996	1999	N/A	Regulation	N/A
UK	1990	1998	Yes, but eliminated	Market-based rates	1990–1998
New Zealand	1993	1994	None mandated	Market-based rates	None mandated

Notes:
* The results of the Illinois default supply auction in late 2006 were struck down by regulators, effectively halting progress towards full retail competition in that state.
** Rate caps expired at different times for different utilities within a state.
*** Default utilities in New York were required to submit customized rate plans to regulators. Many, but not all, included some form of rate cap.

Sources: EC (2005); European Commission, *Internal Market Fact Sheets* (various years and countries); Rose (2006); Individual websites of US state electricity regulators.

electricity competition earlier than the US, with many countries opening their electricity markets beginning in the early to mid-1990s. Within the US, some states acted early and implemented retail competition for all (or nearly all) customers simultaneously. California, Pennsylvania and New Jersey are the two most prominent 'early adopters', though California has been omitted from the table since it cancelled its retail competition program three years after it began (Sweeney 2002). Illinois represents an interesting exception, in taking nearly 10 years to implement full retail competition for all electricity customers (as the note in the table indicates, as of 2008 the process of retail market design in Illinois is not yet complete).

Another significant difference between retail electric market designs in various countries has been the treatment of so-called 'default service' pricing (as discussed above). For those customers who do not or are not able to choose a competitive generation supplier, many European countries have retained some sort of rate regulation. Finland and the UK have been exceptions to this rule, placing default customers on a market-based tariff. New Zealand also has market-based pricing for default service customers. A wider variety of approaches have been implemented in the US. Only a few states have chosen to keep default customers on regulated service rates; once the full transition to competition has been made, these default rates are likely to somehow reflect market prices. Some other states, such as Texas, New York and Massachusetts currently use a market-based rate structure for default customers. More popular in the US has been to set default service rates through an auction process run by the state, though the outcomes of these auctions have at times been controversial, as in Maryland and Illinois (Apt et al. 2007).

5   Performance of Retail Competition

We have discussed a number of reasons why countries and regions have undertaken significant reforms in electricity pricing. Perhaps the most significant reform on the retail side of the industry is not pricing, per se, but competitive retail access. Without getting too far ahead of ourselves, we do note that significant reform in retail price determination is one necessary element for the success of retail competition (Kiesling 2006). Particularly with the cross-subsidization of large industrial customers by smaller residential and commercial customers, traditional electric utility rate-of-return regulation (not to mention the allowance of a geographic monopoly) represents a significant barrier to retail electric-rate reform.

We ultimately wish to be able to provide policy-makers with a set of policy choices that are most likely to lead to healthy switching activity and competition at the retail level. In this section, we review the performance of retail electricity markets in several countries. While prices will merit some mention in this section, the primary metric we use to evaluate the success of retail competition is the level of demand or number of customers in each rate class served by competitive suppliers, as opposed to the default utility. The behavior of retail prices under competition is an important issue, but is fairly complex (Kwoka 2006).

Retail electricity markets in the United States
Sixteen of the United States, plus the District of Columbia, have opened their retail electricity markets to competition for all customer classes (Rose 2006). Fourteen of these have also embraced restructuring at the wholesale level, including participation in centralized regional electricity markets, having their utilities' transmission networks operated by an independent regional transmission organization (RTO), and pursuing market-based ratemaking for generators and utility divestiture. The two exceptions are Arizona and Oregon. These states are not a part of any official RTO, but their utilities have been active in over-the-counter bilateral electricity trading for decades.[4]

It is nearly impossible to underestimate the effect of California's electricity crisis on electricity restructuring in the United States. Since the onset of the crisis in 2000, no US state has announced plans for restructuring, except those that had already started the process. In addition, a number of regulated states halted their restructuring plans. At least two US states (Montana and Virginia) reversed course, abandoning restructuring and retail competition, and re-instituting regulated ratemaking.[5] Despite these market setbacks, several states have introduced reasonably successful retail competition programs, in terms of the amount of load shifting to competitive suppliers.

Industrial customers in the US were expected to be the primary beneficiaries of retail competition (Apt 2005). As the largest individual loads, they were thought to have more incentive than others to shop around for competitive generation supply. However, having benefited for years from cross-subsidized electric rates, increased price transparency would hit these consumers the hardest. In the US, many large industrial customers were able to sign long-term deals at below-market prices in the year or two prior to restructuring taking effect (Apt et al. 2007). The reason why many utilities were willing to sign these contracts was the expectation that prices would fall precipitously under competition. Many of these particular long-term contracts lasted three to five years, meaning that they expired just before the US natural gas pricing bubble.

Data from US states suggest that even if industrial customers have not benefited the most from retail competition, they certainly have been among the most active participants in shopping for generation suppliers.

Figure 28.5 shows the percentage of industrial load in several different states served by a competitive supplier. The clear leader in industrial load switching (in the US) has been Texas, where more than 85 percent of the state's commercial and industrial load has left the default utility for a competitive supplier. (The 15 percent still with the default utility represents smaller commercial customers; 100 percent of large customers have switched to a competitive provider.) Other states have also seen measurable success in industrial switching: in Massachusetts, Maine, New York and Illinois more than 50 percent of industrial load had switched to a competitive supplier by the end of 2006.

The biggest disappointments in the US for industrial load switching appear to be states such as Pennsylvania and Ohio. That Pennsylvania has seen extremely low levels of industrial load leaving the default supplier is, at first glance, somewhat surprising given the enthusiasm with which the state embraced restructuring in the mid-1990s. Virtually all of the switching activity among industrial customers has been in the Duquesne Light service territory surrounding Pittsburgh, where default service price caps were lifted and the transition period ended far earlier than in the remainder of the state.

We do not include data for California here, since that state suspended its 'Direct Access' retail competition program in the midst of the power crisis in 2001. Retail competition on the industrial side was initially moderately successful, with approximately 30 percent of industrial load choosing a competitive supplier prior to the suspension of Direct Access (California Energy Commission, various years).

As shown in Figure 28.6, residential switching has been a much more difficult process in the US. With the exception of Texas, which has nearly 40 percent of residential load served by competitive suppliers (and the number appears to be rising over time), only Ohio has surpassed the 10 percent switching level for residential customers. Further, in most states the percentage of residential load participating in retail competition has

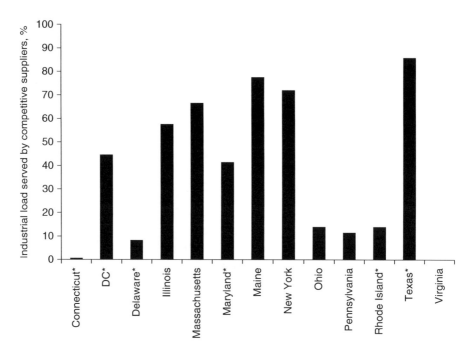

Note: States marked with a (*) include some commercial load in their statistics for large customers.

Source: Rose (2006); individual state electricity regulators.

Figure 28.5 US industrial load served by competitive electric suppliers, 2005

actually been falling. Apart from Texas, only Massachusetts and New York have seen a significant increase in residential switching activity (Connecticut has seen a small increase, but less than 3 percent of residential load in that state is served by a competitive supplier).

Why has it been so difficult, for the most part, to get residential customers to switch electric generation providers, particularly when compared to the industrial customer class? One reason is that residential customers are fairly homogeneous, and the product they demand is also generally homogeneous. Apart from perhaps 10 percent of US households that would demand green power if it were offered, very few residential customers have idiosyncratic demands for electricity. This stands in contrast to large commercial or industrial customers, who may have very specific requirements for voltage, power quality, or reliability related to their business or production process. There is thus much more of an opportunity for competitive suppliers to offer differentiated products to industrial loads than to residential loads.

A difficulty with serving residential load competitively is that the transaction costs for individual customers may simply be too high. Most residential customers in the US simply do not spend a significant proportion of their income on electricity. Based on data from the US Energy Information Administration, we calculate that the average residential electric consumer in the US spent US$1100 on electricity in 2006, compared to an

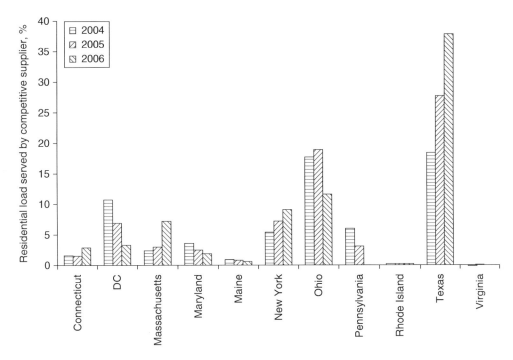

Note: Many states have zero residential consumers signed up with competitive suppliers, or have not had competitive suppliers enter the market for residential customers; these states are omitted from the figure.

Sources: Rose (2006); individual state electric regulatory agencies.

Figure 28.6 US residential load served by competitive electric suppliers, 2004–2006

average income of around US$60 000.[6] Thus, the average consumer spends less than 2 percent of his/her income on electricity.

Since energy and transmission/distribution make up most of the typical US residential electric bill, unless the default electric price is set at significantly above-market levels, residential consumers do not stand to save very much by switching electric suppliers. Further, in some states, retail competition has led to price convergence among competitive suppliers, so there is not very much competition on price (Apt et al. 2007). In addition, the types of differentiated products that could be offered to residential consumers (such as time-of-day rates, interruptible load contracts, and so forth) may involve high transaction costs for many customers in the form of active participation and demand management. Large industrial customers, on the other hand, often have designated energy managers with a specific responsibility to interface with the electricity provider.[7]

States for which separate data are available for commercial customers generally report lower levels of switching activity than for industrials, but higher levels than residential customers. The commercial rate class is highly heterogeneous, with customers ranging from large office buildings to small businesses. Particularly for large commercial customers, it is somewhat surprising that switching levels have been so low. In some ways, large commercial customers stand to benefit from retail competition even more than large industrial customers, as discussed in a study of competition in Pennsylvania by Apt et al. (2007) Large commercial customers with a long payment history, good future prospects, and highly predictable loads (such as hospital complexes and universities) have been able to find prices from competitive suppliers far below the default service rate. These customers have a much lower credit risk from the perspective of the competitive suppliers, and since their loads have low volatility, they are easy to serve using standard products available through the wholesale or bilateral markets. Large manufacturing facilities (steel mills, for example) tend to have highly volatile loads and require larger amounts of ancillary services (principally reactive power and voltage support). This increases costs for the competitive suppliers, who can easily buy or provide generation services, but may have higher costs in procuring ancillary services. These higher costs should be reflected in higher prices offered to industrial customers by competitive suppliers.

Retail competition in Europe and the United Kingdom
The European Commission Electricity Directive has mandated that all customers in all member countries must be allowed to choose their electric supplier by July 2007.[8] However, a number of countries began the transition to retail competition much earlier. Unlike some US states (particularly Pennsylvania and California), most European countries have chosen to progressively phase-in competitive retail pricing over a number of years, starting with the largest customers. Some of these transition periods were fairly short, as in Norway (Beato and Fuente 1999; Andersson 2005) while others stretched four years or longer, as in Spain and the English and Welsh markets.

As with the US, the European experience with competition has been quite mixed. Figure 28.7 shows the market penetration of competitive suppliers in several European countries for large customers (large commercial and industrial) and smaller customers (smaller commercial establishments and residential customers). The most switching activity has been seen in the UK and the Scandinavian countries (most notably Finland and Sweden). Germany has also seen a substantial amount of industrial load move from the old incumbent utility to competitive suppliers. As with the US, industrial customers in Europe have thus far been more eager to switch electricity suppliers than residential customers or small businesses. Perhaps an unusual outcome of the Scandinavian markets has been the interest of residential consumers in switching to a competitive supplier, particularly those customers with high electric demand. Andersson (2005) also notes that Scandinavian residential customers consume significantly more electricity than those in the UK – 20 MWh per year for Scandinavia versus 3.6 MWh per year for the UK.

Being an early adopter of retail competition has not necessarily been associated with success in the number of customers choosing a supplier other than the distribution utility. Spain, which began its transition to retail competition in 1998, has seen only about 25 percent of large customers switch suppliers. Analysis by Hoffmaister (2006) suggests that this may be due to the dominance of regional distribution utilities; in particular the two largest distributors, Endesa and Iberdrola.

The same thing might be true of France, which seems to have engaged in a number of policies specifically designed to bolster the market position of Électricité de France (EDF) (Finon 2002). France has created a highly credible regulatory structure, particularly with respect to open transmission access. Yet, as shown by the recent example of

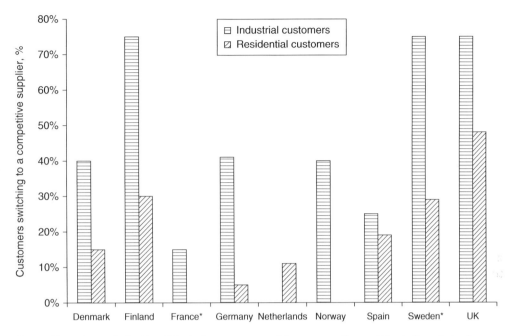

Note: Countries marked with a (*) include some commercial customers. France did not allow choice for residential customers until 2007.

Source: European Commission, *Internal Market Fact Sheets* (various countries).

Figure 28.7 Customer switching in European countries, 2005

an independent retail supplier, Direct Energie, competing with EDF in retail supply is still not easy.[9]

Policy surrounding retail competition in Europe has focused on reducing switching costs, particularly for residential customers. Despite the fact that the European Union does allow for the recovery of stranded costs by the default distribution utility, the UK has not instituted a competitive transition surcharge for customers. Other features thought to limit competition in the US do not exist in the UK or in Scandinavia. There are no price caps in either NETA (New Electricity Trading Arrangements) or the Nord Pool market (price caps were removed from the UK market in 2002 following a roughly eight-year transition period). Retail prices are also unregulated in both markets. The default supplier may offer a regulated 'price to beat', but competitive suppliers do not face any price constraints. Importantly for Sweden, costly metering requirements (which would have essentially reduced a household's 'profit' from switching electric suppliers) were dropped.

Retail competition in New Zealand
New Zealand was one of the first countries to introduce full retail access for all customer classes, beginning in 1994. As Bergara and Spiller (1996) note, New Zealand is also unique in that, at least initially, it did not create a specific regulatory body charged with electricity market oversight. The electricity market in New Zealand operated along the

principles of antitrust law until 2003, when the Electricity Commission was established in response to concerns of vertical integration among suppliers and price gouging during the 2001 drought (Lindell 2004). The New Zealand wholesale and retail markets have generally operated based on principles of open information, rather than heavy-handed market monitoring or control. There are no explicit price controls in the New Zealand retail market, for example, although under the new regulatory regime, consumers and traders can file complaints related to pricing, asset management, or conduct. Open access to distribution systems exists and is governed by a simple license fee (although the return on distribution assets is still regulated).

Given the low transactions costs in the New Zealand retail electricity market, the low levels of customer switching (compared to, say, Texas and the UK) are surprising. Over all customer classes, the average switching rate has hovered around 30 percent of customers, although the rate of market penetration by competitive suppliers has increased by around 5 percent in the past few years. The exact reasons are uncertain, although Beato and Fuente (1999) suggest that incumbent distribution-owning suppliers may be engaging in cross-subsidization to retain high-revenue customers. Another possibility is that since New Zealand has not had a repeat of the 2001 drought and price spikes (in terms of the magnitude and duration of the spikes), with few exceptions, prices have not been sufficiently high or volatile to entice consumers (particularly households) to switch.

6   Critical Design Elements for Successful Retail Competition

While the ability for competitive electric suppliers to offer differentiated products is clearly the goal, the means to this end are unclear. As surprising as it may sound, there is simply no theory accepted among economists for how to organize a competitive retail electricity market. Some economic analyses exist, such as Borenstein and Holland (2005) and Joskow and Tirole (2007), but focus more on efficiency and welfare properties than on specific policy recommendations. Based on the discussion in this chapter, we therefore conclude by offering a set of policy prescriptions for successful retail electricity markets. Our 'rules of thumb' are based not on any theoretical analysis, but on what specific policies appear to have worked well in existing retail markets in Europe, the US and elsewhere.

First, recognizing the link between competitive retail markets and competitive wholesale markets, open access for transmission and distribution in some form appears necessary. The dominant model for ensuring open access is the independent transmission system operator (TSO, called an RTO in the US), which manages the transmission grid for a region or country but does not own any generating assets or customer load to take a market position. This is the model used by the US and the UK, for example.

Open access to the transmission grid is necessary to avoid giving any one supplier a competitive advantage solely because of the configuration of the transmission grid. It is, however, interesting to note that Germany, which has seen some success in retail competition, has neither a single TSO nor a formal mechanism for open transmission access. Third parties (for example, competitive suppliers) who would like to serve customers in Germany must sign bilateral agreements with specific transmission owners.

Second, default service prices must not be set at artificially low levels or in such a way as to erect an ad hoc barrier to entry by competitive suppliers. Supply procurement auctions for default service are one possible way to satisfy this criterion, although care must be taken by regulators that generators are not exercising any market power in the bidding process. Here the auction structure itself is also extremely important.

Another possibility is to pursue an 'ugly' default service policy and set prices for default supply at artificially high above-market levels. From an efficiency standpoint, if the auction can be made competitive, the various risks associated with default supply for different customer classes are more likely to be correctly captured through an auction than through a regulator simply setting the default rate at a high level.

A third related requirement for success of retail competition programs is that price caps on the incumbent supplier should last as little time as possible, and should be indexed or otherwise linked to market prices or fuel costs. Doing so avoids two problems that have plagued restructuring efforts in the US. The first is that fixing prices during a period of low prices benefits consumers when prices rise, but also forces competitive suppliers out of the market. This is essentially the story of the Pennsylvania experience. Retail rate caps were set in the late 1990s for a transition period that was allowed to last up to 12 years. When wholesale natural gas and electricity prices started rising in 2001, suppliers were not able to compete and most withdrew from the Pennsylvania market. The second problem with capping retail prices (especially for long periods) is that the expiration of price caps may amount to a rude awakening if prices must instantly adjust to different market conditions. There have been many highly publicized instances of this in the US.

Fourth, rules on frequency of switching should be chosen carefully. Allowing unrestricted switching provides a benefit to consumers who actively seek to switch suppliers. However, it imposes a cost on those customers who do not choose a competitive supplier. The default utility must plan in advance and procure power for its expected amount of default service load. Frequent switching in and out of the default utility service plan increases the volatility of the default utility's load. The increased risk is then passed on to the remaining default customers. Thus, there is a free-rider problem associated with unrestricted switching that may negatively affect the competitive supplier as well. For example, a particular customer facing a choice between a competitive supplier and a flat average-cost rate from the default utility might switch once per season, choosing the competitive supplier when system load is low and prices are below average, and choosing the default supplier when system load is high and prices are above average. The UK, for example, has dealt with this problem by requiring customers to provide six months of prior notice before switching. In the US, Massachusetts has imposed restrictions on how often customers can switch, with penalties for violating the restrictions. Pennsylvania is an example of a state that allows customers to switch electric providers nearly at will. Another option, suggested by Apt et al. (2007) would be to price electric service in a similar fashion as mobile phones. Customers would sign agreements to stay with a given supplier for a certain amount of time, with penalties for early cancellation.

Finally, the types of service that default utilities can offer their *default* customers must be chosen carefully. One option (perhaps considered by some to be equivalent to 'ugly' default service) is to place all default customers on a market-based rate. Risk-averse customers can then choose a fixed-price contract option from a different supplier if desired. Another approach allows the default service provider to offer one or more long-term (usually fixed-price) contract options. In some states (such as New Jersey and Illinois), the contract options allowed to the default utility correspond to the supply contract lengths found in the default supply auctions. Since there is (or should be) a link between spot and forward prices in electricity markets, the exact length of the contract options offered may not be important in and of itself. The crucial point is to limit the number of contract options that any one default supplier can offer. If the default supplier is allowed to crowd the space of electricity-related products, it will surely keep competitive suppliers out of the market.

An additional remark can be made that retail competition will not succeed, and will not produce the desired consumer benefits and efficiency gains, without the ability of competitive suppliers to offer differentiated products to suit the heterogeneous tastes of consumers. A number of aspects of product differentiation exist, the most apparent of which is the ability to sell 'green power' to customers willing to pay a premium to subsidize renewable generation resources such as solar and wind power.[10] Other possibilities include bundling electricity and other services such as natural gas or telecommunications.

The important possibility of product differentiation is offered by the difference in the attitudes of customers towards risk. Particularly risk-averse customers may prefer a flat rate, reflecting expectations of average costs; these customers should also be willing to pay a premium for the risk-reduction service that a flat rate provides (under the standard regulated utility tariff, all customers get this service for free, whether they demand it or not). Customers with more risk tolerance might be better served with some sort of time-varying electricity pricing. Time-differentiated pricing is sometimes viewed as a necessary, but not sufficient, condition for retail electricity competition to emerge (Kiesling 2006).

Notes

1. This regulatory body goes by a number of different names in various parts of the world. Public Utility Commission or PUC is the name of the body adopted in the US.
2. The intuition behind the metric is that the average cost of serving each customer class is roughly identical (in the US, each of the customer classes accounts for approximately one-third of electric demand). Even if this is not necessarily the case, equalization of average rates does suggest the reduction of cross-subsidies.
3. Some customers may consciously choose a supplier who also happens to be the default supplier. In this case, the default retail tariff applies, and these consumers are treated identically to consumers who do not choose a particular supplier.
4. The Western Systems Power Pool (WSPP) was the first coordinated wholesale electricity trading forum in the US. It was granted an experimental license to allow market-based ratemaking in the 1980s, and was formally approved following the passage of the US Energy Policy Act of 1992 (van Vactor 2004).
5. As of 2008, a number of other states (principally Ohio, Maine, Illinois and Pennsylvania) were seriously considering re-regulation. In many ways, Montana and Virginia were special cases; it is highly unlikely that significant re-regulation efforts will succeed elsewhere in the US (Lave et al. 2007).
6. We acknowledge the difficulty of using average income figures, given the skewed distribution of income in the US. However, data on the median electric bill are not available for the US.
7. Kiesling (2006) argues that advances in telecommunications should reduce these transaction costs significantly for residential customers. While this may be true, the US has generally been slow to roll out the advanced metering and communication systems required to support communication between the utility and specific residential customers or appliances.
8. Text of the directive is available at: http://europa.edu.int/comm/energy/electricity/legislation/index_en.htm.
9. See French Competition Authority (Conseil de la concurrence), 28 June 2007.
10. There is an interesting technical issue with green power. Because of the physics of AC power flow, there is no way to direct the electrons from renewable resources to those who are willing to pay a premium for

this type of generation. What consumers are really purchasing, therefore, is a form of 'green account-ing', where energy payments are directed to the owners of renewable generation facilities. It is not clear whether there is a connection between the actual output of these facilities and the payments made to these companies by consumers who do sign up for green power.

References

Andersson, B. (2005), 'Retail competition: experiences from Scandinavia', presentation to Harvard Policy Group, Harvard University, Cambridge, MA, September 22.
Apt, J. (2005), 'Competition has not lowered U.S. industrial electricity prices', *Electricity Journal*, **18**(2), 52–61.
Apt, J., S. Blumsack and L.B. Lave (2007), 'Competitive Energy Options for Pennsylvania', report to the Team Pennsylvania Foundation, Harrisburg, PA.
Averch, H. and L. Johnson (1962), 'Behavior of the firm under regulatory constraint', *American Economic Review*, **52** (December), 1052–69.
Beato, P. and C. Fuente (1999), 'Retail competition in electricity', Inter-American Development Bank Working Paper, Washington, DC.
Bergara, M. and P. Spiller (1996), 'The introduction of direct access in New Zealand's electricity market', *Utility Policy*, **6**(2), 97–106.
Bergstrom, T. and J. Mackie-Mason (1991), 'Some simple analytics of peak-load pricing', *RAND Journal of Economics*, **22**(2), 241–9.
Blumsack, S., J. Apt and L.B. Lave (2007), 'Electricity restructuring and the environment for commercial and industrial customers in Pennsylvania', *Papers and Proceedings of the Regional Science Association*, Savannah, GA.
Boisseleau, F. and R. Hakvoort (2003), 'The liberalisation of the European electricity market(s): an unstruc-tured restructuring process?', Working Paper, Delft University of Technology, The Netherlands.
Borenstein, S. (2005), 'The long run efficiency of real-time electricity pricing', *The Energy Journal*, **26**(3), 93–116.
Borenstein, S. and S. Holland (2005), 'On the efficiency of competitive electricity markets with time-invariant retail prices', *RAND Journal of Economics*, **36**(3), 469–93.
California Energy Commission, 'Direct Access Service Reports', various years, Sacramento, CA.
Caves, D., L. Christensen and J. Herriges (1984), 'Consistency of residential customer response in time-of-use electricity pricing experiments', *Journal of Econometrics*, **26**, 179–204.
de Vries, L. (2004), *Securing the Public Interest in Electricity Generation Markets*, Delft: DUP Science.
Edison Electric Institute, *Average Rates and Typical Bills*, various years.
European Commission, *Internal Market Fact Sheets*, various years and EU member countries, available at: http://ec.europa.eu.
European Commission (2005), 'Report on Progress in Creating the Internal Gas and Electricity Market', available at: http://ec.europa.eu/energy/electricity/report_2005/doc/2005_report_en.pdf (accessed March 10, 2009).
Faruqui, A. and R. Hledik (2007), 'The State of Demand Response in California', report for the California Energy Commission, Sacramento, CA.
Finon, D. (2002), 'Introducing competition in the French electricity supply industry: the destabilisation of a public hierarchy in an open market', CEER Working Paper 02-009, Centre for Energy and Environmental Policy Research, Cambridge, MA.
Flaim, T. (2001), 'Are retail markets working?', presentation to Harvard Electricity Policy Group, Harvard University, Cambridge, MA, February 1.
French Competition Authority (Autorité de la concurrence) (2007), Decision no. 07-MC-04 regarding a demand from Direct Energie (relatives à une demande de mesures conservatoires de la société Direct Energie), June 28, available at: http://www.autoritedelaconcurrence.fr/pdf/avis/07mc04.pdf (accessed March 10, 2009).
Hirsh, R. (1999), *Power Loss: The Origins of Deregulation and Restructuring in the American Electric Utility System*, Cambridge, MA: MIT Press.
Hoffmaister, A. (2006), 'Barriers to retail competition and prices: evidence from Spain', IMF Working Paper WP/06/231, International Monetary Fund, Washington, DC.
Joskow, P. and J. Tirole (2007), 'Reliability and competitive electricity markets', *RAND Journal of Economics*, **38**(1), 60–84.
Joskow, P. and R. Schmalensee (1983), *Markets for Power: An Analysis of Electric Utility Deregulation*, Cambridge, MA: MIT Press.
Kahn, E. (1988), *The Economics of Regulation: Principles and Institutions*, Cambridge, MA: MIT Press.

Kiesling, L. (2006), 'The role of retail pricing in electricity restructuring', in A. Kleit (ed.), *Electric Choices: Deregulation and the Future of Electric Power*, Totowa, NJ: Rowman & Littlefield, pp. 39–62.

Knittel, C. (2003), 'Market structure and the pricing of electricity and natural gas', *Journal of Industrial Economics*, **51**(2), 167–91.

Kwoka, J. (2006), 'Restructuring the U.S. Electric Power Sector: A Review of Recent Studies', report prepared for the American Public Power Association, Washington, DC.

Lave, L.B., J. Apt and S. Blumsack (2007), 'Deregulation/restructuring, Part I: re-regulation will not fix the problems', *Electricity Journal*, **20**(8), 9–22.

Lindell, C. (2004), 'Retail choice in New Zealand', Carnegie Mellon Electricity Industry Center, Pittsburgh, PA, available at: http://wpweb2.tepper.cmu.edu/ceic/presentations/Lindell_6_10_04.pdf (accessed March 10, 2009).

Morgan, M.G., J. Apt and L.B. Lave (2005), 'The U.S. Electric Power Sector and Climate Change Mitigation', report prepared for the Pew Center on Global Climate Change, Arlington, VA, available at http://www.pewclimate.org/docUploads/Electricity_Final.pdf (accessed March 10, 2009).

Rose, K. (2006), 'Performance Review of Competitive Electricity Markets', report for the Virginia State Corporation Commission, Richmond, VA.

Spann, R. (1974), 'Rate of return regulation and efficiency in production: an empirical test of the Averch–Johnson thesis', *Bell Journal of Economics*, **5**(1), 38–52.

Spees, K. and L.B. Lave (2007), 'Impacts of responsive load in PJM: load shifting and real-time pricing', Carnegie Mellon Electricity Industry Center Working Paper CEIC-07-02, Pittsburgh, PA.

Steiner, P. (1957), 'Peak loads and efficient pricing', *Quarterly Journal of Economics*, **71**(4), 585–610.

Sweeney, J. (2002), *The California Electricity Crisis*, Stanford, CA: Hoover Institution Press.

Taylor, L. (1975), 'The demand for electricity: a survey', *Bell Journal of Economics*, **6**(1), 74–110.

van Vactor, S. (2004), 'The transformation of energy markets', PhD dissertation, University of Cambridge, UK.

Wolak, F. (2006), 'Residential customer response to real-time pricing: the Anaheim critical peak pricing experiment', CSEM Working Paper 151, Center for the Study of Energy Markets, University of California Energy Institute, Berkeley, CA.

29 Emissions trading and the convergence of electricity and transport markets in Australia
*Luke J. Reedman and Paul W. Graham**

1 Introduction

Consistent with most developed economies, Australia's greenhouse gas (GHG) inventory is dominated by energy-related GHG emissions. In 2005, stationary energy, transport and fugitive emissions accounted for around 70 per cent of total GHG emissions (AGO 2007). In the absence of new measures, continued growth in energy demand is projected to lead to national emissions rising to 127 per cent of 1990 levels by 2020. This growth will be driven primarily by the stationary energy sector, where emissions in 2020 are projected to be 84 per cent higher than 1990 levels (Prime Ministerial Task Group on Emissions Trading 2007).

Despite the large share of GHG emissions attributable to the stationary energy sector, it is generally accepted that an emissions trading scheme (ETS) that has universal coverage of all economic sectors, is best placed to locate lowest-cost abatement opportunities. The recent report from the Prime Ministerial Task Group on Emissions Trading (2007) endorsed this principle, but recommended that measurement uncertainties and compliance cost issues meant that agricultural and land-use emissions be initially excluded from an ETS. Similarly, the National Emissions Trading Taskforce (NETT) recently expanded its terms of reference to consider an economy-wide scheme beyond its original scope of the stationary energy sector (NETT 2007).

To determine the extent of least-cost abatement opportunities in the energy sector, we employ a model of the energy sector to investigate the proportion that electricity and transport may contribute given the relative cost of abatement in those sectors, for specified emission targets. A related issue is the potential convergence of the two sectors through greater uptake of electrically powered road transport in the form of electric vehicles (EVs) and plug-in hybrid electric vehicles (PHEVs).

Our expectation is that previous analyses that have studied emissions trading in electricity separately to transport in the Australian context (for example, CRA International 2006 and The Climate Institute 2007a), have underestimated both the potential for electricity to play a positive role in transport sector emission abatement, and the likely permit price to achieve a given CO_2e abatement target.

This chapter proceeds as follows. Section 2 examines the relative cost of GHG abatement in the Australian electricity and transport sectors. Section 3 outlines the partial equilibrium model used in this chapter. Section 4 formulates our three emission-reduction scenarios based on the information contained in the recent fourth assessment report of the Intergovernmental Panel on Climate Change (IPCC) and contemporary debate in Australia. Section 5 briefly discusses the key assumptions impacting on the modelling results. Section 6 discusses the modelling results and Section 7 concludes.

2   Cost of Greenhouse Gas Abatement in the Electricity and Transport Sectors

Electricity and transport account for approximately 35 and 14 per cent of total Australian GHG emissions, respectively (AGO 2007). While Australia's share of transport sector emissions is similar to the average for the rest of the world, its share of electricity generation-related emissions is significantly higher owing to its reliance on brown and black coal as electricity generation fuels and the presence of energy-intensive mining and metals manufacturing industries (Baumert et al. 2005).

Electricity generation in Australia currently has an average emission factor of approximately $1 \, tCO_2e/MWh$[1] (ESAA 2007). Wholesale electricity prices in the National Electricity Market (NEM)[2] in the absence of emissions trading are around A\$40/MWh[3] (NEMMCO 2008). Accordingly, the introduction of a CO_2-equivalent (CO_2e) permit price will increase the wholesale cost of electricity generation by A\$1/MWh for each A\$1 increase in the CO_2e permit price. Lower emission electricity generation technologies are available at costs of A\$50–100/MWh (Graham et al. 2008). Therefore, one can conclude that, given enough time for existing generation stock to be retired, electricity sector emissions could be substantially reduced by deployment of new technology for an abatement cost of A\$10–60/tCO_2e.

In contrast, it is expected that technology uptake in the transport sector will be less responsive to CO_2e permit prices. The long-run marginal cost (LRMC) of transport includes not just fuel costs but capital (vehicle), registration, insurance, maintenance and any relevant fuel taxes. For a medium passenger Australian road vehicle, this whole cost of transport is around 60c/km (NRMA Motoring and Services 2007). Of that, fuel contributes only 10c/km. The largest cost component is the cost of the vehicle.

A CO_2e permit price of A\$50/tCO_2e increases the retail petrol price by about 11c/L. This adds an additional 1c/km or 1.8 per cent to the overall cost of transport. It is apparent from this example that the Australian transport sector is not likely to be very sensitive to CO_2e permit prices. That is, it will take a fairly high CO_2e permit price in order to create a price differential for consumers that causes a shift to another fuel or type of vehicle or switch to another mode of transport.

Our modelling suggests, given the low responsiveness of the transport sector, that CO_2e permit prices needed may be much higher, potentially over A\$100/tCO_2e in the long term to bring about significant GHG emission reduction across the whole economy. This is substantially higher than previous studies have suggested. There are two main reasons for this. First, in some cases the emission targets analysed in previous studies were not as stringent as those modelled here (for example, Turton et al. 2002; Australian Climate Group 2004; Allen Consulting 2006; Graham et al. 2008). Second, some previous studies only considered the cost of abatement in the electricity sector (for example: CRA International 2006; The Climate Institute 2007a; Graham et al. 2008).

As discussed, the cost of abatement is lower in the electricity sector than other sectors such as transport. For example, CRA International (2006) and The Climate Institute (2007a) posit substantial electricity sector abatement at projected CO_2e permit prices of around A\$10–80/tCO_2e to 2050. It is the cost of the last tonne of abatement that will set the CO_2e permit price. Assuming that these studies are correct, and that the cost of abatement in the electricity sector is relatively low, the electricity sector is likely to become a near-zero emission sector. However, it cannot supply all the necessary emissions reduction since it accounts for less than half of national emissions. Therefore, the cost of abatement will be set by another, higher cost abatement sector. Some studies which have included the costs of abatement in all sectors have found higher CO_2e permit prices (for example, Energy Futures Forum 2006 and The Climate Institute 2007b).

A recent study by McKinsey & Company (2008) finds that stringent emission targets of 30 per cent below 1990 levels by 2030 can be achieved at a marginal abatement cost of A\$65/tCO_2e. This finding would appear to go against the previous arguments that higher abatement costs should be expected. However, there are two reasons why one could consider the McKinsey & Company finding to be an underestimate of the costs of abatement.

First, the methodology employed in McKinsey & Company does not consider the value in utilising existing assets. The methodology considers only the relative LRMCs of high versus low emission technologies and the CO_2e permit price needed to make low emission technologies more cost competitive. However, decisions to close existing assets are not made on their LRMCs, they are made on their short-run marginal costs (SRMCs).

Consider low emission technology X that has an LRMC of A\$80 per unit of output and a zero emission factor and high emission technology Y that has an LRMC of A\$40 per unit of output, an SRMC of A\$10 per unit of output and an emission factor of 0.8 tCO_2e per unit of output. In order to make low emission technology X competitive, the CO_2e permit price must rise to be equal to the difference in their costs divided by the difference in their emissions which is $(80-40)/(0.8-0) = $ A\$50/tCO_2e. This makes technology X competitive, but does not shut down production from technology Y. In order to shut down production from technology Y, the CO_2e permit price must rise to $(80-10)/(0.8-0) = $ A\$88/tCO_2e. Since much of the present emission-intensive technology in Australia will still be operating in 2020 and 2030, it would appear that this higher cost of abatement is likely to be the determinant of costs if very deep emissions cuts are required such as those discussed in McKinsey & Company.

A second concern about the abatement costs in McKinsey & Company is the abatement opportunities often cited as negative costs (those that save emissions and money for the consumer or end-user). While there may be some negative abatement cost opportunities in Australia, it is often overlooked that taking up such options usually requires a change in consumer preferences. An example relevant to transport is vehicle size. If consumers chose to purchase and use smaller vehicles then they would save money through lower fuel costs, and reduce emissions. However, this requires consumers to make a change in preferences. While such a change is possible, there is little consideration of what could make the preference change occur. Therefore, it may not be appropriate to include such opportunities as abatement achieved simply because they appear to be lower cost. It is likely that such choices are driven by non-price factors and that the introduction of emissions trading will not be sufficient to see that abatement occur.

3   Outline of Economic Modelling Approach

Economic modelling of energy policy issues is often discussed in the literature as being either 'top down' or 'bottom up' (see Hourcade et al. 2006 for a recent review of the literature). Top-down models provide a comprehensive representation of the operation of all sectors of the economy from the global, national or regional viewpoint. Regardless of viewpoint, bottom-up models tend to model particular sectors of the economy, such as the energy sector, but do so in considerable detail. Bottom-up models more accurately describe and discriminate between the characteristics of the technologies and processes associated with the operation of energy markets.

As this chapter is concerned with the relative share of CO_2 abatement between the electricity and transport sectors, and the potential for convergence between the two sectors via specific technological developments relating to hybridisation of vehicles to incorporate electric drivetrains, a bottom-up modelling approach is deemed appropriate.

The Energy Sector Model (ESM) is an Australian model co-developed by the Commonwealth Scientific and Industrial Research Organisation (CSIRO) and the Australian Bureau of Agricultural and Resource Economics (ABARE) as a scenario analysis tool. The ESM is a partial equilibrium (bottom-up) model of the electricity and transport sectors. The model has a robust economic decision-making framework around the cost of alternative fuels and vehicles as well as detailed fuel and vehicle technical performance characterisation such as fuel efficiencies and emission factors by transport mode, vehicle type, engine type and age. It also has a detailed representation of the electricity generation sector. Competition for resources between the two sectors and relative costs of abatement are resolved simultaneously within the model.

The ESM is solved as a linear program where the objective function is to maximise welfare, which is the sum of consumer and producer surplus over time. The sum of consumer and producer surplus is calculated as the integral of the demand functions minus the integral of the supply functions which are both disaggregated into many components across the electricity and transport markets. The objective function is maximised subject to constraints which control the physical limitations of fuel resources, the stock of electricity plant and vehicles, GHG emissions as prescribed by legislation, and various market- and technology-specific constraints such as the need to maintain a minimum number of peaking plants to meet rapid changes in the electricity load. (See Graham and Williams, 2003 for an example of the equations required to construct a similar partial equilibrium model.)

The main components of the ESM include:

- coverage of all States and Territories of Australia;
- trade in electricity between NEM States;
- nine road transport modes: light, medium and heavy passenger cars; light, medium and heavy commercial vehicles; rigid trucks; articulated trucks and buses;
- twelve road transport fuels: petrol; diesel; liquefied petroleum gas (LPG); compressed natural gas (CNG); petrol with 10 per cent ethanol blend; diesel with 20 per cent biodiesel blend; ethanol and biodiesel at high concentrations; gas to liquids diesel; coal to liquids diesel; hydrogen (from renewables) and electricity;
- rail, air and shipping sectors: governed by much less detailed fuel substitution possibilities;
- four engine types: internal combustion; hybrid electric/internal combustion; hybrid plug-in electric/internal combustion; and fully electric;
- seventeen centralised generation (CG) electricity plant types: black coal pulverised fuel; black coal integrated gasification combined cycle (IGCC); black coal with

partial CO_2 capture and sequestration (CCS) (50 per cent capture rate); black coal with full CCS (85 per cent capture rate); brown coal pulverised fuel; brown coal IGCC; brown coal with partial CCS (50 per cent capture rate); brown coal with full CCS (85 percent capture rate); natural gas combined cycle; natural gas peaking plant; natural gas with full CCS (85 per cent capture rate); biomass; hydro; wind; solar thermal; hot fractured rocks (geothermal) and nuclear;

- fourteen distributed generation (DG) electricity plant types: internal combustion diesel; internal combustion gas; gas turbine; gas micro turbine; gas combined heat and power (CHP); biomass CHP; gas micro turbine CHP; gas reciprocating engine CHP; solar photovoltaic; biomass; wind; biogas reciprocating engine; natural gas fuel cell and hydrogen fuel cell;
- all vehicles and centralised electricity generation plants are assigned a vintage based on when they were first purchased or installed in annual increments;
- four electricity end-use sectors: industrial; commercial and services; rural; and residential; and
- time is represented in annual frequency (2006, 2007, . . ., 2050).

All technologies are assessed on the basis of their relative costs subject to constraints such as the turnover of capital stock, existing or new policies such as subsidies and taxes.

For given time paths of the exogenous (or input) variables that define the economic environment, the ESM determines the time paths of the endogenous (output) variables. Key output variables include:

- fuel, engine and electricity generation technology uptake;
- primary and final fuel consumption;
- cost of transport services (for example, c/km);
- price of fuels;
- GHG and criteria air pollutant emissions;
- wholesale and retail electricity prices;
- CO_2e permit prices; and
- demand for transport and electricity services.

Some of these outputs can also be defined as fixed inputs depending upon the design of the scenario.

The endogenous variables are determined using demand and production relationships, commodity balance definitions and assumptions of competitive markets at each time step for fuels, electricity and transport services, and over time for assets such as vehicles and plant capacities. With respect to asset markets, the assumption is used that market participants know future outcomes of their joint actions over the entire time horizon of the model.

The model aims to mirror real-world investment decisions by simultaneously taking into account:

- the requirement to earn a reasonable return on investment over the life of a plant or vehicle;

- that the actions of one investor or user affect the financial viability of all other investors or users simultaneously and dynamically;
- that consumers react to price signals;
- that the consumption of energy resources by one user affects the price and availability of that resource for other users, and the overall cost of energy and transport services; and
- energy and transport market policies and regulations.

The model evaluates uptake on the basis of cost effectiveness but at the same time takes into account the key constraints with regard to the operation of energy and transport markets, current excise and mandated fuel mix legislation, GHG emission limits, existing plant and vehicle stock in each State, and lead times in the availability of new vehicles or plant. It does not take into account issues such as community acceptance of technologies but these can be controlled by user inputs.

4   Scenario Description

Contemporary debate on emissions trading in Australia has shifted substantially in recent times. The Federal government elected in November 2007 has an aspirational goal to reduce emissions by 60 per cent on 2000 levels by 2050 but has not committed to a legislated emission target prior to the findings of a commissioned report (Garnaut Climate Change Review 2008). This aspirational goal is consistent with a global agreement to achieve 450 parts per million by volume (ppmv) where all countries have the same target or a global target of 550 ppmv where developed countries (Annex 1) have a differentiated (deeper) target which allows developing countries (Non-Annex 1) to have a less-stringent GHG abatement task.

However, the recent fourth assessment report of the IPCC posits that more-stringent emission reduction targets are required to limit the chance of exceeding 2°C increase in global mean temperatures. It noted that: 'Using the "best estimate" assumption of climate sensitivity, the most-stringent scenarios (stabilising at 445–490 ppmv CO_2-equivalent) could limit global mean temperature increases to 2–2.4°C above the pre-industrial level, at equilibrium, requiring emissions to peak before 2015 and to be around 50 percent of current levels by 2050' (Fisher et al. 2007, p. 173). This implies that: 'developed countries as a group would need to reduce their emissions to below 1990 levels in 2020 (on the order of –10% to 40% below 1990 levels . . .) and to still lower levels by 2050 (40 percent to 95 percent below 1990 levels), even if developing countries make substantial reductions' (Gupta et al. 2007, p. 775).

The position that developed countries may need to reduce emissions at a greater rate in the medium term is a departure from the straight-line reduction path that is typically modelled in emission reduction scenarios. Examples of the straight-line approach in the Australian context include the Business Roundtable on Climate Change examining 60 per cent below 2000 levels by 2050 (Allen Consulting 2006) preceded by earlier studies that adopted 60 per cent below 'current' levels by 2050 (for example, Turton et al. 2002; Australian Climate Group 2004).

Debate on the proposed timing of global emissions trading is still ongoing. However, it is increasingly recognised that 'early action' is preferential to 'delayed action' to limit the chance of exceeding 2°C increase in global mean temperatures. This is consistent with economic analysis that delay in taking action on climate change would make it necessary to accept more climate change (greater probability of exceeding 2°C), and, eventually lead to higher mitigation costs (for example, Allen Consulting 2006; Energy Futures Forum 2006; Stern et al. 2006). In the Australian context, the Australian Government has endorsed this principle, recommending that Australia commence emissions trading in 2010 (Treasury 2008) with the first emission reduction target set in 2011.

Given the state of the current debate summarised above, we shall examine three emission reduction scenarios (ERSs) for the Australian energy sector:

- a smooth trajectory to 60 per cent below 1990 emission levels by 2050 (ERS1990-60);
- a reduction path to 10 per cent below 1990 levels by 2020 and a smooth path to 80 per cent below 1990 levels by 2050 (ERS1990-80A); and
- a reduction path to 40 per cent below 1990 levels by 2020 and a smooth path to 80 per cent below 1990 levels by 2050 (ERS1990-80B).

Figure 29.1 shows the GHG emission reduction paths for the combined electricity and transport sector.[4] The ESM projects combined electricity and transport sector GHG emissions to be approximately 288 million tonnes (mt) in 2010 at the commencement of emissions trading.

All three ERSs represent significant amounts of abatement. In the absence of emissions trading, ESM projects combined electricity and transport sector GHG emissions

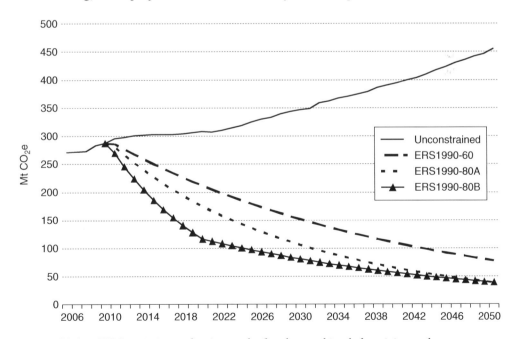

Figure 29.1   GHG emission reduction paths for the combined electricity and transport sectors

to be approximately 456 mt in 2050. GHG emissions under the ERS1990-60 scenario are projected to decline to around 78 mt by 2050, constituting approximately 378 mt of abatement. Emissions are presumed to decline at a constant rate in ERS1990-60. In contrast, both ERS1990-80A and ERS1990-80B track alternative reduction paths with targets of around 39 mt by 2050.

As discussed in Section 2, the ESM does not contain a detailed representation of the non-road transport sector (for example: rail, air and sea). Although the road transport task currently accounts for 90 per cent of transport sector emissions, it is expected that the share of emissions from domestic and international air travel will increase in the future (AGO 2006). It is assumed that there are only limited abatement opportunities in the non-road sector. Increasing electrification of rail, greater use of biofuels and better overall fuel efficiency are the best opportunities available for reduced emission intensity. However, the assumed uptake of abatement options can only deliver emission reduction of the order of around 20 to 40 per cent, which is more than offset by growth in the demand for non-road travel.

A flaw in our approach is that, in reality, the movements in the CO_2e permit price will be determined by the cost of abatement available in other sectors, including the purchase of international credits. For the moderate emission reduction scenarios the assumed cost of abatement from other sectors begins at around A\$50/tCO_2e in 2010 and increases at a constant percentage rate to A\$200/tCO_2e in 2050, consistent with mid-range estimates of carbon prices reviewed by the IPCC (see Fisher et al. 2007). For our deeper ERSs, a higher credit price path is assumed to take account of the steeper rate of reduction to 2020 and the possible increased competition for abatement certificates in domestic and international markets under such scenarios. The cost of abatement from other sectors is shown in Figure 29.2.

Another important issue in the design of an ETS is the extent to which existing relatively high emission-intensive assets may be quarantined from a CO_2e penalty for the purposes of compensation or other equity considerations. The modelling in this chapter assumes that no grandfathering of emissions takes place (that is, no free auction of permits) and all GHG emitting generators must bid for permits.

5   Key Assumptions

Given our use of a 'bottom-up' energy sector model, there are a number of assumptions underpinning the modelling reported in this chapter. The model includes many assumptions for parameters that are in reality uncertain and in some cases evolving rapidly. Parameters of most concern include, for example, possible breakthroughs in so-called 'second-generation' biofuel production technologies and the unknown quality and cost of future offerings of fully and partially electrified vehicles. The following list briefly identifies the key assumptions:

- *Oil prices*   We use the projections from the Energy Information Administration (EIA) 'high oil price' scenario that has oil prices rising from current levels in real terms to 2030. We extrapolate this path from 2030 to 2050 given our longer projection period. In 2006 prices, this equates to an oil price of around US\$145 per barrel in 2050.

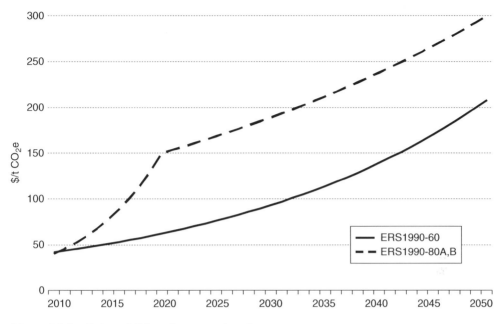

Figure 29.2 Price of CO$_2$e abatement in other sectors

- *Transport demand* Passenger road growth of 0.5 per cent per annum out to 2050 is assumed compared to current growth of 1.2 per cent per annum. This decline in growth is assumed partly due to saturation of vehicle ownership and use given expected population growth as well as other factors such as increased population density, greater use of mass transport modes and lifestyle changes. Commercial road growth of 2.2 per cent per annum out to 2050 is assumed compared to current growth of 3 per cent per annum. Bus growth of 4.6 per cent per annum out to 2050 is assumed compared to current growth of 2.3 per cent per annum. Aviation growth of 1.6 per cent per annum out to 2050 is assumed compared to current growth of 2.4 per cent pa. Rail growth of 2.9 per cent per annum out to 2050 is assumed compared to current growth of 1.2 per cent per annum. This assumed increased in the rate of growth in rail is consistent with recent observed increase in rail patronage in response to higher oil prices.
- *Hybrid vehicles* In 2006, passenger and light commercial vehicles were deemed to require only 65 per cent of the litres (or volume of gas) used by vehicles with only internal combustion engines for each 100 km travelled. This ratio is assumed to improve to 50 per cent of internal combustion engine fuel requirements by 2050. In keeping with the assumption of only mild hybridisation, the current fuel per 100 km requirement is assumed to be 95 per cent for trucks and buses, improving to 85 per cent by 2050.
- *Plug-in hybrid electric vehicles (PHEVs)* PHEVs are assumed to be powered by electric battery for 80 per cent of their kilometres in a given year, reflecting typical travel patterns and average trip length (NSW Ministry of Transport 2007). PHEVs are assumed to be available in the medium (1200 to 1500 kg) and heavy (greater

than 1500 kg) passenger and commercial vehicle categories. When operating on battery mode, the fuel efficiency of medium-weighted PHEVs is 0.22 kWh/km and heavy-weighted PHEVs is 0.31 kWh/km.

- *Electric vehicles (EVs)*   EVs operate with a fuel efficiency of 0.2 kWh/km. They are assumed available in the light passenger and commercial vehicle categories (less than 1200 kg).
- *Availability and cost of biofuels*   With regard to first-generation biofuels, estimates are obtained from O'Connell et al. (2007). With regard to second-generation biofuels, lignocellulosic ethanol production is assumed to be available from 2020 at similar to current cost of ethanol from first-generation technologies and feedstocks. It is assumed that biodiesel can be produced from algae from 2020 at twice the cost of biodiesel from canola.
- CO_2 *capture and sequestration (CCS)*   CCS is assumed to be commercially available from 2020 onwards. We have employed a cap of 115 $mtCO_2$ per year that can be stored nationally as estimated by Bradshaw et al. (2004). For captured CO_2, a transport and storage cost of $10/t has been applied to any CO_2 stored, consistent with the estimate from Hooper et al. (2005).
- *Electricity generation technologies*   Assumptions of technical performance and cost data for centralised and distributed electricity generation technologies are contained in Graham et al. (2008).
- *Transport costs*   Vehicle costs are calculated by adding up the major items based on a representative vehicle for that weight or vehicle category. Vehicle costs are based on the most common engine type for the representative vehicle in the category and all other options are calculated relative to that vehicle. For example, the most common type of medium passenger vehicle is a spark ignition petrol-fuelled vehicle. A diesel-fuelled compression ignition medium passenger vehicle might have an on-cost relative to the representative vehicle of $1500 due to the higher cost of compression ignition engines. Other items such as maintenance, registration and insurance are calculated from quoted prices from their respective service providers.
- *Full fuel cycle CO_2 emission factors*   Estimates for fossil fuels are taken from AGO (2002a,b). Estimates for biofuels are obtained from O'Connell et al. (2007).
- *Policy settings*   It is assumed that the state renewable energy targets are replaced by the recently expanded Mandatory Renewable Energy Target (MRET). MRET seeks to increase the contribution of renewable energy sources in Australia's electricity mix to 45000 GWh by 2020. The Queensland 13 per cent gas target is assumed to remain in place until 2020. The New South Wales (NSW) Greenhouse Gas Abatement Scheme is not extended beyond 2010 due to the introduction of emissions trading. Currently stated excise policy for transport fuels is assumed to remain in place. The NSW ethanol mandate is applied in the model as a constraint on the minimum use of petrol with 10 per cent ethanol blend (E10) in fuel consumption.

6   Modelling Results

The main results of interest are the extent of CO_2e abatement achieved in the electricity and transport sectors from our scenarios and the degree to which there is convergence

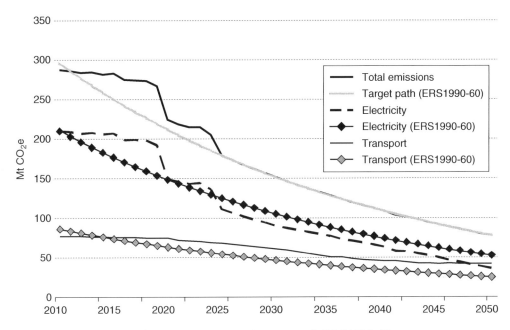

Figure 29.3   Estimated GHG emissions and target path ERS1990-60

between the two sectors with regard to electric-powered transport. Figures 29.3–5 show the estimated annual GHG emissions under the three ERSs and the extent to which emissions are reduced in both sectors.

Figures 29.3–5 show that there are periods when the combined electricity and transport sectors fail to meet the emission reduction target. Under ERS1990-60, the sector is unable to reduce emissions in line with the target at a lower abatement cost compared to other sectors between 2013 and 2024. However, due to the higher cost of abatement outside the energy sector under ERS1990-80A (see Figure 29.2), the combined electricity and transport sectors meets its target for most of the projection period. In contrast, the electricity and transport sectors struggle to meet the aggressive emission reductions required in the initial years under ERS1990-80B.

The volume of credits purchased from other sectors, reflecting the deviation of total energy sector emissions from its target path, is shown in Figure 29.6. It clearly shows that reducing energy sector GHG emissions under the assumed emissions targets is a challenging task. This is mainly due to the large stock of relatively high emission-intensive electricity generation plant. Australia's electricity supply is currently dominated by centralised coal-fired plants, accounting for around 81 per cent of national electricity generation (ESAA 2007). The long lead-times in the availability of new low-emission technologies, the sunk cost of existing electricity generation assets and the slow turnover of the road vehicle stock, mean that lower cost abatement is located in other sectors.

The estimated CO_2e permit prices displayed in Figure 29.7 reflect the marginal cost of abatement in a given year for the three scenarios. The marginal abatement costs are derived directly from the model, and calculated as a result of the imposition of an overall

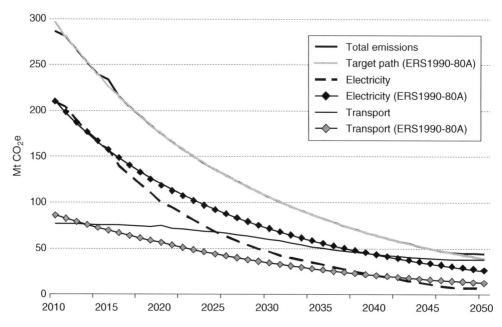

Figure 29.4   Estimated GHG emissions and target path ERS1990-80A

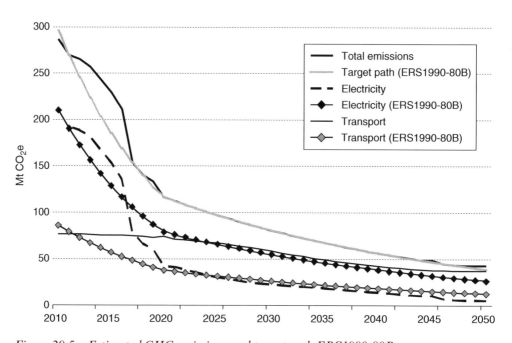

Figure 29.5   Estimated GHG emissions and target path ERS1990-80B

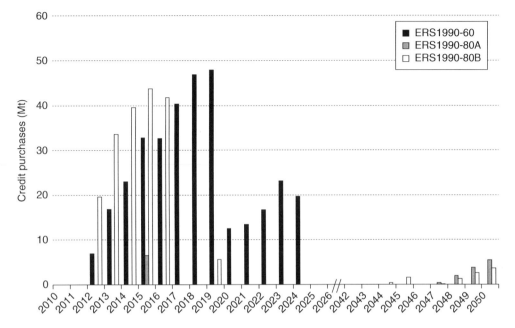

Figure 29.6   Purchase of CO$_2$e permits from other sectors

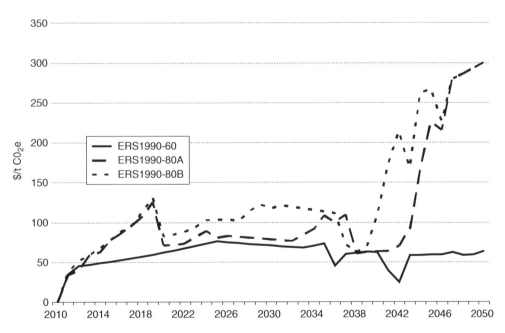

Figure 29.7   Estimated CO$_2$e permit prices

GHG emissions constraint. They represent the costs of abating the final tonne of CO_2e to meet a given constraint.

Figure 29.7 shows that CO_2e prices average around A\$60/tCO_2e under the mild emission target, ERS1990-60. CO_2e prices fall below this average around 2036 and 2042 due to the retirement of high emission coal-fired plant before reverting back to the average. The marginal cost of abatement between 2012 and 2025 is equal to the marginal cost of abatement outside of the energy sector. The dynamics resemble those discussed in Section 2. During that period, the electricity sector can source lower cost abatement opportunities from other sectors compared to the forced retirement of high emission assets. The retirement of approximately 5 GW of coal-fired plant around 2025 brings electricity sector emissions below its equal share (see Figure 29.3) and establishes its role as the source of least-cost abatement for the remainder of the projection period.

The estimated CO_2e prices in the other scenarios exhibit greater volatility. For ERS1990-80A, the higher cost of CO_2e abatement outside the energy sector (see Figure 29.2) combined with the need for significant emission reductions in the initial stages of emissions trading, produces rapidly increasing CO_2e prices to shut down high emission plant operating on SRMC. High CO_2e prices also induce a negative elastic demand response until near-zero emission CCS technologies are available in 2020. Declining from their initial peak, CO_2e prices stabilise between A\$70 and A\$80/tCO_2e. However, the increasing stringency of the target induces significant deployment of zero emission non-hydro renewable technologies leading to rapidly escalating CO_2e prices. Near the end of the projection period, the least-cost source of CO_2e abatement is located outside the energy sector.

These dynamics are also apparent in ERS1990-80B with the greater need for emissions reductions prior to 2020 requiring significant purchase of credits (see Figure 29.6) from other sectors.

It must be reiterated that the marginal cost of CO_2e abatement is heavily influenced by the assumed abatement cost outside the energy sector (Figure 29.2) and the cost and availability assumptions of technology options within the energy sector. Similarly, structural design issues of the ETS with regard to borrowing and banking of CO_2e permits would also impact on the estimated CO_2e permit prices.

The preceding discussion indicates that, in general, the electricity generation sector has greater lower cost abatement options when compared to the transport sector. This is reflected in electricity sector emissions being below its 'equal share' of abatement in the medium term whereas the transport sector is above its 'equal share' (see Figures 29.3–5). To provide perspective on the low-emission technologies being deployed in the electricity sector, Figures 29.8–10 show the electricity generation mix for the three scenarios.

The electricity generation profiles show that:

- in the near term (2010 to 2020), the proportion of high-emission electricity generation (coal pulverised fuel) is reduced in favour of gas-fired generation (centralised combined cycle plants and distributed (less than 30 MW rated capacity and close to load) gas turbines with CHP), gas with full CCS, and wind farms;
- in the medium term (2020 to 2030), there is significant deployment of coal and gas-fired generation with CCS in the ERS1990-60 scenario;

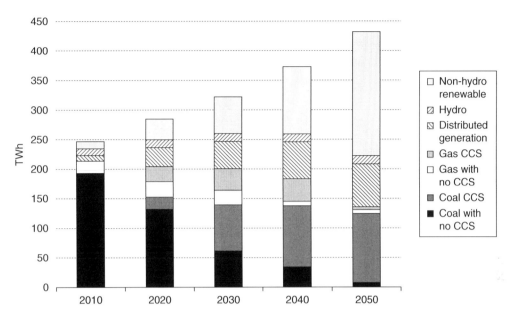

Figure 29.8   Electricity generation profile ERS1990-60

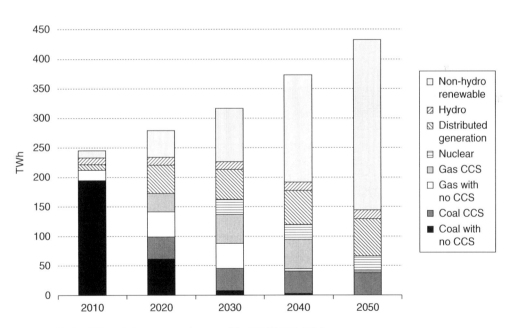

Figure 29.9   Electricity generation profile ERS1990-80A

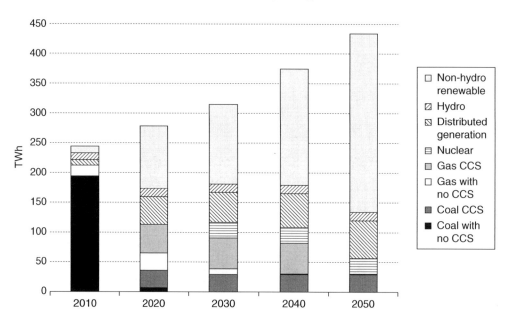

Figure 29.10   Electricity generation profile ERS1990-80B

- in the medium term under the more-stringent emission mitigation scenarios, there is greater deployment of zero-emission technologies including non-hydro renewables (mainly hot fractured rocks and wind generation) and nuclear power; and
- over the long term (2040 to 2050), non-hydro renewables dominate the electricity generation mix.

With regard to the degree of convergence between the two sectors, Figure 29.11 shows the extent of electric-powered road transport. The figure shows that over time, there is a progression away from internal combustion engines towards PHEVs and EVs. It shows that initially under all scenarios, CO_2e prices are not high enough to radically alter the engine type mix by 2020. The stabilisation of transport sector emissions up until that time (see Figures 29.3–5) is mainly due to improvements in the efficiency of internal combustion engines and increased consumer preferences for lighter vehicles. However, the declining capital costs of alternative vehicle technologies over time and the lower greenhouse intensity of electricity leads to significant uptake of hybrid and electric vehicles under all scenarios. By 2050, PHEVs have the greatest share of road transport propulsion, followed by light electric vehicles, highly efficient diesel engines and non-plug-in hybrid vehicles.

Figure 29.11 shows a moderate to high degree of convergence between the electricity and transport markets under the scenarios modelled. By 2050, electricity accounts for approximately 50 per cent of fuel use in the road sector in ERS1990-60 and approximately 60 per cent of fuel use in the road sector in ERS1990-80A and ERS1990-80B. In the three scenarios modelled, this equates to around 13 per cent of total electricity generation being used to power road transport.

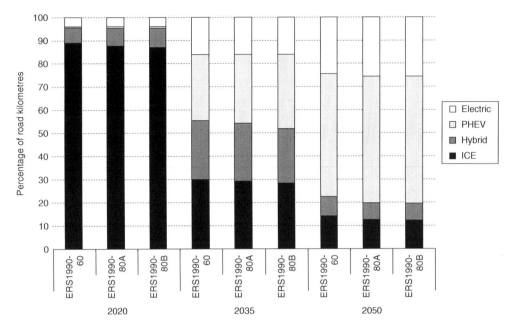

Figure 29.11 Engine type in road transport under ERS scenarios

7 Conclusion

Our expectation was that analyses that have studied emissions trading in electricity separately to transport in the Australian context, would have underestimated both the potential for electricity to play a positive role in transport sector emission abatement and the likely CO_2e permit price to achieve a given abatement target. Under the modelling assumptions used, the key findings of this chapter are:

- CO_2e permit prices in excess of A\$100/tCO_2e are required to achieve rapid and deep GHG emission abatement targets;
- the presumption that the majority of energy sector CO_2e abatement will take place in the electricity sector is, in the main, supported by the modelling results in this chapter;
- although the transport sector does not meet its 'equal share' of energy sector abatement, its emissions do decline over the projection period principally through improvements in fuel economy, increasing preference for smaller vehicles and the convergence between electricity and transport markets via the deployment of electric-powered vehicles (EVs and PHEVs). The increased use of electrically powered transport may proxy quasi-transport sector CO_2e abatement;
- the electricity sector almost fully decarbonises by 2050 under the ERS1990-80A and ERS1990-80B scenarios. This finding is consistent with other studies that have examined similar abatement targets in Australia (for example, The Climate Institute 2007b) and the UK (for example, DEFRA 2007);

- without further measures, the combined electricity and transport sectors are unable to meet aggressive cuts in CO_2e emissions in the near term. The long lead-times in the availability of new low-emission technologies, the sunk cost of existing electricity generation assets and the slow turnover of the road vehicle stock, mean that lower cost abatement is located in other sectors;
- over the medium and long terms, the electricity generation sector has greater lower cost abatement options when compared to the transport sector; and
- more-stringent targets reveal that the electricity and transport sectors have significant abatement options, but do require additional CO_2e permits from other sectors.

The modelling results need to be considered with some caution. A key limitation is that it only considers cost effectiveness and a limited set of constraints in projecting technology uptake. In reality, community concerns and many other non-price factors not included in the modelling will influence the future technology choices that individuals and businesses make.

Development of the integrated model used in this chapter is ongoing. Avenues for further research include:

- more detailed representation of the non-road transport sector to test our assumption that the extent of CO_2e abatement in the non-road transport sector is limited;
- incorporation of marginal CO_2e abatement functions for other sectors to better understand their role in whole of economy emission reduction relative to the energy sector; and
- exploration of sensitivities around key assumptions including oil prices, changing consumer preferences on transport mode choice and the timing of the availability of low-emission technology options and biofuels.

Notes

*   An earlier version of the work in this chapter was presented at the Australian Agricultural and Resource Economics (AARES) annual conference in Canberra on 6 February 2008 and the authors thank the participants for helpful comments on improving the modelling framework.
1. The GHG emission intensity of electricity generation in Australia in 2005/06 was 0.97 tCO_2e/MWh. This was rounded to 1 tCO_2e/MWh to simplify the example.
2. The NEM commenced operation in 1998 with New South Wales, Victoria, Queensland and South Australia. Tasmania joined the NEM in 2005.
3. To take account of transitory high wholesale prices in the 2006/07 financial year due to drought conditions affecting the water allocation to some coal-fired plants, this figure is the NEM volume-weighted average annual price over the last three financial years.
4. The ESM does not contain a representation of the stationary energy outside of the electricity generation sector.

References

Allen Consulting Group (2006), *Deep Cuts in Greenhouse Gas Emissions: Economic, Social and Environmental Impacts*, Report to the Business Roundtable on Climate Change, March.
Australian Climate Group (2004), *Climate Change: Solutions for Australia*, Sydney: World Wildlife Fund Australia.
Australian Greenhouse Office (AGO) (2002a), *Australia's National Greenhouse Gas Inventory 1990, 1995 and*

1999 End Use Allocation of Emissions, Report to the Australian Greenhouse Office by George Wilkenfeld & Associates Pty Ltd and Energy Strategies, Vol. 1, Canberra: AGO.

Australian Greenhouse Office (AGO) (2002b), *Australia's National Greenhouse Gas Inventory 1990, 1995 and 1999 End Use Allocation of Emissions*, Report to the Australian Greenhouse Office by George Wilkenfeld & Associates Pty Ltd and Energy Strategies, Vol. 2, Canberra: AGO.

Australian Greenhouse Office (AGO) (2006), *Transport Sector Greenhouse Gas Emissions Projections 2006*, Canberra: AGO, December.

Australian Greenhouse Office (AGO) (2007), *National Greenhouse Gas Inventory 2005: Accounting for the 108% Target*, Canberra: AGO, March.

Baumert, K.A., T. Herzog and J. Pershing (2005), *Navigating the Numbers: Greenhouse Gas Data and International Climate Policy*, Washington, DC: World Resources Institute.

Bradshaw, J., G. Allinson, B. Bradshaw, V. Nguyen, A. Rigg, L. Spencer and P. Wilson (2004), 'Australia's CO_2 geological storage potential and matching of emission sources to potential sinks', *Energy*, **29** (9–10), 1623–31.

CRA International (2006), *Analysis of Greenhouse Gas Policies for the Australian Electricity Sector: A Report for the National Generators Forum*, Melbourne: CRA International, September.

Department for Environment, Food and Rural Affairs, UK (DEFRA) (2007), *MARKAL Macro Analysis of Long Run Costs of Climate Change Mitigation Targets*, London: UK Department for Environment, Food and Rural Affairs, November.

Energy Futures Forum (2006), *The Heat Is On: The Future of Energy in Australia*, a Report by the Energy Futures Forum, Canberra: CSIRO.

Energy Supply Association of Australia (ESAA) (2007), *Electricity Gas Australia 2007*, Melbourne: ESAA.

Fisher, B., N. Nakicenovic, K. Alfsen, J. Corfee Morlot, F. de la Chesnaye, J.-C. Hourcade, K. Jiang, M. Kainuma, E. La Rovere, A. Matysek, A. Rana, K. Riahi, R. Richels, S. Rose, D. van Vuuren and R. Warren (2007), 'Issues related to mitigation in the long term context', in B. Metz, O. Davidson, P. Bosch, R. Dave and L. Meyer (eds), *Climate Change 2007: Mitigation, Contribution of Working Group III to the Fourth Assessment Report of the Inter-governmental Panel on Climate Change*, Cambridge: Cambridge University Press, pp. 169–250.

Garnaut Climate Change Review (2008), *Interim Report to the Commonwealth, State and Territory Governments of Australia*, February.

Graham, P.W., L.J. Reedman and P. Coombes (2008), *Options for Electricity Generation in Australia – 2007 Update (Includes Supplement on Revised Real Option Modeling Results and the Impact of CO_2e Permit Price Uncertainty on Investment)*, Technology Assessment Report No. 72, Cooperative Research Centre for Coal in Sustainable Development (CCSD), Pullenvale, QLD: CCSD, March.

Graham, P. and D. Williams (2003), 'Optimal technological choices in meeting Australian energy policy goals', *Energy Economics*, **25** (6), 691–712.

Gupta, S., D.A. Tirpak, N. Burger, J. Gupta, N. Höhne, A.I. Boncheva, G.M. Kanoan, C. Kolstad, J.A. Kruger, A. Michaelowa, S. Murase, J. Pershing, T. Saijo and A. Sari (2007), 'Policies, instruments and co-operative arrangements', in B. Metz, O. Davidson, P. Bosch, R. Dave and L. Meyer (eds), *Climate Change 2007: Mitigation, Contribution of Working Group III to the Fourth Assessment Report of the Inter-governmental Panel on Climate Change*, Cambridge: Cambridge University Press, pp. 745–807.

Hooper, B., L. Murray and C. Gibson-Poole (eds) (2005), *Latrobe Valley CO_2 Storage Assessment: Final Report*, Report No. RPT05-0108, Canberra: Cooperative Research Centre for Greenhouse Gas Technologies, November.

Hourcade, J.-C., M. Jaccard, C. Bataille and F. Ghersi (eds) (2006), 'Hybrid modelling of energy–environment policies: reconciling bottom-up and top-down', *Special Issue of The Energy Journal*, Cleveland: International Association for Energy Economics.

McKinsey & Company (2008), *An Australian Cost Curve for Greenhouse Gas Reduction*, Sydney: McKinsey & Company.

National Electricity Market Management Company (NEMMCO) (2008), 'Average annual prices (per financial year)', available at: http://www.nemmco.com.au/data/avg_price/averageprice_main.shtm (accessed 10 March 2008).

National Emissions Trading Taskforce (NETT) (2007), 'Terms of reference for the National Emissions Trading Taskforce' (amended July 2007), available at: http://www.emissionstrading.nsw.gov.au/key_docu ments/nett_terms_of_reference,_july_2007 (accessed 18 January 2008).

New South Wales (NSW) Ministry of Transport (2007), *TransFigures: Travel in Sydney, Newcastle and Illawarra*, Sydney: NSW Ministry of Transport.

NRMA Motoring and Services (2007), *Private Whole of Life Vehicle Operating Costs Survey*, Sydney: NRMA Motoring and Service.

O'Connell, D., D. Batten, M. O'Connor, B. May, J. Raison, B. Keating, T. Beer, A. Braid, V. Haritos, C. Begley, M. Poole, P. Poulton, S. Graham, M. Dunlop, T. Grant, P. Campbell and D. Lamb (2007),

Biofuels in Australia – Issues and Prospects: A Report for the Rural Industries Research and Development Corporation, Canberra: RIRDC, May.

Prime Ministerial Task Group on Emissions Trading (2007), *Report of the Task Group on Emissions Trading*, Canberra: Department of Prime Minister and Cabinet.

Stern, N., S. Peters, V. Bakhshi, A. Bowen, C. Cameron, S. Catovsky, D. Crane, S. Cruickshank, S. Dietz, N. Edmondson, S.-L. Garbett, L. Hamid, G. Hoffman, D. Ingram, B. Jones, N. Patmore, H. Radcliffe, R. Sathiyarajah, M. Stock, C. Taylor, T. Vernon, H. Wanjie and D. Zenghelis (2006), *Stern Review on the Economics of Climate Change*, Cambridge: Cambridge University Press.

The Climate Institute (2007a), *Making the Switch: Australian Clean Energy Policies*, Sydney: The Climate Institute, May.

The Climate Institute (2007b), *Leader, Follower or Free Rider? The Economic Impacts of Different Australian Emission Targets*, Sydney: The Climate Institute, November.

Treasury, Commonwealth Department of (2008), *Australia's Law Pollution Future: The Economics of Climate Change Mitigation*, Canberra: Canprint Communications.

Turton, H., J. Ma, H. Saddler and C. Hamilton (2002), 'Long-term greenhouse gas scenarios: a pilot study of how Australia can achieve deep cuts in emissions', Discussion Paper No. 48, Canberra: Australia Institute, October.

30 International energy derivatives markets
*Ronald D. Ripple**

1 Introduction

Energy derivatives are relatively new to global energy and financial markets. The first exchange traded energy futures contract was heating oil on the New York Mercantile Exchange (NYMEX) in November 1978. This contract was followed by its European counterpart, a gasoil futures contract traded on the International Petroleum Exchange, in April 1981. Since then a wide range of energy derivatives have been listed on numerous exchanges around the world. The energy commodities covered by derivatives contracts that followed these initial offerings include a range of crude oil, refined oil products, electricity, coal, and natural gas. Perhaps the best known of these is the NYMEX futures contract on light, sweet crude oil, which began trading in March, 1983. This futures contract has grown to be the largest traded futures contract of all commodity futures traded anywhere in the world (see Table 30.5, below).

Prior to the 1970s, virtually all energy commodities either traded under long-term contracts with set quantities and sticky prices, or they were regulated by government. The inherent lack of price fluctuations under these types of regime meant that there was no need for such risk mitigating, hedging instruments. The crude oil disruptions of the mid-1970s and early 1980s, along with a shift away from sticky prices in term contracts, meant that energy prices became more volatile, and market risk mitigation tools and instruments were necessary.

Market participants do not have to hold physical positions in the underlying commodity. Speculators (who do not hold a physical position) who expect to profit from a directional price movement, typically will hold the derivative instrument as part of a diversified portfolio of financial, and perhaps other physical, assets. Therefore investment decisions regarding the derivative instrument are influenced by its relationship with all of the other assets in the speculator's portfolio. Thus, non-physical participants may be willing to accept the risk the hedgers want to shed, not because they are less risk averse, but rather because their portfolio is diversified in such a way that the particular risk characteristics of the derivative assist in reducing the overall portfolio risk faced.

This chapter provides background to the introduction of these financial instruments into the energy markets and an outline of the current products available on the various exchanges. In Section 2, the types of derivatives available to assist market participants with risk mitigation are outlined. Section 3 covers the underlying economics of these instruments and their market valuations with some examples. More detail is provided about the reporting of trades in Section 4, and in Section 5 there is a discussion of the international energy derivatives exchanges. Section 6 evaluates the evolution of both price volatility and the relative roles of hedgers and investors/speculators in these markets. Section 7 concludes.

2   Derivative Instruments

The fundamental purpose for derivatives is to facilitate risk mitigation and to aid in price discovery of the underlying asset. The basic derivative instruments are forwards, swaps, futures, and options.[1] They come in plain vanilla and exotic formats, and trading occurs in the over-the-counter (OTC)[2] 'markets' and on organized exchanges. Forwards, most swaps, and some options trade in the OTC markets, while futures and many options trade on organized exchanges. One can say that all futures are forwards, but the reverse is not true; swaps may be viewed as a sequence of forwards; and options are distinct from the others in that they provide protection from adverse market movements while preserving the possibility of participation in positive movements, albeit for a price. Each is discussed in turn.

Forward contracts are typically employed both to establish a price for a forward date and to secure supplies and placements of the commodity. A forward contract, tailor-made for the parties to the bilateral agreement, specifies the terms of the agreement between the parties (the commodity, quantity, price to be paid at the pre-set future maturity date, the terms for delivery and receipt and settlement of payment). A long forward position implies that the trader will take delivery of the commodity, while a short position implies the sale and delivery of the commodity. For hedging purposes, a trader takes a long position in anticipation of acquiring the underlying commodity in the future so as to lock in future price and gain certainty over future cash flows. The short trader to a forward expects to have quantities of the underlying commodity available for sale in the future and desires to reduce uncertainty (market risk) regarding the price to be received. Since each forward contract is specific to the needs of the parties who initiated the arrangement, unwinding the position is difficult as it involves finding another party with exactly the same requirements for the same commodity at the same time in the same place. In addition, because of the exposure to default risk that forward contracts exhibit, neither party may simply find someone else to take their obligation. They will first have to gain the approval of the initial counterparty, which may not be forthcoming.

Futures contracts differ from forward contracts in many significant ways. Traded on organized exchanges, future contracts have standardized specifications for each commodity traded. Contract standardization significantly enhances liquidity. However, it is rarely the case that a single contract, or even multiples of such contracts, will exactly match the quantities desired by either party. Also, the commodity that underlies the contract itself will rarely be the commodity that the short holds or the long wants. Instead, the underlying commodity will likely be a close substitute whose price movements tend to mirror those of the commodity of specific interest to the parties in the physical market.

As all contracts are identical, there is the basis for a ready secondary market. So any party may purchase or sell a contract at any time when trading is underway to unwind an existing position; the trader need only enter into a trade in the opposite direction to the initial position to close it out and eliminate the obligation. In addition, most exchanges provide a clearinghouse operation whereby the clearinghouse takes the opposite side to every transaction and insures against default. To maintain investor/hedger discipline, the exchange requires that each trader establish a margin account that provides the basis for its provision of insurance against default, and initiates periodic margin calls when the balance falls below acceptable levels.

Non-physical traders are attracted to highly liquid markets which facilitates revelation of relevant market information that may affect the price of the underlying commodity and thus the value of the derivatives/futures contract. Most exchange traded futures contracts in energy commodities tend to be closed out prior to the final trading day, so that the contracts do not go to delivery.[3] As such, futures contracts tend to be employed primarily to manage market price risk and for price discovery, not for securing or placing physical volumes of the commodities.

Swaps may be characterized as a sequence of forwards designed to meet the specific needs of the parties to the swap and tend to be traded over the counter although some exchanges provide clearing services. Swaps originated in the interest rate and currency markets and were later incorporated into the energy markets. The typical structure of a swap is to exchange a floating for a fixed cashflow. A company faced with uncertain future cashflows may wish to exchange (swap) its uncertain cashflow for one that is certain so as to facilitate long-term planning. Swaps may also be employed to secure certainty of cashflow to provide backing for project development funding, that is collateral, for bank loans or other sources of project financing.[4]

Forwards, futures and swaps all place an obligation on both parties to perform at some specified later date. However, an option places the only obligation on the writer of the option; the buyer of the option acquires a right, but no obligation, thus a premium is paid to acquire an option, where no price is paid to enter into a forward, futures, or swap contract.[5] Options may be traded on either organized exchanges or over the counter; if the option is traded on an organized exchange, the writer will typically be required to establish a margin account. However, when a call-option writer can demonstrate that the option is fully covered, that is, the writer owns sufficient unencumbered units of the underlying commodity/asset to meet the obligation should the call be exercised, this covered call option requires no margin account.

To acquire or dispose of a commodity, the buyer of the option must exercise the option. Options come in two basic forms: calls and puts. A call option gives the holder (the purchaser) the right to purchase the underlying commodity at a predetermined price (the exercise or strike price). If the holder of a call option chooses to exercise the option at the appropriate time, the writer of the call option is obliged to deliver the agreed quantity of the specified commodity for the exercise price. The holder of a put option has acquired the right to sell the specified commodity to the writer of the put for the exercise price established at the time the option was entered.

Generally, a call option has value (is 'in the money') and will be exercised when at the maturity of the option the spot price in the market for the commodity is higher than the exercise price. This means that the holder of the option is able to acquire the commodity for less than its current market value, providing an immediate profit, whereby the holder exercises the option, acquires the commodity at the exercise price, and immediately sells in the market for the higher current market price. Or, if the commodity is used in the trader's production process, this means that the trader is able to acquire required inputs for less than the current market price, which may provide for a competitive advantage if competitors have not done the same.

However, if at maturity the market price for the commodity is below the exercise price, the holder of the option will allow the option to expire (it is out of the money). If the holder of the call option is a trader who uses the commodity in its productive process, it will be better to acquire the commodity in the market at the lower current spot price. The reverse set of exercise and market price relationships will dictate the exercise decision for a put.

The time when an option may be exercised depends on the type or style of option. Options typically are styled either as American or European. The designation has nothing to do with the geographic location of the market or exchange where the option is traded, but rather it designates whether an option may be exercised prior to the maturity of the option or only on that maturity date. An American option may be exercised by the holder at anytime during the life of the option. Alternatively, a European option may only be exercised on the maturity date of the option. The distinction translates into different valuations between the two styles for options on the same commodity for the same maturity. The American option will always have a higher value than the European option, simply because it carries with it the superior right to exercise any time up until maturity.

Energy commodity options are typically written with the underlying asset being a futures contract on the physical commodity rather than on the commodity itself. For example, if the holder of an option on NYMEX crude oil exercises the option, the holder will receive a futures contract (one futures contract per option contract). This may then be closed out for profit, if the option was in the money where the current price for the futures contract will be greater than the exercise price for the option, or taken to delivery to acquire feedstock for productive processes.

In the next section we shall briefly review valuation models for futures/forwards and options. We shall also examine an example of how to value a swap, and we shall provide an example of how to construct a crack spread using futures contracts.

3   Valuing Derivative Instruments

The value of a futures or a forward is tied to the value of the underlying asset's spot value, the time to maturity, and the cost to carry the asset from the current period to the maturity of the contract. The simplest expression of the value of a futures contract is the following:

$$F_t^T = S_t e^{rT}, \tag{30.1}$$

where:

 F is the futures price;
 S is the spot price of the commodity;
 r is the interest rate; and
 T is the time to maturity measured in years and fractions thereof.

For most energy commodities (with the exception of electricity) there are also storage costs that must be factored into the value of the futures/forward. The futures price must reflect the full cost to carry the commodity to the maturity date otherwise there will be arbitrage opportunities. If storage costs are valued as a percentage of the spot price of the commodity, the value of the futures is then as follows:

$$F_t^T = S_t e^{(r+\mu)T}, \tag{30.2}$$

where μ is the percent of the spot price associated with storage costs. This provides an expression often referred to as the 'cost of carry model'. However, the convenience yield is an additional nuance necessary to capture the potential value that may accrue to the holder of inventories of the commodity that is used in the production process. In the valuation model the convenience yield offsets some or all of the interest rate and storage costs. The formulation is as follows:

$$F_t^T = S_t e^{(r+\mu-\delta)T}, \tag{30.3}$$

where δ represents convenience yield, which is subtracted from the components of carrying cost. Convenience yield is typically credited as the basis for 'backwardation', the downward-sloping forward curve, which is likely for most energy commodities including crude oil (where backwardation is the norm). If the convenience yield from holding physical inventories is sufficiently large, and $\delta > (r + \mu)$, the futures price will be less than the spot price, and the forward curve will be in backwardation.

Convenience yield is not an observable quantity, it is derived as a residual of this valuation model; with knowledge of the current futures price, the spot price, the interest rate, storage cost, and the time to maturity, the convenience yield can be calculated.[6] Differences will occur between the value of a futures and the value of a forward for the same commodity over the same horizon. The primary reason for the difference is that futures contracts, which are traded on organized exchanges, carry the requirement to establish a margin account and the obligation to meet periodic margin calls. Forward contracts have no such requirement or obligation; the interest costs, and opportunity costs, of these margin accounts place a wedge between values of futures and forwards.

Option valuation is typically carried out using the following Black–Scholes model:

$$c = S_0 N(d_1) - X e^{-rT} N(d_2),$$

$$p = X e^{-rT} N(-d_2) - S_0 N(-d_1),$$

where:

$$d_1 = \frac{\ln(S_0/X) + (r + \sigma^2/2)T}{\sigma\sqrt{T}},$$

$$d_2 = d_1 - \sigma\sqrt{T}, \tag{30.4}$$

where:

c is the value of a call option;
p is the value of a put option;
S is the spot price of the underlying asset;
X is the exercise price;
σ^2 is the variance of the price of the underlying asset;
r is the risk-free interest rate for the time horizon;

T is the time to maturity; and
N and the *d*s effectively represent the probability, taken from the lognormal distribution, that the option will be in the money.

There is a tendency for energy commodity options to be on futures contracts rather than to the underlying commodity. When this is the case, the Black–Scholes model is incorrect. The futures price agreed to today will not be paid until maturity, and, thus, it too must be discounted, just as the exercise price is in the basic formulation. That is, we cannot simply substitute a value for *F* in place of *S* and solve. The required valuation model for an option on a futures contract is as follows:

$$c = e^{-rT}[F_0 N(d_1) - XN(d_2)],$$

$$p = e^{-rT}[XN(-d_2) - F_0 N(-d_1)],$$

where:

$$d_1 = \frac{\ln(F_0/X) + (r + \sigma^2/2)T}{\sigma\sqrt{T}},$$

$$d_2 = d_1 - \sigma\sqrt{T}. \tag{30.5}$$

The futures price set 'today' but paid at time *T* is discounted, just as the exercise price is. Options on futures, just as with other options, may also be valued employing binomial tree methods and other techniques, but with any method the fact that the futures price will be paid in the future must be accounted for. We next examine a method for valuing a swap, using jet fuel as an example.

A swap is an arrangement whereby one party typically swaps a floating price for a fixed price which is set by agreement between the parties. Payments are then made between the parties according to the difference between the fixed price and an agreed reference price. The reference price is typically a price reported by a respected price data vendor who tracks actual market prices.

A jet fuel swap is a derivative arrangement that is common in the airline industry. Fuel costs are the single most important cost to this industry, and it is therefore important to hedge as much risk as possible to bring certainty to the cashflows associated with the largest part of the budget. Ideally an airline would like to swap the floating (uncertain) price of jet fuel for a fixed and certain price, around which it may better plan. For example, if the fixed price for jet fuel was set at US$2.50 per gallon (or US$105.00 per barrel), this is the price that the airline will be paying. If at a specified payment date, which may be monthly or quarterly, the reference price happened to be US$2.50, neither party would owe the other anything, so no payment is required. However, if the price on assessment day was US$2.60 per gallon, the party who sold the fixed price to the airline would be obliged to pay the airline US$0.10 per gallon. If the reference price was US$2.40, the airline would be obliged to pay the other party US$0.10 per gallon. In each case, the net effect is that the airline effectively pays US$2.50 per gallon, regardless of what happens to the market price over the life of the swap.

One way of establishing the fixed price is to assess the relationship between jet fuel

Table 30.1   Three-year jet fuel valuation for a swap (prices in US$/bbl)

	2008	2009	2010
WTI (swap value)	92.69	88.90	87.35
WTI/HO crack value	12.38	12.62	11.76
Jet/HO differential	5.50	5.90	5.00
2008		92.69 + 12.38 + 5.50 = 110.57	
2009		88.90 + 12.62 + 5.90 = 107.42	
2010		87.35 + 11.76 + 5.00 = 104.11	

Note: Average of the three years = US$107.37 per barrel (or roughly US$2.56 per gallon).

and close substitutes that are widely and frequently priced. One combination effectively links the value of jet fuel to crude oil through the crack spread between crude oil and heating oil. Both crude and heating oil are frequently traded and highly liquid markets, and thus provide a sound basis for establishing the value of jet fuel, which is chemically quite similar to heating oil.

To price a three-period swap it is simple to employ annual values, using the swap values for crude oil in each of the three forward years, determine the crude oil/heating oil crack for each year based on market values for the two, and employ an estimated jet fuel–heating oil differential to estimate values for jet fuel in each of the periods. An average is taken and adjusted for risk considerations to establish the fixed price. Then for each year, sum the swap value for crude oil with the market value for the same period for the crack between crude oil and heating oil, and finally add to this figure the estimated value of the jet fuel–heating oil differential. Thus three annual values for jet fuel are linked to the values of the underlying feedstock (crude oil) and a near substitute (heating oil). Table 30.1 displays a hypothetical swap valuation based on prices consistent with the markets in December 2007.

Based on this valuation process, a reasonable price for the swap may be set at US$2.56 per gallon (US$107.37 per barrel), or this estimate may be adjusted upwards for risk. This value then will be the fixed leg of the swap around which the reference price will move, determining payments to be made by the parties to the swap.

Crack and spark spreads employ associated futures contracts on the relevant energy commodities. Crack and spark spreads relate to the value of relations between and among input commodities and output commodities. For example, crude oil is run through a refinery and 'cracked' to produce a range of refined products, each of which has a market-determined price. The basic idea of a crack spread has to do with the difference in the value of the weighted average of the refined product outputs and the cost of the crude oil input. Spark spreads relate to the electricity industry, and the relationship is between the input fuel price (such as natural gas or coal) and the electricity output price.

A refinery example: if the total output of a refinery operation consists of gasoline (G), diesel (D), and fuel oil (FO), in proportions a, b, and c (where $a + b + c = 1$), for a barrel of crude oil (C) input, the crack spread will be based on the price of each and is calculated as follows:

$$Spread = (aP_G + bP_D + cP_{FO}) - P_C. \qquad (30.6)$$

All of these prices are market determined, so they will move over time. Moreover, it is quite possible for the markets to move such that the spread goes to zero or turns negative, so the refiner faces market price risk. This price risk may be mitigated by the use of futures contracts. A typical crack spread strategy, especially in North America, is referred to as the 3-2-1,[7] which consists of three barrels of crude oil, two barrels of gasoline, and one barrel of distillate. While a refinery will produce more than just these two products, for a highly complex refinery these two products will typically make up the vast majority of the refined product output. So, if a refiner hedges and protects against adverse market movements between these two products and crude oil, it should be relatively well hedged and insulated from significant losses due to market fluctuations.

A refiner may sell a 3-2-1 crack spread consisting of three long crude oil futures contracts and two short contracts on gasoline and one short contract on distillate; this crack spread is said to be 'sold' because the 'premium' side of the spread (the products) is being sold. A refiner will only tend to do this if the net is positive, because this structure locks in the difference. So, if the net happened to be negative, the refiner would be locking in a certain loss. However, if a refiner strongly believed that the actual net at the maturity of the contracts (the hedging horizon) would be even more negative than the currently available crack spread, s/he may decide to enter into the arrangements to lock in what is believed to be a smaller than expected loss.[8] Alternatively, a refiner may employ an option on the crack spread, which incurs an upfront known cost but leaves open the possibility of participating in positive moves of the spread.

Crack spread hedges also exhibit a temporal aspect. Since crude oil is purchased for delivery prior to the time it is refined, the refined products must be sold in a later period. Therefore, to retain the temporal relation between the cost of the input and the value of the output, the refiner will purchase crude oil futures with a maturity a month earlier than that for the product contracts sold.

While the 3-2-1 crack spread strategy may be typical in North America, it is unlikely to be the 'correct' strategy in Europe or Asia. Figure 30.1 shows the general refinery output proportions for North America, Europe, and Asia. The output mix for North America in 2006 was 45 percent light distillates, 29 percent middle distillates, and the remaining 26 percent is split between fuel oil and other. The ratio of light to middle distillates is 1.55:1, so the 3:2 ratio imbedded in the 5-3-2 crack spread may appear to provide a more efficient hedge than the 3-2-1. Nevertheless, it is likely that the more complex refineries will exhibit a product ratio closer to 2:1, and they may be expected to make more use of sophisticated risk management tools such as crack spreads.

Europe and Asia present quite different circumstances for crack spread strategies. Europe's light-to-middle distillate ratio is almost the reverse of North America's, and this is due to the much higher reliance on diesel fuel for transport in Europe than in North America. The light-to-middle ratio for Europe is 0.46, which suggests a better crack spread strategy for European refiners will be 3-2-1, with heating oil in the '2' position and gasoline in the '1' position. Asia, on the other hand, exhibits a close enough split between light and middle distillates that the best strategy may well be a 2-1-1 crack spread.

Crack spreads provide hedging protection from adverse price movements between the input and the key outputs. The concern for a refiner is that the price of the output products will fall relative to the crude oil input, thus narrowing the gross margin spread.

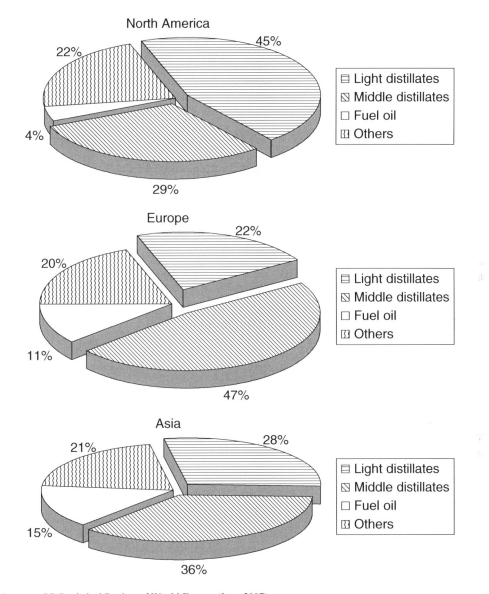

North America

45%

22%

4%

29%

☐ Light distillates
☒ Middle distillates
☐ Fuel oil
☐ Others

Europe

22%

20%

11%

47%

☐ Light distillates
☒ Middle distillates
☐ Fuel oil
☐ Others

Asia

28%

21%

15%

36%

☐ Light distillates
☒ Middle distillates
☐ Fuel oil
☐ Others

Source: BP Statistical Review of World Energy (June 2007).

Figure 30.1   General refinery output in North America, Europe and Asia

A refiner may employ a 3-2-1 crack spread strategy to lock in a spread that s/he deems satisfactory. Table 30.2 provides an example.

A hypothetical refiner, on December 11, 2007, is obligated to purchase 30000 barrels of light, sweet crude oil on March 15, 2008, and s/he is also obligated to supply 20000 barrels (840000 gallons) of gasoline and 10000 barrels (420000 gallons) of heating oil in April, 2008. The refiner is concerned that between December and March, the price

*Table 30.2   A 3–2–1 crack spread hedge strategy for exposure to 30 000 bbl of crude oil,
20 000 bbl of gasoline, and 10 000 bbl of heating oil*

Futures contract (delivery month)	Buy/sell	No of contracts	Price per bbl
Crude oil (April)	Buy	30	$87.40
Gasoline (May)	Sell	20	$102.86 ($2.4491/gal)
Heating oil (May)	Sell	10	$99.83 ($2.3769/gal)

Note: Crack spread established by this strategy: {[(20 × $102.86) + (10 × $99.83)] – (30 × $87.40)}/30 =
$14.45 per bbl.

of crude oil may rise and the prices of the refined products may fall; this will narrow
the spread between the price of the input and the value of the outputs. The refiner may
lock in a spread now by purchasing 30 crude oil futures contracts and selling 20 gasoline
and 10 heating oil futures contracts. The refiner is then short hedging his/her exposure
to market price risk. The prevailing prices on 11 December 2007 for these contracts are:
$87.40 per barrel for NYMEX light, sweet crude oil for April delivery, and US$2.4491
per gallon for NYMEX gasoline-RBOB and US$2.3769 per gallon for NYMEX heating
oil for May delivery. Entering into this hedge strategy will lock in a crack spread of
US$14.45 per barrel, or 16.5 percent of the crude oil cost.[9]

Crack spreads exhibit the same characteristic as all futures hedged positions. If losses
are incurred in the cash position, there will be an offsetting gain in the futures position,
and vice versa. Therefore, the crack spread established with the 3-2-1 hedging strategy
will provide a very high degree of certainty regarding cash flows for the operation of
the refinery and meeting contractual obligations for purchases of crude oil and sale of
products.

4   Energy Commodities Derivatives Contracts

Exchanges around the world list derivatives contracts on a range of energy commodities.
Not all exchanges list all energy commodities; some specialize in specific energy sectors,
like power/electricity, while others offer something for all sectors. Each exchange-
traded contract will carry with it a set of specifications, which clearly identify exactly
what is being traded and what the conditions of trading will be. Specifications for a
futures contract (from the NYMEX light, sweet crude oil contract) include trading unit,
price quotation, trading hours and months, trading at settlement figure, minimum and
maximum daily price fluctuations, the last date traded, settlement type, delivery period
and procedure, deliverable grades, exchange of futures for physicals, inspection, position
accountability levels and limits, margin requirements and trading symbol. Not all these
specifications are reported for all contracts. Virtually all specification lists will include
the trading units, which identify how many units of the commodity are covered by a
single contract. For example, the NYMEX light, sweet crude oil contract represents
1000 barrels (42 gallons each) of crude oil. The deliverable grades characteristic identifies
which crude oils may be delivered against this contract. This contract settles with physical delivery (as opposed to cash settlement), and the value of the contract is underpinned

by the restrictions on the crude oils that may be delivered against it. Crude oil grades that are not specifically listed may not be used to settle an obligation entered into via these contracts, and even some of those that are deliverable under the contract specifications receive either a discount or a premium relative to the actual settlement price set by the exchange. These differentials are specified in the contract and based on quality differentials related to either API (American Petroleum Institute) gravity or sulfur content, or both.

Another key specification is the last trading day. This is an important date for traders, since if a position remains open at the close of the last trading day the holder of the position is obliged to either take delivery (if a long position is held) or make delivery (if a short position is held) and make payment for the value of the commodity, if the trader had been long. Precision in specifying the last trading day for crude oil is important so that there is time for a trader making delivery to nominate pipeline capacity during the delivery month to move the crude oil to an acceptable storage location.

Most commodity futures contracts specify a set quantity that is covered by the contract, and this amount is inflexible. The 'original' electricity futures contracts traded on the NYMEX (and clones of these on the Sydney Futures Exchange: SFE) had rigidly set megawatt hour (MWh) amounts specified, but these tended not to consistently match the exposure of any physical market participants. The contracts all failed, primarily because they failed to provide a solid foundation for physical market participants to hedge effectively.

These contracts have now been replaced by contracts with variable megawatt hour terms dependent upon the specific period of time being covered. The electricity contracts currently traded on the SFE provide a good example of this type of contract. The contract traded on the SFE is actually owned and listed by d-cypha Trade, where the SFE provides the trading platform and settlement and clearing services. There are several electricity futures contracts traded on the SFE covering both base- and peak-load power markets and specific geographical markets for four state wholesale markets that participate in the National Electricity Market (NEM), managed by the National Electricity Market Management Company (NEMMCO). The variability/flexibility in these contracts is due to the fact that each quarter potentially contains a different number of hours during which the market participants must actually operate. The variability in hours from quarter to quarter means that each quarter may present the participants with different market risk exposure that cannot be met by a contract with a rigid MWh specification. Table 30.3 provides a breakdown of the range of the MWh covered by these contracts, reflecting the differences in the possible number of days within a quarter.

The range for peak load is much wider than that for base load because peak load is sensitive to the number of weekends and holidays that fall within a quarter. It is clear that a single contract with a single contract trading unit will not meet the market risk exposure requirements of physical market participants. For example, the original base-load contract on the SFE (originally listed in September, 1997) was for monthly contracts with the trading units being 500 MWh per month. This bears no resemblance, in terms of risk mitigation, to the exposure that market participants face or to the coverage of the current contracts.

Futures contracts will also typically specify the form of the price quotation, in terms of the currency of denomination and whether it is in cents or dollars (or other currency

Table 30.3   d-cypha Trade's electricity contract units for base load and peak load (quarters)

	Contract units
Base load	A 90-day contract quarter will equate to 2160 MWh
	A 91-day contract quarter will equate to 2184 MWh
	A 92-day contract quarter will equate to 2208 MWh
Peak load	A 59-day contract quarter will equate to 885 MWh
	A 60-day contract quarter will equate to 900 MWh
	A 61-day contract quarter will equate to 915 MWh
	A 62-day contract quarter will equate to 930 MWh
	A 63-day contract quarter will equate to 945 MWh
	A 64-day contract quarter will equate to 960 MWh
	A 65-day contract quarter will equate to 975 MWh
	A 66-day contract quarter will equate to 990 MWh

Source: d-cypha Trade; http://d-cyphatrade.com.au/products/electricity_futures.

units) per barrel, ton, MWh, mmBtu, and so on. The minimum price movement will be defined, and the daily maximum price movement, if any, will be stated. This latter specification will differ from exchange to exchange, and it may differ from commodity to commodity within an exchange. The purpose of the daily maximum price limit is to provide the market with a bit of a 'time out' when there has been a very significant price movement from the previous day's close. The limit is typically set at a size such that it will very rarely be an actual constraint, but it is there as a safety valve to disrupt a runaway market, moving primarily on psychology rather than fundamentals.

An example of two different approaches and limit sizes may be seen by comparing the daily limits for the NYMEX and the Tokyo Commodity Exchange (TOCOM) with respect to crude oil. The daily maximum on the NYMEX is $10.00 per barrel (or $10000 per contract), and the limit for TOCOM is ¥2700 per kiloliter (or ¥135000 per contract). Converted to US dollars per barrel, this amounts to roughly US$3.82 per barrel. Therefore, the daily maximum fluctuation on TOCOM is much tighter than that for the NYMEX. Moreover, on TOCOM when the limit is reached trading is suspended until bids and offers move back within the limits. On the other hand, on the NYMEX, if the US$10.00 limit is reached, trading ceases for 5 minutes, and when trading resumes the limit is increased by an additional US$10.00 per barrel. This process continues indefinitely, so while there are temporary slowdowns there is no effective maximum movement limit during a trading session. Because the maximum was being exceeded on the TOCOM during the oil price run-up in mid-2007, the limit was increased from ¥1800 to ¥2700 in September 2007.

The same ¥2700 per kiloliter limit holds on TOCOM for gasoline and kerosene, while on the NYMEX gasoline (now RBOB: reformulated gasoline for oxygen blending) and heating oil have daily limits stated as US$0.25 per gallon (or US$10500 per contract, implying US$10.50 per barrel). The same conditions and processes hold if the limit is reached for these commodities during a trading session for both exchanges as for the respective crude oil contracts.

Since most exchange traded options on energy commodities have a futures contract as the underlying asset, these specifications carry over to the options contract, as well. The exchanges that trade energy-related futures and options globally are outlined next.

5 International Energy Derivatives Exchanges

OTC transactions are, by definition, rather opaque to the rest of the market, since they are structured to meet the specific needs of the two parties to the agreement, and what secondary market there may be is extremely illiquid. Such trading activities, regardless of the specific instrument being traded, carry significant default risk, which is further exacerbated by the effective lack of a liquid secondary market and typically no formal clearinghouse to mitigate default risk. This is why OTC trades tend to be restricted to high creditworthy participants.

Organized exchanges are designed to eliminate the default risk, and the instruments traded on such exchanges are designed to significantly enhance the liquidity of the secondary market. Instruments are designed to meet the needs of physical market participants and liquidity providers, alike. A balance must be struck on specifications because it is highly unlikely that an equal number of offsetting long and short physical traders will exist. Hence, the non-physical, liquidity providers are essential and must be attracted for markets to operate successfully.

Twelve organized exchanges trade energy commodity derivatives contracts. These exchanges provide risk management and price discovery for a wide range of energy commodities; some local or regional and some global. Table 30.4 provides summary information of each of the 12 exchanges which are discussed in turn.

The vast majority of all derivative contracts on energy commodities are traded on the New York Mercantile Exchange (NYMEX), the Intercontinental Exchange (ICE),[10] the Nord Pool, the Sydney Futures Exchange (SFE), and the Tokyo Commodity Exchange (TOCOM) which all began trading energy derivatives prior to 2000.

The NYMEX exchange listed the first energy commodity futures contract in 1978, when it launched its futures contract in heating oil. This was followed in 1983 with the futures contract on light sweet crude oil (LSCO: originally, and colloquially since, referred to as the WTI (West Texas Intermediate) contract). This contract is based on delivery into storage or pipelines at Cushing, Oklahoma. The LSCO contract has grown to be the dominant commodity futures contract globally. As Table 30.5 shows, this contract reports 101 526 321 trades for 2007 through the end of October, at 1000 barrels per contract. The 2007 volume represents about a 70 percent increase over the trading volume for 2006. The 2007 trades equates to roughly 483 000 contracts traded each business day, which means 483 000 000 barrels of oil, nominally.[11] With the average futures settlement price for 2007 (through October) being about US$68.60,[12] a rough estimate of the value of all of the trades through October is nearly US$7 trillion dollars on the NYMEX alone, for just the LSCO contract; that is, roughly US$33 billion of notional value per business day. There is also a healthy options trade on the LSCO contracts, with more than 23 million options traded in 2007, through October.

Natural gas has risen, in terms of contract trading volume, to surpass both heating oil and gasoline. The NYMEX natural gas futures contract is priced for delivery into storage or pipelines at Henry Hub, in Louisiana. The natural gas trading volume for

Table 30.4   Exchanges trading energy commodity derivatives contents

Exchange name	Instruments	Traded since	Price data available
NYMEX	Light Sweet Crude Oil Futures	30/03/1983	No
(www.nymex.com)	Brent Crude Oil Futures	5/09/2001	No
	Natural Gas Futures	3/04/1990	No
	Gasoline Futures	3/12/1984	No
	Heating Oil Futures	14/11/1979	No
	Fuel Oil Futures		No
	Electricity Futures		No
	Coal Futures	12/07/2001	No
	Crude Oil Options	14/11/1986	No
	Natural Gas Options	2/10/1992	No
	Gasoline Options	13/03/1989	No
	Heating Oil Options	26/06/1987	No
	Electricity Options		No
ICE	WTI Crude Futures	3/02/2006	No
(www.theice.com)	Brent Crude Futures	23/06/1988	Yes (for a fee)
	Middle East Sour Crude Oil Futures	21/05/2007	No
	Gasoil Futures	6/04/1981	Yes (for a fee)
	Gasoline Futures	21/04/2006	No
	Heating Oil Futures	21/04/2006	No
	Natural Gas Futures	31/12/1997	Yes (for a fee)
	Electricity Futures	31/12/2001	Yes (for a fee)
	Coal Futures	17/07/2006	No
	WTI Crude Oil Options	20/04/2007	No
	Brent Crude Options	11/05/1989	No
	Gasoil Options	20/07/1987	No
	Crude Oil Forward		No
	Natural Gas Forwards		No
	Electricity Forwards		No
TOCOM	Crude Oil Futures	10/09/2001	Yes
www.(locom or jp)	Gasoline Futures	5/07/1999	Yes
	Kerosene Futures	5/07/1999	Yes
Nord Pool	Electricity Futures	1993	Yes (for a fee)
(www.nordpool.com)	Electricity Forward & Options	10/1997	Yes (for a fee)
Sydney Futures Exchange (www.asx.com.in)	Electricity Futures	1997	No (only for full participants and market data vendors)
	Electricity Options		No (only for full participants and market data vendors)
EEX	Electricity Futures	1/07/2002	Yes (free starting from 2005)
(www.eex.com)	Electricity Options	1/07/2002	No
	Coal Futures	2/05/2006	Yes
	Natural Gas Futures	2/07/2007	Yes

Trading volumes available	Regulatory body
Daily Average and Annual Volume	Commodity futures trading commission
Daily Average and Annual Volume	
Daily Average and Annual Volume	
Daily Average and Annual Volume	
Daily Average and Annual Volume	
No	
No	
No	
Daily Average and Annual Volume	
Daily Average and Annual Volume	
Daily Average and Annual Volume	
Daily Average and Annual Volume	
No	
Yes	ICE Futures Europe Financial Service Authority
Yes	
Yes	
Yes	ICE OTC Commodity Futures Trading Commission
Yes	
Yes	
Yes	
Yes	ICE Futures US Commodity Futures Trading Commission
Yes	
Yes	
Yes	
Yes	
No	
No	
No	
Yes	Ministry of Economy Trade and Industry
Yes	
Yes	
Yes (for a fee)	Kreditisynet (Financial Supervisory Authority)
Yes (for a fee)	NVE (Energy Regulator)
No (only for full participants and market data vendors)	Australian Securities and Investments Commission
No (only for full participants and market data vendors)	Australian Composition and Consumer Commission
Yes (free starting from 2005)	Saxon Ministry for Economic Affairs and Labour

Table 30.4   (continued)

Exchange name	Instruments	Traded since	Price data available
POWERNEXT (www.powernext.com. in)	Electricity Futures	18/06/2004	Yes
Shanghai Futures Exchange (www.shfe.com.in)	Fuel Oil Futures	25/08/2004	Yes
NCDEX (www.ncdex.com)	Crude Oil Futures	15/09/2005	Yes
MCX (www.mcxindia.com)	Crude Oil Futures	9/02/2005	Yes
	Brent Crude Oil Futures	20/06/2005	Yes
	Furnace Oil Futures	20/10/2005	Yes
	Middle East Sour Crude Oil Futures	28/03/2006	Yes
	Natural Gas Futures	11/07/2006	Yes
ENDEX	Natural Gas Futures		No
(www.endex.in)	Electricity Futures		No
	Electricity Forwards		No
DME (www.dubaimerc.com)	Crude Oil Futures	1/06/2007	Yes

Source: The information is drawn directly from the respective exchange websites.

2007 of 24.9 million contracts had an average value of about US$1.8 trillion. The table shows a split and shift for gasoline, primarily during 2006. A change in gasoline specification in the US led to the need to design a new contract with the underlying commodity being RBOB. The uncertainties surrounding how the switchover would go depressed the total trading volume in 2006, but it appears to have rebounded in 2007, with nearly 17 million contracts trading through October.

The table also shows that the NYMEX has listed a contract on Brent crude oil, which to date has not been successful, and that the propane contract is in steep decline. While not shown in the table, the NYMEX was one of the first exchanges to list futures contracts on electricity in 1995 (along with the listing the same year by Nord Pool). The initial contract had a fixed trading unit size of 736 MWh per month. It failed, in large part, because the inflexible unit structure did not match the market risk exposure of physical market participants, as noted above. NYMEX also trades a range of options on most of its futures contracts.

The International Petroleum Exchange (IPE) first listed a contract for gasoil[13] in 1981, gasoil options in 1987 and futures contracts on Brent crude oil were introduced in 1988. The trading volume for gasoil futures contracts on the ICE, which acquired the IPE in 2001, surpassed that for the heating oil contract on the NYMEX in 2006 (Table 30.6). The contracts traded by ICE and NYMEX are different unit sizes. The NYMEX contract unit is 1000 barrels; while the ICE contract unit is 100 metric tonnes (there are 7.5 barrels per tonne meaning that the contracts trade 750 barrels-equivalent with each trade). On that basis, in 2007 the two exchanges traded about equally.

Trading volumes available	Regulatory body
Yes	The Commission de Régulation de l'Energie (CRE) and the DIDEME (French Ministry of Finance)
Yes	China Securities Regulatory Commission
Yes	Forward Markets Commission
Yes	Forward Markets Commission
Yes	
Yes	
Yes	
Yes	
No	Netherlands Authority for the Financial Markets
No	(AFM) and Dutch Office of Energy Regulation (Dfe)
No	
Yes	Dubai Financial Service Authority

The Brent contract unit size is 1000 barrels, and by November 2007 traded 55.6 million contracts.

The ICE launched the WTI futures contract in February, 2006 and these contracts are trading in volumes close to that for Brent. A Middle East sour crude oil futures contract was introduced in May, 2007. Both of these contracts are cash settled only, with the ICE WTI futures being priced off the NYMEX LSCO contract, against the penultimate settlement for the NYMEX contract. This timing is in line with the ICE contract specifying a last trading day one day prior to the last trading day on the NYMEX LSCO contract.

The natural gas futures contract traded on the ICE was listed in 1997, and it trades in multiples of five lots, each equal to 1000 therms per day. This provides for a variable trading unit instrument to account for variations in the number of days in a month, and hence the specific exposure faced in each month. Given 100000 British thermal units (Btu) per therm, for a 30-day month, a contract will equal 15000 mmBtu (million Btu), compared to the 10000 mmBtu contract unit size for the NYMEX Henry Hub futures contract.

The ICE also lists electricity, coal, heating oil, and RBOB gasoline, with an array of options contracts with ICE futures contracts as their underlying commodity.

TOCOM represents the first Asian-based futures exchange to successfully list energy-related futures contracts.[14] TOCOM first listed gasoline and kerosene[15] in July 1999, a crude oil futures contract in 2001 and a gasoil contract in 2003 (which was suspended in 2006 due to lack of trading interest) (Table 30.7).

The TOCOM contracts trade exhibits unusual characteristics. The pattern of trade

Table 30.5 NYMEX (annual trading volumes)

Year	Futures Contracts							Options Contracts				
	Light, sweet crude oil	Brent crude oil	Heating oil	New York Harbor gasoline	New York Harbor RBOB gasoline	Natural gas	Propane	Crude oil	Heating oil	RBOB gasoline	Natural gas	New York Harbor gasoline
2007 (October)	101 526 321		15 067 891		16 916 991	24 960 139	318	23 243 726	493 557	904 521	4 655 138	
2006	71 053 203	1442	13 990 589	8 620 908	3 883 261	23 029 988	1127	21 016 562	595 427		9 581 663	583 342
2005	59 650 468	986 534	13 135 581	13 166 417	1964	19 142 549	4010	14 726 263	983 388		9 168 354	973 849
2004	52 883 220	135 385	12 884 511	12 777 442		17 441 942	14 764	11 512 918	800 277		8 074 967	904 466
2003	45 436 931		11 581 670	11 172 050		19 037 118	14 710	10 237 121	668 859		8 742 277	616 245
2002	45 679 468		10 695 202	10 979 736		24 357 792	12 826	11 460 857	602 170		10 966 023	721 932
2001	37 530 568		9 264 472	9 264 472		16 468 355	10 566	7 726 076	704 972		5 974 240	1 040 030
2000	36 882 692		9 631 376	8 645 182		17 875 013	26 075	7 460 052	1 385 968		5 335 800	1 012 460
1999	37 860 064		9 200 703	8 701 216		19 165 096	37 544	8 161 976	695 558		3 849 454	600 009
1998	30 495 647		8 863 764	7 992 269		15 978 286	43 868	7 448 095	669 725		3 115 765	730 421
1997	24 771 375		8 370 964	7 475 145		11 923 628	40 255	5 790 333	1 147 034		2 079 607	1 033 778
1996	23 487 821		8 341 877	6 312 339		8 813 867	53 903	5 271 456	1 108 935		1 234 691	655 965
1995	23 613 994		8 266 783	7 071 787		8 086 718	49 532	3 975 611	703 388		921 520	766 557
1994	26 812 262		8 986 835	7 470 836		6 357 560	45 100	5 675 072	699 325		493 491	573 502
1993	24 868 602		8 625 061	7 407 809		4 671 533	44 923	7 156 518	803 216		345 814	660 886
1992	21 109 562		8 005 462	6 674 757		1 920 986	50 601	6 562 163	1 247 891		80 756	860 086
1991	21 005 867		6 680 171	5 509 926		418 410	55 854	4 968 742	863 143			573 767
1990	23 686 897		6 376 871	5 205 995		132 820	38 636	5 254 612	406 810			435 685
1989	20 534 865		5 740 967	4 484 558			14 664	5 685 953	298 136			332 094
1988	18 858 948		4 935 015	3 292 055			23 749	5 480 281	125 812			
1987	14 581 614		4 293 395	2 056 238			15 312	3 117 037	143 605			
1986	8 313 529		3 275 044	439 352				135 266				
1985	3 980 867		2 207 733	132 611								
1984	1 840 342		2 091 546	2736								
1983	323 153		1 868 322									
1982			1 745 526									

Table 30.6 ICE (annual trading volumes)

Year	Futures Contracts								Options Contracts		
	Brent	Gasoil	WTI	Heating oil	RBOB gasoline	Coal	Natural gas	Electricity	Brent	WTI	Gasoil
2007 (November)	55 608 322	22 696 604	48 115 940	193 292	12 484	9575	1 154 415	3415	70 349	10 161	153 790
2006	44 346 077	18 290 177	28 672 654	199 187	9692	900	602 125	9570	33 249		104 320
2005	30 412 027	10 971 719					444 230	14 200	44 421		74 055
2004	25 458 259	9 355 767					648 640	4250	28 688		45 154
2003	24 012 969	8 429 981					815 435		49 520		33 339
2002	21 493 486	8 156 358					583 800		146 809		61 001
2001	18 396 069	7 230 408					471 285		252 217		60 240
2000	17 297 723	7 115 434					523 365		452 284		100 631
1999	15 982 337	6 150 912					301 195		495 798		104 813
1998	13 674 664	4 974 171					326 940		337 999		104 523
1997	10 301 918	4 031 608					81 820		249 976		68 195
1996	10 675 474	4 361 062							374 233		110 226
1995	9 773 468	4 491 512							569 943		116 294

723

Table 30.7   TOCOM (annual trading volumes)

Year	Futures Contracts			
	Crude oil	Gasoil	Gasoline	Kerosene
2007 (November)	1 414 122	0	7 074 956	2 218 296
2006	1 961 190	2	12 932 848	4 492 904
2005	1 981 389	6312	17 448 561	7 295 741
2004	2 284 572	235 844	23 648 587	13 036 277
2003	1 809 711	372 977	25 677 079	13 208 350
2002	2 037 215		20 866 237	10 482 433
2001	911 597		16 441 056	8 301 559
2000			14 370 266	6 741 173
1999			3 973 668	1 441 163

across maturities is effectively opposite (inverted) of that for nearly all other futures exchanges. The typical trading pattern concentrates the greatest trading volume and open interest imbedded in the near-month contract(s), with trading activity tailing off as contract maturities increase. On the TOCOM exchange, the norm is for the longest or next to longest maturity contracts to carry the majority of both trading volume and open interest, with the taper in activity coming forward to the near-month contract, which is typically the least active. There does not seem to be a very good explanation for this phenomenon.

While the trading volumes on the TOCOM seem relatively stable in the past few years, albeit with some decline, this is a bit misleading on the positive side. In 2005, the TOCOM changed the unit size for its oil-related contracts from 100 kiloliters (kl) to 50 kl. Therefore, while the number of transactions on the exchange may have not reduced significantly, the volume of notional oil products covered has been halved.

Another difference in specifications is that TOCOM contracts never have a maturity exceeding six months. While the NYMEX has contracts listed through December of 2016, the longest-dated TOCOM contract in December 2007, was for delivery in May 2008 for crude oil and June 2008 for gasoline and kerosene, due to differences in last trading day and delivery month specifications for the contracts.

The TOCOM crude oil contract is based on Middle East crude oil and priced off of the average of Dubai and Oman crude oil. The contract is cash settled with no delivery, and it is denominated in yen per kiloliters, which makes this the only exchange traded crude oil futures contract globally that is not priced in US dollars per barrel. The 50 kl unit size also makes these rather small in notional physical volumes represented – 50 kl equates to roughly 314 barrels, making these contracts less than a third the size of crude oil contracts traded elsewhere.

The notional volumes of gasoline represented by the trading on TOCOM, before the unit size was reduced, were actually quite remarkable. For example, the peak trading year was 2003, with 25.7 million contracts traded. Each contract represented 100 kl, and each kilolitre equates to about 6.28 barrels, implying that a 100 kl contract represents about 628 barrels. Thus, in barrel equivalents, the 2003 TOCOM futures trade in gasoline represented 16 billion notional barrels, while the NYMEX trade in the same year for gasoline represented 11 billion barrels. The notional physical volumes represented

Table 30.8   NORD POOL (annual trading volumes)

Year	Electricity Futures Market (TWh)	Bilateral Clearing Volume (TWh)
2007	N/A	N/A
2006	766	2220
2005	786	2156
2004	590	1207
2003	545	1219
2002	1019	2089
2001	910	1748
2000	359	1180
1999	216	684
1998	89	373
1997	53	147
1996	43	
1995	15	
1994	7	
1993	3	

Note: TWh equals 1 000 000 MWh.

by trading on TOCOM since the reduction in the unit size have been reduced to about a quarter of that for 2003.

The first electricity futures contracts were listed and traded on the Nord Pool in 1995. However, the bilateral trading activity, which Nord Pool facilitates by providing clearing services, dominates the trading activities. This is likely rooted in the foundations of the exchange which is physical markets for trading electricity. Table 30.8 reports volumes of trades in terawatt hours (TWh; where 1 TWh is equal to 1 000 000 MWh).

Since the futures contracts specify variable contract units (in MWh) due to different numbers of days per month or quarter or due to holidays, it is not straightforward to determine the numbers of contracts traded. However, a ballpark estimate of the numbers of contracts involved in the trading activity may be arrived at by accepting an average number of hours for base-load quarters, an average for peak-load quarters, multiply this sum by four, and divide this value into the number of MWh traded. On this basis, the 766 TWh of electricity traded on Nord Pool during 2006 represents roughly 61 000 contracts traded. However, if the bilateral clearing activity is assessed in the same way, the 2006 activity in this component of Nord Pool's operations accounted for roughly 177 000 units traded.

The SFE first listed electricity futures in 1997. The contracts had rigid monthly MWh unit sizes, which did not adequately address physical market participant market risk exposure. As a result the contracts failed.

The initial contracts were for 500 MWh per month, base load, and there were separate contracts for each state power supply system participating in the NEM. There ceased to be any contracts actively traded in electricity on the SFE by the end of 2000.

Currently, the SFE provides a trading platform for electricity futures contract listed by d-cypha Trade. The new contracts, listed in 2002, provide flexible trading units depending on the number of days in a quarter for base-load, and the number of peak days in a quarter for the peak-load contracts (see Table 30.3, above). The growth in trade has been quite strong; in 2006, 50 709 contracts traded and the total trades to November 2007 were 131 078. Each traded contract is a 1 MW quarter equivalent.

The traded contracts include base- and peak-load contracts for each of the four states that participate in the NEM. Contracts are traded for the quarters March, June, September, and December and for up to four-and-a-quarter years forward.

The European Energy Exchange (EEX) was originally based in Frankfurt and first traded electricity futures in late 2000, along with spot trade in electricity. In 2002, the Frankfurt EEX merged with LPX (the Leipzig Power Exchange) and the new exchange, still named EEX took up operations in Leipzig. In 2005, 400 futures contracts traded just over 1.6 million MWh (1.6 TWh) of electricity; rising in 2006 to trade 950 contracts (and just over 1.9 million MWh or (1.9 TWh) of electricity). Futures contracts were also traded for coal (with 557 contracts traded approximately 1.9 million tonnes in 2006) and natural gas (with 2910 contracts traded 3.4 million units in 2007). The variable contract units structure of the original EEX electricity contract appears to be the forerunner of all such contracts that now trade globally.

Also in 2002, the French-based PowerNext exchange was established in response to the changes in the European electricity market. In addition to futures on electricity, PowerNext also provides day-ahead trading allowing market participants' access to short-term hedging facilities. Annual trading volumes of electricity on PowerNext have increased from around 12.8 million MWh (12.8 TWh) in 2004 to just over 83.1 million MWh (83.1 TWh) in 2006. Futures contracts are listed for maturities of a month, quarter, and year, and the unit size is variable according to the number of days in each period for base load and the number of peak-period days for peak load. Employing the same approximation used for Nord Pool, the volume of electricity traded up to December 2007 (73.9 million MWh) equates to roughly 5900 contract units traded.

A third exchange set-up in 2002 was the Amsterdam-based European Energy Derivatives Exchange (ENDEX). The exchange offers a natural gas futures contract for delivery to the TTF hub. This contract is priced in €/MWh, so the volume of natural gas associated with each contract is dependent upon the thermal efficiency and conversion rates between natural gas and electricity. The contract units vary, as with electricity contracts, depending on the days in the month, quarter, and so on. The basic contract size is 1 MWh per hour times the number of days and hours, and the minimum volume is 10 MWh/h for quarter, season, and calendar/year contracts, and 30 MWh/h for month contracts. The contract series include three individual months, four individual quarters (March, June, September, December), two individual seasons (April–September and October–March), and three individual calendars/years (January–December).

The ENDEX also trades three futures contracts for electricity. There are base- and peak-load contracts for the Dutch market and a base-load contract for the Belgian market. The basic contract size is 1 MW per day per hour for base load, and 1 MW per peak delivery day in the contract period times 16 hours for each day for the peak-load contract. The Dutch contracts are for physical delivery to the TenneT hub, and the Belgian contract is for delivery at the ELIA hub. All three are priced as €/MWh.

The Shanghai Futures Exchange (SHFE) primarily traded futures on metals and rubber prior to listing the fuel oil futures contract in 2004. The SHFE is the only futures exchange in China to list an oil-related product since such contracts were banned in the late 1990s due to instances of market manipulation and fraud in such markets. Trade has risen from 5.6 million fuel oil futures contracts during the first year of trading to 25.4 million by 2006.

Each contract is relatively small in barrel equivalence at 10 tons, which equates to roughly 75 barrels per contract. Contracts are listed for 12 months ahead, but no trading or delivery occurs during the Spring Festival, which typically falls in February. The contracts are denominated in yuan per ton, and they are deliverable to SHFE-approved storage.

The SFHE futures contract trading pattern previously resembled that discussed for TOCOM, that is, the greatest trading activity and open interest were in the more-distant maturity contracts. This pattern held for all contracts traded on the SFHE, including those for metals and rubber. Since 2004, the trading pattern across the exchange has shifted. Now for all contracts, including the fuel oil contract, the greatest trading activity and open interest occurs typically for maturities three months out, with trading activity increasing to that 'peak' month and then trailing off to the more-distant maturities. It is not clear what has led to this transition to a pattern more closely resembling that seen on Western exchanges, but during this time the SFHE has engaged in relationship enhancement through several memoranda of understanding with foreign futures and options exchanges such as the Chicago Board of Options Exchange, the Chicago Mercantile Exchange, the NYMEX, and TOCOM, and perhaps the Western influence is being observed in part through the changed trading pattern.

The National Commodity and Derivatives Exchange (NCDEX) based in Mumbai, India traded oil-related futures contracts since 2005. The exchange lists three futures contracts: Brent crude oil (since September 2005), furnace oil (since October 2005), and LSCO (since August 2007). The two crude oil contracts are rather small in size, at 100 barrels, but delivery requires 50000 barrels; however, delivery is into Mumbai. These two crude oil contracts are tied to the same crude oils that underlie the ICE and NYMEX contracts.

The traded volume of crude oil was approximately 124000 contracts in the first year and in 2007 148837 contracts had traded by November, which amounts to a total of 14883700 barrels, or the equivalent of 14884 contracts on either NYMEX or ICE; by comparison this volume of contracts would change hands in roughly 10 minutes on the NYMEX and 20 minutes on the ICE. A furnace oil contract was launched in 2005 and traded 6154 contracts. However, trading fell away in 2006 (4219 contracts in total) with trades occurring only in the first three months. A smattering of very small trades late in 2007 produced a total of 10 contract trades by November. In the first four months of trading the LSCO contract reported 25473 contracts traded.

The Multi Commodity Exchange of India (MCX) was inaugurated as an independent de-mutualized exchange in November 2003. It began listing oil-related futures contracts in 2005, and followed these with a natural gas futures contract in 2006. The specifications for the oil contracts are very similar to those for NCDEX, with contracts on Brent crude oil (90880 contracts traded in 2006 and 150 contracts traded in the year to December 2007), crude oil (which is WTI specification oil, 13 million contracts traded in the year to December 2007), and furnace oil (592 contracts traded in 2006, however, only two contracts traded in the year to December 2007). They also list a contract on Middle East sour oil (in 2006, 21 170 contracts were traded). An additional contract listed on the MCX exchange is for natural gas (1 953 756 contracts traded in 2006 and 1 677 610 contracts traded in the year to December 2007). It too is for relatively small quantities.

The trading unit size for natural gas is 500 mmBtu, compared to the 10 000 mmBtu contracts on NYMEX and 15 000 mmBtu on ICE for a 30-day month. The delivery location for the natural gas contracts is at Hazira, in Gujarat State in Western India. There is a large Shell LNG terminal in this port.

The first exchange based in the Middle East to offer futures trading on a benchmark Middle East crude oil is the Dubai Mercantile Exchange (DME) which began trading Oman crude oil futures contracts in June 2007. By November 2007, Oman crude oil traded 196 131 futures contracts, Brent–Oman 13 616 financial spread contracts and WTI–Oman 8663 financial spread contracts. The exchange is a joint venture between Tatweer Dubai Ltd (a member of Dubai Holding), the NYMEX, and the Oman Investment Fund.

The contract unit size is 1000 barrels, and it is priced in US dollars per barrel. It is deliverable FOB to the seller's vessel at Mina Al Fahal Terminal, Oman, and the last trading day is the last business day of the month two months prior to the delivery month. The contract is cleared through the NYMEX clearinghouse.

During the first six months of trading the DME traded 196 131 contracts, representing 196 131 000 barrels of Omani crude oil. That averages about 33 000 contracts a month; with 42 658 contracts traded during November, their volumes are continuing to grow rapidly, with a nearly 7 percent increase month-on-month between October and November.

In addition to the benchmark Oman crude oil futures contract, the DME has also listed two financial spread contracts. The cash settled spread contracts allow risk managers to hedge the spread between Oman crude oil and either Brent or WTI. However, these two contracts appear to be declining in activity.

In the next section we examine price trends, volatility, and the role of market participants in various energy-related derivatives contracts.

6   Price Trends, Volatility and the Role of Market Participants

Futures contracts provide valuable price discovery and are frequently used as the basis for analyzing energy price volatility. The price series for WTI is presented in Figure 30.2; at first glance it may seem that price volatility has increased, and this apparent increase is typically attributed to non-commercial traders (speculators).

However, the volatility that typically matters to speculators is the volatility on returns, that is, the volatility of the day-to-day percentage changes of the prices. Analysis of the daily returns for NYMEX crude oil futures prices between January 2000 and December 2007 presented in Figure 30.3 shows virtually no slope in either direction and fewer big spikes in these daily returns as we come forward to the present.

Another comparable method to evaluate the volatility is to plot a rolling measure of the coefficient of variation[16] over the period as in Figure 30.4. The plotted linear trendline clearly slopes downward and the volatility of the coefficient of variation appears to decline over the period.

This phenomenon of decreasing volatility over the period is not observed by chance

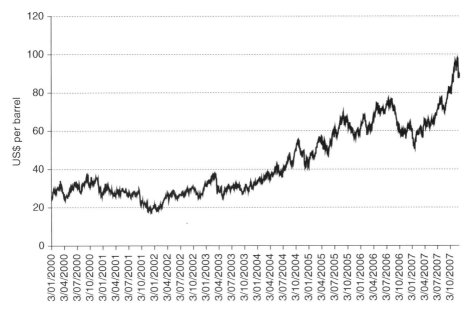

Source: Datastream.

Figure 30.2 NYMEX crude oil futures price series

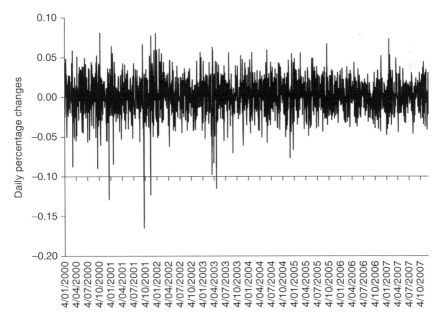

Source: Datastream International and author calculations.

Figure 30.3 NYMEX crude oil daily returns

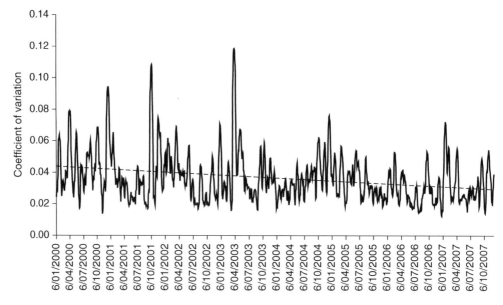

Source: Datastream International and author calculations.

Figure 30.4   Coefficient of variation – NYMEX crude oil futures (daily)

nor is it limited to the specific NYMEX crude oil price series. The decrease in volatility is across the board. Figures 30.5 and 30.6 show the price series for NYMEX natural gas futures and its corresponding rolling coefficient of variation. These are followed by the rolling coefficient of variation graphs in Figures 30.7–9 for Saudi Arabian light, Dubai, and Brent; these are based on Thursday-to-Thursday price observations since several crude oils tend to report only weekly prices. For those that report more frequently, using the Thursday prices takes observations after the markets have been able to digest the regular Wednesday inventory reports. Their price series look much like that for the NYMEX crude oil futures, above.

Similar results will be found when examining the volatility of other petroleum products such as diesel and gasoline, both within the US and globally. One exception is gasoline in the US, which has shown a rise in volatility, while gasoline in the UK shows flat to mildly downward trending coefficients of variation.

Another aspect of the apparent misleading interpretation of the energy commodity price series is the role of non-commercial traders. It is sometimes suggested that there has been a great influx of this class of trader, especially into the futures markets, at the expense of traders with physical requirements. An analysis of the share of open interest held by this class of traders, along with an analysis of the relations between trading volumes and open interest, suggest a different conclusion.

The Commodity Futures Trading Commission (CFTC) is the US regulatory body responsible for all US derivatives markets. It collects and reports weekly long and short open interest positions for all derivatives traded separating the trader classes into commercial, non-commercial,[17] and non-reporting.

The trader classifications do not equate directly to the concepts of hedgers versus

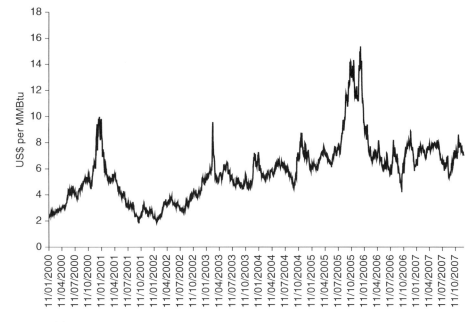

Source: EIA/DOE.

Figure 30.5 NYMEX natural gas futures price series (daily)

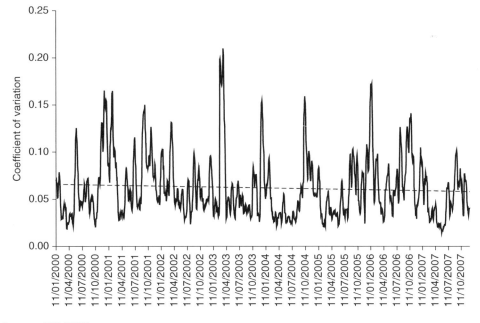

Source: EIA/DOE.

Figure 30.6 Coefficient of variation – NYMEX natural gas futures prices (daily)

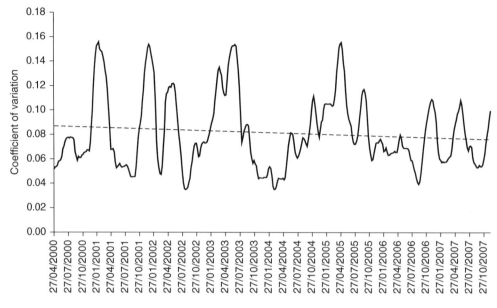

Source: Datastream International and author calculations.

Figure 30.7   Coefficient of variation – Saudi light (Thursday to Thursday)

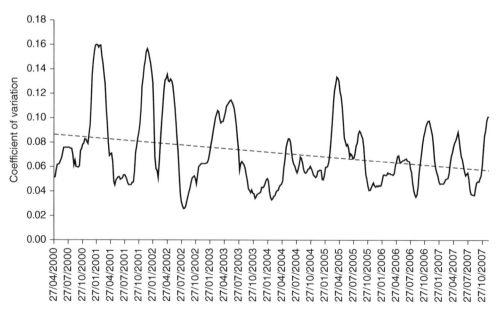

Source: Datastream International and author calculations.

Figure 30.8   Coefficient of variation – Dubai (Thursday to Thursday)

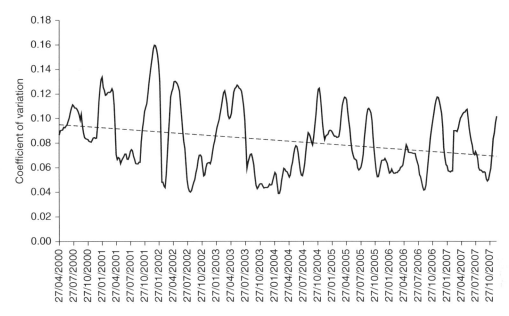

Source: Datastream International and author calculations.

Figure 30.9 *Coefficient of variation – Brent (Thursday to Thursday)*

speculators/investors, but it provides a relatively close linkage to these concepts. The class of non-reporting trader is a residual amount that captures small traders with open interest positions smaller than the CFTC's reporting threshold.[18] Figures 30.10–15 report the percentages of open interest held by commercials, non-commercials, and non-reporters. The figures shown are for long positions, only, but the short positions figures look much the same. The commodities covered include crude oil, natural gas, and gasoline; all traded on the NYMEX.

Both longer time period views (Figure 30.10) and short period views (Figure 30.11) show that there has been relatively little change in the typical share of the open interest held by commercial traders for NYMEX crude oil; the average share held by commercials for the 1986–2007 period is 66 percent, while the average for the 2000–07 period is 61 percent. Moreover, most of the apparent gains in share of open interest by non-commercials have been at the expense of the small trader, non-reporting group. At least in crude oil futures, the non-commercials do not appear to have forced out the commercials. Indeed, what appears to have occurred here is that the non-commercial group, which provides liquidity in these markets, seems to have elevated the amount of liquidity provided to meet the overall growth in the industry.

The CL line in the figures represents the commercial long position holders, NCL represents the non-commercial long position, and all others combines NCL and non-reporting traders. The closing of the gap between all others and NCL shows the gains of non-commercials over non-reporting traders.

Figures 30.12 and 30.13 show the same long-period, short-period information for

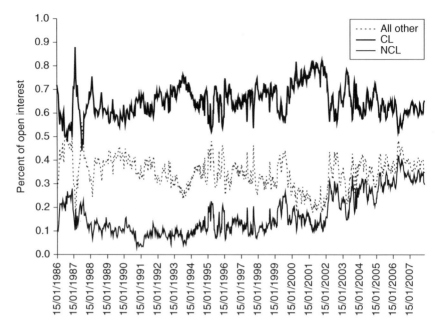

Source: CFTC.

Figure 30.10   Crude oil open interest – long: commercials versus all others (1)

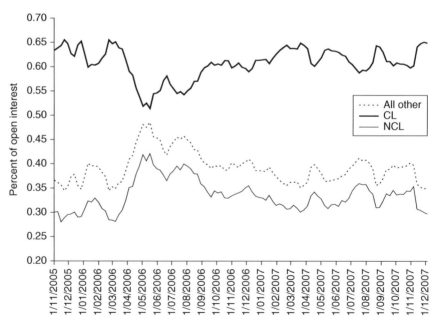

Source: CFTC.

Figure 30.11   Crude oil open interest – long: commercials versus all others (2)

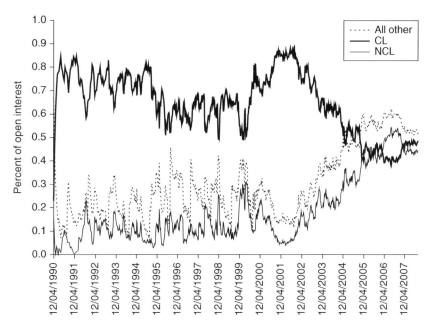

Source: CFTC.

Figure 30.12 Natural gas open interest – long: commercials versus all others (1)

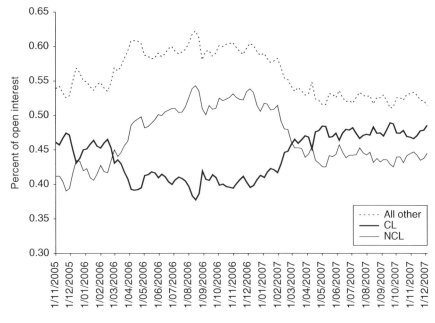

Source: CFTC.

Figure 30.13 Natural gas open interest – long: commercials versus all others (2)

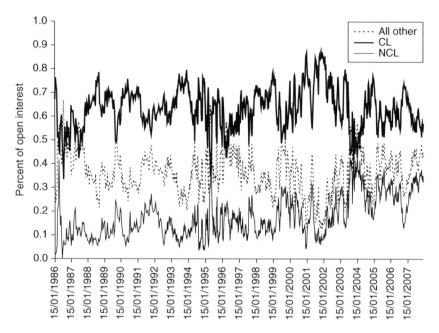

Note: Data for gasoline and RBOB are spliced with the overlapping values summed: February
14–December 5, 2006.

Source: CFTC.

Figure 30.14   Gasoline – RBOB open interest – long: commercials versus all others (1)

NYMEX natural gas futures, and NYMEX gasoline futures is covered in Figures 30.14
and 30.15.

It is clear that there are significant differences in the roles of the different categories
of traders depending on the product. The natural gas futures trade has been dominated
in 2006/07 by non-commercial traders, while the gasoline long market has fluctuated
and seems to be on a rebound to even stronger shares held by commercial traders. (The
character of the short side of the market for gasoline is quite different from its long
side, which is in contrast to the other markets. The commercials have consistently held
roughly 80 percent of the short positions since 2005, and this is an increase from the
range of 65–70 percent in the earlier periods.)

The final aspect of this investigation into the role of traders is to examine the relations
between trading activity and open interest. One would expect that if non-commercials
were operating like the bad version of speculators is expected to, we would see an
increase in the amount of trading volume for a given level of open interest. Open interest captures the number of contracts that are still open in the market that have not been
closed out and may still be traded. Because of the nature of futures markets, where there
is no set number of contracts that are available for trading, new contracts come into
existence simply because two traders desire to open positions (one long and one short).
However, these positions need not remain open, and one would expect that a significant

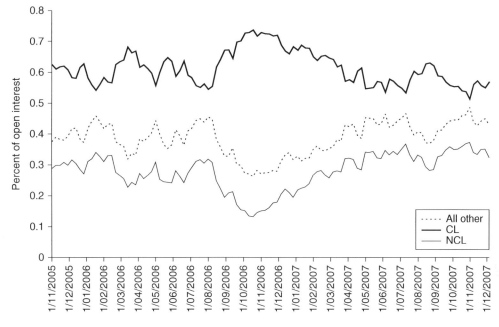

Note: Data for gasoline and RBOB are spliced with the overlapping values summed: February 14–December 5, 2006.

Source: CFTC.

Figure 30.15 Gasoline – RBOB open interest – long: commercials versus all others (2)

influx of 'bad' speculators would be accompanied by an increase in trading volume relative to open interest.

The trading volumes for crude oil on the NYMEX were reported above, and these may be compared to the average weekly open interest positions as reported by the CFTC for this contract. Figure 30.16 reports this analysis.

The annual trades relative to average weekly open interest during 2006 were anomalous, but in the downward direction, with just 66.8 contracts traded per open contract. The trades per average open interest during 2007, of 72.7, appear to be quite in line with the recent past. The level of open interest seems to have grown to match the growth in trade in the industry; average weekly open interest increased from 468 109 in 2000 to 1 397 265 in 2007 (through October).

Thus, contrary to typical commentary, there is little evidence of either increased price volatility or an increase in the relative role of non-commercial traders.

7 Conclusion

The vast majority of energy derivatives are traded bilaterally; however, there is a steadily increasing number of exchanges and products that are available for market participants to hedge their market risk in a growing number of exchanges across the world.

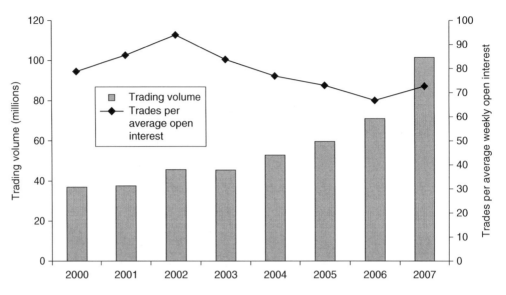

Figure 30.16   Trading activity relative to open interest: NYMEX crude oil futures contract

Notes

*   The author would like to thank Ilke Onur for his wide-ranging research assistance and Phanh Oudomlith for his deft data support.
1.   See Fusaro (1998), Hull (2002), Kolb (2003) and Kaminski (2005) for detailed information on the instruments discussed below, as well as for more exotic alternatives.
2.   The OTC 'markets' represent bilateral arrangements typically between high creditworthy market participants, usually facilitated by an investment banker or other financial intermediary.
3.   It is estimated that less than 1 percent of the contracts for energy commodities on the NYMEX go to delivery.
4.   If the risk of future cashflows can be eliminated, the rates charged by financiers will typically be reduced significantly.
5.   Under forwards, futures, and swaps, both parties enter into equal and opposite obligations to perform in the future at the agreed price. There is no imbalance in value, so no funds need change hands to establish the arrangement. For exchange traded futures contracts a margin account needs to be established by each party. The margin account is held and monitored by the exchange/clearinghouse and provides the basis for the clearinghouse to be able to insure against default.
6.   A mistake is sometimes encountered, however, when a time series of convenience yields is constructed. The tendency is to assume that storage costs are constant over the period of analysis, and doing so will often produce negative estimates for convenience yield. The nature of the concept of convenience yield, introduced in Kaldor (1939), is such that it is either positive or zero. Negative values for convenience yield are simply an artefact of the assumption that storage costs are constant when they are not.
7.   Alternatives to the 3-2-1 also exist, such as 5-3-2 or 2-1-1, and the best strategy will depend on a given refiner's conversion characteristics.
8.   To take such a decision to lock in a certain loss would be a brave decision, indeed. No matter how strongly supported by competent analysis, if the market even once shifted such that a positive margin (or even a smaller loss) would have resulted, the Board of Directors and shareholders would likely ask for the head of the relevant decision maker(s).
9.   It is worth noting that this is a gross margin, and it is not high by historical standards. For the same structure priced on December 13, 2005, the locked-in spread was US$13.43 against a US$63.21 barrel of crude oil, or 21.2 percent; and priced on December 12, 2006 it was US$13.09 against a US$63.63 barrel of crude oil, or 20.6 percent.

10. ICE became an established derivatives exchange in 2000 and acquired the International Petroleum Exchange (IPE) in 2001.
11. The size of this number, and others like it in the energy futures trade, has led some to suggest that the futures markets are dominated by non-commercial speculators. Since the physical trade in crude oil globally is in the order of 87 million barrels per day, this number seems to suggest that something over five times the physical volume is traded. This is a misleading way to assess these numbers since the 483 million number included trades for delivery *months* out through 2016, while the daily use number relates only to an average *day*. When the futures trading volume is placed into comparable daily terms, the apparent multiple shrinks to a fraction of roughly 16 percent of the daily physical usage for both crude oil and natural gas (see Ripple, 2006).
12. The forward curve for much of 2007 has returned to backwardation, which means that the overall average for these trades will be something less than the US$68.60, which is based on the average for the near-month contract. However, since most of the trading action does occur near the front of the curve, the average total should be a fair representation of the actual.
13. 'Gasoil' is the European term commensurate with the heating oil range of distillates.
14. The Singapore Futures Exchange has attempted several times to list oil-related contracts, but all have failed. It is suggested that a key element of this failure is that the Asian oil trade has a long history of forwards trade whereby the trading units are full cargoes, and the smaller parcels represented by standardized futures contracts have failed to break through this market momentum.
15. Kerosene is an important home heating fuel for Japan.
16. The coefficient of variation is calculated by taking the ratio of the standard deviation and the mean of the series. The plot employs a rolling 20-day calculation of both the standard deviation and the mean.
17. An additional category labeled 'spreads' captures net calendar spread positions for the non-commercials.
18. It is interesting to note, and it is visible in the figures, that in the early days of trading, the non-reporting traders significantly outnumbered the non-commercial traders.

References

Fusaro, Peter C. (1998), *Energy Risk Management*, New York: McGraw-Hill.
Hull, John C. (2002), *Fundamentals of Futures and Options Markets*, 4th edn, Upper Saddle River, NJ: Prentice-Hall/Pearson Education.
Kaldor, Nicholas (1939), 'Speculation and economic stability', *Review of Economic Studies*, **7** (1), 1–27.
Kaminski, Vincent (ed.) (2005), *Managing Energy Price Risk: The New Challenges and Solutions*, London: Risk Books.
Kolb, Robert W. (2003), *Future, Options, and Swaps*, 4th edn, Malden, MA: Blackwell.
Ripple, Ronald D. (2006), 'Energy futures market trading versus physical commodity usage: a playground for manipulation or a miscalculation?', Macquarie Economic Research Papers, 3/2006, May.

31 The economics of energy in developing countries
*Reinhard Madlener**

1 Introduction

The social, economic and environmental development of many developing countries (DCs)[1] is threatened by a lack of sufficient, reliable and sustainable supplies of energy. By improving health and education, access to energy contributes both to social development and the productivity of labour and capital, and thus also fosters economic development (Auer, 1981; Dunkerley, 1985; Pachauri and Pachauri, 1985; IEA, 1994). Training and education enabled by the provision of modern energy services are important prerequisites for a prosperous broader economic development, 'requiring far-reaching legal, institutional and regulatory reforms' (Birol, 2007, p. 5). In the presence of rising fossil energy prices and increasing prices for capital-intensive energy infrastructures (for example, power generation plants, distribution grids, oil refineries), as experienced in recent years, economic problems of many DCs (especially those chronically short of foreign currency) are likely to grow again considerably. Climate change issues and the overutilisation of traditional fuel sources beyond sustainable levels pose new additional restrictions and aggravate the problem further.

As many as 1.6 billion people in DCs have no access to electricity today. Some 2.5 billion people (or 40 per cent of the world's population) – especially in rural areas, where population growth is high, incomes low, and increases in agricultural productivity crucial for the entire country concerned – are dependent on non-commercial ('traditional') fuels, such as fuelwood, charcoal, agricultural crop residues, and animal dung. A major problem is that the efficiency of using non-commercial biomass is particularly low (for example, indoor cooking). Whereas the number of people in poor countries relying on traditional biomass fuels is expected to rise, the number of people lacking access to electricity will fall relatively modestly (Birol, 2007).[2] The main uses of traditional biomass fuels are cooking, lighting, running of appliances, and in some cases space heating (IEA, 2006). Without access to clean and efficient ('modern') energy supply, such as liquid fuels, electricity and modern biomass, it is very difficult for people in DCs to engage effectively in productive activities and to improve the standard of living. In the absence of new policies, the International Energy Agency estimates that in 2030 some 2.7 billion people (or one-third of the world's population) will still rely on traditional use of biomass for cooking and heating – an enormous burden for the environment and impediment for social and economic development (IEA, 2002).

While energy is an essential input for economic growth and development, it can cause severe environmental problems. For DCs, development means satisfying basic human needs, such as jobs, food, health services, education, housing, and sewage treatment (Goldemberg, 1995). Lack of such services to satisfy basic human needs creates political unrest and despair, emigration and so on, and political leaders are judged by whether

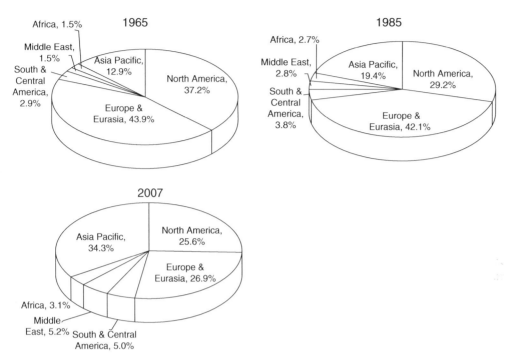

Notes: Primary energy (measured here in Mtoe) comprises commercially traded fuels only. In other words, fuels such as wood, peat and animal waste which, though important in many countries (especially DCs), are unreliably documented in terms of consumption statistics. Also excluded are: wind, geothermal and solar power generation.

Source: BP (www.bp.com/statisticalreview), author's illustration.

Figure 31.1   Total primary energy consumption shares by world region, 1965, 1985 and 2007

they are successful in promoting economic growth. Moreover, transitions in DCs are different from those in developed countries. Multiple fuel strategies are one feature; that is, the simultaneous use of different energy sources (Marcotullio and Schulz, 2007). Another feature is that energy consumption in DCs typically grows much faster than in developed countries (IEA, 1992, 2007b), despite the fact that DCs are more efficient in terms of economic growth. In other words, total energy consumption relative to GDP increase is lower than for developed countries.

World total primary energy consumption (TPEC) is rising fast, from a total of 3826.6 million tonnes of oil equivalent (mtoe) in 1965 to 7165.5 mtoe in 1985 and 11 099.3 mtoe in 2007, and shares of world regions with predominantly DCs increase as well (Figure 31.1). For a detailed analysis of earlier world energy consumption patterns, covering the 1950–92 period, see Goldstein et al. (1997).

Fossil fuels are to an increasing extent also needed by DCs. Therefore, distribution of energy supplies is increasingly a global problem, especially in the case of supply shortages or the need for rationing.

Climate change is another severe issue. Excessive CO_2 emissions, which have almost doubled over the last 25 years, are a consequence of the world's insatiable demand for fossil fuels, and DCs are catching up fast. Consequently, the relative contribution of Organisation for Economic Co-operation and Development (OECD) and non-OECD countries to global greenhouse gas (GHG) emissions has changed dramatically. Whereas in 1973 the OECD accounted for some 65.9 per cent of all CO_2 emission arising from fuel combustion, this share dropped to 47.6 per cent in 2005 (IEA, 2007a; see Figure 31.2).

Per capita consumption of commercial energy is a popular indicator of development in the literature, although it should not be forgotten that non-commercial energy in DCs often makes up an additional 50 per cent of total energy consumption. Another very popular indicator among energy and energy policy analysts is energy intensity, commonly measured as energy consumption per unit of GDP. Typically it rises in DCs and decreases in industrial countries. Reasons for the increase in DCs include industrialisation, urbanisation, transport services, infrastructure development, and lifestyle changes.

There is much research on the relationship and especially the causality between energy consumption and economic growth in the energy economics literature on DCs. If unidirectional causality is found to run from energy consumption to economic growth, then energy conservation or energy efficiency measures could actually hamper economic growth. Conversely, if causality runs from economic growth to energy consumption, then energy-saving policy measures may be implemented with little or no negative impact on economic growth. Unfortunately, empirical evidence gained so far is ambiguous, and thus does not permit any clear policy recommendations. Generally, a GDP increase can influence energy consumption in two different ways. First, private households could spend the additional income earned on energy-intensive activities. Second, economic growth could expand production, and energy is an important input factor especially for

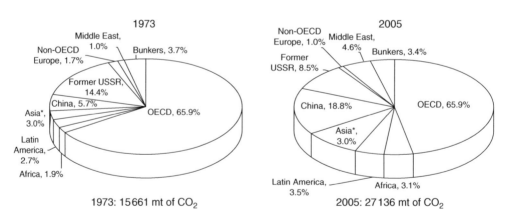

Notes: Total figures include international aviation and international marine bunkers, which are shown together in the pie charts as 'Bunkers'. CO_2 figures calculated by using IEA's Energy Balance Tables and the Revised 1996 IPCC Guidelines. CO_2 emissions are from fuel combustion only. 'Asia' excludes China.

Source: IEA (2007a).

Figure 31.2   Shares of CO_2 emissions in OECD versus non-OECD regions, 1973 and 2005

DCs. Energy inputs are especially important for energy-exporting countries, as they also use energy intensively in the extraction and production of energy. Net energy exporters in DCs often enjoy inexpensive energy for domestic use (artificially kept low by means of tariffs and consumer subsidies), resulting in waste. These inefficiencies are responsible for the fact that energy consumption does not translate to GDP growth as in more-efficient economies (for a useful discussion of these issues, see Mahadevan and Asafu-Adjaye, 2007).

If DCs remain at low levels of development, this can create serious political problems, unchecked population growth, and ultimately only aggravate problems of non-sustainability. While large development projects can cause serious environmental problems, so can underdevelopment. Hence there is a need to strike a delicate balance between (long-term) economic growth and environmental problems.

Technological leapfrogging is a popular notion when discussions come to the issue of sustainable energy development. Obviously, leapfrogging is also an important issue when it comes to the use of energy technologies, especially for energy-intensive industries and countries. However, the actual relevance of leapfrogging in different sectors of the economy is not undisputed. For instance, based on evidence on three joint ventures between US and Chinese passenger car manufacturers, Gallagher (2006) argues that at least for the Chinese automobile industry, little energy leapfrogging occurred until the late 1990s. For an inspiring, more general discussion on leapfrogging, see Dao (2006).

Given the enormous capital requirements for the energy infrastructure needed in DCs, financing issues are very important as well. Often public finances are in vain, so much of the investment has to be funded by the private sector. This requires that basic principles of good governance also be applied in the energy sector.

Based upon the important thematic issues raised, the literature on the economics of energy and policy aspects in DCs has been grouped into eight different thematic blocks: (1) technology transfer and diffusion aspects; (2) energy intensity and energy–GDP causality studies; (3) energy market transitions and energy market reforms; (4) energy and the environmental impact of structural change; (5) oil price development; (6) energy planning, societal and economic development aspects; (7) investment and financing aspects; and (8) energy modelling issues related to DCs. Any such breakdown must of course be arbitrary, and implies considerable overlaps, especially if the published work is broader in scope. Nonetheless, with this survey we hope to somewhat facilitate the access to a literature that is extensive and often crosses disciplinary boundaries. Also, apart from emphasising studies that primarily (but not necessarily exclusively) focus on economic aspects and analysis, we deliberately included policy studies, as these account for a significant part of the rapidly growing literature dealing with energy use in DCs. A useful and quite comprehensive reference book with many case studies, in which a multidisciplinary approach is adopted to accommodate the many facets of sustainable development issues, is Meier and Munasinghe (2005); another useful albeit somewhat dated reference on energy planning issues in DCs is Baum (1984).

2 Technological Transfer and Market Diffusion Aspects

One dimension for studying the economics and policy aspects of energy supply and use in DCs is the technological sphere, and in particular how technologies diffuse the market and how modern technologies can effectively be transferred to DCs for fostering sustainable development.[3]

Barnett (1990), for instance, surveys and synthesises experience regarding the diffusion of energy conversion technologies in rural areas of DCs. The paper draws on a set of papers compiled in a Special Issue of *World Development*, as well as on further literature. Specifically, Barnett discusses the shift of the focus from socio-psychological concerns in the early years of technology transfer and development aid, to concerns about the nature of the technology itself, the political economy of the users and producers, and (co-)evolutionary views of the process of technical change. From the analysis, he derives some basic principles for policy makers and researchers that may help to improve the prospects for the diffusion of rural energy technology.

Cook and Surrey (1989) tackle government policy issues related to energy technologies. Specifically, they focus on how technological capability in the energy sector of DCs can be enhanced. The authors argue that technological capabilities depend largely upon experience and learning, and that learning involves cooperation within subcontracting networks, in which buyers and sellers are linked by complex contractual relationships.

Gowen (1989) studies sectoral differences between the economics of fossil fuels versus biofuels in DCs with regard to production costs, economies of scale, subsidies, and other economic incentives. The author finds that competitive biofuel systems based on residues should be encouraged by national and international agencies, especially in the rural industrial sectors, whereas other biofuel systems are shown to have a limited or even negative impact, higher financial risks, and higher administrative and operational complexity than fossil-fuel systems. For the 1990s the author predicts that, even for high fossil-fuel prices, biofuels will neither replace fossil fuels significantly, nor will biofuels be displaced rapidly by fossil fuels in rural industrial or residential uses. In the author's opinion, a great potential for technological innovation exists in the rural cooking sector.

In a similar vein, Ramsay (1985), Hall et al. (1992) and Demirbas and Demirbas (2007) study the socioeconomic and technological aspects of bioenergy use in DCs. Specifically, Ramsay investigates the role of bioenergy, the resource base for future development, promising biomass cultivation and genetic engineering methods, more-efficient energy conversion technologies, and constraints on the further development of bioenergy in DCs. In contrast, Hall and his colleagues report on four different case studies (ethanol production in Brazil and Zimbabwe, community biogas in a rural village in India, and land rehabilitation for fuel and fodder in Kenya) where they have gained long-term direct experience of evaluation at the local, national and international levels, and point to the importance of social factors in energy programmes. Demirbas and Demirbas, in a recent study, argue that the local production of renewable energy can facilitate economic and social development in communities, provided that the projects are designed in an intelligent way and carefully planned with local input and cooperation. The authors warn, however, that in poor rural areas the costs of renewable energy projects are likely to absorb a significant part of participants' small incomes.

Sanstad et al. (2006), in another recent study, empirically investigate energy-related technological change for DCs. They present estimates of sectoral productivity trends and energy-augmenting technological change for several energy-intensive industries in India and South Korea (and, for comparison, the US) that can help to improve the parameterisation of integrated assessment models. The authors find substantial heterogeneity among both the industries and the countries studied, and a number of cases of declining energy efficiency. They argue for closer attention to the empirical basis for common modelling assumptions, an issue that they consider is becoming even more acute with the increasing popularity of induced or endogenous technological change models. In Roy et al. (2006), the same authors use pooled data across several DCs and the US to estimate substitution and price elasticities on a sectoral level (paper, iron and steel, and aggregate manufacturing industries).

3   Energy Intensity and Causality Relationships between Energy and GDP

Energy intensities, and specifically the causality relationship between energy consumption and GDP, has attracted considerable attention in the energy economics literature (for example, Akarka and Long, 1980; Yu and Hwang, 1984; Yu and Choi, 1985; Hwang and Gum, 1992; Masih and Masih, 1996, 1997, 1998; Cheng and Lai, 1997; Glasure and Lee, 1997; Yang, 2000; Altinay and Karagol, 2004, 2005; Oh and Lee, 2004ab; Al-Iriani, 2006; Lee and Chang, 2007). A useful overview on estimation methods used, countries and time periods covered, and causality findings, is provided in Mahadevan and Asafu-Adjaye (2007, p. 2482). Also related to energy intensities is the study of the economics of energy efficiency and energy conservation, which for DCs is still relatively rare (for discussions of the main issues, see Anandalingam, 1985; World Bank, 1993).

Three types of studies can be distinguished, those using econometric techniques; those computing simple energy/GDP ratios; and studies that compute the responsiveness of energy consumption relative to GDP (GDP elasticity of energy consumption). We select example studies covering groups of countries, rather than individual countries, to give a flavour of the variation of approaches chosen and the empirical evidence gained. Since there is mixed evidence as to whether the impact of energy consumption on economic growth is neutral or not, the issue remains controversial.

Econometric studies of causality

Kraft and Kraft (1978) is the first of numerous empirical studies conducted on the causality between energy consumption and GDP (an income proxy), and sometimes also energy consumption and employment, that have often yielded contradictory results (for a useful overview, see Soytas and Sari, 2003, and Sari and Soytas, 2007). A large part of the disparate empirical findings can be attributed to differences in the approach chosen and statistical testing procedures. Failure to account for the non-stationarity of the variables involved may lead to wrong conclusions, as Glasure and Lee (1997) have demonstrated for the causality between GDP and energy consumption in South Korea and Singapore. The authors find bidirectional causality only when using modern econometric techniques (cointegration analysis), but not when using the standard Granger test.[4]

Asafu-Adjaye (2000) econometrically investigates the causality relations between energy consumption and income for four Asian DCs (India, Indonesia, Thailand and the Philippines). Using cointegration and error-correction modelling techniques and a trivariate model (for energy, income and price), he finds evidence that in the short run, uni-directional Granger causality runs from energy consumption to income (India and Indonesia) and bi-directional Granger causality from energy consumption to income

(Thailand, the Philippines). For Thailand and the Philippines he further finds that energy, income and price are mutually causal. The findings corroborate the view that energy consumption and income are mutually non-neutral, albeit for Indonesia he finds short-run neutrality between energy consumption and income (which the author attributes to the fact that Indonesia is the only energy exporter in the sample studied). The finding of bi-variate causality has important policy implications: a high level of economic growth leads to a high level of energy demand (and vice versa). Based on these findings, the author recommends that policy makers must find ways of reducing energy demand, rather than curtailing energy use, in order not to jeopardise economic growth, and suggests an appropriate mix of energy taxes and subsidies.

Following up on earlier work (Mielnik and Goldemberg, 2000), Mielnik and Goldemberg (2002), in a simple analysis, study foreign direct investment (FDI) and the decoupling between primary energy consumption and GDP for an aggregate sample of 20 DCs. Their hypothesis is that the trend towards a common pattern of energy use between developed and developing countries can at least partly be attributed to the increase of FDI in DCs. For DCs, FDI is an important channel of access to new technologies, which also supports the expansion of domestic industries by increasing productivity via the spillover of these advanced technologies. Hence, they presume that it is a combination between more modern technology and advanced management skills that can explain the higher efficiency resulting from FDI. By simple ordinary least squares regression between energy intensity and the share of FDI on gross domestic investment (GDI) over the period from 1987 to 1998, the authors find the coefficient of determination to be 0.8692, that is, that nearly 87 per cent of the variation in energy intensity can be explained by the FDI/GDI ratio.

Soytas and Sari (2003) study the causality relationship between energy consumption and GDP for the top 10 emerging markets (excluding China due to a lack of data) and the G7 countries. They find bi-directional causality for Argentina, and causality running from GDP to energy consumption in Italy and Korea, and from energy consumption to GDP for France, Germany, Japan, and Turkey (for six out of the nine emerging markets and for three of the seven developed countries they cannot find evidence of a causal relationship). The latter causality indicates that for those four countries, energy conservation may harm economic growth in the long run. Sari and Soytas (2007) re-examine the changing relation between energy consumption and aggregate income over time for six very heterogeneous DCs (Indonesia, Iran, Malaysia, Pakistan, Singapore and Tunisia) within a production function framework. They find that in all six countries studied, energy is an important input factor of production (in terms of explaining the forecast error variance of income growth), in some countries more important than labour and/or capital. The authors conclude that neutrality of energy does not hold. Note that for this kind of analysis, in recent years, some researchers have started to utilise energy consumption data that are disaggregated by energy source (for example, Yang, 2000; Sari and Soytas, 2004), to disaggregate between economic sectors (for example, Hondroyiannis et al., 2002; Wolde-Rufael, 2004), and to focus on electricity consumption only (for example, Jumbe, 2004; Shiu and Lam, 2004; Wolde-Rufael, 2006; Yoo, 2006), but the evidence for developing and transition countries is still scarce to date.

Lee (2005) studies the co-movement and causality relationship between energy consumption and GDP in 18 DCs, using data from 1975 to 2001. He uses panel cointegration and panel-based error correction models (ECMs). The empirical results provide clear evidence for a long-term relationship when heterogeneous country effects are allowed. Long- and short-run causalities are shown to run from energy consumption to GDP, but not vice versa, indicating that energy conservation may actually harm economic growth in DCs both in the short and the long runs.

Wolde-Rufael (2005) investigates the long-run relation between energy consumption and real GDP (both measured per capita) for 19 African countries over the 1971–2001 period. Using bounds testing and a Granger causality test that is independent of the degree of integration of the time series, the author finds evidence for a long-run relationship between the two variables for eight countries, and causality for 10 countries.

Mahadevan and Asafu-Adjaye (2007) study the interrelatedness between energy consumption, economic growth and prices by means of a vector ECM both for developed and developing countries (20 in total), and state-of-the-art panel techniques to test for unit roots, cointegration, and causality. The sample equally contains both net energy-exporting and energy-importing countries.[5] The authors find empirical evidence for bi-directional causality between economic growth and energy consumption in the developed countries, both for the short and the long runs. For DCs, they find some evidence that energy consumption stimulates economic growth only in the short run. Moreover, they find evidence that the industrialised countries' response of economic growth to an increase in energy consumption is larger and the income elasticity lower (in fact less than unity) than for DCs.

Descriptive studies
Energy intensity analysis is of particular interest to policy makers, as DCs often lack the infrastructure that enables them to use energy efficiently, and rely more heavily on traditional energy sources. Consequently the process of industrialisation is often very energy intensive. However, simple extrapolation of energy–GDP ratios can be misleading, as the impact of increasing mechanisation as a consequence of development is not taken into account, thus neglecting an important factor affecting energy consumption. Econometric analysis can account for this kind of structural change.

In a note specifically focusing on the energy intensity of DCs, Goldemberg (1996) summarises the extensive study undertaken by Nilsson (1993), who has investigated 31 developed and developing countries for the period from 1950 to 1988 (using purchasing power parity (PPP) dollars for GDP and commercial and non-commercial primary energy data extracted from UN, 1988). The study finds that energy intensities of most developed countries are decreasing and that energy intensities of DCs are in general smaller than in developed countries (and increasing). Sun (2003), in a follow-up study to Sun (2002) for 11 DCs, points out the scope for additional insights that can be gained from different interpretations of the concept of total primary energy consumption, and suggests that there are three types of energy intensity declines, one of which is related to the restricted utilisation of renewables and wastes for combustion.

GDP elasticity of energy consumption and capital intensity studies
Zilberfarb and Adams (1981) first investigated the GDP elasticity of energy consumption in DCs by using a demand approach to study the impact of changes in personal income and energy prices on energy demand. Gross elasticity of energy consumption

with respect to GDP was found to be greater than unity, implying that energy consumption must rise faster than GDP to enable future economic growth, and that a reduction in energy demand due to energy price increases would seriously hamper output.

Using the same countries and time span covered as Zilberfarb and Adams, Desai (1986) uses a production function approach, explaining energy consumption in terms of economic activity, capital intensity, and the structure of the economy. On a per capita basis, the elasticity of energy consumption with respect to GDP found is less than unity, suggesting that earlier estimates were biased. Moreover, the inclusion of either an agriculture dummy (to account for a dominance of the labour force employed in agriculture) or an energy-export dummy (to account for a surplus in foreign trade of energy) reduces the elasticity by about 0.10, while inclusion of a region dummy reduces the elasticity of energy consumption with respect to GDP by 0.19.

4   Energy Market Transitions and Market Reforms

Research on energy market transitions in DCs deals with a diversity of topics, including electricity market reform, supply-side energy policies for oil-importing DCs, energy pricing issues, transport energy consumption, the assessment of investment projects that help to lower vulnerability and dependence of DCs with respect to oil imports, and rural energy policies.

An increasing number of developing and transition countries are set to reform their electric power markets. Besant-Jones (2006) reports on the lessons learned so far. DeLucia and Lesser (1985) address the issue of energy pricing policies, which have multiple and often conflicting objectives, including economic efficiency, government revenues, maintenance or improvement of income distribution, promotion of specific sectors, demand management, and security of supply.

Geltner (1985) finds some evidence that transport energy consumption in DCs is influenced by information and training programmes; subsidies; pricing and taxing; and administrative regulation. While the marked energy price changes between the mid-1970s and the mid-1980s did not have any major impact on the transport sector, there is still scope to improve energy efficiency.

Cost–benefit analysis (CBA) is a popular means of assessing energy projects in oil-importing DCs. Anand and Nalebuff (1987) deal with the theoretical uncertainty issues associated with CBA, exhaustibility, externalities from exploration and the options for oil-importing DCs to reduce their vulnerability and dependence on imported oil.

Market-oriented approaches suited for making the energy markets both accessible and attractive to local investors, communities, and consumers alike should be the instruments of choice for the governments of DCs. Preferred policies aim at fostering such enabling conditions, such as secure land tenure, the absence of gross inequalities in land holding, and agricultural research and extension, which allow for broad-based income growth in both rural and urban areas (Barnes and Floor, 1996).

There is a strong link between electrification and the uptake of modern cooking fuels (Heltberg, 2004). Marcotullio and Schulz (2007) find that DCs experience energy-related transitions at lower levels of income, with faster change in conditions over time, and in a more simultaneous fashion than the US. Also, over similar income ranges, current DCs use less energy per capita than the US historically did and the more-efficient economic growth of DCs translates into lower systemic environmental impact per capita than that of the US.

5 Energy and the Environmental Impact of Structural Change

Structural change in the economies of DCs will likely play an important role in the driving forces of global CO_2 emissions in the next century. CO_2 intensity transitions are of concern in both developed and transitional economies. Lindmark (2004) shows that a majority of high-income countries have experienced environmental Kuznets curves with respect to CO_2 intensity, while such patterns are absent in the poorer countries. Furthermore, the historical pattern is one of convergence with respect to CO_2 intensities. These findings are robust when including time-specific (vintage) technology.

Jung et al. (2000) assess the dynamics of structural shifts along a number of driving forces, such as the utilisation of natural domestic resources, size of land and population, population growth and composition, patterns of urbanisation, economic and industrial structures, technological diffusion, and institutional and legal mechanisms. Boyd and Ibarrarán (2002) study the impact of a carbon tax on Mexico, the fifteenth largest emitter of greenhouse gases in the world. They find that a double dividend is very unlikely (that is, benefits for the environment and revenues for the government) but that due to a progressive effect of the carbon tax on welfare levels, lower-income population groups would benefit most.

Cao (2003) finds evidence that emission reductions in DCs can be achieved only if policies are supportive and well targeted, if standards and incentives are realistic and flexible, and if the public is indeed willing to actively respond to environmental degradation. Furthermore, he finds that it is important to eliminate fossil-fuel subsidies, internalise externalities, and promote both energy efficiency and renewables.

Templet (1999) studies two distinct development strategies, one which promotes energy use and one which emphasises diversity, arguing that DCs generally rely more on increasing energy use to increase output, while developed countries tend to diversify as a means of increasing economic output. In the empirical analysis for 64 countries, economic diversity is measured by the Shannon–Weaver formula (Shannon and Weaver, 1949), while the development capacity is computed by multiplying diversity with the energy throughput. Government taxing policies aimed at increasing energy prices to high energy-use sectors seem to lead to long-term improvements in public welfare and economic competitiveness in the long run, while artificially lowered energy prices are short-term strategies, jeopardising the environment and thus ultimately hampering development. Therefore governments must implement policies that minimise energy consumption and at the same time encourage diversity, to follow the best long-term sustainability strategy.

6 Oil Price Development

The oil price shocks of the 1970s affected oil-importing and -exporting DCs very differently, and triggered a plethora of articles on this subject. No doubt the increase in the oil price level and volatility experienced in 2007 will prompt a new walk of literature on the economics of oil in DCs. Oil-importing DCs are a critical segment of the global energy, economic and environmental scene. Hence developments in these countries can be expected to have a significant impact on oil prices, thus affecting *all* (both rich and poor) oil-importing countries. Dunkerley and Ramsay (1982) find that the high levels of debt necessary to finance increasing import bills threaten the stability of the international financial markets, and that if DCs are unable to afford more oil, economic growth will be hampered, thus threatening important export markets of developed countries. Hence, they argue, careful management of world financial flows and trade agreements is required along with an expansion of capital assistance, the provision of technical assistance, and scientific and technical transfer of know-how. Pindyck (1979) provides a detailed and early econometric study on the impact of energy price on real GDP, modelling the energy price elasticity of output for a range of countries within a translog function framework. Westoby (1986) addresses a methodological point about whether the openness of a DC economy or the cost share of oil in GDP is the more relevant explanatory variable.

Dick et al. (1984) assess the impact of oil price shocks on DCs to find that the short-run policy impact of maintaining real domestic absorption with a fixed exchange rate will be large external imbalances, whereas the long-run simulations indicate the size of the required expenditure reduction, expenditure switching, and wage reduction for achieving a balanced external trade and to neutralise the impact of the oil price shock on employment.

Finally, higher petroleum prices were found to have only a minor impact on DCs' total energy consumption, and oil-importing DCs experienced a substantial substitution of other fuels for petroleum (Choe, 1985).

7   Energy Planning, Societal and Economic Development

Broadly based energy planning in DCs (that is, designing and implementing strategies for energy development and management) are necessary as a means for cushioning the adverse effects of high energy price volatility on both DCs and the world economy (Baum, 1984; Foell, 1985).

There are a number of independent mechanisms by which urbanisation – one of the main phenomena of economic development (others include agricultural intensification and industrialisation) – changes energy consumption patterns. High densities in population and economic activity, such as in cities, require the substitution of modern energy for traditional forms. Jones (1991), based on an empirical study (regression analysis) for 50 DCs in 1980, finds that urbanisation is an important source of energy consumption increase that must be addressed, as the elasticity of energy consumption with respect to GDP per dollar (and roughly also per capita) turns out to be between 0.35, for modern and traditional energy, and 0.48, if only modern energy is considered. Thus, if per capita income and the degree of industrialisation are kept constant, a 10 per cent increase in the proportion of the population living in cities would increase consumption of modern energy per dollar of GDP markedly by some 4.8 per cent. Parikh and Shukla (1995) consider three types of energy use: direct conversion from one form to another; indirect energy consumption in goods production and transport activities; and direct energy consumption in final uses such as transportation to estimate national GHG emissions and the evolving profiles of energy use disaggregated by final sector and fuel type. The estimated GHG emissions correlate positively with the countries' urbanisation levels;

aggregate energy use rises with urbanisation (confirming the strong link between energy consumption and GHG emissions with development); disaggregate energy use profiles suggest that the sectoral and fuel use shifts accompanying urbanisation have a GHG-augmenting potential (arising particularly from the graving electricity and transport needs accruing from development, a reason for which they think higher living standards and higher access to amenities such as electricity and water could play a main role). The dominance of petroleum-based fuels in transportation is found to contribute to high levels of per capita energy consumption, and electricity use to strongly influence final energy demand levels for significant sectors of the economy. Economic and institutional barriers often constrain the effectiveness of both long- and short-term energy policies in DCs (Abdalla, 1994).

Pachauri (2004) studies changes of individual lifestyles of households using micro-level household survey data by investigating cross-sectional variations in total household energy requirements in India (patterns and volumes of consumption). Total household expenditure per capita has the largest (positive) impact on energy consumption per capita, while household location is somewhat less relevant. Per capita energy requirements of rural households are found to be slightly higher than those of urban households. The impacts of household, family and demographic characteristics were also found to have measurable effects on per capita energy consumption. For example, an increase in household size is found to correlate with lower per capita energy requirements, and families in a later stage of the family life cycle tend to have higher energy requirements than younger families.

Conventional top-down and bottom-up energy policy models applied to DCs need to address equity and sustainability issues (Pandey, 2002). They should also account for the existence of a large traditional energy sector, the transition of the population from traditional to modern markets, ongoing changes in the regulatory and competitive structure of energy industries, the existence of multiple social and economic barriers to capital flow and technology diffusion, the likelihood of huge energy supply investments in the next few decades, long-term uncertainty in domestic policy regimes, and the importance of decentralised planning.

Birol (2007) tackles the neglect of energy inequity and poverty in the energy economics literature, and identifies three major strategic challenges for the global energy system: the growing risk of disruptions to energy supply; the threat of environmental damage; and persistent energy poverty. Strong and coordinated governmental policy action and public support are the only means by which the goals of energy security, environmental protection and expansion of energy access to the world's poor can be reconciled. Aside from the moral aspect, it is of vital interest also for the rich developed countries to help DCs to reduce energy poverty, since important and long-term economic, political and energy security interests are affected. Increasing the welfare of poor countries may cost much less, he argues, than dealing with the instability and insecurity that poverty creates.

The use of traditional biomass has a number of harmful consequences for human health and socioeconomic development. Mostly women and children spend many hours per day gathering such fuels, which reduces the time they can devote to more productive activities, such as education and farming (Birol, 2007). It is estimated that about 1.3 million people each year die in DCs as a result of fumes from indoor biomass stoves (WHO, 2006).

Energy poverty and inequity typically has implications on the environmental and social dimension of sustainability. Kemmler and Spreng (2007) develop lead indicators for sustainable development of DCs that explicitly include poverty and equity as issues equally important to environmental issues. They show that the explanatory power of their single-dimensional energy poverty indicator is comparable to other poverty indicators, and that energy indicators can also be relevant for social (and not just for environmental) issues. In a related earlier study, Pachauri et al. (2004) investigate energy poverty in Indian households from 1983 to 2000 by means of a new two-dimensional measure of energy poverty and energy distribution.

The socioeconomic impact of the demand for cooking through increased access to energy and changes in cooking stoves in rural areas in India is studied quantitatively by Kanagawa and Nakata (2007). They find that in the absence of income generation (reflected by opportunity cost) rural households do not adopt improved wood and gas devices; with increasing opportunity cost, improved wood- and gas-fired cooking stoves will be adopted, and increased income might change patterns and amounts of energy consumption in rural households; and due to the increase in opportunity cost, the average respirable suspended particulate matter exposure is reduced to international standards.

8   Investment and Financing Aspects

Financing aspects are not sufficiently addressed in the energy economics literature. The key question is how to attract capital to DCs, and what financing models and structures to choose.

'Business-as-usual' financing methods are no longer adequate for meeting the unprecedented demands for capital to finance energy sector expansion in DCs (Dunkerley, 1995). Many DCs are opening up their power sectors to private investment, initially through independent power projects, but also by means of sector privatisation, and there is a growing need for external finance. Sectoral reorganisation, including tariff reforms, is also needed to attract the scale of resources required, especially from domestic investors.

Estimated values of cost estimates for construction and scheduling of power generation projects in DCs approved for financing by the World Bank between 1965 and 1986, and completed in 1994, were significantly biased below actual values; moreover, the large variance in the inaccuracy of estimated values precludes the use of a simple adjustment factor as a correction to the estimates (Bacon and Besant-Jones, 1998).

Lamech and Saeed (2003) report on a survey conducted among 48 international investors looking for investment opportunities in DCs with respect to what they see as factors determining success or failure of their investments in DCs. Despite a decline in private investment in DCs, international investors remain very much interested in investing in such markets, although they want to see adequate cash flows in a sector before making firm commitments. International investors are not uniformly dissatisfied with their engagement in the power sectors of DCs, and those countries with smaller systems do not seem to be disadvantaged. What apparently matters most to investors is the country's business environment and the growth potential of the sector in which they (intend to) invest. Governments should therefore ensure adequate cash flows in the sector, for example, by adequate tariff levels and collection discipline; maintain the stability and enforceability of laws and contracts, for example by fixed 'rules of the game'; improve the responsiveness to the needs and timeframes of investors, for example by better preparation of transactions before investors are invited; and minimise government interference, for example by ensuring effective operational and management control and the independence of regulatory processes from government interference.

Siddayao (1992) discusses the energy investment issues relevant to DCs, particularly policy and institutional issues, the measurement of (social) costs and benefits, and the role of opportunity costs in the context of a country's energy investment strategies (energy planning).

The mix of public versus private ownership and the way risk–return is apportioned so to attract private power projects is studied in Bond and Carter (1995). The IAEA (1993) outlines the difficulties in attracting financing for nuclear power projects in DCs in particular, and discusses costs and economic feasibility as well as alternative approaches for mobilising capital for power plant projects in DCs.

In India the liberalised power market is open for privatisation. The Dabhol power project, developed by Enron and financed on a common limited recourse basis, is a good example for problems in developing and financing independent power projects in India. The main barriers are: high country/political risk, an unstable economic/fiscal environment, a highly bureaucratic system, poor credibility of power purchasers, fuel suppliers and power transmitters (state-owned monopolies), and immature capital markets (especially long-term debt markets). Gupta and Sravat (1998) recommend the development of clear and prudent policies regarding the investment in private power projects; to improve the credibility and financial viability of the State electricity boards as the sole power purchasers; enable competitive bidding with greater transparency; to better structure and improve the macroeconomic and fiscal environment (interest rate, inflation, currency exchange rate); to develop and implement credit enhancement mechanisms until the necessary sectoral reforms are in place; to develop capital markets in order to sustain privatisation and provide incentives for statutory funds to invest in private power projects; to streamline the bureaucratic process and regulatory regime in order to achieve fast clearance for the projects, preferably by a 'single window clearance'; and to implement the legally enforceable and fair commercial contracts between fuel suppliers and transmitters. Financial institutions also have to play a vital supportive role in developing capital markets, fulfilling the need for underwriting various loans and securitisation of the debts, in order to attract the necessary funds for the projects. Participation of multilateral financial institutions by way of equity capital would enhance investors' confidence and the success of project financing.

There may be good chances to innovate in the financing of agricultural electrification projects in DCs (Rodríguez and San Segundo, 2007). New sources of financing could be mobilised, and financial mechanisms be adapted to the special characteristics of decentralised energy production systems that also include renewable energy technologies, which are often very capital intensive.

There has been a substantial reduction in overseas development assistance (ODA) flows since 1990, despite the fact that total ODA flows have generally been increasing (Tharakan et al., 2007). In expectation of large amounts of private capital inflows, reductions in ODA and other forms of assistance have exacerbated the negative impacts of falling private investment in energy projects in DCs. Hence total aid flows to DCs should be increased; aid should be linked to performance and used to create a favourable enabling environment, to develop innovative solutions, and to provide implementation support.

9   Energy Models for DCs

Energy models should to be designed specifically to meet the needs and characteristics of DCs. Meier and Mubayi (1983) describe the so-called Brookhaven Energy Economic Assessment Model (BEEAM), developed at Brookhaven National Laboratory for energy assessments in DCs. It is designed to avoid many problems and pitfalls related to models developed for industrialised countries that are inappropriately adapted to the specific circumstances and data limitations of DCs.

The consequences of (actual or anticipated) energy shortages in both developed and developing countries is modelled by Park and Kubursi (1983). Oil price rises often lead to energy shortages that are compounded by a shortage of foreign exchange caused by escalated import bills. The modelling approach introduces an unconstrained dynamic multi-sector input–output (I–O) model (market equilibrium approach) that allows testing for multi-sectoral and inter-temporal energy balances associated with given development plans and alternative hypotheses concerning energy coefficients and technologies. It also employs a constrained dynamic I–O model, that is, a dynamic I–O system that is integrated into a linear programming framework, for investigating the optimal inter-temporal development policy in response to anticipated changes in the energy situation, thus allowing for a selection of necessary changes in technologies and commodities consistent with the objectives and constraints of the particular economy studied.

Urban et al. (2007) analyse 12 different energy models with regard to their suitability for DCs, scrutinising whether the main characteristics of DCs are adequately incorporated. They find that many models are biased towards the developed countries, and ought to be made better suited for DCs, in that they neglect important characteristics of DCs – such as the informal economy, supply shortages, electrification, poor performance of the power sector, structural economic change, the role of traditional biomass fuels, and the urban–rural divide.

10   Conclusions

In this survey we have highlighted some of the major themes and strands of research on the economics of energy supply and use in DCs. Considerable attention in the literature has been dedicated to the study of the relationship between energy consumption and economic growth (with contradictory evidence); the impact of rapid fossil-fuel price rises on development; and interfuel substitution (for example, of fossil fuels for biofuels and vice versa, solar energy and modern biofuels for traditional biofuels).

The rise in crude oil prices experienced over the last few years, and improved data availability, are likely to increase the research activity on the impact of energy price rises on sustainable development of DCs (that is, the impact on the environment, society, and the economy), and appropriate remedies. Issues of equity and energy poverty should also be addressed. Continuation of the Kyoto process and recent price developments will foster the debate on energy issues in DCs, and hopefully also research efforts by energy economists.

Notes

* Fruitful comments received from Shonali Pachauri and research assistance by Nina Bednarz, André Bertolace and Oliver Dick are gratefully acknowledged by the author.
1. The term 'developing countries' is used throughout this chapter as a convenient expression for a loosely defined and very heterogeneous set of countries in the phase of economic development, with a relatively low standard of living, an undeveloped industrial base, and a moderate to low Human Development Index (HDI) score and per capita income (the HDI, developed by Indian Nobel prize winner Amartya Sen and associates in 1990, is a normalised measure of life expectancy, literacy, education, living standard, and GDP per capita for countries worldwide, and can be used to classify countries into developed, developing, or underdeveloped countries). It should be noted that some of these countries actually have higher income per capita or energy consumption per capita than some OECD countries (for example, Singapore, South Korea, Taiwan), and that some of them have in the meantime become members of the OECD (for example, Mexico).
2. The IEA estimates that while two billion people are expected to gain access to electricity until 2030, a large part will be offset by the rising world population, so that barely 200 million people less than today will have gained access to electricity (IEA, 2007b).
3. A comprehensive treatment of methodological and technological issues related to leapfrogging and technology transfer to DCs technological change is provided in IPCC (2000).
4. See Granger (1969); an alternative bivariate causality test has been proposed by Sims (1972).
5. The countries included in the sample can be clustered in four groups: (1) Australia, Norway and the UK as net energy-exporting developed countries; (2) Argentina, Indonesia, Kuwait, Malaysia, Nigeria, Saudi Arabia and Venezuela as energy-exporting DCs; (3) Japan, Sweden and the US as net energy-importing developed countries; and (4) Ghana, India, Senegal, South Africa, South Korea, Singapore and Thailand as net energy-importing DCs.

References

Abdalla, K.L. (1994), 'Energy policies for sustainable development in developing countries', *Energy Policy*, **22**(1), 29–36.

Akarka, A.T. and Long, T.V. (1980), 'On the relationship between energy and GNP: a re-examination', *Journal of Energy and Development*, **5**, 326–31.

Al-Iriani, M.A. (2006), 'Energy–GDP relationship revisited: an example from GCC countries using panel causality', *Energy Policy*, **34**(17), 3342–50.

Altinay, G. and Karagol, E. (2004), 'Structural break, unit root, and the causality between energy consumption and GDP in Turkey', *Energy Economics*, **26**(6), 985–94.

Altinay, G. and Karagol, E. (2005), 'Electricity consumption and economic growth: evidence from Turkey', *Energy Economics*, **27**(6), 849–56.

Anand, S. and Nalebuff, B. (1987), 'Issues in the application of cost–benefit analysis to energy projects in developing countries', *Oxford Economic Papers*, **39**(1), 190–222.

Anandalingam, G. (1985), 'Energy conservation in the industrial sector of developing countries', *Energy Policy*, **13**(4), 335–9.

Asafu-Adjaye, J. (2000), 'The relationship between energy consumption, energy prices and economic growth: time series evidence from Asian developing countries', *Energy Economics*, **22**(6), 615–25.

Auer, P. (ed.) (1981), *Energy and the Developing Nations*, Pergamon Press, New York.

Bacon, R.W. and Besant-Jones, J.E. (1998), 'Estimating construction costs and schedules: experience with power generation projects in developing countries', *Energy Policy*, **26**(4), 317–33.

Barnes, D.F. and Floor, W.M. (1996), 'Rural energy in developing countries: a challenge for economic development', *Annual Review of Energy and the Environment*, **21**, 497–530.

Barnett, A. (1990), 'The diffusion of energy technology in the rural areas of developing countries: a synthesis of recent experience', *World Development*, **18**(4), 539–53.

Baum, V. (1984), *Energy Planning in Developing Countries*, Oxford University Press (in cooperation with the United Nations), Oxford/New York.

Besant-Jones, J.E. (2006), 'Reforming power markets in developing countries: what have we learned?', Energy and Mining Sector Board Discussion Paper No. 19, World Bank, Washington, DC, September.

Birol, F. (2007), 'Energy economics: a place for energy poverty in the agenda?', *The Energy Journal*, **28**(3), 1–6.

Bond, G. and Carter, L. (1995), 'Financing energy projects: experience of the International Finance Corporation', *Energy Policy*, **23**(11), 967–75.

Boyd, R. and Ibarrarán, M.E. (2002), 'Costs of compliance with the Kyoto Protocol: a developing country perspective', *Energy Economics*, **24**(1), 21–39.

Cao, X. (2003), 'Climate change and energy development: implications for developing countries', *Resources Policy*, **29**(1–2), 61–7.

Cheng, B.S. and Lai, T.W. (1997), 'An investigation of co-integration and causality between energy consumption and economic activity in Taiwan', *Energy Economics*, **19**(4), 435–44.

Choe, B.-J. (1985), 'World energy markets and the developing countries', *Energy Policy*, **13**(4), 304–9.

Cook, P.L. and Surrey, J. (1989), 'Energy technology in developing countries: the scope for government policy', *Technovation*, **9**(5), 431–51.

Dao, F. (2006), 'The leapfrog factor: it's a mistake for Third World nations to strive to become exactly like their First World rivals. There is a better way', *Across the Board*, **43**(3), 31–3.

DeLucia, R.J. and Lesser, M.C. (1985), 'Energy pricing policies in developing countries', *Energy Policy*, **13**(4), 345–9.

Demirbas, A.H. and Demirbas, I. (2007), 'Importance of rural bioenergy for developing countries', *Energy Conversion and Management*, **48**(8), 2386–98.

Desai, D. (1986), 'Energy–GDP relationship and capital intensity in LDCs', *Energy Economics*, **8**(2), 113–17.

Dick, H., Gupta, S., Vincent, D. and Voigt, H. (1984), 'The effect of oil price increases on four oil-poor developing countries: a comparative analysis', *Energy Economics*, **6**(1), 59–70.

Dunkerley, J. (1985), 'Energy in developing countries: Editor's introduction', *Energy Policy*, **13**(4), 299–300.

Dunkerley, J. (1995), 'Financing the energy sector in developing countries: context and overview', *Energy Policy*, **23**(11), 929–39.

Dunkerley, J. and Ramsay, W. (1982), 'Energy and the oil-importing developing countries', *Science*, **216**(4546), 590–95.

Foell, W.K. (1985), 'Energy planning in developing countries', *Energy Policy*, **13**(4), 350–54.

Gallagher, K.S. (2006), 'Limits to leapfrogging in energy technologies? Evidence from the Chinese automobile industry', *Energy Policy*, **34**(4), 383–93.

Geltner, D. (1985), 'Transport and energy in developing countries', *Energy Policy*, **13**(4), 340–44.

Glasure, Y.U. and Lee, A.R. (1997), 'Cointegration, error-correction, and the relationship between GDP and energy: the case of South Korea and Singapore', *Resource and Energy Economics*, **20**(1), 17–25.

Goldemberg, J. (1995), 'Energy needs in developing countries and sustainability', *Science*, **269**(5227), 1058–9.

Goldemberg, J. (1996), 'A note on the energy intensity of developing countries', *Energy Policy*, **24**(8), 759–61.

Goldstein, J.S., Huang, X. and Akan, B. (1997), 'Energy in the world economy, 1950–1992', *International Studies Quarterly*, **41**(2), 241–66.

Gowen, M.M. (1989), 'Biofuel v fossil fuel economics in developing countries. How green is the pasture?', *Energy Policy*, **17**(5), 455–70.

Granger, C.W.J. (1969), 'Investigating causal relations by econometric models and cross-spectral methods', *Econometrica*, **37**(3), 424–38.

Gupta, J.P. and Sravat, A.K. (1998), 'Development and project financing of private power projects in developing countries: a case study of India', *International Journal of Project Management*, **16**(2), 99–105.

Hall, D.O., Rosillo-Calle, F. and de Groot, P. (1992), 'Biomass energy. Lessons from case studies in developing countries', *Energy Policy*, **20**(1), 62–73.

Heltberg, R. (2004), 'Fuel switching: evidence from eight developing countries', *Energy Economics*, **26**(5), 869–87.

Hondroyiannis, G., Lolos, S. and Papapetrou, E. (2002), 'Energy consumption and economic growth: assessing the evidence from Greece', *Energy Economics*, **24**(4), 319–36.

Hwang, D.B.K. and Gum, B. (1992), 'The causal relationship between energy and GNP: the case of Taiwan', *Journal of Energy and Development*, **16**, 219–26.

Intergovernmental Panel on Climate Change (IPCC) (2000), *Methodological and Technological Issues in Technology Transfer*, A Special Report of IPCC Working Group III published for the IPCC, Cambridge University Press, Cambridge.

International Atomic Energy Agency (IAEA) (1993), *Financing Arrangements for Nuclear Power Projects in Developing Countries: A Reference Book*, Technical Report Series No. 353, IAEA, Vienna.

International Energy Agency (IEA) (1992), *Global Energy: The Changing Outlook*, IEA/OECD, Paris.

International Energy Agency (IEA) (1994), *Energy in Developing Countries. A Sectoral Analysis*, IEA/OECD, Paris.

International Energy Agency (IEA) (2002), *World Energy Outlook: Energy and Poverty*, OECD/IEA, Paris.

International Energy Agency (IEA) (2006), *World Energy Outlook 2006: Fact Sheet – Energy for Cooking in Developing Countries*, IEA/OECD, Paris.

International Energy Agency (IEA) (2007a), *Key World Energy Statistics 2007*, IEA/OECD, Paris.

International Energy Agency (IEA) (2007b), *World Energy Outlook 2007*, IEA/OECD, Paris.

Jones, D.W. (1991), 'How urbanization affects energy-use in developing countries', *Energy Policy*, **19**(7), 621–30.

Jumbe, C.B.L. (2004), 'Cointegration and causality between electricity consumption and GDP: empirical evidence from Malawi', *Energy Economics*, **26**(1), 61–8.

Jung, T.Y., La Rovere, E.L., Gaj, H., Shukla, P.R. and Zhou, D. (2000), 'Structural changes in developing countries and their implication for energy-related CO_2 emissions', *Technological Forecasting and Social Change*, **63**(2–3), 111–36.

Kanagawa, M. and Nakata, T. (2007), 'Analysis of the energy access improvement and its socioeconomic impacts in rural areas of developing countries', *Ecological Economics*, **62**(2), 319–29.

Kemmler, A. and Spreng, D. (2007), 'Energy indicators for tracking sustainability in developing countries', *Energy Policy*, **35**(4), 2466–80.

Kraft, J. and Kraft, A. (1978), 'On the relationship between energy and GNP', *Journal of Energy and Development*, **3**, 401–3.

Lamech, R. and Saeed, K. (2003), 'What international investors look for when investing in developing countries', Energy and Mining Sector Board Discussion Paper No. 6, World Bank, Washington, DC, May.

Lee, C.-C. (2005), 'Energy consumption and GDP in developing countries: a cointegrated panel analysis', *Energy Economics*, **27**(3), 415–27.

Lee, C.-C. and Chang, C.-P. (2007), 'Energy consumption and GDP revisited: a panel analysis of developed and developing countries', *Energy Economics*, **29**(6), 1206–23.

Lindmark, M. (2004), 'Patterns of historical CO_2 intensity transitions among high- and low-income countries', *Explorations in Economic History*, **46**(4), 426–47.

Mahadevan, R. and Asafu-Adjaye, J. (2007), 'Energy consumption, economic growth and prices: a reassessment using panel VECM for developed and developing countries', *Energy Policy*, **35**(4), 2481–90.

Marcotullio, P.J. and Schulz, N.B. (2007), 'Comparison of energy transitions in the United States and developing and industrializing economies', *World Development*, **35**(10), 1650–83.

Masih, A.M.M. and Masih, R. (1996), 'Energy consumption, real income and temporal causality: results from a multi-country study based on cointegration and error-correction modelling techniques', *Energy Economics*, **18**(13), 165–83.

Masih, A.M.M. and Masih, R. (1997), 'On the temporal causal relationship between energy consumption, real income, and prices: some new evidence from Asian-energy dependent NICs based on a multivariate cointegration/vector error-correction approach', *Journal of Policy Modeling*, **19**(4), 417–40.

Masih, A.M.M. and Masih, R. (1998), 'A multivariate cointegrated modeling approach in testing temporal causality between energy consumption, real income and prices with an application to two Asian LDCs', *Applied Economics*, **30**(10), 1287–98.

Meier, P. and Mubayi, V. (1983), 'Modelling energy–economic interactions in developing countries: a linear programming approach', *European Journal of Operational Research*, **13**(1), 41–59.

Meier, P. and Munasinghe, M. (2005), *Sustainable Energy in Developing Countries. Policy Analysis and Case Studies*, Edward Elgar, Cheltenham, UK and Northampton, MA, USA.

Mielnik, O. and Goldemberg, J. (2000), 'Converging to a common pattern of energy use in developing and industrialised countries', *Energy Policy*, **28**(8), 503–8.

Mielnik, O. and Goldemberg, J. (2002), 'Foreign direct investment and decoupling between energy and gross domestic product in developing countries', *Energy Policy*, **30**(2), 87–9.

Nilsson, L. (1993), 'Energy intensity in 31 industrial and developed countries 1950–88', *Energy*, **18**(4), 309–22.

Oh, W. and Lee, K. (2004a), 'Causal relationship between energy consumption and GDP revisited: the case of Korea 1970–1999', *Energy Economics*, **26**(1), 51–9.

Oh, W. and Lee, K. (2004b), 'Energy consumption and economic growth in Korea: testing the causality relation', *Journal of Policy Modeling*, **26**(8–9), 973–81.

Pachauri, R.K. and Pachauri, R. (1985), 'Energy problems and policies in developing countries', *Energy Policy*, **13**(4), 301–3.

Pachauri, S. (2004), 'An analysis of cross-sectional variations in total household energy requirements in India using micro survey data', *Energy Policy*, **32**(15), 1723–35.

Pachauri, S., Mueller, A., Kemmler, A. and Spreng, D. (2004), 'On measuring energy poverty in Indian households', *World Development*, **32**(12), 2083–104.

Pandey, R. (2002), 'Energy policy modelling: agenda for developing countries', *Energy Policy*, **30**(2), 97–106.

Parikh, J. and Shukla, V. (1995), 'Urbanization, energy use and greenhouse effects in economic development. Results from a cross-national study of developing countries', *Global Environmental Change*, **5**(2), 87–103.

Park, S.-H. and Kubursi, A.A. (1983), 'The energy constraint and development. Consistency and optimality over time', *Energy Economics*, **5**(1), 9–15.

Pindyck, R.S. (1979), *Structure of World Energy Demand*, MIT Press, Cambridge, MA and London.

Ramsay, W. (1985), 'Biomass energy in developing countries', *Energy Policy*, **13**(4), 326–9.

Rodríguez Monroy, C. and San Segundo Hernández, A. (2007), 'Strengthening financial innovation in energy supply projects for rural exploitations in developing countries', *Renewable and Sustainable Energy Reviews* (in print, online available since 22 May 2007).

Roy, J., Sanstad, A.H., Sathaye, J.A. and Khaddaria, R. (2006), 'Substitution and price elasticity estimates using inter-country pooled data in a translog cost model', *Energy Economics*, **28**(5–6), 706–19.

Sanstad, A.H., Roy, J. and Sathaye, J.A. (2006), 'Estimating energy-augmenting technological change in developing country industries', *Energy Economics*, **28**(5–6), 720–29.

Sari, R. and Soytas, U. (2004), 'Disaggregate energy consumption, employment, and income in Turkey', *Energy Economics*, **26**(3), 335–44.

Sari, R. and Soytas, U. (2007), 'The growth of income and energy consumption in six developing countries', *Energy Policy*, **35**(2), 889–98.

Shannon, C.E. and Weaver, W. (1949), *The Mathematical Theory of Communication*, University of Illinois Press, Urbana, IL.

Shiu, A. and Lam, P.L. (2004), 'Electricity consumption and economic growth in China', *Energy Policy*, **32**(1), 47–54.

Siddayao, C.M. (1992), 'Energy investments and environmental implications. Key policy issues in developing countries', *Energy Policy*, **20**(3), 223–32.

Sims, C.A. (1972), 'Money, income, and causality', *American Economic Review*, **62**(4), 540–52.

Soytas, U. and Sari, R. (2003), 'Energy consumption and GDP: causality relationship in G-7 countries and emerging markets', *Energy Economics*, **25**(1), 33–7.

Sun, J.W. (2002), 'The natural and social property of CO_2 emission intensity', *Energy Policy*, **31**(3), 203–9.

Sun, J.W. (2003), 'Three types of decline in energy intensity – an explanation for the decline of energy intensity in some developing countries', *Energy Policy*, **31**(6), 519–26.

Templet, P.H. (1999), 'Energy, diversity and development in economic systems; an empirical analysis', *Ecological Economics*, **30**(2), 223–33.

Tharakan, P.J., de Castro, J. and Kroeger, T. (2007), 'Energy sector assistance in developing countries: current trends and policy recommendations', *Energy Policy*, **35**(1), 734–8.

United Nations (UN) (1988), *Energy Statistics Yearbook 1986*, United Nations Statistics Office, New York.

Urban, F., Benders, R.M.J. and Moll, H.C. (2007), 'Modelling energy systems for developing countries', *Energy Policy*, **35**(6), 3473–82.

Westoby, R. (1986), 'Effect of oil price incrases on developing countries – a comment', *Energy Economics*, **8**(1), 46–7.

Wolde-Rufael, Y. (2004), 'Disaggregated industrial energy consumption and GDP: the case of Shanghai, 1952–1999', *Energy Economics*, **26**(1), 69–75.

Wolde-Rufael, Y. (2005), 'Energy demand and economic growth: the African experience', *Journal of Policy Modeling*, **27**(8), 891–903.

Wolde-Rufael, Y. (2006), 'Electricity consumption and economic growth: a time series experience for 17 African countries', *Energy Policy*, **34**(10), 1106–14.

World Bank (1993), 'Energy efficiency and conservation in the developing world: the World Bank's role', World Bank policy paper, World Bank, Washington, DC.

World Health Organization (WHO) (2006), *Fuel for Life*, World Health Organization, Geneva.

Yang, H.Y. (2000), 'A note on the causal relationship between energy and GDP in Taiwan', *Energy Economics*, **22**(3), 309–17.

Yoo, S.-H. (2006), 'The causal relationship between electricity consumption and economic growth in the ASEAN countries', *Energy Policy*, **34**(18), 3573–82.

Yu, E.S.H. and Choi, J.Y. (1985), 'The causal relationship between energy and GNP: an international comparison', *Journal of Energy and Development*, **10**, 249–72.

Yu, E.S.H. and Hwang, B.-K. (1984), 'The relationship between energy and GNP: further results', *Energy Economics*, **6**(3), 186–90.

Zilberfarb, B. and Adams, F.G. (1981), 'The energy–GDP relationship in developing countries', *Energy Economics*, **3**(4), 244–8.

32 Energy visions to address energy security and climate change
Christoph W. Frei

1 Introduction

Energy policy varies along national boundaries reflecting energy use and social concern. Technological innovation in energy is therefore often linked to social innovation and consequently energy policy is a form of social action. Different stakeholders have specific interests and visions to contribute to the debate about the path ahead. There are many approaches to energy policy formation. When defining strategies to achieve a climate-friendly energy future, *the ideal types* concept described by Weber (1947, 1949) is informative and therefore used as the basis for this analysis. As a social action, energy policy needs to be understood at the level of individual behaviors and underlying motivations. Weber classified social behaviors according to four 'ideal types': the individual acts in accordance with a rational goal; by conviction (faith, ideology, ethical values); guided by a great emotion or passion; or by custom or habit. Weber used ideal types as a tool in the context of political science to identify types of government, depending on their type of legitimacy (charismatic authority, traditional authority, rational and legal authority).

The *ideal types* concept helps the understanding and interpretation of social behavior of individuals participating in a given social action. To advance our comprehension of the feasibility of energy policies and formulate meaningful strategies, arguably a thorough understanding of the different interest groups' vision ideal types is important. Vision ideal types may be used to test the robustness of energy policies. Before setting out different energy vision ideal types, the two issues that determine the viability of any energy vision, energy security and climate change, are briefly discussed.

2 Energy Security

Energy policy needs to be concerned with security of revenues and security of supply. The former is the main concern of hydrocarbon-producing countries, while the latter worries energy-consuming countries during times of high prices and high price volatility. While one led to the foundation of the Organization of the Petroleum Exporting Countries (OPEC), the other was the motivation for the creation of the International Energy Agency (IEA). OPEC and the IEA were founded to address concerns that mattered at a specific moment in time. Likewise, their respective missions reflect perspectives regarding energy security that preceded their creation. Missions for OPEC and the IEA were specified when they were established in 1960 and 1973–74, respectively. Changes over time related to supply, demand, geopolitics, and market structure call for energy policy changes to ensure energy security.

759

There is increasing concentration on the supply side. Since 1970, many of the non-Middle Eastern oilfields have matured. In 1970, roughly half of the oil reserves were located in the Middle East, while in 2006 it was more than two-thirds. The maturity of many of the oldest oilfields implies that the supply of easily accessible conventional oil is dwindling and in conjunction with the changing climate, will impact on the way in which the energy crisis is addressed. The emergence of natural gas after the 1970s led to further concentration. Today, gas resources are concentrated in three countries: Russia, Iran and Qatar. In addition, Russia, the one new key player on the supply side, increasingly influences OPEC and plays a powerful role in the gas market.

The demand side is mainly characterized by new key players, China and India, neither of whom can, under current rules, be a member of the IEA as the agency can only have members that are also members of the OECD. Overall, demand has grown steadily while the energy density has fallen: in 2005, it took four times less oil to produce one unit of world GDP than it did in 1970. Meanwhile total demand has increased by 50 percent. Natural gas demand even grew by over 150 percent during that same period, leaving behind its role as a stepchild of the energy family. Today it is hard to believe that it was a shock for Qatar when it discovered natural gas instead of the expected oil in the 1980s.

Energy markets have seen waves of liberalization and globalization since the 1970s. As a consequence, they have become more intertwined while comfortable reserve margins have dried out. Critical infrastructure – pipelines, refineries, transmission and distribution grids, nuclear power plants – is aging. Oil prices in particular and energy prices in general have reached their highest levels since the oil shocks, further aggravated by painful levels of volatility. Such uncertainties and high prices have rekindled economic nationalism and protectionism. A large number of examples in countries including Venezuela, Bolivia, Russia, as well as Europe and the US, provide the evidence.

Energy producing countries react with (re-)nationalization efforts and closer state control of strategic oil and gas sectors.[1] The tight markets strengthen the negotiation position of state-owned companies in resource-rich countries and lead to a shift of market power from the international oil companies, traditionally built on strong project management skills and technological know-how, to the national oil companies. Consuming countries, meanwhile, usually start to protect their domestic energy utilities when they become concerned about their energy security. This has been particularly visible in the US and in Europe.[2] Counter strategies to swap assets and build joint ventures are rare and seem more likely in the new and more dynamic world than in industrialized countries.[3] This drift away from efficient and competitive markets is accentuated by mergers, which further concentrate power in the hands of a few giant companies. We can summarize these trends as 'system stretch', accompanied by emerging strong and powerful market actors.

3 Climate Change

Arguably, there is little doubt that human-made climate change deserves our full attention. There are non-conventional hydrocarbons and coal that, with coal to liquid technology, could replace a decline in oil production; however, we must consider our greenhouse gas mitigation in our energy future.

As energy security and a healthy climate are both global public goods, there is opportunity for windfalls and free riding. The global society benefits from these public goods, but markets need a suitable regulatory and energy policy framework, including both social and economic considerations. Economic theory suggests that the state intervenes to provide public goods, including the mitigation of large collective risks, whenever there are potential impacts on social welfare. Therefore a global coordinated framework to deliver these public goods should be considered.

In 2009, there were still too few incentives to invest in a global low-carbon infrastructure and energy security still outranks climate change on most national policy agendas. The political weight of an issue is vastly different whether the issue is environment, economics, or security. Overall key issues on national energy policy agendas are access to energy, supply security, energy costs, environmental issues and social acceptance. These are not subject to trade-off, but to a hierarchy that requires satisfying lower-order needs before addressing the higher-order ones. Figure 32.1 illustrates that energy policy priorities can be stratified similarly to the way Maslow (1954) structured his pyramid of human needs. The pyramid is a schematic representation of policy priorities. As such, this structure has no normative value, but history tells us that going against it may lead to policies beyond political feasibility, as discussed by Frei (2004).

The pyramid tells us that understanding the energy security issue is crucial. Unless there is clear public understanding and agreement on an appropriate level of energy security, lobbies that feel threatened by higher-order needs will use the 'fear tactic'. They will insist that the existing level of supply security is inadequate, thereby sharpening the focus on pure supply/demand issues and sweeping higher-level issues off the agenda. This is a simple tactic and energy policy history is full of such examples. Thus, the public understanding of the critical aspects energy security is the foundation on which a robust

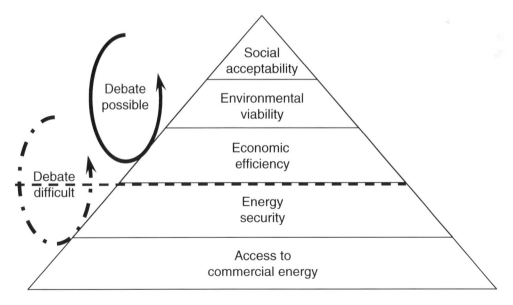

Source: Adapted from Maslow (1954).

Figure 32.1   Energy policy: Maslow pyramid

and balanced energy policy can be built. Customer contracts may be used; a utility may offer the choice between two contracts with different electricity service qualities. Service without interruption has a certain price, however, service with a one-hour interruption per month (most laptops or refrigerators can bridge such gaps) has a lower price. The customer can make an economic choice between the two contracts. Models that help to access these storage capacities systematically can help to make systems more resilient and increase consumer awareness without diminishing economic welfare.

The relative position of an issue in the pyramid may change over time. Climate change in Europe has moved from the environmental agenda (in the 1990s) to the economic agenda, where carbon markets have translated emissions into direct costs for companies since 2005. Climate change is also a security issue, potentially leading to accelerated migration or more frequent environmental disasters. The precautionary principle has led most countries to invest large amounts in armies for the hypothetical case in which they have to defend themselves against aggression. The same principle should make us invest similar amounts in preventing climate change from happening.

Business delivers the link between climate change and energy security. Utilities and technology companies will deliver or operate infrastructure that has yet to be built to secure our energy future under a degree of regulatory uncertainty. The risk premium related to this regulatory uncertainty is difficult to manage. Any change in the carbon framework will affect the profitability of long-term investments related to greenhouse gas emissions. Maintained uncertainty over the framework reduces or delays investments in energy facilities, leads to suboptimal decisions and therefore delivers a suboptimal energy infrastructure from a general welfare perspective. Reinelt and Keith (2007) suggest that regulatory uncertainty raises the social cost of abatement by almost 50 percent, while delay has an upside opportunity in potential technological innovations that deliver cheap alternatives.

Confronted with an aging infrastructure and a growing demand, business and the public need a sound energy policy. Before replacing the aging infrastructure and investing in new facilities, business needs predictability to prevent stranded investments. Competition and consistency, or at least transparency about how rules are applied across the globe, is necessary. It may be today's most pressing challenge for the global communities to agree on and implement a robust post-2012 carbon framework. Whatever decisions the G20 governments take over the next few years, it will fundamentally affect the future energy system.

Energy security and a healthy climate are both public goods therefore environmentalists should be proactive in making sure that the climate framework provides energy security effectively (see Figure 32.1). For example, clean development mechanisms need to be economically viable. Any carbon framework that fails to reconcile economics and the environment will be pushed off the political agenda with the emergence of an energy crisis; and along with it all the other social or environmental issues. This also implies that industrialized countries have to accept a larger share of the burden than rapidly growing economies such as China or India for whom energy security is more difficult to realize. Further, the global community needs to agree on incentives for these countries to use the best-available technology. Also, without revenue security for oil exporting countries, the picture is not complete either. Positive vision for a low-carbon energy future is necessary for the setting up of such a framework.

4   Energy Vision Ideal Types

The IEA estimates that US$20 trillion of investment in energy infrastructure by 2030 is necessary to deliver the world's energy needs (IEA, 2006). The observed rate of investment, however, is lower than required by the IEA's figure due to resource protectionism uncertainty. See Frei (2007) for further discussion of these issues.

The growing energy demand is mainly driven by income growth that leads to an increasing demand for mobility and electricity. An estimated 60 percent of the demand growth over the 2005–15 period will come from the transport sector (IEA, 2006). Dargay et al. (2007) project that the total vehicle stock will increase from about 800 million in 2002 to more than two billion units in 2030, and 56 percent of the world's vehicles will be owned by non-OECD countries, compared with 24 percent in 2002. In particular, China's vehicle stock will increase nearly 20-fold, to 390 million by 2030. This huge rate of vehicle ownership expansion implies rapid growth in liquid fuel demand. However, there is also significant potential for demand growth mitigation between the most- and least-efficient vehicles on the market.

Much of the US$20 trillion is required for massive long-term projects and distribution infrastructure to supply electricity and fuel mobility. Pipelines, hydro dams, and nuclear power plants are built to last for more than half a century. Hence, such investment decisions will seal our long-term energy future. An energy vision and the investment strategy that leads to it should be considered together. If we had a clear vision of our energy future in 50 to 100 years from now, we would obviously align investments to be made with this vision. Investment locks in our energy future and therefore we propose a way to differentiate complementary and contrasting energy vision ideal types. We suggest that the dimensions that fundamentally oppose different types of future electricity and mobility infrastructure expand the vision space. The key question in electricity is whether we shall produce in a centralized or decentralized pattern. The key question on the mobility side is whether we can continue to use our liquid fuel infrastructure or whether we need to replace it, for instance to distribute hydrogen. These two dimensions, 'centralized–localized' and 'liquid fuels–hydrogen economy', expand our vision space (see Figure 32.2). In the figure we sketch an ideal type for each of the quadrants of the vision space: the 'Clean Coal Society', the 'Nuclear Society', the 'Bio Society' and the 'Energy 2.0 Society'.

Energy vision type 1: the Clean Coal Society

Clean coal technologies and carbon capture and sequestration (CCS) are the pillars of the Clean Coal Society energy system. Electricity is generated by coal or coal-derivate-fired power plants. Conventional fossil fuels provide mobility, including an increasing share of liquefied coal, based on coal-to-liquid (CTL) technologies (improved process sequence of gasification and subsequent Fischer–Tropsch conversion to synthetic diesel). The infrastructure to distribute fuels and electricity is not fundamentally different from today's infrastructure. High car emission standards limit the pollution in cities, and cars are equipped with carbon capture devices. Underground geological, oceanic, biological and mineral sequestration of carbon has become proven technology with limited ecological impact.

Coal is the most abundant of all fossil resources. Yet, climate change poses a big challenge for the Clean Coal Society. A big unknown is the potential mitigation of greenhouse

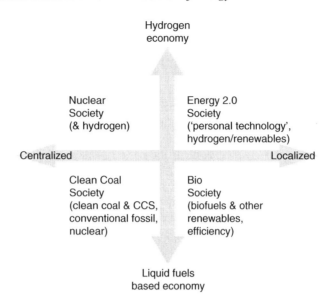

Figure 32.2   Vision space and energy vision ideal types

gas emissions through CCS. The technology for carbon capture from stationary sources such as coal-fired power plants is available and affordable – at least for industrialized countries. The role of carbon capture from mobile sources including cars will become increasingly important to make this vision climate friendly over time. This technology still has to overcome a number of logistical and technological hurdles. Pollution in the large cities is also a concern. Urban traffic fueled by fossil energy is the source for most of that pollution. Measures to reduce this source of pollution include the promotion of public transport financed by congestion charges, the development of car-sharing models, the introduction of differentiated tax models according to the engine size, the promotion of alternative or more-efficient technologies including hybrid and efficient diesel engines, and the provision of freely available bicycles all over the city. Another challenge is that CTL technology delivers liquid fuels based on coal that can replace conventional fossil fuels. It provides an interesting alternative for energy-hungry countries with large coal and too little or decreasing oil resources.

Energy vision type 2: the Nuclear Society
Nuclear energy is the source of electricity and hydrogen production for this vision. Hydrogen is centrally produced by the heat of nuclear plants and, locally, with distributed electricity via electrolysis. While the former is more energy efficient, the latter prevents the need for a massive hydrogen distribution infrastructure. Virtually unlimited amounts of cheap nuclear energy make it cost efficient to distribute electricity and produce hydrogen directly where needed to fuel vehicles. Key issues of nuclear fission and fusion technologies are high reactor safety and the capability to transmute and incinerate nuclear waste. The nuclear fuel cycle is no longer in the hands of individual countries but is tightly controlled and governed by the International Atomic Energy Agency, IAEA (which includes all countries as members).

Concerns regarding nuclear waste, proliferation and accidents make the nuclear option the most controversial of all energy alternatives, certainly since the Chernobyl accident of 1986. Nuclear power is back on the intergovernmental agendas as one means to address the climate change problem. The support for future nuclear generations depends on breakthroughs in waste reduction. The risk of a serious nuclear accident needs to be mitigated if large-scale nuclear power is to be a serious contender.

The infrastructure challenge related to the centralized Nuclear/Hydrogen Society remains. A centralized production scheme that provides hydrogen as the dominant fuel for mobility requires a full hydrogen distribution chain. Infrastructure requirements can be reduced if energy is distributed as electricity instead and the hydrogen production takes place locally via electrolysis. This is less energy efficient but if nuclear energy is abundant and cheap it may be a viable option.

Energy vision type 3: the Bio Society
The Bio Society vision benefits from existing infrastructure and technology and consequently is the least contentious. Politicians and potential objectors have understood that this is the space to which we can move with the least resistance. A diversified agriculture supplies food and resources for energy needs. The agricultural sector has massively boosted its productivity, mainly driven by biotechnology innovation. Second-generation biofuel technologies derive liquid fuels from waste and fast-growing cellulosic biomass (including wood and grass). Electricity is produced from various renewable energies and relies on biomass and hydropower plants to adjust supply and demand. The international trade of agricultural products no longer faces asymmetric barriers but imposes severe quality standards to guarantee the sustainability of traded commodities.

Biofuel potentials are very different across geographical regions; for example, sugar cane can only be produced in equatorial regions. China, the fastest-growing and soon the most energy-hungry country, is home to four times more people on roughly the same surface area as the US. It has only one fertile coastline while the US has two and so is likely to be an importer. For some developing countries the growing demand for biofuels which are imported causes the risk of a relative price change of basic commodities that ensure food security. Another risk is that of potential ecological damage if agricultural land use is displaced. Since the Mexican 'Tortilla Crisis' of early 2007 due in part to droughts and related harvest losses, biofuels have become subject to a highly controversial media coverage for their role in the crisis. Critical links between food production, biofuel production and water consumption are still not understood or managed well enough. Any country that sees in biofuels an export opportunity, or a contribution to the national energy security strategy, or a way to mitigate greenhouse gas emissions, needs to proactively mitigate these risks.

Trade rules need to be such that only 'good biofuels' are encouraged to find their way onto markets. Furthermore, large food commodity and energy companies may avoid negative publicity by agreeing on and implementing security valves that can take the pressure from food-and-fuel commodity markets in moments of high prices and tight supply. The development of principles for sustainable biofuels to define import/export conditions or trade rules, to support food and energy companies' supply chain management, or to develop labels that improve consumer awareness and choice is ongoing.[4] In the absence of successful efforts in these domains, public opinion may turn against the Bio Society. In which case it will be the research and development efforts for second-generation biofuels from cellulosic biomass and waste that will make progress towards this vision viable.

Energy vision type 4: the Energy 2.0 Society
The infrastructure backbone for this vision is the electricity 'smart-grid' or 'electrnet': an information technology (IT) upgraded version of the electricity grid that coordinates demand and supply by commanding decentralized generation and storage devices. It recognizes a client where – and whenever – he/she plugs in. Net metering accounts positively for the electricity the client supplies to the grid through his/her personal power plants and storage devices and negatively for his/her individual consumption. A multitude of distributed power plants produce electricity in an uncoordinated random pattern. The grid is run with overcapacity to cope with aleatory input and produce excess amounts of hydrogen, enough to fuel mobility. Personal power plants based on waste, solar, wind, or movement, complemented by portable hydrogen batteries and personal energy optimization incentive schemes characterize this society.

The Energy 2.0 Society which involves localization, personification, consumerization, and democratization finds a new alliance in cities, non-governmental organizations (NGOs) and venture capitalists via radical sudden technological change or the multiplier effects of a sequence of small technological changes. The upgrade of the power grid and of power devices with storage potential has created the possibility of managing decentralized storage capacity and handling locally produced power. This efficiency improvement, combined with the decreased cost of solar cells, the capability of decentralized storage and utilization of a variety of secondary energy carriers including hydrogen or compressed air, bodes well for the future. As a common element in many of these revolutions we can recognize a 'personalization of technology' pattern. Energy 2.0 creates potential for the development of personal power plants and storage systems, mobile instantaneous individual energy consumption monitors, or personal energy credit cards.

Externally imposed constraints can create the conditions for innovation. South African's history of isolation led to technological progress; the country has become a leader in CTL technology. Also, huge power constraints have forced innovation on the load management side. The incentives are there to further develop the capability of accessing and managing storage capacity in the network as peak-load capacity is simply difficult to build. There is plenty of storage capacity in the grid, the challenge lies in accessing and managing it. Introducing machine-to-machine interaction that can dispatch all this storage capacity in a dynamic way is vastly different from manual dispatch. All that is needed is a power network that has sophisticated IT and that holds a steering signal (such as the instantaneous price of electricity). This is the smart grid that is also capable of handling locally produced electricity from distributed micro and mini power plants.

Comment
There will be coexistence of the various visions over the next decades. However, we shall come to a point where it will no longer be efficient to pursue all these visions and maintain complementary infrastructure types in parallel. While visions situated in neighboring

quadrants have infrastructure synergies, visions in diagonally opposed quadrants may be too different to coexist in the long term. Nuclear and Bio Societies seem far from each other, and so are Clean Coal and Energy 2.0 Societies. Closest may be the Nuclear and Energy 2.0 Societies, which share the hydrogen infrastructure, or the Clean Coal and Bio Societies, which share the liquid fuel infrastructure. Similarly, the Nuclear and Clean Coal Societies share the 'Leviathan' mindset, while the Bio Society and the Energy 2.0 Society are an expression of a strong localized culture.

Multi-stakeholder theory including all interest groups potentially affected by an issue can be more informative than a group consisting of *relevant* stakeholders only (parties thought to have a potential influence on the issue). While some groups will have more influence on future energy policy than others, there is the potential for broader analysis.

Governments who define national and international energy policies are significantly influenced by large energy companies who own the critical infrastructure. NGOs, such as Greenpeace or the Worldwide Fund for Nature (WWF), are also benchmarks for public opinion on issues including nuclear or renewable energies, and work together with scientists to raise public awareness of climate change and related issues. Consumer purchasing power should not be underestimated; an individual decision to buy a hybrid car, for example, or use public transport, all contribute to our energy future. Venture capitalists' capacity to bear the risk and thereby enable the development of green technologies will significantly shape the future energy scenario. Cities become increasingly important and by 2030 it is estimated that almost two-thirds of the world's population will live in urban areas (Worldwatch Institute, 2007). Local government has a significant impact on the energy uses of the local communities and is crucial in the mitigation of greenhouse gas emissions. Not all stakeholders (big business, consumers, local government, national government, NGOs, venture capitalists and academia) are relevant in each of the political decision-making contexts considered.

Stakeholders view the various energy vision ideal types differently. The representative consumer may initially be confused by the complexity of the idea of the Energy 2.0 Society. The pollution that results from urban traffic is a concern of the local government of each city. It is best dealt with locally rather than being left to a national scheme upon which the local government has little influence. Localized solutions are preferable as they empower cities and local communities. National governments administer national energy policy and in doing so aim to minimize their political exposure. Government visions will vary depending on the country-specific access to natural resources, control over the nuclear fuel cycle, and availability of crops for use in the energy process.

NGOs and other community-based organizations have been very active over the past two decades in bringing the issues of climate change onto the public agenda, and in so doing have influenced energy policy. They usually operate under a democratic structure and often prioritize intergenerational and global risks in a different order from the government. Large risks from large technologies receive more attention than dispersed risks from dispersed technologies (including, for example, local pollution, transportation accidents). CCS and bio-vision related concerns now find pragmatic conditional support. Nuclear energy still faces a bold 'NO' from Greenpeace and the WWF.[5] Overall, localized visions find more support than the centralized visions, and on the localized side it is the Energy 2.0 Society that best reflects the NGOs' aspirations. Key concerns across visions include the availability of sufficient capacity and long-term security of CCS, the storage of nuclear waste, nuclear proliferation and accident risks, as well as food-competition and bio-diversity risks related to an increased use of bioenergy.

Large projects of big business are fundamental to any centralized vision. The profit motive prompts business to favor liquid fuels in the short to medium term as compared to the development of hydrogen, because the existing and large infrastructure can be reused. Venture capitalists like to scale up emerging disruptive technologies, where the regulatory environment is favorable and not too restrictive. Hydrogen appliances, second-generation biofuels, as well as the Energy 2.0 Society offer a lot of possibilities. The present energy challenges provide a platform where true interdisciplinary work has the potential to provide a way forward. The Bio Society vision benefits from using existing infrastructure and technology and consequently is the least contentious. Politicians and potential objectors have thought that this is the space to which we can move with the least resistance. As a result, ambitious policies and aggressive targets for the large-scale introduction of biofuels have been set, and international trade of biofuels is promoted through bilateral trade agreements. However, an in-depth fuel-versus-food discussion has yet to show which regions can afford the utilization of crops to fuel this vision.

Energy efficiency has become very popular and more recently made it on to the policy agendas of organizations including the G8. Numerous technologies and concepts for efficiency improvements exist or are being developed. Many of them are profitable, if not in the short term, at least in the mid term. Nevertheless, it is critical that we create an actionable constituency for energy efficiency. At the local level, we see interesting energy-saving initiatives in cities, including decentralized energy generation in Woking, UK, London's congestion charge, and Cape Town's energy-efficient lighting initiative. Efficiency plays a different role in the different energy visions. The efficient use of locally available resources is a pillar of the Energy 2.0 Society. The Clean Coal Society will invest a lot of energy in CCS, and in the Bio Society, food and water security provide incentives for energy efficiency.

5   Conclusion

Climate change makes it imperative that we implement energy-secure low-carbon visions as a matter of urgency. Therefore we need an energy policy to deliver the respective infrastructure. Clean Coal, Nuclear, Bio and Energy 2.0 Society visions all have their challenges and are all costly. Competition is necessary for innovation as well as new alliances between municipalities and venture capitalists. Yet we must be aware that water, food and energy are, and will increasingly be, the critical and scarce commodities necessary for the survival of our planet. We are far from understanding interlinkages between the three, and our energy future needs to balance requirements for water and food security to be sustainable. Technological and fundamental behavioral change is vital as well as the understanding that we have gone beyond a purely state-driven resource management and policy paradigm. We cannot just wait for state governments to react. In the new paradigm, as a result of the shifting power equation, cities and individuals play a much stronger role, and with more power comes more responsibility. In order to better understand this role, Weber argues that we should invest in energy sociology for taking viable energy policy decisions (Weber, 1947).

Notes

1. Examples for producing countries that have started to re-nationalize or take closer state control of their oil and gas sectors include: Russia (2005: Yukos; 2006: Sakkhalin 2), Venezuela (2005) and Bolivia (2006).
2. Examples for national(-istic) protection efforts for domestic utilities: 2005: Unocal-CNOOC/Chevron; 2006/07: Endesa-E.On/Gas Natural/Enel/Acciona, GdF-Enel/Suez, Centrica-Gazprom.
3. An example may be the building of a consumer brand of Saudi Aramco in a joint venture with Sinopec and Exxon Mobil in 2007 in China.
4. See, for example, www.bioenergywiki.org.
5. See www.mdi.lu.
6. See http://www.greenpeace.org/international/campaigns/nuclear; http://www.panda.org/about_wwf/what_we_do/climate_change/solutions/energy_solutions/nuclear_power/index.cfm.

References

Dargay, J., D. Gately and M. Sommer (2007), 'Vehicle ownership and income growth, worldwide: 1960–2030', *The Energy Journal*, **28** (4), 143–70.

Frei, C.W. (2004), 'The Kyoto Protocol – a victim of supply security? Or: if Maslow were in energy politics', *Energy Policy*, **32** (11), July, 1253–6.

Frei, C.W. (2007), 'Different energy visions and implications for the energy future', *Commonwealth Ministers Reference Book 2007*, Henley Media Group, June.

International Energy Agency (IEA) (2006), *World Energy Outlook*, OECD/IEA, Paris.

Maslow, A.H. (1943), 'A theory of human motivation', *Psychological Review*, **50**, 370–96.

Maslow, A.H. (1954), *Motivation and Personality*, New York: Harper.

Reinelt, P.S. and D.W. Keith (2007), 'Carbon capture retrofits and the cost of regulatory uncertainty', *The Energy Journal*, **28** (4), 143–70.

Weber, M. (1947), *The Theory of Social and Economic Organization*, trans. A.M. Henderson and Talcott Parsons, Oxford University Press, Oxford and New York.

Weber, M. (1949), *The Methodology of the Social Sciences*, trans. Edward Shils and Henry Finch, Free Press, New York.

Worldwatch Institute (2007), *State of the World 2007*, Washington, DC.

33 Current issues in the design of energy policy
Thomas Weyman-Jones

1 Introduction

Often energy policy is treated in a partial equilibrium framework concentrating on particular fuels; however, there is also a strong tradition of treating the energy sector as part of a general equilibrium model. In this chapter we address two fundamental yet related areas of concern: the cost–benefit analysis of social discount rates and the nature of integrated assessment models (IA models) which embed the energy sector in a macroeconomic growth model. The issues that arise in the economics of energy policy are considered. The basis for an energy policy is the attempt to correct market failures, which can occur in three principal forms: asymmetric information, market power and externality. Normative economic policy towards asymmetric information issues is treated separately in Chapter 21 on regulation, and the emphasis in this chapter is on the positive economics of market power and externality.

2 Energy Market Policy

Helm (1991) discusses various categories of *market failure* as the basis of energy policy. In general, any form of microeconomic policy implies government intervention to distort the private market outcome for resource allocation. A very general, and politically orientated, basis for policy is to redistribute income by altering the structure of prices set by private markets. Economists tend to ignore this basis for policy as being outside their special expertise. Instead they focus on efficiency reasons for distorting market outcomes, by identifying market failures as:

- monopoly;
- efficient pricing with asymmetric information;
- security of supply and risk; and
- externality.

The issue of market power has been investigated in the previous chapters, but the other sources of market failure in energy supply are likely to be just as important. Asymmetric information and efficient pricing are major concerns addressed by incentive regulation or performance-based regulation of the natural monopoly parts of the energy industries, which are examined in Chapter 21.

Security of supply and risk is very widely cited as a basis for energy policy. There are two economic issues: does society realise the cost of buying from an uncertain energy source; should the government be risk averse? The standard scenario concerns import of energy, for example, oil from foreign suppliers who might interrupt the supply for political or profit-maximising reasons (for example, to exercise market power). Figure 33.1

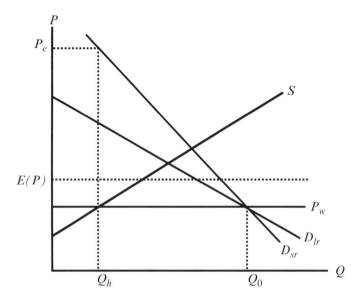

Note: Expected price: $E(P) = 1 - \pi P_w + \pi P_e = P_w + \pi (P_e - P_w)$.

Figure 33.1   The risk premium in uncertain oil prices

illustrates the expected price $E(P)$ when the probability of supply interruption is π. At the world price, P_w, home output is Q_h and consumption is Q_0. In a supply interruption, the price P_e rations demand to Q_h. The expected value of price is $E(P)$, which weights P_w and P_e by their respective probabilities. If consumers and firms use this price to invest in reserves and capacity, they will stockpile in excess of Q_H, and consume less than Q_0. Note that the short-run elasticity of demand is less than the long-run elasticity, and the short-run supply is vertical.

Is it sensible to tax energy consumption or imports? In this model, the answer is no, unless the government has good reason to believe that consumers and firms in general underestimate π. This is an example of an externality. Stretching this idea, there is one case where an import tariff actually benefits the importing country – that is where the country itself is so large a consumer that it has a degree of monopsonistic buying power.

Bohi and Toman (1996) analyse this idea sceptically, among others. The basis for the argument is that where a single economy demands a large share of world trade in a commodity, the price at which it can purchase more rises as its demand rises. There is therefore a marginal supply price curve derived from the average supply price curve. The country maximises 'profit' (which here counts directly as GNP) by restricting its purchases and forcing the supply price down. Following the Organization for Petroleum Exporting Countries (OPEC) price rises of 1974 and 1980 there was an attempt to foster a 'Western economies' joint purchasing monopsony, which foundered on prisoner's dilemma lines.[1]

The optimum tariff argument is shown in Figure 33.2. Suppose we have a typical good that uses oil as an input. However, the economy's demand for oil is such a large part of world demand that, whenever its use of oil rises, that in turn pulls up the world price. The economy moves along the world oil supply schedule rather than taking the world

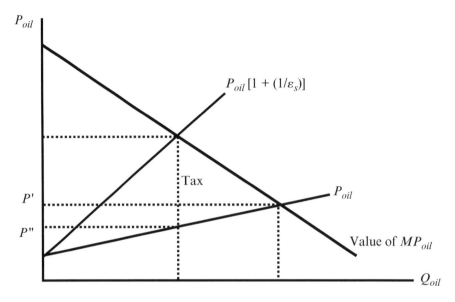

Figure 33.2   Monopsonistic equilibrium and optimal tariff

oil price as given. Usually an oil consumer requiring oil as an input will buy oil until the price of oil equals the value of its marginal product:

$$VMP_{oil} = P_{oil}.$$

However, when the consumer has monopsony power it makes more sense to restrict consumption to force down the price along the supply curve:

$$VMP_{oil} = P_{oil}\left(1 + \frac{1}{\varepsilon_s}\right).$$

Here ε_s is the elasticity of world supply. If individual purchasers are unaware of their aggregate power then the government can exercise it for them by imposing an 'optimum tariff' that reflects the elasticity of supply. In Figure 33.2, the tariff reduces the price to P''.

The formal analysis is as follows. A firm produces output y using oil, Q_{oil}, and sells it at price p. The price of oil, P_{oil}, rises if the country consumes more oil, $P'_{oil}(Q_{oil}) > 0$. The firm's profit-maximisation problem is: $\max \pi = py(Q_{oil}) - Q_{oil}P_{oil}(Q_{oil})$. The first-order condition is:

$$\frac{d\pi}{dQ_{oil}} = py'(Q_{oil}) - P_{oil} - Q_{oil}P'_{oil}(Q_{oil}) = 0.$$

This rearranges to:

$$py'(Q_{oil}) = P_{oil}\left[1 + \frac{Q_{oil}P'_{oil}(Q_{oil})}{P_{oil}}\right].$$

This is simply the expression:

$$VMP_{oil} = P_{oil}\left(1 + \frac{1}{\varepsilon_s}\right).$$

The assumption there is that consumers as a group are risk neutral. However, they may be risk averse so that the variance of price is itself a 'bad'. Strictly, governments are not supposed to be risk averse even if individual consumers are, because any small income changes are spread over the whole population so that, from the government's point of view, the risk to any single individual is negligible. It is unlikely to be correlated with GNP as a whole. (This is the Arrow–Lind theorem, see Lind, 1982.) This might not be the case if an energy policy decision actually affects GNP significantly. Suppose the government believed that over-reliance on one particular fuel type actually increased the risk of supply interruption (increased the variance of price) then there might be a case for diversifying the fuel mix portfolio.

Externality relates primarily to the social cost of environmental emissions associated with energy consumption. Following the work of the Intergovernmental Panel on Climate Change, massive research effort has been devoted to investigate the use of carbon taxes and tradable permits for emissions. There is currently in existence an emissions trading scheme for the European Union, which had a relatively troubled start as national governments treated their incumbent suppliers relatively generously in distributing permits. Permits are already used to search for more-efficient ways of reducing power station emission in the United States (Ellerman et al., 2005). There are three general theoretical issues connected to externality which do impact on the economics of energy, and these are considered in the following sections of this chapter: (i) integrated assessment models, (ii) the debate on the use of carbon permits versus carbon taxes that was initiated by the classic paper of Weitzman (1974) on whether *prices* or *quantities* are the proper target of economic policy, and (iii) value judgements in the choice of social discount rate raised by the widely debated Stern (2006) report on the economics of climate change. Central to all of these concerns is the knowledge that the production processes in most of the energy industries produce carbon dioxide and other greenhouse gases as a byproduct. A key value therefore is the social cost of carbon, and the analysis must start from this point.

3 Modelling the Social Cost of Carbon

Two key references on the social cost of carbon are Pearce (2003) and Mendelsohn (2005). Pearce (2003) demonstrates that the social cost of carbon requires a present value calculation since the damage is caused by an accumulating stock of carbon in the atmosphere. The principal insight is that the social cost of carbon is the present value of a long-term flow of damages, so that its present value depends on both technological factors and the choice of social discount rate. This differs from many environmental analyses where pollution damage is treated only as flow concept. Pearce is then able to show how the social discount rate plays a critical role in determining the size of the social cost of carbon. A similar result underpins the model of Mendelsohn (2005).

Carbon emissions per period are a continuous flow in tonnes per year: $q(t)$. These add to the stock of accumulated carbon in the atmosphere: $S(t)$ through the equation:

$$\dot{S}(t) \equiv dS(t)/dt = q(t) - \lambda S(t),$$

where λ is the constant rate of decay of the stock. Carbon emissions can be abated at a total cost of:

$$A(q): A'(q) < 0, A''(q) > 0.$$

The stock of emissions causes damage to the environment valued at:

$$D(S): D'(S) > 0, D''(S) > 0.$$

The public sector discount rate is constant: ρ, and the social welfare function is to minimise the environmental cost, subject to the accumulation constraint:

$$\max - \int_0^\infty [A(q) + D(S)]\exp(-\rho t)dt,$$

$$\text{s.t. } \dot{S}(t) \equiv dS(t)/dt = q(t) - \lambda S(t).$$

Treat this as an infinite horizon optimal control problem with the following designations:

state variable: $S(t)$;
control variable: $q(t)$, $q(t) \in$ R, the set of real numbers; and
co-state variable: $p(t)$.

The solution proceeds by setting up the Hamiltonian function for the problem:

$$H = -\{A(q(t)) + D(S(t))\}\exp(-\rho t) + p(t)[q(t) - \lambda S(t)].$$

Applying the Pontryagin maximum principle, we obtain a control equation and a pair of differential equations:

$$\max_q H \Rightarrow \partial H/\partial q = -A'(q)\exp(-\rho t) + p(t) = 0,$$

and

$$-\partial H/\partial S = \dot{p}(t) = \exp(-\rho t)D'(S) + \lambda p,$$

$$\partial H/\partial p = \dot{S}(t) = q - \lambda S.$$

Then:

$$p(t) = A'(q)\exp(-\rho t),$$

giving:

$$\dot{p}(t) = -\rho A'(q)\exp(-\rho t).$$

Use these results to write:

$$-\rho A'(q)\exp(-\rho t) - \lambda[A'(q)\exp(-\rho t)] = \exp(-\rho t)D'(S).$$

Consequently:

$$-\exp(-\rho t)A'(q)[\lambda + \rho] = \exp(-\rho t)D'(S)$$

and

$$-A'(q) = D'(S)/[\lambda + \rho].$$

We interpret this as follows. Along the equilibrium time path, the marginal cost of abatement is set equal to the discounted present value of the additional damage to the environment arising from a marginal addition to the accumulated stock of emissions. This marginal damage is constant for the given stock (but rises as the stock rises) and lasts forever. The marginal damage is discounted at a rate given by the social rate of time discount plus the rate of decay of the stock of emissions. This discounted present value of marginal damage is the finite *(marginal) social cost of carbon.*

4   Carbon Permits versus Carbon Taxes

In a classic paper, Weitzman (1974) considered whether the proper target of economic policy should be prices or quantities. This has a straightforward application to the question of whether tradable carbon permits or carbon taxes are the appropriate way to tackle the emissions issue. Weitzman offers a social cost–benefit analysis, but other considerations might be applied instead. For example, Green (2007) considers the impact on the incumbent producers in energy markets. The optimal tax or tradable permit price in Weitzman's treatment can be determined from the trade-off between the social cost of carbon analysed above and the marginal cost of carbon abatement, as shown in Figure 33.3. Note that the marginal carbon abatement cost curve doubles up as the demand for carbon permits curve, since at the margin a firm must choose between abatement of the last unit of carbon emissions using its own costly technology or buying an additional permit at the current market price of permits. Here the marginal cost of abatement curve is written $A'(q) \equiv B'(q)$ to signify that it measures the marginal benefit of reduced damage, q. The marginal social cost of carbon curve is labelled $C'(q)$ to represent the cost of additional damage expressed in terms of the flow of emissions. The intersection of the marginal cost of abatement and the marginal social cost of carbon indicates both the optimal price of permits and the optimal rate of carbon tax.

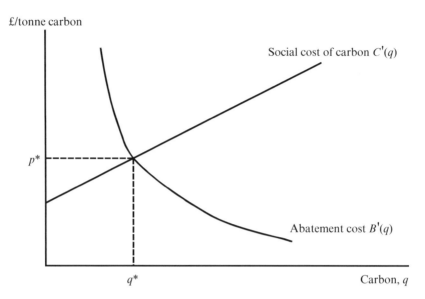

£/tonne carbon

Social cost of carbon $C'(q)$

$p*$

Abatement cost $B'(q)$

$q*$

Carbon, q

Figure 33.3   Optimal carbon tax, p* and number of permits, q* under certainty

With certainty of information, it does not matter whether we set permits at the level $q*$, and allow them to be traded, or set the carbon tax at the level $p*$, since the result is the same.

Now consider a range of uncertainty: where is the optimal $(q*, p*)$ combination? As Figure 33.4 demonstrates, by including unknown information (η) with variance σ_η^2 in the abatement cost (demand for permits) curve, and unknown information (θ) with variance σ_θ^2 in the social cost of carbon curve, Weitzman (1974) shows that the optimum is very difficult to determine.

When carbon is treated as an undesirable output, σ_θ^2 affects the abatement cost and social cost of carbon curves symmetrically, but σ_η^2 impacts asymmetrically, and critically affects the choice between a price-based instrument (carbon tax) and a quantity-based instrument (carbon permits). Weitzman concludes that the relative advantage (Δ) of a price-based instrument (carbon tax) over a quantity-based instrument (carbon permits) depends on two effects:

$$\Delta = \textit{Informational uncertainty} \times \text{curvature effect.}$$

The first term depends on σ_η^2, and the second term depends on the [slope of $B'(q)$ + slope of $C'(q)$]. In Figure 33.5, only the curvature effect is shown.

In the figure, triangle Δ *def* measures the welfare loss from a 50 per cent error on the determination of the number of carbon permits. When the positions of the curves are unknown because of informational uncertainty, there is lower likelihood of welfare loss due to policy error from using permits the greater the likely curvature of the social cost of carbon, that is, [slope of $C'(q)$] relative to the likely curvature of the abatement cost, that is, [slope of $B'(q)$]. A social cost of carbon that is virtually constant, and abatement cost that rises very sharply as carbon is eliminated (right-hand figure), favour the

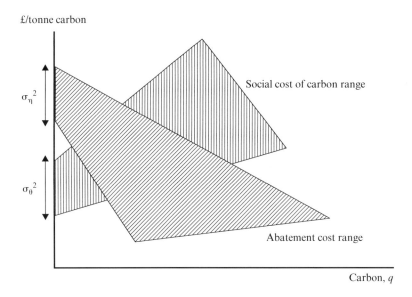

Figure 33.4   Range of uncertainty in Weitzman (1974) model of permits versus taxes

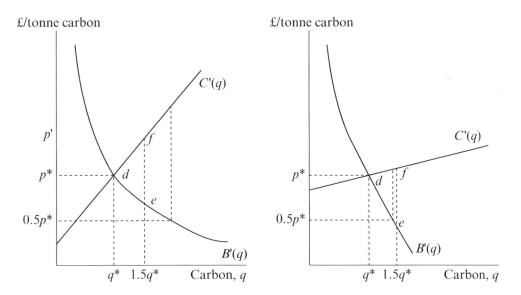

Note: $B'(q)$: carbon abatement cost, £/tonne C, $C'(0)$: social cost of carbon, £/ tonne C.
Δdef measures the welfare loss from a 50% excess supply of permits – contrast with the welfare loss from a carbon tax that is 50% too low.

Figure 33.5   Weitzman analysis of permits versus tax under uncertainty

use of the carbon tax when there is great uncertainty; triangle of welfare damage Δ *def* lies outside the welfare loss from a 50 per cent error on the carbon tax. Otherwise, for instance, a social cost of carbon that rises sharply as carbon emissions increase, and an abatement cost that rises relatively slowly as carbon is eliminated (left-hand figure), means that a policy of carbon permits is likely to prove less costly than a carbon tax if the wrong level is chosen because triangle of welfare damage Δ *def* lies inside the welfare loss from a 50 per cent error on the carbon tax. The advantage of permits in this case is reduced if the number of independent polluters is large.

5   Integrated Assessment Models of Climate Change

Examples of models of the economics of climate policy include those of Nordhaus and Boyer (2000) and the analysis of Kolstad and Toman (2001) for Resources for the Future. Much of this analysis is based on what are known as integrated assessment (IA) models drawn from the original analysis of Ramsey (1928). We have already seen the essential idea in the application of social discount rates in cost–benefit analysis. However the climate application needs to be discussed.

We can get a broad idea of how such IA models are constructed from the following components:

- U: Individual utility function, U, which describes how a typical individual values more consumption.
- Y: Aggregate production function, Y, which describes how GDP is generated from the stock of resources including the economy's capital, K.
- K: Resource accumulation equation, K, which describes how the next generation's stock of resources and capital is added to by saving by the present generation, and possibly reduced by the present generation's pollution or emissions.
- W: Social welfare function, W, which describes how succeeding generations are to count in our social welfare calculations.

Consider how a simple IA model could be constructed.[2] U increases with consumption of goods but at a diminishing rate. We can represent this by a single parameter: η = the elasticity of marginal utility with respect to consumption. An important idea is that if the consumption levels of two different generations are equal, then the individual utility levels of each member of the two generations are also the same:

$$C_0 = C_1 \Rightarrow U(C_0) = U(C_1).$$

An example could be: $U(C) = C^{1-\eta}/(1 - \eta)$.

For production we assume diminishing returns: GDP, Y, rises as the stock of capital including resources, K, increases but at a diminishing rate. This description of the economy's technology sets out the production possibilities for each generation, since: GDP for the current generation is a function of the stock of resources and capital available.

The slope of the aggregate production function is the marginal product of capital:

MP_K. The critical parameter is α the elasticity of output with respect to the stock of resources and capital. Note: $MP_K = \alpha Y/K$:

$$Y = f(K), \text{ for example, } Y = K^\alpha \text{ and } 0 < \alpha < 1.$$

Therefore it is critical how much capital the current generation inherits from the previous generation.

The availability of resources and capital for the next generation depends on the initial stock and how much the previous generation has added by not consuming the whole of GDP:

$$\text{next period's capital equals this period's capital} + \text{saving,}$$

$$K_1 = K_0 + Y_0 - C_0.$$

Alternatively we can supplement the model by adding emissions damage and wastage into this framework. Assuming that a proportion γ of the inherited stock of resources and capital is actually destroyed by the act of consuming goods and services:

Next period's capital = this period's capital − resource loss due to consumption
+ saving,

$$K_1 = K_0 - \gamma C_0 + Y_0 - C_0.$$

Finally we must decide what constitutes social and economic welfare across generations. We assume that social welfare depends on the amount of utility that individual generations receive from consumption of goods:

$$W = U(C_0) + (1 + \delta)^{-1}U(C_1).$$

We have added the multiplicative factor $(1 + \delta)^{-1}$ to the next generation's utility to allow it to be weighted more or less than the current generation's utility:

$(1 + \delta)^{-1} > 1$: weight attached to future generation's utility is greater than for the present generation;
$(1 + \delta)^{-1} = 1$: weight attached to future generation's utility is the same as the present generation; and
$(1 + \delta)^{-1} < 1$: weight attached to future generation's utility is less than for the present generation.

The first step is to construct the economy's intergenerational consumption or production possibility frontier (PPF). The key to understanding this is to realise that next period's maximum consumption possibility depends on three factors: the productivity of capital and resources, the initial stock of capital and resources, and how much saving is done in the current period. By saving more in this period, we shift up the production possibility frontier relating to the next period. The slope of the production possibility frontier is: – (1 + marginal product of capital).

We now add the indifference curves of social welfare and arrive at a sequence of consumption through time by finding the tangency of the production possibility frontier and the highest social welfare indifference curve. This is exactly the same solution technique used to analyse the social discount rate. We begin by looking at what happens if we have different weights on the future generation's utility. The slope of each contour is given by:

$$\{\text{marginal utility of current generation} / [(1 + \delta)^{-1} \times \text{marginal utility of future generation}]\}.$$

As $(1 + \delta)^{-1}$ becomes larger the curve becomes less steep so that flat contours favour the future generation (therefore showing large future consumption and small present consumption) and steep contours favour the present generation. In all cases, however, the tangency ensures that at the optimum:

$$\text{(marginal utility of current generation} / [(1 + \delta)^{-1} \times \text{marginal utility of future generation}]\} = -(1 + \text{marginal product of capital}).$$

The larger is $(1 + \delta)^{-1}$ the more capital is built up for the future so that the marginal product of capital at the optimum is then lower. However, it is always positive so that we always discount the future even when favouring future generations over the present generation since it is always true that:

$$(1 + \text{social discount rate}) = (\text{slope of PPF at optimum}) = (\text{slope of welfare contour}).$$

The important factor in the IA–Ramsey model is that the *PPF* constraint is determined endogenously by society's own investment and consumption decisions. Since consumption imposes emissions damage this must also affect the position of the PPF. The optimal outcome is then to trade off the preferred amount of emissions damage against the cost of eliminating the consequences of the damage. This would mean that the emissions reduction target is chosen endogenously rather than being imposed arbitrarily. This means that we treat the loss of welfare from climate change as the benefit of emissions control (see Kolstad and Toman, 2001, p. 14). In the optimal outcome the energy and emissions permits markets implicit in the model will generate optimal taxes and permit prices that equate the marginal benefits of emissions reduction with the marginal cost. In our simple example we can see that:

Extra output sacrificed in period 1 by one more £ of consumption in period 0 is: $MP_K(1 + \gamma)$ with emissions damage but only MP_K with no damage.

Consequently this additional cost can be used to justify a permits market or set an optimal carbon tax or alter the social discount rate (SDR) to favour delayed consumption and more saving. In our simple framework the optimal policy response postpones consumption so as to delay the environmental damage (see ibid., pp. 27–8, where there is a similar model).

Table 33.1   Results of maximising social welfare

Variable	$\gamma = 0$	$\gamma = 0.25$
C_0	1.72	1.69
C_1	2.29	2.33
$(1 + \text{SDR}) = 1 + (1+\gamma)\,\text{MP}_K$	1.059	1.06
K_1	10.28	9.36

The following is a simple example of such a model. Our initial assumptions are based on an inherited resource and capital stock of $K_0 = 10$. In addition we assume:

Elasticity of utility wrt consumption	η	0.8
Elasticity of output wrt resources and capital	α	0.3
Resource loss per unit of current consumption	γ	0 or 0.25
Relative weight given to future generation	$(1 + \delta)^{-1}$	1

Now solve the model by choosing different amounts of resource loss per unit of consumption. The results of maximising social welfare with these assumptions are shown in Table 33.1.

The interpretation is as follows. Even with no resource loss from present consumption it makes sense to consume less in the present than in the future. This is because there is a positive return to investment in new capital and resources. Consequently we should build up the capital stock. With a 2.5 per cent loss of resources for every 10 per cent increase in consumption it is even more sensible to postpone consumption while still allowing the next generation to consume more than we do. The stock of capital and resources is slightly smaller because of the resource loss but is bigger than if we did not postpone consumption. We build up less capital but it is more than would be the case without choosing an optimal policy. The lower capital and resource stock has a slightly higher marginal product of capital so the social discount rate rises slightly. There is a non-optimal policy to compare with here. Suppose we reduced resource pollution so as to maintain the capital stock at 10. The solution of the model shows that we would have to reduce current consumption far more than is optimal for maximising welfare even when future generations are weighted equally. However, the overall conclusion of the many IAMs analysed by Kolstad and Toman (2001) is that the path of emissions deceleration is extremely sensitive to the choice of social discount rate. This is the final topic for consideration.

6   The Stern Review on the Economics of Climate Change

The Stern Review (2006) is the most significant contribution to the interaction between energy economics, growth and sustainability for many years. It has attracted a massive amount of debate and attention, in particular because it argues unambiguously for a very strong and immediate response to the threat of global warming. It does so on the basis of calculations of the choice of social discount rate which are much lower than many other economists and policy makers have adopted in recent years. Alternative empirical calculations of the social discount rate and its component parameters are given in Pearce and Ulph (1995) and Evans (2005).

The following expression was derived for the social discount factor:

$$1 + SDR = 1 + [\delta + \eta(\Delta \log C)] = 1 + (\alpha Y/K).$$

The basis for this is an intertemporal social welfare analysis analogous to the IA–Ramsey sustainability models. A similar, richer model is incorporated in the Stern Review. The sensitivity of the results to the choice of social discount rate cannot be overestimated. Following established practice in the UK Treasury and among many economists, Stern chooses to estimate the rate of social time preference rather than the social opportunity cost of capital:

$$STP = \delta + \eta \Delta \log C.$$

There are therefore three critical parameters:

δ: the rate of pure time preference;
η: the elasticity of marginal utility of consumption; and
$\Delta \log C$: the expected long-term growth rate of consumption per head.

These are not principally determined by revealed behaviour as is the case in some studies but by introspection and argument. The Stern Review uses: $\eta = 1$, $\Delta \log C = 0.013$, $\delta = 0.001$, giving a social time preference rate of: $STP = 0.014$, that is, 1.4 per cent. How is this argued?

The objective of using the pure rate of time preference is to weight future generations' consumption by the probability of being alive when the consumption occurs. This gives the expression:

$$C_0 \times P(alive)_0 + C_1 \times P(alive)_1 + \cdots + C_t \times P(alive)_t + \cdots$$

What is the probability that a randomly chosen member of society will still be living t years from now?

Mortality is a random event; mortality tables indicate that the death rate in the population is $100\,\delta\%$ per year, for example, $\delta = 0.01 \Rightarrow 1\%$ die each year. If this random event is a small proportion of the population and occurrences are independent of each other, then the Poisson distribution can be used to suggest that if the probability of X occurrences of mortality in the next t years is:

$$P(X) = \frac{(\delta t)^X \exp(-\delta t)}{X!},$$

then the probability of being alive for the next t years is the probability of 0 occurrences in t years:

$$P(0) = \frac{(\delta t)^0 \exp(-\delta t)}{0!} = \exp(-\delta t) \approx \frac{1}{(1 + \delta)^t}.$$

An alternative intuitive argument is this. If the forecast population in the next period is N, then the ratio of the population under normal circumstances to the population with no deaths at all is:

$$\frac{N}{N(1 + \delta)} = \frac{1}{(1 + \delta)}.$$

This can be interpreted as the betting odds that a randomly selected member of the population will belong to the larger group with no deaths, that is, the chance that he/she will not die in the next period.

Consequently, the consumption profile weighted by probability of being alive is:

$$C_0 + [C_1/(1 + \delta)] + [C_2/(1 + \delta)^2] + \cdots + [C_t/(1 + \delta)^t] + \cdots,$$

and this is equivalent to discounting by the rate of pure time preference, δ.

Now consider Stern's social welfare function expressed over individuals (i) and time (t) (see Stern Review, 2006, pp. 30 and 44 and Bliss, 2007):

$$W = \sum_i \sum_t U(C_{it}).$$

For the moment let us ignore the mortality aspect of the discounting, assume $\delta = 0$, and concentrate on the diminishing marginal utility aspect.

For two individuals over two periods:

$$W = U(C_{10}) + U(C_{11}) + U(C_{20}) + U(C_{21}),$$

then

$$\Delta W = MU_{10}\Delta C_{10} + MU_{11}\Delta C_{11} + MU_{20}\Delta C_{20} + MU_{21}\Delta C_{21}.$$

Three cases are:

$$U(C_{it}) = C_{it} \Rightarrow MU_{it} = 1, \text{ linear, i.e., } \eta = 0,$$

$$U(C_{it}) = \log C_{it} \Rightarrow MU_{it} = 1/C_{it}, \text{ logarithmic, i.e., } \eta = 1,$$

$$U(C_{it}) = C_{it}^{1-\eta}/(1 - \eta) \Rightarrow MU_{it} = 1/C_{it}^{\eta}, \text{ iso} - \text{elastic utility, i.e., } \eta > 1.$$

The linear case is the standard cost–benefit analysis assumption: £1 taken from any individual (for example, in producer surplus) at a given time is exactly compensated by giving £1 (for example, in consumer surplus) to any other individual at the same time.

Stern assumes the logarithmic case:

$$\eta = 1 \Rightarrow W = \sum_i \sum_t \log C_{it}.$$

Now consider the implications. At a given time, what is the welfare trade-off between two individuals: f and g:

$$dW = \sum_i \sum_t (1/C_{it})dC_{it}$$

$$dW = 0 \Rightarrow \frac{dC_{gt}}{dC_{ft}} = -\frac{(1/C_{ft})}{(1/C_{gt})} = -\frac{C_{gt}}{C_{ft}}.$$

Welfare is unchanged if: $-dC_{gt} = (C_{gt}/C_{ft})dC_{ft}$. Assume that individual g is very rich and individual f is a poor farmer (see Bliss, 2007). Since the rich person's consumption far exceeds the farmer's consumption, C_{gt}/C_{ft} must be a large number, say 1000. Society's welfare is unchanged by (that is, it remains indifferent about) taking $dC = £1$ from the rich person and giving $£(C_{gt}/C_{ft})dC_{ft} = £1000$ to the poor farmer or taking $dC = £1$ from a farmer and giving $£(C_{ft}/C_{gt})dC_{gt} = £0.001$ to the person whose consumption is 1000 times higher. Bliss describes this as 'moderate aversion to inequality'; it implies that the amount taken from the future wealthy society and given to the present poor society should be in proportion to their relative consumption forecasts.

Dasgupta (2006) says that this is much too hard on poor people alive today, and he argues for a factor: $\eta = 3$. In other words, Dasgupta says that today's population is a very deserving poor group and the future generations should be diverting wealth towards those living today. Other economists have contributed to the debate, including Mendelsohn (2006), Nordhaus (2007) and Weitzman (2007). Each demonstrates that the Stern Review conclusions are critically dependent on the value judgements made in choosing the parameters: δ and η. The deepest discussion is by Weitzman, and it is worth considering in detail.

Weitzman begins by noting that the Stern Review's call to environment–energy action on climate change policy is much more urgent and immediate than what he argues is the consensus among economists. Although the Stern Review contains a complex IA model at its core, Weitzman argues that the key analysis concerns the social discount rate as measured by the social time preference rate, r:

$$r = \delta + \eta g,$$

where $g = \Delta logC$ is the expected growth rate of consumption per head.

Stern adopts $\eta = 1$, $\Delta logC = g = 0.013$, $\delta = 0.001$, giving a social time preference rate of: $STP = r = 0.014$, that is, 1.4 per cent.
Weitzman states that a consensus among economists would choose a trio of twos: $\eta = 2$, $\Delta logC = g = 0.02$, $\delta = 0.02$, leading to:

$$r = 0.02 + 2(0.02) = 0.06,$$

that is, 6 per cent. This has a fundamental impact. Weitzman states that the Stern Review can be summarised in a simple trade-off. The projected cost of climate change damages (D) in 100 years is of the order of 5 per cent of GDP. Policies to adapt to and mitigate climate change could save this sum if adopted now at a cost of about 1 per cent of GDP. Weitzman states the Stern Review cost–benefit analysis succinctly as follows, where Y stands for GDP:

- cost now (year 0): $C = 0.01 Y_0$ and
- benefit in 100 years[3] (year 100): $B = |D| = 0.05 Y_{100} = 0.05[Y_0\exp(g100)]$ if the economy grows at the rate g.

The benefit–cost ratio is:

$$\frac{B}{C} = \frac{\{0.05[Y_0\exp(g100)]\}\exp(-r100)}{0.01 Y_0} = 5\exp[(g - r)100].$$

Then calculating:

Stern:

$$g - r = -0.001, \; B/C \approx 4.5$$

Weitzman-consensus:

$$g - r = -0.04, \; B/C \approx 0.09.$$

On this basis, the Stern conclusion, that the benefit–cost ratio of early action on climate change substantially exceeds one, is unwarranted.

However, Weitzman asks if the Stern recommendation can be defended on other grounds, specifically the issue of risk and uncertainty; he refers to the Stern Review as the 'greatest application of subjective uncertainty theory the world has ever seen' (2007, p. 718). Before considering uncertainty, Weitzman considers risk. This is possible if we are able to attach probabilities to uncertain events; in that case extreme climate change damage can be treated as a *high-impact but low-probability* event.

Weitzman's argument proceeds in stages. To begin, take the mean of the discount factors for a 100 year delay (s for Stern and c for consensus) and convert this to a discount rate:

$$r = -\ln\{[\tfrac{1}{2}\exp(-r_s t)] + \tfrac{1}{2}\exp(-r_c t)\}/t$$

$$= -\ln\{[\tfrac{1}{2}\exp(-1.4)] + \tfrac{1}{2}\exp(-6)\}/100$$

$$= 0.0208,$$

that is, roughly 2 per cent, relatively close to Stern's calculation. Stern is more right than wrong if his estimate is as likely as the consensus. This is a facile argument, so Weitzman introduces a more systematic risk by considering $\Delta \log C = g$, the growth rate of consumption per head, as a random variable. It could be normally distributed with mean: $E[g] = \mu$ and variance: $\text{var}[g] = \sigma^2$. For example, his assumed 'not-implausible' numerical quartet of twos has: $\delta = 0.02, \eta = 2, \mu = 0.02, \sigma = 0.02$. This means that the discount rate is a random variable, with mean $E[r]$ and variance $\text{var}[r]$:

$$E[r] = E[\delta + \eta g] = \delta + \eta E[g] = \delta + \eta\mu = 0.06$$

and

$$\mathrm{var}[r] = \mathrm{var}[\delta + \eta g] = \eta^2 \sigma^2 = 0.0016.$$

Corresponding to this random discount rate there is an economy-wide risk-free rate, calculated in finance theory, as:

$$r^f = E[r] - \tfrac{1}{2}\mathrm{var}[r] = \delta + \eta\mu - \tfrac{1}{2}\eta^2\sigma^2.$$

Using the consensus values from the quartet of twos:

$$r^f = 0.06 - 0.5(4)\,(0.02)^2 = 0.059.$$

You could imagine that this rate is available on loans to the government by holding government bonds. Suppose now that every citizen can also buy shares (equity) in GDP production, then it can be shown that the economy-wide rate of return on this equity is also a random variable with mean:[4]

$$\bar{r}^e = r^f + \eta\sigma^2.$$

Inserting the quartet of twos gives:

$$\bar{r}^e = 0.059 + 2(0.02)^2 = 0.06,$$

and the equity risk premium, that is, the extra reward needed to invest in shares in GDP production instead of lending to the government, is: $\bar{r}^e - r^f = 0.001$ or 0.1 per cent. Even using a standard deviation of $\Delta \log C = g$ that is three times higher still leaves an equity risk premium of less than 1 per cent. In practice in developed economies such as the USA and the UK, the equity risk premium averaged over many years is closer to $\bar{r}^e - r^f = 0.07 - 0.01 = 0.06$, that is, 6 per cent, if the risk-free rate is represented by the real[5] rate of return on short-term Treasury Bills and the equity rate of return represented by something like the long-term average on the FTSE All-Shares index. Weitzman refers to this as the 'equity premium puzzle'; it is an unresolved issue in financial economics that the spread between the return on shares and the risk-free rate is higher in practice than theory would predict.

Which of these rates, $\bar{r}^e$ or r^f should be used in climate change policy? The literature is surveyed in massive detail in Lind (1982), who says (p. 77):[6] 'unless there is substantial evidence to the contrary, the returns associated with public projects should be assumed to be highly correlated with returns to the economy as a whole . . . therefore, the after tax return on the market portfolio should be used to discount benefits and costs for both time and risk'. It matters therefore how much of climate change policy and damage is correlated with the production of GDP.

Weitzman distinguishes between outdoor economic activities which include enjoyment of the unthreatened natural environment (concern for this and people's welfare from this may rise as they become wealthier) and indoor economic activities which may not be correlated with greenhouse gas emission damages.[7] If the correlation of climate change damages and GDP is β, then the correct discount rate to use is:

$$r = -\ln\{[\beta \, exp(-\bar{r}^e t)] + (1 - \beta)exp(-r^f t)\}/t.$$

If β = 0.5 and the empirically observed (rather than theoretical) rates are used, then:

$$r = -\ln(\{0.5 \exp[-0.07(100)]\} + 0.5 \exp[-0.01(100)])/100 = 0.0169,$$

that is, about 1.7 per cent, very close to the Stern value. Weitzman concludes (p. 714): 'in this case, investments for mitigating global climate change become attractive as an insurance policy that secures food supplies, preserves coastal areas, and maintains natural environments in a world where future aggregate growth rates are uncertain'.

So far, Weitzman has considered *risk*, that is, cases where informed probability judgements can be made. The necessary conditions that enable us to attach probabilities to outcomes are either (i) that we know a robust mathematical model for the data-generating process so that we can appeal to such factors as the law of large numbers and the central limit theorem that enable us to make precise inferences on the basis of sample information, or (ii) that we have sufficient past experience in the form of occurrences of the event in question that we can construct an empirical probability distribution of outcomes (by bootstrapping procedures, for example). However, Weitzman contrasts this with uncertainty, where we have no prior mathematical model to provide a data-generating process, nor do we have sufficient or indeed any experience of previous occurrences from which we can synthesise a frequency distribution. This is the problem of *high-impact but unknown and unknowable probability*.

Weitzman argues that the observed equity premium puzzle noted above means that investors are 'disproportionately afraid of rare disasters . . . These disasters are not fully reflected in the available data samples' and that '. . . people are willing to pay high premiums for relatively safe stores of value that might represent "catastrophe insurance" against out-of-sample or newly evolved rare disasters' (p. 715). Of course, cost–benefit analysis can handle uncertainty by using the standard mathematical models of probability. However, there is a sampling theory principle that the rarer an event the more difficult it is to assess its probability. The result is, according to Weitzman, that 'climate change and especially the economics of climate change, is as close to being a pure case of modeling probabilities by subjective judgments as we economists are ever likely to encounter in practice' (p. 716). Previous experience, past observations, the law of large numbers and so on means that we can construct a reasonable guess about the central parts of the probability distribution of Δ log C = g, but our knowledge of the tails of the distribution is weak because we know so little about the frequencies of rare events in the tail. This uncertainty about uncertainty means that the left tail of the distribution of Δ log C = g corresponding to rare disasters beyond our experience becomes thicker than the thin-tailed distributions that arise in standard probability calculations. Weitzman uses an analogy with the *t*-distribution. If, instead of being sure about the population parameters of the Δ log C = g distribution, we have to estimate them from sample data: $\hat{\mu}, \hat{\sigma}^2$ then there is an equivalent effect to the use of estimated variance in hypothesis testing about the mean as opposed to use of population variance. The effect of switching from a distribution whose parameters are known to one whose parameters must be estimated from small samples is that the expected marginal utility of an extra unit of sure consumption could turn out to be so high that we feel the need for catastrophe insurance: 'from experience alone one cannot acquire sufficiently accurate information about the probabilities of tail disasters to prevent the expected marginal utility of an extra sure unit of consumption becoming unbounded' (p. 719). Weitzman argues that the economic models of climate change need to recognise that the thick left tail of the $\Delta \log C = g$ distribution representing rare disasters under uncertainty should be the primary and decisive focus in the analysis.

Weitzman points out a dilemma in the Stern parameter for η which is simultaneously the coefficient of egalitarianism and the measure of risk aversion. Stern worries about the disproportionate effect of climate change damage on the poorer populations of the world, and therefore should opt for a relatively high value of η, as Dasgupta (2006) recommends. However, Stern also wants a consumption smoothing profile whereby a slight lowering of consumption now by today's relatively poor generation is used to compensate for larger but uncertain lowering later on by the much wealthier generation living 100 years from now, and this requires the lowest possible value of η. Weitzman argues:

> [I]t is much better to go directly through the front door with the legitimate concern that there is a chance, whose subjective probability is small but diffuse (thereby resulting in a dangerously thickened left tail of comprehensive consumption growth rates), that global warming may eventually cause disastrous temperatures and environmental catastrophes . . . global climate change is as likely an arena as any for valid application of the general principle that thickened tails from uncertain structural parameters must dominate expected discounted utility questions. (p. 721)

Weitzman's policy conclusions are as follows:

- gradualist ramping up of ever-tighter greenhouse gas reductions that comes from mainstream mid-distribution probability analysis;
- plus the option value of waiting for better information about the thick-tailed disasters; and
- confront honestly the option of taking politically incorrect emergency measures if a worst-case scenario materialises – this means putting serious funding into contingency planning for worst-case disasters.

The Stern Review has its heart in the right place; it does not want to bequeath 'the enormously unsettling uncertainty of a very small but essentially unknown (and perhaps unknowable) probability of a planet earth . . . wrecked on our watch' (p. 722). 'The overarching problem is that we lack a commonly accepted usable economic framework for dealing with these . . . thick-tailed extreme disasters whose probability distributions are inherently difficult to estimate'. The debate between Stern and the critics is about 'tails vs middle' and 'catastrophe insurance vs consumption smoothing' (p. 723).

Weitzman believes that the Stern Review predetermines the outcome by picking SDR parameters that are extreme bounds; but we can see that genuine uncertainty about the discount rate brings it down from conventional values to close to 2–4 per cent – intermediate between Stern and consensus. This intermediate position is 'still grounded in a conventional consumption-smoothing approach to the economic analysis of climate change that avoids formally confronting the issue of what to do about catastrophe insurance against the possibility of thick-tailed rare disasters' (p. 723).

The Stern Review's achievements are:

- it raises the level of public discourse;
- it argues for global carbon tax: 'the pricing of carbon, implemented through tax, trading or regulation is required for an effective global response' (*Review*, p. xvii);
- it discusses adaptation as well as mitigation;
- it popularises the usefulness of cost–benefit analysis; and
- it highlights the problem of genuine uncertainty.

The Stern Review's failure is:

- the claim that best-available economic analysis supports conclusions instead of admitting that recommendations depend on extreme assumptions and controversial discount rates.

Weitzman (p. 724) feels that the report's tone of morality and alarm comes from a not formally articulated fear of what 'might be out there' with greenhouse warming in the 'inherently thickened left tail' of the probability distribution of the growth rate of consumption, including consumption of the natural environment. History will judge whether Stern was right for the wrong reasons, because of his intuitive argument that it might be very important to avoid possibly large uncertainties that are difficult to quantify. Spending money to combat global warming should be less about consumption smoothing, and more about how much insurance to buy to offset a small chance of ruinous catastrophe that is difficult to compensate by ordinary savings.

The chief point of all the Stern critiques is that there are many reasons to regard the Review's calculation of the social discount rate as well below the consensus of the majority of other economic analyses, and that it is partly at least an exercise in political economy.

7 Conclusion

Market failure is the basis for interventionist energy policy. The problem of greenhouse gas emissions is clearly critical here, and economists have made important theoretical contributions in terms of optimal tax and tradable permits. The nature of the social cost of carbon was shown to be best captured by the present value of additions to the stock of damage, highlighting again the importance of the social discount rate. Weitzman's (1974) celebrated analysis of uncertainty was used to explain the choice between carbon permits and carbon taxes, before the analysis finally turned to consider the debate over the 2006 *Stern Review on the Economics of Climate Change*, which has come to set the context of the current debate on energy economics and policy.

Notes

1. The history of the idea of an optimum oil import tariff against OPEC is described in. Weyman-Jones (1986, pp. 71–8).

2. This is a highly simplified version of some of the analyses in Kolstad and Toman (2001).
3. Calculations use continuous growth and discounting factors instead of annual factors.
4. The parameter η now acts as a measure of risk aversion.
5. All rates are expressed in real terms, that is, the nominal rate of return minus the expected rate of inflation.
6. Weitzman gives the first part of the quotation from Lind, I have added the second for clarity.
7. Weitzman notes that most climate change models assume that climate change damage and GDP production have a correlation coefficient of 1.

References

Bliss, C. (2007), 'The Stern Report: is it the answer?', presentation to The Hayek Society, London, January 31.
Bohi, D.R. and M.A. Toman (1996), *The Economics of Energy Security*, Boston, MA: Kluwer Academic.
Dasgupta, Partha (2006), 'Comments on Stern's Review on the Economics of Climate Change', presentation to The Royal Society, London, November 8.
Ellerman, A.D., P.L. Joskow, R. Schmalensee, J.-P. Montero and E.M. Bailey (2005), *Markets for Clean Air: The US Acid Rain Program*, Cambridge: Cambridge University Press.
Evans, D.J. (2005), 'The elasticity of marginal utility of consumption: estimates for 20 OECD countries', *Fiscal Studies*, **26** (2), 197–224.
Green, R. (2007), 'Carbon tax or carbon permits: the impact on generators' risks', Department of Economics Discussion Paper 07–02, University of Birmingham.
Helm, D. (1991), 'The assessment: energy policy', *Oxford Review of Economic Policy*, **7** (2), 1–55.
Kolstad, C.D. and M.D. Toman (2001), 'The economics of climate policy', Discussion Paper 00-40REV, Washington, DC: Resources for the Future, June.
Lind, R. (ed.) (1982), *Discounting for Time and Risk in Energy Policy*, Washington, DC: Resources for the Future.
Mendelsohn, R. (2005), 'The social cost of greenhouse gases: their values and their policy implications', in Dieter Helm (ed.), *Climate Change Policy*, Oxford: Oxford University Press, pp. 134–52.
Mendelsohn, R. (2006), 'A Critique of the Stern Report', *Regulation*, winter, 42–6.
Nordhaus, W. (2007), 'The Stern Review on the Economics of Climate Change', *Journal of Economic Literature*, **XLV**, September, 686–702.
Nordhaus, W. and J. Boyer (2000), *Warming the World*, Cambridge, MA: MIT Press.
Pearce, D.W. (2003), 'The social cost of carbon and its policy implications', *Oxford Review of Economic Policy*, **19** (3), 362–84.
Pearce, D. and D. Ulph (1995), 'A social discount rate for the United Kingdom', CSERGE Working Paper GEC 95–01, Centre for Social and Economic Research on the Global Environment, University College London.
Ramsey, F.P. (1928), 'A mathematical theory of saving', *Economic Journal*, **38** (152), December, 543–59.
Stern, N. (2006), *Stern Review on the Economics of Climate Change*, London: H.M. Treasury.
Weitzman, M.L. (1974), 'Prices vs quantities', *Review of Economic Studies*, **41**, 477–91.
Weitzman, M.L. (2007), 'A Review of the *Stern Review on the Economics of Climate Change*', *Journal of Economic Literature*, **45**, September, 703–24.
Weyman-Jones, T. (1986), *Energy in Europe: Issues and Policies*, London: Methuen.

Index

812   *International handbook on the economics of energy*

550, 552, 553, 554, 555, 563, 566, 740, 741, 759, 760, 763
international energy derivatives exchanges 717–28
    see also ICE (Intercontinental Exchange); Nord Pool; NYMEX (New York Mercantile Exchange)
international energy markets 11–12, 14, 16, 267, 268–9
    see also international derivatives markets
international investment 752–3
international oil companies (IOCs) 411–17
international petroleum fiscal regimes 411–17
international relations 75–6, 384
international trade 4, 361, 447–8
    see also coal exports; coal imports; elasticity of export demand; energy-exporting countries; energy imports; fossil fuel import prices; fossil fuel imports; oil-exporting countries; oil import control; oil import premium; oil-importing developing countries
investment
    and CGE models 361
    and climate change and energy security 762
    and corporate income tax 411
    developing countries 752–4
    and electricity ratemaking regulation 664
    and electricity transmission expansion mechanisms 584, 585, 586, 587–90
    and energy–economy–environment modelling 371, 374–5, 376
    and general equilibrium theory 192
    and low-emissions technologies 762, 763
    and neoclassical growth theory 175, 188
    petroleum tax 401–2
    and resource rent tax 410–411
    and theoretical foundations of the rebound effect 184, 188
investment decisions 29–32, 61–2, 65–6
investment rule, and peak-load pricing 33–4
investor-owned utilities (IOUs)
    and electricity distribution industry in North America 565
    and electricity transmission costs 502, 503, 506–7
    and electricity transmission industry in North America 544, 545, 546, 547, 548
    and energy network industry structure 471, 472–3
    and hidden action game 478–9
    and wholesale electricity markets 464–5
investors 405, 406, 408, 410
IPCC (Intergovernmental Panel on Climate Change) 203, 690, 773

Iran 75, 760
Iraq 75, 386
Ireland 525, 529, 535, 554, 560, 568, 572
iron industry 6–7
Islamic fundamentalism 74, 75–6
Italy
    coal production 445
    efficiency measurement in electricity and gas distribution industries 611, 615
    electricity distribution regulation 535
    electricity transmission regulation 525–6, 529
    market structure of electricity distribution industry 568, 572
    market structure of electricity transmission industry 554–5, 560
    wholesale electricity markets 627, 628, 637, 638, 641–2

Jaccard, M. 258, 269, 272, 315, 316, 317–18, 321, 322, 324, 328, 376, 377
Jacoby, H.D. 277, 362
Japan
    coal international trade 447, 448
    coal production 85, 445
    derivatives markets 716
    electricity distribution regulation 534, 535
    electricity transmission regulation 528, 530
    energy policy 76
    and history of energy 3
    market structure of electricity distribution industry 571, 573
    market structure of electricity transmission industry 562–3, 564
    oil consumption 131, 133
    oil prices 131, 132
    see also TOCOM (Tokyo Commodities Exchange)
jet fuel swaps 710–11
Johansen, S. 128–9
Johnston, D. 412, 413, 414
Jones, D.W. 750
Joskow, P.L. 39, 40, 41, 45, 48, 84, 457, 463, 476, 480, 489, 536, 582, 583–4, 588, 636, 638, 650, 651, 654, 668, 680
Joutz, F.L. 128, 129
Jung, T.Y. 749

Kahn, E. 636, 638, 664, 665
Kanagawa, M. 752
Kannan, R. 293, 295
Kaufmann, R.K. 215, 218–19, 228, 378
Kehoe, P.J. 333
Kehoe, T.J. 333, 343, 347
Kemfert, C. 376

marginal opportunity cost of access, and
access pricing problem 45, 46
marginal prices, and competition in wholesale
energy markets 40
marginal productivity, and theoretical
foundations of the rebound effect 192–3
marginal revenue 56, 482–3, 484, 485, 487, 488,
489
marginal social cost of carbon 775–6
marginal social return to capital, and social
discount rate in cost–benefit analysis 26,
27
marginal user cost (MUC), and extraction of
depletable resources 53, 54, 55, 60
marginal utility, and social discount rate in
cost–benefit analysis 25, 28
MARKAL-ELASTIC DEMAND
(MARKAL-ED) 262, 289
MARKAL-ETL (MARKAL-Endogenous
Technology Learning) 262
MARKAL–MACRO 272, 273, 288, 289,
293
MARKAL-MICRO (MICRO) 262
MARKAL models 260–64, 279, 285–9, 376
see also UK MARKAL model
MARKAL Stochastic 262–3
market clearance, and CGE models 334, 335,
336, 337, 339, 341, 342, 343, 346, 353
market-demand prorationing, and US energy
policy 77–8
market entry 23, 44–5
market failures 73–7, 82–3, 384–5, 770–73
see also cartels; duopolies; energy security;
externalities; information asymmetry;
market power; monopolies; oligopolies
market heterogeneity, and CIMS 318–19,
322–3, 324
market monitoring 639, 645–6
market power 384, 385, 387–8, 464–5, 588, 631,
633–9, 770
see also cartels; monopolies; oligopolies
market prices, and options 707–8
market share 270, 288, 316, 318–19, 325
market splitting, and wholesale electricity
markets 628
market structure of electricity distribution
industry
Europe 566–70, 572
industry structure 471, 472–3, 563, 565
North America 565–6, 572
Pacific Region 570–71, 573
market structure of electricity transmission
industry
Europe 547, 549–59, 560
industry structure 471–2, 473, 541–2, 543

North America 542, 544–7, 548
Pacific Region 559, 561–3, 564
markets 368, 458–61
see also behaviour of crude oil futures
markets; capital markets; cash
markets; competition; currency
markets; electricity markets; energy
markets; futures energy markets; goods
markets; international derivatives
markets; market structure of electricity
distribution industry; market structure
of electricity transmission industry;
money markets; natural gas markets;
wholesale electricity markets
Marron, D.B. 84
Maryland 669, 670, 674
see also PJM (Pennsylvania–New Jersey–
Maryland)
Maslow's pyramid of human needs 761–2
Massachusetts 673, 674, 675, 676, 681
materials
and CGE models 343, 344, 345
and energy–economy–environment
modelling 371
and energy efficiency in a stylised small open
economy 157, 158
and modelling energy demand 98
and multi-equation approaches to modelling
energy demand 117, 118, 120
Mathiesen, L. 340, 346
Meyer, M. 41
Mayo, J.W. 614–15
McFadden, D. 600
McGregor, P. 227
McKinsey & Company 687
MCX (Multi Commodity Exchange of India)
720–21, 727–8
MDM-E3 model, and rebound effect 224, 226
Medlock, K.B., III 71, 93, 102, 126
Meier, P. 743, 754
Mendelsohn, R. 63, 774, 784
merchant transmission investment of
electricity transmission expansion 583,
587–90, 591–4
MERGE 260
MERGE 4.5 272, 273
MESSAGE 264, 272, 376
MESSAGE Stochastic 264
Mexico 765
microeconomics 367–8, 373
Middle East
benchmark crude oil prices 420–21
conflict 384, 392, 393, 422
oil crises 9, 10, 11, 74–5, 77, 79
and oil in history of energy 9, 10

Sorrell, S. 144, 147, 173, 174, 179, 193–4, 203, 208, 209, 211, 213–14, 215, 228, 235, 373
South Africa 445, 446, 447, 448
South America 667, 741
South Korea 744–5
Soviet Union 445, 446
see also Caspian States; Russia
Soytas, U. 745, 746
space cooling 213, 214, 215, 244, 248, 249–52, 444
space heating
and fossil fuels 444
and history of energy 2, 4, 5, 6, 7–8, 9, 10, 12
and modelling energy savings and environmental benefits of new technologies 244, 248, 249–52
and non-commercial fuels in developing countries 740
and rebound effect 208, 213, 214, 215, 220–21
Spain
coal production 445
competitive electricity retail pricing 667
electricity distribution regulation 533, 535
electricity transmission regulation 527, 529
market structure of electricity distribution industry 569, 572
market structure of electricity transmission industry 557–8, 560
wholesale electricity markets 627, 628, 631, 634, 638, 641, 642
spark spread, and futures valuation 711
special petroleum tax 413
speculators 425
spot markets 456, 461, 463, 467, 655
spot prices 32–9, 462, 463, 467, 654–5, 707, 708–9
Spreng, D. 752
Spulber, D.F. 83, 462
Sravat, A.K. 753
stability, as tax principle 405, 406, 408
stakeholders 767
Standard Oil 9
standard scenario analysis, and life-cycle costs approach to modelling energy savings 238
stated preferences, and CIMS 321, 323–4
static model of firm's energy demand 97–9
steam engines 6, 7, 10
steel industry energy demand 85, 422, 437–8
Stern, D.I. 228, 373, 374, 377, 378
Stern Review 25, 28, 144, 203, 691, 773, 781–9
stochastic changes, and electricity transmission expansion mechanisms 588
stock market crashes, and behaviour of crude oil futures markets 430

stock of pollution, and energy–economy–environment modelling 374
stockpiling 384, 442–3, 771
Stone price index 123, 124
storage costs, and valuing derivative instruments 708–9
Strachan, N. 285, 289, 290, 293, 295, 309
stranded cost allowance 671, 673, 679
strategic petroleum reserve (SPR) expenditures 386
structural measures, and market power in wholesale electricity markets 635–6
STSM (structural time series model), and non-stationarity in modelling energy demand 130–31
subsidies 85–6, 151, 348–50
substitution potential
and CGE models 344–5, 354
and energy–economy–environment modelling 373–4
and ITC (induced technological change) policy models 312, 316
natural gas 443
oil 443
and optimization models 259
and rebound effect 166–7, 168–70, 173, 174, 175–6, 178, 182, 189, 190, 195, 196, 197, 202, 204, 206, 215, 219, 225
see also capital–energy substitution elasticity; elasticities of substitution; energy elasticity of substitution (ESUB); factor substitution; inter-fuel substitution
subtransmission facilities, and electricity transmission costs 502–3
Sue Wing, I. 277, 278, 347, 351, 357, 358, 362, 364, 376
Suez Canal crisis 396
sulphur dioxide emissions 291, 296, 444
Sun, J.W. 747
supply curve, and cost–benefit analysis and market structure 22
Surface Mining Control and Reclamation Act 1977 (SRCRA) 449, 451
Surrey, J. 744
sustainability 144, 145–7, 149, 751, 752, 765, 768, 781, 782
Swales, J. K. 227
swaps 707, 710–11
Sweden
electricity distribution regulation 535
electricity retail competition and pricing 678, 679
electricity transmission regulation 527, 529
market structure of electricity distribution industry 570, 572